frétiller [fretije] ⟨1a⟩ wriggle

Informations sur les conjugaisons françaises

Information on French conjugations

gâteau [gɑto] *m* (*pl* -x) cake

gérant, ~e [ʒerɑ̃, -t] *m/f* manager

insulaire [ɛ̃sylɛr] **1** *adj* island *atr* **2** *m/f* islander

Informations grammaticales

Grammatical information

menacer ⟨1k⟩ threaten (**de** with; **de faire** to do)

portable [pɔrtabl] **1** *adj* portable **2** *m* *ordinateur* laptop; *téléphone* cell phone, cell, *Br* mobile

Articles divisés en catégories grammaticales

Entries divided into grammatical categories

acolyte [akɔlit] *m péj* crony

maint, ~e [mɛ̃, -t] *fml* many

minet, ~te [minɛ, -t] *m/f* F pussy (cat); *fig* darling, sweetie pie F

Indicateurs de registre de langue

Register labels

moustache [mustaʃ] *f* mustache, *Br* moustache

courgette [kurʒɛt] *f* BOT zucchini, *Br* courgette

Variantes britanniques

British variants

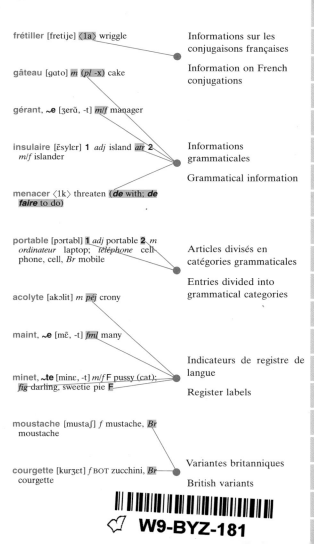

W9-BYZ-181

French
Compact Dictionary

French – English
Anglais – Français

Berlitz Publishing
New York · Munich · Singapore

Original edition edited by the Langenscheidt editorial staff

Compiled by LEXUS Ltd.

Inset cover photo: © Punchstock/Medioimages

© 2006 Berlitz Publishing/APA Publications GmbH & Co. Verlag KG
Singapore Branch, Singapore

Trademark Reg. U.S. Patent Office and other countries.
Marca Registrada.
Used under license from Berlitz Investment Corporation.

Berlitz Publishing
193 Morris Avenue
Springfield, NJ 07081
USA

Printed in Germany
ISBN-13: 978-981-246-877-2
ISBN-10: 981-246-877-3 (vinyl edition)
ISBN-13: 978-981-246-881-9
ISBN-10: 981-246-881-1 (UK paperback edition)

11 10 09 08 07

2. 3. 4. 5. 6.

Preface

Here is a new dictionary of English and French, a tool with some 50,000 references for those who work with the English and French languages at beginner's or intermediate level.

Focusing on modern usage, the dictionary offers coverage of everyday language and this means including vocabulary from areas such as computer use and business. English means both American and British English.

The editors have provided a reference tool to enable the user to get straight to the translation that fits a particular context of use. Indicating words are given to identify senses. Is the *box* you use to store things in, for example, the same in French as the *box* you enter data in on a form? Is *flimsy* referring to furniture the same in French as *flimsy* referring to an excuse? This dictionary is rich in sense distinctions like this and in translation options tied to specific, identified senses.

Vocabulary needs grammar to back it up. So in this dictionary you'll find irregular verb forms, in both English and French, irregular English plural forms, guidance on French feminine endings and French plurals and on prepositional usage with verbs.

Since some vocabulary items are often only clearly understood when contextualized, a large number of idiomatic phrases are given to show how the two languages correspond in particular contexts.

All in all, this is a book full of information, which will, we hope, become a valuable part of your language toolkit.

Préface

Nous vous présentons un tout nouveau dictionnaire d'anglais et de français, proposant plus de 50 000 mots et expressions à l'attention de tous ceux qui utilisent les langues anglaise et française à un niveau débutant ou intermédiaire.

Axé sur l'usage moderne, ce dictionnaire est consacré à la langue de tous les jours et couvre ainsi de multiples domaines, parmi lesquels l'informatique ou encore le commerce. Ici, anglais signifie à la fois anglais américain et anglais britannique.

Les rédacteurs ont conçu un ouvrage de référence permettant à l'utilisateur de trouver directement la traduction adaptée à un contexte particulier. Des indicateurs contextuels et sémantiques permettent de distinguer les différents sens d'un mot. Par exemple, est-ce que l'*égalité* des hommes se traduit en anglais de la même façon que l'*égalité* dans un match de tennis ? Est-ce que l'on dit la même chose en anglais pour *plaquer* un meuble ou *plaquer* sa copine ? Le dictionnaire regorge de distinctions sémantiques de ce type et de choix de traductions liés à un sens spécifique et identifié.

Le vocabulaire ne se suffisant pas à lui-même pour communiquer dans une langue, il doit être complété par des connaissances grammaticales. C'est pourquoi vous trouverez dans ce dictionnaire des formes verbales irrégulières, aussi bien en anglais qu'en français, des pluriels irréguliers anglais ainsi que des indications sur les terminaisons des féminins et pluriels français et sur l'usage des prépositions avec les verbes.

Étant donné que certains mots de vocabulaire ne peuvent être vraiment compris qu'en contexte, le dictionnaire propose un grand nombre d'expressions idiomatiques pour montrer les correspondances entre les deux langues dans des contextes particuliers.

En résumé, voici un ouvrage rempli d'informations qui, nous espérons, vous sera d'une aide précieuse pour tous vos échanges en anglais.

Contents

How to use the dictionary

To get the most out of your dictionary you should understand how and where to find the information you need. Whether you are yourself writing text in a foreign language or wanting to understand text that has been written in a foreign language, the following pages should help.

1. How and where do I find a word?

1.1 French and English headwords. The word list for each language is arranged in alphabetical order and also gives irregular forms of verbs and nouns in their correct alphabetical order.

Sometimes you might want to look up terms made up of two separate words, for example **shooting star**, or hyphenated words, for example **hands-on**. These words are treated as though they were a single word and their alphabetical ordering reflects this.

The only exception to this strict alphabetical ordering is made for English phrasal verbs – words like **go off**, **go out**, **go up**. These are positioned in a block directly after their main verb (in this case **go**), rather than being split up and placed apart.

French headwords belonging to a group of related words are run on in a block. All headwords are given in blue:

> **fumée** [fyme] *f* smoke; **fumer** ⟨1a⟩ smoke; *défense de* ~ no smoking; **fumeur, -euse** *m/f* smoker; **fumeux, -euse** *fig* hazy

1.2 French feminine headwords are shown as follows:

> **commentateur, -trice** *m/f* commentator
> **danseur, -euse** *m/f* dancer
> **débutant, ~e** [debytã, -t] *m/f* beginner
> **délégué, ~e** *m/f* delegate
> **dentiste** *m/f* dentist
> **échotier, -ère** [ekɔtje, -er] *m/f* gossip columnist

When a French headword has a feminine form which translates differently from the masculine form, the feminine is entered as a separate headword in alphabetical order:

dépanneur *m* repairman; *pour voitures* mechanic; **dépanneuse** *f* wrecker, *Br* tow truck

1.3 Running heads

If you are looking for a French or English word you can use the **running heads** printed in bold in the top corner of each page. The running head on the left tells you the *first* headword on the left-hand page and the one on the right tells you the *last* headword on the right-hand page.

1.4 How is the word spelt?

You can look up the spelling of a word in your dictionary in the same way as you would in a spelling dictionary. British spelling variants are marked *Br*.

2. How do I split a word?

French speakers find English hyphenation very difficult. All you have to do with this dictionary is look for the bold dots between syllables. These dots show you where you can split a word at the end of a line. But you should avoid having just one letter before or after the hyphen as in **a·mend** or **thirst·y**. In such cases it is better to take the entire word over to the next line.

2.1 When an English or a French word is written with a hyphen, then this dictionary makes a distinction between a hyphen which is given just because the dictionary line ends at that point and a hyphen which is actually part of the word. If the hyphen is a real hyphen then it is repeated at the start of the following line. So, for example:

> **radio** [radjo] *f* radio; (*radiographie*) X-
> -ray; **~** *privée* commercial radio; **pas-**
> **ser une ~** have an X-ray

Here the hyphen in *X-ray* is a real hyphen; the hyphen in *passer* is not.

3. Swung dashes

3.1 A swung dash (**~**) replaces the entire headword, when the headword is repeated within an entry:

8

face [feɪs] **1** *n* visage *m*, figure *f*; *of mountain* face *f*; **~ to ~** en personne; **lose ~** perdre la face

Here **~ to ~** means **face to face**.

pont [põ] *m* bridge; MAR deck; **~ aérien** airlift; **faire le ~** make a long weekend of it

Here **faire le ~** means **faire le pont**.

3.2 When a headword changes form in an entry, for example if it is put in the past tense or in the plural, then the past tense or plural ending is added to the swung dash – but only if the rest of the word doesn't change:

flame [fleɪm] *n* flamme *f*; **go up in ~s** être détruit par le feu
compliment [kõplimã] *m* compliment; **mes ~s** congratulations

But:

sur·vive [sər'vaɪv] **1** *v/i* survivre; **how are you? – I'm surviving** comment ça va? – pas trop mal
affirmatif, -ive [afirmatif, -iv] ... **répondre par l'affirmative** answer in the affirmative

3.3 Double headwords are replaced by a single swung dash:

'**cash flow** COM trésorerie *f*; **I've got ~ problems** j'ai des problèmes d'argent
'**one-track mind** *hum*: **have a ~** ne penser qu'à ça

4. What do the different typefaces mean?

4.1 All French and English headwords and the Arabic numerals differentiating between parts of speech appear in **bold**:

'**outline 1** *n* silhouette *f*; *of plan, novel* esquisse *f* **2** *v/t plans etc* ébaucher
antagoniste 1 *adj* antagonistic **2** *m/f* antagonist

4.2 *Italics* are used for :

a) abbreviated grammatical labels: *adj, adv, v/i, v/t* etc
b) gender labels: *m, f, mpl* etc
c) all the indicating words which are the signposts pointing to the correct translation for your needs. Here are some examples of indicating words in italics:

squeak [skwiːk] **1** *n of mouse* couinement *m*; *of hinge* grincement *m*

♦ **work out 1** *v/t solution*, *(find out)* trouver; *problem* résoudre **2** *v/i at gym* s'entraîner; *of relationship, arrangement etc* bien marcher

spirituel, ~le spiritual; *(amusant)* witty

agrafe [agraf] *f d'un vêtement* fastener, hook; *de bureau* staple

réussir ⟨2a⟩ **1** *v/i d'une personne* succeed; *~ à faire qch* manage to do sth, succeed in doing sth **2** *v/t vie, projet* make a success of; *examen* be successful in

Note: subjects of verbs are given with *of* or *d'un, d'une* etc.

4.3 All phrases (examples and idioms) are given in ***bold italics***:

shave [ʃeɪv] **1** *v/t* raser **2** *v/i* se raser **3** *n*: ***have a ~*** se raser; ***that was a close ~*** on l'a échappé belle

porte [pɔrt] *f* door; *d'une ville* gate; ***entre deux~s*** very briefly; ***mettre qn à la ~*** throw s.o. out, show s.o. the door

4.4 The normal typeface is used for the translations.

4.5 If a translation is given in italics, and not in the normal typeface, this means that the translation is more of an *explanation* in the other language and that an explanation has to be given because there just is no real equivalent:

con·trol freak F *personne qui veut tout contrôler*

andouille [ɑ̃duj] *f* CUIS *type of sausage*

5. Stress

To indicate where to put the **stress** in English words, the stress marker ' appears before the syllable on which the main stress falls:

rec·ord[1] ['rekərd] *n* MUS disque *m*; SP *etc* record *m*

rec·ord[2] [rɪ'kɔːrd] *v/t electronically* enregistrer; *in writing* consigner

Stress is shown either in the pronunciation or, if there is no pronunciation given, in the actual headword or compound itself:

'rec·ord hold·er recordman *m*, recordwoman *f*

6. What do the various symbols and abbreviations tell you?

6.1 A solid blue diamond is used to indicate a phrasal verb:

♦ **crack down on** *v/t* sévir contre

6.2 A white diamond is used to divide up longer entries into more easily digested chunks of related bits of text:

> **on** [ō] (*après* **que, et, où, qui, si** *souvent* **l'on**) *pron personnel* ◊ (*nous*) we;
> **~ y a été hier** we went there yesterday; **~ est en retard** we're late
> ◊ (*tu, vous*) you; **alors, ~ s'amuse bien?** having fun?
> ◊ (*quelqu'un*) someone; **~ m'a dit que** I was told that ...; **~ a volé mon passeport** somebody has stolen my passport, my passport has been stolen
> ◊ (*eux, les gens*) they, people; **que pensera-t-~ d'un tel comportement?** what will they *ou* people think of such behavior?
> ◊ *autorités* they; **~ va démolir ...** they are going to demolish ...
> ◊ *indéterminé* you; **~ ne sait jamais** you never know, one never knows *fml*

6.3 The abbreviation F tells you that the word or phrase is used colloquially rather than in formal contexts. The abbreviation V warns you that a word or phrase is vulgar or taboo. Words or phrases labeled P are slang. Be careful how you use these words.

These abbreviations, F, V and P are used both for headwords and phrases (placed after) and for the translations of headwords/phrases (placed after). If there is no such label given, then the word or phrase is neutral.

6.4 A colon before an English or French word or phrase means that usage is restricted to this specific example (at least as far as this dictionary's translation is concerned):

> **catch-22** [kætʃtwentɪˈtuː]: **it's a ~ situation** c'est un cercle vicieux
> **opiner** [ɔpine] ⟨1a⟩: **~ de la tête** *ou* **du bonnet** nod in agreement

7. Does the dictionary deal with grammar too?

7.1 All English headwords are given a part of speech label:

> **tooth·less** [ˈtuːθlɪs] *adj* édenté
> **top·ple** [ˈtɑːpl] **1** *v/i* s'écrouler **2** *v/t government* renverser

But if a headword can only be used as a noun (in ordinary English) then no part of speech is given, since none is needed:

> **'tooth·paste** dentifrice *m*

7.2 French gender markers are given:

oursin [ursɛ̃] *m* ZO sea urchin
partenaire [partənɛr] *m/f* partner

If a French word can be used both as a noun and as an adjective, then this is shown:

patient, ⁓e *m/f & adj* patient

No part of speech is shown for French words which are only adjectives or only transitive verbs or only intransitive verbs, since no confusion is possible. But where confusion might exist, grammatical information is added:

patriote [patrijɔt] **1** *adj* patriotic **2** *m/f* patriot
verbaliser ⟨1a⟩ **1** *v/i* JUR bring a charge **2** *v/t (exprimer)* verbalize

7.3 If an English translation of a French adjective can only be used in front of a noun, and not after it, this is marked with *atr*:

villageois, ⁓e 1 *adj* village *atr* **2** *m/f* villager
vinicole [vinikɔl] wine *atr*

7.4 If the French, unlike the English, doesn't change form if used in the plural, this is marked with *inv*:

volte-face [vɔltəfas] *f (pl inv)* about-turn *(aussi fig)*
appuie-tête *m (pl inv)* headrest

7.5 If the English, in spite of appearances, is not a plural form, this is marked with *nsg*:

bil·liards [ˈbɪljərdz] *nsg* billard *m*
mea·sles [ˈmiːzlz] *nsg* rougeole *f*

English translations are given a *pl* or *sg* label (for plural or singular) in cases where this does not match the French:

bagages [bagaʒ] *mpl* baggage *sg*
balance [balɑ̃s] *f* scales *pl*

7.6 Irregular English plurals are identified and French plural forms are given in cases where there might well be uncertainty:

the·sis [ˈθiːsɪs] *(pl **theses** [ˈθiːsiːz])* thèse *f*
thief [θiːf] *(pl **thieves** [θiːvz])* voleur(-euse) *m(f)*
trout [traʊt] *(pl **trout**)* truite *f*
fédéral, ⁓e [federal] *(mpl -aux)* federal

festival [fɛstival] *m* (*pl* -s) festival
pneu [pnø] *m* (*pl* -s) tire, *Br* tyre

7.7 Words like **physics** or **media studies** have not been given a label to say if they are singular or plural for the simple reason that they can be either, depending on how they are used.

7.8 Irregular and semi-irregular verb forms are identified:

sim·pli·fy ['sɪmplɪfaɪ] *v/t* (*pret & pp* **-ied**) simplifier
sing [sɪŋ] *v/t & v/i* (*pret **sang**, pp **sung***) chanter
la·bel ['leɪbl] **1** *n* étiquette *f* **2** *v/t* (*pret & pp* **-ed**, *Br* **-led**) *also fig* étiqueter

7.9 Cross-references are given to the tables of French conjugations on page 694:

balbutier [balbysje] ⟨1a⟩ stammer, stutter
abréger ⟨1g⟩ abridge

7.10 Grammatical information is provided on the prepositions you'll need in order to create complete sentences:

un·hap·py [ʌn'hæpɪ] *adj* malheureux*; *customers etc* mécontent (**with** de)
un·re·lat·ed [ʌnrɪ'leɪtɪd] *adj* sans relation (**to** avec)
accoucher ⟨1a⟩ give birth (**de** to)
accro [akro] F addicted (**à** to)

7.11 In the English-French half of the dictionary an asterisk is given after adjectives which do not form their feminine form just by adding an **-e**. The feminine form of these adjectives can be found in the French-English half of the dictionary:

un·true [ʌn'truː] *adj* faux*
faux, fausse [fo, fos] **1** *adj* false ...

Comment utiliser le dictionnaire

Pour exploiter au mieux votre dictionnaire, vous devez comprendre comment et où trouver les informations dont vous avez besoin. Que vous vouliez écrire un texte en langue étrangère ou comprendre un texte qui a été écrit en langue étrangère, les pages suivantes devraient vous aider.

1. Comment et où trouver un terme ?

1.1 Entrées françaises et anglaises. Pour chaque langue, la nomenclature est classée par ordre alphabétique et présente également les formes irrégulières des verbes et des noms dans le bon ordre alphabétique.

Vous pouvez parfois avoir besoin de rechercher des termes composés de deux mots séparés, comme **shooting star**, ou reliés par un trait d'union, comme **hands-on**. Ces termes sont traités comme un mot à part entière et apparaissent à leur place dans l'ordre alphabétique.

Il n'existe qu'une seule exception à ce classement alphabétique rigoureux : les verbes composés anglais, tels que **go off**, **go out** et **go up**, sont rassemblés dans un bloc juste après le verbe (ici **go**), au lieu d'apparaître séparément.

Les entrées françaises appartenant à un groupe de mots apparentés sont présentées dans un même bloc et apparaissent toutes en bleu.

> **fumée** [fyme] *f* smoke; **fumer** (1a) smoke; ***défense de*** ~ no smoking; **fumeur,-euse** *m/f* smoker; **fumeux, -euse** *fig* hazy

1.2 Les formes féminines des entrées françaises sont présentées de la façon suivante :

> **commentateur, -trice** *m/f* commentator
> **danseur, -euse** *m/f* dancer
> **débutant, ~e** [debytɑ̃, -t] *m/f* beginner
> **délégué, ~e** *m/f* delegate
> **dentiste** *m/f* dentist
> **échotier, -ère** [ekɔtje, -ɛr] *m/f* gossip columnist

Lorsque la forme féminine d'une entrée française ne correspond pas à la même traduction que le masculin, elle est traitée comme une entrée à part entière et classée par ordre alphabétique.

> **dépanneur** *m* repairman; *pour voitures* mechanic; **dépanneuse** *f* wrecker, *Br* tow truck

1.3 Titres courants

Pour rechercher un terme anglais ou français, vous pouvez utiliser les **titres courants** qui apparaissent en gras dans le coin supérieur de chaque page. Le titre courant à gauche indique la *première* entrée de la page de gauche tandis que celui qui se trouve à droite indique la *dernière* entrée de la page de droite.

1.4 Orthographe des mots

Vous pouvez utiliser votre dictionnaire pour vérifier l'orthographe d'un mot exactement comme dans un dictionnaire d'orthographe. Les variantes orthographiques britanniques sont signalées par l'indication *Br*.

2. Comment couper un mot ?

Les francophones trouvent généralement que les règles de coupure des mots en anglais sont très compliquées. Avec ce dictionnaire, il vous suffit de repérer les ronds qui apparaissent entre les syllabes. Ces ronds vous indiquent où vous pouvez couper un mot en fin de ligne, mais évitez de ne laisser qu'une seule lettre avant ou après le tiret, comme dans **a·mend** ou **thirst·y**. Dans ce cas, il vaut mieux faire passer tout le mot à la ligne suivante.

2.1

Lorsqu'un terme anglais ou français est écrit avec le signe « - », ce dictionnaire indique s'il s'agit d'un tiret servant à couper le mot en fin de ligne ou d'un trait d'union qui fait partie du mot. S'il s'agit d'un trait d'union, il est répété au début de la ligne suivante. Par exemple :

> **radio** [radjo] *f* radio; (*radiographie*) X-
> -ray; ~ **privée** commercial radio; **pas-**
> **ser une** ~ have an X-ray

Dans ce cas, le tiret de *X-ray* est un trait d'union, mais pas celui de *passer*.

3. Signe ~ (ou tilde)

3.1 L'entrée est remplacée par un tilde (~) lorsqu'elle est répétée dans le corps de l'article :

> **face** [feɪs] **1** *n* visage *m*, figure *f*; *of mountain* face *f*; **~ to ~** en personne; **lose ~** perdre la face

Ici, **~ to ~** signifie **face to face**.

> **pont** [pɔ̃] *m* bridge; *mar deck*; **~ aérien** airlift; **faire le ~** make a long weekend of it

Ici, **faire le ~** signifie **faire le pont**.

3.2 Lorsqu'une entrée change de forme au sein d'un article, par exemple si elle est conjuguée au passé ou mise au pluriel, la terminaison du passé ou du pluriel est ajoutée au tilde, à condition que le reste du mot reste identique :

> **flame** [fleɪm] *n* flamme *f*; **go up in ~s** être détruit par le feu
> **compliment** [kɔ̃plimɑ̃] *m* compliment; **mes ~s** congratulations

Mais :

> **sur·vive** [sər'vaɪv] **1** *v/i* survivre; **how are you? – I'm surviving** comment ça va? – pas trop mal
> **affirmatif, -ive** [afirmatif, -iv] ... **répondre par l'affirmative** answer in the affirmative

3.3 Les entrées doubles sont remplacées par un seul tilde :

> **'cash flow** COM trésorerie *f*; **I've got ~ problems** j'ai des problèmes d'argent
> **'one-track mind** *hum*: **have a ~** ne penser qu'à ça

4. Que signifient les différents styles typographiques ?

4.1 Les entrées françaises et anglaises ainsi que les numéros signalant les différentes catégories grammaticales apparaissent tous en **gras** :

> **'out·line 1** *n* silhouette *f*; *of plan, novel* esquisse *f* **2** *v/t plans etc* ébaucher
> **antagoniste 1** *adj* antagonistic **2** *m/f* antagonist

4.2 L'*italique* est utilisé pour :

a) les indicateurs grammaticaux abrégés : *adj*, *adv*, *v/i*, *v/t*, *etc.*

b) les indicateurs de genre : *m, f, mpl, etc.*

c) tous les indicateurs contextuels et sémantiques qui vous permettent de déterminer quelle traduction choisir. Voici quelques exemples d'indicateurs en italique :

squeak [skwiːk] **1** *n of mouse* couinement *m*; *of hinge* grincement *m*
♦ **work out 1** *v/t solution*, (*find out*) trouver; *problem* résoudre **2** *v/i at gym* s'entraîner; *of relationship, arrangement etc* bien marcher
spirituel, ⁓le spiritual; (*amusant*) witty
agrafe [agraf] *f d'un vêtement* fastener, hook; *de bureau* staple
réussir (2a) **1** *v/i d'une personne* succeed; *⁓ à faire qch* manage to do sth, succeed in doing sth **2** *v/t vie, projet* make a success of; *examen* be successful in

Remarque : les sujets de verbes sont précédés de *of* ou *d'un, d'une*, etc.

4.3 Toutes les locutions (exemples et expressions) apparaissent en ***gras et italique*** :

shave [ʃeɪv] **1** *v/t* raser **2** *v/i* se raser **3** *n*: ***have a ⁓*** se raser; ***that was a close ⁓*** on l'a échappé belle
porte [pɔrt] *f* door; *d'une ville* gate; ***entre deux ⁓s*** very briefly; ***mettre qn à la ⁓*** throw s.o. out, show s.o. the door

4.4 Le style normal est utilisé pour les traductions.

4.5 Si une traduction apparaît en italique et non en style normal, ceci signifie qu'il s'agit plus d'une *explication* dans la langue d'arrivée que d'une traduction à proprement parler et qu'il n'existe pas vraiment d'équivalent.

con'trol freak F *personne qui veut tout contrôler*
andouille [ɑ̃duj] *f* CUIS *type of sausage*

5. Accent

Pour indiquer où mettre l'**accent** dans les mots anglais, l'indicateur d'accent « ' » est placé devant la syllabe sur laquelle tombe l'accent tonique.

rec·ord[1] ['rekərd] *n* MUS disque *m*; SP *etc* record *m*
rec·ord[2] [rɪ'kɔːrd] *v/t electronically* enregistrer; *in writing* consigner

L'accent apparaît dans la prononciation ou, s'il n'y a pas de prononciation, dans l'entrée ou le mot composé.

'rec·ord hold·er recordman *m*, recordwoman *f*

6. Que signifient les différents symboles et abréviations ?

6.1 Un losange plein bleu indique un verbe composé :

♦**crack down on** *v/t* sévir contre

6.2 Un losange blanc sert à diviser des entrées particulièrement longues en plusieurs blocs plus accessibles afin de regrouper des informations apparentées.

on [ō] (*après* **que, et, où, qui, si** *souvent* l'**on**) *pron personnel* ◊ (*nous*) we; **~ y a été hier** we went there yesterday; **~ est en retard** we're late ◊ (*tu, vous*) you; **alors, ~ s'amuse bien?** having fun? ◊ (*quelqu'un*) someone; **~ m'a dit que …** I was told that …; **~ a volé mon passeport** somebody has stolen my passport, my passport has been stolen

6.3 L'abréviation F indique que le mot ou la locution s'emploie dans un registre familier plutôt que dans un contexte solennel. L'abréviation V signale qu'un mot ou une locution est vulgaire ou injurieux. L'abréviation P désigne des mots ou locutions argotiques. Employez ces mots avec prudence.

Ces abréviations, F, V et P, sont utilisées pour les entrées et les locutions ainsi que pour les traductions des entrées/locutions, et sont toujours placées après les termes qu'elles qualifient. S'il n'y a aucune indication, le mot ou la locution est neutre.

6.4 Un signe « : » (deux-points) précédant un mot ou une locution signifie que l'usage est limité à cet exemple précis (au moins pour les besoins de ce dictionnaire) :

catch-22 [kætʃtwentɪ'tuː]: *it's a ~ situation* c'est un cercle vicieux **opiner** [ɔpine] (1a): **~ de la tête** *ou* **du bonnet** nod in agreement

7. Est-ce que le dictionnaire traite aussi de la grammaire ?

7.1 Les entrées anglaises sont, en règle générale, assorties d'un indicateur grammatical :

tooth·less ['tuːθlɪs] *adj* édenté
top·ple ['tɑːpl] **1** *v/i* s'écrouler **2** *v/t government* renverser

18

Par contre, si une entrée peut uniquement être utilisée en tant que nom (en anglais courant), l'indicateur grammatical est omis, car inutile :

    'tooth‧paste dentifrice *m*

7.2   Le genre des entrées françaises est indiqué :

    oursin [ursɛ̃] *m* ZO sea urchin
    partenaire [partənɛr] *m/f* partner

Le dictionnaire précise également si un mot français peut être utilisé à la fois en tant que nom et en tant qu'adjectif :

    patient, ‿e *m/f & adj* patient

La catégorie grammaticale est omise pour les mots français qui ne peuvent être utilisés qu'en tant qu'adjectifs, verbes transitifs ou verbes intransitifs, étant donné qu'il n'y a pas de confusion possible. Par contre, lorsqu'il y a un risque de confusion, la catégorie grammaticale est précisée :

    patriote [patrijɔt] **1** *adj* patriotic **2** *m/f* patriot
    verbaliser (1a) **1** *v/i* JUR bring a charge **2** *v/t* (*exprimer*) verbalize

7.3   Si la traduction anglaise d'un adjectif français ne peut être placée que devant un nom, et pas après, la traduction est suivie de l'indication *atr* :

    villageois, ‿e 1 *adj* village *atr* **1** *m/f* villager
    vinicole [vinikɔl] wine *atr*

7.4   *inv* indique que le terme français, contrairement à l'anglais, ne s'accorde pas au pluriel :

    volte-face [vɔltəfas] *f (pl inv)* about-turn (*aussi fig*)
    appuie-tête *m (pl inv)* headrest

7.5   *nsg* indique que l'anglais, en dépit des apparences, n'est pas au pluriel :

    bil‧liards ['bɪljərdz] *nsg* billard *m*
    mea‧sles ['miːzlz] *nsg* rougeole *f*

Les traductions anglaises sont assorties d'un indicateur *pl* ou *sg* (pluriel ou singulier) en cas de différence avec le français :

    bagages [bagaʒ] *mpl* baggage *sg*

balance [baläs] *f* scales *pl*

7.6 Les pluriels irréguliers sont indiqués pour les entrées anglaises. Du côté français, le pluriel est donné à chaque fois qu'il peut y avoir un doute.

> **the·sis** ['θiːsɪs] (*pl* ***theses*** ['θiːsiːz]) thèse *f*
> **thief** [θiːf] (*pl* ***thieves*** [θiːvz]) voleur(-euse) *m(f)*
> **trout** [traʊt] (*pl* ***trout***) truite *f*
> **fédéral**, **~e** [federal] (*mpl* -aux) federal
> **festival** [fɛstival] *m* (*pl* -s) festival
> **pneu** [pnø] *m* (*pl* -s) tire, *Br* tyre

7.7 Pour certains termes, tels que **physics** ou **media studies**, aucune indication ne précise s'ils sont singuliers ou pluriels, pour la simple et bonne raison qu'ils peuvent être les deux, selon leur emploi.

7.8 Les formes verbales qui ne suivent pas les modèles réguliers apparaissent après le verbe :

> **sim·pli·fy** ['sɪmplɪfaɪ] *v/t* (*pret & pp* **-ied**) simplifier
> **sing** [sɪŋ] *v/t & v/i* (*pret* ***sang***, *pp* ***sung***) chanter
> **la·bel** ['leɪbl] **1** *n* étiquette *f* **2** *v/t* (*pret & pp* **-ed**, *Br* **-led**) *also fig* étiqueter

7.9 Pour les verbes français, des renvois vous permettent de vous reporter au tableau de conjugaison correspondant (page 694) :

> **balbutier** [balbysje] ⟨1a⟩ stammer, stutter
> **abréger** ⟨1g⟩ abridge

7.10 Les prépositions dont vous aurez besoin pour construire une phrase sont également indiquées :

> **un·hap·py** [ʌn'hæpɪ] *adj* malheureux*; *customers etc* mécontent (***with*** de)
> **un·re·lat·ed** [ʌnrɪ'leɪtɪd] *adj* sans relation (***to*** avec)
> **accoucher** ⟨1a⟩ give birth (***de*** to)
> **accro** [akro] *F* addicted (***à*** to)

7.11 Dans la partie anglais-français du dictionnaire, un astérisque signale les adjectifs qui ne forment pas leur féminin en ajoutant simplement un **-e** au masculin. Vous trouverez le féminin de ces adjectifs dans la partie français-anglais du dictionnaire.

> **un·true** [ʌn'truː] *adj* faux*
> **faux, fausse** [fo, fos] **1** *adj* false …

Pronunciation / La Prononciation

Equivalent sounds, especially for vowels and diphthongs can only be approximations. *Les équivalences, surtout pour les voyelles et les diphtongues, ne peuvent être qu'approximatives.*

1. Consonants / Les consonnes

bouche	[b]	bag	*reine*	[r]	right (*la*	*chat*	[ʃ] she
dans	[d]	dear	(r from	*langue*		*cha-cha-cha*	[tʃ] chair
foule	[f]	fall	the	*vers le*		*adjuger*	[dʒ] join
gai	[g]	give	throat)	*haut*)		*juge*	[ʒ] leisure
et hop	[h]	hole	*sauf*	[s]	sun	*langue entre*	[θ] think
radio	[j]	yes	*table*	[t]	take	*les dents*	
qui	[k]	come	*vain*	[v]	vain	*langue derrière*	[ð] the
la	[l]	land	*oui*	[w]	wait	*les dents*	
mon	[m]	mean	*rose*	[z]	rose	*du haut*	
nuit	[n]	night	*feeling*	[ŋ]	bring	*huit*	[ɥ] roughly
pot	[p]	pot	*agneau*	[ɲ]	onion		sweet

2. Les voyelles anglaises

âme	[ɑ:]	far	*i très*	[ɪ]	stick	*entre à*	[ʌ] mother
salle	[æ]	man	*court*			*et eux*	
sec	[e]	get	*si*	[i:]	need	*bouquin*	[ʊ] book
le	[ə]	utter	*phase*	[ɒ:]	in-laws	(*très court*)	
beurre	[ɜ:]	absurd	*essor*	[ɔ:]	more	*sous*	[u:] hoot

3. Les diphtongues anglaises

aïe	[aɪ]	time	cow-boy	[ɔɪ] point
ciao	[aʊ]	cloud	*eau suivi d'un u court*	[oʊ] so
nez suivi d'un y court	[eɪ]	name		

4. French vowels and nasals

abats	[a]	fat	*poche*	[ɔ]	hot (*British accent*)
âme	[ɑ]	Mars	*leur*	[œ]	fur
les	[e]	pay (*no y sound*)	*meute, nœud*	[ø]	learn (*no r sound*)
père, sec	[ɛ]	bed	*souci*	[u]	tool
le, dehors	[ə]	letter	*tu, eu*	[y]	mouth ready to say
ici, style	[i]	peel			oo, then say ee
beau, au	[o]	bone			

dans, entrer	[ã]	roughly as in song (*no ng*)
vin, bien	[ɛ̃]	roughly as in van (*no n*)
ton, pompe	[õ]	roughly as in song (*no ng but with mouth more rounded*)
un, aucun (*also pronounced as* ɛ̃)	[œ̃]	roughly as in huh

5. ['] means that the following syllable is stressed: *ability* [əˈbɪlətɪ]

Some French words starting with h have ' before the h. This ' is not part of the French word. It shows i) that a preceding vowel does not become an apostrophe and ii) that no elision takes place. (This is called an aspirated h).

'hanche: la hanche, les hanches [leãʃ] **but habit: l'habit, les habits** [lezabi]

Abbreviations / Abréviations

and	&	et
see	→	voir
registered trademark	®	marque déposée
abbreviation	*abbr*	abréviation
abbreviation	*abr*	abréviation
adjective	*adj*	adjectif
adverb	*adv*	adverbe
agriculture	AGR	agriculture
anatomy	ANAT	anatomie
architecture	ARCH	architecture
article	*art*	article
astronomy	ASTR	astronomie
astrology	ASTROL	astrologie
attributive	*atr*	devant le nom
motoring	AUTO	automobiles
aviation	AVIAT	aviation
biology	BIOL	biologie
botany	BOT	botanique
British English	*Br*	anglais britannique
chemistry	CHIM	chimie
commerce, business	COMM	commerce
computers, IT term	COMPUT	informatique
conjunction	*conj*	conjonction
cooking	CUIS	cuisine
economics	ÉCON	économie
education	EDU	éducation
education	ÉDU	éducation
electricity	ÉL	électricité
electricity	ELEC	électricité
especially	*esp*	surtout
euphemism	*euph*	euphémisme
familiar, colloquial	F	familier
feminine	*f*	féminin
figurative	*fig*	figuré
finance	FIN	finance
formal	*fml*	langage formel
feminine plural	*fpl*	féminin pluriel
geography	GEOG	géographie
geography	GÉOGR	géographie
geology	GÉOL	géologie
geometry	GÉOM	géométrie
grammar	GRAM	grammaire
historical	HIST	historique
humorous	*hum*	humoristique
IT term	INFORM	informatique
interjection	*int*	interjection
invariable	*inv*	invariable
ironic	*iron*	ironique
law	JUR	juridique
law	LAW	juridique
linguistics	LING	linguistique

literary	*litt*	littéraire
masculine	*m*	masculin
nautical	MAR	marine
mathematics	MATH	mathématiques
medicine	MED	médecine
medicine	MÉD	médecine
masculine and feminine	*m/f*	masculin et féminin
military	MIL	militaire
motoring	MOT	automobiles
masculine plural	*mpl*	masculin pluriel
music	MUS	musique
noun	*n*	nom
nautical	NAUT	marine
plural noun	*npl*	nom pluriel
singular noun	*nsg*	nom singulier
oneself	o.s.	se, soi
popular, slang	P	populaire
pejorative	*pej*	péjoratif
pejorative	*péj*	péjoratif
pharmacy	PHARM	pharmacie
photography	PHOT	photographie
physics	PHYS	physique
plural	*pl*	pluriel
politics	POL	politique
past participle	*pp, p/p*	participe passé
preposition	*prep*	préposition
preposition	*prép*	préposition
preterite	*pret*	prétérit
pronoun	*pron*	pronom
psychology	PSYCH	psychologie
something	*qch*	quelque chose
someone	*qn*	quelqu'un
radio	RAD	radio
railroad	RAIL	chemin de fer
religion	REL	religion
singular	*sg*	singulier
someone	s.o.	quelqu'un
sports	SP	sport
something	*sth*	quelque chose
subjunctive	*subj*	subjonctif
noun	*subst*	substantif
theater	THEA	théâtre
theater	THÉÂT	théâtre
technology	TECH	technique
telecommunications	TÉL	télécommunications
telecommunications	TELEC	télécommunications
typography, typesetting	TYP	typographie
television	TV	télévision
vulgar	V	vulgaire
auxiliary verb	*v/aux*	verbe auxiliaire
intransitive verb	*v/i*	verbe intransitif
transitive verb	*v/t*	verbe transitif
zoology	ZO	zoologie

A

à [a] *prép* ◊ *lieu* in; **~ la campagne** in the country; **~ Chypre / Haïti** on Cyprus / Haiti; **aux Pays-Bas** in the Netherlands; **au bout de la rue** at the end of the street; **~ 2 heures d'ici** 2 hours from here

◊ *direction* to; **~ l'étranger** to the country; **aux Pays-Bas** to the Netherlands

◊ *temps*: **~ cinq heures** at five o'clock; **~ Noël** at Christmas; **~ tout moment** at any moment; **~ demain** until tomorrow

◊ *but*: **tasse** *f* **~ café** coffee cup; **machine** *f* **~ laver** washing machine

◊ *fonctionnement*: **un moteur ~ gazoil** a diesel engine; **une lampe ~ huile** an oil lamp

◊ *appartenance*: **c'est ~ moi** it's mine, it belongs to me; **c'est ~ qui?** whose is this?, who does this belong to?; **un ami ~ moi** a friend of mine

◊ *caractéristiques* with; **aux cheveux blonds** with blonde hair

◊ : **~ toi de décider** it's up to you; **ce n'est pas ~ moi de ...** it's not up to me to ...

◊ *mode*: **~ pied** on foot, by foot; **~ la russe** Russian-style; **~ quatre mains** MUS for four hands; **~ dix euros** at *ou* for ten euros; **goutte ~ goutte** drop by drop; **vendre qch au kilo** sell sth by the kilo; **on y est allé ~ trois** three of us went

◊ *objet indirect*: **donner qch ~ qn** give sth to s.o.

◊ *en tennis* all; **trente ~** thirty all

abaissement [abɛsmã] *m d'un store, d'un prix, d'un niveau* lowering; (*humiliation*) abasement; **abaisser** ⟨1b⟩ *rideau, prix, niveau* lower; *fig* (*humilier*) humble; **s'~** drop; *fig* demean o.s.

abandon [abãdõ] *m* abandonment; (*cession*) surrender; (*détente*) abandon; SP withdrawal; **laisser à l'~** abandon; **abandonner** ⟨1a⟩ abandon; *pouvoir, lutte* give up; SP withdraw from; **s'~** (*se confier*) open up; **s'~ à** give way to

abasourdi, ~e [abazurdi] amazed, dumbfounded; **abasourdir** ⟨2a⟩ *fig* astonish, amaze

abat-jour [abaʒur] *m* (*pl inv*) (lamp-)shade

abats [aba] *mpl* variety meat *sg*

abattage [abataʒ] *m de bois* felling; *d'un animal* slaughter; **abattement** *m* COMM rebate; PSYCH depression; **abattoir** *m* slaughterhouse, *Br* abattoir; **abattre** ⟨4a⟩ *arbre* fell; AVIAT bring down, shoot down; *animal* slaughter; *péj* (*tuer*) kill, slay; *fig* (*épuiser*) exhaust; (*décourager*) dishearten; **je ne me laisserai pas ~** I won't let myself be discouraged; **~ beaucoup de besogne** get through a lot of work; **s'~** collapse; **abattu, ~e** (*fatigué*) weak, weakened; (*découragé*) disheartened, dejected

abbaye [abei] *f* abbey

abbé [abe] *m* abbot; (*prêtre*) priest

abcès [apsɛ] *m* abscess

abdomen [abdɔmɛn] *m* abdomen; **abdominal, ~e** abdominal

abeille [abɛj] *f* bee

aberrant, ~e [aberã, -t] F absurd; **aberration** *f* aberration

abêtir [abetir] ⟨2a⟩ make stupid; **abêtissant, ~e**: **être ~** addle the brain

abîme [abim] *m* abyss; **abîmer** ⟨1a⟩ spoil, ruin; **s'~** be ruined; *d'aliments* spoil, go off

abject, ~e [abʒɛkt] abject; *personne, comportement* despicable; **abjection** *f* abjectness

abjurer [abʒyre] ⟨1a⟩ *foi* renounce

aboiement [abwamɑ̃] *m* barking

abois [abwa]: *être aux ~* fig have one's back to the wall

abolir [abɔlir] ⟨2a⟩ abolish; **abolition** *f* abolition

abominable [abɔminabl] appalling

abondance [abɔ̃dɑ̃s] *f* abundance, wealth; *société f d'~* affluent society; **abondant**, **~e** abundant; **abonder** ⟨1a⟩ be plentiful, abound; **~ en** have an abundance of

abonné, **~e** [abɔne] *m/f aussi* TÉL subscriber; **abonnement** *m* subscription; *de transport, de spectacles* season ticket; **abonner** ⟨1a⟩: *s'~ à une revue* subscribe to a magazine

abord [abɔr] *m*: *être d'un ~ facile* approachable; *d'~* first; *tout d'~* first of all; *dès l'~* from the outset; *au premier ~*, *de prime ~* at first sight; *~s* surroundings; **abordable** approachable; **abordage** *m* MAR (*collision*) collision; (*assaut*) boarding; **aborder** ⟨1a⟩ **1** *v/t* (*prendre d'assaut*) board; (*heurter*) collide with; *fig*: *question* tackle; *personne* approach **2** *v/i* land (*à* at)

aboutir [abutir] ⟨2a⟩ *d'un projet* succeed, be successful; *~ à / dans* end at / in; *~ à* fig lead to; **aboutissement** *m* (*résultat*) result

aboyer [abwaje] ⟨1h⟩ bark

abrasif, **-ive** [abrazif, -iv] TECH **1** *adj* abrasive **2** *m* abrasive

abrégé [abreʒe] *m d'un roman* abridgement; **abréger** ⟨1g⟩ abridge

abreuver [abrœve] ⟨1a⟩ water; *s'~* F drink; **abreuvoir** *m* watering place

abréviation [abrevjasjɔ̃] *f* abbreviation

abri [abri] *m* shelter; *à l'~ de* sheltered from, protected from; *mettre à l'~ de* shelter from, protect from; *être sans ~* be homeless

abribus [abribys] *m* bus shelter

abricot [abriko] *m* apricot; **abricotier** *m* apricot (tree)

abriter [abrite] ⟨1a⟩ (*loger*) take in, shelter; *~ de* (*protéger*) shelter from, protect from; *s'~* take shelter, take cover

abroger [abrɔʒe] ⟨1l⟩ JUR repeal

abrupt, **~e** [abrypt] *pente* steep; *personne*, *ton* abrupt

abruti, **~e** [abryti] stupid; **abrutir** ⟨2a⟩: *~ qn* turn s.o.'s brain to mush; (*surmener*) exhaust s.o.; **abrutissant**, **~e** *bruit* deafening; *travail* exhausting

absence [apsɑ̃s] *f* absence; **absent**, **~e** absent; *air* absent-minded; **absentéisme** *m* absenteeism; **absenter** ⟨1a⟩: *s'~* leave, go away

absolu, **~e** [apsɔly] absolute; **absolument** *adv* (*à tout prix*, *tout à fait*) absolutely

absolution [apsɔlysjɔ̃] *f* REL absolution

absorbant, **~e** [apsɔrbɑ̃, -t] absorbent; **absorber** ⟨1a⟩ absorb; *nourriture* eat; *boisson* drink; *s'~ dans qch* be absorbed *ou* engrossed in sth; **absorption** *f* absorption

absoudre [apsudr] ⟨4b⟩ absolve

abstenir [apstənir] ⟨2h⟩: *s'~* POL abstain; *s'~ de faire qch* refrain from doing sth; **abstention** *f* POL abstention; **abstentionniste** *m* POL abstainer

abstraction [apstraksjɔ̃] *f* abstraction; *faire ~ de qch* disregard sth; *~ faite de* leaving aside

abstrait, **~e** [apstrɛ, -t] abstract

absurde [apsyrd] absurd; **absurdité** *f* absurdity; **~(s)** nonsense *sg*

abus [aby] *m* abuse; *~ de confiance* breach of trust; **abuser** ⟨1a⟩ overstep the mark, be out of line; *~ de qch* misuse *ou* abuse sth; *s'~* be mistaken; *si je ne m'abuse* if I'm not mistaken; **abusif**, **-ive** excessive; *emploi d'un mot* incorrect

académicien [akademisjɛ̃] *m* academician (*especially of the Académie française*); **académie** *f* academy; **académique** academic

acajou [akaʒu] *m* mahogany

acariâtre [akarjɑtr] bad-tempered

accablant, **~e** [akablɑ̃, -t] *preuve* overwhelming; *chaleur* oppressive; **accabler** ⟨1a⟩: *être accablé de problèmes*, *soucis* be weighed down by, be overwhelmed by; *~ qn de qch* repro-

ches shower s.o. with sth, heap sth on s.o.

accalmie [akalmi] *f aussi fig* lull

accaparer [akapaʀe] ⟨1a⟩ ÉCON, *fig* monopolize; ~ **le** *marché* corner the market; **accapareur**: *il est* ~ he doesn't like sharing

accéder [aksede] ⟨1f⟩: ~ **à** reach, get to; INFORM access; *au pouvoir* gain, achieve; *d'un chemin* lead to

accélérateur [akseleratœʀ] *m* AUTO gas pedal, *Br* accelerator; **accélération** *f* acceleration; **accélérer** ⟨1f⟩ *aussi* AUTO accelerate, speed up

accent [aksɑ̃] *m* accent; *(intonation)* stress; *mettre l'~ sur qch fig* put the emphasis on sth; **accentuation** *f* stressing; *fig* growth; **accentuer** ⟨1n⟩ *syllabe* stress, accentuate

acceptable [akseptabl] acceptable; **acceptation** *f* acceptance; **accepter** ⟨1a⟩ accept; *(reconnaître)* agree; ~ **de** *faire qch* agree to do sth; *je n'accepte pas que tu fasses ça* I won't have you doing that

acception [aksɛpsjɔ̃] *f* sense

accès [aksɛ] *m aussi* INFORM access; MÉD fit; **accessible** *région, lecture, sujet* accessible (*à* to); *prix* affordable; ~ **à tous** accessible to all, within everyone's reach; **accession** *f* accession (*à* to)

accessoire [aksɛswaʀ] **1** *adj* incidental **2** *m* detail; ~**s** accessories; ~**s de théâtre** props

accident [aksidɑ̃] *m* accident; *événement fortuit* mishap; ~ **de** *terrain* bump, unevenness in the ground; ~ **de** *travail* accident in the workplace, work-related accident; *par* ~ by accident, accidentally; *dans un* ~ in an accident; ~ *avec délit de fuite* hit-and-run accident; ~ *mortel* fatality, fatal accident; **accidenté,** ~**e** damaged (in an accident); *terrain* uneven; **accidentel,** ~**le** accidental; **accidentellement** *adv* accidentally

acclamation [aklamasjɔ̃] *f* acclamation; ~**s** cheers, cheering *sg*; **acclamer** ⟨1a⟩ cheer

acclimatation [aklimatasjɔ̃] *f* acclimatization; **acclimater** ⟨1a⟩: *s'~* become acclimatized

accointances [akwɛ̃tɑ̃s] *fpl souvent péj* contacts; *avoir des* ~ *avec qn* have dealings with s.o.

accolade [akɔlad] *f* embrace; *signe* brace, *Br* curly bracket

accommodation [akɔmɔdasjɔ̃] *f* adaptation; **accommodement** *m* compromise; **accommoder** ⟨1a⟩ adapt; CUIS prepare; *s'~ à* adapt to; *s'~ de* put up with, make do with

accompagnateur, -trice [akɔ̃paɲatœʀ, -tʀis] *m/f* guide; MUS accompanist; **accompagnement** *m* MUS accompaniment; **accompagner** ⟨1a⟩ go with, accompany; MUS accompany

accompli, ~**e** [akɔ̃pli] accomplished; **accomplir** ⟨2a⟩ accomplish; *souhait* realize, carry out; **accomplissement** *m* accomplishment

accord [akɔʀ] *m* agreement, consent; *(pacte)* agreement; MUS chord; *d'~* OK, alright; *être d'~* agree (*avec* with); *tomber d'~* come to an agreement, reach agreement; *avec l'~ de* with the agreement of; *en* ~ *avec* in agreement with; *donner son* ~ give one's consent, agree; ~ *d'extradition* extradition treaty

accordé, ~**e** [akɔʀde]: *(bien)* ~ in tune

accordéon [akɔʀdeɔ̃] *m* accordion

accorder [akɔʀde] ⟨1a⟩ *crédit, délai* grant, give; GRAM make agree; MUS tune; ~ *un sursis à* reprieve, grant a reprieve to; *s'~* get on; GRAM agree; *s'~ pour faire qch* agree to do sth; *s'~ qch* allow o.s. sth

accostage [akɔstaʒ] *m* MAR bringing alongside; **accoster** ⟨1a⟩ **1** *v/i* MAR come alongside **2** *v/t* personne approach

accotement [akɔtmɑ̃] *m* shoulder

accouchement [akuʃmɑ̃] *m* birth; **accoucher** ⟨1a⟩ give birth (*de* to); **accoucheur, -euse** *m/f* midwife; *médecin* obstetrician

accouder [akude] ⟨1a⟩: *s'~* lean (one's elbows); **accoudoir** *m* armrest

accouplement [akupləmã] *m* connection; BIOL mating; **accoupler** ⟨1a⟩ connect; **s'~** BIOL mate

accourir [akurir] ⟨2i⟩ come running

accoutrement [akutrəmã] *m* péj get--up; **accoutrer** ⟨1a⟩: **s'~** dress

accoutumance [akutymãs] f MÉD dependence; **accoutumé, ~e** usual; **être ~ à qch** be used to sth; **accoutumer** ⟨1a⟩: **~ qn à qch** get s.o. used to sth, accustom s.o. to sth; **s'~ à qch** get used to sth

accréditer [akredite] ⟨1a⟩ give credence to

accro [akro] F addicted (*à* to)

accroc [akro] *m* (*déchirure*) tear; (*obstacle*) hitch

accrochage [akrɔʃaʒ] *m* AUTO (minor) collision, fender-bender F; **accrocher** ⟨1a⟩ *tableau* hang (up); *manteau* hang up; AUTO collide with; **~ le regard** be eye-catching; **s'~ à** hang on to, hold tight to; *fig* cling to; **accrocheur, -euse** eye-catching

accroissement [akrwasmã] *m* increase; **~ démographique** population growth; **accroître** ⟨4w⟩ increase; **s'~** grow

accroupir [akrupir] ⟨2a⟩: **s'~** crouch, squat; **accroupis** squatting on their haunches

accru, ~e [akry] **1** p/p → **accroître 2** *adj* increased, greater

accu [aky] *m* F battery

accueil [akœj] *m* reception, welcome; **accueillant, ~e** friendly, welcoming; **accueillir** ⟨2c⟩ greet, welcome

accumulateur [akymylatœr] *m* battery; **accumulation** f accumulation; **accumuler** ⟨1a⟩ accumulate; **s'~** accumulate, pile up

accusateur, -trice [akyzatœr, -tris] *m/f* accuser; **accusation** f accusation; JUR prosecution; *plainte* charge; **accusé, ~e** *m/f* **1** JUR: *l'~* the accused **2** COMM: *accusé m de réception* acknowledgement (of receipt); **accuser** ⟨1a⟩ (*incriminer*) accuse (*de* of); (*faire ressortir*) emphasize; **~ réception de qch** COMM acknowledge receipt of sth

acerbe [asɛrb] caustic

acéré, ~e [asere] sharp (*aussi fig*)

acétique [asetik] acetic; **acide** *m ~* acetic acid; **acétone** f CHIM acetone

achalandage [aʃalãdaʒ] *m* custom

acharné, ~e [aʃarne] *combat, efforts* desperate; **~ à faire qch** desperate to do sth; **acharnement** *m* grim determination, desperation; **acharner** ⟨1a⟩: **s'~ à faire qch** be bent on doing sth; **s'~ sur** *ou* **contre qn** pick on s.o., have it in for s.o.

achat [aʃa] *m* purchase; **pouvoir** *m* **d'~** purchasing power; **prix** *m* **d'~** purchase price; **faire des ~s** go shopping

acheminer [aʃmine] ⟨1a⟩ *paquet* dispatch; **s'~ vers** make one's way toward

acheter [aʃte] ⟨1e⟩ buy; **~ qch à qn** (*pour qn*) buy sth for s.o.; (*de qn*) buy sth from s.o.; **~ qn** bribe s.o., buy s.o. off F; **acheteur, -euse** *m/f* buyer, purchaser

achèvement [aʃɛvmã] *m* completion

achever [aʃve] ⟨1d⟩ finish; **~ de faire qch** finish doing sth; **s'~** finish; **~ qn** *fig* finish s.o. off

acide [asid] **1** *adj* sour; CHIM acidic **2** *m* CHIM acid; **acidité** f sourness; CHIM acidity

acier [asje] *m* steel; **d'~** *regard* steely; **aciérie** [asjeri] f steel plant

acné [akne] f acne

acolyte [akɔlit] *m* péj crony

acompte [akõt] *m* installment, Br instalment; **par ~s** in installments

à-côté [akote] *m* (*pl* à-côtés) side issue; **~s de revenus** extras, perks F

à-coup [aku] *m* (*pl* à-coups) jerk; **par ~s** in fits and starts

acoustique [akustik] **1** *adj* acoustic; **appareil** *m ~* hearing aid **2** f acoustics

acquéreur [akerœr] *m* purchaser; **acquérir** ⟨2l⟩ acquire; *droit* win; *coutume* acquire, get into

acquiescer [akjese] ⟨1k⟩: **~ à** agree to

acquis, ~e [aki] **1** p/p → **acquérir 2** *adj* acquired; *résultats* achieved; **c'est un point ~** it's an established

fact; **considérer qn / qch comme ~**
take s.o. / sth for granted
acquisition [akizisjɔ̃] *f* acquisition
acquit [aki] *m* COMM: **pour~** received
with thanks; **par ~ de conscience**
fig to set my / his *etc* mind at rest
acquittement [akitmɑ̃] *m d'une dette*
discharge; JUR acquittal; **acquitter**
⟨1a⟩ *facture, dette* pay; JUR acquit;
s'~ de carry out; *dette* pay
acres [ɑkr] *mpl* acreage *sg*
âcre [ɑkr] acrid; *goût, fig* bitter;
âcreté *f au goût, fig* bitterness
acrimonieux, -euse [akrimɔnjø, -z]
acrimonious
acrobate [akrɔbat] *m/f* acrobat; **acrobatie** *f* acrobatics *pl*; **acrobatique**
acrobatic
acronyme [akrɔnim] *m* acronym
acrylique [akrilik] *m* acrylic
acte [akt] *m (action)* action, deed; *(document officiel)* deed; THÉÂT act;
faire ~ de présence put in an appearance; **dresser un ~** draw up a
deed; **prendre ~ de qch** note sth;
~ de décès death certificate; **~ de
mariage** marriage certificate; **~ de
naissance** birth certificate; **~ de
vente** bill of sale
acteur, -trice [aktœr, -tris] *m/f* actor;
actress
actif, -ive [aktif, -iv] **1** *adj* active **2** *m*
COMM assets *pl*; **activiste** *m/f* activist
action [aksjɔ̃] *f aussi* JUR action;
COMM share; **~s** stock *sg*, shares *pl*;
actionnaire *m/f* shareholder
actionnement [aksjɔnmɑ̃] *m* TECH
operation; *d'une alarme etc* activation; **actionner** ⟨1a⟩ TECH operate;
alarme etc activate
activer [aktive] ⟨1a⟩ *(accélérer)* speed
up
activité [aktivite] *f* activity
actualiser [aktyalize] update, bring
up to date
actualité [aktyalite] *f* current events
pl; **d'~** topical; **~s** TV news *sg*
actuel, ~le [aktyɛl] *(présent)* current,
present; *(d'actualité)* topical; **actuellement** *adv* currently, at present
acuité [akyite] *f des sens* shrewdness;

d'une douleur intensity, acuteness
acupuncteur, -trice [akypɔ̃ktœr,
-tris] *m/f* acupuncturist; **acupuncture** *f* acupuncture
adaptabilité [adaptabilite] *f* adaptability, versatility; **adaptable** adaptable; **adaptateur** *m* ÉL adapter;
adaptation *f* adaptation; **adapter**
⟨1a⟩ adapt; **s'~ à** adapt to
additif [aditif] *m* additive
addition [adisjɔ̃] *f aussi* MATH addition; *au restaurant* check, *Br* bill; **additionnel, ~le** additional; **additionner** ⟨1a⟩ MATH add (up); *(ajouter)*
add
adepte [adɛpt] *m/f* supporter; *d'une
activité, d'un sport* fan
adéquat, ~e [adekwa, -t] suitable;
montant adequate
adhérence [aderɑ̃s] *f* adherence; *des
pneus* grip; **adhérent, ~e** *m/f* member; **adhérer** ⟨1f⟩ stick, adhere (**à**
to); **~ à une doctrine** agree with
ou support a doctrine; **~ à un parti**
be a member of a party, belong to
a party; **~ à la route** grip *ou* hold
the road
adhésif, -ive [adezif, -iv] **1** *adj* sticky,
adhesive **2** *m* adhesive; **adhésion** *f*
membership; *(consentement)* support
(**à** for), agreement (**à** with)
adieu [adjø] *m* goodbye; **dire ~ à qn**
say goodbye to s.o., take one's leave
of s.o.; **~x** farewells; **faire ses ~x** say
one's goodbyes (**à qn** to s.o.)
adipeux, -euse [adipø, -z] fatty, adipose
adjacent, ~e [adʒasɑ̃, -t] adjacent
adjectif [adʒɛktif] *m* GRAM adjective
adjoindre [adʒwɛ̃dr] ⟨4b⟩: **~ à** add to;
s'~ qn hire *ou* recruit s.o.; **adjoint,
~e 1** *adj* assistant *atr*, deputy *atr*
2 *m/f* assistant, deputy; **~ au maire**
deputy mayor
adjudication [adʒydikasjɔ̃] *f dans
vente aux enchères* sale by auction; *travaux* award; *(attribution)* adjudication
adjuger [adʒyʒe] ⟨1l⟩ award
admettre [admɛtr] ⟨4p⟩ *(autoriser)* allow; *(accueillir)* admit, allow in; *(reconnaître)* admit; **~ que** (+ *ind ou subj*)

admit that; **admettons que, en admettant que** (+ *subj*) supposing *ou* assuming that

administrateur, -trice [administratœr, -tris] *m/f* administrator; **~ judiciaire** (official) receiver; **administratif, -ive** administrative; **administration** *f* administration; (*direction*) management, running; **administrer** ⟨1a⟩ administer; (*diriger*) manage

admirable [admirabl] admirable; **admirateur, -trice 1** *adj* admiring, of admiration **2** *m/f* admirer; **admiratif, -ive** admiring; **admiration** *f* admiration; **admirer** ⟨1a⟩ admire

admis [admi] admissible; **admissible** *candidat* eligible; **ce n'est pas ~** that's unacceptable

admission [admisjõ] *f* admission

A.D.N. [adeɛn] *m abr* (= **acide désoxyribonucléique**) DNA (=desoxyribonucleic acid)

adolescence [adɔlesɑ̃s] *f* adolescence; **adolescent, ~e** *m/f* adolescent, teenager

adonner [adɔne] ⟨1a⟩: **s'~ à qch** devote o.s. to sth; **s'~ à la boisson** drink, hit the bottle F

adopter [adɔpte] ⟨1a⟩ adopt; **adoptif, -ive** *enfant* adopted; *parent* adoptive; **adoption** *f* adoption; **patrie** *f* **d'~** adopted country

adorable [adɔrabl] adorable; **adorateur, -trice** *m/f* worshipper; (*admirateur*) admirer; **adoration** *f* adoration; **adorer** ⟨1a⟩ REL worship; *fig* (*aimer*) adore

adosser [adose] ⟨1a⟩ lean; **s'~ contre** *ou* **à** lean against *ou* on

adoucir [adusir] ⟨2a⟩ soften; **s'~ du temps** become milder; **adoucissant** *m* softener

adrénaline [adrenalin] *f* adrenalin

adresse [adrɛs] *f domicile* address; (*habileté*) skill; **à l'~ de qn** aimed at s.o., meant for s.o.; **~ électronique** e-mail address; **~ personnelle** home address; **adresser** ⟨1b⟩ *lettre* address (*à* to); *compliment, remarque* aim, direct (*à* at); **~ la parole à qn** address s.o., speak to s.o.; **s'~ à qn** apply to

s.o.; (*être destiné à*) be aimed at s.o.

adroit, ~e [adrwa, -t] skillful, *Br* skilful

adulateur, -trice [adylatœr, -tris] *m/f* idolizer; **aduler** ⟨1a⟩ idolize

adulte [adylt] **1** *adj* adult; *plante* mature **2** *m/f* adult, grown-up

adultère [adylter] **1** *adj* adulterous **2** *m* adultery

advenir [advənir] ⟨2h⟩ happen; **advienne que pourra** come what may

adverbe [adverb] *m* GRAM adverb

adversaire [adverser] *m/f* opponent, adversary

adverse [advers] adverse

adversité [adversite] *f* adversity

aérateur [aeratœr] *m* ventilator; **aération** *f* ventilation; **aérer** ⟨1f⟩ ventilate; *literie, pièce qui sent le renfermé* air; **aérien, ~ne** air *atr*, vue aerial; **pont** *m* **~** airlift

aérobic [aerobik] *f* aerobics

aéroclub [aerɔklœb] *m* flying club; **aérodrome** *m* airfield; **aérodynamique** aerodynamic; **aérogare** *f* air terminal, terminal building; **aéroglisseur** *m* hovercraft; **aéronautique 1** *adj* aeronautical **2** *f* aeronautics; **aéronef** *m* aircraft; **aéroport** *m* airport; **aéroporté** *troupes* airborne; **aérosol** *m* aerosol

affable [afabl] affable

affaiblir [afeblir] ⟨2a⟩ weaken; **s'~** weaken, become weaker; **affaiblissement** *m* weakening; (*déclin*) decline

affaire [afer] *f* (*question*) matter, business; (*entreprise*) business; *marché* deal; (*bonne occasion*) bargain; JUR case; (*scandale*) affair, business; **avoir ~ à qn** deal with s.o.; **se tirer d'~** get out of trouble; **~s** *biens personnels* things, belongings; **ce sont mes ~s** that's my business; **occupe-toi de tes affaires!** mind your own business!; **le monde des ~s** the business world; **les ~s étrangères** foreign affairs; **qui marche** going concern

affairé, ~e [afere] busy; **affairer** ⟨1b⟩: **s'~** busy o.s.

affaissement [afesmɑ̃] *m*: **~ de ter-**

rain subsidence; **affaisser** ⟨1b⟩: *s'~ du terrain* subside; *d'une personne* collapse

affamé, ~e [afame] hungry; *~ de gloire* hungry for fame

affectation [afɛktasjõ] *f d'une chose* allocation; *d'un employé* assignment, appointment; MIL posting; *(pose)* affectation; **affecté, ~e** affected; **affecter** ⟨1a⟩ *(destiner)* allocate, allot; *employé* assign, appoint; MIL post; *(émouvoir)* affect; *~ la forme de* have the shape of

affectif, -ive [afɛktif, -iv] emotional

affection [afɛksjõ] *f* affection; MÉD complaint

affectueux, -euse [afɛktɥø, -z] affectionate

affermir [afɛrmir] ⟨2a⟩ strengthen

affichage [afiʃaʒ] *m* billposting; INFORM display; *panneau m d'~* bulletin board; *Br* notice board; *~ à cristaux liquides* liquid crystal display; *~ numérique* digital display; *montre f à ~ numérique* digital watch

affiche [afiʃ] *f* poster; **afficher** ⟨1a⟩ *affiche* put up, stick up; *attitude* flaunt, display; INFORM display; *~ des bénéfices* post profits; **afficheur** *m* billposter

affilée [afile]: *d'~* at a stretch; **affiler** ⟨1a⟩ sharpen

affilier [afilje] ⟨1a⟩: *s'~ à* club, parti join; *être affilié à un parti* be a member of a party

affiner [afine] ⟨1a⟩ refine

affinité [afinite] *f* affinity

affirmatif, -ive [afirmatif, -iv] *réponse* affirmative; *personne* assertive; *répondre par l'affirmative* answer in the affirmative

affirmation [afirmasjõ] *f* statement; **affirmer** ⟨1a⟩ *(prétendre)* maintain; *volonté, autorité* assert

affligeant, ~e [afliʒã, -t] distressing, painful; **affliger** ⟨1l⟩ distress

affluence [aflyãs] *f*: *heures fpl d'~* rush hour *sg*; **affluent** [-ã] *m* tributary; **affluer** ⟨1a⟩ come together

afflux [afly] *m de capitaux* influx

affolement [afɔlmã] *m* panic; **affoler** ⟨1a⟩ *(bouleverser)* madden, drive to distraction; *d'une foule, d'un cheval* panic; *s'~* panic, get into a panic; *être affolé* be in a panic, be panic-stricken

affranchir [afrãʃir] ⟨2a⟩ *(libérer)* free; *lettre* meter, *Br* frank; **affranchissement** *m* montant postage

affréter [afrete] ⟨1f⟩ MAR, AVIAT charter

affreux, -euse [afrø, -z] horrible; *peur, mal de tête* terrible

affront [afrõ] *m* insult, affront; **affrontement** *m* POL confrontation; **affronter** ⟨1a⟩ confront, face; SP meet; *situation* face; *s'~* confront *ou* face each other; SP meet

affût [afy] *m*: *être à l'~ de qch* fig be on the lookout for sth

afin [afɛ̃]: *~ de faire qch* in order to do sth, so as to do sth; *~ que* (+ *subj*) so that; *~ de ne pas se mouiller* so as not to get wet; *~ qu'il soit mis au courant* so that he can be put in the picture

africain, ~e [afrikɛ̃, -ɛn] **1** *adj* African **2** *m/f* **Africain, ~e** African; **Afrique** *f*: *l'~* Africa

agaçant, ~e [agasã, -t] infuriating, annoying; **agacement** *m* annoyance; **agacer** ⟨1k⟩ annoy; *(taquiner)* tease

âge [aʒ] *m* age; *Moyen-Âge* Middle Ages *pl*; *personnes fpl du troisième ~* senior citizens; *retour m d'~* MÉD change of life; *quel ~ a-t--il?* how old is he?, what age is he?; *limite f d'~* age limit; *~ de la retraite* retirement age; *âgé, ~e* elderly; *~ de deux ans* aged two, two years old

agence [aʒãs] *f* agency; *d'une banque* branch; *~ immobilière* realtor, *Br* estate agent's; *~ de placement* employment agency; *~ de presse* news agency; *~ de publicité* advertising agency; *~ de voyages* travel agency

agencement [aʒãsmã] *m* layout, arrangement; **agencer** ⟨1k⟩ arrange

agenda [aʒɛ̃da] *m* diary; *~ électronique* (personal) organizer

agenouiller [aʒnuje] ⟨1a⟩ *s'~* kneel (down)

agent [aʒɑ̃] *m* agent; **~ d'assurance** insurance broker; **~ de change** stockbroker; **~ de la circulation** traffic policeman; **~ immobilier** realtor, *Br* real estate agent; **~ de police** police officer; **~ secret** secret agent

agglomération [aglɔmerasjɔ̃] *f* built-up area; *concentration de villes* conurbation; *l'~ parisienne* Greater Paris, the conurbation of Paris

aggloméré [aglɔmere] *m planche* chipboard, composite

aggraver ⟨1a⟩ make worse; **s'~** worsen, deteriorate

agile [aʒil] agile; **agilité** *f* agility

agios [aʒjo] *mpl* ÉCON bank charges

agir [aʒir] ⟨2a⟩ act; **~ sur qn** affect s.o.; *il s'agit de* it's about; *il s'agit de votre santé* it's a question *ou* a matter of your health; *il s'agit de ne pas faire d'erreurs* it's important not to make any mistakes

agitateur, -trice [aʒitatœr, -tris] *m/f* agitator, rabble-rouser; **agitation** [aʒitasjɔ̃] *f* hustle and bustle; POL unrest; *(nervosité)* agitation; **agité, ~e** agitated, restless; *mer* rough; **agiter** ⟨1a⟩ *bouteille, liquide* shake; *mouchoir, main* wave; *(préoccuper, énerver)* upset; **s'~** *d'un enfant* fidget; *(s'énerver)* get upset

agneau [aɲo] *m (pl -x)* lamb

agnostique [agnɔstik] *m/f* agnostic

agonie [agɔni] *f* death throes *pl*

agrafe [agraf] *f d'un vêtement* fastener, hook; *de bureau* staple; **agrafer** ⟨1a⟩ *vêtements* fasten; *papier* staple; **agrafeuse** *f* stapler; *à tissu* staple gun

agrandir [agrɑ̃dir] ⟨2a⟩ *photographie, ouverture* enlarge; **agrandissement** *m* enlargement; *d'une ville* expansion; **agrandisseur** *m* enlarger

agréable [agreabl] pleasant (*à* to); **agréer** ⟨1a⟩: *veuillez ~, Monsieur, mes salutations distinguées* Yours truly

agrégation [agregasjɔ̃] *f d'un compétitive examination for people wanting to teach at college and university level*

agrément [agremɑ̃] *m (consentement)* approval, consent; *les ~s (attraits)* the delights

agresser [agrese] ⟨1b⟩ attack; **agresseur** *m* attacker; *pays* aggressor; **agressif, -ive** aggressive; **agression** *f* attack; PSYCH stress; **agressivité** *f* aggressiveness

agricole [agrikɔl] agricultural, farm *atr*, **ouvrier** *m* **~** agricultural laborer *ou Br* labourer, farm worker

agriculteur [agrikyltœr] *m* farmer; **agriculture** *f* agriculture, farming

agripper [agripe] ⟨1a⟩ clutch; **s'~ à qch** clutch sth, cling to sth

agroalimentaire [agroalimɑ̃ter] *f* food industry, agribusiness

agronome [agrɔnɔm] *m* agronomist, agricultural economist; **ingénieur** *m* **~** agricultural engineer

agrumes [agrym] *mpl* citrus fruit *sg*

aguerri, ~e [ageri] *(expérimenté)* veteran

aguets [age]: *être aux ~* be on the lookout

ahuri, ~e [ayri] astounded, thunderstruck; **ahurir** ⟨2a⟩ astound; **ahurissant, ~e** astounding

aide [ed] **1** *f* help, assistance; *à l'~ de qch* with the help of sth, using sth; *avec l'~ de qn* with s.o.'s help; *appeler à l'~* shout for help **2** *m/f (assistant)* assistant; **~-soignant** *m* orderly; **aider** ⟨1b⟩ *v/t* help; **s'~ de qch** use sth **2** *v/i* help; **~ à qch** contribute to sth

aïeul, ~e [ajœl] *m/f* ancestor; **aïeux** ancestors

aigle [egl] *m* eagle

aiglefin [egləfɛ̃] *m* haddock

aigre [egr] sour; *vent* bitter; *paroles, critique* sharp; *voix* shrill; **aigre-doux, aigre-douce** CUIS sweet and sour

aigreur [egrœr] *f* sourness; *fig* bitterness; **aigrir** ⟨2a⟩ turn sour; *fig* make bitter, embitter

aigu, ~ë [egy] sharp; *son* high-pitched; *conflit* bitter; *intelligence* keen; MÉD, GÉOM, GRAM acute

aiguille [egɥij] *f* needle; *d'une montre* hand; *tour* spire; **~ à tricoter** knitting needle; **aiguiller** ⟨1a⟩ *fig* steer, guide; **aiguilleur** *m* AVIAT: *~ du ciel* air-traffic controller

aiguillon [eguijõ] *m* (*dard*) sting; **aiguillonner** ⟨1a⟩ *fig* spur (on)

aiguiser [egize] ⟨1a⟩ sharpen; *fig: appétit* whet

ail [aj] *m* (*pl* ails, *parfois* aulx [o]) garlic; **gousse** *f* **d'~** clove of garlic

aile [el] *f* wing; AUTO fender, *Br* wing

ailier [elje] *m* SP wing, winger

ailleurs [ajœr] somewhere else, elsewhere; *d'~* besides; *par ~* moreover; *nulle part ~* nowhere else

aimable [emabl] kind

aimant[1], **~e** [emã, -t] loving

aimant[2] [emã] *m* magnet; **aimanter** ⟨1a⟩ magnetize

aimer [eme] ⟨1b⟩ like; *parent, enfant, mari etc* love; *~ mieux* prefer, like ... better; *~ faire qch* like to do sth; *~ mieux faire qch* prefer to do sth; *je l'aime bien* I like him (a lot), I really like him

aine [en] *f* groin

aîné, ~e [ene] **1** *adj de deux* elder; *de trois ou plus* eldest **2** *m/f* elder / eldest; *il est mon ~* he is older than me; *il est mon ~ de deux ans* he is two years older than me

ainsi [ẽsi] this way, thus *fml*; *~ que* and, as well as; *~ soit-il!* so be it; *pour ~ dire* so to speak

aïoli [ajɔli] *m* CUIS *mayonnaise flavored with garlic*

air [er] *m* atmosphérique, vent air; aspect, expression look; MUS tune; *en plein ~* in the open; *menace f en l'~* empty threat; *avoir l'~ fatigué* look tired; *il a l'~ de ne pas écouter* he looks as if he isn't listening, he appears not to be listening; *se donner des ~s* give o.s. airs; *~ conditionné* air conditioning

airbag [erbag] *m* airbag

aire [er] *f* area; *~ de jeu* playground; *~ de repos* picnic area

aisance [ezãs] *f* (*naturel*) ease; (*richesse*) wealth

aise [ez] *f* ease; *à l'~, à son ~* comfortable; *être à l'~* be comfortable; *dans une situation* be comfortable, feel at

ease; *être mal à l'~* be uncomfortable; *dans une situation* be uncomfortable, feel ill at ease; *se mettre à l'~* make o.s. comfortable; *en faire à son ~* do as one pleases; *prendre ses ~s* make o.s. at home; aisé, *~e* (*facile*) easy; (*assez riche*) comfortable; **aisément** *adv* easily

aisselle [esel] *f* armpit

ajournement [aʒurnəmã] *m* postponement; JUR adjournment; **ajourner** ⟨1a⟩ postpone (*d'une semaine* for a week); JUR adjourn

ajouter [aʒute] ⟨1a⟩ add; *s'~ à* be added to

ajusté, ~e [aʒyste]: (*bien*) *~* close-fitting; **ajustement** *m* adjustment; **ajuster** ⟨1a⟩ adjust; *vêtement* alter; (*viser*) aim at; (*joindre*) fit (*à* to)

alarmant, ~e [alarmã, -t] alarming; **alarme** *f* signal, *inquiétude* alarm; *donner l'~* raise the alarm; *~ antivol* burglar alarm; **alarmer** ⟨1a⟩ alarm; *s'~ de* be alarmed by; **alarmiste** *m/f* alarmist

Albanie [albani] *f: l'~* Albania; **albanais, ~e 1** *adj* Albanian **2** *m langue* Albanian **3** *m/f* **Albanais, ~e** Albanian

album [albɔm] *m* album; *~ photos* photo album

alcool [alkɔl] *m* alcohol; **alcoolémie** *f: taux m d'~* blood alcohol level; **alcoolique** *adj & m/f* alcoholic; **alcoolisé, ~e** alcoholic; **alcoolisme** alcoholism

alco(o)test [alkɔtest] *m* Breathalyzer®, *Br* Breathalyser®

aléas [alea] *mpl* risks, hazards; **aléatoire** uncertain; INFORM, MATH random

alentour [alãtur] **1** *adv* around about **2**: *~s mpl* surroundings; *aux ~s de* in the vicinity of; (*autour de*) about

alerte [alert] **1** *adj* alert **2** *f* alert; *donner l'~ à qn* alert s.o.; *~ à la bombe* bomb scare; **alerter** ⟨1a⟩ alert

algèbre [alʒebr] *f* algebra

Algérie [alʒeri] *f: l'~* Algeria; **algérien, ~ne 1** *adj* Algerian **2** *m/f* Algérien, ~ne Algerian

algue [alg] *f* BOT seaweed

alibi [alibi] *m* alibi

aliéner ⟨1f⟩ alienate

alignement [aliɲmɑ̃] *m* alignment (**sur** with); (*rangée*) line, row; **aligner** ⟨1a⟩ TECH align, line up (**sur** with); (*mettre sur une ligne*) line up; *s'~* line up; *s'~ sur qch* align o.s. with sth

aliment [alimɑ̃] *m* foodstuff; *~s* food *sg*; *~s diététiques* health food; *~s surgelés* deep-frozen food; **alimentaire** food *atr*; **chaîne** *f ~* food chain; **alimentation** *f* food; *en eau, en électricité* supply; *~ de base* staple diet; *~ en courant (électrique)* power supply; *~ énergique* energy supply; **alimenter** ⟨1a⟩ feed; *en eau, en électricité* supply (**en** with); *conversation* keep going

alinéa [alinea] *m* paragraph

aliter [alite] ⟨1a⟩: *être alité(e)* be in bed; *s'~* take to one's bed

allaiter [alete] ⟨1b⟩ breast-feed

allant [alɑ̃] *m* energy, drive

allécher [aleʃe] ⟨1f⟩ tempt

allée [ale] *f* (*avenue*) path; *~s et venues* comings and goings; *des ~s et venues continuelles* a constant to-and-fro *sg*

allégation [alegasjɔ̃] *f* allegation

allégé, ~e [aleʒe] *yaourt* low-fat; *confiture* low-sugar; *~ à 5% de ...* 95% ...-free; **alléger** ⟨1g⟩ lighten, make lighter; *impôt* reduce; *tension* alleviate

allègre [alɛgr] cheerful; **allégrement** *adv* cheerfully

alléguer [alege] ⟨1f⟩ *excuse* put forward, offer

Allemagne [almaɲ] *f*: *l'~* Germany; **allemand, ~e 1** *adj* German **2** *m langue* German **3** *m/f* Allemand, ~e German

aller [ale] ⟨1o⟩ **1** *v/i* (*aux être*) go; *~ en voiture* drive, go by car; *~ à ou en bicyclette* cycle, go by bike; *~ chercher* go for, fetch; *~ voir qn* go and see s.o.; *comment allez-vous?* how are you?; *je vais bien* I'm fine; *ça va?* is that OK?; (*comment te portes-tu?*) how are you?, how are things?; *ça va bien merci* fine, thanks; *~ bien avec* go well with; *cela me va pour projet, proposition* that's fine by me, that suits me; *il y a de sa réputation* his reputation is at stake; *on y va!* F let's go!; *il va sans dire* needless to say, it goes without saying; *allez!* go on!; *allons!* come on!; *allons donc!* come now!; *s'en ~* leave; *d'une tâche* disappear; *cette couleur te va bien* that color really suits you **2** *v/aux*: *je vais partir demain* I'm going to leave tomorrow, I'm leaving tomorrow; *j'allais dire* I was going to say, I was about to say

3 *m*: *~ et retour* round trip, *Br* return trip; *billet* round-trip ticket, *Br* return (ticket); *~ simple* one-way ticket, *Br* single; *match m ~* away game; *au pis ~* if the worst comes to the worst

allergie [alɛrʒi] *f* allergy; **allergique** allergic (*à* to)

alliage [aljaʒ] *m* CHIM alloy; **alliance** *f* POL alliance; (*mariage*) marriage; (*anneau*) wedding ring; **tante** *f par ~* aunt by marriage; **allié, ~e 1** *adj* allied; *famille* related by marriage **2** *m/f* ally; *famille* relative by marriage; **allier** ⟨1a⟩ combine (*à* with, and); *s'~ à qn* ally o.s. with s.o.

allô [alo] hello

allocation [alɔkasjɔ̃] *f* allowance; *~s familiales* dependents' allowance *sg*, *Br* child benefit *sg*; *~ chômage* workers' compensation, *Br* unemployment benefit

allocution [alɔkysjɔ̃] *f* speech

allonger [alɔ̃ʒe] ⟨1l⟩ lengthen, make longer; *bras, jambes* stretch out; *~ le pas* lengthen one's stride, step out; *s'~* get longer; (*s'étendre*) lie down; *être allongé* be lying down, be stretched out

allouer [alwe] ⟨1a⟩ allocate

allumage [alymaʒ] *m* AUTO ignition; **allumer** ⟨1a⟩ *v/t cigarette, feu, bougie* light; *chauffage, télévision etc* turn on, switch on **2** *v/i* turn *ou* switch on the lights on; **allumette** *f* match

allure [alyr] f (*démarche*) walk; (*vitesse*) speed; (*air*) appearance; **prendre des ~s de mannequin** act *ou* behave like a model; **avoir de l'~** have style *ou* class; **à toute ~** at top speed

allusion [alyzjõ] f allusion; **faire ~ à** allude to

alors [alɔr] (*à ce moment-là*) then; (*par conséquence*) so; **ça ~!** well!!; **~?** so?; **~ que** *temps* when; *opposition* while

alouette [alwɛt] f lark

alourdir [alurdir] ⟨2a⟩ make heavy

aloyau [alwajo] m sirloin

Alpes [alp] *fpl*: **les ~** the Alps

alpestre [alpɛstr] alpine

alphabet [alfabe] m alphabet; **alphabétique** alphabetical; **alphabétiser** teach to read and write

alpin, ~e [alpɛ̃, -in] alpine; **alpinisme** m mountaineering; **alpiniste** m/f mountaineer

Alsace [alzas] f: **l'~** Alsace; **alsacien, ~ne 1** *adj* of / from Alsace, Alsatian **2** m LING Alsace dialect **3** m/f **Alsacien, ~ne** inhabitant of Alsace

altercation [altɛrkasjõ] f argument, altercation *fml*

altérer [altere] ⟨1f⟩ *denrées* spoil; *couleur* fade; *vérité* distort; *texte* change, alter

altermondialiste [altɛrmõdjalist] m/f & *adj* alternative globalist

alternance [altɛrnɑ̃s] f alternation; *de cultures* rotation; **alternatif, -ive** alternative; **alternative** f alternative; **alternativement** alternately, in turn; **alterner** ⟨1a⟩ alternate

altimètre [altimetr] m altimeter; **altitude** f altitude

alto [alto] m MUS *saxophone, voix* alto; *instrument à cordes* viola

altruisme [altryism] m altruism; **altruiste 1** *adj* altruistic **2** m/f altruist

aluminium [alyminjɔm] m aluminum, *Br* aluminium

alunir [alynir] ⟨2a⟩ land on the moon; **alunissage** m moon landing

amabilité [amabilite] f kindness

amadouer [amadwe] ⟨1a⟩ softsoap

amaigri, ~e [amegri] thinner; **amaigrir** ⟨2a⟩: **~ qn** *de maladie* cause

s.o. to lose weight; **s'~** lose weight, get thinner

amalgame [amalgam] m mixture, amalgamation; **amalgamer** ⟨1a⟩ amalgamate

amande [amɑ̃d] f BOT almond

amant [amɑ̃] m lover

amarre [amar] f MAR mooring line; **amarrer** ⟨1a⟩ MAR moor

amas [ama] m pile, heap; **amasser** ⟨1a⟩ amass

amateur [amatœr] m *qui aime bien* lover; *non professionnel* amateur; **~ d'art** art lover; **en ~** *péj* as a hobby; **d'~** *péj* amateurish

ambages [ɑ̃baʒ] *fpl*: **sans ~** without beating about the bush

ambassade [ɑ̃basad] f embassy; **ambassadeur, -drice** m/f ambassador

ambiance [ɑ̃bjɑ̃s] f (*atmosphère*) atmosphere; **ambiant, ~e: température ~e** room temperature

ambidextre [ɑ̃bidekstr] ambidextrous

ambigu, ~ë [ɑ̃bigy] ambiguous; **ambiguïté** f ambiguity

ambitieux, -euse [ɑ̃bisjø, -z] **1** *adj* ambitious **2** m ambitious person; **ambition** f ambition; **ambitionner** ⟨1a⟩: **~ de faire qch** want to do sth

ambivalence [ɑ̃bivalɑ̃s] f ambivalence; **ambivalent, ~e** ambivalent

ambulance [ɑ̃bylɑ̃s] f ambulance; **ambulancier** m paramedic, *Br aussi* ambulance man

ambulant, ~e [ɑ̃bylɑ̃, -t] traveling, *Br* travelling, itinerant

âme [ɑm] f soul; **état m d'~** state of mind; **rendre l'~** breathe one's last; **~ charitable** do-gooder

amélioration [ameljɔrasjõ] f improvement; **améliorer** ⟨1a⟩ improve; **s'~** improve, get better

aménagé, ~e [amenaʒe]: **cuisine f ~e** fitted kitchen; **aménagement** m arrangement, layout; *d'une vieille maison* conversion; **aménager** ⟨1l⟩ *appartement* arrange, lay out; *terrain* develop; *vieille maison* convert

amende [amɑ̃d] f fine; **sous peine d'~** or you will be liable to a fine

amendement [amɑ̃dmɑ̃] m improve-

ment; POL amendment; **amender**
⟨1a⟩ improve; *projet de loi* amend
amener [amne] ⟨1d⟩ bring; *(causer)*
cause; **~ qn à faire qch** get s.o. to
do sth; **s'~** turn up
amer, -ère [amɛr] bitter
américain, ~e [amerikɛ̃, -ɛn] **1** *adj*
American **2** *m* LING American English **3** *m/f* **Américain, ~e** American;
américaniser Americanize
amérindien, ~ne [amerɛ̃djɛ̃, -ɛn] **1**
adj Native American, Amerindian;
2 *m/f* **Amérindien, ~ne** Native
American, Amerindian
Amérique [amerik] *f:* **l'~** America; **l'~
centrale** Central America; **l'~ latine**
Latin America; **l'~ du Nord** North
America; **l'~ du Sud** South America;
les Amériques the Americas
amerrir [amerir] ⟨2a⟩ AVIAT splash
down; **amerrissage** *m* splashdown
amertume [amɛrtym] *f* bitterness
ameublement [amœbləmɑ̃] *m (meubles)* furniture
ameuter [amøte] ⟨1a⟩ rouse
ami, ~e [ami] **1** *m/f* friend; *(amant)*
boyfriend; *(maîtresse)* girlfriend; **petit
~** boyfriend; **petite ~e** girlfriend; **devenir ~ avec qn** make friends with
s.o. **2** *adj* friendly; **amiable: à l'~**
amicably; JUR out of court; *arrangement* amicable, friendly; JUR out-
-of-court
amiante [amjɑ̃t] *m* asbestos
amical, ~e [amikal] *(mpl -aux)* **1** *adj*
friendly **2** *f* association; **amicalement** in a friendly way
amincir [amɛ̃sir] ⟨2a⟩ **1** *v/t chose*
make thinner; *d'une robe* make look
thinner **2** *v/i* get thinner
amiral [amiral] *m (pl -aux)* admiral
amitié [amitje] *f* friendship; **~s** best
wishes, regards
amnésie [amnezi] *f* amnesia
amnistie [amnisti] *f* amnesty
amoindrir [amwɛ̃drir] ⟨2a⟩ diminish,
lessen; *mérite* detract from; **s'~** diminish; **amoindrissement** *m* decline, decrease
amollir [amɔlir] ⟨2a⟩ soften
amonceler [amɔ̃sle] ⟨1c⟩ pile up

amont [amɔ̃]: **en ~** upstream (**de** from)
amoral, ~e [amɔral] *(mpl -aux)* amoral
amorce [amɔrs] *f (début)* beginning;
amorcer ⟨1k⟩ begin; INFORM boot
up
amorphe [amɔrf] *sans énergie* listless
amortir [amɔrtir] ⟨2a⟩ *choc* cushion;
bruit muffle; *douleur* dull; *dettes* pay
off; **amortisseur** *m* AUTO shock absorber
amour [amur] *m* love; **mon ~** my love,
darling; **~s** love life *sg*; **faire l'~** make
love; **amoureux, -euse** *regard* loving; *vie* love *atr*; *personne* in love
(**de** with); **tomber ~** fall in love
amour-propre [amurprɔpr] *m* pride
amovible [amɔvibl] *housse* removable
amphibie [ɑ̃fibi] amphibious
amphithéâtre [ɑ̃fiteɑtr] *m d'université*
lecture hall; *(théâtre classique)* am-
phitheater, *Br* amphitheatre
ample [ɑ̃pl] *vêtements* loose, roomy;
sujet, matière broad, wide; *ressources*
ample; **pour de plus ~s informations** for more *ou* further information; **amplement** *décrire, expliquer*
fully; **c'est ~ suffisant** it's more than
enough; **ampleur** *f d'un désastre* extent, scale; *d'une manifestation* size
amplificateur [ɑ̃plifikatœr] *m* TECH
amplifier; **amplification** *f* TECH amplification; *fig* growth, expansion;
amplifier ⟨1a⟩ TECH amplify; *fig:
problème, scandale* magnify; *idée* expand, develop
amplitude [ɑ̃plityd] *f* PHYS amplitude
ampoule [ɑ̃pul] *f sur la peau* blister; *de
médicament* ampoule; *lampe* bulb
amputation [ɑ̃pytasjɔ̃] *f* amputation;
amputer ⟨1a⟩ amputate; *fig* cut
amusant, ~e [amyzɑ̃, -t] funny, entertaining, amusing
amuse-gueule [amyzgœl] *m (pl inv)*
appetizer, nibble F
amusement [amyzmɑ̃] *m* amusement; **amuser** ⟨1a⟩ amuse; *(divertir)*
entertain, amuse; **s'~** have a good
time, enjoy o.s.; **amuse-toi bien!**
have fun!, enjoy yourself!; **s'~ à faire
qch** have fun doing sth, enjoy doing

sth; *faire qch pour s'~* do sth for fun; *s'~ de* make fun of

amygdale [ami(g)dal] *f* ANAT tonsil; **amygdalite** *f* tonsillitis

an [ɑ̃] *m* year; *le jour ou le premier de l'~* New Year's Day, New Year's; *bon ~, mal ~* averaged out over the years; *deux fois par ~* twice a year; *20 000 euros par ~* 20,000 euros a year ou per annum; *elle a 15 ~s* she's 15 (years old); *tous les ~s* every year; *l'~ prochain* next year; *l'~ dernier* last year

anachronisme [anakrɔnism] *m* anachronism

analgésique [analʒezik] *m* PHARM analgesic, pain killer

analogie [analɔʒi] *f* analogy; **analogique** INFORM analog; **analogue** analogous (*à* with), similar (*à* to)

analphabète [analfabɛt] *m/f* illiterate; **analphabétisme** *m* illiteracy

analyse [analiz] *f* analysis; *de sang* test; **analyser** ⟨1a⟩ analyze, *Br* analyse; *sang* test; **analyste** *m/f* analyst; **analytique** analytical

ananas [anana(s)] *m* BOT pineapple

anarchie [anarʃi] *f* anarchy; **anarchiste** *m* anarchist

anatomie [anatɔmi] *f* anatomy

ancêtres [ɑ̃sɛtr] *mpl* ancestors

anchois [ɑ̃ʃwa] *m* anchovy

ancien, ~ne [ɑ̃sjɛ̃, -ɛn] old; (*précédent*) former, old; *de l'Antiquité* ancient; *~ combattant* (war) veteran, vet F; **anciennement** *adv* formerly; **ancienneté** *f* dans une profession seniority

ancre [ɑ̃kr] *f* anchor; **ancrer** ⟨1a⟩ anchor; *être ancré* be at anchor; *fig* embedded, be firmly rooted

Andorre [ɑ̃dɔr] *f*: *l'~* Andorra

andouille [ɑ̃duj] *f* CUIS *type of sausage*; *fig* F idiot, noodle F

âne [ɑn] *m* donkey; *fig* ass

anéantir [aneɑ̃tir] ⟨2a⟩ annihilate; **anéantissement** *m* annihilation

anecdote [anɛgdɔt] *f* anecdote

anémie [anemi] *f* MÉD anemia, *Br* anaemia; **anémique** anemic, *Br* anaemic

anesthésiant [anɛstezjɑ̃] *m* anesthetic, *Br* anaesthetic; **anesthésie** *f* MÉD anesthesia, *Br* anaesthesia; *~ générale / locale* general / local anesthetic; **anesthésier** ⟨1a⟩ anesthetize, *Br* anaesthetize; **anesthésique** *m* anesthetic, *Br* anaesthetic; **anesthésiste** *m/f* anesthesiologist, *Br* anaesthetist

ange [ɑ̃ʒ] *m* angel; *être aux ~s fig* be in seventh heaven; *~ gardien* guardian angel; **angélique** angelic

angine [ɑ̃ʒin] *f* MÉD throat infection; *~ de poitrine* angina

anglais, ~e [ɑ̃glɛ, -z] **1** *adj* English **2** *m langue* English **3** *m/f* **Anglais, ~e** Englishman; Englishwoman; *les ~* the English

angle [ɑ̃gl] *m* angle; (*coin*) corner; *~ droit* right angle; *~ mort* blind spot

Angleterre [ɑ̃glətɛr] *f*: *l'~* England

anglicisme [ɑ̃glisism] *m* anglicism

anglophone [ɑ̃glɔfon] English-speaking; **anglo-saxon** Anglo-Saxon

angoissant, ~e painful, distressing; **angoisse** *f* anguish, distress; **angoisser** ⟨1a⟩ distress

anguille [ɑ̃gij] *f* eel

anguleux, -euse [ɑ̃gylø, -z] angular

anicroche [anikrɔʃ] *f* hitch

animal [animal] (*mpl* -aux) **1** *m* animal; *~ domestique* pet **2** *adj* (*f ~e*) animal *atr*

animateur, -trice [animatœr, -tris] *m/f* d'une émission de radio, de télévision host, presenter; d'une discussion moderator; d'activités culturelles organizer, leader; d'une entreprise leader; **animation** de dessin animé animator; *f* (*vivacité*) liveliness; de mouvements hustle and bustle; de dessin animé animation; *~ (culturelle)* community-based activities *pl*; **animé, ~e** rue, quartier busy; conversation lively, animated; **animer** ⟨1a⟩ conversation, fête liven up; (*stimuler*) animate; discussion, émission host; *s'~* d'une rue, d'un quartier come to life, come alive; d'une personne become animated

animosité [animozite] *f* animosity

anis [anis] *m* aniseed; *liqueur aniseed-*

flavored alcoholic drink; **anisette** f aniseed-flavored alcoholic drink

anneau [ano] m (pl -x) ring

année [ane] f year; **les ~s 90** the 90s; **bonne ~!** happy New Year!; **~ fiscale** fiscal year; **~ sabbatique** sabbatical (year); **année-lumière** f light year

annexe [anɛks] f d'un bâtiment annex; d'un document appendix; d'une lettre enclosure, Br attachment; **annexer** ⟨1a⟩ document enclose, Br attach; pays annex

annihiler [aniile] ⟨1a⟩ annihilate

anniversaire [aniversɛr] m birthday; d'un événement anniversary; **~ de mariage** wedding anniversary

annonce [anõs] f (nouvelle) announcement; dans journal ad(vertisement); (présage) sign; **petites ~s** classified advertisements, classifieds; **annoncer** ⟨1k⟩ announce; **s'~ bien / mal** be off to a good / bad start; **annonceur** m dans un journal advertiser; TV, à la radio announcer

annotation [anɔtasjõ] f annotation; **annoter** ⟨1a⟩ annotate

annuaire [anɥɛr] m yearbook; **~ du téléphone** phone book

annuel, ~le [anɥɛl] annual, yearly

annulaire [anɥlɛr] m ring finger

annulation [anɥlasjõ] f cancellation; d'un mariage annulment; **annuler** ⟨1a⟩ cancel; mariage annul

anodin, ~e [anɔdɛ̃, -in] harmless; personne insignificant; blessure slight

anomalie [anɔmali] f anomaly

anonymat [anɔnima] m anonymity; **anonyme** anonymous; **société f ~** incorporated ou Br limited company

anorak [anɔrak] m anorak

anorexie [anɔrɛksi] f anorexia; **anorexique** anorexic

anormal, ~e [anɔrmal] abnormal

anse [ɑ̃s] f d'un panier etc handle; GÉOGR cove, bay

antagonisme [ɑ̃tagɔnism] m antagonism; **antagoniste 1** adj antagonistic **2** m/f antagonist

antarctique [ɑ̃tarktik] **1** adj Antarctic **2** m **l'Antarctique** Antarctica, the Antarctic

antécédents [ɑ̃teseda] mpl history sg

antenne [ɑ̃tɛn] f ZO antenna, feeler; TV, d'une radio antenna, Br aerial; **être à l'~** be on the air

antérieur, ~e [ɑ̃terjœr] (de devant) front; (d'avant) previous, earlier; **~ à** prior to, before

anthologie [ɑ̃tɔlɔʒi] f anthology

anthropologie [ɑ̃trɔpɔlɔʒi] f anthropology; **anthropologue** m/f anthropologist

antiadhésif, -ive [ɑ̃tiadezif, -iv] non-stick

antibiotique [ɑ̃tibjɔtik] m antibiotic

antibrouillard [ɑ̃tibrujar] m fog lamp

antibruit [ɑ̃tibrɥi] soundproof

antichoc [ɑ̃tiʃɔk] shock-proof

anticipation [ɑ̃tisipasjõ] f anticipation; **payer par ~** pay in advance; **d'~** film, roman science-fiction; **anticipé, ~e** early; paiement advance; **anticiper** ⟨1a⟩ anticipate; **~ un paiement** pay in advance

anticlérical, ~e [ɑ̃tiklerikal] (mpl -aux) anticlerical

anticonceptionnel, ~le [ɑ̃tikõsɛpsjɔnɛl] contraceptive

anticonstitutionnel, ~le [ɑ̃tikõstitysjɔnɛl] unconstitutional

anticorps [ɑ̃tikɔr] m antibody

antidater [ɑ̃tidate] ⟨1a⟩ backdate

antidérapant, ~e [ɑ̃tiderapɑ̃, -t] AUTO **1** adj non-skid **2** m non-skid tire, Br non-skid tyre

antidote [ɑ̃tidɔt] m MÉD antidote

antigel [ɑ̃tiʒɛl] m antifreeze

antillais, ~e [ɑ̃tije, -z] **1** adj West Indian **2** m/f **Antillais, ~e** West Indian; **Antilles** f / pl: **les ~** the West Indies

antimondialiste [ɑ̃timõdjalist] m/f & adj antiglobalist

antipathie [ɑ̃tipati] f antipathy; **antipathique** unpleasant

antipelliculaire [ɑ̃tipelikylɛr]: **shampoing** m **~** dandruff shampoo

antipode [ɑ̃tipɔd] m: **aux ~s** fig poles apart (de from)

antipollution [ɑ̃tipɔlysjõ] anti-pollution

antiquaire [ãtikɛr] *m* antique dealer; **antique** ancient; *meuble* antique; *péj* antiquated; **antiquités** *fpl* meubles, objets d'art antiques

antirouille [ãtiruj] antirust

antisocial, ~e [ãtisɔsjal] antisocial

antisémite [ãtisemit] **1** *adj* anti-Semitic **2** *m/f* anti-Semite

antiseptique [ãtisɛptik] *m & adj* antiseptic

antiterroriste [ãtiterɔrist] anti-terrorist

antivol [ãtivɔl] *m* anti-theft device

anxiété [ãksjete] *f* anxiety; **anxieux, -euse** anxious; **être ~ de faire qch** be anxious to do sth

août [u(t)] *m* August

apaiser [apeze] ⟨1b⟩ *personne* pacify, calm down; *douleur* soothe; *soif* slake; *faim* satisfy

apathie [apati] *f* apathy

apercevoir [apɛrsəvwar] ⟨3a⟩ see; **s'~ de qch** notice sth; **aperçu 1** *p/p* → **apercevoir 2** *m* broad outline

apéritif [aperitif] *m* aperitif; **apéro** *m* F → **apéritif**

apesanteur [apəzãtœr] *f* weightlessness

à-peu-près [apøprɛ] *m* (*pl inv*) approximation

apeuré, ~e [apœre] frightened

apitoyer [apitwaje] ⟨1h⟩: **~ qn** move s.o. to pity; **s'~ sur qn** feel sorry for s.o.

aplanir [aplanir] ⟨2a⟩ flatten, level; *fig: différend* smooth over; *difficultés* iron out

aplatir [aplatir] ⟨2a⟩ flatten; **s'~** (*s'écraser*) be flattened; **s'~ devant qn** kowtow to s.o.

aplomb [aplõ] *m* (*confiance en soi*) self-confidence; (*audace*) nerve; **d'~** vertical, plumb; **je ne suis pas d'~** *fig* I don't feel a hundred percent; **avec ~** confidently

apogée [apɔʒe] *m fig* height, peak

apolitique [apɔlitik] apolitical

apostrophe [apɔstrɔf] *f* (*interpellation*) rude remark; *signe* apostrophe; **apostropher** ⟨1a⟩: **~ qn** F shout at s.o., tear s.o. off a strip

apôtre [apotr] *m* apostle

apparaître [aparɛtr] ⟨4z⟩ appear; **faire ~** bring to light; **il apparaît que** it appears *ou* seems that, it would appear that

appareil [aparɛj] *m* device; AVIAT plane; **qui est à l'~?** TÉL who's speaking?, who's this?; **~ (dentaire)** brace; **~ ménager** household appliance; **~ photo** camera; **appareiller** ⟨1a⟩ match (*à* with); MAR set sail (*pour* for)

apparemment [aparamã] apparently

apparence [aparãs] *f* appearance; **en ~** on the face of things; **sauver les ~s** save face; **selon toute ~** judging by appearances; **apparent, ~e** (*visible*) visible; (*illusoire*) apparent

apparenté, ~e [aparãte] related (*à* to)

apparition [aparisjõ] *f* appearance

appartement [apartəmã] *m* apartment, *Br* flat

appartenance [apartənãs] *f à une association, à un parti* membership; **appartenir** ⟨2h⟩ belong (*à qn* to s.o.); **il ne m'appartient pas d'en décider** it's not up to me to decide

appât [apɑ] *m aussi fig* bait; **appâter** ⟨1a⟩ lure

appauvrir [apovrir] ⟨2a⟩ impoverish; **s'~** become impoverished; **appauvrissement** *m* impoverishment

appel [apɛl] *m* call; TÉL (telephone) call; (*exhortation*) appeal, call; MIL (*recrutement*) draft, *Br* call-up; JUR appeal; ÉDU roll-call; **faire ~** JUR appeal; **sans ~** final; **faire ~ à qch** (*nécessiter*) require; **faire ~ à qn** appeal to s.o.; **~ d'offres** invitation to tender; **appelé** *m* MIL conscript; **appeler** ⟨1c⟩ call; (*nécessiter*) call for; **en ~ à qn** approach s.o., turn to s.o.; **comment t'appelles-tu?** what's your name?, what are you called?; **je m'appelle ...** my name is ..., I'm called ...

appendice [apẽdis] *m* appendix; **appendicite** *f* MÉD appendicitis

appesantir [apəzãtir]: **s'~** grow heavier; **s'~ sur** dwell on

appétissant, ~e [apetisã, -t] appetizing; **appétit** *m* appetite; **bon ~!** enjoy (your meal)!

applaudir [aplodir] ⟨2a⟩ applaud, clap; **applaudissements** *mpl* applause *sg*, clapping *sg*

applicable [aplikabl] applicable; **applicateur** *m* applicator; **application** *f* application; **appliqué, ~e** *science* applied; **appliquer** ⟨1m⟩ apply; *loi* apply, enforce; **s'~ d'une personne** apply o.s., work hard; **~ Y sur X** smear X with Y, smear Y on X; **s'~ à qch** apply to sth; **s'~ à faire qch** take pains to do sth with

appointements [apwɛtmɑ̃] *mpl* salary *sg*

apport [apɔr] *m* contribution; **apporter** ⟨1a⟩ bring; **~ du soin à qch** take care over sth; **~ de l'attention à qch** pay attention to sth; **~ des raisons** provide reasons

apposer [apoze] ⟨1a⟩: **~ sa signature** append one's signature

appréciable [apresjabl] significant, appreciable; **appréciation** *f d'un prix, d'une distance* estimate; *(jugement)* comment, opinion; COMM appreciation; **apprécier** ⟨1a⟩ *valeur, distance* estimate; *personne, musique, la bonne cuisine* appreciate

appréhender [apreɑ̃de] ⟨1a⟩: **~ qch** be apprehensive about sth; **~ qn** JUR arrest s.o.; **appréhensif, -ive** apprehensive; **appréhension** *f* apprehension

apprendre [aprɑ̃dr] ⟨4q⟩ *leçon* learn; *nouvelle* learn, hear (*par qn* from s.o.); **~ qch à qn** *(enseigner)* teach s.o. sth; *(raconter)* tell s.o. sth; **~ à lire** learn to read

apprenti, ~e [aprɑ̃ti] *m/f* apprentice; *fig* beginner, novice; **~ conducteur** student driver, *Br* learner driver; **apprentissage** *m d'un métier* apprenticeship; *processus psychologique* learning

apprêté, ~e [aprete] affected; **apprêter** ⟨1a⟩ prepare; **s'~ à faire qch** prepare to do sth, get ready to do sth

apprivoiser [aprivwaze] ⟨1a⟩ tame

approbateur, -trice [aprɔbatœr, -tris] approving; **approbation** *f* approval

approche [aprɔʃ] *f* approach; **approcher** ⟨1a⟩ **1** *v/t* bring closer (*de* to) **2** *v/i* approach; **s'~ de** approach

approfondi, ~e [aprɔfɔ̃di] thorough, detailed; **approfondir** ⟨2a⟩ deepen; *(étudier)* go into in detail

approprié, ~e [aprɔprije] appropriate, suitable (*à* for); **approprier** ⟨1a⟩ **s'~ qch** appropriate sth

approuver [apruve] ⟨1a⟩ *projet, loi* approve; *personne, manières* approve of

approvisionnement [aprɔvizjɔnmɑ̃] *m* supply (*en* of); **approvisionner** ⟨1a⟩ supply; **~ un compte bancaire** pay money into a bank account

approximatif, -ive [aprɔksimatif, -iv] approximate; **approximation** *f* approximation; **approximativement** *adv* approximately

appui [apɥi] *m* support; *d'une fenêtre* sill; **prendre ~ sur** lean on; **à l'~ de** in support of; **preuves** *fpl* **à l'appui** supporting evidence *sg*; **appuie-tête** *m* (*pl* inv) headrest; **appuyer** ⟨1h⟩ **1** *v/t* lean; *(tenir debout)* support; *fig candidat, idée* support, back **2** *v/i*: **~ sur** *bouton* press, push; *fig* stress; **s'~ sur** lean on; *fig* rely on

âpre [apr] bitter

après [aprɛ] **1** *prép* after; **l'un ~ l'autre** one after the other; **~ coup** after the event; **~ quoi** and then, after that; **~ tout** after all; **~ avoir lu le journal, il ...** after reading the paper he ..., after having read the paper, he ...; **d'~ (ce que disent) les journaux** according to the papers, going by what the papers say **2** *adv* afterward, *Br aussi* afterwards **3** *conj*: **~ que** after; **~ qu'il soit** (*subj*) **parti nous avons ...** after he left we ...; **~ qu'il soit** (*subj*) **parti nous aurons ...** after he leaves we will have ...

après-demain [apredmɛ̃] the day after tomorrow

après-guerre [apreger] *m* (*pl* après--guerres) post-war period

après-midi [apremidi] *m ou f* (*pl inv*) afternoon

après-rasage [aprɛraza3]: *lotion* f ~ aftershave

après-vente [aprɛvɑ̃t]: *service* m ~ after-sales service

apr. J.-C. *abr* (= *après Jésus-Christ*) AD (= anno Domini)

à-propos [apropo] m aptness

apte [apt] apt (*à* to)

aptitude [aptityd] f aptitude

aquarelle [akwarɛl] f watercolor, Br watercolour

aquarium [akwarjɔm] m aquarium

aquatique [akwatik] aquatic; *oiseau* water *atr*

aqueduc [akdyk] m aqueduct

arabe [arab] **1** *adj* Arab **2** m *langue* Arabic **3** m/f **Arabe** Arab; **Arabie** f: *l'*~ **Saoudite** Saudi (Arabia)

arachide [araʃid] f BOT peanut

araignée [arɛɲe] f spider

arbitrage [arbitra3] m arbitration; *à la Bourse* arbitrage

arbitraire [-ɛr] arbitrary

arbitre [arbitr] m referee; *libre* ~ m free will; **arbitrer** ⟨1a⟩ arbitrate

arbre [arbr] m tree; TECH shaft; ~ **généalogique** family tree; ~ **de Noël** Christmas tree

arbuste [arbyst] m shrub

arc [ark] m ARCH arch; GÉOM arc

arcades [arkad] fpl ARCH arcade sg

arc-boutant [arkbutɑ̃] m (*pl* arcs-boutants) ARCH flying buttress

arc-en-ciel [arkɑ̃sjɛl] m (*pl* arcs-en-ciel) rainbow

archange [arkɑ̃3] m REL archangel

arche [arʃ] f arch; *Bible* Ark

archéologie [arkeɔlɔ3i] f archeology, Br archaeology; **archéologique** archeological, Br archaeological; **archéologue** m/f archeologist, Br archaeologist

archet [arʃɛ] m archer; MUS bow

archevêque [arʃəvɛk] m archbishop

architecte [arʃitɛkt] m/f architect; **architecture** f architecture

archives [arʃiv] fpl records, archives

arctique [arktik] **1** *adj* Arctic **2** m *l'*Arctique the Arctic

ardent, ~**e** [ardɑ̃, -t] *soleil* blazing; *désir* burning; *défenseur* fervent; ar-

deur f *fig* ardor, Br ardour

ardoise [ardwaz] f slate

ardu, ~**e** [ardy] arduous

arène [arɛn] f arena; ~**s** arena sg

arête [arɛt] f *d'un poisson* bone; *d'une montagne* ridge

argent [ar3ɑ̃] m silver; (*monnaie*) money; ~ **liquide** *ou* **comptant** cash; ~ **du ménage** housekeeping; ~ **de poche** allowance, Br pocket money; **argenterie** f silver(ware)

argentin, ~**e** [ar3ɑ̃tɛ̃, -in] **1** *adj* Argentinian **2** m/f **Argentin**, ~**e** Argentinian; **Argentine** f: *l'*~ Argentina

argile [ar3il] f GÉOL clay

argot [argo] m slang; **argotique** slang *atr*

argument [argymɑ̃] m argument; **argumenter** ⟨1a⟩ argue

aride [arid] arid, dry; *sujet* dry; **aridité** f aridity, dryness

aristocrate [aristɔkrat] m/f aristocrat; **aristocratie** f aristocracy; **aristocratique** aristocratic

arithmétique [aritmetik] **1** *adj* arithmetical **2** f arithmetic

armateur [armatœr] m shipowner

armature [armatyr] f structure, framework

arme [arm] f weapon (*aussi fig*); ~**s** (*blason*) coat of arms sg; ~ **à feu** firearm; **armé**, ~**e** armed (*de* with); *fig* equipped (*contre* for; *de* with); **armée** f army; ~ **de l'air** airforce; **Armée du Salut** Salvation Army; **armement** m arming; ~**s** *moyens d'un pays* armaments; **course** f **aux** ~**s** armaments race; **armer** ⟨1a⟩ arm (*de* with); *fig* equip (*de* with)

armistice [armistis] m armistice; *l'***Armistice** Veterans' Day, Br Remembrance Day

armoire [armwar] f cupboard; *pour les vêtements* closet, Br wardrobe

arnaque [arnak] f F rip-off F, con F; **arnaquer** ⟨1b⟩ F rip off F; **arnaqueur**, -**euse** m/f F hustler F

aromate [arɔmat] m herb; (*épice*) spice; **aromathérapie** m aromatherapy; **aromatique** aromatic; **arome**,

arôme *m* flavor, *Br* flavour; *(odeur)* aroma

arpenter [arpɑ̃te] ⟨1a⟩ measure; *fig: salle* pace up and down; **arpenteur** *m* surveyor

arrache-pied [araʃpje]: ***travailler d'~*** slave; **arracher** ⟨1a⟩ pull out; *pommes de terre* pull up, lift; *page* pull out, tear out; **~ qch à qn** snatch sth from s.o.; **~ un aveu à qn** extract a confession from s.o.; **s'~ à** *ou* **de qch** free o.s. from sth; **s'~ qch** fight over sth; **s'~ les cheveux** pull one's hair out

arrangeant, **~e** [arɑ̃ʒɑ̃] obliging; **arrangement** *m (disposition, accord)* MUS arrangement; **arranger** ⟨1l⟩ arrange; *objet* mend, fix; *différend* settle; F **~ qn** *(maltraiter)* beat s.o. up; ***cela m'arrange*** that suits me; **s'~ avec qn pour faire qch** come to an arrangement with s.o. about sth; ***tout s'arrange*** everything works out in the end; **s'~ pour faire qch** manage to do sth; **s'~ de qch** put up with sth

arrestation [arɛstasjõ] *f* arrest; ***en état d'~*** under arrest

arrêt [arɛ] *m (interruption)* stopping; *d'autobus* stop; JUR judgment; **sans ~** constantly; AUTO **à l'~** stationary; **~(s) de jeu** overtime, *Br* injury *ou* stoppage time; **~ de travail** work stoppage; **arrêté** *m* decree; **arrêter** ⟨1b⟩ **1** *v/i* stop **2** *v/t* stop; *moteur* turn off, switch off; *voleur* arrest; *jour, date* set, fix; **~ de faire qch** stop doing sth; **s'~** stop

arrhes [ar] *fpl* COMM deposit

arrière [arjɛr] **1** *adv* back; **en ~** backward; *regarder* back; *(à une certaine distance)* behind; **en ~ de** behind, at the back of **2** *adj inv feu* rear *atr*; **siège** *m* **~** back seat **3** *m* AUTO, SP back; **à l'~** in back, at the back

arriéré, **~e** [arjere] **1** *adj paiement* late, in arrears; *enfant, idées* backward **2** *m* COMM arrears *pl*

arrière-goût [arjɛrgu] *m* aftertaste

arrière-grand-mère [arjɛrɡrɑ̃mɛr] *f* (*pl* arrière-grand⟨s⟩-mères) great-grandmother; **arrière-grand-père** *m* (*pl* arrière-grands-pères) great-grandfather

arrière-pays [arjɛrpei] *m* hinterland

arrière-pensée [arjɛrpɑ̃se] *f* (*pl* arrière-pensées) ulterior motive, hidden agenda

arrière-petit-fils [arjɛrp(ə)tifis] *m* (*pl* arrière-petits-fils) great-grandson

arrière-plan [arjɛrplɑ̃] *m* background

arrière-saison [arjɛrsezõ] *f* fall, *Br* autumn

arrimer [arime] ⟨1a⟩ *chargement* stow

arrivage [arivaʒ] *m* consignment; **arrivée** *f* arrival; SP finish line, *Br* finishing line; **arriver** ⟨1a⟩ *(aux être)* arrive; *d'un événement* happen; **~ à un endroit** reach a place, arrive at a place; ***ses cheveux lui arrivent aux épaules*** her hair comes down to her shoulders; ***qu'est-ce qui est arrivé?*** what happened?; **~ à faire qch** manage to do sth; **~ à qn** happen to s.o.; ***il arrive qu'il soit (subj) en retard*** he's late sometimes; ***j'arrive!*** (I'm) coming!

arriviste [arivist] *m/f* social climber

ar(r)obase [arɔbaz] *f* INFORM at, at sign

arrogance [arɔgɑ̃s] *f* arrogance; **arrogant**, **~e** arrogant

arrondir [arõdir] ⟨2a⟩ *somme d'argent*: *vers le haut* round up; *vers le bas* round down; **arrondissement** *m* *d'une ville* district

arroser [aroze] ⟨1a⟩ water; **~ qch** *fig* have a drink to celebrate sth; **arrosoir** *m* watering can

arsenal [arsənal] *m* (*pl* -aux) MAR naval dockyard; MIL arsenal

arsenic [arsənik] *m* arsenic

art [ar] *m* art; **avoir l'~ de faire qch** have a knack *ou* a gift for doing sth; **~s décoratifs** decorative arts; **~s graphiques** graphic arts; **~s plastiques** fine arts

artère [artɛr] *f* ANAT artery; *(route)* main road

artériel, **~le** [arterjɛl]: **tension** *f* **artérielle** blood pressure; **artériosclérose** *f* MÉD hardening of the arteries

arthrite [artrit] *f* arthritis

artichaut [artiʃo] *m* artichoke; *cœur m d'~* artichoke heart

article [artikl] *m* article, item; JUR article, clause; *de presse*, GRAM article; **~ de fond** *presse* feature article; **~s de luxe** luxury goods

articulation [artikylasjõ] *f* ANAT joint; *d'un son* articulation; **articulé, ~e** *son* articulate; **articuler** ⟨1a⟩ *son* articulate

artifice [artifis] *m* trick; **artificiel, ~le** artificial

artillerie [artijri] *f* artillery

artisan [artizã] *m* craftsman; **artisanal, ~e** (*mpl* -aux) *tapis, poterie etc* hand-made; *fromage, pain etc* traditional; **artisanat** *m* crafts *pl*; **~ d'art** arts and crafts *pl*

artiste [artist] **1** *m/f* artist; *comédien, chanteur* performer **2** *adj* artistic; **artistique** artistic

as [as] *m* ace

asbeste [asbɛst] *m* asbestos

ascendance [asãdãs] *f* ancestry; **ascendant, ~e 1** upward **2** *m* influence (**sur** on, over)

ascenseur [asãsœr] *m* elevator, *Br* lift; **ascension** *f* *d'un alpiniste, d'une fusée, d'un ballon* ascent; *fig* (*progrès*) rise; *l'Ascension* REL Ascension

asiatique [azjatik] **1** *adj* Asian **2** *m/f* **Asiatique** Asian; **Asie** *f*: *l'~* Asia

asile [azil] *m* (*refuge*) shelter; POL asylum; **~ de vieillards** old people's home; **demande** *f* **d'~** request for asylum; **demandeur** *m* **d'~** asylum seeker

asocial, ~e [asɔsjal] antisocial

aspect [aspɛ] *m* (*vue*) look; (*point de vue*) angle, point of view; *d'un problème* aspect; (*air*) appearance; **sous cet ~** looked at that way; **à l'~ de** at the sight of

asperge [aspɛrʒ] *f* BOT stalk of asparagus; **asperges** asparagus *sg*

asperger [aspɛrʒe] ⟨1l⟩ sprinkle; **~ qn de qch** spray s.o. with sth

asphalte [asfalt] *m* asphalt

asphyxie [asfiksi] *f* asphyxiation; **as-phyxier** ⟨1a⟩ asphyxiate

aspirateur [aspiratœr] *m* vacuum (cleaner); **aspiration** *f* suction; *fig* aspiration (**à** to)

aspirer [aspire] ⟨1a⟩ *de l'air* breathe in, inhale; *liquide* suck up; **~ à qch** aspire to sth; **~ à faire qch** aspire to doing sth

aspirine [aspirin] *f* aspirin

assagir [asaʒir] ⟨2a⟩: **s'~** settle down

assaillant, ~e [asajã, -t] *m/f* assailant; **assaillir** ⟨2c, *futur* 2a⟩ *vedette* mob; *être assailli de* *de doutes* be assailed by; *de coups de téléphone* be bombarded by

assainir [asenir] ⟨2a⟩ (*nettoyer*) clean up; *eau* purify

assaisonnement [asɛzɔnmã] *m* seasoning; **assaisonner** ⟨1a⟩ season

assassin [asasɛ̃] *m* murderer; *d'un président* assassin; **assassinat** *m* assassination; **assassiner** ⟨1a⟩ murder; *un président* assassinate

assaut [aso] *m* assault, attack

assécher [aseʃe] ⟨1f⟩ drain

assemblage [asãblaʒ] *m* assembly; *fig* collection; **assemblée** *f* gathering; (*réunion*) meeting; **~ générale** annual general meeting; **Assemblée nationale** POL National Assembly; **assembler** ⟨1a⟩ (*unir*) assemble, gather; TECH assemble; **s'~** assemble, gather

assentiment [asãtimã] *m* consent

asseoir [aswar] ⟨3l⟩: **s'~** sit down

assermenté, ~e [asɛrmãte] *fonctionnaire* sworn; *témoin* on oath

assertion [asɛrsjõ] *f* assertion

assez [ase] *adv* enough; (*plutôt*) quite; **~ d'argent** enough money (*pour faire qch* to do sth); *la maison est ~ grande* the house is quite big; *la maison est ~ grande pour tous* the house is big enough for everyone; *j'en ai ~!* I've had enough!

assidu, ~e [asidy] *élève* hard-working

assiéger [asjeʒe] ⟨1g⟩ besiege (*aussi fig*)

assiette [asjɛt] *f* plate; *ne pas être dans son ~* *fig* be under the weather; **~ anglaise** cold cuts *pl*, *Br* cold meat

assignation [asiɲasjõ] f allocation; ~ (à comparaître) JUR summons sg; assigner ⟨1a⟩ à un rôle, un emploi, une tâche assign; ~ à comparaître subpoena

assimiler [asimile] ⟨1a⟩ (comparer) compare; connaissances, étrangers assimilate; il s'assimile à ... he thinks he's like ..., he compares himself with ...

assis, ~e [asi, -z] 1 p/p → asseoir 2 adj: place f ~e seat; être ~ be sitting; assise f fig basis; assises fpl JUR: cour f d'~ court of assizes

assistance [asistɑ̃s] f (public) audience; (aide) assistance; être placé à l'Assistance Publique be taken into care; assistant, ~e m/f assistant; ~e sociale social worker; assister ⟨1a⟩ 1 v/i: ~ à qch attend sth, be (present) at sth 2 v/t: ~ qn assist s.o.; assisté(e) par ordinateur computer-aided

association [asɔsjasjõ] f association; ~ de parents d'élèves parent-teacher association, PTA; associé, ~e m/f partner; associer ⟨1a⟩ associate (à with); s'~ join forces; COMM go into partnership; s'~ à douleur share in

assoiffé, ~e [aswafe] thirsty; ~ de fig hungry for

assombrir [asõbrir] ⟨2a⟩: s'~ darken

assommant, ~e [asɔmɑ̃, -t] F deadly boring; assommer ⟨1a⟩ stun; F bore to death

Assomption [asõpsjõ] f REL Assumption

assorti, ~e [asɔrti] matching; gants ~s au bonnet matching hat and gloves; fromages mpl ~s cheese platter sg, assortiment of cheeses; ~ de accompanied by; assortiment m assortment; assortir ⟨2a⟩ match

assoupir [asupir] ⟨2a⟩ send to sleep; fig: douleur, sens dull; s'~ doze off; fig die down

assouplissant [asuplisɑ̃] fabric softener

assourdir [asurdir] ⟨2a⟩ (rendre comme sourd) deafen; bruit muffle

assouvir [asuvir] ⟨2a⟩ satisfy (aussi fig)

assujettir [asyʒetir] ⟨2a⟩ subjugate; ~ qn à qch subject s.o. to sth; assujetti à l'impôt subject to tax; assujettissement m subjugation

assumer [asyme] ⟨1a⟩ take on, assume

assurance [asyrɑ̃s] f (confiance en soi) assurance, self-confidence; (promesse) assurance; (contrat) insurance; ~ auto car insurance; ~ maladie health insurance; ~ responsabilité civile public liability insurance; ~ tous risques all-risks insurance; ~ au tiers third party insurance; ~ vie life insurance; assuré, ~e 1 (sûr) confident 2 m/f insured party; assurément adv certainly; assurer ⟨1a⟩ victoire, succès ensure, make sure of; (couvrir par une assurance) insure; ~ à qn que assure s.o. that; ~ qch à qn provide s.o. with sth; s'~ take out insurance (contre against); s'~ de qch (vérifier) make sure of sth, check sth

astérisque [asterisk] m asterisk

asthmatique [asmatik] asthmatic; asthme m asthma

astiquer [astike] ⟨1m⟩ meuble polish; casserole scour

astre [astr] m star

astreindre [astrɛ̃dr] ⟨4b⟩ compel (à faire qch to do sth)

astrologie [astrolɔʒi] astrology; astrologue m/f astrologer

astronaute [astronot] m/f astronaut; astronome m/f astronomer; astronomie f astronomie; astronomique astronomical (aussi fig)

astuce [astys] f (ingéniosité) astuteness, shrewdness; (truc) trick; astucieux, -euse astute, shrewd

atelier [atəlje] m workshop; d'un artiste studio

athée [ate] m/f atheist; athéisme m atheism

athlète [atlɛt] m/f athlete; athlétique athletic; athlétisme m athletics sg

atlantique [atlɑ̃tik] 1 adj Atlantic; l'océan m Atlantique the Atlantic

Ocean **2** *m*: **l'Atlantique** the Atlantic

atlas [atlɑs] *m* (*pl inv*) atlas

atmosphère [atmɔsfɛr] *f* atmosphere; **atmosphérique** atmospheric

atome [atom] *m* atom; **atomique** atomic; **bombe** *f* ∼ atom bomb; **atomiseur** *m* spray, atomizer

atout [atu] *m fig* asset

atroce [atrɔs] dreadful, atrocious; **atrocité** *f* atrocity

attabler [atable] ⟨1a⟩: **s'**∼ sit at the table

attachant, ~e [ataʃɑ̃, -t] captivating; **attache** *f* fastener, tie; **~s** *fig* ties; attaché, ~e: être ∼ à qn / qch be attached to s.o. / sth; **attaché-case** *m* executive briefcase; **attacher** ⟨1a⟩ **1** *v/t* attach, fasten; *animal* tie up; *prisonnier* secure; *chaussures* do up; ∼ **de l'importance à qch** *fig* attach importance to sth **2** *v/i* CUIS (*coller*) stick; **s'**∼ à *personne, objet* become attached to

attaquant, ~e [atakɑ̃, -t] *m/f* SP striker; **attaque** *f* attack; ∼ **à la bombe** bomb attack; **attaquer** ⟨1m⟩ attack; *travail, difficulté* tackle; **s'**∼ à attack; *problème* tackle

attarder [atarde] ⟨1a⟩: **s'**∼ linger; **s'**∼ à *ou* **sur qch** dwell on sth

atteindre [atɛ̃dr] ⟨4b⟩ reach; *but* reach, achieve; *d'un projectile, d'un coup* strike, hit; *d'une maladie* affect; **être atteint du cancer** have cancer; **atteinte** *f* fig attack; **porter** ∼ **à qch** undermine sth; **hors d'**∼ out of reach

atteler [atle] ⟨1c⟩ *cheval* harness

attenant, ~e [atnɑ̃, -t] adjoining; ∼ **à** adjacent to

attendant [atɑ̃dɑ̃]: **en** ∼ in the meantime; **en** ∼ **qu'il arrive** (*subj*) while waiting for him to arrive; **attendre** ⟨4a⟩ wait; ∼ **qn** wait for s.o.; **j'attends que les magasins ouvrent** (*subj*) I'm waiting for the shops to open; **s'**∼ **à qch** expect sth; ∼ **qch de qn, qch** expect sth from s.o. / sth; ∼ **un enfant** be expecting a baby

attendrir [atɑ̃drir] ⟨2a⟩ *fig*: *personne* move; *cœur* soften; **s'**∼ be moved (**sur** by); **attendrissement** *m* tenderness

attendu, ~e [atɑ̃dy] **1** *adj* expected **2** *prép* in view of; ∼ **que** considering that

attentat [atɑ̃ta] *m* attack; ∼ **à la bombe** bombing, bomb attack; ∼ **à la pudeur** indecent assault; ∼ **suicide** suicide bomb attack; ∼ **terroriste** terrorist attack

attente [atɑ̃t] *f* wait; (*espoir*) expectation

attenter [atɑ̃te] ⟨1a⟩: ∼ **à la vie de qn** make an attempt on s.o.'s life

attentif, -ive [atɑ̃tif, -iv] attentive (**à** to); **attention** *f* attention; (*fais*) ∼! look out!, (be) careful!; **faire** ∼ **à qch** pay attention to sth; **faire** ∼ (**à ce**) **que** (+ *subj*) make sure that; **à l'**∼ **de** for (the attention of)

atténuant, ~e [atenɥɑ̃, -t] JUR: **circonstances** *fpl* **atténuantes** mitigating *ou* extenuating circumstances; **atténuer** ⟨1n⟩ reduce, diminish; *propos, termes* soften, tone down

atterrer [atere] ⟨1b⟩: **être atterré par** be staggered by

atterrir [aterir] ⟨2a⟩ AVIAT land; **en catastrophe** crash-land; **atterrissage** *m* AVIAT landing; ∼ **forcé** crash landing

attestation [atɛstasjɔ̃] *f* certificate; **attester** ⟨1a⟩ certify; (*prouver*) confirm

attirail [atiraj] *m péj* gear

attirance *f* attraction; **attirer** ⟨1a⟩ attract; ∼ **l'attention de qn sur qch** draw s.o.'s attention to sth; **s'**∼ **des critiques** come in for criticism, be criticized

attiser [atize] ⟨1b⟩ *émotions* whip up

attitude [atityd] *f* attitude; *d'un corps* pose

attractif, -ive [atraktif, -iv] attractive; **attraction** *f* attraction; ∼ **touristique** tourist attraction

attrait [atrɛ] *m* attraction, appeal

attrape-nigaud [atrapnigo] *m* (*pl* attrape-nigauds*) trick, scam F

attraper [atrape] ⟨1a⟩ catch; (*duper*)

take in; **~ un rhume** catch (a) cold

attrayant, **~e** [atrɛjɑ̃, -t] attractive

attribuer [atribɥe] ⟨1n⟩ attribute; *prix* award; *part, rôle, tâche* assign, allot; *valeur, importance* attach; **s'~** take; **attribut** *m* attribute; **attribution** *f* allocation; *d'un prix* award; **~s** (*compétence*) competence *sg*

attrister [atriste] ⟨1a⟩ sadden

attroupement [atrupmɑ̃] *m* crowd; **attrouper** ⟨1a⟩: **s'~** gather

aubaine [obɛn] *f* stroke of luck

aube [ob] *f* dawn; **à l'~** at dawn

auberge [obɛrʒ] *f* inn; **~ de jeunesse** youth hostel

aubergine [obɛrʒin] *f* BOT eggplant, *Br* aubergine

aubergiste [obɛrʒist] *m/f* innkeeper

aucun, **~e** [okɛ̃, -yn] **1** *adj* ◊ *avec négatif* no, not …any; *il n'y a ~e raison* there is no reason, there isn't any reason; *sans ~ doute* without a *ou* any doubt; *en ~ cas* under no circumstances
◊ *avec positif, interrogatif* any; *plus qu'~ autre* more than any other **2** *pron* ◊ *avec négatif* none; **~ des deux** neither of the two
◊ *avec positif, interrogatif* anyone, anybody; *d'~s litt* some (people)

aucunement [okynəmɑ̃] *adv* not at all, not in the slightest

audace [odas] *f* daring, audacity; *péj* audacity; **audacieux, -euse** (*courageux*) daring, audacious; (*insolent*) insolent

au-delà [ou(ə)la] **1** *adv* beyond; **~ de** above **2** *m* REL hereafter

au-dessous [odsu] **1** *adv* below **2** *prép*: **~ de** below

au-dessus [odsy] **1** *adv* above **2** *prép*: **~ de** above

au-devant [odvɑ̃]: *aller~ de personne, danger* meet; *désirs* anticipate

audible [odibl] audible

audience [odjɑ̃s] *f* (*entretien*) audience; *d'un tribunal* hearing

audiovisuel, **~le** [odjɔvizɥɛl] audiovisual

audit *m* FIN audit

auditeur, **-trice** [oditœr, -tris] *m/f* listener; FIN auditor; **audition** *f* audition; (*ouïe*) hearing; *de témoins* examination; **auditionner** ⟨1a⟩ audition; **auditoire** *m* audience

augmentation [ogmɑ̃tasjɔ̃] *f* increase; *de salaire* raise, *Br* rise; **augmenter** ⟨1a⟩ *v/t* increase; *salarié* give a raise *ou Br* rise to **2** *v/i* increase, rise

augure [ɔgyr] *m* omen; *être de bon / mauvais ~* be a good / bad sign *ou* omen

aujourd'hui [oʒurdɥi] today; (*de nos jours*) nowadays, these days, today

auparavant [oparavɑ̃] *adv* beforehand; *deux mois ~* two months earlier

auprès [oprɛ] *prép*: **~ de** beside, near

auquel [okɛl] → **lequel**

aura [ɔra] *f* aura

auréole [ɔreɔl] *f* halo; (*tâche*) ring

auriculaire [ɔrikylɛr] *m* little finger

aurore [ɔrɔr] *f* dawn

ausculter [oskylte, ɔs-] ⟨1a⟩ MÉD sound

aussi [osi] **1** *adv* too, also; *c'est ~ ce que je pense* that's what I think too *ou* also; *il est ~ grand que moi* he's as tall as me; **~ jeune qu'elle soit** (*subj*) young though she may be, as young as she is **2** *conj* therefore

aussitôt [osito] immediately; **~ que** as soon as

austère [ostɛr] austere; **austérité** *f* austerity

austral, **~e** [ostral] (*mpl* -s) GÉOGR southern

Australie [ostrali] *f*: *l'~* Australia; **australien, ~ne 1** *adj* Australian **2 Australien, ~ne** *m/f* Australian

autant [otɑ̃] ◊ (*tant*) as much (*que* as); *avec pluriel* as many (*que* as); *je ne pensais pas manger ~* I didn't mean to eat as *ou* so much
◊ *comparatif*: **~ de … que …** as much … as …; *avec pluriel* as many … as …
◊: (*pour*) **~ que je sache** (*subj*) as far as I know; *en faire ~* do the same, do likewise; *d'~ plus / moins / mieux que* all the more / less / bet-

ter because; *mais elles ne sont pas plus satisfaites pour* ~ but that doesn't make them any happier, but they aren't any the happier for that; *~ parler à un sourd* you might as well be talking to a brick wall

autel [otɛl] *m* altar

auteur [otœr] *m/f* (*écrivain*) author; *d'un crime* perpetrator; **auteur-compositeur** *m* songwriter

authenticité [otɑ̃tisite] *f* authenticity; **authentique** authentic

autiste [otist] autistic

auto [oto] *f* car, automobile; *~ tamponneuse* dodgem

autobiographie [otobjografi] *f* autobiography

autobus [otobys] *m* bus

autocar [otokar] *m* bus

autochtone [otokton] *adj* & *m/f* native

autocollant, ~e [otokɔlɑ̃, -t] **1** *adj* adhesive **2** *m* sticker

autocrate [otokrat] *m* autocrat; **autocratique** autocratic

autodéfense [otodefɑ̃s] *f* self-defense, *Br* self-defence

autodétermination [otodetɛrminasjɔ̃] *f* self-determination

autodidacte [otodidakt] self-taught

auto-école [otoekɔl] *f* (*pl* auto-écoles) driving school

autogéré, ~e [otoʒere] self-managed; **autogestion** *f* self-management

autographe [otograf] *m* autograph

automatique [otomatik] **1** *adj* automatic **2** *m pistolet* automatic; **automatiquement** *adv* automatically; **automatisation** *f* automation; **automatiser** ⟨1a⟩ automate

automnal, ~e [otɔn] fall *atr*, *Br* autumn *atr*, autumnal; **automne** *m* fall, *Br* autumn; *en ~* in fall

automobile [otomɔbil] **1** *adj* automobile *atr*, car *atr* **2** *f* car, automobile; **automobilisme** *m* motoring; **automobiliste** *m/f* driver

autonome [otɔnɔm] independent; POL autonomous; **autonomie** *f* independence; POL autonomy

autopsie [otɔpsi] *f* autopsy

autoradio [otoradjo] *m* car radio

autorisation [otɔrizasjɔ̃] *f* authorization, permission; **autoriser** ⟨1a⟩ authorize, allow

autoritaire [otɔritɛr] authoritarian; **autorité** *f* authority; *faire ~ en qch* be an authority on sth

autoroute [otorut] *f* highway, *Br* motorway; **autoroutier, -ère**: *réseau m ~* highway *ou Br* motorway network

auto-stop [otostɔp] *m*: *faire de l'~* hitchhike, thumb a ride; **auto-stoppeur, -euse** *m/f* (*pl* auto-stoppeurs, -euses) hitchhiker

autour [otur] *adv* around; *~ de* around

autre [otr] **1** *adj* other; *un / une ~ ...* another ...; *l'~ jour* the other day; *nous ~s Américains* we Americans; *rien d'~* nothing else; *~ part* somewhere else; *d'~ part* on the other hand; *de temps à ~* from time to time; *elle est tout ~ maintenant* she's quite different now **2** *pron*: *un / une ~* another (one); *l'~* the other (one); *les ~s* the others; (*autrui*) other people; *d'~s* others; *l'un l'~, les uns les ~* each other, one another; *tout ~ que lui* anyone other than him

autrefois [otrəfwa] in the past

autrement [otrəmɑ̃] *adv* (*différemment*) differently; (*sinon*) otherwise; *~ dit* in other words

Autriche [otriʃ] *f*: *l'~* Austria; **autrichien, ~ne** **1** *adj* Austrian **2** *m/f* Autrichien, ~ne Austrian

autrui [otrɥi] other people *pl*, others *pl*; *l'opinion d'~* what other people think

auvent [ovɑ̃] *m* awning

auxiliaire [oksiljɛr] **1** *adj* auxiliary **2** *m/f* (*assistant*) helper, auxiliary; *~ médical(e)* paramedic **3** *m* GRAM auxiliary

auxquelles, auxquels [okɛl] → *lequel*

av. *abr* (= *avenue*) Ave (= avenue)

aval [aval] *adv*: *en ~* downstream (*de* from); FIN guarantee; *donner son ~* give one's backing

avalanche [avalɑ̃ʃ] *f* avalanche

avaler [avale] ⟨1a⟩ swallow

avance [avɑ̃s] *f* advance; *d'une course* lead; **à l'~, par ~, d'~** in advance, ahead of time; **en ~** ahead of time; **~ rapide** fast forward; **avancé** advanced; *travail* well-advanced; **avancement** *m* (*progrès*) progress; (*promotion*) promotion; **avancer** ⟨1k⟩ **1** *v/t chaise* bring forward; *main* put out, stretch out; *argent* advance; *date, rendez-vous* bring forward; *proposition, thèse* put forward **2** *v/i* make progress; *il est parti en ~* he went on ahead; *s'~ vers* come up to

avant [avɑ̃] **1** *prép* before; **~ six mois** within six months; **~ tout** above all; **~ de faire qch** before doing sth **2** *adv temps* before; *espace* in front of; **en ~** forward; *il est parti en ~* he went on ahead; **en ~!** let's go!; **en ~, marche!** forward march! **3** *conj*: **~ que** (+ *subj*) before; **~ que cela ne se rompe** before it breaks **4** *adj*: *roue f~* front wheel **5** *m* front; *d'un navire* bow; SP forward

avantage [avɑ̃taʒ] *m* advantage; **~s sociaux** fringe benefits; **avantager** ⟨1l⟩ suit; (*favoriser*) favor, *Br* favour; **avantageux, -euse** advantageous; *prix* good

avant-bras [avɑ̃bra] *m* (*pl inv*) forearm

avant-coureur [avɑ̃kurœr] (*pl avant-coureurs*): *signe m ~* precursor

avant-dernier, -ère [avɑ̃dɛrnje, -ɛr] (*pl avant-derniers, avant-dernières*) last but one

avant-goût [avɑ̃gu] *m fig* foretaste

avant-hier [avɑ̃tjɛr] *adv* the day before yesterday

avant-poste [avɑ̃pɔst] *m* (*pl avant-postes*) outpost

avant-première [avɑ̃prəmjɛr] *f* preview

avant-projet [avɑ̃prɔʒɛ] *m* (*pl avant-projets*) preliminary draft

avant-propos [avɑ̃prɔpo] *m* (*pl inv*) foreword

avant-veille [avɑ̃vɛj] *f*: *l'~* two days before

avare [avar] **1** *adj* miserly; *être ~ de qch* be sparing with sth **2** *m* miser; **avarice** *f* miserliness

avarié, -e [avarje] *nourriture* bad

avec [avɛk] **1** *prép* with; *et ~ cela?* (will there be) anything else? **2** *adv*: *tu viens ~?* F are you coming too?

avenant, ~e [avnɑ̃, -t] *fml* **1** *adj* pleasant **2** *adv*: *le reste est à l'~* the rest is in keeping with it

avènement [avɛnmɑ̃] *m* advent

avenir [avnir] *m* future; *à l'~* in future; *dans un ~ prochain* in the near future; *d'~* promising

Avent [avɑ̃] *m* Advent; *calendrier m de l'~* Advent calendar

aventure [avɑ̃tyr] *f* adventure; (*liaison*) affair; **aventurer** ⟨1a⟩: *s'~* venture (*dans* into); **aventureux, -euse** adventurous; *projet* risky

avenu [avny]: *nul et non ~* null and void

avenue [avny] *f* avenue

avérer [avere] ⟨1f⟩: *s'~* (+ *adj*) prove

averse [avɛrs] *f* shower

aversion [avɛrsjɔ̃] *f* aversion (*pour ou contre* to); *prendre qn en ~* take a dislike to s.o.

averti, ~e [avɛrti] informed; **avertir** ⟨2a⟩ inform (*de* of); (*mettre en garde*) warn (*de* of); **avertissement** *m* warning; **avertisseur** *m* AUTO horn; *~ d'incendie* fire alarm

aveu [avø] *m* (*pl -x*) confession, admission

aveuglant, ~e [avœglɑ̃, -t] blinding; **aveugle** [avœgl] **1** *adj* blind **2** *m/f* blind man; blind woman; **aveuglement** *m fig* blindness; **aveuglément** *adv* blindly; **aveugler** ⟨1a⟩ blind; *d'une lumière* blind, dazzle; **aveuglette**: *à l'~ fig* blindly

aviateur, -trice [avjatœr, -tris] *m/f* pilot; **aviation** *f* aviation, flying

avide [avid] greedy, avid (*de* for); **avidité** *f* greed

avilir [avilir] ⟨2a⟩ degrade; **avilissant** degrading

avion [avjɔ̃] *m* (air)plane, *Br* (aero)plane; *aller en ~* fly, go by plane;

par ~ (by) airmail; *~-cargo* freighter, freight plane; ~ *de chasse* , *de combat* fighter (aircraft); ~ *commercial* commercial aircraft; ~ *furtif* stealth bomber; *~ de ligne* passenger aircraft *ou* plane

aviron [avirõ] *m* oar; SP rowing

avis [avi] *m* (*opinion*) opinion; (*information*) notice; *à mon* ~ in my opinion; *je suis du même* ~ *que vous* I share your opinion, I agree with you; *changer d'~* change one's mind; *sauf* ~ *contraire* unless I / you / *etc* hear anything to the contrary, unless otherwise stated; ~ *de réception* acknowledgment of receipt; *~ de tempête* storm warning; **avisé,** *~e* sensible; *être bien* ~ *de faire qch* be well-advised to do sth; **aviser** ⟨1a⟩: ~ *qn de qch* advise *ou* inform s.o. of sth; ~ *à qch* think about sth; *s'~ de qch* notice sth; *s'~ de faire qch* take it into one's head to do sth

av. J.-C. *abr* (= *avant Jésus-Christ*) BC (= before Christ)

avocat, *~e* [avɔka, -t] **1** *m/f* lawyer; (*défenseur*) advocate **2** *m* BOT avocado

avoine [avwan] *f* oats *pl*

avoir [avwar] ⟨1⟩ **1** *v/t* ◊ (*posséder*) have, have got; *il a trois filles* he has three daughters, he's got three daughters

◊ (*obtenir*) *permis etc* get; *il a eu de bonnes notes* he had *ou* he got good grades

◊ F (*duper*): ~ *qn* take s.o. for a ride

F; *on vous a eu* you've been had

◊: *j'ai froid / chaud* I am cold / hot

◊: ~ *20 ans* be 20, be 20 years old

◊: *elle eut un petit cri* she gave a little cry

◊: *tu n'as qu'à ...* all you have to do is ...

◊: *il y a* there is; *avec pluriel* there are; *qu'est-ce qu'il y a?* what's the matter?; *il y a un an* a year ago; *il y a deux mois jusqu'à ...* it is *ou* it's two months until ...

2 *v/aux* have; *j'ai déjà parlé* I have *ou* I've already spoken; *il a déjà parlé* he has *ou* he's already spoken; *je lui ai parlé hier* I spoke to him yesterday; *je ne lui ai pas parlé hier* I didn't speak to him yesterday

3 *m* COMM credit; (*possessions*) property, possessions *pl*

avoisinant, *~e* [avwazinã, -t] neighboring, *Br* neighbouring; **avoisiner** ⟨1a⟩: ~ *qch* border *ou* verge on sth

avorté, *~e* [avɔrte] abortive; **avortement** *m* miscarriage; *provoqué* abortion; **avorter** ⟨1a⟩ **1** *v/t femme* terminate the pregnancy of; *se faire* ~ have an abortion *ou* a termination **2** *v/i* miscarry; *fig* fail; **avorteur, -euse** *m/f* abortionist

avouer [avwe] ⟨1a⟩ confess; ~ *avoir fait qch* confess to having done sth

avril [avril] *m* April

axe [aks] *m* axle; GÉOM axis; *fig* basis; **axer** ⟨1a⟩ base (*sur* on); *être axé sur qch* center *ou Br* centre on sth

azote [azɔt] *m* CHIM nitrogen

B

baba [baba] **1** *m*: ~ *au rhum* rum baba **2** *adj inv* F: *en rester* ~ be staggered

babillage [babijaʒ] *m* babble; **babil-** **ler** ⟨1a⟩ babble

babiole [babjɔl] *f* trinket; *fig* trifle

bâbord [babɔr] *m* MAR: *à* ~ to port

baby-foot [bebifut] *m* (*pl inv*) table

B

football

baby-sitter [bebisitœr] *m/f* (*pl baby--sitters*) baby-sitter

bac[1] [bak] *m bateau* ferry; *récipient* container

bac[2] [bak] *m* F, **baccalauréat** [bakalɔrea] *m exam that is a prerequisite for university entrance*

bâche [bɑʃ] *f* tarpaulin

bacille [basil] *m* BIOL, MÉD bacillus

bâcler [bɑkle] ⟨1a⟩ F botch

bactérie [bakteri] *f* BIOL, MÉD bacteria *pl*, bacterium *fml*; **~s** bacteria

badaud [bado] *m* onlooker, rubberneck F

badge [badʒ] *m* badge

badigeonner [badiʒɔne] ⟨1a⟩ paint (*aussi* MÉD), slap some paint on *péj*

badinage [badinaʒ] *m* banter

badiner [badine] ⟨1a⟩ joke; *ne pas ~ avec qch* not treat sth as a joke

baffe [baf] *f* F slap

bafouer [bafwe] ⟨1a⟩ ridicule

bafouiller [bafuje] ⟨1a⟩ **1** *v/t* stammer **2** *v/i* F talk nonsense

bâfrer [bɑfre] ⟨1a⟩ F pig out F

bagages [bagaʒ] *mpl* baggage *sg*, luggage *sg*; *fig* (*connaissances*) knowledge *sg*; *faire ses ~* pack one's bags; *~ à main* hand baggage, hand luggage; **bagagiste** *m* baggage handler

bagarre [bagar] *f* fight, brawl; **bagarrer** ⟨1a⟩ F: *se ~* fight, brawl; **bagarreur, -euse 1** *adj* scrappy, pugnacious **2** *m* F brawler

bagatelle [bagatɛl] *f* trifle

bagne [baɲ] *m* prison

bagnole [baɲɔl] *f* F car

bague [bag] *f* ring; *~ de fiançailles* engagement ring

baguette [bagɛt] *f* stick; MUS baton; *pain* French stick; *~s pour manger* chopsticks; *~ magique* magic wand

baie[1] [be] *f* BOT berry

baie[2] [be] *f* (*golfe*) bay; *Baie d'Hudson* Hudson Bay

baignade [beɲad] *f action* swimming; **baigner** ⟨1b⟩ *enfant* bathe, *Br* bath; *se ~* go for a swim; **baigneur** *m* doll; **baignoire** *f* (*bath*)tub

bail [baj] *m* (*pl* baux [bo]) lease

bâiller [bɑje] ⟨1a⟩ yawn; *d'un trou* gape; *d'une porte* be ajar

bailleur, -eresse [bajœr, -rɛs] *m/f* lessor; *~ de fonds* backer

bâillon [bɑjõ] *m* gag; **bâillonner** ⟨1a⟩ gag (*aussi fig*)

bain [bɛ̃] *m* bath; *salle f de ~s* bathroom; *être dans le ~ fig* (*au courant*) be up to speed; *prendre un ~* take a bath; *prendre un ~ de soleil* sunbathe; *~ de bouche* mouthwash; *~ moussant* bubble bath; *~ de sang* bloodbath; **bain-marie** *m* (*pl* bains-marie) double boiler

baïonnette [bajɔnɛt] *f* MIL bayonet

baiser [beze] **1** *m* kiss **2** *v/t* ⟨1b⟩ kiss; V screw V; *se baiser ~* V be screwed V

baisse [bes] *f* drop, fall; *être en ~* be dropping *ou* falling; **baisser** ⟨1b⟩ **1** *v/t* tête, voix, yeux, store, prix etc lower; *radio, chauffage* turn down **2** *v/i de forces* fail; *de lumière* fade; *d'un niveau, d'une température, d'un prix, d'actions* drop, fall; *de vue* deteriorate; *se ~* bend down

bal [bal] *m* (*pl* bals) dance; *formel* ball

balade [balad] *f* walk, stroll; *faire une ~* go for a walk *ou* stroll; **balader** ⟨1a⟩ walk; *se ~* go for a walk *ou* stroll

baladeur [baladœr] *m* Walkman®

balafre [balafr] *f* (*blessure*) gash; (*cicatrice*) scar

balai [bale] *m* broom; *donner un coup de ~ à qch* give sth a sweep; *un coup de ~ fig* F dismissals *pl*, job losses *pl*; **balai-brosse** *m* (*pl* balais-brosses) long-handled scrubbing brush

balance [balɑ̃s] *f* scales *pl*; COMM balance; ASTROL Libra; *~ commerciale* trade balance; **balancer** ⟨1k⟩ *bras, jambes* swing; F (*lancer*) throw, chuck F; F (*jeter*) chuck out F; *se ~* swing; *je m'en balance* F I don't give a damn F; **balancier** *m* (*pendule*) pendulum; **balançoire** *f* swing

balayer [baleje] ⟨1i⟩ sweep; *fig: gouvernement* sweep from power; *soucis* sweep away, get rid of; *~ devant sa porte* put one's own house in order; **balayette** *f* handbrush; **ba-**

layeur, -euse *m/f* street sweeper
balbutier [balbysje] ⟨1a⟩ stammer, stutter
balcon [balkõ] *m* balcony
Baléares [balear] *fpl*: **les ~** the Balearic Islands, the Balearics
baleine [balɛn] *f* whale
balise [baliz] *f* MAR (marker) buoy; AVIAT (marker) light
balivernes [balivern] *fpl* nonsense *sg*
balkanique [balkanik] Balkan; **Balkans** *mpl*: **les ~** the Balkans
ballade [balad] *f* ballad
balle [bal] *f* ball; *d'un fusil* bullet; *de marchandises* bale; **renvoyer la ~ à qn** *fig* answer s.o. back; **500 ~s** P 500 euros / francs; **~ de golf** golf ball; **~ de match** match point; **~ de tennis** tennis ball
ballerine [balrin] *f* ballerina
ballet [balɛ] *m* ballet
ballon [balõ] *m* ball; *pour enfants*, AVIAT balloon; **~ rond** soccer ball, *Br* football; SP soccer, *Br* football; **ballonné, ~e** *ventre* bloated
ballot [balo] *m* bundle; *fig* F jerk F, idiot; **ballottage** *m*: (**scrutin** *m* **de**) **~** second ballot; **ballotter** ⟨1a⟩ **1** *v/t* buffet **2** *v/i* bounce up and down
balnéaire [balneɛr]: **station** *f* **~** seaside resort
balourd, ~e [balur, -d] clumsy
balte [balt] Baltic; **les pays ~s** the Baltic countries
Baltique [baltik]: **la (mer) ~** the Baltic (Sea)
balustrade [balystrad] *f* balustrade
bambin [bãbɛ̃] *m* child
bambou [bãbu] *m* BOT bamboo
banal, ~e [banal] (*mpl* -als) banal; **banalité** *f* banality
banane [banan] *f* banana; *sac* fanny pack, *Br* bum bag; **bananier** *m* banana tree
banc¹ [bã] *m* bench, seat; **~ des accusés** dock; **~ d'essai** test bed; **~ de sable** sandbank
banc² [bã] *m de poissons* shoal
bancaire [bãker] bank *atr*; **chèque** *m* **~** check, *Br* cheque

bancal, ~e [bãkal] (*mpl* -als) *table* wobbly
bandage [bãdaʒ] *m* MÉD bandage
bande [bãd] *f de terrain*, *de tissu* strip; MÉD bandage; (*rayure*) stripe; (*groupe*) group; *péj* gang, band; **~ annonce** trailer; **~ dessinée** comic strip; **~ magnétique** magnetic tape; **~ originale** sound track; **~ son** sound track; **bandeau** *m* (*pl* -x) *sur le front* headband; *sur les yeux* blindfold; **bander** ⟨1a⟩ MÉD bandage; P have an erection *ou* hard-on P; **les yeux à qn** blindfold s.o.
banderole [bãdrɔl] *f* banner
bandit [bãdi] *m* bandit; (*escroc*) crook
bandoulière [bãduljɛr] *f*: **en ~** across the shoulder
banlieue [bãljø] *f* suburbs *pl*; **de ~** suburban; **trains** *mpl* **de** suburban *ou* commuter trains; **banlieusard, ~e** *m/f* suburbanite
bannière [banjɛr] *f* banner; **~ étoilée** Stars and Stripes *sg ou pl*
bannir [banir] ⟨2a⟩ banish
banque [bãk] *f* bank; **Banque centrale européenne** European Central Bank; **~ de données** data bank; **Banque mondiale** World Bank; **~ du sang** blood bank; **~ du sperme** sperm bank
banqueroute [bãkrut] *f* bankruptcy
banquet [bãkɛ] *m* banquet
banquette [bãkɛt] *f* seat
banquier [bãkje] *m* banker
banquise [bãkiz] *f* pack ice
bans [bã] *mpl* banns
baptême [batɛm] *m* baptism; **baptiser** ⟨1a⟩ baptize
baquet [bakɛ] *m* tub
bar [bar] *m établissement*, *comptoir* bar; *meuble* cocktail cabinet
baragouin [baragwɛ̃] *m* gibberish
baraque [barak] *f* shack; (*maison*) house; **baraqué, ~e** F: (**bien**) **~** well-built
baratin [baratɛ̃] *m* F spiel F; **baratiner** ⟨1a⟩ sweet-talk; *fille* chat up
barbant, ~e [barbã, -t] F boring
barbare [barbar] **1** *adj* barbaric **2** *m/f* barbarian; **barbarie** *f* barbarity

barbe [barb] *f* beard; *quelle ~!* F what a drag! F; *~ à papa* cotton candy, *Br* candy floss

barbecue [barbəkju, -ky] *m* barbecue

barbelé, ~e [barbəle] **1** *adj*: *fil m de fer ~* barbed wire **2** *m*: *~s* barbed wire *sg*

barber [barbe] ⟨1a⟩ F bore rigid F

barbiturique [barbityrik] *m* PHARM barbiturate

barboter [barbɔte] ⟨1a⟩ *dans l'eau* paddle

barbouiller [barbuje] ⟨1a⟩ *(peindre grossièrement)* daub; *visage* smear (*de* with); *avoir l'estomac barbouillé* feel nauseous

barbu, ~e [barby] bearded

barda [barda] *m* kit

barder [barde] ⟨1a⟩ F: *ça va ~* there's going to be trouble

barème [barɛm] *m* scale

baril [baril] *m* barrel

bariolé, ~e [barjɔle] gaudy

baromètre [barɔmɛtr] *m* barometer

baron [barõ] *m* baron; **baronne** *f* baroness

baroque [barɔk] ART, MUS baroque; *(bizarre)* weird

barque [bark] *f* MAR boat; *mener la ~ fig* be in charge

barrage [baraʒ] *m ouvrage hydraulique* dam; *(barrière)* barrier; *~ de police* roadblock

barre [bar] *f* bar; MAR helm; *(trait)* line; *~ d'espacement* INFORM space-bar; *~ d'état* INFORM status bar; *~ des témoins* JUR witness stand, *Br* witness box; *~ oblique* oblique, slash; **barreau** *m* (*pl* -x) *bar*; *d'échelle* rung; *le ~* JUR the bar; *derrière les ~x* behind bars; **barrer** ⟨1a⟩ *(obstruer)* block, bar; *route* cross out; *chèque Br* cross; *se ~* F leave, take off

barrette [barɛt] *f pour cheveux* barrette, *Br* hairslide

barreur [barœr] *m* helmsman

barricade [barikad] *f* barricade; **barricader** ⟨1a⟩ barricade

barrière [barjɛr] *f* barrier; *(clôture)* fence; *~s douanières* customs barriers; *~ linguistique* language bar-

rier

barrique [barik] *f* barrel

bar-tabac [bartaba] *m* bar-cum-tobacco store

baryton [baritõ] *m* baritone

bas, ~se [bɑ, -s] **1** *adj* low (*aussi fig*); GÉOGR lower; *instrument* bass; *voix* deep; *à voix ~se* in a low voice, quietly **2** *adv* ~ low; *parler* in a low voice, quietly; *à ~ ...!* down with ...!; *en ~* downstairs; *là-~* there **3** *m* (*partie inférieure*) bottom; (*vêtement*) stocking; *au ~ de* at the bottom *ou* foot of

basané, ~e [bazane] weather-beaten; *naturellement* swarthy

bas-côté [bɑkote] *m* (*pl* bas-côtés) *d'une route* shoulder

bascule [baskyl] *f jeu* teeter-totter, *Br* seesaw; *(balance)* scales *pl*; *à ~ cheval, fauteuil* rocking *atr*; **basculer** ⟨1a⟩ topple over

base [baz] *f* base; *d'un édifice* foundation; *fig: d'une science, de discussion* basis; *de ~* basic; *à ~ de lait* milk-based; *être à la ~ de* form the basis of

base-ball [bezbol] *m* baseball

base *f* **de données** [bazdadɔne] database

baser [baze] ⟨1a⟩ base (*sur* on); *se ~ sur* draw on; *d'une idée* be based on

bas-fond [bafõ] *m* (*pl* bas-fonds) MAR shallow; *~s fig: d'une ville* sleazy area

basilic [bazilik] *m* BOT basil

basilique [bazilik] *f* ARCH basilica

basket(-ball) [basket(bol)] *m* basketball; **baskets** *fpl* sneakers, *Br* trainers; **basketteur, -euse** *m/f* basketball player

basque [bask] **1** *adj* Basque **2** *m langue* Basque **3** *m/f* **Basque** Basque

basse [bɑs] *f voix, musicien, instrument* bass; *(contrebasse)* double bass

basse-cour [bɑskur] *f* (*pl* basses-cours) AGR farmyard; *animaux* poultry

bassin [basɛ̃] *m* basin; *dans un jardin* pond; ANAT pelvis; MAR dock; *~ de radoub* dry dock; **bassine** *f* bowl

bassiste [basist] *m/f* bass (player)

basson [basõ] *m* MUS *instrument* bassoon; *musicien* bassoonist

bastide [bastid] *f country house in the South of France*

bastingage [bastɛ̃gaʒ] *m* MAR rail

bastion [bastjõ] *m* bastion

bas-ventre [bavɑ̃tr] *m* lower abdomen

bataille [bataj] *f* battle; *livrer ~* give battle; *batailler* ⟨1a⟩ *fig* battle, fight; *bataillon m* MIL battalion

bâtard, ~e [batar, -d] *m enfant* bastard; *chien* mongrel

bateau [bato] *m* (*pl* -x) boat; *faire du ~* (*faire de la voile*) go sailing, sail; *mener qn en ~ fig* put s.o. on, *Br* have s.o. on; *bateau-mouche m* (*pl bateaux-mouches*) *boat that carries tourists up and down the Seine*

bâti, ~e [bati] **1** *adj* built on; *bien ~ personne* well-built **2** *m* frame

bâtiment [batimã] *m* (*édifice*) building; *secteur* construction industry; MAR ship

bâtir [batir] ⟨2a⟩ build

batisse [batis] *f souvent péj* (ugly) big building

bâton [batõ] *m* stick; *parler à ~s rompus* make small talk; *~ de rouge* lipstick; *~ de ski* ski pole *ou* stick

battage [bataʒ] *m* (*publicité*) hooha, ballyhoo; *~ médiatique* media hype

battant, ~e [batã, -t] **1** *adj pluie* driving; *le cœur ~* with pounding heart **2** *m d'une porte* leaf; *personne* fighter

batte [bat] *f de base-ball* bat

battement [batmã] *m de cœur* beat; *intervalle de temps* interval, window

batterie [batri] *f* ÉL battery; MUS drums *pl*; *dans un orchestre* percussion; *batteur m* CUIS whisk; *électrique* mixer; MUS drummer; *en base-ball* batter

battre [batr] ⟨4a⟩ **1** *v/t* beat; *monnaie* mint; *cartes* shuffle; *~ son plein* be in full swing; *~ des cils* flutter one's eyelashes; *~ en retraite* retreat **2** *v/i* beat; *d'une porte, d'un volet* bang; *se ~* fight; *battu, ~e* **1** *p/p* → *battre* **2** *adj* beaten

bavard, ~e [bavar, -d] **1** *adj* talkative

2 *m/f* chatterbox; *bavardage m* chatter; *bavarder* ⟨1a⟩ chatter; (*divulguer un secret*) talk, blab F

bave [bav] *f* drool, slobber; *d'escargot* slime; *baver* ⟨1a⟩ drool, slobber; *bavette f* bib; *baveux, -euse omelette* runny

Bavière [bavjer]: *la ~* Bavaria

bavure [bavyr] *f fig* blunder, blooper F; *sans ~* impeccable

BCBG [besebeʒe] *adj abr* (= *bon chic bon genre*) preppie

B.C.E. [besea] *f abr* (= *Banque centrale européenne*) ECB (= European Central Bank)

Bd *abr* (= *boulevard*) Blvd (= Boulevard)

B.D. [bede] *f abr* (= *bande dessinée*) comic strip

béant, ~e [beã, -t] gaping

béat, ~e [bea, -t] *péj: sourire* silly

beau, bel, belle [bo, bɛl] (*mpl* beaux) beautiful, lovely; *homme* handsome, good-looking; *il fait ~* (*temps*) it's lovely weather; *il a ~ dire / faire ...* it's no good him saying / doing ...; *l'échapper belle* have a narrow escape; *bel et bien* well and truly; *de plus belle* more than ever; *un ~ jour* one (fine) day; *le ~ monde* the beautiful people *pl*

beaucoup [boku] a lot; *~ de* lots of, a lot of; *~ de gens* lots *ou* a lot of people, many people; *~ d'argent* lots *ou* a lot of money; *je n'ai pas ~ d'amis* I don't have a lot of *ou* many friends; *je n'ai pas ~ d'argent* I don't have a lot of *ou* much money; *~ trop cher* much too expensive

beau-fils [bofis] *m* (*pl* beaux-fils) *m* son-in-law; *d'un remariage* stepson; *beau-frère m* (*pl* beaux-frères) brother-in-law; *beau-père m* (*pl* beaux-pères) father-in-law; *d'un remariage* stepfather

beauté [bote] *f* beauty

beaux-arts [bozar] *mpl*: *les ~* fine art *sg*

beaux-parents [boparã] *mpl* parents-in-law

bébé [bebe] *m* baby; *bébé-éprouv-*

B

ette *m* (*pl* bébés-éprouvettes) test-tube baby

bec [bɛk] *m* d'un oiseau beak; d'un récipient spout; MUS mouthpiece; F mouth; **un ~ fin** a gourmet

bécane [bekan] *f* F bike

béchamel [beʃamɛl] *f* CUIS: (**sauce**) **~** béchamel (sauce)

bêche [bɛʃ] *f* spade; **bêcher** ⟨1b⟩ dig

bedaine [bədɛn] *f* (beer) belly, paunch

bée [be]: **bouche ~** open-mouthed

beffroi [befrwa] *m* belfry

bégayer [begeje] ⟨1i⟩ stutter, stammer

béguin [begɛ̃] *m* fig F: **avoir le ~ pour qn** have a crush on s.o.

B.E.I. [beəi] *f* abr (= **Banque européenne d'investissement**) EIB (= European Investment Bank)

beige [bɛʒ] beige

beignet [bɛɲɛ] *m* CUIS fritter

bêler [bele] ⟨1b⟩ bleat

belette [bəlɛt] *f* weasel

belge [bɛlʒ] **1** *adj* Belgian **2** *m/f* **Belge** Belgian; **Belgique** [bɛlʒik]: **la ~** Belgium

bélier [belje] *m* ZO ram; ASTROL Aries

belle → *beau*

belle-famille [bɛlfamij] *f* in-laws *pl*

belle-fille [bɛlfij] *f* (*pl* belles-filles) daughter-in-law; d'un remariage stepdaughter; **belle-mère** *f* (*pl* belles-mères) mother-in-law; d'un remariage stepmother; **belle-sœur** *f* (*pl* belles-sœurs) sister-in-law

belligérant, ~e [beliʒerɑ̃, -t] belligerent

belliqueux, -euse [belikø, -z] warlike

belvédère [bɛlvedɛr] *m* viewpoint, lookout point

bémol [bemɔl] *m* MUS flat

bénédictin [benediktɛ̃] *m* Benedictine (monk)

bénédiction [benediksjõ] *f* blessing

bénéfice [benefis] *m* benefit, advantage; COMM profit; **bénéficiaire 1** *adj* marge profit atr **2** *m/f* beneficiary; **bénéficier** ⟨1a⟩: **~ de** benefit from; **bénéfique** beneficial

Bénélux [benelyks]: **le ~** the Benelux countries *pl*

bénévolat [benevɔla] voluntary work; **bénévole 1** *adj* travail voluntary **2** *m/f* volunteer, voluntary worker

bénin, -igne [benɛ̃, -iɲ] tumeur benign; accident minor

bénir [benir] ⟨2a⟩ bless; **bénit, ~e** consecrated; **eau** *f* **~e** holy water; **bénitier** *m* stoup

benne [bɛn] *f* d'un téléphérique (cable) car; **~ à ordures** garbage truck, *Br* bin lorry

B.E.P. [beəpe] *m* abr (= **brevet d'études professionnelles**) type of vocational qualification

B.E.P.C. [beəpese] *m* abr (= **brevet d'études du premier cycle**) equivalent of high school graduation

béquille [bekij] *f* crutch; d'une moto stand

bercail [bɛrkaj] *m* (sans pl) fold

berceau [bɛrso] *m* (*pl* -x) cradle; **bercer** ⟨1k⟩ rock; **~ qn de promesses** fig delude s.o. with promises; **se ~ d'illusions** delude o.s.; **berceuse** *f* lullaby; (chaise à bascule) rocking chair

béret [bere] *m* beret

berge [bɛrʒ] *f* bank

berger [bɛrʒe] *m* shepherd; **chien** German shepherd, *Br aussi* Alsatian; **bergère** *f* shepherd

berline [bɛrlin] *f* AUTO sedan, *Br* saloon

berlingot [bɛrlɛ̃go] *m* bonbon humbug; emballage pack

Bermuda(s) [bɛrmyda] *m*(*pl*) Bermuda shorts *pl*

Bermudes [bɛrmyd] *fpl*: **les ~** Bermuda *sg*

berner [bɛrne] ⟨1a⟩: **~ qn** fool s.o., take s.o. for a ride

besogne [bəzɔɲ] *f* job, task

besoin [bəzwɛ̃] *m* need; **avoir ~ de qch** need sth; **avoir ~ de faire qch** need to do sth; **il n'est pas ~ de dire** needless to say; **au ~** if necessary, if need be; **si ~ est** if necessary, if need be; **être dans le ~** be in need; **faire ses ~s** relieve o.s.; d'un animal do its business

best-seller [bɛstsɛlɛr] *m* best-seller

bestial, **~e** [bɛstjal] (*mpl* -iaux) bestial; **bestialité** *f* bestiality; **bestiaux** *mpl* cattle *pl*; **bestiole** *f* small animal; (*insecte*) insect, bug F

bétail [betaj] *m* (*sans pl*) livestock

bête [bɛt] **1** *adj* stupid **2** *f* animal; (*insecte*) insect, bug F; **~s** (*bétail*) livestock *sg*; **chercher la petite ~** nitpick, quibble; **bêtement** *adv* stupidly; **bêtise** *f* stupidity; **dire des ~s** talk nonsense; **une ~** a stupid thing to do / say

béton [betõ] *m* concrete; **~ armé** reinforced concrete; **bétonnière** *f* concrete mixer

betterave [betrav] *f* beet, *Br* beetroot; **~ à sucre** sugar beet

beugler [bøgle] ⟨1a⟩ *de bœuf* low; F *d'une personne* shout

beur [bœr] *m/f* F French-born person of North African origin

beurre [bœr] *m* butter; **~ de cacahuètes** peanut butter; **beurrer** ⟨1a⟩ butter; **beurrier** *m* butter dish

beuverie [bœvri] *f* drinking session, booze-up *Br* F

bévue [bevy] *f* blunder; **commettre une ~** blunder, make a blunder

biais [bjɛ] **1** *adv*: **en ~** traverser, couper diagonally; **de ~** regarder sideways **2** *m fig* (*aspect*) angle; **par le ~ de** through

bibelots [biblo] *mpl* trinkets

biberon [bibrõ] *m* (baby's) bottle; **nourrir au ~** bottlefeed

Bible [bibl] *f* bible

bibliographie [biblijɔgrafi] *f* bibliography

bibliothécaire [biblijɔtekɛr] *m/f* librarian; **bibliothèque** *f* library; *meuble* bookcase

biblique [biblik] *adj* biblical

bic® [bik] *m* ballpoint (pen)

bicarbonate [bikarbɔnat] *m* CHIM: **~ de soude** bicarbonate of soda

bicentenaire [bisɑ̃tənɛr] *m* bicentennial, *Br* bicentenary

biceps [bisɛps] *m* biceps *sg*

biche [biʃ] *f* ZO doe; **ma ~** *fig* my love

bichonner [biʃɔne] ⟨1a⟩ pamper

bicolore [bikɔlɔr] two-colored, *Br* two-coloured

bicoque [bikɔk] *f* tumbledown house

bicyclette [bisiklɛt] *f* bicycle; **aller en** *ou* **à ~** cycle

bidet [bidɛ] *m* bidet

bidon[1] [bidõ] *m*: **~ à essence** gas *ou Br* petrol can

bidon[2] [bidõ] *fig* F **1** *adj* phony **2** *m* baloney

bidonville [bidõvil] *m* shanty town

bidule [bidyl] *m* F gizmo F

bien [bjɛ̃] **1** *m* good; (*possession*) possession, item of property; **le ~** *ce qui est juste* good; **faire le ~** do good; **le ~ public** the common good; **faire du ~ à qn** do s.o. good; **dire du ~ de** say nice things about, speak well of; **c'est pour son ~** it's for his own good; **~s** (*possessions*) possessions, property *sg*; (*produits*) goods; **~s de consommation** consumer goods **2** *adj* good; (*beau, belle*) good-looking; **être ~** feel well; (*à l'aise*) be comfortable; **être ~ avec qn** be on good terms *ou* get on well with s.o.; **ce sera très ~ comme ça** that will do very nicely; **se sentir ~** feel well; **avoir l'air ~** look good; **des gens ~** respectable *ou* decent people **3** *adv* well; (*très*) very; **~ jeune** very young; **~ sûr** of course, certainly; **tu as ~ de la chance** you're really *ou* very lucky; **~ des fois** lots of times; **eh ~** well; **oui, je veux ~** yes please; **~ comprendre** understand properly **4** *conj*: **~ que** (+ *subj*) although

bien-être [bjɛ̃nɛtr] *m matériel* welfare; *sensation agréable* well-being

bienfaisance [bjɛ̃fəzɑ̃s] *f charity*; **bienfaisant**, **~e** (*salutaire*) beneficial; **bienfait** *m* benefit; **bienfaiteur**, **-trice** *m/f* benefactor

bien-fondé [bjɛ̃fõde] *m* legitimacy

bien-fonds [bjɛ̃fõ] *m* (*pl* biens-fonds) JUR land, property

bienheureux, **-euse** [bjɛ̃nørø, -z] happy; REL blessed

biennal, **~e** [bjenal] (*mpl* -aux) *contrat* two-year *atr*; *événement* biennial

B

bienséance [bjɛ̃seɑ̃s] *f* propriety; **bi-enséant, ~e** proper

bientôt [bjɛ̃to] soon; **à ~!** see you (soon)!

bienveillance [bjɛ̃vejɑ̃s] *f* benevolence; **bienveillant, ~e** benevolent

bienvenu, ~e [bjɛ̃vny] **1** *adj* welcome **2** *m/f*: **être le ~ / la ~e** be welcome **3** *f*: **souhaiter la ~e à qn** welcome s.o.; **~e en France!** welcome to France!

bière [bjɛr] *f boisson* beer; **~ blanche** wheat beer; **~ blonde** beer, *Br* lager; **~ brune** dark beer, *Br* bitter; **~ pression** draft (beer), *Br* draught (beer)

bifteck [biftɛk] *m* steak

bifurcation [bifyrkasjõ] *f* fork; **bifurquer** ⟨1m⟩ fork; **~ vers** fork off onto; *fig* branch out into

bigame [bigam] **1** *adj* bigamous **2** *m/f* bigamist; **bigamie** *f* bigamy

bigarreau [bigaro] *m type of cherry*

bigot [bigo, -ɔt] **1** *adj* excessively pious **2** *m/f* excessively pious person

bijou [biʒu] *m* (*pl* -x) jewel; **~x** jewelry *sg*, *Br* jewellery *sg*; **bijouterie** *f* jewelry store, *Br* jeweller's; **bijoutier, -ère** *m/f* jeweler, *Br* jeweller

bikini [bikini] *m* bikini

bilan [bilɑ̃] *m* balance sheet; *fig* (*résultat*) outcome; **faire le ~ de** take stock of; **déposer son ~** file for bankruptcy; **~ de santé** check-up

bilatéral, ~e [bilateral] (*mpl* -aux) bilateral

bile [bil] *f* F: **se faire de la ~** fret, worry

bilingue [bilɛ̃g] bilingual; **bilinguisme** *m* bilingualism

billard [bijar] *m* billiards *sg*; *table* billiard table; **~ américain** pool

bille [bij] *f* marble; *billard* (billiard) ball; **stylo** *m* (**à**) **~** ball-point (pen)

billet [bijɛ] *m* ticket; (*petite lettre*) note; **~** (**de banque**) bill, *Br* (bank)note; **billeterie** *f* ticket office; *automatique* ticket machine; FIN ATM, automated teller machine; *Br* cash dispenser

billion [biljõ] *m* trillion

bimensuel, ~le [bimɑ̃sɥel] bimonthly, twice a month

binaire [binɛr] binary

binocles [binɔkl] *mpl* F specs F

biochimie [bjɔʃimi] *f* biochemistry; **biochimique** biochemical; **biochimiste** *m/f* biochemist

biodégradable [bjɔdegradabl] biodegradable

biodiversité [bjɔdiversite] *f* biodiversity

biographie [bjɔgrafi] *f* biography; **biographique** biographical

biologie [bjɔlɔʒi] *f* biology; **biologique** biological; *aliments* organic; **biologiste** *m/f* biologist

biopsie [bjɔpsi] *f* biopsy

biorythme [bjɔritm] *m* biorhythm

biotechnologie [bjɔtɛknɔlɔʒi] *f* biotechnology

bipartisme [bipartism] *m* POL two-partysystem; **bipartite** POL bipartite

biplace [biplas] *m* two-seater

bipolaire [bipɔlɛr] bipolar

bis [bis] **1** *adj*: **24 ~** 24A **2** *m* (*pl inv*) encore

bisannuel, ~le [bizanɥel] biennial

biscornu, ~e [biskɔrny] *fig* weird

biscotte [biskɔt] *f* rusk

biscuit [biskɥi] *m* cookie, *Br* biscuit

bise [biz] *f*: **faire la ~ à qn** kiss s.o., give s.o. a kiss; **grosses ~s** love and kisses

bisexuel, ~le [bisɛksɥel] bisexual

bison [bizõ] *m* bison, buffalo

bisou [bizu] *m* F kiss

bissextile [bisɛkstil]: **année** *f* **~** leap year

bistro(t) [bistro] *m* bistro

bit [bit] *m* INFORM bit

bitume [bitym] *m* asphalt

bivouac [bivwak] *m* bivouac

bizarre [bizar] strange, bizarre; **bizarrerie** *f* peculiarity

blafard, ~e [blafar, -d] wan

blague [blag] *f* (*plaisanterie*) joke; (*farce*) trick, joke; **sans ~!** no kidding!; **blaguer** ⟨1a⟩ joke

blaireau [blɛro] *m* (*pl* -x) ZO badger; *pour se raser* shaving brush

blâme [blɑm] *m* blame; (*sanction*) reprimand; **blâmer** ⟨1a⟩ blame; (*sanctionner*) reprimand

blanc, blanche [blɑ̃, -ʃ] **1** *adj* white; *feuille, page* blank; **examen** *m* ~ practice exam, *Br* mock exam; **mariage** *m* ~ unconsummated marriage; **nuit** *f* **blanche** sleepless night; **en** ~ blank; **chèque** *m* **en** ~ blank check, *Br* blank cheque **2** *m* white; *de poulet* white meat; *Br* breast; *vin* white (wine); *textile* (household) linen; *par opposé aux couleurs* whites *pl*; *dans un texte* blank; ~ **(d'œuf)** (egg) white; **tirer à** ~ shoot blanks **3** *m/f* **Blanc, Blanche** white, White

blanc-bec [blɑ̃bɛk] *m* (*pl* blancs-becs) greenhorn

blanchâtre [blɑ̃ʃɑtr] whiteish

Blanche-Neige [blɑ̃ʃnɛʒ] *f* Snow-white

blanchir [blɑ̃ʃir] ⟨2a⟩ **1** *v/t* whiten; *mur* white-wash; *linge* launder, wash; *du soleil* bleach; CUIS blanch; *fig: innocenter* clear; ~ **de l'argent** launder money **2** *v/i* go white; **blanchisserie** *f* laundry

blasé, ~e [blaze] blasé

blason [blazɔ̃] *m* coat of arms

blasphème [blasfɛm] *m* blasphemy; **blasphémer** ⟨1f⟩ blaspheme

blé [ble] *m* wheat, *Br* corn

bled [blɛd] *m* F *péj* dump F, hole F

blême [blɛm] pale; **blêmir** ⟨2a⟩ turn pale

blessant [blesɑ̃] hurtful; **blessé, ~e 1** *adj* hurt (*aussi fig*); *dans un accident* injured; *avec une arme* wounded **2** *m/f* **les ~s** the injured, the casualties; *avec une arme* the wounded, the casualties; **je me suis blessé à la main** I injured *ou* hurt my hand; **blessure** *f d'accident* injury; *d'arme* wound

bleu, ~e [blø] (*mpl* -s) **1** *adj* blue; *viande* very rare, practically raw **2** *m* blue; *fromage* blue cheese; *marque sur la peau* bruise; *fig (novice)* new recruit, rookie F; TECH blueprint; ~ **(de travail), bleus** *pl*, overalls *pl*; ~ **marine** navy blue; **avoir**

une peur ~e be scared stiff

bleuet [blø ɛ] *m* BOT cornflower

blindage [blɛ̃daʒ] *m* armor, *Br* armour; **blindé, ~e 1** *adj* MIL armored, *Br* armoured; *fig* hardened **2** *m* MIL armored *ou Br* armoured vehicle; **blinder** ⟨1a⟩ armor, *Br* armour; *fig* F harden

bloc [blɔk] *m* block; POL bloc; *de papier* pad; **en** ~ in its entirety; ~ **opératoire** operating room, *Br* operating theatre

blocage [blɔkaʒ] *m* jamming; *d'un compte en banque, de prix* freezing; PSYCH block

bloc-notes [blɔknɔt] *m* (*pl* blocs-notes) notepad

blocus [blɔkys] *m* blockade

blond, ~e [blɔ̃, -d] **1** *adj cheveux* blonde; *tabac* Virginian; *sable* golden; **bière** *f* **~e** beer, *Br* lager **2** *m/f* blonde **3** *f bière* beer, *Br* lager

bloquer [blɔke] ⟨1m⟩ block; *mécanisme* jam; *roues* lock; *compte, crédits* freeze; *(regrouper)* group together; ~ **le passage** be in the way, bar the way

blottir [blɔtir] ⟨2a⟩: **se** ~ huddle (up)

blouse [bluz] *f* MÉD white coat; *de chirurgien* (surgical) robe; *d'écolier* lab coat; *(chemisier)* blouse

blouson [bluzɔ̃] *m* jacket, blouson; ~ **noir** *fig* young hoodlum

bluff [blœf] *m* bluff; **bluffer** ⟨1a⟩ bluff

B. O. [beo] *f abr* (= **bande originale**) sound track

bobard [bobar] *m* F tall tale, *Br* tall story

bobine [bɔbin] *f* reel

bobsleigh [bɔbslɛg] *m* bobsled, *Br aussi* bobsleigh

bocal [bɔkal] *m* (*pl* -aux) (glass) jar

bock [bɔk] *m*: **un** ~ a (glass of) beer

bœuf [bœf] *m* animal; *Br* mâle castré steer; *viande* beef; **~s** cattle *pl*; ~ **bourguignon** CUIS kind of beef stew

bof! [bɔf] *indifférence* yeah, kinda

bogue [bɔg] *m* INFORM bug

bohème [bɔɛm] *m/f* Bohemian; **bohémien, ~ne** *m/f* gipsy

B

boire [bwar] ⟨4u⟩ drink; (*absorber*) soak up; **~ un coup** F have a drink; **~ comme un trou** F drink like a fish F

bois [bwa] *m matière, forêt* wood; **en ou de ~** wooden; **~ de construction** lumber; **boisé, ~e** wooded; **boiserie** *f* paneling, *Br* panelling

boisson [bwasõ] *f* drink; **~s alcoolisées** alcohol *sg*, alcoholic drinks

boîte [bwat] *f* box; *en tôle* can, *Br* tin; F (*entreprise*) company; **sa ~** his company, the place where he works; **~ (de nuit)** nightclub; **en ~** canned, *Br aussi* tinned; **~ de conserves** can, *Br aussi* tin; **~ à gants** glove compartment; **~ aux lettres** mailbox, *Br* letterbox; **~ noire** black box; **~ postale** post office box; **~ de vitesses** AUTO gearbox; **~ vocale** INFORM voicemail

boiter [bwate] ⟨1a⟩ limp; *fig: de raisonnement* be shaky, not stand up very well; **boiteux, -euse** *chaise, table etc* wobbly; *fig: raisonnement* shaky; **être ~** *d'une personne* have a limp

boîtier [bwatje] *m* case, housing

bol [bɔl] *m* bowl

bolide [bɔlid] *m* meteorite; AUTO racing car

Bolivie [bɔlivi]: **la ~** Bolivia; **bolivien, ~ne** *adj* Bolivian **2** *m/f* **Bolivien, ~ne** Bolivian

bombardement [bõbardəmã] *m* bombing; *avec obus* bombardment; **bombarder** ⟨1a⟩ bomb; *avec obus, questions* bombard; **bombardier** *m avion* bomber; **bombe** *f* MIL bomb; (*atomiseur*) spray; **~ atomique** atom bomb; **~ incendiaire** incendiary device; **~ à retardement** time bomb

bombé, ~e [bõbe] *front, ventre* bulging; **bomber** ⟨1a⟩ bulge

bon, ~ne [bõ, bɔn] **1** *adj* good; *route, adresse, moment* right, correct; *brave* kind, good-hearted; **de ~ne foi** *personne* sincere; **de ~ne heure** early; **(à) ~ marché** cheap; **être ~ à qch** be good at sth; **~ à rien** good-for-nothing; **elle n'est pas ~ne à grand-chose** she's not much use;

pour de ~ for good; **il est ~ que ...** (+ *subj*) it's a good thing that ..., it's good that ...; **à quoi ~?** what's the point?, what's the use?; **~ mot** witty remark, witticism; **~ anniversaire!** happy birthday!; **~ voyage!** have a good trip!, bon voyage!; **~ne chance!** good luck!; **~ne année!** Happy New Year!; **~ne nuit!** good night!; **ah ~** really

2 *adv*: **sentir ~** smell good; **tenir ~** not give in, stand one's ground; **trouver ~ de faire qch** think it right to do sth; **il fait ~ vivre ici** it's good living here

3 *m* COMM voucher; **avoir du ~** have its good points; **~ d'achat** gift voucher; **~ de commande** purchase order; **~ du Trésor** Treasury bond

bonbon [bõbõ] *m* candy, *Br* sweet; **~s** candy *sg*, *Br* sweets

bonbonne [bõbɔn] *f* cannister; **~ d'oxygène** oxygen tank

bond [bõ] *m* jump, leap; *d'une balle* bounce

bondé, ~e [bõde] packed

bondir [bõdir] ⟨2a⟩ jump, leap (**de** with)

bonheur [bɔnœr] *m* happiness; (*chance*) luck; **par ~** luckily, fortunately; **porter ~ à qn** bring s.o. luck; **au ~** at random; **se promener au ~** stroll *ou* wander around

bonhomie [bɔnɔmi] *f* good nature, bonhomie; **bonhomme** *m* (*pl* bonshommes) *m* F (*type*) guy F, man; **~ de neige** snowman

bonification [bɔnifikasjõ] *f* improvement; *assurance* bonus; **bonifier** ⟨1a⟩ improve

boniment [bɔnimã] *m battage* spiel F, sales talk; F (*mensonge*) fairy story

bonjour [bõʒur] *m* hello; *avant midi* hello, good morning; **dire ~ à qn** say hello to s.o.; **donne le ~ de ma part à ta mère** tell your mother I said hello, give your mother my regards

bonne [bɔn] *f* maid

bonnement [bɔnmã] *adv*: **tout ~** simply

bonnet [bɔnɛ] *m* hat; **gros ~** *fig* F big

boucler

shot F; **~ de douche** shower cap

bonsoir [bõswar] *m* hello, good evening

bonté [bõte] *f* goodness; **avoir la ~ de faire qch** be good *ou* kind enough to do sth

bonus [bɔnys] *m* no-claims bonus

boom [bum] *m* boom

bord [bɔr] *m* edge; *(rive)* bank; *d'une route* side; *d'un verre* brim; *au ~ de la mer* at the seaside; *être au ~ des larmes* be on the verge *ou* brink of tears; *être un peu bête sur les ~s* *fig* F be a bit stupid; *tableau m de ~* AUTO dash(board); *à ~ d'un navire / d'un avion* on board a ship / an aircraft; *monter à ~* board, go on board; *jeter qch par-dessus ~* throw sth overboard; *virer de ~* turn, go about; *fig: d'opinion* change one's mind; *de parti* switch allegiances

bordeaux [bɔrdo] **1** *adj inv* wine-colored, *Br* wine-coloured, claret **2** *m vin* claret, Bordeaux

bordel [bɔrdɛl] *m* F brothel; *(désordre)* mess F, shambles *sg*

bordelais, ~e [bɔrdəlɛ, -z] of / from Bordeaux, Bordeaux *atr*

bordélique [bɔrdelik] F chaotic; *c'est vraiment ~* it's a disaster area F

border [bɔrde] ⟨1a⟩ *(garnir)* edge *(de* with); *(être le long de)* line, border; *enfant* tuck in

bordereau [bɔrdəro] *m (pl -x)* COMM schedule, list; **~ d'expédition** dispatch note

bordure [bɔrdyr] *f* border, edging; *en ~ de forêt, ville* on the edge of

boréal, ~e [bɔreal] *(mpl -aux)* northern

borgne [bɔrɲ] *m* one-eyed

borne [bɔrn] *f* boundary marker; ÉL terminal; *~s fig* limits; **sans ~s** unbounded; **dépasser les ~s** go too far; **~ kilométrique** milestone; **borné, ~e** narrow-minded; **borner** ⟨1a⟩: **se ~ à (faire) qch** restrict o.s. to (doing) sth

bosniaque [bɔznjak] **1** *adj* Bosnian **2** *m/f* **Bosniaque** Bosnian; **Bosnie** *f* Bosnia

bosquet [bɔskɛ] *m* copse

bosse [bɔs] *f (enflure)* lump; *d'un bossu, d'un chameau* hump; *du sol* bump; *en ski* mogul; **avoir la ~ de** F have a gift for

bosser [bɔse] ⟨1a⟩ F work hard

bossu, ~e [bɔsy] *m/f* [bɔsy] hunchback

botanique [bɔtanik] **1** *adj* botanical **2** *f* botany; **botaniste** *m/f* botanist

botte[1] [bɔt] *f de carottes, de fleurs, de radis* bunch

botte[2] [bɔt] *f chaussure* boot

botter [bɔte] ⟨1a⟩: **~ le derrière à qn** F give s.o. a kick up the rear end, let s.o. feel the toe of one's boot; **ça me botte** F I like it

bottin [bɔtɛ̃] *m* phone book

bottine [bɔtin] *f* ankle boot

bouc [buk] *m* goat; **~ émissaire** *fig* scapegoat

boucan [bukã] *m* F din, racket

bouche [buʃ] *f* mouth; *de métro* entrance; **~ d'aération** vent; **~ d'incendie** (fire) hydrant; **bouche-à-bouche** *m* MÉD mouth-to-mouth resuscitation

bouché, ~e [buʃe] blocked; *nez* blocked, stuffed up; *temps* overcast

bouchée [buʃe] *f* mouthful; **~ à la reine** vol-au-vent

boucher[1] [buʃe] ⟨1a⟩ block; *trou* fill (in); **se ~** *d'un évier, d'un tuyau* get blocked; **se ~ les oreilles** put one's hands over one's ears; *fig* refuse to listen, turn a deaf ear; **se ~ le nez** hold one's nose

boucher[2], **-ère** [buʃe, -er] *m/f* butcher *(aussi fig)*

boucherie [buʃri] *f magasin* butcher's; *fig* slaughter

bouche-trou [buʃtru] *m (pl* bouche-trous) stopgap

bouchon [buʃõ] *m* top; *de liège* cork; *fig: trafic* hold-up, traffic jam

boucle [bukl] *f* loop *(aussi* INFORM); *de ceinture, de sandales* buckle; *de cheveux* curl; **~ d'oreille** earring; **bouclé, ~e** *cheveux* curly; **boucler** ⟨1a⟩ *ceinture* fasten; *porte, magasin* lock; MIL surround; *en prison* lock away; **boucle-la!** F shut up! F

B

bouclier [buklije] *m* shield (*aussi fig*)

bouddhisme [budism] *m* Buddhism; **bouddhiste** *m* Buddhist

bouder [bude] ⟨1a⟩ **1** *v/i* sulk **2** *v/t:* ~ **qn** / **qch** give s.o. / sth the cold shoulder; **boudeur, -euse** sulky

boudin [budɛ̃] *m:* ~ (**noir**) blood sausage, *Br* black pudding

boudiné, ~e [budine] *doigts* stubby; **elle est ~ e dans cette robe** that dress is too small for her

boue [bu] *f* mud

bouée [bwe] *f* MAR buoy; ~ (**de sauvetage**) lifebuoy, lifebelt

boueux, -euse [bwø, -z] muddy

bouffe [buf] *f* F grub F, food

bouffée [bufe] *f de fumée* puff; *de vent* puff, gust; *de parfum* whiff; **une ~ d'air frais** a breath of fresh air; ~ **de chaleur** MÉD hot flash, *Br* hot flush

bouffer [bufe] ⟨1a⟩ F eat

bouffi, ~e [bufi] bloated

bougeoir [buʒwar] *m* candleholder

bougeotte [buʒɔt] *f:* **avoir la ~** fidget, be fidgety; **bouger** ⟨1l⟩ move; *de prix* change

bougie [buʒi] *f* candle; AUTO spark plug

bougonner [bugɔne] ⟨1a⟩ F grouse F

bouillabaisse [bujabɛs] *f* CUIS bouillabaisse, fish soup

bouillant, ~e [bujɑ̃, -t] *qui bout* boiling; (*très chaud*) boiling hot

bouillie [buji] *f* baby food

bouillir [bujir] ⟨2e⟩ boil; *fig* be boiling (with rage); **faire ~** boil; **bouilloire** *f* kettle

bouillon [bujɔ̃] *m* (*bulle*) bubble; CUIS stock, broth; **bouillonner** ⟨1a⟩ *de source, de lave etc* bubble; *fig: d'idées* seethe

bouillotte [bujɔt] *f* hot water bottle

boulanger, -ère [bulɑ̃ʒe, -er] *m/f* baker; **boulangerie** *f* bakery, baker's

boule [bul] *f* (*sphère*) ball; **jeu** *m* **de ~s** bowls *sg*; ~ **de neige** snowball; **faire ~ de neige** snowball

bouleau [bulo] *m* (*pl* -x) BOT birch (tree)

bouledogue [buldɔg] *m* bulldog

bouler [bule] ⟨1a⟩ F: **envoyer ~ qn** kick s.o. out, send s.o. packing

boulette [bulɛt] *f de papier* pellet; ~ (**de viande**) meatball

boulevard [bulvar] *m* boulevard; ~ **périphérique** belt road, *Br* ring road

bouleversement [bulvɛrsəmɑ̃] *m* upheaval; **bouleverser** ⟨1a⟩ (*mettre en désordre*) turn upside down; *traditions, idées* overturn; *émotionnellement* shatter, deeply move

boulimie [bulimi] *f* bulimia

boulon [bulɔ̃] *m* TECH bolt; **boulonner** ⟨1a⟩ **1** *v/t* TECH bolt **2** *v/i fig* F slave away F

boulot¹, ~te [bulo, -ɔt] plump

boulot² [bulo] *m* F work

bouquet [bukɛ] *m* bouquet, bunch of flowers; *de vin* bouquet

bouquin [bukɛ̃] *m* F book; **bouquiner** ⟨1a⟩ read; **bouquiniste** *m/f* bookseller

bourbe [burb] *f* mud; **bourbeux, -euse** muddy; **bourbier** *m* bog; *fig* quagmire

bourde [burd] *f* blunder, booboo F, blooper F

bourdon [burdɔ̃] *m* ZO bumblebee; **faux ~** drone

bourdonnement [burdɔnmɑ̃] *d'insectes* buzzing; *de moteur* humming; **bourdonner** ⟨1a⟩ *d'insectes* buzz; *de moteur* hum; *d'oreilles* ring

bourg [bur] *m* market town; **bourgade** *f* village

bourgeois, ~e [burʒwa, -z] **1** *adj* middle-class; *péj* middle-class, bourgeois **2** *m/f* member of the middle classes; *péj* member of the middle classes *ou* the bourgeoisie; **bourgeoisie** *f* middle classes *pl*; *péj* middle classes *pl*, bourgeoisie; **haute ~** upper middle classes *pl*; **petite ~** lower middle classes *pl*

bourgeon [burʒɔ̃] *m* BOT bud

Bourgogne [burgɔɲ] *f:* **la ~** Burgundy; **bourgogne** *m* burgundy; **bourguignon, ~ne 1** *adj* Burgundian, of / from Burgundy **2** *m/f* **Bourguignon, ~ne** Burgundian

bourlinguer [burlɛ̃ge] ⟨1m⟩: **il a pas**

mal bourlingué F he's been around
bourrage [buʀaʒ] *m* F: **~ de crâne**
brain-washing
bourrasque [buʀask] *f* gust
bourratif, -ive [buʀatif, -iv] stodgy
bourré, ~e [buʀe] full (*de* of), packed
(*de* with), crammed (*de* with); F (*ivre*)
drunk, sozzled F
bourreau [buʀo] *m* (*pl* -x) execu-
tioner; **~ de travail** workaholic
bourrer [buʀe] ⟨1a⟩ *coussin* stuff; *pipe*
fill; *se* **~ de qch** F stuff o.s. with sth
bourrique [buʀik] *f fig* (*personne têtue*)
mule
bourru, ~e [buʀy] surly, bad-tempered
bourse [buʀs] *f d'études* grant; (*porte-
monnaie*) coin purse, *Br* purse;
Bourse (*des valeurs*) Stock Exchange; *la Bourse monte / baisse*
stock *ou Br* share prices are rising / falling; **boursicoter** ⟨1a⟩ dabble on the Stock Exchange; **boursier, -ère 1** *adj* stock exchange *atr*
2 *m/f* grant recipient
boursouf(f)lé, ~e [buʀsufle] swollen
bousculade [buskylad] *f* crush; (*précipitation*) rush; **bousculer** ⟨1a⟩
(*heurter*) jostle; (*presser*) rush; *fig*: *traditions* overturn, upset
bouse [buz] *f*: **~ (de vache)** cowpat
bousiller [buzije] ⟨1a⟩ F *travail* screw
up F, bungle; (*détruire*) wreck
boussole [busɔl] *f* compass; *perdre la
~* F lose one's head
bout¹ [bu] *m* (*extrémité*) end; *de doigts,
de nez, de bâton* end, tip; (*morceau*)
piece; **~ à ~** end to end; *tirer à ~ portant* fire at point-blank range; *au ~
de* at the end of; *au ~ du compte*
when all's said and done; *d'un ~ à
l'autre* right the way through; *aller
jusqu'au ~ fig* see it through to the
bitter end; *être à ~* be at an end; *être
à ~ de ...* have no more ... (left); *venir à ~ de qch / qn* overcome sth /
s.o.; *connaître qch sur le ~ des
doigts* have sth at one's fingertips;
manger un ~ eat something, have
a bite (to eat)
bout² [bu] → *bouillir*
boutade [butad] *f* joke

bouteille [butɛj] *f* bottle; *d'air
comprimé, de butane* cylinder
boutique [butik] *f* store, *Br* shop; *de
mode* boutique
bouton [butɔ̃] *m* button; *de porte* handle; ANAT spot, zit F; BOT bud; **bou-
ton-d'or** *m* (*pl* boutons-d'or) BOT
buttercup; **boutonner** ⟨1a⟩ button;
BOT bud; **boutonneux, -euse**
spotty; **boutonnière** *f* buttonhole;
bouton-pression *m* (*pl* boutons-
-pression) snap fastener, *Br* press
stud fastener
bouture [butyʀ] *f* BOT cutting
bovin, ~e [bɔvɛ̃, -in] **1** *adj* cattle *atr*
2 *mpl* **~s** cattle *pl*
bowling [bulin] *m* bowling, *Br* ten-pin
bowling; *lieu* bowling alley
box [bɔks] *m* (*pl* boxes) *f* JUR: **~ des
accusés** dock
boxe [bɔks] *f* boxing; **boxer** ⟨1a⟩ box;
boxeur *m* boxer
boycott [bɔjkɔt] *m* boycott; **boycot-
tage** *m* boycott; **boycotter** ⟨1a⟩
boycott
B.P. [bepe] *abr* (*= boîte postale*) PO
Box
bracelet [bʀaslɛ] *m* bracelet
braconner [bʀakɔne] ⟨1a⟩ poach;
braconnier *m* poacher
brader [bʀade] ⟨1a⟩ sell off
braguette [bʀagɛt] *f* fly
braille [bʀaj] *m* braille
brailler [bʀaje] ⟨1a⟩ bawl, yell
braire [bʀɛʀ] ⟨4s⟩ *d'un âne* bray; F
bawl, yell
braise [bʀɛz] *f* embers *pl*; **braiser**
⟨1b⟩ CUIS braise
brancard [bʀɑ̃kaʀ] *m* (*civière*) stretcher; **brancardier, -ère** *m/f* stretcher-
-bearer
branche [bʀɑ̃ʃ] *f* branch; *de céleri* stick
brancher [bʀɑ̃ʃe] ⟨1a⟩ connect up
(*sur* to); *à une prise* plug in; *être
branché fig* (*informé*) be clued
up; (*en vogue*) be trendy F
brandir [bʀɑ̃diʀ] ⟨2a⟩ brandish
brandy [bʀɑ̃di] *m* brandy
branle [bʀɑ̃l] *m*: *mettre en* **~** set in motion; **branle-bas** *m fig* commotion;
branler ⟨1a⟩ shake

B

braquage [brakaʒ] *m* AUTO turning; **rayon** *m* **de ~** turning circle; **braquer** ⟨1m⟩ **1** *v/t arme* aim, point (*sur* at); **~ qn contre qch / qn** turn s.o. against sth / s.o. **2** *v/i* AUTO: **~ à droite** turn the wheel to the right

bras [bra, brɑ] *m* arm; **être le ~ droit de qn** *fig* be s.o.'s right-hand man; **~ de mer** arm of the sea; **dessus dessous** arm in arm; **avoir le ~ long** *fig* have influence *ou* F clout; **avoir qn / qch sur les ~** *fig* F have s.o. / sth on one's hands; **accueillir qn / qch à ~ ouverts** welcome s.o. / sth with open arms; **cela me coupe ~ et jambes** F I'm astonished; *de fatigue* it knocks me out F

brasier [brazje] *m* blaze

brassage [brasaʒ] *m* brewing

brassard [brasar] *m* armband

brasse [bras] *f* stroke; **~ papillon** butterfly (stroke)

brasser [brase] ⟨1a⟩ *bière* brew; **~ de l'argent** turn over huge sums of money; **brasserie** *f* brewery; *établissement* restaurant; **brasseur** *m* brewer

brave [brav] **1** *adj* (*after the noun: courageux*) brave; (*before the noun: bon*) good **2** *m:* **un ~** a brave man; **braver** ⟨1a⟩ (*défier*) defy; **bravoure** *f* bravery

break [brɛk] *m* AUTO station wagon, *Br* estate (car)

brebis [brəbi] *f* ewe

brèche [brɛʃ] *f* gap; *dans les défenses* breach; **être toujours sur la ~** *fig* be always on the go

bredouille [brəduj]: **rentrer ~** return empty-handed; **bredouiller** ⟨1a⟩ mumble

bref, -ève [brɛf, -ɛv] **1** *adj* brief, short **2** *adv* briefly, in short

Brésil [brezil]: **le ~** Brazil; **brésilien, ~ne 1** *adj* Brazilian **2** *m/f* **Brésilien, ~ne** Brazilian

Bretagne [brətaɲ]: **la ~** Britanny

bretelle [brətɛl] *f de lingerie* strap; *d'autoroute* ramp, *Br* slip road; **~s** *de pantalon* suspenders, *Br* braces

breton, ~ne [brətõ, -ɔn] **1** *adj* Breton **2** *m langue* Breton **3** *m/f* **Breton, ~ne** Breton

breuvage [brœvaʒ] *m* drink

brevet [brəvɛ] *m diplôme* diploma; *pour invention* patent; **breveter** ⟨1c⟩ patent

bribes [brib] *fpl de conversation* snippets

bric-à-brac [brikabrak] *m* (*pl inv*) bric-a-brac

bricolage [brikɔlaʒ] *m* do-it-yourself, DIY

bricole [brikɔl] *f* little thing

bricoler [brikɔle] ⟨1a⟩ do odd jobs; **bricoleur, -euse** *m/f* handyman, DIY expert

bride [brid] *f* bridle

bridé, ~e [bride]: **yeux** *mpl* **~s** almond-shaped eyes, slant eyes

bridge [bridʒ] *m* bridge

brièvement [brijɛvmã] *adv* briefly; **brièveté** *f* briefness, brevity

brigade [brigad] *f* MIL brigade; *de police* squad; *d'ouvriers* gang; **brigadier** *m* MIL corporal

brillamment [brijamã] *adv* brilliantly; **brillant, ~e** shiny; *couleur* bright; *fig* brilliant; **briller** ⟨1a⟩ shine (*aussi fig*); **faire ~** *meuble* polish

brimer [brime] ⟨1a⟩ bully

brin [brɛ̃] *m d'herbe* blade; *de corde* strand; *de persil* sprig; **un ~ de** *fig* a bit of

brindille [brɛ̃dij] *f* twig

brio [brijo] *m:* **avec ~** with panache

brioche [brijɔʃ] *f* CUIS brioche; F (*ventre*) paunch

brique [brik] *f* brick

briquet [brikɛ] *m* lighter

brise [briz] *f* breeze

brisé, ~e [brize] broken

brise-glace(s) [brizglas] *m* (*pl inv*) icebreaker; **brise-lames** *m* (*pl inv*) breakwater

briser [brize] ⟨1a⟩ **1** *v/t chose, grève, cœur, volonté* break; *résistance* crush; *vie, amitié, bonheur* destroy; (*fatiguer*) wear out **2** *v/i de la mer* break; **se ~** *de verre etc* break, shatter; *de la voix* break, falter; *des espoirs* be shattered

brise-tout [briztu] *m* (*pl inv*) klutz F, clumsy oaf

briseur [brizœr] *m*: **~ de grève** strike-breaker

britannique [britanik] **1** *adj* British **2** *m/f* **Britannique** Briton, Britisher, Brit F; **les ~s** the British

broc [bro] *m* pitcher

brocante [brɔkãt] *f magasin* second-hand store; **brocanteur, -euse** *m/f* second-hand dealer

brocart [brɔkar] *m* brocade

broche [brɔʃ] *f* CUIS spit; *bijou* brooch

brochet [brɔʃɛ] *m* pike

brochette [brɔʃɛt] *f* CUIS skewer; *plat* shish kebab

brochure [brɔʃyr] *f* brochure

brocolis [brɔkɔli] *mpl* broccoli *sg*

broder [brɔde] ⟨1a⟩ embroider

broderie [brɔdri] *f* embroidery

bronches [brɔ̃ʃ] *fpl* ANAT bronchial tubes, bronchials

broncher [brɔ̃ʃe] ⟨1a⟩: **sans ~** without batting an eyelid

bronchite [brɔ̃ʃit] *f* MÉD bronchitis

bronze [brɔ̃z] *m* bronze

bronzé, ~e [brɔ̃ze] tanned; **bronzer** ⟨1a⟩ **1** *v/t peau* tan **2** *v/i* get a tan; **se ~** sunbathe

brosse [brɔs] *f* brush; *coiffure* crew-cut; **~ à dents / cheveux** toothbrush / hairbrush; **brosser** ⟨1a⟩ brush; **se ~ les dents / cheveux** brush one's teeth / hair; **~ un tableau de la situation** *fig* outline the situation

brouette [bruɛt] *f* wheelbarrow

brouhaha [bruaa] *m* hubbub

brouillage [brujaʒ] *m* interference; *délibéré* jamming

brouillard [brujar] *m* fog; **il y a du ~** it's foggy

brouille [bruj] *f* quarrel; **brouillé, ~e**: **être ~ avec qn** have quarreled *ou Br* quarrelled with s.o.; **œufs** *mpl* **~s** CUIS scrambled eggs; **brouiller** ⟨1a⟩ *œufs* scramble; *cartes* shuffle; *papiers* muddle, jumble; *radio* jam; *involontairement* cause interference to; *amis* cause to fall out; **se ~ du ciel** cloud over, become overcast; *de vi-*tres, lunettes mist up; *d'idées* get muddled *ou* jumbled; *d'amis* fall out, quarrel

brouillon [brujõ] *m* draft; **papier** *m* **~** scratch paper, *Br* scrap paper

broussailles [brusaj] *fpl* undergrowth *sg*; **broussailleux, -euse** *cheveux, sourcils* bushy

brousse [brus] *f* GÉOGR bush; **la ~** F *péj* the boonies F, the back of beyond

brouter [brute] ⟨1a⟩ graze

broutille [brutij] *f* trifle

broyer [brwaje] ⟨1h⟩ grind; **~ du noir** *fig* be down

broyeur *m*: **~ à ordures** garbage *ou Br* waste disposal unit

bru [bry] *f* daughter-in-law

brugnon [bryɲõ] *m* BOT nectarine

bruine [brɥin] *f* drizzle; **bruiner** ⟨1a⟩ drizzle; **bruineux, -euse** drizzly

bruissement [brɥismã] *m* rustle, rustling

bruit [brɥi] *m* sound; *qui dérange* noise; (*rumeur*) rumor, *Br* rumour; **un ~** a sound, a noise; **faire du ~** make a noise; *fig* cause a sensation; **faire grand ~ de qch** make a lot of fuss about sth; **le ~ court que …** there's a rumor going around that …; **~ de fond** background noise; **bruitage** *m à la radio, au théâtre* sound effects *pl*

brûlant, ~e [brylã, -t] burning (*aussi fig*); (*chaud*) burning hot; *liquide* scalding; **brûlé, ~e 1** *adj* burnt; **sentir le ~** taste burnt **2** *m/f* burns victim

brûle-pourpoint [brylpurpwɛ̃]: **à ~** point-blank

brûler [bryle] ⟨1a⟩ **1** *v/t* burn; *d'eau bouillante* scald; *vêtement en repassant* scorch; *électricité* use; **~ un feu rouge** go through a red light; **~ les étapes** *fig* cut corners **2** *v/i* burn; **~ de fièvre** be burning up with fever; **se ~** burn o.s.; *d'eau bouillante* scald o.s.; **se ~ la cervelle** blow one's brains out; **brûleur** *m* burner; **brûlure** *f sensation* burning; *lésion* burn; **~s d'estomac** heartburn *sg*

brume [brym] *f* mist; **brumeux, -euse** misty

brun, ~e [brɛ̃ *ou* brœ̃, bryn] **1** *adj* brown; *cheveux, peau* dark **2** *m/f* dark-haired man / woman; **une ~e** a brunette **3** *m couleur* brown; **brunâtre** brownish; **brunir** ⟨2a⟩ tan

brushing® [brœʃiŋ] *m* blow-dry

brusque [brysk] (*rude*) abrupt, brusque; (*soudain*) abrupt, sudden; **brusquement** *adv* abruptly, suddenly; **brusquer** ⟨1m⟩ *personne, choses* rush; **brusquerie** *f* abruptness

brut, ~e [bryt] **1** *adj* raw, unprocessed; *bénéfice, poids, revenu* gross; *pétrole* crude; *sucre* unrefined; *champagne* very dry **2** *m* crude (petroleum) **3** *f* brute; **brutal, ~e** (*mpl* -aux) brutal; **brutalement** *adv* brutally; **brutaliser** ⟨1a⟩ ill-treat; **brutalité** *f* brutality

Bruxelles [bry(k)sɛl] Brussels

bruyamment [brɥijamɑ̃] *adv* noisily; **bruyant, ~e** noisy

bruyère [bryjɛr, brɥijɛr] *f* BOT heather; *terrain* heath

bu, ~e [by] *p/p* → **boire**

buanderie [bɥɑ̃dri] *f* laundry room

bûche [byʃ] *f* log; **~ de Noël** Yule log

bûcher[1] [byʃe] *m* woodpile; (*échafaud*) stake

bûcher[2] [byʃe] ⟨1a⟩ work hard; ÉDU F hit the books, *Br* swot; **bûcheur, -euse** *m/f* ÉDU grind, *Br* swot

budget [bydʒɛ] *m* budget; **~ de la Défense** defense budget

budgétaire [bydʒetɛr] budget *atr*; **déficit** *m* **~** budget deficit

buée [bɥe] *f sur vitre* steam, condensation

buffet [byfɛ] *m de réception* buffet; *meuble* sideboard; **~ (de la gare)** (station) buffet

buffle [byfl] *m* buffalo

buisson [bɥisɔ̃] *m* shrub, bush; **buissonnière: faire l'école ~** play truant

bulbe [bylb] *f* BOT bulb

bulldozer [buldozœr] *m* bulldozer

bulgare [bylgar] **1** *adj* Bulgarian **2** *m langue* Bulgarian **3** *m/f* Bulgare Bulgarian; **Bulgarie: la ~** Bulgaria

bulle [byl] *f* bubble; *de bande dessinée* (speech) bubble *ou* balloon; **~ de savon** soap bubble

bulletin [byltɛ̃] *m* (*formulaire*) form; (*rapport*) bulletin; *à l'école* report card, *Br* report; **~ (de vote)** ballot (paper); **~ météorologique** weather report; **~ de salaire** paystub, *Br* payslip

bureau [byro] *m* (*pl* -x) office; *meuble* desk; **~ de change** exchange office, *Br* bureau de change; **~ de location** box office; **~ de poste** post office; **~ de tabac** tobacco store, *Br* tobacconist's; **~ de vote** polling station

bureaucrate [byrokrat] *m/f* bureaucrat; **bureaucratie** *f* bureaucracy; **bureaucratique** bureaucratic

bureautique [byrotik] *f* office automation

bus [bys] *m* bus

busqué, ~e [byske] *nez* hooked

buste [byst] *m* bust

but [by(t)] *m* (*cible*) target; *fig* (*objectif*) aim, goal; *d'un voyage* purpose; SP goal; **de ~ en blanc** point-blank; **dans le ~ de faire qch** with the aim of doing sth; **j'ai pour seul ~ de ...** my sole ambition is to ...; **marquer un ~** score (a goal); **errer sans ~** wander aimlessly; **à ~ lucratif** profit-making; **à ~ non lucratif** not-for-profit, *Br* non-profit making

butane [bytan] *m* butane gas

buté, ~e [byte] stubborn; **buter** ⟨1a⟩: **~ contre qch** bump into sth, collide with sth; **~ sur un problème** come up against a problem, hit a problem; **se ~** *fig* dig one's heels in

buteur [bytœr] *m* goalscorer

butin [bytɛ̃] *m* booty; *de voleurs* haul

butte [byt] *f* (*colline*) hillock; **être en ~ à** be exposed to

buvable [byvabl] drinkable; **buvette** *f* bar; **buveur, -euse** *m/f* drinker

C

c' [s] → ce

CA [sea] *abr* (= *chiffre d'affaires*) turnover; ÉL (= *courant alternatif*) AC (= alternating current)

ça [sa] that; *~, c'est très bon* that's very good; *nous attendons que ~ commence* we're waiting for it to start; *~ va?* how are things?; *(d'accord?)* ok?; *~ y est* that's it; *c'est ~!* that's right!; *~ alors!* well I'm damned!; *et avec ~?* anything else?; *où / qui ~?* where's / who's that?

çà [sa] *adv*: *~ et là* here and there

cabale [kabal] *f* (*intrigue*) plot

cabane [kaban] *f* (*baraque*) hut; **cabanon** *m cellule* padded cell; *en Provence* cottage

cabaret [kabarε] *m* (*boîte de nuit*) night club

cabas [kaba] *m* shopping bag

cabillaud [kabijo] *m* cod

cabine [kabin] *f* AVIAT, MAR cabin; *d'un camion* cab; *~ d'essayage* changing room; *~ de pilotage* AVIAT cockpit; *~ téléphonique* phone booth

cabinet [kabinε] *m petite pièce* small room; *d'avocat* chambers *pl*; *de médecin* office, *Br* surgery; (*clientèle*) practice; POL Cabinet; *~s* toilet *sg*

câble [kabl] *m* cable; *~ de remorque* towrope; *le ~, la télévision par ~* cable (TV)

cabosser [kabɔse] ⟨1a⟩ dent

cabrer [kɑbre] ⟨1a⟩: *se ~ d'un animal* rear

cabriolet [kabrijɔlε] *m* AUTO convertible

caca [kaka] *m* F poop F, *Br* poo F; *faire ~* do a poop

cacahuète [kakawεt, -ɥεt] *f* BOT peanut

cacao [kakao] *m* cocoa; BOT cocoa bean

cache-cache [kaʃkaʃ] *m* hide-and--seek; *jouer à ~* play hide-and-seek

cache-col [kaʃkɔl] *m* (*pl inv*) scarf

cachemire [kaʃmir] *m tissu* cashmere

cache-nez [kaʃne] *m* (*pl inv*) scarf

cacher [kaʃe] ⟨1a⟩ hide; *se ~ de qn* hide from s.o.; *il ne cache pas que* he makes no secret of the fact that; *~ la vérité* hide the truth, cover up

cachet [kaʃε] *m* seal; *fig* (*caractère*) style; PHARM tablet; (*rétribution*) fee; *~ de la poste* postmark

cacheter [kaʃte] ⟨1c⟩ seal

cachette [kaʃεt] *f* hiding place; *en ~* secretly

cachot [kaʃo] *m* dungeon

cachotterie [kaʃɔtri] *f*: *faire des ~s* be secretive; **cachottier, -ère** secretive

cactus [kaktys] *m* cactus

c.-à-d. *abr* (= *c'est-à-dire*) ie (= id est)

cadavre [kadavr] *m d'une personne* (dead) body, corpse; *d'un animal* carcass

caddie[1]® [kadi] *m* cart, *Br* trolley

caddie[2] [kadi] *m* GOLF caddie

cadeau [kado] *m* (*pl -x*) present, gift; *faire un ~ à qn* give s.o. a present *ou* a gift; *faire ~ de qch à qn* give s.o. sth (as a present *ou* gift)

cadenas [kadna] *m* padlock; **cadenasser** ⟨1a⟩ padlock

cadence [kadɑ̃s] *f tempo* rhythm; *de travail* rate; **cadencé, ~e** rhythmic

cadet, ~te [kadε, -t] *m/f de deux* younger; *de plus de deux* youngest; *il est mon ~ de trois ans* he's three years my junior, he's three years younger than me

cadran [kadrɑ̃] *m* dial; *~ solaire* sundial

cadre [kɑdr] *m* frame; *fig* framework;

d'une entreprise executive; (*environnement*) surroundings *pl*; **s'inscrire dans le ~ de** form part of, come within the framework of; **~s supérieurs / moyens** senior / middle management *sg*; **cadrer** ⟨1a⟩: **~ avec** tally with

CAF [kaf] **1** *f abr* (= **Caisse d'allocations familiales**) Benefits Agency **2** *m abr* (= **Coût, Assurance, Fret**) CIF (= cost insurance freight)

cafard [kafar] *m* ZO cockroach; **avoir le ~** F be feeling down; **donner le ~ à qn** depress s.o., get s.o. down

café [kafe] *m boisson* coffee; *établissement* café; **~ crème** coffee with milk, *Br* white coffee; **~ noir** black coffee

caféine [kafein] *f* caffeine

cafeteria [kafeterja] *f* cafeteria

cafetière [kaftjɛr] *f* coffee pot; **~ électrique** coffee maker, coffee machine

cage [kaʒ] *f* cage; **~ d'ascenseur** elevator shaft, *Br* lift shaft; **~ d'escalier** stairwell

cageot [kaʒo] *m* crate

cagibi [kaʒibi] *m* F storage room

cagneux, -euse [kaɲø, -z] *personne* knock-kneed

cagnotte [kaɲɔt] *f* kitty

cagoule [kagul] *f de moine* cowl; *de bandit* hood; (*passe-montagne*) balaclava

cahier [kaje] *m* notebook; ÉDU exercise book

cahot [kao] *m* jolt; **cahoter** ⟨1a⟩ jolt; **cahoteux, -euse** bumpy

caille [kaj] *f* quail

cailler [kaje] ⟨1a⟩ *du lait* curdle; *du sang* clot; **ça caille!** *fig* F it's freezing!

caillot [kajo] *m* blood clot

caillou [kaju] *m* (*pl* -x) pebble, stone

caisse [kɛs] *f* chest; *pour le transport* crate; *de déménagement* packing case; *de champagne, vin* case; (*argent*) cash; (*guichet*) cashdesk; *dans un supermarché* checkout; **tenir la ~** look after the money; **grosse ~** MUS bass drum; **~ enregistreuse** cash register; **~ d'épargne** savings bank; **~ noire** slush fund; **~ de retraite** pension fund; **caissier, -ère** *m/f* cashier

cajoler [kaʒɔle] ⟨1a⟩ (*câliner*) cuddle

cake [kɛk] *m* fruit cake

calamité [kalamite] *f* disaster, calamity

calandre [kalɑ̃dr] *f* AUTO radiator grille

calcaire [kalkɛr] **1** *adj massif* limestone *atr*; *terrain* chalky; *eau* hard **2** *m* GÉOL limestone

calcium [kalsjɔm] *m* calcium

calcul[1] [kalkyl] *m* calculation (*aussi fig*); **~ mental** mental arithmetic

calcul[2] [kalkyl] *m* MÉD stone *m*; **~ biliaire** gallstone; **~ rénal** kidney stone

calculateur, -trice [kalkylatœr, -tris] **1** *adj* calculating **2** *f*: **~ (de poche)** (pocket) calculator

calculer [kalkyle] ⟨1a⟩ calculate; **calculette** *f* pocket calculator

cale [kal] *f* MAR hold; *pour bloquer* wedge; **~ sèche** dry dock

calé, ~e [kale] F: **être ~ en qch** be good at sth

caleçon [kalsɔ̃] *m d'homme* boxer shorts *pl*, boxers *pl*; *de femme* leggings *pl*

calembour [kalɑ̃bur] *m* pun, play on words

calendrier [kalɑ̃drije] *m* calendar; *emploi du temps* schedule, *Br* timetable

calepin [kalpɛ̃] *m* notebook

caler [kale] ⟨1a⟩ **1** *v/t moteur* stall; TECH wedge **2** *v/i d'un moteur* stall

calibre [kalibr] *m d'une arme, fig* caliber, *Br* calibre; *de fruits, œufs* grade

califourchon [kalifurʃɔ̃]: **à ~** astride

câlin, ~e [kalɛ̃, -in] **1** *adj* affectionate **2** *m* (*caresse*) cuddle; **câliner** ⟨1a⟩ (*caresser*) cuddle

calmant, ~e [kalmɑ̃, -t] **1** *adj* soothing; MÉD (*tranquillisant*) tranquilizing, *Br* tranquillizing; *contre douleur* painkilling **2** *m* tranquilizer, *Br* tranquillizer; *contre douleur* painkiller

calmar [kalmar] *m* squid

calme [kalm] **1** *adj* calm; *Bourse, vie* quiet **2** *m* calmness, coolness; MAR calm; (*silence*) peace and quiet, quietness; **calmement** *adv* calmly, coolly; **calmer** ⟨1a⟩ *personne* calm down; *douleur* relieve; **se ~** calm down

calomnie [kalɔmni] *f* slander; *écrite* libel; **calomnier** ⟨1a⟩ insult; *par écrit* libel; **calomnieux, -euse** slanderous *par écrit* libelous

calorie [kalɔri] *f* calorie; *régime basses ~s* low-calorie diet

calque [kalk] *m* TECH tracing; *fig* exact copy; **calquer** ⟨1m⟩ trace; *~ qch sur fig* model sth on

calva [kalva] *m* F, **calvados** [kalvadɔs] *m* Calvados, apple brandy

calvaire [kalver] *m* REL wayside cross; *fig* agony

calvitie [kalvisi] *f* baldness

camarade [kamarad] *m/f* friend; POL comrade; *~ de jeu* playmate; **camaraderie** *f* friendship, camaraderie

Cambodge [kɑ̃bɔdʒ]: *le ~* Cambodia; **cambodgien, ~ne 1** *adj* Cambodian **2** *m langue* Cambodian **3** *m/f* **Cambodgien, ~ne** Cambodian

cambouis [kɑ̃bwi] *m* (dirty) oil

cambrer [kɑ̃bre] ⟨1a⟩ arch

cambriolage [kɑ̃brijolaʒ] *m* break-in, burglary; **cambrioler** ⟨1a⟩ burglarize, *Br* burgle; **cambrioleur, -euse** *m/f* house-breaker, burglar

cambrousse [kɑ̃brus] *f* F *péj: la ~* the back of beyond, the sticks *pl*

came [kam] *f* TECH cam; *arbre m à ~s* camshaft

camelote [kamlɔt] *f* F junk

camembert [kamɑ̃ber] *m* Camembert; *diagramme* pie chart

caméra [kamera] *f* camera; *~ vidéo* video camera

Cameroun [kamrun]: *le ~* Cameroon; **camerounais, ~e 1** *adj* Cameroonian **2** *m/f* **Camerounais, ~e** Cameroonian

camion [kamjɔ̃] *m* truck, *Br aussi* lorry; *~ de livraison* delivery van; **camion-citerne** *m* (*pl* camions-citernes) tanker

camionnette [kamjɔnet] *f* van; **camionneur** *m conducteur* truck driver, *Br aussi* lorry driver; *directeur d'entreprise* trucker, *Br* haulier

camomille [kamɔmij] *f* BOT camomile

camouflage [kamuflaʒ] *m* camouflage; **camoufler** ⟨1a⟩ camouflage; *fig: intention, gains* hide; *faute* cover up

camp [kɑ̃] *m* camp (*aussi* MIL, POL); *~ de concentration* concentration camp; *~ militaire* military camp *m*; *~ de réfugiés* refugee camp; *~ de vacances* summer camp, *Br* holiday camp; *ficher le ~* F clear off, get lost F

campagnard, ~e [kɑ̃paɲar, -d] **1** *adj* country *atr* **2** *m/f* person who lives in the country

campagne [kɑ̃paɲ] *f* country, countryside; MIL, *fig* campaign; *à la ~* in the country; *en pleine ~* deep in the countryside; *~ de diffamation* smear campaign; *~ électorale* election campaign; *~ publicitaire* advertising campaign

campement [kɑ̃pmɑ̃] *m action* camping; *installation* camp; *lieu* campground; **camper** ⟨1a⟩ camp; *se ~ devant* plant o.s. in front of; **campeur, -euse** *m/f* camper

camping [kɑ̃piŋ] *m* camping; (*terrain m de*) campground, campsite; *faire du ~* go camping; **camping-car** *m* (*pl* camping-cars) camper; **camping-gaz** ® *m* campstove

Canada [kanada] *le ~* Canada; **canadien, ~ne 1** *adj* Canadian **2** *m/f* **Canadien, ~ne** Canadian

canal [kanal] *m* (*pl* -aux) channel; (*tuyau*) pipe; (*bras d'eau*) canal; *~ d'irrigation* irrigation canal; *le ~ de Suez* the Suez Canal

canalisation [kanalizasjɔ̃] *f* (*tuyauterie*) pipes *pl*, piping; **canaliser** *fig* channel

canapé [kanape] *m* sofa; CUIS canapé; **canapé-lit** *m* sofa-bed

canard [kanar] *m* duck; F *newpaper*; *il fait un froid de ~* F it's freezing

canari [kanari] *m* canary

cancans [kɑ̃kɑ̃] *mpl* gossip *sg*

cancer [kɑ̃ser] *m* MÉD cancer; *avoir un ~ du poumon* have lung cancer; *le Cancer* ASTROL Cancer

cancéreux, -euse [kɑ̃serø, -z] **1** *adj tumeur* cancerous **2** *m/f* person with cancer, cancer patient; **cancérigène, -ogène** carcinogenic; **cancérologue** *m/f* cancer specialist

candeur [kɑ̃dœr] *f* ingenuousness

candidat, ~e [kɑ̃dida, -t] *m/f* candidate; **candidature** *f* candidacy; *à un poste* application; **~ spontanée** unsolicited application; **poser sa ~ à un poste** apply for a position

candide [kɑ̃did] *adj* ingenuous

cane [kan] *f* (female) duck; **caneton** *m* duckling

canette [kanɛt] *f* (*bouteille*) bottle

canevas [kanva] *m* canvas; *de projet* outline

caniche [kaniʃ] *m* poodle

canicule [kanikyl] *f* heatwave

canif [kanif] *m* pocket knife

canin, ~e [kanɛ̃, -in] *adj* dog *atr*, canine

canine [kanin] *f* canine

caniveau [kanivo] *m* (*pl* -x) gutter

canne [kan] *f pour marcher* cane, stick; **~ à pêche** fishing rod; **~ à sucre** sugar cane

cannelle [kanɛl] *f* cinnamon

canoë [kanɔe] *m* canoe; *activité* canoeing; **canoéiste** *m/f* canoeist

canon [kanɔ̃] *m* MIL gun; HIST cannon; *de fusil* barrel; **~ à eau** water cannon

canoniser [kanɔnize] ⟨1a⟩ REL canonize

canot [kano] *m* small boat; **~ pneumatique** rubber dinghy; **~ de sauvetage** lifeboat

cantatrice [kɑ̃tatris] *f* singer

cantine [kɑ̃tin] *f* canteen

cantonner [kɑ̃tɔne] ⟨1a⟩ MIL billet; **se ~** shut o.s. away; **se ~ à** *fig* confine o.s. to

canular [kanylar] *m* hoax

caoutchouc [kautʃu] *m* rubber; (*bande élastique*) rubber band; **~ mousse** foam rubber

cap [kap] *m* GÉOGR cape; AVIAT, MAR course; **franchir le ~ de la quarantaine** *fig* turn forty; **mettre le ~ sur** head for, set course for

C.A.P. [seape] *m abr* (= **certificat d'aptitude professionnelle**) vocational training certificate

capable [kapabl] capable; **~ de faire qch** capable of doing sth; **capacité** *f* (*compétence*) ability; (*contenance*) capacity; **~ d'absorption** absorbency; **~ de production** production capacity; **~ de stockage** storage capacity

cape [kap] *f* cape; **rire sous ~** *fig* laugh up one's sleeve

capillaire [kapilɛr] capillary; *lotion, soins* hair *atr*

capitaine [kapitɛn] *m* captain

capital, ~e [kapital] (*mpl* -aux) **1** *adj* essential; **peine** *f* **~e** capital punishment **2** *m* capital; **capitaux** capital *sg*; **capitaux propres** equity *sg* **3** *f* ville capital (city); *lettre* capital (letter)

capitalisme [kapitalism] *m* capitalism; **capitaliste** *m/f & adj* capitalist

capiteux, -euse [kapitø, -z] *parfum, vin* heady

capitonner [kapitɔne] ⟨1a⟩ pad

capitulation [kapitylasjɔ̃] *f* capitulation; **capituler** ⟨1a⟩ capitulate

caporal [kapɔral] *m* (*pl* -aux) MIL private first class, *Br* lance-corporal; **caporal-chef** corporal

capot [kapo] *m* AUTO hood, *Br* bonnet; **capote** *f vêtement* greatcoat; AUTO top, *Br* hood; **~** (**anglaise**) F condom, rubber F; **capoter** ⟨1a⟩ AVIAT, AUTO overturn

câpre [kɑpr] *f* CUIS caper

caprice [kapris] *m* whim; **capricieux, -euse** capricious

Capricorne [kaprikɔrn] *m*: **le ~** ASTROL Capricorn

capsule [kapsyl] *f* capsule; *de bouteille* top; **~ spatiale** space capsule

capter [kapte] ⟨1a⟩ *attention, regard* catch; RAD, TV pick up; **capteur** *m*: **~ solaire** solar panel

captif, -ive [kaptif, -iv] *m/f & adj* captive; **captivant, ~e** *personne* captivating, enchanting; *histoire, lecture* gripping; **captiver** ⟨1a⟩ *fig* captivate; **captivité** *f* captivity

capture [kaptyr] *f* capture; (*proie*) catch; **capturer** ⟨1a⟩ capture

capuche [kapyʃ] *f* hood; **capuchon**

m de vêtement hood; *de stylo* top, cap

capucine [kapysin] *f* BOT nasturtium

car¹ [kar] *m* bus, *Br* coach

car² [kar] *conj* for

carabine [karabin] *f* rifle; **carabiné**, **~e** F: *un … carabiné* one hell of a … F

caractère [karaktɛr] *m* character; *en* **~s gras** in bold; **~s d'imprimerie** block capitals; *avoir bon ~* be good-natured; *avoir mauvais ~* be bad-tempered

caractériel [karakterjɛl] *troubles* emotional; *personne* emotionally disturbed

caractérisé, **~e** [karakterize] *affront, agression* outright; **caractériser** ⟨1a⟩ be characteristic of; **caractéristique** *f & adj* characteristic

carafe [karaf] *f* carafe

caraïbe [karaib] **1** *adj* Caribbean **2** *fpl* **les Caraïbes** the Caribbean *sg*; *la mer des ~* the Caribbean (Sea)

carambolage [karɑ̃bɔlaʒ] *m* AUTO pile-up; **caramboler** ⟨1a⟩ AUTO collide with

caramel [karamɛl] *m* caramel

carapace [karapas] *f* ZO, *fig* shell

carat [kara] *m* carat; *or (à) 18 ~s* 18-carat gold

caravane [karavan] *f* AUTO trailer, *Br* caravan; **caravaning** *m* caravanning

carbone [karbɔn] *m* CHIM carbon; **carbonique** CHIM carbonic; *neige f ~* dry ice; *gaz m ~* carbon dioxide; **carboniser** ⟨1a⟩ burn; **carbonisé** F burnt to a crisp

carburant [karbyrɑ̃] *m* fuel; **carburateur** *m* TECH carburet(t)or

carcasse [karkas] *f d'un animal* carcass; *d'un bateau* shell

cardiaque [kardjak] MÉD **1** *adj* cardiac, heart *atr*; *être ~* have a heart condition; *arrêt m ~* heart failure **2** *m/f* heart patient

cardinal, **~e** [kardinal] (*mpl* -aux) **1** *adj* cardinal; *les quatre points mpl cardinaux* the four points of the compass **2** *m* REL cardinal

cardiologie [kardjɔlɔʒi] *f* cardiology; **cardiologue** *m/f* cardiologist, heart

specialist; **cardio-vasculaire** cardiovascular

carême [karɛm] *m* REL Lent

carence [karɑ̃s] *f* (*incompétence*) inadequacy, shortcoming; (*manque*) deficiency; *~ alimentaire* nutritional deficiency; *maladie f par ~* deficiency disease; *~ affective* emotional deprivation

caresse [karɛs] *f* caress; **caresser** ⟨1b⟩ caress; *projet, idée* play with; *espoir* cherish

cargaison [kargɛzõ] *f* cargo; *fig* load

cargo [kargo] *m* MAR freighter, cargo boat

caricature [karikatyr] caricature; **caricaturer** ⟨1a⟩ caricature

carie [kari] *f* MÉD: *~ dentaire* tooth decay; *une ~* a cavity

carié, **~e** [karje] *dent* bad

carillon [karijõ] *m air, sonnerie* chimes *pl*

caritatif, **~ive** [karitatif, -iv] charitable

carlingue [karlɛ̃g] *f* AVIAT cabin

carnage [karnaʒ] *m* carnage

carnassier, **-ère** [karnasje, -ɛr] carnivorous

carnation [karnasjõ] *f* complexion

carnaval [karnaval] *m* (*pl* -als) carnival

carnet [karnɛ] *m* notebook; *de tickets, timbres* book; *~ d'adresses* address book; *~ de chèques* checkbook, *Br* chequebook; *~ de rendez-vous* appointments diary

carnivore [karnivɔr] **1** *adj* carnivorous **2** *m* carnivore

carotte [karɔt] *f* carrot; *poil de ~* ginger

carpe [karp] *f* ZO carp

carpette [karpɛt] *f* rug

carré, **~e** [kare] **1** *adj* square; *fig: personne, réponse* straightforward; *mètre m ~* square meter **2** *m* square; *élever au ~* square

carreau [karo] *m* (*pl* -x) *de faïence etc* tile; *fenêtre* pane (of glass); *motif* check; *cartes* diamonds; *à ~x tissu* check(ed)

carrefour [karfur] *m* crossroads *sg*

(*aussi fig*)

carrelage [karlaʒ] *m* (*carreaux*) tiles *pl*; **carreler** ⟨1c⟩ tile

carrément [karemɑ̃] *adv répondre, refuser* bluntly, straight out

carrière [karjɛr] *f* quarry; *profession* career; **militaire** *m* **de ~** professional soldier

carrossable [karɔsabl] suitable for cars

carrosse [karɔs] *m* coach; **carrosserie** *f* AUTO bodywork

carrousel [karuzɛl] *m* AVIAT carousel

carrure [karyr] *f* build

cartable [kartabl] *m* schoolbag; *à bretelles* satchel

carte [kart] *f* card; *dans un restaurant* menu; GÉOGR map; MAR, *du ciel* chart; **donner ~ blanche à qn** give s.o. a free hand; **à la ~** à la carte; **~ d'abonnement** membership card; **~ bancaire** cash card; **~ bleue** credit card; **~ de crédit** credit card; **~ d'embarquement** boarding pass; **~ d'étudiant** student card; **~ de fidélité** loyalty card; **~ graphique** graphics card; **~ grise** AUTO registration document; **~ d'identité** identity card; **~ à mémoire** INFORM smartcard; *la* ~ INFORM motherboard; **~ postale** postcard; **~ à puce** INFORM smart card; **~ routière** road map; **~ de séjour** residence permit; **~ son** sound card; **~ vermeil** senior citizens' railpass; **~ de vœux** greeting card; **~** (**de visite**) card; **~ des vins** wine list

carte-clé *f* key card

cartel [kartɛl] *m* ÉCON cartel

carter [kartɛr] *m* TECH casing; AUTO sump

cartilage [kartilaʒ] *m* cartilage

carton [kartõ] *m matériau* cardboard; *boîte* cardboard box, carton; **~ (à dessin)** portfolio; **~ ondulé** corrugated cardboard; **~ jaune / rouge** *en football* yellow / red card; **cartonné, ~e: livre** ~ hardback

cartouche [kartuʃ] *f* cartridge; *de cigarettes* carton; **cartouchière** *f* cartridge belt

cas [kɑ, ka] *m* case; **en aucun ~** under no circumstances; **dans ce ~-là, en ce ~** in that case; **en tout ~** in any case; **au ~ où il voudrait faire de la natation** in case he wants to go swimming, if he should want to go swimming; **en ~ de** in the event of; **en ~ de besoin** if need be; **le ~ échéant** if necessary; **faire (grand) ~ de** have a high opinion of; **faire peu de ~** not think a lot of

casanier, -ère [kazanje, -ɛr] *m/f* stay-at-home

cascade [kaskad] *f* waterfall; *fig* cascade

cascadeur *m* stuntman; **cascadeuse** *f* stuntwoman

case [kɑz] *f* (*hutte*) hut; (*compartiment*) compartment; *dans formulaire* box; *dans mots-croisés, échiquier* square; **retourner à la ~ départ** go back to square one

caser [kaze] ⟨1a⟩ (*ranger*) put; (*loger*) put up; **se ~** (*se marier*) settle down

caserne [kazɛrn] *f* barracks *sg ou pl*; **~ de pompiers** fire station

cash [kaʃ]: **payer ~** pay cash

casier [kazje] *m pour courrier* pigeonholes *pl*; *pour bouteilles, livres* rack; **~ judiciaire** criminal record

casino [kazino] *m* casino

casque [kask] *m* helmet; *de radio* headphones *pl*; **les ~s bleus** the Blue Berets, the UN forces; **casquer** ⟨1m⟩ P pay up, cough up P

casquette [kaskɛt] *f* cap

cassable [kasabl] breakable; **cassant, ~e** fragile; *fig* curt, abrupt

cassation [kasasjõ] *f* JUR quashing; **Cour** *f* **de ~** final court of appeal

casse [kas] *f* AUTO scrapyard; **mettre à la ~** scrap; **payer la ~** pay for the damage

casse-cou [kasku] *m* (*pl inv*) daredevil

casse-croûte [kaskrut] *m* (*pl inv*) snack

casse-noisettes [kasnwazɛt] *m* (*pl inv*) nutcrackers *pl*

casse-pieds [kaspje] *m/f* (*pl inv*) F pain in the neck F

casser [kase] ⟨1a⟩ **1** *v/t* break; *noix* crack; JUR quash; **~ les pieds à qn**

F bore the pants off s.o. F; (*embêter*) get on s.o.'s nerves F; **~ les prix** COMM slash prices; **~ la croûte** have a bite to eat; **~ la figure** *ou* **gueule à qn** F smash s.o.'s face in F; **se ~** break; **se ~ la figure** *ou* **gueule** F fall over; *fig* fail; **se ~ la tête** rack one's brains; **ne pas se ~** F not exactly bust a gut **2** *v/i* break

casserole [kasrɔl] *f* (*sauce*)pan

casse-tête [kastɛt] *m* (*pl inv*) *fig*: *problème* headache

cassette [kasɛt] *f* (*bande magnétique*) cassette; **magnétophone** *m* **à ~** cassette recorder; **~ vidéo** video

casseur, -euse *m/f* rioter; AUTO scrap metal merchant

cassis [kasis] *m* BOT blackcurrant; (*crème f de*) ~ blackcurrant liqueur

cassoulet [kasulɛ] *m* CUIS *casserole of beans, pork, sausage and goose*

cassure [kasyr] *f* (*fissure*) crack; *fig* (*rupture*) split, break-up

caste [kast] *f* caste

castor [kastɔr] *m* beaver

castrer [kastre] ⟨1a⟩ castrate

cataclysme [kataklism] *m* disaster

catalogue [katalɔg] *m* catalog, *Br* catalogue; **cataloguer** ⟨1m⟩ catalog, *Br* catalogue; F *péj* label, pigeonhole

catalyseur [katalizœr] *m* catalyst (*aussi fig*); **catalytique** AUTO: **pot** *m* **~** catalytic converter

catapulte [katapylt] *f* catapult; **catapulter** ⟨1a⟩ catapult (*aussi fig*)

cataracte [katarakt] *f* (*cascade*) waterfall; MÉD cataract

catastrophe [katastrɔf] *f* disaster, catastrophe; **en ~** in a rush; **~ naturelle** act of God; **catastrophé, ~e** stunned; **catastrophique** disastrous, catastrophic

catch [katʃ] *m* wrestling

catéchisme [kateʃism] *m* catechism

catégorie [kategɔri] *f* category; **~ d'âge** age group; **catégorique** categorical; **catégoriser** ⟨1a⟩ categorize

cathédrale [katedral] *f* cathedral

catholicisme [katɔlisism] *m* (Roman) Catholicism; **catholique 1** *adj* (Roman) Catholic; **pas très ~** *fig* F a bit

dubious **2** *m/f* Roman Catholic

catimini [katimini] F: **en ~** on the quiet

cauchemar [koʃmar] *m* nightmare (*aussi fig*); **cauchemardesque** nightmarish

causant, ~e [kozɑ̃, -t] talkative

cause [koz] *f* cause; JUR case; **à ~ de** because of; **pour ~ de** owing to, on account of; **sans ~** for no reason; **pour ~** with good reason; **faire ~ commune avec qn** join forces with s.o.; **être en ~** d'honnêteté, de loyauté be in question; **mettre en ~** honnêteté, loyauté question; *personne* suspect of being involved

causer ⟨1a⟩ **1** *v/t* (*provoquer*) cause **2** *v/i* (*s'entretenir*) chat (**avec qn de** with s.o. about); **causerie** *f* talk; **causette** *f* chat; **faire la ~** have a chat; **causeur, -euse** *m/f* speaker

caustique [kostik] CHIM, *fig* caustic

cautériser [koterize] ⟨1a⟩ MÉD cauterize

caution [kosjɔ̃] *f* security; *pour logement* deposit; JUR bail; *fig* (*appui*) backing, support; **libéré sous ~** released on bail; **cautionner** ⟨1a⟩ stand surety for; JUR bail; *fig* (*se porter garant de*) vouch for; (*appuyer*) back, support

cavale [kaval] *f* F break-out F, escape; **être en ~** be on the run; **cavaler** ⟨1a⟩ F: **~ après qn** chase after s.o.; **cavalerie** *f* cavalry; **cavalier, -ère 1** *m/f pour cheval* rider; *pour bal* partner **2** *m aux échecs* knight **3** *adj* offhand, cavalier

cave [kav] *f* cellar; **~ (à vin)** wine cellar; **caveau** *m* (*pl* -x) *d'enterrement* vault

caverne [kavɛrn] *f* cave

caviar [kavjar] *m* caviar

cavité [kavite] *f* cavity

CC [sese] *abr* (= *courant continu*) DC (= direct current); (= *charges comprises*) all inclusive

CD [sede] *m abr* (= *compact disc*) CD; **CD-Rom** *m* CD-Rom

CE *f abr* (= *Communauté f européenne*) EC (= European Community)

ce [sə] *m* (*cet m*, **cette** *f*, **ces** *pl*) **1** *adj* this, *pl* these; **~ matin / soir** this morning / evening; **en ~ moment** at the moment; **~ livre-ci** this book; **~ livre-là** that book; **ces jours-ci** these days; **cette vie est difficile** it's a hard life;
2 *pron* ◊ : **c'est pourquoi** that is *ou* that's why; **c'est triste** it's sad; **~ sont mes enfants** these are my children; **c'est un acteur** he is *ou* he's an actor; **c'est une actrice** she is *ou* she's an actress; **c'est la vie** that's life; **c'est à qui ce manteau?** whose coat is this?; **c'est elle qui me l'a dit** she's the one who told me, it was her that told me; **qui est-~?** who is it?; **c'est que...** it's that ...; **c'est que tu as grandi!** how you've grown!
◊: **~ que tu fais** what you're doing; **~ qui me plaît** what I like; **ils se sont mis d'accord, ~ qui n'arrive pas souvent** they reached an agreement, which doesn't often happen; **~ qu'il est gentil!** isn't he nice!
◊: **pour ~ faire** to do that; **sur ~** with that

ceci [səsi] this; **~ ou cela** this or that
cécité [sesite] *f* blindness
céder [sede] ⟨1f⟩ **1** *v/t* give up; **cédez le passage** AUTO yield, *Br* give way **2** *v/i* give in (**à** to); (*se casser*) give way; **elle ne lui cède en rien** she is every bit as good as he is
cédille [sedij] *f* cedilla
cèdre [sɛdr] *m* BOT cedar
ceinture [sɛ̃tyr] *f* belt; ANAT waist; **se serrer la ~** *fig* tighten one's belt; **~ de sauvetage** lifebelt; **~ de sécurité** seatbelt; **~ verte** green belt
cela [s(ə)la] that; **il y a cinq ans de ~** that was five years ago; **à ~ près** apart from that
célébration [selebrasjõ] *f* celebration
célèbre [selɛbr] famous
célébrer [selebre] ⟨1f⟩ celebrate; **~ la mémoire de qn** be a memorial to s.o.; **célébrité** *f* fame; *personne* celebrity
céleri [sɛlri] *m* BOT: **~ (en branche)**

celery; **~(-rave)** celeriac
célérité [selerite] *f litt* speed
céleste [selɛst] heavenly
célibat [seliba] *m* single life; *d'un prêtre* celibacy; **célibataire 1** *adj* single, unmarried **2** *m* bachelor **3** *f* single woman
celle, celles [sɛl] → **celui**
cellier [selje] *m* cellar
cellophane [selɔfan] *f* cellophane
cellule [selyl] *f* cell
cellulite [selylit] *f* MÉD cellulite
cellulose [selyloz] *f* cellulose
Celsius [sɛljys]: **20 degrés ~** 20 degrees Celsius
celtique [sɛltik] Celtic
celui [səlɥi] *m* (**celle** *f*, **ceux** *mpl*, **celles** *fpl*) the one, *pl* those; **~ dont je parle** the one I'm talking about; **meilleurs que ceux que ma mère fait** better than the ones *ou* than those my mother makes; **~ qui ... personne** he who ...; *chose* the one which; **tu peux utiliser celle de Claude** you can use Claude's; **celui-ci** this one; **celui-là** that one
cendre [sɑ̃dr] *f* ash; **~s** ashes; **~s de cigarette** cigarette ash *sg*
cendré, ~e [sɑ̃dre] ash-gray, *Br* ash-grey; **cendrée** *f* SP cinder track; **cendrier** *m* ashtray
cène [sɛn] *f* REL: **la ~** (Holy) Communion; **la Cène** *peinture* the Last Supper
censé, ~e [sɑ̃se]: **il est ~ être malade** he's supposed to be sick; **censeur** *m* censor; ÉDU vice-principal, *Br* deputy head; *fig* critic
censure [sɑ̃syr] *f* censorship; *organe* board of censors; **motion** *f* **de ~** POL motion of censure; **censurer** ⟨1a⟩ censor
cent [sɑ̃] **1** *adj* hundred **2** *m* a hundred, one hundred; *monnaie* cent; **pour ~** per cent; **deux ~s personnes** two hundred people; **centaine** *f*: **une ~ de personnes** a hundred or so people; **des ~s de personnes** hundreds of people; **centenaire 1** *adj* hundred-year-old **2** *m fête* centennial, *Br* centenary

centième [sɑ̃tjɛm] hundredth; **centilitre** *m* centiliter, *Br* centilitre; **centime** *m* centime; **centimètre** *m* centimeter, *Br* centimetre; *ruban* tape measure

central, ~e [sɑ̃tral] (*mpl* -aux) **1** *adj* central **2** *m* TÉL telephone exchange **3** *f* power station; **centrale nucléaire** *ou* **atomique** nuclear power station; **centralisation** centralization; **centraliser** ⟨1a⟩ centralize

centre [sɑ̃tr] *m* center, *Br* centre; **~ d'accueil** temporary accommodations *pl*; **~ d'appel** call center; **~ d'attention** center of attention; **~ commercial** shopping mall, *Br aussi* shopping centre; **~ de gravité** center of gravity; **~ d'intérêt** center of interest; **~ de loisirs** leisure center; **~ de planning familial** family planning clinic; **centrer** ⟨1a⟩ center, *Br* centre

centre-ville *m* downtown area, *Br* town centre

centrifuge [sɑ̃trify ʒ] centrifugal

centrifugeuse *f* juicer, juice extractor

centuple [sɑ̃typl] *m*: **au ~** a hundredfold

cep [sɛp] *m* vine stock; **cepage** *m* wine variety

cèpe [sɛp] *m* BOT cèpe, boletus

cependant [səpɑ̃dɑ̃] yet, however

céramique [seramik] *f* ceramic

cercle [sɛrkl] *m* circle; **~ vicieux** vicious circle

cercueil [sɛrkœj] *m* casket, *Br* coffin

céréales [sereal] *fpl* (breakfast) cereal *sg*

cérébral, ~e [serebral] (*mpl* -aux) cerebral

cérémonial [seremɔnjal] *m* ceremonial; **cérémonie** *f* ceremony; **sans ~** *repas etc* informal; *se présenter etc* informally; *mettre à la porte* unceremoniously; **cérémonieux, -euse** *manières* formal

cerf [sɛr] *m* deer

cerfeuil [sɛrfœj] *m* BOT chervil

cerf-volant [sɛrvɔlɑ̃] *m* (*pl* cerfs-volants) kite

cerise [s(ə)riz] *f* cherry; **cerisier** *m* cherry(-tree)

cerne [sɛrn] *m*: **avoir des ~s** have bags under one's eyes; **cerner** ⟨1a⟩ (*encercler*) surround; *fig*: *problème* define

certain, ~e [sɛrtɛ̃, -ɛn] **1** *adj* ◇ (*après le subst*) certain; **être ~ de qch** be certain of sth; ◇ (*devant le subst*) certain; **d'un ~ âge** middle-aged; **~s enfants** certain *ou* some children **2** *pron*: **certains, -aines** some (people); **certains d'entre eux** some of them

certainement [sɛrtɛnmɑ̃] *adv* certainly; (*sûrement*) probably; **~ pas!** definitely not

certes [sɛrt] *adv* certainly

certificat [sɛrtifika] *m* certificate; **~ de mariage** marriage certificate; **~ médical** medical certificate; **certifier** ⟨1a⟩ guarantee; **copie** *f* **certifiée conforme** certified true copy; **~ qch à qn** assure s.o. of sth

certitude [sɛrtityd] *f* certainty

cerveau [sɛrvo] *m* (*pl* -x) brain

cervelas [sɛrvəla] *m* saveloy

cervelle [sɛrvɛl] *f* brains *pl*; **se brûler la ~** *fig* blow one's brains out

ces [se] → *ce*

césarienne [sezarjɛn] *f* MÉD cesarian, *Br* caesarian

cessation [sɛsasjɔ̃] *f* cessation; **après leur ~ de commerce** when they ceased trading; **~ de paiements** suspension of payments; **cesse**: **sans ~** constantly; **cesser** ⟨1b⟩ stop; **~ de faire qch** stop doing sth; **cessez-le-feu** *m* (*pl inv*) ceasefire

cession [sɛsjɔ̃] *f* disposal

c'est-à-dire [sɛtadir] that is, that is to say

cet, cette [sɛt] → *ce*

ceux [sø] → *celui*

CFC [seɛfse] *mpl abr* (= *chlorofluorocarbones*) CFCs (= chlorofluorocarbons)

chacun, ~e [ʃakœ̃ *ou* ʃakœ̃, -yn] *m/f* each (one); **~ de nous** *ou* **d'entre nous** each (one) of us; **c'est ~ pour soi** it's every man for himself; **accessible à tout un ~** available to each and every person; **~ le sait** every-

C

body knows it

chagrin [ʃagrɛ̃] *m* grief; *faire du ~ à qn* upset s.o.; *un ~ d'amour* an unhappy love affair; **chagriner** ⟨1a⟩ sadden

chahut [ʃay] *m* F racket, din; **chahuter** ⟨1b⟩ heckle

chaîne [ʃɛn] *f* chain; *radio*, TV channel; *~s* AUTO snow chains; *~ hi-fi* hi-fi; *~ (de montage)* assembly line; *travail m à la ~* assembly line work; *~ payante* TV pay channel; *~ de montagnes* range of mountains

chair [ʃɛr] *f* flesh; *en ~ et en os* in the flesh; *avoir la ~ de poule* have goosebumps, *Br aussi* have goosepimples; *être bien en ~* be plump

chaire [ʃɛr] *f dans église* pulpit; *d'université* chair

chaise [ʃɛz] *f* chair; *~ longue (transatlantique)* deck chair; *~ électrique* electric chair; *~ roulante* wheelchair

châle [ʃɑl] *m* shawl

chalet [ʃalɛ] *m* chalet

chaleur [ʃalœr] *f* heat; *plus modérée* warmth (*aussi fig*); **chaleureusement** warmly; **chaleureux, -euse** warm

chaloupe [ʃalup] *f* boat

chalumeau [ʃalymo] *m* (*pl* -x) blowtorch

chalutier [ʃalytje] *m* MAR trawler

chamailler [ʃamaje] ⟨1a⟩ F: *se ~* bicker

chambouler [ʃãbule] ⟨1a⟩ turn upside down

chambranle [ʃãbrɑ̃l] *m* frame

chambre [ʃãbr] *f* (bed)room; JUR, POL chamber; *~ à air de pneu* inner tube; *Chambre du Commerce et de l'Industrie* Chamber of Commerce; *~ à coucher* bedroom; *~ à un lit* single (room); *~ à deux lits* twin-bedded room; *~ d'amis* spare room, guest room; *~ noire* PHOT darkroom

chambré [ʃãbre] *vin* at room temperature

chameau [ʃamo] *m* (*pl* -x) camel

chamois [ʃamwa] *m* ZO chamois; *cuir* shammy

champ [ʃã] *m* field (*aussi fig*); *à travers ~* across country; *laisser le ~ libre à qn* give s.o. a free hand; *~ de bataille* battlefield; *~ de courses* racecourse; *~ de mines* minefield; *~ pétrolifère* oilfield

champagne [ʃãpaɲ] *m* champagne

champêtre [ʃãpɛtr] country *atr*

champignon [ʃãpiɲõ] *m* BOT, MÉD fungus; *nourriture* mushroom; *~ de Paris* button mushroom; *~ vénéneux* toadstool

champion, ~ne [ʃãpjõ, -ɔn] *m/f* champion (*aussi fig*); **championnat** *m* championship

chance [ʃãs] *f* (*sort*) luck, fortune; (*occasion*) chance; *il y a des ~s que cela se produise (subj)* there is a chance that it might happen; *bonne ~!* good luck!; *avoir de la ~* be lucky; *c'est une ~ que (+ subj)* it's lucky that; *il y a peu de ~s pour que cela se produise (+ subj)* there is little chance of that happening

chanceler [ʃãsle] ⟨1c⟩ stagger; *d'un gouvernement* totter

chancelier [ʃãsəlje] *m* chancellor

chanceux, -euse [ʃãsø, -z] lucky

chandail [ʃãdaj] *m* (*pl* -s) sweater

chandelier [ʃãdəlje] *m* candlestick

chandelle [ʃãdɛl] *f* candle

change [ʃãʒ] *m* exchange; *taux m de ~* exchange rate, rate of exchange; *contrôle m des ~s* exchange control; *~ du jour* current rate of exchange; *donner le ~ à qn* deceive s.o.; **changeable** changeable; **changeant, ~e** changeable; **changement** *m* change; *~ de vitesse* AUTO gear shift

changer [ʃãʒe] ⟨11⟩ **1** *v/t* change (*en* into); (*échanger*) exchange (*contre* for) **2** *v/i* change; *~ de qch* change sth; *~ d'adresse* change address; *~ d'avis* change one's mind; *~ de place avec qn* change places with s.o.; *~ de sujet* change the subject; *~ de train* change trains; *~ de vitesse* shift gear(s), *Br* change gear(s); *se ~* change

chanson [ʃãsõ] *f* song; **chansonnier**

m singer

chant [ʃɑ̃] *m* song; *action de chanter* singing; *d'église* hymn

chantage [ʃɑ̃taʒ] *m* blackmail; **faire du ~ à qn** blackmail s.o.

chanter [ʃɑ̃te] ⟨1a⟩ **1** *v/i* sing; *d'un coq* crow; **faire ~ qn** blackmail s.o.; **si cela te chante** if you feel like it **2** *v/t* sing; **chanteur, -euse** *m/f* singer

chantier [ʃɑ̃tje] *m* building site; **~ naval** shipyard

chantonner [ʃɑ̃tɔne] ⟨1a⟩ sing under one's breath

chanvre [ʃɑ̃vr] *m* BOT hemp

chaos [kao] *m* chaos; **chaotique** chaotic

chapardage [ʃapardaʒ] *m* F pilfering; **chaparder** ⟨1a⟩ F pinch F

chapeau [ʃapo] *m* (*pl* -x) hat; **~!** congratulations!; **chapeauter** *fig* head up

chapelet [ʃaplɛ] *m* REL rosary

chapelle [ʃapɛl] *f* chapel

chapelure [ʃaplyr] *f* CUIS breadcrumbs *pl*

chaperon [ʃaprõ] *m* chaperone; **chaperonner** chaperone

chapiteau [ʃapito] *m* (*pl* -x) *de cirque* big top; ARCH capital

chapitre [ʃapitr] *m* chapter; *division de budget* heading; *fig* subject

chapon [ʃapõ] *m* capon

chaque [ʃak] each

char [ʃar] *m* cart; *de carnaval* float; MIL tank; **~ funèbre** hearse

charabia [ʃarabja] *m* F gibberish

charbon [ʃarbõ] *m* coal; **~ de bois** charcoal; **être sur des ~s ardents** be like a cat on a hot tin roof

charcuterie [ʃarkytri] *f* CUIS cold cuts *pl*, *Br* cold meat; *magasin* pork butcher's; **charcutier** *m* pork butcher

chardon [ʃardõ] *m* BOT thistle

charge [ʃarʒ] *f* (*fardeau*) load; *fig* burden; ÉL, JUR, MIL, *d'explosif* charge; (*responsabilité*) responsibility; **à la ~ de qn** dependent on s.o.; FIN chargeable to s.o.; **avoir des enfants à ~** have dependent children; **prendre en ~** take charge of; *passager* pick up; **~s** charges; (*impôts*) costs; **~s fiscales** taxation *sg*; **~s sociales** social security contributions paid by the employer, FICA, *Br* national insurance contributions

chargé, ~e [ʃarʒe] **1** *adj* loaded; *programme* full; **être ~ de faire qch** have been given the job of doing sth **2** *m* EDUC: **~ de cours** lecturer; **chargement** *m* loading; *ce qui est chargé* load; **charger** ⟨11⟩ **1** *v/t* *voiture, navire, arme* load; *batterie,* JUR charge; (*exagérer*) exaggerate; **~ qn de qch** put s.o. in charge of sth; **se ~ de qch / qn** look after sth / s.o. **2** *v/i* charge; **chargeur** *m*: **~ (de batterie)** battery charger

chariot [ʃarjo] *m* *pour bagages, achats* cart, *Br* trolley; (*charrette*) cart

charismatique [karismatik] charismatic; **charisme** *m* charisma

charitable [ʃaritabl] charitable; **charité** *f* charity; **faire la ~ à qn** give s.o. money; **fête de ~** charity sale *ou* bazaar

charivari [ʃarivari] *m* din, racket

charlatan [ʃarlatɑ̃] *m* *péj* charlatan

charmant, ~e [ʃarmɑ̃, -t] charming, delightful; *prince ~* Prince Charming; (*mari idéal*) Mr Right; **charme** *m* charm; **charmer** ⟨1a⟩ charm

charnel, ~le [ʃarnɛl] carnal

charnier [ʃarnje] *m* mass grave

charnière [ʃarnjɛr] *f* hinge

charnu [ʃarny] fleshy

charognard [ʃarɔɲar] *m* scavenger; **charogne** *f* P bastard; *femme* bitch

charpente [ʃarpɑ̃t] *f* framework; **charpentier** *m* carpenter

charrette [ʃarɛt] *f* cart; **charrier** ⟨1a⟩ **1** *v/t* (*transporter*) carry; (*entraîner*) carry along **2** *v/i* F (*exagérer*) go too far

charrue [ʃary] *f* plow, *Br* plough

charte [ʃart] *f* charter

charter [ʃarter] *m* charter

chasse[1] [ʃas] *f* hunting; (*poursuite*) chase; **prendre en ~** chase (after); **la ~ est ouverte / fermée** the hunting season has started / finished; **~ à courre** hunting; **~ à l'homme** manhunt; **~ privée** private game reserve; **~ aux sorcières** witchhunt

chasse² [ʃas]: **~ d'eau** flush; **tirer la ~** flush the toilet, pull the chain

chasse-neige [ʃasnɛʒ] *m* (*pl inv*) snowplow, *Br* snowplough

chasser [ʃase] ⟨1a⟩ *gibier* hunt; (*expulser*) drive away; *employé* dismiss; **chasseur** *m* hunter; AVIAT fighter; *dans un hôtel* bellhop, *Br* bellboy; **~ de têtes** headhunter

châssis [ʃasi] *m* frame; AUTO chassis

chaste [ʃast] chaste; **chasteté** *f* chastity

chat¹ [ʃa] *m* cat

chat² [tʃat] *m* INFORM chatroom; *conversation* (online) chat

châtaigne [ʃatɛɲ] *f* chestnut; **châtaignier** *m* chestnut (tree); **châtain** *adj inv* chestnut

château [ʃato] *m* (*pl* -x) castle; **~ fort** (fortified) castle; **~ d'eau** water tower *m*; **le ~ de Versailles** the Palace of Versailles; **construire des ~x en Espagne** *fig* build castles in Spain

châtié, ~e [ʃatje] *style* polished

châtier [ʃatje] ⟨1a⟩ punish; **châtiment** *m* punishment

chatoiement [ʃatwamã] *m* shimmer

chaton [ʃatõ] *m* kitten

chatouiller [ʃatuje] ⟨1a⟩ tickle; **chatouilleux, -euse** ticklish; *fig* touchy

chatoyer [ʃatwaje] ⟨1h⟩ shimmer

chatte [ʃat] *f* cat

chatter [tʃate] INFORM chat (online)

chaud, ~e [ʃo, -d] **1** *adj* hot; *plus modéré* warm; **tenir ~** keep warm; **il fait ~** it's hot / warm **2** *m* heat; *plus modéré* warmth; **j'ai ~** I'm hot / warm; **chaudière** *f* boiler

chaudron [ʃodrõ] *m* cauldron

chauffage [ʃofaʒ] *m* heating; **~ central** central heating

chauffard [ʃofar] *m* F roadhog

chauffe-eau [ʃofo] *m* (*pl inv*) water heater; **chauffe-plats** *m* (*pl inv*) hot plate

chauffer [ʃofe] ⟨1a⟩ **1** *v/t* heat (up), warm (up); *maison* heat; **se ~** warm o.s.; *d'un sportif* warm up **2** *v/i d'eau,*

d'un four warm *ou* heat up; *d'un moteur* overheat; **faire ~ eau** heat; *moteur* warm up; **chaufferie** *f* boiler room

chauffeur [ʃofœr] *m* driver; *privé* chauffeur, driver; **~ de taxi** taxi *ou* cab driver

chaume [ʃom] *m* AGR *champ* stubble; **toit** *m* **de ~** thatched roof; **chaumière** *f* thatched cottage

chaussée [ʃose] *f* pavement, *Br* roadway

chausse-pied [ʃospje] *m* (*pl* chausse-pieds) shoehorn; **chausser** ⟨1a⟩ *bottes* put on; **~ qn** put shoes on s.o.; **se ~** put one's shoes on; **~ du 40** take a size 40

chaussette [ʃoset] *f* sock; **chausson** *m* slipper; **~ (de bébé)** bootee *m*; **~ aux pommes** CUIS apple turnover; **chaussure** *f* shoe; **~s de marche** hiking boots; **~s de ski** ski boots

chauve [ʃov] bald

chauve-souris [ʃovsuri] *f* (*pl* chauves-souris) bat

chauvin, ~e [ʃovɛ̃, -in] **1** *adj* chauvinistic **2** *m/f* chauvinist; **chauvinisme** *m* chauvinism

chaux [ʃo] *f* lime

chavirer [ʃavire] ⟨1a⟩ MAR capsize; **~ qn** *fig* overwhelm s.o.

chef [ʃef] *m* (*meneur*) leader; POL leader; (*patron*) boss, chief; *d'une entreprise* head; *d'une tribu* chief; CUIS chef; **au premier ~** first and foremost; **de mon propre ~** on my own initiative; **rédacteur** *m* **en ~** editor-in-chief; **~ d'accusation** JUR charge, count; **~ d'équipe** foreman; **~ d'État** head of State; **~ de famille** head of the family; **~ de gare** station manager; **~ d'orchestre** conductor

chef-d'œuvre [ʃedœvr] *m* (*pl* chefs-d'œuvre) masterpiece; **chef-lieu** *m* (*pl* chefs-lieux) capital (*of département*)

chemin [ʃ(ə)mɛ̃] *m* way; (*route*) road; (*allée*) path; **~ de fer** railroad, *Br* railway; **se mettre en ~** set out; **elle n'y est pas allée par quatre ~s** she didn't beat about the bush, she got straight to the point

cheminée [ʃ(ə)mine] *f* chimney; (*âtre*) fireplace; (*encadrement*) mantelpiece; *de bateau* funnel; *d'usine* smokestack, chimney

cheminement [ʃ(ə)minmɑ̃] *m* progress; **~ de la pensée** *fig* thought processes *pl*; **cheminer** ⟨1a⟩ walk, make one's way; *d'une idée* take root; **cheminot** *m* rail worker

chemise [ʃ(ə)miz] *f* shirt; (*dossier*) folder; **~ de nuit** *de femme* nightdress; *d'homme* nightshirt; **chemisette** *f* short-sleeved shirt; **chemisier** *m* blouse

chenal [ʃ(ə)nal] *m* (*pl* -aux) channel

chêne [ʃɛn] *m* BOT oak (tree)

chenil [ʃ(ə)ni(l)] *m* kennels *pl*

chenille [ʃ(ə)nij] *f* ZO caterpillar; **véhicule m à ~s** tracked vehicle

chèque [ʃɛk] *m* COMM check, *Br* cheque; **~ barré** crossed check; **~ sans provision** bad check, rubber check F; **~ de voyage** traveler's check, *Br* traveller's cheque; **chéquier** *m* checkbook, *Br* chequebook

cher, chère [ʃɛr] **1** *adj* dear (*à qn* to s.o.); *coûteux* dear, expensive **2** *adv*: **payer qch ~** pay a lot for sth; *fig* pay a high price for sth; **nous l'avons vendu ~** we got a lot *ou* a good price for it **3** *m/f* **mon cher, ma chère** my dear

chercher [ʃɛrʃe] ⟨1a⟩ look for; **~ à faire qch** try to do sth; **aller ~** fetch, go for; **venir ~** collect, come for; **envoyer ~** send for; **chercheur, -euse** *m/f* researcher

chère [ʃɛr] *f* food; **aimer la bonne ~** love good food

chéri, ~e [ʃeri] beloved, darling; **(mon)** darling; **chérir** ⟨2a⟩ cherish

chérubin [ʃerybɛ̃] *m* cherub

chétif, -ive [ʃetif, -iv] puny

cheval [ʃ(ə)val] *m* (*pl* -aux) horse; AUTO horsepower, HP; **aller à ~** ride; **faire du ~** SP ride; **être à ~ sur qch** straddle sth; **à ~** on horseback; **~ à bascule** rocking horse; **~ de bataille** *fig* hobby-horse; **~ de course** racehorse; **chevaleresque** chivalrous;

chevalerie *f* chivalry

chevalet [ʃ(ə)valɛ] *m* *de peinture* easel

chevalier [ʃ(ə)valje] *m* HIST knight; **chevalière** *f* signet ring; **chevalin, ~e** horse *atr*; **boucherie f ~e** horse butcher's; **cheval-vapeur** *m* horsepower

chevaucher [ʃ(ə)voʃe] ⟨1a⟩ ride; **se ~** overlap

chevelu, ~e [ʃəvly] *personne* longhaired; **cuir** *m* **~** scalp; **chevelure** *f* hair; **avoir une belle ~** have beautiful hair

chevet [ʃəvɛ] *m* bedhead; **table f de ~** nightstand, *Br aussi* bedside table; **être au ~ de qn** be at s.o.'s bedside

cheveu [ʃ(ə)vø] *m* (*pl* -x) hair; **~x** hair *sg*; **aux ~x courts** short-haired; **avoir les ~x courts** have short hair; **couper les ~x en quatre** *fig* split hairs

cheville [ʃ(ə)vij] *f* ANAT ankle; TECH peg

chèvre [ʃɛvr] *f* goat

chevreau [ʃəvro] *m* kid

chèvrefeuille [ʃɛvrəfœj] *m* BOT honeysuckle

chevreuil [ʃəvrœj] *m* deer; CUIS venison

chevronné, ~e [ʃəvrɔne] experienced

chez [ʃe] ◇: **~ lui** at his place; *direction* to his place; **tout près de ~ nous** close to our place, close to where we live; **~ Marcel** at Marcel's; **quand nous sommes ~ nous** when we are at home; **rentrer ~ soi** go home ◇: **aller ~ le coiffeur** go to the hairdresser *ou Br* hairdresser's; **~ le boucher** at the butcher's shop *ou Br* butcher's ◇: **~ Molière** in Molière ◇ (*parmi*) amongst; **courant ~ les personnes âgées** common amongst *ou* with old people; **beaucoup admiré ~ les Américains** much admired by Americans

chez-soi *m* home

chiant, ~e [ʃjɑ̃, -t] *adj* F boring

chic [ʃik] **1** *m* (*élégance*) style; **avoir le ~ pour faire qch** have a gift for doing sth **2** *adj* chic; (*sympathique*) decent, nice; **~!** F great! F

chicane [ʃikan] *f* (*querelle*) squabble; **chicaner** ⟨1a⟩ quibble (*sur* over)

chiche [ʃiʃ] mean; BOT **pois** ~ chickpea; **tu n'es pas** ~ **de le faire** F you're too chicken to do it F

chicorée [ʃikɔre] *f* BOT chicory; ~ (**endive**) endive

chien [ʃjɛ̃] *m* dog; **temps de** ~ fig F filthy weather; ~ **d'arrêt** retriever; ~ **d'aveugle** seeing-eye dog, Br guide dog; ~ **de berger** sheepdog; ~ **de garde** guard dog; ~ **policier** police dog; **chien-loup** *m* (*pl* chiens-loups) wolfhound; **chienne** *f* dog; **le chien et la** ~ the dog and the bitch

chier [ʃje] ⟨1a⟩ P shit P; **ça me fait** ~ P it pisses me off P

chiffon [ʃifɔ̃] *m* rag; ~ (**à poussière**) duster; **chiffonner** ⟨1a⟩ crumple; *fig* F bother

chiffre [ʃifr] *m* numeral; (*nombre*) number; (*code*) cipher; ~ **d'affaires** COMM turnover; **chiffrer** ⟨1a⟩ *revenus, somme* work out (**à** at); (*encoder*) encipher; **se** ~ **à** amount to

chignon [ʃiɲɔ̃] *m* bun

Chili [ʃili] **le** ~ Chili; **chilien**, **-ne 1** *adj* Chilean **2** *m/f* **Chilien**, **~ne** Chilean

chimère [ʃimɛr] *f* fantasy

chimie [ʃimi] *f* chemistry; **chimiothérapie** *f* chemotherapy

chimique [ʃimik] chemical; **chimiste** *m/f* chemist

Chine [ʃin] **la** ~ China; **chinois**, **~e 1** *adj* Chinese **2** *m langue* Chinese **3** *m/f* **Chinois**, **~e** Chinese

chiot [ʃjo] *m* pup

chiper [ʃipe] ⟨1a⟩ F pinch

chipoter [ʃipɔte] ⟨1b⟩ haggle (**sur** for, over)

chips [ʃip(s)] *mpl* chips, Br crisps

chirurgical, **~e** [ʃiryrʒikal] (*mpl* -aux) surgical; **chirurgie** *f* surgery; ~ **esthétique** plastic surgery; **chirurgien**, **~ne** *m/f* surgeon; ~ **dentiste** dental surgeon; ~ **esthétique** cosmetic surgeon

chlorofluorocarbone [klɔrɔflyɔrɔkarbɔn] *m* chlorofluorocarbon

choc [ʃɔk] *m* impact, shock; MÉD, PSYCH shock; *d'opinions, intérêts* clash

chocolat [ʃɔkɔla] *m* chocolate; ~ **au lait** milk chocolate

chœur [kœr] *m* choir (*aussi* ARCH); THÉÂT chorus; **en** ~ in chorus

choisir [ʃwazir] ⟨2a⟩ **1** *v/t* choose, select **2** *v/i* (*se décider*) choose; ~ **de faire qch** decide to do sth; **choix** *m* choice; (*sélection, assortiment*) range, selection; **c'est au** ~ you have a choice; **de** (**premier**) ~ choice; **avoir le** ~ have the choice

cholestérol [kɔlesterɔl] *m* cholesterol

chômage [ʃomaʒ] *m* unemployment; **être au** ~ be unemployed, be out of work; ~ **de longue durée** long-term unemployment; ~ **partiel** short time; **chômer** ⟨1a⟩ be unemployed, be out of work; **chômeur**, **-euse** *m/f* unemployed person; **les** ~**s** the unemployed *pl*

chope [ʃɔp] *f* beer mug

choquant, **~e** [ʃɔkɑ̃, -t] shocking; **choquer** ⟨1a⟩: ~ **qch** knock sth; ~ **qn** shock s.o.

chorale [kɔral] *f* choir; **choriste** *m/f* chorister

chose [ʃoz] *f* thing; **autre** ~ something else; **c'est peu de** ~ it's nothing; **quelque** ~ something; **c'est** ~ **faite** it's done; **voilà où en sont les** ~**s** that's where things stand

chou [ʃu] *m* (*pl* -x) BOT cabbage; ~**x de Bruxelles** Brussels sprouts; **mon** (**petit**) ~ *fig* my love

choucroute [ʃukrut] *f* sauerkraut

chouette [ʃwɛt] **1** *f* owl **2** *adj* F great

chou-fleur [ʃuflœr] *m* (*pl* choux-fleurs) cauliflower

choyer [ʃwaje] ⟨1h⟩ coddle

chrétien, **~ne** [kretjɛ̃, -ɛn] **1** *adj* Christian **2** *m/f* Christian; **chrétienté** *f* Christendom

Christ [krist] *m*: **le** ~ Christ

christianiser [kristjanize] ⟨1a⟩ Christianize; **christianisme** *m* Christianity

chrome [krom] *m* chrome; **chromé**, **~e** chrome-plated

chronique [krɔnik] **1** *adj* chronic **2** *f*

d'un journal column; *reportage* report; **la ~ locale** the local news *sg*; **chroniqueur** *m pour un journal* columnist
chronologique [krɔnɔlɔʒik] chronological
chronomètre [krɔnɔmɛtr] *m* stopwatch; **chronométrer** ⟨1f⟩ time
chuchoter [ʃyʃɔte] ⟨1a⟩ whisper
chut [ʃyt]: **~!** hush
chute [ʃyt] *f* fall; **~ des cheveux** hair loss; **~ de pluie** rainfall; **faire une ~ de bicyclette** fall off one's bike
Chypre [ʃipr]: **l'île f de ~** Cyprus; **chypriote 1** *adj* Cypriot **2** *m/f* **Chypriote** Cypriot
ci [si] *après **ce*** (+ *subst*); **à cette heure-~** at this time; **comme ~ comme ça** F so-so; **par-~ par-là** here and there
ci-après [siaprɛ] below
cible [sibl] *f* target; **cibler** ⟨1b⟩ target
ciboulette [sibulɛt] *f* BOT chives *pl*
cicatrice [sikatris] *f* scar (*aussi fig*); **cicatriser** ⟨1a⟩: **(se) ~** heal
ci-contre [sikɔ̃tr] opposite; **ci-dessous** below; **ci-dessus** above
cidre [sidr] *m* cider
ciel [sjɛl] *m* (*pl* cieux [sjø]) sky; REL heaven; **au ~** in heaven
cierge [sjɛrʒ] *m dans église* candle
cigale [sigal] *f* cicada
cigare [sigar] *m* cigar; **cigarette** *f* cigarette
ci-gît [siʒi] here lies
cigogne [sigɔɲ] *f* stork
ci-inclus [siɛ̃kly] enclosed; **ci-joint** enclosed, attached
cil [sil] *m* eyelash
ciller [sije] ⟨1a⟩ blink
cime [sim] *f d'une montagne* top, summit; *d'un arbre* top
ciment [simɑ̃] *m* cement; **cimenter** ⟨1a⟩ cement (*aussi fig*)
cimetière [simtjɛr] *m* cemetery
ciné [sine] *m* F movie theater, *Br* cinema; **cinéaste** *m* film-maker; **cinéma** *m* movie theater, *Br* cinema; *art* cinema, movies *pl*; **cinématographique** cinematic; **cinéphile** *m/f* moviegoer
cinglé, ~e [sɛ̃gle] F mad, crazy; **cingler** ⟨1a⟩ **1** *v/t* lash **2** *v/i*: **~ vers**

MAR make for
cinq [sɛ̃k] five; → **trois**
cinquantaine [sɛ̃kɑ̃tɛn] *f* about fifty; **une ~ de personnes** about fifty people *pl*; **elle approche la ~** she's almost fifty, she's getting on for fifty; **cinquante** fifty; **cinquantième** fiftieth
cinquième [sɛ̃kjɛm] fifth; **cinquièmement** *adv* fifthly
cintre [sɛ̃tr] *m* ARCH arch; *pour vêtements* coathanger; **cintré, ~e veste** waisted; ARCH arched
cirage [siraʒ] *m pour parquet* wax, polish; *pour chaussures* polish
circoncision [sirkɔ̃sizjɔ̃] *f* REL circumcision
circonférence [sirkɔ̃ferɑ̃s] *f* circumference
circonscription [sirkɔ̃skripsjɔ̃] *f*: **~ électorale** district, *Br* constituency; **circonscrire** ⟨4f⟩ MATH circumscribe; *fig*: *sujet* delimit
circonspect, ~e [sirkɔ̃spɛ, -kt] circumspect; **circonspection** *f* circumspection
circonstance [sirkɔ̃stɑ̃s] *f* circumstance; **dans ces ~s** in the circumstances; **circonstancié, ~e** detailed
circuit [sirkɥi] *m* circuit; *de voyage* tour; SP track; **court ~** short circuit; **~ intégré** INFORM integrated circuit
circulaire [sirkylɛr] *adj & f* circular
circulation [sirkylasjɔ̃] *f* circulation; *voitures* traffic; **~ du sang** MÉD circulation (of the blood); **libre ~** freedom of movement; **~ à double sens** two-way traffic; **circuler** ⟨1a⟩ circulate; *de personnes, véhicules aussi* move about; **faire ~ nouvelles** spread
cire [sir] *f* wax; **ciré, ~e 1** *adj* polished **2** *m* MAR oilskin; **cirer** ⟨1a⟩ *chaussures* polish; *parquet* polish, wax
cirque [sirk] *m* circus
cirrhose [siroz] *f*: **~ du foie** cirrhosis of the liver
cisaille(s) [sizaj] *f(pl)* shears *pl*; **ciseau** *m* (*pl* -x) chisel; **ciseaux** *mpl* scissors; **une paire de ~** a pair of scissors, some scissors; **~ à ongles** nail scissors; **ciseler** ⟨1d⟩ chisel; *fig* hone

citadelle [sitadɛl] f citadel; fig stronghold

citadin, ~e [sitadɛ̃, -in] 1 adj town atr, city atr 2 m/f town-dweller, city-dweller

citation [sitasjɔ̃] f quotation; JUR summons for

cité [site] f city; ~ universitaire fraternity house, Br hall of residence; ~ ouvrière workers' accommodations pl; droit m de ~ freedom of the city; cité-dortoir f (pl cités-dortoirs) dormitory town

citer [site] ⟨1a⟩ quote; JUR summons; ~ qch en exemple hold sth up as an example

citerne [sitɛrn] f tank

citoyen, ~ne [sitwajɛ̃, -ɛn] m/f citizen; citoyenneté f citizenship

citron [sitrɔ̃] m lemon; ~ vert lime; citronnier m lemon (tree)

citrouille [sitruj] f pumpkin

civet [sivɛ] m CUIS: ~ de lièvre stew made with hare

civière [sivjɛr] f stretcher

civil, ~e [sivil] 1 adj civil; non militaire civilian; responsabilité f ~e public liability; état m ~ marital status; bureau m de l'état ~ registry office; mariage m ~ civil marriage; service m ~ community service 2 m civilian; en ~ in civilian clothes; policier in plain clothes; civilement adv se marier in a registry office

civilisation [sivilizasjɔ̃] f civilization; civiliser ⟨1a⟩ civilize

civique [sivik] civic; civisme m public-spiritedness

clair, ~e [klɛr] 1 adj clear; couleur light; chambre bright; vert ~ light green 2 adv voir clearly; dire, parler plainly 3 m: ~ de lune moonlight

clairière [klɛrjɛr] f clearing

clairon [klɛrɔ̃] m MUS bugle

clairsemé, ~e [klɛrsəme] sparse

clairvoyance [klɛrvwajɑ̃s] f perceptiveness; clairvoyant, ~e perceptive

clameur [klamœr] f clamor, Br clamour

clan [klɑ̃] m clan; fig clique

clandestin, ~e [klɑ̃dɛstɛ̃, -in] secret, clandestine; passager m ~ stowaway

clapotement [klapɔtmɑ̃] m, clapotis [klapɔti] m lapping; clapoter ⟨1a⟩ lap

claque [klak] f slap; claquement m d'une porte, d'un volet slamming, banging; de fouet crack; de dents chattering; de doigts snap; claquer ⟨1m⟩ 1 v/t porte slam, bang; argent F blow; ~ des doigts snap one's fingers; faire ~ sa langue click one's tongue 2 v/i d'un fouet crack; des dents chatter; d'un volet slam, bang; claquettes fpl tap dancing sg

clarifier [klarifje] ⟨1a⟩ clarify

clarinette [klarinɛt] f clarinet

clarté [klarte] f (lumière) brightness; (transparence) clarity, clearness; fig clarity

classe [klas] f d'école, fig class; local class(room); de première ~ first-class; il a de la ~ he's got class; faire la ~ teach; ~ affaires business class; ~ économique economy class; ~ de neige school study trip to the mountains; ~ sociale social class

classement [klasmɑ̃] m position, place; BOT, ZO classification; de lettres filing; elle était seconde au ~ SP she took second place

classer [klase] ⟨1a⟩ classify; actes, dossiers file; ~ une affaire consider a matter closed; ~ qn F size s.o. up; être classé monument historique be a registered historic site, Br be a listed building; classeur m cahier binder; meuble file cabinet, Br filing cabinet

classicisme [klasisism] m classicism

classification [klasifikasjɔ̃] f classification; classifier ⟨1a⟩ classify

classique [klasik] 1 adj classical; (traditionnel) classic 2 m en littérature classical author; MUS classical music; film, livre classic

claudication [klodikasjɔ̃] f limp

clause [kloz] f clause; ~ pénale penalty clause

clavecin [klavsɛ̃] m harpsichord

clavicule [klavikyl] f collarbone, clavicle fml

clavier [klavje] *m d'un ordinateur, d'un piano* keyboard

clé [kle] *f* key; TECH wrench; **~ de fa** MUS bass clef; **fermer à ~** lock; **sous ~** under lock and key; **prendre la ~ des champs** *fig* take off; **mot** *m* **~** key word; **position** *f* **~** key position; **~ de contact** ignition key; **~s de voiture** car keys

clef [kle] *f →* **clé**

clémence [klemɑ̃s] *f* clemency; **clément, ~e** merciful

clerc [klɛr] *m de notaire* clerk; REL cleric

clergé [klɛrʒe] *m* clergy

clérical, ~e [klerikal] (*mpl* -aux) clerical

clic [klik] *m bruit,* INFORM click

cliché [kliʃe] *m* cliché; (*photo*) negative

client, ~e [klijɑ̃, -t] *m/f* (*acheteur*) customer; *d'un médecin* patient; *d'un avocat* client; **clientèle** *f* customers *pl*, clientèle; *d'un médecin* patients *pl*; *d'un avocat* clients *pl*

cligner [kliɲe] ⟨1a⟩: **~ (des yeux)** blink; **~ de l'œil à qn** wink at s.o.

clignotant [kliɲɔtɑ̃] *m* turn signal, *Br* indicator; **clignoter** ⟨1a⟩ *d'une lumière* flicker

climat [klima] *m* climate; *fig* atmosphere, climate; **climatique** climatic; **station** *f* **~** health resort; **changement** *m* **~** climate change

climatisation [klimatizasjɔ̃] *f* air conditioning; **climatisé, ~e** air conditioned

clin [klɛ̃] *m*: **~ d'œil** wink; **en un ~ d'œil** in a flash, in the twinkling of an eye

clinique [klinik] **1** *adj* clinical **2** *f* clinic

clique [klik] *f péj* clique

cliquer [klike] ⟨1a⟩ INFORM click (**sur** on)

cliqueter [klikte] ⟨1c⟩ *de clés* jingle; *de verres* clink, chink; **cliquetis** *m* jingling; *de verres* chinking

clivage [klivaʒ] *m fig* split

clochard, ~e [klɔʃar, -d] *m/f* hobo, *Br* tramp

cloche [klɔʃ] *f* bell; F (*idiot*) nitwit; **clocher 1** *m* steeple; **esprit** *m* **de ~** *fig* parochialism **2** *v/i* ⟨1a⟩ F: **ça cloche** something's not right; **clochette** *f* (small) bell

cloison [klwazɔ̃] *f* partition; **cloisonner** ⟨1b⟩ partition off

cloître [klwatr] *m* monastery; ARCH cloisters *pl*; **cloîtrer** ⟨1a⟩ *fig*: **se ~** shut o.s. away

clope [klɔp] *m ou f* F (*cigarette*) cigarette, *Br* F fag; (*mégot*) cigarette end

clopin-clopant [klɔpɛ̃klɔpɑ̃] *adv* F limping, with a limp

clopinettes [klɔpinet] *fpl* F peanuts F

cloque [klɔk] *f* blister

clore [klɔr] ⟨4k⟩ *débat, compte* close

clos, ~e [klo, -z] *p/p →* **clore**

clôture [klotyr] *f d'un débat* closure; *d'un compte* closing; (*barrière*) fence; **clôturer** ⟨1a⟩ *espace* enclose, fence off; *débat, compte* close

clou [klu] *m* nail; *fig* main attraction; MÉD boil; **~s** F crosswalk, *Br* pedestrian crossing; **~ de girofle** clove; **clouer** ⟨1a⟩ nail; **être cloué au lit** be confined to bed; **clouté, ~e** studded; **passage** *m* **~** crosswalk, *Br* pedestrian crossing

clown [klun] *m* clown

club [klœb] *m* club; **~ de golf** golf club; **~ de gym** gym

coaguler [kɔagyle] ⟨1a⟩ *du lait* curdle; *du sang* coagulate

coaliser [kɔalize] ⟨1a⟩ POL: **se ~** form a coalition; **coalition** *f* POL coalition

coasser [kɔase] ⟨1a⟩ croak

cobaye [kɔbaj] *m* ZO, *fig* guinea pig

coca [kɔka] *m* Coke®

cocagne [kɔkaɲ] *f*: **pays** *m* **de ~** land flowing with milk and honey

cocaïne [kɔkain] *f* cocaine

cocasse [kɔkas] F ridiculous, comical

coccinelle [kɔksinel] *f* ladybug, *Br* ladybird; F AUTO Volkswagen® beetle

cocher [kɔʃe] ⟨1a⟩ *sur une liste* check, *Br aussi* tick off

cochère [kɔʃer]: **porte** *f* **~** carriage entrance

cochon [kɔʃɔ̃] **1** *m* ZO, *fig* pig; **~ d'Inde** guinea pig **2** *adj* **cochon,**

~ne F dirty, smutty; **cochonnerie** f F: **des ~s** filth sg; *nourriture* junk food sg

cocktail [kɔktɛl] m cocktail; *réception* cocktail party

coco [kɔko] m: **noix f de ~** coconut

cocon [kɔkõ] m cocoon

cocotier [kɔkɔtje] m coconut palm

cocotte [kɔkɔt] f CUIS casserole; F *darling*; *péj* tart; **~ minute** pressure cooker

cocu [kɔky] m F deceived husband, cuckold

code [kɔd] m code; **~ civil** civil code; **~ pénal** penal code; **~ de la route** traffic regulations, Br Highway Code; **se mettre en ~s** switch to low beams, Br aussi dip one's headlights; **phares** mpl **~s** low beams, Br aussi dipped headlights; **~ (à) barres** bar code; **~ postal** zipcode, Br postcode; **~ secret** secret code

coéquipier, -ière [koekipje, -ɛr] m/f team mate

cœur [kœr] m heart; **à ~ joie** rire, s'en donner whole-heartedly; **au ~ de** in the heart of; **de bon ~** gladly, willingly; **apprendre qch par ~** learn sth by heart; **connaître qch par ~** know sth by heart; **j'ai mal au ~** I'm nauseous, Br aussi I feel sick; **cela lui tient à ~** he feels quite strongly about it; **avoir bon ~** have a good heart

coexistence [kɔɛgzistɑ̃s] f co-existence; **coexister** ⟨1a⟩ co-exist

coffre [kɔfr] m *meuble* chest; FIN safe; AUTO trunk, Br boot; **coffre-fort** m (pl coffres-forts) safe

coffret [kɔfrɛ] m box

cogérer [kɔʒere] ⟨1f⟩ co-manage; **cogestion** f joint management; *avec les ouvriers* worker participation

cognac [kɔɲak] m brandy, cognac

cognée [kɔɲe] f ax, Br axe; **cogner** ⟨1a⟩ d'un moteur knock; **~ à ou contre qch** bang against sth; **se ~ à ou contre qch** bump into sth

cohabitation [kɔabitasjõ] f living together, cohabitation; POL cohabitation; **cohabiter** ⟨1a⟩ cohabit

cohérence [kɔerɑ̃s] f d'une théorie consistency, coherence; **cohérent, ~e** théorie consistent, coherent

cohésion [kɔezjõ] f cohesiveness

cohue [kɔy] f crowd, rabble

coiffer [kwafe] ⟨1a⟩: **~ qn** do s.o.'s hair; **~ qn de qch** put sth on s.o.('s head); **~ un service** head a department; **se ~** do one's hair; **coiffeur** m hairdresser, hair stylist; **coiffeuse** f hairdresser, hair stylist; *meuble* dressing table; **coiffure** f de cheveux hairstyle

coin [kwɛ̃] m corner (aussi fig); *cale* wedge; **au ~ du feu** by the fireside; **les gens du ~** the locals

coincer [kwɛ̃se] ⟨1k⟩ squeeze; *porte, tiroir* jam, stick; **~ qn** fig (acculer) corner s.o.; **être coincé dans un embouteillage** be stuck in a traffic jam

coïncidence [kɔɛ̃sidɑ̃s] f coincidence; **coïncider** ⟨1a⟩ coincide (**avec** with)

col [kɔl] m d'une robe, chemise collar; d'une bouteille, d'un pull neck; GÉOGR col; **~ blanc / bleu** white-collar / blue-collar worker

colère [kɔlɛr] f anger; **se mettre en ~** get angry; **coléreux, -euse**: **être ~** have a terrible temper; **colérique** irritable

colimaçon [kɔlimasõ] m snail; **escalier** m **en ~** spiral staircase

colin [kɔlɛ̃] m hake

colique [kɔlik] f colic; (diarrhée) diarrhea, Br diarrhoea

colis [kɔli] m parcel, package

collaborateur, -trice [kɔlabɔratœr, -tris] m/f collaborator (aussi POL péj); **collaboration** f collaboration, cooperation; POL péj collaboration; **collaborer** ⟨1a⟩ collaborate, cooperate (**avec** with; **à** on); POL péj collaborate

collant, ~e [kɔlɑ̃, -t] **1** adj sticky; *vêtement* close-fitting; F *personne* clingy **2** m pantyhose pl, Br tights pl

collation [kɔlasjõ] f CUIS light meal

colle [kɔl] f glue; fig P *question* tough question; (retenue) detention

collecte [kɔlɛkt] f collection; **collec-**

tif, **-ive** collective, joint; **billet** m ~ group ticket; **voyage** m ~ group tour

collection [kɔlɛksjɔ̃] f collection; **collectionner** ⟨1a⟩ collect; **collectionneur, -euse** m/f collector

collectivité [kɔlɛktivite] f community

collège [kɔlɛʒ] m école junior high, Br secondary school; (assemblée) college; **collégien, ~ne** m/f junior high student, Br secondary school pupil

collègue [kɔlɛg] m/f colleague, co--worker

coller [kɔle] ⟨1a⟩ **1** v/t stick, glue **2** v/i stick (à to); ~ **à la peau** d'un vêtement be close-fitting; **ça colle bien entre eux** F they get on well; **se ~ contre** mur press o.s against; personne cling to

collet [kɔlɛ] m d'un vêtement collar; pour la chasse snare; **prendre qn au ~** fig catch s.o.

collier [kɔlje] m bijou necklace; de chien collar

colline [kɔlin] f hill

collision [kɔlizjɔ̃] f collision; **entrer en ~ avec** collide with

colloque [kɔlɔk] m seminar

collyre [kɔlir] m eye drops pl

colocataire [kɔlɔkater] m/f room-mate, Br flatmate

Cologne [kɔlɔɲ]: **eau f de ~** eau de Cologne

colombe [kɔlɔ̃b] f dove (aussi fig)

Colombie [kɔlɔ̃bi] **la ~** Colombia; **colombien, ~ne 1** adj Colombian **2** m/f **Colombien, ~ne** Colombian

colon [kɔlɔ̃] m colonist

colonel [kɔlɔnɛl] m colonel

colonial, ~e [kɔlɔnjal] (mpl -iaux) colonial; **colonialisme** m colonialism; **colonie** f colony; ~ **de vacances** summer camp, Br holiday camp; **colonisation** f colonization; **coloniser** ⟨1a⟩ colonize

colonne [kɔlɔn] f column; ~ **vertébrale** spine, spinal column

colorant, ~e [kɔlɔrɑ̃, -t] **1** adj shampoing color atr, Br colour atr **2** m dye; dans la nourriture coloring, Br colouring; **coloration** f coloring, Br colouring; **coloré, ~e** teint ruddy;

colorer ⟨1a⟩ color, Br colour; **coloris** m color, Br colour

colossal, ~e [kɔlɔsal] (mpl -aux) colossal, gigantic; **colosse** m colossus

colza [kɔlza] m BOT rape

coma [kɔma] m coma

combat [kɔ̃ba] m fight; MIL aussi battle; **mettre hors de ~** put out of action; **aller au ~** go into battle; ~ **à mains nues** unarmed combat

combattant, ~e [kɔ̃batɑ̃, -t] **1** adj fighting **2** m combatant; **ancien ~** veteran, Br aussi ex-serviceman; **combattre** ⟨4a⟩ fight; ~ **contre qn pour qch** fight s.o. for sth

combien [kɔ̃bjɛ̃] **1** adv quantité how much; avec pl how many; ~ **de fois** how many times, how often; ~ **de personnes** how many people; ~ **de temps** how long; ~ **est-ce que ça coûte?** how much is this?; ~ **je regrette ...** how I regret ...
2 m: **tous les ~** how often; **on est le ~ aujourd'hui?** what date is it today?

combinaison [kɔ̃binɛzɔ̃] f combination; (astuce) scheme; de mécanicien coveralls pl, Br boiler suit; lingerie (full-length) slip; ~ **de plongée** wet suit; ~ **de ski** ski suit

combiné [kɔ̃bine] m TÉL receiver

combine [kɔ̃bin] f F trick; **combiner** ⟨1a⟩ combine; voyage, projet plan

comble [kɔ̃bl] **1** m fig: sommet height; **~s** pl attic sg; **de fond en ~** from top to bottom; **ça, c'est le ~!** that's the last straw! **2** adj full (to capacity); **combler** ⟨1a⟩ trou fill in; déficit make good; personne overwhelm; ~ **une lacune** fill a gap; ~ **qn de qch** shower s.o. with sth

combustible [kɔ̃bystibl] **1** adj combustible **2** m fuel; **combustion** f combustion

comédie [kɔmedi] f comedy; ~ **musicale** musical; **comédien, ~ne** m/f actor; qui joue le genre comique comic actor

comestible [kɔmɛstibl] **1** adj edible **2** mpl **~s** food sg

comète [kɔmɛt] f comet

comique [kɔmik] **1** adj THÉÂT comic; (drôle) funny, comical **2** m comedian; acteur comic (actor); genre comedy

comité [kɔmite] m committee; ~ d'entreprise plant committee, Br works council; ~ d'experts think tank

commandant [kɔmɑ̃dɑ̃] m MIL commanding officer; MAR captain; ~ de bord AVIAT captain; ~ en chef commander-in-chief

commande [kɔmɑ̃d] f COMM order; TECH control; INFORM command; **commandement** m MIL command; (ordre) command, order; REL commandment; **commander** ⟨1a⟩ **1** v/t COMM order; (ordonner) command, order; MIL be in command of, command; TECH control **2** v/i (diriger) be in charge; (passer une commande) order

commanditaire [kɔmɑ̃diter] m silent partner, Br sleeping partner; **commandite**: société f en ~ limited partnership; **commanditer** ⟨1a⟩ entreprise fund, finance

commando [kɔmɑ̃do] m MIL commando

comme [kɔm] **1** adv like; chanter ~ un oiseau sing like a bird; noir ~ la nuit as black as night; ~ cela like that; ~ ci ~ ça F so-so; ~ vous voulez as you like; ~ si as if
◇ (en tant que) as; il travaillait ~ ... he was working as a ...
◇ (ainsi que) as well as; moi, ~ les autres, je ... like the others, I ...
◇: j'ai ~ l'impression que ... F I've kind of got the feeling that ... F
◇: qu'est-ce qu'on a ~ boissons? what do we have in the way of drinks?, what sort of drinks do we have?
2 conj (au moment où, parce que) as; ~ elle sortait de la banque as she was coming out of the bank; ~ tu m'as aidé autrefois as ou since you helped me once before

commémoratif, -ive [kɔmemɔratif, -iv] plaque etc memorial, commemmorative; **commémoration** f cérémonie commemoration; **commémorer** ⟨1a⟩ commemorate

commencement [kɔmɑ̃smɑ̃] m beginning, start; **commencer** ⟨1k⟩ **1** v/t begin, start; ~ qch par qch start sth with sth; ~ à faire qch start to do sth, start doing sth **2** v/i begin, start; ~ par faire qch start by doing sth; ~ par le commencement start at the beginning; ~ mal get off to a bad start

comment [kɔmɑ̃] adv how; ~? (qu'avez-vous dit?) pardon me?, Br sorry?; ~! surpris what!; le pourquoi et le ~ the whys and the wherefores pl

commentaire [kɔmɑ̃ter] m comment; RAD, TV commentary; **commentateur, -trice** m/f commentator; **commenter** ⟨1a⟩ comment on; RAD, TV commentate on

commérages [kɔmeraʒ] mpl gossip sg

commerçant, ~e [kɔmersɑ̃, -t] **1** adj: rue f ~e shopping street **2** m/f merchant, trader

commerce [kɔmers] m activité trade, commerce; (magasin) store, Br shop; fig (rapports) dealings pl; **commercer** ⟨1k⟩ trade, do business

commercial, ~e [kɔmersjal] (mpl -iaux) commercial; **commercialiser** ⟨1a⟩ market

commère [kɔmer] f gossip

commettre [kɔmetr] ⟨4p⟩ commit; erreur make

commis [kɔmi] m dans l'administration clerk; d'un magasin clerk, Br (shop) assistant; ~ voyageur commercial traveler ou Br traveller

commissaire [kɔmiser] m commission member; de l'UE Commissioner; SP steward; ~ aux comptes COMM auditor; **commissaire-priseur** m (pl commissaires-priseurs) auctioneer

commissariat [kɔmisarja] m commissionership; ~ (de police) police station

commission [kɔmisjɔ̃] f (comité, mission), COMM commission; (message) message; faire les ~s go shopping; **commissionnaire** m COMM agent; dans un hôtel commissionaire

commode [kɔmɔd] **1** *adj* handy; *arrangement* convenient; *pas ~ personne* awkward; *~ d'accès* lieu easy to get to **2** *f* chest of drawers; **commodité** *f d'arrangement* convenience; *toutes les ~s* all mod cons

commotion [kɔmɔsjõ] *f* MÉD: *~ cérébrale* stroke

commun, ~e [kɔmɛ̃ *ou* kɔmœ̃, -yn] **1** *adj* common; *œuvre* joint; *transports mpl en ~*, mass transit *sg*, *Br* public transport *sg*; *mettre en ~ argent* pool **2** *m*: *hors du ~* out of the ordinary

communal, ~e [kɔmynal] (*mpl* -aux) (*de la commune*) local

communautaire [kɔmynotɛr] community *atr*; **communauté** *f* community; *de hippies* commune; *~ européenne* European Community; *la ~ internationale* the international community; *~ des biens* JUR common ownership of property

commune [kɔmyn] *f* commune

communément [kɔmynemã] *adv* commonly

communicatif, -ive [kɔmynikatif, -iv] *personne* communicative; *rire, peur* contagious; **communication** *f* communication; (*message*) message; *~s routes, téléphone* communications; *~ téléphonique* telephone call; *la ~ a été coupée* the line is dead; *se mettre en ~ avec qn* get in touch with s.o.

communier [kɔmynje] ⟨1a⟩ REL take Communion; **communion** *f* REL Communion

communiqué [kɔmynike] *m* POL press release

communiquer [kɔmynike] ⟨1m⟩ **1** *v/t* communicate; *nouvelle, demande* convey, pass on; *maladie* pass on, give (*à qn* to s.o.) **2** *v/i* communicate

communisme [kɔmynism] *m* communism; **communiste** *m/f & adj* Communist

commutateur [kɔmytatœr] *m* TECH switch; **commutation** *f* JUR: *bénéficier d'une ~ de peine* have one's sentence reduced

compact, ~e [kɔ̃pakt] compact; **compact disc** *m* compact disc

compagne [kɔ̃paɲ] *f* companion; *dans couple* wife; **compagnie** *f* company; *en ~ de* accompanied by; *tenir ~ à qn* keep s.o. company; *~ aérienne* airline; *~ d'assurance* insurance company; *~ pétrolière* oil company; **compagnon** *m* companion; *dans couple* husband; *employé* journeyman

comparable [kɔ̃parabl] comparable (*à* to, *avec* with); **comparaison** *f* comparison; *en ~ de, par ~ à, par ~ avec* compared with; *par ~* by comparison

comparaître [kɔ̃parɛtr] ⟨4z⟩ appear (*en justice* in court)

comparer [kɔ̃pare] ⟨1a⟩ compare (*à* to, *avec* with); **comparatif, -ive** comparative

compartiment [kɔ̃partimã] *m* compartment; *de train* car, *Br* compartment; *~ fumeurs* smoking car

comparution [kɔ̃parysjõ] *f* JUR appearance

compas [kɔ̃pa] *m* MATH, MAR compass

compassion [kɔ̃pasjõ] *f* compassion; **compatibilité** [kɔ̃patibilite] *f* compatibility; **compatible** compatible

compatir [kɔ̃patir] *v/i*: *~ à* sympathize with, feel for

compatriote [kɔ̃patrijɔt] *m/f* compatriot

compensation [kɔ̃pãsasjõ] *f* compensation; *en ~* by way of compensation; **compenser** ⟨1a⟩ compensate for; *paresse, terreur* make up for

compétence [kɔ̃petãs] *f* (*connaissances*) ability, competence; JUR jurisdiction; **compétent, ~e** competent, skillful, *Br* skilful; JUR competent

compétitif, -ive [kɔ̃petitif, -iv] competitive; **compétition** *f* competition; **compétitivité** *f* competitiveness

compiler [kɔ̃pile] ⟨1a⟩ compile

complainte [kɔ̃plɛ̃t] *f* lament

complaire [kɔ̃plɛr] ⟨4a⟩: *se ~ dans qch / à faire qch* delight in sth / in doing sth

complaisance [kɔ̃plεzɑ̃s] f (amabilité) kindness; péj complacency; **complaisant, ~e** kind (pour, envers qn to s.o.); péj complacent

complément [kɔ̃plemɑ̃] m remainder; MAT complement; **complémentaire** article, renseignement further, additional

complet, -ète [kɔ̃plε, -t] 1 adj complete; hôtel, description, jeu de cartes full; pain whole wheat, Br wholemeal 2 m suit; **complètement** adv completely; **compléter** ⟨1f⟩ complete; **se ~** complement each other

complexe [kɔ̃plεks] 1 adj complex; (compliqué) complex, complicated 2 m complex; **~ d'infériorité** inferiority complex; **complexé, ~e** uptight, full of complexes; **complexité** f complexity

complication [kɔ̃plikasjɔ̃] f complication

complice [kɔ̃plis] 1 adj JUR: **être ~ de qch** be an accessory to sth 2 m/f accomplice; **complicité** f collusion

compliment [kɔ̃plimɑ̃] m compliment; **mes ~s** congratulations; **complimenter** ⟨1a⟩ pour coiffure etc compliment (pour on); pour réussite etc congratulate (pour on)

compliqué, ~e [kɔ̃plike] complicated; **compliquer** ⟨1m⟩ complicate; **se ~** become complicated; **pourquoi se ~ la vie?** why complicate things?, why make life difficult?

complot [kɔ̃plo] m plot; **comploter** plot

comportement [kɔ̃pɔrtəmɑ̃] m behavior, Br behaviour; **comporter** ⟨1a⟩ (comprendre) comprise; (impliquer) involve, entail; **se ~** behave (o.s)

composant [kɔ̃pozɑ̃] m component; **composé, ~e** 1 adj corps, mot compound 2 m compound; **composer** ⟨1a⟩ 1 v/t (former) make up; MUS compose; livre, poème write; **être composé de** be made up of, consist of; **~ un numéro** dial a number 2 v/i transiger come to terms (avec with); **se ~ de** be made up of, consist of

composite [kɔ̃pozit] composite

compositeur, -trice [kɔ̃pozitœr, -tris] m/f composer; **composition** f composition (aussi MUS); de livre, poème writing; d'un plat, une équipe make-up

composter [kɔ̃pɔste] ⟨1a⟩ billet punch; **composteur** m punch

compote [kɔ̃pɔt] f: **~ de pommes / poires** stewed apples / pears

compréhensible [kɔ̃preɑ̃sibl] (intelligible) understandable, comprehensible; (concevable) understandable; **compréhensif, -ive** understanding; **compréhension** f understanding, comprehension; (tolérance) understanding

comprendre [kɔ̃prɑ̃dr] ⟨4q⟩ understand, comprehend fml; (inclure) include; (comporter) comprise; **faire ~ qch à qn** (expliquer) make s.o. understand sth; (suggérer) give s.o. to understand sth; **se faire ~** make o.s. understood

compresse [kɔ̃prεs] f MÉD compress

compresseur [kɔ̃prεsœr] m TECH compressor; **compression** f compression; de dépenses, effectifs reduction

comprimé [kɔ̃prime] m tablet; **comprimer** ⟨1a⟩ air, substance compress; dépenses, effectifs cut (back), reduce

compris, ~e [kɔ̃pri, -z] (inclus) included (dans in); **y ~** including

compromettre [kɔ̃prɔmεtr] ⟨4p⟩ compromise; **compromis** m compromise

comptabilité [kɔ̃tabilite] f accountancy; (comptes) accounts pl; **comptable** m/f accountant; **comptant** COMM 1 adj: **argent** m **~** cash 2 m: **acheter qch au ~** pay cash for sth

compte [kɔ̃t] m account; (calcul) calculation; **~s** accounts; **à bon ~** acheter qch for a good price; **en fin de ~** at the end of the day, when all's said and done; **faire le ~ de qch** count up sth; **rendre ~ de qch** give an account of sth; (expliquer) account for sth; **se rendre ~ de qch** realize sth; **tenir ~ de qch** take sth into account, bear sth in mind; **~ tenu de**

bearing in mind, in view of; *pour mon* ~ for my part, as far as I'm concerned; *prendre qch à son* ~ take responsibility for sth; *mets-le sur le* ~ *de la fatigue* put it down to fatigue; *s'installer à son* ~ set up on one's own, go into business for o.s.; ~ *chèque postal* post office account; ~ *courant* checking account, *Br* current account; ~ *de dépôt* savings account, *Br* deposit account; ~ *à rebours* countdown; ~ *rendu* report; *de réunion* minutes *pl*; *faire le* ~ *rendu d'une réunion* take the minutes of a meeting

compte-gouttes [kõtgut] dropper; *je lui donne son argent au* ~ *fig* I give him his money in dribs and drabs

compter [kõte] ⟨1a⟩ **1** *v/t* count; (*prévoir*) allow; (*inclure*) include; ~ *faire qch* plan on doing sth; ~ *que* hope that; *ses jours sont comptés* his days are numbered; *sans* ~ *le chien* not counting the dog **2** *v/i* (*calculer*) count; (*être important*) matter, count; ~ *avec* reckon with; ~ *sur* rely on; *il ne compte pas au nombre de mes amis* I don't regard him as a friend; *à* ~ *de demain* starting (from) tomorrow, (as) from tomorrow

compte-tours [kõt(ə)tur] *m* (*pl inv*) TECH rev counter

compteur [kõtœr] *m* meter; ~ *de vitesse* speedometer

comptine [kõtin] *f* nursery rhyme

comptoir [kõtwar] *m d'un café* bar; *d'un magasin* counter

compulsif, -ive [kõpylsif, -iv] *comportement* compulsive

comte [kõt] *m en France* count; *en Grande-Bretagne* earl; **comté** *m* county; **comtesse** *f* countess

con, ~ne [kõ, kɔn] P **1** *adj* damn stupid F **2** *m/f* damn idiot F; *espèce de* ~*!* V fucking bastard! V

concave [kõkav] concave

concéder [kõsede] ⟨1f⟩ (*accorder*) grant; (*consentir*) concede; ~ *que* admit that

concentration [kõsɑ̃trasjõ] *f* concentration (*aussi fig*); **concentrer** ⟨1a⟩

concentrate; *se* ~ concentrate (*sur on*)

concept [kõsɛpt] *m* concept

conception [kõsɛpsjõ] *f* (*idée*) concept; (*planification*) design; BIOL conception; *avoir la même* ~ *de la vie* have the same outlook on life, share the same philosophy

concernant [kõsɛrnɑ̃] *prép* concerning, about; **concerner** ⟨1a⟩ concern, have to do with; *en ce qui me concerne* as far as I'm concerned; *cela ne vous concerne pas du tout* it's none of your concern, it has nothing to do with you

concert [kõsɛr] *m* MUS concert; *de* ~ *avec* together with; *agir de* ~ take concerted action

concerter [kõsɛrte] ⟨1a⟩ agree on; *se* ~ consult

concerto [kõsɛrto] *m* concerto

concession [kõsɛsjõ] *f* concession; AUTO dealership; **concessionnaire** *m* dealer

concevable [kõsəvabl] conceivable; **concevoir** ⟨3a⟩ (*comprendre*) understand, conceive; (*inventer*) design; BIOL, *plan, idée* conceive

concierge [kõsjɛrʒ] *m/f d'immeuble* superintendent, *Br* caretaker; *d'école* janitor, *Br aussi* caretaker; *d'un hôtel* concierge

concilier ⟨1a⟩ *idées, théories* reconcile

concis, ~e [kõsi, -z] concise; **concision** *f* concision, conciseness

concitoyen, ~ne [kõsitwajɛ̃, -ɛn] *m/f* fellow citizen

concluant, ~e [kõklyɑ̃, -t] conclusive; **conclure** ⟨4l⟩ **1** *v/t* (*finir*, *déduire*) conclude; ~ *un contrat* enter into a contract **2** *v/i*: ~ *à* JUR return a verdict of; ~ *de* conclude from; **conclusion** *f* conclusion

concombre [kõkõbr] *m* BOT cucumber

concordance [kõkɔrdɑ̃s] *f* agreement; **concorder** ⟨1a⟩ (*correspondre*) tally (*avec* with); (*convenir*) match; ~ *avec* (*convenir avec*) go with

concourir [kõkurir] ⟨2i⟩: ~ *à qch* contribute to sth; **concours** *m* competition; (*assistance*) help; **avec le ~ de qn** with the help of s.o.; **~ de circonstances** combination of circumstances; **~ hippique** horse show

concret, -ète [kɔ̃krɛ, -t] concrete; **concrétiser** ⟨1a⟩ *idée, rêve* turn into reality; *projet* make happen; (*illustrer*) give concrete form to; **le projet se concrétise** the project is taking shape

conçu, ~e [kɔ̃sy] *p/p* → **concevoir**

concubin [kɔ̃kybɛ̃] *m* common-law husband; **concubinage** *m* co-habitation; **concubine** *f* common-law wife

concurrence [kɔ̃kyrɑ̃s] *f* competition; **faire ~ à** compete with; **jusqu'à ~ de 300 000 euros** to a maximum of 300,000 euros; **concurrent, ~e 1** *adj* competing, rival **2** *m/f d'un concours* competitor; COMM competitor, rival; **concurrentiel, ~le** competitive

condamnable [kɔ̃danabl] reprehensible; **condamnation** *f* sentence; *action* sentencing; *fig* condemnation; **~ à perpétuité** life sentence; **condamner** ⟨1a⟩ JUR sentence; *malade* give up; (*réprouver*) condemn; *porte* block up

condenser [kɔ̃dɑ̃se] ⟨1a⟩ condense (*aussi fig*); **se ~** condense

condescendance [kɔ̃desɑ̃dɑ̃s] *f péj* condescension; **condescendre** ⟨4a⟩: **~ à faire qch** condescend to do sth

condiment [kɔ̃dimɑ̃] *m* seasoning

condition [kɔ̃disjɔ̃] *f* condition; **~ préalable** prerequisite; **~ requise** precondition; **à (la) ~ que** (+ *subj*) on condition that, **à (la) ~ de faire qch** on condition of doing sth; **~s de travail** working conditions; **conditionnel, ~le 1** *adj accord etc* conditional **2** GRAM conditional; **conditionnement** *m* (*emballage*) packaging; PSYCH conditioning; **conditionner** ⟨1a⟩ (*emballer*) package; PSYCH condition

condoléances [kɔ̃dɔleɑ̃s] *fpl* condolences

conducteur, -trice [kɔ̃dyktœr, -tris] **1** *adj* ÉL *matériau* conductive **2** *m/f* driver **3** *m* PHYS conductor

conduire [kɔ̃dųir] ⟨4c⟩ **1** *v/t* (*accompagner*) take; (*mener*) lead; *voiture* drive; *eau* take, carry; ÉL conduct; **~ qn à faire qch** lead s.o. to do sth; **se ~** behave **2** *v/i* AUTO drive; (*mener*) lead (**à** to); **permis** *m* **de ~** driver's license, *Br* driving licence

conduit [kɔ̃dųi] *m d'eau, de gaz* pipe; **~ d'aération** ventilation shaft; **~ lacrymal** ANAT tear duct; **conduite** *f* (*comportement*) behavior, *Br* behaviour; *direction* management; *d'eau, de gaz* pipe; AUTO driving; **~ en état d'ivresse** drunk driving

cône [kon] *m* cone

confection [kɔ̃fɛksjɔ̃] *f d'une robe, d'un plat etc* making; *industrie* clothing industry; **une tarte de sa ~** a tart she'd made (herself); **confectionner** ⟨1a⟩ make

confédération [kɔ̃federasjɔ̃] *f* confederation

conférence [kɔ̃ferɑ̃s] *f* (*congrès*) conference; (*exposé*) lecture; **être en ~** be in a meeting; **~ de presse** press conference; **~ au sommet** POL summit conference; **conférencier, -ère** *m/f* speaker; **conférer** ⟨1f⟩ (*accorder*) confer

confesser [kɔ̃fese] ⟨1b⟩ confess (*aussi* REL); **~ qn** REL hear s.o.'s confession; **se ~** REL go to confession; **confession** *f* confession (*aussi* REL); (*croyance*) (religious) denomination, faith; **confessionnal** *m* (*pl* -aux) confessional

confiance [kɔ̃fjɑ̃s] *f* (*foi, sécurité*) confidence, trust; (*assurance*) confidence; **avoir ~ en qch / qn** have faith in s.o. / sth, trust s.o. / sth; **faire ~ à qn** trust s.o.; **~ en soi** self-confidence; **confiant, ~e** (*crédule*) trusting; (*optimiste*) confident; (*qui a confiance en soi*) (self-)confident

confidence [kɔ̃fidɑ̃s] *f* confidence; **faire une ~ à qn** confide in s.o.; **confident, ~e** *m/f* confidant; **confidentiel, ~le** confidential

confier [kõfje] ⟨1a⟩: ~ **qch à qn** (*laisser*) entrust s.o. (with sth); **se ~ à** confide in

configuration [kõfigyrasjõ] *f* configuration

confiner [kõfine] ⟨1a⟩ **1** *v/t*: ~ **à** confine to **2** *v/i*: ~ **à** border (on); **confins** *mpl* borders; **aux ~ de** on the border between

confirmation [kõfirmasjõ] *f* confirmation (*aussi* REL); **confirmer** ⟨1a⟩ confirm (*aussi* REL); **l'exception confirme la règle** the exception proves the rule

confiscation [kõfiskasjõ] *f* confiscation

confiserie [kõfizri] *f* confectionery; *magasin* confectioner's; **~s** candy *sg*, *Br* sweets

confisquer [kõfiske] ⟨1m⟩ confiscate (*qch à qn* sth from s.o.)

confit, ~e [kõfi, -t] *fruits* candied

confiture [kõfityr] *f* jelly, *Br* jam

conflictuel, ~le [kõfliktɥel] adversarial; **conflit** *m* conflict; *d'idées* clash; ~ **des générations** generation gap; ~ **social** industrial dispute

confluent [kõflyã] *m* tributary

confondre [kõfõdr] ⟨4a⟩ *mêler dans son esprit* confuse (**avec** with); (*déconcerter*) take aback; **se ~** (*se mêler*) merge, blend; **se ~ en excuses** apologize profusely

conforme [kõfɔrm]: ~ **à** in accordance with; **copie ~ à l'original** exact copy of the original; **conformément** *adv*: ~ **à** in accordance with; **conformer** ⟨1a⟩: ~ **à qch** adapt to; **se ~ à qch** comply with sth; **conformisme** *m* conformity; **conformiste** *m/f* conformist; **conformité** *f* caractère de ce qui est semblable similarity; **en ~ avec** in accordance with

confort [kõfɔr] *m* comfort; **tout ~** with every convenience

confortable [kõfɔrtabl] comfortable; *somme* sizeable

confrère [kõfrɛr] *m* colleague

confrontation [kõfrõtasjõ] *f* confrontation; (*comparaison*) comparison; **confronter** ⟨1a⟩ confront; (*comparer*) compare

confus, ~e [kõfy, -z] *amas, groupe* confused; *bruit* indistinct; *souvenirs* vague; *personne* (*gêné*) embarrassed; **confusion** *f* confusion; (*embarras*) embarrassment

congé [kõʒe] *m* (*vacances*) vacation, *Br* holiday; MIL leave; *avis de départ* notice; **prendre ~ de qn** take one's leave of s.o.; **être en ~** be on vacation; ~ **de maladie** sick leave; ~ **de maternité** maternity leave; **congédier** ⟨1a⟩ dismiss

congélateur [kõʒelatœr] *m* freezer; **congélation** *f* freezing; **congelé, ~e** *aliment* frozen; **congeler** ⟨1d⟩ freeze

congénère [kõʒenɛr] *m*: **avec ses ~s** with its own kind

congénital, ~e [kõʒenital] (*mpl* -aux) congenital

congère [kõʒɛr] *f* (snow)drift

congestion [kõʒɛstjõ] *f* MÉD congestion; ~ **cérébrale** stroke; **congestionner** ⟨1a⟩ *rue* cause congestion in, block; **congestionné, ~e** *visage* flushed

congrès [kõgrɛ] *m* convention, conference; **Congrès** *aux États-Unis* Congress; **congressiste** *m/f* conventioneer, *Br* conference member

conifère [kɔnifɛr] *m* BOT conifer

conique [kɔnik] conical

conjecture [kõʒɛktyr] *f* conjecture; **conjecturer** ⟨1a⟩ conjecture about

conjoint, ~e [kõʒwẽ, -t] **1** *adj* joint **2** *m/f* spouse

conjonction [kõʒõksjõ] *f* GRAM conjunction

conjonctivite [kõʒõktivit] *f* MÉD conjunctivitis

conjoncture [kõʒõktyr] *f* situation, circumstances *pl*; ÉCON economic situation

conjugaison [kõʒygɛzõ] *f* GRAM conjugation

conjugal, ~e [kõʒygal] (*mpl* -aux) conjugal; *vie* married; **quitter le domicile ~** desert one's wife / husband

conjuguer [kõʒyge] ⟨1m⟩ *efforts* combine; GRAM conjugate

conjuration [kõʒyrasjõ] *f (conspiration)* conspiracy; **conjurer** ⟨1a⟩: ~ **qn de faire qch** implore s.o. to do sth; **se ~ contre** conspire against

connaissance [kɔnɛsɑ̃s] *f (savoir)* knowledge; *(conscience)* consciousness; *personne connue* acquaintance; ~**s** *d'un sujet* knowledge *sg*; **avoir ~ de qch** know about sth, be aware of sth; **prendre ~ de qch** acquaint o.s. with sth; **perdre ~** lose consciousness; **reprendre ~** regain consciousness, come to; **faire ~ avec qn, faire la ~ de qn** make s.o.'s acquaintance, meet s.o.; **à ma ~** to my knowledge, as far as I know; **connaisseur** *m* connoisseur; **connaître** ⟨4z⟩ know; *(rencontrer)* meet; **s'y ~ en qch** know all about sth, be an expert on sth; **il s'y connaît** he's an expert

connecter [kɔnɛkte] ⟨1a⟩ TECH connect; **se ~** INFORM log on

connerie [kɔnri] *f* P damn stupidity; **une ~** a damn stupid thing to do / say; **dire des ~s** talk crap P

connexion [kɔnɛksjõ] *f* connection *(aussi* ÉL*)*; **hors ~** INFORM off-line

connivence [kɔnivɑ̃s] *f* connivance; **être de ~ avec qn** connive with s.o.

connu, ~e [kɔny] **1** *p/p* → **connaître** **2** *adj* well-known

conquérant [kõkerɑ̃] *m* winner; **Guillaume le Conquérant** William the Conqueror; **conquérir** ⟨21⟩ *peuple, pays* conquer; *droit, indépendance, estime* win, gain; *marché* capture, conquer; *personne* win over; **conquête** *f* conquest

consacrer [kõsakre] ⟨1a⟩ REL consecrate; *(dédier)* dedicate; *temps, argent* spend; **se ~ à qch / qn** dedicate *ou* devote o.s. to sth / s.o.; **une expression consacrée** a fixed expression

consanguin, ~e [kõsɑ̃gɛ̃, -in]: **frère ~** half-brother *(who has the same father)*; **unions** *fpl* ~**es** inbreeding *sg*

conscience [kõsjɑ̃s] *f moral* conscience; *physique,* PSYCH consciousness; **avoir bonne / mauvaise ~** have a clear / guilty conscience; **prendre ~ de qch** become aware of sth; **perdre ~** lose consciousness; **consciencieux, -euse** conscientious; **conscient, ~e** conscious; **être ~ de qch** be aware *ou* conscious of sth

consécration [kõsekrasjõ] *f* REL consecration; *(confirmation)* confirmation

consécutif, -ive [kõsekytif, -iv] consecutive; ~ **à** resulting from; **consécutivement** *adv* consecutively

conseil [kõsɛj] *m (avis)* advice; *(conseiller)* adviser; *(assemblée)* council; **un ~** a piece of advice; ~ **municipal** town council; ~ **d'administration** board of directors; ~ **des ministres** Cabinet; **Conseil de Sécurité de l'ONU** Security Council

conseiller[1] [kõseje] ⟨1b⟩ *personne* advise; ~ **qch à qn** recommend sth to s.o.

conseiller[2]**, -ère** [kõseje, -ɛr] *m* adviser; ~ **en gestion** management consultant; ~ **municipal** councilman, *Br* town councillor

consentement [kõsɑ̃tmɑ̃] *m* consent; **consentir** ⟨2b⟩ **1** *v/i* consent, agree *(à* to); ~ **à faire qch** agree *ou* consent to do sth; ~ **à ce que qn fasse** *(subj)* **qch** agree to s.o.'s doing sth **2** *v/t prêt, délai* grant, agree

conséquence [kõsekɑ̃s] *f* consequence; **en ~** *(donc)* consequently; **en ~ de** as a result of; **conséquent, ~e** *(cohérent)* consistent; **par ~** consequently

conservateur, -trice [kõsɛrvatœr, -tris] **1** *adj* POL conservative **2** *m/f* POL conservative; *d'un musée* curator **3** *m* CUIS preservative; **conservation** *f* preservation; *des aliments* preserving

conservatoire [kõsɛrvatwar] *m* school, conservatory

conserve [kõsɛrv] *f* preserve; *en boîte* canned food, *Br aussi* tinned food; **en ~** *(en boîte)* canned, *Br aussi* tinned; **conserver** ⟨1a⟩ *(garder)* keep; *aliments* preserve

considérable [kõsiderabl] considerable; **considérablement** *adv* considerably; **considération** f consideration; **en ~ de** in consideration of; **prendre en ~** take into consideration; **considérer** ⟨1f⟩ consider; **~ comme** consider as, look on as

consigne [kõsiɲ] f orders pl; d'une gare baggage checkroom, Br left luggage office; pour bouteilles deposit; ÉDU detention; **consigner** ⟨1a⟩ (noter) record; écolier keep in; soldat confine to base, Br confine to barracks; **bouteille** f **consignée** returnable bottle

consistance [kõsistãs] f consistency; **consistant, ~e** liquide, potage thick; mets substantial; **consister** ⟨1a⟩: **~ en / dans qch** consist of sth; **~ à faire qch** consist in doing sth

consolant, ~e [kõsɔlɑ̃, -t] consoling; **consolation** f consolation

console [kõsɔl] f (table) console table; INFORM console; **jouer à la ~** play computer games

consoler [kõsɔle] ⟨1a⟩ console, comfort; **se ~ de qch** get over sth

consolider [kõsɔlide] ⟨1a⟩ strengthen, consolidate; COMM, FIN consolidate

consommateur, -trice [kõsɔmatœr, -tris] m/f consumer; dans un café customer; **consommation** f consumption; dans un café drink

consommé [kõsɔme] m CUIS consommé, clear soup; **consommer** ⟨1a⟩ **1** v/t bois, charbon, essence etc consume, use **2** v/i dans un café drink

consonne [kõsɔn] f consonant

conspirateur, -trice [kõspiratœr, -tris] m/f conspirator; **conspiration** f conspiracy; **conspirer** ⟨1a⟩ conspire

constamment [kõstamɑ̃] adv constantly

constance [kõstãs] f (persévérance) perseverance; en amour constancy

constant, ~e [kõstã, -t] **1** adj ami steadfast, staunch; efforts persistent; souci, température, quantité constant; intérêt unwavering **2** f constant

constat [kõsta] m JUR report

constatation [kõstatasjõ] f observa-

tion; **constater** ⟨1a⟩ observe

constellation [kõstelasjõ] f constellation

consternation [kõsternasjõ] f consternation; **consterner** ⟨1a⟩ fill with consternation, dismay; **consterné, ~e** dismayed

constipation [kõstipasjõ] f constipation; **constipé, ~e** constipated

constituer [kõstitɥe] ⟨1a⟩ constitute; comité, société form, set up; rente settle (à on); **être constitué de** be made up of; **se ~** collection, fortune amass, build up; **se ~ prisonnier** give o.s. up

constitution [kõstitɥsjõ] f (composition) composition; ANAT, POL constitution; d'un comité, d'une société formation, setting up; **constitutionnel, ~le** constitutional

constructeur [kõstryktœr] m de voitures, d'avions, d'ordinateurs manufacturer; de maisons builder; **~ mécanicien** m mechanical engineer; **~ naval** shipbuilder; **constructif, -ive** constructive; **construction** f action, bâtiment construction, building; **construire** ⟨4c⟩ construct, build; théorie, roman construct

consul [kõsyl] m consul; **consulat** m consulate

consultatif, -ive [kõsyltatif, -tiv] consultative; **consultation** f consultation; (**heures** fpl **de**) **~** MÉD office hours, Br consulting hours; **consulter** ⟨1a⟩ **1** v/t consult **2** v/i be available for consultation

consumer [kõsyme] ⟨1a⟩ de feu, passion consume

contact [kõtakt] m contact; **lentilles** fpl ou **verres** mpl **de ~** contact lenses, contacts F; **entrer en ~ avec qn** (first) come into contact with s.o.; **prendre ~ avec qn, se mettre en ~ avec qn** contact s.o., get in touch with s.o.; **mettre / couper le ~** AUTO switch the engine on / off

contagieux, -euse [kõtaʒjø, -z] contagious; rire infectious; **contagion** f contagion

container [kõtener] m container; **~ à**

verre bottle bank

contamination [kɔ̃taminasjɔ̃] *f* contamination; MÉD *d'une personne* infection; **contaminer** ⟨1a⟩ contaminate; MÉD *personne* infect

conte [kɔ̃t] *m* story, tale; **~ de fées** fairy story *ou* tale

contemplation [kɔ̃tɑ̃plasjɔ̃] *f* contemplation; **contempler** ⟨1a⟩ contemplate

contemporain, ~e [kɔ̃tɑ̃pɔrɛ̃, -ɛn] *m/f* & *adj* contemporary

contenance [kɔ̃tnɑ̃s] *f* (*capacité*) capacity; (*attitude*) attitude; **perdre ~** lose one's composure; **conteneur** *m* container; **~ à verre** *m* bottle bank; **contenir** ⟨2h⟩ contain; *foule* control, restrain; *larmes* hold back; *peine* suppress; **se ~** contain o.s., control o.s.

content, ~e [kɔ̃tɑ̃, -t] pleased, content (*de* with); **contentement** *m* contentment; **contenter** ⟨1a⟩ *personne, curiosité* satisfy; **se ~ de qch** be content with sth; **se ~ de faire qch** be content with doing sth

contentieux [kɔ̃tɑ̃sjø] *m* disputes *pl*; *service* legal department

contenu [kɔ̃tny] *m* content

conter [kɔ̃te] ⟨1a⟩ tell

contestable [kɔ̃testabl] *décision* questionable; **contestataire** POL **1** *adj propos* of protest **2** *m/f* protester; **contestation** *f* discussion; (*opposition*) protest; **contester** ⟨1a⟩ challenge

contexte [kɔ̃tekst] *m* context

contigu, ~ë [kɔ̃tigy] adjoining

continent [kɔ̃tinɑ̃] *m* continent

contingent [kɔ̃tɛ̃ʒɑ̃] *m* (*part*) quota; **contingenter** ⟨1a⟩ apply a quota to

continu, ~e [kɔ̃tiny] continuous; ÉL *courant* direct; **continuation** *f* continuation; **continuel, ~le** continual; **continuer** ⟨1n⟩ **1** *v/t voyage, travaux* continue (with), carry on with; *rue, ligne* extend **2** *v/i* continue, carry *ou* go on; *de route* extend; **~ à** *ou* **de faire qch** continue to do sth, carry *ou* go on doing sth; **continuité** *f* continuity; *d'une tradition* continuation

contorsion [kɔ̃tɔrsjɔ̃] *f* contorsion

contour [kɔ̃tur] *m* contour; *d'une fenêtre, d'un visage* outline; **~s** (*courbes*) twists and turns; **contourner** ⟨1a⟩ *obstacle* skirt around; *fig: difficulté* get around

contraceptif, -ive [kɔ̃traseptif, -iv] contraceptive; **contraception** *f* contraception

contracter [kɔ̃trakte] ⟨1a⟩ *dette* incur; *maladie* contract, incur; *alliance, obligation* enter into; *assurance* take out; *habitude* acquire; **contractuel, ~le 1** *adj* contractual **2** *m/f* traffic officer, *Br* traffic warden

contradiction [kɔ̃tradiksjɔ̃] *f* contradiction; **contradictoire** contradictory

contraindre [kɔ̃trɛ̃dr] ⟨4b⟩: **~ qn à faire qch** force *ou* compel s.o. to do sth; **contrainte** *f* constraint; **agir sous la ~** act under duress; **sans ~** freely, without restraint

contraire [kɔ̃trɛr] **1** *adj sens* opposite; *principes* conflicting; *vent* contrary; **~ à** contrary to **2** *m*: **le ~ de** the opposite *ou* contrary of; **au ~** on the contrary; **contrairement** *adv*: **~ à** contrary to; **~ à toi** unlike you

contrarier [kɔ̃trarje] ⟨1a⟩ *personne* annoy; *projet, action* thwart; **contrariété** *f* annoyance

contraste [kɔ̃trast] *m* contrast; **contraster** ⟨1a⟩ contrast (*avec* with)

contrat [kɔ̃tra] *m* contract; **~ de location** rental agreement

contravention [kɔ̃travɑ̃sjɔ̃] *f* (*infraction*) infringement; (*procès-verbal*) ticket; **~ pour excès de vitesse** speeding fine

contre [kɔ̃tr] **1** *prép* against; SP *aussi* versus; (*en échange*) (in exchange) for; **tout ~ qch** right next to sth; **joue ~ joue** cheek to cheek; **par ~** on the contrary; **quelque chose ~ la diarrhée** something for diarrhea **2** *m*: **le pour et le ~** the pros and the cons *pl*

contre-attaque [kɔ̃tratak] *f* counterattack

contrebalancer [kɔ̃trəbalɑ̃se] ⟨1k⟩ counterbalance

contrebande [kɔ̃trəbɑ̃d] *f* smuggling; *marchandises* contraband; **faire la ~ de qch** smuggle sth; **contrebandier** *m* smuggler

contrebasse [kɔ̃trəbas] *f* double bass

contrecarrer [kɔ̃trəkare] ⟨1a⟩ *projets* thwart

contrecœur [kɔ̃trəkœr]: **à ~** unwillingly, reluctantly

contrecoup [kɔ̃trəku] *m* after-effect

contre-courant [kɔ̃trəkurɑ̃] *m*: **nager à ~** swim against the current

contredire [kɔ̃trədir] ⟨4m⟩ contradict

contrée [kɔ̃tre] *f* country

contre-espionnage [kɔ̃trɛspjɔnaʒ] *m* counterespionage

contrefaçon [kɔ̃trəfasɔ̃] *f action* counterfeiting; *de signature* forging; *objet* fake, counterfeit; **contrefaire** ⟨4n⟩ *(falsifier)* counterfeit; *signature* forge; *personne, gestes* imitate; *voix* disguise; **contrefait, ~e** *(difforme)* deformed

contre-interrogatoire [kɔ̃trɛ̃terɔgatwar] *m* cross-examination

contre-jour [kɔ̃trəʒur] PHOT backlighting; **à ~** against the light

contremaître [kɔ̃trəmɛtr] *m* foreman

contre-mesure [kɔ̃trəm(ə)zyr] *f (pl* contre-mesures) countermeasure

contre-nature [kɔ̃trənatyr] unnatural

contre-offensive [kɔ̃trɔfɑ̃siv] *f* counteroffensive

contrepartie [kɔ̃trəparti] *f* compensation; **en ~** in return

contre-pied [kɔ̃trəpje] *m* opposite; **prendre le ~ d'un avis** ask for advice and then do the exact opposite

contre-plaqué [kɔ̃trəplake] *m* plywood

contrepoids [kɔ̃trəpwa] *m* counterweight

contre-productif, -ive [kɔ̃trəprɔdyktif, -iv] counterproductive

contrer [kɔ̃tre] ⟨1b⟩ counter

contresens [kɔ̃trəsɑ̃s] *m* misinterpretation; **prendre une route à ~** AUTO go down a road the wrong way

contresigner [kɔ̃trəsiɲe] ⟨1a⟩ countersign

contretemps [kɔ̃trətɑ̃] *m* hitch

contre-terrorisme [kɔ̃trəterɔrism] *m* counterterrorism

contrevenir [kɔ̃trəv(ə)nir] ⟨2h⟩ JUR: **~ à qch** contravene sth

contribuable [kɔ̃tribɥabl] *m* taxpayer; **contribuer** ⟨1n⟩ contribute *(à* to); **~ à faire qch** help to do sth; **contribution** *f* contribution; *(impôt)* tax

contrôle [kɔ̃trol] *m (vérification)* check; *(domination)* control; *(maîtrise de soi)* self-control; **perdre le ~ de son véhicule** lose control of one's vehicle; **~ aérien** air-traffic control; **~ des bagages** baggage check; **~ douanier** customs inspection; **~ des naissances** birth control; **~ des passeports** passport control; **~ qualité** quality control; **~ radar** radar speed check, radar trap; **~ de soi** self-control; **contrôler** ⟨1a⟩ *comptes, identité, billets etc* check; *(maîtriser, dominer)* control; **se ~** control o.s.; **contrôleur, -euse** *m/f* controller; *de train* ticket inspector; **~ de trafic aérien** air-traffic controller

controverse [kɔ̃trɔvers] *f* controversy; **controversé, ~e** controversial

contumace [kɔ̃tymas] *f* JUR: **être condamné par ~** be sentenced in absentia

contusion [kɔ̃tyzjɔ̃] *f* MÉD bruise, contusion

convaincant, ~e [kɔ̃vɛ̃kɑ̃, -t] convincing; **convaincre** ⟨4i⟩ *(persuader)* convince; JUR convict *(de* of); **~ qn de faire qch** persuade s.o. to do sth; **convaincu, ~e** convinced

convalescence [kɔ̃valesɑ̃s] *f* convalescence; **convalescent, ~e** *m/f* convalescent

convenable [kɔ̃vnabl] suitable, fitting; *(correct) personne* respectable, decent; *tenue* proper, suitable; *salaire* adequate; **convenance** *f*: **les ~s** the proprieties; **quelque chose à ma ~** something to my liking

convenir [kɔ̃vnir] ⟨2h⟩: **~ à qn** suit s.o.; **~à qch** be suitable for sth; **~ de qch** *(décider)* agree on sth;

(*avouer*) admit sth; **~ que** (*reconnaître que*) admit that; **il convient de respecter les lois** the laws must be obeyed; **il convient que tu ailles** (*subj*) **voir ta grand-mère** you should go and see your grandmother; **il a été convenu de ...** it was agreed to ...; **comme convenu** as agreed

convention [kɔ̃vɑ̃sjɔ̃] *f* (*accord*) agreement, convention; POL convention; **les ~s** the conventions; **~ collective** collective agreement; **conventionné, ~e: médecin *m* ~** doctor who charges according to a nationally agreed fee structure; **conventionnel, ~le** conventional

convergence [kɔ̃vɛrʒɑ̃s] *f* ÉCON convergence; **converger** ⟨1l⟩ converge (*aussi fig*)

conversation [kɔ̃vɛrsasjɔ̃] *f* conversation; **~ téléphonique** telephone conversation, phonecall; **converser** ⟨1a⟩ converse, talk

conversion [kɔ̃vɛrsjɔ̃] *f* conversion (*aussi* REL)

convertible [kɔ̃vɛrtibl] COMM convertible; **convertir** ⟨2a⟩ convert (*en* into); REL convert (*à* to)

conviction [kɔ̃viksjɔ̃] *f* conviction

convier [kɔ̃vje] ⟨1a⟩ *fml*: **~ qn à qch** invite s.o. to sth; **~ qn à faire qch** urge s.o. to do sth

convive [kɔ̃viv] *m/f* guest; **convivial, ~e** convivial, friendly; INFORM user-friendly; **convivialité** *f* conviviality, friendliness; INFORM user-friendliness

convocation [kɔ̃vɔkasjɔ̃] *f d'une assemblée* convening; JUR summons *sg*

convoi [kɔ̃vwa] *m* convoy

convoiter [kɔ̃vwate] ⟨1a⟩ covet; **convoitise** *f* covetousness

convoquer [kɔ̃vɔke] ⟨1m⟩ *assemblée* convene; JUR summons; *candidat* notify; *employé, écolier* call in, summon

convoyer [kɔ̃vwaje] ⟨1h⟩ MIL escort

convulser [kɔ̃vylse] ⟨1a⟩ convulse; **convulsion** *f* convulsion

coopérant [kɔɔperɑ̃] *m* aid worker

coopératif, -ive [kɔɔperatif, -iv] cooperative; **coopération** *f* cooperation; **être en ~** be an aid worker

coopérer [kɔɔpere] ⟨1f⟩ cooperate (*à* in)

coordinateur, -trice [kɔɔrdinatœr, -tris] *m/f* coordinator; **coordination** *f* coordination

coordonner [kɔɔrdɔne] ⟨1a⟩ coordinate; **coordonnées** *fpl* MATH coordinates; *d'une personne* contact details; **je n'ai pas pris ses ~** I didn't get his address or phone number

copain [kɔpɛ̃] *m* F pal, *Br* mate; **être ~ avec** be pally with

copie [kɔpi] *f* copy; ÉDU paper; **~ de sauvegarde** INFORM back-up (copy); **~ sur papier** hard copy

copier [kɔpje] ⟨1a⟩ **1** *v/t* copy **2** *v/i* ÉDU copy (*sur qn* from s.o.); **copieur, -euse** *m/f* copier, copy cat F

copieux, -euse [kɔpjø, -z] copious

copilote [kɔpilɔt] *m* co-pilot

copinage [kɔpinaʒ] *m* cronyism

copine [kɔpin] *f* F pal, *Br* mate

coproduction [kɔprɔdyksjɔ̃] *f d'un film* coproduction

copropriétaire [kɔprɔprijetɛr] *m/f* co-owner; **copropriété** *f* joint ownership; **un immeuble en ~** a condo

copyright [kɔpirajt] *m* copyright

coq [kɔk] *m* rooster, *Br* cock

coque [kɔk] *f d'œuf, de noix* shell; MAR hull; AVIAT fuselage; **œuf *m* à la ~** soft-boiled egg

coquelicot [kɔkliko] *m* BOT poppy

coqueluche [kɔklyʃ] *f* whooping cough

coquet, ~te [kɔkɛ, -t] flirtatious; (*joli*) charming; (*élégant*) stylish; **une somme ~te** a tidy amount

coquetier [kɔktje] *m* eggcup

coquetterie [kɔkɛtri] *f* flirtatiousness; (*élégance*) stylishness

coquillage [kɔkijaʒ] *m* shell; **des ~s** shellfish *sg*

coquille [kɔkij] *f d'escargot, d'œuf, de noix etc* shell; *erreur* misprint, typo; **~ Saint-Jacques** CUIS scallop

coquin, ~e [kɔkɛ̃, -in] **1** *adj enfant* naughty **2** *m/f* rascal

cor [kɔr] *m* MUS horn; MÉD corn

corail [kɔraj] *m* (*pl* coraux) coral

Coran [kɔrɑ̃]: *le ~* the Koran
corbeau [kɔrbo] *m* (*pl* -x) ZO crow
corbeille [kɔrbɛj] *f* basket; *au théâtre* circle; *~ à papier* wastebasket, *Br* wastepaper basket
corbillard [kɔrbijar] *m* hearse
corde [kɔrd] *f* rope; MUS, *de tennis* string; *~ raide* high wire; *~s* MUS strings; *~s vocales* vocal cords; **cordée** *f en alpinisme* rope
cordial, *~e* [kɔrdjal] (*mpl* -iaux) cordial; **cordialité** *f* cordiality
cordon [kɔrdɔ̃] *m* cord; *~ littoral* offshore sand bar; *~ ombilical* umbilical cord; **cordon-bleu** *m* (*pl* cordons-bleus) cordon bleu chef
cordonnier [kɔrdɔnje] *m* shoe repairer, *Br aussi* cobbler
Corée [kɔre]: *la ~* Korea; **coréen**, *~ne* **1** *adj* Korean **2** *m langue* Korean **3** *m/f* **Coréen**, *~ne* Korean
coriace [kɔrjas] tough (*aussi fig*); *être ~ en affaires* be a hard-headed businessman
corne [kɔrn] *f* horn; *avoir des ~s fig* be a cuckold; **cornée** *f* cornea
corneille [kɔrnɛj] *f* crow
cornemuse [kɔrnəmyz] *f* bagpipes *pl*
corner [kɔrner] *m en football* corner
cornet [kɔrnɛ] *m sachet* (paper) cone; MUS cornet
corniche [kɔrniʃ] *f* corniche; ARCH cornice
cornichon [kɔrniʃɔ̃] *m* gherkin
corniste [kɔrnist] *m* MUS horn player
coronaire [kɔrɔnɛr] coronary
coroner [kɔrɔner] *m* coroner
corporation [kɔrpɔrasjɔ̃] *f* body; HIST guild
corporel, *~le* [kɔrpɔrɛl] *hygiène* personal; *châtiment* corporal; *art body atr*; *odeur ~le* BO, body odor *or Br* odour
corps [kɔr] *m* body; *mort* (dead) body, corpse; MIL corps; *prendre ~* take shape; *le ~ diplomatique* the diplomatic corps; *le ~ électoral* the electorate; *~ étranger* foreign body; *~ expéditionnaire* task force; *~ médical* medical profession
corpulence [kɔrpylɑ̃s] *f* stoutness,

corpulence; **corpulent**, *~e* stout, corpulent
correct, *~e* [kɔrɛkt] correct; *personne* correct, proper; *tenue* right, suitable; F (*convenable*) acceptable, ok F
correcteur [kɔrɛktœr] *m*: *~ orthographique* spellchecker
correction [kɔrɛksjɔ̃] *f qualité* correctness; (*modification*) correction; (*punition*) beating
corrélation [kɔrelasjɔ̃] *f* correlation
correspondance [kɔrɛspɔ̃dɑ̃s] *f* correspondence; *de train etc* connection; **correspondant**, *~e* **1** *adj* corresponding **2** *m/f* correspondent
correspondre [kɔrɛspɔ̃dr] ⟨4a⟩ *de choses* correspond; *de salles* communicate; *par courrier* correspond (*avec* with); *~ à réalité* correspond with; *preuves* tally with; *idées* fit in with
corridor [kɔridɔr] *m* corridor
corriger [kɔriʒe] ⟨1l⟩ correct; *épreuve* proof-read; (*battre*) beat; *~ le tir* adjust one's aim
corroborer [kɔrɔbɔre] ⟨1a⟩ corroborate
corroder [kɔrɔde] ⟨1a⟩ corrode
corrompre [kɔrɔ̃pr] ⟨4a⟩ (*avilir*) corrupt; (*soudoyer*) bribe; **corrompu**, *~e* **1** *p/p* → **corrompre 2** *adj* corrupt
corrosif, **-ive** [kɔrozif, -iv] **1** *adj* corrosive; *fig* caustic **2** *m* corrosive; **corrosion** *f* corrosion
corruption [kɔrypsjɔ̃] *f* corruption; (*pot-de-vin*) bribery
corsage [kɔrsaʒ] *m* blouse
corse [kɔrs] **1** *adj* Corsican **2** *m/f* **Corse** Corsican **3** *f* **la Corse** Corsica
corsé, *~e* [kɔrse] *vin* full-bodied; *sauce* spicy; *café* strong; *facture* stiff; *problème* tough
corset [kɔrsɛ] *m* corset
cortège [kɔrtɛʒ] *m* cortège; (*défilé*) procession; *~ funèbre* funeral cortège; *~ nuptial* bridal procession
cortisone [kɔrtizon] *f* PHARM cortisone
corvée [kɔrve] *f* chore; MIL fatigue
cosmétique [kɔsmetik] *m & adj* cos-

metic

cosmique [kɔsmik] cosmic

cosmonaute [kɔsmonot] *m/f* cosmonaut

cosmopolite [kɔsmɔpɔlit] cosmopolitan

cosmos [kɔsmɔs] *m* cosmos

cosse [kɔs] *f* BOT pod

cossu, ~e [kɔsy] *personne* well-off; *château* opulent

costaud [kɔsto] (*f inv*) F sturdy

costume [kɔstym] *m* costume; *pour homme* suit; **costumer** ⟨1a⟩: **se ~** get dressed up (**comme** as)

cote [kɔt] *f en Bourse* quotation; *d'un livre, document* identification code; **avoir la ~** *fig* F be popular; **~ de popularité** POL popularity (rating)

côte [kot] *f* ANAT rib; (*pente*) slope; *à la mer* coast; *viande* chop; **~ à ~** side by side

Côte d'Azur [kotdazyr] French Riviera

Côte-d'Ivoire [kotdivwar]: **la ~** the Ivory Coast

côté [kote] *m* side; **à ~** (*près*) nearby; **à ~ de l'église** next to the church, beside the church; **de ~** aside; **de l'autre ~ de la rue** on the other side of the street; **du ~ de** in the direction of; **sur le ~** on one's / its side; **laisser de ~** leave aside; **mettre de ~** put aside; **de tous ~s** from all sides

coteau [koto] *m* (*pl* -x) (*colline*) hill; (*pente*) slope

côtelette [kotlɛt] *f* CUIS cutlet

coter [kote] ⟨1a⟩ *en Bourse* quote; **valeurs cotées en Bourse** listed *ou* quoted stocks

côtier, -ère [kotje, -ɛr] coastal

cotisation [kɔtizasjõ] *f* contribution; *à une organisation* subscription; **cotiser** ⟨1a⟩ contribute; *à une organisation* subscribe

coton [kɔtõ] *m* cotton; **~ hydrophile** absorbent cotton, *Br* cotton wool

côtoyer [kotwaje] ⟨1h⟩: **~ qn** rub shoulders with s.o.; **~ qch** border sth; *fig* be verging on sth

cottage [kɔtaʒ] *m* cottage

cou [ku] *m* (*pl* -s) neck

couchage [kuʃaʒ] *m*: **sac m de ~** sleeping bag; **couchant 1** *m* west **2** *adj*: **soleil m ~** setting sun

couche [kuʃ] *f* layer; *de peinture aussi* coat; *de bébé* diaper, *Br* nappy; **fausse ~** MÉD miscarriage; **~ d'ozone** ozone layer; **~s sociales** social strata *pl*

couché, ~e [kuʃe] lying down; (*au lit*) in bed; **coucher** ⟨1a⟩ **1** *v/t* (*mettre au lit*) put to bed; (*héberger*) put up; (*étendre*) put *ou* lay down **2** *v/i* sleep; **~ avec qn** F sleep with s.o., go to bed with s.o.; **se ~** go to bed; (*s'étendre*) lie down; *du soleil* set, go down **3** *m*: **~ du soleil** sunset

couchette [kuʃɛt] *f* couchette

coucou [kuku] **1** *m* cuckoo; (*pendule*) cuckoo clock **2** *int*: **~!** hi!

coude [kud] *m* ANAT elbow; *d'une route* turn; **jouer des ~s** elbow one's way through; *fig* hustle

cou-de-pied [kudpje] *m* (*pl* cous-de-pied) instep

coudre [kudr] ⟨4d⟩ sew; *bouton* sew on; *plaie* sew up

couenne [kwan] *f* rind

couette [kwɛt] *f* comforter, *Br* quilt

couffin [kufɛ̃] *m* basket

couilles [kuj] *fpl* V balls V

couillon [kujõ] *m* F jerk F

couinement [kwinmã] *m* squeak

coulant, ~e [kulã, -t] *style* flowing; *fig* easy-going; **couler** ⟨1a⟩ **1** *v/i* flow, run; *d'eau de boue* run; *d'un bateau* sink; **l'argent lui coule entre les doigts** money slips through his fingers **2** *v/t* *liquide* pour; (*mouler*) cast; *bateau* sink

couleur [kulœr] *f* color, *Br* colour

couleuvre [kulœvr] *f* grass snake

coulisse [kulis] *f* TECH runner; **à ~** sliding; **~s** *d'un théâtre* wings; **dans les ~s** *fig* behind the scenes

couloir [kulwar] *m* *d'une maison* passage, corridor; *d'un bus, avion, train* aisle; **place f côté ~** aisle seat

coup [ku] *m* blow; *dans jeu* move; **à ~s de marteau** using a hammer; **boire qch à petits ~s** sip sth; **boire un ~** F have a drink; **~ droit** TENNIS fore-

C

hand; ~ *franc* SP free kick; ~ *monté* frame-up; *à* ~ *sûr* certainly; *du* ~ and so; *du même* ~ at the same time; *d'un seul* ~ *tout d'un coup* all at once; *pour le* ~ as a result; *cette fois* this time; *après* ~ after the event; *tout d'un* ~, *tout à* ~ suddenly, all at once; ~ *sur* ~ *coup* in quick succession; *être dans le* ~ be with it; *être impliqué* be involved; *tenir le* ~ stick it out, hang in there; *coup d'État* coup (d'état); *coup de balai* fig: *donner un* ~ *dans le couloir* give the passage a sweep; *donner un* ~ fig have a shake-up; *coup de chance* stroke of luck; *coup de couteau* stab; *il a reçu trois coups de couteau* he was stabbed three times; *coup d'envoi* kickoff; *coup de feu* shot; *coup de foudre*: *ce fut le* ~ it was love at first sight; *coup de main*: *donner un* ~ *à qn* give s.o. a hand; *coup de maître* master stroke; *coup d'œil*: *au premier* ~ at first glance; *coup de pied* kick; *coup de poing* punch; *donner un* ~ *à* punch; *coup de pub* F plug; *coup de téléphone* (phone) call; *coup de tête* whim; *coup de tonnerre* clap of thunder; *coup de vent* gust of wind; *coup de soleil*: *avoir un* ~ have sun stroke

coupable [kupabl] **1** *adj* guilty **2** *m/f* culprit, guilty party; *le* / *la* ~ JUR the guilty man / woman, the guilty party
coupe[1] [kup] *f de cheveux, d'une robe* cut
coupe[2] [kup] *f (verre)* glass; SP cup; *de fruits, glace* dish
coupe-circuit [kupsirkɥi] *m (pl inv)* ÉL circuit breaker
coupe-ongles [kupɔ̃gl] *m (pl inv)* nail clippers *pl*
couper [kupe] ⟨1a⟩ **1** *v/t* cut; *morceau, eau* cut off; *viande* cut (up); *robe, chemise* cut out; *vin* dilute; *animal* castrate **2** *v/i* cut; *se* ~ cut o.s.; *(se trahir)* give o.s. away; ~ *court à qch* put a stop to sth; ~ *la parole à qn* interrupt s.o.; ~ *par le champ* cut across the field

couplage [kupla3] *m* TECH coupling
couple [kupl] *m* couple; **coupler** ⟨1a⟩ couple
couplet [kuple] *m* verse
coupole [kupɔl] *f* ARCH cupola
coupon [kupõ] *m de tissu* remnant; COMM coupon; *(ticket)* ticket
coupure [kupyr] *f blessure, dans un film, dans un texte* cut; *de journal* cutting, clipping; *(billet de banque)* bill, Br note; ~ *de courant* power outage, Br power cut
cour [kur] *f* court; ARCH courtyard; *faire la* ~ *à qn* court s.o.; *Cour internationale de justice* International Court of Justice
courage [kura3] *m* courage, bravery; **courageux, -euse** brave, courageous
couramment [kuramã] *adv parler, lire* fluently
courant, ~e [kurã, -t] **1** *adj* current; *eau* running; *langage* everyday **2** *m* current (*aussi* ÉL); ~ *d'air* draft, Br draught; *être au* ~ *de qch* know about sth; *tiens-moi au* ~ keep me informed *ou* posted; ~ *alternatif* alternating current; ~ *continu* direct current
courbature [kurbatyr] *f* stiffness; *avoir des* ~*s* be stiff
courbe [kurb] **1** *adj* curved **2** *f* curve, bend; GÉOM curve; **courber** ⟨1a⟩ bend; *se* ~ *(se baisser)* stoop, bend down; **courbure** *f* curvature
coureur [kurœr] *m* runner; *péj* skirt-chaser; ~ *de jupons* womanizer
courge [kur3] *f* BOT squash, Br marrow
courgette [kur3et] *f* BOT zucchini, Br courgette
courir [kurir] ⟨2i⟩ **1** *v/i* run (*aussi d'eau*); *d'un bruit* go around; *monter* / *descendre en courant* run up / down **2** *v/t*: ~ *les magasins* go around the stores; ~ *les femmes* run after *ou* chase women; ~ *un risque* / ~ *un danger* run a risk / a danger
couronne [kurɔn] *f* crown; *de fleurs* wreath; **couronné, ~e** crowned (*de*

with); **couronnement** *m* coronation; **couronner** ⟨1a⟩ crown; *fig: auteur, livre* award a prize to; **vos efforts seront couronnés de succès** your efforts will be crowned with success

courrier [kurje] *m* mail, *Br aussi* post; (*messager*) courier; **par retour de ~** by return of mail, *Br* by return of post; **le ~ des lecteurs** readers' letters; **~ électronique** electronic mail, e-mail

courroie [kurwa] *f* belt

cours [kur] *m d'un astre, d'une rivière* course (*aussi temporel*); ÉCON price; *de devises* rate; ÉDU course; (*leçon*) lesson; *à l'université* class, *Br aussi* lecture; **au ~ de** in the course of; **donner libre ~ à qch** give free rein to sth; **donner des ~** ÉDU lecture; **en ~ de route** on the way; **~ du change** exchange rate; **~ d'eau** waterway; **~ du soir** ÉDU evening class

course [kurs] *f à pied* running; SP race; *en taxi* ride; (*commission*) errand; **~s** (*achats*) shopping *sg*; **faire des ~s** go shopping; **la ~ aux armements** the arms race; **coursier** *m* messenger; *à moto* biker, courrier

court[1] [kur] *m* (*aussi ~ de tennis*) (tennis) court

court[2], **~e** [kur, -t] short; **à ~ de** short of

courtage [kurtaʒ] *m* brokerage

court-circuit [kursirkɥi] *m* (*pl* courts-circuits) ÉL short circuit

courtier [kurtje] *m* broker

courtisane [kurtizan] *f* courtesan; **courtiser** *femme* court, woo

courtois, **~e** [kurtwa, -z] courteous; **courtoisie** *f* courtesy

couru, **~e** [kury] *p/p* 1 → **courir** 2 *adj* popular

couscous [kuskus] *m* CUIS couscous

cousin, **~e** [kuzɛ̃, -in] *m/f* cousin

coussin [kusɛ̃] *m* cushion

coussinet [kusinɛ] *m* small cushion; TECH bearing

coût [ku] *m* cost; **~s de production** production costs; **coûtant** [kutɑ̃]: **au prix ~** at cost (price)

couteau [kuto] *m* (*pl* -x) knife; **~ de poche** pocket knife

coûter ⟨1a⟩ 1 *v/t* cost; **combien ça coûte?** how much is it?, what does it *ou* how much does it cost?; **cette décision lui a coûté beaucoup** it was a very difficult decision for him; **coûte que coûte** at all costs; **~ les yeux de la tête** cost a fortune, cost an arm and a leg 2 *v/i* cost; **~ cher** be expensive; **~ cher à qn** *fig* cost s.o. dear

coûteux, **-euse** expensive, costly

coutume [kutym] *f* custom; **avoir ~ de faire qch** be in the habit of doing sth

couture [kutyr] *f activité* sewing; *d'un vêtement, bas etc* seam; **haute ~** fashion, haute couture; **battre à plates ~s** take apart; **couturier** *m* dress designer, couturier; **couturière** *f* dressmaker

couvée [kuve] *f* clutch; *fig* brood

couvent [kuvɑ̃] *m* convent

couver [kuve] ⟨1a⟩ 1 *v/t* hatch; *fig: projet* hatch; *personne* pamper; **~ une grippe** be coming down with flu 2 *v/i d'un feu* smolder, *Br* smoulder; *d'une révolution* be brewing

couvercle [kuvɛrkl] *m* cover

couvert, **~e** [kuver, -t] 1 *p/p* → **couvrir** 2 *adj ciel* overcast; **~ de** covered with *ou* in; **être bien ~** be warmly dressed 3 *m à table* place setting; **~s** flatware *sg*, *Br* cutlery *sg*; **mettre le ~** set the table; **sous le ~ de faire qch** *fig* on the pretext of doing sth; **se mettre à ~ de l'orage** take shelter from the storm

couverture [kuvɛrtyr] *f* cover; *sur un lit* blanket; **~ chauffante** electric blanket; **~ médiatique** media coverage

couveuse [kuvøz] *f* broody hen; MÉD incubator

couvre-feu [kuvrəfø] *m* (*pl* couvre-feux) curfew; **couvre-lit** *m* (*pl* couvre-lits) bedspread

couvreur [kuvrœr] *m* roofer

couvrir [kuvrir] ⟨2f⟩ cover (**de** with *ou*

in); **~ qn** fig (protéger) cover (up) for s.o.; **se ~** (s'habiller) cover o.s. up; du ciel cloud over

CPAM [sepeaɛm] f abr (= **Caisse primaire d'assurance maladie**) local health authority

cow-boy [kɔbɔj] m cowboy

crabe [krab] m crab

crachat [kraʃa] m spit; MÉD sputum; **un ~** a gob of spit

cracher [kraʃe] ⟨1a⟩ **1** v/i spit **2** v/t spit; injures spit, hurl; F argent cough up F

crachin [kraʃɛ̃] m drizzle

crack [krak] m F genius; drogue crack

craie [krɛ] f chalk

craindre [krɛ̃dr] ⟨4b⟩ (avoir peur de) fear, be frightened of; **cette matière craint la chaleur** this material must be kept away from heat; **craint la chaleur** COMM keep cool; **~ de faire qch** be afraid of doing sth; **~ que (ne)** (+ subj) be afraid that

crainte [krɛ̃t] f fear; **de ~ de** for fear of

craintif, -ive [krɛ̃tif, -iv] timid

cramoisi, ~e [kramwazi] crimson

crampe [krɑ̃p] f MÉD cramp; **avoir des ~s d'estomac** have cramps, Br have stomach cramps

crampon [krɑ̃põ] m d'alpinisme crampon; **cramponner** ⟨1a⟩: **se ~** hold on (à to)

cran [krɑ̃] m notch; **il a du ~** F he's got guts F

crâne [krɑn] m skull; **crâner** F (pavaner) show off; **crâneur, -euse** big-headed

crapaud [krapo] m ZO toad

crapule [krapyl] f villain

craquelé, ~e [krakle] cracked; **craquelure** f crack; **craquement** m crackle; **craquer** ⟨1m⟩ crack; d'un parquet creak; de feuilles crackle; d'une couture give way, split; fig: d'une personne (s'effondrer) crack up; **plein à ~** full to bursting

crasse [kras] **1** adj ignorance crass **2** f dirt; **crasseux, -euse** filthy

cratère [kratɛr] m crater

cravache [kravaʃ] f whip

cravate [kravat] f necktie, Br tie

crawl [krol] m crawl

crayon [krɛjõ] m pencil; **~ à bille** ball-point pen; **~ de couleur** crayon; **~ feutre** felt-tipped pen, felt-tip

créance [kreɑ̃s] f COMM debt; **créancier, -ère** m/f creditor

créateur, -trice [kreatœr, -tris] **1** adj creative **2** m/f creator; de produit designer; **créatif, -ive** creative; **création** f creation; de mode, design design; **créativité** f creativity

créature [kreatyr] f creature

crèche [krɛʃ] f day nursery; de Noël crèche, Br crib

crédibilité [kredibilite] f credibility; **crédible** credible

crédit [kredi] m credit; (prêt) loan; (influence) influence; **acheter à ~** buy on credit; **faire ~ à qn** give s.o. credit; **il faut bien dire à son ~ que** fig it has to be said to his credit that; **crédit-bail** m leasing; **créditer** ⟨1a⟩ credit (de with); **créditeur, -trice 1** m/f creditor **2** adj solde credit atr; **être ~** be in credit

crédule [kredyl] credulous; **crédulité** f credulity

créer [kree] ⟨1a⟩ create; institution set up; COMM produit nouveau design

crémaillère [kremajɛr] f: **pendre la ~** fig have a housewarming party

crémation [kremasjõ] f cremation; **crématorium** [krematɔrjəm] m crematorium

crème [krɛm] **1** f cream; **~ anglaise** custard; **~ dépilatoire** hair remover; **~ fouettée** ou **Chantilly** whipped cream; **~ glacée** CUIS ice cream; **~ de nuit** night cream; **~ pâtissière** pastry cream; **~ solaire** suntan cream **2** m coffee with milk, Br white coffee **3** adj inv cream; **crémerie** f dairy; **crémeux, -euse** creamy

créneau [kreno] m (pl -x) AUTO space; COMM niche; **faire un ~** reverse into a tight space

crêpe [krɛp] **1** m tissu crêpe; **semelle f de ~** crêpe sole **2** f CUIS pancake, crêpe

crêper [krepe] ⟨1b⟩ cheveux backcomb

crépi [krepi] *m* roughcast; **crépir** ⟨2a⟩ roughcast

crépiter [krepite] ⟨1a⟩ crackle

crépu, ~e [krepy] frizzy

crépuscule [krepyskyl] *m* twilight

cresson [krɛsɔ̃ *ou* krəsɔ̃] *m* BOT cress

Crète [krɛt]: **la ~** Crete

crête [krɛt] *f* crest; *d'un coq* comb

crétin, ~e [kretɛ̃, -in] **1** *adj* idiotic, cretinous **2** *m/f* idiot, cretin

crétois, ~e [kretwa, -z] **1** *adj* Cretan **2** *m/f* **Crétois, ~e** Cretan

creuser [krøze] ⟨1a⟩ (*rendre creux*) hollow out; *trou* dig; *fig* look into; **ça creuse** it gives you an appetite; **se ~ la tête** rack one's brains

creuset [krøze] *m* TECH crucible; *fig* melting pot

creux, -euse [krø, -z] **1** *adj* hollow; **assiette f creuse** soup plate; **heures fpl creuses** off-peak hours **2** *adv*: **sonner ~** ring hollow **3** *m* hollow; **le ~ de la main** the hollow of one's hand

crevaison [krəvɛzɔ̃] *f* flat, *Br* puncture

crevant, ~e [krəvɑ̃, -t] F (*épuisant*) exhausting; (*drôle*) hilarious

crevasse [krəvas] *f* de la peau, du sol crack; GÉOL crevasse; **crevasser** ⟨1a⟩ *peau, sol* crack; **des mains crevassées** chapped hands; **se ~** crack

crever [krəve] ⟨1d⟩ **1** *v/t ballon* burst; *pneu* puncture **2** *v/i* burst; F (*mourir*) kick the bucket; F AUTO have a flat, *Br* have a puncture; **je crève de faim** F I'm starving; **~ d'envie de faire qch** be dying to do sth

crevette [krəvɛt] *f* shrimp

cri [kri] *m* shout, cry; **c'est le dernier ~** *fig* it's all the rage

criant, ~e [krijɑ̃, -t] *injustice* flagrant; *mensonge* blatant; **criard, ~e** *voix* shrill; *couleur* gaudy, garish

crible [kribl] *m* sieve; **cribler** ⟨1a⟩ sieve; **criblé de** *fig* riddled with

cric [krik] *m* jack

criée [krije] *f*: **vente f à la ~** sale by auction; **crier** ⟨1a⟩ **1** *v/i* shout; *d'une porte* squeak; **~ au scandale** protest **2** *v/t* shout, call; **~ ven-**

geance call for revenge; **~ qch sur les toits** shout sth from the rooftops

crime [krim] *m* crime; (*assassinat*) murder; **~ organisé** organized crime; **criminalité** *f* crime; **~ informatique** computer crime; **criminel, ~le 1** *adj* criminal **2** *m/f* criminal; (*assassin*) murderer

crin [krɛ̃] *m* horsehair

crinière [krinjɛr] *f* mane

crique [krik] *f* creek

criquet [krike] *m* ZO cricket

crise [kriz] *f* crisis; MÉD attack; **~ cardiaque** heart attack; **avoir une ~ de nerfs** have hysterics

crisper [krispe] ⟨1a⟩ *muscles* tense; *visage* contort; F *fig* irritate; **se ~** go tense, tense up

crisser [krise] ⟨1a⟩ squeak

cristal [kristal] *m* (*pl* -aux) crystal; **~ de roche** rock crystal; **cristallin, ~e** *eau* crystal clear; *son, voix* clear; **cristalliser** ⟨1a⟩: **se ~** crystallize

critère [kriter] *m* criterion; **~s** criteria

critique [kritik] **1** *adj* critical **2** *m* critic **3** *f* criticism; *d'un film, livre, pièce* review; **critiquer** ⟨1m⟩ criticize; (*analyser*) look at critically

croasser [krɔase] ⟨1a⟩ crow

croc [kro] *m* (*dent*) fang; *de boucherie* hook

croche-pied [krɔʃpje] *m* (*pl* croche-pieds): **faire un ~ à qn** trip s.o. up

crochet [krɔʃe] *m* hook; *pour l'ouvrage* crochet hook; *ouvrage* crochet; *d'une route* sharp turn; **~s en typographie** square brackets; **faire du ~** (do) crochet; **faire un ~ d'une route** bend sharply; *d'une personne* make a detour; **crochu, ~e** *nez* hooked

crocodile [krɔkɔdil] *m* crocodile

crocus [krɔkys] *m* crocus

croire [krwar] ⟨4v⟩ **1** *v/t* believe; (*penser*) think; **~ qch de qn** believe sth about s.o.; **je vous crois sur parole** I'll take your word for it; **on le croyait médecin** people thought he was a doctor; **à l'en ~** if you believed him / her; **à en ~ les journaux** judging by the newspapers **2** *v/i*: **~ à qch** believe in sth; **~ en**

qn believe in s.o.; **~ en Dieu** believe in God **3**: *il se croit intelligent* he thinks he's intelligent

croisade [krwazad] *f* crusade *(aussi fig)*

croisé, ~e [krwaze] **1** *adj veston* double-breasted **2** *m* crusader; **croisement** *m action* crossing *(aussi* BIOL*)*; *animal* cross; **croiser** ⟨1a⟩ **1** *v/t* cross *(aussi* BIOL*)*; **~ qn dans la rue** pass s.o. in the street **2** *v/i* MAR cruise; **se ~ de routes** cross; *de personnes* meet; *leurs regards se croisèrent* their eyes met; **croiseur** *m* MAR cruiser; **croisière** *f* MAR cruise

croissance [krwasãs] *f* growth; **~ zéro** zero growth; **croissant** *m de lune* crescent; CUIS croissant

croître [krwatr] ⟨4w⟩ grow

croix [krwa] *f* cross; *la Croix-Rouge* the Red Cross; *mettre une ~ sur qch fig* give sth up; *chemin m de ~* way of the cross

croquant, ~e [krɔkã, -t] crisp, crunchy

croque-monsieur [krɔkməsjø] *m (pl inv)* CUIS sandwich of ham and melted cheese

croque-mort [krɔkmɔr] *m* F *(pl* croque-morts) mortician, *Br* undertaker

croquer [krɔke] ⟨1m⟩ **1** *v/t* crunch; *(dessiner)* sketch **2** *v/i* be crunchy

croquis [krɔki] *m* sketch

crosse [krɔs] *f d'un évêque* crosier; *d'un fusil* butt

crotte [krɔt] *f* droppings *pl*; **crottin** *m* road apples *pl*, *Br* dung

croulant, ~e [krulã, -t] **1** *adj* crumbling, falling to bits **2** *m/f* F oldie F; **crouler** ⟨1a⟩ *(s'écrouler)* collapse *(aussi fig)*

croupe [krup] *f* rump

croupir [krupir] ⟨2a⟩ *d'eau* stagnate *(aussi fig)*

croustillant, ~e [krustijã, -t] crusty

croûte [krut] *f de pain* crust; *de fromage* rind; MÉD scab; **croûter** ⟨1a⟩ F eat; **croûton** *m* crouton

croyable [krwajabl] believable; **croy-**

ance *f* belief; **croyant, ~e** *m/f* REL believer

CRS [seɛrɛs] *abr (= compagnie républicaine de sécurité): les ~ mpl* the riot police; *un ~* a riot policeman

cru, ~e [kry] **1** *p/p → croire* **2** *adj légumes* raw; *lumière, verité* harsh; *paroles* blunt **3** *m (domaine)* vineyard; *de vin* wine; *de mon ~ fig* of my own (devising)

cruauté [kryote] *f* cruelty

cruche [kryʃ] *f* pitcher

crucial, ~e [krysjal] *(mpl -aux)* crucial

crucifiement [krysifimã] *m* crucifixion; **crucifier** ⟨1a⟩ crucify; **crucifix** *m* crucifix; **crucifixion** *f* crucifixion

crudité [krydite] *f* crudeness; *de paroles* bluntness; *de lumière* harshness; *de couleur* gaudiness, garishness; **~s** CUIS raw vegetables

crue [kry] *f* flood; *être en ~* be in spate

cruel, ~le [kryɛl] cruel

crûment [krymã] *adv parler* bluntly; *éclairer* harshly

crustacés [krystase] *mpl* shellfish *pl*

crypte [kript] *f* crypt

Cuba [kyba] *f* Cuba

cubage [kybaʒ] *m (volume)* cubic capacity

cubain, ~e **1** *adj* Cuban; **2** *m/f* **Cubain, ~e** Cuban

cube [kyb] MATH **1** *m* cube **2** *adj* cubic; **cubique** cubic; **cubisme** *m* cubism; **cubiste** *m* cubiste

cueillette [kœjɛt] *f* picking; **cueillir** ⟨2c⟩ pick

cuiller, cuillère [kɥijɛr] *f* spoon; **~ à soupe** soupspoon; **~ à café** coffee spoon; **cuillerée** *f* spoonful

cuir [kɥir] *m* leather; **~ chevelu** scalp

cuirasse [kɥiras] *f* armor, *Br* armour; **cuirasser** ⟨1a⟩ *navire* armorplate, *Br* armourplate

cuire [kɥir] ⟨4c⟩ cook; *au four* bake; *rôti* roast; *faire ~ qch* cook sth

cuisine [kɥizin] *f* cooking; *pièce* kitchen; *faire la ~* do the cooking; *la ~ italienne* Italian cooking *ou* cuisine *ou* food

cuisiné [kɥizine]: *plat m ~* ready-to-eat meal; **cuisiner** ⟨1a⟩ cook; **cuisinier** m cook; **cuisinière** f cook; (*fourneau*) stove; **~ à gaz** gas stove

cuisse [kɥis] f ANAT thigh; CUIS *de poulet* leg

cuisson [kɥisɔ̃] f cooking; *du pain* baking; *d'un rôti* roasting

cuit, ~e [kɥi, -t] **1** p/p → **cuire 2** adj *légumes* cooked, done; *rôti, pain* done; **pas assez ~** underdone; **trop ~** overdone

cuivre [kɥivr] m copper; **~ jaune** brass; **~s** brasses

cul [ky] m P ass P, Br arse P

culasse [kylas] *d'un moteur* cylinder head

culbute [kylbyt] f somersault; (*chute*) fall; **faire la ~** do a somersault; (*tomber*) fall

culbuteur [kylbytœr] m tumbler

cul-de-sac [kydsak] m (*pl* culs-de-sac) blind alley; *fig* dead end

culinaire [kyliner] culinary

culminant [kylminɑ̃]: **point** m **~ d'une** *montagne* highest peak; *fig* peak; **culminer** ⟨1a⟩ *fig* peak, reach its peak; **~ à 5 000 mètres** be 5,000 metres high at its highest point

culot [kylo] m F nerve, Br cheek

culotte [kylɔt] f short pants pl, Br short trousers pl; *de femme* panties pl, Br aussi knickers pl; **culotté, ~e** F: **être ~** be nervy, Br have the cheek of the devil

culpabilité [kylpabilite] f guilt

culte [kylt] m (*vénération*) worship; (*religion*) religion; (*service*) church service; *fig* cult

cultivable [kyltivabl] AGR suitable for cultivation; **cultivateur, -trice** m/f farmer; **cultivé, ~e** cultivated (*aussi fig*); **cultiver** ⟨1a⟩ AGR *terre* cultivate (*aussi fig*); *légumes, tabac* grow; **se ~** improve one's mind

culture [kyltyr] f culture; AGR *action* cultivation; *de légumes, fruits etc* growing; **~ générale** general knowledge; **~ physique** physical training; **~ de la vigne** wine-growing; **culturel, ~le** cultural; **choc** m **~** culture shock

culturisme [kyltyrism] m body build-

ing

cumin [kymɛ̃] m BOT cumin

cumulatif, -ive [kymylatif, -iv] cumulative; **cumuler** ⟨1a⟩: **~ des fonctions** hold more than one position; **~ deux salaires** have two salaries (coming in)

cupide [kypid] adj greedy; **cupidité** f greed, cupidity

curable [kyrabl] curable

curateur [-atœr] m JUR *de mineur* guardian

cure [kyr] f MÉD course of treatment; **~ de repos** rest cure; **~ thermale** stay at a spa (in order to take the waters); **je n'en ai ~** I don't care

curé [kyre] m curate

cure-dent [kyrdɑ̃] m (*pl* cure-dents) tooth pick

curer [kyre] ⟨1a⟩ *cuve* scour; *dents* pick; **se ~ le nez** pick one's nose

curieux, -euse [kyrjø, -z] curious

curiosité [kyrjozite] f curiosity; *objet bizarre, rare* curio; **une région pleine de ~s** an area full of things to see

curiste [kyrist] m/f person taking a 'cure' at a spa

curriculum vitae [kyrikylɔmvite] m (*pl inv*) resumé, Br CV

curry [kyri] m curry

curseur [kyrsœr] m INFORM cursor

cutané, ~e [kytane] skin atr

cuticule [kytikyl] f cuticle

cuve [kyv] f tank; *de vin* vat; **cuvée** f *de vin* vatful; *vin* wine, vintage; **cuver** ⟨1a⟩ **1** v/i mature **2** v/t: **~ son vin** fig sleep it off

cuvette [kyvɛt] f (*bac*) basin; *de cabinet* bowl

C.V. [seve] m abr (= **curriculum vitae**) résumé, Br CV (= curriculum vitae)

cybercafé [siberkafe] m Internet café

cyberespace [siberespas] m cyberspace

cybernétique [sibɛrnetik] f cybernetics

cyclable [siklabl]: **piste** f **~** cycle path

cyclamen [siklamɛn] m BOT cyclamen

cycle [sikl] m nature, ÉCON, littérature, véhicule cycle

cyclisme [siklism] m cycling; **cycliste**

m/f cyclist

cyclomoteur [siklɔmɔtœr] *m* moped; **cyclomotoriste** *m/f* moped rider

cyclone [siklon] *m* cyclone

cygne [siɲ] *m* swan

cylindre [silɛ̃dr] *m* MATH, TECH cylinder; **cylindrée** *f* AUTO cubic capacity; **cylindrer** ⟨1a⟩ roll; **cylindrique** cylindrical

cymbale [sɛ̃bal] *f* MUS cymbal

cynique [sinik] **1** *adj* cynical **2** *m/f* cynic; **cynisme** *m* cynicism

cyprès [sipre] *m* cypress

cystite [sistit] *f* MÉD cystitis

D

dactylo [daktilo] *f* typing; *personne* typist; **dactylographie** *f* typing

dada [dada] *m* F hobby horse

dahlia [dalja] *m* BOT dahlia

daigner [dɛɲe] ⟨1b⟩: ~ **faire qch** deign *ou* condescend to do sth

daim [dɛ̃] *m* ZO deer; *peau* suede

dallage [dalaʒ] *m* flagstones *pl*; *action* paving; **dalle** *f* flagstone; **daller** ⟨1a⟩ pave

daltonien, ~ne [daltɔnjɛ̃, -ɛn] color-blind, *Br* colourblind

dame [dam] *f* lady; *aux échecs, cartes* queen; *jeu* **de** ~**s** checkers *sg*, *Br* draughts *sg*; **damier** *m* checkerboard, *Br* draughts board

damnation [danasjõ] *f* damnation; **damner** ⟨1a⟩ damn

dancing [dãsiŋ] *m* dance hall

dandiner [dãdine] ⟨1a⟩: *se* ~ shift from one foot to the other

Danemark [danmark]: *le* ~ Denmark

danger [dãʒe] *m* danger; ~ **de mort!** danger of death!; *mettre en* ~ endanger, put in danger; *courir un* ~ be in danger

dangereux, -euse [dãʒrø, -z] dangerous

danois, ~e [danwa, -z] **1** *adj* Danish **2** *m langue* Danish **3** *m/f* **Danois, ~e** Dane

dans [dã] ◊ *lieu* in; *direction* in(to); ~ *la rue* in the street; ~ *le train* on the train; ~ *Molière* in Molière; *être* ~ *le commerce* be in business; *boire* ~ *un verre* drink from a glass; *il l'a pris* ~ *sa poche* he took it out of his pocket ◊ *temps* in; ~ *les 24 heures* within *ou* in 24 hours; ~ *trois jours* in three days, in three days' time; ◊ *mode:* ~ *ces circonstances* in the circumstances; *avoir* ~ *les 50 ans* be about 50

dansant, ~e [dãsã, -t]: *soirée f* ~*e* party (with dancing); **danse** *f* dance; *action* dancing; ~ *classique* ballet, classical dancing; ~ *folklorique* folk dance; **danser** ⟨1a⟩ dance; **danseur, -euse** *m/f* dancer

dard [dar] *m d'une abeille* sting

dare-dare [dardar] *adv* F at the double

date [dat] *f* date; *quelle* ~ *sommes-nous?* what date is it?, what's today's date?; *de longue* ~ *amitié* long-standing; ~ *d'expiration* expiration date, *Br* expiry date; ~ *limite* deadline; ~ *limite de conservation* use-by date; ~ *de livraison* delivery date; **dater** ⟨1a⟩ **1** *v/t* date **2** *v/i:* ~ *de* date from; *à* ~ *de ce jour* from today; *cela ne date pas d'hier* that's nothing new

datte [dat] *f* date; **dattier** *m* date palm

daube [dob] *f* CUIS: *bœuf m en* ~ braised beef

dauphin [dofɛ̃] *m* ZO dolphin; *le Dauphin* HIST the Dauphin

davantage [davãtaʒ] *adv* more; *en veux-tu* ~*?* do you want (some) more?

de [də] **1** *prép* ◇ *origine* from; *il vient* **~ *Paris*** he comes from Paris; *du centre à la banlieue* from the center to the suburbs

◇ *possession* of; *la maison ~ mon père* my father's house; *la maison ~ mes parents* my parents' house; *la maison des voisins* the neighbors' house

◇ *fait par* by; *un film ~ Godard* a movie by Godard, a Godard movie

◇ *matière* (made) of; *fenêtre ~ verre coloré* colored glass window, window made of colored glass

◇ *temps*: **~ *jour*** by day; *je n'ai pas dormi ~ la nuit* I lay awake all night; **~ ... *à*** from ... to

◇ *raison*: *trembler ~ peur* shake with fear

◇ *mode* **~ *force*** by force

◇: **~ *plus en plus grand*** bigger and bigger; **~ *moins en moins valable*** less and less valid

◇: *la plus grande ... du monde* the biggest ... in the world

◇ *mesure*: *une planche ~ 10 cm large* a board 10 centimeters wide

◇ *devant inf*: *cesser ~ travailler* stop working; *décider ~ faire qch* decide to do sth

2 *partitif*: *du pain* (some) bread; *des petits pains* (some) rolls; *je n'ai pas d'argent* I don't have any money, I have no money; *est-ce qu'il y a des disquettes?* are there any diskettes?

dé [de] *m jeu* dice; **~ (*à coudre*)** thimble

dealer [dilœr] *m* dealer

déambulateur [deɑ̃bylatœr] *m* walker; **déambuler** ⟨1a⟩ stroll

débâcle [debakl] *f de troupes* rout; *d'une entreprise* collapse

déballer [debale] ⟨1a⟩ unpack

débandade [debɑ̃dad] *f* stampede

débarbouiller [debarbuje] ⟨1a⟩: **~ *un enfant*** wash a child's face

débarcadère [debarkadɛr] *m* MAR landing stage

débardeur [debardœr] *m vêtement* tank top

débarquement [debarkəmɑ̃] *m de marchandises* unloading; *de passagers* landing; MIL disembarkation; **débarquer** ⟨1m⟩ **1** *v/t marchandises* unload; *passagers* land, disembark **2** *v/i* land, disembark; MIL disembark; **~ *chez qn*** *fig* F turn up at s.o.'s place

débarras [debara] *m* **1** F: *bon ~* good riddance **2** (*cagibi*) storage room, *Br aussi* boxroom; **débarrasser** ⟨1a⟩ *table etc* clear; **~ *qn de qch*** take sth from *ou* off s.o.; *se ~ de qn / qch* get rid of s.o. / sth

débat [deba] *m* debate, discussion; POL debate; (*polémique*) argument

débattre [debatr] ⟨4a⟩: **~ *qch*** discuss *ou* debate sth; *se ~* struggle

débauche [deboʃ] *f* debauchery; **débauché, ~e 1** *adj* debauched **2** *m/f* debauched person; **débaucher** ⟨1a⟩ (*licencier*) lay off; F lead astray

débile [debil] **1** *adj* weak; F idiotic **2** *m*: **~ *mental*** mental defective; **débilité** *f* weakness; **~ *mentale*** mental deficiency

débiner [debine] ⟨1a⟩ F badmouth, *Br* be spiteful about; *se ~* run off

débit [debi] *m* (*vente*) sale; *d'un stock* turnover; *d'un cours d'eau* rate of flow; *d'une usine, machine* output; (*élocution*) delivery; FIN debit; **~ *de boissons*** bar; **~ *de tabac*** smoke shop, *Br* tobacconist's; **débiter** ⟨1a⟩ *marchandises, boisson* sell (retail); *péj: fadaises* talk; *texte étudié* deliver, *péj* recite; *d'une pompe: liquide, gaz* deliver; *d'une usine, machine, de produits* output; *bois, viande* cut up; FIN debit; **~ *qn d'une somme*** debit s.o. with an amount; **débiteur, -trice 1** *m/f* debtor **2** *adj compte* overdrawn; *solde* debit

déblais [deblɛ] *mpl* (*décombres*) rubble *sg*

déblatérer [deblatere] ⟨1f⟩: **~ *contre qn*** run s.o. down

déblayer [deblɛje] ⟨1i⟩ *endroit* clear; *débris* clear (away), remove

déblocage [deblɔkaʒ] *m* TECH release; ÉCON *des prix, salaires* unfreezing

débloquer [deblɔke] ⟨1m⟩ **1** *vt* TECH release; ÉCON *prix, compte* unfreeze; *fonds* release **2** *vi* F be crazy; *se ~ d'une situation* be resolved, get sorted out

déboguer [debɔge] ⟨1m⟩ debug

déboires [debwar] *mpl* disappointments

déboisement [debwazmɑ̃] *m* deforestation; **déboiser** ⟨1a⟩ deforest, clear

déboîter [debwate] ⟨1a⟩ **1** *vt* MÉD dislocate **2** *v/i* AUTO pull out; *se ~ l'épaule* dislocate one's shoulder

débonnaire [debɔnɛr] kindly

débordé, ~e [debɔrde] snowed under (*de* with); *~ par les événements* overwhelmed by events; **débordement** *m* overflowing; *~s fig* excesses; **déborder** ⟨1a⟩ *d'une rivière* overflow its banks; *du lait, de l'eau* overflow; *c'est la goutte d'eau qui fait ~ le vase fig* it's the last straw; *~ de santé* be glowing with health

débouché [debuʃe] *m d'une vallée* entrance; COMM outlet; *~s d'une profession* prospects; **déboucher** ⟨1a⟩ **1** *v/t tuyau* unblock; *bouteille* uncork **2** *v/i: ~ de* emerge from; *~ sur* lead to (*aussi fig*)

débourser [deburse] ⟨1a⟩ *(dépenser)* spend

déboussolé, ~e [debusɔle] disoriented

debout [dəbu] standing; *objet* upright, on end; *être ~* stand; *(levé)* be up, be out of bed; *tenir ~ fig* stand up; *voyager ~* travel standing up; *se mettre ~* stand up, get up

déboutonner [debutɔne] ⟨1a⟩ unbutton

débraillé, ~e [debraje] untidy

débrancher [debrɑ̃ʃe] ⟨1a⟩ ÉL unplug

débrayage [debrejaʒ] *m* AUTO declutching; *fig* work stoppage; **débrayer** ⟨1i⟩ AUTO declutch; *fig* down tools

débridé, ~e [debride] unbridled

débris [debri] *mpl* debris *sg; fig* remains

débrouillard, ~e [debrujar, -d] resourceful; **débrouillardise** *f* resourcefulness

débrouiller [debruje] ⟨1a⟩ *affaire, intrigue* clear up; *se ~* cope, manage

début [deby] *m* beginning, start; *~s* THÉÂT debut *sg*, first appearance *sg;* POL debut *sg; ~ mai* at the beginning *ou* start of May

débutant, ~e [debytɑ̃, -t] *m/f* beginner; **débuter** ⟨1a⟩ begin, start

déca [deka] *m* F decaff F

décacheter [dekaʃte] ⟨1c⟩ *lettre* open

décadence [dekadɑ̃s] *f* decadence; **décadent, ~e** decadent

décaféiné, ~e [dekafeine]: *café m ~* decaffeinated coffee, decaff F

décalage [dekalaʒ] *m dans l'espace* moving, shifting; *(différence)* difference; *fig* gap; *~ horaire* time difference; **décaler** ⟨1a⟩ *rendez-vous* reschedule, change the time of; *dans l'espace* move, shift

décalquer [dekalke] ⟨1m⟩ transfer

décamper [dekɑ̃pe] ⟨1a⟩ F clear out

décapant [dekapɑ̃] *m* stripper; **décaper** ⟨1a⟩ *surface métallique* clean; *meuble vernis* strip

décapiter [dekapite] ⟨1a⟩ decapitate

décapotable [dekapɔtabl] **1** *adj* convertible **2** *f:* (*voiture f*) *~* convertible

décapsuler [dekapsyle] ⟨1a⟩ take the top off, open; **décapsuleur** *m* bottle opener

décarcasser [dekarkase] ⟨1a⟩: *se ~* F bust a gut F

décédé, ~e [desede] dead; **décéder** ⟨1f⟩ die

déceler [desle] ⟨1d⟩ *(découvrir)* detect; *(montrer)* point to

décembre [desɑ̃br] *m* December

décemment [desamɑ̃] *adv (convenablement)* decently, properly; *(raisonnablement)* reasonably

décence [desɑ̃s] *f* decency

décennie [deseni] *f* decade

décent, ~e [desɑ̃, -t] decent, proper; *salaire* decent, reasonable

décentralisation [desɑ̃tralizasjɔ̃] *f* decentralization; **décentraliser**

⟨1a⟩ decentralize

déception [desɛpsjõ] *f* disappointment

décerner [desɛrne] ⟨1a⟩ *prix* award

décès [desɛ] *m* death

décevant, ~e [desəvã, -t] disappointing; **décevoir** ⟨3a⟩ disappoint

déchaînement [deʃɛnmã] *m passions, fureur* outburst; **déchaîner** ⟨1b⟩ *fig* provoke; **se ~** *d'une tempête* break; *d'une personne* fly into an uncontrollable rage

déchanter [deʃãte] ⟨1a⟩ change one's tune

décharge [deʃarʒ] *f* JUR acquittal; *dans fusillade* discharge; **à la ~ de qn** in s.o.'s defense *ou* Br defence; **~ publique** dump; **~ électrique** electric shock; **déchargement** *m* unloading; **décharger** ⟨1l⟩ unload; *batterie* discharge; *arme (tirer)* fire, discharge; *accusé* acquit; *colère* vent (**contre** on); **~ qn de qch** relieve s.o. of sth; **~ sa conscience** get it off one's chest

décharné, ~e [deʃarne] skeletal

déchausser [deʃose] ⟨1a⟩: **~ qn** take s.o.'s shoes off; **se ~** take one's shoes off; **avoir les dents qui se déchaussent** have receding gums

déchéance [deʃeãs] *f* decline; JUR forfeiture

déchets [deʃɛ] *mpl* waste *sg*; **~ industriels** industrial waste; **~ nucléaires** atomic waste; **~ radioactifs** radioactive waste; **~ toxiques** toxic waste

déchiffrer [deʃifre] ⟨1a⟩ decipher; *message aussi* decode

déchiqueté, ~e [deʃikte] *montagne, côte* jagged; **déchiqueter** ⟨1c⟩ *corps, papier* tear to pieces

déchirant, ~e [deʃirã, -t] heart-rending, heart-breaking; **déchirement** *m* tearing; *fig (chagrin)* heartbreak; **déchirer** ⟨1a⟩ *tissu* tear; *papier* tear up; *fig: silence* pierce; **se ~** *d'une robe* tear; **se ~ un muscle** tear a muscle; **déchirure** *f* tear, rip

déchu, ~e [deʃy] *roi* dethroned; **ange** *m* **~** fallen angel

décidé, ~e [deside] *(résolu)* deter-

mined; **c'est (une) chose ~e** it's settled; **être ~ à faire qch** be determined to do sth; **décidément** *adv* really; **décider** ⟨1a⟩ **1** *v/t* decide on; *question* settle, decide; **~ que** decide that; **~ qn à faire qch** convince *ou* decide s.o. to do sth; **~ de qch** decide on sth; **~ de faire qch** decide to do sth **2** *v/i* decide; **se ~** make one's mind up, decide (**à faire qch** to do sth); **décideur** *m* decision-maker

décimal, ~e [desimal] *(mpl* -aux) decimal

décimer [desime] ⟨1a⟩ decimate

décimètre [desimɛtr] *m*: **double ~** ruler

décisif, -ive [desizif, -iv] decisive; **décision** *f* decision; *(fermeté)* determination

déclamer [deklame] ⟨1a⟩ declaim

déclaration [deklarasjõ] *f* declaration, statement; *(fait d'annoncer)* declaration; *d'une naissance* registration; *de vol, perte* report; **~ d'impôts** tax return; **déclarer** ⟨1a⟩ declare; *naissance* register; **se ~** declare o.s.; *(faire une déclaration d'amour)* declare one's love; *d'un feu, d'une épidémie* break out; **~ une personne innocente / coupable** find a person innocent / guilty

déclenchement [deklãʃmã] *m* triggering; **déclencher** ⟨1a⟩ *(commander)* trigger, set off; *(provoquer)* trigger; **se ~** be triggered; **déclencheur** *m* PHOT shutter release

déclic [deklik] *m bruit* click

déclin [deklɛ̃] *m* decline

déclinaison [deklinɛzõ] *f* GRAM declension; **décliner** ⟨1a⟩ **1** *v/i du soleil* go down; *du jour, des forces, du prestige* wane; *de la santé* decline **2** *v/t offre* decline *(aussi* GRAM); **~ ses nom, prénoms, titres et qualités** state one's full name and qualifications; **la société décline toute responsabilité pour** the company will not accept any liability for

décocher [dekɔʃe] ⟨1a⟩ *flèche, regard* shoot

décoder [dekɔde] ⟨1a⟩ decode; **dé-**

codeur *m* decoder

décoiffer [dekwafe] ⟨1a⟩ *cheveux* ruffle

décollage [dekɔlaʒ] *m* AVIAT takeoff; **décoller** ⟨1a⟩ **1** *v/t* peel off **2** *v/i* AVIAT take off; **se ~** peel off

décolleté, ~e [dekɔlte] **1** *adj robe* low-cut **2** *m en V, carré etc* neckline

décolonisation [dekɔlɔnizasjõ] *f* decolonization; **décoloniser** ⟨1a⟩ decolonize

décolorer [dekɔlɔre] ⟨1a⟩ *tissu, cheveux* bleach; **se ~** fade

décombres [dekõbr] *mpl* rubble *sg*

décommander [dekɔmãde] ⟨1a⟩ cancel; **se ~** cancel

décomposer [dekõpoze] ⟨1a⟩ *mot, produit* break down (**en** into); CHIM decompose; **se ~** *d'un cadavre* decompose; *d'un visage* become contorted; **décomposition** *f* breakdown; *d'un cadavre* decomposition

décompresser [dekõprese] ⟨1b⟩ F unwind, relax, chill out F

décompte [dekõt] *m* deduction; *d'une facture* breakdown; **décompter** ⟨1a⟩ deduct

déconcentrer [dekõsãtre] ⟨1a⟩: **~ qn** make it hard for s.o. to concentrate

déconcertant, ~e [dekõsertã, -t] disconcerting; **déconcerter** ⟨1a⟩ disconcert

déconfit, ~e [dekõfi, -t] *air, mine* disheartened; **déconfiture** *f* collapse

décongeler [dekõʒle] ⟨1d⟩ *aliment* thaw out

décongestionner [dekõʒɛstjɔne] ⟨1a⟩ *route* relieve congestion on, decongest; *nez* clear

déconnecter [dekɔnɛkte] ⟨1a⟩ unplug, disconnect

déconner [dekɔne] ⟨1a⟩ P *(faire des conneries)* fool around, *Br aussi* bugger around P; *(dire des conneries)* talk nonsense *ou* crap P

déconseiller [dekõseje] ⟨1b⟩ advise against; **je te déconseille ce plat** I wouldn't advise you to have this dish; **c'est tout à fait déconseillé dans votre cas** it's definitely inadvisable in your case

décontenancer [dekõtnãse] ⟨1k⟩ disconcert

décontracté, ~e [dekõtrakte] relaxed; F relaxed, laid-back F; **décontracter** relax; **se ~** relax

déconvenue [dekõvny] *f* disappointment

décor [dekɔr] *m d'une maison* decor; *fig (cadre)* setting, surroundings *pl*; **~s de théâtre** sets, scenery *sg*; **décorateur, -trice** *m/f* decorator; THÉÂT set designer; **décoratif, -ive** decorative; **décoration** *f* decoration; **décorer** ⟨1a⟩ decorate (**de** with)

décortiquer [dekɔrtike] ⟨1m⟩ shell; *texte* analyze, *Br* analyse

découcher [dekuʃe] ⟨1a⟩ not sleep in one's own bed

découdre [dekudr] ⟨4d⟩ *ourlet* unstitch; **se ~** *d'un pantalon* come apart at the seams

découler [dekule] ⟨1a⟩: **~ de** arise from

découper [dekupe] ⟨1a⟩ *(diviser en morceaux)* cut up; *photo* cut out (**dans** from); **se ~ sur** *fig* stand out against

décourageant, ~e [dekuraʒã, -t] discouraging; **découragement** *m* discouragement; **décourager** ⟨1l⟩ discourage; **~ qn de faire qch** discourage s.o. from doing sth; **se ~** lose heart, become discouraged

décousu, ~e [dekuzy] coming apart at the seams; *fig: propos* incoherent, disjointed

découvert, ~e [dekuver, -t] **1** *adj tête, épaules* bare, uncovered; **à ~** FIN overdrawn **2** *m* overdraft **3** *f* discovery; **découvreur, -euse** *m/f* discoverer; **découvrir** ⟨2f⟩ uncover; *(trouver)* discover; *ses intentions* reveal; **je découvre que** *(je comprends que)* I find that; **~ les épaules** *d'un vêtement* leave the shoulders bare; **se ~** *d'une personne* take off a couple of layers (of clothes); *(enlever son chapeau)* take off one's hat; *du ciel* clear

décrépit, ~e [dekrepi, -t] decrepit

décret [dekrɛ] *m* decree; **décréter** ⟨1f⟩ decree

décrire [dekrir] ⟨4f⟩ describe; ~ *une orbite autour de* orbit; ~ *X comme* (*étant*) *Y* describe X as Y

décrocher [dekrɔʃe] ⟨1a⟩ *tableau* take down; *fig* F *prix, bonne situation* land F; ~ *le téléphone pour ne pas être dérangé* take the phone off the hook; *pour répondre, composer un numéro* pick up the receiver

décroissant, ~e [dekrwasɑ̃, -t] decreasing

décroître [dekrwɑtr] ⟨4w⟩ decrease, decline

décrypter [dekripte] ⟨1a⟩ decode

déçu, ~e [desy] **1** *p/p* → **décevoir 2** *adj* disappointed

décupler [dekyple] ⟨1a⟩ increase tenfold

dédaigner [dedɛɲe] ⟨1b⟩ **1** *v/t* scorn; *personne* treat with scorn; *un avantage qui n'est pas à ~* an advantage that's not to be sniffed at **2** *v/i*: ~ *de faire qch* disdain to do sth; **dédaigneux, -euse** disdainful; **dédain** *m* disdain

dédale [dedal] *m* labyrinth, maze

dedans [dədɑ̃] **1** *adv* inside; *là-~* in it; *en ~* on the inside; *de ~* from the inside, from within **2** *m* inside; *au ~* (*de*) inside

dédicace [dedikas] *f* dedication; **dédicacer** ⟨1k⟩ dedicate

dédier [dedje] ⟨1a⟩ dedicate

dédire [dedir] ⟨4m⟩: *se ~* cry off

dédommagement [dedɔmaʒmɑ̃] *m* compensation; **dédommager** ⟨1l⟩ compensate (*de* for)

dédouanement [dedwanmɑ̃] *m* customs clearance; **dédouaner** ⟨1a⟩: ~ *qch* clear sth through customs; ~ *qn fig* clear s.o.

dédoublement [dedubləmɑ̃] *m*: ~ *de personnalité* split personality; **dédoubler** ⟨1a⟩ split in two; *se ~* split

dédramatiser [dedramatize] ⟨1a⟩ *situation* play down, downplay

déductible [dedyktibl] COMM deductible; ~ *des impôts* tax-deductible; **déduction** *f* COMM, (*conclusion*) deduction; *avant* / *après* ~*s* before / after tax; **déduire** ⟨4c⟩ COMM deduct; (*conclure*) deduce (*de* from)

déesse [dees] *f* goddess

défaillance [defajɑ̃s] *f* weakness; *fig* failing, shortcoming; *technique* failure; **défaillant, ~e** *santé* failing; *forces* waning; **défaillir** ⟨2n⟩ (*faiblir*) weaken; (*se trouver mal*) feel faint

défaire [defɛr] ⟨4n⟩ undo; (*démonter*) take down, dismantle; *valise* unpack; *se ~* come undone; *se ~ de qn* / *de qch* get rid of s.o. / sth; **défait, ~e** *visage* drawn; *chemise, valise* undone; *armée, personne* defeated; **défaite** *f* defeat; **défaitisme** *m* defeatism; **défaitiste** *m/f* defeatist

défaut [defo] *m* (*imperfection*) defect, flaw; (*faiblesse morale*) shortcoming, failing; TECH defect; (*manque*) lack; JUR default; *à ~ de glace je prendrai ...* if there isn't any ice cream, I'll have ...; *faire ~* be lacking, be in short supply; *par ~* INFORM default *atr*; ~ *de caractère* character flaw; ~ *de conception* design fault; ~ *d'élocution* speech impediment

défaveur [defavœr] *f* disfavor, *Br* disfavour

défavorable [defavɔrabl] unfavorable, *Br* unfavourable; *être défavorisé* disadvantaged; *les milieux ~s* the underprivileged classes; **défavoriser** ⟨1a⟩ put at a disadvantage

défection [defɛksjɔ̃] *f* desertion; POL defection; *d'un invité* cancellation; **défectueux, -euse** defective; **défectuosité** *f* defectiveness; (*défaut*) defect

défendable [defɑ̃dabl] defensible

défendre [defɑ̃dr] ⟨4a⟩ (*protéger*) defend (*aussi* JUR, *fig*); ~ *à qn de faire qch* forbid s.o. to do sth; *le médecin lui a défendu l'alcool* the doctor has forbidden him to drink, the doctor has ordered him to stop drinking

défense [defɑ̃s] *f* defense, *Br* defence *f* (*aussi* JUR *fig*); *d'un éléphant* tusk; ~ *d'entrer* / *de fumer* / *de stationner* no entry / smoking / parking; **défenseur** *m* (*protecteur*) defender; *d'une cause* supporter; JUR defense attorney, *Br* counsel for the defence;

défensif, -ive 1 adj defensive **2** f defensive; **être sur la ~** be on the defensive

déférence [deferɑ̃s] f deference; **déférent, ~e** deferential; **déférer** ⟨1f⟩ v/t: **~ qn à la justice** prosecute s.o.

déferler [deferle] ⟨1a⟩ de vagues break; **~ sur tout le pays** fig sweep the entire country

défi [defi] m challenge; (bravade) defiance

défiance [defjɑ̃s] f distrust, mistrust; **défiant, ~e** distrustful

déficience [defisjɑ̃s] f deficiency; **~ immunitaire** immune deficiency

déficit [defisit] m deficit; **déficitaire** balance des paiements showing a deficit; compte in debit

défier [defje] ⟨1a⟩ (provoquer) challenge; (braver) defy; **des prix qui défient toute concurrence** unbeatable prices; **~ qn de faire qch** dare s.o. to do sth

défigurer [defigyre] ⟨1a⟩ disfigure; fig: réalité, faits misrepresent; **~ la campagne** be a blot on the landscape

défilé [defile] m parade; GÉOGR pass; **~ de mode** fashion show; **défiler** ⟨1a⟩ parade, march

défini, ~e [defini] definite (aussi GRAM); **article** m **~** definite article; **bien ~** well defined; **définir** ⟨2a⟩ define; **définitif, -ive** definitive; **en définitive** in the end; **définition** definition; **définitivement** adv definitely; (pour de bon) for good

défiscaliser [defiskalize] ⟨1a⟩ lift the tax on

déflagration [deflagrasjɔ̃] f explosion

déflation [deflasjɔ̃] f deflation

défoncer [defɔ̃se] ⟨1k⟩ voiture smash up, total; porte break down; terrain break up; **défoncé, ~e** route potholed

déformation [deformasjɔ̃] f deformation; fig: d'un fait distortion, misrepresentation; de pensées, idées misrepresentation; **déformer** ⟨1a⟩ deform; chaussures stretch (out of shape); visage, fait distort; idée misre-

present; **se ~ de chaussures** lose their shape

défouler [defule] ⟨1a⟩: **se ~** give vent to one's feelings

défraîchi, ~e [defreʃi] dingy

défricher [defriʃe] ⟨1a⟩ AGR clear

défroisser [defrwase] ⟨1a⟩ vêtement crumple, crease

défunt, ~e [defœ̃, -œ̃t] **1** adj late **2** m/f: **le ~** the deceased

dégagé, ~e [degaʒe] route, ciel clear; vue unimpeded; air, ton relaxed; **dégagement** m d'une route clearing; de chaleur, vapeur release; **voie f de ~** filter lane; **dégager** ⟨1l⟩ (délivrer) free; route clear; odeur give off; chaleur, gaz give off, release; personne d'une obligation release, free; **se ~** free o.s.; d'une route, du ciel clear; une odeur désagréable se dégageait de la cuisine an unpleasant smell was coming from the kitchen

dégarnir [degarnir] ⟨2a⟩ empty; **se ~** d'un arbre lose its leaves; **ses tempes se dégarnissent** he's going a bit thin on top

dégât [dega] m damage; **~s** damage sg

dégel [deʒel] m thaw (aussi POL)

dégeler [deʒle] ⟨1d⟩ **1** v/t frigidaire defrost; crédits unfreeze **2** v/i d'un lac thaw

dégénérer [deʒenere] ⟨1f⟩ degenerate (en into)

dégivrer [deʒivre] ⟨1a⟩ defrost; TECH de-ice; **dégivreur** m de-icer

déglinguée, ~e [deglɛ̃ge] F beat-up F

déglutir [deglytir] ⟨2a⟩ swallow

dégonflé, ~e [degɔ̃fle] pneu deflated; **dégonfler** ⟨1a⟩ let the air out of, deflate; **se ~** deflate; fig F lose one's nerve

dégot(t)er [degɔte] ⟨1a⟩ F travail find; livre, objet de collection track down

dégouliner [deguline] ⟨1a⟩ trickle

dégourdi, ~e [degurdi] resourceful; **dégourdir** ⟨2a⟩ membres loosen up, get the stiffness out of; **se ~ les jambes** stretch one's legs

dégoût [degu] m disgust; **dégoûtant, ~e** disgusting; **dégoûter** ⟨1a⟩ disgust; **~ qn de qch** put s.o. off sth;

se ~ de qch take a dislike to sth

dégradant, ~e [degradã, -t] degrading; **dégrader** ⟨1a⟩ MIL demote; *édifice* damage; *(avilir)* degrade; **se ~** *d'une situation, de la santé* deteriorate; *d'un édifice* fall into disrepair; *d'une personne (s'avilir)* demean o.s.

degré [dəgre] *m* degree; *(échelon)* level; **de l'alcool à 90 ~s** 90 degree proof alcohol; **un cousin au premier ~** a first cousin

dégressif, -ive [degresif, -iv] *tarif* tapering

dégrèvement [degrɛvmã] *m*: **~ d'impôt** tax relief

dégriffé, ~e [degrife] *vêtements* sold at a cheaper price with the designer label removed

dégringoler [degrɛ̃gɔle] ⟨1a⟩ fall

dégriser [degrize] ⟨1a⟩ sober up

déguerpir [degerpir] ⟨2a⟩ take off, clear off

dégueulasse [degœlas] P disgusting, F sick-making; *il a été ~ avec nous* P he was a real bastard to us P

dégueuler [degœle] ⟨1a⟩ F puke F, throw up

déguisement [degizmã] *m* disguise; *pour bal masqué,* Halloween etc costume; **déguiser** ⟨1a⟩ disguise; *enfant* dress up **(en** as); **se ~** disguise o.s. **(en** as); *pour bal masqué etc* dress up

dégustation [degystasjõ] *f* tasting; **~ de vins** wine tasting; **déguster** ⟨1a⟩ taste

dehors [dəɔr] **1** *adv* outside; **jeter ~** throw out **2** *prép*: **en ~ de la maison** outside the house; **un problème en ~ de mes compétences** a problem I'm not competent to deal with, a problem beyond my area of competence **3** *m* exterior

déjà [deʒa] already; **je l'avais ~ vu** I'd seen it before, I'd already seen it; **c'est qui ~?** F who's he again?

déjanté, ~e [deʒãte] F crazy, whacky F

déjeuner [deʒœne] **1** *v/i* ⟨1a⟩ *midi* (have) lunch; *matin* (have) breakfast **2** *m* lunch; **petit ~** breakfast; **~ d'affaires** business lunch

déjouer [deʒwe] ⟨1a⟩ thwart

DEL [del] *f abr* **(= diode électroluminescente)** LED **(=** light-emitting diode)

delà [dəla] → **au-delà**

délabré, ~e [delabre] dilapidated; **délabrement** *m* decay

délacer [delase] ⟨1k⟩ loosen, unlace

délai [delɛ] *m* *(temps imparti)* time allowed; *(date limite)* deadline; *(prolongation)* extension; **sans ~** without delay, immediately; **dans les ~s** within the time allowed, within the allotted time; **dans les plus courts ~s** as soon as possible; **dans un ~ de 8 jours** within a week; **~ de réflexion** cooling-off period

délaisser [delese] ⟨1b⟩ *(abandonner)* leave; *(négliger)* neglect

délassement [delasmã] *m* relaxation; **délasser** ⟨1a⟩ relax; **se ~** relax

délateur, -trice [delatœr, -tris] *m/f* informer; **délation** *f* denunciation

délavé, ~e [delave] faded

délayer [deleje] ⟨1i⟩ dilute, water down; *fig: discours* pad out

délectation [delɛktasjõ] *f* delight; **délecter** ⟨1a⟩: **se ~ de** take delight in

délégation [delegasjõ] *f* delegation; **délégué, ~e** *m/f* delegate; **délégué(e) syndical(e)** *m/f* union representative, *Br* shop steward; **déléguer** ⟨1f⟩ *autorité, personne* delegate

délestage [delestaʒ] *m*: **itinéraire m de ~** diversion, alternative route (to ease congestion); **délester** ⟨1a⟩ remove ballast from; **~ qn de qch** *iron* relieve s.o. of sth

délibération [deliberasjõ] *f* *(débat)* deliberation, discussion; *(réflexion)* consideration, deliberation; *(décision)* resolution

délibéré, ~e [delibere] *(intentionnel)* deliberate; **délibérément** *adv* deliberate

délibérer [delibere] ⟨1f⟩ deliberate, discuss; *(réfléchir)* consider, deliberately

délicat, ~e [delika, -t] *(fin, fragile)* situation delicate; *problème* tricky; *(plein de tact)* tactful; **délicatesse** *f* delicacy; (*tact*) tact; **délicatement** delicately

délice [delis] *m* delight; **délicieux, -euse** delicious; *sensation* delightful

délier [delje] ⟨1a⟩ loosen, untie; **~ la langue à qn** loosen s.o.'s tongue

délimiter [delimite] ⟨1a⟩ define

délinquance [delɛ̃kɑ̃s] *f* crime, delinquency; **~ juvénile** juvenile delinquency; **délinquant, ~e 1** *adj* delinquent **2** *m/f* criminal, delinquent

délire [delir] *m* delirium; *enthousiasme, joie* frenzy; **foule f en ~** ecstatic crowd; **c'est du ~!** *fig* F it's sheer madness!; **délirer** ⟨1a⟩ be delirious; F *être fou* be stark raving mad; **~ de joie** be delirious with joy

délit [deli] *m* offense, *Br* offence; **commettre un ~ de fuite** leave the scene of an accident; **~ d'initié** insider dealing

délivrance [delivrɑ̃s] *f* release; (*soulagement*) relief; (*livraison*) delivery; *d'un certificat* issue; **délivrer** ⟨1a⟩ release; (*livrer*) deliver; *certificat* issue

délocaliser [delokalize] ⟨1a⟩ relocate

déloger [delɔʒe] ⟨1l⟩ *ennemi* dislodge

déloyal, ~e [delwajal] (*mpl* -aux) *ami* disloyal; **concurrence f ~e** unfair competition

delta [dɛlta] *m* GÉOGR delta

deltaplane [dɛltaplan] *m* hang-glider; **faire du ~** go hang-gliding

déluge [delyʒ] *m* flood

déluré, ~e [delyre] sharp; *péj* forward

demain [d(ə)mɛ̃] *adv* tomorrow; **à ~!** see you tomorrow!; **~ matin / soir** tomorrow morning / evening

demande [d(ə)mɑ̃d] *f* (*requête*) request; *écrite* application; ÉCON demand; **sur** *ou* **à la ~ de qn** at the request of s.o.; **~ d'emploi** job application; **~ en mariage** proposal; **~ de renseignements** inquiry

demandé, ~e [d(ə)mɑ̃de] popular, in demand; **demander** ⟨1a⟩ ask for; *somme d'argent* ask; (*nécessiter*) call for, take; **~ qch à qn** ask s.o. for sth; (*vouloir savoir*) ask s.o. sth; **~ à qn de faire qch** ask s.o. to do sth; **il demande que le vol soit** (*subj*) re-

tardé he's asking for the flight to be delayed; **je ne demande qu'à le faire** I'd be only too delighted; **se ~ si** wonder if; **il est demandé au téléphone** he's wanted on the phone, there's a call for him; **on demande un programmeur** *offre d'emploi* programmer wanted

démangeaison [demɑ̃ʒɛzõ] *f* itch; **démanger** ⟨1l⟩: **le dos me démange** my back itches, I have an itchy back; **ça me démange depuis longtemps** I've been itching to do it for ages

démanteler [demɑ̃tle] ⟨1d⟩ dismantle

démaquillant [demakijɑ̃] *m* cleanser; *lait m ~* cleansing milk; **démaquiller** ⟨1a⟩: **se ~** take off *ou* remove one's make-up

démarcation [demarkasjõ] *f* demarcation; **ligne f de ~** boundary, demarcation line

démarchage [demarʃaʒ] *m* selling

démarche [demarʃ] *f* step (*aussi fig*); **faire des ~s** take steps

démarquer [demarke] ⟨1a⟩: **se ~** stand out (*de* from)

démarrage [demaraʒ] *m* start (*aussi fig*); **~ à froid** INFORM cold start; **démarrer** ⟨1a⟩ **1** *v/t* AUTO start (up) (*aussi fig*); INFORM boot up, start up **2** *v/i* AUTO start (up); **~ bien** *fig* get off to a good start; **démarreur** *m* AUTO starter

démasquer [demaske] ⟨1m⟩ unmask

démêlé [demele] *m* argument; **avoir des ~s avec la justice** be in trouble with the law; **démêler** ⟨1b⟩ disentangle; *fig* clear up

déménagement [demenaʒmɑ̃] *m* move; **déménager** ⟨1l⟩ move; **déménageurs** *mpl* movers, *Br* removal men

démence [demɑ̃s] *f* dementia; **dément, ~e** demented; **c'est ~** *fig* F it's unbelievable

démener [demøne] ⟨1d⟩: **se ~** struggle; (*s'efforcer*) make an effort

démenti [demɑ̃ti] *m* denial

démentiel, ~le [demɑ̃sjɛl] insane

démentir [demɑ̃tir] ⟨2b⟩ (*nier*) deny;

(*infirmer*) belie

démerder [demerde] ⟨1a⟩: *se ~* F manage, sort things out

démesure [demǝzyr] f excess; **démesuré, ~e** *maison* enormous; *orgueil* excessive

démettre [demetr] ⟨4p⟩ *pied, poignet* dislocate; *~ qn de ses fonctions* dismiss s.o. from office; *se ~ de ses fonctions* resign one's office

demeurant [dǝmœrɑ̃]: *au ~* moreover

demeure [dǝmœr] f residence; **demeurer** ⟨1a⟩ (*habiter*) live; (*rester*) stay, remain; **demeuré, ~e** retarded

demi, ~e [d(ǝ)mi] **1** *adj* half; *une heure et ~e* an hour and a half; *il est quatre heures et ~e* it's four thirty, it's half past four **2** *adv* half; *à ~* half **3** *m* half; *bière* half a pint; *en football, rugby* halfback; *~ de mêlée* scrum half; *~ d'ouverture* stand-off (half), fly half

demi-cercle [d(ǝ)misɛrkl] *m* semi-circle

demi-finale [d(ǝ)mifinal] f (*pl* demi-finales) semi-final

demi-frère [d(ǝ)mifrer] *m* (*pl* demi-frères) half-brother

demi-heure [d(ǝ)mijœr] f (*pl* demi-heures) half-hour

démilitariser [demilitarize] ⟨1a⟩ de-militarize

demi-litre [d(ǝ)militr] *m* half liter *ou Br* litre

demi-mot [d(ǝ)mimo]: *il nous l'a dit à ~* he hinted at it to us

demi-pension [d(ǝ)mipɑ̃sjɔ̃] f American plan, *Br* half board

demi-pression [d(ǝ)mipresjɔ̃] f half-pint of draft *ou Br* draught

demi-sel [d(ǝ)misɛl] *m* slightly salted butter

demi-sœur [d(ǝ)misœr] f (*pl* demi-sœurs) half-sister

démission [demisjɔ̃] f resignation; *fig* renunciation; *donner sa ~* hand in one's resignation, hand in one's notice; **démissionner** ⟨1a⟩ **1** *vi* resign; *fig* give up **2** *vt* sack

demi-tarif [d(ǝ)mitarif] *m* half price

demi-tour [d(ǝ)mitur] *m* AUTO U-turn; *faire ~ fig* turn back

démocrate [demɔkrat] democrat; *US* POL Democrat; **démocratie** f democracy; **démocratique** democratic

démodé, ~e [demɔde] old-fashioned

démographique [demɔgrafik] demographic; *poussée f ~* population growth

demoiselle [d(ǝ)mwazɛl] f (*jeune fille*) young lady; *~ d'honneur* bridesmaid

démolir [demɔlir] ⟨2a⟩ demolish (*aussi fig*); **démolition** f demolition

démon [demɔ̃] *m* demon

démonstratif, -ive [demɔ̃stratif, -iv] demonstrative; **démonstration** f (*preuve*) demonstration, proof; *d'un outil, sentiment* demonstration

démonter [demɔ̃te] ⟨1a⟩ dismantle; *fig* disconcert

démontrer [demɔ̃tre] ⟨1a⟩ (*prouver*) demonstrate, prove; (*faire ressortir*) show

démoraliser [demɔralize] ⟨1a⟩ de-moralize

démordre [demɔrdr] ⟨4a⟩: *il n'en démordra pas* he won't change his mind

démotiver [demɔtive] ⟨1a⟩ demotivate

démuni, ~e [demyni] penniless; **démunir** ⟨2a⟩: *~ qn de qch* deprive s.o. of sth

dénaturé, ~e [denatyre] unnatural; **dénaturer** ⟨1a⟩ distort

déneigement [denɛʒmɑ̃] *m* snow removal *ou* clearance

dénicher [denife] ⟨1a⟩ find

dénier [denje] ⟨1a⟩ deny; *~ à qn le droit de faire qch* deny s.o. the right to do sth

dénigrer [denigre] ⟨1a⟩ denigrate

dénivellation [denivelasjɔ̃] f difference in height

dénombrement [denɔ̃brǝmɑ̃] *m* count; **dénombrer** ⟨1a⟩ count

dénominateur [denɔminatœr] *m* MATH denominator; **dénomination** f name

dénoncer [denɔ̃se] ⟨1k⟩ denounce; *à la police* report; *contrat* terminate; *se*

~ **à la police** give o.s. up to the police; **dénonciateur, -trice** *m/f* informer; **dénonciation** *f* denunciation

dénoter [denɔte] ⟨1a⟩ indicate, point to, denote

dénouement [denumɑ̃] *m d'une pièce de théâtre, affaire difficile* ending, denouement *fml*; **dénouer** ⟨1a⟩ loosen; **se ~** *fig d'une scène* end; *d'un mystère* be cleared up

dénoyauter [denwajote] ⟨1a⟩ pit, *Br* stone

denrée [dɑ̃re] *f:* **~s (alimentaires)** foodstuffs; **une ~ rare** *fig* a rare commodity

dense [dɑ̃s] dense; *brouillard, forêt* dense, thick; **densité** *f* density; *du brouillard, d'une forêt* denseness, thickness

dent [dɑ̃] *f* tooth; ~ **de sagesse** wisdom tooth; **j'ai mal aux ~s** I've got toothache; **faire ses ~s** *d'un enfant* be teething; **avoir une ~ contre qn** have a grudge against s.o.; ~ **de lait** milk tooth; **dentaire** dental

dentelé, ~e [dɑ̃tle] jagged

dentelle [dɑ̃tɛl] *f* lace

dentier [dɑ̃tje] *m* (dental) plate, false teeth *pl*; **dentifrice** *m* toothpaste; **dentiste** *m/f* dentist; **dentition** *f* teeth *pl*

dénuder [denyde] ⟨1a⟩ strip

dénué, ~e [denɥe]: ~ **de qch** devoid of sth; ~ **de tout** deprived of everything; **dénuement** *m* destitution

déodorant [deɔdɔrɑ̃] *m* deodorant; ~ **en aérosol** spray deodorant; ~ **à bille** roll-on deodorant

dépannage [depanaʒ] *m* AUTO *etc* repairs *pl*; *(remorquage)* recovery; **service m de ~** breakdown service; **dépanner** ⟨1a⟩ repair; *(remorquer)* recover; ~ **qn** *fig* F help s.o. out of a spot; **dépanneur** *m* repairman; *pour voitures* mechanic; **dépanneuse** *f* wrecker, *Br* tow truck

dépareillé, ~e [depareje] odd

départ [depar] *m d'un train, bus, avion* departure; SP start *(aussi fig)*; **au ~** at first, to begin with; **point m de ~** starting point

départager [departaʒe] ⟨1l⟩ decide between

département [departəmɑ̃] *m* department; **départemental, ~e** departmental; **route ~e** secondary road

dépassé, ~e [depase] out of date, old-fashioned; **dépasser** ⟨1a⟩ *personne* pass; AUTO pass; *Br* overtake; *but, ligne d'arrivée etc* overshoot; *fig* exceed; **cela me dépasse** it's beyond me, I can't understand it; **tu dépasses les limites** you're overstepping the mark; **se ~** surpass o.s.

dépaysé, ~e [depeize]: **se sentir ~** feel out of place; **dépaysement** *m* disorientation; *changement agréable* change of scene

dépecer [depəse] ⟨1d *aussi* 1k⟩ cut up

dépêche [depɛʃ] *f* dispatch; **dépêcher** ⟨1b⟩ dispatch; **se ~ de faire qch** hurry to do sth; **dépêche-toi!** hurry up!

dépeindre [depɛ̃dr] ⟨4b⟩ depict

dépendance [depɑ̃dɑ̃s] *f* dependence, dependency; **~s** *bâtiments* outbuildings; **entraîner une (forte) ~** be (highly) addictive; **dépendant, ~e** dependent; **dépendre** ⟨4a⟩: ~ **de** depend on; *moralement* be dependent on; **cela dépend** it depends

dépens [depɑ̃] *mpl:* **aux ~ de** at the expense of

dépense [depɑ̃s] *f* expense, expenditure; *de temps, de forces* expenditure; *d'essence, d'électricité* consumption, use; **~s** expenditure *sg*; **~s publiques** public *ou* government spending; **dépenser** ⟨1a⟩ spend; *son énergie, ses forces* use up; *essence* consume, use; **se ~** be physically active; *(faire des efforts)* exert o.s.; **dépensier, -ère 1** *adj* extravagant, spendthrift **2** *m/f* spendthrift

dépérir [deperir] ⟨2a⟩ *d'un malade, d'une plante* waste away; *fig d'une entreprise* go downhill

dépeuplement [depœpləmɑ̃] *m* depopulation; **dépeupler** ⟨1a⟩ depopulate

dépilatoire [depilatwar]: **crème f ~** hair remover, depilatory cream

dépistage [depista3] *m d'un criminel* tracking down; MÉD screening; **~ du sida** Aids screening; **dépister** ⟨1a⟩ MÉD screen for; *(établir la présence de)* detect, discover

dépit [depi] *m* spite; **en ~ de** in spite of; **dépité, ~e** crestfallen

déplacé, ~e [deplase] out of place; *(inconvenant)* uncalled for; POL displaced; **déplacement** *m d'un meuble* moving; *du personnel* transfer; *(voyage)* trip; **frais mpl de ~** travel expenses; **déplacer** ⟨1k⟩ move; *personnel* transfer; *problème, difficulté* shift the focus of; **se ~** move; *(voyager)* travel

déplaire [depler] ⟨4a⟩: **~ à qn** *(fâcher)* offend s.o.; **elle me déplaît** *(ne me plaît pas)* I don't like her, I dislike her; **cela lui déplaît de faire ...** he dislikes doing ..., he doesn't like doing ...; **ça ne me déplaît pas** I quite like it

déplaisant, ~e [deplezɑ̃, -t] unpleasant

dépliant [deplijɑ̃] *m* leaflet; **déplier** ⟨1a⟩ unfold, open out

déploiement [deplwamɑ̃] *m* MIL deployment; *de forces, courage* display

déplorable [deplorabl] deplorable; **déplorer** ⟨1a⟩ deplore

déployer [deplwaje] ⟨1h⟩ *aile, voile* spread; *carte, drap* open out, unfold; *forces, courage etc* display

déportation [deportasjõ] *f* POL deportation; **déporter** ⟨1a⟩ POL deport; **se ~** *d'un véhicule* swing

déposer [depoze] ⟨1a⟩ **1** *v/t* put down; *armes* lay down; *passager* drop; *roi* depose; *argent, boue* deposit; *projet de loi* table; *ordures* dump; *plainte* lodge; **~ ses bagages à la consigne** leave one's bags at the baggage checkroom; **~ le bilan** file for bankruptcy **2** *v/i d'un liquide* settle; JUR **~ contre / en faveur de qn** testify against / on behalf of s.o.; **se ~** *de la boue* settle; **déposition** *f* JUR testimony, deposition

déposséder [deposede] ⟨1f⟩ deprive **(de** of)

dépôt [depo] *m* deposit; *action* depositing; *chez le notaire* lodging; *d'un projet de loi* tabling; *des ordures* dumping; *(entrepôt)* depot

dépotoir [depotwar] *m* dump, *Br* tip *(aussi fig)*

dépouille [depuj] *f*: **la ~ (mortelle)** the (mortal) remains *pl*

dépouillé, ~e [depuje] *style* pared down; **~ de** deprived of; **dépouiller** ⟨1a⟩ *animal* skin; *(voler)* rob **(de** of); *(examiner)* go through; **~ le scrutin ou les votes** count the votes

dépourvu, ~e [depurvy]: **~ de** devoid of; **prendre qn au ~** take s.o. by surprise

dépoussiérer [depusjere] ⟨1a⟩ dust; *fig* modernize

dépravation [depravasjõ] *f* depravity; **dépraver** ⟨1a⟩ deprave

déprécier [depresje] ⟨1a⟩ *chose* lower *ou* decrease the value of; *personne* disparage, belittle; **se ~** depreciate, lose value; *d'une personne* belittle o.s.

dépressif, -ive [depresif, -iv] depressive; **dépression** *f* depression; **faire une ~** be depressed, be suffering from depression

déprimant, ~e [deprimɑ̃, -t] depressing; **déprime** *f* depression; **déprimer** ⟨1a⟩ depress

dépuceler [depysle] ⟨1c⟩ deflower

depuis [depɥi] **1** *prép* ◇ since; **j'attends ~ une heure** I have been waiting for an hour; **~ quand es-tu là?** how long have you been there?; **~ quand permettent-ils que tu ...?** since when do they allow you to ...?; **je ne l'ai pas vu ~ des années** I haven't seen him in years

◇ *espace* from; **il est venu en courant ~ chez lui** he came running all the way from his place

2 *adv* since; **elle ne lui a pas reparlé ~** she hasn't spoken to him again since

3 *conj*: **~ que** since; **~ qu'elle habite ici** since she has been living here

député [depyte] *m* POL MP, Member of Parliament; **~ européen** *m* Euro MP, *Br aussi* MEP

déraciner [derasine] ⟨1a⟩ *arbre, personne* uproot; *(extirper)* root out, eradicate

dérailler [deraje] ⟨1a⟩ go off the rails; *fig* F *d'un mécanisme* go on the blink; *(déraisonner)* talk nonsense; **dérailleur** *m d'un vélo* derailleur

déraisonnable [derezɔnabl] unreasonable

dérangeant [derãʒã] disturbing

dérangement [derãʒmã] *m* disturbance; **déranger** ⟨1l⟩ disturb

déraper [derape] ⟨1a⟩ AUTO skid

déréglé, ~e [deregle] *vie* wild

déréglementation [dereglemãtasjõ] *f* deregulation; **déréglementer** ⟨1a⟩ deregulate

dérégler [deregle] ⟨1f⟩ *mécanisme* upset

dérision [derizjõ] *f* derision; **tourner en ~** deride

dérisoire [derizwar] derisory, laughable

dérivatif [derivatif] *m* diversion; **dérivation** *f* derivation

dérive [deriv] *f* MAR drift; *aller à la ~ fig* drift; *à la ~* adrift; **dériver** ⟨1a⟩ **1** *v/t* MATH derive; *cours d'eau* divert **2** *v/i* MAR, AVIAT drift; *~ de d'un mot* be derived from; **dériveur** *m* dinghy

dermatologue [dɛrmatɔlɔg] *m/f* dermatologist

dernier, -ère [dɛrnje, -ɛr] last; *(le plus récent)* mode, film, roman etc latest; *extrême* utmost; *ce ~* the latter; **dernièrement** adv recently, lately

dérobée [derɔbe]: *à la ~* furtively; **dérober** ⟨1a⟩ steal; *~ qch à qn* rob s.o. of sth, steal sth from s.o.; *se ~ à discussion* shy away from; *obligations* shirk

dérogation [derɔgasjõ] *f* JUR exception; *~ à* exception to, departure from; **déroger** ⟨1l⟩ JUR: *~ à* make an exception to, depart from

déroulement [derulmã] *m* unfolding; **pour faciliter le ~ du projet** to facilitate the smooth running of the project; **dérouler** ⟨1a⟩ unroll; *bobine, câble* unwind; **se ~** take place; *d'une cérémonie* go (off)

déroutant, ~e [derutã, -t] disconcerting; **dérouter** ⟨1a⟩ *(déconcerter)* disconcert

derrière [dɛrjɛr] **1** *adv* behind; *être assis ~ en voiture* be sitting in back *ou Br* in the back **2** *prép* behind **3** *m* back; ANAT bottom, rear end; *de ~ patte etc* back *atr*

des [de] → **de**

dès [dɛ] *prép* from, since; *~ lors* from then on; *(par conséquent)* consequently; *~ demain* tomorrow; *(à partir de)* as of tomorrow, as from tomorrow; *~ lundi* as of Monday, as from Monday; *~ qu'il part* the moment (that) he leaves, as soon as he leaves

désabusé, ~e [dezabyze] disillusioned; **désabuser** ⟨1a⟩ disillusion

désaccord [dezakɔr] *m* disagreement

désaccordé, ~e [dezakɔrde] out of tune

désaffecté, ~e [dezafɛkte] disused; *église* deconsecrated

désagréable [dezagreabl] unpleasant, disagreeable

désagréger [dezagreʒe] ⟨1g⟩: *se ~* disintegrate

désagrément [dezagremã] *m* unpleasantness, annoyance

désaltérant, ~e [dezalterã, -t] thirst-quenching

désamorcer [dezamɔrse] ⟨1k⟩ *bombe, mine* defuse *(aussi fig)*

désappointement [dezapwɛtmã] *m* disappointment; **désappointer** ⟨1a⟩ disappoint

désapprobateur, -trice [dezaprobatœr, -tris] disapproving

désapprouver [dezapruve] ⟨1a⟩ disapprove of

désarmement [dezarmemã] *m* MIL disarmament; **désarmer** ⟨1a⟩ disarm *(aussi fig)*

désarroi [dezarwa] *m* disarray

désastre [dezastr] *m* disaster; **désastreux, -euse** disastrous

désavantage [dezavãtaʒ] *m* disadvantage; **désavantager** ⟨1l⟩ put at a disadvantage; **désavantageux, -euse** disadvantageous

désaveu [dezavø] *m* disowning; *d'un*

propos retraction; **désavouer** ⟨1a⟩ disown; *propos* retract

descendance [desɑ̃dɑ̃s] *f* descendants *pl*; **descendant, ~e** *m/f* descendant

descendre [desɑ̃dr] ⟨4a⟩ **1** *v/i* (*aux être*) (*aller vers le bas*) go down; (*venir vers le bas*) come down; *d'un train, un autobus* get off; *d'une voiture* get out; *d'un cheval* get off, dismount; (*baisser*) go down; *de température, prix* go down, fall; *d'un chemin* drop; AVIAT descend; **~ à l'hôtel / chez qn** stay at the hotel / with s.o.; **~ de qn** be descended from s.o.; **~ d'une voiture** get out of a car; **~ de son cheval** get off one's horse, dismount; **~ du troisième étage en ascenseur / à pied** take the elevator down / walk down from the fourth floor; **~ dans la rue** *pour manifester* take to the streets; **~ bien bas** (*baisser*) sink very low; **le manteau lui descend jusqu'aux pieds** the coat comes down to her feet **2** *v/t* (*porter vers le bas*) bring down; (*emporter*) take down; *passager* drop off; F (*abattre*) shoot down, bring down; *vallée, rivière* descend; **~ les escaliers** come / go downstairs;

descente *f* descent; (*pente*) slope; *en parachute* jump; **~ de lit** bedside rug

description [dɛskripsjɔ̃] *f* description; **~ d'emploi** job description

désemparé, ~e [dezɑ̃pare] at a loss

désenchanté, ~e [dezɑ̃ʃɑ̃te] disenchanted

déséquilibre [dezekilibr] *m* imbalance; **déséquilibré, ~e** PSYCH unbalanced; **déséquilibrer** ⟨1a⟩ unbalance (*aussi fig*)

désert, ~e [dezɛr, -t] **1** *adj* deserted; **une île ~e** a desert island **2** *m* desert

déserter [dezɛrte] ⟨1a⟩ desert (*aussi* MIL); **déserteur** *m* MIL deserter

désertification [dezɛrtifikasjɔ̃] *f* desertification

désertion [dezɛrsjɔ̃] *f* desertion

désertique [dezɛrtik] desert *atr*

désespérant, ~e [dezɛsperɑ̃, -t] *temps*

etc depressing; **d'une bêtise ~e** depressingly *ou* hopelessly stupid

désespéré, ~e [dezɛspere] desperate; *air, lettre, regard* desperate, despairing; **désespérément** *adv* (*en s'acharnant*) desperately; (*avec désespoir*) despairingly; **désespérer** ⟨1f⟩ **1** *v/t* drive to despair **2** *v/i* despair, lose hope; **~ de** despair of

désespoir [dezɛspwar] *m* despair; **il fait le ~ de ses parents** his parents despair of him; **en ~ de cause** in desperation

déshabillé [dezabije] *m* negligee; **déshabiller** ⟨1a⟩ undress; **se ~** get undressed

désherbant [dezɛrbɑ̃] *m* weedkiller, herbicide

déshériter [dezerite] ⟨1a⟩ disinherit

déshonorant, ~e [dezɔnɔrɑ̃, -t] dishonorable, *Br* dishonourable; **déshonorer** ⟨1a⟩ disgrace, bring dishonor *ou Br* dishonour on

déshydraté, ~e [dezidrate] *aliments* dessicated; *personne* dehydrated; **déshydrater** ⟨1a⟩: **se ~** become dehydrated

design [dizajn] *m*: **~ d'intérieurs** interior design

désigner [deziɲe] ⟨1a⟩ (*montrer*) point to, point out; (*appeler*) call; (*nommer*) appoint (*pour* to), designate; **~ qch du doigt** point at sth

désillusion [dezilyzjɔ̃] disillusionment

désinfectant [dezɛ̃fɛktɑ̃] *m* disinfectant; **désinfecter** ⟨1a⟩ disinfect

désintégration [dezɛ̃tegrasjɔ̃] *f* breakup, disintegration; PHYS disintegration

désintéressé, ~e [dezɛ̃terese] (*impartial*) disinterested, impartial; (*altruiste*) selfless; **désintéressement** *m* impartiality; (*altruisme*) selflessness; **désintéresser** ⟨1b⟩: **se ~ de** lose interest in

désintoxication [dezɛ̃tɔksikasjɔ̃] *f*: **faire une cure de ~** go into detox

désinvolte [dezɛ̃vɔlt] casual; **désinvolture** *f* casualness

désir [dezir] *m* desire; (*souhait*) wish;

le ~ de changement / de plaire the desire for change / to please; **désirable** desirable; **désirer** ⟨1a⟩ want; *sexuellement* desire; ~ *faire qch* want to do sth; *nous désirons que vous veniez* (*subj*) *avec nous* we want you to come with us; **dési- reux, - euse** eager (*de faire* to do)

désister [deziste] ⟨1a⟩ POL: *se ~* withdraw, stand down

désobéir [dezɔbeir] disobey; ~ *à qn / à la loi / à un ordre* disobey s.o. / the law / an order; **désobéissant, ~e** disobedient

désobligeant, ~e [dezɔbliʒɑ̃, -t] disagreeable

désodorisant [dezɔdɔrizɑ̃] *m* deodorant

désœuvré, ~e [dezœvre] idle

désolé, ~e [dezɔle] upset (*de* about, over); *je suis ~* I am so sorry; **désoler** ⟨1a⟩ upset

désopilant, ~e [dezɔpilɑ̃, -t] hilarious

désordonné, ~e [dezɔrdɔne] untidy

désordre [dezɔrdr] *m* untidiness; *en ~* untidy

désorganisé, ~e [dezɔrganize] disorganized

désorienter [dezɔrjɑ̃te] ⟨1a⟩ disorient, *Br* disorientate

désormais [dezɔrmɛ] *adv* now; *à partir de maintenant* from now on

désosser [dezɔse] ⟨1a⟩ bone, remove the bones from

despote [dɛspɔt] *m* despot; **despotique** despotic; **despotisme** *m* despotism

desquels, desquelles [dekɛl] → *lequel*

dessécher [deseʃe] ⟨1f⟩ *d'un sol, rivière, peau* dry out; *de fruits* dry

dessein [desɛ̃] *m* intention; *à ~* intentionally, on purpose; *dans le ~ de faire qch* with the intention of doing sth

desserrer [desɛre] ⟨1b⟩ loosen

dessert [desɛr] *m* dessert

desservir [desɛrvir] ⟨2b⟩ *des transport publics* serve; (*s'arrêter à*) call at, stop at; *table* clear; ~ *qn* do s.o. a disservice

dessin [desɛ̃] *m* drawing; (*motif*) design; ~ *animé* cartoon

dessinateur, -trice [desinatœr, -tris] *m/f* drawer; TECH draftsman, *Br* draughtsman; *de mode* designer; **dessiner** ⟨1a⟩ draw

dessoûler [desule] ⟨1a⟩ F sober up

dessous [d(ə)su] **1** *adv* underneath; *en ~* underneath; *agir en ~ fig* act in an underhanded way; *ci-~* below **2** *m* (*face inférieure*) underside; *les voisins du ~* the downstairs neighbors, the people in the apartment beneath; *des ~ en dentelle* lace underwear *sg*; *les ~ de la politique fig* the side of politics people don't get to hear about; *avoir le ~* get the worst of it; **dessous-de-plat** *m* (*pl inv*) table mat

dessus [d(ə)sy] **1** *adv*: *le nom est écrit ~* the name's written on top; *sens ~ dessous* upside down; *en ~* on top; *par-~* over; *ci-~* above; *il nous est tombé ~ fig* F he came down on us like a ton of bricks F; *il a le nez ~* it's right under his nose **2** *m* top; *les voisins du ~* the upstairs neighbors, the people in the apartment above; *avoir le ~ fig* have the upper hand; **dessus-de-lit** *m* (*pl inv*) bedspread

destabilisant, ~e [destabilizɑ̃, -t] unnerving; **déstabiliser** ⟨1a⟩ destabilize

destin [destɛ̃] *m* destiny, fate

destinataire [destinatɛr] *m* addressee; **destination** *f* destination; **destinée** *f* destiny; **destiner** ⟨1a⟩ mean, intend (*à* for)

destituer [destitɥe] ⟨1a⟩ dismiss; MIL discharge; *destitué de ses fonctions* relieved of his duties

destroyer [dɛstrwaje] *m* destroyer

destructeur, -trice [dɛstryktœr, -tris] destructive; **destruction** *f* destruction

désuet, -ète [desɥɛ, -t] obsolete; *mode* out of date; **désuétude** *f*: *tomber en ~* fall into disuse

désuni, ~e [desɥni] disunited

détachable [detaʃabl] detachable

détaché, **~e** [detaʃe] *fig* detached; **détacher** ⟨1a⟩ detach; *ceinture* undo; *chien* release, unchain; *employé* second; *(nettoyer)* clean, remove the spots from; **je ne pouvais pas ~ mes yeux de ...** I couldn't take my eyes off ...; **se ~ sur** stand out against

détail [detaj] *m* detail; COMM retail trade; **vendre au ~** sell retail; **prix** *m* **de ~** retail price; **en ~** detailed

détaillant [detajɑ̃] *m* retailer

détartrage [detartraʒ] *m* descaling; **détartrer** ⟨1a⟩ descale

détecter [detɛkte] ⟨1a⟩ detect; **détecteur** *m* sensor

détective [detɛktiv] *m* detective

déteindre [detɛ̃dr] ⟨4b⟩ fade; **~ sur** come off on; *fig* rub off on

détendre [detɑ̃dr] ⟨4a⟩ slacken; **~ l'atmosphère** *fig* make the atmosphere less strained, take the tension out of the atmosphere; **se ~ d'une corde** slacken; *fig* relax; **détendu**, **~e** relaxed; *pull* baggy

détenir [detnir] ⟨2h⟩ hold; JUR detain, hold

détente [detɑ̃t] *f d'une arme* trigger; *fig* relaxation; POL détente; **détenteur** *m* holder; **détention** *f* holding; JUR detention; **~ préventive** preventive detention

détenu, **~e** [detny] *m/f* inmate

détergent [detɛrʒɑ̃] *m* detergent

détériorer [deterjɔre] ⟨1a⟩ *appareil, machine, santé* damage; **se ~** deteriorate

déterminant, **~e** [detɛrminɑ̃, -t] decisive; **détermination** *f* determination; **déterminer** ⟨1a⟩ establish, determine; **son expérience passée l'a déterminée à se marier** her past experience made her decide to get married

déterrer [detɛre] ⟨1b⟩ dig up

détestable [detɛstabl] detestable; **détester** ⟨1a⟩ detest, hate

détonation [detɔnasjɔ̃] *f* detonation; **détonner** ⟨1a⟩ MUS sing off-key; *fig: de couleurs* clash; *d'un meuble* be *ou* look out of place

détour [detur] *m* detour; *d'un chemin, fleuve* bend; **sans ~** *fig:* dire qch frankly, straight out; **détourné**, **~e** *fig* indirect; **par des moyens ~s** by indirect means; **détournement** *m* diversion; **~ d'avion** hijack(ing); **~ de fonds** misappropriation of funds, embezzlement; **détourner** ⟨1a⟩ *trafic* divert; *avion* hijack; *tête, yeux* turn away; *de l'argent* embezzle, misappropriate; **~ la conversation** change the subject; **se ~** turn away

détracteur, **-trice** [detraktœr, -tris] *m/f* detractor

détraqué, **~e** [detrake] *montre, radio etc* broken, kaput F; *estomac* upset

détrempé, **~e** [detrɑ̃pe] soggy

détresse [detrɛs] *f* distress

détriment [detrimɑ̃] *m*: **au ~ de** to the detriment of

détritus [detritys] *m* garbage, *Br* rubbish

détroit [detrwa] *m* strait

détromper [detrɔ̃pe] ⟨1a⟩ put right

détrôner [detrone] ⟨1c⟩ dethrone

détruire [detrɥir] ⟨4c⟩ destroy; *(tuer)* kill

dette [dɛt] *f* COMM, *fig* debt; **~ publique** national debt; **avoir des ~s** be in debt

DEUG [dœg] *m abr* (= **diplôme d'études universitaires générales**) *university degree obtained after two years' study*

deuil [dœj] *m* mourning; **être en ~** be in mourning; **porter le ~** be in mourning, wear mourning; **il y a eu un ~ dans sa famille** there's been a bereavement in his family

deux [dø] **1** *adj* two; **les ~** both; **les ~ maisons** the two houses, both houses; **tous (les) ~** both; **tous les ~ jours** every two days, every second day; **nous ~** the two of us, both of us; **~ fois** twice **2** *m* two; **à nous ~ on y arrivera** we'll manage between the two of us; **en ~** in two, in half; **~ à ~** *ou* **par ~** in twos, two by two; → **trois**

deuxième second; *étage* third, *Br* second; **deuxièmement** *adv* secondly

deux-pièces [døpjɛs] *m* (*pl inv*) bikini two-piece swimsuit; *appartement* two-room apartment

deux-points [døpwɛ̃] *m* (*pl inv*) colon

deux-roues [døru] *m* (*pl inv*) two-wheeler

dévaliser [devalize] ⟨1a⟩ *banque* rob, raid; *maison* burglarize, *Br* burgle; *personne* rob; *fig: frigo* raid

dévalorisant, **~e** [devalɔrizɑ̃, -t] demeaning; **dévalorisation** *f* ÉCON drop in value, depreciation; *fig* belittlement; **dévaloriser** ⟨1a⟩ ÉCON devalue; *fig* belittle

dévaluation [devaluɑsjɔ̃] *f* ÉCON devaluation; **dévaluer** ⟨1a⟩ devalue

devancer [d(ə)vɑ̃se] ⟨1k⟩ (*dépasser, surpasser*), *âge, siècle* be ahead of; *désir, objection* anticipate; **~ qn de deux mètres / trente minutes** be two meters / thirty minutes ahead of s.o.

devant [d(ə)vɑ̃] **1** *adv* in front; **se fermer ~** *d'un vêtement* do up at the front, do up in front; **droit ~** straight ahead **2** *prép* in front of; **passer ~ l'église** go past the church; **~ Dieu** before God; **~ un tel mensonge** *fig* when faced with such a lie **3** *m* front; **de ~** front *atr*; **prendre les ~s** take the initiative

devanture [d(ə)vɑ̃tyr] *f* shop window

dévaster [devaste] ⟨1a⟩ devastate

développement [devlɔpmɑ̃] *m* ÉCON, ANAT development, growth; PHOT development; **pays ~ en voie de ~** developing country; **développer** ⟨1a⟩ develop (*aussi* PHOT); *entreprise, affaire* expand, grow; **se ~** develop

devenir [dəvnir] ⟨2h⟩ (*aux être*) become; **il devient agressif** he's getting aggressive; **que va-t-il ~?** what's going to become of him?

dévergondé, **~e** [devɛrgɔ̃de] *sexuellement* promiscuous

déverser [devɛrse] ⟨1a⟩ *ordures* dump; *passagers* disgorge

dévêtir [devetir] ⟨2g⟩ undress

déviation [devjɑsjɔ̃] *f d'une route* detour; (*écart*) deviation

dévier [devje] ⟨1a⟩ **1** *v/t circulation, convoi* divert, reroute **2** *v/i* deviate

(**de** from)

devin [dəvɛ̃] *m*: **je ne suis pas ~!** I'm not a mind-reader; **pour l'avenir** I can't tell the future; **deviner** ⟨1a⟩ guess; **devinette** *f* riddle

devis [d(ə)vi] *m* estimate

dévisager [devizaʒe] ⟨1l⟩ look intently at, stare at

devise [d(ə)viz] *f* FIN currency; (*moto, règle de vie*) motto; **~s étrangères** foreign currency *sg*

dévisser [devise] ⟨1a⟩ unscrew

dévoiler [devwale] ⟨1a⟩ unveil; *secret* reveal, disclose

devoir [dəvwar] ⟨3a⟩ **1** *v/t de l'argent, respect* owe **2** *v/aux nécessité* have to; **il doit le faire** he has to do it, he must do it, he has *ou* he's got to do it; **tu as fait ce que tu devais** you did what you had to

◇ *obligation*: **il aurait dû me le dire** he should have told me; **tu devrais aller la voir** you should go and see her

◇ *conseil*: **tu devrais l'acheter** you should buy it

◇ *supposition*: **ça doit être cuit** it should be done; **je crois que ça doit suffire** I think that should be enough; **tu dois te tromper** you must be mistaken

◇: *prévision*: **l'usine doit fermer le mois prochain** the plant is (due) to close down next month

3 *m* duty; *pour l'école* homework; **faire ses ~s** do one's homework

dévorer [devɔre] ⟨1a⟩ devour

dévotion [devosjɔ̃] *f* devoutness; *péj* sanctimoniousness

dévoué, **~e** [devwe] devoted; **dévouement** *m* devotion; **dévouer** ⟨1a⟩: **se ~ pour** *cause* dedicate one's life to

dextérité [dɛksterite] *f* dexterity, skill

diabète [djabɛt] *m* diabetes *sg*; **diabétique** *m/f* diabetic

diable [djabl] *m* devil

diabolique [djabɔlik] diabolical

diagnostic [djagnɔstik] *m* MÉD diagnosis; **diagnostiquer** ⟨1m⟩ MÉD diagnose

diagonal, **~e** [djagɔnal] (*mpl* -aux)
1 *adj* diagonal 2 *f* diagonal (line);
en ~e diagonally; **lire un texte en
~e** *fig* skim (through) a text

diagramme [djagram] *m* diagram

dialecte [djalɛkt] *m* dialect

dialogue [djalɔg] *m* dialog, *Br* dialogue; **dialoguer** ⟨1m⟩ communicate, enter into a dialog *ou Br* dialogue with

dialyse [djaliz] *f* dialysis

diamant [djamɑ̃] *m* diamond

diamétralement [djametralmɑ̃] *adv* diametrically

diamètre [djamɛtr] *m* diameter; **faire
10 centimètres de ~** be 10 centimeters in diameter

diapason [djapazɔ̃] *m* MUS tuning fork; **se mettre au ~ de qn** *fig* follow s.o.'s lead

diaphragme [djafragm] *m* ANAT, PHOT, *contraceptif* diaphragm

diapositive [djapozitiv] *f* slide

diarrhée [djare] *f* diarrhea, *Br* diarrhoea

dictateur [diktatœr] *m* dictator; **dictatorial**, **~e** dictatorial; **dictature** *f* dictatorship

dictée [dikte] *f* dictation; **dicter** ⟨1a⟩ dictate

diction [diksjɔ̃] *f* diction

dictionnaire [diksjɔner] *m* dictionary

dicton [diktɔ̃] *m* saying

dièse [djez] *m* MUS sharp

diesel [djezɛl] *m* diesel

diète [djet] *f* diet

diététicien, **~ne** [djetetisjɛ̃, -ɛn] *m/f* dietitian

Dieu [djø] *m* God; **~ merci!** thank God!

diffamation [difamasjɔ̃] *f* defamation (of character), slander; **diffamatoire** defamatory; **diffamer** ⟨1a⟩ slander

différence [diferɑ̃s] *f* difference (*aussi* MATH); **à la ~ de sa femme** unlike his wife; **différencier** ⟨1a⟩ differentiate; **différend** *m* dispute; **différent**, **~e** different; **~es personnes** various people; **différentiel** *m* AUTO differential

différer [difere] ⟨1f⟩ 1 *v/t* (*renvoyer*)

defer; **en différé** *émission* recorded
2 *v/i* differ

difficile [difisil] difficult; (*dur*) difficult, hard; (*exigeant*) particular, hard to please

difficulté [difikylte] *f* difficulty

difforme [difɔrm] deformed; *chaussures* shapeless; **difformité** *f* deformity

diffuser [difyze] ⟨1a⟩ *chaleur, lumière* spread, diffuse; RAD, TV broadcast; *idées, nouvelle* spread; **diffusion** *f* spread; RAD, TV broadcast; *de chaleur, lumière* diffusion

digérer [diʒere] ⟨1f⟩ digest

digeste [diʒest] digestible; **digestif**, **-ive** *adj* digestive 2 *m* liqueur; **digestion** *f* digestion

digital, **~e** [diʒital] (*mpl* -aux) digital; **empreinte** *f* **~e** fingerprint

digne [diɲ] (*plein de dignité*) dignified; **~ de** worthy of; **~ de foi** reliable, **~ d'intérêt** interesting; **dignitaire** *m* dignitary; **dignité** *f* dignity; (*charge*) office

digression [digresjɔ̃] *f* digression

digue [dig] *f* dyke

dilapider [dilapide] ⟨1a⟩ fritter away, squander

dilatation [dilatasjɔ̃] *f* expansion; *de pupille* dilation; **dilater** ⟨1a⟩ expand; *pupille* dilate

dilemme [dilɛm] *m* dilemma

diluer [dilɥe] ⟨1n⟩ dilute

dimanche [dimɑ̃ʃ] *m* Sunday

dimension [dimɑ̃sjɔ̃] *f* size, dimension; MATH dimension; *d'une faute* magnitude

diminuer [diminɥe] ⟨1n⟩ 1 *v/t* nombre, prix, vitesse reduce; *joie, enthousiasme, forces* diminish; *mérites* detract from; *souffrances* lessen, decrease; **la maladie l'a diminuée** the illness has weakened her 2 *v/i* decrease; **les jours diminuent** the days are drawing in, the nights are getting longer; **diminutif** *m* diminutive; **diminution** *f* decrease, decline; *d'un nombre, prix* reduction

dinde [dɛ̃d] *f* turkey; **dindon** *m* turkey

dîner [dine] 1 *v/i* ⟨1a⟩ dine 2 *m* dinner; **~ dansant** dinner-dance

dingue [dɛ̃g] F crazy, nuts F

dinosaure [dinozɔr] m dinosaur

diplomate [diplɔmat] m diplomat; **diplomatie** f diplomacy; **diplomatique** diplomatic

diplôme [diplom] m diploma; *universitaire* degree; **diplômé, ~e** m diploma holder; *de l'université* graduate

dire [dir] **1** *v/t & v/i* ⟨4m⟩ say; *(informer, révéler, ordonner)* tell; *(penser)* think; *poème* recite; **elle dit le connaître** she says she knows him; **dis-moi où il est** tell me where he is; **~ à qn de faire qch** tell s.o. to do sth; **que dis-tu d'une pizza?** how about a pizza?; **on dirait qu'elle a trouvé ce qu'elle cherchait** it looks as if she's found what she was looking for; **vouloir ~** mean; **à vrai ~** to tell the truth; **ça veut tout ~** that says it all; **et ~ que** and to think that; **cela va sans ~** that goes without saying; **cela ne me dit rien de faire …** I'm not particularly keen on doing …, I don't feel like doing … **2** m: **au(x) ~(s) de qn** according to s.o.

direct, ~e [dirɛkt] direct; **train** m **~** through train; **en ~** *émission* live; **directement** adv directly

directeur, -trice [dirɛktœr, -tris] **1** adj *comité* management **2** m/f manager; *plus haut dans la hiérarchie* director; ÉDU principal, Br head teacher; **direction** f *(sens)* direction; *(gestion, directeurs)* management; AUTO steering; **sous la ~ de Simon Rattle** MUS under the baton of Simon Rattle, conducted by Simon Rattle; **~ assistée** power steering; **directive** f instruction; *de l'UE* directive

dirigeable [diriʒabl] m airship; **dirigeant** m *surtout* POL leader; **diriger** ⟨1l⟩ manage, run; *pays* lead; *orchestre* conduct; *voiture* steer; *arme, critique* aim (**contre** at); *regard, yeux* turn (**vers** to); *personne* direct; **se ~ vers** head for

discernement [disɛrnəmɑ̃] m discernment; **discerner** ⟨1a⟩ *(percevoir)* make out; **~ le bon du mauvais** tell good from bad

disciplinaire [disiplinɛr] disciplinary; **discipline** f discipline; **discipliné, ~e** disciplined

disc-jockey [diskʒɔke] m disc jockey, DJ

disco [disko] m disco

discontinu, ~e [diskɔ̃tiny] *ligne* broken; *effort* intermittent

discordant, ~e [diskɔrdɑ̃, -t] discordant, unmusical; **discorde** f discord

discothèque [diskɔtɛk] f *(boîte)* discotheque, disco; *collection* record library

discours [diskur] m speech; **faire** ou **prononcer un ~** give a speech

discréditer [diskredite] ⟨1a⟩ discredit

discret, -ète [diskrɛ, -t] *(qui n'attire pas l'attention)* unobtrusive; *couleur* quiet; *robe* plain, simple; *(qui garde le secret)* discreet; **discrétion** f discretion; **à la ~ de qn** at s.o.'s discretion

discrimination [diskriminasjɔ̃] f discrimination

disculper [diskylpe] ⟨1a⟩ clear, exonerate; **se ~** clear o.s.

discussion [diskysjɔ̃] f discussion; *(altercation)* argument; **discutable** debatable; **discuter** ⟨1a⟩ discuss; *(contester)* question

diseur, -euse [dizœr, øz] m/f: **~ de bonne aventure** fortune-teller

disgracier [disgrasje] ⟨1a⟩ dismiss

disjoindre [disʒwɛ̃dr] ⟨4b⟩ separate

disjoncter [disʒɔ̃kte] ⟨1a⟩ **1** vt ÉL break **2** vi F be crazy; **disjoncteur** m circuit breaker

disparaître [disparɛtr] ⟨4z⟩ disappear; *(mourir)* die; *d'une espèce* die out; **faire ~** get rid of

disparité [disparite] f disparity

disparition [disparisjɔ̃] f disappearance; *(mort)* death; **être en voie de ~** be dying out, be becoming extinct; **espèce en voie de ~** endangered species

dispensaire [dispɑ̃sɛr] m clinic; **dispenser** ⟨1a⟩: **~ qn de (faire) qch** *(exempter)* excuse s.o. from (doing) sth; **je vous dispense de vos**

commentaires I can do without your comments; *je peux me ~ de faire la cuisine* I don't need to cook

disperser [dispɛrse] ⟨1a⟩ disperse; *se ~ (faire trop de choses)* spread o.s. too thin

disponibilité [disponibilite] *f* availability; **disponible** available

dispos [dispo]: *frais et ~* bright-eyed and bushy-tailed F

disposé, ~e [dispoze] disposed; **disposer** ⟨1a⟩ *(arranger)* arrange; *~ de qn / qch* have s.o. / sth at one's disposal; *se ~ à faire qch* get ready to do sth; **dispositif** *m* device; **disposition** *f (arrangement)* arrangement; *d'une loi* provision; *(humeur)* mood; *(tendance)* tendency; *être à la ~ de qn* be at s.o.'s disposal; *avoir qch à sa ~* have sth at one's disposal; *prendre ses ~s pour faire qch* make arrangements to do sth; *avoir des ~s pour qch* have an aptitude for sth

disproportionné, ~e [disproporsjone] disproportionate

dispute [dispyt] *f* quarrel, dispute; **disputer** ⟨1a⟩ *match* play; *~ qch à qn* compete with s.o for sth.; *se ~* quarrel, fight

disqualification [diskalifikasjõ] *f* disqualification; **disqualifier** ⟨1a⟩ disqualify

disque [disk] *m* disk, *Br* disc; *SP* discus; *MUS* disk, *Br* record; *INFORM* disk; *~ compact* compact disc; *~ dur* hard disk; **disquette** *f* diskette, disk, floppy; *~ de démonstration* demo disk

dissension [disãsjõ] *f le plus souvent au pl* **~s** dissension *sg*

disséquer [diseke] ⟨1f *et* 1m⟩ dissect

dissertation [disɛrtasjõ] *f* ÉDU essay

dissident, ~e [disidã, -t] *m/f* dissident

dissimuler [disimyle] ⟨1a⟩ conceal, hide *(à* from)

dissiper [disipe] ⟨1a⟩ dispel; *brouillard* disperse; *fortune* squander; *se ~ du brouillard* clear

dissociation [disɔsjasjõ] *f fig* separation

dissolu, ~e [disɔly] dissolute

dissolution [disɔlysjõ] *f* POL dissolution

dissolvant [disɔlvã] *m* CHIM solvent; *pour les ongles* nail polish remover

dissoudre [disudr] ⟨4bb⟩ dissolve

dissuader [disɥade] ⟨1a⟩: *~ qn de faire qch* dissuade s.o. from doing sth, persuade s.o. not to do sth; **dissuasif, -ive** off-putting; **dissuasion** *f* dissuasion; *~ nucléaire* POL nuclear deterrent

distance [distãs] *f* distance *(aussi fig)*; *commande f à ~* remote control; *tenir qn à ~* keep s.o. at a distance; *prendre ses ~s avec qn* distance o.s. from s.o.; **distancer** ⟨1k⟩ outdistance; **distant, ~e** distant *(aussi fig)*

distiller [distile] ⟨1a⟩ distill; **distillerie** *f* distillery

distinct, ~e [distɛ̃, -kt] distinct; *~ de* different from; **distinctement** *adv* distinctly

distinctif, -ive [distɛ̃ktif, -iv] distinctive; **distinction** *f* distinction

distingué, ~e [distɛ̃ge] distinguished; **distinguer** ⟨1m⟩ *(percevoir)* make out; *(différencier)* distinguish *(de* from); *se ~ (être différent)* stand out *(de* from)

distraction [distraksjõ] *f (passe-temps)* amusement, entertainment; *(inattention)* distraction

distraire [distrɛr] ⟨4s⟩ *du travail, des soucis* distract *(de* from); *(divertir)* amuse, entertain; *se ~* amuse o.s.; **distrait, ~e** absent-minded; **distraitement** *adv* absent-mindedly

distribuer [distribɥe] ⟨1n⟩ distribute; *courrier* deliver; **distributeur** *m* distributor; *~ automatique* vending machine; *~ de billets* ticket machine; *~ de boissons* drinks machine; **distribution** *f* distribution; *du courrier* delivery

district [distrikt] *m* district

dit, ~e [di, -t] **1** *p/p* → **dire 2** *adj (surnommé)* referred to as; *(fixé)* appointed

divaguer [divage] ⟨1m⟩ talk nonsense

dont

divan [divã] *m* couch

divergence [diverʒãs] *f* *d'opinions* difference; **diverger** ⟨1l⟩ *de lignes* diverge; *d'opinions* differ

divers, ~e [diver, -s] *(différent)* different, varied; *au pl* *(plusieurs)* various

diversification [diversifikasjõ] *f* diversification; **diversifier** ⟨1a⟩ diversify

diversion [diversjõ] *f* diversion

diversité [diversite] *f* diversity

divertir [divertir] ⟨2a⟩ amuse, entertain; **divertissant, ~e** entertaining; **divertissement** *m* amusement, entertainment

dividende [dividãd] *m* dividend

divin, ~e [divɛ̃, -in] divine; **divinité** *f* divinity

diviser [divize] ⟨1a⟩ divide *(aussi fig, MATH)*; *tâche, somme, domaine* divide up; *se ~* be divided *(en* into); **division** *f* division

divorce [divors] *m* divorce; **demander le ~** ask for a divorce; **divorcé, ~e** *m/f* divorcee; **divorcer** ⟨1k⟩ get a divorce *(d'avec* from)

divulguer [divylge] ⟨1m⟩ divulge, reveal

dix [dis] *fem*; → **trois**; **dix-huit** eighteen; **dix-huitième** eighteenth; **dixième** tenth; **dix-neuf** nineteen; **dix-neuvième** nineteenth; **dix-sept** seventeen; **dix-septième** seventeenth

dizaine [dizɛn] *f*: **une ~ de** about ten *pl*, ten or so *pl*

D.J. [didʒe] *m/f abr* *(= disc-jockey)* DJ, deejay *(= disc jockey)*

do [do] *m* MUS C

docile [dosil] docile

docteur [doktœr] *m* doctor; **doctorat** *m* doctorate, PhD; **doctoresse** *f* F woman doctor

doctrine [doktrin] *f* doctrine

document [dokymã] *m* document; **documentaire** *m* & *adj* documentary; **documentation** *f* documentation; **documenter** ⟨1a⟩: **se ~** collect information

dodo [dodo] *m* F: **faire ~** go to beddy-byes F

dodu, ~e [dody] chubby

dogmatique [dogmatik] dogmatic; **dogme** *m* dogma

doigt [dwa] *m* finger; **~ de pied** toe; **croiser les ~s** keep one's fingers crossed; **savoir qch sur le bout des ~s** have sth at one's fingertips; **doigté** *m* MUS fingering; *fig* tact

dollar [dolar] *m* dollar

domaine [domɛn] *m* estate; *fig* domain

dôme [dom] *m* dome

domestique [domestik] **1** *adj* domestic; *animal* **~** pet **2** *m* servant; **domestiquer** ⟨1m⟩ tame

domicile [domisil] *m* place of residence; **domicilié, ~e** *à* resident at

dominant, ~e [dominã, -t] dominant; **dominateur, -trice** domineering; **domination** *f* domination; **dominer** ⟨1a⟩ **1** *v/t* dominate *(aussi fig)* **2** *v/i* *(prédominer)* be predominant; *se* **~** control o.s.

dommage [domaʒ] *m*: **(quel) ~!** what a pity!; **c'est ~ que** (+ *subj*) it's a pity; **~s et intérêts** JUR damages

dompter [dõte] ⟨1a⟩ *animal* tame; *rebelle* subdue; **dompteur** *m* trainer

DOM-TOM [domtom] *mpl abr* *(= départements et territoires d'outre-mer)* overseas departments and territories of France

don [dõ] *m* *(donation)* donation; *charité* donation, gift; *(cadeau)* gift, present; *(aptitude)* gift; **~ du ciel** godsend; **donation** *f* donation

donc [dõk] *conclusion* so; **écoutez ~!** do listen!; **comment ~?** how (so)?; **allons ~!** come on!

donjon [dõʒõ] *m* keep

donné, ~e [done] **1** *p/p* → **donner 2** *adj* given; **étant ~** given; **c'est ~** I'm / he's / etc giving it away; **données** *fpl* data *sg*, information *sg*; INFORM data *sg*; **donner** ⟨1a⟩ **1** *v/t* give **2** *v/i*: **~ sur la mer** overlook the sea, look onto the sea; **donneur** *m* MÉD donor

dont [dõ]: **le film ~ elle parlait** the movie she was talking about; **une famille ~ le père est parti** a family whose father has left; **la manière ~**

elle me regardait the way (in which) she was looking at me; *celui ~ il s'agit* the one it is about; *ce ~ j'ai besoin* what I need; *plusieurs sujets, ~ le sexe* several subjects including sex

dopage [dɔpaʒ] *m* drug taking; **doper** ⟨1a⟩ drug; *se ~* take drugs

doré, ~e [dɔre] *bijou* gilt, gilded; *couleur* golden

dorénavant [dɔrenavã] from now on

dorer [dɔre] ⟨1a⟩ gild

dorloter [dɔrlɔte] ⟨1a⟩ pamper

dormeur, -euse [dɔrmœr, -øz] *m/f* sleeper; **dormir** ⟨2b⟩ sleep; *histoire f à ~ debout* tall tale, *Br* tall story

dortoir [dɔrtwar] *m* dormitory

dos [do] *m* back; *d'un chèque* back, reverse; *~ d'âne m* speed bump; *pont* hump-backed bridge

dosage [dozaʒ] *m* MÉD dose

dose [doz] *f* MÉD dose; PHARM proportion; **doser** ⟨1a⟩ measure out

dossier [dosje] *m d'une chaise* back; *de documents* file, dossier; *~ médical* medical record(s)

doter [dote] ⟨1a⟩ endow

douane [dwan] *f* customs *pl*; **douanier, -ère** [dwanje, -ɛr] **1** *adj* customs *atr* **2** *m/f* customs officer

doublage [dublaʒ] *m d'un vêtement* lining; *d'un film* dubbing; **double** [dubl] **1** *adj* double **2** *m deuxième exemplaire* duplicate; *au tennis* doubles (match); *le ~* double, twice as much; **doubler** ⟨1a⟩ **1** *v/t* double; AUTO pass, *Br* overtake; *film* dub; *vêtement* line **2** *v/i* double; **doublon** *m* double; **doublure** *f d'un vêtement* lining

doucement [dusmã] *adv* gently; *(bas)* softly; *(lentement)* slowly; **douceur** *f d'une personne* gentleness; *~s (jouissance)* pleasures; *(sucreries)* sweet things

douche [duʃ] *f* shower; *prendre une ~* shower, take a shower

doué, ~e [dwe] ⟨1a⟩ gifted; *~ de qch* endowed with sth

douille [duj] *f* ÉL outlet, *Br* socket

douillet, ~te [duje, -t] *lit, vêtement, intérieur* cozy, *Br* cosy; *personne* baby-

ish

douleur [dulœr] *f* pain

douloureux, -euse [dulurø, -z] painful

doute [dut] *m* doubt; *sans ~* without doubt; *sans aucun ~* undoubtedly; **douter** ⟨1a⟩: *~ de qn / qch* doubt s.o. / sth; *se ~ de qch* suspect sth; *se ~ que* suspect that, have an idea that; **douteux, -euse** doubtful

doux, douce [du, -s] sweet; *temps* mild; *personne* gentle; *au toucher* soft

douzaine [duzen] *f* dozen; **douze** twelve; → *trois*; **douzième** twelfth

Dow-Jones [dowdʒons] *m*: *indice m ~* Dow Jones Average

doyen [dwajē] *m* doyen; *d'une université* dean

draconien, ~ne [drakɔnjē, -ɛn] draconian

dragée [draʒe] *f* sugared almond

dragon [dragõ] *m* dragon

draguer [drage] *rivière* dredge; *F femmes* try to pick up; **dragueur** *m F* ladies' man

drainage [drenaʒ] *m* drainage; **drainer** ⟨1a⟩ drain

dramatique [dramatik] dramatic *(aussi fig)*; **dramatiser** ⟨1a⟩ dramatize; **dramaturge** *m* playwright; **drame** *m* drama; *fig* tragedy, drama

drap [dra] *m de lit* sheet

drapeau [drapo] *m (pl -x)* flag

drap-housse [draus] *m* fitted sheet

dressage [dresaʒ] *m d'un échafaudage, d'un monument* erection; *d'une tente* pitching; *d'un animal* training; **dresser** ⟨1b⟩ put up; *échafaudage, monument* erect, put up; *tente* pitch, put up; *contrat* draw up; *animal* train; *~ qn contre qn* set s.o. against s.o.; *se ~* straighten up; *d'une tour* rise up; *d'un obstacle* arise

drogue [drɔg] *f* drug; *~ douce* soft drug; *~ récréative* recreational drug; **drogué, ~e** *m/f* drug addict; **droguer** ⟨1a⟩ drug; MÉD *(traiter)* give medication to; *se ~* take drugs; MÉD *péj* pop pills; **droguerie** *f* hardware store

droit, ~e [drwa, -t] **1** *adj côté* right; *li-*

gne straight; (*debout*) erect; (*honnête*) upright **2** *adv* **tout ~** straight ahead **3** *m* right; (*taxe*) fee; JUR law; **de ~** de facto; **à qui de ~** to whom it may concern; **être en ~ de faire qch** be entitled to do sth; **~s d'auteur** royalties; **~ international** international law

droite [drwat] *f* right; **côté** right-hand side; **à ~** on the right(-hand side); **droitier, -ère: être ~** be right-handed; **droiture** *f* rectitude

drôle [drol] (*amusant, bizarre*) funny; **une ~ d'idée** a funny idea; **drôlement** *adv* F awfully

dromadaire [drɔmadɛr] *m* dromedary

dru, ~e [dry] thick

drugstore [drœgstɔr] *m* drugstore

D.S.T. [deɛste] *f abr* (= **direction de la surveillance du territoire**) French secret service

du [dy] → **de**

dû, due [dy] *p/p* → **devoir**

dubitatif, -ive [dybitatif, -iv] doubtful; **dubitativement** *adv* doubtfully

duc [dyk] *m* duke

duchesse [-ɛs] *f* duchess

duel [dɥɛl] *m* duel

dûment [dymã] *adv* duly

dune [dyn] *f* (sand) dune

Dunkerque [dɛ̃kɛrk] Dunkirk

duo [dyo] *m* MUS duet

dupe [dyp] *f* dupe; **être ~ de qch** be taken in by sth; **duper** ⟨1a⟩ dupe

duplex [dyplɛks] *m* duplex

duplicata [dyplikata] *m* duplicate

duquel [dykɛl] → **lequel**

dur, ~e [dyr] **1** *adj* hard (*aussi difficile, sévère*); *climat* harsh; *viande* tough **2** *adv travailler, frapper* hard; **durable** durable, lasting; *croissance, utilisation de matières premières* sustainable; **durant** *prép* during; **des années ~** for years

durcir [dyrsir] ⟨2a⟩ **1** *v/t* harden (*aussi fig*) **2** *v/i*: **se ~** harden; **durcissement** *m* hardening (*aussi fig*)

durée [dyre] *f* duration; **~ de vie** life; *d'une personne* life expectancy

durement [dyrmã] *adv* harshly; **être frappé ~ par** be hard hit by

durer [dyre] ⟨1a⟩ last; *d'un objet, vêtement aussi* wear well

dureté [dyrte] *f* hardness

duvet [dyvɛ] *m* down; (*sac de couchage*) sleeping bag; **duveteux, -euse** fluffy

DVD [devede] *m abr* DVD (= digitally versatile disk); **DVD-Rom** *m* DVD-Rom

dynamique [dinamik] **1** *adj* dynamic **2** *f* dynamics; **dynamisme** *m* dynamism

dynamite [dinamit] *f* dynamite

dynamo [dinamo] *f* dynamo

dynastie [dinasti] *f* dynasty

dyslexie [dislɛksi] *f* dyslexia; **dyslexique** dyslexic

E

eau [o] *f* (*pl* -x) water; **~x internationales** international waters; **tomber à l'~** fall in the water; *fig* fall through; **faire ~** MAR take in water; **mettre à l'~** *navire* launch; **~ courante** running water; **~ gazeuse** carbonated water, *Br* fizzy water; **~ de Javel** bleach; **~ minérale** mineral water

eau-de-vie [odvi] *f* (*pl* eaux-de-vie) brandy

ébahi, ~e [ebai] dumbfounded

ébattre [ebatr] ⟨4a⟩: **s'~** frolic

ébauche [eboʃ] *f* *d'une peinture* sketch; *d'un roman* outline; *d'un texte* draft; **ébaucher** ⟨1a⟩ *tableau, roman* rough out; *texte* draft; **~ un sourire**

smile faintly

ébène [ebɛn] *f* ebony

ébéniste [ebenist] *m* cabinetmaker

éberlué, ~e [ebɛrlɥe] F flabbergasted F

éblouir [ebluir] ⟨2a⟩ dazzle (*aussi fig*); **éblouissement** *m* glare, dazzle; **éblouissant, ~e** dazzling

éboueur [ebwœr] *m* garbageman, *Br* dustman

éboulement [ebulmã] *m* landslide; **éboulis** *m* pile

ébouriffé, ~e [eburife] tousled; **ébouriffer** ⟨1a⟩ *cheveux* ruffle

ébranler [ebrãle] ⟨1a⟩ shake; **s'~** move off

ébréché, ~e [ebreʃe] chipped

ébriété [ebrijete] *f* inebriation; **en état d'~** in a state of inebriation

ébruiter [ebrɥite] ⟨1a⟩ *nouvelle* spread

ébullition [ebylisjõ] *f* boiling point; **être en ~** be boiling

écaille [ekaj] *f de coquillage, tortue* shell; *de poisson* scale; *de peinture, plâtre* flake; *matière* tortoiseshell; **écailler** ⟨1a⟩ *poisson* scale; *huître* open; **s'~** *de peinture* flake (off); *de vernis à ongles* chip

écarlate [ekarlat] *f & adj* scarlet

écarquiller [ekarkije] ⟨1a⟩: **~ les yeux** open one's eyes wide

écart [ekar] *m* (*intervalle*) gap; (*différence*) difference; *moral* indiscretion; **à l'~** at a distance (*de* from)

écarteler [ekartəle] ⟨1d⟩ *fig*: **être écartelé** be torn

écartement [ekartəmã] *m* space; *action* spacing; **écarter** ⟨1a⟩ *jambes* spread; *fig: idée, possibilité* reject; *danger* avert; **s'~ de** (*s'éloigner*) stray from

ecclésiastique [eklezjastik] ecclesiastical

écervelé, ~e [esɛrvəle] scatterbrained

échafaudage [eʃafodaʒ] *m* scaffolding; **échafauder** ⟨1a⟩ **1** *v/i* erect scaffolding **2** *v/t fig*: *plan* put together

échalote [eʃalɔt] *f* BOT shallot

échancré, ~e [eʃãkre] low-cut; **échancrure** *d'une robe* neckline; *d'une côte* cove

échange [eʃãʒ] *m* exchange; **~s extérieurs** foreign trade *sg*; **en ~** in exchange (*de* for); **échanger** ⟨1l⟩ exchange, trade (*contre* for); *regards, lettres* exchange (*avec* with); **échangeur** *m* interchange; **échangisme** *m* partner swapping

échantillon [eʃãtijõ] *m* COMM sample; **~ gratuit** free sample

échappatoire [eʃapatwar] *f* way out; **échappée** *f de vue* vista; **en cyclisme** breakaway; **échappement** *m* AUTO exhaust; *tuyau m d'~* tail pipe; **échapper** ⟨1a⟩: **~ à qn** *d'une personne* escape from s.o.; **~ à qch** escape sth; *l'~ belle* have a narrow escape; **s'~** escape; *le verre lui échappa des mains* the glass slipped from his fingers; *un cri lui échappa, il laissa ~ un cri* he let out a cry

écharde [eʃard] *f* splinter

écharpe [eʃarp] *f* scarf; *de maire* sash; **en ~** MÉD in a sling

échasse [eʃas] *f* stilt

échauffement [eʃofmã] *m* heating; SP warm-up; **échauffer** ⟨1a⟩ heat; **s'~** SP warm up; **~ les esprits** get people excited

échéance [eʃeãs] *f* COMM, JUR *d'un contrat* expiration date, *Br* expiry date; *de police* maturity; **à brève / longue ~** short- / long-term; **arriver à ~** fall due

échéant, ~e [eʃeã, -t]: *le cas ~* if necessary

échec [eʃɛk] *m* failure; *essuyer ou subir un ~* meet with failure

échecs [eʃɛk] *mpl* chess *sg*; *jouer aux ~* play chess

échelle [eʃɛl] *f* ladder; *d'une carte, des salaires* scale; *sur une grande ~* on a grand scale; *à l'~ mondiale* on a global scale; **~ des salaires** salary scale

échelon [eʃlõ] *m* rung; *fig* level; *de la hiérarchie* grade, echelon; **échelonner** ⟨1a⟩ *paiements* spread, stagger (*sur un an* over a year)

échevelé, ~e [eʃəvle] disheveled, *Br* dishevelled

125

écoute

échine [eʃin] *f* spine (*aussi fig*); **plier ou courber l'~** give in; **échiner** ⟨1a⟩ F: **s'~ à faire qch** go to great lengths to do sth

échiquier [eʃikje] *m* chessboard

écho [eko] *m* echo

échographie [ekografi] *f* ultrasound (scan)

échoir [eʃwar] ⟨3m⟩ *d'un délai* expire

échotier, -ère [ekotje, -ɛr] *m/f* gossip columnist

échouer [eʃwe] ⟨1a⟩ fail; **(s')~** *d'un bateau* run aground

éclabousser [eklabuse] ⟨1a⟩ spatter

éclair [eklɛr] *m* flash of lightning; CUIS éclair; **comme un ~** in a flash; **éclairage** *m* lighting

éclaircie [eklɛrsi] *f* clear spell; **éclaircir** ⟨2a⟩ lighten; *fig: mystère* clear up; **s'~** *du ciel* clear, brighten

éclairer [eklere] ⟨1b⟩ **1** *v/t* light; **~ qn** light the way for s.o.; *fig:* **~ qn sur qch** enlighten s.o. about sth **2** *v/i:* **cette ampoule n'éclaire pas assez** this bulb doesn't give enough light; **éclaireur** *m* scout

éclat [ekla] *m de verre* splinter; *de métal* gleam; *des yeux* sparkle; *de couleurs, fleurs* vividness; **~ de rire** peal of laughter; **faire un ~** *scandale* make a fuss; **un ~ d'obus** a piece of shrapnel

éclatant, ~e [eklatɑ̃, -t] dazzling; *couleur* vivid; *rire* loud; **éclater** ⟨1a⟩ *d'une bombe* blow up; *d'une chaudière* explode; *d'un ballon, pneu* burst; *d'un coup de feu* ring out; *d'une guerre, d'un incendie* break out; *fig: d'un groupe, parti* break up; **~ de rire** burst out laughing; **~ en sanglots** burst into tears; **~ de santé** be blooming

éclipse [eklips] *f* eclipse; **éclipser** ⟨1a⟩ eclipse (*aussi fig*); **s'~** F vanish, disappear

éclore [eklɔr] ⟨4k⟩ *d'un oiseau* hatch out; *de fleurs* open

écluse [eklyz] *f* lock

écœurant, ~e [ekœrɑ̃, -t] disgusting, sickening; *aliment* sickly; *(décourageant)* discouraging, disheartening; **écœurement** *m* disgust; *(décourage-*ment)* discouragement; **il a mangé de la crème jusqu'à l'~** he ate cream until he felt sick; **écœurer** ⟨1a⟩ disgust, sicken; *(décourager)* discourage, dishearten; **~ qn** *d'un aliment* make s.o. feel nauseous, *Br aussi* make s.o. feel sick

école [ekɔl] *f* school; **~ maternelle** nursery school; **~ primaire** elementary school, *Br* primary school; **~ privée (du secondaire)** private school; **~ publique** state school; **~ secondaire** secondary school; **écolier** *m* schoolboy; **écolière** *f* schoolgirl

écolo [ekɔlo] *m* F Green

écologie [ekɔlɔʒi] *f* ecology; **écologique** ecological; **écologiste** *m/f* ecologist

économe [ekɔnɔm] economical, thrifty

économie [ekɔnɔmi] *f* economy; *science* economics *sg*; *vertu* economy, thriftiness; **~ de marché** market economy; **~ planifiée** planned economy; **~ souterraine** black economy; **~s** savings; **faire des ~s** save; **économique** economic; *(avantageux)* economical; **économiser** ⟨1a⟩ **1** *v/t* save **2** *v/i* save; **~ sur qch** save on sth; **économiseur** *m* **d'écran** INFORM screen saver; **économiste** *m/f* economist

écorce [ekɔrs] *f d'un arbre* bark; *d'un fruit* rind

écorcher [ekɔrʃe] ⟨1a⟩ *animal* skin; *(égratigner)* scrape; *fig: nom, mot* murder

écossais, ~e [ekɔsɛ, -z] **1** *adj* Scottish **2** *m/f* **Écossais, ~e** Scot; **Écosse** *f:* **l'~** Scotland

écosser [ekɔse] ⟨1a⟩ shell

écosystème [ekɔsistɛm] *m* ecosystem

écoulement [ekulmɑ̃] *m* flow; COMM sale; **système** *m* **d'~ des eaux usées** drainage; **écouler** ⟨1a⟩ COMM sell; **s'~** flow; *du temps* pass; COMM sell

écourter [ekurte] ⟨1a⟩ shorten; *vacances* cut short

écoute [ekut] *f:* **être à l'~** be always

listening out; *aux heures de grande* ~ RAD at peak listening times; TV at peak viewing times; *mettre qn sur table d'*~ TÉL tap s.o.'s phone; **écouter** ⟨1a⟩ **1** *v/t* listen to **2** *v/i* listen; **écouteur** *m* TÉL receiver; ~**s** RAD headphones

écran [ekrã] *m* screen; *porter à l'*~ TV adapt for television; *le grand* ~ the big screen; *le petit* ~ the small screen; ~ *d'aide* INFORM help screen; ~ *radar* radar screen; ~ *solaire* sunblock; ~ *tactile* touch screen; ~ *total* sunblock

écrasant, ~**e** [ekrazã, -t] overwhelming; **écraser** ⟨1a⟩ (*broyer, accabler, anéantir*) crush; *cigarette* stub out; (*renverser*) run over; *s'*~ *au sol* *d'un avion* crash

écrémé, ~**e** [ekreme]: *lait m* ~ skimmed milk; **écrémer** ⟨1f⟩ skim

écrevisse [ekrəvis] *f* crayfish

écrier [ekrije] ⟨1a⟩: *s'*~ cry out

écrin [ekrɛ̃] *m* jewel case

écrire [ekrir] ⟨4f⟩ write; *comment est-ce que ça s'écrit?* how do you spell it?

écrit [ekri] *m* document; *l'*~ *examen* the written exam; *par* ~ in writing

écriteau [ekrito] *m* (*pl* -x) notice; **écriture** *f* writing; COMM entry; *les* (*Saintes*) *Écritures* Holy Scripture *sg*

écrivain [ekrivɛ̃] *m* writer

écrou [ekru] *m* (*pl* -s) nut

écrouer [ekrue] ⟨1a⟩ JUR imprison

écrouler [ekrule] ⟨1a⟩: *s'*~ collapse

écru, ~**e** [ekry] *couleur* natural

écueil [ekœj] *m* reef; *fig* pitfall

écuelle [ekɥɛl] *f* bowl

éculé, ~**e** [ekyle] *chaussure* down-at--heel, worn-out; *fig* hackneyed

écume [ekym] *f* foam; **écumer** ⟨1a⟩ **1** *v/i* foam; ~ *de rage* be foaming at the mouth **2** *v/t* skim; *fig* scour; **écumeux**, -**euse** frothy

écureuil [ekyrœj] *m* squirrel

écurie [ekyri] *f* stable (*aussi* SP)

écusson [ekysõ] *m* coat of arms

écuyer, -**ère** [ekɥije, -ɛr] *m/f* rider

eczéma [egzema] *m* MÉD eczema

édenté, ~**e** [edãte] toothless

édifiant, ~**e** [edifjã, -t] edifying; **édification** *f* ARCH erecting; *fig*: *d'empire etc* creation; **édifice** *m* building; **édifier** ⟨1a⟩ ARCH erect; *fig* build up

Édimbourg [edɛ̃bur] Edinburgh

éditer [edite] ⟨1a⟩ *livre* publish; *texte* edit; **éditeur**, -**trice** *m/f* publisher; (*commentateur*) editor; **édition** *f action, métier* publishing; *action de commenter* editing; (*tirage*) edition; **maison** *f* **d'**~ publishing house; **éditorial** *m* (*pl* -iaux) editorial

édredon [edredõ] *m* eiderdown

éducateur, -**trice** [edykatœr, -tris] *m/f* educator; ~ *spécialisé* special needs teacher; **éducatif**, -**ive** educational; **éducation** *f* (*enseignement*) education; (*culture*) upbringing; *il manque d'*~ he has no manners

édulcorer [edylkɔre] ⟨1a⟩ sweeten

éduquer [edyke] ⟨1m⟩ (*enseigner*) educate; (*élever*) bring up

effacé, ~**e** [efase] self-effacing

effacer [efase] ⟨1k⟩ erase; *s'*~ *d'une inscription* wear away; *d'une personne* fade into the background

effarant, ~**e** [efarã, -t] frightening; **effarement** *m* fear; **effarer** ⟨1a⟩ frighten

effaroucher [efaruʃe] ⟨1a⟩ *personne* scare; *gibier* scare away

effectif, -**ive** [efɛktif, -iv] **1** *adj* effective **2** *m* manpower, personnel; **effectivement** *adv* true enough

effectuer [efɛktɥe] ⟨1a⟩ carry out

efféminé, ~**e** [efemine] *péj* effeminate

effervescence [efɛrvesãs] *f* POL ferment; **effervescent**, ~**e** *boisson* effervescent; *fig: foule* excited

effet [efɛ] *m* effect; COMM bill; *à cet* ~ with that in mind, to that end; *en* ~ sure enough; *faire de l'*~ have an effect; ~**s** (*personal*) effects; ~ *de serre* greenhouse effect; ~**s** *spéciaux* special effects

effeuiller [efœje] ⟨1a⟩ leaf through

efficace [efikas] *remède, médicament* effective; *personne* efficient; **efficacité** *f* effectiveness; *d'une personne* efficiency

effigie [efiʒi] *f* effigy

effilé, **~e** [efile] tapering

efflanqué, **~e** [eflɑ̃ke] thin

effleurer [eflœre] ⟨1a⟩ brush against; (*aborder*) touch on; **~ qch du bout des doigts** brush one's fingers against sth

effondrement [efɔ̃drǝmɑ̃] *m* collapse; **effondrer** ⟨1a⟩: **s'~** collapse

efforcer [eforse] ⟨1k⟩: **s'~ de faire qch** try very hard to do sth

effort [efor] *m* effort; **faire un ~** make an effort, try a bit harder

effraction [efraksjɔ̃] *f* JUR breaking and entering

effrayant, **~e** [efrejɑ̃, -t] frightening; **effrayer** ⟨1i⟩ frighten; **s'~** be frightened (**de** at)

effréné, **~e** [efrene] unbridled; *course* frantic

effriter [efrite] ⟨1a⟩: **s'~** crumble away (*aussi fig*)

effroi [efrwa] *m* fear

effronté, **~e** [efrɔ̃te] impertinent; **effronterie** *f* impertinence, effrontery

effroyable [efrwajabl] terrible, dreadful

effusion [efyzjɔ̃] *f*: **~ de sang** bloodshed; **~s** *litt* effusiveness *sg*

égal, **~e** [egal] (*mpl* -aux) **1** *adj* equal; *surface* even; *vitesse* steady; **ça lui est ~** it's all the same to him **2** *m* equal; **d'~ à ~** between equals; **sans ~** unequaled, *Br* unequalled; **également** *adv* (*pareillement*) equally; (*aussi*) as well, too; **égaler** ⟨1a⟩ equal; **égaliser 1** *v/t* ⟨1a⟩ *haies*, *cheveux* even up; *sol* level **2** *v/i* SP tie the game, *Br* equalize; **égalité** *f* equality; *en tennis* deuce; **être à ~** be level; *en tennis* be at deuce

égard [egar] *m*: **à cet ~** in that respect; **à l'~ de qn** to(ward) s.o.; **se montrer patient à l'~ de qn** be patient with s.o.; **par ~ pour** out of consideration for; **~s** respect *sg*; **manque** *m* **d'~s** lack of consideration

égarer [egare] ⟨1a⟩ *personne* lead astray; *chose* lose; **s'~** get lost; *du sujet* stray from the point

égayer [egeje] ⟨1i⟩ cheer up; *chose*, *pièce aussi* brighten up

églantine [eglɑ̃tin] *f* dog rose

église [egliz] *f* church

égocentrique [egosɑ̃trik] egocentric

égoïsme [egoism] *m* selfishness, egoism; **égoïste 1** *adj* selfish **2** *m/f* egoist; **~! **you're so selfish!

égorger [egorʒe] ⟨1l⟩: **~ qn** cut s.o.'s throat

égosiller [egozije] ⟨1a⟩: **s'~** shout

égout [egu] *m* sewer

égoutter [egute] ⟨1a⟩ drain; **égouttoir** *m* (**à vaisselle**) drain board, *Br* draining board

égratigner [egratiɲe] ⟨1a⟩ scratch; **s'~** scratch; **égratignure** *f* scratch

égrener [egrǝne] ⟨1d⟩ *épi* remove the kernels from; *grappe* pick the grapes from

Égypte [eʒipt] *f*: **l'~** Egypt; **égyptien**, **~ne 1** *adj* Egyptian **2** *m/f* Égyptien, **~ne** Egyptian

éhonté, **~e** [eɔ̃te] barefaced, shameless

éjecter [eʒɛkte] ⟨1a⟩ TECH eject; F *personne* kick out

élaboré, **~e** [elabore] sophisticated; **élaborer** ⟨1a⟩ *projet* draw up

élaguer [elage] ⟨1m⟩ *arbre* prune

élan[1] [elɑ̃] *m* momentum; SP run-up; *de tendresse* upsurge; *de générosité* fit; (*vivacité*) enthusiasm

élan[2] [elɑ̃] *m* ZO elk

élancement [elɑ̃smɑ̃] *m* twinge; *plus fort* shooting pain; **élancer** ⟨1k⟩ *v/i*: **ma jambe m'élance** I've got shooting pains in my leg; **s'~** dash; SP take a run-up

élargir [elarʒir] ⟨2a⟩ widen, broaden; *vêtement* let out; *débat* widen, extend the boundaries of

élasticité [elastisite] *f* elasticity

élastique [elastik] **1** *adj* elastic **2** *m* elastic; *de bureau* rubber band, *Br aussi* elastic band

électeur, **-trice** [elɛktœr, -tris] *m/f* voter; **élection** *f* election; **électoral**, **~e** (*mpl* -aux) election *atr*; **électorat** *m* droit franchise; *personnes* electorate

électricien, **~ne** [elɛktrisjɛ̃, -ɛn] *m/f*

electrician; **électricité** *f* electricity; **~ statique** static (electricity); **électrification** *f* electrification; **électrifier** ⟨1a⟩ electrify; **électrique** electric; **électriser** ⟨1a⟩ electrify

électrocardiogramme [elɛktrokardjɔgram] *m* MÉD electrocardiogram, ECG

électrocuter [elɛktrɔkyte] ⟨1a⟩ electrocute

électroménager [elɛktromenaʒe]: **appareils** *mpl* **~s** household appliances

électronicien, ~ne [elɛktrɔnisjɛ̃, -ɛn] *m/f* electronics expert; **électronique 1** *adj* electronic **2** *f* electronics

électrophone [elɛktrɔfɔn] *m* record player

électrotechnicien, ~ne [elɛktroteknisjɛ̃, -ɛn] *m/f* electrical engineer; **électrotechnique** *f* electrical engineering

élégamment [elegamɑ̃] *adv* elegantly; **élégance** *f* elegance; **élégant, ~e** elegant

élément [elemɑ̃] *m* element; (*composante*) component; *d'un puzzle* piece; **~s** (*rudiments*) rudiments; **élémentaire** elementary

éléphant [elefɑ̃] *m* elephant

élevage [elvaʒ] *m* breeding, rearing; **~ (du bétail)** cattle farming; **~ en batterie** battery farming

élévation [elevasjɔ̃] *f* elevation; *action de lever* raising; *d'un monument, d'une statue* erection; (*montée*) rise

élève [elɛv] *m/f* pupil

élevé, ~e [elve] high; *esprit* noble; *style* elevated; **bien / mal ~** well / badly brought up; **c'est très mal ~ de faire ça** it's very rude to do that; **élever** ⟨1d⟩ raise; *prix, température* raise, increase; *statue, monument* put up, erect; *enfants* bring up, raise; *animaux* rear, breed; **s'~** rise; *d'une tour* rise up; *d'un cri* go up; **s'~ contre** rise up against; **s'~ à** amount to; **éleveur, -euse** *m/f* breeder

éligible [eliʒibl] eligible

élimé, ~e [elime] threadbare

élimination [eliminasjɔ̃] *f* elimination; *des déchets* disposal; **éliminatoire** *f* qualifying round; **éliminer** ⟨1a⟩ eliminate; *difficultés* get rid of

élire [elir] ⟨4x⟩ elect

élite [elit] *f* elite

elle [ɛl] *f* ◊ *personne* she; *après prép* her; **c'est pour ~** it's for her; **je les ai vues, ~ et sa sœur** I saw them, her and her sister; **~ n'aime pas ça, ~** she doesn't like that; **ta grand-mère a-t-~ téléphoné?** did your grandmother call?

◊ *chose* it; **ta robe?, ~ est dans la machine à laver** your dress?, it's in the washing machine

elle-même [ɛlmɛm] herself; *chose* itself

elles [ɛl] *fpl* they; *après prép* them; **les chattes sont~ rentrées?** have the cats come home?; **je les ai vues hier, ~ et leurs maris** I saw them yesterday, them and their husbands; **~, elles ne sont pas contentes** they are not happy; **ce sont ~ qui** they are the ones who

elles-mêmes [ɛlmɛm] themselves

élocution [elɔkysjɔ̃] *f* way of speaking; **défaut** *m* **d'~** speech defect

éloge [elɔʒ] *m* praise; **faire l'~ de** praise; **élogieux, -euse** full of praise

éloigné, ~e [elwaɲe] remote

éloignement [elwaɲmɑ̃] *m* distance, remoteness; **éloigner** ⟨1a⟩ move away, take away; *soupçon* remove; **s'~** move away (*de* from); **s'~ de qn** distance o.s. from s.o.

élongation [elɔ̃gasjɔ̃] *f* MÉD pulled muscle

éloquemment [elɔkamɑ̃] *adv* eloquently; **éloquence** *f* eloquence; **éloquent, ~e** eloquent

élu, ~e 1 *p/p* → **élire 2** *adj*: **le président ~** the President elect **3** *m/f* POL (elected) representative; **l'heureux ~** the lucky man

élucider [elyside] ⟨1a⟩ *mystère* clear up; *question* clarify, elucidate *fml*

éluder [elyde] ⟨1a⟩ *fig* elude

Élysée [elize]: **l'~** the Elysée Palace (*where the French president lives*)

émacié, ~e [emasje] emaciated

e-mail [imɛl] *m* e-mail; ***envoyer un ~ à qn*** send s.o. an e-mail, e-mail s.o.

émail [emaj] *m* (*pl* émaux) enamel

émancipation [emɑ̃sipasjɔ̃] *f* emancipation; **émanciper** ⟨1a⟩ emancipate; ***s'~*** become emancipated

émaner [emane] ⟨1a⟩: ***~ de*** emanate from

emballage [ɑ̃balaʒ] *m* packaging; **emballer** ⟨1a⟩ package; *fig* F thrill; ***s'~ d'un moteur*** race; *fig* F get excited; ***emballé sous vide*** vacuum packed

embarcadère [ɑ̃barkadɛr] *m* MAR landing stage; **embarcation** *f* boat

embargo [ɑ̃bargo] *m* embargo

embarquement [ɑ̃barkəmɑ̃] *m* MAR *d'une cargaison* loading; *de passagers* embarkation; **embarquer** ⟨1m⟩ **1** *v/t* load **2** *v/i ou* ***s'~*** embark; ***s'~ dans*** F get involved in

embarras [ɑ̃bara] *m* difficulty; (*gêne*) embarrassment; ***être dans l'~*** be in an embarrassing position; *sans argent* be short of money; ***n'avoir que l'~ du choix*** be spoiled for choice

embarrassant, ~e [ɑ̃barasɑ̃, -t] (*gênant*) embarrassing; (*encombrant*) cumbersome; **embarrassé, ~e** (*gêné*) embarrassed; **embarrasser** ⟨1a⟩ (*gêner*) embarrass; (*encombrer*) *escaliers* clutter up

embauche [ɑ̃boʃ] *f* recruitment, hiring; ***offre f d'~*** job offer; **embaucher** ⟨1a⟩ take on, hire

embaumer [ɑ̃bome] ⟨1a⟩ *corps* embalm; ***~ la lavande*** smell of lavender

embellir [ɑ̃belir] ⟨1a⟩ **1** *v/t* make more attractive; *fig* embellish **2** *v/i* become more attractive

embêtant, ~e [ɑ̃bɛtɑ̃, -t] F annoying; **embêtement** *m* F: ***avoir des ~s*** be in trouble; **embêter** F ⟨1a⟩ (*ennuyer*) bore; (*contrarier*) annoy; ***s'~*** be bored

emblée [ɑ̃ble]: ***d'~*** right away, immediately

emblème [ɑ̃blɛm] *m* emblem

emboîter [ɑ̃bwate] ⟨1a⟩ insert; ***~ le pas à qn*** fall into step with s.o. (*aussi fig*); ***s'~*** fit together

embolie [ɑ̃bɔli] *f* embolism; ***~ pulmonaire*** pulmonary embolism

embonpoint [ɑ̃bɔ̃pwɛ̃] *m* stoutness, embonpoint *fml*

embouchure [ɑ̃buʃyr] *f* GÉOGR mouth; MUS mouthpiece

embourber [ɑ̃burbe] ⟨1a⟩: ***s'~*** get bogged down

embouteillage [ɑ̃buteja3] *m* traffic jam; **embouteiller** ⟨1b⟩ *rue* block

emboutir [ɑ̃butir] ⟨2a⟩ crash into

embranchement [ɑ̃brɑ̃ʃmɑ̃] *m* branch; (*carrefour*) intersection, *Br* junction

embrasser [ɑ̃brase] ⟨1a⟩ kiss; *période, thème* take in, embrace; *métier* take up; ***~ du regard*** take in at a glance

embrasure [ɑ̃brazyr] *f* embrasure; ***~ de porte*** doorway

embrayage [ɑ̃breja3] *m* AUTO clutch; *action* letting in the clutch

embrouiller [ɑ̃bruje] ⟨1a⟩ muddle; ***s'~*** get muddled

embruns [ɑ̃brœ̃, -œ̃] *mpl* MAR spray *sg*

embryon [ɑ̃brijɔ̃] *m* embryo; **embryonnaire** embryonic

embûches [ɑ̃byʃ] *fpl fig* traps

embuer [ɑ̃bɥe] ⟨1a⟩ *vitre* steam up

embuscade [ɑ̃buskad] *f* ambush

éméché, ~e [emeʃe] F tipsy

émeraude [ɛmrod] *f* & *adj* emerald

émerger [emɛrʒe] ⟨1l⟩ emerge

émerveillement [emɛrvɛjmɑ̃] *m* wonder; **émerveiller** ⟨1a⟩ amaze; ***s'~*** be amazed (***de*** by)

émetteur [emɛtœr] *m* RAD, TV transmitter

émettre [emɛtr] ⟨4p⟩ *radiations etc* give off, emit; RAD, TV broadcast, transmit; *opinion* voice; COMM *action*, FIN *nouveau billet, nouvelle pièce* issue; *emprunt* float

émeute [emøt] *f* riot; ***~ raciale*** race riot

émietter [emjete] ⟨1b⟩ crumble

émigrant, ~e [emigrɑ̃, -t] *m/f* emigrant; **émigration** *f* emigration; **émigré, ~e** *m/f* emigré; **émigrer** ⟨1a⟩ emigrate

émincer [emɛ̃se] ⟨1k⟩ cut into thin slices

éminence [eminɑ̃s] *f* (*colline*) hill;

Éminence Eminence; éminent, ~e eminent

émirat [emira] m: **les Émirats arabes unis** the United Arab Emirates

émissaire [emiser] m emissary; **émission** f emission; RAD, TV program, Br programme; COMM, FIN issue

emmagasiner [ãmagazine] ⟨1a⟩ store

emmêler [ãmele] ⟨1a⟩ fils tangle; fig muddle

emménager [ãmenaʒe] ⟨1l⟩: ~ **dans** move into

emmener [ãmne] ⟨1d⟩ take

emmerder [ãmɛrde] ⟨1a⟩ F: ~ **qn** get on s.o.'s nerves; **s'~** be bored rigid

emmitoufler [ãmitufle] ⟨1a⟩ wrap up; **s'~** wrap up

émoi [emwa] m commotion

émotif, -ive [emotif, -iv] emotional

émotion [emosjõ] f emotion; F (frayeur) fright; **émotionnel, ~le** emotional

émousser [emuse] ⟨1a⟩ blunt, take the edge off (aussi fig)

émouvant, ~e [emuvã, -t] moving; **émouvoir** ⟨3d⟩ (toucher) move, touch; **s'~** be moved, be touched

empailler [ãpaje] ⟨1a⟩ animal stuff

empaqueter [ãpakte] ⟨1c⟩ pack

emparer [ãpare] ⟨1a⟩: **s'~ de** seize; clés, héritage grab; des doutes, de la peur overcome

empâter [ãpate] ⟨1a⟩: **s'~** thicken

empêchement [ãpɛʃmã] m: **j'ai eu un~** something has come up; **empêcher** ⟨1b⟩ prevent; ~ **qn de faire qch** prevent ou stop s.o. doing sth; **(il) n'empêche que** nevertheless; **je n'ai pas pu m'en ~** I couldn't help it

empereur [ãprœr] m emperor

empester [ãpɛste] ⟨1a⟩: **elle empeste le parfum** she reeks ou stinks of perfume

empêtrer [ãpɛtre] ⟨1b⟩: **s'~ dans** get tangled ou caught up in

emphase [ãfaz] f emphasis

empiéter [ãpjete] ⟨1f⟩: ~ **sur** encroach on

empiffrer [ãpifre] ⟨1a⟩ F: **s'~** stuff o.s.

empiler [ãpile] ⟨1a⟩ pile (up), stack (up)

empire [ãpir] m empire; fig (maîtrise) control

empirer [ãpire] ⟨1a⟩ get worse, deteriorate

empirique [ãpirik] empirical

emplacement [ãplasmã] m site

emplette [ãplɛt] f purchase; **faire des ~s** go shopping

emplir [ãplir] ⟨2a⟩ fill; **s'~** fill (de with)

emploi [ãplwa] m (utilisation) use; ÉCON employment; ~ **du temps** schedule, Br timetable; **plein ~** full employment; **un ~** a job; **chercher un ~** be looking for work ou for a job

employé, ~e [ãplwaje] m/f employee; ~ **de bureau** office worker; ~ **à temps partiel** part-timer; **employer** ⟨1h⟩ use; personnel employ; **s'~ à faire qch** strive to do sth; **employeur, -euse** m/f employer

empocher [ãpoʃe] ⟨1a⟩ pocket

empoigner [ãpwaɲe] ⟨1a⟩ grab, seize

empoisonnement [ãpwazɔnmã] m: ~ **du sang** blood poisoning; **empoisonner** ⟨1a⟩ poison

emporter [ãpɔrte] ⟨1a⟩ take; prisonnier take away; (entraîner, arracher) carry away ou off; du courant sweep away; d'une maladie carry off; **l'~** win the day; **l'~ sur qn / qch** get the better of s.o. / sth; **s'~** fly into a rage

empoté, ~e [ãpote] clumsy

empreinte [ãprɛt] f impression; fig stamp; ~ **digitale** fingerprint; ~ **génétique** genetic fingerprint

empressement [ãprɛsmã] m eagerness; **empresser** ⟨1b⟩: **s'~ de faire qch** rush to do sth; **s'~ auprès de qn** be attentive to s.o.

emprise [ãpriz] f hold

emprisonnement [ãprizɔnmã] m imprisonment; **emprisonner** ⟨1a⟩ imprison

emprunt [ãprɛ̃, -œ̃] m loan; **emprunté, ~e** fig self-conscious; **emprunter** ⟨1a⟩ borrow (à from); chemin, escalier take

ému, ~e [emy] **1** p/p → **émouvoir 2** adj moved, touched

en[1] [ã] *prép* ◊ *lieu* in; **~ France** in France; **~ ville** in town

◊ *direction* to; **~ France** to France; **~ ville** to ou into town

◊ *temps* in; **~ 1789** in 1789; **~ l'an 1789** in the year 1789; **~ été** in summer; **~ 10 jours** in 10 days

◊ *mode: agir* **~ ami** act as a friend; **~ cercle** in a circle; **~ vente** for ou on sale; **~ français** in French; **habillé ~ noir** dressed in black; **se déguiser ~ homme** disguise o.s. as a man

◊ *transport* by; **~ voiture / avion** by car / plane

◊ *matière:* **~ or** of gold; **une bague ~ or** a gold ring

◊ *après verbes, adj, subst: croire* **~ Dieu** believe in God; **riche ~ qch** rich in sth; **avoir confiance ~ s.o.** have confidence in s.o.

◊ *avec gérondif:* **en même temps** while, when; *mode* by; **~ détachant soigneusement les ...** by carefully detaching the ...; **~ rentrant chez moi, j'ai remarqué que ...** when I came home ou on coming home I noticed that ...; **je me suis cassé une dent ~ mangeant ...** I broke a tooth while ou when eating ...

en[2] [ã] *pron* ◊: **qu'~ pensez-vous?** what do you think about it?; **tu es sûr de cela? - oui, j'~ suis sûr** are you sure about that? - yes, I'm sure; **j'~ suis** count me in

◊: **il y ~ a deux** there are two (of them); **il n'y ~ a plus** there's none left; **j'~ ai** I have some; **j'~ ai cinq** I have five; **je n'~ ai pas** I don't have any; **qui ~ est le propriétaire?** who's the owner?, who does it belong to?; **voici trois** here are three (of them)

◊ *cause:* **je n'~ suis pas plus heureux** I'm none the happier for it; **il ~ est mort** he died of it

◊ *provenance:* **le gaz ~ sort** the gas comes out (of it); **tu as vu le grenier? - oui, j'~ viens** have you seen the attic? - yes, I've just been up there

encadrer [ãkadre] ⟨1a⟩ *tableau* frame; **encadré de deux gendarmes** *fig*

flanked by gendarmes, with a gendarme on either side

encaisser [ãkese] ⟨1b⟩ COMM take; *chèque* cash; *fig* take

encart [ãkar] *m* insert

en-cas [ãka] *m* (*pl inv*) CUIS snack

encastrable [ãkastrabl] *four etc* which can be built in; **encastrer** ⟨1a⟩ TECH build in

enceinte[1] [ãsɛ̃t] pregnant

enceinte[2] [ãsɛ̃t] *f* enclosure; **~ (acoustique)** speaker

encens [ãsã] *m* incense

encéphalopathie *f* **spongiforme bovine** [ãsefalɔpatispɔ̃ʒifɔrmbɔvin] *f* bovine spongiform encephalitis

encercler [ãsɛrkle] ⟨1a⟩ encircle

enchaînement [ãʃɛnmã] *m* d'événements series *sg*; **enchaîner** ⟨1b⟩ *chien, prisonnier* chain up; *fig: pensées, faits* connect, link up

enchanté, ~e [ãʃãte] enchanted; **~!** how do you do?; **enchantement** *m* enchantment; (*ravissement*) delight; **enchanter** ⟨1a⟩ (*ravir*) delight; (*ensorceler*) enchant

enchère [ãʃɛr] *f* bid; **vente** *f* **aux ~s** auction; **mettre aux ~s** put up for auction; **vendre aux ~s** sell at auction, auction off

enchevêtrer [ãʃ(ə)vetre] ⟨1b⟩ tangle; *fig: situation* confuse; **s'~ de fils** get tangled up; *d'une situation* get muddled

enclave [ãklav] *f* enclave

enclencher [ãklãʃe] ⟨1a⟩ engage; **s'~** engage

enclin, ~e [ãklɛ̃, -in]: **être ~ à faire qch** be inclined to do sth

enclos [ãklo] *m* enclosure

enclume [ãklym] *f* anvil

encoche [ãkɔʃ] *f* notch

encoller [ãkɔle] ⟨1a⟩ glue

encolure [ãkɔlyr] *f* neck; *tour de cou* neck (size)

encombrant, ~e [ãkɔ̃brã, -t] cumbersome; **être ~** d'une personne be in the way; **encombrement** *m* trafic congestion; *d'une profession* overcrowding; **encombrer** ⟨1a⟩ *maison* clutter up; *rue, passage* block; **s'~ de** load o.s.

down with

encontre [ãkõtr]: *aller à l'~ de* go against, run counter to

encore [ãkɔr] **1** *adv* ◊ *de nouveau* again; *il nous faut essayer ~ (une fois)* we'll have to try again ◊ *temps (toujours)* still; *est-ce qu'il pleut ~?* is it still raining?; *elles ne sont pas ~ rentrées* they still haven't come back, they haven't come back yet; *non, pas ~* no, not yet ◊ *de plus*: *~ une bière?* another beer?; *est-ce qu'il y a ~ des …?* are there any more …?; *~ plus rapide / belle* even faster / more beautiful

2 *conj*: *~ que* (+ *subj*) although

encourageant, ~e [ãkuraʒã, -t] encouraging; **encouragement** *m* encouragement; **encourager** ⟨1l⟩ encourage; *projet, entreprise* foster

encourir [ãkurir] ⟨2i⟩ incur

encrasser [ãkrase] ⟨1a⟩ dirty; *s'~* get dirty

encre [ãkr] *f* ink; **encrier** *m* inkwell

encroûter [ãkrute] ⟨1a⟩: *s'~ fig* get stuck in a rut

encyclopédie [ãsiklɔpedi] *f* encyclopedia

endetter [ãdete] ⟨1b⟩: *s'~* get into debt

endeuillé, ~e [ãdœje] bereaved

endiablé, ~e [ãdjable] *fig* frenzied, demonic

endimanché, ~e [ãdimãʃe] in one's Sunday best

endive [ãdiv] *f* BOT, CUIS chicory

endoctriner [ãdɔktrine] ⟨1a⟩ indoctrinate

endolori, ~e [ãdɔlɔri] painful

endommager [ãdɔmaʒe] ⟨1l⟩ damage

endormi, ~e [ãdɔrmi] asleep; *fig* sleepy; **endormir** ⟨2b⟩ send *ou* lull to sleep; *douleur* dull; *s'~* fall asleep

endosser [ãdose] ⟨1a⟩ *vêtement* put on; *responsabilité* shoulder; *chèque* endorse

endroit [ãdrwa] *m* (*lieu*) place; *d'une étoffe* right side

enduire [ãdɥir] ⟨4c⟩: *~ de* cover with;

enduit m de peinture coat

endurance [ãdyrãs] *f* endurance

endurcir [ãdyrsir] ⟨2a⟩ harden; *fig* toughen up, harden; **endurcissement** *m* hardening

endurer [ãdyre] ⟨1a⟩ endure

énergétique [enerʒetik] energy *atr*; *repas* energy-giving; **énergie** *f* energy; *~ solaire* solar energy; **énergique** energetic; *protestation* strenuous; **énergiquement** *adv* energetically; *nier* strenuously

énervant, ~e [enervã, -t] irritating; **énervé, ~e** (*agacé*) irritated; (*à bout de nerfs*) on edge, edgy; **énerver** ⟨1a⟩: *~ qn* (*agacer*) get on s.o.'s nerves; (*agiter*) make s.o. excited; *s'~* get excited

enfance [ãfãs] *f* childhood

enfant [ãfã] *m ou f* child; *~ modèle* model child, goody-goody *péj*; *~ prodige* child prodigy; *~s à charge* dependent children *pl*

enfantillage [ãfãtijaʒ] *m* childishness; **enfantin, ~e** *air* childlike; *voix* of a child, child's; (*puéril*) childish; (*très simple*) elementary; *c'est ~* it's child's play

enfer [ãfer] *m* hell (*aussi fig*)

enfermer [ãferme] ⟨1a⟩ shut *ou* lock up; *champ* enclose; *s'~* shut o.s. up

enfiler [ãfile] ⟨1a⟩ *aiguille* thread; *perles* string; *vêtement* slip on; *rue* turn into

enfin [ãfɛ̃] (*finalement*) at last; (*en dernier lieu*) lastly, last; (*bref*) in a word; *mais ~, ce n'est pas si mal* come on, it's not that bad; *nous étions dix, ~ onze* there were ten of us, well eleven; *~ et surtout* last but not least

enflammer [ãflame] ⟨1a⟩ set light to; *allumette* strike; MÉD inflame; *fig: imagination* fire; *s'~* catch; MÉD become inflamed; *fig: de l'imagination* take flight

enfler [ãfle] ⟨1a⟩ *membre* swell; **enflure** *f* swelling

enfoncer [ãfõse] ⟨1k⟩ **1** *v/t clou, pieu* drive in; *couteau* thrust, plunge (*dans* into); *porte* break down **2** *v/i dans sable etc* sink (*dans* into); *s'~* sink; *s'~ dans la forêt* go deep into the forest

enfouir [ɑ̃fwir] ⟨2a⟩ bury

enfourcher [ɑ̃furʃe] ⟨1a⟩ *cheval, bicyclette* mount

enfourner [ɑ̃furne] ⟨1a⟩ put in the oven; *fig* F (*avaler*) gobble up

enfreindre [ɑ̃frɛ̃dr] ⟨4b⟩ infringe

enfuir [ɑ̃fɥir] ⟨2d⟩: **s'~** run away

enfumé, ~e [ɑ̃fyme] smoky

engagé, ~e [ɑ̃gaʒe] **1** *adj* committed **2** *m* MIL volunteer

engagement [ɑ̃gaʒmɑ̃] *m* (*obligation*) commitment; *de personnel* recruitment; THÉÂT booking; (*mise en gage*) pawning

engager [ɑ̃gaʒe] ⟨1l⟩ (*lier*) commit (*à* to); *personnel* hire; TECH (*faire entrer*) insert; *conversation, discussion* begin; (*entraîner*) involve (*dans* in); THÉÂT book; (*mettre en gage*) pawn; **cela ne vous engage à rien** this in no way commits you; **s'~** (*se lier*) commit o.s. (*à faire qch* to doing sth), promise (*à faire qch* to do sth); (*commencer*) begin; MIL enlist; **s'~ dans** get involved in; *rue* turn into

engelure [ɑ̃ʒlyr] *f* chillblain

engendrer [ɑ̃ʒɑ̃dre] ⟨1a⟩ *fig* engender

engin [ɑ̃ʒɛ̃] *m* machine; MIL missile; F *péj* thing

englober [ɑ̃glɔbe] ⟨1a⟩ (*comprendre*) include, encompass

engloutir [ɑ̃glutir] ⟨2a⟩ (*dévorer*) devour, wolf down; *fig* engulf, swallow up

engorger [ɑ̃gɔrʒe] ⟨1l⟩ *rue* block

engouement [ɑ̃gumɑ̃] *m* infatuation

engouffrer [ɑ̃gufre] ⟨1a⟩ devour, wolf down; **s'~ dans** *de l'eau* pour in; *fig*: *dans un bâtiment* rush into; *dans une foule* be swallowed up by

engourdir [ɑ̃gurdir] ⟨2a⟩ numb; **s'~** go numb

engrais [ɑ̃grɛ] *m* fertilizer; **engraisser** ⟨1a⟩ *bétail* fatten

engrenage [ɑ̃grənaʒ] *m* TECH gear

engueuler [ɑ̃gœle] ⟨1a⟩ F bawl out; **s'~** have an argument *ou* a fight

énigmatique [enigmatik] enigmatic; **énigme** *f* (*mystère*) enigma; (*devinette*) riddle

enivrement [ɑ̃nivrəmɑ̃] *m fig* exhilaration; **enivrer** ⟨1a⟩ intoxicate; *fig* exhilarate

enjambée [ɑ̃ʒɑ̃be] *f* stride; **enjamber** ⟨1a⟩ step across; *d'un pont* span, cross

enjeu [ɑ̃ʒø] *m* (*pl* -x) stake; **l'~ est important** *fig* the stakes are high

enjoliver [ɑ̃ʒɔlive] ⟨1a⟩ embellish; **enjoliveur** *m* AUTO wheel trim, hub cap

enjoué, ~e [ɑ̃ʒwe] cheerful, good-humored, *Br* good-humoured

enlacer [ɑ̃lase] ⟨1k⟩ *rubans* weave (*dans* through); (*étreindre*) put one's arms around; **s'~** *de personnes* hug

enlaidir [ɑ̃ledir] ⟨2a⟩ make ugly

enlèvement [ɑ̃lɛvmɑ̃] *m* (*rapt*) abduction, kidnap; **enlever** ⟨1d⟩ take away, remove; *tache* take out, remove; *vêtement* take off, remove; (*kidnapper*) abduct, kidnap; **~ qch à qn** take sth away from s.o.

enliser [ɑ̃lize] ⟨1a⟩: **s'~** get bogged down (*aussi fig*)

enneigé, ~e [ɑ̃neʒe] *route* blocked by snow; *sommet* snow-capped

ennemi, ~e [enmi] **1** *m/f* enemy **2** *adj* enemy *atr*

ennui [ɑ̃nɥi] *m* boredom; **~s** problems; **on lui a fait des ~s à la douane** he had a bit of bother *ou* a few problems at customs; **ennuyé, ~e** (*contrarié*) annoyed; (*préoccupé*) bothered; **ennuyer** ⟨1h⟩ (*contrarier, agacer*) annoy; (*lasser*) bore; **s'~** be bored; **ennuyeux, -euse** (*contrariant*) annoying; (*lassant*) boring

énoncé [enɔse] *m* statement; *d'une question* wording; **énoncer** ⟨1k⟩ state; **~ des vérités** state the obvious

enorgueillir [ɑ̃nɔrgœjir] ⟨2a⟩: **s'~ de qch** be proud of sth

énorme [enɔrm] enormous; **énormément** *adv* enormously; **~ d'argent** F an enormous amount of money; **énormité** *f* enormity; **dire des ~s** say outrageous things

enquérir [ɑ̃kerir] ⟨2l⟩: **s'~ de** enquire about

enquête [ɑ̃kɛt] *f* inquiry; *policière aus-*

si investigation; (*sondage d'opinion*) survey; **enquêter** ⟨1b⟩: **~ sur** investigate

enraciné, ~e [ɑ̃ʀasine] deep-rooted

enragé, ~e [ɑ̃ʀaʒe] MÉD rabid; *fig* fanatical

enrayer [ɑ̃ʀeje] ⟨1i⟩ jam; *fig: maladie* stop

enregistrement [ɑ̃ʀəʒistʀəmɑ̃] *m dans l'administration* registration; *de disques* recording; AVIAT check-in; **~ des bagages** check-in; **~ vidéo** video recording; **enregistrer** ⟨1a⟩ register; *disques* record; *bagages* check in; **enregistreur** *m*: **~ de vol** flight recorder, black box

enrhumé, ~e [ɑ̃ʀyme]: **être ~** have a cold; **enrhumer** ⟨1a⟩: **s'~** catch (a) cold

enrichir [ɑ̃ʀiʃiʀ] ⟨2a⟩ enrich; **s'~** get richer

enrôler [ɑ̃ʀole] ⟨1a⟩ MIL enlist

enroué, ~e [ɑ̃ʀwe] husky, hoarse; **enrouer** ⟨1a⟩: **s'~** get hoarse

enrouler [ɑ̃ʀule] ⟨1a⟩ *tapis* roll up; **~ qch autour de qch** wind sth around sth

ensanglanté, ~e [ɑ̃sɑ̃ɡlɑ̃te] bloodstained

enseignant, ~e [ɑ̃sɛɲɑ̃, -t] *m/f* teacher

enseigne [ɑ̃sɛɲ] *f* sign

enseignement [ɑ̃sɛɲmɑ̃] *m* education; *d'un sujet* teaching; **enseigner** ⟨1a⟩ teach; **~ qch à qn** teach s.o. sth; **~ le français** teach French

ensemble [ɑ̃sɑ̃bl] **1** *adv* (*simultanément*) together; *aller* **~** go together **2** *m* (*totalité*) whole; (*groupe*) group, set; MUS, *vêtement* ensemble; MATH set; **l'~ de la population** the whole *ou* entire population; **dans l'~** on the whole; **vue** *f* **d'~** overall picture

ensevelir [ɑ̃səvliʀ] ⟨2a⟩ bury

ensoleillé, ~e [ɑ̃soleje] sunny

ensommeillé, ~e [ɑ̃someje] sleepy, drowsy

ensorceler [ɑ̃sɔʀsəle] ⟨1c⟩ cast a spell on; *fig* (*fasciner*) bewitch

ensuite [ɑ̃sɥit] then; (*plus tard*) after

ensuivre [ɑ̃sɥivʀ] ⟨4h⟩: **s'~** ensue

entacher [ɑ̃taʃe] ⟨1a⟩ smear

entaille [ɑ̃taj] *f* cut; (*encoche*) notch; **entailler** ⟨1a⟩ notch; **s'~ la main** cut one's hand

entamer [ɑ̃tame] ⟨1a⟩ *pain, travail* start on; *bouteille, négociations* open, start; *conversation* start; *économies* make

entasser [ɑ̃tase] ⟨1a⟩ *choses* pile up, stack; *personnes* cram

entendre [ɑ̃tɑ̃dʀ] ⟨4a⟩ hear; (*comprendre*) understand; (*vouloir dire*) mean; **~ faire qch** intend to do sth; **on m'a laissé ~ que** I was given to understand that; **~ dire que** hear that; **avez-vous entendu parler de …?** have you heard of …?; **s'~** (*être compris*) be understood; **s'~** (*avec qn*) get on (with s.o.); (*se mettre d'accord*) come to an agreement (with s.o.); **cela s'entend** that's understandable

entendu, ~e [ɑ̃tɑ̃dy] *regard, sourire* knowing; **bien ~** of course; **très bien, c'est ~** it's settled then

entente [ɑ̃tɑ̃t] *f* (*accord*) agreement

enterrement [ɑ̃tɛʀmɑ̃] *m* burial; *cérémonie* funeral; **enterrer** ⟨1b⟩ bury

en-tête [ɑ̃tɛt] *m* (*pl* en-têtes) heading; INFORM header; COMM letterhead; *d'un journal* headline; **papier** *m* **à ~** headed paper

entêté, ~e [ɑ̃tɛte] stubborn; **entêtement** *m* stubbornness; **entêter** ⟨1b⟩: **s'~** persist (*dans* in; **à faire qch** in doing sth)

enthousiasme [ɑ̃tuzjasm] *m* enthusiasm; **enthousiasmer** ⟨1a⟩: **cette idée m'enthousiasme** I'm enthusiastic about *ou Br aussi* keen on the idea; **s'~ pour** be enthusiastic about; **enthousiaste** enthusiastic

enticher [ɑ̃tiʃe] ⟨1a⟩: **s'~ de** *personne* become infatuated with; *activité* develop a craze for

entier, -ère [ɑ̃tje, -ɛʀ] whole, entire; (*intégral*) intact; *confiance, satisfaction* full; **le livre en ~** the whole book, the entire book; **lait** *m* **~** whole milk; **entièrement** *adv* entirely

entonner [ɑ̃tone] ⟨1a⟩ *chanson* start

to sing

entonnoir [ɑ̃tɔnwar] *m* funnel

entorse [ɑ̃tɔrs] *f* MÉD sprain; *faire une ~ au règlement fig* bend the rules

entortiller [ɑ̃tɔrtije] ⟨1a⟩ (*envelopper*) wrap (*autour de* around; *dans* in)

entourage [ɑ̃tura3] *m* entourage; (*bordure*) surround; **entourer** ⟨1a⟩: **~ de** surround with; **s'~ de** surround o.s. with

entracte [ɑ̃trakt] *m* intermission

entraide [ɑ̃trɛd] *f* mutual assistance; **entraider** ⟨1b⟩: **s'~** help each other

entrailles [ɑ̃traj] *fpl d'un animal* intestines, entrails

entrain [ɑ̃trɛ̃] *m* liveliness; **entraînant, ~e** lively

entraînement [ɑ̃trɛnmɑ̃] *m* SP training; TECH drive; **entraîner** ⟨1b⟩ (*charrier, emporter*) sweep along; SP train; *fig* result in; *frais* entail; *personne* drag; TECH drive; **~ qn à faire qch** lead s.o. to do sth; **s'~** train; **entraîneur** *m* trainer

entrave [ɑ̃trav] *f fig* hindrance; **entraver** ⟨1a⟩ hinder

entre [ɑ̃tr] between; **~ les mains de qn** in s.o.'s hands; **le meilleur d'~ nous** the best of us; **~ autres** among other things; **il faut garder ce secret ~ nous** we have to keep the secret to ourselves; **~ nous, ...** between you and me, ...

entrebâiller [ɑ̃trəbaje] ⟨1a⟩ half open

entrechoquer [ɑ̃trəʃɔke] ⟨1m⟩: **s'~** knock against one another

entrecôte [ɑ̃trəkot] *f* rib steak

entrecouper [ɑ̃trəkupe] ⟨1a⟩ interrupt (*de* with)

entrecroiser [ɑ̃trəkrwaze] ⟨1a⟩ (**s'~**) crisscross

entrée [ɑ̃tre] *f lieu d'accès* entrance, way in; *accès au théâtre, cinéma* admission; (*billet*) ticket; (*vestibule*) entry (way); CUIS starter; INFORM *touche* enter (key); *de données* input, inputting; **d'~** from the outset; **~ gratuite** admission free; **~ interdite** no admittance

entrefilet [ɑ̃trəfilɛ] *m* short news item

entrejambe [ɑ̃trə3ɑ̃b] *m* crotch

entrelacer [ɑ̃trəlase] ⟨1k⟩ interlace, intertwine

entremêler [ɑ̃trəmele] ⟨1b⟩ mix; **entremêlé de** *fig* interspersed with

entremets [ɑ̃trəmɛ] *m* CUIS dessert

entremise [ɑ̃trəmiz] *f*: *par l'~ de* through (the good offices of)

entreposer [ɑ̃trəpoze] ⟨1a⟩ store; **entrepôt** *m* warehouse

entreprenant, ~e [ɑ̃trəprənɑ̃, -t] enterprising

entreprendre [ɑ̃trəprɑ̃dr] ⟨4q⟩ undertake; **entrepreneur, -euse** *m/f* entrepreneur; **~ des pompes funèbres** mortician, *Br* undertaker; **entreprise** *f* enterprise; (*firme*) company, business; *libre ~* free enterprise; *petites et moyennes ~s* small and medium-sized businesses

entrer [ɑ̃tre] ⟨1a⟩ **1** *v/i* (*aux être*) come / go in, enter; **~ dans** *pièce, gare etc* come / go into, enter; *voiture* get into; *pays* enter; *catégorie* fall into; *l'armée, le parti socialiste etc* join; *faire ~ visiteur* show in; *entrez!* come in!; **elle est entrée par la fenêtre** she got in through the window **2** *v/t* bring in; INFORM *données, texte* input, enter

entre-temps [ɑ̃trətɑ̃] *adv* in the meantime

entretenir [ɑ̃trətnir] ⟨2h⟩ *route, maison, machine etc* maintain; *famille* keep, support; *amitié* keep up; **s'~ de qch** talk to each other about sth

entretien [ɑ̃trətjɛ̃] *m* maintenance, upkeep; (*conversation*) conversation

entretuer [ɑ̃trətɥe] ⟨1n⟩: **s'~** kill each other

entrevoir [ɑ̃trəvwar] ⟨3b⟩ glimpse; *fig* foresee; **entrevue** *f* interview

entrouvrir [ɑ̃truvrir] ⟨2f⟩ half open

énumération [enymerasjõ] *f* list, enumeration; **énumérer** ⟨1f⟩ list, enumerate

envahir [ɑ̃vair] ⟨2a⟩ invade; *d'un sentiment* overcome, overwhelm; **envahissant, ~e** *personne* intrusive; *sentiments* overwhelming; **envahisseur** *m* invader

enveloppe [ãvlɔp] *f d'une lettre* envelope; *enveloper* ⟨1a⟩ wrap; *enveloppé de brume, mystère* enveloped in

envenimer [ãvnime] ⟨1a⟩ poison (*aussi fig*)

envergure [ãvɛrgyr] *f d'un oiseau, avion* wingspan; *fig* scope; *d'une personne* caliber, *Br* calibre

envers [ãvɛr] **1** *prép* toward, *Br* towards; *son attitude ~ ses parents* her attitude toward *ou* to her parents **2** *m d'une feuille* reverse; *d'une étoffe*: *wrong side; à l'~* pull inside out; (*en désordre*) upside down

enviable [ãvjabl] enviable

envie [ãvi] *f* (*convoitise*) envy; (*désir*) desire (*de* for); *avoir ~ de qch* want sth; *avoir ~ de faire qch* want to do sth; *envier* ⟨1a⟩ envy; *~ qch à qn* envy s.o. sth; *envieux, -euse* envious

environ [ãvirõ] **1** *adv* about **2** *mpl*: *~s* surrounding area *sg*; *dans les ~s* in the vicinity; *aux ~s de ville* in the vicinity of; *Pâques* around about; *environnant, ~e* surrounding; *environnement m* environment

envisager [ãvizaʒe] ⟨1l⟩ (*considérer*) think about, consider; (*imaginer*) envisage; *~ de faire qch* think about doing sth

envoi [ãvwa] *m* consignment, shipment; *action* shipment, dispatch; *d'un fax* sending

envoler [ãvɔle] ⟨1a⟩: *s'~* fly away; *d'un avion* take off (*pour* for); *fig: du temps* fly

envoûter [ãvute] ⟨1a⟩ bewitch

envoyé [ãvwaje] *m* envoy; *d'un journal* correspondent; *~ spécial* special envoy; *envoyer* ⟨1p⟩ send; *coup, gifle* give; *~ chercher* send for

éolienne [eɔljɛn] *f* wind turbine; *champ m d'~s* wind farm

épagneul [epaɲœl] *m* spaniel

épais, ~se [epɛ, -s] thick; *forêt, brouillard* thick, dense; *foule* dense; *épaisseur f* thickness; *épaissir* ⟨2a⟩ thicken

épancher [epãʃe] ⟨1a⟩: *s'~* pour out one's heart (*auprès de* to)

épanoui, ~e [epanwi] *femme, sourire* radiant; (*ouvert*) open; *épanouir* ⟨2a⟩: *s'~ d'une fleur* come up; (*se développer*) blossom; *épanouissement m* opening; (*développement*) blossoming

épargne [eparɲ] *f action* saving; *~s* (*économies*) savings; *épargne-logement f: plan d'~* savings plan for would-be house buyers; *épargneur, -euse m/f* saver

épargner [eparɲe] ⟨1a⟩ **1** *v/t* save; *personne* spare; *~ qch à qn* spare s.o. sth; *ne pas ~ qch* be generous with sth **2** *v/i* save

éparpiller [eparpije] ⟨1a⟩ scatter

épars, ~e [epar, -s] sparse

épatant, ~e [epatã, -t] F great, terrific; *épater* ⟨1a⟩ astonish

épaule [epol] *f* shoulder; *épauler* ⟨1a⟩ shoulder; *fig* support; *épaulette f* (*bretelle*) shoulderstrap; *de veste, manteau* shoulder pad; MIL epaulette

épave [epav] *f* wreck (*aussi fig*)

épée [epe] *f* sword

épeler [eple] ⟨1c⟩ spell

éperdu, ~e [epɛrdy] *besoin* desperate; *~ de* beside o.s. with

éperon [eprõ] *m* spur; *éperonner* ⟨1a⟩ spur on (*aussi fig*)

éphémère [efemer] *fig* short-lived, ephemeral

épi [epi] *m* ear; *stationnement m en ~* AUTO angle parking

épice [epis] *f* spice; *épicer* ⟨1k⟩ spice; *épicerie f* grocery store, *Br* grocer's; *épicier, -ère m/f* grocer

épidémie [epidemi] *f* epidemic

épier [epje] ⟨1a⟩ spy on; *occasion* watch for

épilation [epilasjõ] *f* removal of unwanted hair (*de* from); *épiler* ⟨1a⟩ remove the hair from

épilepsie [epilɛpsi] *f* epilepsy; *crise f d'~* epileptic fit; *épileptique m/f* epileptic

épilogue [epilɔg] *m* epilog, *Br* epilogue

épinards [epinar] *mpl* spinach *sg*

épine [epin] *f d'une rose* thorn; *d'un hérisson* spine, prickle; ~ **dorsale** backbone; **épineux, -euse** *problème* thorny

épingle [epɛ̃gl] *f* pin; ~ **de sûreté** ou **de nourrice** safety pin; *tiré à quatre* ~**s** *fig* well turned-out; **épingler** ⟨1a⟩ pin

Épiphanie [epifani] *f* Epiphany

épique [epik] epic

épisode [epizɔd] *m* episode

épitaphe [epitaf] *f* epitaph

éploré, ~e [eplɔre] tearful

éplucher [eplyʃe] ⟨1a⟩ peel; *fig* scrutinize; **épluchures** *fpl* peelings

éponge [epɔ̃ʒ] *f* sponge; **éponger** ⟨1l⟩ sponge down; *flaque* sponge up; *déficit* mop up

épopée [epɔpe] *f* epic

époque [epɔk] *f* age, epoch; *meubles mpl d'*~ period ou antique furniture *sg*

époumoner [epumɔne] ⟨1a⟩: *s'*~ F shout o.s. hoarse

épouse [epuz] *f* wife, spouse *fml*; **épouser** ⟨1a⟩ marry; *idées, principe etc* espouse

épousseter [epuste] ⟨1c⟩ dust

époustouflant, ~e [epustuflɑ̃, -t] F breathtaking

épouvantable [epuvɑ̃tabl] dreadful

épouvantail [epuvɑ̃taj] *m* (*pl* -s) scarecrow

épouvante [epuvɑ̃t] *f* terror, dread; *film m d'*~ horror film; **épouvanter** ⟨1a⟩ horrify; *fig* terrify

époux [epu] *m* husband, spouse *fml*; *les* ~ the married couple

éprendre [eprɑ̃dr] ⟨4q⟩: *s'*~ *de* fall in love with

épreuve [eprœv] *f* trial; SP event; *imprimerie* proof; *photographie* print; *à toute* ~ *confiance etc* never-failing; *à l'*~ *du feu* fireproof; *mettre à l'*~ put to the test, try out

éprouvant, ~e [epruvɑ̃, -t] trying; **éprouver** ⟨1a⟩ (*tester*) test, try out; (*ressentir*) feel, experience; *difficultés* experience; **éprouvette** *f* test tube

EPS *abr* (= **éducation physique et**

sportive) PE (= physical education)

épuisant, ~e [epɥizɑ̃, -t] punishing; **épuisé, ~e** exhausted; *livre* out of print; **épuisement** *m* exhaustion; **épuiser** ⟨1a⟩ exhaust; ~ *les ressources* be a drain on resources; *s'*~ tire o.s. out (*à faire qch* doing sth); *d'une source* dry up

épuration [epyrasjɔ̃] *f* purification; *station f d'*~ sewage plant; **épurer** ⟨1a⟩ purify

équateur [ekwatœr] *m* equator

Équateur [ekwatœr] *m*: *l'*~ Ecuador

équation [ekwasjɔ̃] *f* MATH equation

équatorien, ~ne [ekwatɔrjɛ̃, -en] **1** *adj* Ecuador(i)an **2** *m* **Équatorien, ~ne** Ecuador(i)an

équerre [eker] *f à dessin* set square

équestre [ekɛstr] *statue* equestrian

équilibre [ekilibr] *m* balance, equilibrium (*aussi fig*); **équilibré, ~e** balanced; **équilibrer** ⟨1a⟩ balance

équinoxe [ekinɔks] *m* equinox

équipage [ekipaʒ] *m* AVIAT, MAR crew

équipe [ekip] *f* team; *d'ouvriers* gang; *travail m en* ~ teamwork; ~ *de jour / de nuit* day / night shift; ~ *de secours* rescue party; **équipement** *m* equipment; **équiper** ⟨1a⟩ equip (*de* with)

équitable [ekitabl] just, equitable

équitation [ekitasjɔ̃] *f* riding, equestrianism

équité [ekite] *f* justice, equity

équivalence [ekivalɑ̃s] *f* equivalence; **équivalent, ~e 1** *adj* equivalent (*à* to) **2** *m* equivalent; **équivaloir** ⟨3h⟩: ~ *à* be equivalent to

équivoque [ekivɔk] **1** *adj* equivocal, ambiguous **2** *f* (*ambiguïté*) ambiguity; (*malentendu*) misunderstanding

érable [erabl] *m* BOT maple

érafler [erafle] ⟨1a⟩ *peau* scratch; **éraflure** *f* scratch

ère [er] *f* era

érection [erɛksjɔ̃] *f* erection

éreintant, ~e [erɛ̃tɑ̃, -t] exhausting, back-breaking; **éreinter** ⟨1a⟩ exhaust; *s'*~ exhaust o.s. (*à faire qch* doing sth)

E

ergothérapeute [ɛrgoterapøt] *m/f* occupational therapist; **ergothérapie** *f* occupational therapy

ériger [erize] ⟨1l⟩ erect; **s'~ en** set o.s. up as

ermite [ɛrmit] *m* hermit

éroder [erɔde] ⟨1a⟩ *(aussi fig)* erode; **érosion** *f* erosion

érotique [erɔtik] erotic; **érotisme** *m* eroticism

errant, ~e [ɛrɑ̃, -t] *personne, vie* roving; *chat, chien* stray; **errer** ⟨1b⟩ roam; *des pensées* stray

erreur [ɛrœr] *f* mistake, error; **par ~** by mistake; **~ de calcul** miscalculation; **~ judiciaire** miscarriage of justice; **erroné, ~e** wrong, erroneous *fml*

érudit, ~e [erydi, -t] erudite; **érudition** *f* erudition

éruption [erypsjɔ̃] *f* eruption; MÉD rash

ès [ɛs] *prép:* **docteur** *m* **~ lettres** PhD

escabeau [ɛskabo] *m (pl -x) (tabouret)* stool; *(marchepied)* stepladder

escadron [ɛskadrɔ̃] *m* squadron

escalade [ɛskalad] *f* climbing; **~ de violence etc** escalation in; **escalader** ⟨1a⟩ climb

escalator [ɛskalatɔr] *m* escalator

escale [ɛskal] *f* stopover; **faire ~ à** MAR call at; AVIAT stop over in

escalier [ɛskalje] *m* stairs *pl*, staircase; **dans l'~** on the stairs; **~ roulant** escalator; **~ de secours** fire escape; **~ de service** backstairs *pl*

escalope [ɛskalɔp] *f* escalope

escamotable [ɛskamɔtabl] retractable; **escamoter** ⟨1a⟩ *(dérober)* make disappear; *antenne* retract; *fig: difficulté* get around

escapade [ɛskapad] *f:* **faire une ~** get away from it all

escargot [ɛskargo] *m* snail

escarpé, ~e [ɛskarpe] steep; **escarpement** *m* slope; GÉOL escarpment

escarpin [ɛskarpɛ̃] *m* pump, *Br* court shoe

escient [ɛsjɑ̃] *m:* **à bon ~** wisely

esclaffer [ɛsklafe] ⟨1a⟩: **s'~** guffaw, laugh out loud

esclandre [ɛsklɑ̃dr] *m* scene

esclavage [ɛsklavaʒ] *m* slavery; **esclave** *m/f* slave

escompte [ɛskɔ̃t] *m* ÉCON, COMM discount; **escompter** ⟨1a⟩ discount; *fig* expect

escorte [ɛskɔrt] *f* escort; **escorter** ⟨1a⟩ escort

escrime [ɛskrim] *f* fencing; **escrimer** ⟨1a⟩: **s'~** fight, struggle (*à* to)

escroc [ɛskro] *m* crook, swindler

escroquer [ɛskrɔke] ⟨1m⟩ swindle; **~ qch à qn, ~ qn de qch** swindle s.o. out of sth; **escroquerie** *f* swindle

espace [ɛspas] *m* space; **~ aérien** airspace; **~s verts** green spaces; **espacer** ⟨1k⟩ space out; **s'~** become more and more infrequent

espadrille [ɛspadrij] *f* espadrille, rope sandal

Espagne [ɛspaɲ] *f* Spain; **espagnol, ~e 1** *adj* Spanish **2** *m langue* Spanish **3** *m/f* **Espagnol, ~e** Spaniard

espèce [ɛspɛs] *f* kind, sort (*de* of); BIOL species; **~ d'abruti!** *péj* idiot!; **en ~s** COMM cash

espérance [ɛsperɑ̃s] *f* hope; **~ de vie** life expectancy

espérer [ɛspere] ⟨1f⟩ **1** *v/t* hope for; **~ que** hope that; **~ faire qch** hope to do sth; **je n'en espérais pas tant** it's more than I'd hoped for **2** *v/i* hope; **~ en** trust in

espiègle [ɛspjɛgl] mischievous

espion, ~ne [ɛspjɔ̃, -ɔn] *m/f* spy; **espionnage** *m* espionage, spying; **espionner** ⟨1a⟩ spy on

esplanade [ɛsplanad] *f* esplanade

espoir [ɛspwar] *m* hope

esprit [ɛspri] *m* spirit; *(intellect)* mind; *(humour)* wit; **faire de l'~** show off one's wit; **perdre l'~** lose one's mind; **~ d'équipe** team spirit

Esquimau, ~de [ɛskimo, -d] *(mpl -x) m/f* Eskimo

esquinter [ɛskɛ̃te] ⟨1a⟩ F *voiture* smash up, total; *(fatiguer)* wear out

esquisse [ɛskis] *f* sketch; *fig: d'un roman* outline; **esquisser** ⟨1a⟩ sketch; *fig: projet* outline

esquiver [ɛskive] ⟨1a⟩ dodge; **s'~** slip away

essai [esɛ] *m* (*test*) test, trial; (*tentative*) attempt, try; *en rugby* try; *en littérature* essay; **à l'~, à titre d'~** on trial

essaim [esɛ̃] *m* swarm

essayage [esɛjaʒ] *m*: **cabine** *f* **d'~** changing cubicle; **essayer** ⟨1i⟩ try; (*mettre à l'épreuve, évaluer*) test; *plat, vin* try, taste; *vêtement* try on; **~ de faire qch** try to do sth; **s'~ à qch** try one's hand at sth

essence [esɑ̃s] *f* essence; *carburant* gas, *Br* petrol; BOT species *sg*

essentiel, ~le [esɑ̃sjɛl] **1** *adj* essential **2** *m*: **l'~** the main thing; *de sa vie* the main part; **n'emporter que l'~** take only the essentials

essieu [esjø] *m* (*pl* -x) axle

essor [esɔr] *m fig* expansion; **prendre un ~** expand rapidly

essorer [esɔre] ⟨1a⟩ *linge, à la main* wring out; *d'une machine à laver* spin; **essoreuse** *f* spindryer

essoufflé, ~e [esufle] out of breath, breathless; **essoufflement** *m* breathlessness

essuie-glace [esɥiglas] *m* (*pl inv ou* essuie-glaces) AUTO (windshield) wiper, *Br* (windscreen) wiper; **essuie-mains** *m* (*pl inv*) handtowel; **essuie-tout** kitchen towel *ou* paper

essuyer [esɥije] ⟨1h⟩ wipe; (*sécher*) wipe, dry; *fig* suffer

est [ɛst] **1** *m* east; **vent** *m* **d'~** east wind; **à l'~ de** (to the) east of **2** *adj* east, eastern; **côte** *f* **~** east *ou* eastern coast

estampe [ɛstɑ̃p] *f en cuivre* engraving, print

est-ce que [ɛskə] *pour formuler des questions*: **~ c'est vrai?** is it true?; **est-ce qu'ils se portent bien?** are they well?

esthéticienne [ɛstetisjɛn] *f* beautician

esthétique [ɛstetik] esthetic, *Br* aesthetic

estimable [ɛstimabl] estimable; *résultats, progrès* respectable; **estimatif, -ive** estimated; **devis** *m* **~** estimate; **estimation** *f* estimation; *des coûts* estimate

estime [ɛstim] *f* esteem; **estimer** ⟨1a⟩ *valeur, coûts* estimate; (*respecter*) have esteem for; (*croire*) feel, think; **s'~ heureux** consider o.s. lucky (**d'être accepté** to have been accepted)

estival, ~e [ɛstival] (*mpl* -aux) summer *atr*; **estivant, ~e** *m/f* summer resident

estomac [ɛstɔma] *m* stomach; **avoir mal à l'~** have stomach-ache

estomper [ɛstɔ̃pe] ⟨1a⟩: **s'~ de souvenirs** fade

Estonie [ɛstɔni] *f* Estonia; **estonien, ~ne 1** *adj* Estonian **2** *m langue* Estonian **3** *m/f* **Estonien, ~ne** Estonian

estrade [ɛstrad] *f* podium

estragon [ɛstragɔ̃] *m* tarragon

estropier [ɛstrɔpje] ⟨1a⟩ cripple

estuaire [ɛstɥɛr] *m* estuary

et [e] *and*; **~ ... ~ ...** both ... and ...

étable [etabl] *f* cowshed

établi [etabli] *m* workbench

établir [etablir] ⟨2a⟩ *camp, entreprise* establish, set up; *relations, contact, ordre* establish; *salaires, prix* set, fix; *facture, liste* draw up; *record* set; *culpabilité* establish, prove; *raisonnement, réputation* base (**sur** on); **s'~** (*s'installer*) settle; **s'~ à son compte** set up (in business) on one's own; **établissement** *m* establishment; *de salaires, prix* setting; *d'une facture, liste* drawing up; *d'un record* setting; *d'une loi, d'un impôt* introduction; **~ scolaire** educational establishment; **~ bancaire / hospitalier** bank / hospital; **~ industriel** factory; **~ thermal** spa

étage [etaʒ] *m* floor, story, *Br* storey; *d'une fusée* stage; **premier / deuxième ~** second / third floor, *Br* first / second floor

étagère [etaʒɛr] *f meuble* bookcase, shelves *pl*; *planche* shelf

étain [etɛ̃] *m* pewter

étalage [etalaʒ] *m* display; **faire ~ de qch** show sth off; **étaler** ⟨1a⟩ *carte* spread out, open out; *peinture, margarine* spread; *paiements* spread out (**sur** over); *vacances* stagger; *marchandises* display, spread out; *fig* (*exhiber*) show off; **s'~ de peinture**

spread; *de paiements* be spread out (*sur* over); (*s'afficher*) show off; (*se vautrer*) sprawl; *par terre* fall flat

étalon [etalɔ̃] *m* ZO stallion; *mesure* standard

étanche [etɑ̃ʃ] watertight; **étancher** ⟨1a⟩ TECH make watertight; *litt: soif* quench

étang [etɑ̃] *m* pond

étape [etap] *f lieu* stopover, stopping place; *d'un parcours* stage, leg; *fig* stage

état [eta] *m* state; *de santé, d'une voiture, maison* state, condition; (*liste*) statement, list; **~ civil** *bureau* registry office; *condition* marital status; **~ d'esprit** state of mind; **en tout ~ de cause** in any case, anyway; **être dans tous ses ~s** be in a right old state; **être en ~ de faire qch** be in a fit state to do sth; **hors d'~** out of order; **état-major** *m* (*pl* états-majors) MIL staff; **État-providence** *m* welfare state; **États-Unis** *mpl*: **les ~** the United States

étau [eto] *m* (*pl* -x) vise, *Br* vice

étayer [eteje] ⟨1i⟩ shore up

été[1] [ete] *m* summer; **en ~** in summer; **~ indien** Indian summer

été[2] [ete] *p/p* → **être**

éteindre [etɛ̃dr] ⟨4b⟩ *incendie, cigarette* put out, extinguish; *électricité, radio, chauffage* turn off; **s'~** *de feu, lumière* go out; *de télé etc* go off; *euph* (*mourir*) pass away

étendre [etɑ̃dr] ⟨4a⟩ *malade, enfant* lay (down); *beurre, enduit* spread; *peinture* apply; *bras* stretch out; *linge* hang up; *influence, pouvoir* extend; **s'~** extend, stretch (*jusqu'à* as far as, to); *d'une personne* lie down; *d'un incendie, d'une maladie* spread; *d'un tissu* stretch; **s'~ sur qch** dwell on sth

étendue [etɑ̃dy] *f extent; d'une eau* expanse; *de connaissances, affaires* extent, scope; *d'une catastrophe* extent, scale

éternel, ~le [etɛrnɛl] eternal; **éterniser** ⟨1a⟩ drag out; **s'~** drag on; **éternité** *f* eternity

éternuement [etɛrnymɑ̃] *m* sneeze; **éternuer** ⟨1n⟩ sneeze

Éthiopie [etjɔpi] *f*: **l'~** Ethiopia; **éthiopien, ~ne 1** *adj* Ethiopian **2** *m langue* Ethiopic **3** *m/f* **Éthiopien, ~ne** Ethiopian

éthique [etik] **1** *adj* ethical **2** *f* ethics

ethnie [ɛtni] *f* ethnic group; **ethnique** ethnic

étinceler [etɛ̃sle] ⟨1c⟩ sparkle; **étincelle** *f* spark

étiqueter [etikte] ⟨1c⟩ label (*aussi fig*)

étiquette [etikɛt] *f d'un vêtement, cahier* label; (*protocole*) etiquette

étirer [etire] ⟨1a⟩: **s'~** stretch

étoffe [etɔf] *f* material; **avoir l'~ de qch** *fig* have the makings of sth; **étoffer** ⟨1a⟩ *fig* flesh out

étoile [etwal] *f star (aussi fig)*; **~ filante** falling star, *Br aussi* shooting star; **à la belle ~** out of doors; *dormir* under the stars; **~ de mer** starfish

étonnant, ~e [etɔnɑ̃, -t] astonishing, surprising; **étonné, ~e** astonished, surprised (*de* at, by); **étonnement** *m* astonishment, surprise; **étonner** ⟨1a⟩ astonish, surprise; **s'~ de** astonished *ou* surprised at; **s'~ que** (+ *subj*) be surprised that

étouffant, ~e [etufɑ̃, -t] stifling, suffocating; **étouffée** CUIS: **à l'~** braised; **étouffer** ⟨1a⟩ suffocate; *avec un oreiller* smother, suffocate; *fig: bruit* quash; *révolte* put down, suppress; *cri* smother; *scandale* hush up

étourderie [eturdəri] *f caractère* foolishness; *action* foolish thing to do

étourdi, ~e [eturdi] foolish, thoughtless; **étourdir** ⟨2a⟩ daze; **~ qn** *d'alcool, de succès* go to s.o.'s head; **étourdissement** *m* (*vertige*) dizziness, giddiness

étourneau [eturno] *m* starling

étrange [etrɑ̃ʒ] strange

étranger, -ère [etrɑ̃ʒe, -er] **1** *adj* strange; *de l'étranger* foreign **2** *m/f* stranger; *de l'étranger* foreigner **3** *m*: **à l'~** *aller, vivre* abroad; *investissement* foreign, outward

étranglement [etrɑ̃gləmɑ̃] *m* strangulation; **étrangler** ⟨1a⟩ strangle; *fig*:

critique, liberté stifle

être [ɛtr] ⟨1⟩ **1** *v/i* ◊ be; **~ ou ne pas ~** to be or not to be; *il est avocat* he's a lawyer; *il est de Paris* he is *ou* he's from Paris, he comes from Paris; *nous sommes lundi* it's Monday
◊ *passif* be; *nous avons été éliminé* we were eliminated; *il fut assassiné* he was assassinated
◊: **~ à qn** appartenir *à* belong to s.o.; *ce n'est pas à moi de le faire* it's not up to me to do it
◊ (*aller*) go; *j'ai été lui rendre visite* I have *ou* I've been to visit her; *est-ce tu as jamais été à Rouen?* have you ever been to Rouen?
2 *v/aux* have; *elle n'est pas encore arrivée* she hasn't arrived yet; *elle est arrivée hier* she arrived yesterday
3 *m* being; *personne* person

étreindre [etrɛ̃dr] ⟨4b⟩ grasp; *ami* embrace, hug; *de sentiments* grip; **étreinte** *f* hug, embrace; *de la main* grip

étrenner [etrene] ⟨1a⟩ use for the first time

étrennes [etrɛn] *fpl* New Year's gift *sg*

étrier [etrije] *m* stirrup

étriqué, ~e [etrike] *pull, habit* too tight, too small; *fig* narrow

étroit, ~e [etrwa, -t] narrow; *amitié* close; *être ~ d'esprit* be narrow-minded

étroitesse [etrwates] *f* narrowness; **~ d'esprit** narrow-mindedness

Ets. *abr* (= **établissements**): **~ Morin** Morin's

étude [etyd] *f study*; MUS étude; *salle à l'école* study room; *de notaire* office; *activité* practice; *un certificat d'~s* an educational certificate; *faire des ~s* study; **~ de faisabilité** feasibility study; **~ de marché** market research; *une ~ de marché* a market study

étudiant, ~e [etydjã, -t] *m/f* student; **étudié, ~e** *discours* well thought out; (*affecté*) affected; **étudier** ⟨1a⟩ study

étui [etɥi] *m* case

étuvée [etyve] CUIS: **à l'~** braised

eu, ~e [y] *p/p* → *avoir*

euphémisme [øfemism] *m* understatement; *pour ne pas choquer* euphemism

euphorie [øfɔri] *f* euphoria; **euphorique** euphoric

euro [øro] *m* euro

Europe [ørɔp] *f:* **l'~** Europe; **européen, ~ne 1** *adj* European **2** *m/f* **Européen, ~ne** European

euthanasie [øtanazi] *f* euthanasia

eux [ø] *mpl* they; *après prép* them; *je les ai vues hier, ~ et leurs femmes* I saw them yesterday, them and their wives; **~, ils ne sont pas contents** they are not happy; *ce sont ~ qui* they are the ones who

eux-mêmes [ømɛm] themselves

évacuation [evakɥasjõ] *f* evacuation; **~ne** ⟨1n⟩ evacuate

évacuer ⟨1n⟩ evacuate

évadé [evade] *m* escaped prisoner, escapee; **évader** ⟨1a⟩: **s'~** escape

évaluer [evalɥe] ⟨1n⟩ (*estimer*) evaluate, assess; *tableau, meuble* value; *coût, nombre* estimate

Évangile [evãʒil] *m* Gospel

évanouir [evanwir] ⟨2a⟩: **s'~** faint; *fig* vanish, disappear; **évanouissement** *m* faint; *fig* disappearance

évaporation [evaporasjõ] *f* evaporation; **évaporer** ⟨1a⟩: **s'~** evaporate

évasé, ~e [evaze] *vêtement* flared; **évasif, -ive** evasive; **évasion** *f* escape

évêché [eveʃe] *m* bishopric; *édifice* bishop's palace

éveil [evɛj] *m* awakening; *en ~* alert; **éveillé, ~e** awake; **éveiller** ⟨1b⟩ wake up; *fig* arouse; **s'~** wake up; *fig* is aroused

événement [evɛnmã] *m* event; **~ médiatique** media event

éventail [evãtaj] *m* (*pl* -s) fan; *fig: de marchandises* range; **en ~** fan-shaped

éventé, ~e [evãte] *boisson* flat; **éventer** ⟨1a⟩ fan; *fig: secret* reveal

éventualité [evãtɥalite] *f* eventuality, possibility

éventuel, ~le [evãtɥel] possible; **éventuellement** possibly

évêque [evɛk] *m* bishop

évertuer [evɛʀtɥe] ⟨1n⟩: **s'~ à faire qch** try one's hardest *ou* damnedest F to do sth

éviction [eviksjɔ̃] *f* eviction

évidemment [evidamɑ̃] (*bien sûr*) of course

évidence [evidɑ̃s] *f* evidence; **en ~** plainly visible; **mettre en ~** *idée, fait* highlight; *objet* emphasize; **de toute ~** obviously, clearly; **évident, ~e** obvious, clear

évier [evje] *m* sink

évincer [evɛ̃se] ⟨1k⟩ oust

évitable [evitabl] avoidable; **éviter** ⟨1a⟩ avoid; **~ qch à qn** spare s.o. sth; **~ de faire qch** avoid doing sth

évocation [evɔkasjɔ̃] *f* evocation

évolué, ~e [evɔlɥe] developed, advanced; **évoluer** ⟨1n⟩ (*progresser*) develop, evolve; **évolution** *f* development; BIOL evolution

évoquer [evɔke] ⟨1m⟩ *esprits* conjure up (*aussi fig*); **~ un problème** bring up a problem

exacerber [ɛgzasɛrbe] ⟨1a⟩ exacerbate

exact, ~e [ɛgza(kt), ɛgzakt] *nombre, poids, science* exact, precise; *compte, reportage* accurate; *calcul, date, solution* right, correct; *personne* punctual; **l'heure ~e** the right time; **c'est ~** that's right *ou* correct; **exactitude** *f* accuracy; (*ponctualité*) punctuality

ex æquo [ɛgzeko]: **être ~** tie, draw

exagération [ɛgzaʒerasjɔ̃] *f* exaggeration; **exagérer** ⟨1f⟩ exaggerate

exalter [ɛgzalte] ⟨1a⟩ excite; (*vanter*) exalt

examen [ɛgzamɛ̃] *m* exam; MÉD examination; **passer un ~** take an exam, *Br aussi* sit an exam; **être reçu à un ~** pass an exam; **~ d'entrée** entrance exam; **mise f en ~** JUR indictment

examinateur, -trice [ɛgzaminatœr, -tris] *m/f* examiner; **examiner** ⟨1a⟩ examine (*aussi* MÉD)

exaspérant, ~e [ɛgzaspeʀɑ̃, -t] exasperating; **exaspérer** ⟨1f⟩ exasperate

exaucer [ɛgzose] ⟨1k⟩ *prière* answer; *vœu* grant; **~ qn** grant s.o.'s wish

excavation [ɛkskavasjɔ̃] *f* excavation

excédent [ɛksedɑ̃] *m* excess; *budgétaire, de trésorerie* surplus; **~ de bagages** excess baggage; **excéder** ⟨1f⟩ *mesure* exceed, be more than; *autorité, pouvoirs* exceed; (*énerver*) irritate

excellence [ɛksɛlɑ̃s] *f* excellence; **Excellence** *titre* Excellency; **par ~** par excellence; **excellent, ~e** excellent; **exceller** ⟨1b⟩ excel (**dans** in; **en** in, at; **à faire qch** at doing sth)

excentré, ~e [ɛksɑ̃tre] not in the center *ou* Br centre

excentrique [ɛksɑ̃trik] eccentric

excepté, ~e [ɛksɛpte] **1** *adj*: **la Chine ~e** except for China, with the exception of China **2** *prép* except; **~ que** except for the fact that; **~ si** unless, except if; **excepter** ⟨1a⟩ exclude, except

exception [ɛksɛpsjɔ̃] *f* exception; **à l'~ de** with the exception of; **d'~** exceptional; **exceptionnel, ~le** exceptional

excès [ɛksɛ] *m* excess; **à l'~** to excess, excessively; **~ de vitesse** speeding; **excessif, -ive** excessive

excitant, ~e [ɛksitɑ̃] *m/f* stimulant

excitation [ɛksitasjɔ̃] *f* excitement; (*provocation*) incitement (**à** to); *sexuelle* arousal; **excité, ~e** excited; *sexuellement* aroused; **exciter** ⟨1a⟩ excite; (*provoquer*) incite (**à** to); *sexuellement, envie, passion* arouse, excite; *appétit* whet; *imagination* stir

exclamation [ɛksklamasjɔ̃] *f* exclamation; **exclamer** ⟨1a⟩: **s'~** exclaim

exclu, ~e [ɛkskly] *m/f* outcast; **exclure** ⟨4l⟩ exclude

exclusif, -ive [ɛksklyzif, -iv] exclusive

exclusion [ɛksklyzjɔ̃] *f* expulsion; **à l'~ de** to the exclusion of; (*à l'exception de*) with the exception of

exclusivement [ɛksklyzivmɑ̃] *adv* exclusively; **exclusivité** *f* COMM exclusivity, sole rights *pl*; **en ~** exclusively

excommunier [ɛkskɔmynje] ⟨1a⟩ excommunicate

excrément [ɛkskremɑ̃] *m* excrement

excursion [ɛkskyrsjɔ̃] *f* trip, excursion

excuse [ɛkskyz] *f* (*prétexte, justification*) excuse; **~s** apology *sg*; **faire ses ~s** apologize, make one's apologies; **excuser** ⟨1a⟩ excuse; **s'~** apologize (*de* for); **excusez-moi** excuse me; **excusez-moi de vous déranger** I'm sorry to bother you

exécrable [ɛgzekrabl] horrendous, atrocious

exécuter [ɛgzekyte] ⟨1a⟩ *ordre, projet* carry out; MUS perform, execute; JUR *loi, jugement* enforce; *condamné* execute; **exécutif, -ive 1** *adj* executive **2** *m*: *l'~* the executive; **exécution** *f d'un ordre, projet* carrying out, execution; MUS performance, execution; JUR *d'une loi, un jugement* enforcement; *d'un condamné* execution; **mettre à ~** *menaces, plan* carry out

exemplaire [ɛgzɑ̃plɛr] **1** *adj* exemplary; **une punition ~** a punishment intended to act as an example **2** *m* copy; (*échantillon*) sample; **en deux / trois ~s** in duplicate / triplicate

exemple [ɛgzɑ̃pl] *m* example; **par ~** for example; **donner / ne pas donner l'~** set a good / bad example

exempt, ~e [ɛgzɑ̃, -t] exempt (*de* from); *inquiétude, souci* free (*de* from); **exempter** ⟨1a⟩ exempt (*de* from); **exemption** *f* exemption; **~ d'impôts** tax exemption

exercer [ɛgzɛrse] ⟨1k⟩ *corps* exercise; *influence* exert, use; *pouvoir* use; *profession* practise; *mémoire* train; MIL drill; **elle exerce la médecine** she's a doctor; **s'~** (*s'entraîner*) practise

exercice [ɛgzɛrsis] *m* exercise (*aussi* ÉDU); *d'une profession* practice; COMM *fiscal year*, *Br* financial year; MIL drill; **~ d'évacuation** evacuation drill

exhaler [ɛgzale] ⟨1a⟩ exhale

exhaustif, -ive [ɛgzostif, -iv] exhaustive

exhiber [ɛgzibe] ⟨1a⟩ exhibit; *document* produce; **s'~** make an exhibition of o.s.; **exhibitionniste** *m* exhibitionist

exhumer [ɛgzyme] ⟨1a⟩ exhume

exigeant, ~e [ɛgziʒɑ̃, -t] demanding; **exigence** *f* (*revendication*) demand; **exiger** ⟨1l⟩ (*réclamer*) demand; (*nécessiter*) need

exigu, ~ë [ɛgzigy] tiny

exil [ɛgzil] *m* exile; **exilé, ~e** *m/f* exile; **exiler** ⟨1a⟩ exile; **s'~** go into exile

existence [ɛgzistɑ̃s] *f* existence; **exister** ⟨1a⟩ exist; **il existe** there is, *pl* there are

exode [ɛgzɔd] *m* exodus

exonérer [ɛgzɔnere] ⟨1f⟩ exempt

exorbitant, ~e [ɛgzɔrbitɑ̃, -t] exorbitant

exorbité, ~e *yeux* bulging

exotique [ɛgzɔtik] exotic

expansif, -ive [ɛkspɑ̃sif, -iv] expansive (*aussi* PHYS); **expansion** *f* expansion; **~ économique** economic expansion *ou* growth

expatrier [ɛkspatrije] ⟨1a⟩ *argent* move abroad *ou* out of the country; **s'~** settle abroad

expectative [ɛkspɛktativ] *f*: **rester dans l'~** wait and see

expédient [ɛkspedjɑ̃] *m* expedient

expédier [ɛkspedje] ⟨1a⟩ send; COMM ship, send; *travail* do quickly

expéditeur, -trice [ɛkspeditœr, -tris] *m/f* sender; COMM shipper, sender; **expéditif, -ive** speedy; *péj* hasty; **expédition** *f* sending; COMM shipment; (*voyage*) expedition

expérience [ɛksperjɑ̃s] *f* experience; *scientifique* experiment

expérimenté, ~e [ɛksperimɑ̃te] experienced; **expérimenter** ⟨1a⟩ (*tester*) test

expert, ~e [ɛkspɛr, -t] **1** *adj* expert; **être ~ en la matière** be an expert in the matter **2** *m/f* expert; **expert-comptable** *m* (*pl* experts-comptables) certified public accountant, *Br* chartered accountant; **expert légiste** *m* forensic scientist

expertise [ɛkspɛrtiz] *f* (*estimation*) valuation; JUR expert testimony; **expertiser** ⟨1a⟩ *tableau, voiture* value

expier [ɛkspje] ⟨1a⟩ expiate

expiration [ɛkspirasjɔ̃] *f d'un contrat*,

délai expiration, *Br* expiry; *de souffle* exhalation; **expirer** ⟨1a⟩ *d'un contrat, délai* expire; *(respirer)* exhale; *(mourir)* die, expire *fml*

explicatif , -ive [ɛksplikatif, -iv] explanatory; **explication** *f* explanation; *nous avons eu une ~* we talked things over

explicite [ɛksplisit] explicit; **explicitement** *adv* explicitly

expliquer [ɛksplike] ⟨1m⟩ explain; *s'~* explain o.s.; *s'~ qch* account for sth, find an explanation for sth; *s'~ avec qn* talk things over with s.o.

exploit [ɛksplwa] *m sportif, médical* feat, achievement; *amoureux* exploit; **exploitant , ~e** *m/f agricole* farmer

exploitation [ɛksplwatasjõ] *f d'une ferme, ligne aérienne* operation, running; *du sol* working, farming; *de richesses naturelles* exploitation; *(entreprise)* operation, concern; *péj: des ouvriers* exploitation; *~ minière* mining; **exploiter** ⟨1a⟩ *ferme, ligne aérienne* operate, run; *sol* work, farm; *richesses naturelles* exploit (*aussi péj*)

explorateur , -trice [ɛksplɔratœr, -tris] *m/f* explorer; **exploration** *f* exploration; **explorer** ⟨1a⟩ explore

exploser [ɛksploze] ⟨1a⟩ explode (*aussi fig*); *~ de rire* F crack up F; **explosif , -ive 1** *adj* explosive (*aussi fig*) **2** *m* explosive; **explosion** *f* explosion (*aussi fig*)

exportateur , -trice [ɛkspɔrtatœr, -tris] **1** *adj* exporting **2** *m* exporter; **exportation** *f* export; **exporter** ⟨1a⟩ export

exposant , ~e *m/f* exhibitor

exposé [ɛkspoze] *m* account, report; *ÉDU* presentation; **exposer** ⟨1a⟩ *art, marchandise* exhibit, show; *problème, programme* explain; *à l'air, à la chaleur* expose (*aussi PHOT*); **exposition** *f d'art, de marchandise* exhibition; *d'un problème* explanation; *au soleil* exposure (*aussi PHOT*)

exprès[1] [ɛksprɛ] *adv (intentionnellement)* deliberately, on purpose; *(spécialement)* expressly, specially

exprès[2] **, -esse** [ɛksprɛs] **1** *adj* ex-

press **2** *adj inv* **lettre** *f* **exprès** express letter

express [ɛksprɛs] **1** *adj inv* express; *voie* *f* ~ expressway **2** *m train* express; *café* espresso

expressément [ɛkspresemã] *adv* expressly

expressif , -ive [ɛkspresif, -iv] expressive; **expression** *f* expression

expresso [ɛkspreso] *m* espresso (coffee)

exprimer [ɛksprime] ⟨1a⟩ express; *s'~* express o.s.

exproprier [ɛksprɔprije] ⟨1a⟩ expropriate

expulser [ɛkspylse] ⟨1a⟩ expel; *d'un pays* deport; **expulsion** *f* expulsion; *d'un pays* deportation

exquis , ~e [ɛkski, -z] exquisite

extase [ɛkstaz] *f* ecstasy; **extatique** ecstatic

extensible stretchable; **extensif , -ive** *AGR* extensive; **extension** *f des bras, jambes* stretching; *(prolongement)* extension; *d'une épidémie* spread; *IN-FORM* expansion

exténuer [ɛkstenɥe] ⟨1n⟩ exhaust

extérieur , ~e [ɛksterjœr] **1** *adj paroi, mur* outside, external; *ÉCON, POL* foreign, external; *(apparent)* external **2** *m (partie externe)* outside, exterior; *à l'~ (dehors)* outside, out of doors; *à l'~ de* outside; **extérieurement** *adv* externally, on the outside; **extérioriser** ⟨1a⟩ express, let out; *s'~ d'un sentiment* show itself, find expression; *d'une personne* express one's emotions

exterminer [ɛkstɛrmine] ⟨1a⟩ exterminate

externe [ɛkstɛrn] external

extincteur [ɛkstɛ̃ktœr] *m* extinguisher

extinction [ɛkstɛ̃ksjõ] *f* extinction (*aussi fig*)

extirper [ɛkstirpe] ⟨1a⟩ *mauvaise herbe* pull up; *MÉD* remove; *fig renseignement* drag out

extorquer [ɛkstɔrke] ⟨1m⟩ extort

extorsion [ɛkstɔrsjõ] *f* extortion

extra [ɛkstra] **1** *adj inv* great, terrific

façon

2 *m*: **un ~** something special

extraconjugal, ~e [ɛkstrakɔ̃ʒygal] extramarital

extraction [ɛkstraksjɔ̃] *f de pétrole, d'une dent* extraction

extrader [ɛkstrade] ⟨1a⟩ extradite; **extradition** *f* JUR extradition

extraire [ɛkstrɛr] ⟨4s⟩ extract

extrait [ɛkstrɛ] *m* extract

extraordinaire [ɛkstraɔrdinɛr] extraordinary

extrapoler [ɛkstrapɔle] ⟨1a⟩ extrapolate

extrascolaire [ɛkstraskɔlɛr] extracurricular

extraterrestre [ɛkstraterɛstr] *m/f* extraterrestrial, alien

extravagance [ɛkstravagɑ̃s] *f* extravagance; *d'une personne, d'une idée, d'un habit* eccentricity; **extravagant,**

~e extravagant; *habits, idées, personne* eccentric

extraverti, ~e [ɛkstraverti] extrovert

extrême [ɛkstrɛm] **1** *adj* extreme **2** *m* extreme; **à l'~** to extremes; **extrêmement** *adv* extremely; **extrême-onction** *f* REL extreme unction; **Extrême-Orient** *m*: **l'~** the Far East

extrémiste [ɛkstremist] *m/f* POL extremist; **~ de droite** right-wing extremist; **extrémité** *f d'une rue* (very) end; *d'un doigt* tip; *(situation désespérée)* extremity; **~s** ANAT extremities

exubérance [ɛgzyberɑ̃s] *f d'une personne* exuberance; **exubérant, ~e** exuberant

exulter [ɛgzylte] exult

exutoire [ɛgzytwar] *m fig* outlet

eye-liner [ajlajnœr] *m* eyeliner

F

F *abr* (= **franc(s)**) FF (= French franc(s))

fa [fa] *m* MUS F

fable [fabl] *f* fable

fabricant, ~e [fabrikɑ̃, -t] *m/f* manufacturer, maker; **fabrication** *f* making; *industrielle* manufacture; **~ en série** mass production

fabrique [fabrik] *f* factory; **fabriquer** ⟨1m⟩ make; *industrielle aussi* manufacture; *histoire* fabricate

fabuler ⟨1m⟩ make things up

fabuleux, -euse [fabylø, -z] *f* fabulous

fac [fak] *f abr* (= **faculté**) uni, university

façade [fasad] *f* façade *(aussi fig)*

face [fas] *f* face; *d'une pièce* head; **de ~** from the front; **en ~ de** opposite; **~ à qch** facing sth; *fig* faced with sth; **~ à ~** face to face; **en ~** opposite; **faire ~ à** *problèmes, responsabilités* face (up to); **face-à-face** *m (pl inv)* face-to-

-face (debate)

facétieux, -euse [fasesjø, -z] mischievous

facette [fasɛt] *f* facet

fâché, ~e [faʃe] annoyed; **fâcher** ⟨1a⟩ annoy; **se ~** get annoyed; **se ~ avec qn** fall out with s.o.; **fâcheux, -euse** annoying; *(déplorable)* unfortunate

facho [faʃo] F fascist

facile [fasil] easy; *personne* easy-going; **~ à faire / utiliser** easy to do / use; **facilement** *adv* easily; **facilité** *f* easiness; *à faire qch* ease; **elle a beaucoup de ~s à l'école** she shows a lot of strengths at school; **~s de paiement** easy terms; **~ d'utilisation** ease of use; **faciliter** ⟨1a⟩ make easier, facilitate

façon [fasɔ̃] *f (manière)* way, method; **de ~ (à ce) que** (+*subj*) so that; **de toute ~** anyway, anyhow; **de cette ~** (in) that way; **à la ~ de chez nous**

like we have at home; **à la ~ de Monet** in the style of Monet; **~s** (*comportement*) behavior *sg*, *Br* behaviour *sg*, manners; **faire des ~s** make a fuss; **sans ~** simple, unpretentious

façonner [fasɔne] ⟨1a⟩ shape, fashion

facteur [faktœr] *m de la poste* mailman, letter carrier, *Br* postman; MATH, *fig* factor

factice [faktis] artificial

faction [faksjõ] *f* (*groupe*) faction

factrice [faktris] *f* mailwoman, *Br* postwoman

factuel, ~le [faktɥɛl] factual

facture [faktyr] *f* bill; COMM invoice; **facturer** ⟨1a⟩ invoice

facultatif, -ive [fakyltatif, -iv] optional; **arrêt** *m* **~ d'autobus** request stop

faculté [fakylte] *f* faculty (*aussi université*); **~ d'adaptation** adaptability

fade [fad] insipid (*aussi fig*)

Fahrenheit [farenajt] Fahrenheit

faible [fɛbl] **1** *adj* weak; *bruit, lumière, voix, espoir* faint; *avantage* slight **2** *m pour personne* soft spot; *pour chocolat etc* weakness; **faiblesse** *f* weakness; **faiblir** ⟨2a⟩ weaken

faïence [fajɑ̃s] *f* earthenware

faille [faj] *f* GÉOL fault; *dans théorie, raisonnement* flaw

faillible [fajibl] fallible; **faillir** ⟨2n⟩: **il a failli gagner** he almost won, he nearly won; **faillite** *f* COMM bankruptcy; **faire ~** go bankrupt; **être en ~** be bankrupt

faim [fɛ̃] *f* hunger; **avoir ~** be hungry; **manger à sa ~** eat one's fill; **mourir de ~** starve (*aussi fig*)

fainéant, ~e [fɛneɑ̃, -t] **1** *adj* idle, lazy **2** *m/f* idler

faire [fɛr] ⟨4n⟩ **1** *v/t* ◇ do; *gâteau, robe, meuble, repas, liste* make; **qu'est-ce que vous faites dans la vie?** what do you do for a living?; **tu ferais bien** *ou* **mieux de te dépêcher** you had better hurry up; **elle ne fait que parler** she does nothing but talk; **~ la cuisine** cook; **~ du tennis** play tennis; **~ de la natation / du bateau / du ski** swim / sail / ski,

go swimming / sailing / skiing; **~ son droit** study law, take a law degree; **~ un voyage** make *ou* take a trip; **~ jeune** look young; **~ le malade / le clown** act *ou* play the invalid / the fool; **ça fait 100 euros** that's *ou* that makes 100 euros; **cinq plus cinq font dix** five and five are *ou* make ten; **ça ne fait rien** it doesn't matter; **qu'est-ce que ça peut te ~?** what business is it of yours?; **on ne peut rien y ~** we can't do anything about it; **ce qui fait que** which means that; **... fit-il** ... he said

◇ *avec inf*: **~ rire qn** make s.o. laugh; **~ venir qn** send for s.o.; **chauffer de l'eau** heat some water; **~ peindre la salle de bain** have the bathroom painted

2 *v/i*: **~ vite** hurry up, be quick; **fais comme chez toi** make yourself at home; **~ avec** make do

3 *impersonnel*: **il fait chaud / froid** it is *ou* it's warm / cold; **ça fait un an que je ne l'ai pas vue** I haven't seen her in a year

4 ◇ **se ~** become; *amis, ennemis, millions* make (for o.s.); *d'une réputation* be made; **cela se fait beaucoup** it's quite common; **ça ne se fait pas** it's not done; **tu t'es fait couper les cheveux?** have you had your hair cut?; **se ~ rare** become rarer and rarer; **je me fais vieux** I'm getting old

◇ **se ~ à qch** get used to sth

◇ **je ne m'en fais pas** I'm not worried *ou* bothered

faire-part [fɛrpar] *m* (*pl inv*) announcement

faisable [fəzabl] feasible

faisan [fəzɑ̃] *m* pheasant

faisceau [fɛso] *m* (*pl -x*) bundle; *de lumière* beam

fait¹ [fɛ] *m* fact; (*action*) act; (*événement*) development; **au ~** by the way, incidentally; **de ~** in fact; **de ce ~** consequently; **en ~** in fact; **du ~ de** because of; **en ~ de** by way of; **tout à ~** absolutely; **un ~ divers** a brief news item; **prendre qn sur le**

~ catch s.o. in the act; *tous ses ~s et gestes* his every move

fait², **~e** [fɛ, fɛt] **1** *p/p* → *faire* **2** *adj*: *être ~ pour qn / qch* be made for s.o. / sth; *être ~ F* be done for; *bien ~ personne* good-looking; *c'est bien ~ pour lui* serves him right!

falaise [falɛz] *f* cliff

falloir [falwar] ⟨3c⟩ ◊ : *il faut un visa* you need a visa, you must have a visa; *combien te faut-il?* how much do you need?; *il faut l'avertir* we have to warn him, he has to be warned; *il me faut un visa* I need a visa; *il me faut sortir, il faut que je sorte* (*subj*) I have to go out, I must go out; *s'il le faut* if necessary, if need be; *il aurait fallu prendre le train* we should have taken the train; *il faut vraiment qu'elle soit* (*subj*) *fatiguée* she must really be tired; *comme il faut* respectable ◊ *avec négatif*: *il ne faut pas que je sorte* (*subj*) *avant ...* I mustn't go out until ... ◊ : *il s'en fallait de 20 euros / 3 points* another 20 euros / 3 points was all that was needed; *il a failli nous heurter* il s'en est fallu de peu he came within an inch of hitting us; *il s'en est fallu de peu que je vienne* (*subj*) I almost came; *...il s'en faut de beaucoup* not by a long way

falsification [falsifikasjɔ̃] *f* forgery; *document* falsification; **falsifier** ⟨1a⟩ *argent* forge; *document* falsify; *vérité* misrepresent

famé, **~e** [fame] : *mal ~* disreputable

famélique [famelik] starving

fameux, **-euse** [famø, -z] (*célèbre*) famous; (*excellent*) wonderful, marvelous, *Br* marvellous; *c'est un ~ ...* it's quite a ...

familial, **~e** [familjal] (*mpl* -aux) family *atr*

familiariser [familjarize] ⟨1a⟩ familiarize (*avec* with); **familiarité** *f* familiarity (*avec* with); **familier**, **-ère** (*impertinent, connu*) familiar; *langage* colloquial, familiar

famille [famij] *f* family; ~ *monoparentale* single-parent family; ~ *nombreuse* large family

famine [famin] *f* famine

fan [fan] *m/f*, **fana** [fana] *m/f* F fan; **fanatique 1** *adj* fanatical **2** *m/f* (*obsédé*) fanatic; **fanatisme** *m* fanaticism

faner [fane] ⟨1a⟩: *se ~* fade, wither

fanfare [fɑ̃far] *f* (*orchestre*) brass band; (*musique*) fanfare; **fanfaron**, **~ne 1** *adj* boastful, bragging **2** *m* boaster

fantaisie [fɑ̃tezi] *f* imagination; (*caprice*) whim; *bijoux mpl ~* costume jewelry, *Br* costume jewellery; **fantaisiste** *m/f & adj* eccentric

fantasme [fɑ̃tasm] *m* fantasy; **fantasmer** fantasize

fantasque [fɑ̃task] *personne* strange, weird

fantastique [fɑ̃tastik] **1** *adj* fantastic; (*imaginaire*) imaginary **2** *m*: *le ~* fantasy

fantoche [fɑ̃tɔʃ] *m fig* puppet

fantôme [fɑ̃tom] *m* ghost; *train m ~* ghost train; *ville f ~* ghost town

FAQ [ɛfaky] *f abr* (= *Foire aux questions*) FAQ (= frequently asked question(s))

farce [fars] *f au théâtre* farce; (*tour*) joke; CUIS stuffing; **farceur**, **-euse** *m/f* joker; **farcir** ⟨2a⟩ CUIS stuff; *fig* cram

fard [far] *m* make-up; ~ *à paupières* eye shadow

fardeau [fardo] *m* (*pl* -x) burden (*aussi fig*)

farder [farde] ⟨1a⟩: *se ~* make up

farfelu, **~e** [farfəly] odd, weird

farfouiller [farfuje] ⟨1a⟩ F rummage around

farine [farin] *f* flour; ~ *de maïs* corn starch, *Br* cornflour; **farineux**, **-euse** floury

farouche [faruʃ] (*timide*) shy; (*violent*) *volonté, haine* fierce

fart [far(t)] *m* ski wax

fascicule [fasikyl] *m* installment, *Br* instalment

fascinant, **~e** [fasinɑ̃, -t] fascinating; **fascination** *f* fascination; **fasciner**

⟨1a⟩ fascinate

fascisme [faʃism] *m* fascism; **fasciste** *m/f & adj* Fascist

faste [fast] *m* pomp, splendor, *Br* splendour

fast-food [fastfud] *m* fast food restaurant

fastidieux, -euse [fastidjø, -z] tedious

fastoche [fastɔʃ] F dead easy

fastueux, -euse [fastɥø, -z] lavish

fatal, ~e [fatal] (*mpl* -s) fatal; (*inévitable*) inevitable; **fatalement** *adv* fatally; **fatalisme** *m* fatalism; **fataliste 1** *adj* fatalistic **2** *m/f* fatalist; **fatalité** *f* fate; **la ~ de l'hérédité** the inescapability of heredity

fatidique [fatidik] fateful

fatigant, ~e [fatigɑ̃, -t] *tiring*; (*agaçant*) tiresome; **fatigue** *f* tiredness, fatigue; **mort de ~** dead on one's feet; **fatigué, ~e** *m/f* tired; **fatiguer** ⟨1m⟩ tire; (*importuner*) annoy; **se ~** tire o.s. out, get tired

faubourg [fobur] *m* (working-class) suburb

fauché, ~e [foʃe] F broke F; **faucher** ⟨1a⟩ *fig* mow down; F (*voler*) pinch F, lift F

faucille [fosij] *f* sickle

faucon [fokõ] *m* falcon

faufiler [fofile] ⟨1a⟩: **se ~ dans une pièce** slip into a room; **se ~ entre les voitures** thread one's way through the traffic

faune [fon] *f* wildlife, fauna

faussaire [foser] *m* forger; **faussement** *adv* falsely; *accuser, condamner* wrongly; *croire* wrongly; **fausser** ⟨1a⟩ *calcul, données* skew, distort; *sens, vérité* distort, twist; *clef* bend; **~ compagnie à qn** skip out on s.o.

faute [fot] *f* mistake; (*responsabilité*) fault; **c'est (de) ta ~** it's your fault, you're the one to blame; **à qui la ~?** whose fault is that?; **par sa ~** because of him; **être en ~** be at fault; **~ de** for lack of; **sans ~** without fail; **~ professionnelle** professional misconduct

fauteuil [fotœj] *m* armchair; **~ de jar-**
din garden chair; **~ roulant** wheelchair

fautif, -ive [fotif, -iv] (*coupable*) guilty; (*erroné*) incorrect

fauve [fov] **1** *adj* tawny; **bêtes** *fpl* **~s** big cats **2** *m félin* big cat

faux, fausse [fo, fos] **1** *adj* false; (*incorrect*) *aussi* wrong; *bijoux* imitation, fake; **fausse couche** *f* miscarriage; **~ billet** forged *ou* dud bill; **~ numéro** wrong number; **~ témoignage** perjury **2** *adv*: **chanter ~** sing off-key, sing out of tune **3** *m copie* forgery, fake

faux-filet [fofile] *m* (*pl* faux-filets) CUIS sirloin

faux-monnayeur [fomonejœr] *m* counterfeiter, forger

faux-semblant [fosɑ̃blɑ̃] *m* pretense, *Br* pretence

faveur [favœr] *f* favor, *Br* favour; **de ~** *traitement* preferential; *prix* special; **en ~ de** in favor of; **favorable** favorable, *Br* favourable; **favorablement** *adv* favorably, *Br* favourably

favori, ~te [favɔri, -t] *m/f & adj* favorite, *Br* favourite; **favoriser** ⟨1a⟩ favor, *Br* favour; *faciliter, avantager* promote, encourage; **favoritisme** *m* favoritism, *Br* favouritism

fax [faks] *m* fax; **faxer** ⟨1a⟩ fax

fébrile [febril] feverish

fécond, ~e [fekõ, -d] fertile (*aussi fig*); **fécondation** *f* fertilization; **~ artificielle** artificial insemination; **féconder** ⟨1a⟩ fertilize; **fécondité** *f* fertility

fécule [fekyl] *f* starch; **féculent** *m* starchy food

fédéral, ~e [federal] (*mpl* -aux) federal; **fédéralisme** *m* federalism; **fédéraliste** *m/f & adj* federalist; **fédération** *f* federation

fée [fe] *f* fairy

feeling [filiŋ] *m* feeling; **avoir un bon ~ pour qch** have a good feeling about sth

féerique [fe(e)rik] *fig* enchanting

feignant [feɲɑ̃, -ɑ̃t] → **fainéant**

feindre [fɛ̃dr] ⟨4b⟩: **~ l'étonnement / l'indifférence** pretend to be astonished / indifferent, feign astonishment / indifference; **~ de faire qch** pretend to do sth; **feinte** f feint

fêlé, **~e** [fele] *aussi fig* cracked; **fêler** ⟨1b⟩: **se ~** crack

félicitations [felisitasjɔ̃] *fpl* congratulations; **féliciter** ⟨1a⟩: **~ qn de** *ou* **pour qch** congratulate s.o. on sth; **se ~ de qch** congratulate o.s. on sth

félin, **~e** [felɛ̃, -in] *m & adj* feline

fêlure [felyr] f crack

femelle [fəmɛl] f & adj female

féminin, **~e** [feminɛ̃, -in] **1** *adj* feminine; *sexe* female; *problèmes, maladies, magazines, mode* women's **2** *m* GRAM feminine; **féminisme** *m* feminism; **féministe** *m/f & adj* feminist; **féminité** f femininity

femme [fam] f woman; (*épouse*) wife; **jeune ~** young woman; **~ d'affaires** businesswoman; **~ battue** battered wife; **~-enfant** childlike woman; **~ au foyer** homemaker, *Br* housewife; **~ de ménage** cleaning woman

fendre [fɑ̃dr] ⟨4a⟩ split; (*fissurer*) crack; *cœur* break; **se ~** split; (*se fissurer*) crack

fenêtre [f(ə)nɛtr] f window

fenouil [fənuj] *m* BOT fennel

fente [fɑ̃t] f crack; *d'une boîte à lettres, jupe* slit; *pour pièces de monnaie* slot

fer [fɛr] *m* iron; **volonté** *ou* **discipline de ~** *fig* iron will / discipline; **~ à cheval** horseshoe; **~ à repasser** iron

férié [ferje]: *jour m ~* (public) holiday

ferme¹ [fɛrm] **1** *adj* firm; **terre** f **~** dry land, terra firma **2** *adv* travailler hard; **s'ennuyer ~** be bored stiff; **discuter ~** be having a fierce debate

ferme² [fɛrm] f farm

fermé, **~e** [fɛrme] closed, shut; *robinet* off; *club, milieu* exclusive

fermement [fɛrməmɑ̃] *adv* firmly

fermentation [fɛrmɑ̃tasjɔ̃] f fermentation; **fermenter** ⟨1a⟩ ferment

fermer [fɛrme] ⟨1a⟩ **1** *v/t* close, shut; *définitivement* close down, shut down; *eau, gaz, robinet* turn off; *manteau* fasten; *frontière, port, chemin* close; **~ boutique** close down, go out of business; **~ à clef** lock; **ferme-la!** shut up!

2 *v/i* close, shut; *définitivement* close down, shut down; *d'un manteau* fasten; **se ~** close, shut

fermeté [fɛrməte] f firmness

fermette [fɛrmɛt] f small farmhouse

fermeture [fɛrmətyr] f closing; *définitive* closure; *mécanisme* fastener; **~ éclair** zipper, *Br* zip (fastener)

fermier [fɛrmje, -jɛr] **1** *adj œufs, poulet* free-range **2** *m* farmer; **fermière** f farmer; *épouse* farmer's wife

fermoir [fɛrmwar] *m* clasp

féroce [ferɔs] fierce, ferocious; **férocité** f fierceness, ferocity

ferraille [fɛraj] f scrap; **mettre à la ~** scrap, throw on the scrapheap

ferré, **~e** [fɛre]: **voie ~e** f (railroad *ou* *Br* railway) track

ferroviaire [fɛrɔvjɛr] railroad *atr*, *Br* railway *atr*

ferry-boat [feribot] *m* (*pl* ferry-boats) ferry

fertile [fɛrtil] fertile; **~ en** full of, packed with; **fertilisant** *m* fertilizer; **fertilité** f fertility

fervent, **~e** [fɛrvɑ̃, -t] *prière, admirateur* fervent; **ferveur** f fervor, *Br* fervour

fesse [fes] f buttock; **~s** butt *sg*, *Br* bottom *sg*; **fessée** f spanking

festif, **-ive** [fɛstif -iv] festive

festin [fɛstɛ̃] *m* feast

festival [fɛstival] *m* (*pl* -s) festival

festivités [fɛstivite] *fpl* festivities

fêtard [fɛtar] *m* F reveller, *Br* reveller

fête [fɛt] f party; (*soirée*) party; *publique* holiday; REL feast (day), festival; *jour d'un saint* name day; **les ~s** (**de fin d'année**) the holidays, Christmas and New Year; **faire la ~** party; **être en ~** be in party mood; **~ foraine** fun fair; **Fête des mères** Mother's Day; **Fête nationale** Bastille Day; **fêter** ⟨1b⟩ celebrate; (*accueillir*) fête

fétiche [fetif] *m* fetish; (*mascotte*) mascot; **numéro** / **animal ~** lucky number / animal

feu [fø] *m* (*pl* -x) fire; AUTO, AVIA, MAR light; *de circulation* (traffic) light, *Br* (traffic) lights *pl*; *d'une cuisinière* burner; *fig* (*enthousiasme*) passion; *au coin du ~* by the fireside; *coup m de ~* shot; *~ d'artifice* fireworks *pl*, firework display; *mettre le ~ à qch* set sth on fire, set fire to sth; *prendre ~* catch fire; *en ~* on fire; *à ~ doux / vif* over a low / high heat; *faire ~ sur* MIL fire *ou* shoot at; *vous avez du ~?* got a light?; *~ rouge* red light, stoplight; *~ vert* green light (*aussi fig*); *~ arrière* AUTO tail light, *Br* rear light; *~ stop* brake light, stoplight; *~ de position* side light; *~x de croisement* low beams, *Br* dipped headlights; *~x de route* headlights on high *ou Br* full beam; *~x de signalisation* traffic light, *Br* traffic lights *pl*; *~x de stationnement* parking lights

feuillage [fœjaʒ] *m* foliage; **feuille** *f* leaf; *de papier* sheet; *~ d'impôt* tax return; *~ de maladie* form used to claim reimbursement of medical expenses; *~ de paie* payslip; **feuillet** *m* leaf; **feuilleter** ⟨1c⟩ *livre etc* leaf through; CUIS *pâte f feuilletée* puff pastry; **feuilleton** *m d'un journal* serial; TV soap opera

feutre [føtr] *m* felt; *stylo* felt-tipped pen; *chapeau* fedora; **feutré**, *~e bruit* muffled

fève [fɛv] *f* BOT broad bean

février [fevrije] *m* February

FF *m abr* (= *franc(s) français*) FF (= French franc(s))

fiabilité [fjabilite] *f* reliability; **fiable** reliable

fiançailles [fi(j)ãsaj] *fpl* engagement *sg*; **fiancé**, *~e m/f* fiancé, fiancée; **fiancer** ⟨1k⟩: *se ~ avec* get engaged to

fiasco [fjasko] *m* fiasco

fibre [fibr] *f* fiber, *Br* fibre; *avoir la ~ paternelle fig* be a born father; *faire jouer la ~ patriotique* play on patriotic feelings; *~ optique* optical fiber; *le domaine des ~s optiques* fiber optics; *~ de verre* fiberglass, *Br* fibreglass

ficeler [fisle] ⟨1c⟩ tie up; **ficelle** *f* string; *pain* thin French stick

fiche [fiʃ] *f pour classement* index card;

formulaire form; ÉL plug; **ficher** ⟨1a⟩ F (*faire*) do; (*donner*) give; (*mettre*) stick; *par la police* put on file; *fiche-moi la paix!* leave me alone *ou* in peace!; *fiche-moi le camp!* clear out!, go away!; *je m'en fiche* I don't give a damn

fichier [fiʃje] *m* INFORM file; *~ joint* attachment

fichu, *~e* [fiʃy] F (*inutilisable*) kaput F, done-for F; (*sale*) filthy; *être mal ~ santé* be feeling rotten; *être ~* (*condamné*) have had it F

fictif, *-ive* [fiktif, -iv] fictitious; **fiction** *f* fiction

fidéicommis [fideikɔmi] *m* trust; **fidéicommissaire** *m/f* trustee

fidèle [fidɛl] **1** *adj* faithful; *ami, supporter* faithful, loyal **2** *m/f* REL, *fig*: *les fidèles* the faithful *pl*; **fidéliser** ⟨1a⟩: *~ la clientèle* create customer loyalty; **fidélité** *f* faithfulness

fier[1] [fje] ⟨1a⟩: *se ~ à* trust

fier[2], *-ère* [fjer] proud (*de* of); **fièrement** *adv* proudly; **fierté** *f* pride

fièvre [fjɛvr] *f* fever; *avoir de la ~* have a fever, *Br* have a temperature; *avoir 40° de ~* have a temperature of 40°; **fiévreux**, *-euse* feverish (*aussi fig*)

figer [fiʒe] ⟨1l⟩ congeal; *se ~ fig*: *d'un sourire, d'une expression* become fixed

fignoler [fiɲɔle] ⟨1a⟩ put the finishing touches to

figue [fig] *f* fig; **figuier** *m* fig tree

figurant, *~e* [figyrã, -t] *m/f de théâtre* walk-on; *de cinéma* extra; **figuratif**, *-ive* figurative; **figure** *f* figure; (*visage*) face; *se casser la ~* F fall flat on one's face; **figuré**, *~e* figurative; **figurer** ⟨1a⟩ figure; *se ~ qch* imagine sth

fil [fil] *m* thread; *de métal*, ÉL, TÉL wire; *coup m de ~* TÉL (phone) call; *au bout du ~* TÉL on the phone *ou* line; *au ~ des jours* with the passage of time; *~ dentaire* (dental) floss; *~ électrique* wire; *~ de fer barbelé* barbed wire; **filament** *m* ÉL filament

filature *f* spinning; *usine* mill; **prendre**

qn en ~ *fig* tail s.o.

file [fil] *f* line; *d'une route* lane; ~ **(d'attente)** line, *Br* queue; **à la** ~ one after the other; **filer** ⟨1a⟩ **1** *v/t* spin; *F (donner)* give; *(épier)* tail **2** *v/i F (partir vite)* fly, race off; *du temps* fly past

filet [file] *m d'eau* trickle; *de pêche, tennis* net; *CUIS* fillet; ~ **(à provisions)** string bag

filial, ~e [filjal] *(mpl* -aux) **1** *adj* filial **2** *f* COMM subsidiary

filière [filjer] *f (career) path;* **la** ~ **administrative** official channels *pl;* **~s scientifiques / littéraires** science / arts subjects

filigrane [filigran] *m d'un billet de banque* watermark

fille [fij] *f girl;* parenté daughter; **vieille** ~ old maid; **jeune** ~ girl, young woman; **petite** ~ little girl; **fillette** *f* little girl

filleul [fijœl] *m* godson, godchild; **filleule** *f* goddaughter, godchild

film [film] *m* movie, *Br aussi* film; **couche** film; ~ **policier** detective movie *ou Br aussi* film; **se faire un** ~ see a movie; **se faire des ~s** *fig* imagine things; **filmer** ⟨1a⟩ film

filon [filɔ̃] *m* MIN seam, vein; **trouver un bon** ~ *fig* strike it rich

fils [fis] *m* son; ~ **à papa** (spoilt) rich kid

filtre [filtr] *m* filter; **filtrer** ⟨1a⟩ **1** *v/t* filter; *fig* screen **2** *v/i d'une liquide, de lumière* filter through; *fig* leak

fin¹ [fɛ̃] *f* end; **à la** ~ in the end, eventually; **en** ~ **de compte** when all's said and done; **à cette** ~ for that purpose; **mettre** ~ **à qch** put an end to sth; **tirer à sa** ~ come to an end, draw to a close; **sans** ~ *soirée, histoire* endless; *parler* endlessly

fin², ~**e** [fɛ̃, fin] **1** *adj thin;* (*mince*) thin; *taille, cheville* slender, neat; *esprit* refined; (*rusé, malin*) sharp, intelligent; **fines herbes** *fpl* mixed herbs; **au** ~ **fond de** right at the bottom of; *de garage etc* right at the back of **2** *adv* fine(ly)

final, ~e [final] *(mpl* -s) **1** *adj* final;

point *m* ~ period, *Br* full stop **2** *m:* ~**e** MUS finale **3** *f* SP final; **finalement** *adv* finally; **finaliser** ⟨1a⟩ finalize; **finaliste** *m/f* finalist

finance [finãs] *f* finance; **~s** finances, **Ministre** *m* **des ~s** Finance Minister, Minister of Finance; **financement** *m* funding, financing; **financer** ⟨1k⟩ fund, finance; **financier, -ère 1** *adj* financial **2** *m* financier; **financièrement** *adv* financially

finesse [fines] *f* (*délicatesse*) fineness

fini, ~e [fini] **1** *adj* finished, over *attr;* MATH finite **2** *m* finish; **finir** ⟨2a⟩ **1** *v/t* finish **2** *v/i* finish; ~ **de faire qch** finish doing sth; **en** ~ **avec qch** put an end to sth; ~ **par faire qch** end up *ou* finish up doing sth; ~ **à l'hôpital** end up *ou* finish up in the hospital; **finition** *f* action finishing; *qualité* finish

finlandais, ~e [fɛ̃lãdɛ, -z] **1** *adj* Finnish **2** *m langue* Finnish **3** *m/f* Finlandais, ~**e** Finn; **Finlande** *f:* **la** ~ Finland

finnois, ~e [finwa, -z] → **finlandais**

fioul [fjul] *m* fuel oil

firme [firm] *f* firm

fisc [fisk] *m* tax authorities *pl;* **fiscal, ~e** *(mpl* -aux) tax *attr;* **fiscalité** *f* tax system; (*charges*) taxation

fission [fisjɔ̃] *f* PHYS fission; **fissure** *f (craquelure)* crack; (*crevasse*) crack, fissure

fixateur [fiksatœr] *m* PHOT fixer; *pour cheveux* hair spray; **fixation** *f* fastening; (*détermination*) fixing, setting; *en ski* binding; PSYCH fixation; **fixe 1** *adj* fixed; *adresse, personnel* permanent; *prix m* ~ fixed *ou* set price **2** *m* basic salary; **fixer** ⟨1a⟩ fasten; (*déterminer*) fix, set; PHOT fix; (*regarder*) stare at; **se** ~ (*s'établir*) settle down

flacon [flakɔ̃] *m* bottle

flageolet [flaʒɔle] *m* flageolet bean

flagrant, ~e [flagrã, -t] flagrant; **en** ~ **délit** red-handed, in the act

flair [fler] *m d'un animal* sense of smell; *fig* intuition; **flairer** ⟨1b⟩ smell (*aussi fig*)

flamand, ~e [flamã, -d] **1** *adj* Flemish

2 *m/f* **Flamand, ~e** Fleming **3** *m langue* Flemish

flamant [flamɑ̃] *m*: **~ rose** flamingo

flambant, ~e [flɑ̃bɑ̃, -t]: **~ neuf** (*f inv ou* flambant neuve) brand new; **flambeau** *m* (*pl* -x) *f* torch; **flambée** *f* blaze; *fig* flare-up; **~ des prix** surge in prices; **flamber** ⟨1a⟩ **1** *v/i* blaze **2** *v/t* CUIS flambé; **flamboyant, ~e** flamboyant

flamme [flam] *f* flame; *fig* fervor, *Br* fervour; **en ~s** in flames

flan [flɑ̃] *m* flan

flanc [flɑ̃] *m* side; MIL flank

flancher [flɑ̃ʃe] ⟨1a⟩ quail

Flandre [flɑ̃dr]: **la ~** Flanders *sg*

flanelle [flanɛl] *f* flannel

flâner [flɑne] ⟨1a⟩ stroll

flanquer [flɑ̃ke] ⟨1m⟩ flank; F (*jeter*) fling; *coup* give

flaque [flak] *f* puddle

flash [flaʃ] *m* flash; *de presse* newsflash

flasque [flask] flabby

flatter [flate] ⟨1a⟩ flatter; **se ~ de qch** congratulate o.s. on sth; **flatterie** *f* flattery; **flatteur, -euse 1** *adj* flattering **2** *m/f* flatterer

flatulences [flatylɑ̃s] *fpl* flatulence *sg*

fléau [fleo] *m* (*pl* -x) *fig* scourge

flèche [flɛʃ] *f* arrow; *d'un clocher* spire; **monter en ~ de prix** skyrocket

fléchir [fleʃir] ⟨2a⟩ **1** *v/t* bend; (*faire céder*) sway **2** *v/i* *d'une poutre* bend; *fig* (*céder*) give in; (*faiblir*) weaken; *d'un prix, de ventes* fall, decline

flegmatique [flɛɡmatik] phlegmatic

flemme [flɛm] *f* F laziness; **j'ai la ~ de le faire** I can't be bothered (to do it)

flétrir [fletrir] ⟨2a⟩: **se ~** wither

fleur [flœr] *f* flower; *d'un arbre* blossom; **en ~ arbre** in blossom, in flower; **à ~s** flowery, flowered; **fleuri, ~e** *arbre* in blossom; *dessin, style* flowery, flowered; **fleurir** ⟨2a⟩ flower, bloom; *fig* flourish; **fleuriste** *m/f* florist

fleuve [flœv] *m* river

flexibilité [flɛksibilite] *f* flexibility; **flexible** flexible

flic [flik] *m* F cop F

flinguer [flɛ̃ɡe] ⟨1a⟩ F gun *ou* shoot down

flippant, ~e [flipɑ̃, -t] F (*effrayant*) creepy F

flipper 1 *m* [flipœr] pinball machine; *jeu* pinball **2** *v/i* [flipe] F freak out F

flirter [flœrte] ⟨1a⟩ flirt; **flirteur, -euse** flirtatious

flocon [flɔkɔ̃] *m* flake; **~ de neige** snowflake

floraison [flɔrɛzɔ̃] *f* flowering; **en pleine ~** in full bloom; **floral, ~e** (*mpl* -aux) flower *atr*, floral; **exposition** *f* **~e** flower show; **floralies** *fpl* flower show *sg*

flore [flɔr] *f* flora

Floride [flɔrid] *f* Florida

florissant, ~e [flɔrisɑ̃, -t] *fig* flourishing

flot [flo] *m* flood (*aussi fig*); **~s** waves; **~s de larmes** floods of tears; **entrer à ~s** flood in; **à ~** MAR afloat; **remettre à ~** refloat (*aussi fig*)

flottant, ~e [flɔtɑ̃, -t] floating; *vêtements* baggy

flotte [flɔt] *f* fleet; F (*eau*) water; F (*pluie*) rain; **flotter** ⟨1a⟩ *d'un bateau, bois* float; *d'un drapeau* flutter; *d'un sourire, air* hover; *fig* waver; **flotteur** *m* TECH float

flou, ~e [flu] blurred, fuzzy; *robe* loose-fitting

fluctuation [flyktɥasjɔ̃] *f* fluctuation; **fluctuer** ⟨1n⟩ COMM fluctuate

fluide [flɥid] **1** *adj* fluid; *circulation* moving freely **2** *m* PHYS fluid; **fluidité** *f* fluidity

fluorescent, ~e [flyɔresɑ̃, -t] fluorescent

flûte [flyt] *f* MUS, *verre* flute; *pain* thin French stick; **~ à bec** recorder; **~ traversière** flute; **flûtiste** *m/f* flutist, *Br* flautist

fluvial, ~e [flyvjal] (*mpl* -aux) river *atr*

flux [fly] *m* MAR flow

F.M. [ɛfɛm] *abr* (= **frequency modulation**) FM

FMI [ɛfɛmi] *m abr* (= **Fonds monétaire international**) IMF (= International Monetary Fund)

focaliser [fɔkalize] ⟨1a⟩ focus

fœtal, ~e [fetal] (*mpl* -aux) fetal, *Br aussi* foetal; **fœtus** *m* fetus, *Br aussi* foetus

foi [fwa] *f* faith; *être de bonne / mauvaise ~* be sincere / insincere; *ma ~!* goodness!

foie [fwa] *m* liver; *une crise de ~* a stomach upset, an upset stomach

foin [fwɛ̃] *m* hay

foire [fwar] *f* fair; *~-expo(sition)* (trade) fair

fois [fwa] *f* time; *une ~* once; *deux ~* twice; *trois / quatre ~* three / four times; *il était une ~ ...* once upon a time there was ...; *une ~ pour toutes* once and for all; *encore une ~* once again; *quatre ~ six* four times six; *à la ~* at the same time; *des ~* sometimes; *chaque ~ que je le vois* every time *ou* whenever I see him; *une ~ que* once

foisonner [fwazɔne] ⟨1a⟩ be abundant; *~ en ou de* abound in *ou* with

folie [fɔli] *f* madness; *faire des ~s achats* go on a spending spree

folk [fɔlk] *m* folk (music)

folklore [fɔlklɔr] folklore; **folklorique** folk *atr*

folle [fɔl] → *fou*; **follement** *adv* madly

fomenter [fɔmɑ̃te] ⟨1a⟩ foment

foncé, ~e [fɔ̃se] *couleur* dark; **foncer** ⟨1k⟩ *de couleurs* darken; AUTO speed along; *~ sur* rush at

foncier, -ère [fɔ̃sje, -ɛr] COMM land

foncièrement *adv* fundamentally

fonction [fɔ̃ksjɔ̃] *f* function; (*poste*) office; *~ publique* public service, *Br* civil service; *faire ~ de* act as; *être en ~* be in office; *en ~ de* according to; *~s* duties; *prendre ses ~s* take up office

fonctionnaire [fɔ̃ksjɔner] *m/f* public servant, *Br* civil servant

fonctionnel, ~le [fɔ̃ksjɔnel] functional; **fonctionnement** *m* functioning; **fonctionner** ⟨1a⟩ work; *du gouvernement, système* function

fond [fɔ̃] *m* bottom; *d'une salle, armoire* back; *d'une peinture* background; (*contenu*) content; *d'un problème* heart; *d'un pantalon* seat; *au ~ du couloir* at the end of the corridor; *de ~ en comble* from top to bottom; *à ~* thoroughly; *au ~, dans le ~* basically; *~ de teint* foundation

fondamental, ~e [fɔ̃damɑ̃tal] (*mpl* -aux) fundamental; **fondamentalement** *adv* fundamentally; **fondamentalisme** *m* fundamentalism; **fondamentaliste** *m/f* fundamentalist

fondateur, -trice [fɔ̃datœr, -tris] *m/f* founder; **fondation** *f* foundation; *~s d'un édifice* foundations; **fondé, ~e 1** *adj reproche, accusation* well-founded, justified; *mal ~* groundless, ill-founded **2** *m: ~ de pouvoir* authorized representative; **fondement** *m fig* basis; *sans ~* groundless; **fonder** ⟨1a⟩ found; *~ qch sur* base sth on; *se ~ sur d'une personne* base o.s. on; *d'une idée* be based on

fondre [fɔ̃dr] ⟨4a⟩ **1** *v/t neige* melt; *dans l'eau* dissolve; *métal* melt down **2** *v/i de la neige* melt; *dans l'eau* dissolve; *~ en larmes fig* burst into tears; *~ sur proie* pounce on

fonds [fɔ̃] *m* **1** *sg* fund; *d'une bibliothèque, collection* collection; *~ de commerce* business; *Fonds monétaire international* International Monetary Fund **2** *pl* (*argent*) funds *pl*; *~ publics* public funds; *convoyeur m de ~* security guard

fondu, ~e [fɔ̃dy] **1** *p/p* → *fondre* **2** *adj* melted

fondue [fɔ̃dy] *f* CUIS fondue; *~ bourguignonne* beef fondue

fontaine [fɔ̃tɛn] *f* fountain; (*source*) spring

fonte [fɔ̃t] *f métal* cast iron; *~ des neiges* spring thaw

foot [fut] *m* F → *football*

football [futbol] *m* soccer, *Br aussi* football; *~ américain* American football, *Br* American football; **footballeur, -euse** *m/f* soccer player, *Br aussi* footballer

footing [futiŋ] *m* jogging; *faire du ~* jog, go jogging

forage [fɔraʒ] *m pour pétrole* drilling

force [fɔrs] *f* strength; (*violence*) force; *à ~ de travailler* by working; *de ~* by force, forcibly; *de toutes ses ~s* with all one's strength; **~ de frappe** strike force; **~s armées** armed forces; **un cas de ~ majeure** an act of God; **forcé, ~e** forced; **atterrissage** m **~** forced ou emergency landing; **forcément** adv (*inévitablement*) inevitably; **pas ~** not necessarily

forcené, ~e [fɔrsəne] m/f maniac, lunatic

forceps [fɔrsɛps] m forceps

forcer [fɔrse] ⟨1k⟩ force; **~ qn à faire qch** force s.o. to do sth; **~ la note** fig go too far; **se ~** force o.s.

forer [fɔre] ⟨1a⟩ drill

forestier, -ère [fɔrɛstje, -ɛr] **1** adj forest atr **2** m ranger, Br forest warden; **forêt** f forest (aussi fig); **~ tropicale** (**humide**) rain forest

forfait [fɔrfɛ] m COMM package; (*prix*) all-in price, flat rate; **déclarer ~** withdraw; **forfaitaire** prix all-in

forgeron [fɔrʒərõ] m blacksmith

formaliser [fɔrmalize] ⟨1a⟩: **se ~ de qch** take offense ou Br offence at sth; **formalité** f formality

format [fɔrma] m format; **formatage** m INFORM formatting; **formater** ⟨1a⟩ format

formateur, -trice [fɔrmatœr, -tris] **1** adj formative **2** m/f trainer; **formation** f formation (aussi MIL, GÉOL); (*éducation*) training; **~ continue** continuing education; **~ professionnelle** vocational training; **~ sur le tas** on-the-job training

forme [fɔrm] f form; (*figure, contour*) shape, form; **sous ~ de** in the form of; **en ~ de ...** ...-shaped, in the shape of ...; **pour la ~** for form's sake; **être en ~** be in form, be in good shape; **prendre ~** take shape; **garder la ~** keep fit; **formel, ~le** formal; (*explicite*) categorical; **formellement** adv expressly; **~ interdit** strictly forbidden; **former** ⟨1a⟩ form; (*façonner*) shape, form; (*instruire*) train; **se ~** form

formidable [fɔrmidabl] enormous; F terrific, great F

formulaire [fɔrmylɛr] m form

formulation [fɔrmylasjõ] f wording

formule [fɔrmyl] f formula; **~ magique** magic spell; **formuler** ⟨1a⟩ formulate; *vœux, jugement* express

fort, ~e [fɔr, -t] **1** adj strong; (*gros*) stout; *coup, pluie* heavy; *somme, différence* big; **à plus ~e raison** all the more reason; **être ~ en qch** be good at sth; **2** adv *crier, parler* loud, loudly; *pousser, frapper* hard; (*très*) extremely; (*beaucoup*) a lot **3** m strong point; MIL fort; **fortement** adv *pousser* hard; (*beaucoup*) greatly

forteresse [fɔrtərɛs] f fortress

fortifiant [fɔrtifjã] m tonic

fortification [fɔrtifikasjõ] f fortification; **fortifier** ⟨1a⟩ *corps, construction* strengthen; MIL strengthen, fortify

fortuit, ~e [fɔrtɥi, -t] chance

fortune [fɔrtyn] f luck; **de ~** makeshift

fosse [fos] f *grand trou* pit; (*tombe*) grave; **fossé** m ditch; fig gulf; **fossette** f dimple

fossile [fɔsil] m & adj fossil; **fossilisé, ~e** fossilized

fou, folle [fu, fɔl] **1** adj mad, crazy, insane; (*incroyable*) staggering, incredible; **être ~ de qn / qch** be mad ou crazy about s.o. / sth; **~ de joie, colère** etc beside o.s. with; **une crise de ~ rire** a fit of the giggles; **~ à lier** raving mad **2** m/f madman; madwoman

foudre [fudr] f lightning; **coup** m **de ~** fig love at first sight

foudroyant, ~e [fudrwajã, -t] *regard* withering; *nouvelles, succès* stunning; **foudroyer** ⟨1h⟩ strike down; **~ qn du regard** give s.o. a withering look

fouet [fwɛ] m whip; CUIS whisk; **fouetter** ⟨1b⟩ *avec fouet* whip, flog; CUIS whisk

fougère [fuʒɛr] f fern

fougue [fug] f passion; **fougueux, -euse** fiery

fouille [fuj] f search; **~s** en archéologie dig sg; **fouiller** ⟨1a⟩ **1** v/i dig; (*chercher*) search **2** v/t de police search; en archéologie excavate; **fouilleur, -euse** m/f en archéologie excavator

fouiner [fwine] ⟨1a⟩ nose around

foulard [fular] m scarf

foule [ful] *f* crowd; *éviter la* ~ avoid the crowds; *une* ~ *de* masses of; *en* ~ in vast numbers

fouler [fule] ⟨1a⟩ trample; *sol* set foot on; ~ *aux pieds* *fig* trample underfoot; *se* ~ *la cheville* twist one's ankle; *ne pas se* ~ *fig* F not overexert o.s.; **foulure** *f* sprain

four [fur] *m* oven; TECH kiln; *fig* F (*insuccès*) turkey F, flop F; *faire un* ~ flop; *petits* ~*s* cookies, candies *etc* served at the end of a meal

fourbe [furb] deceitful

fourbu, ~e [furby] exhausted

fourche [furʃ] *f* fork; **fourchette** *f* fork; (*éventail*) bracket; **fourchu** (*cheveux* *mpl* ~*s* split ends

fourgon [furgõ] *m camion* van; RAIL baggage car, *Br* luggage van; **fourgonnette** *f* small van

fourmi [furmi] *f* ant; *avoir des* ~*s* (*dans les pieds*) have pins and needles (in one's feet); **fourmilière** *f* anthill; *c'est une véritable* ~ it's a real hive of activity; **fourmillements** *mpl* pins and needles; **fourmiller** ⟨1a⟩ swarm (*de* with)

fournaise [furnɛz] *f fig* oven; **fourneau** *m* (*pl* -x) furnace; CUIS stove; *haut* ~ blast furnace; **fournée** *f* batch (*aussi fig*)

fourni, ~e [furni]: *bien* ~ well stocked; **fournir** ⟨2a⟩ supply (*de, en* with); *occasion* provide; *effort* make; ~ *qch à qn* provide s.o. with sth; **fournisseur** *m* supplier; ~ *d'accès* (*Internet*) Internet service provider, ISP; **fourniture** *f* supply; ~*s de bureau* office supplies; ~*s scolaires* school stationery and books

fourrage [furaʒ] *m* fodder

fourré¹ [fure] *m* thicket

fourré², ~e [fure] CUIS filled; *vêtement* lined

fourrer [fure] ⟨1a⟩ stick, shove; (*remplir*) fill; ~ *son nez partout* stick one's nose into everything; *se* ~ *dans* get into; **fourre-tout** *m* (*pl inv*) (*sac*) carry-all, *Br* holdall

fourrière [furjɛr] *f* pound

fourrure [furyr] *f* fur

fourvoyer [furvwaje] ⟨1h⟩: *se* ~ go astray

foutre [futr] F ⟨4a⟩ do; (*mettre*) put, shove; *coup* give; *se* ~ *de qn* make fun of s.o.; *indifférence* not give a damn about s.o.; ~ *la paix à qn* stop bothering s.o.; ~ *le camp* get the hell out F; *je m'en fous!* I don't give a damn!; *va te faire* ~! go to hell F, fuck off V; **foutu, ~e 1** *p/p* → **foutre 2** *adj* → **fichu**

foyer [fwaje] *m* fireplace; *d'une famille* home; *d'une jeunes* club; (*pension*) hostel; *d'un théâtre* foyer; *d'un incendie* seat; *d'une infection* source; *femme f au* ~ home-maker, *Br* housewife

fracas [fraka] *m* crash; **fracassant, ~e** *effet, propos* shattering; **fracasser** ⟨1a⟩ shatter

fraction [fraksjõ] *f* fraction; **fractionner** ⟨1a⟩ divide (up) (*en* into)

fracture [fraktyr] *f* MÉD *m* fracture; **fracturer** ⟨1a⟩ *coffre* break open; *jambe* fracture

fragile [fraʒil] fragile; *santé* frail; *cœur, estomac* weak; **fragiliser** ⟨1a⟩ weaken; **fragilité** *f* fragility

fragment [fragmã] *m* fragment

fraîchement [frɛʃmã] *adv cueilli* freshly; *arrivé* recently, newly; *accueilli* coolly; **fraîcheur** *f* freshness; (*froideur*) coolness (*aussi fig*); **fraîchir** ⟨2a⟩ *du vent* freshen; *du temps* get cooler

frais¹, fraîche [frɛ, frɛʃ] **1** *adj* fresh; (*froid*) cool; *nouvelles fraîches* recent news; *servir* ~ serve chilled; *il fait* ~ it's cool; *peinture fraîche* wet paint **2** *adv* freshly, newly **3** *m*: *prendre le* ~ get a breath of fresh air; *au* ~ garder in a cool place

frais² [frɛ] *mpl* expenses; COMM costs; *faire des* ~ incur costs; *oh, tu as fait des* ~! hey, you've been spending a lot of money!, *Br aussi* you've been lashing out!; *à mes* ~ at my (own) expense; ~ *bancaires* bank charges; ~ *de déplacement* travel expenses; ~ *d'expédition* shipping costs; ~ *généraux* overhead *sg*, *Br* overheads; ~ *de port* postage

fraise [frɛz] *f* strawberry; **fraisier** *m* strawberry plant; *gâteau* strawberry cake

framboise [frãbwaz] *f* raspberry

franc[1], **franche** [frã, frãʃ] (*sincère*) frank; *regard* open; COMM free

franc[2] [frã] *m* franc

français, **~e** [frãsɛ, -z] **1** *adj* French **2** *m langue* French **3** *m* **Français** Frenchman; **les ~** the French *pl* **4** *f* **Française** Frenchwoman; **France** *f*: **la ~** France

franchement [frãʃmã] *adv* frankly; (*nettement*) really

franchir [frãʃir] ⟨2a⟩ cross; *obstacle* negotiate, get over

franchise [frãʃiz] *f caractère* frankness; (*exemption*) exemption; COMM franchise; *d'une assurance* deductible, *Br* excess; **franchiser** franchise

franco [frãko] *adv*: **~** (**de port**) carriage free; **y aller ~** *fig* F go right ahead

francophile [frãkɔfil] *m/f & adj* Francophile

francophobe [frãkɔfɔb] *m/f & adj* Francophobe

francophone [frãkɔfɔn] **1** *adj* French-speaking **2** *m/f* French speaker; **francophonie** *f*: **la ~** the French-speaking world

franc-parler [frãparle] *m* outspokenness

frange [frãʒ] *f* bangs *pl*, *Br* fringe

frangin [frãʒɛ̃] *m* F brother, broth F; **frangine** *f* F sister, sis F

frangipane [frãʒipan] *f* frangipane

franglais [frãglɛ] *m* Frenglish, mixture of English and French

franquette [frãkɛt] F: **à la bonne ~** simply

frappant, **~e** [frapã, -t] striking; **frappe** *f* INFORM keying, keyboarding; *sur machine à écrire* typing; **faute f de ~** typo, typing error; **frapper** ⟨1a⟩ **1** *v/t* hit, strike; (*impressionner*) strike, impress; **être frappé d'une maladie** be struck by a disease; **être frappé de surprise** be surprised; **~ qn d'un impôt / d'une amende** tax / fine s.o. **2** *v/i* (*agir*) strike; *à la* *porte* knock (**à** at); **~ dans ses mains** clap (one's hands)

fraternel, **~le** [fratɛrnɛl] brotherly, fraternal; **fraterniser** ⟨1a⟩ fraternize; **fraternité** *f* brotherhood

fraude [frod] *f* fraud; ÉDU cheating; **~ fiscale** tax evasion; **passer en ~** smuggle; **frauder** ⟨1a⟩ **1** *v/t fisc*, *douane* defraud **2** *v/i* cheat; **frauduleusement** *adv* fraudulently; **frauduleux**, **-euse** fraudulent

frayer [freje] ⟨1i⟩: **se ~** *chemin* clear

frayeur [frejœr] *f* fright

fredonner [frədɔne] ⟨1a⟩ hum

free-lance [frilãs] *m/f & adj* (*adj inv*) freelance

frein [frɛ̃] *m* brake; **mettre un ~ à** *fig* curb, check; **sans ~** *fig* unbridled; **~ à main** parking brake, *Br* handbrake; **freiner** ⟨1b⟩ **1** *v/i* brake **2** *v/t fig* curb, check

frêle [frɛl] frail

frelon [frəlõ] *m* hornet

frémir [fremir] ⟨2a⟩ shake; *de feuilles* quiver; *de l'eau* simmer; **frémissement** *m* shiver; *de feuilles* quivering

frêne [frɛn] *m* BOT ash (tree)

frénésie [frenezi] *f* frenzy; **avec ~** frantically, frenetically; **frénétique** *applaudissements* frenzied

fréquemment [frekamã] *adv* frequently; **fréquence** *f* frequency (*aussi* PHYS); **quelle est la ~ des bus?** how often do the buses go?; **fréquent**, **~e** frequent; *situation* common

fréquentation [frekãtasjõ] *f d'un théâtre*, *musée* attendance; **tes ~s** (*amis*) the company you keep; **fréquenter** ⟨1a⟩ *endroit* go to regularly, frequent; *personne* see; *bande, groupe* go around with

frère [frɛr] *m* brother

fresque [frɛsk] *f* fresco

fret [frɛ] *m* freight

frétiller [fretije] ⟨1a⟩ wriggle

freudien, **~ne** [frødjɛ̃, -ɛn] Freudian

friable [frijabl] crumbly, friable

friand, **~e** [frijã, -d]: **être ~ de qch** be fond of sth; **friandises** *fpl* sweet things

fric [frik] *m* F money, cash, dosh F

friche [friʃ] *f* AGR: **en ~** (lying) fallow

friction [friksjõ] *f* TECH, *fig* friction; *de la tête* scalp massage; **frictionner** ⟨1a⟩ massage

frigidaire [friʒidɛr] *m* refrigerator

frigide [friʒid] frigid; **frigidité** *f* frigidity

frigo [frigo] *m* F icebox, fridge; **frigorifier** ⟨1a⟩ refrigerate; **frigorifique** *camion, wagon* refrigerated

frileux, -euse [frilø, -z]: **être ~** feel the cold

frimer [frime] ⟨1a⟩ show off; **frimeur, -euse** show-off

fringale [frɛ̃gal] *f* F: **avoir la ~** be starving

fringues [frɛ̃g] *fpl* F clothes, gear F *sg*

friper [fripe] ⟨1a⟩ crease

fripouille [fripuj] *f* F rogue

frire [frir] ⟨4m⟩ **1** *v/i* fry **2** *v/t*: **faire ~** fry

frisé, ~e [frize] curly; **friser** ⟨1a⟩ *cheveux* curl; *fig: le ridicule* verge on; **~ la soixantaine** be pushing sixty, be verging on sixty

frisson [frisõ] *m* shiver; **frissonner** ⟨1a⟩ shiver

frit, ~e [fri, -t] **1** *p/p* → **frire 2** *adj* fried; (**pommes**) **frites** *fpl* (French) fries, *Br aussi* chips; **friteuse** *f* deep fryer; **friture** *f poissons Br* whitebait, small fried fish; *huile* oil; *à la radio,* TÉL interference

frivole [frivɔl] frivolous; **frivolité** *f* frivolity

froid, ~e [frwa, -d] **1** *adj* cold (*aussi fig*); **j'ai ~** I'm cold; **il fait ~** it's cold; **prendre ~** catch (a) cold **2** *m* cold; **démarrage** *m* **à ~** cold start; **à ~** *fig* just like that; (*par surprise*) off guard; **humour** *m* **à ~** dry humor; **froidement** *adv fig* coldly; (*calmement*) coolly; *tuer* in cold blood; **froideur** *f* coldness

froissement [frwasmã] *m bruit* rustle; **froisser** ⟨1a⟩ crumple; *fig* offend; **se ~** crumple; *fig* take offense *ou Br* offence

frôler [frole] ⟨1a⟩ brush against; *fig: catastrophe, mort* come close to

fromage [frɔmaʒ] *m* cheese; **~ blanc** fromage frais; **~ de chèvre** goat's cheese; **~ râpé** grated cheese; **~ à tartiner** cheese spread

froment [frɔmã] *m* wheat

froncement [frõsmã] *m*: **~ de sourcils** frown; **froncer** ⟨1k⟩ gather; **~ les sourcils** frown

fronde [frõd] *f* slingshot, *Br* catapult

front [frõ] *m* ANAT forehead; MIL, *météorologie* front; *de ~* from the front; *fig* head-on; **~ de mer** sea front; **marcher de ~** walk side by side; **faire ~ à** face up to; **frontalier, -ère** frontier *atr*, border *atr*; **frontière** *f* frontier, border

frottement [frɔtmã] *m* rubbing; **frotter** ⟨1a⟩ **1** *v/i* rub **2** *v/t* rub (*de* with); *meuble* polish; *sol* scrub; *allumette* strike; **frottis** *m* MÉD: **~ (vaginal)** Pap test, *Br* smear

frousse [frus] *f* F fear; **avoir la ~** be scared

fructifier [fryktifje] ⟨1a⟩ BOT bear fruit; *d'un placement* yield a profit; **fructueux, -euse** fruitful

frugal, ~e [frygal] (*mpl* -aux) frugal

fruit [frɥi] *m* fruit; **un ~** some fruit; **~s** fruit *sg*; **~s de mer** seafood *sg*; **fruité, ~e** [frɥite] fruity; **fruitier, -ère**: **arbre** *m* **~** fruit tree

frustrant [frystrã] frustrating; **frustration** *f* frustration; **frustrer** ⟨1a⟩ frustrate

fuel [fjul] *m* fuel oil

fugace [fygas] fleeting

fugitif, -ive [fyʒitif, -iv] **1** *adj* runaway; *fig* fleeting **2** *m/f* fugitive, runaway

fugue [fyg] *f d'un enfant* escapade; MUS fugue; **faire une ~** run away; **fuguer** ⟨1a⟩ run away

fuir [fɥir] ⟨2d⟩ **1** *v/i* flee; *du temps* fly; *d'un tonneau, tuyau* leak; *d'un robinet* drip; *d'un liquide* leak out **2** *v/t* shun; *question* avoid; **fuite** *f* flight (*devant* from); *d'un tonneau, d'un tuyau, d'informations* leak; **mettre en ~** put to flight; **prendre la ~** take flight

fulgurant, ~e [fylgyrã, -t] dazzling; *vitesse* lightning

fumé, **~e** [fyme] smoked; *verre* tinted

fume-cigarette [fymsigaret] *m* (*pl inv*) cigarette holder

fumée [fyme] *f* smoke; **défense de ~** no smoking; **fumeur**, **-euse** *m/f* smoker; **fumeux**, **-euse** *fig* hazy

fumier [fymje] *m* manure

funèbre [fynebr] funeral *atr*; (*lugubre*) gloomy

funérailles [fyneraj] *fpl* funeral *sg*

funeste [fynest] *erreur*, *suite* fatal

funiculaire [fynikyler] *m* incline railway, *Br* funicular (railway)

fur [fyr]: **au ~ et à mesure** as I / you *etc* go along; **au ~ et à mesure que** as

furet [fyre] *m* ferret; **fureter** ⟨1e⟩ ferret around

fureur [fyrœr] *f* fury; **entrer dans une ~ noire** fly into a towering rage; **faire ~** be all the rage

furibond, **~e** [fyribõ, -d] furious, livid

furie [fyri] (*colère*) fury; *femme* shrew; **furieux**, **-euse** furious (*contre qn* with s.o.; *de qch* with *ou* at sth)

furoncle [fyrõkl] *m* boil

furtif, **-ive** [fyrtif, -iv] furtive, stealthy; **furtivement** *adv* furtively, stealthily

fusain [fyzẽ] *m* charcoal

fuseau [fyzo] *m* (*pl* -x): **~ horaire** time zone

fusée [fyze] *f* rocket; **~ de détresse** distress rocket

fuselage [fyzlaʒ] *m* fuselage

fuser [fyze] ⟨1a⟩ *fig* come thick and fast

fusible *m* [fysibl] ÉL fuse

fusil [fyzi] *m* rifle; **~ de chasse** shotgun; **fusillade** *f* firing, gun fire; **fusiller** ⟨1a⟩ execute by firing squad; **fusil-mitrailleur** *m* (light) machine gun

fusion [fyzjõ] *f* COMM merger; PHYS fusion; **fusionner** ⟨1a⟩ COMM merge

futé, **~e** [fyte] cunning, clever

futile [fytil] *chose* futile, trivial; *personne* frivolous; **futilité** *f* futility

futur, **~e** [fytyr] *m* & *adj* future; **futuriste** futuristic

fuyant, **~e** [fɥijã, -t] *menton* receding; *regard* evasive

G

gabarit *m* size; TECH template

gâcher [gaʃe] ⟨1a⟩ *fig* spoil; *travail* bungle; *temps*, *argent* waste

gâchette [gaʃet] *f* MIL trigger

gâchis [gaʃi] *m* (*désordre*) mess; (*gaspillage*) waste

gadget [gadʒet] *m* gadget

gaffe [gaf] *f* F blooper F, blunder; **faire ~ à** F be careful of, take care of; **gaffer** ⟨1a⟩ F make a gaffe *ou* blooper F

gag *m* joke

gage [gaʒ] *fig* forfeit; (*preuve*) token; **tueur** *m* **à ~s** hired killer, hitman; **mettre en ~** pawn

gagnant, **~e** [gaɲã, -t] **1** *adj* winning **2** *m/f* winner

gagne-pain [gaɲpẽ] *m* (*pl inv*) livelihood

gagner [gaɲe] ⟨1a⟩ *salaire*, *réputation*, *amitié* earn; *place*, *temps* gain, save; *endroit* reach; *de peur*, *sommeil* overcome; **~ sa vie** earn one's living

gai, **~e** [ge, gɛ] cheerful; *un peu ivre* tipsy; **gaiement** *adv* cheerfully; **gaieté** *f* cheerfulness; **de ~ de cœur** willingly

gain [gẽ] *m* gain; (*avantage*) benefit; **~s** profits; *d'un employé* earnings; **~ de temps** time-saving

gaine [gɛn] f sheath

gala [gala] m gala

galant, **~e** [galɑ̃, -t] galant; **homme ~** gentleman; **rendez-vous ~** (romantic) rendez-vous; **galanterie** f galantry

galaxie [galaksi] f galaxy

galbé, **~e** [galbe] jambes shapely

galère [galɛr] f: **il est dans la ~** fig F he's in a mess; **galérer** F sweat

galerie [galri] f gallery; AUTO roof-rack; **~ d'art** art gallery; **~ marchande** mall, Br aussi (shopping) arcade

galet [galɛ] m pebble

galette [galɛt] f type of flat cake; **~ des rois** cake traditionally eaten to celebrate Twelfth Night (6 January)

galipette [galipɛt] f F somersault

Galles [gal] fpl: **le pays m de ~** Wales; **gallois**, **~e 1** adj Welsh **2** m langue Welsh **3** **Gallois**, **~e** m/f Welshman; Welsh woman

galon [galõ] m braid; MIL stripe

galop [galo] m gallop; **galopant** inflation galloping; **galoper** ⟨1a⟩ gallop

galopin [galɔpɛ̃] m urchin

galvaniser [galvanize] ⟨1a⟩ galvanize

gambader [gɑ̃bade] gambol, leap

gamelle [gamɛl] f MIL mess tin

gamin, **~e** [gamɛ̃, -in] **1** m/f kid **2** adj childlike

gamme [gam] f MUS scale; fig range; **haut de ~** top-of-the-line, Br top-of-the-range; **bas de ~** downscale, Br downmarket

ganglion [gɑ̃glijõ] m: **avoir des ~s** have swollen glands

gang [gɑ̃g] m gang

gangrène [gɑ̃grɛn] f gangrene

gangster [gɑ̃gstɛr] m gangster

gant [gɑ̃] m glove; **~ de boxe** boxing glove; **~ de toilette** washcloth, Br facecloth

garage [garaʒ] m garage; **garagiste** m auto mechanic, Br car mechanic; propriétaire garage owner

garant, **~e** [garɑ̃, -t] m/f guarantor; **se porter ~ de** answer for; JUR stand guarantor for; **garantie** f guarantee; **sous ~** COMM under guarantee ou warranty; **garantir** ⟨2a⟩ guarantee

garce [gars] f F bitch

garçon [garsõ] m boy; (serveur) waiter; **~ d'honneur** best man; **~ manqué** tomboy; **petit ~** little boy; **garçonnière** f bachelor apartment ou Br flat

garde[1] [gard] f care (de of); MIL soldats guard; **chien m de ~** guard dog; **droit m de ~** JUR custody; **prendre ~** be careful; **être sur ses ~s** be on one's guard; **de ~** médecin, pharmacien duty atr; **être de ~** be on duty; **monter la ~** mount guard; **mettre qn en ~** warn s.o., put s.o. on their guard; **la relève de la ~** MIL the changing of the guard; **à vue** police custody

garde[2] [gard] m guard; **~ du corps** bodyguard; **~ forestier** (forest) ranger; **~ des Sceaux** Minister of Justice; **garde-à-vous** m MIL attention

garde-boue [gardəbu] m (pl inv) AUTO fender, Br mudguard

garde-chasse [gardəʃas] m (pl gardes-chasse⟨s⟩) gamekeeper

garde-côte [gardəkot] m (pl garde-côte⟨s⟩) coastguard boat

garde-fou [gardəfu] m (pl garde-fous) railing

garde-malade [gardəmalad] m/f (pl gardes-malade⟨s⟩) nurse

garde-manger [gardəmɑ̃ʒe] m (pl inv) larder

garde-meuble [gardəmœbl] m (pl garde-meuble⟨s⟩) furniture repository

garder [garde] ⟨1a⟩ objet keep; vêtement keep on; (surveiller) guard; malade, enfant, animal look after, take care of; **~ pour soi** renseignements keep to o.s.; **~ le silence** remain silent; **~ la chambre** stay in ou keep to one's room; **se ~ de faire qch** be careful not to do sth; **garderie** f daycare center, Br daycare centre

garde-robe [gardərɔb] f (pl garde-robes) armoire closet, Br wardrobe; vêtements wardrobe

gardien, **~ne** [gardjɛ̃, -ɛn] m/f de prison guard, Br warder; d'un musée attendant; *d'un immeuble, d'une école* janitor, *Br aussi* caretaker; *fig* guardian; **~ (de but)** goalkeeper, goalie F; **~ de la paix** police officer

gare¹ [gar] *f* station; **~ routière** bus station

gare² [gar]: **~ à ...!** watch out for ...!; **~ à toi!** watch out!; *ça va mal se passer* you'll be for it!

garer [gare] ⟨1a⟩ *f* park; **se ~** park; *pour laisser passer* move aside

gargariser [gargarize] ⟨1a⟩: **se ~** gargle

gargouille [garguj] *f* ARCH gargoyle; **gargouiller** ⟨1a⟩ gurgle; *de l'estomac* rumble

garnement [garnəmã] *m* rascal

garnir [garnir] ⟨2a⟩ *(fournir)* fit *(de* with); *(orner)* trim *(de* with); **garni de légumes** CUIS served with vegetables

garnison [garnizõ] *f* MIL garrison

garniture [garnityr] *f* CUIS *légumes* vegetables *pl*

gars [gɑ] *m* F guy F

Gascogne [gaskɔɲ] *f* Gascony; **golfe** *m* **de ~** Bay of Biscay

gasoil [gazwal, gazɔjl] *m* gas oil, *Br* diesel

gaspillage [gaspijaʒ] *m* waste; **gaspiller** ⟨1a⟩ waste, squander; **gaspilleur, -euse** **1** *adj* wasteful **2** *m/f* waster

gastrique [gastrik] gastric

gastroentérite [gastrɔãterit] *f* gastroenteritis

gastronome [gastrɔnɔm] *m/f* gourmet; **gastronomie** *f* gastronomy; **gastronomique** gourmet *atr*

gâté, ~e [gate] spoilt

gâteau [gato] *m (pl -x)* cake; **~ sec** cookie, *Br* biscuit; **~ d'anniversaire** birthday cake

gâter [gate] ⟨1a⟩ spoil; **se ~** *d'un aliment* spoil; *du temps* deteriorate

gâteux, -euse [gatø, -z] senile, gaga F

gauche [goʃ] **1** *adj* left, left-hand; *manières* gauche, awkward **2** *f* left; **à ~** on the left *(de* of); **tourner à ~** turn left *ou* to the left; **la ~** POL the left (wing); **de ~** POL on the left,

leftwing; **gaucher, -ère 1** *adj* left-handed **2** *m/f* left-hander, lefty F; **gauchiste** *m/f* POL leftist

gaufre [gofr] *f* waffle; **gaufrette** *f* wafer

Gaule [gol]: **la ~** Gaul

gaulliste [golist] Gaullist

gaulois, ~e [golwa, -z] **1** *adj* Gallic; *fig* spicy **2** *m langue* Gaulish **3** *m/f* **Gaulois, ~e** Gaul

gaver [gave] ⟨1a⟩ *oie* force-feed; **~ qn de qch** *fig* stuff s.o. full of sth; **se ~ de qch** stuff o.s. with sth

gaz [gɑz] *m* gas; **~ naturel** natural gas; **mettre les ~** step on the gas, *Br* put one's foot down; **~** *pl* **d'échappement** AUTO exhaust *sg*, exhaust fumes; **~ à effet de serre** greenhouse gas; **~ lacrymogène** tear gas

gaze [gɑz] *f* gauze

gazelle [gazɛl] *f* gazelle

gazeux, -euse [gazø, -z] *boisson, eau* carbonated, *Br* fizzy

gazinière [gazinjɛr] *f* gas cooker

gazoduc [gazɔdyk] *m* gas pipeline

gazole [gazɔl] *m* gas oil, *Br* diesel

gazon [gɑzõ] *m* grass

gazouiller [gazuje] ⟨1a⟩ *oiseaux* twitter

geai [ʒɛ] *m* jay

géant, ~e [ʒeɑ̃, -t] **1** *adj* gigantic, giant *atr* **2** *m/f* giant

geindre [ʒɛ̃dr] ⟨4b⟩ groan

gel [ʒɛl] *m* frost; *fig: des salaires, prix* freeze; *cosmétique* gel

gélatine [ʒelatin] *f* gelatine

gelée [ʒəle] *f* frost; CUIS aspic; *confiture* jelly, *Br* jam; **geler** ⟨1d⟩ *v/t* freeze **2** *v/i d'une personne* freeze; **il gèle** there's a frost

gélule [ʒelyl] *f* PHARM capsule

Gémeaux [ʒemo] *mpl* ASTROL Gemini

gémir [ʒemir] ⟨2a⟩ groan; **gémissement** *m* groan

gênant, ~e [ʒɛnɑ̃, -t] *(embarrassant)* embarrassing

gencive [ʒɑ̃siv] *f* gum

gendarme [ʒɑ̃darm] *m* policeman, gendarme; **gendarmerie** *f* police force; *lieu* police station

gendre [ʒɑ̃dr] *m* son-in-law

gène [ʒɛn] *m* BIOL gene

gêne [ʒɛn] *f* (*embarras*) embarrassment; (*dérangement*) inconvenience; *physique* difficulty; **sans ~** shameless; **gêné, ~e** embarrassed; **gêner** ⟨1b⟩ bother; (*embarrasser*) embarrass; (*encombrer*) be in the way; **~ le passage** be in the way

généalogique [ʒenealɔʒik] genealogical; **arbre ~** family tree

général, ~e [ʒeneral] (*mpl* -aux) **1** *adj* general; **en ~** generally, in general; (*habituellement*) generally, usually **2** *m* MIL general **3** *f* THÉÂT dress rehearsal; **généralement** *adv* generally; **généralisation** *f* generalization; *d'un cancer* spread; **généraliser** ⟨1a⟩ generalize; **se ~** spread; **généraliste** *m* MÉD generalist; **généralités** *fpl* generalities

générateur [ʒeneratœr] *m* generator; **génération** [ʒenerasjɔ̃] *f* generation; **générer** ⟨1a⟩ generate

généreux, -euse [ʒenerø, -z] generous

générique [ʒenerik] **1** *adj* generic **2** *m* de cinéma credits *pl*

générosité [ʒenerozite] *f* generosity

genêt [ʒ(ə)nɛ] *m* BOT broom, gorse

généticien, ~ne [ʒenetisjɛ̃, -ɛn] *m/f* geneticist; **génétique 1** *adj* genetic **2** *f* genetics; **génétiquement** *adv* genetically; **~ modifié** genetically modified, GM

Genève [ʒ(ə)nɛv] Geneva

génial, ~e [ʒenjal] (*mpl* -iaux) of genius; (*formidable*) great, terrific; **génie** *m* TECH engineering; **de ~** of genius; *idée* which shows genius; **avoir du ~** be a genius; **~ civil** civil engineering; **~ génétique** genetic engineering

génisse [ʒenis] *f* heifer

génital, ~e [ʒenital] (*mpl* -aux) genital

génocide [ʒenɔsid] *m* genocide

génoise [ʒenwaz] *f* sponge cake

genou [ʒ(ə)nu] *m* (*pl* -x) knee; **à ~x** on one's knees; **se mettre à ~x** kneel (down), go down on one's knees; **genouillère** *f* kneepad

genre [ʒɑ̃r] *m* kind, sort; GRAM gender; **bon chic, bon ~** preppie *atr*

gens [ʒɑ̃] *mpl* people *pl*

gentil, ~le [ʒɑ̃ti, -j] nice; (*aimable*) kind, nice; *enfant* good; REL Gentile; **gentillesse** *f* (*amabilité*) kindness; **gentiment** *adv* (*aimablement*) kindly, nicely; (*sagement*) nicely, well

géographie [ʒeɔgrafi] *f* geography; **géographique** geographic

géologie [ʒeɔlɔʒi] *f* geology; **géologique** geological; **géologue** *m/f* geologist

géomètre [ʒeɔmetr] *m/f* geometrician; **géométrie** *f* geometry; **géométrique** geometric

géophysique [ʒeɔfizik] *f* geophysics *sg*

géopolitique [ʒeɔpɔlitik] *f* geopolitics

gérable [ʒerabl] manageable; **gérance** *f* management

géranium [ʒeranjɔm] *m* BOT geranium

gérant, ~e [ʒerɑ̃, -t] *m/f* manager

gerbe [ʒɛrb] *f* de blé sheaf; de fleurs spray

gercé, ~e [ʒɛrse] *lèvres* chapped

gérer [ʒere] ⟨1f⟩ manage

gériatrie [ʒerjatri] *f* geriatrics; **gériatrique** geriatric

germain, ~e [ʒɛrmɛ̃, -ɛn]: **cousin ~**, **cousine** *f* **~e** (first) cousin

germanique [ʒɛrmanik] Germanic

germe [ʒɛrm] *m* germ (*aussi fig*); **germer** ⟨1a⟩ germinate

gestation [ʒɛstasjɔ̃] *f* gestation

geste [ʒɛst] *m* gesture; **gesticuler** ⟨1a⟩ gesticulate

gestion [ʒɛstjɔ̃] *f* management; **gestionnaire** *m/f* manager; **~ de fichiers** file manager

ghetto [ɡeto] *m* ghetto

gibet [ʒibɛ] *m* gallows *pl*

gibier [ʒibje] *m* game

giboulée [ʒibule] *f* wintry shower

gicler [ʒikle] ⟨1a⟩ spurt

gifle [ʒifl] *f* slap (in the face); **gifler** ⟨1a⟩ slap (in the face)

gigantesque [ʒiɡɑ̃tɛsk] gigantic

gigaoctet [ʒiɡaɔkte] *m* gigabyte

gigot [ʒiɡo] *m* CUIS d'agneau leg

gigoter [ʒigɔte] ⟨1a⟩ F fidget

gilet [ʒilɛ] *m* vest, *Br* waistcoat; (*chandail*) cardigan; **~ pare-balles** bulletproof vest; **~ de sauvetage** lifejacket

gin [dʒin] *m* gin; **~ tonic** gin and tonic, G and T

gingembre [ʒɛ̃ʒɑ̃br] *m* BOT ginger

girafe [ʒiraf] *f* giraffe

giratoire [ʒiratwar]: **sens** *m* **~** traffic circle, *Br* roundabout

girofle [ʒirɔfl] *m* CUIS: **clou** *m* **de ~** clove

girouette [ʒirwɛt] *f* weather vane

gisement [ʒizmɑ̃] *m* GÉOL deposit; **~ pétrolifère** *ou* **de pétrole** oilfield

gitan, ~e [ʒitɑ̃, -an] **1** *adj* gypsy *atr* **2** *m/f* gypsy

gîte [ʒit] *m* (*rental*) cottage, *Br* holiday cottage *ou* home

givre [ʒivr] *m* frost; **givré, ~e** covered with frost; *avec du sucre* frosted; F (*fou*) crazy; **orange** *f* **~e** orange sorbet

glaçage [glasaʒ] *m* d'un gâteau frosting, *Br* icing; *d'une tarte* glazing; **glace** *f* ice (*aussi fig*); (*miroir*) mirror; AUTO window; (*crème glacée*) ice cream; *d'un gâteau* frosting, *Br* icing; *d'une tarte* glaze; **glacé, ~e** (*gelé*) frozen; *vent, accueil* icy; *boisson* iced; *papier* glossy; **glacer** ⟨1k⟩ freeze; (*intimider*) petrify; *gâteau* frost, *Br* ice; *tarte* glaze; **se ~** freeze; *du sang* run cold; **glacial, ~e** (*mpl* -iaux *ou* -ials) icy (*aussi fig*); **glacier** *m* glacier; *vendeur* ice cream seller; **glacière** *f* cool bag; *fig* icebox; **glaçon** *m* icicle; *artificiel* icecube

glaise [glɛz] *f* (*aussi* **terre** *f* **~**) clay

gland [glɑ̃] *m* acorn

glande [glɑ̃d] *f* gland

glander [glɑ̃de] ⟨1a⟩ F hang around F; **glandeur, -euse** *m/f* F layabout F

glaner [glane] ⟨1a⟩ *fig* glean

glapir [glapir] ⟨2a⟩ shriek

glas [glɑ] *m* death knell

glauque [glok] *eau* murky; *couleur* blue-green

glissade [glisad] *f* slide; *accidentelle* slip; **faire des ~s** slide; **glissant, ~e** slippery, slippy; **glissement** *m*

~ de terrain landslide; **glisser** ⟨1a⟩ **1** *v/t* slip (**dans** into) **2** *v/i* slide; *sur l'eau* glide (**sur** over); (*déraper*) slip; *être glissant* be slippery *ou* slippy; **se ~ dans** slip into; **glissière** *f* TECH runner; **à ~ porte** sliding; **fermeture** *f* **à ~** zipper, *Br* zip; **~ de sécurité** crash barrier

global, ~e [glɔbal] (*mpl* -aux) global; *prix, somme* total, overall; **globalement** *adv* globally; **globalisation** *f* globalization; **globe** *m* globe; **~ oculaire** eyeball; **~ terrestre** globe

globule [glɔbyl] *m* globule; MÉD blood cell, corpuscle; **globuleux, -euse** *yeux* bulging

gloire [glwar] *f* glory; **glorieux, -euse** glorious; **glorifier** ⟨1a⟩ glorify

glossaire [glɔsɛr] *m* glossary

gloussement [glusmɑ̃] *m* clucking; *rire* giggle; **glousser** ⟨1a⟩ cluck; *rire* giggle

glouton, ~ne [glutɔ̃, -ɔn] **1** *adj* greedy, gluttonous **2** *m/f* glutton; **gloutonnerie** *f* gluttony

gluant, ~e [glyɑ̃, -t] sticky

glucide [glysid] *m* CHIM carbohydrate

glucose [glykoz] *m* glucose

gluten [glytɛn] *m* CHIM gluten

glycine [glisin] *f* wisteria

gnangnan [ɲɑ̃ɲɑ̃] (*fem inv*) F *film, livre* sloppy F, sentimental

G.O. *abr* (= **grandes ondes**) LW (= long wave)

goal [gol] *m* goalkeeper

gobelet [gɔblɛ] *m* tumbler; *en carton, plastique* cup

gober [gɔbe] ⟨1a⟩ gobble; F *mensonge* swallow

godasse [gɔdas] *f* F shoe

godet [gɔdɛ] *m récipient* pot; *de vêtements* flare

goéland [gɔelɑ̃] *m* (sea)gull

goélette [gɔelɛt] *f* MAR schooner

gogo [gogo] F: **à ~** galore

goguenard, ~e [gɔgnar, -d] mocking

goinfre [gwɛ̃fr] **1** *m* glutton **2** *adj* gluttonous; **goinfrer** ⟨1a⟩: **se ~** *péj* stuff o.s.

golf [gɔlf] *m* SP golf; *terrain* golf course

golfe [gɔlf] *m* GÉOGR gulf

golfeur, -euse [gɔlfœr, -øz] *m/f* golfer

gomme [gɔm] *f* gum; *pour effacer* eraser; **gommer** ⟨1a⟩ *(effacer)* erase *(aussi fig)*

gond [gõ] *m* hinge; **sortir de ses ~s** fly off the handle

gondole [gõdɔl] *f* gondola; **gondoler** ⟨1a⟩: **se ~** *du papier* curl; *du bois* warp

gonflable [gõflabl] inflatable; **gonflement** *m* swelling; **gonfler** ⟨1a⟩ **1** *v/i* swell **2** *v/t* blow up, inflate; *(exagérer)* exaggerate

gong [gõg] *m* gong

gonzesse [gõzɛs] *f* F *péj* chick F

gorge [gɔrʒ] *f* throat; *(poitrine)* bosom; GÉOGR gorge; **avoir mal à la ~** have a sore throat; **gorgée** *f* mouthful; **gorger** ⟨1a⟩: **se ~** gorge o.s. *(de* with*)*

gorille [gɔrij] *m* gorilla; *fig* F bodyguard, minder F

gosier [gozje] *m* throat

gosse [gɔs] *m/f* F kid F

gothique [gɔtik] **1** *adj* Gothic **2** *m/f* Goth

gouache [gwaʃ] *f* gouache

goudron [gudrõ] *m* tar; **goudronner** ⟨1a⟩ asphalt, *Br* tar

gouffre [gufr] *m* abyss; *fig* depths *pl*

goujat [guʒa] *m* boor

goulot [gulo] *m* neck; **boire au ~** drink from the bottle

goulu, ~e [guly] greedy

gourd, ~e [gur, -d] numb (with the cold)

gourde [gurd] *f récipient* water bottle; *fig* F moron

gourdin [gurdɛ̃] *m* club

gourer [gure] ⟨1a⟩ F: **se ~** goof F, *Br* boob

gourmand, ~e [gurmã, -d] **1** *adj* greedy **2** *m/f* person who likes to eat, gourmand; **gourmandise** *f* greediness; **~s** *mets* delicacies; **gourmet** *m* gourmet

gourmette [gurmɛt] *f* chain

gourou [guru] *m* guru

gousse [gus] *f* pod; **~ d'ail** clove of garlic

goût [gu] *m* taste; **de bon ~** tasteful, in good taste; **de mauvais ~** tasteless,

in bad taste; **avoir du ~** have taste; **prendre ~ à qch** develop a taste *ou* liking for sth; **goûter 1** *v/t* ⟨1a⟩ taste; *fig* enjoy, appreciate **2** *v/i prendre un goûter* have an afternoon snack **3** *m* afternoon snack

goutte [gut] *f* drop; **tomber ~ à ~** drip; **~ de pluie** raindrop; **goutte-à- -goutte** *m* MÉD drip; **gouttelette** *f* little drop; **goutter** ⟨1a⟩ drip; **gouttière** *f* gutter

gouvernail [guvɛrnaj] *m* (*pl* -s) tiller, helm

gouverne [guvɛrn] *f* MAR steering; **pour ta / sa ~** for your / his guidance

gouvernement [guvɛrnəmã] *m* government; **gouvernemental, ~e** (*mpl* -aux) government *air*, governmental; **gouverner** ⟨1a⟩ *pays* govern; *passions* master, control; MAR steer; **gouverneur** *m* governor

grabuge [grabyʒ] *m* F stink F

grâce [grɑs] *f* grace; *(bienveillance)* favor, *Br* favour; JUR pardon; **de bonne ~** with good grace, willingly; **de mauvaise ~** grudgingly, unwillingly; **faire ~ à qn de qch** spare s.o. sth; **rendre ~ à Dieu** give thanks to God; **~ à** thanks to; **être dans les bonnes ~s de qn** be in s.o.'s good books; **un délai de ~ de deux jours** two days' grace; **gracier** [grasje] ⟨1a⟩ reprieve; **gracieusement** *adv* gracefully; **gracieux, -euse** graceful; **à titre ~** free

grade [grad] *m* rank; **gradé** *m* MIL noncommissioned officer

gradins *mpl* SP bleachers, *Br* terraces

graduel, ~le [gradyɛl] gradual; **graduellement** *adv* gradually; **graduer** ⟨1n⟩ *(augmenter)* gradually increase; *instrument* graduate

graffitis [grafiti] *mpl* graffiti *sg ou pl*

grain [grɛ̃] *m* grain; MAR squall; **poulet** *m* **de ~** cornfed chicken; **~ de beauté** mole, beauty spot; **~ de café** coffee bean; **~ de poivre** peppercorn; **~ de raisin** grape

graine [grɛn] *f* seed

graissage [grɛsaʒ] *m* lubrication,

greasing; **graisse** f fat; TECH grease; **graisser** ⟨1b⟩ grease, lubricate; (*salir*) get grease on; **graisseux, -euse** greasy

grammaire [gramer] f grammar; **grammatical, ~e** (*mpl* -aux) grammatical

gramme [gram] m gram

grand, ~e [grã, -d] **1** *adj* big, large; (*haut*) tall; (*adulte*) grown-up; (*long*) long; (*important, glorieux*) great; *frère, sœur* big; **quand je serai ~** when I grow up; **les ~es personnes** fpl grown-ups, adults; **au ~ air** in the open air; **~ malade** m seriously ill patient; **il est ~ temps** it's high time; **~e surface** f supermarket, Br superstore; **il n'y avait pas ~ monde** there weren't many people; **les ~es vacances** fpl the summer vacation sg, Br the summer holidays; **~ ensemble** new development, Br (*housing*) estate **2** *adv* ouvrir wide; **voir ~** think big; **~ ouvert** wide open **3** m giant, great man; **les ~s de ce monde** those in high places

grand-chose [grãʃoz]: **pas ~** not much

Grande-Bretagne [grãdbrətaɲ]: **la ~** Great Britain

grandement [grãdmã] *adv* (*beaucoup*) greatly; **grandeur** f (*taille*) size; **~ nature** lifesize; **grandiose** *spectacle, vue* magnificent; **grandir** ⟨2a⟩ **1** *v/i* (*croître*) grow; (*augmenter*) grow, increase **2** *v/t*: **~ qn** make s.o. look taller; *de l'expérience* strengthen s.o.

grand-mère [grãmer] f (pl grand(s)-mères) grandmother

grand-père [grãper] m (pl grands-pères) grandfather

grand-route [grãrut] f (pl grand(s)-routes) highway, main road

grand-rue [grãry] f (pl grand(s)-rues) main street

grands-parents [grãparã] mpl grand-parents

grange [grãʒ] f barn

granit(e) [granit] m granite

granuleux, -euse [granylø, -z] granular

graphique [grafik] **1** *adj* graphic **2** m chart; MATH graph; INFORM graphic; **graphiste** m/f graphic designer

grappe [grap] f cluster; **~ de raisin** bunch of grapes

grappin [grapɛ̃] m: **mettre le ~ sur qn** get one's hands on s.o.

gras, ~se [grɑ, -s] **1** *adj* fatty, fat; *personne* fat; *cheveux, peau* greasy; **faire la ~se matinée** sleep late, Br have a lie-in **2** m CUIS fat; **grassouillet, ~te** plump, cuddly

gratification [gratifikasjõ] f (*prime*) bonus; PSYCH gratification; **gratifiant, ~e** gratifying; **gratifier** ⟨1a⟩: **~ qn de qch** present s.o. with sth

gratin [gratɛ̃] m dish served with a coating of grated cheese; **gratiné, ~e** CUIS with a sprinkling of cheese; *fig* F *addition* colossal

gratis [gratis] free (of charge)

gratitude [gratityd] f gratitude

gratte-ciel [gratsjɛl] m (pl inv) skyscraper

gratter [grate] ⟨1a⟩ scratch; (*enlever*) scrape; (*griffer, piquer*) scratch; (*enlever*) scrape off; *mot, signature* scratch out; **se ~** scratch; **grattoir** m scraper

gratuit, ~e [gratɥi, -t] free; *fig* gratuitous; **gratuitement** adv for nothing, free of charge; *fig* gratuitously

gravats [grava] mpl rubble sg

grave [grav] (*sérieux*) serious, grave; *maladie, faute* serious; *son* deep; **ce n'est pas ~** it's not a problem, it doesn't matter; **gravement** adv gravely, seriously; **~ malade** seriously ill

graver [grave] ⟨1a⟩ engrave; *disque* cut; **gravé dans sa mémoire** engraved on one's memory

gravier [gravje] m gravel

gravillon [gravijõ] m grit; **~s** gravel sg, Br loose chippings pl

gravir [gravir] ⟨2a⟩ climb

gravité [gravite] f gravity, seriousness; *d'une maladie, d'un accident* seriousness; PHYS gravity; **graviter** ⟨1a⟩ PHYS: **~ autour de** revolve around

gravure [gravyr] f ART engraving; (*reproduction*) print

grommeler

gré [gre] *m*: **bon ~, mal ~** like it or not; **à mon ~** to my liking; **contre mon ~** against my will; **de bon ~** willingly; **de son plein ~** of one's own free will; **savoir ~ de qch à qn** be grateful to s.o. for sth

grec, ~que [grɛk] **1** *adj* Greek **2** *m langue* Greek **3** *m/f* **Grec, ~que** Greek; **Grèce: la ~** Greece

gredin [grədɛ̃] *m* scoundrel

gréement [gremɑ̃] *m* MAR rigging

greffe [grɛf] AGR, *de peau, tissu* graft; **~ du cœur** MÉD heart transplant; **greffer** ⟨1b⟩ AGR, *peau, tissu* graft; *cœur, poumon* transplant

greffier [grɛfje] *m* clerk of the court

grêle[1] [grɛl] *jambes* skinny; *voix* shrill

grêle[2] [grɛl] *f* hail; **grêler** ⟨1a⟩: **il grêle** it's hailing; **grêlon** *m* hailstone

grelot [grəlo] *m* (small) bell

grelotter [grəlɔte] ⟨1a⟩ shiver

grenade [grənad] *f* BOT pomegranate; MIL grenade; **grenadine** *f* grenadine, pomegranate syrup

grenier [grənje] *m* attic

grenouille [grənuj] *f* frog

grès [grɛ] *m* sandstone; *poterie* stoneware

grésiller [grezije] ⟨1a⟩ sizzle; RAD crackle

grève[1] [grɛv] *f* strike; **être en ~, faire ~** be on strike; **se mettre en ~** go on strike; **~ de la faim** hunger strike; **~ du zèle, ~ perlée** slowdown, *Br* go-slow

grève[2] [grɛv] *f* (*plage*) shore

grever [grəve] ⟨1d⟩ *budget* put a strain on

gréviste [grevist] *m/f* striker

gribouillage [gribujaʒ] *m* scribble; (*dessin*) doodle; **gribouiller** ⟨1a⟩ scribble; (*dessiner*) doodle; **gribouillis** *m* scribble

grief [grijɛf] *m* grievance

grièvement [grijɛvmɑ̃] *adv blessé* seriously

griffe [grif] *f* claw; COMM label; *fig* (*empreinte*) stamp; **griffer** ⟨1a⟩ scratch

griffonnage [grifonaʒ] *m* scribble; **griffonner** ⟨1a⟩ scribble

grignoter [griɲɔte] ⟨1a⟩ **1** *v/t* nibble on; *économies* nibble away at, eat into **2** *v/i* nibble

grill [gril] *m* broiler, *Br* grill; **grillade** *f* broil, *Br* grill

grillage [grijaʒ] *m* wire mesh; (*clôture*) fence; **grille** *f* *d'une fenêtre* grille; (*clôture*) railings *pl*; *d'un four* rack; (*tableau*) grid; **grille-pain** *m* (*pl inv*) toaster; **griller** ⟨1a⟩ **1** *v/t viande* broil, *Br* grill; *pain* toast; *café, marrons* roast **2** *v/i d'une ampoule* burn out; **~ un feu rouge** go through a red light

grillon [grijɔ̃] *m* cricket

grimace [grimas] *f* grimace; **faire des ~s** pull faces; **grimer** ⟨1a⟩: (**se**) **~** make up

grimper [grɛ̃pe] ⟨1a⟩ climb

grincement [grɛ̃smɑ̃] *m de porte* squeaking; **grincer** ⟨1k⟩ *d'une porte* squeak; **~ des dents** grind one's teeth

grincheux, -euse [grɛ̃ʃø, -z] bad-tempered, grouchy

gringalet [grɛ̃galɛ] *m* F puny little shrimp

griotte [grijɔt] *f* BOT *type of cherry*

grippe [grip] *f* MÉD flu; **prendre qn en ~** take a dislike to s.o.; **~ gastro-intestinale** gastric flu; **grippé, ~e** MÉD: **être ~** have flu

gris, ~e [gri, -z] gray, *Br* grey; *temps, vie* dull; (*ivre*) tipsy; **grisaille** *f* grayness, *Br* greyness

grisant, ~e [grizɑ̃, -t] exhilarating

grisâtre [grizɑtr] grayish, *Br* greyish

griser [grize] ⟨1a⟩: **~ qn** go to s.o.'s head; **se laisser ~ par** get carried away by

grisonner [grizone] ⟨1a⟩ go gray *ou Br* grey

grive [griv] *f* thrush

grivois, ~e [grivwa, -z] bawdy

groggy [grɔgi] *adj inv* F groggy

grognement [grɔɲmɑ̃] *m* (*plainte*) grumbling; *d'un cochon etc* grunt; **grogner** ⟨1a⟩ (*se plaindre*) grumble; *d'un cochon* grunt; **grognon, ~ne**: **être ~** be grumpy

grommeler [grɔmle] ⟨1c⟩ mutter

G

grondement [grõdmã] *m d'un chien* growl; *de tonnerre* rumble; **gronder** ⟨1a⟩ **1** *v/i d'une personne, d'un chien* growl; *du tonnerre* rumble; *d'une révolte* brew **2** *v/t* scold

groom [grum] *m* bellhop, *Br* page

gros, **~se** [gro, -s] **1** *adj* big, large; *(corpulent)* fat; *lèvres* thick; *averse*, *rhume*, *souliers* heavy; *chaussettes* heavy, thick; *plaisanterie* coarse; *vin* rough; **avoir le cœur ~** be heavy-hearted; **~ bonnet** *m* F bigwig F; **toucher le ~ lot** hit the jackpot; **~se mer** *f* MAR rough *ou* heavy sea; **~ mots** *mpl* bad language *sg*, swear words; **~ plan** *m* close-up **2** *adv*: **gagner ~** win a lot; **en ~** *(globalement)* generally, on the whole; COMM wholesale **3** *m personne* fat man; COMM wholesale trade; **prix m de ~** COMM wholesale price; **le ~ de** the bulk of

groseille [grozɛj] *f* BOT currant; **~ à maquereau** gooseberry

grosse [gros] *f* fat woman

grossesse [grosɛs] *f* pregnancy

grosseur [groscɛr] *f (corpulence)* fatness; *(volume)* size; *(tumeur)* growth

grossier, **-ère** [grosje, -ɛr] *(rudimentaire)* crude; *(indélicat)* coarse, crude; *(impoli)* rude; *erreur* big; **grossièrement** *adv* crudely; *(impoliment)* rudely; *(à peu près)* roughly; **grossièreté** *f* crudeness; **dire des ~s** use crude *ou* coarse language

grossir [grosir] ⟨2a⟩ **1** *v/t au microscope* magnify; *nombre*, *rivière* swell; *(exagérer)* exaggerate; **~ qn** *pantalon*, *robe etc* make s.o. look fatter **2** *v/i d'une personne* put on weight

grossiste [grosist] *m/f* COMM wholesaler

grosso modo [grosomodo] *adv* roughly

grotesque [grotɛsk] ludicrous, grotesque

grotte [grot] *f* cave

grouiller [gruje] ⟨1a⟩: **~ de** be swarming with; **se ~** F get a move on

groupe [grup] *m* group; **~ de pression** pressure group; **~ sanguin** blood group; **groupement** *m* group;

action grouping; **grouper** ⟨1a⟩ group; **se ~ autour de qn** gather around s.o.

groupie [grupi] *f* groupie

grue [gry] *f* ZO, TECH crane

grumeau [grymo] *m (pl -x) m* lump; **grumeleux**, **-euse** lumpy

gué [ge] *m* ford

guenilles [gənij] *fpl* rags

guépard [gepar] *m* cheetah

guêpe [gɛp] *f* wasp; **guêpier** *m* wasps' nest; **tomber dans un ~** *fig* fall into a trap; **se mettre dans un ~** *fig* put o.s. in a difficult position

guère [gɛr]: **ne ... ~** hardly; **je ne la connais ~** I hardly know her

guéridon [geridõ] *m* round table

guérilla [gerija] *f* guerrilla warfare; **guérillero** *m* guerrilla

guérir [gerir] ⟨2a⟩ **1** *v/t malade*, *maladie* cure *(de* of); **2** *v/i d'une blessure* heal; *d'un malade*, *d'une maladie* get better; **guérissable** curable; **guérison** *f (rétablissement)* recovery

guerre [gɛr] *f* war; **Seconde Guerre mondiale** Second World War; **en ~** at war; **faire la ~** be at war *(à* with); **faire la ~ à qch** wage war on sth; **~ bactériologique / biologique** germ / biological warfare; **~ civile** civil war; **~ froide** Cold War; **~ des gangs** gang warfare; **~ sainte** holy war; **guerrier**, **-ère 1** *adj* warlike **2** *m* warrior

guet [gɛ] *m*: **faire le ~** keep watch

guet-apens [gɛtapã] *m (pl guets-apens)* ambush

guetter [gete] ⟨1b⟩ watch for, keep an eye open for; *(épier)* watch

gueule [gœl] *f* F mouth; *(visage)* face; **ta ~!** F shut up!, *Br aussi* shut it! F; **~ de bois** hangover; **gueuler** ⟨1a⟩ F yell, shout; **gueuleton** *m* F enormous meal, *Br aussi* blow-out

guichet [giʃɛ] *m de banque*, *poste* wicket, *Br* window; *de théâtre* box office; **~ automatique** automatic teller (machine), ATM, *Br aussi* cash dispenser; **guichetier**, **-ère** *m/f* clerk, *Br* assistant; *dans banque* teller

guide [gid] **1** *m* guide; *ouvrage*

guide(book); **~ de conversation** phrasebook **2** *f* girl scout, *Br* guide **3**: **~s** *fpl* guiding reins; **guider** ⟨1a⟩ guide

guidon [gidɔ̃] *m de vélo* handlebars *pl*

guignol [giɲɔl] *m* Punch; **un spectacle de ~** a Punch-and-Judy show

guillemets [gijmɛ] *mpl* quote marks, *Br aussi* inverted commas

guillotiner [gijɔtine] ⟨1a⟩ guillotine

guindé, ~e [gɛ̃de] *personne, style* stiff, awkward

guirlande [girlɑ̃d] *f* garland; **~ lumineuse** string of lights; **~s de Noël** tinsel *sg*

guise [giz] *f*: **agir à sa ~** do as one pleases; **en ~ de** as, by way of

guitare [gitar] *f* guitar; **guitariste** *m/f* guitarist

guttural, ~e [gytyral] (*mpl* -aux) guttural

guyanais, ~e [gɥijanɛ, -z] **1** *adj département* Guianese; *république* Guyanese **2** *m/f* Guyanais, ~e *département* Guianese; *république* Guyanese; **Guyane: la ~** Guyana

gym [ʒim] *f* gym

gymnase [ʒimnɑz] *m* SP gym; **gymnaste** *m/f* gymnast; **gymnastique** *f* gymnastics *sg*; *corrective, matinale exercises pl*; **faire de la ~** do gymnastics / exercises

gynécologie [ʒinekɔlɔʒi] *f* gynecology, *Br* gynæcology; **gynécologique** gynecological, *Br* gynæcological; **gynécologue** *m/f* MÉD gynecologist, *Br* gynæcologist

gyrophare [ʒirɔfar] *m* flashing light

H

H

h *abr* (= **heure**) hr (= hour)

ha *abr* (= **hectare**) *approx* 2.5 acres

habile [abil] skillful, *Br* skilful; **habileté** *f* skill

habiliter [abilite] ⟨1a⟩ JUR: **être habilité à faire qch** be authorized to do sth

habillement [abijmɑ̃] *m* (*vêtements*) clothes *pl*; **habillé, ~e** (*élégant*) dressy; **habiller** ⟨1a⟩ dress; **s'~** get dressed, dress; *élégamment* get dressed up

habit [abi] *m*: **~s** clothes

habitable [abitabl] inhabitable; **habitacle** *m* AVIAT cockpit; **habitant, ~e** *m/f* inhabitant; **habitat** *m* ZO, BOT habitat; **habitation** *f* living, (*domicile*) residence; **habiter** ⟨1a⟩ **1** *v/t* live in **2** *v/i* live (**à Paris** in Paris); **habité, ~e** inhabited

habitude [abityd] *f* habit, custom; **d'~** usually; **par ~** out of habit; **habitué, ~e** *m/f* regular; **habituel, ~le** usual;

habituer ⟨1a⟩: **~ qn à qch** get s.o. used to sth; **s'~ à** get used to; **s'~ à faire qch** get used to doing sth

'hache [aʃ] *f* ax, *Br* axe; **enterrer la ~ de guerre** bury the hatchet; **'hacher** [aʃe] ⟨1a⟩ chop; **viande** *f* **hachée** ground beef, *Br* mince; **'hachette** *f* hatchet; **'hachis** *m* CUIS *kind of stew in which the meat is covered with mashed potatoes*

'hachisch [aʃiʃ] *m* hashish

'hachoir [aʃwar] *m appareil* meat grinder, *Br* mincer; *couteau* cleaver; *planche* chopping board

haddock [adɔk] *m* smoked haddock

'hagard, ~e [agar, -d] *visage* haggard; *air* wild

'haie [ɛ] *f* hedge; SP hurdle; *pour chevaux* fence, jump; **course** *f* **de ~s** hurdles; *pour chevaux* race over jumps; **une ~ de policiers** *fig* a line of police

'haillons [ajɔ̃] *mpl* rags

'**haine** [ɛn] *f* hatred; '**haineux, -euse**
full of hatred

'**haïr** [air] ⟨2m⟩ hate; '**haïssable** hateful

'**hâle** [ɑl] *m* (sun)tan; '**hâlé, ~e** (sun)-tanned

haleine [alɛn] *f* breath; **hors d'~** out of breath; **c'est un travail de longue ~** *fig* it's a long hard job; **avoir mauvaise ~** have bad breath

'**halètement** [alɛtmɑ̃] *m* gasping; '**haleter** ⟨1e⟩ pant, gasp

'**hall** [ol] *m* d'hôtel, *immeuble* foyer; *de gare* concourse

'**halle** [al] *f* market

halloween [alwin] *f* Halloween

hallucination [alysinasjɔ̃] *f* hallucination

'**halo** [alo] *m* halo

halogène [aloʒɛn] *m*: (**lampe** *f*) ~ halogen light

'**halte** [alt] *f* stop; **faire ~** halt, make a stop; **~!** MIL halt!

haltère [altɛr] *m* dumbbell; **faire des ~s** do weightlifting; **haltérophilie** *f* weightlifting

'**hamac** [amak] *m* hammock

'**hameau** [amo] *m* (*pl* -x) hamlet

hameçon [amsɔ̃] *m* hook

'**hamster** [amster] *m* hamster

'**hanche** [ɑ̃ʃ] *f* hip

'**handicap** [ɑ̃dikap] *m* handicap; '**handicapé, ~e 1** *adj* disabled, handicapped **2** *m/f* disabled *ou* handicapped person; **les ~s** the disabled *pl*, the handicapped *pl*; **~ physique** disabled person, physically handicapped person; **~ mental(e)** mentally handicapped person

'**hangar** [ɑ̃gar] *m* shed; AVIAT hangar

'**hanter** [ɑ̃te] ⟨1a⟩ haunt; '**hantise** *f* fear, dread

'**happer** [ape] ⟨1a⟩ catch; *fig*: *de train, autobus* hit

'**haranguer** [arɑ̃ge] ⟨1a⟩ speak to; *péj* harangue

'**haras** [ara] *m* stud farm

'**harassant, ~e** [arasɑ̃, -t] *travail* exhausting; '**harassé, ~e** exhausted

'**harcèlement** [arsɛlmɑ̃] *m* harassment; **~ sexuel** sexual harassment;

'**harceler** ⟨1d⟩ harass

'**hard** [ard] *m* hardcore; MUS hard rock

'**hardi, ~e** [ardi] bold

'**hardware** [ardwɛr] *m* hardware

'**hareng** [arɑ̃] *m* herring

'**hargne** [arɲ] *f* bad temper; '**hargneux, -euse** venomous; *chien* vicious

'**haricot** [ariko] *m* BOT bean; **~s verts** green beans; **c'est la fin des ~s** F that's the end

harmonica [armɔnika] *m* harmonica

harmonie [armɔni] *f* harmony; **harmonieux, -euse** harmonious; **harmoniser** ⟨1a⟩ match (up); MUS harmonize; **s'~ de couleurs** go together; **s'~ avec** d'une couleur go with

'**harnais** [arnɛ] *m* harness

'**harpe** [arp] *f* MUS harp

'**harpon** [arpɔ̃] *m* harpoon

'**hasard** [azar] *m* chance; **au ~** at random; **par ~** by chance; '**hasarder** ⟨1a⟩ hazard; **se ~ à faire qch** venture to do sth; '**hasardeux, -euse** hazardous

'**haschisch** [aʃiʃ] *m* hashish

'**hâte** [ɑt] *f* hurry, haste; **à la ~** in a hurry, hastily; **en ~** in haste; **avoir ~ de faire qch** be eager to do sth; '**hâter** ⟨1a⟩ hasten; **se ~** hurry up; **se ~ de faire qch** hurry to do sth; '**hâtif, -ive** hasty; AGR early

'**hausse** [os] *f* de prix, cours, température increase, rise; '**hausser** ⟨1a⟩ increase; **~ la voix** raise one's voice; **~ les épaules** shrug (one's shoulders)

'**haut, ~e** [o, ot] **1** *adj* high; *immeuble* tall, high; *cri, voix* loud; *fonctionnaire* high-level, senior; **la ~e Seine** the upper Seine; **à voix ~e** in a loud voice, loudly; **être ~ de 5 mètres** be 5 meters tall; **~ de gamme** upscale, *Br* upmarket **2** *adv* high; **là-~** up there; **de ~ en bas** from top to bottom; *regarder qn* up and down; **~ les mains!** hands up!; **en ~** above; **en ~ de** at the top of; **parler plus ~** speak up, speak louder; **voir plus ~ dans un texte** see above **3** *m* top; **du ~ de** from the top of; **des ~s et des bas** ups and downs

'**hautain**, **~e** [otɛ̃, -ɛn] haughty

'**hautbois** [obwa] *m* MUS oboe

'**hauteur** [otœr] *f* height; *fig* haughtiness; *être à la ~ de qch* be up to sth

'**haut-le-cœur** [olkœr] *m* (*pl inv*): *avoir un ~* retch

'**haut-parleur** [oparlœr] *m* (*pl haut-parleurs*) loudspeaker

'**havre** [avr] *m* haven

'**hayon** [ejõ] *m*: *voiture à ~* hatchback

hebdomadaire [ɛbdɔmadɛr] *m & adj* weekly

hébergement [ebɛrʒəmɑ̃] *m* accommodations *pl*, *Br* accommodation; **héberger** [ebɛrʒe] ⟨1l⟩: *~ qn* put s.o. up; *fig* take s.o. in

hébété, **~e** [ebete] *regard* vacant

hébreu [ebrø] *m*: *l'~* Hebrew

hécatombe [ekatõb] *f* bloodbath

hectare [ɛktar] *m* hectare (*approx 2.5 acres*)

'**hein** [ɛ̃] F eh?; *c'est joli, ~?* it's pretty, isn't it?

'**hélas** [elɑs] alas

'**héler** [ele] ⟨1f⟩ hail

hélice [elis] *f* MAR, AVIAT propeller; *escalier m en ~* spiral staircase

hélicoptère [elikɔptɛr] *m* helicopter, chopper F; **héliport** *m* heliport

hématome [ematom] *m* MÉD hematoma, *Br* hæmatoma

hémisphère [emisfɛr] *m* hemisphere

hémophilie [emɔfili] *f* MÉD hemophilia, *Br* hæmophilia

hémorragie [emɔraʒi] *f* hemorrhage, *Br* hæmorrhage

hémorroïdes [emɔrɔid] *fpl* hemorrhoids, *Br* haemorrhoids, piles

'**hennir** [enir] ⟨2a⟩ neigh; '**hennissement** *m* neigh

hépatite [epatit] *f* hepatitis

'**herbe** [ɛrb] *f* grass; CUIS herb; *mauvaise ~* weed; *fines ~s* herbs; **herbeux**, **-euse** grassy; **herbicide** *m* herbicide, weedkiller

héréditaire [erediter] hereditary; **hérédité** *f* heredity

hérésie [erezi] *f* heresy; **hérétique** **1** *adj* heretical **2** *m/f* heretic

'**hérissé**, **~e** [erise] ruffled, standing

on end; '**hérisson** *m* hedgehog

héritage [eritaʒ] *m* inheritance; **hériter** ⟨1a⟩ **1** *v/t* inherit **2** *v/i*: *~ de qch* inherit sth; *~ de qn* receive an inheritance from s.o.; **héritier**, **-ère** *m/f* heir

hermétique [ɛrmetik] *récipient* hermetically sealed, airtight; *style* inaccessible

hermine [ɛrmin] *f* stoat; *fourrure* ermine

'**hernie** [ɛrni] *f* MÉD hernia; *~ discale* slipped disc

héroïne[1] [erɔin] *f drogue* heroin; **héroïnomane** *m/f* heroin addict

héroïne[2] [erɔin] *f* heroine; **héroïque** heroic; **héroïsme** *m* heroism

'**héron** [erõ] *m* heron

'**héros** [ero] *m* hero

herpès [ɛrpɛs] *m* herpes

hésitant, **~e** [ezitɑ̃, -t] hesitant, tentative; **hésitation** *f* hesitation; **hésiter** ⟨1a⟩ hesitate (*à faire qch* to do sth; *sur* over)

hétéro [etero] F straight F, hetero F

hétérogène [eterɔʒɛn] heterogeneous

hétérosexuel, **~le** [eterosɛksɥel] heterosexual

'**hêtre** [ɛtr] *m* BOT beech

heure [œr] *f durée* hour; *arriver à l'~* arrive on time; *de bonne ~* early; *tout à l'~* (*tout de suite*) just a minute ago, not long ago; (*avant peu*) in a minute; *à tout à l'~!* see you soon!; *à l'~ actuelle* at the moment; *à toute ~* at any time; *quelle ~ est-il?* what time is it?; *il est six ~s* it's six (o'clock); *il est l'~ de partir* it's time to leave; *~ locale* local time; *~s d'ouverture* opening hours; *~s de pointe* rush hour *sg*; *~s supplémentaires* overtime *sg*

heureusement [œrøzmɑ̃] *adv* luckily, fortunately; **heureux**, **-euse** happy; (*chanceux*) lucky, fortunate

'**heurt** [œr] *m de deux véhicules* collision; *fig* (*friction*) clash

'**heurter** [œrte] ⟨1a⟩ collide with; *fig* offend; *se ~* collide (*à* with); *fig* (*s'affronter*) clash (*sur* over)

hexagone [ɛgzagɔn] *m* hexagon; **l'Hexagone** France

hiberner [ibɛrne] ⟨1a⟩ hibernate

'hibou [ibu] *m* (*pl* -x) owl

'hic [ik] *m* F problem

'hideux, -euse [idø, -z] hideous

hier [jɛr] yesterday

'hiérarchie [jerarʃi] *f* hierarchy

hiéroglyphe [jerɔglif] *m* hieroglyph

high-tech [ajtɛk] *adj inv* high tech, hi-tech

hilare [ilar] grinning; **hilarité** *f* hilarity

hindou, ~e Hindu

hippique [ipik] SP equestrian; **concours** *m* ~ horse show; **hippisme** *m* riding; **hippodrome** *m* race course

hippopotame [ipɔpɔtam] *m* hippo, hippopotamus

hirondelle [irɔdɛl] *f* swallow

hirsute [irsyt] hairy, hirsute *fml, hum*

hispanique [ispanik] Hispanic

'hisser [ise] ⟨1a⟩ *drapeau, étendard, voile* hoist; (*monter*) lift, raise; **se ~** pull o.s. up

histoire [istwar] *f* history; (*récit, conte*) story; **faire des ~s** make a fuss; **historien, ~ne** *m/f* historian; **historique 1** *adj* historic **2** *m* chronicle

hiver [ivɛr] *m* winter; **en ~** in winter; **hivernal, ~e** (*mpl* -aux) winter *atr*

H.L.M. [aʃɛlɛm] *m* ou *f abr* (= **habitation à loyer modéré**) low cost housing

'hobby [ɔbi] *m* hobby

'hochement [ɔʃmɑ̃] *m*: ~ **de tête** *en signe d'approbation* nod; *en signe de désapprobation* shake of the head; **'hocher** ⟨1a⟩: ~ **la tête** *en signe d'approbation* nod (one's head); *en signe de désapprobation* shake one's head

'hochet [ɔʃɛ] *m* rattle

'hockey [ɔkɛ] *m sur gazon* field hockey, *Br* hockey; *sur glace* hockey, *Br* ice hockey

'holding [ɔldiŋ] *m* holding company

'hold-up [ɔldœp] *m* holdup

'hollandais, ~e [ɔlɑ̃dɛ, -z] **1** *adj* Dutch **2** *m langue* Dutch **3 Hollandais** *m* Dutchman; **'Hollandaise** *f* Dutchwoman; **'Hollande**: **la ~** Holland

holocauste [ɔlɔkost] *m* holocaust

hologramme [ɔlɔgram] *m* hologram

'homard [ɔmar] *m* lobster

homéopathe [ɔmeɔpat] *m* homeopath; **homéopathie** *f* homeopathy; **homéopathique** homeopathic

homicide [ɔmisid] *m acte* homicide; ~ **involontaire** manslaughter; ~ **volontaire** murder

hommage [ɔmaʒ] *m* homage; **rendre ~ à qn** pay homage to s.o.

homme [ɔm] *m* man; ~ **d'affaires** businessman; ~ **d'État** statesman; ~ **de lettres** man of letters, literary man; ~ **de main** henchman; ~ **de paille** *fig* figurehead; ~ **de la rue** man in the street; **homme-grenouille** *m* (*pl* hommes-grenouilles) frogman; **homme-sandwich** *m* (*pl* hommes-sandwichs) sandwich man

homo [ɔmo] *m/f* gay

homogène [ɔmɔʒɛn] homogenous

homologue [ɔmɔlɔg] *m* counterpart, opposite number; **homologuer** ⟨1m⟩ *record* ratify; *tarif* authorize

homonyme [ɔmɔnim] *m* namesake; LING homonym

homophobe [ɔmɔfɔb] homophobic; **homophobie** *f* homophobia

homosexuel, ~le [ɔmɔsɛksɥɛl] *m/f & adj* homosexual

'Hongrie [ɔ̃gri] *f*: **la ~** Hungary; **'hongrois, ~e 1** *adj* Hungarian **2** *m langue* Hungarian **3** *m/f* **Hongrois, ~e** Hungarian

honnête [ɔnɛt] honest; (*convenable*) decent; (*passable*) reasonable; **honnêtement** *adv* honestly; (*passablement*) quite well; **honnêteté** honesty

honneur [ɔnœr] *m* honor, *Br* honour; **en l'~ de** in honor of; **faire ~ à qch** honor sth; **honorable** honorable, *Br* honourable

honoraire [ɔnɔrɛr] **1** *adj* honorary **2** ~**s** *mpl* fees; **honorer** ⟨1a⟩ honor, *Br* honour; **honorifique** honorific

'honte [ɔ̃t] *f* shame; **avoir ~** be ashamed of; **faire ~ à qn** make s.o. ashamed; **'honteusement** *adv* shamefully; *dire, admettre* shamefacedly;

'honteux, -euse (*déshonorant*) shameful; (*déconfit*) ashamed; *air* shamefaced

'hooligan [uligan] *m* hooligan; 'hooliganisme *m* hooliganism

hôpital [opital] *m* (*pl* -aux) hospital; **à l'~** in the hospital, *Br* in hospital

'hoquet [ɔkɛ] *m* hiccup; **avoir le ~** have (the) hiccups

horaire [ɔrɛr] 1 *adj* hourly 2 *m* *emploi du temps* timetable, schedule; *des avions, trains etc* schedule, *Br* timetable; **~ souple** flextime

horizon [ɔrizõ] *m* horizon; **horizontal, ~e** (*mpl* -aux) horizontal

horloge [ɔrlɔʒ] *f* clock; **horloger, -ère** *m/f* watchmaker

'hormis [ɔrmi] *prép* but

hormonal, ~e [ɔrmɔnal] (*mpl* -aux) hormonal; **hormone** *f* hormone

horodateur [ɔrodatœr] *m* *dans parking* pay and display machine

horoscope [ɔrɔskɔp] *m* horoscope

horreur [ɔrœr] *f* horror; (*monstruosité*) monstrosity; **avoir ~ de qch** detest sth; (*quelle*) **~!** how awful!; **horrible** horrible; **horrifiant, ~e** horrifying; **horrifié, ~e** horrified (*par* by); **horrifique** hair-raising

horripilant, ~e [ɔripilã, -t] infuriating

'hors [ɔr] *prép*: **~ de** (*à l'extérieur de*) outside; **~ de danger** out of danger; **c'est ~ de prix** it's incredibly expensive; **~ sujet** beside the point; **être ~ de soi** be beside o.s.; **~ service** out of service

'hors-bord [ɔrbɔr] *m* (*pl inv*) outboard

'hors-d'œuvre [ɔrdœvr] *m* (*pl inv*) CUIS appetizer, starter

'hors-jeu [ɔrʒœ] *adv* offside

'hors-la-loi [ɔrlalwa] *m* (*pl inv*) outlaw

'hors-piste [ɔrpist] *adv* off-piste

hortensia [ɔrtãsja] *f* hydrangea

horticulture [ɔrtikyltyr] *f* horticulture

hospice [ɔspis] *m* REL hospice; (*asile*) home

hospitalier, -ère [ɔspitalje, -ɛr] hospitable; MÉD hospital *atr*; **hospitaliser** ⟨1a⟩ hospitalize; **hospitalité** *f* hospitality

hostie [ɔsti] *f* REL wafer, host

hostile [ɔstil] hostile; **hostilité** *f* hostility

hosto [ɔsto] *m* F hospital

'hot-dog [ɔtdɔg] *m* hot dog

hôte [ot] *m* (*maître de maison*) host; (*invité*) guest; **table** *f* **d'~** set meal, table d'hôte

hôtel [otel] *m* hotel; **~** (*particulier*) town house; **~ de ville** town hall; **hôtelier, ~e** 1 *adj* hotel *atr* 2 *m/f* hotelier; **hôtellerie** *f*: **l'~** the hotel business

hôtesse [otɛs] *f* hostess; **~ de l'air** air hostess

'hotte [ɔt] *f* (*panier*) large basket carried on the back; *d'aération* hood

'houblon [ublõ] *m* BOT hop

'houille [uj] *f* coal

'houle [ul] *f* MAR swell; 'houleux, -euse *fig* stormy

'houppe [up] *f* *de cheveux* tuft

'hourra [ura] 1 *int* hurrah 2 *m*: **pousser des ~** give three cheers

huile [ɥil] *f* oil; **~ solaire** suntan oil; **huiler** ⟨1a⟩ oil, lubricate; **huileux, -euse** oily

'huis [ɥi] *m*: **à ~ clos** behind closed doors; JUR in camera; **huissier** *m* JUR bailiff

'huit [ɥit] eight; **~ jours** a week; **demain en ~** a week tomorrow; 'huitaine *f*: **une ~ de** about eight, eight or so; **une ~** (*de jours*) a week; 'huitième eighth; **~ m de finale** last sixteen

huître [ɥitr] *f* oyster

humain, ~e [ymɛ̃, -ɛn] human; *traitement* humane; **humaniser** ⟨1a⟩ humanize; **humanitaire** humanitarian; **humanité** *f* humanity

humble [ɛ̃bl] humble

humecter [ymɛkte] ⟨1a⟩ moisten

'humer [yme] ⟨1a⟩ breathe in

humeur [ymœr] *f* mood; (*tempérament*) temperament; **être de bonne / mauvaise ~** be in a good / bad mood

humide [ymid] damp; (*chaud et ~*) humid; humidificateur *m* TECH humidifier; humidifier ⟨1a⟩ moisten; *atmosphère* humidify; humidité *f* dampness; humidity

humiliation [ymiljasjõ] *f* humiliation; humiliant, ~e humiliating; humilier ⟨1a⟩ humiliate

humilité [ymilite] *f* humility

humoriste [ymɔrist] **1** *adj* humorous **2** *m/f* humorist; humoristique humorous; humour *m* humor, *Br* humour; **avoir de l'~** have a (good) sense of humor

'huppé, ~e [ype] exclusive

'hurlement [yrləmã] *m* *d'un loup* howl; *d'une personne* scream; 'hurler ⟨1a⟩ *d'un loup* howl; *d'une personne* scream; **~ de rire** roar with laughter

'hutte [yt] *f* hut

hybride [ibrid] *m* hybrid

hydratant, ~e [idratã, -t] *cosmétique* moisturizing

hydraulique [idrolik] **1** *adj* hydraulic **2** *f* hydraulics

hydravion [idravjõ] *m* seaplane

hydrocarbure [idrɔkarbyr] *m* CHIM hydrocarbon

hydroélectrique [idroelεktrik] hydroelectric

hydrogène [idrɔʒεn] *m* CHIM hydrogen

hydroglisseur [idroglisœr] *m* jetfoil

hyène [jεn] *f* hyena

hygiène [iʒjεn] *f* hygiene; **avoir une bonne ~ de vie** have a healthy lifestyle; **~ intime** personal hygiene; hygiénique hygienic; **papier ~** toilet paper; **serviette ~** sanitary napkin, *Br* sanitary towel

hymne [imn] *m* hymn; **~ national** national anthem

hyperactif, -ive [iperaktif, -iv] hyperactive

hyperbole [iperbɔl] *f* hyperbole; MATH hyperbola

hypermarché [ipermarʃe] *m* supermarket, *Br* hypermarket

hypermétrope [ipermetrɔp] far-sighted, *Br* long-sighted

hypersensible [ipersãsibl] hypersensitive

hypertension [ipertãsjõ] *f* MÉD high blood pressure

hypertexte [ipertεkst]: **lien** *m* **~** hypertext link

hypnose [ipnoz] *f* hypnosis; hypnothérapie *f* hypnotherapy; hypnotiser ⟨1a⟩ hypnotize

hypoallergénique [ipoalερʒenik] hypoallergenic

hypocrisie [ipɔkrizi] *f* hypocrisy; hypocrite **1** *adj* hypocritical **2** *m/f* hypocrite

hypocondriaque [ipɔkõdrijak] *m/f* hypochondriac

hypothèque [ipɔtεk] *f* COMM mortgage; hypothéquer ⟨1m⟩ mortgage

hypothermie [ipɔtεrmi] *f* hypothermia

hypothèse [ipɔtεz] *f* hypothesis; hypothétique hypothetical

hystérectomie [isterεktɔmi] *f* hysterectomy

hystérie [isteri] *f* hysteria; hystérique hysterical

---

iceberg [ajsbεrg] *m* GÉOGR iceberg

ici [isi] here; **jusqu'~** to here; (*jusqu'à maintenant*) so far, till now; **par ~** this way; (*dans le coin*) around about here;

d'~ peu shortly, before long; ***d'~ demain / la semaine prochaine*** by tomorrow / next week; ***d'~ là*** by then, by that time; ***d'~*** from here; ***sors d'~*** get out of here

icône [ikon] *f* icon

id. *abr* (= *idem*) idem

idéal, ~e [ideal] (*mpl* - *ou* -aux) *m & adj* ideal; **idéalement** *adv* ideally; **idéaliser** idealize; **idéalisme** *m* idealism; **idéaliste 1** *adj* idealistic **2** *m/f* idealist

idée [ide] *f* idea; (*opinion*) view; **à l'~ de faire qch** at the idea of doing sth; **avoir dans l'~ de faire qch** be thinking of doing sth; **avoir dans l'~ que** have an idea that; **se faire une ~ de qch** get an idea of sth; ***tu te fais des ~s*** (*tu te trompes*) you're imagining things; **~ fausse** misconception; **~ fixe** obsession; **~ de génie** brainstorm, *Br* brainwave

identification [idãtifikasjɔ̃] *f* identification; **identifier** ⟨1a⟩ identify (**avec, à** with); **s'~ avec** *ou* **à** identify with

identique [idãtik] identical (**à** to); **identité** [idãtite] *f* identity; **carte f d'~** identity *ou* ID card; **pièce f d'~** identity, identity papers *pl*, ID

idéologie [ideɔlɔʒi] *f* ideology; **idéologique** ideological

idiomatique [idjɔmatik] idiomatic; **idiome** *m* idiom

idiot, ~e [idjo, -ɔt] **1** *adj* idiotic **2** *m/f* idiot; **idiotie** *f* idiocy; ***une ~*** an idiotic thing to do / say; ***dire des ~s*** talk nonsense *sg*

idolâtrer [idɔlɑtre] ⟨1a⟩ idolize; **idole** *f* idol

idylle [idil] *f* romance; **idyllique** idyllic

ignare [iɲar] *péj* **1** *adj* ignorant **2** *m/f* ignoramus

ignoble [iɲɔbl] vile

ignorance [iɲɔrɑ̃s] *f* ignorance; **ignorant, ~e** ignorant; **ignorer** ⟨1a⟩ not know; *personne, talent* ignore; ***vous n'ignorez sans doute pas que ...*** you are doubtless aware that ...

il [il] ◇ *sujet* he; *chose* it; ***le chat est-~ rentré?*** did the cat come home? ◇ *impersonnel* it; **~ ne fait pas beau** it's not very nice (weather); **~ va pleuvoir** it is *ou* it's going to rain; **~ était une fois ...** once upon a time there was ...

île [il] *f* island; **~ déserte** desert island; **des ~s** West Indian; **les ~s britanniques** the British Isles; **les Îles Anglo-Normandes** the Channel Islands

illégal, ~e [ilegal] (*mpl* -aux) illegal; **illégalement** illegally

illégitime [ileʒitim] *enfant* illegitimate

illettré, ~e [iletre] **1** *adj* illiterate **2** *m/f* person who is illiterate; **illettrisme** *m* illiteracy

illicite [ilisit] illicit

illico (presto) [iliko (prɛsto)] *adv* **F** pronto **F**

illimité, ~e [ilimite] unlimited

illisible [ilizibl] (*indéchiffrable*) illegible; *mauvaise littérature* unreadable

illogique [ilɔʒik] illogical

illuminer [ilymine] ⟨1a⟩ light up, illuminate; *par projecteur* floodlight

illusion [ilyzjɔ̃] *f* illusion; **se faire des ~s** delude *ou* fool o.s.; **~ d'optique** optical illusion; **illusionniste** *m* illusionist; **illusoire** illusory

illustrateur, -trice [ilystratœr, -tris] *m/f* illustrator; **illustration** *f* illustration; **illustre** illustrious; **illustré 1** *adj* illustrated **2** *m* comic; (*revue*) illustrated magazine; **illustrer** ⟨1a⟩ illustrate; **s'~** distinguish o.s. (**par** by)

îlot [ilo] *m* (small) island; *de maisons* block

ils [il] *mpl* they; **tes grands-parents ont-~ téléphoné?** did your grand-parents call?

image [imaʒ] *f* picture; *dans l'eau, un miroir* reflection, image; (*ressemblance*) image; *représentation mentale* image, picture; **~ de marque** brand image

imaginable [imaʒinabl] imaginable; **imaginaire** imaginary; **imaginatif, -ive** imaginative; **imagination** *f* imagination; **avoir de l'~** be imaginative, have imagination; **imaginer** ⟨1a⟩ imagine; (*inventer*) devise; *s'~ que* imagine that

imbattable [ɛ̃batabl] unbeatable

imbécile [ɛ̃besil] **1** *adj* idiotic **2** *m/f* idiot, imbecile; **imbécillité** *f* stupidity, idiocy; *chose, parole imbécile* idiotic thing

imberbe [ɛ̃bɛrb] beardless

imbiber [ɛ̃bibe] ⟨1a⟩ soak (*de* with)

imbu, ~e [ɛ̃by]: *~ de fig* full of

imbuvable [ɛ̃byvabl] undrinkable; *fig* unbearable

imitateur, -trice [imitatœr, -tris] *m/f* imitator; THÉÂT impersonator; **imitation** *f* imitation; THÉÂT impersonation; **imiter** ⟨1a⟩ imitate; THÉÂT impersonate

immaculé, ~e [imakyle] immaculate, spotless; *réputation* spotless

immangeable [ɛ̃mɑ̃ʒabl] inedible

immatriculation [imatrikylasjõ] *f* registration; *plaque f d'~* AUTO license plate, *Br* number plate; *numéro m d'~* AUTO license plate number, *Br* registration number; **immatriculer** ⟨1a⟩ register

immature [imatyr] immature

immédiat, ~e [imedja, -t] **1** *adj* immediate **2** *m*: *dans l'~* for the moment; **immédiatement** *adv* immediately

immense [imɑ̃s] immense; **immensité** *f* immensity, vastness

immerger [imɛrʒe] ⟨1l⟩ immerse; *s'~ d'un sous-marin* submerge; **immersion** *f* immersion

immeuble [imœbl] *m* building

immigrant, ~e [imigrɑ̃, -t] *m/f* immigrant; **immigration** *f* immigration; **immigré, ~e** *m/f* immigrant; **immigrer** ⟨1a⟩ immigrate

imminent, ~e [iminɑ̃, -t] imminent

immiscer [imise] ⟨1k⟩: *s'~ dans qch* interfere in sth

immobile [imɔbil] motionless, immobile

immobilier, -ère [imɔbilje, -er] **1** *adj* property *atr*; *agence f immobilière* real estate agency; *agent m ~* realtor, *Br* real estate agent; *biens mpl ~s*

real estate *sg* **2** *m* property

immobiliser [imɔbilize] ⟨1a⟩ immobilize; *train, circulation* bring to a standstill; *capital* lock up, tie up; *s'~* (*s'arrêter*) come to a standstill

immonde [imõd] foul

immoral, ~e [imɔral] (*mpl* -aux) immoral; **immoralité** *f* immorality

immortaliser [imɔrtalize] ⟨1a⟩ immortalize; **immortalité** *f* immortality; **immortel, ~le** immortal

immuable [imɥabl] unchanging

immuniser [imynize] ⟨1a⟩ immunize; *immunisé contre fig* immune to; **immunitaire**: *système ~* immune system; **immunité** *f* JUR, MÉD immunity; *~ diplomatique* diplomatic immunity

impact [ɛ̃pakt] *m* impact

impair, ~e [ɛ̃per] **1** *adj* odd **2** *m* blunder

impardonnable [ɛ̃pardɔnabl] unforgiveable

imparfait, ~e [ɛ̃parfe, -t] imperfect

impartial, ~e [ɛ̃parsjal] (*mpl* -aux) impartial

impasse [ɛ̃pas] *f* dead end; *fig* deadlock, impasse

impassible [ɛ̃pasibl] impassive

impatiemment [ɛ̃pasjamɑ̃] *adv* impatiently; **impatience** *f* impatience; **impatient, ~e** impatient; **impatienter** ⟨1a⟩: *s'~* get impatient

impayé, ~e [ɛ̃peje] unpaid

impeccable [ɛ̃pekabl] impeccable; *linge* spotless, impeccable; **impeccablement** *adv* impeccably

impénétrable [ɛ̃penetrabl] *forêt* impenetrable

impensable [ɛ̃pɑ̃sabl] unthinkable, inconceivable

imper [ɛ̃per] *m* F raincoat, *Br* F mac

impératif, -ive [ɛ̃peratif, -iv] **1** *adj* imperative **2** *m* (*exigence*) requirement; GRAM imperative

impératrice [ɛ̃peratris] *f* empress

imperceptible [ɛ̃persɛptibl] imperceptible

imperfection [ɛ̃perfɛksjõ] *f* imperfection

impérial, ~e [ɛ̃perjal] imperial; **im-**

imprimer

périalisme *m* imperialism

impérieux, -euse [ɛ̃perjø, -z] *personne* imperious; *besoin* urgent, pressing

impérissable [ɛ̃perisabl] immortal; *souvenir* unforgettable

imperméabiliser [ɛ̃permeabilize] ⟨1a⟩ waterproof; **imperméable 1** *adj* impermeable; *tissu* waterproof **2** *m* raincoat

impersonnel, ~le [ɛ̃pɛrsɔnɛl] impersonal

impertinence [ɛ̃pɛrtinɑ̃s] *f* impertinence; **impertinent, ~e** impertinent

imperturbable [ɛ̃pɛrtyrbabl] imperturbable

impétueux, -euse [ɛ̃petɥø, -z] impetuous

impitoyable [ɛ̃pitwajabl] pitiless, ruthless; **impitoyablement** *adv* pitilessly, ruthlessly

implacable [ɛ̃plakabl] implacable

implanter [ɛ̃plɑ̃te] ⟨1a⟩ *fig* introduce; *industrie* set up, establish; **s'~** become established; *d'une industrie* set up

implication [ɛ̃plikasjɔ̃] *f* implication; **implicite** implicit; **impliquer** ⟨1m⟩ *personne* implicate; *(entraîner)* mean, involve; *(supposer)* imply

implorer [ɛ̃plɔre] ⟨1a⟩ *aide* beg for; **~ qn de faire qch** implore *ou* beg s.o. to do sth

impoli, ~e [ɛ̃pɔli] rude, impolite; **impolitesse** *f* rudeness

impopulaire [ɛ̃pɔpylɛr] unpopular

importance [ɛ̃pɔrtɑ̃s] *f* importance; *d'une ville* size; *d'une somme d'argent, catastrophe* magnitude; **important, ~e 1** *adj* important; *ville, somme* large, sizeable **2** *m*: **l'~, c'est que ...** the important thing *ou* main thing is that ...

importateur, -trice [ɛ̃pɔrtatœr, -tris] **1** *adj* importing **2** *m* importer; **importation** *f* import; **importer** ⟨1a⟩ **1** *v/t* import; *mode, musique* introduce **2** *v/i* matter, be important *(à* to); **peu m'importe qu'il arrive** *(subj)* **demain** *(cela m'est égal)* I don't care if he arrives tomorrow; **peu m'importe la couleur** the color doesn't

matter, the color isn't important; **ce qui importe, c'est que ...** the important thing is that ...; **n'importe où** wherever; **n'importe qui** whoever; **n'importe quand** any time; **n'importe quoi** just anything; **n'importe quoi!** nonsense!

importun, ~e [ɛ̃pɔrtɛ̃, -yn] troublesome; **importuner** ⟨1a⟩ bother

imposable [ɛ̃pozabl] taxable; **imposant, ~e** imposing; **imposer** ⟨1a⟩ impose; *marchandise, industrie* tax; **en ~** be impressive; **s'~** *(être nécessaire)* be essential; *(se faire admettre)* gain recognition; **imposition** *f* taxation

impossibilité [ɛ̃posibilite] *f* impossibility; **être dans l'~ de faire qch** be unable to do sth; **impossible 1** *adj* impossible **2** *m*: **l'~** the impossible; **faire l'~ pour faire qch** do one's utmost to do sth

imposteur [ɛ̃pɔstœr] *m* imposter

impôt [ɛ̃po] *m* tax; **~ sur le revenu** income tax

impotent, ~e [ɛ̃pɔtɑ̃, -t] crippled

impraticable [ɛ̃pratikabl] *projet* impractical; *rue* impassable

imprécis, ~e [ɛ̃presi, -z] vague, imprecise

imprégner [ɛ̃preɲe] ⟨1f⟩ impregnate *(de* with); **imprégné de** *fig* full of

imprenable [ɛ̃prənabl] *fort* impregnable; **vue ~** unobstructed view

impression [ɛ̃presjɔ̃] *f* impression; *imprimerie* printing; **impressionnable** impressionable; **impressionnant, ~e** impressive; *(troublant)* upsetting; **impressionner** ⟨1a⟩ impress; *(troubler)* upset; **impressionnisme** *m* impressionism; **impressionniste** *m/f & adj* impressionist

imprévisible [ɛ̃previzibl] unpredictable; **imprévu, ~e 1** *adj* unexpected **2** *m*: **sauf ~** all being well, barring accidents

imprimante [ɛ̃primɑ̃t] *f* INFORM printer; **~ laser** laser printer; **~ à jet d'encre** ink-jet (printer); **imprimé** *m* *(formulaire)* form; *tissu* print; *poste* **~s** printed matter *sg*; **imprimer**

⟨1a⟩ print; INFORM print out; *édition* publish; **imprimerie** *f établissement* printing works *sg*; ART printing; **imprimeur** *m* printer

improbable [ɛ̃prɔbabl] unlikely, improbable

improductif, -ive [ɛ̃prɔdyktif, -iv] *terre, travail* unproductive

imprononçable [ɛ̃prɔnɔ̃sabl] unpronounceable

impropre [ɛ̃prɔpr] *mot, outil* inappropriate; **~ à** unsuitable for; **~ à la consommation** unfit for human consumption

improviser [ɛ̃prɔvize] ⟨1a⟩ improvize; **improviste** *adv*: **à l'~** unexpectedly

imprudemment [ɛ̃prydamɑ̃] *adv* recklessly; **imprudence** *f* recklessness, imprudence; **commettre une ~** be careless; **imprudent, ~e** reckless, imprudent

impudence [ɛ̃pydɑ̃s] *f* impudence; **impudent, ~e** impudent

impudique [ɛ̃pydik] shameless

impuissance [ɛ̃pɥisɑ̃s] *f* powerlessness, helplessness; MÉD impotence; **impuissant, ~e** powerless, helpless; MÉD impotent

impulsif, -ive [ɛ̃pylsif, -iv] impulsive; **impulsion** *f* impulse; *à l'économie* boost; **sous l'~ de** urged on by

impunément [ɛ̃pynemɑ̃] *adv* with impunity; **impuni, ~e** unpunished; **rester ~** go unpunished

impur, ~e [ɛ̃pyr] *eau* dirty, polluted; *(impudique)* impure

imputable [ɛ̃pytabl] FIN chargeable; **~ à** attributable to, caused by; **imputer** ⟨1a⟩ attribute (**à** to); FIN charge (**sur** to)

inabordable [inabɔrdabl] *prix* unaffordable

inacceptable [inaksɛptabl] unacceptable

inaccessible [inaksesibl] inaccessible; *personne* unapproachable; *objectif* unattainable

inachevé, ~e [inaʃve] unfinished

inactif, -ive [inaktif, -iv] idle; *population* non-working; *remède, méthode* ineffective; *marché* slack

inadapté, ~e [inadapte] *enfant* handicapped; **~ à** unsuited to

inadéquat, ~e [inadekwa, -t] inadequate; *méthode* unsuitable

inadmissible [inadmisibl] unacceptable

inadvertance [inadvɛrtɑ̃s] *f*: **par ~** inadvertently

inaltérable [inalterabl] *matériel* that does not deteriorate; *fig* unfailing

inanimé, ~e [inanime] inanimate; *(mort)* lifeless; *(inconscient)* unconscious

inanition [inanisjɔ̃] *f* starvation

inaperçu, ~e [inapɛrsy]: **passer ~** go *ou* pass unnoticed

inapplicable [inaplikabl] *règlement* unenforceable

inapproprié, ~e [inaprɔprije] inappropriate

inapte [inapt]: **~ à** unsuited to; MÉD, MIL unfit for

inattaquable [inatakabl] unassailable

inattendu, ~e [inatɑ̃dy] unexpected

inattentif, -ive [inatɑ̃tif, -iv] inattentive; **inattention** *f* inattentiveness; **erreur d'~** careless mistake

inaudible [inodibl] inaudible

inauguration [inogyrasjɔ̃] *f d'un édifice* (official) opening; *fig* inauguration; **inaugurer** ⟨1a⟩ *édifice* (officially) open; *fig* inaugurate

inavouable [inavwabl] shameful

incalculable [ɛ̃kalkylabl] incalculable

incapable [ɛ̃kapabl] incapable (**de qch** of sth; **de faire qch** of doing sth); **nous sommes ~s de vous répondre** we are unable to give you an answer; **incapacité** *f (inaptitude)* incompetence; *de faire qch* inability; **être dans l'~ de faire qch** be incapable of doing sth

incarcérer [ɛ̃karsere] ⟨1f⟩ imprison, incarcerate

incarnation [ɛ̃karnasjɔ̃] *f* embodiment, personification; **incarner** ⟨1a⟩ THÉÂT play; **~ qch** be sth personified

incartade [ɛ̃kartad] *f* indiscretion

incassable [ɛ̃kasabl] unbreakable

incendiaire [ɛ̃sɑ̃djɛr] *adj* incendiary; *discours* inflammatory; **incendie** *m* fire; **~ criminel** arson; **incendier** ⟨1a⟩ set fire to

incertain, ~e [ɛ̃sɛrtɛ̃, -ɛn] uncertain; *temps* unsettled; (*hésitant*) indecisive; **incertitude** *f* uncertainty

incessamment [ɛ̃sesamɑ̃] *adv* any minute now; **incessant, ~e** incessant

inceste [ɛ̃sɛst] *m* incest

inchangé, ~e [ɛ̃ʃɑ̃ʒe] unchanged

incident [ɛ̃sidɑ̃] *m* incident; **~ de parcours** mishap; **~ technique** technical problem

incinération [ɛ̃sinerasjɔ̃] *f* incineration; *d'un cadavre* cremation; **incinérer** ⟨1f⟩ *ordures* incinerate; *cadavre* cremate

incisif, -ive [ɛ̃sizif, -iv] incisive

incision [ɛ̃sizjɔ̃] *f* incision

inciter [ɛ̃site] ⟨1a⟩ encourage (*à faire qch* to do sth); *péj* egg on (*à faire qch* to do sth), incite

inclinable [ɛ̃klinabl] tilting

inclinaison [ɛ̃klinɛzɔ̃] *f* *d'un toit* slope, slant; *d'un terrain* incline, slope; **inclination** *f fig* inclination (*pour* for); **~ de tête** (*salut*) nod; **incliner** ⟨1a⟩ tilt; **s'~** bend; *pour saluer* bow; **s'~ devant qch** (*céder*) yield to sth; **s'~ devant qn** *aussi fig* bow to s.o.

inclure [ɛ̃klyr] ⟨4l⟩ include; *dans une lettre* enclose; **inclus, ~e: ci-inclus** enclosed; **jusqu'au 30 juin ~** to 30th June inclusive

incohérence [ɛ̃kɔerɑ̃s] *f* *de comportement* inconsistency; *de discours, explication* incoherence; **incohérent, ~e** *comportement* inconsistent; *discours, explication* incoherent

incollable [ɛ̃kɔlabl] *riz* non-stick; **elle est ~** *F* she's rock solid

incolore [ɛ̃kɔlɔr] colorless, *Br* colourless

incomber [ɛ̃kɔ̃be] ⟨1a⟩: **il vous incombe de le lui dire** it is your responsibility *ou* duty to tell him

incommoder [ɛ̃kɔmɔde] ⟨1a⟩ bother

incomparable [ɛ̃kɔ̃parabl] incomparable

incompatibilité [ɛ̃kɔ̃patibilite] *f* incompatibility; **incompatible** incompatible

incompétence [ɛ̃kɔ̃petɑ̃s] *f* incompetence; **incompétent, ~e** incompetent

incomplet, -ète [ɛ̃kɔ̃plɛ, -t] incomplete

incompréhensible [ɛ̃kɔ̃preɑ̃sibl] incomprehensible; **incompréhension** *f* lack of understanding; **incompris, ~e** misunderstood (*de* by)

inconcevable [ɛ̃kɔ̃svabl] inconceivable

inconditionnel, ~le [ɛ̃kɔ̃disjɔnɛl] **1** *adj* unconditional **2** *m/f* fan, fanatic

inconfortable [ɛ̃kɔ̃fɔrtabl] uncomfortable

incongru, ~e [ɛ̃kɔ̃gry] incongruous

inconnu, ~e [ɛ̃kɔny] **1** *adj* (*ignoré*) unknown; (*étranger*) strange **2** *m/f* stranger

inconscience [ɛ̃kɔ̃sjɑ̃s] *f* *physique* unconsciousness; **inconscient, ~e** **1** *adj physique*, PSYCH unconscious; (*irréfléchi*) irresponsible **2** *m* PSYCH: **l'~** the unconscious (mind)

inconsidéré, ~e [ɛ̃kɔ̃sidere] rash, thoughtless

inconsistant, ~e [ɛ̃kɔ̃sistɑ̃, -t] inconsistent; *fig: raisonnement* flimsy

inconsolable [ɛ̃kɔ̃sɔlabl] inconsolable

inconstant, ~e [ɛ̃kɔ̃stɑ̃, -t] changeable

incontestable [ɛ̃kɔ̃tɛstabl] indisputable; **incontestablement** *adv* indisputably; **incontesté, ~e** outright

incontournable [ɛ̃kɔ̃turnabl]: **être ~** *d'un monument, d'un événement* be a must

incontrôlable [ɛ̃kɔ̃trolabl] uncontrollable; *pas vérifiable* unverifiable

inconvénient [ɛ̃kɔ̃venjɑ̃] *m* disadvantage *m*; **si vous n'y voyez aucun ~** if you have no objection

incorporer [ɛ̃kɔrpɔre] ⟨1a⟩ incorporate (*à* with, into); MIL draft; **avec flash incorporé** with built-in flash

incorrect, ~e [ɛ̃kɔrɛkt] wrong, incorrect; *comportement, tenue, langage* improper

incorrigible [ɛ̃kɔriʒibl] incorrigible

incorruptible [ɛ̃kɔryptibl] incorruptible

incrédule [ɛ̃kredyl] (*sceptique*) incredulous; **incrédulité** *f* incredulity

increvable [ɛ̃krəvabl] *pneu* punctureproof; F full of energy

incriminer [ɛ̃krimine] ⟨1a⟩ *personne* blame; JUR accuse; *paroles, actions* condemn

incroyable [ɛ̃krwajabl] incredible, unbelievable; **incroyablement** *adv* incredibly, unbelievably

incrustation [ɛ̃krystasjõ] *f ornement* inlay; **incruster**: *s'~ chez qn* be impossible to get rid of

incubateur [ɛ̃kybatœr] *m* incubator; **incubation** *f* incubation

inculpation [ɛ̃kylpasjõ] *f* JUR indictment; **inculpé, ~e** *m/f*: *l'~* the accused, the defendant; **inculper** ⟨1a⟩ JUR charge, indict (*de, pour* with)

inculquer [ɛ̃kylke] ⟨1m⟩: *~ qch à qn* instill sth into s.o.

inculte [ɛ̃kylt] *terre* waste *atr*, uncultivated; (*ignorant*) uneducated

incurable [ɛ̃kyrabl] incurable

incursion [ɛ̃kyrsjõ] *f* MIL raid, incursion; *fig: dans la politique etc* foray, venture (*dans* into)

indécent, ~e [ɛ̃desã, -t] indecent; (*incorrect*) inappropriate, improper

indéchiffrable [ɛ̃deʃifrabl] *message, écriture* indecipherable

indécis, ~e [ɛ̃desi, -z] undecided; *personne, caractère* indecisive; **indécision** *f de caractère* indecisiveness

indéfendable [ɛ̃defãdabl] MIL, *fig* indefensible

indéfini, ~e [ɛ̃defini] indefinite; (*imprécis*) undefined; *article m ~* indefinite article; **indéfiniment** *adv* indefinitely; **indéfinissable** indefinable

indélébile [ɛ̃delebil] indelible

indélicat, ~e [ɛ̃delika, -t] *personne, ac-* *tion* tactless

indemne [ɛ̃dɛmn] unhurt

indemnisation [ɛ̃dɛmnizasjõ] *f* compensation; **indemniser** ⟨1a⟩ compensate (*de* for); **indemnité** *f* (*dédommagement*) compensation; (*allocation*) allowance

indémodable [ɛ̃demɔdabl] classic, timeless

indéniable [ɛ̃denjabl] undeniable

indépendamment [ɛ̃depãdamã] *adv* independently; *~ de en faisant abstraction de* regardless of; (*en plus de*) apart from; **indépendance** *f* independence; **indépendant, ~e** independent (*de* of); *journaliste, traducteur* freelance; **indépendantiste** (pro-)independence *atr*

indescriptible [ɛ̃deskriptibl] indescribable

indésirable [ɛ̃dezirabl] undesirable

indestructible [ɛ̃dɛstryktibl] indestructible

indéterminé, ~e [ɛ̃detɛrmine] unspecified

index [ɛ̃dɛks] *m d'un livre* index; *doigt* index finger

indic [ɛ̃dik] *m/f* F grass F

indicateur, -trice [ɛ̃dikatœr, -tris] *m* (*espion*) informer; TECH gauge, indicator; **indicatif** *m* GRAM indicative; *de radio* signature tune; TÉL code; *à titre ~* to give me / you / *etc* an idea; **indication** *f* indication; (*information*) piece of information; *~s* instructions

indice [ɛ̃dis] *m* (*signe*) sign, indication; JUR clue; *~ des prix* price index; *~ de protection* protection factor

indien, ~ne [ɛ̃djɛ̃, -ɛn] **1** *adj* Indian; *d'Amérique aussi* native American **2** *m/f* **Indien, ~ne** Indian; *d'Amérique aussi* native American

indifféremment [ɛ̃diferamã] *adv* indiscriminately; **indifférence** *f* indifference; **indifférent, ~e** indifferent

indigène [ɛ̃diʒɛn] **1** *adj* native, indigenous **2** *m/f* native

indigeste [ɛ̃diʒɛst] indigestible; **indigestion** *f* MÉD indigestion

inexploré

indignation [ɛ̃diɲasjɔ̃] *f* indignation
indigne [ɛ̃diɲ] unworthy (*de* of); *parents* unfit
indigner [ɛ̃diɲe] ⟨1a⟩ make indignant; *s'~ de qch / contre qn* be indignant about sth / with s.o.
indiqué, ~e [ɛ̃dike] appropriate; *ce n'est pas ~* it's not advisable; **indiquer** ⟨1m⟩ indicate, show; *d'une pendule* show; (*recommander*) recommend; *~ qn du doigt* point at s.o.
indirect, ~e [ɛ̃dirɛkt] indirect; **indirectement** *adv* indirectly
indiscipline [ɛ̃disiplin] *f* lack of discipline, indiscipline; **indiscipliné, ~e** undisciplined; *cheveux* unmanageable
indiscret, -ète [ɛ̃diskrɛ, -t] indiscreet; **indiscrétion** indiscretion
indiscutable [ɛ̃diskytabl] indisputable
indispensable [ɛ̃dispɑ̃sabl] indispensable, essential
indisposer [ɛ̃dispoze] ⟨1a⟩ (*rendre malade*) make ill, sicken; (*fâcher*) annoy
indistinct, ~e [ɛ̃distɛ̃(kt), -ɛ̃kt] indistinct; **indistinctement** *adv* indistinctly; (*indifféremment*) without distinction
individu [ɛ̃dividy] *m* individual (*aussi péj*); **individualisme** *m* individualism; **individualiste** individualistic; **individualité** *f* individuality; **individuel, ~le** individual; *secrétaire* private, personal; *liberté, responsabilité* personal; *chambre* single; *maison* detached; **individuellement** *adv* individually
indivisible [ɛ̃divizibl] indivisible
indolence [ɛ̃dɔlɑ̃s] *f* laziness, indolence; **indolent, ~e** lazy, indolent
indolore [ɛ̃dɔlɔr] painless
indomptable [ɛ̃dɔ̃tabl] *fig* indomitable
Indonésie [ɛ̃dɔnezi] *f*: *l'~* Indonesia; **indonésien, ~ne 1** *adj* Indonesian **2** *m langue* Indonesian **3** *m/f* **Indonésien, ~ne** Indonesian
indu, ~e [ɛ̃dy]: *à une heure ~e* at some ungodly hour

indubitable [ɛ̃dybitabl] indisputable
induire [ɛ̃dɥir] ⟨4c⟩: *~ qn en erreur* mislead s.o.
indulgence [ɛ̃dylʒɑ̃s] *f* indulgence; *d'un juge* leniency; **indulgent, ~e** indulgent; *juge* lenient
industrialisation [ɛ̃dystrijalizasjɔ̃] *f* industrialization; **industrialisé:** *les pays ~s* the industrialized nations; **industrialiser** ⟨1a⟩ industrialize; **industrie** *f* industry; *~ automobile* car industry, auto industry; *~ lourde* heavy industry; **industriel, ~le 1** *adj* industrial **2** *m* industrialist
inébranlable [inebrɑ̃labl] solid (as a rock); *fig: personne, foi aussi* unshakeable
inédit, ~e [inedi, -t] (*pas édité*) unpublished; (*nouveau*) original, unique
inefficace [inefikas] inefficient; *remède* ineffective
inégal, ~e [inegal] (*mpl -aux*) unequal; *surface* uneven; *rythme* irregular; **inégalé, ~e** unequalled; *Br* unequalled; **inégalité** *f* inequality; *d'une surface* unevenness
inéligible [ineliʒibl] ineligible
inéluctable [inelyktabl] unavoidable
inepte [inɛpt] inept; **ineptie** *f* ineptitude; *~s* nonsense *sg*
inépuisable [inepɥizabl] inexhaustible
inerte [inɛrt] *corps* lifeless, inert; PHYS inert; **inertie** *f* inertia (*aussi* PHYS)
inespéré, ~e [inɛspere] unexpected, unhoped-for
inestimable [inɛstimabl] *tableau* priceless; *aide* invaluable
inévitable [inevitabl] inevitable; *accident* unavoidable
inexact, ~e [inɛgza(kt), -akt] inaccurate
inexcusable [inɛkskyzabl] inexcusable, unforgiveable
inexistant, ~e [inɛgzistɑ̃, -t] non-existent
inexpérimenté, ~e [inɛksperimɑ̃te] *personne* inexperienced
inexplicable [inɛksplikabl] inexplicable; **inexpliqué, ~e** unexplained
inexploré, ~e [inɛksplɔre] unexplored

inexprimable [inɛksprimabl] inexpressible

infaillible [ɛ̃fajibl] infallible

infaisable [ɛ̃fəzabl] not doable, not feasible

infâme [ɛ̃fɑm] vile

infanterie [ɛ̃fɑ̃tri] f MIL infantry

infantile [ɛ̃fɑ̃til] *mortalité* infant *atr*; *péj* infantile; **maladie** f **~e** children's illness, childhood illness

infarctus [ɛ̃farktys] m MÉD: **~ du myocarde** coronary (thrombosis), myocardial infarction *fml*

infatigable [ɛ̃fatigabl] tireless, indefatigable

infect, **~e** [ɛ̃fɛkt] disgusting; *temps* foul; **infecter** ⟨1a⟩ infect; *air, eau* pollute; **s'~** become infected; **infectieux, -euse** infectious; **infection** f MÉD infection

inférieur, **~e** [ɛ̃ferjœr] **1** *adj* lower; *qualité* inferior **2** m/f inferior; **infériorité** f inferiority

infernal, **~e** [ɛ̃fɛrnal] (*mpl* -aux) infernal

infester [ɛ̃fɛste] ⟨1a⟩ *d'insectes, de plantes* infest, overrun

infidèle [ɛ̃fidɛl] unfaithful; REL pagan *atr*; **infidélité** f infidelity

infiltrer [ɛ̃filtre] ⟨1a⟩: **s'~ dans** get into; *fig* infiltrate

infime [ɛ̃fim] tiny, infinitesimal

infini, **~e** [ɛ̃fini] **1** *adj* infinite **2** m infinity; **à l'~** to infinity; **infiniment** *adv* infinitely; **infinité** f infinity; **une ~ de** an enormous number of

infinitif [ɛ̃finitif] m infinitive

infirme [ɛ̃firm] **1** *adj* disabled **2** m/f disabled person; **infirmerie** f infirmary; ÉDU infirmary; **infirmier, -ère** m/f nurse; **infirmité** f disability

inflammable [ɛ̃flamabl] flammable; **inflammation** f MÉD inflammation

inflation [ɛ̃flasjɔ̃] f inflation; **inflationniste** inflationary

inflexible [ɛ̃flɛksibl] inflexible

infliger [ɛ̃fliʒe] ⟨1l⟩ *peine* inflict (**à** on); *défaite* impose

influençable [ɛ̃flyɑ̃sabl] easily influenced *ou* swayed; **influence** f influence; **influencer** ⟨1k⟩ influence; in-

fluent, **~e** influential

influer[ɛ̃flye] ⟨1a⟩: **~ sur** affect

info [ɛ̃fo] f F RAD, TV news item; **les ~s** the news *sg*

informateur, -**trice** m/f informant

informaticien, **~ne** [ɛ̃fɔrmatisjɛ̃, -ɛn] m/f computer scientist

informatif, -**ive** [ɛ̃fɔrmatif, -iv] informative; **information** f information; JUR inquiry; **une ~** a piece of information; **des ~s** some information *sg*; RAD, TV a news item; **les ~s** RAD, TV the news *sg*; **traitement** m **de l'~** data processing

informatique [ɛ̃fɔrmatik] **1** *adj* computer **2** f information technology, IT; **informatiser** ⟨1a⟩ computerize

informe [ɛ̃fɔrm] shapeless

informer [ɛ̃fɔrme] ⟨1a⟩ inform (**de** of); **s'~** find out (**de qch auprès de qn** about sth from s.o.)

infraction [ɛ̃fraksjɔ̃] f infringement (**à** of); **~ au code de la route** traffic violation, *Br* traffic offence

infranchissable [ɛ̃frɑ̃ʃisabl] impossible to cross; *obstacle* insurmountable

infrarouge [ɛ̃fraruʒ] infrared

infrastructure [ɛ̃frastryktyr] f infrastructure

infroissable [ɛ̃frwasabl] crease-resistant

infructueux, -**euse** [ɛ̃fryktɥø, -z] unsuccessful

infuser [ɛ̃fyze] ⟨1a⟩ **1** v/t infuse **2** v/i: **faire ~** *thé* brew

infusion [ɛ̃fyzjɔ̃] f herb tea

ingénier [ɛ̃ʒenje] ⟨1a⟩: **s'~ à faire qch** go out of one's way to do sth

ingénierie [ɛ̃ʒenjəri] f engineering; **ingénieur** m engineer; **ingénieux, -euse** ingenious; **ingéniosité** f ingeniousness

ingérence [ɛ̃ʒerɑ̃s] f interference; **ingérer** ⟨1f⟩: **s'~** interfere (**dans** in)

ingrat, **~e** [ɛ̃gra, -t] ungrateful; *tâche* thankless; **ingratitude** f ingratitude

ingrédient [ɛ̃gredjɑ̃] m ingredient

inguérissable [ɛ̃gerisabl] incurable

ingurgiter [ɛ̃gyrʒite] ⟨1a⟩ gulp down

inhabitable [inabitabl] uninhabitable; **inhabité, ~e** uninhabited inhabituel, ~le [inabituɛl] unusual

inhalateur [inalatœr] m MÉD inhaler; inhaler ⟨1a⟩ inhale

inhérent, ~e [inerɑ̃, -t] inherent (à in)

inhibé, ~e [inibe] inhibited; inhibition f PSYCH inhibition

inhospitalier, -ère [inɔspitalje, -ɛr] inhospitable

inhumain, ~e [inymɛ̃, -ɛn] inhuman

inimaginable [inimaʒinabl] unimaginable

inimitable [inimitabl] inimitable

ininflammable [inɛ̃flamabl] non--flammable

ininterrompu, ~e [inɛ̃terɔ̃py] uninterrupted; musique, pluie non-stop; sommeil unbroken

initial, ~e [inisjal] (mpl -aux) 1 adj initial 2 f initial (letter); initiation f initiation; ~ à fig introduction to

initiative [inisjativ] f initiative; prendre l'~ take the initiative

inimitié [inimitje] f enmity

inintelligible [inɛ̃teliʒibl] unintelligible

inintéressant, ~e [inɛ̃teresɑ̃, -t] uninteresting

initié, ~e [inisje] m/f insider; initier ⟨1a⟩ (instruire) initiate (à in); fig introduce (à to)

injecté, ~e [ɛ̃ʒɛkte]: ~ (de sang) blood-shot; injecter ⟨1a⟩ inject; injection f injection

injoignable [ɛ̃ʒwaɲabl] unreachable, uncontactable

injonction [ɛ̃ʒɔ̃ksjɔ̃] f injunction

injure [ɛ̃ʒyr] f insult; ~s abuse sg; injurier ⟨1a⟩ insult, abuse; injurieux, -euse insulting, abusive

injuste [ɛ̃ʒyst] unfair, unjust; injustice f injustice; d'une décision unfairness; injustifié, ~e unjustified

inlassable [ɛ̃lasabl] tireless

inné, ~e [in(n)e] innate

innocence [inɔsɑ̃s] f innocence; innocent, ~e innocent; innocenter ⟨1a⟩ clear

innombrable [inɔ̃brabl] countless; auditoire, foule vast

innovant, ~e [inɔvɑ̃, -t] innovative; innovateur, -trice 1 adj innovative

2 m/f innovator; innovation f innovation

inoccupé, ~e [inɔkype] personne idle; maison unoccupied

inoculer [inɔkyle] ⟨1a⟩ inoculate

inodore [inɔdɔr] odorless, Br odourless

inoffensif, -ive [inɔfɑ̃sif, -iv] harmless; humour inoffensive

inondation [inɔ̃dasjɔ̃] f flood; inonder ⟨1a⟩ flood; ~ de fig inundate with

inopérable [inɔperabl] inoperable

inopiné, ~e [inɔpine] unexpected; inopinément adv unexpectedly

inopportun, ~e [inɔpɔrtœ̃, -yn] ill--timed, inopportune

inorganique [inɔrganik] inorganic

inoubliable [inublijabl] unforgettable

inouï, ~e [inwi] unheard-of

inox® [inɔks] m stainless steel; inoxydable stainless; acier ~ stainless steel

inqualifiable [ɛ̃kalifjabl] unspeakable

inquiet, -ète [ɛ̃kjɛ, -t] anxious, worried (de about); inquiétant, ~e worrying; inquiéter ⟨1f⟩ worry; s'~ worry (de about); inquiétude f anxiety

insaisissable [ɛ̃sezisabl] elusive; différence imperceptible

insalubre [ɛ̃salybr] insalubrious; climat unhealthy

insatiable [ɛ̃sasjabl] insatiable

insatisfaisant, ~e [ɛ̃satisfazɑ̃, -t] unsatisfactory; insatisfait, ~e unsatisfied; mécontent dissatisfied

inscription [ɛ̃skripsjɔ̃] f inscription; (immatriculation) registration; inscrire ⟨4f⟩ (noter) write down, note; dans registre enter; à examen register; (graver) inscribe; s'~ put one's name down; à l'université register; à un cours enroll, Br enrol, put one's name down (à for); s'~ dans un club join a club

insecte [ɛ̃sɛkt] m insect; insecticide m insecticide

insécurité [ɛ̃sekyrite] f insecurity; il faut combattre l'~ we have to tackle the security problem

insémination [ɛ̃seminasjɔ̃] *f*: **~ artifi-cielle** artificial insemination

insensé, ~e [ɛ̃sɑ̃se] mad, insane

insensibiliser [ɛ̃sɑ̃sibilize] ⟨1a⟩ numb; **insensibilité** *f* insensitivity; **insensible** ANAT numb; *personne* insensitive (**à** to)

inséparable [ɛ̃separabl] inseparable

insérer [ɛ̃sere] ⟨1f⟩ insert, put; **~ une annonce dans le journal** put an ad in the paper; **insertion** *f* insertion

insidieux, -euse [ɛ̃sidjø, -z] insidious

insigne [ɛ̃siɲ] *m* (*emblème*) insignia; (*badge*) badge

insignifiant, ~e [ɛ̃siɲifjɑ̃, -t] insignificant

insinuer [ɛ̃sinɥe] ⟨1n⟩ insinuate; **s'~ dans** worm one's way into

insipide [ɛ̃sipid] insipid

insistance [ɛ̃sistɑ̃s] *f* insistence; **insistant, ~e** insistent; **insister** ⟨1a⟩ insist; F (*persévérer*) persevere; **~ pour faire qch** insist on doing sth; **~ sur qch** (*souligner*) stress sth

insolation [ɛ̃sɔlasjɔ̃] *f* sunstroke

insolence [ɛ̃sɔlɑ̃s] *f* insolence; **insolent, ~e** insolent

insolite [ɛ̃sɔlit] unusual

insoluble [ɛ̃sɔlybl] insoluble

insolvable [ɛ̃sɔlvabl] insolvent

insomniaque [ɛ̃sɔmnjak] *m/f* insomniac; **insomnie** *f* insomnia

insonoriser [ɛ̃sɔnɔrize] soundproof

insouciant, ~e [ɛ̃susjɑ̃, -t] carefree

insoumis [ɛ̃sumi] rebellious

insoupçonnable [ɛ̃supsɔnabl] *personne* above suspicion; **insoupçonné, ~e** unsuspected

insoutenable [ɛ̃sutnabl] (*insupportable*) unbearable; *argument, revendication* untenable

inspecter [ɛ̃spɛkte] ⟨1a⟩ inspect; **inspecteur, -trice** *m/f* inspector; **inspection** *f* inspection

inspiration [ɛ̃spirasjɔ̃] *f* fig inspiration; **inspirer** ⟨1a⟩ **1** *v/i* breathe in, inhale **2** *v/t* inspire; **s'~ de** be inspired by

instable [ɛ̃stabl] unstable; *table, échelle* unsteady

installation [ɛ̃stalasjɔ̃] *f* installation;

~ électrique wiring; **~ militaire** military installation; **~s** facilities; **installer** ⟨1a⟩ install; *appartement*: fit out; (*loger, placer*) put, place; **s'~** (*s'établir*) settle down; *à la campagne etc* settle; *d'un médecin, dentiste* set up in practice; **s'~ chez qn** make o.s. at home at s.o.'s place

instance [ɛ̃stɑ̃s] *f* (*autorité*) authority; **ils sont en ~ de divorce** they have filed for a divorce

instant [ɛ̃stɑ̃] *m* instant, moment; **à l'~** just this minute; **en un ~** in an instant *ou* moment; **à l'~ où je vous parle** even as I speak; **ça sera fini d'un ~ à l'autre** it will be finished any minute now; **dans un ~** in a minute; **pour l'~** for the moment

instantané, ~e [ɛ̃stɑ̃tane] **1** *adj* immediate; *café* instant; *mort* instantaneous **2** *m* PHOT snap(shot); **instantanément** *adv* immediately

instaurer [ɛ̃store] ⟨1a⟩ establish

instigateur, -trice [ɛ̃stigatœr, -tris] *m/f* instigator; **instigation** *f*: **à l'~ de qn** at s.o.'s instigation

instinct [ɛ̃stɛ̃] *m* instinct; **instinctif, -ive** instinctive; **instinctivement** *adv* instinctively

instituer [ɛ̃stitɥe] ⟨1n⟩ introduce

institut [ɛ̃stity] *m* institute; **~ de beauté** beauty salon

instituteur, -trice [ɛ̃stitytœr, -tris] *m/f* (primary) school teacher

institution [ɛ̃stitysjɔ̃] *f* institution

instructeur [ɛ̃stryktœr] *m* MIL instructor; **instructif, -ive** instructive; **instruction** *f* (*enseignement, culture*) education; MIL training; JUR preliminary investigation; INFORM instruction; **~s** instructions; **instruire** ⟨4c⟩ ÉDU educate, teach; MIL train; JUR investigate; **instruit, ~e** (well-)educated

instrument [ɛ̃strymɑ̃] *m* instrument; **~ à cordes / à vent / à percussion** string / wind / percussion instrument

insu [ɛ̃sy]: **à l'~ de** unbeknownst to; **à mon ~** unbeknownst to me

insubmersible [ɛ̃sybmɛrsibl] unsinkable

insubordination [ɛ̃sybɔrdinasjõ] *f* insubordination; **insubordonné, ~e** insubordinate

insuffisance *f* deficiency; **~ respiratoire** respiratory problem; **~ cardiaque** heart problem; **insuffisant, ~e** [ɛ̃syfizã, -t] *quantité* insufficient; *qualité* inadequate; **un effort ~** not enough of an effort

insulaire [ɛ̃syler] **1** *adj* island *atr* **2** *m/f* islander

insuline [ɛ̃sylin] *f* insulin

insultant, ~e [ɛ̃syltã, -t] insulting; **insulte** *f* insult; **insulter** ⟨1a⟩ insult

insupportable [ɛ̃sypɔrtabl] unbearable

insurger [ɛ̃syrʒe] ⟨1l⟩: **s'~ contre** rise up against

insurmontable [ɛ̃syrmõtabl] insurmountable

insurrection [ɛ̃syreksjõ] *f* insurrection

intact, ~e [ɛ̃takt] intact

intarissable [ɛ̃tarisabl] *source* inexhaustible

intégral, ~e [ɛ̃tegral] (*mpl* -aux) full, complete; *texte* unabridged; **intégralement** *adv* payer, recopier in full; **intégrant, ~e: faire partie ~e de** be an integral part of; **intégration** *f* (*assimilation*) integration

intègre [ɛ̃tegr] of integrity

intégrer [ɛ̃tegre] ⟨1a⟩ (*assimiler*) integrate; (*incorporer*) incorporate

intégrisme [ɛ̃tegrism] *m* fundamentalism; **intégriste** *m/f* & *adj* fundamentalist

intégrité [ɛ̃tegrite] *f* integrity

intellectuel, ~le [ɛ̃telektɥel] *m/f* & *adj* intellectual

intelligemment [ɛ̃teliʒamã] *adv* intelligently; **intelligence** *f* intelligence; **~ artificielle** artificial intelligence; **intelligent, ~e** intelligent; **intello** *m/f* F egghead F

intempéries [ɛ̃tãperi] *fpl* bad weather *sg*

intempestif, -ive [ɛ̃tãpestif, -iv] untimely

intenable [ɛ̃t(ə)nabl] *situation, froid* unbearable

intense [ɛ̃tãs] intense; **intensif, -ive** intensive; **intensification** *f* intensification; *d'un conflit* escalation; **intensifier** intensify, step up; **s'~** intensify; *d'un conflit* escalate; **intensité** *f* intensity

intenter [ɛ̃tãte] ⟨1a⟩: **~ un procès contre** start proceedings against

intention [ɛ̃tãsjõ] *f* intention; **avoir l'~ de faire qch** intend to do sth; **à l'~ de** for; **c'est l'~ qui compte** it's the thought that counts; **intentionné, ~e: bien ~** well-meaning; **mal ~** ill-intentioned; **intentionnel, ~le** intentional

interactif, -ive [ɛ̃teraktif, -iv] interactive

intercaler [ɛ̃terkale] ⟨1a⟩ insert

intercéder [ɛ̃tersede] ⟨1f⟩: **~ pour qn** intercede for s.o.

intercepter [ɛ̃tersepte] ⟨1a⟩ intercept; *soleil* shut out

interchangeable [ɛ̃terʃãʒabl] interchangeable

interclasse [ɛ̃terklas] *m* ÉDU (short) break

intercontinental [ɛ̃terkõtinãtal] intercontinental

interdépendance [ɛ̃terdepãdãs] *f* interdependence; **interdépendant, ~e** interdependent

interdiction [ɛ̃terdiksjõ] *f* ban; **interdire** ⟨4m⟩ ban; **~ à qn de faire qch** forbid s.o. to do sth; **interdit, ~e** forbidden; (*très étonné*) taken aback

intéressant, ~e [ɛ̃teresã, -t] interesting; (*avide*) selfish; *prix* good; *situation* well-paid; **intéressé, ~e** interested; **les parties ~es** the people concerned; **être ~ aux bénéfices** COMM have a share in the profits; **intéressement** *m aux bénéfices* share; **intéresser** ⟨1b⟩ interest; (*concerner*) concern; **s'~ à** be interested in

intérêt [ɛ̃tere] *m* interest; (*égoïsme*) self-interest; **~s** COMM interest *sg*; **il a ~ à le faire** it's in his interest to do it; **agir par ~** act out of self-interest; **prêt sans ~** interest-free loan

interface [ɛ̃terfas] *f* interface

interférence [ɛ̃tɛrferɑ̃s] f PHYS, fig interference

intérieur, ~e [ɛ̃terjœr] 1 adj poche inside; porte, cour, vie inner; commerce, marché, politique, vol domestic; mer inland 2 m inside; d'un pays, d'une auto interior; **à l'~ (de)** inside; **ministre m de l'Intérieur** Secretary of the Interior, Br Home Secretary

intérim [ɛ̃terim] m interim; travail temporary work; **assurer l'~** stand in; **par ~** acting; intérimaire 1 adj travail temporary 2 m/f temp

intérioriser [ɛ̃terjɔrize] ⟨1a⟩ internalize

interlocuteur, -trice [ɛ̃terlɔkytœr, -tris] m/f: **mon / son ~** the person I / she was talking to

interloquer [ɛ̃terlɔke] ⟨1m⟩ take aback

interlude [ɛ̃terlyd] m interlude

intermède [ɛ̃termɛd] m interlude

intermédiaire [ɛ̃termedjɛr] 1 adj intermediate 2 m/f intermediary, go-between; COMM middleman; **par l'~ de qn** through s.o.

interminable [ɛ̃terminabl] interminable

intermittence [ɛ̃termitɑ̃s] f: **par ~** intermittently; intermittent, ~e intermittent

internat [ɛ̃terna] m ÉDU boarding school

international, ~e [ɛ̃ternasjɔnal] (mpl -aux) m/f & adj international

interne [ɛ̃tern] 1 adj internal; oreille inner; d'une société in-house 2 m/f élève boarder; médecin intern, Br houseman; interné, ~e m/f inmate; interner ⟨1a⟩ intern

Internet [ɛ̃ternet] m Internet; **sur ~** on the Internet ou the Net

interpeller [ɛ̃terpɛle] ⟨1a orthographe, 1c prononciation⟩ call out to; de la police, POL question

interphone [ɛ̃terfɔn] m intercom; d'un immeuble entry phone

interposer [ɛ̃terpoze] ⟨1a⟩ interpose; **par personne interposée** through an intermediary; **s'~** (intervenir) intervene

interprétation [ɛ̃terpretasjɔ̃] f interpretation; au théâtre performance; interprète m/f (traducteur) interpreter; (porte-parole) spokesperson; interpréter ⟨1f⟩ interpret; rôle, MUS play

interrogateur, -trice [ɛ̃terɔgatœr, -tris] questioning; interrogatif, -ive air, ton inquiring, questioning; GRAM interrogative; interrogation f question; (d'un suspect) questioning, interrogation; **point m d'~** question mark; interrogatoire m par police questioning; par juge cross-examination; interroger ⟨1l⟩ question; de la police question, interrogate; d'un juge cross-examine

interrompre [ɛ̃terɔ̃pr] ⟨4a⟩ interrupt; **s'~** break off

interrupteur [ɛ̃teryptœr] m switch; interruption f interruption; **sans ~** without stopping; **~ volontaire de grossesse** termination, abortion

intersection [ɛ̃tersɛksjɔ̃] f intersection

interstice [ɛ̃terstis] m crack

interurbain, ~e [ɛ̃teryrbɛ̃, -ɛn] long-distance

intervalle [ɛ̃terval] m d'espace space, gap; de temps interval

intervenant, ~e [ɛ̃tervɔnɑ̃, -t] m/f participant; intervenir ⟨2h⟩ (aux être) intervene (**en faveur de** on behalf of); d'une rencontre take place

intervention [ɛ̃tervɑ̃sjɔ̃] f intervention; MÉD operation; (discours) speech

interview [ɛ̃tervju] f interview; interviewer ⟨1a⟩ interview

intestin, ~e [ɛ̃testɛ̃, -in] 1 adj internal 2 m intestin; intestinal, ~e (mpl -aux) intestinal

intime [ɛ̃tim] 1 adj intimate; ami close; pièce cozy, Br cosy; vie private 2 m/f close friend

intimidation [ɛ̃timidasjɔ̃] f intimidation; intimider ⟨1a⟩ intimidate

intimité [ɛ̃timite] f entre amis closeness, intimacy; vie privée privacy, private life; **dans l'~** in private; dîner with a few close friends

intituler [ɛ̃tityle] ⟨1a⟩ call; **s'~** be

called

intolérable [ɛ̃tɔlerabl] intolerable; **intolérance** f intolerance; **intolérant, ~e** intolerant

intoxication [ɛ̃tɔksikasjɔ̃] f poisoning; **~ alimentaire** food poisoning; **intoxiquer** ⟨1m⟩ poison; *fig* brainwash

intraduisible [ɛ̃traduizibl] untranslatable; *peine, souffrance* indescribable

intraitable [ɛ̃tretabl] uncompromising

Intranet [ɛ̃tranɛt] m intranet

intransigeant, ~e [ɛ̃trɑ̃ziʒɑ̃, -t] intransigent

intransitif, -ive [ɛ̃trɑ̃zitif, -iv] GRAM intransitive

intraveineux, -euse [ɛ̃travenø, -z] intravenous

intrépide [ɛ̃trepid] intrepid

intrigant, ~e [ɛ̃trigɑ̃, -t] scheming; **intrigue** f plot; **~s** scheming sg, plotting sg; **intriguer** ⟨1m⟩ **1** v/i scheme, plot **2** v/t intrigue

intrinsèque [ɛ̃trɛ̃sɛk] intrinsic

introduction [ɛ̃trɔdyksjɔ̃] f introduction

introduire [ɛ̃trɔduir] ⟨4c⟩ introduce; *visiteur* show in; (*engager*) insert; **s'~ dans** gain entry to

introuvable [ɛ̃truvabl] impossible to find

introverti, ~e [ɛ̃trɔvɛrti] m/f introvert

intrus, ~e [ɛ̃try, -z] m/f intruder; **intrusion** f intrusion

intuitif, -ive [ɛ̃tyitif, -iv] intuitive; **intuition** f intuition; (*pressentiment*) premonition

inusable [inyzabl] hard-wearing

inutile [inytil] *qui ne sert pas* useless; (*superflu*) pointless, unnecessary; **inutilisable** unuseable; **inutilisé, ~e** unused

invaincu, ~e [ɛ̃vɛ̃ky] unbeaten

invalide [ɛ̃valid] **1** *adj* (*infirme*) disabled **2** m/f disabled person; **~ du travail** person who is disabled as the result of an industrial accident; **invalider** ⟨1a⟩ JUR, POL invalidate; **invalidité** f disability

invariable [ɛ̃varjabl] invariable

invasion [ɛ̃vazjɔ̃] f invasion

invendable [ɛ̃vɑ̃dabl] unsellable; **invendus** mpl unsold goods

inventaire [ɛ̃vɑ̃tɛr] m inventory; COMM *opération* stocktaking

inventer [ɛ̃vɑ̃te] ⟨1a⟩ invent; *histoire* make up; **inventeur, -trice** m/f inventor; **inventif, -ive** inventive; **invention** f invention

inverse [ɛ̃vɛrs] **1** *adj* MATH inverse; *sens* opposite; **dans l'ordre ~** in reverse order; **dans le sens ~ des aiguilles d'une montre** counterclockwise, *Br* anticlockwise **2** m opposite, reverse; **inverser** ⟨1a⟩ invert; *rôles* reverse

investigation [ɛ̃vɛstigasjɔ̃] f investigation

investir [ɛ̃vɛstir] ⟨2a⟩ FIN invest; (*cerner*) surround; **investissement** m FIN investment; **investisseur, -euse** m/f investor

invétéré, ~e [ɛ̃vetere] inveterate

invincible [ɛ̃vɛ̃sibl] *adversaire, armée* invincible; *obstacle* insuperable

inviolable [ɛ̃vjɔlabl] inviolable

invisible [ɛ̃vizibl] invisible

invitation [ɛ̃vitasjɔ̃] f invitation; **invité, ~e** m/f guest; **inviter** ⟨1a⟩ invite; **~ qn à faire qch** (*exhorter*) urge s.o. to do sth

invivable [ɛ̃vivabl] unbearable

involontaire [ɛ̃vɔlɔ̃tɛr] unintentional; *témoin* unwilling; *mouvement* involuntary

invoquer [ɛ̃vɔke] ⟨1m⟩ *Dieu* call on, invoke; *aide* call on; *texte, loi* refer to; *solution* put forward

invraisemblable [ɛ̃vrɛsɑ̃blabl] unlikely, improbable

invulnérable [ɛ̃vylnerabl] invulnerable

iode [jɔd] m CHIM iodine

Iran [irɑ̃] m: **l'~** Iran; **iranien, ~ne 1** *adj* Iranian **2** m/f **Iranien, ~ne** Iranian

Iraq [irak] m: **l'~** Iraq; **iraquien, ~ne 1** *adj* Iraqi **2** m/f **Iraquien, ~ne** Iraqi

irascible [irasibl] irascible

iris [iris] m MÉD, BOT iris

irlandais, ~e [irlɑ̃dɛ, -z] **1** *adj* Irish; **2** *m langue* Irish (Gaelic) **3 Irlandais** *m* Irishman; **Irlandaise** *f* Irishwoman; **Irlande** *f*: **l'~** Ireland

ironie [irɔni] *f* irony; **ironique** ironic; **ironiser** ⟨1a⟩ be ironic

irradier [iradje] ⟨1a⟩ **1** *v/i* radiate **2** *v/t* (*exposer aux radiations*) irradiate

irraisonné, ~e [irezɔne] irrational

irrationnel, ~le [irasjɔnel] irrational

irréalisable [irealizabl] *projet* impracticable; *rêve* unrealizable; **irréaliste** unrealistic

irréconciliable [irekɔ̃siljabl] irreconcilable

irrécupérable [irekyperabl] beyond repair; *personne* beyond redemption; *données* irretrievable

irréductible [iredyktibl] indomitable; *ennemi* implacable

irréel, ~le [ireel] unreal

irréfléchi, ~e [irefleʃi] thoughtless, reckless

irréfutable [irefytabl] irrefutable

irrégularité [iregylarite] *f* irregularity; *de surface, terrain* unevenness; **irrégulier, -ère** irregular; *surface, terrain* uneven; *étudiant, sportif* erratic

irrémédiable [iremedjabl] *maladie* incurable; *erreur* irreparable

irremplaçable [irɑ̃plasabl] irreplaceable

irréparable [ireparabl] *faute, dommage* irreparable; *vélo* beyond repair

irrépressible [irepresibl] irrepressible; *colère* overpowering

irréprochable [ireprɔʃabl] irreproachable, beyond reproach

irrésistible [irezistibl] irresistible

irrésolu, ~e [irezɔly] *personne* indecisive; *problème* unresolved

irrespectueux, -euse [irespektɥø, -z] disrespectful

irrespirable [irespirabl] unbreathable

irresponsable [irespɔ̃sabl] irresponsible

irrévérencieux, -euse [ireverɑ̃sjø, -z] irreverent

irréversible [ireversibl] irreversible

irrévocable [irevɔkabl] irrevocable

irrigation [irigasjɔ̃] *f* AGR irrigation;

irriguer ⟨1m⟩ irrigate

irritable [iritabl] irritable; **irritant, ~e** irritating; **irritation** *f* irritation; **irriter** ⟨1a⟩ irritate; **s'~** get irritated

irruption [irypsjɔ̃] *f*: **faire ~ dans une pièce** burst into a room

islam, Islam [islam] *m* REL Islam; **islamique** Islamic; **islamiste** Islamic fundamentalist

islandais, ~e [islɑ̃dɛ, -z] **1** *adj* Icelandic; **2** *m langue* Islandic **3** *m/f* **Islandais, ~e** Icelander; **Islande**: **l'~** Iceland

isolant, ~e [izɔlɑ̃, -t] **1** *adj* insulating **2** *m* insulation; **isolation** *f* insulation; *contre le bruit* soundproofing; **isolé, ~e** *maison, personne* isolated; TECH insulated; **isolement** *m* isolation; **isoler** ⟨1a⟩ isolate; *prisonnier* place in solitary confinement; ÉL insulate; **isoloir** *m* voting booth

isotherme [izɔterm] *camion etc* refrigerated; *sac ~* cool bag

Israël [israel] *m* Israel; **israélien, ~ne 1** *adj* Israeli **2** *m/f* **Israélien, ~ne** Israeli

issu, ~e [isy]: **être ~ de** *parenté* come from; *résultat* stem from

issue [isy] *f* way out (*aussi fig*), exit; (*fin*) outcome; **à l'~ de** at the end of; **voie** *f* **sans ~** dead end; **~ de secours** emergency exit

Italie [itali] *f*: **l'~** Italy; **italien, ~ne 1** *adj* Italian **2** *m langue* Italian **3** *m/f* **Italien, ~ne** Italian

italique *m*: **en ~** in italics

itinéraire [itinerer] *m* itinerary

IUT [iyt] *m abr* (= *Institut universitaire de technologie*) technical college

IVG [iveʒe] *f abr* (= *interruption volontaire de grossesse*) termination, abortion

ivoire [ivwar] *m* ivory

ivoirien, ~ne [ivwarjɛ̃, -ɛn] **1** *adj* Ivorian **2** *m/f* **Ivoirien, ~ne** Ivorian

ivre [ivr] drunk; **~ de** *fig: joie, colère* wild with; **ivresse** *f* drunkenness; **conduite** *f* **en état d'~** drunk driving, *Br aussi* drink driving; **ivrogne** *m/f* drunk

J

j' [ʒ] → **je**

jacasser [ʒakase] ⟨1a⟩ chatter

jachère [ʒaʃɛr] f AGR: **en ~** lying fallow; **mise en ~** set-aside

jacinthe [ʒasɛ̃t] f BOT hyacinth

jackpot [dʒakpɔt] m jackpot

jade [ʒad] m jade

jadis [ʒadis] formerly

jaillir [ʒajir] ⟨2a⟩ *d'eau, de flammes* shoot out (*de* from)

jalousement [ʒaluzmã] adv jealously; **jalousie** f jealousy; (*store*) Venetian blind; **jaloux, -ouse** jealous

jamais [ʒamɛ] ◊ *positif* ever; **avez-vous~ été à Vannes?** have you ever been to Vannes?; **plus que ~** more than ever; **à ~** for ever, for good; ◊ *négatif* **ne ... ~** never; **je ne lui ai ~ parlé** I've never spoken to him; **on ne sait ~** you never know; **~ de la vie!** never!, certainly not!

jambe [ʒãb] f leg

jambon [ʒãbõ] m ham; **~ fumé** gammon

jante [ʒãt] f rim

janvier [ʒãvje] m January

Japon [ʒapõ] m: **le ~** Japan; **japonais, ~e** 1 adj Japanese 2 m/f **Japonais, ~e** Japanese 3 m langue Japanese

jappement [ʒapmã] m yap; **japper** ⟨1a⟩ yap

jaquette [ʒakɛt] f *d'un livre* dust jacket

jardin [ʒardɛ̃] m garden; **~ botanique** botanical gardens pl; **~ d'enfants** kindergarten; **~ public** park

jardinage [ʒardinaʒ] m gardening; **jardiner** garden; **jardinerie** f garden center *ou Br* centre; **jardinier** m gardener; **jardinière** f *à fleurs* window box; *femme* gardener

jargon [ʒargõ] m jargon; *péj* (*charabia*) gibberish

jarret [ʒarɛ] m back of the knee; CUIS shin; **jarretière** f garter

jaser [ʒaze] ⟨1a⟩ gossip

jatte [ʒat] f bowl

jauge [ʒoʒ] f gauge; **~ de carburant** fuel gauge; **jauger** ⟨1l⟩ gauge

jaunâtre [ʒonɑtr] yellowish; **jaune 1** adj yellow **2** adv: **rire ~** give a forced laugh **3** m yellow; F *ouvrier* scab F; **~ d'œuf** egg yolk; **jaunir** ⟨2a⟩ turn yellow; **jaunisse** f MÉD jaundice

Javel [ʒavɛl]: **eau f de ~** bleach

javelot [ʒavlo] m sports javelin

jazz [dʒaz] m jazz; **jazzman** m jazz musician

je [ʒə] I

jean [dʒin] m jeans pl: **veste m en ~** denim jacket

jeep [dʒip] f jeep

je-m'en-foutisme [ʒmãfutism] m F I-don't-give-a-damn attitude

jérémiades [ʒeremjad] fpl complaining sg, moaning sg F

Jésus-Christ [ʒezykri] Jesus (Christ)

jet [ʒɛ] m (*lancer*) throw; (*jaillissement*) jet; *de sang* spurt; **~ d'eau** fountain

jetable [ʒətabl] disposable

jetée [ʒ(ə)te] f MAR jetty

jeter [ʒ(ə)te] ⟨1c⟩ throw; (*se défaire de*) throw away, throw out; **~ un coup d'œil à qch** glance at sth, cast a glance at sth; **~ qn dehors** throw s.o. out

jeton [ʒ(ə)tõ] m token; *de jeu* chip

jeu [ʒø] m (pl -x) play (*aussi* TECH); *activité, en tennis* game; (*série, ensemble*) set; *de cartes* deck, *Br* pack; MUS playing; THÉÂT acting; **un ~ de cartes / d'échecs / de tennis** a game of cards / of chess / of tennis; **le ~** gambling; **faites vos ~x** place your bets; **les ~x sont faits** no more bets please; **mettre en ~** stake; **être en ~** be at stake; **~ éducatif** educational game; **~ de mots** play on words, pun;

Jeux Olympiques Olympic Games, Olympics; **~ de société** board game; **~ vidéo** video game

jeudi [ʒødi] *m* Thursday

jeun [ʒɛ̃, ʒœ̃]: **à ~** on an empty stomach; **être à ~** have eaten nothing, have nothing in one's stomach

jeune [ʒœn] **1** *adj* young; **~s mariés** newly-weds **2** *m/f*: **un ~** a young man; **les ~s** young people *pl*, the young *pl*

jeûne [ʒøn] *m* fast; **jeûner** ⟨1a⟩ fast

jeunesse [ʒœnɛs] *f* youth; *caractère jeune* youthfulness

jingle [dʒiŋgəl] *m* jingle

J.O. [ʒio] *mpl abr* (= *Jeux Olympiques*) Olympic Games

joaillerie [ʒɔajri] *f magasin* jewelry store, *Br* jeweller's; *articles* jewelry, *Br* jewellery; **joaillier, -ère** *m/f* jeweler, *Br* jeweller

jockey [ʒɔkɛ] *m* jockey

jogging [dʒɔgin] *m* jogging; (*survêtement*) sweats *pl*, *Br* tracksuit; **faire du ~** go jogging

joie [ʒwa] *f* joy; **débordant de ~** jubilant

joignable [ʒwaɲabl] contactable

joindre [ʒwɛ̃dr] ⟨4b⟩ *mettre ensemble* join; (*relier, réunir*) join, connect; *efforts* combine; *à un courrier* enclose (*à* with); *personne* contact, get in touch with; *par téléphone* get, reach; *mains* clasp; **se ~ à qn pour faire qch** join s.o. in doing sth; **~ les deux bouts** make ends meet; **pièce f jointe** enclosure; **veuillez trouver ci-joint** please find enclosed

joint [ʒwɛ̃] *m* ANAT joint (*aussi* TECH); *d'étanchéité* seal, gasket; *de robinet* washer

joker [ʒɔkɛr] *m cartes* joker; INFORM wild card

joli, ~e [ʒɔli] pretty

joncher [ʒɔ̃ʃe] ⟨1a⟩ strew (*de* with)

jonction [ʒɔ̃ksjɔ̃] *f* junction

jongler [ʒɔ̃gle] juggle; **~ avec** *fig* juggle; **jongleur** *m* juggler

jonquille [ʒɔ̃kij] *f* BOT daffodil

Jordanie [ʒɔrdani] *f*: **la ~** Jordan; **jordanien, ~ne 1** *adj* Jordanian **2** *m/f*

Jordanien, ~ne Jordanian

joue [ʒu] *f* cheek

jouer [ʒwe] ⟨1a⟩ **1** *v/t* play; *argent, réputation* gamble; THÉÂT *pièce* perform; *film* show; **~ un tour à qn** play a trick on s.o.; **~ la comédie** put on an act **2** *v/i* play; *d'un acteur* act; *d'un film* play, show; *miser de l'argent* gamble; **~ aux cartes / au football** play cards / football; **~ d'un instrument** play an instrument; **~ sur** *cheval etc* put money on; **jouet** *m* toy; *fig* plaything; **joueur, -euse** *m/f* player; *de jeux d'argent* gambler; **être beau / mauvais ~** be a good / bad loser

joufflu, ~e [ʒufly] chubby

jouir [ʒwir] ⟨2a⟩ have an orgasm, come; **~ de qch** enjoy sth; (*posséder*) have sth; **jouissance** *f* enjoyment; JUR possession

jour [ʒur] *m* day; (*lumière*) daylight; (*ouverture*) opening; **le** *ou* **de ~** by day; **un ~** one day; **vivre au ~ le ~** live from day to day; **au grand ~** in broad daylight; **de nos ~s** nowadays, these days; **du ~ au lendemain** overnight; **l'autre ~** the other day; **être à ~** be up to date; **mettre à ~** update, bring up to date; **mettre au ~** bring to light; **se faire ~** *fig*: *de problèmes* come to light; **trois fois par ~** three times a day; **un ~ ou l'autre** one of these days; **il devrait arriver d'un ~ à l'autre** he should arrive any day now; **de ~ en ~** day by day, from day to day; **deux ans ~ pour ~** two years to the day; **il fait ~** it's (getting) light; **à ce ~** to date, so far; **au petit ~** at dawn, at first light; **~ férié** (public) holiday

journal [ʒurnal] *m* (*pl* -aux) (news)paper; *intime* diary, journal; TV, *à la radio* news *sg*; **~ de bord** log(book)

journalier, -ère [ʒurnalje, -ɛr] daily

journalisme [ʒurnalism] *m* journalism; **journaliste** *m/f* journalist, reporter

journée [ʒurne] *f* day; **~ portes ouvertes** open house, open day

jovial, ~e [ʒɔvjal] (*pl* -aux) jovial

joyau [ʒwajo] *m* (*pl* -x) jewel

joyeux, -euse [ʒwajø, -z] joyful; **~**

Noël! Merry Christmas!

jubilation [ʒybilasjɔ̃] *f* jubilation; **jubiler** ⟨1a⟩ be jubilant; *péj* gloat

jucher [ʒyʃe] ⟨1a⟩ perch

judas [ʒyda] *m* spyhole

judiciaire [ʒydisjɛr] judicial, legal; *combat* legal

judicieux, -euse [ʒydisjø, -z] sensible, judicious

judo [ʒydo] *m* judo

juge [ʒyʒ] *m* judge; **~ d'instruction** examining magistrate (*whose job it is to question witnesses and determine if there is a case to answer*); **~ de paix** police court judge; **~ de touche** SP linesman, assistant referee; **jugement** *m* judg(e)ment; *en matière criminelle* sentence; **porter un ~ sur** *qch* pass judg(e)ment on sth; **le Jugement dernier** REL the Last Judg(e)ment; **jugeote** *f* F gumption; **juger** ⟨1l⟩ *v/t* JUR try; (*évaluer*) judge; **~ qch / qn intéressant** consider sth / s.o. to be interesting; **~ que** think that; **~ bon de faire qch** think it right to do sth; **~ de qn / qch** judge s.o. / sth **2** *v/i* judge

juif, -ive [ʒɥif, -iv] **1** *adj* Jewish **2** *m/f* **Juif, -ive** Jew

juillet [ʒɥijɛ] *m* July

juin [ʒɥɛ̃] *m* June

juke-box [dʒukbɔks] *m* jukebox

jumeau, jumelle [ʒymo, ʒymɛl] (*mpl* -x) *m/f & adj* twin; **jumelage** *m de villes* twinning; **jumeler** ⟨1c⟩ *villes* twin; **jumelles** *fpl* binoculars

jument [ʒymɑ̃] *f* mare

jumping [dʒœmpiŋ] *m* show-jumping

jungle [ʒɛ̃glə, ʒɑ̃-] *f* jungle

jupe [ʒyp] *f m* skirt; **jupe-culotte** *f* (*pl* jupes-culottes) culottes *pl*; **jupon** *m* slip, underskirt

juré [ʒyre] *m* JUR juror, member of the jury; **jurer** ⟨1a⟩ **1** *v/t* swear; **~ de faire qch** swear to do sth **2** *v/i* swear; **~ avec qch** clash with sth; **~ de qch**

swear to sth

juridiction [ʒyridiksjɔ̃] *f* jurisdiction

juridique [ʒyridik] legal

jurisprudence [ʒyrisprydɑ̃s] *f* jurisprudence, case law

juron [ʒyrɔ̃] *m* curse

jury [ʒyri] *m* JUR jury; *d'un concours* panel, judges *pl*; ÉDU board of examiners

jus [ʒy] *m* juice; **~ de fruit** fruit juice

jusque [ʒysk(ə)] **1** *prép*: **jusqu'à** *lieu* as far as, up to; *temps* until; **aller jusqu'à la berge** go as far as the bank; **jusqu'au cou / aux genoux** up to the neck / knees; **jusqu'à trois heures** until three o'clock; **jusqu'alors** up to then, until then; **jusqu'à présent** until now, so far; **jusqu'à quand restez-vous?** how long are you staying?; **jusqu'où vous allez?** how far are you going? **2** *adv* even, including; **jusqu'à lui** even him **3** *conj*: **jusqu'à ce qu'il s'endorme** (*subj*) until he falls asleep

justaucorps [ʒystokɔr] *m* leotard

juste [ʒyst] **1** *adj* (*équitable*) fair, just; *salaire, récompense* fair; (*précis*) right, correct; *vêtement* tight **2** *adv* *viser, tirer* accurately; (*précisément*) exactly, just; (*seulement*) just, only; **chanter ~** sing in tune; **justement** *adv* (*avec justice*) justly; (*précisément*) just, exactly; (*avec justesse*) rightly

justesse [ʒystɛs] *f* accuracy; **de ~** only just

justice [ʒystis] *f* fairness, justice; JUR justice; **la ~** the law; **faire** *ou* **rendre ~ à qn** do s.o. justice

justifiable [ʒystifjabl] justifiable; **justification** *f* justification; **justifier** ⟨1a⟩ justify; **~ de qch** prove sth

juteux, -euse [ʒytø, -z] juicy

juvénile [ʒyvenil] youthful; **délinquance ~** juvenile delinquency

juxtaposer [ʒykstapoze] ⟨1a⟩ juxtapose

J

K

kaki [kaki] khaki

kamikaze [kamikaz] *m/f* suicide bomber

kangourou [kãguru] *m* kangaroo

karaté [karate] *m* karate

kébab [kebab] *m* kabob, *Br* kebab

Kenya [kenja]: **le ~** Kenya; **kenyan,**
~e 1 *adj* Kenyan **2** *m/f* **Kenyan,**
~e Kenyan

képi [kepi] *m* kepi

kermesse [kɛrmɛs] *f* fair

kérosène [kerozɛn] *m* kerosene

ketchup [kɛtʃœp] *m* ketchup

kg *abr* (= **kilogramme**) kg (= kilogram)

kidnapping [kidnapiŋ] *m* kidnapping;
kidnapper ⟨1a⟩ kidnap; **kidnap-**
peur, -euse *m/f* kidnapper

kif-kif [kifkif] *adj*: **c'est ~** F it's all the same

kilo(gramme) [kilo, kilɔgram] *m*
kilo(gram)

kilométrage [kilɔmetraʒ] *m* mileage;

kilomètre *m* kilometer, *Br* kilometre; **kilométrique** *distance* in kilometers, *Br* in kilometres

kilo-octet [kilookte] *m* kilobyte, k

kinésithérapeute [kineziterapøt] *m/f*
physiotherapist; **kinésithérapie** *f*
physiotherapy

kiosque [kjɔsk] *m* pavilion; COMM
kiosk; **~ à journaux** newsstand

kit [kit] *m*: **en ~** kit

kiwi [kiwi] *m* ZO kiwi; BOT kiwi (fruit)

klaxon [klaksɔn] *m* AUTO horn; **kla-**
xonner ⟨1a⟩ sound one's horn, hoot

km *abr* (= **kilomètre**) km (= kilometer)

knock-out [nɔkawt] *m* knockout

K-O [kao] *m abr* (= **knock-out**) KO

Ko *m abr* (= **kilo-octet** *m*) k(= kilobyte)

krach [krak] *m* ÉCON crash; **~ bour-**
sier stockmarket crash

Kremlin [krɛmlɛ̃]: **le ~** the Kremlin

kyste [kist] *m* MÉD cyst

L

l' [l] → **le, la**

la¹ [la] → **le**

la² [la] *pron personnel* her; *chose* it; *je*
ne ~ supporte pas I can't stand
her / it

la³ [la] *m* MUS A

là [la] here; *dans un autre lieu qu'ici*
there; *de ~* from there; *causal* hence;
par ~ that way; *que veux-tu dire par*
~? what do you mean by that?; **là-**
-bas (over) there

label [labɛl] *m* COMM label

labeur [labœr] *m* labor, *Br* labour, toil

labyrinthe [labirɛ̃t] *m* labyrinth, maze

laboratoire [labɔratwar] *m* laboratory, lab; **~ de langues** language lab

laborieux, -euse [labɔrjø, -z] *tâche* laborious; *personne* hardworking

labour [labur] *m* plowing, *Br* ploughing; **labourer** ⟨1a⟩ plow, *Br* plough

lac [lak] *m* lake

lacer [lase] ⟨1k⟩ tie

lacérer [lasere] ⟨1f⟩ lacerate

lacet [lasɛ] *m de chaussures* lace; *de la*

route sharp turn; **~s** twists and turns

lâche [lɑʃ] **1** *adj fil* loose, slack; *nœud, vêtement* loose; *personne* cowardly **2** *m* coward

lâcher [lɑʃe] ⟨1a⟩ **1** *v/t* let go of; *(laisser tomber)* drop; *(libérer)* release; *ceinture* loosen; *juron, vérité* let out; SP leave behind **2** *v/i de freins* fail; *d'une corde* break

lâcheté [lɑʃte] *f* cowardice

laconique [lakɔnik] laconic, terse

lacrymogène [lakrimɔʒɛn] *gaz* tear *atr*, *grenade* tear-gas *atr*

lacté, ~e [lakte] milk *atr*

lacune [lakyn] *f* gap

là-dedans [lad(ə)dɑ̃] inside; **là-dessous** underneath; *derrière cette affaire* behind it; **là-dessus** on it, on top; *à ce moment* at that instant; *sur ce point* about it

lagon [lagɔ̃] *m* lagoon

là-haut [lao] up there

laïc [laik] → **laïque**

laid, ~e [lɛ, -d] ugly

laideur [lɛdœr] *f* ugliness; *(bassesse)* meanness, nastiness

lainage [lenaʒ] *m* woolen *ou* Br woollen fabric; *vêtement* woolen; **laine** *f* wool; **laineux, -euse** fleecy

laïque [laik] **1** *adj* REL secular; *(sans confession)* école State *atr* **2** *m/f* lay person

laisse [lɛs] *f* leash; **tenir en ~** *chien* keep on a leash

laisser [lese] ⟨1b⟩ leave; *(permettre)* let; **~ qn faire qch** let s.o. do sth; **se ~ aller** let o.s. go; **se ~ faire** let o.s. be pushed around; **laisse-toi faire!** come on!

laisser-aller [leseale] *m* casualness

laisser-faire [lesefer] *m* laissez faire

laissez-passer [lesepase] *m (pl inv)* pass

lait [lɛ] *m* milk; **laitage** *m* dairy product; **laiterie** *f* dairy; **laitier, -ère 1** *adj* dairy *atr* **2** *m/f* milkman, milkwoman

laiton [letɔ̃] *m* brass

laitue [lety] *f* BOT lettuce

laïus [lajys] *m* F sermon, lecture

lambeau [lɑ̃bo] *m (pl -x)* shred

lambin, ~e [lɑ̃bɛ̃, -in] *m/f* F slowpoke F, Br slowcoach F

lambris [lɑ̃bri] *m* paneling, Br panelling

lame [lam] *f* blade; *(plaque)* strip; *(vague)* wave; **~ de rasoir** razor blade

lamentable [lamɑ̃tabl] deplorable

lamentation [lamɑ̃tasjɔ̃] *f* complaining; **lamenter** ⟨1a⟩: **se ~** complain

laminoir [laminwar] *m* TECH rolling mill

lampadaire [lɑ̃pader] *m meuble* floor lamp, Br *aussi* standard lamp; *dans la rue* street light

lampe [lɑ̃p] *f* lamp; **~ de poche** flashlight, Br torch

lampée [lɑ̃pe] *f* gulp, swallow

lance [lɑ̃s] *f* spear; **~ d'incendie** fire hose

lancé, ~e [lɑ̃se] well-known, established

lancement [lɑ̃smɑ̃] *m* launch(ing) *(aussi* COMM)

lancer [lɑ̃se] ⟨1k⟩ throw; *avec force* hurl; *injure* shout, hurl (**à** at); *cri, regard* give; *bateau, fusée,* COMM launch; INFORM *programme* run; *moteur* start; **se ~ sur** *marché* enter; *piste de danse* step out onto; **se ~ dans** *des activités* take up; *des explications* launch into; *des discussions* get involved in

lancinant, ~e [lɑ̃sinɑ̃, -t] *douleur* stabbing

landau [lɑ̃do] *m* baby carriage, Br pram

lande [lɑ̃d] *f* heath

langage [lɑ̃gaʒ] *m* language; **~ de programmation** programming language; **~ des signes** sign language

lange [lɑ̃ʒ] *m* diaper, Br nappy

langouste [lɑ̃gust] *f* spiny lobster

langue [lɑ̃g] *f* ANAT, CUIS tongue; LING language; **mauvaise ~** gossip; **de ~ anglaise** English-speaking; **~ étrangère** foreign language; **~ maternelle** mother tongue; **~s vivantes** modern languages

languette [lɑ̃gɛt] *f d'une chaussure* tongue

langueur [lɑ̃gœr] *f (apathie)* listless-

L

ness; (*mélancolie*) languidness; **languir** ⟨2a⟩ languish; *d'une conversation* flag

lanière [lanjɛr] *f* strap

lanterne [lɑ̃tɛrn] *f* lantern

laper [lape] ⟨1a⟩ lap up

lapidaire [lapidɛr] *fig* concise; **lapider** ⟨1a⟩ (*assassiner*) stone to death; (*attaquer*) stone

lapin [lapɛ̃] *m* rabbit

laps [laps] *m*: **~ de temps** period of time

laque [lak] *f peinture* lacquer; *pour cheveux* hairspray, lacquer

laquelle [lakɛl] → **lequel**

larcin [larsɛ̃] *m* petty theft

lard [lar] *m* bacon

larder [larde] ⟨1a⟩ CUIS, *fig* lard

lardon [lardɔ̃] *m* lardon, diced bacon

large [larʒ] **1** *adj* wide; *épaules, hanches* broad; *mesure, part, rôle* large; (*généreux*) generous; **~ d'un millimètre** one millimeter wide **2** *m* MAR open sea; **faire trois mètres de ~** be three meters wide; **prendre le ~** take off; **largement** *adv* widely; (*généreusement*) generously; **elle a ~ le temps de finir** she's got more than enough time to finish; **largesse** *f* generosity; **largeur** *f* width; **~ d'esprit** broad-mindedness

larme [larm] *f* tear; **une ~ de** a drop of; **larmoyer** ⟨1h⟩ *des yeux* water; (*se plaindre*) complain

larve [larv] *f* larva; **larvé, ~e** latent

laryngite [larɛ̃ʒit] *f* MÉD laryngitis

larynx [larɛ̃ks] *m* larynx

las, ~se [lɑ, -s] weary, tired; **~ de** *fig* weary of, tired of

laser [lazɛr] *m* laser

lasser [lase] ⟨1a⟩ weary, tire; **se ~ de qch** tire *ou* weary of sth; **lassitude** *f* weariness, lassitude *fml*

latent, ~e [latɑ̃, -t] latent

latéral, ~e [lateral] (*mpl* -aux) lateral, side *atr*

latin, ~e [latɛ̃, -in] Latin

latitude [latityd] *f* latitude; *fig* latitude, scope

latrines [latrin] *fpl* latrines

latte [lat] *f* lath; *de plancher* board; **lattis** *m* lathwork

lauréat, ~e [lɔrea, -t] *m/f* prizewinner

laurier [lɔrje] *m* laurel; **feuille *f* de ~** CUIS bayleaf

lavable [lavabl] washable; **lavabo** *m* (wash)basin; **~s** toilets; **lavage** *m* washing; **~ de cerveau** POL brainwashing; **~ d'estomac** MÉD stomach pump

lavande [lavɑ̃d] *f* BOT lavender

lave [lav] *f* lava

lave-glace [lavglas] *m* (*pl* lave-glaces) windshield wiper, *Br* windscreen wiper

lavement [lavmɑ̃] *m* MÉD enema; **laver** ⟨1a⟩ wash; *tâche* wash away; **se ~ les mains** wash one's hands; **se ~ les dents** brush one's teeth; **laverie** *f*: **~ automatique** laundromat, *Br* laundrette

lavette [lavɛt] *f* dishcloth; *fig péj* spineless individual

laveur, -euse [lavœr, -øz] *m/f* washer; **~ de vitres** window cleaner

lave-vaisselle [lavvɛsɛl] *m* (*pl inv*) dishwasher

laxatif, -ive [laksatif, -iv] *adj & m* laxative

laxisme [laksism] *m* laxness; **laxiste** lax

layette [lɛjɛt] *f* layette

le *pron personnel, complément d'objet direct* ◊ him; *chose* it; **je ne ~ supporte pas** I can't stand him / it ◊: **oui, je ~ sais** yes, I know; **je l'espère bien** I very much hope so

le, *f* **la**, *pl* **les** [lə, la, le] *article défini* ◊ the; **le garçon / les garçons** the boy / the boys ◊ *parties du corps*: **je me suis cassé la jambe** I broke my leg; **elle avait les cheveux très longs** she had very long hair ◊ *généralité*: **j'aime le vin** I like wine; **elle ne supporte pas les enfants** she doesn't like children; **la défense de la liberté** the defense of freedom; **les dinosaures avaient …** dinosaurs had … ◊ *dates*: **le premier mai** May first, *Br* the first of May; *ouvert le samedi* open (on) Saturdays

◇ : *trois euros le kilo* three euros a *ou* euros per kilo; *10 euros les 5* 10 euros for 5

◇ *noms de pays*: *tu connais la France?* do you know France; *l'Europe est …* Europe is …

◇ *noms de saison*: *le printemps est là* spring is here

◇ *noms propres*: *le lieutenant Duprieur* Lieutenant Duprieur; *ah, la pauvre Hélène!* oh, poor Helen!

◇ *langues*: *je ne parle pas l'italien* I don't speak Italian

◇ *avec adjectif*: *la jaune est plus …* the yellow one is …

leader [lidœr] *m* POL leader

leasing [liziŋ] *m* leasing

lécher [leʃe] ⟨1f⟩ lick; *~ les bottes à qn* F suck up to s.o.

lèche-vitrines [lɛʃvitrin]: *faire du ~* go window shopping

leçon [l(ə)sõ] *f* lesson; *~s particulières* private lessons

lecteur, -trice [lɛktœr, -tris] **1** *m/f* reader; *à l'université* foreign language assistant **2** *m* INFORM drive; *~ de disquette(s)* disk drive; *~ de cassettes* cassette player; **lecture** *f* reading; *fichier m en ~ seule* read-only file

ledit, ladite [lədi, ladit] (*pl* lesdits, lesdites) the said

légal, ~e [legal] (*mpl* -aux) legal; **légaliser** ⟨1a⟩ *certificat, signature* authenticate; (*rendre légal*) legalize; **légalité** *f* legality

légataire [legatɛr] *m/f* legatee; *~ universel* sole heir

légendaire [leʒɑ̃dɛr] legendary

légende [leʒɑ̃d] *f* legend; *sous image* caption; *d'une carte* key

léger, -ère [leʒe, -ɛr] *poids, aliment* light; *vent, erreur, retard* slight; *mœurs* loose; (*frivole, irréfléchi*) thoughtless; *à la légère* lightly; **légèrement** *adv* lightly; (*un peu*) slightly; (*inconsidérément*) thoughtlessly; **légèreté** *f* lightness; (*frivolité, irréflexion*) thoughtlessness

légiférer [leʒifere] ⟨1g⟩ legislate

légion [leʒjõ] *f* legion; *~ étrangère* Foreign Legion; **légionnaire** *m* legionnaire

législateur, -trice [leʒislatœr, -tris] *m/f* legislator; **législatif, -ive** legislative; (*élections fpl*) *législatives fpl* parliamentary elections; **législation** *f* legislation; **législature** *f* legislature

légitime [leʒitim] legitimate; *~ défense* self-defense, *Br* self-defence

legs [lɛ(g)] *m* legacy

léguer [lege] ⟨1f *et* 1m⟩ bequeath

légume [legym] *m* vegetable; *~s secs* pulses

Léman [lemɑ̃]: *le lac ~* Lake Geneva

lendemain [lɑ̃dmɛ̃] *m*: *le ~* the next *ou* following day; *le ~ de son élection* the day after he was elected

lent, ~e [lɑ̃, -t] slow; **lentement** *adv* slowly; **lenteur** *f* slowness

lentille [lɑ̃tij] *f* TECH lens; *légume sec* lentil

léopard [leɔpar] *m* leopard

lèpre [lɛpr] *f* leprosy; **lépreux, -euse** *m/f* leper (*aussi fig*)

lequel, laquelle [ləkɛl, lakɛl] (*pl* lesquels, lesquelles) ◇ *pron interrogatif* which (one); *laquelle / lesquelles est-ce que tu préfères?* which (one) / which (ones) do you prefer?

◇ *pron relatif, avec personne* who; *le client pour ~ il l'avait fabriqué* the customer (who) he had made it for, the customer for whom he had made it

◇ *pron relatif, avec chose* which; *les cavernes dans lesquelles ils s'étaient noyés* the caves in which they had drowned, the caves which they had drowned in; *les entreprises auxquelles nous avons envoyé …* the companies to which we sent …, the companies (which) we sent … to; *un vieux château dans les jardins duquel …* an old castle in the gardens of which …

les¹ [le] → *le*

les² [le] *pron personnel* them; *je ~ ai vendu(e)s* I sold them

lesbien, ~ne [lɛsbjɛ̃, -ɛn] **1** *adj* lesbian **2** f lesbian

léser [leze] ⟨1f⟩ (*désavantager*) injure, wrong; *intérêts* damage; *droits* infringe; MÉD injure

lésiner [lezine] ⟨1a⟩ skimp (*sur* on)

lésion [lezjõ] f MÉD lesion

lesquels, lesquelles [lekɛl] → **lequel**

lessive [lɛsiv] f *produit* laundry detergent, Br washing powder; *liquide* detergent; *linge* laundry, Br aussi washing; **faire la ~** do the laundry

lest [lɛst] m ballast

leste [lɛst] (*agile*) agile; *propos* crude

léthargie [letarʒi] f lethargy; **léthargique** lethargic

lettre [lɛtr] f (*caractère, correspondance*) letter; **à la ~, au pied de la ~** literally; **en toutes ~s** in full; *fig* in black and white; **~ de change** bill of exchange; **~s** literature *sg*; *études* arts

lettré, ~e [lɛtre] well-read

leucémie [løsemi] f MÉD leukemia, Br leukaemia

leur [lœr] **1** *adj possessif* their; **~ prof** their teacher; **~s camarades** their friends

2 *pron personnel*: **le / la ~, les ~s** theirs; **meilleur que le / la ~** better than theirs

3 *complément d'objet indirect* (to) them; **je ~ ai envoyé un e-mail** I sent them an e-mail; **je le ~ ai envoyé hier** I sent it (to) them yesterday

leurre [lœr] m bait; *fig* illusion; **leurrer** ⟨1a⟩ *fig* deceive

levé, ~e [l(ə)ve]: **être ~** be up, be out of bed; **levée** f lifting; *d'une séance* adjournment; *du courrier* collection; *aux cartes* trick; **lever** ⟨1d⟩ **1** *v/t* raise, lift; *main, bras* raise; *poids, interdiction* lift; *impôts* collect **2** *v/i de la pâte* rise; **se ~** get up; *du soleil* rise; *du jour* break **3** m: **~ du jour** daybreak; **~ du soleil** sunrise

levier [l(ə)vje] m lever; **~ de vitesse** gear shift, *surtout Br* gear lever

lèvre [lɛvr] f lip

lévrier [levrije] m greyhound

levure [l(ə)vyr] f yeast; **~ chimique** baking powder

lexique [lɛksik] m (*vocabulaire*) vocabulary; (*glossaire*) glossary

lézard [lezar] m lizard

lézarde [lezard] f crack

liaison [ljɛzõ] f connection; *amoureuse* affair; *de train* link; LING liaison; **être en ~ avec qn** be in touch with s.o.

liant, ~e [ljã, -t] sociable

liasse [ljas] f bundle, wad; *de billets* wad

Liban [libã]: **le ~** (the) Lebanon; **libanais, ~e 1** *adj* Lebanese **2** m/f **Libanais, ~e** Lebanese

libeller [libele] ⟨1b⟩ *document, contrat* word; **~ un chèque (au nom de qn)** make out *ou* write a check (to s.o.)

libellule [libelyl] f dragonfly

libéral, ~e [liberal] (*mpl* -aux) liberal; **profession f ~e** profession; **libéralisme** m liberalism; **libéralité** f generosity, liberality

libérateur, -trice [liberatœr, -tris] **1** *adj* liberating **2** m/f liberator; **libération** f *d'un pays* liberation; *d'un prisonnier* release; **conditionnelle** parole; **libérer** ⟨1f⟩ *pays* liberate; *prisonnier* release, free (*de* from); *gaz, d'un engagement* release

liberté [liberte] f freedom, liberty; **mettre en ~** set free, release; **~ d'expression** freedom of speech; **~ de la presse** freedom of the press

libraire [librɛr] m/f bookseller; **librairie** f bookstore, *Br* bookshop

libre [libr] free (**de faire qch** to do sth); **~ concurrence** free competition; **libre-échange** m free trade; **libre-service** m (*pl* libres-services) self-service; *magasin* self-service store

Libye [libi] f Libya; **libyen, ~ne 1** *adj* Libyan **2** m/f **Libyen, ~ne** Libyan

licence [lisãs] f license, *Br* licence; *diplôme* degree; **licencié, ~e** m/f graduate

licenciement [lisãsimã] m layoff; (*renvoi*) dismissal; **licencier** ⟨1a⟩ lay off; (*renvoyer*) dismiss

licencieux, -euse [lisãsjø, -z] licentious

lié, **~e** [lije]: **être ~ par** be bound by; **être très ~ avec qn** be very close to s.o.

liège [ljɛʒ] *m* BOT cork

lien [ljɛ̃] *m* tie, bond; (*rapport*) connection; **ils ont un ~ de parenté** they are related; **lier** ⟨1a⟩ tie (up); *d'un contrat* be binding on; CUIS thicken; *fig*: *pensées, personnes* connect; **~ amitié avec** make friends with

lierre [ljɛr] *m* BOT ivy

lieu [ljø] *m* (*pl* -x) place; **~x** premises; JUR scene *sg*; **au ~ de qch / de faire qch** instead of sth / of doing sth; **avoir ~** take place, be held; **avoir ~ de faire qch** have (good) reason to do sth; **donner ~ à** give rise to; **en premier ~** in the first place, first(ly); **en dernier ~** last(ly); **~ de destination** destination; **il y a ~ de faire qch** there is good reason to do sth; **s'il y a ~** if necessary; **tenir ~ de qch** act *ou* serve as sth

lieu-dit [ljødi] (*pl* lieux-dits) *m* place

lièvre [ljɛvr] *m* hare

ligne [liɲ] *f* line; *d'autobus* number; **à la ~!** new paragraph; **hors ~** top class; **garder la ~** keep one's figure; **entrer en ~ de compte** be taken into consideration; **pêcher à la ~** go angling; **adopter une ~ dure sur** take a hard line on

lignée [liɲe] *f* descendants *pl*

ligue [lig] *f* league; **liguer** ⟨1m⟩: **se ~** join forces (*pour faire qch* to do sth)

lilas [lila] **1** *m* lilac **2** *adj inv* lilac

limace [limas] *f* slug

lime [lim] *f* file; **~ à ongles** nail file; **limer** ⟨1a⟩ file

limier [limje] *m* bloodhound

limitation [limitasjɔ̃] *f* limitation; **~ de vitesse** speed limit

limite [limit] *f* limit; (*frontière*) boundary; **à la ~** if absolutely necessary; **ça va comme ça? - oui, à la ~** is that ok like that? - yes, just about; **je l'aiderai dans les ~s du possible** I'll help him as much as I can; **date f ~** deadline; **vitesse f ~** speed limit; **limiter** ⟨1a⟩ limit (*à* to)

limoger [limoʒe] ⟨1l⟩ POL dismiss

limon [limɔ̃] *m* silt

limonade [limɔnad] *f* lemonade

limousine [limuzin] *f* limousine, limo F

lin [lɛ̃] *m* BOT flax; *toile* linen

linceul [lɛ̃sœl] *m* shroud

linéaire [lineɛr] linear

linge [lɛ̃ʒ] *m* linen; (*lessive*) washing; **~ (de corps)** underwear; **lingerie** *f* lingerie

lingot [lɛ̃go] *m* ingot

linguiste [lɛ̃gɥist] *m/f* linguist; **linguistique 1** *f* linguistics **2** *adj* linguistic

lion [ljɔ̃] *m* lion; ASTROL Leo; **lionne** *f* lioness

lipide [lipid] *m* fat

liqueur [likœr] *f* liqueur

liquidation [likidasjɔ̃] *f* liquidation; *vente au rabais* sale

liquide [likid] **1** *adj* liquid; **argent m ~** cash **2** *m* liquid; **~ de freins** brake fluid

liquider [likide] ⟨1a⟩ liquidate; *stock* sell off; *problème, travail* dispose of

lire [lir] ⟨4x⟩ read

lis [lis] *m* BOT lily

lisibilité [lizibilite] *f* legibility; **lisible** legible

lisière [lizjɛr] *f* edge

lisse [lis] smooth; **lisser** ⟨1a⟩ smooth

listage [listaʒ] *m* printout; **liste** *f* list; **~ d'attente** waiting list; **~ de commissions** shopping list; **~ noire** blacklist; **être sur ~ rouge** TÉL have an unlisted number, *Br* be ex-directory; **lister** ⟨1a⟩ list; **listing** *m* printout

lit [li] *m* bed; **aller au ~** go to bed; **faire son ~** make one's bed; **garder le ~** stay in bed; **~ de camp** cot, *Br* camp bed

litanie [litani] *f* litany; **c'est toujours la même ~** *fig* it's the same old thing over and over again

literie [litri] *f* bedding

litige [litiʒ] *m* dispute; **litigieux, -euse** *cas* contentious

litre [litr] *m* liter, *Br* litre

littéraire [literɛr] literary

L

littéral, ~e [literal] (*mpl* -aux) literal; **littéralement** *adv* literally

littérature [literatyr] *f* literature

littoral, ~e [litɔral] (*mpl* -aux) **1** *adj* coastal **2** *m* coastline

liturgie [lityrʒi] *f* liturgy

livraison [livrezõ] *f* delivery

livre[1] [livr] *m* book; **~ d'images** picture book; **~ de poche** paperback

livre[2] [livr] *f poids, monnaie* pound

livrer [livre] 〈1a〉 *marchandises* deliver; *prisonnier* hand over; *secret, information* divulge; **se ~** (*se confier*) open up; (*se soumettre*) give o.s. up; **se ~ à** (*se confier*) confide in; *activité* indulge in; *la jalousie, l'abattement* give way to

livret [livrɛ] *m* booklet; *d'opéra* libretto; **~ de caisse d'épargne** passbook

livreur [livrœr] *m* delivery man; **~ de journaux** paper boy

lobby [lɔbi] *m* lobby

lobe [lɔb] *m*: **~ de l'oreille** earlobe

local, ~e [lɔkal] (*mpl* -aux) **1** *adj* local **2** *m* (*salle*) premises *pl*; **locaux** premises; **localisation** *f* location; *de software etc* localization; **localiser** 〈1a〉 locate; (*limiter*), *de software* localize; **localité** *f* town

locataire [lɔkatɛr] *m/f* tenant; **location** *f par propriétaire* renting out; *par locataire* renting; (*loyer*) rent; *au théâtre* reservation

locomotive [lɔkɔmɔtiv] *f* locomotive; *fig* driving force

locution [lɔkysjõ] *f* phrase

loge [lɔʒ] *f d'un concierge, de francs-maçons* lodge; *de spectateurs* box

logement [lɔʒmã] *m* accommodation, accommodations *pl*, *Br* accommodation; (*appartement*) apartment, *Br aussi* flat; **loger** 〈1l〉 **1** *v/t* accommodate **2** *v/i* live; **logeur** *m* landlord; **logeuse** *f* landlady

logiciel [lɔʒisjɛl] *m* INFORM software

logique [lɔʒik] **1** *adj* logical **2** *f* logic; **logiquement** *adv* logically

logistique [lɔʒistik] **1** *adj* logistical **2** *f* logistics

logo [logo] *m* logo

loi [lwa] *f* law; **~ martiale** martial law

loin [lwɛ̃] *adv* far; *dans le passé* long ago, a long time ago; *dans l'avenir* far off, a long way off; **au ~** in the distance; **de ~** from a distance; *fig* by far; **~ de** far from

lointain, ~e [lwɛ̃tɛ̃, -ɛn] **1** *adj* distant **2** *m* distance

loisir [lwazir] *m* leisure; **~s** leisure activities; **avoir le ~ de faire qch** have the time to do sth

Londres [lõdr] London

long, longue [lõ, -g] **1** *adj* long; **un voilier ~ de 25 mètres** a 25-meter (long) yacht, a yacht 25 meters in length; **à ~ terme** in the long term *ou* run, long-term; **à la ~ue** in time, eventually; **être ~** (*durer*) take a long time; **être ~ à faire qch** take a long time doing sth **2** *adv*: **en dire ~** speak volumes **3** *m*: **de deux mètres de ~** two meters long, two meters in length; **le ~ de** along; **de ~ en large** up and down; **tout au** *ou* **le ~ de l'année** throughout the year

longe [lõʒ] *f* CUIS loin

longer [lõʒe] 〈1l〉 follow, hug

longévité [lõʒevite] *f* longevity

longitude [lõʒityd] *f* longitude

longtemps [lõtã] *adv* a long time; **il y a ~** a long time ago, long ago; **il y a ~ qu'il habite là** he's been living here for a long time

longuement [lõgmã] *adv* for a long time; *parler* at length

longueur [lõgœr] *f* length; **être sur la même ~ d'onde** be on the same wavelength

longue-vue [lõgvy] *f* (*pl* longues-vues) telescope

lopin [lɔpɛ̃] *m*: **~ de terre** piece of land

loquace [lɔkas] talkative

loque [lɔk] *f* rag; **~ humaine** wreck

loquet [lɔkɛ] *m* latch

lorgner [lɔrɲe] 〈1a〉 (*regarder*) eye; *fig*: *héritage, poste* have one's eye on

lors [lɔr] *adv*: **dès ~** from that moment on, from then on; **dès ~ que vous …** should you …; **~ de** during

lorsque [lɔrsk(ə)] *conj* when

losange [lɔzãʒ] *m* lozenge

lot [lo] *m* (*destin*) fate, lot; *à la loterie* prize; (*portion*) share; COMM batch;

gagner le gros ~ hit the jackpot

loterie [lɔtri] *f* lottery

loti, ~e [lɔti]: **être bien / mal ~** be well / badly off

lotion [losjõ] *f* lotion

lotissement [lɔtismã] *m* (*parcelle*) plot; *terrain loti* housing development, *Br aussi* (housing) estate

loto [lɔto] *m* lotto; *au niveau national* national lottery

louable [lwabl] praiseworthy; **louange** *f* praise

louche[1] [luʃ] sleazy

louche[2] [luʃ] *f* ladle

loucher [luʃe] ⟨1a⟩ squint, have a squint

louer[1] [lwe] ⟨1a⟩ *du locataire: appartement* rent; *bicyclette, canoë* rent, *Br aussi*; *du propriétaire: appartement* rent (out), let; *bicyclette, canoë* rent out, *Br aussi* hire (out)

louer[2] [lwe] ⟨1a⟩ (*vanter*) praise (**de** *ou* **pour qch** for sth)

loufoque [lufɔk] F crazy

loup [lu] *m* wolf

loupe [lup] *f* magnifying glass

louper [lupe] ⟨1a⟩ F *travail* botch; *train, bus* miss

loup-garou [lugaru] *m* (*pl* loups-garous) werewolf

lourd, ~e [lur, -d] heavy; *plaisanterie* clumsy; *temps* oppressive; **lourdaud, ~e 1** *adj* clumsy **2** *m/f* oaf; **lourdement** *adv* heavily; **lourdeur** *f* heaviness

louvoyer [luvwaje] ⟨1h⟩ MAR tack; **entre des problèmes** *fig* sidestep around problems

loyal, ~e [lwajal] (*mpl* -aux) honest; *adversaire* fair-minded; *ami* loyal; **bons et loyaux services** good and faithful service; **loyauté** *f* honesty; *d'un ami* loyalty

loyer [lwaje] *m* rent

lubie [lybi] *f* whim

lubrifiant [lybrifjã] *m* lubricant; **lubrification** *f* lubrication; **lubrifier** ⟨1a⟩ lubricate

lucarne [lykarn] *f* skylight

lucide [lysid] lucid; (*conscient*) conscious; **lucidité** *f* lucidity

lucratif, -ive [lykratif, -iv] lucrative; **à but non ~** not for profit, *Br aussi* non--profit making

lueur [lɥœr] *f* faint light; **une ~ d'espoir** a gleam *ou* glimmer of hope

luge [lyʒ] *f* toboggan; **faire de la ~** go tobogganing

lugubre [lygybr] gloomy, lugubrious

lui [lɥi] *pron personnel* ◊ *complément d'objet indirect, masculin* (to) him; *féminin* (to) her; *chose, animal* (to) it; **~ ai envoyé un e-mail** I sent him / her an e-mail; **je le ~ ai envoyé hier** I sent it (to) him / her yesterday; **le pauvre chien, je ~ ai donné à boire** the poor dog, I gave it something to drink

◊ *après prép, masculin* him; *animal* it; **le jus d'orange, c'est pour ~** the orange juice is for him

◊: **je les ai vues, ~ et sa sœur** I saw them, him and his sister; **il n'aime pas ça, ~** he doesn't like that

lui-même [lɥimɛm] himself; *de chose* itself

luire [lɥir]⟨4c⟩ glint, glisten

lumbago [lœbago] *m* lumbago

lumière [lymjɛr] *f* light (*aussi fig*); **le siècle des ~s** the Enlightenment; **ce n'est pas une ~** *iron* he's not exactly Einstein; **à la ~ de** in the light of

luminaire [lyminɛr] *m* light; **lumineux, -euse** luminous; *ciel, couleur* bright; *affiche* illuminated; *idée* brilliant; **rayon ~** beam of light

lunaire [lynɛr] lunar

lunatique [lynatik] lunatic

lundi [lœdi] *m* Monday; **~ de Pâques** Easter Monday

lune [lyn] *f* moon; **~ de miel** honeymoon

lunette [lynɛt] *f*: **~s** glasses; **~s de soleil** sunglasses; **~s de ski** ski goggles; **~ arrière** AUTO rear window

lurette [lyrɛt] *f* F: **il y a belle ~** an eternity ago

lustre [lystr] *m* (*lampe*) chandelier; *fig* luster, *Br* lustre

lustrer [lystre] ⟨1a⟩ *meuble* polish

lutte [lyt] *f* fight, struggle; SP wrestling; **lutter** ⟨1a⟩ fight, struggle; SP wrestle

luxe [lyks] *m* luxury; **de ~** luxury *atr*

Luxembourg [lyksãbur]: **le ~** Luxemburg; **luxembourgeois, ~e 1** *adj* of / from Luxemburg, Luxemburg *atr* **2** *m/f* **Luxembourgeois, ~e** Luxemburger

luxer [lykse] ⟨1a⟩: **se ~ l'épaule** dislocate one's shoulder

luxueux, -euse [lyksɥø, -z] luxurious; **luxueusement** *adv* luxuriously

luxuriant, ~e [lyksyrjã, -t] luxuriant

luxurieux, -euse [lyksyrjø, -z] luxur-

ious

lycée [lise] *m* senior high, *Br* grammar school; **lycéen, ~ne** *m/f* student (at a lycée)

lyncher [lẽʃe] ⟨1a⟩ lynch

Lyon [ljõ] Lyons

lyophilisé [ljɔfilize] freeze-dried

lyrique [lirik] lyric; **qui a du lyrisme** lyrical; **artiste ~** opera singer; **comédie ~** comic opera; **lyrisme** *m* lyricism

lys [lis] *m* → **lis**

M

m' [m] → **me**

M. *abr* (= **monsieur**) Mr

ma [ma] → **mon**

macabre [makabr] macabre

macaron [makarõ] *m* CUIS macaroon; (*insigne*) rosette

macédoine [masedwan] *f* CUIS: **~ de légumes** mixed vegetables *pl*; **~ de fruits** fruit salad

macérer [masere] ⟨1f⟩ CUIS: **faire ~** marinate

mâche [maʃ] *f* BOT lamb's lettuce

mâcher [maʃe] ⟨1a⟩ chew; **elle ne mâche pas ses mots** *fig* she doesn't mince her words

machin [maʃẽ] *m* F thing, thingamajig F

machinal, ~e [maʃinal] (*mpl* -aux) mechanical; **machinalement** *adv* mechanically

machination [maʃinasjõ] *f* plot; **~s** machinations

machine [maʃin] *f* machine; MAR engine; *fig* machinery; **~ à coudre** sewing machine; **~ à écrire** typewriter; **~ à laver** washing machine; **~ à sous** slot machine; **machine-outil** *f* (*pl* machines-outils) machine tool; **machiniste** *m au théâtre* stage hand

machisme [ma(t)ʃism] *m* machismo;

machiste male chauvinist

macho [matʃo] **1** *adj* male chauvinist **2** *m* macho type

mâchoire [maʃwar] *f* ANAT jaw

mâchonner [maʃɔne] ⟨1a⟩ chew (on); (*marmonner*) mutter

maçon [masõ] *m* bricklayer; *avec des pierres* mason; **maçonnerie** *f* masonry

macro [makro] *f* INFORM macro

maculer [makyle] ⟨1a⟩ spatter

madame [madam] *f* (*pl* mesdames [medam]): **bonjour ~** good morning; **~!** ma'am!, *Br* excuse me!; **Madame Durand** Mrs Durand; **bonsoir mesdames et messieurs** good evening, ladies and gentlemen

mademoiselle [madmwazɛl] *f* (*pl* mesdemoiselles [medmwazɛl]): **bonjour ~** good morning; **~!** miss!, *Br* excuse me!; **Mademoiselle Durand** Miss Durand

Madère [madɛr] *m* Madeira

madone [madɔn] *f* Madonna

magasin [magazẽ] *m* (*boutique*) store, *surtout Br* shop; (*dépôt*) store room; **grand ~** department store; **magasinier** *m* storeman

magazine [magazin] *m* magazine

mage [maʒ] *m*: **les Rois ~s** the Three

Wise Men, the Magi

magicien, **~ne** [maʒisjɛ̃, -ɛn] *m/f* magician

Maghreb [magrɛb]: **le ~** French-speaking North Africa; **maghrébin**, **~e1** *adj* North African **2** *m/f* **Maghrébin**, **~e** North African

magie [maʒi] *f* magic (*aussi fig*); **magique** magic, magical

magistral, **~e** [maʒistral] (*mpl* -aux) *ton* magisterial; *fig* masterly; **cours** *m* **~** lecture

magistrat [maʒistra] *m* JUR magistrate

magnanime [mananim] magnanimous

magnat [maɲa] *m* magnate, tycoon

magner [maɲe]: **se ~** F get a move on, move it F

magnétique [maɲetik] magnetic; **magnétisme** *m* magnetism

magnéto [maɲeto] *m* F (*magnétophone*) tape recorder

magnétophone [maɲetɔfɔn] *m* tape recorder

magnétoscope [maɲetɔskɔp] *m* video (recorder)

magnifique [maɲifik] magnificent

magot [mago] *m fig* F trésor savings *pl*

magouille [maguj] *f* F scheming; **~s électorales** election shenanigans F; **magouiller** ⟨1a⟩ F scheme

magret [magrɛ] *m*: **~ de canard** duck's breast

mai [mɛ] *m* May

maigre [mɛgr] thin; *résultat, salaire* meager, *Br* meagre; **maigreur** *f* thinness; *de profit, ressources* meagerness, *Br* meagreness; **maigrir** ⟨2a⟩ get thin, lose weight

mailing [mɛliŋ] *m* mailshot

maille [maj] *f* stitch

maillet [majɛ] *m* mallet

maillon [majɔ̃] *m d'une chaîne* link

maillot [majo] *m* SP shirt, jersey; *de coureur* vest; **~ (de bain)** swimsuit; **~ jaune** SP yellow jersey

main [mɛ̃] *f* hand; **donner un coup de ~ à qn** give s.o. a hand; **à la ~** *tenir qch* in one's hand; **fait / écrit à la ~** handmade / handwritten; **à ~ armée**

vol, attaque armed; **vote à ~ levée** show of hands; **la ~ dans la ~** hand in hand; **prendre qch en ~** *fig* take sth in hand; **prendre son courage à deux ~s** summon up all one's courage, steel o.s.; **en ~s propres** in person; **en un tour de ~** in no time at all; **haut les ~s!** hands up!; **donner la ~ à qn** hold s.o.'s hand; **perdre la ~** *fig* lose one's touch; **sous la ~** to hand, within reach

main-d'œuvre [mɛ̃dœvr] *f* (*pl inv*) manpower, labor, *Br* labour

main-forte [mɛ̃fɔrt] *f*: **prêter ~ à qn** help s.o.

mainmise [mɛ̃miz] *f* seizure

maint, **~e** [mɛ̃, -t] *fml* many; **à ~es reprises** time and again

maintenance [mɛ̃tnɑ̃s] *f* maintenance

maintenant [mɛ̃tnɑ̃] *adv* now; **~ que** now that

maintenir [mɛ̃t(ə)nir] ⟨2h⟩ *pai* keep, maintain; *tradition* uphold; (*tenir fermement*) hold; *d'une poutre* hold up; (*conserver dans le même état*) keep; (*soutenir*) maintain; **~ l'ordre** maintain *ou* keep law and order; **~ son opinion** stick to one's opinion, not change one's mind; **se ~ d'un prix** hold steady; *d'une tradition* last; *de la paix* hold, last; **se ~ au pouvoir** stay in power; **le temps se maintient au beau fixe** the good weather is holding; **maintien** *m* maintenance; **~ de l'ordre** maintenance of law and order; **~ de la paix** peace keeping

maire [mɛr] *m* mayor; **mairie** *f* town hall

mais [mɛ] **1** *conj* but **2** *adv*: **~ bien sûr!** of course!; **~ non!** no!; **~ pour qui se prend-t-elle?** just who does she think she is?

maïs [mais] *m* BOT corn, *Br aussi* maize; **en boîte** sweet corn

maison [mɛzɔ̃] *f* house; (*chez-soi*) home; COMM company; **à la ~** at home; **je vais à la ~** I'm going home; **pâté** *m* **~** homemade pâté; **Maison Blanche** White House; **~ de campa-**

M

gne country house; **~ close** brothel; **~ mère** parent company; **~ de retraite** retirement home, old people's home

maître [mɛtr] *m* master; (*professeur*) school teacher; (*peintre, écrivain*) maestro; **~ chanteur** blackmailer; **~ d'hôtel** maitre d', *Br* head waiter; **~ nageur** swimming instructor; **maîtresse 1** *f* mistress (*aussi amante*); (*professeur*) schoolteacher; **~ de maison** lady of the house; *qui reçoit des invités* hostess **2** *adj*: **pièce** *f* **~** main piece; **idée** *f* **~** main idea

maîtrise [mɛtriz] *f* mastery; *diplôme* MA, master's (degree); **~ de soi** self-control; **maîtriser** ⟨1a⟩ master; *cheval* gain control of; *incendie* bring under control, get a grip on

maïzena® [maizena] *f* corn starch, *Br* cornflour

majesté [maʒeste] *f* majesty; **majestueux, -euse** majestic

majeur, ~e [maʒœr] **1** *adj* major; **être ~** JUR be of age **2** *m* middle finger

majoration [maʒɔrasjɔ̃] *f des prix, salaires* increase; **majorer** ⟨1a⟩ *prix* increase

majoritaire [maʒɔritɛr] majority; **scrutin** *m* **~** majority vote; **majorité** *f* majority

majuscule [maʒyskyl] *f & adj*: (**lettre** *f*) **~** capital (letter)

mal [mal] **1** *m* (*pl* maux [mo]) evil; (*maladie*) illness; (*difficulté*) difficulty, trouble; **faire ~** hurt; **avoir ~ aux dents** have toothache; **se donner du ~** go to a lot of trouble; **ne voir aucun ~** à not see any harm in; **faire du ~ à qn** hurt s.o.; **j'ai du ~ à faire cela** I find it difficult to do that; **dire du ~ de qn** say bad things about s.o.; **~ de mer** seasickness; **~ du pays** homesickness **2** *adv* badly; **~ fait** badly done; **pas ~** not bad; **il y avait pas ~ de monde** there were quite a lot of people there; **s'y prendre ~** go about it in the wrong way; **se sentir ~** feel ill **3** *adj*: **faire / dire qch de ~** do / say sth bad; **être ~ à l'aise** be ill at

ease, be uncomfortable

malade [malad] ill, sick; **tomber ~** fall ill; **~ mental** mentally ill; **maladie** *f* illness, disease; **maladif, -ive** *personne* sickly; *curiosité* unhealthy

maladresse [maladrɛs] *f* clumsiness; **maladroit, ~e** clumsy

malaise [malɛz] *m physique* physical discomfort; (*inquiétude*) uneasiness, discomfort; POL malaise; **il a fait un ~** he fainted

malaria [malarja] *f* MÉD malaria

malavisé, ~e [malavize] ill-advised

malaxer [malakse] ⟨1a⟩ mix

malchance [malʃɑ̃s] *f* bad luck; **une série de ~s** a series of misfortunes, a string of bad luck; **malchanceux, -euse** unlucky

mâle [mal] *m & adj* male

malédiction [malediksjɔ̃] *f* curse

maléfique [malefik] evil

malencontreux, -euse [malɑ̃kɔ̃trø, -z] unfortunate

malentendant, ~e [malɑ̃tɑ̃dɑ̃, -t] hard of hearing

malentendu [malɑ̃tɑ̃dy] *m* misunderstanding

malfaiteur [malfɛtœr] *m* malefactor

malfamé, ~e [malfame] disreputable

malformation [malfɔrmasjɔ̃] *f* deformity

malgache [malgaʃ] **1** *adj* Malagasy **2** *m/f* **Malgache** Malagasy

malgré [malgre] *prép* in spite of, despite; **~ moi** despite myself; **~ tout** in spite of everything

malhabile [malabil] *personne, geste* awkward; *mains* unskilled

malheur [malœr] *m* misfortune; (*malchance*) bad luck; **par ~** unfortunately; **porter ~** be bad luck; **malheureusement** *adv* unfortunately; **malheureux, -euse** unfortunate; (*triste*) unhappy; (*insignifiant*) silly little

malhonnête [malɔnɛt] dishonest; **malhonnêteté** *f* dishonesty

malice [malis] *f* malice; (*espièglerie*) mischief; **malicieux, -euse** malicious; (*coquin*) mischievous

malin, -igne [malɛ̃, maliɲ] (*rusé*)

manivelle

crafty, cunning; (*méchant*) malicious; MÉD malignant

malle [mal] *f* trunk

malléable [maleabl] malleable

mallette [malɛt] *f* little bag

malmener [malməne] ⟨1d⟩ *personne, objet* treat roughly; (*critiquer*) maul

malnutrition [malnytrisjõ] *f* malnutrition

malodorant, ~e [malodorã, -t] foul-smelling

malpoli, ~e [malpoli] impolite

malpropre [malpropr] dirty

malsain, ~e [malsɛ̃, -ɛn] unhealthy

malt [malt] *m* malt

Malte [malt] *f* Malta; **maltais, ~e 1** *adj* Maltese **2** *m/f* **Maltais, ~e** Maltese

maltraiter [maltrɛte] ⟨1b⟩ mistreat, maltreat

malveillant, ~e [malvejã, -t] malevolent

malvenu, ~e [malvəny]: *c'est ~ de sa part de faire une remarque* it's not appropriate for him to make a comment

malvoyant, ~e [malvwajã, -t] **1** *adj* visually impaired **2** *m/f* visually impaired person

maman [mamã] *f* Mom, *Br* Mum

mamelle [mamɛl] *f de vache* udder; *de chienne* teat

mamelon [mamlõ] *m* ANAT nipple

mamie [mami] *f* F granny

mammifère [mamifɛr] *m* mammal

manager [manadʒœr] *m* manager

manche[1] [mãʃ] *m d'outils, d'une casserole* handle; *d'un violon* neck

manche[2] [mãʃ] *f* sleeve; **la Manche** the English Channel; *la première / deuxième ~* the first / second round; *faire la ~* play music on the street, *Br* busk

manchette [mãʃɛt] *f* cuff; *d'un journal* headline; **manchon** *m* muff; TECH sleeve

manchot, ~e [mãʃo, -ot] **1** *adj* one-armed **2** *m/f* one-armed person **3** *m* ZO penguin

mandarine [mãdarin] *f* mandarin (orange)

mandat [mãda] *m d'un député* term of office, mandate; (*procuration*) proxy; *de la poste* postal order; *~ d'arrêt* arrest warrant; *~ de perquisition* search warrant; **mandataire** *m/f à une réunion* proxy

manège [manɛʒ] *m* riding school; (*carrousel*) carousel, *Br* roundabout; *fig* game

manette [manɛt] *f* TECH lever

mangeable [mãʒabl] edible, eatable; **mangeoire** *f* manger

manger [mãʒe] ⟨1l⟩ **1** *v/t* eat; *fig: argent, temps* eat up; *mots* swallow **2** *v/i* eat **3** *m* food; **mangeur, -euse** *m/f* eater

mangue [mãg] *f* mango

maniable [manjabl] *voiture, bateau* easy to handle

maniaque [manjak] fussy; **manie** *f* mania

manier [manje] ⟨1a⟩ handle

manière [manjɛr] *f* way, manner; *~s* manners; *affectées* airs and graces, affectation *sg*; *à la ~ de* in the style of; *de cette ~* (in) that way; *de toute ~* anyway, in any case; *d'une ~ générale* generally speaking, on the whole; *de ~ à faire qch* so as to do sth; *de telle ~ que* in such a way that; **maniéré, ~e** affected

manifestant, ~e [manifɛstã, -t] *m/f* demonstrator; **manifestation** *f de joie etc* expression; POL demonstration; *culturelle, sportive* event

manifeste [manifɛst] **1** *adj* obvious **2** *m* POL manifesto; COMM manifest

manifester [manifɛste] ⟨1a⟩ **1** *v/t courage, haine* show; *se ~ de maladie, problèmes* manifest itself / themselves **2** *v/i* demonstrate

manigance [manigãs] *f* scheme, plot

manipulateur, -trice [manipylatœr, -tris] manipulative; **manipulation** *f d'un appareil* handling; *d'une personne* manipulation; *~ génétique* genetic engineering; **manipuler** ⟨1a⟩ handle; *personne* manipulate; **manipulé génétiquement** genetically engineered

manivelle [manivɛl] *f* crank

M

mannequin [mankɛ̃] *m de couture* (tailor's) dummy; *dans un magasin* dummy; *femme, homme* model

manœuvre [manœvr] **1** *f* maneuver, *Br* manoeuvre; *d'un outil, une machine etc* operation **2** *m* unskilled laborer *ou Br* labourer; **manœuvrer** ⟨1a⟩ maneuver, *Br* manoeuvre

manoir [manwar] *m* manor (house)

manque [mɑ̃k] *m* lack (**de** of); *par* **~** **de** for lack of; *~***s** *fig* failings; *être* **en ~** *d'un drogué* be experiencing withdrawal symptoms; *~* **à gagner** COMM loss of earnings; **manqué,** **~e** unsuccessful; *rendez-vous* missed; **manquement** *m* breach (**à** of)

manquer [mɑ̃ke] ⟨1m⟩ **1** *v/i* (*être absent*) be missing; (*faire défaut*) be lacking; (*échouer*) fail; **tu me manques** I miss you; **~ à** *parole, promesse* fail to keep; *devoir* fail in; **~ de** *qch* lack sth, be lacking in sth **2** *v/t* (*rater, être absent à*) miss; *examen* fail; *~* **son coup** *au tir* miss; *fig* miss one's chance; **ne** **pas** **~ de faire** *qch* make a point of doing sth; **elle a manqué (de)** **faire écraser** she was almost run over **3** *impersonnel* **il manque des** **preuves** there isn't enough evidence, there's a lack of evidence; **il** **manque trois personnes** three people are missing

mansarde [mɑ̃sard] *f* attic

manteau [mɑ̃to] *m* (*pl* -x) coat; *de neige* blanket, mantle; **sous le ~** clandestinely; **~ de cheminée** mantelpiece

manucure [manykyr] *f* manicure

manuel, **~le** [manɥɛl] **1** *adj* manual **2** *m* manual; **~ d'utilisation** instruction manual

manufacture [manyfaktyr] *f* manufacture; *usine* factory; **manufacturé,** **~e:** *produits mpl* **~s** manufactured goods, manufactures

manuscrit, **~e** [manyskri, -t] **1** *adj* handwritten **2** *m* manuscript

manutention [manytɑ̃sjɔ̃] *f* handling

mappemonde [mapmɔ̃d] *f* (*carte*) map of the world; (*globe*) globe

maquereau [makro] *m* (*pl* -x) ZO

mackerel; F (*souteneur*) pimp

maquette [makɛt] *f* model

maquillage [makijaʒ] *m* make-up; **maquiller** ⟨1a⟩ make up; *crime, vérité* conceal, disguise; **toute maquillée** all made up; **se ~** make up, put one's make-up on

maquis [maki] *m* maquis, member of the Resistance

maraîcher, **-ère** [marɛʃe, -ɛr] *m/f* truck farmer, *Br* market gardener

marais [marɛ] *m* swamp, *Br aussi* marsh

marasme [marasm] *m* ÉCON slump

marathon [maratɔ̃] *m* marathon

marbre [marbr] *m* marble; **marbré,** **~e** marbled

marc [mar] *m*: **~ de café** coffee grounds *pl*

marcassin [markasɛ̃] *m* young wild boar

marchand, **~e** [marʃɑ̃, -d] **1** *adj prix,* *valeur* market *atr*, *rue* shopping *atr*; *marine, navire* merchant *atr* **2** *m/f* merchant, storekeeper, *Br* shopkeeper; **~ de vin** wine merchant

marchandage [marʃɑ̃daʒ] *m* haggling, bargaining; **marchander** ⟨1a⟩ haggle, bargain

marchandise [marʃɑ̃diz] *f*: **~s** merchandise *sg*; **train m de ~s** freight train, *Br aussi* goods train

marche [marʃ] *f activité* walking; *d'escalier* step; MUS, MIL march; *des événements* course; (*démarche*) walk; **assis dans le sens de la ~** *dans un* *train* sitting facing the engine; **~ arrière** AUTO reverse; **mettre en ~** start (up)

marché [marʃe] *m* market (*aussi* COMM); (*accord*) deal; (**à**) **bon ~** cheap; (**à**) **meilleur ~** cheaper; **pardessus le ~** into the bargain; **~ boursier** stock market; **le Marché** **Commun** POL the Common Market; **~ noir** black market; **~ aux puces** flea market; **~ de titres** securities market; **le Marché unique** the Single Market

marcher [marʃe] ⟨1a⟩ *d'une personne* walk; MIL march; *d'une machine* run, work; F (*réussir*) work; *être en service*: *d'un bus, train* run; **et il a marché!** F and he fell for it!; *faire ~ qn* pull s.o.'s leg, have s.o. on *{fam}*; *~ sur les pieds de qn* tread on; *pelouse* walk on; **défense de ~ sur la pelouse** keep off the grass

mardi [mardi] *m* Tuesday; *Mardi gras* Mardi Gras, *Br* Shrove Tuesday

mare [mar] *f* pond; *~ de sang* pool of blood

marécage [mareka3] *m* swamp, *Br aussi* marsh; **marécageux, -euse** swampy, *Br aussi* marshy

maréchal [mareʃal] *m* (*pl* -aux) marshal; **maréchal-ferrant** *m* (*pl* maréchaux-ferrants) blacksmith

marée [mare] *f* tide; *~ basse* low tide; *~ haute* high tide; *~ noire* oil slick

marelle [marel] *f* hopscotch

margarine [margarin] *f* margarine

marge [marʒ] *f* margin (*aussi fig*); *~ bénéficiaire ou ~ de profit* profit margin; *notes fpl en ~* marginal notes; *en ~ de* on the fringes of; *laisser de la ~ à qn fig* give s.o. some leeway

marginal, ~e [marʒinal] (*mpl* -aux) **1** *adj* marginal **2** *m* person who lives on the fringes of society

marguerite [margərit] *f* daisy

mari [mari] *m* husband

mariage [marjaʒ] *m fête* wedding; *état* marriage; *demander qn en ~* ask for s.o.'s hand in marriage; *marié, ~e* **1** *adj* married **2** *m* (bride)groom; *les jeunes ~s* the newly weds, the bride and groom; **mariée** *f* bride; **marier** ⟨1a⟩ *du maire, du prêtre, des parents* marry (*qn avec ou à qn* s.o. to s.o.); *se ~* get married; *se ~ avec qn* marry s.o., get married to s.o.

marijuana [marirwana] *f* marihuana, marijuana

marin, ~e [marɛ̃, -in] **1** *adj* sea *atr; animaux* marine **2** *m* sailor

marine *f* MIL navy; (*bleu*) *~* navy (blue)

mariner [marine] ⟨1a⟩ CUIS marinate

marionnette [marjɔnɛt] *f* puppet; *avec des ficelles aussi* marionnette

maritime [maritim] *climat, droit* maritime; *port* sea *atr; ville* seaside *atr*

marmelade [marməlad] *f* marmalade

marmite [marmit] *f* (large) pot

marmonner [marmɔne] ⟨1a⟩ mutter

marmotte [marmɔt] *f* marmot

Maroc [marɔk]: *le ~* Morocco; **marocain, ~e 1** *adj* Moroccan **2** *m/f* **Marocain, ~e** Moroccan

maroquinerie [marɔkinri] *f* leather goods shop; *articles* leather goods *pl*

marquant, ~e [markɑ̃, -t] remarkable, outstanding

marque [mark] *f* mark; COMM brand; *de voiture* make; COMM (*signe*) trademark; *à vos ~s!* on your marks!; *~ déposée* registered trademark; *de ~* COMM branded; *fig: personne* distinguished; *une ~ de fig* (*preuve de*) a token of

marquer [marke] ⟨1m⟩ mark; (*noter*) write down, note down; *personnalité* leave an impression *ou* its mark on; *d'un baromètre* show; (*exprimer*) indicate, show; (*accentuer*) *taille* emphasize; *~ un but* score (a goal); *ma montre marque trois heures* my watch says three o'clock, it's three o'clock by my watch

marqueterie [markɛtri] *f* marquetry

marqueur [markœr] *m* marker pen

marquis [marki] *m* marquis; **marquise** *f* marchioness

marraine [marɛn] *f* godmother

marrant, ~e [marɑ̃, -t] F funny

marre [mar] F: *j'en ai ~* I've had it up to here F

marrer [mare] ⟨1a⟩ F: *se ~* have a good laugh

marron [marɔ̃] **1** *m* chestnut **2** *adj inv* brown; **marronnier** *m* chestnut tree

mars [mars] *m* March

Marseille [marsɛj] Marseilles

marsupiaux [marsypjo] *mpl* marsupials

marteau [marto] (*pl* -x) **1** *m* hammer; *~ piqueur* pneumatic drill **2** *adj* F crazy, nuts F

marteler [martəle] ⟨1d⟩ hammer

martial, ~e [marsjal] (*mpl* -aux) martial; *cour f ~* court martial; *arts mpl martiaux* martial arts

martien 204

martien, ~ne [marsjɛ̃, -ɛn] Martian
martyr, ~e[1] [martir] *m/f* martyr
martyre[2] [martir] *m* martyrdom; **martyriser** ⟨1a⟩ abuse; *petit frère, camarade de classe* bully
marxisme [marksism] *m* Marxism; **marxiste** *m/f & adj* Marxist
mas [mɑ *ou* mas] *m farmhouse in the south of France*
mascara [maskara] *m* mascara
mascarade [maskarad] *f* masquerade; *fig* (*mise en scène*) charade
mascotte [maskɔt] *f* mascot
masculin, ~e [maskylɛ̃,-in] **1** *adj* male; GRAM masculine **2** *m* GRAM masculine
masque [mask] *m* mask (*aussi fig*); **masquer** ⟨1m⟩ mask; *cacher à la vue* hide, mask; *bal m* **masqué** costume ball
massacre [masakr] *m* massacre; **massacrer** ⟨1a⟩ massacre (*aussi fig*)
massage [masaʒ] *m* massage
masse [mas] *f* masse; ÉL ground, *Br* earth; **en ~** in large numbers, en masse; *manifestation* massive: *une ~ de choses à faire* masses *pl* (of things) to do; *taillé dans la ~* carved from the solid rock; *être à la ~* F be off one's rocker F
masser [mase] ⟨1a⟩ (*assembler*) gather; *jambes* massage; **masseur, -euse** *m/f* masseur; masseuse
massif, -ive [masif, -iv] **1** *adj* massif; *or, chêne* solid **2** *m* massif; *~ de fleurs* flowerbed
massue [masy] *f* club
mastic [mastik] *m* mastic; *autour d'une vitre* putty
mastiquer [mastike] ⟨1m⟩ chew, masticate; *vitre* put putty around
mastodonte [mastɔdɔ̃t] *m* colossus, giant
masure [mazyr] *f péj* hovel
mat[1], **~e** [mat] matt; *son* dull
mat[2] [mat] *adj inv aux échecs* checkmated
mât [mɑ] *m* mast
match [matʃ] *m* game, *Br aussi* match; *~ aller* first game; *~ retour* return game; *~ nul* tied game, *Br* draw

matelas [matla] *m* mattress; *~ pneumatique* air bed; **matelassé, ~e** quilted
matelot [matlo] *m* sailor
matérialiser [materjalize] ⟨1a⟩: *se ~* materialize; **matérialisme** *m* materialism; **matérialiste** **1** *adj* materialistic **2** *m/f* materialist
matériau [materjo] *m* (*pl* -x) material; **matériel, ~le** **1** *adj* material **2** *m* MIL matériel; *de camping*, SP equipment; INFORM hardware
maternel, ~le [matɛrnɛl] **1** *adj* maternal, motherly; *instinct, grand-père* maternal; *lait m* **~** mother's milk **2** *f* nursery school; **materner** ⟨1a⟩ mother; **maternité** *f* motherhood; *établissement* maternity hospital; (*enfantement*) pregnancy; **congé** *m* (*de*) **~** maternity leave
mathématicien, ~ne [matematisjɛ̃, -ɛn] *m/f* mathematician; **mathématique 1** *adj* mathematical **2** *fpl*: *~s* mathematics; **math(s)** *fpl* math *sg*, *Br* maths *sg*
matière [matjɛr] *f* PHYS matter; (*substance*) material; (*sujet*) subject; *c'est une bonne entrée en ~* it's a good introduction; *en la ~* on the subject; *en ~ de* when it comes to; *~ grasse* shortening; *~ grise* gray *ou Br* grey matter, brain cells *pl*; *~ première* raw material
matin [matɛ̃] *m* morning; *le ~* in the morning; *ce ~* this morning; *du ~ au soir* from morning till night; *~ et soir* morning and evening; *tous les lundis* **~**s every Monday morning; *demain* **~** tomorrow morning; **matinal, ~e** (*mpl* -aux) morning *atr*; *être* **~** be an early riser; *tu es bien* **~!** you're an early bird!, you're up early!; **matinée** *f* morning; (*spectacle*) matinée
matou [matu] *m* tom cat
matraque [matrak] *f* blackjack, *Br* cosh
matrice [matris] *f* ANAT uterus; TECH die, matrix; MATH matrix
matricule [matrikyl] *m* number
matrimonial, ~e [matrimɔnjal] (*mpl*

-aux) matrimonial; *agence f ~e* marriage bureau

mature [matyr] mature; maturité f maturity

maudire [modir] ⟨2a et 4m⟩ curse; maudit, ~e F blasted F, damn F

mausolée [mozole] m mausoleum

maussade [mosad] *personne* sulky; *ciel, temps* dull

mauvais, ~e [mɔvɛ, -z] **1** *adj* bad, poor; (*méchant*) bad; (*erroné*) wrong **2** *adv* bad; *il fait ~* the weather is bad; *sentir ~* smell (bad)

mauve [mov] mauve

mauviette [movjɛt] F wimp F

maux [mo] *pl de* mal

maximal, ~e [maksimal] (*mpl* -aux) maximum; maximum **1** *adj* (*mpl et fpl aussi* maxima) maximum **2** *m* maximum; *au ~* (*tout au plus*) at most, at the maximum

mayonnaise [majɔnɛz] *f* CUIS mayonnaise, mayo F

mazout [mazut] *m* fuel oil; mazouté, ~e *oiseau* covered in oil

McDrive® [makdrajv] *m* drive-in McDonald's

me [mə] *pron personnel* ◊ *complément d'objet direct* me; *il ne m'a pas vu* he didn't see me

◊ *complément d'objet indirect* (to) me; *elle m'en a parlé* she spoke to me about it; *tu vas ~ chercher mon journal?* will you fetch me my paper?

◊ *avec verbe pronominal* myself; *je ~ suis coupé* I cut myself; *je ~ lève à ...* I get up at ...

mec [mɛk] *m* F guy F

mécanicien [mekanisjɛ̃] *m* mechanic; mécanique **1** *adj* mechanical **2** *f* mechanics; mécaniquement *adv* mechanically; mécaniser ⟨1a⟩ mechanize; mécanisme *m* mechanism

méchanceté [meʃɑ̃ste] *f caractère* nastiness; *action, parole* nasty thing to do / say; méchant, ~e **1** *adj* nasty; *enfant* naughty F; *les gentils et les ~s* the goodies and the baddies

mèche [mɛʃ] *f d'une bougie* wick; *d'explosif* fuse; *d'une perceuse* bit; *de che-*

veux strand, lock

méconnaissable [mekɔnɛsabl] unrecognizable; méconnaître ⟨4z⟩ (*mésestimer*) fail to appreciate

mécontent, ~e [mekɔ̃tɑ̃, -t] unhappy, displeased (*de* with); mécontenter ⟨1a⟩ displease

Mecque [mɛk]: *la ~* Mecca

médaille [medaj] *f* medal; *~ de bronze / d'argent / d'or* bronze / silver / gold medal; médaillé, ~e *m/f* medalist, *Br* medallist; médaillon *m* medallion

médecin [medsɛ̃] *m* doctor; *~ de famille* family doctor; médecine *f* medicine; *les ~s douces* alternative medicines; *~ légale* forensic medicine; *~ du sport* sports medicine

média [medja] *m* (*pl* média *ou* médias) media *pl*

médiateur, -trice [medjatœr, -tris] *m/f* mediator

médiathèque [medjatɛk] *f* media library

médiation [medjasjɔ̃] *f* mediation

médiatique [medjatik] media *atr*

médical, ~e [medikal] (*mpl* -aux) medical; médicament *m* medicine, drug; médicinal, ~e [medisinal] (*mpl* -aux) medicinal

médiéval, ~e [medjeval] (*mpl* -aux) medieval, *Br* mediaeval

médiocre [medjɔkr] mediocre; *~ en* ÉDU poor at; médiocrité *f* mediocrity

médire [medir] ⟨4m⟩: *~ de qn* run s.o. down; médisance *f* gossip

méditation [meditasjɔ̃] *f* meditation; méditer ⟨1a⟩ **1** *v/t*: *~ qch* think about sth, reflect on sth *fml* **2** *v/i* meditate (*sur* on)

Méditerranée [mediterane]: *la ~* the Mediterranean; méditerranéen, ~ne **1** *adj* Mediterranean **2** *m/f* Méditerranéen, ~ne Mediterranean *atr*

médium [medjɔm] *m* medium

méduse [medyz] *f* ZO jellyfish

meeting [mitiŋ] *m* meeting

méfait [mefɛ] *m* JUR misdemeanor, *Br* misdemeanour; *~s de la drogue* harmful effects

méfiance [mefjãs] *f* mistrust, suspicion; **méfiant**, **~e** suspicious; **méfier** ⟨1a⟩: **se ~ de** mistrust, be suspicious of; (*se tenir en garde*) be wary of

mégalomanie [megalɔmani] *f* megalomania

mégaoctet [megaɔktɛ] *m* INFORM megabyte

mégaphone [megafɔn] *m* bullhorn, Br loudhailer

mégarde [megard] *f*: **par ~** inadvertently

mégère [meʒɛr] *f* shrew

mégot [mego] *m* cigarette butt

meilleur, **~e** [mɛjœr] **1** *adj* better; **le ~** ... the best ... **2** *m*: **le ~** the best

mél [mɛl] *m* e-mail

mélancolie [melãkɔli] *f* gloom, melancholy; **mélancolique** gloomy, melancholy

mélange [melãʒ] *m* mixture; *de tabacs, thés, vins* blend; *action* mixing; *de tabacs, thés, vins* blending; **mélanger** ⟨11⟩ (*mêler*) mix; *tabacs, thés, vins* blend; (*brouiller*) jumble up, mix up

mélasse [melas] *f* molasses *sg*

mêlée [mele] *f* fray, melee; *en rugby* scrum

mêler [mele] ⟨1b⟩ mix; (*réunir*) combine; (*brouiller*) jumble up, mix up; **~ qn à qch** fig get s.o. mixed up in sth, involve s.o. in sth; **se ~ à qch** get involved in sth; **se ~ de qch** interfere in sth; **mêle-toi de ce qui te regarde!** mind your own business!; **se ~ à la foule** get lost in the crowd

mélo [melo] *m* melodrama

mélodie [melɔdi] *f* tune, melody; **mélodieux**, **-euse** tuneful, melodious; *voix* tuneful

mélodramatique [melɔdramatik] melodramatic; **mélodrame** *m* melodrama

melon [m(ə)lõ] *m* BOT melon; (**chapeau** *m*) **~** derby, Br bowler (hat)

membrane [mãbran] *f* membrane

membre [mãbr] *m* ANAT limb; *fig* member; **pays ~** member country

même [mɛm] **1** *adj*: **le / la ~**, **les ~s** the same; **la bonté ~** kindness itself;

il a répondu le jour ~ he replied the same day *ou* that very day; **en ~ temps** at the same time; **~ chose** (the) same again; **ce jour ~** *fml* today **2** *pron*: **le / la ~** the same one; **les ~s** the same ones; **cela revient au ~** it comes to the same thing

3 *adv* even; **~ pas** not even; **~ si** even if; **ici ~** right here; **faire de ~** do the same; **de ~!** likewise!; **de ~ que** just as; **boire à ~ la bouteille** drink straight from the bottle; **être à ~ de faire qch** be able to do sth; **tout de ~** all the same; **quand ~** all the same; **moi de ~** me too; **à ~ le sol** on the ground

mémoire [memwar] **1** *f* (*faculté, souvenir*) memory (*aussi* INFORM); **~ morte** read-only memory, ROM; **~ vive** random access memory, RAM; **de ~** by heart; **à la ~ de** in memory of, to the memory of; **de ~ d'homme** in living memory **2** *m* (*exposé*) report; (*dissertation*) thesis, dissertation; **~s** memoirs

mémorable [memɔrabl] memorable

mémorandum [memɔrãdɔm] *m* memorandum

mémorial [memɔrjal] *m* (*pl* -aux) memorial

mémoriser [memɔrize] memorize

menaçant, **~e** [mənasã, -t] threatening, menacing; **menace** *f* threat; **constituer une ~** pose a threat; **menacer** ⟨1k⟩ threaten (**de** with; **de faire** to do)

ménage [menaʒ] *m* (*famille*) household; (*couple*) (married) couple; **faire le ~** clean house, Br do the housework; **femme** *f* **de ~** cleaning woman, Br aussi cleaner; **~ à trois** ménage à trois, three-sided relationship; **faire bon ~ avec qn** get on well with s.o.

ménagement [menaʒmã] *m* consideration

ménager[1] ⟨1l⟩ (*traiter bien*) treat with consideration; *temps, argent* use sparingly; (*arranger*) arrange

ménager[2], **-ère** [menaʒe, -ɛr] **1** *adj* household *atr* **2** *f* home-maker, housewife

mendiant, **~e** [mɑ̃djɑ̃, -t] *m/f* beggar; **mendier** ⟨1a⟩ **1** *v/i* beg **2** *v/t* beg for

mener [məne] ⟨1d⟩ **1** *v/t* lead (*aussi fig*); (*amener*, *transporter*) take **2** *v/i*: **~ à** d'un chemin lead to; **ne ~ à rien** des efforts de qn come to nothing; **ceci nous mène nulle part** this is getting us nowhere; **meneur** *m* leader; *péj* ringleader; **~ de jeu** RAD, TV question master

menhir [menir] *m* menhir, standing stone

méningite [menɛ̃ʒit] *f* meningitis

ménopause [menopoz] *f* menopause

menotte [mənɔt] *f*: **~s** handcuffs; **menotter** ⟨1a⟩ handcuff

mensonge [mɑ̃sɔ̃ʒ] *m* lie; **mensonger, -ère** false

menstruation [mɑ̃stryasjɔ̃] *f* menstruation

mensualité [mɑ̃sɥalite] *f* somme à payer monthly payment; **mensuel, ~le** monthly

mensurations [mɑ̃syrasjɔ̃] *fpl* measurements; *de femme* vital statistics

mental, ~e [mɑ̃tal] (*mpl* -aux) mental; **calcul** *m* ~ mental arithmetic; **mentalement** *adv* mentally; **mentalité** *f* mentality

menteur, -euse [mɑ̃tœr, -øz] *m/f* liar

menthe [mɑ̃t] *f* BOT mint; **~ poivrée** peppermint; **~ verte** spearmint

mention [mɑ̃sjɔ̃] *f* mention; à un examen grade, *Br aussi* mark; **faire ~ de** mention; **rayer la ~ inutile** delete as appropriate; **mentionner** ⟨1a⟩ mention

mentir [mɑ̃tir] ⟨2b⟩ lie (**à qn** to s.o.)

menton [mɑ̃tɔ̃] *m* chin; **double ~** double chin

mentor [mɑ̃tɔr] *m* mentor

menu, ~e [məny] **1** *adj personne* slight; *morceaux* small; **~e monnaie** *f* change **2** *adv* finely, fine **3** *m* (*liste*) menu (*aussi* INFORM); (*repas*) set meal; **par le ~** in minute detail

menuiserie [mənɥizri] *f* carpentry; **menuisier** *m* carpenter

méprendre [meprɑ̃dr] ⟨4q⟩: **se ~** be mistaken (**sur** about)

mépris [mepri] *m* (*indifférence*) dis-

dain; (*dégoût*) scorn; **au ~ de** regardless of; **méprisable** despicable; **méprisant, ~e** scornful; **mépriser** ⟨1a⟩ *argent, ennemi* despise; *conseil, danger* scorn

mer [mer] *f* sea; **en ~** at sea; **par ~** by sea; **prendre la ~** go to sea; **la Mer du Nord** the North Sea; **mal m de ~** seasickness

mercenaire [mersəner] *m* mercenary

mercerie [mersəri] *f magasin* notions store, *Br* haberdashery; *articles* notions, *Br* haberdashery *pl*

merci [mersi] **1** *int* thanks, thank you (**de, pour** for); **~ beaucoup, ~ bien** thanks a lot, thank you very much; **Dieu ~!** thank God! **2** *f* mercy; **être à la ~ de** be at the mercy of; **sans ~** merciless, pitiless; *adv* mercilessly, pitilessly

mercredi [merkrədi] *m* Wednesday

mercure [merkyr] *m* CHIM mercury, quicksilver

merde [merd] *f* P shit P; **merder** ⟨1a⟩ P screw up P; **merdique** P shitty P, crappy P

mère [mer] *f* mother; **~ célibataire** unmarried mother; **~ porteuse** surrogate mother

méridional, ~e [meridjɔnal] (*mpl* -aux) southern

meringue [mərɛ̃g] *f* CUIS meringue

mérite [merit] *m* merit; **mériter** ⟨1a⟩ deserve; **~ le détour** be worth a visit; **méritoire** praiseworthy

merlan [merlɑ̃] *m* whiting

merle [merl] *m* blackbird

merveille [mervej] *f* wonder, marvel; **à ~** wonderfully well; **merveilleux, -euse** wonderful, marvelous, *Br* marvellous

mes [me] → **mon**

mésange [mezɑ̃ʒ] *f* ZO tit

mésaventure [mezavɑ̃tyr] *f* mishap

mesdames [medam] *pl* → **madame**

mesdemoiselles [medmwazel] *pl* → **mademoiselle**

mésentente [mezɑ̃tɑ̃t] *f* misunderstanding

mesquin, ~e [meskɛ̃, -in] mean, petty; (*parcimonieux*) mean

message [mɛsaʒ] *m* message; **~ d'erreur** error message; **~ téléphonique** telephone message; **messager, -ère** *m/f* messenger, courier; **messagerie** *f* parcels service; *électronique* electronic mail; **~ vocale** voicemail

messe [mɛs] *f* REL mass

messieurs [mesjø] *pl* → **monsieur**

mesurable [məzyrabl] measurable; **mesure** *f* action measurement, measuring; *grandeur* measurement; *disposition* measure, step; MUS (*rythme*) time; **à la ~ de** commensurate with; **à ~ que** as; **dans la ~ où** insofar as; **dans une large ~** to a large extent; **être en ~ de faire qch** be in a position to do sth; *outre* excessive; **fait sur ~** made to measure; **sur ~** *fig* tailor-made; **en ~** in time; **mesurer** ⟨1a⟩ measure; *risque, importance* gauge; *paroles* weigh; **se ~ avec qn** pit o.s. against s.o.

métabolisme [metabolism] *m* metabolism

métal [metal] *m* (*pl* -aux) metal; **métallique** metallic; **métallisé, ~e** metallic; **métallurgie** *f* metallurgy

métamorphose [metamorfoz] *f* metamorphosis; **métamorphoser** ⟨1a⟩: **se ~** metamorphose

métaphore [metafor] *f* metaphor

métaphysique [metafizik] **1** *adj* metaphysical **2** *f* metaphysics

météo [meteo] *f* weather forecast

météore [meteor] *m* meteor; **météorite** *m* meteorite

météorologie [meteorologi] *f science* meteorology; *service* weather office; **météorologiste** *m/f* meteorologist

méthode [metod] *f* method; **méthodique** [metod] methodical

méticuleux, -euse [metikylø, -z] meticulous

métier [metje] *m* (*profession*) profession; (*occupation manuelle*) trade; (*expérience*) experience; *machine* loom

métis, ~se [metis] *m/f & adj* half-caste

métrage [metraʒ] *m d'un film* footage; **court ~** short; **long ~** feature film

mètre [mɛtr] *m* meter, *Br* metre; (*règle*) measuring tape, tape measure;

métrique metric

métro [metro] *m* subway, *Br* underground; **à Paris** metro

métropole [metropol] *f ville* metropolis; *de colonie* mother country; **métropolitain, ~e: la France ~e** metropolitan France

mets [mɛ] *m* dish

metteur [mɛtœr] *m*: **~ en scène** director

mettre [mɛtr] ⟨4p⟩ ◇ put; *sucre, lait* put in; *vêtements, lunettes, chauffage, radio* put on; *réveil* set; *argent dans entreprise* invest, put in; **~ deux heures à faire qch** take two hours to do sth; **~ en bouteilles** bottle; **mettons que je n'aie** (*subj*) **plus d'argent** let's say I have no more money; **~ fin à qch** put an end to sth

◇ **je ne savais pas où me ~** I didn't know where to put myself; **où se mettent les …?** where do the …go?; **se ~ au travail** set to work; **se ~ à faire qch** start to do sth; **je n'ai plus rien à me ~** I have nothing to wear

meuble [mœbl] *m* piece of furniture; **~s** furniture *sg*; **meubler** ⟨1a⟩ furnish

meugler [møgle] ⟨1a⟩ moo

meule [møl] *f* millstone; **~ de foin** haystack

meunier, -ère [mønje, -ɛr] **1** *m/f* miller **2** *f* CUIS: (**à la**) **~** dusted with flour and fried

meurtre [mœrtr] *m* murder; **meurtrier, -ère 1** *adj* deadly **2** *m/f* murderer

meurtrir [mœrtrir] ⟨2a⟩ bruise; **avoir le cœur meurtri** *fig* be heart-broken; **meurtrissure** *f* bruise

meute [møt] *f* pack; *fig* mob

mexicain, ~e [mɛksikɛ̃, -ɛn] **1** *adj* Mexican **2** *m/f* **Mexicain, ~e** Mexican; **Mexique: le ~** Mexico

mezzanine [medzanin] *f* mezzanine (floor)

mi [mi] *m* MUS E

mi-… [mi] half; **à mi-chemin** halfway; (**à la**) **mi-janvier** mid-January

miam-miam [mjammjam] yum-yum

miaou [mjau] *m* miaow

miauler [mjole] ⟨1a⟩ miaow

mi-bas [miba] *mpl* knee-highs, pop socks

miche [miʃ] *f* large round loaf

mi-clos, ~e [miklo, -z] half-closed

micro [mikro] *m* mike; INFORM computer, PC; *d'espionnage* bug

microbe [mikrɔb] *m* microbe

microbiologie [mikrobiolɔʒi] *f* microbiology

microclimat [mikroklima] *m* microclimate

microcosme [mikrokɔsm] *m* microcosm

microélectronique [mikroelεktronik] *f* microelectronics

microfilm [mikrofilm] *m* microfilm

micro-onde [mikrɔ̃d] *m* (*pl* micro-ondes) microwave; (*four m à*) ~**s** *m* microwave (oven)

micro-ordinateur [mikroɔrdinatœr] *m* (*pl* micro-ordinateurs) INFORM microcomputer *m*

micro-organisme [mikroorganism] *m* microorganism

microphone [mikrofɔn] *m* microphone

microprocesseur [mikroprɔsεsœr] *m* INFORM microprocessor

microscope [mikrɔskɔp] *m* microscope; **microscopique** microscopic

midi [midi] *m* noon, twelve o'clock; (*sud*) south; ~ **et demi** half-past twelve; **le Midi** the South of France

mie [mi] *f de pain* crumb

miel [mjεl] *m* honey; **mielleux, -euse** *fig* sugary-sweet

mien, ~ne [mjε̃, mjεn]: **le mien, la mienne, les miens, les miennes** mine

miette [mjεt] *f* crumb

mieux [mjø] **1** *adv* ◊ *comparatif de bien* better; *superlatif de bien* best; **le** ~ best; **le** ~ **possible** the best possible; **de** ~ **en** ~ better and better; **tant** ~ so much the better; **valoir** ~ be better; **vous feriez** ~ **de** … you would *ou* you'd do best to …; ~ **vaut prévenir que guérir** prevention is better than cure; **on ne peut** ~ extre-

mely well

2 *m* (*progrès*) progress, improvement; **j'ai fait de mon** ~ I did my best; **le** ~, **c'est de** … the best thing is to …

mièvre [mjεvr] insipid

mignon, ~ne [miɲõ, miɲɔn] (*charmant*) cute; (*gentil*) nice, good

migraine [migrεn] *f* migraine

migrateur, -trice [migratœr, -tris] *oiseau* migratory; **migration** *f* migration; **migrer** ⟨1a⟩ migrate

mijoter [miʒɔte] ⟨1a⟩ CUIS simmer; *fig* hatch; **qu'est-ce qu'il mijote encore?** what's he up to now?

milice [milis] *f* militia

mildiou [mildju] *m* mildew

milieu [miljø] *m* (*pl* -x) (*centre*) middle; *biologique* environment; *social* environment, surroundings *pl*; **au** ~ **de** in the middle of; **en plein** ~ **de** right in the middle of; **le juste** ~ a happy medium; **le** ~ the underworld; ~**x diplomatiques** diplomatic circles

militaire [militεr] **1** *adj* military; **service** *m* ~ military service **2** *m* soldier; **les** ~**s** the military *sg ou pl*

militant, ~e [militã, -t] active

militariser [militarize] ⟨1a⟩ militarize

militer [milite] ⟨1a⟩: ~ **dans** be an active member of; ~ **pour** / **contre qch** *fig* militate for / against sth

mille [mil] **1** (a) thousand **2** *m mesure* mile; ~ **marin** nautical mile

millénaire [milenεr] **1** *adj* thousand-year old **2** *m* millennium

mille-pattes [milpat] *m* (*pl inv*) millipede

millésime [milezim] *m de timbres* date; *de vin* vintage, year

millet [mije] *m* BOT millet

milliard [miljar] *m* billion; **milliardaire** *m* billionaire

millième [miljεm] thousandth

millier [milje] *m* thousand

milligramme [miligram] *m* milligram

millimètre [milimεtr] *m* millimeter, *Br* millimetre

million [miljõ] *m* million; **millionnaire** *m/f* millionaire

mime [mim] *m* mimic; *de métier* mime;

mimer ⟨1a⟩ mime; *personne* mimic; **mimique** *f* expression

mimosa [mimoza] *m* BOT mimosa

minable [minabl] mean, shabby; *un salaire ~* a pittance

mince [mɛ̃s] *m* thin; *personne* slim, slender; *taille* slender; *espoir* slight; *somme, profit* small; *argument* flimsy; *~ (alors)!* F what the…!, blast!

mine¹ [min] *f* appearance, look; *faire ~ de faire qch* make as if to do sth; *avoir bonne / mauvaise ~* look / not look well

mine² [min] *f* mine (*aussi* MIL); *de crayon* lead; **miner** ⟨1a⟩ undermine; MIL mine

minerai [minrɛ] *m* ore

minéral, ~e [mineral] (*mpl* -aux) *adj & m* mineral

minéralogique [mineralɔʒik] AUTO: *plaque f ~* license plate, *Br* number plate

minet, ~te [minɛ, -t] *m/f* F pussy (cat); *fig* darling, sweetie pie F

mineur¹, ~e [minœr] JUR, MUS minor

mineur² [minœr] *m* (*ouvrier*) miner

miniature [minjatyr] *f* miniature

minibus [minibys] *m* minibus

minichaîne [miniʃɛn] *f* mini (hi-fi)

minier, -ère [minje, -ɛr] mining

mini-jupe [miniʒyp] *f* (*pl* mini-jupes) mini (skirt)

minimal, ~e [minimal] minimum; **minimalisme** *m* minimalism

minime [minim] minimal; *salaire* tiny; **minimiser** ⟨1a⟩ minimize

minimum [minimɔm] **1** *adj* (*mpl et fpl aussi* minima) minimum **2** *m* minimum; *au ~* at the very least; *un ~ de* the least little bit of; *il pourrait avoir un ~ de politesse* he could try to be a little polite; *prendre le ~ de risques* take as few risks as possible, minimize risk-taking

ministère [minister] *m* department; (*gouvernement*) government; REL ministry; **ministériel, ~le** *d'un ministère* departmental; *d'un ministre* ministerial

ministre [ministr] *m* minister; *~ des Affaires étrangères* Secretary of State, *Br* Foreign Secretary; *~ de la Défense* Defense Secretary, *Br* Minister of Defence; *~ de l'Intérieur* Secretary of the Interior, *Br* Home Secretary

minitel [minitɛl] *m* small home terminal connected to a number of data banks

minoritaire [minɔriter] minority; **minorité** *f* JUR, POL minority

minou [minu] *m* F pussy(-cat) F

minuit [minɥi] *m* midnight

minuscule [minyskyl] **1** *adj* tiny, minuscule; *lettre* small, lower case **2** *f* small *ou* lower-case letter

minute [minyt] *f* minute; *tu n'es quand même pas à la ~?* you're surely not in that much of a rush!; *d'une ~ à l'autre* any minute now; **minuterie** *f* time switch

minutie [minysi] *f* attention to detail, meticulousness; **minutieux, -euse** meticulous

mioche [mjɔʃ] *m* F kid F

mirabelle [mirabɛl] *f* mirabelle plum

miracle [mirakl] *m* miracle (*aussi fig*); **miraculeux, -euse** miraculous

mirador [miradɔr] *m* watch tower

mirage [miraʒ] *m* mirage; *fig* illusion

mire [mir] *f*: *point m de ~* target (*aussi fig*)

miroir [mirwar] *m* mirror; **miroiter** ⟨1a⟩ sparkle

mis, ~e [mi, -z] *p/p* → *mettre*

mise [miz] *f au jeu* stake; *de ~* acceptable; *~ en bouteilles* bottling; *~ en marche ou route* start-up; *~ en scène d'une pièce de théâtre* staging; *d'un film* direction; *~ en service* commissioning; *~ en vente* (putting up for) sale

miser [mize] ⟨1a⟩ *au jeu, fig* stake (*sur* on)

misérable [mizerabl] wretched; (*pauvre*) destitute, wretched; **misère** *f* (*pauvreté*) destitution; (*chose pénible*) misfortune; **miséreux, -euse** poverty-stricken

miséricorde [mizerikɔrd] *f* mercifulness; **miséricordieux, -euse** merciful

misogyne [mizɔʒin] **1** *adj* misogynistic **2** *m* misogynist

missel [misɛl] *m* REL missal

missile [misil] *m* MIL missile

mission [misjɔ̃] *f* (*charge*) mission (*aussi* POL, REL); (*tâche*) job, task; **missionnaire** *m* missionary

missive [misiv] *f* brief

mistral [mistral] *m* mistral (*cold north wind on the Mediterranean coast*)

mite [mit] *f* ZO (clothes) moth

mi-temps [mitɑ̃] (*pl inv*) **1** *f* SP half-time **2** *m* part-time job; **à ~** *travail, travailler* part-time

miteux, -euse [mitø, -z] *vêtement* moth-eaten; *hôtel, théâtre* shabby, flea-bitten F

mitigé, ~e [mitiʒe] moderate; *sentiments* mixed

mitonner [mitɔne] ⟨1a⟩ cook on a low flame

mitoyen, ~ne [mitwajɛ̃, -ɛn] *jardin* with a shared wall / hedge; **des maisons ~nes** duplexes, *Br* semi-detached houses; *plus de deux* row houses, *Br* terraced houses

mitrailler [mitraje] ⟨1a⟩ MIL machine gun; *fig* bombard (**de** with); **mitraillette** *f* sub-machine gun; **mitrailleuse** *f* machine gun

mi-voix [mivwa]: **à ~** under one's breath

mixage [miksaʒ] *m* mixing; **mixer, mixeur** *m* CUIS blender; **mixte** mixed; **mixture** *f* péj vile concoction

MM *abr* (= **Messieurs**) Messrs.

Mme *abr* (= **Madame**) Mrs

Mo *m abr* (= **mégaoctet**) Mb (= megabyte)

mobile [mɔbil] **1** *adj* mobile; (*amovible*) movable (*aussi* REL); *feuilles* loose; *reflets, ombres* moving **2** *m* motive; ART mobile; **mobilier, -ère 1** *adj* JUR movable, personal; **valeurs fpl mobilières** FIN securities **2** *m* furniture

mobilisation [mɔbilizasjɔ̃] *f* MIL mobilization (*aussi fig*); **mobiliser** ⟨1a⟩ MIL mobilize (*aussi fig*)

mobilité [mɔbilite] *f* mobility

mobylette® [mɔbilɛt] *f* moped

moche [mɔʃ] F (*laid*) ugly; (*mépri-*

sable) mean, rotten F

modalité [mɔdalite] *f*: **~s de paiement** methods of payment

mode¹ [mɔd] *m* method; **~ d'emploi** instructions (for use); **~ de paiement** method of payment; **~ de vie** lifestyle

mode² [mɔd] *f* fashion; **être à la ~** be fashionable, be in fashion

modèle [mɔdɛl] *m* model; *tricot* pattern; **modeler** ⟨1d⟩ model

modem [mɔdem] *m* INFORM modem

modération [mɔderasjɔ̃] *f* moderation; **modéré, ~e** moderate; **modérer** ⟨1f⟩ moderate; **se ~** control o.s.

moderne [mɔdɛrn] modern; **modernisation** *f* modernization; **moderniser** ⟨1a⟩ modernize

modeste [mɔdɛst] modest; **modestie** *f* modesty

modification [mɔdifikasjɔ̃] *f* alteration, modification; **modifier** ⟨1a⟩ alter, modify

modique [mɔdik] modest

modiste [mɔdist] *f* milliner

modulable [mɔdylabl] *meuble* modular; *horaire* flexible; **modulation** *f* modulation; **~ de fréquence** frequency modulation; **module** *m* TECH module; **moduler** ⟨1a⟩ modulate

moelle [mwal] *f* marrow; **~ épinière** spinal cord

moelleux, -euse [mwalø, -z] *lit, serviette* soft; *chocolat, vin* smooth

mœurs [mœr(s)] *fpl* (*attitude morale*) morals; (*coutumes*) customs; **brigade *f* des ~** vice squad

mohair [mɔɛr] *m* mohair

moi [mwa] *pron personnel* me; **avec ~** with me; **c'est ~ qui l'ai fait** I did it, it was me that did it

moignon [mwaɲɔ̃] *m* stump

moi-même [mwamɛm] myself

moindre [mwɛ̃dr] lesser; *prix, valeur* lower; *quantité* smaller; **le / la ~** the least; **c'est un ~ mal** it's the lesser of two evils

moine [mwan] *m* monk

moineau [mwano] *m* (*pl -x*) sparrow

moins [mwɛ̃] **1** *adv* less; **~ d'argent**

less money; **deux mètres de ~** two meters less; **c'est ~ cher que ...** it's less expensive than ..., it's not as expensive as ...; **au ou du ~** at least; **je ne pourrai pas venir à ~ d'annuler mon rendez-vous** I can't come unless I cancel my meeting, **à ~ que ... ne** (+ *subj*) unless; **de ~ en ~** less and less

2 *m*: **le ~** the least

3 *prép* MATH minus; **dix heures ~ cinq** five of ten, *Br* five to ten; **il fait ~ deux** it's 2 below zero, it's two below freezing

mois [mwa] *m* month; **par ~** a month

moisi, ~e [mwazi] **1** *adj* moldy, *Br* mouldy **2** *m* BOT mold, *Br* mould; **moisir** ⟨2a⟩ go moldy *ou Br* mouldy; **moisissure** *f* BOT mold, *Br* mould

moisson [mwasɔ̃] *f* harvest; **moissonner** ⟨1a⟩ harvest; **moissonneur, -euse** *m/f* harvester **2** *f* reaper; **moissonneuse-batteuse** *f* (*pl* moissonneuses-batteuses) combine harvester

moite [mwat] damp, moist

moitié [mwatje] *f* half; **à ~ vide / endormi** half-empty / -asleep; **~ ~** fifty-fifty; **à ~ prix** (at) half-price; **à la ~ de travail, vie** halfway through

mol [mɔl] → **mou**

molaire [mɔlɛr] *f* molar

môle [mol] *m* breakwater, mole

moléculaire [mɔlekylɛr] molecular; **molécule** *f* molecule

molester [mɔlɛste] ⟨1a⟩ rough up

molette [mɔlɛt] *f de réglage* knob

mollasse [mɔlas] *péj* spineless; (*paresseux*) lethargic

mollement [mɔlmɑ̃] *adv* lethargically; **mollesse** *f d'une chose* softness; *d'une personne, d'actions* lethargy; **mollet¹, ~te** soft; *œuf* soft-boiled

mollet² [mɔlɛ] *m* calf

mollir [mɔlir] ⟨2a⟩ *des jambes* give way; *du vent* die down

mollusque [mɔlysk] *m* mollusc

môme [mom] *m/f* F kid F

moment [mɔmɑ̃] *m* moment; **à ce ~** at that moment; **en ce ~** at the moment; **dans un ~** in a moment; **du ~** of the moment; **d'un ~ à l'autre** at any moment; **par ~s** at times, sometimes; **pour le ~** for the moment, for the time being; **à tout ~** at any moment

momentané, ~e [mɔmɑ̃tane] temporary; **momentanément** *adv* for a short while

momie [mɔmi] *f* mummy

mon *m*, **ma** *f*, **mes** *pl* [mɔ̃, ma, me] my

Monaco [mɔnako]: **la principauté de ~** the principality of Monaco

monarchie [mɔnarʃi] *f* monarchy; **monarque** *m* monarch

monastère [mɔnastɛr] *m* monastery

monceau [mõso] *m* (*pl* -x) pile

mondain, ~e [mõdɛ̃, -ɛn] *soirée, vie* society *atr*; **elle est très ~** she's a bit of a socialite; **mondanités** *fpl* social niceties

monde [mõd] *m* world; *gens* people *pl*; **tout le ~** everybody, everyone; **dans le ~ entier** in the whole world, all over the world; **l'autre ~** the next world; **le beau ~** the beautiful people; **homme *m* du ~** man of the world; **mettre au ~** bring into the world

mondial, ~e [mõdjal] (*mpl* -aux) world *atr*, global; **mondialement** *adv*: **~ connu** known worldwide; **mondialisation** *f* globalization

monégasque [mɔnegask] **1** *adj* of / from Monaco, Monacan **2** *m/f* **Monégasque** Monacan

monétaire [mɔnetɛr] monetary; *marché* money *atr*

moniteur, -trice [mɔnitœr, -tris] *m/f* instructor **2** *m* INFORM monitor

monnaie [mɔnɛ] *f* (*pièces*) change; (*moyen d'échange*) money; (*unité monétaire*) currency; **une pièce de ~** a coin; **~ forte** hard currency; **~ unique** single currency

monologue [mɔnɔlɔg] *m* monolog, *Br* monologue

mononucléose [mɔnɔnykleoz] *f*: **~ infectieuse** glandular fever

monoparental, ~e [mɔnɔparɑ̃tal] single-parent

monoplace [mɔnɔplas] *m & adj* single-seater

monopole [mɔnɔpɔl] *m* monopoly; **monopoliser** ⟨1a⟩ monopolize

monospace [mɔnɔspas] *m* people carrier, MPV

monotone [mɔnɔtɔn] monotonous; **monotonie** *f* monotony

monseigneur [mõsɛɲœr] *m* monsignor

monsieur [məsjø] *m* (*pl* messieurs [mesjø]) *dans lettre* Dear Sir; **bonjour ~** good morning; **~!** sir!; *Br* excuse me!; **Monsieur Durand** Mr Durand; **bonsoir mesdames et messieurs** good evening, ladies and gentlemen

monstre [mõstr] **1** *m* monster (*aussi fig*) **2** *adj* colossal; **monstrueux, -euse** (*géant*) colossal; (*abominable*) monstrous; **monstruosité** *f* (*crime*) monstrosity

mont [mõ] *m* mount; **par ~s et par vaux** up hill and down dale

montage [mõtaʒ] *m* TECH assembly; *d'un film* editing; *d'une photographie* montage; ÉL connecting

montagnard, ~e [mõtaɲar, -d] **1** *adj* mountain *atr* **2** *m/f* mountain dweller; **montagne** *f* mountain; **à la ~** in the mountains; **~s russes** roller coaster *sg*; **en haute ~** in the mountains; **montagneux, -euse** mountainous

montant, ~e [mõtã, -t] **1** *adj robe* high-necked; *mouvement* upward **2** *m somme* amount; *d'un lit* post

monte-charge [mõtʃarʒ] *m* (*pl inv*) hoist

montée [mõte] *f sur montagne* ascent; (*pente*) slope; *de l'eau, des prix, de la température* rise

monter [mõte] ⟨1a⟩ **1** *v/t montagne* climb; *escalier* climb, go / come up; *valise* take / bring up; *machine, échafaudage, étagère* assemble, put together; *tente* put up, erect; *pièce de théâtre* put on, stage; *film, émission* edit; *entreprise, société* set up; *cheval* ride; *diamant, rubis etc* mount **2** *v/i* (*aux être*) come / go upstairs; *d'un avion, d'une route, d'une voiture* climb;

des prix climb, rise, go up; *d'un baromètre, fleuve* rise; **~ dans** *avion, train* get on; *voiture* get in(to); **monte dans ta chambre!** go up to your room!; **~ à bord** go on board, board, **~ en grade** be promoted; **~ à cheval** ride **3**: **se ~ à** *de frais* amount to

monteur, -euse [mõtœr, -øz] *m/f film*, TV editor

montgolfière [mõgɔlfjɛr] *f* balloon

monticule [mõtikyl] *m* (*tas*) heap, pile

montre [mõtr] *f* (wrist)watch; **faire ~ de qch** (*faire preuve de*) show sth; **montre-bracelet** *f* wristwatch

Montréal [mõreal] Montreal

montrer [mõtre] ⟨1a⟩ show; **~ qn / qch du doigt** point at s.o. / sth; **se ~** show o.s.

monture [mõtyr] *f* (*cheval*) mount; *de lunettes* frame; *d'un diamant* setting

monument [mɔnymã] *m* monument; *commémoratif* memorial; **monumental, ~e** monumental

moquer [mɔke] ⟨1m⟩: **se ~ de** (*railler*) make fun of, laugh at; (*dédaigner*) not care about; (*tromper*) fool; **moquerie** *f* mockery

moquette [mɔkɛt] *f* wall-to-wall carpet

moqueur, -euse [mɔkœr, -øz] **1** *adj* mocking **2** *m/f* mocker

moral, ~e [mɔral] **1** *adj* (*mpl* -aux) moral; *souffrance, santé* spiritual; **personne f ~e** JUR legal entity **2** *m* morale **3** *f* morality, morals *pl*; *d'une histoire* moral; **moralisateur, -trice** moralistic, sanctimonious; **moralité** *f* morality

moratoire [mɔratwar] *m* moratorium

morbide [mɔrbid] morbid

morceau [mɔrso] *m* (*pl* -x) piece (*aussi* MUS); *d'un livre* extract, passage

morceler [mɔrsəle] ⟨1c⟩ divide up, parcel up; **morcellement** *m* division

mordant, ~e [mɔrdã, -t] biting; *fig* biting, scathing

mordiller [mɔrdije] ⟨1a⟩ nibble

mordre [mɔrdr] ⟨4a⟩ bite; *d'un acide* eat into; **~ à** *fig* take to

mordu, ~e [mɔrdy] *m/f F* fanatic; **un ~ de sport** a sports fanatic

morfondre [mɔrfõdr] ⟨4a⟩: **se ~** mope; (s'ennuyer) be bored

morgue [mɔrg] f endroit mortuary, morgue

moribond, ~e [mɔribõ, -d] dying

morille [mɔrij] f BOT morel

morne [mɔrn] gloomy

morose [mɔroz] morose; **morosité** f moroseness

morphine [mɔrfin] f morphine

mors [mɔr] m bit

morse[1] [mɔrs] m ZO walrus

morse[2] [mɔrs] m morse code

morsure [mɔrsyr] f bite

mort[1] [mɔr] f death (aussi fig); **à ~** lutte to the death

mort[2], **~e** [mɔr, -t] **1** adj dead; eau stagnant; yeux lifeless; membre numb; **ivre ~** dead drunk; **~ de fatigue** dead tired; **être ~ de rire** F die laughing; **nature** f **~e** still life **2** m/f dead man; dead woman; **les ~s** the dead pl

mortalité [mɔrtalite] f mortality; **taux** m **de ~** death rate, mortality

mortel, ~le [mɔrtɛl] mortal; blessure, dose, maladie fatal; péché deadly

morte-saison [mɔrtəsezõ] f (pl mortes-saisons) off-season

mortier [mɔrtje] m mortar (aussi CUIS, MIL)

mort-né, ~e [mɔrne] (pl mort-nés) still-born

morue [mɔry] f cod

morve [mɔrv] f snot F, nasal mucus; **morveux, -euse** m/f F squirt F

mosaïque [mozaik] f mosaic

Moscou [mɔsku] Moscow

mosquée [mɔske] f mosque

mot [mo] m word; (court message) note; **bon ~** witty remark, witticism; **~ clé** key word; **~ de passe** password; **~s croisés** crossword sg; **gros ~** rude word, swearword; **~ à ~** word for word; traduction literal; **~ pour ~** word for word; **à ~s couverts** in a roundabout way; **au bas ~** at least; **sans ~ dire** without (saying) a word; **en un ~** in a word; **avoir le dernier ~** have the last word; **prendre qn au ~** take s.o. at his / her word

motard [mɔtar] m motorcyclist, biker; de la gendarmerie motorcycle policeman

motel [mɔtɛl] m motel

moteur, -trice [mɔtœr, -tris] **1** adj TECH arbre drive; force driving; ANAT motor; **à quatre roues motrices** voiture with four wheel drive **2** m TECH engine; fig: personne qui inspire driving force (**de** behind); **~ de recherche** INFORM search engine

motif [mɔtif] m motive, reason; (forme) pattern; MUS theme, motif; **en peinture** motif

motion [mosjõ] f POL motion; **~ de censure** motion of censure

motivation [mɔtivasjõ] f motivation; **motiver** ⟨1a⟩ personne motivate; (expliquer) be the reason for, prompt; (justifier par des motifs) give a reason for

moto [mɔto] f motorbike, motorcycle; **faire de la ~** ride one's motorbike

motocyclette [mɔtosiklɛt] f moped; **motocycliste** m/f motorcyclist

motoriser [mɔtorize] ⟨1a⟩ mechanize; **je suis motorisé** F I have a car

motte [mɔt] f de terre clump; **~ de gazon** turf

mou, molle [mu, mɔl] soft; personne spineless; caractère, résistance weak, feeble

mouchard, ~e [muʃar, -d] m/f F informer, grass F; **moucharder** ⟨1a⟩ F inform on, grass on F

mouche [muʃ] f fly; **faire ~** hit the bull's eye (aussi fig)

moucher [muʃe] ⟨1a⟩: **se ~** blow one's nose

moucheron [muʃrõ] m gnat

moucheter [muʃte] ⟨1c⟩ speckle

mouchoir [muʃwar] m handkerchief, hanky F

moudre [mudr] ⟨4y⟩ grind

moue [mu] f pout; **faire la ~** pout

mouette [mwɛt] f seagull

mouffette [mufɛt] f skunk

moufle [mufl] f mitten

mouillé, ~e [muje] wet; (humide) damp; **mouiller** ⟨1a⟩ **1** v/t wet; (hu-

mecter) dampen; *liquide* water down **2** *v/i* MAR anchor

moule [mul] **1** *m* mold, *Br* mould; CUIS tin **2** *f* ZO mussel; **mouler** ⟨1a⟩ mold, *Br* mould; **~ qch sur qch** *fig* model sth on sth

moulin [mulɛ̃] *m* mill; **~ (à vent)** windmill; **~ à café** coffee grinder; **~ à paroles** F wind-bag F; **~ à poivre** peppermill; **moulu, ~e 1** *p/p* → **moudre 2** *adj* ground

moulure [mulyr] *f* molding, *Br* moulding

mourant, ~e [murɑ̃, -t] dying; **mourir** ⟨2k⟩ *(aux être)* die (de of); **~ de froid** freeze to death; **~ de faim** die of hunger, starve

moussant, ~e [musɑ̃, -t]: **bain ~** foam bath; **mousse** *f* foam; BOT moss; CUIS mousse; **~ à raser** shaving foam; **mousser** ⟨1a⟩ lather; **mousseux, -euse 1** *adj* foamy **2** *m* sparkling wine

moustache [mustaʃ] *f* mustache, *Br* moustache

moustique [mustik] *m* mosquito

moutarde [mutard] *f* mustard

mouton [mutɔ̃] *m* sheep *(aussi fig)*; *viande* mutton; *fourrure* sheepskin; **revenons-en à nos ~s** *fig* let's get back to the subject

mouvant, ~e [muvɑ̃, -t]: **sables** *mpl* **~s** quicksand *sg*; **terrain** *m* **~** uncertain ground *(aussi fig)*

mouvement [muvmɑ̃] *m* movement *(aussi* POL, MUS *etc)*; *trafic* traffic; **en ~** moving; **mouvementé, ~e** *existence*, *voyage* eventful; *récit* lively

mouvoir [muvwar] ⟨3d⟩: **se ~** move

moyen, ~ne [mwajɛ̃, -ɛn] **1** *adj* average; *classe* middle; **Moyen Âge** *m* Middle Ages *pl*; **Moyen-Orient** *m* Middle East **2** *m* *(façon, méthode)* means *sg*; *(argent)* means *pl*; *(capacités intellectuelles)* faculties; **au ~ de, par le ~ de** by means of; **vivre au-dessus de ses ~s** live beyond one's means **3** *f* average; *statistique* mean; **en ~ne** on average

moyenâgeux, -euse [mwajɛnɑʒø, -z] medieval

moyennant [mwajɛnɑ̃] for

moyeu [mwajø] *m* hub

MST [emɛste] *f abr* (= **maladie sexuellement transmissible**) STD (= sexually transmitted disease)

Mt *abr* (= **Mont**) Mt (= Mount)

mucus [mykys] *m* mucus

muer [mɥe] ⟨1a⟩ *d'un oiseau* molt, *Br* moult; *d'un serpent* shed its skin; *de voix* break

muet, ~te [mɥɛ, -t] dumb; *fig* silent

mufle [myfl] *m* muzzle; *fig* F boor

mugir [myʒir] ⟨2a⟩ moo; *du vent* moan; **mugissement** *m* mooing; *du vent* moaning

muguet [mygɛ] *m* lily of the valley

mule [myl] *f* mule; **mulet** *m* mule

mulot [mylo] *m* field mouse

multicolore [myltikɔlɔr] multicolored, *Br* multicoloured

multiculturel, ~le [myltikyltyrɛl] multicultural

multimédia [myltimedja] *m & adj* multimedia

multinational, ~e [myltinasjɔnal] **1** *adj* multinational **2** *f*: **multinationale** multinational

multiple [myltipl] many; *(divers)* multifaceted; **multiplication** *f* MATH multiplication; **la ~ de** *(augmentation)* the increase in the number of; **multiplicité** *f* multiplicity; **multiplier** ⟨1a⟩ MATH multiply; **~ les erreurs** make one mistake after another; **se ~ d'une espèce** multiply

multiracial, ~e [myltirasjal] multiracial

multirisque [myltirisk] *assurance* all-risks

multitude [myltityd] *f*: **une ~ de** a host of; **la ~** *péj* the masses *pl*

multiusages [myltiyzaʒ] versatile

municipal, ~e [mynisipal] *(mpl -aux)* town *atr*, municipal; *bibliothèque*, *piscine* public; **municipalité** *f* *(commune)* municipality; *conseil* town council

munir [mynir] ⟨2a⟩: **~ de** fit with; *personne* provide with; **se ~ de qch** *d'un parapluie*, *de son passeport* take sth

munitions [mynisjɔ̃] *fpl* ammunition

M

sg

mur [myr] *m* wall; *mettre qn au pied du ~* have s.o. with his / her back against the wall

mûr, **~e** [myr] ripe

muraille [myrɑj] *f* wall

mural, **~e** [myrɑl] *m* (*mpl* -aux) wall *atr*

mûre [myr] *f* BOT *des ronces* blackberry; *d'un mûrier* mulberry

murer [myre] ⟨1a⟩ *enclos* wall in; *porte* wall up

mûrier [myrje] *m* mulberry (tree)

mûrir [myrir] ⟨2a⟩ ripen

murmure [myrmyr] *m* murmur; **murmurer** ⟨1a⟩ (*chuchoter, se plaindre*) murmur; (*médire*) talk

muscade [myskad] *f*: *noix* (*de*) ~ nutmeg

muscadet [myskadɛ] *m* muscadet

muscat [myska] *m raisin* muscatel grape; *vin* muscatel wine

muscle [myskl] *m* muscle; **musclé**, **~e** muscular; *politique* tough; **musculaire** muscle *atr*; **musculation** *f* body-building

muse [myz] *f* muse

museau [myzo] *m* (*pl* -x) muzzle

musée [myze] *m* museum

museler [myzle] ⟨1c⟩ muzzle (*aussi fig*); **muselière** *f* muzzle

musical, **~e** [myzikal] (*mpl* -aux) musical; **musicien**, **~ne 1** *adj* musical

2 *m/f* musician; **musique** *f* music; **~** *de chambre* chamber music; **~** *de fond* piped music

must [mœst] *m* must

musulman, **~e** [myzylmɑ̃, -an] *m/f* & *adj* Muslim

mutation [mytasjõ] *f* change; BIOL mutation; *d'un fonctionnaire* transfer, relocation; **muter** ⟨1a⟩ *fonctionnaire* transfer, relocate

mutilation [mytilasjõ] *f* mutilation; **mutiler** ⟨1a⟩ mutilate

mutinerie [mytinri] *f* mutiny

mutisme [mytism] *m fig* silence

mutuel, **~le** [mytɥɛl] mutual

myope [mjɔp] shortsighted, myopic *fml*; **myopie** *f* shortsightedness, myopia *fml*

myosotis [mjɔzɔtis] *m* forget-me-not

myrtille [mirtij] *f* bilberry

mystère [mistɛr] *m* mystery; **mystérieusement** *adv* mysteriously; **mystérieux**, **-euse** mysterious

mysticisme [mistisism] *m* mysticism

mystifier [mistifje] ⟨1a⟩ fool, take in

mystique [mistik] **1** *adj* mystical **2** *m/f* mystic **3** *f* mystique

mythe [mit] *m* myth; **mythique** mythical; **mythologie** *f* mythology; **mythologique** mythological

mythomane [mitɔman] *m/f* pathological liar

n' [n] → **ne**

nabot [nabo] *m péj* midget

nacelle [nasɛl] *f d'un ballon* basket

nacre [nakr] *f* mother-of-pearl

nage [naʒ] *f* swimming; *style* stroke; *~* **sur le dos** backstroke; *~* **libre** freestyle; *traverser une rivière à la ~* swim across a river; *être en ~ fig* be soaked in sweat

nageoire [naʒwar] *f* fin

nager [naʒe] ⟨1l⟩ **1** *v/i* swim **2** *v/t*: *la* **brasse** do the breaststroke; **nageur**, **-euse** *m/f* swimmer

naguère [nagɛr] *adv* formerly

naïf, **naïve** [naif, naiv] naive

nain, **~e** [nɛ̃, nɛn] *m/f* & *adj* dwarf

naissance [nɛsɑ̃s] *f* birth (*aussi fig*); **date** *f* **de ~** date of birth; **donner ~** **à** give birth to; *fig* give rise to

naître [nɛtr] ⟨4g⟩ (*aux être*) be born

(aussi fig); **je suis née en 1968** I was born in 1968; **faire ~** *sentiment* give rise to

naïvement [naivmã] *adv* naively; **naïveté** *f* naivety

nana [nana] *f* F chick F, girl

nanti, ~e [nãti] **1** *adj* well-off, rich; **~ de** provided with **2** *mpl* **les ~s** the rich *pl*; **nantir** ⟨2a⟩ provide (**de** with)

nappe [nap] *f* tablecloth; GÉOL *de gaz, pétrole* layer; **~ d'eau** (**souterraine**), **~ phréatique** water table; **napperon** *m* mat

narcodollars [narkɔdɔlar] *mpl* drug money *sg*

narcotique [narkɔtik] *m* & *adj* narcotic

narguer [narge] ⟨1m⟩ taunt

narine [narin] *f* nostril

narquois, ~e [narkwa, -z] taunting

narrateur, -trice [naratœr, -tris] *m/f* narrator; **narratif, -tive** narrative; **narration** *f* narration

nasal, ~e [nazal] (*mpl* -aux) **1** *adj* nasal **2** *f*: **nasale** nasal; **nasaliser** ⟨1a⟩ nasalize; **nasillard, ~e** nasal

natal, ~e [natal] (*mpl* -aux) *pays, région etc* of one's birth, native; **natalité** *f*: (**taux** *m* **de**) **~** birth rate

natation [natasjõ] *f* swimming; **faire de la ~** swim

natif, -ive [natif, -v] native

nation [nasjõ] *f* nation; **les Nations Unies** the United Nations

national, ~e [nasjɔnal] (*mpl* -aux) **1** *adj* national; **route** *f* **~e** highway **2** *mpl*: **nationaux** nationals **3** *f* highway; **nationalisation** *f* nationalization; **nationaliser** ⟨1a⟩ nationalize; **nationalisme** *m* nationalism; **nationaliste 1** *adj* nationalist; *péj* nationalistic **2** *m/f* nationalist; **nationalité** *f* nationality; **de quelle ~ est-elle?** what nationality is she?

nativité [nativite] *f* ART, REL Nativity

natte [nat] *f* (*tapis*) mat; *de cheveux* braid, plait

naturalisation [natyralizasjõ] *f* naturalization; **naturaliser** ⟨1a⟩ naturalize

nature [natyr] **1** *adj yaourt* plain; *thé,*

café without milk or sugar; *personne* natural **2** *f* nature; *genre, essence* kind, nature; **être artiste de ~** be a natural artist, be an artist by nature; **de ~ à faire qch** likely to do sth; **~ morte** ART still life; **naturel, ~le 1** *adj* natural **2** *m* (*caractère*) nature; (*spontanéité*) naturalness; **naturellement** *adv* naturally

naufrage [nofraʒ] *m* shipwreck; **faire ~** be shipwrecked; **naufragé, ~e** person who has been shipwrecked

nauséabond, ~e [nozeabõ, -d] nauseating, disgusting; **nausée** *f* nausea (*aussi fig*); **j'ai la ~** I'm nauseous, *Br* I feel sick; **~s du matin** morning sickness *sg*; **nauséeux, -euse** nauseous

nautique [notik] nautical; *ski* water *atr*; **nautisme** *m* water sports and sailing

naval, ~e [naval] (*mpl* -als) naval; *construction* ship *atr*; **chantier** *m* **~** shipyard

navet [nave] *m* rutabaga, *Br* swede; *fig* turkey F, *Br* flop

navette [navet] *f* shuttle; **faire la ~** shuttle backward and forward; **~ spatiale** space shuttle

navigable [navigabl] navigable; **navigant**: **le personnel ~** the navigation crew; **navigateur** *m* AVIATT navigator; MAR sailor; INFORM browser; **navigation** *f* sailing; (*pilotage*) navigation; **~ aérienne** air travel; **~ spatiale** space travel; **naviguer** ⟨1m⟩ *d'un navire, marin* sail; *d'un avion* fly; (*conduire*) navigate; INFORM navigate; **~ sur Internet** surf the Net

navire [navir] *m* ship; **~ de guerre** battleship

navrant, ~e [navrã, -t] distressing, upsetting; **navré, ~e**: **je suis ~** I am so sorry

ne [n(ə)] ◊: **je n'ai pas d'argent** I don't have any money, I have no money; **je ~ comprends pas** I don't understand, I do not understand; **afin de ~ pas l'oublier** so as not to forget

◊: **~ ... guère** hardly; **~ ... jamais**

never; ~ ... **personne** nobody; ~ ...
plus no longer; not any more; ~ ...
que only; ~ ... **rien** nothing; *voir aussi*
guère, jamais etc
◊: **à moins que je ~ lui parle** (*subj*)
unless I talk to him; **avant qu'il ~**
meure (*subj*) before he dies

né, **~e** [ne] **1** *p/p de* **naître 2** *adj* born;
~e Lepic née Lepic

néanmoins [neɑ̃mwɛ̃] *adv* nevertheless

néant [neɑ̃] *m* nothingness

nébuleux, **-euse** [nebylø, -z] cloudy;
fig hazy; **nébulosité** *f* cloudiness; *fig*
haziness

nécessaire [neseser] **1** *adj* necessary
2 *m* necessary; **le strict ~** the bare
minimum; **~ de toilette** toiletries *pl*
nécessité [nesesite] *f* need, necessity;
~s necessities; **par ~** out of necessity;
nécessiter ⟨1a⟩ require, necessi-
tate; **nécessiteux**, **-euse** needy

nécrologie [nekrɔlɔʒi] *f* deaths column, obituaries *pl*

néerlandais, **~e** [neɛrlɑ̃dɛ, -z] **1** *adj*
Dutch **2** *m langue* Dutch **3** *m/f* **Néer-**
landais, **~e** Dutchman; Dutchwoman

nef [nɛf] *f* nave

néfaste [nefast] harmful

négatif, **-ive** [negatif, -iv] **1** *adj* negative **2** *m* negative; **négation** *f* nega-
tion; GRAM negative

négligé [negliʒe] *adj travail* careless,
sloppy; *tenue* untidy; *épouse, enfant*
neglected **2** *f* negligee; **négligeable**
negligible; **négligence** *f* negligence,
carelessness; *d'une épouse, d'un enfant* neglect; (*nonchalance*) casualness; **négligent**, **~e** careless, negligent; *parent* negligent; *geste* casual;
négliger ⟨1l⟩ *personne, vêtements, intérêts* neglect; *occasion* miss; *avis* disregard; **~ de faire qch** fail to do sth
négoce [negɔs] *m* trade

négociable [negɔsjabl] negotiable
négociant [negɔsjɑ̃] *m* merchant
négociateur, **-trice** [negɔsjatœr,
-tris] *m/f* negotiator; **négociation** *f*
negotiation; **négocier** ⟨1a⟩ negotiate

négrier, **-ère** [negrije, -er] *m/f* F slave-
driver

neige [nɛʒ] *f* snow; **neiger** ⟨1l⟩ snow;
neigeux, **-euse** snowy

nénuphar [nenyfar] *m* BOT waterlily

néon [neɔ̃] *m* neon

nerf [nɛr] *m* nerve; (*vigueur*) energy,
verve; **être à bout de ~s** be at the
end of one's tether

nerveusement [nɛrvøzmɑ̃] *adv* ner-
vously; **nerveux**, **-euse** nervous; (*vigoureux*) full of energy; AUTO re-
sponsive; **nervosité** *f* nervousness

n'est-ce pas [nɛspa]: **il fait beau**, **~?**
it's a fine day, isn't it?; **tu la connais**,
~? you know her, don't you?

net, **~te** [nɛt] **1** *adj* (*propre*) clean;
(*clair*) clear; *différence, amélioration*
distinct; COMM net **2** *adv* (*aussi* **net-**
tement) *tué* outright; *refuser* flatly;
parler plainly

nétiquette [netiket] *f* netiquette

netteté [nɛtte] *f* cleanliness; (*clarté*)
clarity

nettoyage [netwajaʒ] *m* cleaning; **~**
ethnique ethnic cleansing; **~ de**
printemps spring-cleaning; **~ à sec**
dry cleaning; **nettoyer** ⟨1h⟩ clean;
F (*ruiner*) clean out F; **~ à sec** dry-
clean

neuf[1] [nœf, *avec liaison* nœv] nine; →
trois

neuf[2], **neuve** [nœf, nœv] new; **refaire**
à ~ maison etc renovate; *moteur* recondition, rebuild; **quoi de ~?**
what's new?, what's happening?

neurochirurgie [nørɔʃiryrʒi] *f* brain
surgery; **neurochirurgien**, **~ne** *m/f*
brain surgeon

neurologie [nørɔlɔʒi] *f* neurology;
neurologue *m/f* neurologist

neutraliser [nøtralize] ⟨1a⟩ neutra-
lize; **neutralité** *f* neutrality

neutre [nøtr] neutral; GRAM neuter

neuvième [nœvjɛm] ninth

neveu [n(ə)vø] (*pl* -x) *m* nephew

névralgie [nevralʒi] *f* MÉD neuralgia;
névralgique MÉD neuralgic

névrose *f* PSYCH neurosis; **névrosé**,
~e *m/f* neurotic

nez [ne] *m* nose; **avoir du ~** have a

good sense of smell; *fig* have a sixth sense; *raccrocher au ~ de qn* hang up on s.o.; *au ~ et à la barbe de qn* (right) under s.o.'s nose

ni [ni] neither, nor; *~ ... ~* (*ne before verb*) neither ... nor; *je n'ai ~ intérêt ~ désir* I have neither interest nor inclination; *sans sucre ~ lait* without sugar or milk, with neither sugar nor milk; *~ l'un ~ l'autre* neither (one nor the other); *~ moi non plus* neither *ou* nor do I, me neither

niais, *~e* [njɛ, -z] stupid; **niaiserie** *f* stupidity

niche [niʃ] *f dans un mur* niche; *d'un chien* kennel; **nicher** ⟨1a⟩ nest; *fig* F live

nicotine [nikɔtin] *f* nicotine

nid [ni] *m* nest; *~ d'amoureux fig* love nest; *~ de poule fig* pothole

nièce [njɛs] *f* niece

nier [nje] deny; *~ avoir fait qch* deny doing sth

nigaud, *~e* [nigo, -d] **1** *adj* silly **2** *m* idiot, fool

nippon, *~(n)e* [nipõ, -ɔn] Japanese

nitouche [nituʃ] *f* F: *sainte ~* hypocrite

niveau [nivo] *m* (*pl* -x) level; ÉDU standard; *outil* spirit level; *~ d'eau* water level; *~ de vie* standard of living

niveler [nivle] ⟨1c⟩ *terrain* grade, level; *fig: différences* even out; **nivellement** *m* grading, leveling, *Br* levelling; *fig* evening out

noble [nɔbl] noble; **noblesse** *f* nobility

noce [nɔs] *f wedding*; *faire la ~* F paint the town red; *~s d'argent* silver wedding anniversary *sg*

nocif, *-ive* [nɔsif, -iv] harmful, noxious; **nocivité** *f* harmfulness

noctambule [nɔktãbyl] *m/f* night owl

nocturne [nɔktyrn] **1** *adj* night *atr*; ZO nocturnal **2** *f*: *ouvert en ~* open till late; *le match sera joué en ~* it's going to be an evening match

Noël [nɔel] *m* Christmas; *joyeux ~!* Merry Christmas!; *le père ~* Santa Claus, *Br aussi* Father Christmas; *à*

~ at Christmas

nœud [nø] *m* knot (*aussi* MAR); (*ruban*) ribbon; *fig: d'un débat, problème* nub; *~ coulant* slipknot; *de bourreau* noose; *~ papillon* bow tie; *~ plat* sailor's knot, *Br* reef knot

noir, *~e* [nwar] **1** *adj* black; (*sombre*) dark; F (*ivre*) sozzled; *il fait ~* it's dark **2** *m* black; (*obscurité*) dark; *travail au ~* moonlighting; *travailler au ~* moonlight; **Noir** *m* black man

noirceur [nwarsœr] *f* blackness; **noircir** ⟨2a⟩ blacken

Noire [nwar] *f* black woman

noisetier [nwaztje] *m* hazel; **noisette 1** *f* hazelnut **2** *adj inv* hazelnut

noix [nwa] *f* walnut; *~ de coco* coconut

nom [nõ] *m* name; GRAM noun; *au ~ de qn* ou *Br* on behalf of s.o.; *du ~ de* by the name of; *~ déposé* registered trade mark; *~ de famille* surname, family name; *~ de guerre* pseudonym; *~ de jeune fille* maiden name

nombre [nõbr] *m* number; (*bon*) *~ de mes amis* a good many of my friends; *ils sont au ~ de trois* there are three in number; *être du ~ de ...* be one of the ...; *sans ~* countless; **nombreux**, *-euse* numerous, many; *famille* large

nombril [nõbri(l)] *m* navel; **nombrilisme** *m* navel-gazing

nominal, *~e* [nɔminal] (*mpl* -aux) *autorité, chef* nominal; *valeur* face *atr*; **nomination** *f* appointment; *à un prix* nomination

nommément [nɔmemã] *adv* by name; (*en particulier*) especially; **nommer** ⟨1a⟩ name, call; *à une fonction* appoint; *se ~* be called

non [nõ] no; *dire que ~* say no; *j'espère que ~* I hope not; *moi ~ plus* me neither; *et ~ sa sœur* and not her sister; *c'est normal, ~?* that's normal, isn't it?; *elle vient, ~?* she is coming, isn't she?; *~ que ...* (+ *subj*) not that ...

non-alcoolisé [nõnalkɔlize] non-alcoholic

nonante [nõnãt] *Belgique, Suisse* ninety

non-assistance f: **~ à personne en danger** failure to assist a person in danger (*a criminal offense in France*)

nonchalant, **~e** [nõʃalã, -t] nonchalant, casual

non-fumeur, **-euse** [nõfymœr, -øz] m/f non-smoker

non-intervention [nõnɛ̃tervãsjõ] f POL non-intervention

nonobstant [nɔnɔpstã] *prép* notwithstanding

non-polluant, **~e** [nõpɔlyã, -t] environmentally friendly, non-polluting

non-sens [nõsãs] m (pl inv) (absurdité) nonsense; *dans un texte* meaningless word

non-violence [nõvjɔlãs] f POL non-violence

nord [nɔr] **1** m north; **vent** m **du ~** north wind; **au ~ de** (to the) north of; **perdre le ~** fig F lose one's head **2** adj north; *hemisphère* northern; **côte** f **~** north ou northern coast

nord-africain, **~e** [nɔrdafrikɛ̃, -ɛn] **1** adj North-African **2** m/f Nord-Africain, **~e** North-African

nord-américain, **~e** [nɔramerikɛ̃, -ɛn] **1** adj North-American **2** m/f Nord-Américain, **~e** North-American

nord-est [nɔrɛst] m north-east

nordique [nɔrdik] Nordic

Nordiste [nɔrdist] m/f & adj HIST Unionist, Yankee

nord-ouest [nɔrwɛst] m north-west

normal, **~e** [nɔrmal] (mpl -aux) **1** adj normal **2** f: **inférieur / supérieur à la ~e** above / below average; **normalement** adv normally; **normalisation** f normalization; TECH standardization; **normalité** f normality

normand, **~e** [nɔrmã, -d] **1** adj Normandy atr **2** m/f Normand, **~e** Norman; **Normandie**: **la ~** Normandy

norme [nɔrm] f norm; TECH standard

Norvège [nɔrvɛʒ]: **la ~** Norway; **norvégien**, **~ne 1** adj Norwegian **2** m *langue* Norwegian **3** m/f Norvégien, **~ne** Norwegian

nos [no] → **notre**

nostalgie [nɔstalʒi] f nostalgia; **avoir la ~ de son pays** be homesick

notabilité [nɔtabilite] f VIP; notable

notable [nɔtabl] **1** adj noteworthy **2** m local worthy

notaire [nɔter] m notary

notamment [nɔtamã] adv particularly

notarié, **~e** [nɔtarje] notarized

notation [nɔtasjõ] f notation; (*note*) note; ÉDU grading, Br marking

note [nɔt] f note; à l'école grade, Br mark; (*facture*) check, Br bill; **prendre ~ de qch** note sth; **prendre des ~s** take notes; **~ de bas de page** footnote; **~ de frais** expense account; **~ de service** memo; **noter** ⟨1a⟩ (*écrire*) write down, take down; (*remarquer*) note; **notice** f note; (*mode d'emploi*) instructions pl

notification [nɔtifikasjõ] f notification; **notifier** ⟨1a⟩ v/t: **~ qch à qn** notify s.o. of sth

notion [nosjõ] f (*idée*) notion, concept; **~s** basics pl

notoire [nɔtwar] well-known; *criminel, voleur* notorious

notre [nɔtr], pl **nos** [no] our

nôtre [nɔtr]: **le, la ~**, **les ~s** ours

nouer [nwe] ⟨1a⟩ tie; *relations, amitié* establish; **noueux**, **-euse** gnarled

nougat [nuga] m nougat

nouilles [nuj] fpl noodles

nounou [nunu] f F nanny

nounours [nunurs] m teddy bear

nourrice [nuris] f childminder; **nourrir** ⟨2a⟩ feed; *fig: espoir, projet* nurture; **nourrissant** nourishing

nourrisson [nurisõ] m infant

nourriture [nurityr] f food

nous [nu] *pron personnel* ◊ *sujet* we; **à ~ deux ~ pourrons le faire** the two of us can do it, we can do it between the two of us

◊ *complément d'objet direct* us; **il ~ regarde** he is looking at us

◊ *complément d'objet indirect* (to) us; **donnez-le-~** give it to us; **il ~ a dit que ...** he told us that ...

◊ *emphatique*: **~**, **~ préférons ...** we prefer ...; **~ autres Français** we French

◊ *réfléchi*: **~ ~ sommes levés tôt ce**

matin we got up early this morning; ~ *aimons beaucoup* we love each other very much

nouveau, nouvelle (*m* **nouvel** *before a vowel or silent h; mpl* **nouveaux**) [nuvo, -ɛl] **1** *adj* new; **rien de** ~ nothing new; **de** *ou* **à** ~ again; ~ *venu, nouvelle venue* newcomer; **Nouvel An** *m* New Year('s); **Nouveau Monde** *m* New World; **Nouvelle--Angleterre** *f* New England; **Nouvelle-Orléans** New Orleans; **Nouvelle Zélande** *f* New Zealand **2** *m* **voilà du ~!** that's new! **2** *m/f* new person

nouveau-né, ~e [nuvone] **1** *adj* new-born **2** *m* (*pl* nouveau-nés) newborn baby

nouveauté [nuvote] *f* novelty

nouvelle [nuvɛl] *f* (*récit*) short story; *une ~ dans les médias* a piece of news

nouvelles [nuvɛl] *fpl* news *sg*

nouvellement [-mã] *adv* newly

novateur, -trice [nɔvatœr, -tris] **1** *adj* innovative **2** *m/f* innovator

novembre [nɔvãbr] *m* November

novice [nɔvis] **1** *m/f* novice, beginner; REL novice **2** *adj* inexperienced

noyade [nwajad] *f* drowning

noyau [nwajo] *m* (*pl* -x) pit, stone; BIOL, PHYS nucleus; *fig* (*groupe*) (small) group; **noyauter** ⟨1a⟩ POL infiltrate

noyer[1] [nwaje] ⟨1h⟩ drown; AUTO flood; *se* ~ drown; *se suicider* drown o.s.

noyer[2] [nwaje] *m arbre, bois* walnut

nu, ~e [ny] **1** *adj* naked; *plaine, arbre, bras, tête etc* bare **2** *m* ART nude

nuage [nɥaʒ] *m* cloud; *être dans les ~s fig* be daydreaming; **nuageux, -euse** cloudy

nuance [nɥãs] *f* shade; *fig* slight difference; (*subtilité*) nuance; **nuancé, ~e** subtle; **nuancer** ⟨1k⟩ qualify

nucléaire [nykleɛr] **1** *adj* nuclear **2** *m:*

le ~ nuclear power

nudisme [nydism] *m f* nudism; **nudiste** *m/f & adj* nudist; **nudité** *f* nudity

nues [ny] *fpl fig: porter aux* ~ praise to the skies; *tomber des* ~ be astonished

nuée [nɥe] *f d'insectes* cloud; *de journalistes* horde

nuire [nɥir] ⟨4c⟩: ~ *à* hurt, harm, be harmful to

nuisible [nɥizibl] harmful

nuit [nɥi] *f* night; *de* ~ night *atr; la ~, de* ~ *voyager* at night; ~ *blanche* sleepless night; *il fait* ~ (*noire*) it's (pitch) dark

nul, ~le [nyl] **1** *adj* no; (*non valable*) invalid; (*sans valeur*) hopeless; (*inexistant*) nonexistent, nil; ~ *le part* nowhere; *match m* ~ tie, draw **2** *pron* no-one; **nullement** *adv* not in the slightest *ou* the least; **nullité** *f* JUR invalidity; *fig* hopelessness; *personne* loser

numéraire [nymerɛr] *m* cash; **numéral, ~e** (*mpl* -aux) *adj & m* numeral; **numération** *f:* ~ *globulaire* blood count; **numérique** numerical; INFORM digital

numéro [nymero] *m* number; ~ *de compte* account number; ~ *de série* serial number; ~ *sortant* winning number; ~ *vert* toll-free number, *Br* Freefone number

numérotage [nymerɔtaʒ] *m* numbering; **numéroter** ⟨1a⟩ **1** *v/t* number **2** *v/i* TÉL dial

nu-pieds [nypje] *adj inv* barefoot

nuptial, ~e [nypsjal] (*mpl* -aux) wedding *atr; chambre* bridal; *messe* nuptial

nuque [nyk] *f* nape of the neck

nurse [nœrs] *f* nanny

nu-tête [nytɛt] *adj inv* bare-headed

nutritif, -ive [nytritif, -iv] nutritional; *aliment* nutritious; **nutrition** *f* nutrition; **nutritionniste** *m/f* nutritionist

nylon [nilõ] *m* nylon

N

O

oasis [ɔazis] *f* oasis

obéir [ɔbeir] ⟨2a⟩ obey; **~ à** obey

obéissance [ɔbeisɑ̃s] *f* obedience; **obéissant, ~e** obedient

obèse [ɔbɛz] obese; **obésité** *f* obesity

objecter [ɔbʒɛkte] ⟨1a⟩: **~ qch pour ne pas faire qch** give as a reason; **~ que** object that; **objecteur** *m*: **~ de conscience** conscientious objector

objectif, -ive [ɔbʒɛktif, -iv] **1** *adj* objective **2** *m* objective, aim; MIL objective; PHOT lens

objection [ɔbʒɛksjõ] *f* objection

objectivité [ɔbʒɛktivite] *f* objectivity

objet [ɔbʒɛ] *m* object; **de réflexions, d'une lettre** subject

obligation [ɔbligasjõ] *f* obligation; COMM bond; **être dans l'~ de faire qch** be obliged to do sth; **obligatoire** compulsory, obligatory

obligé, ~e [ɔbliʒe] obliged; **obligeance** *f* obligingness; **obligeant, ~e** obliging; **obliger** ⟨1l⟩ oblige; (*forcer*) compel, force; **~ qn à faire qch** compel *ou* force s.o. to do sth; **être obligé de faire qch** be obliged to do sth

oblique [ɔblik] oblique; **obliquer** ⟨1m⟩: **~ vers la droite / la gauche** veer (to the) left / right

oblitérer [ɔblitere] ⟨1f⟩ *timbre* cancel

oblong, oblongue [ɔblõ, -g] oblong

obscène [ɔpsɛn] obscene; **obscénité** *f* obscenity

obscur, ~e [ɔpskyr] obscure; *nuit, rue* dark; **obscurcir** ⟨2a⟩ darken; **s'~** grow dark, darken; **obscurcissement** *m* darkening; **obscurité** *f* obscurity; *de la nuit, d'une rue* darkness

obsédé, ~e [ɔpsede] *m/f* sex maniac; **obséder** ⟨1f⟩ obsess; **être ~ par** be obsessed by

obsèques [ɔpsɛk] *fpl* funeral *sg*

observateur, -trice [ɔpsɛrvatœr, -tris] *m/f* observer; **observation** *f* observation; (*remarque*) remark, observation; *d'une règle* observance; **observatoire** *m* observatory

observer [ɔpsɛrve] ⟨1a⟩ (*regarder*) watch, observe; *règle* observe; *changement, amélioration* notice; **faire ~ qch à qn** point sth out to s.o.

obsession [ɔpsesjõ] *f* obsession; **obsessionnel, ~le** obsessive

obstacle [ɔpstakl] *m* obstacle; SP hurdle; *pour cheval* fence, jump; **faire ~ à qch** stand in the way of sth

obstétricien, ~ne [ɔpstetrisjɛ̃, -ɛn] *m/f* obstetrician; **obstétrique** *f* obstetrics

obstination [ɔpstinasjõ] *f* obstinacy; **obstiné, ~e** obstinate; **obstiner** ⟨1a⟩: **s'~ à faire qch** persist in doing sth, be set on doing sth

obstruction [ɔpstryksjõ] *f* obstruction; *dans tuyau* blockage; **obstruer** ⟨1n⟩ obstruct, block

obtempérer [ɔptɑ̃pere] ⟨1f⟩: **~ à** obey

obtenir [ɔptønir] ⟨2h⟩ get, obtain; **obtention** *f* obtaining; **~ d'un diplôme** graduation

obturateur [ɔptyratœr] *m* PHOT shutter; **obturation** *f* sealing; *d'une dent* filling; **obturer** ⟨1a⟩ seal; *dent* fill

obtus, ~e [ɔpty, -z] MATH, *fig* obtuse

obus [ɔby] *m* MIL shell

occasion [ɔkazjõ] *f* opportunity; *marché* bargain; **d'~** second-hand; **à l'~** when the opportunity arises; **à l'~ de sa fête** on his name day; **en toute ~** all the time; **occasionnel, ~le** occasional; (*fortuit*) chance; **occasionner** ⟨1a⟩ cause

Occident [ɔksidɑ̃] *m*: **l'~** the West; **occidental, ~e** (*m / pl* -aux) **1** *adj* western **2** *m/f* **Occidental, ~e** westerner

occlusion [ɔklyzjõ] *f* MÉD blockage;

buccale occlusion

occulte [ɔkylt] occult

occupant, ~e [ɔkypɑ̃, -t] 1 *adj* occupying 2 *m* occupant; **occupation** *f* occupation; **occupé, ~e** *personne* busy; *pays, appartement* occupied; *chaise* taken; TÉL busy, *Br aussi* engaged; *toilettes* occupied, *Br* engaged; **occuper** ⟨1a⟩ occupy; *place* take up, occupy; *temps* fill, occupy; *personnel* employ; **s'~ de** *politique, littérature* take an interest in; *malade* look after; *organisation* deal with

occurrence [ɔkyrɑ̃s] *f*: **en l'~** as it happens

océan [ɔseɑ̃] *m* ocean; **océanographie** *f* oceanography

octante, ~e [ɔktɑ̃t] *Belgique, Suisse* eighty

octet [ɔktɛ] *m* INFORM byte

octobre [ɔktɔbr] *m* October

oculaire [ɔkylɛr] eye *atr*; **oculiste** *m/f* eye specialist

odeur [ɔdœr] *f* smell, odor, *Br* odour; *parfum* smell, scent; **mauvaise ~** bad smell; **~ corporelle** body odor, BO

odieux, -euse [ɔdjø, -z] hateful, odious

odorant, ~e [ɔdɔrɑ̃, -t] scented; **odorat** *m* sense of smell

œil [œj] *m* (*pl* **yeux** [jø]) eye; **à mes yeux** in my opinion, in my eyes; **à vue d'~** visibly; **avoir l'~** be sharp-eyed; **coup m d'~** glance, look; **avoir les yeux bleus** have blue eyes; **fermer les yeux sur qch** close one's eyes to sth, turn a blind eye to sth; **œillade** *f* glance, look; **œillères** *fpl* blinders, *Br* blinkers (*aussi fig*)

œillet [œjɛ] *m* BOT carnation; TECH eyelet

œsophage [ezɔfaʒ] *m* esophagus, *Br* œsophagus

œuf [œf] *m* (*pl* -s [ø]) egg; **~s brouillés** scrambled eggs; **~ à la coque** soft-boiled egg; **~ sur le plat** fried egg; **~ de Pâques** Easter egg; **dans l'~** *fig* in the bud

œuvre [œvr] 1 *f* work; **~ d'art** work of art; **se mettre à l'~** set to work; **mettre en ~** (*employer*) use; (*exécuter*) carry out, implement 2 *m* ART, *litté-*

rature works *pl*; **gros ~** TECH fabric

offense [ɔfɑ̃s] *f* (*insulte*) insult; (*péché*) sin; **offenser** ⟨1a⟩ offend; **s'~ de qch** take offense at sth *ou Br* offence at sth; **offensif, -ive** 1 *adj* offensive 2 *f* offensive

office [ɔfis] *m* (*charge*) office; (*bureau*) office, agency; REL service; **bons ~s** good offices; **d'~** automatically; **faire ~ de** act as

officiel, ~le [ɔfisjɛl] official

officier [ɔfisje] *m* officer; **~ de police** police officer

officieux, -euse [ɔfisjø, -z] semi-official

officinal, ~e [ɔfisinal] (*mpl* -aux) *plante* medicinal; **officine** *f* PHARM dispensary

offrande [ɔfrɑ̃d] *f* REL offering; **offre** *f* offer; **~ d'emploi** job offer; **offrir** ⟨2f⟩ offer; *cadeau* give; **~ à boire à qn** offer s.o. a drink; **s'~ qch** treat o.s. to sth

offusquer [ɔfyske] ⟨1m⟩ offend

ogive [ɔʒiv] *f* MIL head; ARCH *m* rib; **~ nucléaire** nuclear warhead

OGM [oʒeɛm] *m abr* (= **organisme génétiquement modifié**) GMO (= genetically modified organism)

oie [wa] *f* goose

oignon [ɔɲɔ̃] *m* onion; BOT bulb

oiseau [wazo] *m* (*pl* -x) bird; **à vol d'~** as the crow flies

oiseux, -euse [wazø, -z] idle

oisif, -ive [wazif, -iv] idle; **oisiveté** *f* idleness

oléoduc [ɔleɔdyk] *m* (oil) pipeline

olfactif, -ive [ɔlfaktif, -iv] olfactory

olive [ɔliv] *f* olive; **olivier** *m* olive (tree); *bois* olive (wood)

O.L.P. [oɛlpe] *f abr* (= **Organisation de libération palestinienne**) PLO (= Palestine Liberation Organization)

olympique [ɔlɛ̃pik] Olympic

ombrage [ɔ̃braʒ] *m* shade; **ombragé, ~e** shady

ombrageux, -euse [ɔ̃braʒø, -z] *cheval* skittish; *personne* touchy

ombre [ɔ̃br] *f* (*ombrage*) shade; (*projection de silhouette*) shadow (*aussi*

O

fig); *fig* (*anonymat*) obscurity; *de regret* hint, touch; **à l'~** in the shade; **être dans l'~ de qn** be in s.o.'s shadow, be overshadowed by s.o.; **ombrelle** *f* sunshade

omelette [ɔmlɛt] *f* omelet, *Br* omelette

omettre [ɔmetr] ⟨4p⟩ *détail, lettre* leave out, omit; **~ de faire qch** fail *ou* omit to do sth

omission [ɔmisjɔ̃] *f* omission

omnibus [ɔmnibys] *m*: (**train** *m*) **~** slow train

on [ɔ̃] (*après que, et, où, qui, si souvent* l'on) *pron personnel* ◇ (*nous*) we; **~ y a été hier** we went there yesterday; **~ est en retard** we're late ◇ (*tu, vous*) you; **alors, ~ s'amuse bien?** having fun? ◇ (*quelqu'un*) someone; **~ m'a dit que...** I was told that...; **a volé mon passeport** somebody has stolen my passport, my passport has been stolen ◇ (*eux, les gens*) they, people; **que pensera-t-~ d'un tel comportement?** what will they *ou* people think of such behavior? ◇ *autorités* they; **~ va démolir ...** they are going to demolish ... ◇ *indéterminé* you; **~ ne sait jamais** you never know, one never knows *fml*

oncle [ɔ̃kl] *m* uncle

onction [ɔ̃ksjɔ̃] *f* REL unction

onctueux, -euse [ɔ̃ktɥø, -z] smooth, creamy; *fig* smarmy F, unctuous

onde [ɔ̃d] *f* wave; **sur les ~s** RAD on the air; **~s courtes** short wave *sg*; **grandes ~s** long wave *sg*; **~s moyennes** medium wave *sg*

ondée [ɔ̃de] *f* downpour

on-dit [ɔ̃di] *m* (*pl inv*) rumor, *Br* rumour

ondoyer [ɔ̃dwaje] ⟨1h⟩ *du blés* sway

ondulation [ɔ̃dylasjɔ̃] *f de terrain* undulation; *de coiffure* wave; **ondulé, ~e** *cheveux* wavy; *tôle* corrugated; **onduler** ⟨1a⟩ *d'ondes* undulate; *de cheveux* be wavy; **onduleux, -euse** undulating; *rivière* winding

onéreux, -euse [ɔnerø, -z] expensive; **à titre ~** for a fee

ONG [ɔɛnʒe] *f abr* (= **Organisation non gouvernementale**) NGO (= non-governmental organization)

ongle [ɔ̃gl] *m* nail; ZO claw

onguent [ɔ̃gɑ̃] *m* cream, salve

O.N.U. [ɔny *ou* ɔeny] *f abr* (= **Organisation des Nations Unies**) UN (= United Nations)

onze [ɔ̃z] eleven; **le ~** the eleventh; → **trois**; **onzième** eleventh

O.P.A. [ɔpea] *f abr* (= **offre publique d'achat**) takeover bid

opale [ɔpal] *f* opal

opaque [ɔpak] opaque

OPEP [ɔpɛp] *f abr* (= **Organisation des pays exportateurs de pétrole**) OPEC (= Organization of Petroleum Exporting Countries)

opéra [ɔpera] *m* opera; *bâtiment* opera house

opérable [ɔperabl] MÉD operable

opérateur, -trice [ɔperatœr, -tris] *m/f* operator; *en cinéma* cameraman; FIN trader

opération [ɔperasjɔ̃] *f* operation; *action* working; FIN transaction; **opérationnel, ~le** MIL, TECH operational; **opératoire** MÉD *choc* post-operative; *bloc* operating; **opérer** ⟨1f⟩ **1** *v/t* MÉD operate on; (*produire*) make; (*exécuter*) implement, put in place **2** *v/i* MÉD operate; (*avoir effet*) work; (*procéder*) proceed; **se faire ~** have an operation

opérette [ɔperet] *f* operetta

ophtalmie [ɔftalmi] *f* MÉD ophthalmia; **ophtalmologiste**, **ophtalmologue** *m/f* ophthalmologist

opiner [ɔpine] ⟨1a⟩: **~ de la tête** *ou* **du bonnet** nod in agreement

opiniâtre [ɔpinjɑtr] stubborn; **opiniâtreté** *f* stubbornness

opinion [ɔpinjɔ̃] *f* opinion

opium [ɔpjɔm] *m* opium

opportun, ~e [ɔpɔrtœ̃ *ou* ɔpɔrtœ, -yn] opportune; *moment* right; **opportunisme** *m* opportunism; **opportuniste** *m/f* opportunist; **opportunité** *f* timeliness; (*occasion*) opportunity

orgueilleux

opposant, **~e** [ɔpozɑ̃, -t] **1** *adj* opposing **2** *m/f* opponent; **les ~s** the opposition *sg*; **opposé**, **~e 1** *adj maisons, pôles* opposite; *goûts, opinions* conflicting; **être ~ à qch** be opposed to sth **2** *m* opposite; **à l'~** in the opposite direction (**de** from); **à l'~ de qn** unlike s.o.; **opposer** ⟨1a⟩ *personnes, pays* bring into conflict; *argument* put forward; **s'~ à qn / à qch** oppose s.o. / sth; **opposition** *f* opposition; (*contraste*) contrast; **par ~ à** in contrast to, unlike

oppresser [ɔprese] ⟨1b⟩ oppress, weigh down; **oppresseur** *m* oppressor; **oppressif**, **-ive** *adj* oppressive; **oppression** *f* (*domination*) oppression

opprimer [ɔprime] ⟨1a⟩ oppress

opter [ɔpte] ⟨1a⟩: **~ pour** opt for

opticien, **~ne** [ɔptisjɛ̃, -ɛn] *m/f* optician

optimal, **~e** [ɔptimal] (*mpl* -aux) optimum; **optimisme** *m* optimism; **optimiste 1** *adj* optimistic **2** *m/f* optimist; **optimum** *m* optimum

option [ɔpsjɔ̃] *f* option

optique [ɔptik] **1** *adj nerf* optic; *verre* optical **2** *f science* optics; *fig* viewpoint

opulent, **~e** [ɔpylɑ̃, -t] (*riche*) wealthy; *poitrine* ample

or[1] [ɔr] *m* gold; **d'~**, **en ~** gold *atr*; **plaqué ~** gold-plated

or[2] [ɔr] *conj* now

oracle [ɔrakl] *m* oracle

orage [ɔraʒ] *m* storm (*aussi fig*); **orageux**, **-euse** stormy (*aussi fig*)

oraison [ɔrezɔ̃] *f* REL prayer; **~ funèbre** eulogy

oral, **~e** [ɔral] (*mpl* -aux) **1** *adj* oral **2** *m* oral (exam)

orange [ɔrɑ̃ʒ] **1** *f* orange **2** *adj inv* orange; **oranger** *m* orange tree

orateur, **-trice** [ɔratœr, -tris] *m/f* orator

orbital, **~e** [ɔrbital] (*mpl* -aux) *navigation spatiale* orbital

orbite [ɔrbit] *f* ANAT eyesocket; ASTR orbit (*aussi fig*)

orchestre [ɔrkestr] *m* orchestra; *de théâtre* orchestra, *Br* stalls *pl*

orchidée [ɔrkide] *f* BOT orchid

ordinaire [ɔrdiner] **1** *adj* ordinary **2** *m essence* regular; **comme à l'~** as usual; **d'~** ordinarily

ordinateur [ɔrdinatœr] *m* computer; **assisté par ~** computer-assisted

ordonnance [ɔrdɔnɑ̃s] *f* arrangement, layout; (*ordre*) order (*aussi* JUR); MÉD prescription; **ordonné**, **~e** tidy; **ordonner** ⟨1a⟩ *choses, pensées* organize; (*commander*) order; MÉD prescribe

ordre [ɔrdr] *m* order; **~ du jour** agenda; **~ établi** established order, status quo; **par ~ alphabétique** in alphabetical order, alphabetically; **de l'~ de** in the order of; **de premier ~** first-rate; **en ~** in order; **mettre en ~ pièce** tidy (up); **jusqu'à nouvel ~** until further notice

ordures [ɔrdyr] *fpl* (*détritus*) garbage *sg*, *Br* rubbish *sg*; *fig* filth *sg*; **ordurier**, **-ère** filthy

oreille [ɔrɛj] *f* ANAT ear; *d'un bol* handle; **être dur d'~** be hard of hearing

oreiller [ɔreje] *m* pillow

oreillons [ɔrejɔ̃] *mpl* MÉD mumps *sg*

ores: **d'~ et déjà** [dɔrzedeʒa] already

orfèvre [ɔrfɛvr] *m* goldsmith

organe [ɔrgan] *m* organ; (*voix, porte-parole*) voice; *d'un mécanisme* part; **~s génitaux** genitals; **~s vitaux** vital organs

organigramme [ɔrganigram] *m* organization chart; **~ de production** production flowchart

organique [ɔrganik] organic

organisateur, **-trice** [ɔrganizatœr, -tris] *m/f* organizer; **organisation** *f* organization; **organiser** ⟨1a⟩ organize; **s'~ d'une personne** organize o.s., get organized; **organiseur** *m* INFORM personal organizer

organisme [ɔrganism] *m* organism; ANAT system; (*organisation*) organization, body

organiste [ɔrganist] *m/f* organist

orgasme [ɔrgasm] *m* orgasm

orge [ɔrʒ] *f* BOT barley

orgue [ɔrg] *m* (*pl f*) organ

orgueil [ɔrgœj] *m* pride; **orgueilleux**,

O

-euse proud

Orient [ɔrjɑ̃] m: **l'~** the East; *Asie* the East, the Orient; **oriental, ~e** (*mpl* -aux) **1** *adj* east, eastern; *d'Asie* eastern, Oriental **2** *m/f* **Oriental, ~e** Oriental

orientation [ɔrjɑ̃tasjɔ̃] f direction; *d'une maison* exposure; **orienté, ~e** (*engagé*) biassed; **être ~ à l'est** face east; **orienter** ⟨1a⟩ orient, *Br* orientate; (*diriger*) direct; **s'~** get one's bearings; **s'~ vers** fig go in for; **s'~ à gauche** lean to the left

orifice [ɔrifis] m TECH opening

originaire [ɔriʒinɛr] original; **être ~ de** come from

original, ~e [ɔriʒinal] (*mpl* -aux) **1** *adj* original; *péj* eccentric **2** *m ouvrage* original; *personne* eccentric; **originalité** f originality

origine [ɔriʒin] f origin; **à l'~** originally; **d'~ française** of French origin, French in origin; **avoir son ~ dans qch** have its origins in sth; **originel, ~le** original; **péché** m ~ REL original sin

orme [ɔrm] m BOT elm

ornement [ɔrnəmɑ̃] m ornament; **ornemental, ~e** (*mpl* -aux) ornamental, decorative; **ornementer** ⟨1a⟩ ornament

orner [ɔrne] ⟨1a⟩ decorate (**de** with)

ornière [ɔrnjɛr] f rut

ornithologie [ɔrnitɔlɔʒi] f ornithology

orphelin, ~e [ɔrfəlɛ̃, -in] m/f orphan; **orphelinat** m orphanage

orteil [ɔrtɛj] m toe

orthodoxe [ɔrtɔdɔks] orthodox

orthographe [ɔrtɔgraf] f spelling

orthopédique [ɔrtɔpedik] orthopedic; **orthopédiste** m/f orthopedist

orthophonie [ɔrtɔfɔni] f speech therapy; **orthophoniste** m/f speech therapist

ortie [ɔrti] f BOT nettle

os [ɔs; *pl* o] m bone; **trempé jusqu'aux ~** F soaked to the skin

O.S. [ɔɛs] m abr (= **ouvrier spécialisé**) semi-skilled worker

oscillation [ɔsilasjɔ̃] f PHYS oscillation; *fig* swing; **osciller** ⟨1a⟩ PHYS

oscillate; *d'un pendule* swing; **~ entre** fig waver ou hesitate between

osé, ~e [oze] daring

oseille [ozɛj] f BOT sorrel

oser [oze] ⟨1a⟩: **~ faire** dare to do

osier [ozje] m BOT osier; **en ~** wicker

ossature [ɔsatyr] f skeleton, bone structure

ossements [ɔsmɑ̃] mpl bones; **osseux, -euse** ANAT bone atr; *visage, mains* bony

ostensible [ɔstɑ̃sibl] evident; **ostentation** [ɔstɑ̃tasjɔ̃] f ostentation

otage [ɔtaʒ] m hostage

OTAN [ɔtɑ̃] f abr (= **Organisation du Traité de l'Atlantique Nord**) NATO (= North Atlantic Treaty Organization)

ôter [ote] ⟨1a⟩ remove, take away; *vêtement, chapeau* take off; MATH take away; *tâche* remove

oto-rhino(-laryngologiste) [ɔtorino (larɛ̃gɔlɔʒist)] m ENT specialist, ear-nose-and-throat specialist

ou [u] conj or; **~ bien** or (else); **~ ... ~** ... either ... or

où [u] adv where; *direction* **~ vas-tu?** where are you going (to)?; **d'~ vient-il?** where does he come from?; **d'~ l'on peut déduire que ...** from which it can be deduced that ...; **par ~ es-tu passé?** which way did you go?; **~ que** (+ *subj*) wherever; **le jour / soir ~ ...** the day / evening when ...

ouais [wɛ] F yeah F

ouate [wat] f absorbent cotton, *Br* cotton wool; **ouater** ⟨1a⟩ pad, quilt

oubli [ubli] m forgetting; (*omission*) oversight; **tomber dans l'~** sink into oblivion; **un moment d'~** a moment's forgetfulness; **oublier** ⟨1a⟩ forget; **~ de faire qch** forget to do sth

ouest [wɛst] **1** m west; **vent m d'~** west wind; **à l'~ de** (to the) west of **2** *adj* west, western; **côte** f ~ west ou western coast

oui [wi] yes; **je crois que ~** I think so; **mais ~** of course; **tu aimes ça? - ~** do you like this? - yes, I do

ouï-dire [widir]: **par ~** by hearsay

ouïe [wi] *f* hearing; **~s** ZO gills
ouragan [uragɑ̃] *m* hurricane
ourdir [urdir] ⟨2a⟩ *fig*: **~ un complot** hatch a plot
ourler [urle] ⟨1a⟩ hem; **ourlet** *m* hem
ours [urs] *m* bear; **ourse** *f* she-bear; **la Grande Ourse** ASTR the Great Bear
oursin [ursɛ̃] *m* ZO sea urchin
oust(e)! [ust] F (get) out!
outil [uti] *m* tool; **~ pédagogique** teaching aid; **outillage** *m* tools *pl*
outrage [utraʒ] *m* insult; **outrager** ⟨1l⟩ insult; **outrageusement** *adv* excessively
outrance [utrɑ̃s] *f* excessiveness; **à ~** excessively
outre [utr] **1** *prép* (*en plus de*) apart from, in addition to; **~ mesure** excessively **2** *adv*: **en ~** besides; **passer ~ à qch** ignore sth
outré, **~e** [utre]: **être ~ de** *ou* **par qch** be outraged by sth
outre-Atlantique *adv* on the other side of the Atlantic
outre-Manche *adv* on the other side of the Channel
outre-mer [utrəmɛr]: **d'~** overseas *atr*
outrepasser [utrəpase] ⟨1a⟩ exceed
outsider [awtsajdœr] *m* outsider
ouvert, **~e** [uvɛr, -t] open (*aussi fig*); **à**

bras ~s with open arms; **ouverte-ment** *adv* openly; **ouverture** *f* opening; MUS overture; **des ~s** *fig* overtures; **ouvrable** working; **jour** *m* **~** workday, *Br aussi* working day
ouvrage [uvraʒ] *m* work; **ouvragé**, **~e** ornate
ouvrant [uvrɑ̃] AUTO: **toit** *m* **~** sun roof
ouvre-boîtes [uvrəbwat] *m* (*pl inv*) can opener, *Br aussi* tin opener; **ouvre-bouteilles** *m* (*pl inv*) bottle opener
ouvrier, **-ère** [uvrije, -er] **1** *adj* working-class; *classe* working **2** *m/f* worker; **~ qualifié** skilled worker
ouvrir [uvrir] ⟨2f⟩ *v/t* open; *radio, gaz* turn on **2** *v/i d'un magasin, musée* open; **s'~** open; *fig* open up
ovaire [ɔvɛr] *m* BIOL ovary
ovale [ɔval] *m & adj* oval
ovation [ɔvasjɔ̃] *f* ovation
ovni [ɔvni] *m abr* (= **objet volant non identifié**) UFO (= unidentified flying object)
oxyder [ɔkside] ⟨1a⟩: (**s'**)**~** rust
oxygène [ɔksiʒen] *m* oxygen
ozone [ozɔ(o)n] *m* ozone; **trou** *m* **de la couche d'~** hole in the ozone layer

P

p. *abr* (= **page**) p; (= **pages**) pp
pacemaker [pesmekœr] *m* pacemaker
pacifier [pasifje] ⟨1a⟩ pacify
pacifique [pasifik] **1** *adj personne* peace-loving; *coexistence* peaceful; **l'océan Pacifique** the Pacific Ocean **2** *m* **le Pacifique** the Pacific; **pacifisme** *m* pacifism; **pacifiste** *m/f & adj* pacifist
pacotille [pakɔtij] *f péj* junk
pacte [pakt] *m* pact; **pactiser** ⟨1a⟩: **~ avec** come to terms with

pagaie [pagɛ] *f* paddle
pagaie, **pagaille** [pagaj] *f* F mess
paganisme [paganism] *m* paganism
pagayer [pageje] ⟨1i⟩ paddle
page [paʒ] *f* page; **être à la ~** *fig* be up to date; **tourner la ~** make a new start, start over; **~ d'accueil** INFORM home page; **~s jaunes** yellow pages
paie, **paye** [pɛ] *f* pay
paiement [pemɑ̃] *m* payment
païen, **~ne** [pajɛ̃, -ɛn] *m/f & adj* pagan
paillard, **~e** [pajar, -d] bawdy

paillasson [pɑjasõ] *m* doormat

paille [pɑj] *f* straw

paillette [pɑjɛt] *f* sequin

pain [pɛ̃] *m* bread; **un ~** a loaf; **~ de savon** bar of soap; **~ au chocolat** chocolate croissant; **~ de campagne** farmhouse loaf; **~ complet** whole wheat *ou Br* wholemeal bread; **~ d'épice** gingerbread; **petit ~** roll; **~ de mie** sandwich loaf

pair, ~e [pɛr] **1** *adj nombre* even **2** *m*: **hors ~** *succès* unequaled, *Br* unequalled; *artiste, cuisinier* unrivaled, *Br* unrivalled; **aller de ~** go hand in hand; **fille** *f* **au ~** au pair; **être au ~** be an au pair

paire [pɛr] *f*: **une ~ de** a pair of

paisible [pezibl] peaceful; *personne* quiet; **paisiblement** *adv* peacefully

paître [pɛtr] ⟨4z⟩ graze

paix [pɛ] *f* peace; *(calme)* peace and quiet; **faire la ~** make peace; **fiche--moi la ~!** F leave me alone *ou* in peace!

Pakistan [pakistɑ̃]: **le ~** Pakistan; pakistanais, **~e 1** *adj* Pakistani **2** *m/f* **Pakistanais, ~e** Pakistani

palais [palɛ] *m* palace, ANAT palate; **~ de justice** law courts *pl*

pale [pal] *f* blade

pâle [pɑl] pale; *fig*: *style* colorless, *Br* colourless; *imitation* pale

palefrenier, -ère [palfrənje, ɛr] *m/f* groom

Palestine [palɛstin]: **la ~** Palestine; palestinien, **~ne 1** *adj* Palestinian **2** *m/f* **Palestinien, ~ne** Palestinian

palette [palɛt] *f de peinture* palette

pâleur [pɑlœr] *f* paleness, pallor

palier [palje] *m d'un escalier* landing; TECH bearing; *(phase)* stage; **par ~s** in stages

pâlir [pɑlir] ⟨2a⟩ *d'une personne* go pale, pale; *de couleurs* fade

palissade [palisad] *f* fence

pallier [palje] ⟨1a⟩ alleviate; *manque* make up for

palmarès [palmarɛs] *m d'un concours* list of prizewinners; MUS charts *pl*

palme [palm] *f* BOT palm; *de natation* flipper

palmeraie [palmərɛ] *f* palm grove; **palmier** *m* BOT palm tree

palombe [palõb] *f* wood pigeon

pâlot, ~te [pɑlo, -ɔt] pale

palpable [palpabl] palpable; **palper** ⟨1a⟩ feel; MÉD palpate

palpitant, ~e [palpitɑ̃, -t] *fig* exciting, thrilling; **palpitations** *fpl* palpitations; **palpiter** ⟨1a⟩ *du cœur* pound

paludisme [palydism] *m* MÉD malaria

pamphlet [pɑ̃flɛ] *m* pamphlet

pamplemousse [pɑ̃pləmus] *m* grapefruit

pan [pɑ̃] *m de vêtement* tail; *de mur* section

panache [panaʃ] *m* plume; **avoir du ~** have panache; **panaché** *m* shandygaff, *Br* shandy

pancarte [pɑ̃kart] *f* sign; *de manifestation* placard

pancréas [pɑ̃kreas] *m* ANAT pancreas

paner [pane] ⟨1a⟩ coat with breadcrumbs; **poisson** *m* **pané** breaded fish

panier [panje] *m* basket; **~ à provisions** shopping basket

panique [panik] **1** *adj*: **peur** *f* **~** panic **2** *f* panic; **paniquer** ⟨1a⟩ panic

panne [pan] *f* breakdown; **être** *ou* **rester en ~** break down; **tomber en ~ sèche** run out of gas *ou Br* petrol; **en ~** broken down; **~ d'électricité** power outage, *Br* power failure

panneau [pano] *m (pl -x)* board; TECH panel; **~ d'affichage** billboard; **~ publicitaire** billboard, *Br aussi* hoarding; **~ de signalisation** roadsign; **~ solaire** solar panel

panonceau [panõso] *m (pl -x)* plaque

panoplie [panɔpli] *f fig* range

panorama [panɔrama] *m* panorama; **panoramique** panoramic

panse [pɑ̃s] *f* F belly

pansement [pɑ̃smɑ̃] *m* dressing; **panser** ⟨1a⟩ *blessure* dress; *cheval* groom

pantalon [pɑ̃talõ] *m* pants *pl*, *Br* trousers *pl*; **un ~** a pair of pants

pantelant, ~e [pɑ̃tlɑ̃, -t] panting

panthère [pɑ̃tɛr] *f* panther

pantin [pɑ̃tɛ̃] *m péj* puppet

pantois [pɑ̃twa] *adj inv*: **rester ~** be

speechless

pantouflard [pɑ̃tuflar] *m* F stay-at--home

pantoufle [pɑ̃tufl] *f* slipper

PAO [peao] *f abr* (= **publication assistée par ordinateur**) DTP (= desk-top publishing)

paon [pɑ̃] *m* peacock

papa [papa] *m* dad

papal, ~e [papal] (*mpl* -aux) REL papal; **papauté** *f* REL papacy

pape [pap] *m* REL pope

paperasse [papras] *f* (*souvent au pl* **~s**) *péj* papers *pl*

papeterie [papetri] *f magasin* stationery store, *Br* stationer's; *usine* paper mill; **papetier, -ère** *m/f* stationer

papi, papy [papi] *m* F grandpa

papier [papje] *m* paper; **~s** papers, documents; **~** (**d'**)**aluminium** kitchen foil; **~ hygiénique** toilet tissue; **~s d'identité** identification, ID; **~ à lettres** notepaper; **~ peint** wallpaper

papillon [papijɔ̃] *m* butterfly; TECH wing nut; *F* (*contravention*) (parking) ticket; **nœud ~** bow tie; (*brasse f*) **~** butterfly (stroke)

papoter [papɔte] ⟨1a⟩ F shoot the breeze, *Br* chat

paquebot [pakbo] *m* liner

pâquerette [pakrɛt] *f* BOT daisy

Pâques [pak] *m / sg ou fpl* Easter; **à ~** at Easter; **joyeuses ~!** happy Easter

paquet [pakɛ] *m* packet; *de sucre, café* bag; *de la poste* parcel, package

par [par] *prép* ◊ *lieu* through; **~ la porte** through the door; **regarder ~ la fenêtre** de *l'extérieur* look in at the window; *de l'intérieur* look out of the window; **tomber ~ terre** fall down; **assis ~ terre** sitting on the ground; **passer ~ Denver** go through *ou* via Denver

◊ *temps*: **beau temps** in fine weather; **~ une belle journée** one fine day

◊ *raison*: **~ conséquent** consequently; **~ curiosité** out of curiosity; **~ hasard** by chance; **~ malheur** unfortunately;

◊ *agent du passif* by; **il a été ren-**

versé **~ une voiture** he was knocked over by a car; **faire qch ~ soi-même** do sth by o.s.

◊ *moyen* by; **~ bateau** by boat; **partir ~ le train** leave by train; **~ la poste** by mail

◊ *mode* by; **~ centaines** in their hundreds; **~ avion** by airmail; **~ cœur** by heart; **~ écrit** in writing; **prendre qn ~ la main** take s.o. by the hand

◊ MATH: **diviser ~ quatre** divide by four;

◊ *distributif*: **~ an** a year, per annum; **~ jour** a day; **~ tête** each, a *ou* per head;

◊ : **commencer / finir ~ faire qch** start / finish by doing sth

◊ : **de ~ le monde** all over the world; **de ~ sa nature** by his very nature

para [para] *m* MIL *abr* → **parachutiste**

parabole [parabɔl] *f* parable; MATH parabola; **parabolique: antenne f ~ satellite** dish

paracétamol [parasetamɔl] *m* paracetamol

parachute [paraʃyt] *m* parachute; **sauter en ~** parachute out; **parachuter** ⟨1a⟩ parachute; **parachutiste** *m/f* parachutist; MIL paratrooper

parade [parad] *f* (*défilé*) parade; *en escrime* parry; **à un argument** counter

paradis [paradi] *m* heaven, paradise

paradoxal, ~e [paradɔksal] (*mpl* -aux) paradoxical; **paradoxe** *m* paradox

parages [paraʒ] *mpl*: **dans les ~ de** in the vicinity of; **est-ce que Philippe est dans les ~?** is Philippe around?

paragraphe [paragraf] *m* paragraph

paraître [parɛtr] ⟨4z⟩ appear; *d'un livre* come out, be published; **il paraît que** it seems that, it would appear that; **à ce qu'il paraît** apparently; **elle paraît en pleine forme** she seems to be in top form; **cela me paraît bien compliqué** it looks very complicated to me; **laisser ~** show

parallèle [paralɛl] **1** *adj* parallel (**à** to) **2** *f* MATH parallel (line) **3** *m* GÉOGR parallel (*aussi fig*)

P

paralyser [paralize] ⟨1a⟩ paralyse; *fig*: *circulation, production, ville* paralyse, bring to a standstill; **paralysie** *f* paralysis; **paralytique** paralytic

paramédical, **~e** [paramedikal] paramedical

paramètre [parametr] *m* parameter

parano [parano] F paranoid

paranoïaque [paranɔjak] *m/f & adj* paranoid

paranormal, **~e** [paranɔrmal] paranormal

parapente [parapɑ̃t] *m* paraglider; *activité* paragliding

parapet [parapɛ] *m* parapet

parapharmacie [parafarmasi] *f* (non--dispensing) pharmacy; *produits* toiletries *pl*

paraphrase [parafrɑz] *f* paraphrase

paraplégique [paraplezik] *m/f & adj* paraplegic

parapluie [paraplɥi] *m* umbrella

parapsychique [parapsiʃik] psychic

parascolaire [paraskɔlɛr] extracurricular

parasite [parazit] **1** *adj* parasitic **2** *m* parasite; *fig* parasite, sponger; **~s** *radio* interference *sg*

parasol [parasɔl] *m* parasol; *de plage* beach umbrella

paratonnerre [paratɔnɛr] *m* lightning rod, *Br* lightning conductor

paravent [paravɑ̃] *m* windbreak

parc [park] *m* park; *pour enfant* playpen; **~ de stationnement** parking lot, *Br* car park

parcelle [parsɛl] *f de terrain* parcel

parce que [parsk] *conj* because

parchemin [parʃəmɛ̃] *m* parchment

par-ci [parsi] *adv*: **~, par-là** *espace* here and there; *temps* now and then

parcimonie [parsimɔni] *f*: **avec ~** sparingly, parcimoniously

parcmètre [parkmɛtr] *m* (parking) meter

parcourir [parkurir] ⟨2i⟩ *région* travel through; *distance* cover; *texte* read quickly, skim

parcours [parkur] *m* route; *course d'automobiles* circuit; **accident** *m* **de ~** snag

par-derrière [pardɛrjɛr] *adv* from behind

par-dessous [pardəsu] *prép & adv* underneath

pardessus [pardəsy] *m* overcoat

par-dessus [pardəsy] *prép & adv* over

par-devant [pardəvɑ̃] *adv* emboutir from the front

pardon [pardɔ̃] *m* forgiveness; **~!** sorry!; **~?** excuse me?, *Br aussi* sorry?; **demander ~ à qn** say sorry to s.o.; **pardonner** ⟨1a⟩: **~ qch à qn** forgive s.o. sth

pare-brise [parbriz] *m* (*pl inv*) AUTO windshield, *Br* windscreen

pare-chocs [parʃɔk] *m* (*pl inv*) AUTO bumper

pareil, **~le** [parɛj] **1** *adj* (*semblable*) similar (**à** to); (*tel*) such; **sans ~** without parallel; **elle est sans ~le** there's nobody like her; **c'est du ~ au même** F it comes to the same thing; **c'est toujours ~** it's always the same **2** *adv*: **habillés ~** similarly dressed, dressed the same way

parent, **~e** [parɑ̃, -t] **1** *adj* related **2** *m/f* relative; **~s** (*mère et père*) parents; **parental** parental; **parenté** *f* relationship

parenthèse [parɑ̃tɛz] *f* parenthesis, *Br* (round) bracket; (*digression*) digression; **entre ~s** in parentheses; *fig* by the way

parer [pare] ⟨1a⟩ *attaque* ward off; *en escrime* parry

pare-soleil [parsɔlɛj] *m* sun visor

paresse [parɛs] *f* laziness; **paresser** ⟨1b⟩ laze around; **paresseux, -euse** lazy

parfait [parfɛ] ⟨1b⟩ perfect; *travail* complete; **parfait**, **~e 1** *adj* perfect; *before the noun* complete **2** *m* GRAM perfect (tense); **parfaitement** *adv* perfectly; *comme réponse* absolutely

parfois [parfwa] *adv* sometimes, on occasions

parfum [parfɛ̃, -œ̃] *m* perfume; *d'une glace* flavor, *Br* flavour

parfumé, **~e** [parfyme] scented; *femme* wearing perfume; **parfumer**

⟨1a⟩ (*embaumer*) scent; **parfumerie** *f* perfume store; *produits* perfumes *pl*
pari [pari] *m* bet
paria [parja] *m fig* pariah
parier [parje] ⟨1a⟩ bet
Paris [pari] *m* Paris; **parisien, ~ne 1** *adj* Parisian, of / from Paris **2** *m/f* **Parisien, ~ne** Parisian
paritaire [pariter] parity *atr*; **parité** *f* ÉCON parity
parjure [parʒyr] *litt* **1** *m* perjury **2** *m/f* perjurer
parka [parka] *m* parka
parking [parkiŋ] *m* parking lot, *Br* car park; *édifice* parking garage, *Br* car park
parlant, ~e [parlɑ̃, -t] *comparaison* striking; *preuves, chiffres* decisive; *parlé, ~e* spoken
Parlement [parləmɑ̃] *m* Parliament; **parlementaire 1** *adj* Parliamentary **2** *m/f* Parliamentarian
parlementer [parləmɑ̃ter] ⟨1a⟩ talk (*avec qn de qch* to s.o. about sth)
parler [parle] ⟨1a⟩ **1** *v/i* speak, talk (*à, avec* to; *de* about); *sans ~ de* not to mention; *tu parles!* F you bet!; *refus* you're kidding! **2** *v/t*: *~ affaires* talk business; *~ anglais* speak English; *~ politique* talk politics **3** *m* speech; *~ régional* regional dialect; **parloir** *m* REL parlor, *Br* parlour
parmi [parmi] *prép* among; *ce n'est qu'un exemple ~ tant d'autres* it's just one example (out of many)
parodie [parɔdi] *f* parody; **parodier** ⟨1a⟩ parody
paroi [parwa] *f* partition
paroisse [parwas] *f* REL parish; **paroissien, ~ne** *m/f* REL parishioner
parole [parɔl] *f* (*mot, engagement*) word; *faculté* speech; *~ d'honneur* word of honor *ou Br* honour; *donner la ~ à qn* give s.o. the floor; *donner sa ~* give one's word; *~s de chanson* words, lyrics; **parolier, -ère** *m/f* lyricist
parquer [parke] ⟨1m⟩ *bétail* pen; *réfugiés* dump
parquet [parke] *m* (parquet) floor; JUR public prosecutor's office

parrain [parɛ̃] *m* godfather; *dans un club* sponsor; **parrainer** ⟨1b⟩ sponsor
parsemer [parsəme] ⟨1d⟩ sprinkle (*de* with)
part [par] *f* share; (*fraction*) part, portion; *pour ma ~* for my part, as far as I'm concerned; *faire ~ de qch à qn* inform s.o. of sth; *faire la ~ des choses* make allowances; *prendre ~ à* take part in; *chagrin* share (in); *de la ~ de qn* from s.o., in *ou* Br on behalf of s.o.; *d'une ~ ... d'autre ~* on the one hand ... on the other hand; *autre ~* elsewhere; *nulle ~* nowhere; *quelque ~* somewhere; *~ traiter etc* separately; *un cas à ~* a case apart; *à ~ cela* apart from that; *prendre qn à ~* take s.o. to one side
partage [partaʒ] *m* division; *~ des tâches (ménagères)* sharing the housework; **partager** ⟨1l⟩ share; (*couper, diviser*) divide (up)
partance [partɑ̃s] *f*: *en ~ bateau* about to sail; *avion* about to take off; *train* about to leave; *en ~ pour ...* bound for ...
partant [partɑ̃] *m* SP starter
partenaire [partəner] *m/f* partner
parterre [parter] *m de fleurs* bed; *au théâtre* rear orchestra, *Br* rear stalls *pl*
parti[1] [parti] *m* side; POL party; *prendre ~ pour* side with, take the side of; *prendre ~ contre* side against; *prendre le ~ de faire qch* decide to so sth; *tirer ~ de qch* turn sth to good use; *~ pris* preconceived idea
parti[2]**, ~e** [parti] **1** *p/p* → *partir* **2** *adj* F: *être ~ (ivre)* be tight
partial, ~e [parsjal] (*mpl* -aux) biassed, prejudiced; **partialité** *f* bias, prejudice
participant, ~e [partisipɑ̃, -t] *m/f* participant; **participation** *f* participation; *~ aux bénéfices* profit sharing; *~ aux frais* contribution; **participer** ⟨1a⟩: *~ à* participate in, take part in; *bénéfices* share; *frais* contribute to; *douleur, succès* share in
particularité [partikylarite] *f* special feature, peculiarity

particule [partikyl] *f* particle

particulier, -ère [partikylje, -er] **1** *adj* particular, special; *privé* private; **~ à** characteristic of, peculiar to; **en ~** in particular **2** *m* (private) individual; **particulièrement** *adv* particularly

partie [parti] *f* part (*aussi* MUS); *de boules, cartes, tennis* game; JUR party; *lutte* struggle; **en ~** partly; **faire ~ de qch** be part of sth

partiel, ~le [parsjel] partial; **un** (*examen*) **~** an exam

partir [partir] ⟨2b⟩ (*aux être*) leave (**à, pour** for); SP start; *de la saleté* come out; **~ de qch** (*provenir de*) come from sth; **si on part du fait que ...** if we take as our starting point the fact that ...; **en partant de** (starting) from; **à ~ de** (starting) from, with effect from

partisan, ~e [partizã, -an] *m/f* supporter; MIL partisan; **être ~ de qch** be in favor *ou* Br favour of sth

partition [partisjõ] *f* MUS score; POL partition

partout [partu] *adv* everywhere

paru, ~e [pary] *p/p* → **paraître**

parure [paryr] *f* finery; *de bijoux* set; **~ de lit** set of bed linen

parution [parysjõ] *f d'un livre* appearance

parvenir [parvənir] ⟨2h⟩ (*aux être*) arrive; **~ à un endroit** reach a place, arrive at a place; **faire ~ qch à qn** forward sth to s.o.; **à ~ à faire qch** manage to do sth, succeed in doing sth

parvenu, ~e [parvəny] *m/f* upstart, parvenu *fml*

pas[1] [pɑ] *m* step, pace; **faux ~** stumble; *fig* blunder, faux pas; **~ à ~** step by step; **le Pas de Calais** the Straits *pl* of Dover

pas[2] [pɑ] *adv* ◊ not; **~ lui** not him; **tous les autres sont partis, mais ~ lui** all the others left, but not him *ou* but he didn't

◊: **ne ... ~** not; **il ne pleut ~** it's not raining; **il n'a ~ plu** it didn't rain; **j'ai décidé de ne ~ accepter** I decided not to accept

passable [pasabl] acceptable

passage [pasaʒ] *m* passage; *fig* (*changement*) changeover; **~ à niveau** grade crossing, Br level crossing; **de ~** passing; **~ clouté** crosswalk, Br pedestrian crossing; **passager, -ère 1** *adj* passing, fleeting **2** *m/f* passenger; **~ clandestin** stowaway

passant, ~e [pasã, -t] *m/f* passerby

passe [pɑs] *f* SP pass

passé, ~e [pase] **1** *adj* past **2** *prép*: **~ dix heures** past *ou* after ten o'clock **3** *m* past; **~ composé** GRAM perfect

passe-partout [paspartu] *m* (*pl inv*) skeleton key

passe-passe [paspas] *m*: **tour *m* de ~** conjuring trick

passeport [paspɔr] *m* passport

passer [pase] ⟨1a⟩ **1** *v/i* (*aux être*) *d'une personne, du temps, d'une voiture* pass, go past; *d'une loi* pass; *d'un film* show; **~ avant qch** take precedence over sth; **je suis passé chez Sophie** I dropped by Sophie's place; **~ dans une classe supérieure** move up to a higher class; **~ de mode** go out of fashion; **~ devant la boulangerie** go past the bakery; **~ en seconde** AUTO shift into second; **~ pour qch** pass as sth; **~ sur qch** go over sth; **faire ~ personne** let past; *plat, journal* pass, hand; **laisser ~ personne** let past; *lumière* let in *ou* through; *chance* let slip; **en passant** in passing

2 *v/t rivière, frontière* cross; (*omettre*) *ligne* miss (out); *temps* spend; *examen* take, Br *aussi* sit; *vêtement* slip on; CUIS strain; *film* show; *contrat* enter into; **~ qch à qn** pass s.o. sth, pass sth to s.o.; **~ l'aspirateur** vacuum; **~ qch sous silence** pass over sth in silence

3: **se ~** (*se produire*) happen; **se ~ de qch** do without sth

passerelle [pasrel] *f* footbridge; MAR gangway; AVIAT steps *pl*

passe-temps [pastã] *m* (*pl inv*) hobby, pastime

passible [pasibl] JUR: **être ~ d'une peine** be liable to a fine

passif, -ive [pasif, -iv] **1** *adj* passive **2** *m* GRAM passive; COMM liabilities *pl*

passion [pasjõ] *f* passion

passionnant, ~e [pasjonã, -t] thrilling, exciting; **passionné, ~e 1** *adj* passionate **2** *m/f* enthusiast; **être un ~ de...** be crazy about ...; **passionner** ⟨1a⟩ thrill, excite; **se ~ pour qch** have a passion for sth, be passionate about sth

passivité [pasivite] *f* passiveness, passivity

passoire [paswar] *f* sieve

pastel [pastɛl] *m* pastel; **couleurs ~** pastel colors

pastèque [pastɛk] *f* BOT watermelon

pasteur [pastœr] *m* REL pastor

pasteuriser [pastœrize] ⟨1a⟩ pasteurize

pastiche [pastiʃ] *m* pastiche

pastille [pastij] *f* pastille

patate [patat] *f* potato, spud F

patauger [patoʒe] ⟨1l⟩ flounder

pâte [pat] *f* paste; CUIS *à pain* dough; *à tarte* pastry; **~s** pasta *sg*; **~ d'amandes** almond paste; **~ dentifrice** toothpaste; **~ feuilletée** flaky pastry

pâté [pate] *m* paté; **~ de maisons** block of houses

patère [patɛr] *f* coat peg

paternaliste [patɛrnalist] paternalistic; **paternel, ~le** paternal; **paternité** *f* paternity; **congé de ~** paternity leave

pâteux, -euse [patø, -z] doughy; *bouche* dry

pathétique [patetik] touching; F *(mauvais)* pathetic

pathologie [patɔlɔʒi] *f* pathology; **pathologique** pathological; **pathologiste** *m/f* pathologist

patibulaire [patibylɛr] sinister

patience [pasjãs] *f* patience; **patient, ~e** *m/f & adj* patient; **patienter** ⟨1a⟩ wait

patin [patɛ̃] *m*: **faire du ~** go skating; **~ (à glace)** (ice)skate; **~ à roulettes** roller skate; **patinage** *m* skating; **~ artistique** figure skating; **patiner** ⟨1a⟩ skate; AUTO skid; *de roues* spin;

patineur, -euse *m/f* skater; **patinoire** *f* skating rink

pâtisserie [patisri] *f magasin* cake shop; *gâteaux* pastries, cakes; **pâtissier, -ère** *m/f* pastrycook

patois [patwa] *m* dialect

patraque [patrak] F: **être ~** be feeling off-color *ou* Br off-colour

patriarche [patrijarʃ] *m* patriarch

patrie [patri] *f* homeland

patrimoine [patrimwan] *m* heritage *(aussi fig)*; **~ culturel** *fig* cultural heritage

patriote [patrijɔt] **1** *adj* patriotic **2** *m/f* patriot; **patriotique** patriotic; **patriotisme** *m* patriotism

patron [patrõ] *m* boss; *(propriétaire)* owner; *d'une auberge* landlord; REL patron saint; TECH stencil; *de couture* pattern; **patronal, ~e** *m* employers' *atr*; **patronat** *m* POL employers; **patronne** *f* boss; *(propriétaire)* owner; *d'une auberge* landlady; REL patron saint; **patronner** ⟨1a⟩ sponsor

patrouille [patruj] *f* MIL, *de police* patrol; **patrouiller** ⟨1a⟩ patrol

patte [pat] *f* paw; *d'un oiseau* foot; *d'un insecte* leg; F hand, paw *péj*; **graisser la ~ à qn** F grease s.o.'s palm; **~s d'oie** crow's feet

pâturage [patyraʒ] *m* pasturage

paume [pom] *f* palm; **(jeu** *m* **de) ~** royal tennis

paumé, ~e [pome] F lost; **paumer** ⟨1a⟩ F lose

paupière [popjɛr] *f* eyelid

pause [poz] *f (silence)* pause; *(interruption)* break; **~-café** coffee break; **~-déjeuner** lunch break

pauvre [povr] **1** *adj* poor; **~ en calories** low in calories **2** *m/f* poor person; **les ~s** the poor *pl*; **pauvreté** *f* poverty

pavaner [pavane] ⟨1a⟩: **se ~** strut around

pavé [pave] *m* paving; *(chaussée)* pavement, Br road surface; *pierres rondes* cobbles *pl*, cobblestones *pl*; **un ~** a paving stone; **rond** a cobblestone; **paver** ⟨1a⟩ pave

pavillon [pavijõ] *m (maisonnette)*

small house; MAR flag

pavot [pavo] *m* BOT poppy

payable [pɛjabl] payable

payant, ~e [pɛjɑ̃, -t] *spectateur* paying; *parking* which charges; *fig* profitable, worthwhile

paye [pɛj] *f* → **paie**

payement [pɛjmɑ̃] *m* → **paiement**

payer [pɛje] ⟨1⟩ **1** *v/t* pay; **~ qch dix euros** pay ten euros for sth; **~ qch à qn** buy sth for s.o. **2** *v/i* pay **3**: **se ~ qch** treat o.s. to sth

pays [pei] *m* country; **~ membre** *de l'UE* member country; **mal** *m* **du ~** homesickness; **le Pays basque** the Basque country

paysage [peizaʒ] *m* landscape; **paysager, -ère** landscaped; **bureau** *m* **~** open plan office; **paysagiste** *m/f*: **(architecte** *m***) ~** landscape architect

paysan, ~ne [peizɑ̃, -an] **1** *m/f* small farmer; HIST peasant **2** *adj mœurs* country *atr*

Pays-Bas [peibɑ] *mpl*: **les ~** the Netherlands

PC [pese] *m abr* (= **personal computer**) PC (= personal computer); (= **Parti communiste**) CP (= Communist Party)

PCV [peseve] *m abr* (= **paiement contre vérification**): **appel en ~** collect call

PDG [pedeʒe] *m abr* (= **président-directeur général**) President, CEO (= Chief Executive Officer),

péage [peaʒ] *m* AUTO tollbooth; **autoroute à ~** turnpike, toll road

peau [po] *f* (*pl* -x) skin; *cuir* hide, leather

pêche[1] [pɛʃ] *f* BOT peach

pêche[2] [pɛʃ] *f* fishing; *poissons* catch

péché [peʃe] *m* sin; **~ mignon** peccadillo; **pécher** ⟨1f⟩ sin; **~ par** suffer from an excess of

pêcher[1] [peʃe] *m* BOT peach tree

pêcher[2] [peʃe] ⟨1b⟩ **1** *v/t* fish for; (*attraper*) catch **2** *v/i* fish; **~ à la ligne** go angling

pécheur, -eresse [peʃœr, -ʃ(ə)rɛs] *m/f* sinner

pêcheur [peʃœr] *m* fisherman; **~ à la ligne** angler

pécule [pekyl] *m* nest egg

pécuniaire [pekynjɛr] pecuniary

pédagogie [pedagɔʒi] *f* education, teaching; **pédagogique** educational; *méthode* teaching; **pédagogue** *m/f* educationalist; (*professeur*) teacher

pédale [pedal] *f* pedal; **~ de frein** brake pedal; **pédaler** ⟨1a⟩ pedal

pédalo [pedalo] *m* pedal boat, pedalo

pédant, ~e [pedɑ̃, -t] pedantic

pédé [pede] *m* F faggot F, Br poof F

pédéraste [pederast] *m* homosexual, pederast

pédestre [pedɛstr]: **sentier** *m* **~** footpath; **randonnée** *f* **~** hike

pédiatre [pedjatr] *m/f* MÉD pediatrician; **pédiatrie** *f* pediatrics

pédicure [pedikyr] *m/f* podiatrist, Br chiropodist

pedigree [pedigre] *m* pedigree

pègre [pɛgr] *f* underworld

peigne [pɛɲ] *m* comb; **peigner** ⟨1b⟩ comb; **se ~** comb one's hair; **peignoir** *m* robe, Br dressing gown

peindre [pɛ̃dr] ⟨4b⟩ paint; (*décrire*) depict

peine [pɛn] *f* (*punition*) punishment; (*effort*) trouble; (*difficulté*) difficulty; (*chagrin*) grief, sorrow; **~ capitale** capital punishment; **ce n'est pas la ~** there's no point, it's not worth it; **valoir la ~ de faire qch** be worth doing sth; **avoir de la ~ à faire qch** have difficulty doing sth, find it difficult to do sth; **prendre la ~ de faire qch** go to the trouble to do sth; **faire de la ~ à qn** upset s.o.; **à ~** scarcely, hardly

peiner [pɛne] ⟨1b⟩ **1** *v/t* upset **2** *v/i* labor, Br labour

peintre [pɛ̃tr] *m* painter

peinture [pɛ̃tyr] *f* painting; *action, tableau* painting; *description* depiction

péjoratif, -ive [peʒɔratif, -iv] pejorative

pelage [pəlaʒ] *m* coat

pêle-mêle [pɛlmɛl] *adv* pell-mell

peler [pəle] ⟨1d⟩ peel

pèlerin [pɛlrɛ̃] *m* pilgrim; **pèlerinage** *m* pilgrimage; *lieu* place of pilgrimage

pélican [pelikɑ̃] *m* pelican

pelle [pɛl] *f* spade; **~ à gâteau** cake slice; **... à la ~** huge quantities of ...

pelleteuse [pɛltøz] *f* mechanical shovel, digger

pellicule [pelikyl] *f* film; **~s** dandruff *sg*

pelote [p(ə)lɔt] *f* de fil ball

peloter [p(ə)lɔte] ⟨1a⟩ F grope, feel up

peloton [p(ə)lɔtɔ̃] *m* ball; MIL platoon; SP pack, bunch; **pelotonner** ⟨1a⟩ wind into a ball; **se ~** curl up; **se ~ contre qn** snuggle up to s.o.

pelouse [p(ə)luz] *f* lawn

peluche [p(ə)lyʃ] *f jouet* cuddly *ou* soft toy; **faire des ~s** *d'un pull etc* go fluffy *ou* picky; **ours** *m* **en ~** teddy bear

pelure [p(ə)lyr] *f* de fruit peel

pénal, ~e [penal] (*mpl -aux*) JUR penal; **pénalisation** *f* SP penalty; **pénaliser** ⟨1a⟩ penalize; **pénalité** *f* penalty

penalty [penalti] *m* SP penalty

penaud, ~e [pəno, -d] hangdog, sheepish

penchant [pɑ̃ʃɑ̃] *m fig (inclination)* liking, penchant

pencher [pɑ̃ʃe] ⟨1a⟩ **1** *v/t pot* tilt; *penché écriture* sloping; **~ la tête en avant** bend *ou* lean forward **2** *v/i* lean; *d'un plateau* tilt; *d'un bateau* list; **~ pour qch** *fig* lean *ou* tend toward sth; **se ~ au dehors** lean out; **se ~ sur** *fig: problème* examine

pendaison [pɑ̃dɛzɔ̃] *f* hanging

pendant[1] [pɑ̃dɑ̃] **1** *prép* during; *avec chiffre* for; **elle a habité ici ~ trois ans** she lived here for three years **2** *conj:* **~ que** while

pendant[2], **~e** [pɑ̃dɑ̃, -t] *oreilles* pendulous; *(en instance)* pending; **pendentif** *m* pendant

penderie [pɑ̃dri] *f armoire, Br* wardrobe

pendiller [pɑ̃dije] ⟨1a⟩ dangle

pendre [pɑ̃dr] ⟨4a⟩ **1** *v/t* hang (up); *condamné* hang **2** *v/i* hang; **se ~** hang

o.s.

pendule [pɑ̃dyl] **1** *m* pendulum **2** *f (horloge)* clock

pénétration [penetrasjɔ̃] *f* penetration; *fig (acuité)* shrewdness; **pénétrer** ⟨1f⟩ **1** *v/t liquide, lumière* penetrate; *pensées, personne* fathom out **2** *v/i:* **~ dans** penetrate; *maison, bureaux* get into

pénible [penibl] *travail* laborious; *vie* hard; *nouvelle, circonstances* painful; *caractère* difficult; **péniblement** *adv (avec difficulté)* laboriously; *(à peine)* only just, barely; *(avec douleur)* painfully

péniche [peniʃ] *f* barge

pénicilline [penisilin] *f* penicillin

péninsule [penɛ̃syl] *f* peninsula

pénis [penis] *m* penis

pénitence [penitɑ̃s] *f* REL penitence; *(punition)* punishment; **pénitencier** *m* penitentiary, *Br* prison

pénombre [penɔ̃br] *f* semi-darkness

pense-bête [pɑ̃sbɛt] *m* reminder

pensée [pɑ̃se] *f* thought; BOT pansy

penser [pɑ̃se] ⟨1a⟩ **1** *v/i* think; **~ à** *(réfléchir à, s'intéresser à)* think of, think about; **faire ~ à qch** be reminiscent of sth; **faire ~ à qn à faire qch** remind s.o. to do sth **2** *v/t* think; *(imaginer)* imagine; **~ faire qch** *(avoir l'intention)* be thinking of doing sth; **~ de** think of, think about; **penseur** *m* thinker; **pensif, -ive** thoughtful

pension [pɑ̃sjɔ̃] *f (allocation)* allowance; *logement* rooming house, *Br* boarding house; *école* boarding school; **~ alimentaire** alimony; **~ complète** American plan, *Br* full board; **pensionnaire** *m/f d'un hôtel* guest; *écolier* boarder; **pensionnat** *m* boarding school

pente [pɑ̃t] *f* slope; **en ~** sloping; **être sur une mauvaise ~** *fig* be on a slippery slope

Pentecôte [pɑ̃tkot]: **la ~** Pentecost

pénurie [penyri] *f* shortage *(de* of)

pépin [pepɛ̃] *m* de fruit seed; **avoir un ~** F have a problem

pépinière [pepinjɛr] *f* nursery

pépite [pepit] *f* nugget

perçant, **~e** [persã, -t] *regard, froid* piercing; **percée** f breakthrough

percepteur [perseptœr] m tax collector; **perceptible** perceptible; **perception** f perception; *des impôts* collection; *bureau* tax office

percer [perse] ⟨1k⟩ **1** v/t *mur, planche* make a hole in; *porte* make; (*transpercer*) pierce **2** v/i *du soleil* break through; **perceuse** f drill

percevoir [persəvwar] ⟨3a⟩ perceive; *argent, impôts* collect

perche [pɛrʃ] f ZO perch; *en bois, métal* pole; **percher** ⟨1a⟩: (**se**) **~** *d'un oiseau* perch; F live; **perchiste** m pole vaulter; **perchoir** m perch

percolateur [perkɔlatœr] m percolator

percussion [perkysjõ] f MUS percussion; **percutant, ~e** fig powerful; **percuter** ⟨1a⟩ crash into

perdant, **~e** [perdã, -t] **1** adj losing **2** m/f loser

perdre [perdr] ⟨4a⟩ **1** v/t lose; **~ courage** lose heart; **~ une occasion** miss an opportunity, let an opportunity slip; **~ son temps** waste one's time; **~ connaissance** lose consciousness; **se ~** *disparaître* disappear, vanish; *d'une personne* get lost **2** v/i: **~ au change** lose out

perdrix [perdri] f partridge

perdu, **~e** [perdy] **1** p/p → **perdre 2** adj lost; *occasion* missed; *endroit* remote; *balle* stray; *emballage, verre* non-returnable

père [per] m father (*aussi* REL)

perfection [perfeksjõ] f perfection; **perfectionnement** m perfecting; **perfectionner** ⟨1a⟩ perfect; **se ~ en anglais** improve one's English; **perfectionniste** m/f & adj perfectionist

perfide [perfid] treacherous; **perfidie** f treachery

perforatrice [perfɔratris] f *pour cuir, papier* punch; **perforer** ⟨1a⟩ perforate; *cuir* punch

performance [perfɔrmãs] f performance; **performant, ~e** high-performance

perfusion [perfyzjõ] f MÉD drip

péril [peril] m peril; **périlleux, -euse** perilous

périmé, **~e** [perime] out of date

périmètre [perimetr] m MATH perimeter; **dans un ~ de 25 km** within a 25km radius

période [perjɔd] f period (*aussi* PHYS); **~ de transition** transitional period ou phase; **en ~** in times of; **périodique 1** adj periodic **2** m periodical

péripéties [peripesi] fpl ups and downs

périphérie [periferi] f *d'une ville* outskirts pl; **périphérique** m & adj: (**boulevard** m) **~** beltway, Br ring-road

périple [peripl] m long journey

périr [perir] ⟨2a⟩ perish

périscope [periskɔp] m periscope

périssable [perisabl] perishable

péritel [peritel]: **prise** f **~** scart

perle [perl] f pearl; (*boule percée*) bead; *fig: personne* gem; *de sang* drop; **perler** ⟨1a⟩: **la sueur perlait sur son front** he had beads of sweat on his forehead

permanence [permanãs] f permanence; **être de ~** be on duty; **en ~** constantly; **permanent, ~e 1** adj permanent **2** f *coiffure* perm

perméable [permeabl] permeable

permettre [permetr] ⟨4p⟩ allow, permit; **~ à qn de faire qch** allow s.o. to do sth; **~ qch à qn** allow s.o. sth; **se ~ qch** allow o.s. sth

permis [permi] m permit; **passer son ~** sit one's driving test; **~ de conduire** driver's license, Br driving licence; **~ de séjour** residence permit; **~ de travail** work permit

permissif, **-ive** [permisif, -iv] permissive; **permission** f permission; MIL leave

Pérou [peru]: **le ~** Peru

perpendiculaire [perpãdikyler] perpendicular (**à** to)

perpétrer [perpetre] ⟨1f⟩ JUR perpetrate

perpétuel, **~le** [perpetɥel] perpetual;

perpétuellement *adv* perpetually;
perpétuer ⟨1n⟩ perpetuate; **perpé-**
tuité *f*: **à ~** in perpetuity; JUR
condamné to life imprisonment
perplexe [pɛrpleks] perplexed,
puzzled; **laisser ~** puzzle; **perple-**
xité *f* perplexity
perquisitionner [pɛrkizisjɔne] ⟨1a⟩
JUR carry out a search
perron [pɛrõ] *m* steps *pl*
perroquet [pɛrɔkɛ] *m* parrot
perruche [pɛryʃ] *f* ZO budgerigar
perruque [pɛryk] *f* wig
persan, ~e [pɛrsã, -an] **1** *adj* Persian
2 *m/f* Persan, ~e Persian
persécuter [pɛrsekyte] ⟨1a⟩ perse-
cute; **persécution** *f* persecution
persévérance [pɛrseverãs] *f* perseverance; **persévérant, ~e** persever-
ing; **persévérer** ⟨1f⟩ persevere
persienne [pɛrsjɛn] *f* shutter
persil [pɛrsi] *m* BOT parsley
Persique [pɛrsik]: **golfe** *m* **~** Persian
Gulf
persistance [pɛrsistãs] *f* persistence;
persister ⟨1a⟩ persist; **~ dans sa**
décision stick to one's decision; **~**
à faire qch persist in doing sth
personnage [pɛrsɔnaʒ] *m* character;
(dignitaire) important person
personnaliser [pɛrsɔnalize] ⟨1b⟩
personalize
personnalité [pɛrsɔnalite] *f* personality
personne[1] [pɛrsɔn] *f* person; **deux~s**
two people; **grande ~** grown-up; **en**
~ in person, personally; **par~** per person, each; **les ~s âgées** the old *pl*,
old people *pl*
personne[2] [pɛrsɔn] *pron* ◇ no-one,
nobody; **~ ne le sait** no-one *ou* nobody knows; **il n'y avait ~** no-one
was there, there wasn't anyone there;
je ne vois jamais ~ I never see anyone
◇ *qui que ce soit* anyone, anybody;
sans avoir vu ~ without seeing anyone *ou* anybody
personnel, ~le [pɛrsɔnɛl] **1** *adj* personal; *conversation, courrier* private
2 *m* personnel *pl*, staff *pl*; **person-**

nellement *adv* personally
personnifier [pɛrsɔnifje] ⟨1a⟩ perso-
nify
perspective [pɛrspɛktiv] *f* perspective; *fig: pour l'avenir* prospect; *(point*
de vue) viewpoint, perspective; **avoir**
qch en ~ have sth in prospect
perspicace [pɛrspikas] shrewd; **per-**
spicacité *f* shrewdness
persuader [pɛrsɥade] ⟨1a⟩ persuade
(de faire qch to do sth; **de qch** of
sth); **je ne suis pas persuadé que**
... I'm not convinced that; **se ~**
de qch convince o.s. of sth; **se ~**
que convince o.s. that; **persuasif,**
-ive persuasive; **persuasion** *f* persuasion; *don* persuasiveness
perte [pɛrt] *f* loss; *fig (destruction)* ruin;
à ~ *vendre* at a loss; **à ~ de vue** as far
as the eye can see; **une ~ de temps** a
waste of time
pertinent, ~e [pɛrtinã, -t] relevant
perturbateur, -trice [pɛrtyrbatœr,
-tris] disruptive; **être un élément ~**
be a disruptive influence; **perturba-**
tion *f* météorologique, politique disturbance; *de trafic* disruption; **per-**
turber ⟨1a⟩ *personne* upset; *trafic* disrupt
péruvien, ~ne [peryvjẽ, -ɛn] **1** *adj*
Peruvian **2** *m/f* Péruvien, ~ne Peruvian
pervers, ~e [pɛrvɛr, -s] *sexualité* perverse; **perversion** *f* sexuelle perversion; **pervertir** ⟨2a⟩ pervert
pesamment [pəzamã] *adv* heavily;
pesant, ~e heavy (*aussi fig*); **pesan-**
teur *f* PHYS gravity
pesée [pəze] *f* weighing
pèse-personne [pɛzpɛrsɔn] *f* (*pl*
pèse-personnes) scales *pl*
peser [pəze] ⟨1d⟩ **1** *v/t* weigh; *fig*
weigh up; *mots* weigh **2** *v/i* weigh; **~**
sur de poids, responsabilité weigh
on; **~ à qn** weigh heavy on s.o.
pessimisme [pesimism] *m* pessi-
mism; **pessimiste 1** *adj* pessimistic
2 *m/f* pessimist
peste [pɛst] *f* MÉD plague; *fig* pest;
pester ⟨1a⟩: **~ contre qn / qch**
curse s.o. / sth

P

pesticide [pɛstisid] *m* pesticide

pet [pɛ] *m* F fart F

pétale [petal] *f* petal

pétanque [petɑ̃k] *f* type of bowls

pétarader [petarade] ⟨1a⟩ AUTO backfire

pétard [petar] *m* firecracker; F (*bruit*) racket

péter [pete] ⟨1f⟩ F fart F

pétillant, ~e [petijɑ̃, -t] sparkling; **pétiller** ⟨1a⟩ *du feu* crackle; *d'une boisson, d'yeux* sparkle

petit, ~e [p(ə)ti, -t] **1** *adj* small, little; **en ~** in a small size; **à ~** gradually, little by little; **~ nom** *m* first name; **~ ami** *m* boyfriend; **~e amie** *f* girlfriend; **au ~ jour** at dawn; **~ déjeuner** breakfast **2** *m/f* child; **les ~s** the children; **une chatte et ses ~s** a cat and her young; **attendre des ~s** be pregnant

petit-bourgeois, petite-bourgeoise [p(ə)tiburʒwa, p(ə)titburʒwaz] petty-bourgeois

petite-fille [p(ə)titfij] *f* (*pl* petites-filles) granddaughter

petitesse [p(ə)tites] *f* smallness; *fig* pettiness

petit-fils [p(ə)tifis] *m* (*pl* petits-fils) grandson

pétition [petisjɔ̃] *f* petition

petits-enfants [p(ə)tizɑ̃fɑ̃] *mpl* grandchildren

pétrifier [petrifje] ⟨1a⟩ turn to stone; *fig* petrify

pétrin [petrɛ̃] *m fig* F mess; **pétrir** ⟨2a⟩ knead

pétrochimie [petroʃimi] *f* petrochimistry; **pétrochimique** petrochemical

pétrole [petrɔl] *m* oil, petroleum; **~ brut** crude (oil); **pétrolier, -ère 1** *adj* oil *atr* **2** *m* tanker

peu [pø] **1** *adv* ◇ : **~ gentil / intelligent** not very nice / intelligent; **~ après** a little after; **j'ai ~ dormi** I didn't sleep much
◇: **~ de pain** not much bread; **il a eu ~ de chance** he didn't have much luck; **il reste ~ de choses à faire** there aren't many things left to do; **~ de gens** few people; **dans ~ de**

temps in a little while
◇: **un ~** a little, a bit; **un tout petit ~** just a very little, just a little bit; **un ~ de chocolat / patience** a little chocolate / patience, a bit of chocolate / patience; **un ~ plus long** a bit *ou* little longer
◇: **de ~** rater le bus etc only just; **à ~** little by little, gradually; **à ~ près** (*plus ou moins*) more or less; (*presque*) almost; **elle travaille depuis ~** she has only been working for a little while, she hasn't been working for long; **quelque ~** a little; **pour ~ que** (+ *subj*) if; **sous ~** before long, by and by
2 *m*: **le ~ d'argent que j'ai** what little money I have

peuple [pœpl] *m* people

peupler [pøple, pœ-] ⟨1a⟩ *pays, région* populate; *maison* live in

peuplier [pøplije, pœ-] *m* BOT poplar

peur [pœr] *f* fear (*de* of); **avoir ~** be frightened, be afraid (*de* of); **prendre ~** take fright; **faire ~ à qn** frighten s.o.; **je ne veux pas y aller de ~ qu'il ne soit** (*subj*) **là** I don't want to go there in case he's there; **peureux, -euse** fearful, timid

peut-être [pøtɛtr] perhaps, maybe

phalange [falɑ̃ʒ] *f* ANAT, MIL phalanx

phare [far] *m* MAR lighthouse; AVIAT beacon; AUTO headlight, headlamp; **se mettre en (pleins) ~s** switch to full beam

pharmaceutique [farmasøtik] pharmaceutical; **pharmacie** *f* local pharmacy, *Br aussi* chemist's; *science* pharmacy; *médicaments* pharmaceuticals *pl*; **pharmacien, ~ne** *m/f* pharmacist

phase [faz] *f* phase

phénoménal, ~e [fenomenal] phenomenal; **phénomène** *m* phenomenon

philippin, ~e [filipɛ̃, -in] **1** *adj* Filippino **2**: **Philippin, ~e** *m/f* Filippino

philosophe [filozof] *m* philosopher; **philosophie** *f* philosophy; **philosophique** philosophical

phobie [fobi] *f* PSYCH phobia

phonétique [fɔnetik] **1** *adj* phonetic **2** *f* phonetics

phoque [fɔk] *m* seal

phosphate [fɔsfat] *m* phosphate

photo [fɔto] *f* photo; *l'art* photography; **faire de la ~** take photos; **prendre qn en ~** take a photo of s.o.

photocopie [fɔtɔkɔpi] *f* photocopy; **photocopier** ⟨1a⟩ photocopy; **photocopieur** *m*, **photocopieuse** *f* photocopier

photogénique [fɔtɔʒenik] photogenic

photographe [fɔtɔgraf] *m/f* photographer; **photographie** *f* photograph; *l'art* photography; **photographier** ⟨1a⟩ photograph; **photographique** photographic

photomaton® [fɔtomatɔ̃] *m* photo booth

phrase [fraz] *f* GRAM sentence; MUS phrase; **sans ~s** in plain English, straight out; **faire de grandes ~s** use a lot of pompous *ou* high-falutin language

physicien, ~ne [fizisjɛ̃, -ɛn] *m/f* physicist

physionomie [fizjɔnɔmi] *f* face

physique [fizik] **1** *adj* physical **2** *m* physique **3** *f* physics; **~ nucléaire** nuclear physics; **~ quantique** quantum physics; **physiquement** *adv* physically

piailler [pjaje] ⟨1a⟩ *d'un oiseau* chirp; F *d'un enfant* scream, shout

pianiste [pjanist] *m/f* pianist; **piano** *m* piano; **~ à queue** grand piano; **pianoter** ⟨1a⟩ F *sur piano* play a few notes; *sur table, vitre* drum one's fingers

piaule [pjol] *f* F pad F

PIB [peibe] *m abr* (= **produit intérieur brut**) GDP (= gross domestic product)

pic [pik] *m instrument* pick; *d'une montagne* peak; **à ~ tomber** steeply; **arriver à ~** *fig* F come at just the right moment

pichet [piʃɛ] *m* pitcher, *Br* jug

pickpocket [pikpɔkɛt] *m* pickpocket

pick-up [pikœp] *m* pick-up (truck)

picorer [pikɔre] ⟨1a⟩ peck

pie [pi] *f* ZO magpie

pièce [pjɛs] *f* piece; *de machine* part; (*chambre*) room; (*document*) document; *de monnaie* coin; *de théâtre* play; **deux ~s** *vêtement* two-piece; **à la ~** singly; **cinq euros** (**la**) **~** five euros each; **mettre en ~s** smash to smithereens; **une ~ d'identité** proof of identity; **~ jointe** enclosure; **~ de monnaie** coin; **~ de rechange** spare part; **~ de théâtre** play

pied [pje] *m* foot; *d'un meuble* leg; *d'un champignon* stalk; **~ de vigne** vine; **à ~** on foot; **~s nus** barefoot; **au ~ de** at the foot of; **de ~ en cap** from head to foot; **mettre sur ~** set up

pied-à-terre [pjetatɛr] *m* (*pl inv*) pied-à-terre

piédestal [pjedɛstal] *m* (*pl* -aux) pedestal

pied-noir [pjenwar] *m/f* (*pl* pieds-noirs) F French Algerian (*French person who lived in Algeria but returned to France before independence*)

piège [pjɛʒ] *m* trap; **piégé, ~e: voiture** *f* **~e** car bomb; **piéger** ⟨1b⟩ trap; **voiture** booby-trap

piercing [pɛrsiŋ] *m* body piercing

pierre [pjɛr] *f* stone; **~ précieuse** precious stone; **~ tombale** gravestone; **pierreux, -euse** *sol, chemin* stony

piété [pjete] *f* REL piety

piétiner [pjetine] ⟨1a⟩ **1** *v/t* trample; *fig* trample underfoot **2** *v/i fig* (*ne pas avancer*) mark time

piéton, ~ne [pjetɔ̃, -ɔn] **1** *m/f* pedestrian **2** *adj*: **zone** *f* **~ne** pedestrianized zone, *Br* pedestrian precinct; **piétonnier, -ère** pedestrian *atr*

pieu [pjø] *m* (*pl* -x) stake; F pit F

pieuvre [pjœvr] *f* octopus

pieux, -euse [pjø, -z] pious; **~ mensonge** *m fig* white lie

pif [pif] *m* F nose, honker F, *Br* hooter F; **au ~** by guesswork

pigeon [piʒɔ̃] *m* pigeon; **pigeonnier** *m* dovecot

piger [piʒe] ⟨1l⟩ F understand, get F

pigment [pigmɑ̃] *m* pigment

pignon [piɲɔ̃] *m* ARCH gable; TECH

gearwheel

pile¹ [pil] *f* (*tas*) pile; ÉL battery; *monnaie* tails; *à* ~ *ou face?* heads or tails?

pile² [pil] *adv:* **s'arrêter** ~ stop dead; *à* **deux heures** ~ at two o'clock sharp, at two o'clock on the dot

piler [pile] ⟨1a⟩ *ail* crush; *amandes* grind

pilier [pilje] *m* ARCH pillar (*aussi fig*)

pillage [pijaʒ] *m* pillage, plunder; **piller** ⟨1a⟩ pillage, plunder

pilotage [pilotaʒ] *m* AVIAT flying, piloting; MAR piloting; **pilote 1** *m* MAR, AVIAT pilot; AUTO driver; ~ **automatique** automatic pilot **2** *adj:* **usine** *f* ~ pilot plant; **piloter** ⟨1a⟩ AVIAT, MAR pilot; AUTO drive

pilule [pilyl] *f* pill; **la** ~ (**contraceptive**) the pill; **prendre la** ~ be on the pill, take the pill

piment [pimɑ̃] *m* pimento; *fig* spice

pimenter [pimɑ̃te] ⟨1a⟩ spice up

pimpant, ~**e** [pɛ̃pɑ̃, -t] *adj* spruce

pin [pɛ̃] *m* BOT pine

pinard [pinar] *m* F wine

pince [pɛ̃s] *f* pliers *pl*; *d'un crabe* pincer; ~ *à épiler* tweezers *pl*; ~ *à linge* clothespin, *Br* clothespeg

pincé, ~**e** [pɛ̃se] *lèvres* pursed; *air* stiff

pinceau [pɛ̃so] *m* (*pl* -x) brush

pincée [pɛ̃se] *f* CUIS: **une** ~ **de sel** a pinch of salt

pincer [pɛ̃se] ⟨1k⟩ pinch; MUS pluck; **se** ~ **le doigt dans la porte** catch one's finger in the door

pince-sans-rire [pɛ̃ssɑ̃rir] *m/f* (*pl inv*) person with a dry sense of humor *ou Br* humour

pingouin [pɛ̃gwɛ̃] *m* penguin

ping-pong [piŋpõg] *m* ping-pong

pingre [pɛ̃gr] miserly

pinson [pɛ̃sõ] *m* chaffinch

pintade [pɛ̃tad] *f* guinea fowl

pioche [pjɔʃ] *f* pickax, *Br* pickaxe; **piocher** ⟨1a⟩ dig

piolet [pjɔlɛ] *m* ice ax, *Br* ice axe

pion [pjõ] *m* piece, man; *aux échecs* pawn

pioncer [pjõse] ⟨1k⟩ F sleep, *Br* kip F

pionnier [pjɔnje] *m* pioneer

pipe [pip] *f* pipe; *fumer la* ~ smoke a pipe

pipeau [-o] *m* (*pl* -x) pipe

pipi [pipi] *m* F pee F; *faire* ~ do a pee

piquant, ~**e** [pikɑ̃, -t] **1** *adj* prickly; *remarque* cutting; CUIS hot, spicy **2** *m épine* spine, spike; *fig* spice

pique [pik] *m aux cartes* spades

pique-assiette [pikasjɛt] *m* (*pl* pique-assiette)) F freeloader

pique-nique [piknik] *m* (*pl* pique-niques) picnic; **pique-niquer** ⟨1m⟩ picnic

piquer [pike] ⟨1m⟩ *d'une abeille, des orties* sting; *d'un moustique, serpent* bite; *d'une barbe* prickle; *d'épine* prick; *fig: curiosité* excite; *fig* F (*voler*) pinch F; ~ *qn* MÉD give s.o. an injection, inject s.o.; **se** ~ prick o.s.; *se faire une piqûre* inject o.s.; *la fumée me pique les yeux* the smoke makes my eyes sting; **se** ~ **le doigt** prick one's finger

piquet [pikɛ] *m* stake; ~ *de tente* tent peg; ~ *de grève* picket line

piquette [pikɛt] *f* cheap wine

piqûre [pikyr] *f d'abeille* sting; *de moustique* bite; MÉD injection

pirate [pirat] *m* pirate; ~ **informatique** hacker; ~ *de l'air* hijacker; **pirater** ⟨1a⟩ pirate

pire [pir] worse; *le / la* ~ the worst

pirouette [pirwɛt] *f* pirouette

pis-aller [pizale] *m* (*pl inv*) stopgap

pisciculture [pisikyltyr] *f* fish farming

piscine [pisin] *f* (swimming) pool; ~ **couverte** indoor (swimming) pool; ~ **en plein air** outdoor (swimming) pool

pissenlit [pisɑ̃li] *m* BOT dandelion

pisser [pise] ⟨1a⟩ F pee F, piss F; **pissotière** *f* F urinal

pistache [pistaʃ] *f* BOT pistachio (nut)

piste [pist] *f* track; *d'animal, fig* track, trail; AVIAT runway; SP track; *ski alpin* piste; *ski de fond* trail; ~ *d'atterrissage* landing strip; ~ *cyclable* cycle path; ~ *de danse* dance floor; ~ *magnétique* magnetic stripe

pistolet [pistolɛ] *m* pistol

piston [pistõ] *m* TECH piston; *elle est*

rentrée dans la boîte par ~ *fig* F she got the job through contacts; **pistonner** ⟨1a⟩ F: ~ *qn* pull strings for s.o., give s.o. a leg-up F

piteux, -euse [pitø, -z] pitiful

pitié [pitje] *f* pity; *avoir* ~ *de qn* take pity on s.o.

piton [pitõ] *m d'alpiniste* piton; (*pic*) peak

pitoyable [pitwajabl] pitiful

pitre [pitr] *m: faire le* ~ clown around

pittoresque [pitɔrɛsk] picturesque

pivert [pivɛr] *m* woodpecker

pivoine [pivwan] *f* BOT peony

pivot [pivo] *m* TECH pivot; *vous êtes le* ~ *de ce projet fig* the project hinges on you; **pivoter** ⟨1a⟩ pivot

pizza [pidza] *f* pizza

PJ *abr* (= *pièce(s) jointe(s)*) enclosure(s)

placage [plakaʒ] *m d'un meuble* veneer; *au rugby* tackle

placard [plakar] *m* (*armoire*) cabinet, *Br* cupboard; (*affiche*) poster; **placarder** ⟨1a⟩ *avis* stick up, post

place [plas] *f de village, ville* square; (*lieu*) place; (*siège*) seat; (*espace libre*) room, space; (*emploi*) position, place; *sur* ~ on the spot; *à la* ~ *de* instead of; *être en* ~ have everything in place; ~ *assise* seat; ~ *forte* fortress

placé, ~e [plase]: *être bien* ~ *d'une maison* be well situated; *être bien* ~ *pour savoir qch* be in a good position to know sth; **placement** *m* (*emploi*) placement; (*investissement*) investment; *agence f de* ~ employment agency; **placer** ⟨1k⟩ (*mettre*) put, place; (*procurer emploi à*) find a job for; *argent* invest; *dans une famille etc* find a place for; *je n'ai pas pu* ~ *un mot* I couldn't get a word in edgewise *ou Br* edgeways; *se* ~ take one's place

placide [plasid] placid

plafond [plafõ] *m aussi fig* ceiling; **plafonner** ⟨1a⟩ *de prix* level off; **plafonnier** *m* ceiling lamp

plage [plaʒ] *f* beach; *lieu* seaside resort; ~ *horaire* time slot

plagiat [plaʒja] *m* plagiarism; **plagier**

plaider [plede] ⟨1b⟩ **1** *v/i* JUR *d'un avocat* plead **2** *v/t*: ~ *la cause de qn* defend s.o.; *fig* plead s.o.'s cause; ~ *coupable / non coupable* plead guilty / not guilty; **plaidoirie** *f* JUR speech for the defense *ou Br* defence; **plaidoyer** *m* JUR speech for the defense *ou Br* defence; *fig* plea

plaie [plɛ] *f* cut; *fig* wound; *quelle* ~! *fig* what a nuisance!

plaignant, ~e [plɛɲɑ̃, -t] *m/f* JUR plaintiff

plaindre [plɛ̃dr] ⟨4b⟩ pity; *se* ~ complain (*de* about; *à* to); *se* ~ (*de ce*) *que* complain that

plaine [plɛn] *f* plain

plain-pied [plɛ̃pje]: *de* ~ *maison etc* on one level

plainte [plɛ̃t] *f* (*lamentation*) moan; *mécontentement*, JUR complaint; *porter* ~ lodge a complaint (*contre* about); **plaintif, -ive** plaintive

plaire [plɛr] ⟨4a⟩: *il ne me plaît pas* I don't like him; *s'il vous plaît, s'il te plaît* please; *je me plais à Paris* I like it in Paris; *Paris me plaît* I like Paris; *ça me plairait d'aller* … I would like to go …; *ils se sont plu tout de suite* they were immediately attracted to each other

plaisance [plɛzɑ̃s] *f: navigation f de* ~ boating; *port m de* ~ marina; **plaisant, ~e** (*agréable*) pleasant; (*amusant*) funny

plaisanter [plɛzɑ̃te] ⟨1a⟩ joke; **plaisanterie** *f* joke; **plaisantin** *m* joker

plaisir [plezir] *m* pleasure; *avec* ~ with pleasure, gladly; *par* ~, *pour le* ~ for pleasure, for fun; *faire* ~ *à qn* please s.o.; *prendre* ~ *à* take pleasure in sth

plan, ~e [plɑ̃, plan] **1** *adj* flat, level **2** *m* (*surface*) surface; (*projet, relevé*) plan; *premier* ~ foreground; *de premier* ~ *personnalité* prominent; *sur ce* ~ in that respect, on that score; *sur le* ~ *économique* in economic terms, economically speaking; ~ *d'eau* stretch of water; ~ *de travail* work surface

planche [plɑ̃ʃ] *f* plank; ~ *à voile* sailboard

plancher [plɑ̃ʃe] *m* floor

planer [plane] ⟨1a⟩ hover; *fig* live in another world

planétaire [planetɛr] planetary; **planète** *f* planet

planeur [planœr] *m* glider

planification [planifikasjɔ̃] *f* planning; **planifier** ⟨1a⟩ plan

planning [planiŋ] *m*: ~ **familial** family planning

planque [plɑ̃k] *f* F *abri* hiding place; *travail* cushy job F

planquer [plɑ̃ke] ⟨1m⟩ F hide; **se** ~ hide

plant [plɑ̃] *m* AGR seedling; (*plantation*) plantation; **plantation** *f* plantation

plante¹ [plɑ̃t] *f* plant

plante² [plɑ̃t] *f*: ~ **du pied** sole of the foot

planter [plɑ̃te] ⟨1a⟩ *jardin* plant up; *plantes, arbres* plant; *poteau* hammer in; *tente* erect, put up; ~ **là qn** dump s.o.

plantureux, -euse [plɑ̃tyrø, -z] *femme* voluptuous

plaque [plak] *f* plate; (*inscription*) plaque; **~ électrique** hotplate; **~ minéralogique, ~ d'immatriculation** AUTO license plate, *Br* number plate; **~ tournante** turntable; *fig* hub; **être à côté de la** ~ be wide of the mark

plaqué [plake] *m*: ~ **or** gold plate; **plaquer** ⟨1m⟩ *argent, or* plate; *meuble* veneer; *fig* pin (*contre* to, against); F (*abandonner*) dump F; *au rugby* tackle

plaquette [plakɛt] *f de pilules* strip; *de beurre* pack; **~ de frein** brake pad

plastic [plastik] *m* plastic explosive

plastifier ⟨1a⟩ laminate

plastique [plastik] **1** *adj* plastic; **arts** *mpl* **~s** plastic arts **2** *m* plastic; **une chaise en** ~ a plastic chair

plat, ~e [pla, plat] **1** *adj* flat; *eau* still, non-carbonated **2** *m vaisselle, mets* dish

platane [platan] *m* BOT plane tree

plateau [plato] *m* (*pl* -x) tray; *de théâtre* stage; TV, *d'un film* set; GÉOGR

plateau; **~ à** ou **de fromages** cheeseboard

plate-bande [platbɑ̃d] *f* (*pl* plates-bandes) flower bed

plate-forme [platfɔrm] *f* (*pl* plates-formes) platform; **~ électorale** POL election platform; **~ de forage** drilling platform; **~ de lancement** launch pad

platine [platin] **1** *m* CHIM platinum **2** *f*: **~ disques** turntable; **~ laser** ou **CD** CD player

platitude [platityd] *f fig: d'un livre etc* dullness; (*lieu commun*) platitude

platonique [platɔnik] platonic

plâtre [plɑtr] *m* plaster; MÉD plaster cast; **plâtrer** ⟨1a⟩ plaster

plausible [plozibl] plausible

plein, ~e [plɛ̃, -ɛn] **1** *adj* full (**de** of); **à ~ temps** full time; **en ~ air** in the open (air), out of doors; **en ~ été** at the height of summer; **en ~ Paris** in the middle of Paris; **en ~ jour** in broad daylight **2** *adv*: **en ~ dans** right in; **~ de** F loads of F, lots of F, a whole bunch of F; **j'en ai ~ le dos!** *fig* F I've had it up to here! **3** *m*: **battre son ~** be in full swing; **faire le ~** AUTO fill up; **faire le ~ de** *vin, eau, nourriture* stock up on; **pleinement** *adv* fully

plein-emploi [plɛ̃nɑ̃plwa] *m* ÉCON full employment

pleurer [plœre] ⟨1a⟩ **1** *v/i* cry, weep; **~ sur qch** complain about sth, bemoan sth *fml*; **~ de rire** cry with laughter **2** *v/t* (*regretter*) mourn; **pleureur** BOT: **saule** ~ weeping willow

pleurnicher [plœrniʃe] ⟨1a⟩ F snivel

pleurs [plœr] *mpl litt*: **en ~** in tears

pleuvoir [pløvwar] ⟨3e⟩ rain; **il pleut** it is raining

pli [pli] *m* fold; *d'une jupe* pleat; *d'un pantalon* crease; (*enveloppe*) envelope; (*lettre*) letter; *au jeu de cartes* trick; (**faux**) ~ crease; **mise** *f* **en ~s** coiffure set

pliant, ~e [plijɑ̃, -t] folding

plier [plije] ⟨1a⟩ **1** *v/t* (*rabattre*) fold; (*courber, ployer*) bend **2** *v/i d'un arbre, d'une planche* bend; *fig* (*céder*) give in;

se ~ à (*se soumettre*) submit to; *caprices* give in to

plisser [plise] ⟨1a⟩ pleat; (*froisser*) crease; *front* wrinkle

plomb [plɔ̃] *m* lead; *soleil m de ~* scorching hot sun; *sans ~ essence* unleaded

plombage [plɔ̃baʒ] *m action, amalgame* filling; **plomber** ⟨1a⟩ *dent* fill; **plomberie** *f* plumbing; **plombier** *m* plumber

plongée [plɔ̃ʒe] *f* diving; *faire de la ~* go diving; **plongeoir** *m* diving board; **plongeon** *m* SP dive; **plonger** ⟨1l⟩ **1** *v/i* dive **2** *v/t* plunge; *se ~ dans* bury *ou* immerse o.s. in; **plongeur, -euse** *m/f* diver

ployer [plwaje] ⟨1h⟩ *litt* (*se courber*) bend; (*fléchir*) give in

pluie [plɥi] *f* rain; *fig* shower; *sous la ~* in the rain; *~s acides* acid rain *sg*

plumage [plymaʒ] *m* plumage

plume [plym] *f* feather; **plumer** ⟨1a⟩ pluck; *fig* fleece

plupart [plypar]: *la ~ des élèves* most of the pupils *pl*; *la ~ d'entre nous* most of us; *pour la ~* for the most part, mostly; *la ~ du temps* most of the time

pluridisciplinaire [plyridisiplinɛr] multidisciplinary

pluriel, ~le [plyrjɛl] **1** *adj* plural **2** *m* GRAM plural; *au ~* in the plural

plus 1 *adv* ◇ [ply] *comparatif* more (*que, de* than); *~ grand / petit* bigger / smaller (*que* than); *~ efficace / intéressant* more efficient / interesting (*que* than); *de en ~* more and more; *~ il vieillit il dort* the older he gets the more he sleeps

◇ [ply] *superlatif*: *le ~ grand / petit* the biggest / smallest; *le ~ efficace / intéressant* the most efficient / interesting; *le ~* the most; *au ~ tard* at the latest; (*tout*) *au ~* [plys] at the (very) most

◇ [plys] *davantage* more; *tu en veux ~?* do you want some more?; *rien de ~* nothing more; *je l'aime bien, sans ~* I like her, but it's no more than that

ou but that's as far as it goes; *20 euros de ~* another 20 euros, 20 euros more; *et de ~ ...* (*en outre*) and moreover ...; *en ~* on top of that

◇ [ply] *négation, quantité*: *nous n'avons ~ d'argent* we have no more money, we don't have any more money

◇ [ply] *temps*: *elle n'y habite ~* she doesn't live there any more, she no longer lives there; *je ne le reverrai ~* I won't see him again; *je ne le reverrai ~ jamais* I won't see him ever again, I will never see him again

◇ [ply]: *lui, il n'a pas compris non ~* he didn't understand either; *je n'ai pas compris - moi non ~* I didn't understand - neither *ou* nor did I, I didn't either, me neither; *je ne suis pas prêt - moi non ~* I'm not ready - neither *ou* nor am I, me neither **2** *prép* [plys] MATH plus; *trois ~ trois* three plus *ou* and three **3** *m* [plys] MATH plus (sign)

plusieurs [plyzjœr] *adj & pron* several

plus-que-parfait [plyskəparfɛ] *m* GRAM pluperfect

plutôt [plyto] *adv*; *il est ~ grand* he's rather tall; *~ que de partir tout de suite* rather than leave *ou* leaving straight away

pluvieux, -euse [plyvjø, -z] rainy

PME [peemø] *abr* (= *petite(s) et moyenne(s) entreprise(s)*) SME (= small and medium-sized enterprise(s)); *une ~* a small business

PMU [peemy] *m abr* (= *Pari mutuel urbain*) state-run betting system

PNB [peenbe] *m abr* (= *produit national brut*) GDP (= gross domestic product)

pneu [pnø] *m* (*pl* -s) tire, *Br* tyre; **pneumatique 1** *adj marteau* pneumatic; *matelas* air **2** *m* → *pneu*

pneumonie [pnømɔni] *f* pneumonia

poche [pɔʃ] *f* pocket; ZO pouch; *livre m de ~* paperback; *~ revolver* back pocket; *argent de ~* pocket money; *avoir des ~s sous les yeux* have bags under one's eyes; **pocher**

⟨1a⟩ CUIS *œufs* poach

pochette [pɔʃɛt] *f pour photos, feuilles de papier* folder; *d'un disque,* CD sleeve; *(sac)* bag

podium [pɔdjɔm] *m* podium

poêle [pwal] **1** *m* stove **2** *f* frypan, *Br* frying pan

poêlon [pwalɔ̃] *m* pan

poème [pɔɛm] *m* poem

poésie [pɔezi] *f* poetry; *(poème)* poem

poète [pɔɛt] *m* poet; *femme f ~* poet, female poet; **poétique** poetic; *atmosphère* romantic

pognon [pɔɲɔ̃] *m* F dough F

poids [pwa] *m* weight; *fig (charge, fardeau)* burden; *(importance)* weight; *~ lourd boxeur* heavyweight; AUTO heavy truck, *Br* heavy goods vehicle; *perdre / prendre du ~* lose / gain weight; *lancer m du ~* putting the shot; *de ~* influential; *ne pas faire le ~ fig* not be up to it

poignant, ~e [pwaɲɑ̃, -t] *souvenir* poignant

poignard [pwaɲar] *m* dagger; **poignarder** ⟨1a⟩ stab

poignée [pwaɲe] *f quantité, petit nombre* handful; *d'une valise, d'une porte* handle; *~ de main* handshake

poignet [pwaɲɛ] *m* wrist

poil [pwal] *m* hair; *à ~* naked, in the altogether F

poilu, ~e [pwaly] hairy

poinçon [pwɛ̃sɔ̃] *m (marque)* stamp; **poinçonner** ⟨1a⟩ *or, argent* hallmark; *billet* punch

poing [pwɛ̃] *m* fist; *coup m de ~* punch

point[1] [pwɛ̃] *m* point; *de couture* stitch; *deux ~s* colon *sg*; *être sur le ~ de faire qch* be on the point of doing sth; *mettre au ~ caméra* focus; TECH finalize; *(régler)* adjust; *à ~ viande* medium; *au ~ d'être...* to the point of being...; *jusqu'à un certain ~* to a certain extent; *sur ce ~* on this point; *faire le ~ fig* take stock; *à ce ~* so much; *~ de côté* MÉD stitch (in one's side); *~ d'exclamation* exclamation point, *Br* exclamation mark; *~ d'interrogation* question mark; *~*

du jour dawn, daybreak; *~ de vue* point of view, viewpoint

point[2] [pwɛ̃] *adv litt: il ne le fera ~* he will not do it

pointe [pwɛ̃t] *f* point; *d'asperge* tip; *sur la ~ des pieds* on tippy-toe, *Br aussi* on tiptoe; *en ~* pointed; *de ~ technologie* leading-edge; *secteur* high-tech; *une ~ de* a touch of; **pointer** ⟨1a⟩ **1** *v/t sur liste* check, *Br* tick off **2** *v/i d'un employé* clock in

pointillé [pwɛ̃tije] *m*: *les ~s* the dotted line *sg*

pointilleux, -euse [pwɛ̃tijø, -z] fussy

pointu, ~e [pwɛ̃ty] pointed; *voix* high-pitched

pointure [pwɛ̃tyr] *f* (shoe) size; *quelle est votre ~?* what size are you?, what size (shoe) do you take?

point-virgule [pwɛ̃virgyl] *m (pl points-virgules)* GRAM semi-colon

poire [pwar] *f* BOT pear; F *visage, naïf* mug F

poireau [pwaro] *m (pl -x)* BOT leek

poireauter [pwarote] ⟨1a⟩ F be kept hanging around

poirier [pwarje] *m* BOT pear (tree)

pois [pwa] *m* BOT pea; *petits ~* garden peas; *à ~* polka-dot

poison [pwazɔ̃] **1** *m* poison **2** *m/f fig* F nuisance, pest

poisse [pwas] *f* F bad luck

poisson [pwasɔ̃] *m* fish; *~ d'avril* April Fool; *Poissons mpl* ASTROL Pisces; **poissonnerie** *f* fish shop, *Br* fishmonger's

poitrine [pwatrin] *f* chest; *(seins)* bosom; *tour f de ~* chest measurement; *d'une femme* bust measurement

poivre [pwavr] *m* pepper; *~ et sel cheveux* pepper-and-salt; **poivrer** ⟨1a⟩ pepper; **poivrière** *f* pepper shaker

poivron [pwavrɔ̃] *m* bell pepper, *Br* pepper

poker [pɔker] *m* poker

polaire [pɔlɛr] polar

polar [pɔlar] *m* F whodunnit F

polariser [pɔlarize] ⟨1a⟩ PHYS polarize; *~ l'attention / les regards fig* be the focus of attention

polaroïd® [pɔlarɔid] *m* polaroid

pôle [pol] *m* pole; *fig* center, *Br* centre, focus; **~ Nord** North Pole; **~ Sud** South Pole

polémique [polemik] **1** *adj* polemic **2** *f* controversy

poli, ~e [poli] (*courtois*) polite; *métal, caillou* polished

police[1] [polis] *f* police; **~ judiciaire** *branch of the police force that carries out criminal investigations*

police[2] [polis] *f d'assurances* policy; **~ d'assurance** insurance policy

polichinelle [poliʃinɛl] *m* Punch; **secret *m* de ~** open secret

policier, -ère [polisje, -ɛr] **1** *adj* police *atr*; *film, roman* detective *atr* **2** *m* police officer

polio [poljo] *f* polio

polir [polir] ⟨2a⟩ polish

polisson, ~ne [polisõ, -on] **1** *adj* (*coquin*) mischievous; (*grivois*) bawdy **2** *m/f* mischievous child

politesse [polites] *f* politeness

politicard [politikar] *m* F *péj* unscrupulous politician, politico F

politicien, ~ne [politisjɛ̃, -ɛn] *m/f* politician

politique [politik] **1** *adj* political; **homme *m* ~** politician; **économie *f* ~** political economy **2** *f d'un parti, du gouvernement* policy; (*affaires publiques*) politics *sg*; **~ monétaire** monetary policy **3** *m* politician

politisation [politizasjõ] *f* politicization; **politiser** ⟨1a⟩ politicize

politologie [politɔlɔʒi] *f* political science

pollen [polɛn] *m* pollen

polluant, ~e [polɥɑ̃, -t] **1** *adj* polluting **2** *m* pollutant; **polluer** ⟨1n⟩ pollute; **pollution** *f* pollution; **~ atmosphérique** air pollution

polo [polo] *m* polo

Pologne [polɔɲ]: **la ~** Poland; **polonais, ~e 1** *adj* Polish **2** *m langue* Polish **3** *m/f* Polonais, ~e Pole

poltron, ~ne [poltrõ, -on] *m/f* coward; **poltronnerie** *f* cowardice

polyclinique [poliklinik] *f* (general) hospital

polycopié [polikɔpje] *m* (photocopied) handout

polyester [poliɛstɛr] *m* polyester

polyéthylène [polietilɛn] *m* polyethylene

polygamie [poligami] *f* polygamy

polyglotte [poliglɔt] polyglot

Polynésie [polinezi] *f* Polynesia; **polynésien, ~ne 1** *adj* Polynesian **2** *m* LING Polynesian **3** *m/f* Polynésien, ~ne Polynesian

polystyrène [polistirɛn] *m* polystyrene

polyvalence [polivalɑ̃s] *f* versatility; **polyvalent** multipurpose; *personne* versatile

pommade [pomad] *f* MÉD ointment

pomme [pom] *f* apple; **tomber dans les ~s** F pass out; **~ d'Adam** Adam's apple; **~ de pin** pine cone; **~ de terre** potato

pommeau [pomo] *m* (*pl* -x) handle; *d'une selle* pommel

pommette [pomɛt] *f* ANAT cheekbone

pommier [pomje] *m* BOT apple tree

pompe[1] [põp] *f faste* pomp; **~s funèbres** funeral director, *Br aussi* undertaker's

pompe[2] [põp] *f* TECH pump; **~ à essence** gas pump, *Br* petrol pump; **~ à eau** water pump; **pomper** ⟨1a⟩ pump; *fig* (*épuiser*) knock out

pompeux, -euse [põpø, -z] pompous

pompier [põpje] *m* firefighter, *Br aussi* fireman; **~s** fire department *sg*, *Br* fire brigade *sg*

pompiste [põpist] *m* pump attendant

pompon [põpõ] *m* pompom; **pomponner** ⟨1a⟩ F: **se ~** get dolled up F

ponce [põs]: **pierre *f* ~** pumice stone; **poncer** ⟨1k⟩ sand; **ponceuse** *f* sander

ponctualité [põktɥalite] *f* punctuality

ponctuation [põktɥasjõ] *f* GRAM punctuation

ponctuel, ~le [põktɥel] *personne* punctual; *fig: action* one-off; **ponctuer** ⟨1n⟩ GRAM punctuate (*aussi fig*)

pondération [põderasjõ] *f d'une personne* level-headedness; *de forces* balance; ÉCON weighting; **pondéré, ~e** *personne* level-headed; *forces* balanced; ÉCON weighted

pondre [põdr] ⟨4a⟩ *œufs* lay; *fig* F come up with; *roman* churn out

poney [pɔnɛ] *m* pony

pont [põ] *m* bridge; MAR deck; **~ aérien** airlift; **faire le ~** make a long weekend of it; **pont-levis** *m* (*pl* ponts-levis) drawbridge

pontage [põtaʒ] *m*: **~ coronarien** (heart) bypass

pontife [põtif] *m* pontiff

ponton [põtõ] *m* pontoon

pop [pɔp] *f* MUS pop

popote [pɔpɔt] *f* F: **faire la ~** do the cooking

populace [pɔpylas] *f péj* rabble

populaire [pɔpylɛr] *popular*; **populariser** ⟨1a⟩ popularize; **popularité** *f* popularity

population [pɔpylasjõ] *f* population

porc [pɔr] *m* hog, pig; *fig* pig; *viande* pork

porcelaine [pɔrsəlɛn] *f* porcelain

porcelet [pɔrsəlɛ] *m* piglet

porc-épic [pɔrkepik] *m* (*pl* porcs-épics) porcupine

porche [pɔrʃ] *m* porch

porcherie [pɔrʃəri] *f élevage* hog *ou* pig farm

pore [pɔr] *m* pore; **poreux, -euse** porous

porno [pɔrno] F porno F

pornographie [pɔrnografi] *f* pornography; **pornographique** pornographic

port[1] [pɔr] *m* port; **~ de commerce** commercial port; **~ de pêche** fishing port

port[2] [pɔr] *m d'armes* carrying; *courrier* postage; **le ~ du casque est obligatoire** safety helmets must be worn; **en ~ dû** carriage forward

portable [pɔrtabl] **1** *adj* portable **2** *m ordinateur* laptop; *téléphone* cellphone, cell, *Br* mobile

portail [pɔrtaj] *m* (*pl* -s) ARCH portal; *d'un parc* gate

portant, ~e [pɔrtã, -t] *mur* load-bearing; **à bout ~** at point-blank range; **bien ~** well; **mal ~** not well, poorly; **portatif, -ive** portable

porte [pɔrt] *f* door; *d'une ville* gate; **entre deux ~s** very briefly; **mettre qn à la ~** throw s.o. out, show s.o. the door; **porte-à-porte** *m*: **faire du ~ vendre** be a door-to-door salesman

porte-avions [pɔrtavjõ] *m* (*pl inv*) aircraft carrier

porte-bagages [pɔrt(ə)bagaʒ] *m* AUTO roof rack; *filet* luggage rack

porte-bonheur [pɔrt(ə)bɔnœr] *m* (*pl inv*) lucky charm

porte-cigarettes [pɔrt(ə)sigarɛt] *m* (*pl inv*) cigarette case

porte-clés [pɔrtəkle] *m* (*pl inv*) keyring

porte-documents [pɔrt(ə)dɔkymã] *m* (*pl inv*) briefcase

portée [pɔrte] *f* ZO litter; *d'une arme* range; (*importance*) significance; **à ~ de la main** within arm's reach; **à la ~ de qn** *fig* be accessible to s.o.; **à la ~ de toutes les bourses** affordable by all; **hors de ~ de voix** out of hearing

porte-fenêtre [pɔrt(ə)fənɛtr] *f* (*pl* portes-fenêtres) French door, *Br* French window

portefeuille [pɔrtəfœj] *m* portfolio (*aussi* POL, FIN); (*porte-monnaie*) billfold, *Br* wallet

porte-jarretelles [pɔrt(ə)ʒartɛl] *m* (*pl inv*) garter belt, *Br* suspender belt

portemanteau [pɔrt(ə)mãto] *m* (*pl* -x) coat rack; *sur pied* coatstand

portemine [pɔrtəmin] *m* mechanical pencil, *Br* propelling pencil

porte-monnaie [pɔrt(ə)mɔnɛ] *m* (*pl inv*) coin purse, *Br* purse

porte-parole [pɔrt(ə)parɔl] *m* (*pl inv*) spokesperson

porter [pɔrte] ⟨1a⟩ **1** *v/t* carry; *un vêtement, des lunettes etc* wear; (*apporter*) take; bring; *yeux, attention* turn (**sur** to); *toast* drink; *responsabilité* shoulder; *fruits, nom* bear; **~ les cheveux longs / la barbe** have long hair / a beard; **~ plainte** make a complaint; **~ son attention sur qch** direct one's attention to sth; **être porté sur qch** have a weakness for sth **2** *v/i d'une voix* carry; **~ juste**

d'un coup strike home; **~ sur** (*appuyer sur*) rest on, be borne by; (*concerner*) be about, relate to; **~ sur les nerfs de qn** F get on s.o.'s nerves **3**: *il se porte bien / mal* he's well / not well; *se ~ candidat* be a candidate, run

porte-savon [pɔrtsavõ] *m* (*pl* porte--savon(s)) soap dish

porte-serviettes [pɔrtservjet] *m* (*pl inv*) towel rail

porte-skis [pɔrt(ə)ski] *m* (*pl inv*) ski rack

porteur [pɔrtœr] *m pour une expédition* porter, bearer; *d'un message* bearer; MÉD carrier

porte-voix [pɔrtəvwa] *m* (*pl inv*) bull horn, *Br* megaphone

portier [pɔrtje] *m* doorman

portière [pɔrtjer] *f* door

portion [pɔrsjõ] *f d'un tout* portion; CUIS serving, portion

portique [pɔrtik] *m* ARCH portico; SP beam

porto [pɔrto] *m* port

Porto Rico [pɔrtoriko] Puerto Rico; **portoricain, ~e 1** *adj* Puerto Rican; **2** *m/f* **Portoricain, ~e** Puerto Rican

portrait [pɔrtre] *m* portrait; *faire le ~ de qn* paint / draw a portrait of s.o.; **portrait-robot** *m* (*pl* portraits-robots) composite picture, *Br* Identi-kit® picture

portuaire [pɔrtɥer] port *atr*

portugais, ~e 1 [pɔrtyge, -z] *adj* Portuguese **2** *m langue* Portuguese **3** *m/f* **Portugais, ~e** Portuguese; **Portugal:** *le ~* Portugal

pose [poz] *f d'un radiateur* installation; *de moquette* fitting; *de papier peint, rideaux* hanging; (*attitude*) pose

posé, ~e [poze] poised, composed; **posément** *adv* with composure

poser [poze] ⟨1a⟩ **1** *v/t* (*mettre*) put (down); *compteur, radiateur* install, *Br* instal; *moquette* fit; *papier peint, rideaux* put up, hang; *problème* pose; *~ une question* ask a question; *~ sa candidature à un poste* apply for; *se ~* AVIAT land, touch down; *se ~ en* set o.s. up as **2** *v/i* pose

poseur, -euse [pozœr, -øz] *m/f* **1** show-off, *Br* F pseud **2** *m*: *~ de bombes* person who plants bombs

positif, -ive [pozitif, -iv] positive

position [pozisjõ] *f* position; *prendre ~* take a stand; *~ sociale* (social) standing

positiver [pozitive] ⟨1b⟩ accentuate the positive

posologie [pozɔlɔʒi] *f* PHARM dosage

possédé, ~e [posede] possessed (*de* by); **posséder** ⟨1f⟩ own, possess; **possesseur** *m* owner; **possessif, -ive** possessive; **possession** *f* possession, ownership; *être en ~ de qch* be in possession of sth

possibilité [posibilite] *f* possibility

possible [posibl] **1** *adj* possible; *le plus souvent ~* as often as possible; *autant que ~* as far as possible; *le plus de pain ~* as much bread as possible **2** *m*: *faire tout son ~* do everything one can, do one's utmost

postal, ~e [pɔstal] (*mpl* -aux) mail *atr*, *Br aussi* postal

postdater [pɔstdate] ⟨1a⟩ postdate

poste[1] [pɔst] *f* mail, *Br aussi* post; (*bureau m de*) *~* post office; *mettre à la ~* mail, *Br aussi* post; *~ restante* general delivery, *Br* poste restante

poste[2] [pɔst] *m* post; (*profession*) position; RAD, TV set; TÉL extension; *~ de pilotage* AVIAT cockpit; *~ de secours* first-aid post; *~ supplémentaire* TÉL extension; *~ de travail* INFORM work station

poster [pɔste] ⟨1a⟩ *soldat* post; *lettre* mail, *Br aussi* post

postérieur, ~e [pɔsterjœr] **1** *adj dans l'espace* back *atr*, rear *atr*; *dans le temps* later; *~ à qch* after sth **2** *m* F posterior F, rear end F

postérité [pɔsterite] *f* posterity

posthume [pɔstym] posthumous

postiche [pɔstiʃ] *m* hairpiece

postier, -ère [pɔstje, -er] *m/f* post office employee

postillonner [pɔstijɔne] ⟨1a⟩ splutter

postulant, ~e [pɔstylã, -t] *m/f* candidate; **postuler** ⟨1a⟩ apply for

posture [pɔstyr] *f* (*attitude*) position,

P

posture; *fig* position

pot [po] *m* pot; **~ à eau** water jug; **~ de fleurs** flowerpot; **prendre un ~** F have a drink; **avoir du ~** F be lucky

potable [pɔtabl] fit to drink; **eau ~** drinking water

potage [pɔtaʒ] *m* soup; **potager, -ère: jardin** *m* **~** kitchen garden

potassium [pɔtasjɔm] *m* potassium

pot-au-feu [pɔtofø] *m* (*pl inv*) boiled beef dinner

pot-de-vin [podvɛ̃] *m* (*pl* pots-de-vin) F kickback F, bribe, backhander F

pote [pɔt] *m* F pal, *Br aussi* mate

poteau [pɔto] *m* (*pl* -x) post; **~ indicateur** signpost; **~ télégraphique** utility pole, *Br* telegraph pole

potelé, ~e [pɔtle] chubby

potentiel, ~le [pɔtɑ̃sjɛl] *m* & *adj* potential

poterie [pɔtri] *f* pottery; *objet* piece of pottery; **potier** *m* potter

potins [pɔtɛ̃] *mpl* gossip *sg*

potion [pɔsjɔ̃] *f* potion

potiron [pɔtirɔ̃] *m* BOT pumpkin

pou [pu] *m* (*pl* -x) *m* louse

poubelle [pubɛl] *f* trash can, *Br* dustbin; **mettre qch à la ~** throw sth out

pouce [pus] *m* thumb; **manger sur le ~** grab a quick bite (to eat)

poudre [pudr] *f* powder; **chocolat** *m* **en ~** chocolate powder; **sucre** *m* **en ~** superfine sugar, *Br* caster sugar; **poudrier** *m* powder compact; **poudrière** *f fig* powder keg

pouf [puf] *m* pouffe

pouffer [pufe] ⟨1a⟩: **~ de rire** burst out laughing

poulailler [pulaje] *m* henhouse; *au théâtre* gallery, *Br* gods *pl*

poulain [pulɛ̃] *m* ZO foal

poule [pul] *f* hen; **poulet** *m* chicken

poulie [puli] *f* TECH pulley

poulpe [pulp] *m* octopus

pouls [pu] *m* pulse; **prendre le ~ de qn** take s.o.'s pulse

poumon [pumɔ̃] *m* lung

poupe [pup] *f* MAR poop

poupée [pupe] *f* doll (*aussi fig*)

poupon [pupɔ̃] *m* little baby; **pouponnière** *f* nursery

pour [pur] **1** *prép* ◇ for; **~ moi** for me; **~ ce qui est de ...** as regards ...; **c'est ~ ça que ...** that's why ...; **c'est ~ ça** that's why; **~ moi, ~ ma part** as for me; **aversion ~** aversion to; **avoir ~ ami** have as *ou* for a friend; **être ~ faire qch** be for doing sth, be in favor *ou Br* favour of doing sth; **~ 20 euros de courses** 20 euros' worth of shopping; **~ affaires** on business

◇: **~ ne pas perdre trop de temps** so as not to *ou* in order not to lose too much time; **je l'ai dit ~ te prévenir** I said that to warn you

2 *conj*: **~ que** (+ *subj*) so that, **je l'ai fait exprès ~ que tu saches que ...** I did it deliberately so that you would know that ...; **il parle trop vite ~ que je le comprenne** he speaks too fast for me to understand

3 *m*: **le ~ et le contre** the pros and the cons *pl*

pourboire [purbwar] *m* tip

pourcentage [pursɑ̃taʒ] *m* percentage

pourchasser [purʃase] ⟨1a⟩ chase after, pursue

pourparlers [purparle] *mpl* talks, discussions

pourpre [purpr] purple

pourquoi [purkwa] why; **c'est ~, voilà ~** that's why; **le ~** the whys and the wherefores *pl*

pourri, ~e [puri] rotten (*aussi fig*); **pourrir** ⟨2a⟩ **1** *v/i* rot; *fig: d'une situation* deteriorate **2** *v/t* rot; *fig* (*corrompre*) corrupt; (*gâter*) spoil; **pourriture** *f* rot (*aussi fig*)

poursuite [pursɥit] *f* chase, pursuit; *fig* pursuit (**de** of); **~s** JUR proceedings; **poursuivant, ~e** *m/f* pursuer; **poursuivre** ⟨4h⟩ pursue, chase; *fig: honneurs, but, bonheur* pursue; *de pensées, images* haunt; JUR sue; *malfaiteur, voleur* prosecute; (*continuer*) carry on with, continue

pourtant [purtɑ̃] *adv* yet

pourtour [purtur] *m* perimeter

pourvoir [purvwar] ⟨3b⟩ **1** *v/t emploi* fill; **~ de** *voiture, maison* equip *ou* fit

précipiter

with **2** v/i: **~ à besoins** provide for; **se
~ de** provide for; provide o.s. with; **se ~
en cassation** JUR appeal

pourvu [purvy]: **~ que** (+ *subj*) provided that; *exprimant désir* hopefully

pousse [pus] f AGR shoot; **poussée** f
thrust; MÉD outbreak; *de fièvre* rise;
fig: de racisme etc upsurge; **pousser**
⟨1a⟩ **1** v/t push; *du vent, de la marée*
drive; *cri, soupir* give; *fig: travail, recherches* pursue; **~ qn à faire qch** (*inciter*) drive s.o. to do sth; **se ~ d'une
foule** push forward; **pour faire de la
place** move over; **sur banc** move up
2 v/i push; *de cheveux, plantes* grow

poussette [puset] f *pour enfants* stroller, *Br* pushchair

poussière [pusjɛr] f dust; *particule*
speck of dust; **poussiéreux, -euse**
dusty

poussin [pusɛ̃] m chick

poutre [putr] f beam

pouvoir [puvwar] **1** ⟨3f⟩ be able to,
can; **est-ce que vous pouvez m'aider?** can you help me?; **puis-je
vous aider?** can I ou may I help
you?; **je ne peux pas aider** I can't
ou cannot help; **je suis désolé de
ne pas ~ vous aider** I am sorry
not to be able to help you; **je ne pouvais pas accepter** I couldn't accept,
I wasn't able to accept; **il ne pourra
pas ~** he will not ou won't be able to
…; **j'ai fait tout ce que j'ai pu** I did
all I could; **je n'en peux plus** I can't
take any more; **si l'on peut dire** in a
manner of speaking, if I may put it
that way; **il peut arriver que** (+ *subj*)
it may happen that; **il se peut que**
(+ *subj*) it's possible that
◊ *permission* can, be allowed to; **elle
ne peut pas sortir seule** she can't
go out alone, she is not allowed to
go out alone
◊: **tu aurais pu me prévenir!** you
could have ou might have warned
me!

2 m power; *procuration* power of attorney; **les ~s publics** the authorities; **~s exceptionels** special
powers; **~ d'achat** purchasing power;

être au ~ be in power

pragmatique [pragmatik] pragmatic

prairie [preri] f meadow; *plaine* prairie

praline [pralin] f praline

praticable [pratikabl] *projet* feasible;
route passable

praticien, ~ne [pratisjɛ̃, -ɛn] m/f MÉD
general practitioner

pratiquant, ~e [pratikɑ̃, -t] REL prac-
tising

pratique [pratik] **1** adj practical **2** f
practice; *expérience* practical experience; **pratiquement** adv (*presque*)
practically, virtually; *dans la pratique*
in practice; **pratiquer** ⟨1m⟩ practice,
Br practise; *sports* play; *méthode, technique* use; TECH *trou, passage* make;
se ~ be practiced, *Br* be practised

pré [pre] m meadow

préado [preado] m/f pre-teen

préalable [prealabl] **1** adj (*antérieur*)
prior; (*préliminaire*) preliminary
2 m condition; **au ~** beforehand,
first

préambule [preɑ̃byl] m preamble

préau m (*pl* préaux) courtyard

préavis [preavi] m notice; **sans ~**
without any notice ou warning

précaire [prekɛr] precarious

précaution [prekosjɔ̃] f caution, care;
mesure precaution; **par ~** as a precaution

précédent, ~e [presedɑ̃, -t] **1** adj previous **2** m precedent; **sans ~** unpre-
cedented, without precedent; **précéder** ⟨1f⟩ precede

préchauffer [prefofe] ⟨1a⟩ preheat

prêcher ⟨1b⟩ preach (*aussi fig*)

précieusement [presjøzmɑ̃] adv:
garder qch ~ treasure sth; **précieux,
-euse** precious

précipice [presipis] m precipice

précipitamment [presipitamɑ̃] adv
hastily, in a rush; **précipitation** f
haste; **~s** *temps* precipitation *sg*; **précipiter** ⟨1a⟩ (*faire tomber*) plunge
(**dans** into); (*pousser avec violence*)
hurl; (*brusquer*) precipitate; *pas* hasten; **j'ai dû ~ mon départ** I had to
leave suddenly; **se ~** (*se jeter*) throw
o.s.; (*se dépêcher*) rush

P

précis, ~e [presi, -z] **1** *adj* precise, exact; **à dix heures ~es** at 10 o'clock precisely *ou* exactly **2** *m* précis, summary; **précisément** *adv* precisely, exactly; **préciser** ⟨1a⟩ specify; **~ que** (*souligner*) make it clear that; **précision** *f d'un calcul, d'une montre* accuracy; *d'un geste* preciseness; **pour plus de ~s** for further details; **merci de ses ~s** thanks for that information

précoce [prekɔs] early; *enfant* precocious; **précocité** *f* earliness; *d'un enfant* precociousness

préconçu, ~e [prekɔ̃sy] preconceived

préconiser [prekɔnize] ⟨1a⟩ recommend

précurseur [prekyrsœr] **1** *m* precursor **2** *adj*: **signe** *m* **~** warning sign

prédateur, -trice [predatœr, -tris] **1** *adj* predatory **2** *m/f* predator

prédécesseur [predesesœr] *m* predecessor

prédestiner [predestine] ⟨1a⟩ predestine (**à qch** for sth; **à faire qch** to do sth)

prédicateur [predikatœr] *m* preacher

prédiction [prediksjɔ̃] *f* prediction

prédilection [predilɛksjɔ̃] *f* predilection (**pour** for); **de ~** favorite, *Br* favourite

prédire [predir] ⟨4m⟩ predict

prédominance [predɔminɑ̃s] *f* predominance; **prédominant, ~e** predominant; **prédominer** ⟨1a⟩ predominate

préfabriqué, ~e [prefabrike] prefabricated

préface [prefas] *f* preface

préfecture [prefɛktyr] *f* prefecture, *local government offices*; **~ de police** police headquarters *pl*

préférable [preferabl] preferable (**à** to); **préféré, ~e** favorite, *Br* favourite; **préférence** *f* preference; **de ~** preferably; **de ~ à** in preference to; **donner la ~ à qn / qch** prefer s.o. / sth; **préférentiel, ~le** preferential; **préférer** ⟨1f⟩ prefer (**à** to); **~ faire qch** prefer to do sth; **je préfère que tu viennes** (*subj*) **demain** I

would *ou* I'd prefer you to come tomorrow, I'd rather you came tomorrow

préfet [prefɛ] *m* prefect, *head of a département*; **~ de police** chief of police

préfixe [prefiks] *m* prefix

préhistoire [preistwar] *f* prehistory

préjudice [preʒydis] *m* harm; **porter ~ à qn** harm s.o.; **préjudiciable** harmful (**à** to)

préjugé [preʒyʒe] *m* prejudice

prélasser [prelase] ⟨1a⟩: **se ~** lounge

prélavage [prelavaʒ] *m* prewash

prélèvement [prelɛvmɑ̃] *m sur salaire* deduction; **~ de sang** blood sample

prélever [prelve] ⟨1d⟩ *échantillon* take; *montant* deduct (**sur** from)

préliminaire [preliminɛr] **1** *adj* preliminary **2** *mpl*: **~s** preliminaries

prélude [prelyd] *m* MUS, *fig* prelude (**de** to); **préluder** ⟨1a⟩ *fig*: **~ à qch** be the prelude to sth

prématuré, ~e [prematyre] premature

préméditation [premeditasjɔ̃] *f* JUR premeditation; **préméditer** ⟨1a⟩ premeditate

premier, -ère [prəmje, -ɛr] **1** *adj* first; *rang* front; *objectif, souci, cause* primary; *nombre* prime; **les ~s temps** in the early days, at first; **au ~ étage** on the second floor, *Br* on the first floor; **du ~ coup** at the first attempt; **Premier ministre** Prime Minister; **~ rôle** *m* lead, leading role; **de ~ ordre** first-class, first-rate; **matière** *f* **première** raw material; **le ~ août** August first, *Br* the first of August **2** *m/f*: **partir le ~** leave first **3** *m* second floor, *Br* first floor; **en ~** first **4** *f* THÉÂT first night; AUTO first (gear); *en train* first (class); **premièrement** *adv* firstly

prémisse [premis] *f* premise

prémonition [premɔnisjɔ̃] *f* premonition; **prémonitoire** *rêve* prophetic

prenant, ~e [prənɑ̃, -t] *livre, occupation* absorbing, engrossing

prénatal, ~e [prenatal] antenatal

prendre [prɑ̃dr] ⟨4q⟩ **1** *v/t* take; (*enlever*) take away; *capturer: voleur* catch, capture; *ville* take, capture; *aliments* have, take; *froid* catch; *poids* put on; **qch à qn** take sth (away) from s.o.; **~ bien / mal qch** take sth well / badly; **~ qn chez lui** pick s.o. up, fetch s.o.; **~ de l'âge** get old; **~ qn par surprise** catch *ou* take s.o. by surprise; **~ l'eau** let in water; **~ qn / qch pour** take s.o. / sth for; **à tout ~** all in all, on the whole **2** *v/i* (*durcir*) set; *d'une greffe* take; *d'un feu* take hold, catch; *de mode* catch on; **~ à droite** turn right; **ça ne prend pas avec moi** I don't believe you, I'm not swallowing that F **3**: **se ~** (*se laisser attraper*) get caught; **s'y ~ bien / mal** go about it the right / wrong way; **se ~ d'amitié pour qn** take a liking to s.o.; **s'en ~ à qn** blame s.o.; **se ~ à faire qch** start *ou* begin to do sth

preneur, -euse [prənœr, -øz] *m/f* COMM, JUR buyer; **il y a des ~s?** any takers?; **~ d'otages** hostage taker

prénom [prenõ] *m* first name; **deuxième ~** middle name

prénuptial, ~e [prenypsjal] prenuptial

préoccupant, ~e [preɔkypã, -t] worrying

préoccupation [preɔkypasjõ] *f* concern, worry; **préoccuper** ⟨1a⟩ (*occuper fortement*) preoccupy; (*inquiéter*) worry; **se ~ de** worry about

préparatifs [preparatif] *mpl* preparations; **préparation** *f* preparation; **préparatoire** preparatory; **préparer** ⟨1a⟩ prepare; (*organiser*) arrange; **~ qn à qch** prepare s.o. for sth; **~ un examen** prepare for an exam; **se ~** get ready; **une dispute / un orage se prépare** an argument / a storm is brewing

prépondérant, ~e [prepõderã, -t] predominant

préposé [prepoze] *m* (*facteur*) mailman, *Br* postman; *au vestiaire* attendant; *des douanes* official; **préposée** *f* (*factrice*) mailwoman, *Br* postwoman

préposition *f* GRAM preposition

préretraite [preretret] *f* early retirement

prérogative [prerɔgativ] *f* prerogative

près [pre] **1** *adv* close, near; **tout ~** very close by; **à peu ~** almost; **à peu de choses ~** more or less, pretty much; **à cela ~ que** except that; **de ~** closely; **être rasé de ~** be close-shaven **2** *prép*: **~ de qch** near sth, close to sth; **~ de 500** nearly 500, close to 500; **être ~ de faire qch** be on the point *ou* the brink of doing sth; **je ne suis pas ~ de l'épouser** I'm not about to marry him

présage [preza3] *m* omen

presbyte [prezbit] MÉD farsighted, *Br* long-sighted

prescription [preskripsjõ] *f* rule; MÉD prescription; **il y a ~** JUR the statute of limitations applies

prescrire [preskrir] ⟨4f⟩ stipulate; MÉD prescribe

présence [prezãs] *f* presence; **~ d'esprit** presence of mind; **en ~ de** in the presence of; **en ~** face to face, alone together; **présent, ~e 1** *adj* present **2** *m* present (*aussi* GRAM); **les ~s** those present; **à ~** at present; **à ~ que** now that; **jusqu'à ~** till now

présentable [prezãtabl] presentable

présentateur, -trice [prezãtatœr, -tris] *m/f* TV presenter; **~ météo** weatherman; **présentation** *f* presentation; (*introduction*) introduction; (*apparence*) appearance; **présenter** ⟨1a⟩ present; *chaise* offer; *personne* introduce; *pour un concours* put forward; *billet* show, present; *condoléances, félicitations* offer; *difficultés, dangers* involve; **se ~** introduce o.s.; *pour un poste, un emploi* apply; *aux élections* run, *Br aussi* stand; *de difficultés* come up; **cette réunion se présente bien / mal** it looks like being a good / bad meeting

préservatif [prezervatif] *m* condom

préservation [prezervasjõ] *f* protection; *du patrimoine* preservation; **préserver** ⟨1a⟩ protect, shelter (*de* from); *bois, patrimoine* preserve

présidence [prezidãs] *f* chairmanship; POL presidency; **président,**

~e *m/f d'une réunion, assemblée* chair; POL president; ~**directeur** *m* **général** president, CEO; **présidentiel, ~le** presidential; **présider** ⟨1a⟩ *réunion* chair

présomption [prezɔ̃psjɔ̃] *f* (*supposition*) presumption; (*arrogance aussi*) conceit; **présomptueux, -euse** presumptuous

presque [prɛsk] *adv* almost, nearly

presqu'île [prɛskil] *f* peninsula

pressant, ~e [prɛsɑ̃, -t] *besoin* pressing, urgent; *personne* insistent

presse [prɛs] *f* press; **mise** *f* **sous** ~ going to press

pressé, ~e [prese] *lettre, requête* urgent; *citron* fresh; **je suis** ~ I'm in a hurry *ou* a rush

presse-citron [prɛsitrɔ̃] *m* (*pl presse-citron(s)*) lemon squeezer

pressentiment [prɛsɑ̃timɑ̃] *m* foreboding, presentiment; **pressentir** ⟨2b⟩: ~ *qch* have a premonition that sth is going to happen; ~ *qn pour un poste* approach s.o., sound s.o. out

presse-papiers [prɛspapje] *m* (*pl inv*) paperweight

presser [prese] ⟨1b⟩ **1** *v/t bouton* push, press; *fruit* squeeze, juice; (*harceler*) press; *pas* quicken; *affaire* hurry along, speed up; (*étreindre*) press, squeeze; **se** ~ **contre** press (o.s.) against **2** *v/i* be urgent; **rien ne presse** there's no rush; **se** ~ hurry up, get a move on F

pressing [prɛsiŋ] *m magasin* dry cleaner

pression [prɛsjɔ̃] *f* PHYS, *fig* pressure; *bouton* snap fastener; (*bière f*) ~ draft beer, *Br* draught beer; **être sous** ~ be under pressure; **exercer une** ~ **sur** bring pressure to bear on; **faire** ~ **sur** pressure, put pressure on; ~ **artérielle** blood pressure

pressoir [prɛswar] *m vin* wine press

prestance [prɛstɑ̃s] *f* presence

prestation [prɛstɑsjɔ̃] *f* (*allocation*) allowance; ~**s familiales** child benefit *sg*

prestidigitateur, -trice [prɛsti-

diʒitatœr, -tris] *m/f* conjuror

prestige [prɛstiʒ] *m* prestige; **prestigieux, -euse** prestigious

présumer [prezyme] ⟨1a⟩ **1** *v/t*: ~ *que* presume *ou* assume that **2** *v/i*: ~ *de* overrate, have too high an opinion of

présupposer [presypoze] ⟨1a⟩ presuppose

prêt¹, ~e [prɛ, -t] ready (**à** *qch* for sth; **à faire** *qch* to do sth)

prêt² [prɛ] *m* loan; ~ **immobilier** mortgage, home loan

prêt-à-porter [prɛtaporte] *m* ready-to-wear clothes *pl*, ready-to-wear *sg*

prétendre [pretɑ̃dr] ⟨4a⟩ **1** *v/t* maintain; ~ **faire** *qch* claim to do sth **2** *v/i*: ~ **à** lay claim to; **prétendu, ~e** so-called

prétentieux, -euse [pretɑ̃sjø, -z] pretentious; **prétention** [pretɑ̃sjɔ̃] *f* (*revendication, ambition*) claim, pretention; (*arrogance*) pretentiousness

prêter [prete] ⟨1b⟩ **1** *v/t* lend; *intentions* attribute (**à** to) **2** *v/i*: ~ **à** give rise to; **se** ~ **à** *d'une chose* lend itself to; *d'une personne* be a party to

prétexte [pretɛkst] *m* pretext; **sous** ~ **de faire** *qch* on the pretext of doing sth; **sous aucun** ~ under no circumstances; **prétexter** ⟨1a⟩ claim (*que* that); **il a prétexté une tâche urgente** he claimed he had something urgent to do

prêtre [prɛtr] *m* priest; **prêtresse** *f* woman priest

preuve [prœv] *f* proof, evidence; MATH proof; ~**s** evidence *sg*; **faire** ~ **de courage** show courage

prévaloir [prevalwar] ⟨3h⟩ prevail (**sur** over; **contre** against); **se** ~ **de** *qch* (*tirer parti de*) make use of sth; (*se flatter de*) pride o.s. on sth

prévenance [prevnɑ̃s] *f* consideration; **prévenant, ~e** considerate, thoughtful

prévenir [prevnir] ⟨2h⟩ (*avertir*) warn (**de** of); (*informer*) tell (**de** about), inform (**de** of); *besoin, question* anticipate; *crise, maladie* avert

préventif, -ive [prevɑ̃tif, -iv] preventive; **prévention** *f* prevention; ~ **rou-**

tière road safety

prévenu, **~e** [prevǝny] *m/f* accused

prévisible [previzibl] foreseeable; **prévision** *f* forecast; **~s** predictions; **~s météorologiques** weather forecast *sg*; **en ~ de** in anticipation of

prévoir [prevwar] ⟨3b⟩ *(pressentir)* foresee; *(planifier)* plan; **les sanctions prévues par la loi** the penalties provided for by the law; **comme prévu** as expected; **son arrivée est prévue pour ce soir** he's expected *ou* scheduled to arrive this evening

prévoyance [prevwajãs] *f* foresight; **prévoyant**, **~e** farsighted

prier [prije] ⟨1a⟩ 1 *v/i* REL pray 2 *v/t* *(supplier)* beg; REL pray to; **~ qn de faire qch** ask s.o. to do sth; **~ Dieu** pray to God; **je vous en prie** not at all, don't mention it; **prière** *f* REL prayer; *(demande)* entreaty; **faire sa ~** say one's prayers; **~ de ne pas toucher** please do not touch

primaire [primer] primary; *péj* narrow-minded

primate [primat] *m* ZO primate

prime[1] [prim]: **de ~ abord** at first sight

prime[2] [prim] *f d'assurance* premium; *de fin d'année* bonus; *(cadeau)* free gift

primer [prime] ⟨1a⟩ 1 *v/i* take precedence, come first 2 *v/t* take precedence over, come before

primeur [primœr] *f*: **avoir la ~ de nouvelle** be the first to hear; *objet* have first use of; **~s** early fruit and vegetables

primevère [primver] *f* BOT primrose

primitif, **-ive** [primitif, -iv] primitive; *couleur, sens* original

primordial, **~e** [primɔrdjal] *(mpl* -aux) essential

prince [prɛ̃s] *m* prince; **princesse** princess; **princier**, **-ère** princely

principal, **~e** [prɛ̃sipal] *(mpl* -aux) 1 *adj* main, principal; GRAM main 2 *m*: **le ~** the main thing, the most important thing 3 *m/f* principal, *Br* head teacher

principauté [prɛ̃sipote] *f* principality

principe [prɛ̃sip] *m* principle; **par ~** on principle; **en ~** in theory, in principle

printanier, **-ère** [prɛ̃tanje, -ɛr] spring *atr*

printemps [prɛ̃tã] *m* spring

prioritaire [prijɔriter] priority; **être ~** have priority; *de véhicule aussi* have right of way

priorité [prijɔrite] *f* priority *(sur* over); *sur la route* right of way; **à droite** yield to cars coming from the right, *Br* give way cars to coming from the right; **donner la ~ à** prioritize, give priority to

pris, **~e** [pri, -z] 1 *p/p* → **prendre** 2 *adj* place taken; *personne* busy

prise [priz] *f* hold; *d'un pion, une ville etc* capture, taking; *de poissons* catch; ÉL outlet, *Br* socket; CINÉ take; **être aux ~s avec** be struggling with; **lâcher ~** let go; *fig* give up; **~ de conscience** awareness, realization; **~ de courant** outlet, *Br* socket; **~ d'otage(s)** hostage-taking; **~ de position** stand, stance; **~ de sang** blood sample; **~ de vue** shot

priser [prize] ⟨1a⟩ *litt (apprécier)* value

prison [prizɔ̃] *f* prison; **prisonnier**, **-ère** *m/f* prisoner; **~ de guerre** prisoner of war, POW; **~ politique** political prisoner *ou* detainee

privation [privasjɔ̃] *f* deprivation

privatisation [privatizasjɔ̃] *f* privatization; **privatiser** ⟨1a⟩ privatize

privé, **~e** [prive] 1 *adj* private; **agir à titre ~** act in a private capacity 2 *m* **en ~** in private; **le ~** *(intimité)* private life; *secteur* private sector; **priver** ⟨1a⟩: **~ qn de qch** deprive s.o. of sth; **se ~ de qch** go without sth

privilège [privilɛʒ] *m* privilege; **privilégié**, **privilégiée** [privileʒje] 1 *adj* privileged 2 *m/f*: **les ~s** the privileged *pl*; **privilégier** ⟨1a⟩ favor, *Br* favour

prix [pri] *m* price; *(valeur)* value; *(récompense)* prize; **à tout ~** at all costs; **à aucun ~** absolutely not; **hors de ~** prohibitive; **au ~ de** at the cost of; **~ brut** gross price; **~ fort** full price; **~**

P

Nobel Nobel Prize; *personne* Nobel prizewinner, Nobel laureate; **~ de revient** cost price

pro [pro] *m/f (pl inv)* F pro

probabilité [probabilite] *f* probability; **probable** probable

probant, ~e [probã, -t] convincing; *démonstration* conclusive

problématique [problematik] problematic; **problème** *m* problem; *pas de ~* no problem

procédé [prosede] *m (méthode)* method; TECH process; **~s** *(comportement)* behavior

procéder [prosede] ⟨1f⟩ proceed; **~ à qch** carry out sth; **procédure** *f* JUR procedure

procès [prose] *m* JUR trial

processeur [prosescer] *m* INFORM processor

procession [prosesjõ] *f* procession

processus [prosesys] *m* process

procès-verbal [proseverbal] *m (pl procès-verbaux)* minutes *pl*; *(contravention)* ticket; **dresser un ~** write a ticket

prochain, ~e [profẽ, -ɛn] **1** *adj* next *m/f*: **son ~** one's fellow human being, one's neighbor *ou* Br neighbour; **prochainement** *adv* shortly, soon

proche [prof] **1** *adj* close *(de* to); near; *ami* close; *événement, changement* recent; **~ de** *fig* close to; **dans un futur ~** in the near future **2** *mpl*: **~s** family and friends

proclamation [proklamasjõ] *f d'un événement, résultat* declaration, announcement; *d'un roi, d'une république* proclamation; **proclamer** ⟨1a⟩ *roi, république* proclaim; *résultats, innocence* declare

procréer [prokree] ⟨1a⟩ procreate

procuration [prokyrasjõ] *f* proxy, power of attorney; **procurer** ⟨1a⟩ get, procure *fml*; **procureur** *m*: **~ (de la République)** District Attorney, *Br* public prosecutor

prodige [prodiʒ] *m* wonder, marvel; **enfant** *m* **~** child *ou* infant prodigy; **prodigieux, -euse** enormous, tremendous

prodigue [prodig] extravagant; **prodiguer** ⟨1m⟩ lavish

producteur, -trice [prodyktœr, -tris] **1** *adj* producing; **pays** *m* **~ de pétrole** oil-producing country **2** *m/f* producer; **productif, -ive** productive; **production** *f* production; **productivité** *f* productivity; **produire** ⟨4c⟩ produce; **se ~** happen; **produit** *m* product; *d'un investissement* yield; **~ d'entretien** cleaning product; **~ fini** end product; **~ intérieur brut** ÉCON gross domestic product; **~ national brut** ÉCON gross national product

proéminent, ~e [proeminã, -t] prominent

prof [prof] *m/f abr (= professeur)* teacher

profanation [profanasjõ] *f* desecration

profane [profan] **1** *adj art, musique* secular **2** *m/f fig* lay person

profaner [profane] ⟨1a⟩ desecrate, profane

proférer [profere] ⟨1f⟩ *menaces* utter

professeur [profesœr] *m* teacher; *d'université* professor

profession [profesjõ] *f* profession; **professionnel, ~le** *m/f & adj* professional

professorat [profesora] *m* teaching

profil [profil] *m* profile

profit [profi] *m* COMM profit; *(avantage)* benefit; **au ~ de** in aid of; **tirer ~ de qch** take advantage of sth; **profitable** beneficial; COMM profitable; **profiter** ⟨1a⟩: **~ de qch** take advantage of sth; **~ à qn** be to s.o.'s advantage; **profiteur, -euse** *m/f* profiteer

profond, ~e [profõ, -d] deep; *personne, penseés* deep, profound; *influence* great, profound; **profondément** *adv* deeply, profoundly; **profondeur** *f* depth *(aussi fig)*

profusion [profyzjõ] *f* profusion; **à ~** in profusion

progéniture [proʒenityr] *f litt* progeny; *hum* offspring *pl*

programme [program] *m* program, *Br* programme; INFORM program; **~ an-**

tivirus antivirus program; **~ télé** TV program; **programmer** ⟨1a⟩ TV schedule; INFORM program; **programmeur, -euse** *m/f* programmer

progrès [prɔgrɛ] *m* progress; *d'un incendie, d'une épidémie* spread

progresser [prɔgrese] ⟨1b⟩ make progress, progress; *d'un incendie, d'une épidémie* spread; MIL advance, progress; **progressif, -ive** progressive; **progression** *f* progress; **progressiste** progressive (*aussi* POL); **progressivement** progressively

prohiber [prɔibe] ⟨1a⟩ ban, prohibit; **prohibitif, -ive** *prix* prohibitive; **prohibition** *f* ban; **la Prohibition** HIST Prohibition

proie [prwa] *f* prey (*aussi fig*); **en ~ à** prey to

projecteur [prɔʒɛktœr] *m* (*spot*) spotlight; *au cinéma* projector

projectile [-il] *m* projectile

projection [prɔʒɛksjɔ̃] *f* projection

projet [prɔʒɛ] *m* project; *personnel* plan; (*ébauche*) draft; **~ de loi** bill

projeter [prɔʒ(ə)te, prɔʃte] ⟨1c⟩ (*jeter*) throw; *film* screen; *travail, voyage* plan

prolétariat [prɔletarja] *m/f* proletariat

prolifération [prɔliferasjɔ̃] *f* proliferation; **proliférer** ⟨1f⟩ proliferate; **prolifique** prolific

prologue [prɔlɔg] *m* prologue

prolongation [prɔlɔ̃gasjɔ̃] *f* extension; **~s** SP overtime, *Br* extra time; **prolongement** *m* extension; **prolonger** ⟨1l⟩ prolong; *mur, route* extend; **se ~** go on, continue; *d'une route* continue

promenade [prɔmnad] *f* walk; *en voiture* drive; **promener** ⟨1d⟩ take for a walk; **~ son regard sur** *fig* run one's eyes over; **se ~** go for a walk; *en voiture* go for a drive; **envoyer ~** *fig* F: *personne* send packing; **promeneur, -euse** *m/f* stroller, walker

promesse [prɔmɛs] *f* promise

prometteur, -euse [prɔmɛtœr, -øz] promising; **promettre** ⟨4p⟩ promise (*qch à qn* s.o. sth, sth to s.o., **de faire qch** to do sth); **se ~ de faire qch**

make up one's mind to do sth

promiscuité [prɔmiskɥite] *f* overcrowding; *sexuelle* promiscuity

promontoire [prɔmɔ̃twar] *m* promontory

promoteur, -trice [prɔmɔtœr, -tris] **1** *m/f* (*instigateur*) instigator **2** *m*: **~ immobilier** property developer; **promotion** *f* promotion; *sociale* advancement; ÉDU class, *Br* year; **~ des ventes** COMM sales promotion; **en ~** on special offer

promouvoir [prɔmuvwar] ⟨3d⟩ promote

prompt, ~e [prõ, -t] (*rapide*) prompt, swift; *rétablissement* speedy; (*soudain*) swift

prôner [prone] ⟨1a⟩ advocate

pronom [prɔnõ] *m* GRAM pronoun

prononcé, ~e [prɔnõse] *fig* marked, pronounced; *accent, traits* strong

prononcer [prɔnõse] ⟨1k⟩ (*dire*) say, utter; (*articuler*) pronounce; *discours* give; JUR *sentence* pass, pronounce; **se ~** *d'un mot* be pronounced; (*se déterminer*) express an opinion; **se ~ pour / contre qch** come out in favor *ou Br* favour of / against sth; **prononciation** *f* pronunciation; JUR passing

pronostic [prɔnɔstik] *m* forecast; MÉD prognosis

propagande [prɔpagɑ̃d] *f* propaganda

propagation [prɔpagasjɔ̃] *f* spread; BIOL propagation; **propager** ⟨1l⟩ *idée, nouvelle* spread; BIOL propagate; **se ~** spread; BIOL reproduce

propane [prɔpan] *m* propane

propension [prɔpɑ̃sjɔ̃] *f* propensity (**à qch** for sth)

prophète, prophétesse [prɔfɛt, -etɛs] *m/f* prophet; **prophétie** *f* prophecy

propice [prɔpis] favorable, *Br* favourable; *moment* right; **~ à** conducive to

proportion [prɔpɔrsjɔ̃] *f* proportion; **toutes ~s gardées** on balance; **en ~ de** in proportion to; **proportionnel, ~le** proportional (**à** to); **proportionnellement** *adv* proportionally, in proportion (**à** to)

propos [prɔpo] **1** *mpl* (*paroles*) words **2** *m* (*intention*) intention; **à ~** at the right moment; **à tout ~** constantly; **mal à ~, hors de ~** at the wrong moment; **à ~!** by the way; **à ~ de** (*au sujet de*) about

proposer [prɔpoze] ⟨1a⟩ suggest, propose; (*offrir*) offer; **il m'a proposé de sortir avec lui** he suggested that I should go out with him, he offered to take me out; **se ~ de faire qch** propose doing sth; **se ~** offer one's services; **proposition** *f* (*suggestion*) proposal, suggestion; (*offre*) offer; GRAM clause

propre [prɔpr] **1** *adj* own; (*net, impeccable*) clean; (*approprié*) suitable; **sens** *m* **~** literal meaning; **~ à** (*particulier à*) characteristic of **2** *m*: **mettre au ~** make a clean copy of; **proprement** *adv* carefully; **à ~ parler** properly speaking; **le / la ... ~ dit** the actual ...; **propreté** *f* cleanliness

propriétaire [prɔprijetɛr] *m/f* owner; *qui loue* landlord; *femme* landlady; **~ terrien** land owner; **propriété** *f* (*possession*) ownership; (*caractéristique*) property; **proprio** *m/f* F landlord; landlady

propulser [prɔpylse] ⟨1a⟩ propel; **propulsion** *f* propulsion

prorata [prɔrata]: **au ~ de** in proportion to

proscrire [prɔskrir] ⟨4f⟩ (*interdire*) ban; (*bannir*) banish

prose [proz] *f* prose

prospecter [prɔspɛkte] ⟨1a⟩ prospect

prospectus [prɔspɛktys] *m* brochure; FIN prospectus

prospère [prɔspɛr] prosperous; **prospérer** ⟨1f⟩ prosper; **prospérité** *f* prosperity

prosterner [prɔstɛrne] ⟨1a⟩: **se ~** prostrate o.s.

prostituée [prɔstitɥe] *f* prostitute; **prostituer** ⟨1n⟩: **se ~** prostitute o.s.; **prostitution** *f* prostitution

protagoniste [prɔtagɔnist] *m* hero, protagonist

protecteur, -trice [prɔtɛktœr, -tris] **1** *adj* protective; *péj: ton, expression* patronizing **2** *m/f* protector; (*mécène*) sponsor, patron; **protection** *f* protection; **protectionnisme** *m* ÉCON protectionism; **protectorat** *m* protectorate; **protégé, ~e** *m/f* protégé; *péj* favorite, *Br* favourite; **protéger** ⟨1g⟩ protect (**contre, de** from); *arts, artistes* be a patron of; **protège-slip** *m* (*pl* protège-slips) panty-liner

protéine [prɔtein] *f* protein

protestant, ~e [prɔtɛstã, -t] REL *m/f* & *adj* Protestant

protestation [prɔtɛstasjõ] *f* (*plainte*) protest; (*déclaration*) protestation; **protester** ⟨1a⟩ protest; **~ contre qch** protest sth, *Br* protest against sth; **~ de son innocence** protest one's innocence

prothèse [prɔtɛz] *f* prosthesis

protocole [prɔtɔkɔl] *m* protocol

prototype [prɔtɔtip] *m* prototype

protubérance [prɔtyberãs] *f* protuberance

proue [pru] *f* MAR prow

prouesse [prwɛs] *f* prowess

prouver [pruve] ⟨1a⟩ prove

provenance [prɔvnãs] *f* origin; **en ~ de avion, train** from

provençal, ~e [prɔvãsal] (*mpl* -aux) Provençal

provenir [prɔvnir] ⟨2h⟩ (*aux être*): **~ de** come from

proverbe [prɔvɛrb] *m* proverb

providence [prɔvidãs] *f* providence; **providentiel, ~le** providential

province [prɔvɛ̃s] *f* province; **provincial, ~e** (*mpl* -iaux) provincial (*aussi fig*)

proviseur [prɔvizœr] *m* principal, *Br* head (teacher)

provision [prɔvizjõ] *f* supply (**de** of); **~s** (*vivres*) provisions; (*achats*) shopping *sg*; *d'un chèque* funds *pl*; **chèque** *m* **sans ~** bad check, *Br* bad cheque

provisoire [prɔvizwar] provisional

provocant, ~e [prɔvɔkã, -t], **provocateur, -trice** [prɔvɔkatœr, -tris] provocative; **provocation** *f* provocation; **provoquer** ⟨1m⟩ provoke; *acci-*

dent cause

proxénète [prɔksenɛt] *m* (*souteneur*) pimp

proximité [prɔksimite] *f* proximity; **à ~ de** near, in the vicinity of

prude [pryd] prudish

prudence [prydɑ̃s] *f* caution, prudence; **prudent, ~e** cautious, prudent; *conducteur* careful

prune [pryn] *f* BOT plum

pruneau [pryno] *m* (*pl* -x) prune

prunelle [prynɛl] *f* ANAT pupil; BOT sloe

prunier [prynje] *m* plum (tree)

PS [pɛɛs] *m abr* (= *Parti socialiste*) Socialist Party; (= *Post Scriptum*) postscript

psaume [psom] *m* psalm

pseudonyme [psødɔnim] *m* pseudonym

psychanalyse [psikanaliz] *f* psychoanalysis; **psychanalyser** ⟨1a⟩ psychoanalyze; **psychanalyste** *m/f* psychoanalyst

psychiatre [psikjatr] *m/f* psychiatrist; **psychiatrie** *f* psychiatry

psychique [psiʃik] psychic

psychologie [psikɔlɔʒi] *f* psychology; **psychologique** psychological; **psychologue** *m/f* psychologist

psychopathe [psikɔpat] *m/f* psychopath, psycho F

psychose [psikoz] *f* psychosis

psychosomatique [psikosɔmatik] psychosomatic

puant, ~e [pɥɑ̃, -t] stinking *fig* arrogant; **puanteur** *f* stink

pub [pyb] *f*: **une ~** an ad; *à la télé aussi* a commercial; **faire de la ~** do some advertising *ou* promotion; **je t'ai fait de la ~ auprès de lui** I put in a plug for you with him

puberté [pybɛrte] *f* puberty

public, publique [pyblik] **1** *adj* public **2** *m* public; *d'un spectacle* audience; **en ~** in public

publication [pyblikasjɔ̃] *f* publication

publicitaire [pyblisitɛr] advertising *atr*; **publicité** *f* publicity; COMM advertising; (*affiche*) ad

publier [pyblije] ⟨1a⟩ publish

publipostage [pyblipɔstaʒ] *m* mailshot; **logiciel** *m* **de ~** mailmerge software

puce [pys] *f* ZO flea; INFORM chip; **~ électronique** silicon chip; **marché** *m* **aux ~s** flea market

puceau [pyso] *m* F virgin

pucelle [pysɛl] *f* F *iron* virgin; **la ~ d'Orléans** the Maid of Orleans

pudeur [pydœr] *f* modesty; **pudique** modest; *discret* discreet

puer [pɥe] ⟨1a⟩ **1** *v/i* stink; **~ des pieds** have smelly feet **2** *v/t* stink of

puériculture [pɥerikyltyr] *f* child care

puéril, ~e [pɥeril] childish

puis [pɥi] *adv* then

puiser [pɥize] ⟨1a⟩ draw (**dans** from)

puisque [pɥiskə] *conj* since

puissance [pɥisɑ̃s] *f* power; *d'une armée* strength; **~ nucléaire** nuclear power; **puissant, ~e** powerful; *musculature, médicament* strong

puits [pɥi] *m* well; *d'une mine* shaft; **~ de pétrole** oil well

pull(-over) [pyl(ɔvɛr)] *m* (*pl* pulls, pull-overs) sweater, *Br aussi* pullover

pulluler [pylyle] ⟨1a⟩ swarm

pulmonaire [pylmɔnɛr] pulmonary

pulpe [pylp] *f* pulp

pulsation [pylsasjɔ̃] *f* beat, beating

pulsion [pylsjɔ̃] *f* drive; **~s fpl de mort** death wish *sg*

pulvérisateur [pylverizatœr] *m* spray; **pulvériser** ⟨1a⟩ *solide* pulverize (*aussi fig*); *liquide* spray

punaise [pynɛz] *f* ZO bug; (*clou*) thumbtack, *Br* drawing pin

punch[1] [pɔ̃ʃ] *m boisson* punch

punch[2] [pœnʃ] *m en boxe* punch (*aussi fig*)

punir [pynir] ⟨2a⟩ punish; **punition** *f* punishment

pupille [pypij] **1** *m/f* JUR ward **2** *f* ANAT pupil

pupitre [pypitr] *m* desk

pur, ~e [pyr] pure; *whisky* straight

purée [pyre] *f* purée; **~ (de pommes de terre)** mashed potatoes *pl*

pureté [pyrte] *f* purity

purge [pyrʒ] *f* MÉD, POL purge; **purger** ⟨1l⟩ TECH bleed; POL purge;

JUR *peine* serve
purification [pyrifikasjõ] *f* purification; **~ ethnique** ethnic cleansing;
purifier ⟨1a⟩ purify
puriste [pyrist] *m* purist
puritain, ~e [pyritɛ̃, -en] **1** *adj* purita-
nical **2** *m/f* puritan
pur-sang [pyrsã] *m* (*pl inv*) thor-
oughbred
pus [py] *m* pus
putain [pytɛ̃] *f* P whore; **~!** shit! P; **ce ~
de ...** this god-damn P *ou* Br bloody
F...
pute [pyt] *f* F slut
putréfaction [pytrefaksjõ] *f* putrefac-
tion; **putréfier** ⟨1a⟩ putrefy; **se ~** putrefy

putsch [putʃ] *m* putsch
puzzle [pœzl(ə)] *m* jigsaw (puzzle)
P.-V. [peve] *m abr* (= **procès-verbal**)
ticket
PVC [pevese] *m abr* (= **polychlorure
de vinyle**) PVC (= polyvinyl chloride)
pygmée [pigme] *m* pygmy
pyjama [piʒama] *m* pajamas *pl*, *Br*
pyjamas *pl*
pylône [pilon] *m* pylon
pyramide [piramid] *f* pyramid
Pyrénées [pirene] *fpl* Pyrenees
pyrex [pirɛks] *m* Pyrex®
pyromane [piroman] *m* pyromaniac;
JUR arsonist
python [pitõ] *m* python

Q

Q.I. [kyi] *m abr* (= **Quotient intellectuel**) IQ (= intelligence quotient)
quadragénaire [kwadraʒenɛr] *m/f &
adj* forty-year old
quadrangulaire [kwadrãgylɛr] quad-
rangular
quadrilatère [kwadrilatɛr, ka-] *m*
quadrilateral
quadrillé, ~e [kadrije] *papier* squared;
quadriller ⟨1a⟩ *fig: région* put under
surveillance
quadrupède [kwadryped] *m* quad-
ruped
quadruple [kwadryplə, ka-] quadruple; **quadrupler** ⟨1a⟩ quadruple;
quadruplés, -ées *mpl, fpl* quadru-
plets, quads
quai [ke] *m d'un port* quay; *d'une gare*
platform
qualificatif [kalifikatif] *m fig* term,
word; **qualification** *f* qualification
(*aussi* SP); (*appellation*) name; **~ professionnelle** professional qualification; **qualifié, ~e** qualified; **ouvrier**
m **~ / non ~** skilled / unskilled work-

er; **qualifier** ⟨1a⟩ qualify; (*appeler*)
describe; **~ qn d'idiot** describe s.o.
as an idiot, call s.o. an idiot; **se ~**
SP qualify
qualité [kalite] *f* quality; **de ~** quality
atr; **en ~ d'ambassadeur** as ambassador, in his capacity as ambassador;
~ de la vie quality of life
quand [kã] *adv & conj* when; **~ je serai de retour** when I'm back; **~
même** all the same
quant à [kãta] *prép* as for; **être certain ~ qch** be certain as to *ou* about
sth
quantifier [kãtifje] ⟨1a⟩ quantify
quantité [kãtite] *f* quantity; **une ~ de**
grand nombre a great many; *abondance* a great deal of; **du vin / des
erreurs en ~** lots of wine / mistakes;
~ de travail workload
quarantaine [karãten] *f* MÉD quaran-
tine; **une ~ de personnes** about
forty people *pl*, forty or so people
pl; **avoir la ~** be in one's forties;
quarante forty; **quarantième** for-

tieth

quart [kar] *m* quarter; *de vin* quarter liter, *Br* quarter litre; **~ d'heure** quarter of an hour; **les trois ~s** three--quarters; **~ de finale** quarter-final; **il est trois heures moins le ~** it's a quarter to three, it's two forty-five; **deux heures et~** two fifteen, a quarter after *ou Br* past two

quartier [kartje] *m* (*quart*) quarter; *d'orange, de pamplemousse* segment; *d'une ville* area, neighborhood, *Br* neighbourhood; *de / du ~* local *atr*; **~ général** MIL headquarters *pl*

quartz [kwarts] *m* quartz

quasi [kazi] *adv* virtually; **quasiment** *adv* virtually

quatorze [katɔrz] fourteen; → *trois*; **quatorzième** fourteenth

quatre [katr] four; → *trois*; **quatre--vingt(s)** eighty; **quatre-vingt-dix** ninety

quatrième [katrijɛm] fourth; **quatrièmement** *adv* fourthly

quatuor [kwatɥɔr] *m* MUS quartet

que [kə] **1** *pron relatif* ◊ *personne* who, that; **les étudiants ~ j'ai rencontrés** the students I met, the students who *ou* that I met; **imbécile ~ tu es!** you fool!

◊ *chose, animal* which, that; **les croissants ~ j'ai mangés** the croissants I ate, the croissants which *ou* that I ate

◊: **un jour ~** one day when

2 *pron interrogatif* what; **~ veut-il?** what does he want?; **qu'y a-t-il?** what's the matter?; **qu'est-ce que c'est?** what's that?; **je ne sais ~ dire** I don't know what to say

3 *adv dans exclamations*: **~ c'est beau!** it's so beautiful!, isn't that just beautiful!; **~ de fleurs!** what a lot of flowers!

4 *conj* that; **je croyais ~ tu avais compris** I thought (that) you had understood

◊ *après comparatif* than; **plus grand ~ moi** bigger than me

◊ *dans comparaison* as; **aussi petit ~ cela** as small as that

◊ **ne ... ~** only; **je n'en ai ~ trois** I have only three

◊ *concession*: **qu'il pleuve ou non** whether it rains or not

◊ *désir*: **qu'il entre** let him come in

◊: **~ je sache** as far as I know

◊: **~ coûte ~ coûte** whatever it might cost, cost what it might

◊: **s'il fait beau et ~ ...** if it's fine and (if) ...; **quand j'aurai fini et ~ ...** when I have finished and ...

Québec [kebɛk] Québec, Quebec; **québécois, ~e 1** *adj* from Quebec **2** *m langue* Canadian French **3** *m/f* **Québécois, ~e** Quebecois, Quebecker

quel, ~le [kɛl] *interrogatif* what, which; **~ prof / film as-tu préféré?** which teacher / movie did you prefer?; **~le est la différence?** what's the difference?; **~ est le plus riche des deux?** which is the richer of the two?; **~ est ce misérable qui ...?** *surtout litt* who is this wretched person who ...?

◊ *exclamatif*: **~le femme!** what a woman!; **~les belles couleurs!** what beautiful colors!

◊: **~ que: ~les que soient** (*subj*) **vos raisons** whatever reasons you might have, whatever your reasons might be

quelconque [kɛlkõk] ◊ (*médiocre*) very average, mediocre ◊: **un travail ~** some sort of a job

quelque [kɛlkə, kɛlk] **1** *adj* ◊ some; **~s** some, a few; **à ~ distance** at some distance; **~s jours** a few days; ◊: **~ ... que** (+ *subj*) whatever, whichever; **~ solution qu'il propose** whatever *ou* whichever solution he suggests

2 *adv devant chiffre* some; **~ grands qu'ils soient** (*subj*) however big they are, however big they might be

quelque chose *pron* something; *avec interrogatif, conditionnel aussi* anything; **il y a ~ d'autre** there's something else

quelquefois [kɛlkəfwa] *adv* sometimes

quelqu'un [kɛlkœ̃] *pron* someone,

Q

somebody; *avec interrogatif, conditionnel aussi* anyone, anybody; *il y a ~?* is anyone *ou* somebody there?; *~ d'autre* someone *ou* somebody else; **quelques-uns, quelques-unes** *pron pl* a few, some

quémander [kemɑ̃de] ⟨1a⟩ beg for

querelle [kərɛl] *f* quarrel; **quereller** ⟨1b⟩: *se ~* quarrel; **querelleur, -euse** 1 *adj* quarrelsome 2 *m/f* quarrelsome person

question [kɛstjɔ̃] *f* question; (*problème*) matter, question; *~ travail* as far as work is concerned, when it comes to work; *en ~* in question; *c'est hors de ~* it's out of the question; *il est ~ de* it's a question *ou* a matter of; **questionnaire** *m* questionnaire; **questionner** ⟨1a⟩ question (*sur* about)

quête [kɛt] *f* (*recherche*) search, quest *fml*; (*collecte*) collection; *en ~ de* in search of; **quêter** ⟨1b⟩ collect; (*solliciter*) seek, look for

queue [kø] *f* d'un animal tail; d'un fruit stalk; *d'une casserole* handle; *d'un train, cortège* rear; *d'une classe, d'un classement* bottom; *d'une file* line, Br queue; **faire la ~** stand in line, Br queue (up); **faire une ~ de poisson à qn** AUTO cut in in front of s.o.; *à la ~, en ~* at the rear; *~ de cheval* ponytail

qui [ki] *pron* ◇ *interrogatif* who; *de ~ est-ce qu'il tient ça?* who did he get that from?; *à ~ est-ce?* whose is this?, who does this belong to?; *~ est-ce que tu vas voir?* who are you going to see?; *~ est-ce qui a dit ça?* who said that?

◇ *relatif, personne* who, that; *tous les conducteurs ~ avaient …* all the drivers who *ou* that had …

◇ *relatif, chose, animal* which, that; *toutes les frites ~ restaient* all the fries which *ou* that were left

◇: *je ne sais ~* someone or other

◇: *~ que* (+ *subj*) whoever

quiconque [kikɔ̃k] *pron* whoever, anyone who, anybody who; (*n'importe qui*) anyone, anybody

quille [kij] *f* MAR keel

quincaillerie [kɛ̃kɑjri] *f* hardware, Br *aussi* ironmongery; *magasin* hardware store, Br *aussi* ironmonger's

quinquagénaire [kɛ̃kaʒenɛr] *m/f* & *adj* fifty-year old

quintal [kɛ̃tal] *m* hundred kilos *pl*

quinte [kɛ̃t] *f*: *~ (de toux)* coughing fit

quinzaine [kɛ̃zɛn] *f* de jours two weeks *pl*, Br *aussi* fortnight; *une ~ de personnes* about fifteen people *pl*, fifteen or so people *pl*; **quinze** fifteen; *~ jours* two weeks, Br *aussi* fortnight; *demain en ~* two weeks tomorrow; → *trois*; **quinzième** fifteenth

quittance [kitɑ̃s] *f* receipt

quitte [kit]: *être ~ envers qn* be quits with s.o.; *~ à faire qch* even if it means doing sth

quitter [kite] ⟨1a⟩ *endroit, personne* leave; *vêtement* take off; *se ~* part; *ne quittez pas* TÉL hold the line please

quoi [kwa] *pron* ◇ what; *~?* what?; *à ~ penses-tu?* what are you thinking about?; *après ~, il …* after which he …; *sans ~* otherwise; *à ~ bon?* what's the point?; *avoir de ~ vivre* have enough to live on; *il n'y a pas de ~!* not at all, don't mention it; *il n'y a pas de ~ rire / pleurer* there's nothing to laugh / cry about

◇: *~ que* (+ *subj*) whatever; *~ que tu fasses* whatever you do; *~ que ce soit* anything at all; *~ qu'il en soit* be that as it may

quoique [kwakə] *conj* (+ *subj*) although, though

quote-part [kɔtpar] *f* (*pl* quotes-parts) share

quotidien, ~ne [kɔtidjɛ̃, -ɛn] **1** *adj* daily; *de tous les jours* everyday **2** *m* daily

R

rab [rab] *m* F extra; **faire du ~** do a bit extra

rabâcher [rabaʃe] ⟨1a⟩ keep on repeating

rabais [rabɛ] *m* discount, reduction; **rabaisser** [rabese] ⟨1b⟩ *prix* lower, reduce; *mérites, qualités* belittle

rabat [raba] *m d'un vêtement etc* flap

rabat-joie [rabaʒwa] *m* killjoy

rabattre [rabatr] ⟨4a⟩ **1** *v/t siège* pull down; *couvercle* close, shut; *col* turn down; *gibier* drive **2** *v/i fig:* **se ~ sur** make do with, fall back on; *d'une voiture* pull back into

rabbin [rabɛ̃] *m* rabbi

râblé, ~e [rɑble] stocky

rabot [rabo] *m* plane; **raboter** ⟨1a⟩ plane

rabougri, ~e [rabugri] stunted

rabrouer [rabrue] ⟨1a⟩ snub

racaille [rakaj] *f* rabble

raccommodage [rakɔmɔdaʒ] *m* mending; **raccommoder** ⟨1a⟩ mend; *chaussettes* darn

raccompagner [rakɔ̃paɲe] ⟨1a⟩: **je vais vous ~ chez vous** *à pied* I'll take you home

raccord [rakɔr] *m* join; *de tuyaux aussi* connection; *d'un film* splice; **raccorder** ⟨1a⟩ join, connect

raccourci [rakursi] *m* shortcut; **en ~** briefly; **raccourcir** ⟨2a⟩ **1** *v/t* shorten **2** *v/i* get shorter

raccrocher [rakrɔʃe] ⟨1a⟩ **1** *v/t* put back up; **~ le téléphone** hang up; **se ~ à** cling to **2** *v/i* TÉL hang up

race [ras] *f* race; *(ascendance)* descent; ZO breed

rachat [raʃa] *m* repurchase; *d'un otage* ransoming; REL atonement; *d'une société* buyout; **racheter** ⟨1e⟩ buy back; *otage* ransom; REL *péché* atone for; *fig: faute* make up for; **se ~** make amends

racial, ~e [rasjal] *(mpl -aux)* racial

racine [rasin] *f* root *(aussi fig et* MATH*)*; **prendre ~** take root *(aussi fig)*; **~ carrée** square root

racisme [rasism] *m* racism; **raciste** *m/f & adj* racist

racket [rakɛt] *m* racket

raclée [rɑkle] *f* F beating, *Br aussi* walloping *(aussi fig)*

racler [rɑkle] ⟨1a⟩ scrape; **se ~ la gorge** clear one's throat; **raclette** *f* TECH scraper; CUIS raclette

racoler [rakɔle] ⟨1a⟩ *péj: d'une prostituée* accost; **racoleur, -euse** *péj: affiche* flashy; *sourire* cheesy

raconter [rakɔ̃te] ⟨1a⟩ tell

radar [radar] *m* radar

radeau [rado] *m (pl -x)* raft

radiateur [radjatœr] *m* radiator

radiation [radjasjɔ̃] *f* PHYS radiation; *d'une liste, facture* deletion

radical, ~e [radikal] *(mpl -aux)* **1** *adj* radical **2** *m* radical; **radicalement** *adv* radically; **radicalisme** *m* radicalism

radier [radje] ⟨1a⟩ strike out

radieux, -euse [radjø, -z] radiant; *temps* glorious

radin, ~e [radɛ̃, -in] F mean, tight

radio [radjo] *f* radio; *(radiographie)* X-ray; **~ privée** commercial radio; **passer une ~** have an X-ray

radioactif, -ive [radjoaktif, -iv] radioactive; **radioactivité** *f* radioactivity

radiocassette [radjokasɛt] *f* radio cassette player

radiodiffusion [radjodifyzjɔ̃] *f* broadcasting

radiographie [radjografi] *f procédé* radiography; *photo* X-ray

radiologie [radjɔlɔʒi] *f* radiology; **radiologue** *m/f* radiologist

radiophonique [radjofɔnik] radio *atr*

radioréveil [radjorevɛj] *m* radio alarm

R

radiotélévisé, ~e [radjotelevize] broadcast on both radio and TV

radis [radi] m BOT radish

radoter [radote] ⟨1a⟩ ramble

radoucir [radusir] ⟨2a⟩: *la température du vent* bring milder temperatures; *se ~ du temps* get milder

rafale [rafal] f de vent gust; MIL burst

raffermir [rafermir] ⟨2a⟩ chair firm up; fig: autorité re-assert

raffinage [rafina3] m TECH refining; **raffiné, ~e** refined; **raffinement** m refinement; **raffiner** ⟨1a⟩ refine; **raffinerie** f TECH refinery; **~ de pétrole** oil refinery

raffoler [rafole] ⟨1a⟩: **~ de qch / qn** adore sth / s.o.

rafistoler [rafistole] ⟨1a⟩ F patch up

rafle [rafl] f de police raid; **rafler** ⟨1a⟩ F take

rafraîchir [rafreʃir] ⟨2a⟩ **1** v/t cool down; mémoire refresh **2** v/i du vin chill; **se ~** de la température get cooler; d'une personne have a drink (in order to cool down); **rafraîchissant, ~e** refreshing (aussi fig); **rafraîchissement** m de la température cooling; **~s** (boissons) refreshments

rage [ra3] f rage; MÉD rabies sg; **rageur, -euse** furious

ragot [rago] m F piece of gossip; **des ~s** gossip sg

ragoût [ragu] m CUIS stew

raid [red] m raid

raide [red] personne, membres stiff (aussi fig); pente steep; cheveux straight; (ivre, drogué) stoned; **~ mort** stone dead; **raideur** f d'une personne, de membres stiffness (aussi fig); d'une pente steepness; **raidir** ⟨2a⟩: **se ~** de membres stiffen up

raie [re] f (rayure) stripe; des cheveux part, Br parting; ZO skate

raifort [refor] m BOT horseradish

rail [raj] m rail; **~ de sécurité** crash barrier

railler [raje] ⟨1a⟩ mock; **raillerie** f mockery; **railleur, -euse** mocking

rainure [renyr] f TECH groove

raisin [rezɛ̃] m grape; **~ de Corinthe** currant; **~ sec** raisin

raison [rezõ] f reason; **avoir ~** be right; **avoir ~ de** get the better of; **à ~ de** at a rate of; **à plus forte ~** all the more so, especially; **en ~ de** (à cause de) because of; **~ d'être** raison d'etre; **pour cette ~** for that reason; **~ sociale** company name; **raisonnable** reasonable

raisonné, ~e [rezone] rational; **raisonnement** m reasoning; **raisonner** ⟨1a⟩ **1** v/i reason **2** v/t: **~ qn** make s.o. see reason

rajeunir [raʒœnir] ⟨2a⟩ **1** v/t pensée, thème modernize, bring up to date; **~ qn** d'une coiffure, des vêtements etc make s.o. look (years) younger **2** v/i look younger

rajouter [raʒute] ⟨1a⟩ add

rajustement [raʒystəmã] m adjustment; **rajuster** ⟨1a⟩ adjust; coiffure put straight

ralenti [ralãti] m AUTO slow running, idle; dans un film slow motion; **au ~** fig at a snail's pace; **tourner au ~** AUTO tick over; **ralentir** ⟨2a⟩ slow down; **ralentissement** m slowing down; **ralentisseur** m de circulation speedbump

râler [rɑle] ⟨1a⟩ moan; F beef F, complain; **râleur, -euse** F **1** adj grumbling **2** m/f grumbler

rallier [ralje] ⟨1a⟩ rally; (s'unir à) join; **se ~ à** rally to

rallonge [ralõ3] f d'une table leaf; ÉL extension (cable); **rallonger** ⟨1l⟩ **1** v/t vêtement lengthen **2** v/i get longer

rallumer [ralyme] ⟨1a⟩ télé, lumière switch on again; fig revive

rallye [rali] m rally

RAM [ram] f (pl inv) RAM (= random access memory)

ramassage [ramasa3] m collection; de fruits picking; **car m de ~ scolaire** school bus; **ramasser** ⟨1a⟩ collect; ce qui est par terre pick up; fruits pick; F coup get; **ramassis** m péj pile; de personnes bunch

rambarde [rãbard] f rail

rame [ram] f (aviron) oar; de métro train

rameau [ramo] *m* (*pl* -x) branch (*aussi fig*); **les Rameaux** REL Palm Sunday

ramener [ramne] ⟨1d⟩ take back; (*rapporter*) bring back; *l'ordre, la paix* restore; **~ à** (*réduire*) reduce to; **se ~ à** (*se réduire à*) come down to

ramer [rame] ⟨1a⟩ row; **rameur, -euse** *m/f* rower

ramification [ramifikasjõ] *f* ramification

ramollir [ramɔlir] ⟨2a⟩ soften; **se ~** soften; *fig* go soft

ramoner [ramɔne] ⟨1a⟩ sweep

rampant, ~e [rãpã, -t] crawling; BOT creeping; *fig: inflation* rampant

rampe [rãp] *f* ramp; *d'escalier* banisters *pl*; *au théâtre* footlights *pl*; **~ de lancement** MIL launch pad; **ramper** ⟨1a⟩ crawl (*aussi fig*); BOT creep

rancard [rãkar] *m* F (*rendez-vous*) date

rancart [rãkar] *m*: **mettre au ~** (*jeter*) throw out

rance [rãs] rancid

ranch [rãtʃ] *m* ranch

rancœur [rãkœr] *f* resentment (**contre** toward), *Br* rancour

rançon [rãsõ] *f* ransom; **la ~ de** *fig* the price of

rancune [rãkyn] *f* resentment; **rancunier, -ère** resentful

randonnée [rãdɔne] *f* walk; *en montagne* hike, hill walk; **randonneur** *m* walker; *en montagne* hiker, hillwalker

rang [rã] *m* (*rangée*) row; (*niveau*) rank; **se mettre sur les ~s** *fig* join the fray; **rentrer dans le ~** step back in line; **être au premier ~** be in the forefront

rangé, ~e [rãʒe] *personne* well-behaved; *vie* orderly

rangée [rãʒe] *f* row

rangement *m* tidying; **pas assez de ~s** not enough storage space; **ranger** ⟨1l⟩ put away; *chambre* tidy up; *voiture* park; (*classer*) arrange; **se ~** (*s'écarter*) move aside; AUTO pull over; *fig* (*assagir*) settle down; **se ~ à une opinion** come around to a point of view

ranimer [ranime] ⟨1a⟩ *personne* bring around; *fig: courage, force* revive

rap [rap] *m* MUS rap

rapace [rapas] **1** *adj animal* predatory; *personne* greedy, rapacious **2** *m* bird of prey

rapatriement [rapatrimã] *m* repatriation; **rapatrier** ⟨1a⟩ repatriate

râpe [rap] *f* grater; TECH rasp; **râper** ⟨1a⟩ CUIS grate; *bois* file; **râpé** CUIS grated; *manteau* threadbare

rapetisser [raptise] ⟨1a⟩ **1** *v/t salle, personne* make look smaller; *vêtement* shrink; (*raccourcir*) shorten, cut down; *fig* belittle **2** *v/i d'un tissu, d'une personne* shrink

rapide [rapid] **1** *adj* fast, rapid; *coup d'œil, décision* quick **2** *m dans l'eau* rapid; *train* express, fast train; **rapidité** *f* speed, rapidity

rapiécer [rapjese] ⟨1f *et* 1k⟩ patch

rappel [rapel] *m* reminder; *d'un ambassadeur, produit* recall; THÉÂT curtain call; MÉD booster; **~ de salaire** back pay; **descendre en ~** *d'un alpiniste* abseil down

rappeler [raple] ⟨1c⟩ call back (*aussi* THÉÂT); *ambassadeur* recall; TÉL call back, *Br aussi* ring back; **~ qch / qn à qn** remind s.o. of sth / s.o.; **se ~ qch** remember sth; **se ~ avoir fait qch** remember doing sth

rapport [rapor] *m écrit, oral* report; (*lien*) connection; (*proportion*) ratio, proportion; COMM return, yield; MIL briefing; **~s** (*relations*) relations; **~s** (*sexuels*) intercourse *sg*, sexual relations, sex *sg*; **par ~ à** compared with; **sous tous les ~s** in all respects; **en ~ avec** suited to; **être en ~ avec qn** be in touch *ou* contact with s.o.; **~ qualité-prix** value for money; **rapporter** ⟨1a⟩ return, bring / take back; *d'un chien* retrieve, fetch; COMM bring in; *relater* report; **se ~ à** be connected with; **rapporteur** *m* reporter; *enfant* sneak, telltale; **rapporteuse** *f enfant* sneak, telltale

rapprochement [raprɔʃmã] *m fig* reconciliation; POL rapprochement; *analogie* connection; **rapprocher** ⟨1a⟩ *chose* bring closer *ou* nearer (*de* to); *fig: personnes* bring closer together; *établir un lien* connect, link; **se ~** come closer *ou* nearer (*de qch* to sth)

rapt [rapt] *m* abduction

raquette [raket] *f* racket

rare [rɑr] rare; *marchandises* scarce; (*peu dense*) sparse; *il est ~ qu'il arrive* (*subj*) *en retard* it's rare for him to be late; **raréfier** ⟨1a⟩: **se ~** become rare; *de l'air* become rarefied; **rarement** *adv* rarely; **rareté** *f* rarity

ras, ~e [rɑ, -z] short; *rempli à ~ bord* full to the brim; *en ~e campagne* in open country; *j'en ai ~ le bol* F I've had it up to here F; *faire table ~e* make a clean sweep

raser [rɑze] ⟨1a⟩ shave; *barbe* shave off; (*démolir*) raze to the ground; *murs* hug; F (*ennuyer*) bore; **se ~** shave; **rasoir** *m* razor; **~ électrique** electric shaver

rassasier [rɑsɑzje] ⟨1a⟩ satisfy

rassemblement [rɑsɑ̃bləmɑ̃] *m* gathering; **rassembler** ⟨1a⟩ collect, assemble; **se ~** gather

rasseoir [rɑswar] ⟨3l⟩ replace; **se ~** sit down again

rassis, ~e [rɑsi, -z] stale; *fig* sedate

rassurant, ~e [rɑsyrɑ̃, -t] reassuring; **rassurer** ⟨1a⟩ reassure; **se ~: rassurez-vous** don't be concerned

rat [rɑ] *m* rat

ratatiner [ratatine] ⟨1a⟩: **se ~** shrivel up; *d'une personne* shrink

rate [rat] *f* ANAT spleen

raté, ~e [rate] **1** *adj* unsuccessful; *occasion* missed **2** *m personne* failure; *avoir des ~s* AUTO backfire

râteau [rɑto] *m* (*pl* -x) rake

rater [rate] ⟨1a⟩ **1** *v/t* miss; **~ un examen** fail an exam **2** *v/i d'une arme* misfire; *d'un projet* fail

ratification [ratifikɑsjõ] *f* POL ratification

ration [rɑsjõ] *f* ration; *fig* (*fair*) share

rationalisation [rɑsjonalizɑsjõ] *f* rationalization; **rationaliser** ⟨1a⟩ rationalize; **rationalité** *f* rationality; **rationnel, ~le** rational

rationner [rɑsjone] ⟨1a⟩ ration

raton laveur *m* [ratõlavœr] raccoon

ratisser [ratise] ⟨1a⟩ rake; (*fouiller*) search

R.A.T.P. [eratepe] *f abr* (= **Régie autonome des transports parisiens**) *mass transit authority in Paris*

rattacher [rataʃe] ⟨1a⟩ *chien* tie up again; *cheveux* put up again; *lacets* do up again; *conduites d'eau* connect, join; *idées* connect; **se ~ à** be linked to

rattraper [ratrape] ⟨1a⟩ *animal, fugitif* recapture; *objet qui tombe* catch; (*rejoindre*) catch up (with); *retard* make up; *malentendu, imprudence* make up for; **se ~** make up for it; (*se raccrocher*) get caught

rature [ratyr] *f* deletion, crossing out

rauque [rok] hoarse

ravages [ravaʒ] *mpl* havoc *sg*, devastation *sg*; **les ~ du temps** the ravages of time; **ravager** ⟨1l⟩ devastate

ravaler [ravale] ⟨1a⟩ *aussi fierté etc* swallow; *façade* clean up

rave[1] [rav] *f:* **céleri ~** celeriac

rave[2] [rev] *f* rave

rave-party [revparti] *f* rave

ravi, ~e [ravi] delighted (*de qch* with sth; *de faire qc* to do sth)

ravin [ravẽ] *m* ravine

ravir [ravir] ⟨2a⟩ (*enchanter*) delight

raviser [ravize] ⟨1a⟩: **se ~** change one's mind

ravissant, ~e [ravisɑ̃, -t] delightful, enchanting

ravisseur, -euse [ravisœr, -øz] *m/f* abductor

ravitaillement [ravitajmɑ̃] *m* supplying; *en carburant* refueling, *Br* refuelling; **ravitailler** ⟨1a⟩ supply; *en carburant* refuel

raviver [ravive] ⟨1a⟩ revive

rayé, ~e [reje] striped; *papier* lined; *verre, carrosserie* scratched; **rayer** ⟨1l⟩ *meuble, carrosserie* scratch; *mot* score out

rayon [rejõ] *m* ray; MATH radius; *d'une roue* spoke; (*étagère*) shelf; *de magasin* department; **~s X** X-rays; *dans un ~ de* within a radius of; **~ laser** laser beam; **rayonnage** *m* shelving

rayonnant, ~e [rɛjɔnɑ̃, -t] radiant; **rayonnement** *m* PHYS radiation; **rayonner** ⟨1a⟩ *de chaleur* radiate; *d'un visage* shine; **~ de** *fig: bonheur, santé* radiate

rayure [rɛjyr] *f* stripe; *sur un meuble, du verre* scratch

raz [rɑ] *m*: **~ de marée** tidal wave (*aussi fig*)

R&D *f abr* (= **recherche et développement**) R&D (= research and development)

ré [re] *m* MUS D

réabonner [reabɔne] ⟨1a⟩: **se ~** renew one's subscription

réac [reak] *m/f* F reactionary

réacteur [reaktœr] *m* PHYS reactor; AVIAT jet engine

réaction [reaksjɔ̃] *f* reaction; **avion** *m* **à ~** jet (aircraft); **réactionnaire** *m/f* & *adj* reactionary

réactualiser [reaktɥalize] ⟨1a⟩ update

réagir [reaʒir] ⟨2a⟩ react (**à** to; **contre** against)

réajuster [reaʒyste] ⟨1a⟩ → **rajuster**

réalisable [realizabl] feasible; **réalisateur, -trice** *m/f* director; **réalisation** *f d'un plan, un projet* execution, realization; *création, œuvre* creation; *d'un film* direction; **réaliser** ⟨1a⟩ *plan, projet* carry out; *rêve* fulfill, *Br* fulfil; *vente* make; *film* direct; *bien, capital* realize; *(se rendre compte)* realize; **se ~** *d'un rêve* come true; *d'un projet* be carried out

réalisme [realism] *m* realism; **réaliste 1** *adj* realistic **2** *m/f* realist; **réalité** *f* reality; **en ~** actually, in reality; **~ virtuelle** virtual reality

réanimation [reanimasjɔ̃] *f* MÉD resuscitation; **service** *m* **de ~** intensive care; **réanimer** ⟨1a⟩ resuscitate

réapparaître [reaparetr] ⟨4z⟩ reappear; **réapparition** *f* reappearance

réapprendre [reaprɑ̃dr] ⟨4q⟩ relearn

rebaptiser [rəbatize] ⟨1a⟩ rename

rébarbatif, -ive [rebarbatif, -iv] off--putting, daunting

rebattu, ~e [rəbaty] hackneyed

rebelle [rəbɛl] **1** *adj* rebellious **2** *m/f* rebel; **rebeller** ⟨1a⟩: **se ~** rebel (**contre** against); **rébellion** *f* rebellion

reboiser [rəbwaze] ⟨1a⟩ reforest, *Br* reafforest

rebondi, ~e [r(ə)bɔ̃di] rounded; **rebondir** ⟨2a⟩ *d'un ballon* bounce; *(faire un ricochet)* rebound; **faire ~ qch** *fig* get sth going again; **rebondissement** *m fig* unexpected development

rebord [r(ə)bɔr] *m* edge; *d'une fenêtre* sill

rebours [r(ə)bur] *m*: **compte** *m* **à ~** countdown

rebrousse-poil [r(ə)bruspwal]: **à ~** the wrong way; **prendre qn à ~** rub s.o. up the wrong way; **rebrousser** ⟨1a⟩: **~ chemin** retrace one's footsteps

rebuffade [rəbyfad] *f* rebuff

rebut [r(ə)by] *m* dregs *pl*; **mettre au ~** scrap, get rid of

rebuter [r(ə)byte] ⟨1a⟩ *(décourager)* dishearten; *(choquer)* offend

récalcitrant, ~e [rekalsitrɑ̃, -t] recalcitrant

récapituler [rekapityle] ⟨1a⟩ recap

recel [rəsɛl] *m* JUR receiving stolen property, fencing F

récemment [resamɑ̃] *adv* recently

recensement [r(ə)sɑ̃smɑ̃] *m* census; **recenser** ⟨1a⟩ *population* take a census of

récent, ~e [resɑ̃, -t] recent

récépissé [resepise] *m* receipt

récepteur [reseptœr] *m* TECH, TÉL receiver; **réceptif, -ive** receptive; **réception** *f* reception; *d'une lettre, de marchandises* receipt; **réceptionniste** *m/f* receptionist, desk clerk

récession [resesjɔ̃] *f* ÉCON recession

recette [r(ə)sɛt] *f* COMM takings *pl*; CUIS, *fig* recipe

receveur [rəsvœr] *m des impôts* taxman; *de la poste* postmaster; MÉD recipient; **receveuse** *f* MÉD recipient; **recevoir** ⟨3a⟩ receive; **être reçu à un examen** pass an exam

rechange [r(ə)ʃɑ̃ʒ] *m*: **de ~** spare *atr*; **rechanger** ⟨1l⟩ change again

R

réchapper [reʃape] ⟨1a⟩: **~ à qch** survive sth

rechargeable [rəʃarʒabl] *pile* rechargeable

recharger [r(ə)ʃarʒe] ⟨1l⟩ *camion, arme* reload; *accumulateur* recharge; *briquet, stylo* refill

réchaud [reʃo] *m* stove

réchauffement [reʃofmã] *m* warming; **~ de la planète** global warming; **réchauffer** ⟨1a⟩ warm up

rêche [rɛʃ] *aussi fig* rough

recherche [r(ə)ʃɛrʃ] *f* (*enquête, poursuite*) search (**de** for); *scientifique* research; **~ et développement** research and development, R&D; **~ de la police** search *sg*, hunt *sg*; **recherché, ~e** sought-after; *criminel* wanted; (*raffiné*) refined, recherché; **rechercher** ⟨1a⟩ look for, search for; (*prendre*) fetch

rechute [r(ə)ʃyt] *f* MÉD relapse

récidiver [residive] ⟨1a⟩ relapse

récif [resif] *m* GÉOGR reef

récipient [resipjã] *m* container

réciproque [resiprɔk] reciprocal

récit [resi] *m* account; (*histoire*) story

récital [resital] *m* (*pl* -s) recital

réciter [resite] ⟨1a⟩ recite

réclamation [reklamasjõ] *f* claim; (*protestation*) complaint

réclame [reklam] *f* advertisement

réclamer [reklame] ⟨1a⟩ *secours, aumône* ask for; *son dû, sa part* claim, demand; (*nécessiter*) call for

reclus, ~e [rəkly] *m/f* recluse

réclusion [reklyzjõ] *f* imprisonment

recoiffer [rəkwafe] ⟨1a⟩: **se ~** put one's hair straight

recoin [rəkwɛ̃] *m* nook

récolte [rekɔlt] *f* harvesting; *de produits* harvest, crop; *fig* crop; **récolter** ⟨1a⟩ harvest

recommandable [rəkɔmãdabl] *personne* respectable; **recommandation** *f* recommendation; **recommander** ⟨1a⟩ recommend; *lettre* register

recommencer [r(ə)kɔmãse] ⟨1k⟩ **1** *v/t*: **~ qch** start sth over, start sth again; **~ à faire qch** start doing sth

again, start to do sth again **2** *v/i* start *ou* begin again

récompense [rekõpãs] *f* reward; **récompenser** ⟨1a⟩ reward (**de** for)

réconciliation [rekõsiljasjõ] *f* reconciliation; **réconcilier** ⟨1a⟩ reconcile

reconduire [r(ə)kõdɥir] ⟨4c⟩ JUR renew; **~ qn chez lui** take s.o. home; **~ à la porte** see s.o. out

réconfort [rekõfɔr] *m* consolation, comfort; **réconforter** ⟨1a⟩ console, comfort

reconnaissable [r(ə)kɔnɛsabl] recognizable; **reconnaissance** *f* recognition; *d'une faute* acknowledg(e)ment; (*gratitude*) gratitude; MIL reconnaissance; **~ de dette** IOU; **~ vocale** INFORM voice recognition; **reconnaissant, ~e** grateful (**de** for); **reconnaître** ⟨4z⟩ recognize; *faute* acknowledge; **se ~** recognize o.s.; **ils se sont reconnus tout de suite** they immediately recognized each other; **un oiseau qui se reconnaît à ...** a bird which is recognizable by ...; **reconnu, ~e 1** *p/p* → **reconnaître 2** *adj* known

reconquérir [r(ə)kõkerir] ⟨2l⟩ reconquer; *fig* regain

reconstituer [r(ə)kõstitɥe] ⟨1a⟩ reconstitute; *ville, maison* restore; *événement* reconstruct

reconstruction [r(ə)kõstryksjõ] *f* rebuilding, reconstruction; **reconstruire** ⟨4c⟩ rebuild, reconstruct

reconversion [r(ə)kõvɛr sjõ] *f* retraining; **reconvertir** ⟨2a⟩: **se ~** retrain

recopier [rəkɔpje] ⟨1a⟩ *notes* copy out

record [r(ə)kɔr] *m* record; **recordman** *m* record holder; **recordwoman** *f* record holder

recoudre [rəkudr] ⟨4d⟩ *bouton* sew back on

recouper [rəkupe] ⟨1a⟩ **1** *v/t* re-cut, cut again; *pour vérifier* cross-check **2** *v/i* cut again

recourbé, ~e [r(ə)kurbe] bent

recourir [r(ə)kurir] ⟨2i⟩: **~ à qn** consult s.o.; **~ à qch** resort to sth; **recours** *m* recourse, resort; **avoir ~ à**

qch resort to sth; **en dernier ~** as a last resort

recouvrer [r(ə)kuvre] ⟨1a⟩ recover; *santé* regain

recouvrir [r(ə)kuvrir] ⟨2f⟩ recover; *enfant* cover up again; (*couvrir entièrement*) cover (**de** with); (*cacher*) cover (up); (*embrasser*) cover, span

récréation [rekreasjõ] *f* relaxation; ÉDU recess, *Br* break, *Br* recreation

recréer ⟨1a⟩ recreate

récriminations [rekriminasjõ] *fpl* recriminations

recroqueviller [r(ə)krɔkvije] ⟨1a⟩: **se ~** shrivel (up); *d'une personne* curl up

recrudescence [rəkrydesãs] *f* new outbreak

recrue [r(ə)kry] *f* recruit

recrutement [r(ə)krytmã] *m* recruitment; **recruter** ⟨1a⟩ recruit

rectangle [rektãgl] *m* rectangle; **rectangulaire** rectangular

recteur [rektœr] *m* rector

rectifier [rektifje] ⟨1a⟩ rectify; (*ajuster*) adjust; (*corriger*) correct

rectiligne [rektilin] rectilinear

recto [rekto] *m d'une feuille* front

reçu [r(ə)sy] **1** *p/p → recevoir* **2** *m* receipt

recueil [r(ə)kœj] *m* collection; **recueillement** *m* meditation, contemplation; **recueillir** ⟨2c⟩ collect; *personne* take in; **se ~** meditate

recul [r(ə)kyl] *m d'un canon, un fusil* recoil; *d'une armée* retreat, fall-back; *de la production, du chômage* drop, fall-off (**de** in); *fig* detachment

reculé, ~e [r(ə)kyle] remote; (*passé*) distant; **reculer** ⟨1a⟩ **1** *v/t* push back; *échéance, décision* postpone **2** *v/i* back away, recoil; MIL retreat, fall back; *d'une voiture* back, reverse; **~ devant** *fig* back away from; **reculons: à ~** backward, *Br* backwards

récupération [rekyperasjõ] *f* recovery; *de vieux matériel* salvaging; **~ du temps de travail** taking time off in lieu; **récupérer** ⟨1f⟩ **1** *v/t* recover, retrieve; *ses forces* regain; *vieux matériel* salvage; *temps* make up **2** *v/i* recover

récurer [rekyre] ⟨1a⟩ scour

recyclable [rəsiklabl] recyclable; **recyclage** *m du personnel* retraining; TECH recycling; **recycler** ⟨1a⟩ retrain; TECH recycle

rédacteur, -trice [redaktœr, -tris] *m/f* editor; (*auteur*) writer; **~ en chef** editor-in-chief; **~ politique** political editor; **~ publicitaire** copy-writer; **~ sportif** sports editor; **rédaction** *f* editing; (*rédacteurs*) editorial team

redéfinir [rədefinir] ⟨2a⟩ redefine

redescendre [r(ə)desãdr] ⟨4a⟩ **1** *v/i* (*aux être*) come / go down again; *d'un baromètre* fall again; **~ d'une voiture** get out of a car again, get back out of a car **2** *v/t* bring / take down again; *montagne* come *ou* climb down again

redevable [rədvabl]: **être ~ de qch à qn** owe s.o. sth; **redevance** *f d'un auteur* royalty; TV licence fee

rediffusion [rədifyzjõ] *f* repeat

rédiger [rediʒe] ⟨1l⟩ write

redire [r(ə)dir] ⟨4m⟩ (*répéter*) repeat, say again; (*rapporter*) repeat; **trouver à ~ à tout** find fault with everything

redistribuer [rədistribɥe] ⟨1a⟩ redistribute; *aux cartes* redeal

redonner [r(ə)dɔne] ⟨1a⟩ (*rendre*) give back, return; (*donner de nouveau*) give again

redoubler [r(ə)duble] ⟨1a⟩ **1** *v/t* double **2** *v/i* ÉDU repeat a class, *Br aussi* repeat a year; (*augmenter*) intensify; *d'une tempête* intensify; **~ d'efforts** redouble one's efforts

redoutable [r(ə)dutabl] formidable; *hiver* harsh; **redouter** ⟨1a⟩ dread (**de faire qch** doing sth)

redresser [r(ə)drese] ⟨1b⟩ *ce qui est courbe* straighten; *ce qui est tombé* set upright; **~ l'économie** *fig* get the economy back on its feet; **se ~** *d'un pays* recover, get back on its feet

réduction [redyksjõ] *f* reduction; MÉD setting; **réduire** [redɥir] ⟨4c⟩ *dépenses, impôts* reduce, cut; *personnel* cut back; *vitesse* reduce; **se ~ à** amount to; **réduit, ~e 1** *adj* reduced; *possibilités* limited **2** *m* small room

rééditer [reedite] ⟨1a⟩ republish

rééducation [reedykasjõ] f MÉD rehabilitation; **rééduquer** ⟨1m⟩ MÉD rehabilitate

réel, ~le [reɛl] real

réélection [reelɛksjõ] f re-election; **réélire** ⟨4x⟩ re-elect

réellement [reɛlmã] adv really

rééquilibrer [reekilibre] ⟨1a⟩ pneus balance

réévaluer [reevalɥe] ⟨1n⟩ ÉCON revalue; **réévaluation** f revaluation

refaire [r(ə)fer] ⟨4n⟩ faire de nouveau: travail do over, Br do again; examen take again, retake; erreur make again, repeat; remettre en état: maison do up; **~ le monde** set the world to rights

réfection [refɛksjõ] f repair

réfectoire [refɛktwar] m refectory

référence [referãs] f reference; **ouvrage m de ~** reference work; **~s** (recommandation) reference sg

référendum [referẽdɔm] m referendum

référer [refere] ⟨1f⟩: **en ~ à qn** consult s.o.; **se ~ à** refer to

refermer [rəferme] ⟨1a⟩ shut again; **se ~** shut again; d'une blessure close (up)

refiler [r(ə)file] ⟨1a⟩ F: **~ qch à qn** pass sth on to s.o.

réfléchi, ~e [refleʃi] thoughtful; GRAM reflexive; **réfléchir** ⟨2a⟩ 1 v/t reflect 2 v/i think; **~ à ou sur qch** think about sth

reflet [r(ə)flɛ] m de lumière glint; dans eau, miroir reflection (aussi fig); **refléter** ⟨1f⟩ reflect (aussi fig)

réflexe [reflɛks] m reflex

réflexion [reflɛksjõ] f PHYS reflection; fait de penser thought, reflection; (remarque) remark

réformateur, -trice [reformatœr, -tris] m/f reformer; **réforme** f reform; **la Réforme** REL the Reformation; **réformer** ⟨1a⟩ reform; MIL discharge

reformer [rəfɔrme] ⟨1a⟩ reform; **se ~** reform

refoulé, ~e [r(ə)fule] PSYCH repressed; **refoulement** m pushing back; PSYCH repression; **refouler** ⟨1a⟩ push back; PSYCH repress

refrain [r(ə)frẽ] m refrain, chorus

réfréner [refrene, rə-] ⟨1f⟩ control

réfrigérateur [refriʒeratœr] m refrigerator; **conserver au ~** keep refrigerated

refroidir [r(ə)frwadir] ⟨1a⟩ cool down; fig cool; **se ~** du temps get colder; MÉD catch a chill; **refroidissement** m cooling; MÉD chill

refuge [r(ə)fyʒ] m (abri) refuge, shelter; pour piétons traffic island; en montagne (mountain) hut; **réfugié, ~e** m/f refugee; **réfugier** ⟨1a⟩: **se ~** take shelter

refus [r(ə)fy] m refusal; **refuser** ⟨1a⟩ refuse; **~ qch à qn** refuse s.o. sth; **~ de ou se ~ à faire qch** refuse to do sth

réfuter [refyte] ⟨1a⟩ refute

regagner [r(ə)gaɲe] ⟨1a⟩ win back, regain; endroit get back to, regain

régal [regal] m (pl -s) treat; **régaler** ⟨1a⟩ regale (de with); **je vais me ~!** I'm going to enjoy this!

regard [r(ə)gar] m look; **au ~ de la loi** in the eyes of the law; **regardant, ~e** avec argent careful with one's money; **ne pas être ~ sur qch** not be too worried about sth; **regarder** ⟨1a⟩ 1 v/t look at; télé watch; (concerner) regard, concern; **~ qn faire qch** watch s.o. doing sth 2 v/i look; **~ par la fenêtre** look out (of) the window; **se ~** d'une personne look at o.s.; de plusieurs personnes look at each other

régate [regat] f regatta

régie [reʒi] f entreprise state-owned company; TV, cinéma control room

regimber [r(ə)ʒẽbe] ⟨1a⟩ protest

régime [reʒim] m POL government, régime; MÉD diet; fiscal system; **~ de retraite** pension scheme

régiment [reʒimã] m regiment

région [reʒjõ] f region; **~ sinistrée** disaster area; **régional, ~e** (mpl -aux) regional; **régionalisation** f POL regionalization; **régionalisme** m regionalism

régir [reʒir] ⟨2a⟩ govern

régisseur [reʒisœr] m d'un domaine

managing agent; THÉÂT stage manager; *dans le film* assistant director; **~ de plateau** floor manager

registre [r(ə)ʒistr] *m* register (*aussi* MUS); *d'un discours* tone; **~ de comptes** ledger

réglable [reglabl] adjustable; **réglage** *m* adjustment

règle [regl] *f instrument* ruler; (*prescription*) rule; **de ~** customary; **en ~ papiers** in order; **en ~ générale** as a rule; **~s** (*menstruation*) period *sg*

réglé, ~e [regle] *organisé* settled; *vie* well-ordered; *papier* ruled

règlement [regləmã] *m d'une affaire, question* settlement; COMM payment, settlement; (*règles*) regulations *pl*

réglementaire [regləmãter] in accordance with the rules; *tenue* regulation *atr*; **réglementation** *f* (*règle*) regulations *pl*; **réglementer** ⟨1a⟩ control, regulate

régler [regle] ⟨1f⟩ *affaire* settle; TECH adjust; COMM pay, settle; *épicier etc* pay, settle up with

réglisse [reglis] *f* BOT licorice, *Br* liquorice

règne [rɛɲ] *m* reign; **régner** ⟨1f⟩ reign (*aussi fig*)

regorger [r(ə)gɔrʒe] ⟨1l⟩: **~ de** abound in, have an abundance of

régression [regresjõ] *f* regression

regret [r(ə)grɛ] *m* (*repentir*) regret (**de** about); **à ~** with regret, reluctantly; **avoir le ~** *ou* **être au ~ de faire qch** regret to do sth; **regrettable** regrettable, unfortunate; **regretter** ⟨1b⟩ regret; *personne absente* miss; **~ d'avoir fait qch** regret doing sth, regret having done sth; **je ne regrette rien** I have no regrets; **je regrette mais …** I'm sorry (but) …

regrouper [r(ə)grupe] ⟨1a⟩ gather together

régulariser [regylarize] ⟨1a⟩ *finances, papiers* put in order; *situation* regularize; TECH regulate; **régularité** *f d'habitudes* regularity; *d'élections* legality

régulation [regylasjõ] *f* regulation

régulier, -ère [regylje, -ɛr] regular; *allure, progrès* steady; *écriture* even; (*ré-*

glementaire) lawful; (*correct*) decent, honest; **régulièrement** *adv* regularly

réhabilitation [reabilitasjõ] *f* rehabilitation; *d'un quartier* renovation, redevelopment; **réhabiliter** ⟨1a⟩ rehabilitate; *d'un quartier* renovate, redevelop

réhabituer [reabitɥe] ⟨1a⟩: **se ~ à qch / faire qch** get used to sth / doing sth again

rehausser [rəose] ⟨1a⟩ raise; *fig* (*souligner*) bring out, emphasize

réimpression [reɛ̃presjõ] *f* reprint; **réimprimer** ⟨1a⟩ reprint

rein [rɛ̃] *m* ANAT kidney; **~ artificiel** kidney machine; **~s** lower back *sg*

réincarnation [reɛ̃karnasjõ] *f* reincarnation

reine [rɛn] *f* queen

réinsérer [reɛ̃sere] ⟨1f⟩ *mot etc* reinstate; *délinquant* rehabilitate; **réinsertion** *f d'un mot etc* reinstatement; *d'un délinquant* rehabilitation

réintégrer [reɛ̃tegre] ⟨1f⟩ *employé* reinstate; *endroit* return to

réinvestir [reɛ̃vestir] ⟨2a⟩ reinvest

réitérer [reitere] ⟨1f⟩ reiterate

rejaillir [r(ə)ʒajir] ⟨2a⟩ spurt

rejet [r(ə)ʒɛ] *m* rejection; **rejeter** ⟨1c⟩ reject; (*relancer*) throw back; (*vomir*) bring up; *responsabilité, faute* lay (**sur** on), shift (**sur** onto)

rejoindre [r(ə)ʒwɛ̃dr] ⟨4b⟩ *personne* join, meet; (*rattraper*) catch up with; MIL rejoin; *autoroute* get back onto; **se ~** meet

réjouir [reʒwir] ⟨2a⟩ make happy, delight; **se ~ de qch** be delighted about sth; **réjouissance** *f* rejoicing; **~s publiques** public festivities

relâche [r(ə)lɑʃ] *f*: **sans ~** *travailler* without a break, nonstop; **relâchement** *m d'une corde* loosening; *de discipline* easing; **relâcher** ⟨1a⟩ loosen; *prisonnier* release; **se ~** *d'un élève, de la discipline* get slack

relais [r(ə)lɛ] *m* SP relay (race); ÉL relay; **~ routier** truck stop, *Br aussi* transport café; **prendre le ~ de qn** spell s.o., take over from s.o.

R

relancer [r(ə)lɑ̃se] ⟨1k⟩ *balle* throw back; *moteur* restart; *fig: économie* kickstart; *personne* contact again, get back onto F

relater [r(ə)late] ⟨1a⟩ relate

relatif, -ive [r(ə)latif, -iv] relative (*aussi* GRAM); **~ à qch** relating to sth, about sth; **relation** *f (rapport)* connection, relationship; *(connaissance)* acquaintance; **être en ~ avec qn** be in touch with s.o.; **~s** relations; *(connaissances)* contacts; **~s publiques** public relations, PR *sg*; **relativement** *adv* relatively; **~ à** compared with; *(en ce qui concerne)* relating to; **relativiser** ⟨1a⟩ look at in context *ou* perspective

relax [r(ə)laks] *adj inv* F laid-back F, relaxed; **relaxation** *f* relaxation; **relaxer** ⟨1a⟩: **se ~** relax

relayer [r(ə)leje] ⟨1i⟩ take over from; TV, *radio* relay; **se ~** take turns

reléguer [r(ə)lege] ⟨1f⟩ relegate; **~ qn au second plan** ignore s.o., push s.o. into the background

relent [r(ə)lɑ̃] *m* smell; *de scandale* whiff

relève [r(ə)lɛv] *f* relief; **prendre la ~** take over

relevé, -e [rəlve] **1** *adj manche* turned up; *style* elevated; CUIS spicy **2** *m de compteur* reading; **~ de compte** bank statement; **relever** ⟨1d⟩ **1** *v/t* raise; *(remettre debout)* pick up; *mur* rebuild; *col, chauffage* turn up; *manches* turn up, roll up; *siège* put up, lift; *économie, finances* improve; *(ramasser)* collect; *sauce* spice up; *défi* take up; *faute* find; *adresse, date* copy; *compteur* read; *(relayer)* relieve, take over from; **se ~** get up; *fig* recover; **~ qn de ses fonctions** relieve s.o. of his duties **2** *v/i*: **~ de** *(dépendre de)* report to, be answerable to; *(ressortir de)* be the responsibility of

relief [rəljef] *m* relief; **en ~** in relief; **mettre en ~** *fig* highlight

relier [rəlje] ⟨1a⟩ connect (*à* to), link (*à* with); *livre* bind; **relieur, -euse** *m/f* binder

religieux, -euse [r(ə)liʒjø, -z] **1** *adj*

religious **2** *m* monk **3** *f* nun; **religion** *f* religion

relire [r(ə)lir] ⟨4x⟩ re-read

reliure [rəljyr] *f* binding

reluire [rəlɥir] ⟨4c⟩ shine

remaniement [r(ə)manimɑ̃] *m d'un texte* re-working; POL reorganization, *Br* reshuffle; **remanier** ⟨1a⟩ *texte* rework; POL reorganize, *Br* reshuffle

remarier [r(ə)marje] ⟨1a⟩: **se ~** remarry, get married again

remarquable [r(ə)markabl] remarkable; **remarque** *f* remark; **remarquer** ⟨1m⟩ *(apercevoir)* notice; *(dire)* remark; **faire ~ qch à qn** point sth out to s.o., comment on sth to s.o.; **se ~** *d'une chose* be noticed; **se faire ~** *d'un acteur, sportif etc* get o.s. noticed; *d'un écolier* get into trouble; *se différencier* be conspicuous

rembourrage [rɑ̃buraʒ] *m* stuffing; **rembourrer** ⟨1a⟩ stuff

remboursable [rɑ̃bursabl] refundable; **remboursement** *m* refund; *de dettes, d'un emprunt* repayment; **rembourser** ⟨1a⟩ *frais* refund, reimburse; *dettes, emprunt* pay back

remède [r(ə)med] *m* remedy, cure; **remédier** ⟨1a⟩: **~ à qch** remedy sth

remerciement [r(ə)mersimɑ̃] *m*: **~s** thanks; **une lettre de ~** a thankyou letter, a letter of thanks; **remercier** ⟨1a⟩ thank (*de, pour* for); *(congédier)* dismiss

remettre [r(ə)metr] ⟨4p⟩ *chose* put back; *vêtement, chapeau* put on again, put back on; *peine* remit; *décision* postpone; *(ajouter)* add; **~ à neuf** recondition; **~ qch à qn** hand *ou* give sth to s.o.; **~ à l'heure** put to the right time; **~ au beau** *du temps* brighten up again; **se ~ à qch** take up sth again; **se ~ à faire qch** start doing sth again; **se ~ de qch** recover from sth; **s'en ~ à qn** rely on s.o.

réminiscence [reminisɑ̃s] *f* reminiscence

remise [r(ə)miz] *f (hangar)* shed; *d'une lettre* delivery; *de peine* remission, reduction; COMM discount; *d'une décision* postponement; **~ des bagages**

baggage retrieval; **~ en jeu** goal kick; **~ à neuf** reconditioning; **~ en question** questioning

rémission [remisjō] *f* MÉD remission

remontant [r(ə)mõtã] *m* tonic

remonte-pente [r(ə)mõtpãt] *m* (*pl* remonte-pentes) ski lift

remonter [r(ə)mõte] ⟨1a⟩ **1** *v/i* (*aux être*) come / go up again; *dans une voiture* get back in; *d'un baromètre* rise again; *de prix, température* rise again, go up again; *d'un avion, chemin* climb, rise; **~ à** (*dater de*) go back to **2** *v/t* bring / take back up; *rue, escalier* come / go back up; *montre* wind; TECH reassemble; *col* turn up; *stores* raise; **~ qn** *fig* boost s.o.'s spirits

remords [r(ə)mɔr] *mpl* remorse *sg*

remorque [r(ə)mɔrk] *f véhicule* trailer; *câble* towrope; **remorquer** ⟨1m⟩ *voiture* tow; **remorqueur** *m* tug

remous [r(ə)mu] *m d'une rivière* eddy; *d'un bateau* wash; *fig pl* stir *sg*

rempart [rãpar] *m* rampart

remplaçant, ~e [rãplasã, -t] *m/f* replacement; **remplacement** *m* replacement; **remplacer** ⟨1k⟩ replace; **~ X par Y** replace X with Y, substitute Y for X

remplir [rãplir] ⟨2a⟩ fill (*de* with); *formulaire* fill out; *conditions* fulfill, *Br* fulfil, meet; *tâche* carry out

remplissage [rãplisaʒ] *m* filling

remporter [rãpɔrte] ⟨1a⟩ take away; *prix* win; **~ une victoire** win

remue-ménage [r(ə)mymenaʒ] *m* (*pl inv*) (*agitation*) commotion

remuer [rəmɥe] ⟨1a⟩ **1** *v/t* move (*aussi fig*); *sauce* stir; *salade* toss; *terre* turn over **2** *v/i* move; **se ~** move; *fig* F get a move on F

rémunérateur, -trice [remyneratœr, -tris] well-paid; **rémunération** *f* pay, remuneration; **rémunérer** ⟨1f⟩ pay

renaissance [r(ə)nɛsãs] *f* renaissance, rebirth (*aussi* REL); **la Renaissance** the Renaissance

renaître [r(ə)nɛtr] ⟨4g⟩ (*aux être*) REL be born again; *fig* be reborn

renard [r(ə)nar] *m* fox

renchérir [rãʃerir] ⟨2a⟩ go up; **~ sur qn / qch** outdo s.o. / sth, go one better than s.o. / sth

rencontre [rãkõtr] *f* meeting; **faire la ~ de qn** meet s.o.; **aller à la ~ de qn** go and meet s.o.; **rencontrer** ⟨1a⟩ meet; *accueil* meet with; *difficulté* encounter, run into; *amour* find; (*heurter*) hit; **se ~** meet

rendement [rãdmã] *m* AGR yield; *d'un employé, d'une machine* output; *d'un placement* return

rendez-vous [rãdevu] *m* (*pl inv*) appointment; *amoureux* date; *lieu* meeting place; **prendre ~** make an appointment; **donner ~ à qn** arrange to meet s.o.; **avoir ~ avec qn** have an appointment / date with s.o.

rendormir [rãdɔrmir] ⟨2b⟩: **se ~** fall asleep again, go back to sleep again

rendre [rãdr] ⟨4a⟩ **1** *v/t* (*donner en retour, restituer*) give back; *salut, invitation* return; (*donner*) give; (*traduire*) render; (*vomir*) bring up; MIL surrender; **~ un jugement** pass sentence; **~ visite à qn** visit s.o., pay s.o. a visit; **les choses plus difficiles** make things more difficult **2** *v/i de terre, d'un arbre* yield; **se ~ à un endroit** go; MIL surrender; **se ~ à l'avis de qn** come around to s.o.'s way of thinking; **se ~ présentable / malade** make o.s. presentable / sick

rêne [rɛn] *f* rein

renfermé, ~e [rãferme] **1** *adj* withdrawn **2** *m*: **sentir le ~** smell musty; **renfermer** ⟨1a⟩ (*contenir*) contain; **se ~ dans le silence** withdraw into silence

renforcement [rãfɔrsəmã] *m* reinforcement; **renforcer** ⟨1k⟩ reinforce

renfort [rãfɔr] *m* reinforcements *pl*; **à grand ~ de** with copious amounts of

rengaine [rãgɛn] *f* song; **la même ~** *fig* the same old story

rengorger [rãgɔrʒe] ⟨11⟩: **se ~** strut (*aussi fig*)

renier [rənje] ⟨1a⟩ *personne* disown

renifler [r(ə)nifle] ⟨1a⟩ sniff

renne [rɛn] *m* reindeer

renom [r(ə)nõ] *m* (*célébrité*) fame, renown; (*réputation*) reputation; **re-nommé**, **~e** known, famous (*pour* for); **renommée** *f* fame

renoncement [r(ə)nɔ̃smɑ̃] *m* renunciation (*à* of); **renoncer** ⟨1k⟩: ~ **à qch** give sth up; ~ **à faire qch** give up doing sth

renouer [rənwe] ⟨1a⟩ **1** *v/t fig*: *amitié, conversation* renew **2** *v/i*: ~ **avec qn** get back in touch with s.o.; *après brouille* get back together with s.o.

renouveau [rənuvo] *m* revival

renouveler [rənuvle] ⟨1c⟩ *contrat, passeport etc* renew; (*changer*) change, renew; *demande, promesse* repeat; **se ~** (*se reproduire*) happen again; **renouvellement** *m* renewal

rénovation [renɔvasjɔ̃] *f* renovation; *fig* (*modernisation*) updating; **rénover** ⟨1a⟩ renovate; *fig* bring up to date

renseignement [rɑ̃sɛɲmɑ̃] *m* piece of information (*sur* about); **~s** information *sg*; MIL intelligence *sg*; **prendre des ~s sur** find out about; **renseigner** ⟨1a⟩: ~ **qn sur qch** tell *ou* inform s.o. about sth; **se ~** find out (*auprès de qn* from s.o.; *sur* about)

rentabilité [rɑ̃tabilite] *f* profitability; **rentable** cost-effective; *entreprise* profitable; **ce n'est pas ~** there's no money in it

rente [rɑ̃t] *f revenu d'un bien* private income; (*pension*) annuity; *versée à sa femme etc* allowance

rentrée [rɑ̃tre] *f* return; ~ **des classes** beginning of the new school year; **~s** COMM takings

rentrer [rɑ̃tre] ⟨1a⟩ **1** *v/i* (*aux être*) (*entrer*) go / come in; *de nouveau* go / come back in; *chez soi* go / come home; *dans un récipient etc* go, fit; *de l'argent* come in; ~ **dans** (*heurter*) collide with, run into; *serrure, sac* fit in, go into; *ses responsabilités* be part of; *attributions, fonctions* form part of, come under **2** *v/t* bring / take in; *voiture* put away; *ventre* pull in

renverse [rɑ̃vɛrs] *f*: **tomber à la ~** fall backward *ou Br* backwards; **renversé**, **~e** overturned; *image* re-

versed; *fig* astonished; **renversement** *m* POL *d'un régime* overthrow; **renverser** ⟨1a⟩ *image* reverse; *chaise, verre* (*mettre à l'envers*) upturn; (*faire tomber*) knock over, overturn; *piéton* knock down *ou* over; *liquide* spill; *gouvernement* overthrow; **se ~** *d'une voiture, d'un bateau* overturn; *d'une bouteille, chaise* fall over

renvoi [rɑ̃vwa] *m de personnel* dismissal; *d'un élève* expulsion; *d'une lettre* return; *dans un texte* cross-reference (*à* to); **renvoyer** ⟨1p⟩ (*faire retourner*) send back; *ballon* return; *personnel* dismiss; *élève* expel; *rencontre, décision* postpone; (*réfléchir*) reflect; *dans un texte* refer

réorganiser [reɔrganize] ⟨1a⟩ reorganize

réouverture [reuvɛrtyr] *f* reopening

répandre [repɑ̃dr] ⟨4a⟩ spread; (*renverser*) spill; **se ~** spread; (*être renversé*) spill; **se ~ en excuses** apologize profusely; **répandu**, **~e** widespread

reparaître [r(ə)parɛtr] ⟨4z⟩ reappear

réparateur [reparatœr] *m* repairman; **réparation** *f* repair; (*compensation*) reparation; **en ~** being repaired; **surface f de ~** SP penalty area; **réparer** ⟨1a⟩ repair; *fig* make up for

répartie [reparti] *f* retort; **avoir de la ~** have a gift for repartee

repartir [r(ə)partir] ⟨2b⟩ (*aux être*) *partir de nouveau* leave again; *d'un train* set off again; **il est reparti chez lui** he went back home again; ~ **de zéro** start again from scratch

répartir [repartir] ⟨2a⟩ share out; *chargement* distribute; *en catégories* divide; **répartition** *f* distribution; *en catégories* division

repas [rəpɑ] *m* meal; ~ **d'affaires** business lunch / dinner

repassage [rəpasaʒ] *m* ironing; **repasser** ⟨1a⟩ **1** *v/i* (*aux être*) come / go back again **2** *v/t couteau* sharpen; *linge* iron; *examen* take again

repêcher [r(ə)peʃe] ⟨1b⟩ fish out; *fig* **F** help out; *candidat* let pass

repeindre [rəpɛ̃dr] ⟨4b⟩ repaint

repenser [r(ə)pɑ̃se] ⟨1a⟩ **1** *v/t* rethink **2** *v/i* (*réfléchir*) think again (**à** about)

repentir [r(ə)pɑ̃tir] **1** ⟨2b⟩: *se ~* REL repent; *se ~ de qch* be sorry for sth **2** *m* penitence

répercussions [repɛrkysjõ] *fpl* repercussions; **répercuter** ⟨1a⟩: *se ~* reverberate; *fig* have repercussions (**sur** on)

repère [r(ə)pɛr] *m* mark; (*point m de*) *~* landmark; **repérer** ⟨1f⟩ (*situer*) pinpoint; (*trouver*) find, F spot; (*marquer*) mark

répertoire [repɛrtwar] *m* directory; THÉÂT repertoire

répéter [repete] ⟨1f⟩ repeat; *rôle, danse* rehearse; **répétitif, -ive** repetitive; **répétition** *f* repetition; THÉÂT rehearsal

répit [repi] *m* respite; *sans ~* without respite

replacer [r(ə)plase] ⟨1k⟩ put back, replace

repli [r(ə)pli] *m* fold; *d'une rivière* bend; **replier** ⟨1a⟩ fold; *jambes* draw up; *journal* fold up; *manches* roll up; *se ~* MIL fall back; *se ~ sur soi-même* retreat into one's shell

réplique [replik] *f* retort; (*copie*) replica; **répliquer** ⟨1m⟩ retort; *d'un enfant* answer back

répondeur [repõdœr] *m*: *~ automatique* answering machine; **répondre** ⟨4a⟩ **1** *v/t* answer, reply **2** *v/i* answer; (*réagir*) respond; *~ à* answer, reply to; (*réagir à*) respond to; *besoin* meet; *attente* come up to; *signalement* match; *~ de* answer for

réponse [repõs] *f* answer; (*réaction*) response

reportage [r(ə)pɔrtaʒ] *m* report

reporter[1] [r(ə)pɔrte] ⟨1a⟩ take back; *chiffres, solde* carry over; (*ajourner*) postpone

reporter[2] [r(ə)pɔrter] *m/f* reporter

repos [r(ə)po] *m* rest; **reposer** ⟨1a⟩ **1** *v/t* (*remettre*) put back; *question* ask again; (*détendre*) rest; *se ~* rest; *se ~ sur fig* (*compter sur*) rely on **2** *v/i*: *~ sur* rest on; *fig* (*être fondé sur*) be based on

~e [r(ə)pusɑ̃, -t] repulsive, repellant; **repousser** ⟨1a⟩ **1** *v/t* (*dégoûter*) repel; (*différer*) postpone; *pousser en arrière*, MIL push back; (*rejeter*) reject **2** *v/i* grow again

reprendre [r(ə)prɑ̃dr] ⟨4q⟩ **1** *v/t* take back; (*prendre davantage de*) take more; *ville* recapture; (*recommencer*) resume, start again; (*réprimander*) reprimand; (*corriger*) correct; *entreprise* take over (**à** from); (*recouvrer*) regain; (*remporter*) pick up **2** *v/i* retrouver vigueur recover, pick up; (*recommencer*) start again; *se ~* (*se corriger*) correct o.s.; (*se maîtriser*) pull o.s. together

représailles [r(ə)prezaj] *fpl* reprisals; *exercer des ~* take reprisals

représentant, ~e [r(ə)prezɑ̃tɑ̃, -t] *m/f* representative (*aussi* COMM); **représentatif, -ive** representative; **représentation** *f* representation; *au théâtre* performance; **représenter** ⟨1a⟩ represent; *au théâtre* perform; *se ~ qch* imagine sth; *se ~* POL run again for election

répressif, -ive [represif, -iv] POL repressive; **répression** *f* repression; *mesures fpl de ~* crackdown (*contre* on)

réprimande [reprimɑ̃d] *f* reprimand; **réprimander** ⟨1a⟩ reprimand

réprimer [reprime] ⟨1a⟩ suppress

reprise [r(ə)priz] *f* d'une ville recapture; *d'une marchandise* taking back; *d'un travail, d'une lutte* resumption; *à plusieurs ~s* on several occasions; *~ économique* economic recovery; **repriser** ⟨1a⟩ darn, mend

réprobateur, -trice [reprɔbatœr, -tris] reproachful; **réprobation** *f* reproof

reproche [r(ə)prɔʃ] *m* reproach; **reprocher** ⟨1a⟩ reproach; *~ qch à qn* reproach s.o. for sth

reproducteur, -trice [rəprɔdyktœr, -tris] BIOL reproductive; **reproduction** *f* reproduction; **reproduire** ⟨4c⟩ reproduce; *se ~* happen again; BIOL reproduce, breed

reptile [rɛptil] *m* reptile

républicain, **~e** [repyblikɛ̃, -ɛn] *m/f &*
adj republican; **république** *f* republic

répugnance [repyɲɑ̃s] *f* repugnance
(**pour** for); **répugnant**, **~e** repugnant; **répugner** ⟨1a⟩: **~ à qch** be repelled by sth; **~ à faire qch** be reluctant to do sth

répulsif, -ive [repylsif, -iv] *m* repellent; **répulsion** *f* repulsion

réputation [repytasjɔ̃] *f* reputation;
réputé, **~e** famous; **elle est ~e être**
... she is said *ou* supposed to be ...

requérir [rəkerir] ⟨2l⟩ require

requête [rəkɛt] *f* request

requiem [rekwijem] *m* requiem

requin [rəkɛ̃] *m* shark

requis, **~e** [rəki, -z] necessary

réquisitionner [rekizisjɔne] ⟨1a⟩ requisition

rescapé, **~e** [rɛskape] *m/f* survivor

réseau [rezo] *m* (*pl* -x) network; **~ routier** road network *ou* system

réservation [rezɛrvasjɔ̃] *f* booking, reservation

réserve [rezɛrv] *f* reserve; (*entrepôt*)
stockroom, storeroom; (*provision*)
stock, reserve; *indienne* reservation;
émettre des ~s (**à propos de qch**) express reservations (about sth); **~ naturelle** nature reserve; **en ~** in reserve; **sans ~** unreservedly;
sous ~ de subject to

réservé, **~e** [rezɛrve] reserved (*aussi fig*); **réserver** ⟨1a⟩ reserve; *dans un hôtel, un restaurant* book, reserve;
(*mettre de côté*) put aside; **~ qch à qn** keep *ou* save sth for s.o.; **une surprise à qn** have a surprise for s.o.

réservoir [rezɛrvwar] *m* tank; *lac etc* reservoir

résidence [rezidɑ̃s] *f* residence; **~ universitaire** dormitory, *Br* hall of residence; **résidentiel**, **~le** residential;
résider ⟨1a⟩ live; **~ dans** *fig* lie in

résidu [rezidy] *m* residue; MATH remainder

résignation [reziɲasjɔ̃] *f* resignation;
résigner ⟨1a⟩ *d'une fonction* resign;
se ~ resign o.s. (**à** to)

resiliation [reziljasjɔ̃] *f* cancellation;

resilier ⟨1a⟩ *contrat* cancel

résine [rezin] *f* resin

résistance [rezistɑ̃s] *f* resistance; (*endurance*) stamina; *d'un matériau* strength; **la Résistance** HIST the Resistance; **résistant**, **~e** strong, tough;
~ à la chaleur heatproof, heat-resistant; **résister** ⟨1a⟩ resist; **~ à** *tentation, personne* resist; *sécheresse* withstand, stand up to

résolu, **~e** [rezɔly] determined (**à faire qch** to do sth); **résolution** *f* (*décision*)
resolution; (*fermeté*) determination;
d'un problème solving

résonance [rezɔnɑ̃s] *f* resonance; **résonner** ⟨1a⟩ echo, resound

résorber [rezɔrbe] ⟨1a⟩ absorb

résoudre [rezudr] ⟨4bb⟩ **1** *v/t* problème solve **2** *v/i*: **~ de faire qch** decide to do sth; **se ~ à faire qch** decide to do sth

respect [rɛspɛ] *m* respect; **tenir qn en**
~ fend s.o. off; **par ~ pour** out of respect for

respectable [rɛspɛktabl] *personne,*
somme respectable; **respecter** ⟨1a⟩
respect; **~ le(s) délai(s)** meet the deadline; **~ la priorité** AUTO yield,
Br give way; **se ~** have some self-respect; *mutuellement* respect each other; **se faire ~** command respect

respectif, -ive [rɛspɛktif, -iv] respective; **respectivement** *adv* respectively

respectueux, -euse [rɛspɛktɥø, -z]
respectful

respirateur [rɛspiratœr] *m* respirator;
~ artificiel life support system; **respiration** *f* breathing; **retenir sa ~**
hold one's breath; **~ artificielle**
MÉD artificial respiration; **respirer**
⟨1a⟩ **1** *v/t* breathe; *fig* exude **2** *v/i*
breathe

resplendir [rɛsplɑ̃dir] ⟨2a⟩ glitter

responsabilité [rɛspɔ̃sabilite] *f* responsibility (**de** for); JUR liability; **accepter la ~ de** accept responsibility for; **responsable** responsible (**de** for)

ressaisir [r(ə)sezir] ⟨2a⟩: **se ~** pull o.s.
together

ressemblance [r(ə)sãblãs] f resemblance; **ressembler** ⟨1a⟩: **~ à** resemble, be like; **se ~** resemble each other, be like each other; **ne ~ à rien** *péj* look like nothing on earth

ressemeler [r(ə)səmle] ⟨1c⟩ resole

ressentiment [r(ə)sãtimã] m resentment

ressentir [r(ə)sãtir] ⟨2b⟩ feel; **se ~ de qch** still feel the effects of sth

resserrer [r(ə)sere] ⟨1b⟩ *nœud, ceinture* tighten; *fig: amitié* strengthen

resservir [r(ə)servir] ⟨2b⟩ **1** *v/t:* **puis-je vous ~?** would you like some more? **2** *v/i* be used again

ressort [r(ə)sɔr] m TECH spring; *fig* motive; (*énergie*) energy; (*compétence*) province; JUR jurisdiction; **ce n'est pas de mon ~** that's not my province *ou* responsibility; **en dernier ~** JUR without appeal; *fig* as a last resort

ressortir [r(ə)sɔrtir] ⟨2b⟩ (*aux être*) come / go out again; (*se détacher*) stand out; **faire ~** bring out, emphasize; **il ressort de cela que** it emerges from this that; **~ à** JUR fall within the jurisdiction of

ressortissant, ~e [r(ə)sɔrtisã, -t] m/f national

ressource [r(ə)surs] f resource

ressusciter [resysite] ⟨1a⟩ **1** *v/t* resuscitate; *fig aussi* revive **2** *v/i* come back to life

restant, ~e [restã, -t] **1** *adj* remaining **2** m remainder

restaurant [restɔrã] m restaurant; **restaurateur, -trice** m/f restaurateur; ART restorer; **restauration** f catering; ART restoration; **~ rapide** fast food; **restaurer** ⟨1a⟩ restore

reste [rest] m rest, remainder; **~s** CUIS leftovers; **du ~, au ~** moreover; **être en ~ avec** be in debt to

rester [reste] ⟨1a⟩ **1** *v/i* (*aux être*) (*subsister*) be left, remain; (*demeurer*) stay, remain; **on en reste là** we'll stop there **2** *impersonnel:* **il reste du vin** there's some wine left; **il ne reste plus de pain** there's no bread left; (**il**) **reste que** nevertheless

restituer [restitɥe] ⟨1n⟩ (*rendre*) return; (*reconstituer*) restore; **restitution** f restitution

restoroute [restorut] m freeway *ou* Br motorway restaurant

restreindre [restrẽdr] ⟨4b⟩ restrict

restriction [restriksjõ] f restriction; **sans ~** unreservedly

résultat [rezylta] m result; **résulter** ⟨1a⟩ result (**de** from)

résumé [rezyme] m summary; **résumer** ⟨1a⟩ *article, discours* summarize; *situation* sum up

résurrection [rezyreksjõ] f REL resurrection (*aussi fig*)

rétablir [retablir] ⟨2a⟩ (*restituer*) restore; (*remettre*) re-establish, restore; **se ~** recover; **rétablissement** m restoration; *malade* recovery

retaper [r(ə)tape] ⟨1a⟩ *lettre* re-type; F *maison* do up

retard [r(ə)tar] m lateness; *dans travail, paiement* delay; *dans un développement* backwardness; **avoir deux heures de ~** be two hours late; **avoir du ~ en anglais** be behind in English; **avoir du ~ sur qn** be behind s.o.; **être en ~** be late; *d'une montre* be slow; *fig* be behind; **avec 3 heures de ~** three hours late; **sans ~** without delay; **retardataire** m/f latecomer; (*traînard*) straggler; **retardé, ~e** delayed; *enfant* retarded; **retarder** ⟨1a⟩ **1** *v/t* delay, hold up; *montre* put back **2** *v/i d'une montre* be slow; **~ de cinq minutes** be five minutes slow; **~ sur son temps** *fig* be behind the times

retenir [rətnir] ⟨2h⟩ *personne* keep; *argent* withhold; (*rappeler*) remember; *proposition, projet* accept; (*réserver*) reserve; **se ~** restrain o.s.

retentir [rətãtir] ⟨2a⟩ sound; *d'un canon, du tonnerre* boom; **~ sur** impact on; **retentissant, ~e** resounding (*aussi fig*); **retentissement** m impact

retenu, ~e [rətny] (*réservé*) reserved; (*empêché*) delayed, held up; **retenue** f *sur salaire* deduction; *fig* (*modération*) restraint

réticence [retisãs] f (*omission*) omis-

R

sion; (*hésitation*) hesitation

rétine [retin] *f* ANAT retina

retirer [r(ə)tire] ⟨1a⟩ withdraw; *vêtement, chapeau* take off, remove; *promesse* take back; *profit* derive; ~ **qch de** remove sth from; **se** ~ withdraw; (*prendre sa retraite*) retire

retombées [r(ə)tõbe] *fpl* repercussions, fallout F *sg*; ~ **radioactives** PHYS radioactive fallout; **retomber** ⟨1a⟩ (*aux être*) *tomber de nouveau* fall again; (*tomber*) land; *de cheveux, rideau* fall; ~ **sur qch** *fig* come back to sth; ~ **sur qn** *de responsabilité* fall on s.o; ~ **dans qch** sink back into sth

rétorquer [retɔrke] ⟨1m⟩ retort

rétorsion [retɔrsjõ] POL: **mesure f de** ~ retaliatory measure

retouche [r(ə)tuʃ] *f d'un texte, vêtement* alteration; *d'une photographie* retouch; **retoucher** ⟨1a⟩ *texte, vêtement* alter; *photographie* retouch

retour [r(ə)tur] *m* return; **être de** ~ be back; **en** ~ in return; ; **bon** ~*!* have a good trip home!; **par** ~ **du courrier** by return of mail; **retourner** ⟨1a⟩ **1** *v/i* (*aux être*) return, go back; ~ **sur ses pas** backtrack **2** *v/t matelas, tête* turn; *lettre* return; *vêtement* turn inside out; ~ **qn** *fig* get s.o. to change their mind; **tourner et** ~ *fig:* idée turn over and over in one's mind; **se** ~ *au lit* turn over (*aussi* AUTO); (*tourner la tête*) turn (around); **se** ~ **contre qn** turn against s.o.

rétracter [retrakte] ⟨1a⟩: **se** ~ retract

retrait [r(ə)trɛ] *m* withdrawal; **en** ~ set back

retraite [r(ə)trɛt] *f* retirement; (*pension*) retirement pension; MIL retreat; **prendre sa** ~ retire; **retraité, ~e** *m/f* pensioner, retired person

retrancher [r(ə)trãʃe] ⟨1a⟩ (*enlever*) remove, cut (**de** from); (*déduire*) deduct; **se** ~ MIL dig in; *fig* take refuge

retransmettre [rətrãsmɛtr] ⟨4p⟩ relay; **retransmission** *f* TV broadcast

rétrécir [retresir] ⟨2a⟩ **1** *v/t* shrink; *fig* narrow **2** *v/i* shrink; **se** ~ narrow

rétribuer [retribɥe] ⟨1n⟩ pay; **rétribution** *f* remuneration, payment

rétroactif, -ive [retrɔaktif, -iv] retroactive

rétrograde [retrɔgrad] *mouvement* backward; *doctrine, politique* reactionary; **rétrograder** ⟨1a⟩ **1** *v/t* demote **2** *v/i* retreat; AUTO downshift

rétroprojecteur [retrɔprɔʒɛktœr] *m* overhead projector

rétrospectif, -ive [retrɔspɛktif, -iv] **1** *adj* retrospective **2** *f:* **rétrospective** retrospective

retrousser [r(ə)truse] ⟨1a⟩ *manches* roll up

retrouvailles [r(ə)truvaj] *fpl* F reunion *sg*; **retrouver** ⟨1a⟩ (*trouver*) find; *trouver de nouveau* find again; (*rejoindre*) meet; *santé* regain; **se** ~ meet; **se** ~ **seul** find o.s. alone; **on ne s'y retrouve pas** it's confusing

rétroviseur [retrɔvizœr] *m* AUTO rear-view mirror

réunification [reynifikasjõ] *f* reunification; **réunifier** ⟨1a⟩ reunify

réunion [reynjõ] *f* (*assemblée*) meeting; POL reunion; **être en** ~ be in a meeting; **réunir** ⟨2a⟩ bring together; *pays* reunite; *documents* collect; **se** ~ meet

réussi, ~e [reysi] successful; **réussir** ⟨2a⟩ **1** *v/i d'une personne* succeed; ~ **à faire qch** manage to do sth, succeed in doing sth **2** *v/t vie, projet* make a success of; *examen* be successful in; ~ **un soufflé** make a successful soufflé; **réussite** *f* success; *aux cartes* solitaire, *Br aussi* patience

réutilisable [reytilizabl] reusable; **réutiliser** ⟨1a⟩ reuse

revanche [r(ə)vãʃ] *f* revenge; **en** ~ on the other hand

rêve [rɛv] *m* dream

revêche [rəvɛʃ] harsh

réveil [revɛj] *m* awakening; (*pendule*) alarm (clock); **réveiller** ⟨1b⟩ *personne* waken, wake up; *fig* revive; **se** ~ wake up

réveillon [revɛjõ] *m* special meal eaten on Christmas Eve or New Year's Eve; **réveillonner** ⟨1a⟩ have a réveillon

révélateur, -trice [revelatœr, -tris] revealing; **être ~ de qch** point to sth; **révélation** f revelation; **révéler** ⟨1f⟩ reveal; **se ~ faux** prove to be false

revenant [r(ə)vɑ̃nɑ̃] m ghost

revendeur, -euse [r(ə)vɑ̃dœr, -øz] m/f retailer

revendication [r(ə)vɑ̃dikasjɔ̃] f claim, demand; **revendiquer** ⟨1m⟩ claim, demand; *responsabilité* claim; **~ un attentat** claim responsibility for an attack

revendre [r(ə)vɑ̃dr] ⟨4a⟩ resell; **avoir du temps à ~** have plenty of time to spare

revenir [rəvnir] ⟨2h⟩ (*aux être*) come back, return (*à* to); *d'un mot* crop up; **~ sur** *thème, discussion* go back to; *décision, parole* go back on; **~ sur ses pas** retrace one's footsteps; **~ à qn** *d'une part* be due to s.o.; **sa tête ne me revient pas** I don't like the look of him; **~ de** *évanouissement* come around from; *étonnement* get over, recover from; *illusion* lose; **~ cher** cost a lot; **cela revient au même** it comes to the same thing; **faire ~** CUIS brown

revente [r(ə)vɑ̃t] f resale

revenu [rəvny] m income; **~s** revenue sg

rêver [rɛve] ⟨1a⟩ dream (*de* about); *éveillé* (day)dream (*à* about)

réverbère [reverbɛr] m street lamp

révérence [reverɑ̃s] f (*salut*) bow; *d'une femme* curtsey

rêverie [revri] f daydream

révérifier [reverifje] ⟨1a⟩ double-check

revers [r(ə)vɛr] m reverse, back; *d'une enveloppe, de la main* back; *d'un pantalon* cuff, *Br* turn-up; *fig (échec)* reversal; **~ de la médaille** other side of the coin

revêtement [r(ə)vɛtmɑ̃] m TECH cladding; *d'une route* surface; **revêtir** ⟨2g⟩ *vêtement* put on; *forme, caractère* assume; **~ qn d'une autorité / dignité** lend s.o. authority / dignity; **~ qch de** TECH cover *ou* clad sth in sth; **~ une importance particu-**

lière take on particular importance

rêveur, -euse [rɛvœr, -øz] **1** *adj* dreamy **2** m/f dreamer

revigorer [r(ə)vigɔre] ⟨1a⟩ *fig* reinvigorate

revirement [r(ə)virmɑ̃] m: **~ d'opinion** sudden change in public attitude

réviser [revize] ⟨1a⟩ *texte* revise; *machine* service; **révision** f revision; TECH, AUTO service

revivre [r(ə)vivr] ⟨4e⟩ **1** v/t relive **2** v/i revive

révocation [revɔkasjɔ̃] f revocation; *d'un dirigeant etc* dismissal

revoir [r(ə)vwar] **1** vt ⟨3b⟩ see again; *texte* review; ÉDU review, *Br* revise **2** m: **au ~!** goodbye!

révolte [revɔlt] f revolt; **révolter** ⟨1a⟩ revolt; **se ~** rebel, revolt

révolu, -e [revɔly] bygone

révolution [revɔlysjɔ̃] f revolution; **révolutionnaire** m/f & adj revolutionary; **révolutionner** ⟨1a⟩ revolutionize

revolver [revɔlvɛr] m revolver

révoquer [revɔke] ⟨1m⟩ *fonctionnaire* dismiss; *contrat* revoke

revue [r(ə)vy] f review; **passer en ~** *fig* review

rez-de-chaussée [redʃose] m (*pl inv*) first floor, *Br* ground floor

R.F.A. [ɛrɛfɑ] f abr (= **République fédérale d'Allemagne**) FRG (Federal Republic of Germany)

rhabiller [rabije] ⟨1a⟩: **se ~** get dressed again

rhétorique [retɔrik] f rhetoric

Rhin [rɛ̃] m Rhine

rhinocéros [rinɔserɔs] m rhinoceros, rhino F

Rhône [ron] m Rhone

rhubarbe [rybarb] f BOT rhubarb

rhum [rɔm] m rum

rhumatisant, ~e [rymatizɑ̃, -t] rheumatic; **rhumatismes** mpl rheumatism sg

rhume [rym] m cold; **~ de cerveau** head cold; **~ des foins** hay fever

riant, ~e [rijɑ̃, -t] merry

ricanement [rikanmɑ̃] m sneer; *bête*

snigger; **ricaner** ⟨1a⟩ sneer; *bêtement* snigger

riche [riʃ] rich (**en** in); *sol* fertile; *décoration, meubles* elaborate; **richesse** *f* wealth; *du sol* fertility

ricocher [rikɔʃe] ⟨1a⟩ ricochet

rictus [riktys] *m* grimace

ride [rid] *f* wrinkle, line; **ridé, ~e** wrinkled, lined

rideau [rido] *m* (*pl* -x) drape, *Br* curtain; **~ de fer** POL Iron Curtain

rider [ride] ⟨1a⟩ *peau* wrinkle; **se ~** become wrinkled *ou* lined

ridicule [ridikyl] **1** *adj* ridiculous (*de faire qch* to do sth) **2** *m* ridicule; (*absurdité*) ridiculousness; **tourner qch en ~** poke fun at sth; **ridiculiser** ⟨1a⟩ ridicule; **se ~** make a fool of o.s.

rien² [rjɛ̃] **1** *pron* ◇ nothing; **de ~** *comme réponse* not at all, you're welcome; **ils ne se ressemblent en ~** they are not at all alike; **~ que cela?** just that?, nothing else?; **j'y suis pour ~** I have nothing to do with it ◇ **ne ... ~** nothing, not anything; **il ne sait ~** he knows nothing, he doesn't know anything; **~ de** nothing at all, absolutely nothing; **~ du tout** nothing at all; **il n'en est ~** it's not the case, it's not so ◇ *quelque chose* anything; **sans ~ dire** without saying anything **2** *m* trifle; **en un ~ de temps** in no time; **pour un ~ se fâcher** for nothing, for no reason; **un ~ de** a touch of

rigide [riʒid] rigid (*aussi fig*)

rigolade [rigɔlad] *f* F joke

rigole [rigɔl] *f* (*conduit*) channel

rigoler [rigɔle] ⟨1a⟩ F joke; (*rire*) laugh; **rigolo, ~te** F (*amusant*) funny

rigoureusement [rigurøzmɑ̃] *adv* rigorously; **rigoureux, -euse** rigorous, strict; **rigueur** *f* rigor, *Br* rigour; **à la ~** if absolutely necessary; **de ~** compulsory

rime [rim] *f* rhyme; **rimer** ⟨1a⟩ rhyme; **ne ~ à rien** *fig* not make sense

rinçage [rɛ̃saʒ] *m* rinse; **rincer** ⟨1k⟩ rinse

ring [riŋ] *m en boxe* ring

riposte [ripɔst] *f* riposte, response; *avec armes* return of fire; **riposter** ⟨1a⟩ reply, response; *avec armes* return fire

rire [rir] **1** *vi* ⟨4r⟩ laugh (*de* about, at); (*s'amuser*) have fun; **~ aux éclats** roar with laughter; **pour ~** as a joke, for a laugh; **~ de qn** make fun of s.o., laugh at s.o.; **se ~ de** *fml* laugh at **2** *m* laugh; **~s** laughter *sg*

risée [rize] *f* mockery

risible [rizibl] laughable

risque [risk] *m* risk; **à mes / tes ~s et périls** at my / your own risk; **au ~ de faire qch** at the risk of doing sth; **courir le ~ de faire qch** risk doing sth, run the risk of doing sth; **risqué, ~e** risky; *plaisanterie, remarque* risqué; **risquer** ⟨1m⟩ risk; **~ de faire qch** risk doing sth, run the risk of doing sth; ; **se ~ dans** *pièce* venture into; *entreprise* venture on

rissoler [risɔle] ⟨1a⟩ CUIS brown

rite [rit] *m* REL rite; *fig* ritual; **rituel, ~le** *m & adj* ritual

rivage [rivaʒ] *m* shore

rival, ~e [rival] (*mpl* -aux) *m/f & adj* rival; **rivaliser** ⟨1a⟩ compete, vie; **rivalité** *f* rivalry

rive [riv] *f d'un fleuve* bank; *d'une mer, d'un lac* shore; **la Rive Gauche** *à Paris* the Left Bank

river [rive] ⟨1a⟩ TECH rivet

riverain, ~e [rivrɛ̃, -ɛn] *m/f* resident

rivet [rive] *m* TECH rivet

rivière [rivjɛr] *f* river

rixe [riks] *f* fight, brawl

riz [ri] *m* BOT rice

robe [rɔb] *f* dress; *d'un juge, avocat* robe; **~ de chambre** robe, *Br* dressing gown; **~ de mariée** wedding dress; **~ du soir** evening dress

robinet [rɔbine] *m* faucet, *Br* tap

robot [rɔbo] *m* robot

robuste [rɔbyst] sturdy, robust

roc [rɔk] *m* rock

rocaille [rɔkaj] *f terrain* stony ground; **rocailleux, -euse** stony; *voix* rough

roche [rɔʃ] *f* rock; **rocher** *m* rock; **rocheux, -euse** rocky; **les Montagnes Rocheuses** the Rocky Mountains

rock [rɔk] *m* MUS rock

rococo [rɔkɔko] *m* rococo

rodage [rɔdaʒ] *m* AUTO running in

rôder [rode] ⟨1a⟩ prowl; **rôdeur, -euse** *m/f* prowler

rogne [rɔɲ] *f*: **être en ~** F be in a bad mood

rogner [rɔɲe] ⟨1a⟩ **1** *v/t* cut, trim **2** *v/i*: **~ sur qch** cut *ou* trim sth

rognon [rɔɲɔ̃] *m* CUIS kidney

roi [rwa] *m* king

rôle [rol] *m* role; (*registre*) roll; **à tour de ~** turn and turn about

ROM [rɔm] *f* (*pl inv*) *abr* (= **read only memory**) ROM

romain, ~e [rɔmɛ̃, -ɛn] **1** *adj* Roman **2** *m/f* **Romain, ~e** Roman

roman [rɔmɑ̃] *m* novel

romancier, -ère [rɔmɑ̃sje, -ɛr] *m/f* novelist

romand, ~e [rɔmɑ̃, -d]: **la Suisse ~e** French-speaking Switzerland

romanesque [rɔmanɛsk] (*sentimental*) romantic

romantique [rɔmɑ̃tik] *m/f & adj* romantic; **romantisme** *m* romanticism

romarin [rɔmarɛ̃] *m* BOT rosemary

rompre [rɔ̃pr] ⟨4a⟩ **1** *v/t* break; ~ **avec** *petit ami* break it off with; *tradition* break **2** *v/i*: *habitude* break **2** *v/i* break (*aussi fig*); *relations, négociations, fiançailles* break off; **se ~** break; **rompu, ~e** (*cassé*) broken; ~ **à** used to

ronce [rɔ̃s] *f* BOT: ~**s** brambles

rond, ~e [rɔ̃, -d] **1** *adj* round; *joues, personne* plump; F (*ivre*) drunk **2** *adv*: **tourner ~** *moteur, fig* run smoothly **3** *m* figure circle **m 4** *f*: **faire la ~e** dance in a circle; **faire sa ~e** do one's rounds; *d'un soldat* be on patrol; *d'un policier* be on patrol, *Br aussi* be on the beat; **à la ~e** around; **rondelet, ~te** plump

rondelle [rɔ̃dɛl] *f* disk, *Br* disc; *de saucisson* slice; TECH washer

rondement [rɔ̃dmɑ̃] *adv* (*promptement*) briskly; (*carrément*) frankly

rondeur [rɔ̃dœr] *f* roundness; *des bras, d'une personne* plumpness; *fig* frankness; ~**s** *d'une femme* curves

rondin [rɔ̃dɛ̃] *m* log

rond-point [rɔ̃pwɛ̃] *m* (*pl ronds--points*) traffic circle, *Br* roundabout

ronflement [rɔ̃fləmɑ̃] *m* snoring; *d'un moteur* purr; **ronfler** ⟨1a⟩ snore; *d'un moteur* purr

ronger [rɔ̃ʒe] ⟨1l⟩ gnaw at; *fig* torment; **se ~ les ongles** bite one's nails; **rongeur** *m* ZO rodent

ronronnement [rɔ̃rɔnmɑ̃] *m* purr; **ronronner** ⟨1a⟩ purr

rosace [rozas] *f* ARCH rose window

rosaire [rozɛr] *m* REL rosary

rosbif [rɔzbif] *m* CUIS roast beef

rose [roz] **1** *f* BOT rose **2** *m couleur* pink **3** *adj* pink; **rosé, ~e 1** *m* rosé **2** *adj* pinkish

roseau [rozo] *m* (*pl -x*) BOT reed

rosée [roze] *f* dew

rosier [rozje] *m* rose bush

rossignol [rɔsiɲɔl] *m* ZO nightingale

rot [ro] *m* F belch

rotation [rɔtasjɔ̃] *f* rotation

roter [rɔte] ⟨1a⟩ F belch

rôti [roti, ro-] *m* roast

rôtie [roti, ro-] *f* slice of toast

rotin [rɔtɛ̃] *m* rattan

rôtir [rotir, ro-] ⟨2a⟩ roast; **rôtisserie** *f* grill-room; **rôtissoire** *f* spit

rotule [rɔtyl] *f* ANAT kneecap

rouage [rwaʒ] *m* cogwheel; ~**s** *d'une montre* works; *fig* machinery *sg*

roublard, ~e [rublar, -d] crafty

roucouler [rukule] ⟨1a⟩ *d'un pigeon* coo; *d'amoureux* bill and coo

roue [ru] *f* wheel; **deux ~s** *m* two-wheeler; ~ **libre** freewheel

roué, ~e [rwe] crafty

rouer [rwe]⟨1a⟩: ~ **qn de coups** beat s.o. black and blue

rouge [ruʒ] **1** *adj* red (*aussi* POL) **2** *adv fig*: **voir ~** see red **3** *m couleur, vin* red; ~ **à lèvres** lipstick; ~ **à joues** blusher; **rougeâtre** reddish

rouge-gorge [ruʒgɔrʒ] *m* (*pl rouges--gorges*) robin (redbreast)

rougeole [ruʒɔl] *f* MÉD measles *sg*

rouget [ruʒɛ] *m* mullet

rougeur [ruʒœr] *f* redness; (*irritation*) blotch; **rougir** ⟨2a⟩ go red; *d'une personne aussi* blush (*de* with); *de colère* flush (*de* with)

rouille [ruj] *f* rust; **rouillé, ~e** rusty (*aussi fig*); **rouiller** ⟨1a⟩ rust; **se ~** rust; *fig* go rusty

rouleau [rulo] *m* (*pl* -x) roller; *de papier peint, pellicule* roll; CUIS rolling pin

roulement [rulmã] *m de tambour* roll; *d'un train* rumble; TECH bearing; **~ à billes** TECH ball bearing

rouler [rule] ⟨1a⟩ 1 *v/i* roll; *d'une voiture* travel; **ça roule?** F how are things?, how goes it? F; **~ sur qch** *d'une conversation* be about sth 2 *v/t* roll; **~ qn** F cheat s.o.; **se ~ par terre**: roll on the ground

roulette [rulɛt] *f de meubles* caster; *jeu* roulette

roulis [ruli] *m* MAR swell

roulotte [rulɔt] *f* trailer, *Br* caravan

roumain, ~e [rumɛ̃, -ɛn] 1 *adj* Romanian 2 *m langue* Romanian 3 *m/f* **Roumain, ~e** Romanian; **Roumanie: la ~** Romania

round [rund] *m en boxe* round

rouquin, ~e [rukɛ̃, -in] *m/f* F redhead

rouspéter [ruspete] ⟨1f⟩ F complain

rousseur [rusœr] *f*: **taches** *fpl* **de ~** freckles; **roussir** ⟨2a⟩ 1 *v/t linge* scorch 2 *v/i de feuilles* turn brown; **faire ~** CUIS brown

route [rut] *f* road; (*parcours*) route; *fig* (*chemin*) path; **en ~** on the way; **mettre en ~** *moteur, appareil* start up; **se mettre en ~** set off; *fig* get under way; **faire fausse ~** take the wrong turning; *fig* be on the wrong track; be wrong; **faire ~ vers** be heading for; **routier, -ère** 1 *adj* road *atr* 2 *m* (*conducteur*) truck driver, *Br* long-distance lorry driver; *restaurant* truck stop, *Br aussi* transport café

routine [rutin] *f* routine; **de ~** routine *atr*; **routinier, -ère** routine *atr*

rouvrir [ruvrir] ⟨2f⟩ open again, reopen

roux, rousse [ru, -s] 1 *adj* red-haired; *cheveux* red 2 *m* CUIS roux

royal, ~e [rwajal] (*mpl* -aux) royal; *fig*: *pourboire, accueil* superb, right royal; **royaliste** *m/f* & *adj* royalist

royaume [rwajom] *m* kingdom; **Royaume-Uni** United Kingdom; **royauté** *f* royalty

R.-U. *abr* (= **Royaume-Uni**) UK (= United Kingdom)

ruban [rybã] *m* ribbon; **~ adhésif** adhesive tape

rubéole [rybeɔl] *f* German measles *sg*

rubis [rybi] *m* ruby

rubrique [rybrik] *f* heading

ruche [ryʃ] *f* hive

rude [ryd] *personne, manières* uncouth; *sévère: personne, voix, climat* harsh; *travail, lutte* hard

rudimentaire [rydimãter] rudimentary; **rudiments** *mpl* rudiments, basics

rudoyer [rydwaje] ⟨1h⟩ be unkind to

rue [ry] *f* street; **dans la ~** on the street, *Br* in the street; **en pleine ~** in the middle of the street; **descendre dans la ~** take to the streets; **~ à sens unique** one-way street; **~ piétonne** pedestrianized zone, *Br aussi* pedestrian precinct

ruée [rɥe] *f* rush

ruelle [rɥɛl] *f* alley

ruer [rɥe] ⟨1n⟩ *d'un cheval* kick; **~ dans les brancards** *fig* kick over the traces; **se ~ sur** make a headlong dash for

rugby [rygbi] *m* rugby

rugir [ryʒir] ⟨2a⟩ roar; *du vent* howl; **rugissement** *m* roar

rugueux, -euse [rygø, -z] rough

ruine [rɥin] *f* ruin; **ruiner** ⟨1a⟩ ruin; **ruineux, -euse** incredibly expensive

ruisseau [rɥiso] *m* (*pl* -x) stream (*aussi fig*); (*caniveau*) gutter (*aussi fig*)

ruisseler [rɥisle] ⟨1c⟩ run

rumeur [rymœr] *f* hum; *de personnes* murmuring; (*nouvelle*) rumor, *Br* rumour

ruminer [rymine] ⟨1a⟩ 1 *v/i* chew the cud, ruminate 2 *v/t fig*: **~ qch** mull sth over

rupture [ryptyr] *f* breaking; *fig* split; *de négociations* breakdown; *de relations diplomatiques, fiançailles* breaking off; *de contrat* breach

rural, ~e [ryral] (*mpl* -aux) rural

ruse [ryz] *f* ruse; *la ~* cunning; **rusé, ~e** crafty, cunning

russe [rys] **1** *adj* Russian **2** *m langue* Russian **3** *m/f* **Russe** Russian; **Russie:** *la ~* Russia

rustique [rystik] rustic

rustre [rystr] *péj* **1** *adj* uncouth **2** *m* oaf

rutilant, ~e [rytilɑ̃, -t] (*rouge*) glowing; (*brillant*) gleaming

rythme [ritm] *m* rhythm; (*vitesse*) pace; **rythmique** rhythmical

S

S. *abr* (= *sud*) S (= south)

s' [s] → **se**

sa [sa] → **son¹**

S.A. [ɛsɑ] *f abr* (= *société anonyme*) Inc, *Br* plc

sable [sabl] *m* sand; **sablé** *m* CUIS shortbread biscuit; **sabler** ⟨1a⟩ sand; *~ le champagne* break open the champagne; **sablier** *m* CUIS eggtimer; **sablonneux, -euse** sandy

sabot [sabo] *m* clog; ZO hoof; *~ de Denver* Denver boot, *Br* clamp

sabotage [sabotaʒ] *m* sabotage; **saboter** ⟨1a⟩ sabotage; F *travail* make a mess of; **saboteur, -euse** *m/f* saboteur

sac [sak] *m* bag; *de pommes de terre* sack; *~ de couchage* sleeping bag; *~ à dos* backpack; *~ à main* purse, *Br* handbag; *~ à provisions* shopping bag

saccadé, ~e [sakade] *mouvements* jerky; *voix* breathless

saccager [sakaʒe] ⟨1l⟩ (*piller*) sack; (*détruire*) destroy

saccharine [sakarin] *f* saccharine

sachet [saʃe] *m* sachet; *~ de thé* teabag

sacoche [sakɔʃ] *f* bag; *de vélo* saddlebag

sacre [sakr] *m d'un souverain* coronation

sacré, ~e [sakre] sacred; *devant le substantif* F damn F, *Br aussi* bloody F

sacrement [sakrəmɑ̃] *m* REL sacrement

sacrifice [sakrifis] *m* sacrifice (*aussi fig*); **sacrifier** ⟨1a⟩ sacrifice (*aussi fig*); *~ à la mode fig* be a slave to fashion, be a fashion victim; *se ~* sacrifice o.s.

sacrilège [sakrilɛʒ] **1** *adj* sacrilegious **2** *m* sacrilege

sacro-saint, ~e [sakrɔsɛ̃, -t] *iron* sacrosanct

sadique [sadik] **1** *adj* sadistic **2** *m/f* sadist; **sadisme** *m* sadism

safran [safrɑ̃] *m* BOT, CUIS saffron

saga [saga] *f* saga

sagace [sagas] shrewd; **sagacité** *f* shrewdness

sage [saʒ] **1** *adj* wise; *enfant* good **2** *m* sage, wise man; **sage-femme** *f* (*pl* sages-femmes) midwife; **sagesse** *f* wisdom; *d'un enfant* goodness

Sagittaire [saʒitɛr] *m* ASTROL Sagittarius

saignant, ~e [sɛɲɑ̃, -t] bleeding; CUIS rare; **saignement** *m* bleeding; **saigner** ⟨1b⟩ **1** *v/i* bleed; *je saigne du nez* my nose is bleeding, I have a nosebleed **2** *v/t fig* bleed dry *ou* white

saillant, ~e [sajɑ̃, -t] *pommettes* prominent; *fig* salient; **saillie** *f* ARCH projection; *fig* quip; **saillir** ⟨2c⟩ ARCH project

sain, ~e [sɛ̃, sɛn] healthy (*aussi fig*); *gestion* sound; *~ et sauf* safe and sound; *~ d'esprit* sane

saindoux [sɛ̃du] *m* lard

saint, ~e [sɛ̃, -t] **1** *adj* holy; *vendredi m ~* Good Friday **2** *m/f* saint; **Saint-**

Esprit *m* Holy Spirit; **sainteté** *f* holiness; **Saint-Sylvestre:** *la ~* New Year's Eve

saisie [sezi] *f* JUR, *de marchandises de contrebande* seizure; **~ de données** INFORM data capture; **saisir** ⟨2a⟩ seize; *personne, objet* take hold of, seize; *sens, intention* grasp; *occasion* seize, grasp; INFORM capture; **se ~ de qn / de qch** take hold of *ou* seize s.o. / sth; **saisissant, ~e** striking; *froid* penetrating

saison [sɛzõ] *f* season; **saisonnier, -ère 1** *adj* seasonal **2** *m ouvrier* seasonal worker

salade [salad] *f* salad; **~ de fruits** fruit salad; **saladier** *m* salad bowl

salaire [salɛr] *m d'un ouvrier* wages *pl*; *d'un employé* salary; **~ net** take-home pay

salami [salami] *m* salami

salarial, ~e [salarjal], (*mpl* -aux) wage *atr*; **salarié, ~e 1** *adj travail* paid **2** *m/f ouvrier* wage-earner; *employé* salaried employee

salaud [salo] *m* P bastard F

sale [sal] dirty; *devant le substantif* nasty

salé, ~e [sale] *eau* salt; CUIS salted; *fig: histoire* daring; *prix* steep; **saler** ⟨1a⟩ salt

saleté [salte] *f* dirtiness; **~s** *fig* (*grossièretés*) filthy remarks; F *choses sans valeur, mauvaise nourriture* junk *sg*

salière [saljɛr] *f* salt cellar

salir [salir] ⟨2a⟩: **~ qch** get sth dirty, dirty sth; **salissant, ~e** *travail* dirty; *tissu* easily dirtied

salive [saliv] *f* saliva

salle [sal] *f* room; **~ d'attente** waiting room; **~ de bain(s)** bathroom; **~ de classe** classroom; **~ d'eau** shower room; **~ à manger** dining room; **~ de séjour** living room

salmonellose [salmoneloz] *f* MÉD salmonella (poisoning)

salon [salõ] *m* living room; *d'un hôtel* lounge; (*foire*) show; **~ de l'automobile** auto show, *Br* motor show; **~ de thé** tea room; **~ de coiffure** hair salon, *Br* hairdressing salon

salopard [salopar] P *m → **salaud**; **salope** *f* P bitch; **saloperie** *f* F *chose sans valeur* piece of junk; (*bassesse*) dirty trick

salopette [salopet] *f* dungarees *pl*

salubre [salybr] healthy

saluer [salɥe] ⟨1n⟩ greet; MIL salute; **~ qn (de la main)** wave to s.o.

salut [saly] *m* greeting; MIL salute; (*sauvegarde*) safety; REL salvation; **~!** F hi!; (*au revoir*) bye!

salutaire [salytɛr] salutary; **salutation** *f* greeting; *dans lettre* **recevez mes ~s distinguées** yours truly, *Br* yours sincerely

samedi [samdi] *m* Saturday

sanatorium [sanatɔrjɔm] *m* sanitarium, *Br aussi* sanitorium

sanction [sãksjõ] *f* (*peine, approbation*) sanction; **sanctionner** ⟨1a⟩ (*punir*) punish; (*approuver*) sanction

sanctuaire [sãktɥɛr] *m* sanctuary

sandale [sãdal] *f* sandal

sandwich [sãdwitʃ] *m* (*pl* -s) sandwich

sang [sã] *m* blood; **se faire du mauvais ~** F worry, fret; **sang-froid** *m* composure, calmness; **garder son ~** keep one's cool; **tuer qn de ~** kill s.o. in cold blood; **sanglant, ~e** bloodstained; *combat, mort* bloody

sanglier [sãglije] *m* (wild) boar

sanglot [sãglo] *m* sob; **sangloter** ⟨1a⟩ sob

sanguin, ~e [sãgɛ̃, -in] blood *atr*; *tempérament* sanguine; **groupe** *m* **~** blood group; **sanguinaire** *personne* bloodthirsty; *combat* bloody; **sanguine** *f* BOT blood orange

sanitaire [sanitɛr] sanitary; **installations** *fpl* **~s** sanitary fittings, sanitation *sg*; *tuyauterie* plumbing *sg*

sans [sã] **1** *prép* without; **~ manger / travailler** without eating / working; **~ sucre** sugar-free, without sugar; **~ parapluie / balcon** without an umbrella / a balcony; **~ toi nous serions tous ...** if it hadn't been for you we would all ... **2** *conj:* **~ que je le lui suggère** (*subj*) without me suggesting it to him

sauver

sans-abri [sɑ̃zabri] *m/f* (*pl inv*): **les ~** the homeless *pl*

sans-emploi [sɑ̃zɑ̃plwa] *m* person without a job; **les ~** the unemployed *pl*

sans-façon [sɑ̃fasɔ̃] *m* informality

sans-gêne [sɑ̃ʒɛn] **1** *m/f* (*pl inv*): **être un / une ~** be brazen *ou* impudent **2** *m* shamelessness

sans-souci [sɑ̃susi] *adj inv* carefree

santé [sɑ̃te] *f* health; **être en bonne ~** be in good health; **à votre ~!** cheers!, your very good health!

saoudien, ~ne [saudjɛ̃, -ɛn] **1** *adj* Saudi (Arabian) **2** *m/f* **Saoudien, ~ne** Saudi (Arabian)

saoul [su] → **soûl**

saper [sape] ⟨1a⟩ undermine (*aussi fig*)

sapeur [sapœr] *m* MIL sapper; **sapeur-pompier** *m* (*pl sapeurs-pompiers*) firefighter, *Br aussi* fireman

saphir [safir] *m* sapphire

sapin [sapɛ̃] *m* BOT fir

sarcasme [sarkasm] *m* sarcasm; **sarcastique** sarcastic

Sardaigne [sardɛɲ]: **la ~** Sardinia; **sarde 1** *adj* Sardinian **2** *m/f* **Sarde** Sardinian

sardine [sardin] *f* sardine

sardonique [sardɔnik] sardonic

S.A.R.L. [esaɛrɛl] *f abr* (= **société à responsabilité limitée**) Inc, *Br* Ltd

Satan [satɑ̃] *m* Satan; **satanique** satanic

satellite [satelit] *m* satellite (*aussi fig*); **ville** *f* **~** satellite town

satin [satɛ̃] *m* satin

satire [satir] *f* satire; **satirique** satirical

satisfaction [satisfaksjɔ̃] *f* satisfaction; **satisfaire** ⟨4n⟩ **1** *v/t*: **~ à besoins, conditions** meet; **~ à la demande** COMM keep up with *ou* meet demand **2** *v/t* satisfy; *attente* come up to; **satisfaisant, ~e** satisfactory; **satisfait, ~e** satisfied (*de* with)

saturation [satyrasjɔ̃] *f* saturation; **saturer** ⟨1a⟩ saturate; **je suis saturé de** *fig* I've had more than enough of

sauce [sos] *f* sauce; **~ tomate** tomato sauce

saucisse [sosis] *f* sausage; **saucisson** *m* (dried) sausage

sauf¹ [sof] *prép* except; **~ que** except that; **~ si** except if; **~ le respect que je vous dois** with all due respect

sauf², sauve [sof, sov] safe, unharmed; **sauf-conduit** *m* (*pl sauf-conduits*) safe-conduct

sauge [soʒ] *f* BOT sage

saugrenu, ~e [sogrəny] ridiculous

saule [sol] *m* BOT willow; **~ pleureur** weeping willow

saumon [somɔ̃] *m* salmon

saumure [somyr] *f* brine

sauna [sona] *m* sauna

saupoudrer [sopudre] ⟨1a⟩ sprinkle (**de** with)

saut [so] *m* jump; **faire un ~ chez qn** *fig* drop in briefly on s.o.; **au ~ du lit** on rising, on getting out of bed; **~ à l'élastique** bungee jumping; **~ en hauteur** high jump; **~ en longueur** broad jump, *Br* long jump; **~ à la perche** pole vault; **~ périlleux** somersault in the air

saute [sot] *f* abrupt change; **~ de vent** abrupt change in wind direction

sauté, ~e [sote] CUIS sauté(ed)

sauter [sote] ⟨1a⟩ **1** *v/i* jump; (*exploser*) blow up; ÉL *d'un fusible* blow; *d'un bouton* come off; **~ sur** *personne* pounce on; *occasion, offre* jump at; **faire ~** CUIS sauté; **cela saute aux yeux** it's obvious, it's as plain as the nose on your face **2** *v/t obstacle, fossé* jump (over); *mot, repas* skip

sauterelle [sotrɛl] *f* grasshopper

sautiller [sotije] ⟨1a⟩ hop

sauvage [sovaʒ] **1** *adj* wild; (*insociable*) unsociable; (*primitif, barbare*) savage; *pas autorisé* unauthorized **2** *m/f* savage; (*solitaire*) unsociable person; **sauvagement** *adv* savagely

sauvegarde [sovgard] *f* safeguard; INFORM back-up; **copie** *f* **de ~** backup (copy); **sauvegarder** ⟨1a⟩ safeguard; INFORM back up

sauve-qui-peut [sovkipø] *m* (*pl inv*) (*débandade*) stampede; **sauver** ⟨1a⟩

S

save; *personne en danger* save, rescue; *navire* salvage; **~ les apparences** save face; **~ les meubles** *fig* salvage something from the wreckage; **sauve qui peut** it's every man for himself; **se ~** run away; F (*partir*) be off; (*déborder*) boil over

sauvetage [sovtaʒ] *m* rescue; *de navire* salvaging; **sauveteur** *m* rescuer

sauveur [sovœr] *m* savior, *Br* saviour; **le Sauveur** REL the Savior

savamment [savamɑ̃] *adv* (*habilement*) cleverly; **j'en parle ~** (*en connaissance de cause*) I know what I'm talking about

savant, **~e** [savɑ̃, -t] **1** *adj* (*érudit*) *personne, société, revue* learned; (*habile*) skillful, *Br* skilful **2** *m* scientist

saveur [savœr] *f* taste

savoir [savwar] **1** *v/t & v/i* ⟨3g⟩ know; **sais-tu nager?** can you swim?, do you know how to swim?; **j'ai su que** I found out that; **je ne saurais vous le dire** I couldn't rightly say; **reste à ~ si** it remains to be seen whether; **faire ~ qch à qn** tell s.o. sth; **à ce que je sais**, (**pour autant**) **que je sache** (*subj*) as far as I know; **sans le ~** without realizing it, unwittingly **2** *m* knowledge

savoir-faire [savwarfɛr] *m* expertise, knowhow

savoir-vivre [savwarvivr] *m* good manners *pl*

savon [savõ] *m* soap; **savonner** ⟨1a⟩ soap; **savonnette** *f* bar of toilet soap; **savonneux**, **-euse** soapy

savourer [savure] ⟨1a⟩ savor, *Br* savour; **savoureux**, **-euse** tasty; *fig*: *récit* spicy

saxophone [saksofon] *m* saxophone, sax

scalpel [skalpɛl] *m* scalpel

scandale [skɑ̃dal] *m* scandal; **au grand ~ de** to the great indignation of; **faire ~** cause a scandal; **faire tout un ~** make a scene; **scandaleux**, **-euse** scandalous; **scandaliser** ⟨1a⟩ scandalize; **se ~ de** be shocked by

scandinave [skɑ̃dinav] **1** *adj* Scandinavian **2** *m/f* **Scandinave** Scandinavian; **Scandinavie:** *la* **~** Scandinavia

scanner ⟨1a⟩ **1** *v/t* [skane] INFORM scan **2** *m* [skanɛr] INFORM, MÉD scanner

scaphandre [skafɑ̃dr] *m de plongeur* diving suit; *d'astronaute* space suit; **scaphandrier** *m* diver

scarlatine [skarlatin] *f* scarlet fever

sceau [so] *m* (*pl* -x) seal; *fig* (*marque*, *signe*) stamp

scellé [sele] *m* official seal; **sceller** ⟨1b⟩ seal (*aussi fig*)

scénario [senarjo] *m* scenario; (*script*) screenplay; **~ catastrophe** worst-case scenario; **scénariste** *m/f* scriptwriter

scène [sɛn] *f* scene (*aussi fig*); (*plateau*) stage; **ne me fais pas une ~!** don't make a scene!; **mettre en ~** *pièce*, *film* direct; *présenter* stage; **mise** *f* **en ~** direction; *présentation* staging; **~ de ménage** domestic argument

scepticisme [sɛptisism] *m* skepticism, *Br* scepticism; **sceptique 1** *adj* skeptical, *Br* sceptical **2** *m* skeptic, *Br* sceptic

sceptre [sɛptr] *m* scepter, *Br* sceptre

schéma [ʃema] *m* diagram; **schématique** diagrammatic; **schématisation** *f* oversimplification; **schématiser** ⟨1a⟩ oversimplify

schisme [ʃism] *m fig* split; REL schism

schizophrène [skizofrɛn] schizophrenic

sciatique [sjatik] *f* MÉD sciatica

scie [si] *f* saw; *fig* F bore

sciemment [sjamɑ̃] *adv* knowingly

science [sjɑ̃s] *f* science; (*connaissance*) knowledge; **~s économiques** economics *sg*; **~s naturelles** natural science *sg*; **science-fiction** *f* science-fiction; **scientifique 1** *adj* scientific **2** *m/f* scientist

scier [sje] ⟨1a⟩ saw; *branche etc* saw off

scinder [sɛ̃de] ⟨1a⟩ *fig* split; **se ~** split up

scintiller [sɛ̃tije] ⟨1a⟩ sparkle

scission [sisjõ] *f* split

sciure [sjyr] *f* sawdust

sclérose [skleroz] *f* MÉD sclerosis; **~ artérielle** arteriosclerosis

scolaire [skɔlɛr] school *atr*; *succès*, *échec* academic; **année** *f* **~** school year; **scolarité** *f* education, schooling

scoop [skup] *m* scoop

scooter [skutœr, -tɛr] *m* motor scooter

score [skɔr] *m* SP score; POL share of the vote

scorpion [skɔrpjõ] *m* ZO scorpion; ASTROL **Scorpion** Scorpio

scotch® [skɔtʃ] *m* Scotch tape®, *Br* sellotape®; **scotcher** ⟨1a⟩ tape, *Br* sellotape

scout [skut] *m* scout; **scoutisme** *m* scouting

script [skript] *m* block letters *pl*; *d'un film* script

scrupule [skrypyl] *m* scruple; **scrupuleux, -euse** scrupulous

scrutateur, -trice [skrytatœr, -tris] *regard* searching; **scruter** ⟨1a⟩ scrutinize

scrutin [skrytɛ̃] *m* ballot; **~ de ballottage** second ballot; **~ majoritaire** majority vote system, *Br aussi* first-past-the-post system; **~ proportionnel** proportional representation

sculpter [skylte] ⟨1a⟩ *statue* sculpt; *pierre* carve; **sculpteur** *m* sculptor; **sculpture** *f* sculpture; **~ sur bois** wood carving

se [sə] *pron* ◇ *réfléchi masculin* himself; *féminin* herself; *chose, animal* itself; *pluriel* themselves; *avec 'one'* oneself; **elle s'est fait mal** she hurt herself; **il s'est cassé le bras** he broke his arm
◇ *réciproque* each other, one another; **ils ~ respectent** they respect each other *ou* one another
◇ *passif:* **cela ne ~ fait pas** that isn't done; **comment est-ce que ça ~ prononce?** how is it pronounced?

séance [seɑ̃s] *f* session; (*réunion*) meeting, session; *de cinéma* show, performance; **~ tenante** *fig* immediately

seau [so] *m* (*pl* -x) bucket

sec, sèche [sɛk, sɛʃ] **1** *adj* dry; *fruits, légumes* dried; (*maigre*) thin; *réponse, ton* curt **2** *m:* **tenir au ~** keep dry, keep in a dry place **3** *adv:* **être à ~** *fig* F be broke; **boire son whisky ~** drink one's whiskey neat *ou* straight

sécateur [sekatœr] *m* secateurs *pl*

sèche-cheveux [sɛʃʃəvø] *m* (*pl inv*) hair dryer; **sèche-linge** [-lɛ̃ʒ] *m* clothes dryer; **sécher** ⟨1f⟩ **1** *v/t* dry; *rivière* dry up; **~ un cours** cut a class **2** *v/i* dry; *d'un lac* dry up; **sécheresse** *f* dryness; *manque de pluie* drought; *fig: de réponse, ton* curtness; **séchoir** *m* dryer

second, ~e [s(ə)gõ, -d] **1** *adj* second **2** *m* étage third floor, *Br* second floor; (*adjoint*) second in command **3** *f* second; **en train** second class; **secondaire** secondary; **enseignement** *m* **~** secondary education; **seconder** ⟨1a⟩ *personne* assist

secouer [s(ə)kwe] ⟨1a⟩ shake; *poussière* shake off

secourir [s(ə)kurir] ⟨2i⟩ come to the aid of; **secourisme** *m* first aid; **secouriste** *m/f* first-aider; **secours** *m* help; *matériel* aid; **au ~!** help!; **appeler au ~** call for help; **poste** *m* **de ~** first-aid post; **sortie** *f* **de ~** emergency exit; **premiers ~s** first aid *sg*

secousse [s(ə)kus] *f* jolt; *électrique* shock (*aussi fig*); *tellurique* tremor

secret, -ète [sɔkrɛ, -t] **1** *adj* secret; **garder qch ~** keep sth secret **2** *m* secret; (*discrétion*) secrecy; **en ~** in secret, secretly; **dans le plus grand ~** in the greatest secrecy

secrétaire [s(ə)kretɛr] **1** *m/f* secretary; **~ de direction** executive secretary; **~ d'État** Secretary of State **2** *m* writing desk; **secrétariat** *m* bureau secretariat; *profession* secretarial work

sécréter [sekrete] ⟨1f⟩ MÉD secrete; **sécrétion** *f* secretion

sectaire [sɛktɛr] sectarian; **secte** *f* REL sect

secteur [sɛktœr] *m* sector; (*zone*) area, district; ÉL mains *pl*

S

section [sɛksjõ] *f* section; **sectionner** ⟨1a⟩ (*couper*) sever; *région etc* divide up

séculaire [sekylɛr] a hundred years old; *très ancien* centuries-old

séculier, -ère [sekylje, -er] secular

sécurité [sekyrite] *f* security; (*manque de danger*) safety; **~ routière** road safety; **Sécurité sociale** welfare, *Br* social security; **être en ~** be safe; **des problèmes de ~** security problems

sédatif [sedatif] *m* sedative

sédentaire [sedɑ̃tɛr] *profession* sedentary; *population* settled

sédiment [sedimɑ̃] *m* sediment

séditieux, -euse [sedisjø, -z] seditious; **sédition** *f* sedition

séducteur, -trice [sedyktœr, -tris] **1** *adj* seductive **2** *m/f* seducer; **séduction** *f* seduction; *fig* (*charme*) attraction; **séduire** ⟨4c⟩ seduce; *fig* (*charmer*) appeal to; *d'une personne* charm; **séduisant, ~e** appealing; *personne* attractive

segment [sɛgmɑ̃] *m* segment

ségrégation [segregasjõ] *f* segregation

seigle [sɛgl] *m* AGR rye

seigneur [sɛɲœr] *m* REL: **le Seigneur** the Lord; HIST the lord of the manor

sein [sɛ̃] *m* breast; *fig* bosom; **au ~ de** within

séisme [seism] *m* earthquake

seize [sɛz] sixteen; → **trois**; **seizième** sixteenth

séjour [seʒur] *m* stay; (**salle** *f* **de**) **~** living room; **séjourner** ⟨1a⟩ stay

sel [sɛl] *m* salt

sélect, ~e [selɛkt] select; **sélectif, -ive** selective; **sélection** *f* selection; **sélectionner** ⟨1a⟩ select

selle [sɛl] *f* saddle (*aussi* CUIS); MÉD stool; **être bien en ~** *fig* be firmly in the saddle; **seller** ⟨1b⟩ saddle; **sellette** *f*: **être sur la ~** be in the hot seat

selon [s(ə)lõ] **1** *prép* according to; **~ moi** in my opinion; **c'est ~** it all depends **2** *conj*: **~ que** depending on whether

semaine [s(ə)mɛn] *f* week; **à la ~ louer** weekly, by the week; **en ~** during the week, on weekdays

semblable [sɑ̃blabl] **1** *adj* similar; *tel* such; **~ à** like, similar to **2** *m* (*être humain*) fellow human being

semblant [sɑ̃blɑ̃] *m* semblance; **faire ~ de faire qch** pretend to do sth

sembler [sɑ̃ble] ⟨1a⟩ seem; **~ être / faire** seem to / to do; **il (me) semble que** it seems (to me) that

semelle [s(ə)mɛl] *f* sole; *pièce intérieure* insole

semence [s(ə)mɑ̃s] *f* AGR seed

semer [s(ə)me] ⟨1d⟩ sow; *fig* (*répandre*) spread; **~ qn** F shake s.o. off

semestre [s(ə)mɛstr] *m* half-year; ÉDU semester, *Br* term; **semestriel, ~le** half-yearly

semi-circulaire [səmisirkylɛr] semi-circular

séminaire [seminɛr] *m* seminar; REL seminary

semi-remorque [səmirmɔrk] *m* (*pl* semi-remorques) semi, tractor-trailer, *Br* articulated lorry

semonce [s(ə)mõs] *f* reproach

semoule [s(ə)mul] *f* CUIS semolina

Sénat [sena] *m* POL Senate; **sénateur** *m* senator; **sénatorial, ~e** (*mpl* -aux) senatorial

sénile [senil] senile; **sénilité** *f* senility

sens [sɑ̃s] *m* sense; (*direction*) direction; (*signification*) sense, meaning; **~ interdit** no entry; **~ dessus dessous** [sɑ̃dsydsu] upside down; **dans tous les ~** this way and that; **dans tous les ~ du terme** in the full sense of the word; **en un ~** in a way; **à mon ~** to my way of thinking; **le bon ~, le ~ commun** common sense; **~ giratoire** traffic circle, *Br* roundabout; **~ de l'humour** sense of humor *ou Br* humour; (**rue** *f* **à**) **~ unique** one-way street

sensation [sɑ̃sasjõ] *f* feeling, sensation; *effet de surprise* sensation; **faire ~** cause a sensation; **la presse à ~** the gutter press; **sensationnel, ~le** sensational

sensé, ~e [sɑ̃se] sensible

sensibiliser [sɑ̃sibilize] ⟨1a⟩ MÉD sensitize; ~ **qn à qch** *fig* heighten s.o.'s awareness of sth; **sensibilité** *f* sensitivity; **sensible** sensitive; (*notable*) appreciable; **sensiblement** *adv* appreciably; *plus ou moins* more or less; **sensiblerie** *f* sentimentality

sensualité [sɑ̃sɥalite] *f* sensuality; **sensuel, ~le** sensual

sentence [sɑ̃tɑ̃s] *f* JUR sentence

senteur [sɑ̃tœr] *f litt* scent, perfume

sentier [sɑ̃tje] *m* path

sentiment [sɑ̃timɑ̃] *m* feeling; **sentimental, ~e** (*mpl -aux*) *vie* love *atr*; *péj* sentimental; **sentimentalité** *f* sentimentality

sentinelle [sɑ̃tinɛl] *f* MIL guard

sentir [sɑ̃tir] ⟨2b⟩ **1** *v/t* feel; (*humer*) smell; (*dégager une odeur de*) smell of; **se ~ bien** feel well; ~ **le goût de qch** taste sth; *je ne peux pas la ~* F I can't stand her **2** *v/i*: ~ **bon** smell good

séparable [separabl] separable; **séparateur** *m* delimiter; **séparation** *f* separation; (*cloison*) partition; **séparatisme** *m* POL separatism; **séparatiste** POL separatist

séparé, ~e [separe] separate; *époux* separated; **séparément** *adv* separately; **séparer** ⟨1a⟩ separate; **se ~** separate

sept [sɛt] seven; → *trois*; **septante** *Belgique, Suisse* seventy

septembre [sɛptɑ̃br] *m* September

septennat [sɛptena] *m* term of office (*of French President*)

septentrional, ~e [sɛptɑ̃trijɔnal] (*mpl -aux*) northern

septicémie [sɛptisemi] *f* septicemia

septième [sɛtjɛm] seventh

septique [sɛptik] septic

séquelles [sekɛl] *fpl* MÉD after-effects; *fig* aftermath *sg*

séquence [sekɑ̃s] *f* sequence

serein, ~e [sərɛ̃, -ɛn] calm, serene; *temps* calm

sérénade [serenad] *f* serenade

sérénité [serenite] *f* serenity

sergent [sɛrʒɑ̃] *m* MIL sergeant

série [seri] *f* series *sg*; *de casseroles,*

timbres set; SP (*épreuve*) heat; **hors ~ numéro** special; **en ~** *fabrication* mass *atr*, *produits* mass-produced; **fabriquer en ~** mass-produce

sérieusement [serjøzmɑ̃] *adv* seriously; *travailler* conscientiously; **sérieux, -euse 1** *adj* serious; *entreprise, employé* professional; (*consciencieux*) conscientious **2** *m* seriousness; **prendre au ~** take seriously; **garder son ~** keep a straight face

serin [s(ə)rɛ̃] *m* ZO canary

seringue [s(ə)rɛ̃g] *f* MÉD syringe

serment [sɛrmɑ̃] *m* oath; **prêter ~** take the oath

sermon [sɛrmɔ̃] *m* sermon (*aussi fig*)

séropositif, -ive [seropozitif, -iv] HIV-positive

serpent [sɛrpɑ̃] *m* snake; **serpenter** ⟨1a⟩ wind, meander; **serpentin** *m* paper streamer

serpillière [sɛrpijɛr] *f* floor cloth

serre [sɛr] *f* greenhouse; **~s** ZO talons

serré, ~e [sere] tight; *pluie* heavy; *personnes* closely packed; *café* strong; **avoir le cœur ~** have a heavy heart; **serre-livres** *m* (*pl inv*) bookend; **serrer** ⟨1b⟩ **1** *v/t* (*tenir*) clasp; *ceinture, nœud* tighten; *un vêtement* be too tight for; **~ les dents** clench one's jaw; *fig* grit one's teeth; **~ la main à qn** squeeze s.o.'s hand; *pour saluer* shake s.o.'s hand; **~ les rangs** *fig* close ranks **2** *v/i*: **~ à droite** keep to the right; **se ~** (*s'entasser*) move up, squeeze up; **se ~ contre qn** press against s.o.; **se ~ les uns contre les autres** huddle together

serrure [seryr] *f* lock; **serrurier** *m* locksmith

serveur [sɛrvœr] *m dans un café* bartender, *Br* barman; *dans un restaurant* waiter; INFORM server; **serveuse** *f dans un café* bartender, *Br* barmaid; *dans un restaurant* server, *Br* waitress

serviabilité [sɛrvjabilite] *f* helpfulness; **serviable** helpful

service [sɛrvis] *m* service; (*faveur*) favor, *Br* favour; *au tennis* service, serve; *d'une entreprise, d'un hôpital* department; **être de ~** be on duty;

à votre ~! at your service!; **rendre ~ à qn** do s.o. a favor; **~ compris** service included; **mettre en ~** put into service; **hors ~** out of order

serviette [sɛrvjɛt] *f* serviette; *de toilette* towel; *pour documents* briefcase; **~ hygiénique** sanitary napkin, *Br aussi* sanitary towel; **~ de bain** bath towel

servile [sɛrvil] servile

servir [sɛrvir] ⟨2b⟩ **1** *v/t patrie, intérêts, personne, mets* serve **2** *v/i* serve; (*être utile*) be useful; **~ à qn** be of use to s.o.; **~ à qch / à faire qch** be used for sth / for doing sth; **ça sert à quoi?** what's this for?; **ça ne sert à rien** (*c'est vain*) it's pointless, it's no use; **~ de qch** act as sth; **cette planche me sert de table** I use the plank as a table; **~ d'interprète** act as (an) interpreter **3**: **se ~ à table** help o.s. (**en** to); **se ~ de** (*utiliser*) use

servodirection [sɛrvɔdirɛksjɔ̃] *f* AUTO power steering

servofrein [sɛrvɔfrɛ̃] *m* AUTO servo-brake

ses [se] → **son¹**

set [sɛt] *m au tennis* set; **~ de table** place mat

seuil [sœj] *m* doorstep; *fig* threshold; **~ de rentabilité** break-even (point)

seul, ~e [sœl] **1** *adj* alone; (*solitaire*) lonely; *devant le subst.* only, sole; **d'un ~ coup** with (just) one blow, with a single blow **2** *adv* alone; **faire qch tout ~** do sth all by o.s. *ou* all on one's own; **parler tout ~** talk to o.s. **3** *m/f*: **un ~, une ~e** just one; **seulement** *adv* only; **non ~ ... mais encore** *ou* **mais aussi** not only ... but also

sève [sɛv] *f* BOT sap

sévère [sevɛr] severe; **sévèrement** *adv* severely; **sévérité** *f* severity

sévices [sevis] *mpl* abuse *sg*

sévir [sevir] ⟨2a⟩ *d'une épidémie* rage; **~ contre qn** come down hard on s.o.; **~ contre qch** clamp down on sth

sevrer [savre] ⟨1d⟩ *enfant* wean

sexagénaire [sɛksaʒenɛr] *m/f & adj* sixty-year old

sexe [sɛks] *m* sex; *organes* genitals *pl*; **sexiste** *m/f & adj* sexist; **sexualité** *f* sexuality; **sexuel, ~le** sexual; **sexy** *adj inv* sexy

seyant, ~e [sɛjã, -t] becoming

shampo(o)ing [ʃãpwɛ̃] *m* shampoo

shérif [ʃerif] *m* sheriff

shit [ʃit] *m* F shit F, pot F

short [ʃɔrt] *m* shorts *pl*

si¹ [si] **1** *conj* (**s'il, s'ils**) if; **~ j'achetais celui-ci ...** if I bought this one, if I were to buy this one; **je lui ai demandé ~ ...** I asked him if *ou* whether ...; **~ ce n'est que** apart from the fact that; **comme ~** as if, as though; **même ~** even if ◊: **~ bien que** with the result that, and so **2** *adv* ◊ (*tellement*) so; **de ~ bonnes vacances** such a good vacation; **~ riche qu'il soit** (*subj*) however rich he may be ◊ *après négation* yes; **tu ne veux pas? - mais ~!** you don't want to? - oh yes, I do

si² [si] *m* MUS B

Sicile [sisil]: **la ~** Sicily; **sicilien, ~ne 1** *adj* Sicilian **2** *m/f* **Sicilien, ~ne** Sicilian

sida [sida] *m* MÉD Aids

sidéré, ~e [sidere] F thunderstruck

sidérurgie [sideryrʒi] *f* steel industry; **sidérurgique** steel *atr*

siècle [sjɛkl] *m* century; *fig* (*époque*) age

siège [sjɛʒ] *m* seat; *d'une entreprise, d'un organisme* headquarters *pl*; MIL siege; **~ social** COMM head office; **siéger** ⟨1g⟩ sit; **~ à** *d'une entreprise, d'un organisme* be headquartered in

sien, ~ne [sjɛ̃, sjɛn]: **le sien, la sienne, les siens, les siennes** *d'homme* his; *de femme* hers; *de chose, d'animal* its; *avec 'one'* one's; **il avait perdu la ~ne** he had lost his; **y mettre du ~** do one's bit

sieste [sjɛst] *f* siesta, nap

sifflement [sifləmã] *m* whistle; **siffler** ⟨1a⟩ **1** *v/i* whistle; *d'un serpent* hiss **2** *v/t* whistle; **sifflet** *m* whistle; **~s** whistles, whistling *sg*; **coup** *m* **de ~** blow on the whistle; *il a donné un coup de ~* he blew his whistle

sigle [sigl] *m* acronym

signal [sinal] *m* (*pl* -aux) signal; *~ d'alarme* alarm (signal); *~ de détresse* distress signal

signalement [sinalmã] *m* description

signaler [sinale] ⟨1a⟩ *par un* signal; (*faire remarquer*) point out; (*dénoncer*) report; *se ~ par* distinguish o.s. by

signalisation [sinalizasjõ] *f dans rues* signs *pl*; *feux mpl de ~* traffic light *sg*, *Br* traffic lights *pl*

signataire [sinatɛr] *m* signatory; **signature** *f* signature

signe [sin] *m* sign; *geste* sign, gesture; *en ~ de* as a sign of; *faire ~ à qn* gesture *ou* signal to s.o.; (*contacter*) get in touch with s.o.; *c'est ~ que* it's a sign that; *~ de ponctuation* punctuation mark; *~ extérieur de richesse* ÉCON status symbol; *~s du zodiaque* signs of the zodiac

signer [sine] ⟨1a⟩ sign; *se ~* REL make the sign of the cross, cross o.s.

signet [sinɛ] *m* bookmark

significatif, -ive [sinifikatif, -iv] significant; *~ de* indicative of; **signification** *f* meaning; **signifier** ⟨1a⟩ mean; *~ qch à qn* (*faire savoir*) notify s.o. of sth

silence [silãs] *m* silence; *en ~* in silence, silently; **silencieux, -euse 1** *adj* silent **2** *m d'une arme* muffler, *Br* silencer

silhouette [silwɛt] *f* outline, silhouette; (*figure*) figure

silicium [silisjɔm] *m* silicon

silicone [silikɔn] *f* silicone

sillage [sijaʒ] *m* wake (*aussi fig*)

sillon [sijõ] *m dans un champ* furrow; *d'un disque* groove; **sillonner** ⟨1a⟩ (*parcourir*) criss-cross

silo [silo] *m* silo

simagrées [simagre] *fpl* affectation *sg*; *faire des ~* make a fuss

similaire [similɛr] similar; **similarité** *f* similarity

simili [simili] *m* F imitation; *en ~* imitation *atr*; **similicuir** *m* imitation

leather

similitude [similityd] *f* similarity

simple [sɛpl] **1** *adj* simple; *c'est une ~ formalité* it's merely *ou* just a formality **2** *m au tennis* singles *pl*; **simplement** *adv* simply; **simplet, ~te** (*niais*) simple; *idée* simplistic; **simplicité** *f* simplicity

simplification [sɛplifikasjõ] *f* simplification; **simplifier** ⟨1a⟩ simplify

simpliste [sɛplist] *idée* simplistic

simulacre [simylakr] *m* semblance

simulateur, -trice [simylatœr, -tris] **1** *m/f*: *c'est un ~* he's pretending **2** *m* TECH simulator; **simulation** *f* simulation; **simuler** ⟨1a⟩ simulate

simultané, ~e [simyltane] simultaneous; **simultanéité** *f* simultaneousness; **simultanément** *adv* simultaneously

sincère [sɛser] sincere; **sincérité** *f* sincerity

sinécure [sinekyr] *f* sinecure

singe [sɛʒ] *m* monkey; *singer* ⟨1l⟩ ape; **singerie** *f* imitation; *~s* F antics

singulariser [sɛgylarize] ⟨1a⟩: *se ~* stand out (*de* from); **singularité** *f* (*particularité*) peculiarity; (*étrangeté*) oddness

singulier, -ère [sɛgylje, -ɛr] **1** *adj* odd, strange **2** *m* GRAM singular

sinistre [sinistr] **1** *adj* sinister; (*triste*) gloomy **2** *m* disaster, catastrophe; **sinistré, ~e 1** *adj* stricken **2** *m* victim of a disaster

sinon [sinõ] *conj* (*autrement*) or else, otherwise; (*sauf*) except; (*si ce n'est*) if not

sinueux, -euse [sinyø, -z] *route* winding; *ligne* squiggly; *fig: explication* complicated

sinus [sinys] *m* sinus; **sinusite** *f* sinusitis

sionisme [sjɔnism] *m* POL Zionism

siphon [sifõ] *m* siphon; *d'évier* U-bend

sirène [sirɛn] *f* siren

sirop [siro] *m* syrup; *~ d'érable* maple syrup

siroter [sirɔte] ⟨1a⟩ sip

sis, ~e [si, -z] JUR situated

S

sismique [sismik] seismic; **sismologie** f seismology

sitcom [sitkɔm] m ou f sitcom

site [sit] m (*emplacement*) site; (*paysage*) area; **~ Web** INFORM web site

sitôt [sito] **1** adv: **~ parti, il ...** as soon as he had left he ...; **~ dit, ~ fait** no sooner said than done **2** conj: **~ que** as soon as

situation [situasjō] f situation; (*emplacement, profession*) position; **situé, ~e** situated; **situer** ⟨1n⟩ place, site; *histoire* set; **se ~** be situated; *d'une histoire* be set

six [sis] six; → **trois**; **sixième** sixth; **sixièmement** adv sixthly

skateboard [skɛtbɔrd] m skateboard; *activité* skateboarding; **skateur, -euse** m/f skateboarder

sketch [skɛtʃ] m sketch

ski [ski] m ski; *activité* skiing; **faire du ~** ski, go skiing; **~ alpin** downhill (skiing); **~ de fond** cross-country (skiing); **~ nautique** water-skiing; **skier** ⟨1a⟩ ski; **skieur, -euse** m/f skier

slave [slav] **1** adj Slav **2** m/f **Slave** Slav

slip [slip] m *de femme* panties pl, Br aussi knickers pl; *d'homme* briefs; **~ de bain** swimming trunks pl

slogan [slɔgã] m slogan

slovaque [slɔvak] **1** adj Slovak(ian) **2** m/f **Slovaque** Slovak(ian)

slovène [slɔvɛn] **1** adj Slovene, Slovenian **2** m/f **Slovène** Slovene, Slovenian

S.M.I.C. [smik] m abr (= **salaire minimum interprofessionnel de croissance**) minimum wage

smog [smɔg] m smog

smoking [smɔkiŋ] m tuxedo, Br dinner jacket

SMS [ɛsɛmɛs] m text (message)

S.N.C.F. [ɛsɛnseɛf] f abr (= **Société nationale des chemins de fer français**) French national railroad company

snob [snɔb] **1** adj snobbish **2** m/f snob; **snober** ⟨1a⟩ snub; **snobisme** m snobbery

sobre [sɔbr] sober; *style* restrained; **sobriété** f soberness; *d'un style* re-

straint

sobriquet [sɔbrikɛ] m nickname

sociabilité [sɔsjabilite] f sociability; **sociable** sociable

social, ~e [sɔsjal] (*mpl* -aux) social; COMM company atr; **social-démocrate** m (*pl* sociaux-démocrates) social-democrat

socialisation [sɔsjalizasjō] f socialization; **socialiser** ⟨1a⟩ socialize

socialisme [sɔsjalism] m socialism; **socialiste** m/f & adj socialist

société [sɔsjete] f society; *firme* company; **~ anonyme** corporation, Br public limited company, plc; **~ en commandite** limited partnership; **~ à responsabilité limitée** limited liability company; **~ de vente par correspondance** mail-order firm

sociologie [sɔsjɔlɔʒi] f sociology; **sociologue** m/f sociologist

socle [sɔkl] m plinth

socquette [sɔkɛt] f anklet, Br ankle sock

soda [sɔda] m soda, Br fizzy drink; **un whisky ~** a whiskey and soda

sodium [sɔdjɔm] m CHIM sodium

sœur [sœr] f sister; REL nun, sister

sofa [sɔfa] m sofa

soi [swa] oneself; **avec ~** with one; **ça va de ~** that goes without saying; **en ~** in itself

soi-disant [swadizã] adj inv so-called

soie [swa] f silk

soif [swaf] f thirst (**de** for); **avoir ~** be thirsty

soigné, ~e [swaɲe] *personne* well-groomed; *travail* careful; **soigner** ⟨1a⟩ look after, take care of; *d'un médecin* treat; **se ~** take care of o.s.; **soigneux, -euse** careful(**de** about)

soi-même [swamɛm] oneself

soin [swɛ̃] m care; **~s** care sg; MÉD care sg, treatment sg; **avoir** ou **prendre ~ de** look after, take care of; **être sans ~** be untidy; **~s à domicile** home care sg; **~s dentaires** dental treatment sg; **~s médicaux** health care sg

soir [swar] m evening; **ce ~** this evening; **un ~** one evening; **le ~** in the evening; **soirée** f evening; *(fête)* party; **~ dansante** dance

soit¹ [swat] very well, so be it

soit² [swa] *conj* **~ ..., ...** either ..., or ...; *(à savoir)* that is, ie

soixantaine [swasãtɛn] f about sixty; **soixante** sixty; **~ et onze** seventy-one; **soixante-dix** seventy

soja [sɔʒa] m BOT soy bean, Br soya

sol¹ [sɔl] m ground; *(plancher)* floor; *(patrie)*, GÉOL soil

sol² [sɔl] m MUS G

solaire [sɔlɛr] solar

soldat [sɔlda] m soldier; **~ d'infanterie** infantry soldier, infantryman

solde¹ [sɔld] f MIL pay

solde² [sɔld] m COMM balance; **~ débiteur / créditeur** debit / credit balance; **~s marchandises** sale goods; **vente au rabais** sale sg

solder [sɔlde] ⟨1a⟩ COMM *compte* close, balance; *marchandises* sell off; **se ~ par** end in

sole [sɔl] f ZO sole

soleil [sɔlɛj] m sun; **il y a du ~** it's sunny; **en plein ~** in the sunshine; **coup m de ~** sunburn

solennel, ~le [sɔlanɛl] solemn; **solennité** f solemnity

solfège [sɔlfɛʒ] m sol-fa

solidaire [sɔlidɛr]: **être ~ de qn** support s.o.; **solidariser** ⟨1a⟩: **se ~** show solidarity (**avec** with); **solidarité** f solidarity

solide [sɔlid] 1 *adj porte*, *meubles* solid, strong; *tissu* strong; *argument* sound; *personne* sturdy, robust; *(consistant)* solid 2 m PHYS solid; **solidité** f solidity, strength; *d'un matériau* strength; *d'un argument* soundness

soliste [sɔlist] m/f soloist

solitaire [sɔlitɛr] 1 *adj* solitary 2 m/f loner 3 *diamant* solitaire; **solitude** f solitude

sollicitation [sɔlisitasjõ] f plea; **solliciter** ⟨1a⟩ request; *attention* attract; *curiosité* arouse; **~ qn de faire qch** plead with s.o. to do sth; **~ un emploi** apply for a job

sollicitude [sɔlisityd] f solicitude

solo [sɔlo] m MUS solo

solstice [sɔlstis] m ASTR solstice

soluble [sɔlybl] soluble; **café m ~** instant coffee

solution [sɔlysjõ] f solution

solvabilité [sɔlvabilite] f COMM solvency; **pour offrir un crédit** creditworthiness; **solvable** solvent; **digne de crédit** creditworthy

solvant [sɔlvã] m CHIM solvent

sombre [sõbr] *couleur, ciel, salle* dark; *temps* overcast; *avenir, regard* somber, Br sombre; **sombrer** ⟨1a⟩ sink; **~ dans la folie** fig lapse ou sink into madness

sommaire [sɔmɛr] 1 *adj* brief; *exécution* summary 2 m summary

sommation [sɔmasjõ] f JUR summons sg

somme¹ [sɔm] f sum; *(quantité)* amount; *d'argent* sum, amount; **en ~, ~ toute** in short

somme² [sɔm] m nap, snooze; **faire un ~** have a nap ou snooze

sommeil [sɔmɛj] m sleep; **avoir ~** be sleepy; **sommeiller** ⟨1b⟩ doze

sommelier [sɔməlje] m wine waiter

sommer [sɔme] ⟨1a⟩: **~ qn de faire qch** order s.o. to do sth

sommet [sɔme] m *d'une montagne* summit, top; *d'un arbre, d'une tour, d'un toit* top; *fig* pinnacle; POL summit

sommier [sɔmje] m mattress

sommité [sɔmite] f leading figure

somnambule [sɔmnãbyl] m/f sleepwalker; **somnambulisme** m sleepwalking

somnifère [sɔmnifɛr] m sleeping tablet

somnolence [sɔmnɔlãs] f drowsiness, sleepiness; **somnoler** ⟨1a⟩ doze

somptueux, -euse [sõptɥø, -z] sumptuous; **somptuosité** f sumptuousness

son¹ m, **sa** f, **ses** pl [sõ, sa, se] *d'homme* his; *de femme* her; *de chose, d'animal* its; *avec 'one'* one's; **il / elle a perdu son ticket** he lost his ticket / she lost her ticket

son² [sõ] m sound; **~ et lumière** son et lumière

son³ [sõ] *m* BOT bran

sondage [sõdaʒ] *m* probe; TECH drilling; **~ (d'opinion)** opinion poll, survey

sonde [sõd] *f* probe; **sonder** ⟨1a⟩ MÉD probe; *personne, atmosphère* sound out; **~ le terrain** see how the land lies

songe [sõʒ] *m litt* dream; **songer** ⟨1l⟩: **~ à** think about *ou* of; **~ à faire qch** think about *ou* of doing sth; **songeur, -euse** thoughtful

sonné, ~e [sone] **1:** *il est midi ~* it's gone twelve o'clock **2** *fig*: *il est ~* he's cracked F, he's got a slate loose F

sonner [sone] ⟨1a⟩ **1** *v/i de cloches, sonnette* ring; *d'un réveil* go off; *d'un instrument, d'une voix* sound; *d'une horloge* strike; *dix heures sonnent* it's striking ten, ten o'clock is striking; *midi a sonné* it has struck noon; **~ du cor** blow the horn; **~ creux / faux** *fig* ring hollow / false **2** *v/t cloches* ring; **~ l'alarme** MIL sound the alarm

sonnerie [sonri] *f de cloches* ringing; *mécanisme* striking mechanism; *(sonnette)* bell

sonnet [sone] *m* sonnet

sonnette [sonet] *f* bell

sonore [sonor] *voix* loud; *rire* resounding; *cuivres* sonorous; *onde, film* sound *atr*; **sonorisation** *f appareils* PA system; **sonoriser** ⟨1a⟩ *film* dub; **sonorité** *f* sound, tone; *d'une salle* acoustics *pl*

sophistication [sofistikasjõ] *f* sophistication; **sophistiqué, ~e** sophisticated

soporifique [soporifik] sleep-inducing, soporific *(aussi fig)*

soprano [soprano] **1** *f* soprano **2** *m* treble

sorbet [sorbe] *m* sorbet

sorcellerie [sorselri] *f* sorcery, witchcraft

sorcier [sorsje] *m* sorcerer; **sorcière** *f* witch

sordide [sordid] filthy; *fig* sordid

sornettes [sornet] *fpl* nonsense *sg*

sort [sor] *m* fate; *(condition)* lot; **tirer au ~** draw lots; **jeter un ~ à qn** *fig* cast a spell on s.o.; **le ~ en est jeté** *fig* the die is cast

sortant, ~e [sortã, -t] POL outgoing; *numéro* winning

sorte [sort] *f (manière)* way; *(espèce)* sort, kind; **toutes ~s de** all sorts *ou* kinds of; **une ~ de** a sort *ou* kind of; **de la ~** of the sort *ou* kind; *(de cette manière)* like that, in that way; **en quelque ~** in a way; **de (telle) ~ que** and so; **faire en ~ que** (+*subj*) see to it that

sortie [sorti] *f* exit; *(promenade, excursion)* outing; *d'un livre* publication; *d'un disque* release; *d'une voiture* launch; TECH outlet; MIL sortie; **~s** *argent* outgoings; **~ de bain** bathrobe; **~ (sur) imprimante** printout

sortilège [sortilεʒ] *m* spell

sortir [sortir] ⟨2b⟩ **1** *v/i (aux être)* come / go out; *pour se distraire* go out (*avec* with); *d'un livre, un disque* come out; *au loto* come up; **~ de endroit** leave; *accident, affaire, entretien* emerge from; *(provenir de)* come from **2** *v/t chose* bring / take out; *enfant, chien, personne* take out; COMM bring out; F *bêtises* come out with **3**: **s'en ~** *d'un malade* pull through

S.O.S. [εsoεs] *m* SOS

sosie [sozi] *m* double, look-alike

sot, ~te [so, sot] **1** *adj* silly, foolish **2** *m/f* fool; **sottise** *f d'une action, une remarque* foolishness; *action / remarque* foolish thing to do / say

sou [su] *m fig* penny; **être sans le ~** be penniless; **être près de ses ~s** be careful with one's money

soubresaut [subrəso] *m* jump

souche [suʃ] *f d'un arbre* stump; *d'un carnet* stub

souci [susi] *m* worry, care; **un ~ pour** a worry to; **sans ~** carefree; **avoir le ~ de** care about; **se faire du ~** worry; **soucier** ⟨1a⟩: **se ~ de** worry about; **soucieux, -euse** anxious, concerned (*de* about)

soucoupe [sukup] *f* saucer; **~ volante** flying saucer

soudain, ~e [sudɛ̃, -ɛn] **1** *adj* sudden **2** *adv* suddenly; **soudainement** *adv* suddenly

Soudan [sudɑ̃]: **le ~** the Sudan; **soudanais**, ~e **1** *adj* Sudanese **2** *m/f* **Soudanais**, ~e Sudanese

soude [sud] *f* CHIM, PHARM soda

souder [sude] ⟨1a⟩ TECH weld; *fig* bring closer together

soudoyer [sudwaje] ⟨1h⟩ bribe

soudure [sudyr] *f* TECH welding; *d'un joint* weld

souffle [sufl] *m* breath; *d'une explosion* blast; *second ~ fig* new lease of life; *être à bout de ~* be breathless, be out of breath; *retenir son ~* hold one's breath

soufflé, ~e [sufle] **1** *adj fig*: *être ~* F be amazed **2** *m* CUIS soufflé

souffler [sufle] ⟨1a⟩ **1** *v/i du vent* blow; *(haleter)* puff; *(respirer)* breathe; *(reprendre son souffle)* get one's breath back **2** *v/t chandelle* blow out; ÉDU, *au théâtre* prompt; *ne pas ~ mot* not breathe a word; *~ qch à qn* F *(dire)* whisper sth to s.o.; *(enlever)* steal sth from s.o.

souffleur, ~euse [suflœr, -øz] *m/f au théâtre* prompter

souffrance [sufrɑ̃s] *f* suffering; *en ~ affaire* pending; **souffrant**, ~e unwell; **souffrir** ⟨2f⟩ **1** *v/i* be in pain; *~ de* suffer from **2** *v/t* suffer; *je ne peux pas la ~* I can't stand her

soufre [sufr] *m* CHIM sulfur, *Br* sulphur

souhait [swɛ] *m* wish; *à vos ~s!* bless you!; **souhaitable** desirable; **souhaiter** ⟨1b⟩ wish for; *~ qch à qn* wish s.o. sth; *~ que* (+ *subj*) hope that

souiller [suje] ⟨1a⟩ dirty, soil; *fig*: *réputation* tarnish

soûl, ~e [su, -l] **1** *adj* drunk **2** *m*: *manger tout son ~* F eat to one's heart's content

soulagement [sulaʒmɑ̃] *m* relief; **soulager** ⟨1l⟩ relieve; *~ qn au travail* help out

soûler [sule] ⟨1a⟩ F: *~ qn* get s.o. drunk; *se ~* get drunk

soulèvement [sulɛvmɑ̃] *m* uprising;

soulever ⟨1d⟩ raise; *fig*: *enthousiasme* arouse; *protestations* generate; *problème, difficultés* raise; *se ~* raise o.s.; *(se révolter)* rise up

soulier [sulje] *m* shoe

souligner [suliɲe] ⟨1a⟩ underline; *fig* stress, underline

soumettre [sumɛtr] ⟨4p⟩ *pays, peuple* subdue; *à un examen* subject (*à* to); *(présenter)* submit; *se ~ à* submit to

soumis, ~e [sumi, -z] **1** *p/p* → **soumettre 2** *adj peuple* subject; *(obéissant)* submissive; **soumission** *f* submission; COMM tender

soupape [supap] *f* TECH valve

soupçon [supsɔ̃] *m* suspicion; *un ~ de* a trace *ou* hint of; **soupçonner** ⟨1a⟩ suspect; *~ que* suspect that; **soupçonneux**, -euse suspicious

soupe [sup] *f* CUIS (thick) soup

soupente [supɑ̃t] *f* loft; *sous escaliers* cupboard

souper [supe] **1** *v/i* ⟨1a⟩ have dinner *ou* supper **2** *m* dinner, supper

soupeser [supəze] ⟨1d⟩ weigh in one's hand; *fig* weigh up

soupière [supjɛr] *f* soup tureen

soupir [supir] *m* sigh

soupirail [supiraj] *m* (*pl* -aux) basement window

soupirer [supire] ⟨1a⟩ sigh

souple [supl] supple, flexible; *fig* flexible; **souplesse** *f* flexibility

source [surs] *f* spring; *fig* source; *prendre sa ~ dans* rise in

sourcil [sursi] *m* eyebrow; **sourciller** ⟨1a⟩: *sans ~* without batting an eyelid; **sourcilleux**, -euse fussy, picky

sourd, ~e [sur, -d] deaf; *voix* low; *douleur, bruit* dull; *colère* repressed; *~-muet* deaf-and-dumb; **sourdine** *f* MUS mute; *en ~* quietly; *mettre une ~ à qch fig* tone sth down

souriant, ~e [surjɑ̃, -t] smiling

souricière [surisjɛr] *f* mousetrap; *fig* trap

sourire [surir] **1** *v/i* ⟨4r⟩ smile **2** *m* smile

souris [suri] *f* mouse

sournois, ~e [surnwa, -z] **1** *adj* underhanded **2** *m/f* underhanded person;

sournoiserie f underhandedness

sous [su] prép under; ~ *la main* to hand, within reach; ~ *terre* underground; ~ *peu* shortly, soon; ~ *forme de* in the form of; ~ *ce rapport* in this respect; ~ *mes yeux* under my nose; ~ *la pluie* in the rain; *mettre ~ enveloppe* put in an envelope

sous-alimenté, ~e [suzalimãte] undernourished

sous-bois [subwa] m undergrowth

souscription [suskripsjõ] f subscription; **souscrire** [suskrir] ⟨4f⟩: ~ *à* subscribe to (aussi fig); emprunt approve; ~ *un emprunt* take out a loan

sous-développé, ~e [sudevlɔpe] underdeveloped; **sous-développement** m underdevelopment

sous-emploi [suzãplwa] m underemployment

sous-entendre [suzãtãdr] ⟨4a⟩ imply; **sous-entendu, ~e 1** adj implied **2** m implication

sous-estimer [suzɛstime] ⟨1a⟩ underestimate

sous-jacent, ~e [suʒasã, -t] problème underlying

sous-locataire [sulɔkatɛr] m/f subletter; **sous-location** f subletting

sous-louer [sulwe] ⟨1a⟩ sublet

sous-marin, ~e [sumarɛ̃, -in] 1 adj underwater 2 m submarine, F sub

sous-officier [suzɔfisje] m non-commissioned officer

sous-préfecture [suprefɛktyr] f subprefecture

sous-produit [suprɔdɥi] m by-product

sous-secrétaire [sus(ə)kretɛr] m: ~ *d'État* assistant Secretary of State

soussigné, ~e [susiɲe] m/f: *je, ~ ...* I the undersigned ...

sous-sol [susɔl] m GÉOL subsoil; *d'une maison* basement

sous-titre [sutitr] m subtitle

soustraction [sustraksjõ] f MATH subtraction; **soustraire** [sustrɛr] ⟨4s⟩ MATH subtract (*de* from); fig: *au regard de* remove; *à un danger* protect (*à* from)

sous-traitance [sutrɛtãs] f COMM sub-contracting; **sous-traiteur** m sub-contractor

sous-vêtements [suvɛtmã] mpl underwear sg

soutane [sutan] f REL cassock

soute [sut] f MAR, AVIAT hold

soutenable [sutnabl] tenable

soutenance [sutnãs] f université viva (voce)

souteneur [sutnœr] m protector

soutenir [sutnir] ⟨2h⟩ support; attaque, pression withstand; conversation keep going; opinion maintain; ~ *que* maintain that; *se* ~ support each other; **soutenu, ~e** effort sustained; style elevated

souterrain, ~e [sutɛrɛ̃, -ɛn] 1 adj underground, subterranean 2 m underground passage

soutien [sutjɛ̃] m support (aussi fig); **soutien-gorge** m (pl soutiens-gorge) brassière, bra

soutirer [sutire] ⟨1a⟩: ~ *qch à qn* get sth out of s.o.

souvenir [suvnir] 1 ⟨2h⟩: *se* ~ *de qn / qch* remember s.o. / sth; *se* ~ *que* remember that 2 m memory; objet souvenir

souvent [suvã] often; *assez* ~ quite often; *moins* ~ less often, less frequently; *le plus* ~ most of the time

souverain, ~e [suvrɛ̃, -ɛn] m/f sovereign; **souveraineté** f sovereignty

soviétique [sɔvjetik] HIST 1 adj Soviet 2 m/f **Soviétique** Soviet

soyeux, -euse [swajø, -z] silky

spacieux, -euse [spasjø, -z] spacious

spaghetti [spageti] mpl spaghetti sg

sparadrap [sparadra] m Band-Aid®, Br Elastoplast®

spartiate [sparsjat] spartan

spasme [spasm] m MÉD spasm; **spasmodique** spasmodic

spatial, ~e [spasjal] (mpl -iaux) spatial; ASTR space atr; *recherches* fpl ~*es* space research

spatule [spatyl] f spatula

speaker, ~ine [spikœr, spikrin] m/f radio, TV announcer

spécial, ~e [spesjal] (mpl -aux) special; **spécialement** adv specially;

spécialiser ⟨1a⟩: *se ~* specialize; spécialiste *m/f* specialist; spécialité *f* speciality

spécieux, *-euse* [spesjø, -z] specious

spécifier [spesifje] ⟨1a⟩ specify; spécifique specific

spécimen [spesimɛn] *m* specimen

spectacle [spɛktakl] *m* spectacle; *théâtre, cinéma* show, performance; spectaculaire spectacular; spectateur, *-trice m/f (témoin)* onlooker; SP spectator; *au cinéma, théâtre* member of the audience

spectre [spɛktr] *m* ghost; PHYS spectrum

spéculateur, *-trice* [spekylatœr, -tris] *m/f* speculator; spéculatif, *-ive* speculative; spéculation *f* speculation; spéculer ⟨1a⟩ FIN speculate (*sur* in); *fig* speculate (*sur* on, about)

spéléologie [speleɔlɔʒi] *f* caving

spermatozoïde [spɛrmatozoid] *m* BIOL sperm; sperme *m* BIOL sperm

sphère [sfɛr] *f* MATH sphere (*aussi fig*); sphérique spherical

spirale [spiral] *f* spiral

spirite [spirit] *m/f* spiritualist; spiritisme *m* spiritualism

spiritualité [spirityalite] *f* spirituality; spirituel, *~le* spiritual; *(amusant)* witty

spiritueux [spirityø] *mpl* spirits

splendeur, *~e* [splãdœr] *f* splendor, *Br* splendour; splendide splendid

spongieux, *-euse* [spõʒjø, -z] spongy

sponsor [spõsɔr] *m* sponsor; sponsoriser ⟨1a⟩ sponsor

spontané, *~e* [spõtane] spontaneous; spontanéité *f* spontaneity

sporadique [spɔradik] sporadic

sport [spɔr] 1 *m* sport; faire du *~* do sport; *~s d'hiver* winter sports 2 *adj vêtements* casual *atr*; être *~ d'une personne* be a good sport; sportif, *-ive* 1 *adj résultats, association* sports *atr*; *allure* sporty; *(fair-play)* sporting 2 *m* sportsman 3 *f* sportswoman

sprint [sprint] *m* sprint

spumeux, *-euse* [spymø, -z] foamy

square [skwar] *m* public garden

squash [skwaʃ] *m* SP squash

squatter [skwate] ⟨1a⟩ squat; squatteur, *-euse m/f* squatter

squelette [skəlɛt] *m* ANAT skeleton

St *abr* (= *saint*) St (= saint)

stabilisateur, *-trice* [stabilizatœr, -tris] 1 *adj* stabilizing 2 *m* stabilizer; stabilisation *f des prix, d'une devise* stabilization; stabiliser ⟨1a⟩ stabilize; stabilité *f* stability; *~ des prix* price stability; stable stable

stade [stad] *m* SP stadium; *d'un processus* stage

stage [staʒ] *m* training period; *(cours)* training course; *pour professeur* teaching practice; *(expérience professionnelle)* work placement; stagiaire *m/f* trainee

stagnant, *~e* [stagnã, -t] *eau* stagnant; *être~ fig* be stagnating; stagnation *f* ÉCON stagnation

stalactite [stalaktit] *f* icicle

stalle [stal] *f d'un cheval* box; *~s* REL stalls

stand [stãd] *m de foire* booth, *Br* stand; *de kermesse* stall; *~ de ravitaillement* SP pits *pl*

standard [stãdar] *m* standard; TÉL switchboard

standardisation [stãdardizasjõ] *f* standardization; standardiser ⟨1a⟩ standardize

standardiste [stãdardist] *m/f* TÉL (switchboard) operator

standing [stãdiŋ] *m* status; *de grand ~ hôtel, immeuble* high-class

star [star] *f* star

starter [starter] *m* AUTO choke

station [stasjõ] *f* station; *de bus* stop; *de vacances* resort; *~ balnéaire* seaside resort; *~ de sports d'hiver* winter sport resort, ski resort; *~ de taxis* cab stand, *Br* taxi rank; *~ thermale* spa

stationnaire [stasjɔner] stationary; stationnement *m* AUTO parking; stationner ⟨1a⟩ park

station-service [stasjõservis] *f (pl stations-service)* gas station, *Br* petrol station

statique [statik] static

statisticien, *~ne* [statistisjẽ, -ɛn] *m/f*

S

statistician; **statistique 1** *adj* statistical **2** *f* statistic; *science* statistics *sg*

statue [staty] *f* statue; **Statue de la Liberté** Statue of Liberty

stature [statyr] *f* stature

statut [staty] *m* status; **~ social** social status; **~s** *d'une société* statutes

Ste *abr* (= **sainte**) St (= saint)

sténographie [stenografi] *f* shorthand

stéréo(phonie) [stereo(fɔni)] *f* stereo; **en ~** in stereo; **stéréo(phonique)** stereo(phonic)

stéréotype [stereɔtip] *m* stereotype; **stéréotypé, ~e** stereotype

stérile [steril] sterile; **stériliser** ⟨1a⟩ sterilize; **stérilité** *f* sterility

stéroïde [sterɔid] *m* steroid; **~ anabolisant** anabolic steroid

stéthoscope [stetɔskɔp] *m* MÉD stethoscope

steward [stiwart] *m* flight attendant, steward

stigmate [stigmat] *m* mark; **~s** REL stigmata; **stigmatiser** ⟨1a⟩ *fig* stigmatize

stimulant, ~e [stimylɑ̃, -t] **1** *adj* stimulating **2** *m* stimulant; *fig* incentive, stimulus; **stimulateur** *m* MÉD: **~ cardiaque** pacemaker; **stimuler** ⟨1a⟩ stimulate; **stimulus** *m* (*pl le plus souvent* stimuli) PSYCH stimulus

stipulation [stipylasjɔ̃] *f* stipulation; **stipuler** ⟨1a⟩ stipulate

stock [stɔk] *m* stock; **stockage** *m* stocking; INFORM storage; **~ de données** data storage; **stocker** ⟨1a⟩ stock; INFORM store

stoïcisme [stɔisism] *m* stoicism; **stoïque** stoical

stop [stɔp] *m* stop sign; *écriteau* stop sign; (*feu* m) **~** AUTO brake light; **faire du ~** F thumb a ride, hitchhike; **stopper** ⟨1a⟩ stop

store [stɔr] *m* *d'une fenêtre* shade, *Br* blind; *d'un magasin, d'une terrasse* awning

strabisme [strabism] *m* MÉD squint

strapontin [strapɔ̃tɛ̃] *m* tip-up seat

stratagème [strataʒɛm] *m* stratagem

stratégie [strateʒi] *f* strategy; **straté-**

gique strategic

stratifié, ~e [stratifje] GÉOL stratified; TECH laminated

stress [stres] *m* stress; **stressant, ~e** stressful; **stressé, ~e** stressed(-out)

strict, ~e [strikt] strict; **au sens ~** in the strict sense (of the word); **le ~ nécessaire** the bare minimum

strident, ~e [stridɑ̃, -t] strident

strip-tease [striptiz] *m* strip(tease)

structuration [stryktyrasjɔ̃] *f* structuring; **structure** *f* structure

stuc [styk] *m* stucco

studieux, -euse [stydjø, -z] studious

studio [stydjo] *m* studio; (*appartement*) studio, *Br aussi* studio flat

stupéfaction [stypefaksjɔ̃] *f* stupefaction; **stupéfait, ~e** stupefied; **stupéfiant, ~e 1** *adj* stupefying; **2** *m* drug; **stupéfier** ⟨1a⟩ stupefy

stupeur [stypœr] *f* stupor

stupide [stypid] stupid; **stupidité** *f* stupidity

style [stil] *m* style; **stylisé, ~e** stylized; **styliste** *m* *de mode, d'industrie* stylist; **stylistique 1** *adj* stylistic **2** *f* stylistics

stylo [stilo] *m* pen; **~ à bille, ~-bille** (*pl* stylos à bille, stylos-billes) ballpoint (pen); **~ plume** fountain pen; **stylo-feutre** *m* (*pl* stylos-feutres) felt tip, felt-tipped pen

su, ~e [sy] *p/p* → **savoir**

suave [sɥav] *voix, goût* sweet

subalterne [sybaltern] **1** *adj* junior, subordinate; *employé* junior **2** *m/f* junior, subordinate

subconscient [sybkɔ̃sjɑ̃] *m* subconscious

subdivision [sybdivizjɔ̃] *f* subdivision

subir [sybir] ⟨2a⟩ (*endurer*) suffer; (*se soumettre volontairement à*) undergo; **~ une opération** undergo a an operation

subit, ~e [sybi, -t] sudden; **subitement** *adv* suddenly

subjectif, -ive [sybʒɛktif, -iv] subjective

subjonctif [sybʒɔ̃ktif] *m* GRAM subjunctive

subjuguer [sybʒyge] ⟨1m⟩ *fig* captivate

sublime [syblim] sublime

submerger [sybmɛrʒe] ⟨1l⟩ submerge; *être submergé de travail fig* be up to one's eyes in work, be buried in work

subordination [sybɔrdinasjõ] *f* subordination

subordonné, **~e** [sybɔrdɔne] **1** *adj* subordinate **2** *m/f* subordinate **3** *f* GRAM subordinate clause; **subordonner** ⟨1a⟩ subordinate (*à* to)

subrepticement [sybrɛptismã] *adv* surreptitiously

subside [sybzid, sypsid] *m* subsidy; **subsidiaire** subsidiary

subsistance [sybzistãs] *f* subsistence; **subsister** ⟨1a⟩ survive; *d'une personne aussi* live

substance [sypstãs] *f* substance; **substantiel**, **~le** [sypstãsjɛl] substantial

substituer [sypstitɥe] ⟨1n⟩: *~ X à Y* substitute X for Y; **substitution** *f* substitution

subterfuge [sypterfyʒ] *m* subterfuge

subtil, **~e** [syptil] subtle; **subtiliser** ⟨1a⟩ F pinch F (*à qn* from s.o.); **subtilité** *f* subtlety

suburbain, **~e** [sybyrbɛ̃, -ɛn] suburban

subvenir [sybvənir] ⟨2h⟩: *~ à besoins* provide for

subvention [sybvãsjõ] *f* grant, subsidy; **subventionner** ⟨1a⟩ subsidize

subversif, **-ive** [sybversif, -iv] subversive; **subversion** *f* subversion

suc [syk] *m*: *~s gastriques* gastric juices

succédané [syksedane] *m* substitute

succéder [syksede] ⟨1f⟩: *~ à* follow; *personne* succeed; *se ~* follow each other

succès [syksɛ] *m* success; *avec ~* successfully, with success; *sans ~* unsuccessfully, without success

successeur [syksesœr] *m* successor; **successif**, **-ive** successive; **succession** *f* succession; JUR (*biens dévolus*) inheritance; **successivement** *adv* successively

succomber [sykõbe] ⟨1a⟩ (*mourir*) die, succumb; *~ à* succumb to

succulent, **~e** [sykylã, -t] succulent

succursale [sykyrsal] *f* COMM branch

sucer [syse] ⟨1k⟩ suck; **sucette** *f bonbon* lollipop; *de bébé* pacifier, *Br* dummy

sucre [sykr] *m* sugar; *~ glace* confectioner's sugar, *Br* icing sugar; **sucré**, **~e** sweet; *au sucre* sugared; *péj* sugary; **sucrer** ⟨1a⟩ sweeten; *avec sucre* sugar; **sucreries** *fpl* sweet things; **sucrier** *m* sugar bowl

sud [syd] **1** *m* south; *vent m du ~* south wind; *au ~ de* (to the) south of **2** *adj* south; *hemisphère* southern; *côte f ~* south *ou* southern coast

sud-africain, **~e** [sydafrikɛ̃, -ɛn] **1** *adj* South African **2** *m/f* Sud-Africain, **~e** South African

sud-américain, **~e** [sydamerikɛ̃, -ɛn] **1** *adj* South American **2** *m/f* Sud-Américain, **~e** South American

sud-est [sydɛst] *m* south-east

Sudiste [sydist] *m/f & adj* HIST Confederate

sud-ouest [sydwɛst] *m* south-west

Suède [sɥɛd]: *la ~* Sweden; **suédois**, **~e 1** *adj* Swedish **2** *m langue* Swedish **3** *m/f* Suédois, **~e** Swede

suer [sɥe] ⟨1n⟩ **1** *v/i* sweat **2** *v/t* sweat; *fig* (*dégager*) ooze; **sueur** *f* sweat

suffire [syfir] ⟨4o⟩ be enough; *~ pour faire qch* be enough to do sth; *cela me suffit* that's enough for me; *il suffit que tu le lui dises* (*subj*) all you have to do is tell her; *il suffit de …* all you have to do is …; *ça suffit!* that's enough!, that'll do!

suffisamment [syfizamã] *adv* sufficiently, enough; *~ intelligent* sufficiently intelligent, intelligent enough; *~ de …* enough …, sufficient …; **suffisance** *f* arrogance; **suffisant**, **~e** sufficient, enough; (*arrogant*) arrogant

suffixe [syfiks] *m* LING suffix

suffocant, **~e** [syfɔkã, -t] suffocating; *fig* breathtaking; **suffocation** *f* suffocation; **suffoquer** ⟨1m⟩ **1** *v/i* suf-

S

focate **2** v/t suffocate; **~ qn** fig take s.o.'s breath away

suffrage [syfraʒ] m vote; **remporter tous les ~s** fig get everyone's vote, win all the votes; **~ universel** universal suffrage

suggérer [syg3ere] ⟨1f⟩ suggest (**à** to)

suggestif, -ive [syg3εstjɔ̃] suggestive; **robe** etc revealing; **suggestion** f suggestion

suicide [sɥisid] m suicide; **suicidé, ~e** m/f suicide victim; **suicider** ⟨1a⟩: **se ~** kill o.s., commit suicide

suie [sɥi] f soot

suinter [sɥɛ̃te] ⟨1a⟩ d'un mur ooze

suisse [sɥis] **1** adj Swiss **2** m/f **Suisse** Swiss **3**: **la Suisse** Switzerland

suite [sɥit] f pursuit; (série) series sg; (continuation) continuation; d'un film, un livre sequel; (escorte) retinue, suite; MUS, appartement suite; **la ~ de l'histoire** the rest of the story, what happens next; **~s** (conséquences) consequences, results; d'un choc, d'une maladie after-effects; **faire ~ à qch** follow sth, come after sth; **prendre la ~ de qn** succeed s.o.; **donner ~ à lettre** follow up; **~ à votre lettre du ...** further to ou with reference to your letter of ...; **trois fois de ~** three times in succession ou in a row; **et ainsi de ~** and so on; **par ~ de** as a result of, due to; **tout de ~** immediately, at once; **par la ~** later, subsequently; **à la ~ de qn** in s.o.'s wake, behind s.o.; **à la ~ de qch** following sth, as a result of sth

suivant, ~e [sɥivɑ̃, -t] **1** adj next, following **2** m/f next person; **au ~!** next! **3** prép (selon) according to **4** conj: **~ que** depending on whether

suivi, ~e [sɥivi] travail, effort sustained; relations continuous, unbroken; argumentation coherent

suivre [sɥivr] ⟨4h⟩ **1** v/t follow; cours take **2** v/i follow; à l'école keep up; **faire ~ lettre** please forward; **à ~** to be continued

sujet, ~te [sy3ε, -t] **1** adj: **~ à qch** subject to sth **2** m subject; **à ce ~** on that subject; **au ~ de** on the subject of

sulfureux, -euse [sylfyrø, -z] sultry

summum [sɔmɔm] m fig: **le ~ de** the height of

super [sypεr] **1** adj F great F, neat F **2** m essence premium, Br four-star

superbe [sypεrb] superb

supercarburant [sypεrkarbyrɑ̃] m high-grade gasoline ou Br petrol

supercherie [sypεrʃəri] f hoax

superficie [sypεrfisi] f fig: aspect superficiel surface; (surface, étendue) (surface) area; **superficiel, ~le** superficial

superflu, ~e [sypεrfly] **1** adj superfluous **2** m surplus

supérieur, ~e [sypεrjœr] **1** adj higher; étages, face, mâchoire upper; (meilleur, dans une hiérarchie) superior (aussi péj); **~ à** higher than; (meilleur que) superior to **2** m/f superior; **supériorité** f superiority

superlatif [sypεrlatif] m GRAM, fig superlative

supermarché [sypεrmarʃe] m supermarket

superposer [sypεrpoze] ⟨1a⟩ stack; couches superimpose; **lits mpl superposés** bunk beds; **se ~** stack; d'images be superimposed

super-puissance [sypεrpɥisɑ̃s] f superpower

supersonique [sypεrsɔnik] supersonic

superstitieux, -euse [sypεrstisjø, -z] superstitious; **superstition** f superstition

superstructure [sypεrstryktyr] f superstructure

superviser [sypεrvize] ⟨1a⟩ supervise; **superviseur** m supervisor

supplanter [syplɑ̃te] ⟨1a⟩ supplant

suppléant, ~e [sypleɑ̃, -t] **1** adj acting **2** m/f stand-in, replacement; **suppléer** ⟨1a⟩: **~ à** make up for

supplément [syplemɑ̃] m supplement; **un ~ de ...** additional ou extra ...; **supplémentaire** additional

suppliant, ~e [syplijɑ̃, -t] pleading; **supplication** f plea

supplice [syplis] m torture; fig agony; **supplicier** ⟨1a⟩ torture

supplier [syplije] ⟨1a⟩: **~ qn de faire qch** beg s.o. *ou* plead with s.o. to do sth

support [sypɔr] *m* support; **~ de données** INFORM data carrier; **supportable** bearable; **supporter**[1] ⟨1a⟩ TECH, ARCH support, hold up; *conséquences* stand; *frais* bear; *douleur, personne* bear, put up with; *chaleur, alcool* tolerate

supporter[2] [sypɔrtɛr] *m* SP supporter, fan

supposé, ~e [sypoze] supposed; *nom* assumed; **supposer** ⟨1a⟩ suppose; *(impliquer)* presuppose; **à ~ que, en supposant que** (+ *subj*) supposing that; **supposition** *f* supposition

suppositoire [sypozitwar] *m* PHARM suppository

suppression [sypresjɔ̃] *f* suppression; **supprimer** ⟨1a⟩ *institution, impôt* abolish, get rid of; *emplois* cut; *mot, passage* delete; *cérémonie, concert* cancel; **~ qn** get rid of s.o.

suppurer [sypyre] ⟨1a⟩ suppurate

supranational, ~e [sypranasjɔnal] (*mpl* -aux) supranational

suprématie [sypremasi] *f* supremacy; **suprême** supreme

sur[1] [syr] *prép* ◇ on; *prendre qch* **~ l'étagère** take sth off the shelf; *la clé est* **~ la porte** the key's in the lock; *avoir de l'argent* **~ soi** have some money on one; **~ le moment** at the time

◇ *une fenêtre* **~ la rue** a window looking onto the street

◇ *tirer* **~ qn** shoot at s.o.

◇ *sujet* on, about; *un film* **~** ... a movie on *ou* about ...

◇ *un* **~ dix** one out of ten; *une semaine* **~ trois** one week in three, every three weeks

◇ *mesure* by **4 cms ~ 10** 4 cms by 10; *le plage s'étend* **~ 2 kilomètres** the beach stretches for 2 kilometers

sur[2], **~e** [syr] sour

sûr, ~e [syr] sure; *(non dangereux)* safe; *(fiable)* reliable; *jugement* sound; **~ de soi** sure of o.s., self-confident; **être ~ de son fait** be sure of one's

facts; **bien ~** of course; **à coup ~ il sera ...** he's bound to be ...

surcharge [syrʃarʒ] *f* overloading; *(poids excédentaire)* excess weight; **surcharger** ⟨1l⟩ overload

surchauffer [syrʃofe] ⟨1a⟩ overheat

surclasser [syrklase] ⟨1a⟩ outclass

surcroît [syrkrwa] *m*: **un ~ de travail** extra *ou* additional work; **de ~, par ~** moreover

surdité [syrdite] *f* deafness

surdoué, ~e [syrdwe] extremely gifted

sureau [syro] *m* (*pl* -x) BOT elder

surélever [syrelve] ⟨1d⟩ TECH raise

sûrement [syrmɑ̃] *adv* surely

surenchère [syrɑ̃ʃɛr] *f dans vente aux enchères* higher bid; **surenchérir** ⟨2a⟩ bid more; *fig* raise the ante

surestimer [syrɛstime] ⟨1a⟩ overestimate

sûreté [syrte] *f* safety; MIL security; *de jugement* soundness; **Sûreté** FBI, *Br* CID; **pour plus de ~** to be on the safe side

surexciter [syrɛksite] ⟨1a⟩ overexcite

surexposer [syrɛkspoze] ⟨1a⟩ *photographie* overexpose

surf [sœrf] *m* surfing; *(planche)* surfboard

surface [syrfas] *f* surface; **grande ~** COMM supermarket; **remonter à la ~** resurface; **refaire ~** *fig* resurface, reappear

surfait, ~e [syrfɛ, -t] overrated

surfer [sœrfe] ⟨1a⟩ surf; **~ sur Internet** surf the Net

surgelé, ~e [syrʒəle] **1** *adj* deep-frozen **2** *mpl*: **~s** frozen food *sg*

surgir [syrʒir] ⟨2a⟩ suddenly appear; *d'un problème* crop up

surhumain, ~e [syrymɛ̃, -ɛn] superhuman

sur-le-champ [syrləʃɑ̃] *adv* at once, straightaway

surlendemain [syrlɑ̃dmɛ̃] *m* day after tomorrow

surligner [syrliɲe] ⟨1a⟩ highlight; **surligneur** *m* highlighter

surmenage [syrmənaʒ] *m* overwork; **surmener** ⟨1d⟩ overwork; **se ~** over-

S

work, overdo it F

surmontable [syrmõtabl] surmountable; **surmonter** ⟨1a⟩ dominate; *fig* overcome, surmount

surnaturel, ~le [syrnatyrɛl] supernatural

surnom [syrnõ] *m* nickname

surnombre [syrnõbr] *m*: **en ~** too many; **ils étaient en ~** there were too many of them

surnommer [syrnɔme] ⟨1a⟩ nickname

surpasser [syrpase] ⟨1a⟩ surpass

surpeuplé, ~e [syrpœple] *pays* overpopulated; *endroit* overcrowded; **surpeuplement** *m d'un pays* overpopulation; *d'un endroit* overcrowding

surplomb [syrplõ]: **en ~** overhanging; **surplomber** ⟨1a⟩ overhang

surplus [syrply] *m* surplus; **au ~** moreover

surprenant, ~e [syrprənɑ̃, -t] surprising; **surprendre** ⟨4q⟩ surprise; *voleur* catch (in the act); **se ~ à faire qch** catch o.s. doing sth

surpris, ~e [syrpri, -z] **1** *p/p* → **surprendre 2** *adj* surprised

surprise [syrpriz] *f* surprise; **surprise-partie** *f* (*pl* surprises-parties) surprise party

surréalisme [syrealism] *m* surrealism

sursaut [syrso] *m* jump, start; **sursauter** ⟨1a⟩ jump, give a jump

sursis [syrsi] *m fig* reprieve, stay of execution; **peine de trois mois avec ~** JUR suspended sentence of three months

surtaxe [syrtaks] *f* surcharge

surtension [syrtɑ̃sjõ] *f* ÉL surge

surtout [syrtu] *adv* especially; (*avant tout*) above all; **non, ~ pas!** no, absolutely not!; **~ que** F especially since

surveillance [syrvɛjɑ̃s] *f* supervision; *par la police etc* surveillance; **exercer une ~ constante sur** keep a permanent watch on; **surveillant, ~e** *m/f* supervisor; *de prison* guard, *Br aussi* warder; **surveiller** ⟨1b⟩ keep watch over, watch; (*contrôler*) *élèves, employés* supervise; *de la police etc* observe, keep under surveillance; *sa ligne, son langage* watch; **se ~** *comportement* watch one's step; *poids* watch one's figure

survenir [syrvənir] ⟨2h⟩ (*aux être*) *d'une personne* turn up *ou* arrive unexpectedly; *d'un événement* happen; *d'un problème* come up, arise

survêtement [syrvɛtmɑ̃] *m* sweats *pl*, *Br* tracksuit

survie [syrvi] *f* survival; REL afterlife; **survivant, ~e 1** *adj* surviving **2** *m/f* survivor; **survivre** ⟨4e⟩: **~ à** *personne* survive, outlive; *accident* survive

survoler [syrvɔle] ⟨1a⟩ fly over; *fig* skim over

sus [sy(s)]: **en ~ de** *qch* over and above sth, in addition to sth

susceptibilité [sysɛptibilite] *f* sensitivity, touchiness; **susceptible** sensitive, touchy; **être ~ de faire qch** be likely to do sth

susciter [sysite] ⟨1a⟩ arouse

suspect, ~e [syspɛ(kt), -kt] (*équivoque*) suspicious; (*d'une qualité douteuse*) suspect; **~ de qch** suspected of sth; **suspecter** ⟨1a⟩ suspect

suspendre [syspɑ̃dr] ⟨4a⟩ suspend; (*accrocher*) hang up; **suspendu, ~e** suspended; **~ au plafond** hanging *ou* suspended from the ceiling; **être bien / mal ~** *d'une voiture* have good / bad suspension

suspens [syspɑ̃]: **en ~** *personne* in suspense; *affaire* outstanding

suspense [syspɛns] *m* suspense

suspension [syspɑ̃sjõ] *f* suspension; **points** *mpl* **de ~** suspension points

suspicion [syspisjõ] *f* suspicion

susurrer [sysyre] ⟨1a⟩ whisper

suture [sytyr] *f* MÉD suture

svelte [svɛlt] trim, slender

S.V.P. *abr* (= **s'il vous plaît**) please

sweat(shirt) [swit(ʃœrt)] *m* sweatshirt

sycomore [sikɔmɔr] *m* sycamore

syllabe [silab] *f* syllable

sylviculture [silvikyltyr] *f* forestry

symbiose [sɛ̃bjoz] *f* BIOL symbiosis

symbole [sɛ̃bɔl] *m* symbol; **symbolique** symbolic; **symboliser** ⟨1a⟩

symbolize; **symbolisme** *m* symbolism

symétrie [simetri] *f* symmetry; **symétrique** symmetrical

sympa [sɛ̃pa] F nice, friendly

sympathie [sɛ̃pati] *f* sympathy; (*amitié, inclination*) liking; **sympathique** nice, friendly; **sympathiser** ⟨1a⟩ get on (*avec qn* with s.o.)

symphonie [sɛ̃fɔni] *f* MUS symphony; **symphonique** symphonic

symptôme [sɛ̃ptom] *m* symptom

synagogue [sinagɔg] *f* synagogue

synchronisation [sɛ̃krɔnizasjɔ̃] *f* synchronization; **synchroniser** ⟨1a⟩ synchronize

syncope [sɛ̃kɔp] *f* MUS syncopation; MÉD fainting fit

syndical, ~e [sɛ̃dikal] (*mpl* -aux) labor *atr*, *Br* (trade) union *atr*; **syndicaliser** ⟨1a⟩ unionize; **syndicaliste 1** *adj* labor *atr*, *Br* (trade) union *atr*

2 *m/f* union member; **syndicat** *m* (labor) union, *Br* (trade) union; **~ d'initiative** tourist information office; **syndiqué, ~e** unionized

syndrome [sɛ̃drom] *m* syndrome

synonyme [sinɔnim] **1** *adj* synonymous (*de* with) **2** *m* synonym

syntaxe [sɛ̃taks] *f* GRAM syntax

synthèse [sɛ̃tɛz] *f* synthesis; **synthétique** *m & adj* synthetic; **synthétiseur** *m* MUS synthesizer

syphilis [sifilis] *f* syphilis

Syrie [siri]: *la* ~ Syria; **syrien, ~ne 1** *adj* Syrian **2** *m/f* **Syrien, ~ne** Syrian

systématique [sistematik] systematic; **systématiser** ⟨1a⟩ systematize; **système** *m* system; *le* ~ **D** F (*débrouillard*) resourcefulness; ~ **antidémarrage** immobilizer; ~ **d'exploitation** INFORM operating system; ~ **immunitaire** immune system; ~ **solaire** solar system

T

ta [ta] → *ton²*

tabac [taba] *m* tobacco; *bureau m ou débit m de* ~ tobacco store, *Br* tobacconist's; **tabagisme** *m* smoking

tabasser [tabase] ⟨1a⟩ beat up

table [tabl] *f* table; ~ *pliante* folding table; ~ *des matières* table of contents; *à* ~*!* come and get it!, food's up!; ~ *ronde* round table; *se mettre à* ~ sit down to eat

tableau [tablo] *m* (*pl* -x) *à l'école* board; (*peinture*) painting; *fig* picture; (*liste*) list; (*schéma*) table; ~ *d'affichage* bulletin board, *Br* notice board; ~ *de bord* AVIAT instrument panel

tablette [tablɛt] *f* shelf; ~ *de chocolat* chocolate bar

tableur [tablœr] *m* INFORM spreadsheet

tablier [tablije] *m* apron

tabou [tabu] **1** *m* taboo **2** *adj* (*inv ou f* ~*e, pl* ~(*e*)*s*) taboo

tabouret [taburɛ] *m* stool

tabulation [tabylasjɔ̃] *f* tab

tac [tak] *m*: *répondre du* ~ *au* ~ answer quick as a flash

tache [taʃ] *f* stain (*aussi fig*)

tâche [tɑʃ] *f* task

tacher [taʃe] ⟨1a⟩ stain

tâcher [tɑʃe] ⟨1a⟩: ~ *de faire qch* try to do sth

tacheté, ~e [taʃte] stained

tachymètre [takimɛtr] *m* AUTO speedometer

tacite [tasit] tacit

taciturne [tasityrn] taciturn

tact [takt] *m* tact; *avoir du* ~ be tactful

tactile [taktil] tactile

tactique 1 *adj* tactical **2** *f* tactics *pl*

taffetas [tafta] *m* taffeta

taie [tɛ] *f*: **~ (d'oreiller)** pillowslip

taille¹ [taj] *f* BOT pruning; *de la pierre* cutting

taille² [taj] *f* (*hauteur*) height; (*dimension*) size; ANAT waist; **être de ~ à faire qch** *fig* be capable of doing sth; **de ~** F enormous

taille-crayon(s) [tajkrɛjõ] *m* (*pl inv*) pencil sharpener

tailler [taje] ⟨1a⟩ BOT prune; *vêtement* cut out; *crayon* sharpen; *diamant, pierre* cut; **tailleur** *m* (*couturier*) tailor; *vêtement* (woman's) suit; **~ de diamants** diamond cutter

taillis [taji] *m* coppice

taire [tɛr] ⟨4a⟩ not talk about, hide; **se ~** keep quiet (**sur** about); *s'arrêter de parler* stop talking, fall silent; **tais-toi!** be quiet!, shut up!

Taïwan [tajwan] Taiwan; **taïwanais, ~e 1** *adj* Taiwanese **2** *m/f* **Taïwanais, ~e** Taiwanese

talc [talk] *m* talc

talent [talã] *m* talent; **talentueux, -euse** talented

talon [talõ] *m* ANAT, *de chaussure* heel; *d'un chèque* stub; **~s aiguille** spike heels, *Br* stilettos; **talonner** ⟨1a⟩ (*serrer de près*) follow close behind; (*harceler*) harass; **talonneur** *m en rugby* hooker

talus [taly] *m* bank

tambour [tãbur] *m* MUS, TECH drum; **tambouriner** ⟨1a⟩ drum

tamis [tami] *m* sieve

Tamise [tamiz]: **la ~** the Thames

tamiser [tamize] ⟨1a⟩ sieve; *lumière* filter

tampon [tãpõ] *m d'ouate* pad; *hygiène féminine* tampon; (*amortisseur*) buffer; (*cachet*) stamp; **tamponnement** *m* AUTO collision; **tamponner** ⟨1a⟩ *plaie* clean; (*cacheter*) stamp; AUTO collide with; **tamponneux, -euse**: *auto f* **tamponneuse** Dodgem®

tandem [tãdɛm] *m* tandem; *fig* twosome

tandis que [tãdi(s)k] *conj* while

tangent, ~e [tãʒã, -t] **1** *adj* MATH tangential **2** *f* MATH tangent

tangible [tãʒibl] tangible

tango [tãgo] *m* tango

tanguer [tãge] ⟨1a⟩ lurch

tanière [tanjɛr] *f* lair, den (*aussi fig*)

tank [tãk] *m* tank; **tanker** *m* tanker

tanné, ~e [tane] tanned; *peau* weatherbeaten; **tanner** ⟨1a⟩ tan; *fig* F pester; **tannerie** *f* tannery; **tanneur** *m* tanner

tant [tã] **1** *adv* so much; **~ d'erreurs** so many errors; **~ de vin** so much wine; **~ bien que mal** *réparer* after a fashion; (*avec difficulté*) with difficulty; **~ mieux** so much the better; **~ pis** too bad, tough **2** *conj*: **~ que** *temps* as long as; **~ qu'à faire!** might as well!; **en ~ que Français** as a Frenchman; **~ ... que ...** both ... and ...

tante [tãt] *f* aunt

tantième [tãtjɛm] *m* COMM percentage

tantôt [tãto] this afternoon; **à ~** see you soon; **~ ... now ... now ...**

taon [tã] *m* horsefly

tapage [tapaʒ] *m* racket; *fig* fuss; **faire du ~ nocturne** JUR cause a disturbance; **tapageur, -euse** (*voyant*) flashy, loud; (*bruyant*) noisy

tape [tap] *f* pat

tape-à-l'œil [tapalœj] *adj inv* loud, in-your-face F

tapecul [tapky] *m* AUTO F boneshaker

tapée [tape] *f* F: **une ~ de** loads of

taper [tape] ⟨1a⟩ **1** *v/t personne* hit; *table* bang on; **~ (à la machine)** F type **2** *v/i* hit; *à l'ordinateur* type, key; **~ sur les nerfs de qn** F get on s.o.'s nerves; **~ dans l'œil de qn** catch s.o.'s eye; **~ (dur)** *du soleil* beat down; **se ~** F *gâteaux, vin* put away; *corvée* be landed with

tapi, ~e [tapi] crouched; (*caché*) hidden; **tapir** ⟨2a⟩: **se ~** crouch

tapis [tapi] *m* carpet; SP mat; **mettre sur le ~** *fig* bring up; **~ roulant** TECH conveyor belt; *pour personnes travaling ou Br* travelling walkway; **~ de souris** mouse mat; **~ vert** gaming table

tapisser [tapise] ⟨1a⟩ *avec du papier peint* (wall)paper; **tapisserie** *f* tapestry; *(papier peint)* wallpaper; **tapissier, -ère** *m/f*: ~ **(décorateur)** interior decorator

tapoter [tapɔte] ⟨1a⟩ tap; *personne* pat; *rythme* tap out

taquin, ~e [takɛ̃, -in] teasing; **taquiner** ⟨1a⟩ tease; **taquinerie** *f* teasing

tarabiscoté, ~e [tarabiskɔte] overelaborate

tarabuster [tarabyste] ⟨1a⟩ pester; *(travailler)* worry

tard [tar] **1** *adv* late; **plus ~** later (on); **au plus ~** at the latest; **pas plus ~ que** no later than; ~ **dans la nuit** late at night; **il se fait ~** it's getting late; **mieux vaut ~ que jamais** better late than never **2** *m*: **sur le ~** late in life

tarder [tarde] ⟨1a⟩ delay; **à faire qch** take a long time doing sth; **il me tarde de te revoir** I'm longing to see you again; **tardif, -ive** late

targuer [targe] ⟨1m⟩: **se ~ de qch** *litt* pride o.s. on sth

tarif [tarif] *m* rate; ~ **unique** flat rate

tarir [tarir] ⟨2a⟩ dry up *(aussi fig)*; **se ~** dry up

tarmac [tarmak] *m* tarmac

tartan [tartɑ̃] *m* tartan

tarte [tart] *f* tart; **tartelette** *f* tartlet

tartine [tartin] *f* slice of bread; ~ **de beurre / confiture** slice of bread and butter / jam; **tartiner** ⟨1a⟩ spread; **fromage** *m* **à ~** cheese spread

tartre [tartr] *m* tartar

tas [tɑ] *m* heap, pile; **un ~ de choses** heaps *pl ou* piles *pl* of things; **formation** *f* **sur le ~** on-the-job training

tasse [tɑs] *f* cup; **une ~ de café** a cup of coffee; **une ~ à café** a coffee cup

tassement [tɑsmɑ̃] *m* TECH subsidence, settlement; **tasser** ⟨1a⟩ *(bourrer)* cram; **se ~** settle; **ça va se ~** *fig* F things will sort themselves out

tâter [tɑte] ⟨1a⟩ **1** *v/t* feel; ~ **qn** *fig* sound s.o. out **2** *v/i* F: ~ **de qch** try sth, have a shot at sth

tatillon, ~ne [tatijɔ̃, -ɔn] fussy

tâtonner [tɑtɔne] ⟨1a⟩ grope about;

tâtons *adv*: **avancer à ~** feel one's way forward

tatouage [tatwaʒ] *m action* tattooing; *signe* tattoo; **tatouer** ⟨1a⟩ tattoo

taudis [todi] *m* slum

taule [tol] *f* P *(prison)* jail, slammer P

taupe [top] *f* ZO mole

taureau [tɔro] *m* (*pl* -x) bull; **Taureau** ASTROL Taurus

tauromachie [tɔrɔmaʃi] *f* bullfighting

taux [to] *m* rate; ~ **d'escompte** discount rate; ~ **d'expansion** rate of expansion, expansion rate; ~ **d'intérêt** interest rate

taverne [tavɛrn] *f (restaurant)* restaurant

taxe [taks] *f* duty; *(impôt)* tax; ~ **professionnelle** tax paid by people who are self-employed; ~ **de séjour** visitor tax; ~ **sur** *ou* **à la valeur ajoutée** sales tax, *Br* value added tax, VAT; **taxer** ⟨1a⟩ tax; ~ **qn de qch** *fig (accuser)* accuse s.o. with sth; **il la taxe d'égoïsme** he accuses her of selfishness, he describes her as selfish

taxi [taksi] *m* taxi, cab

taximètre [taksimɛtr] *m* meter

tchèque [tʃɛk] **1** *adj* Czech **2** *m langue* Czech **3** *m/f* **Tchèque** Czech

te [tə] *pron personnel* ◊ *complément d'objet direct* you; **il ne t'a pas vu** he didn't see you
◊ *complément d'objet indirect* (to) you; **elle t'en a parlé** she spoke to you about it; **je vais ~ chercher un ...** I'll go and get you a ...
◊ *avec verbe pronominal* yourself; **tu t'es coupé** you've cut yourself; **si tu ~ lèves à ...** if you get up and ...

technicien, ~ne [tɛknisjɛ̃, -ɛn] *m/f* technician; **technicité** *f* technicality; **technique 1** *adj* technical **2** *f* technique

technocrate [tɛknɔkrat] *m* technocrat; **technocratie** *f* technocracy

technologie [tɛknɔlɔʒi] *f* technology; ~ **informatique** computer technology; ~ **de pointe** high-tech; **technologique** technological

teck [tɛk] *m* teak

teckel [tekɛl] *m* dachshund

tee-shirt [tiʃœrt] *m* T-shirt

TEG [teœʒe] *m abr* (= *taux effectif global*) APR (= annual percentage rate)

teindre [tɛ̃dr] ⟨4b⟩ dye

teint, ~e [tɛ̃, -t] **1** *adj* dyed **2** *m* complexion; *fond m de ~* foundation (cream); *bon ou grand ~* *inv* colorfast, *Br* colourfast **3** *f* tint; *fig* tinge, touch; **teinter** ⟨1a⟩ tint; *bois* stain; **teinture** *f action* dyeing; *produit* dye; PHARM tincture; **teinturerie** *f* dry cleaner's

tel, ~le [tɛl] such; *une ~le surprise* such a surprise; *de ce genre* a surprise like that; *~(s) ou ~le(s) que* such as, like; *~ quel* as it is / was; *rien de ~ que* nothing like, nothing to beat; *à ~ point que* to such an extent that, so much that; *~ jour* on such and such a day

télé [tele] *f* F TV, tube F, *Br* telly F

télébenne [teleben] *f* cable car

télécharger [teleʃarʒe] ⟨1l⟩ INFORM download

télécommande [telekɔmãd] *f* remote control; **télécommander** ⟨1a⟩: *télécommandé* remote-controlled

télécommunications [telekɔmynikasjõ] *f pl* telecommunications

téléconférence [telekõferãs] *f* teleconference

téléférique [teleferik] → *téléphérique*

téléguidage [telegidaʒ] *m* remote control; **téléguider** ⟨1a⟩ operate by remote control

téléinformatique [teleɛ̃fɔrmatik] *f* teleprocessing

téléobjectif [teleɔbʒɛktif] *m* telephoto lens

télépathie [telepati] *f* telepathy

téléphérique [teleferik] *m* cable car

téléphone [telefɔn] *m* phone, telephone; *~ portable* cellphone, *Br* mobile (phone); *abonné m au ~* telephone subscriber; *coup m de ~* (phone)call; *par ~* by phone; *avoir le ~* have a telephone; **téléphoner** ⟨1a⟩ **1** *v/i* phone, telephone; *~ à qn* call s.o., *Br aussi* phone s.o. **2**

v/t phone, telephone; **téléphonique** phone *atr*, telephone *atr*; *appel m ~* phonecall, telephone call; **téléphoniste** *m/f* operator

téléréalité [telerealite] *f* reality TV

télescope [teleskɔp] *m* telescope; **télescoper** ⟨1a⟩ crash into, collide with; *se ~* crash, collide; **télescopique** telescopic

télésiège [telesjeʒ] *m* chair lift

téléski [teleski] *m* ski lift

téléspectateur, -trice [telespektatœr, -tris] *m/f* (TV) viewer

téléthon [teletõ] *m* telethon

télévisé, ~e [televize] televised; **téléviseur** *m* TV (set), television (set); **télévision** *f* television; *~ câblée* cable (TV)

tellement [tɛlmã] *adv* so; *avec verbe* so much; *~ facile* so easy; *il a ~ bu que ...* he drank so much that ...; *tu veux? - pas ~* do you want to? - not really; *~ de chance* so much good luck, such good luck; *~ de filles* so many girls

téméraire [temerɛr] reckless; **témérité** *f* recklessness

témoignage [temwaɲaʒ] *m* JUR testimony, evidence; *rapport* account; *fig: d'affection, d'estime* token; **témoigner** ⟨1a⟩ **1** *v/t: ~ que* testify that **2** *v/i* JUR testify, give evidence; *~ de* (*être le témoignage de*) show, demonstrate

témoin [temwɛ̃] *m* witness; *être (le) ~ de qch* witness sth; *appartement m ~* show apartment *ou Br* flat; *~ oculaire* eyewitness

tempe [tãp] *f* ANAT temple

tempérament [tãperamã] *m* temperament; *à ~* in installments *ou Br* instalments; *achat m à ~* installment plan, *Br* hire purchase

tempérance [tãperãs] *f* moderation

température [tãperatyr] *f* temperature; *avoir de la ~* have a fever, *Br aussi* have a temperature; **tempéré, ~e** moderate; *climat* temperate; **tempérer** ⟨1f⟩ moderate

tempête [tãpɛt] *f* storm (*aussi fig*)

temple [tãpl] *m* temple; *protestant*

church

tempo [tɛmpo] *m* MUS tempo

temporaire [tɑ̃pɔrɛr] temporary

temporel, ~le [tɑ̃pɔrɛl] REL, GRAM temporal

temporiser [tɑ̃pɔrize] ⟨1a⟩ stall, play for time

temps [tɑ̃] *m* time; *atmosphérique* weather; TECH stroke; *mesure f à trois ~* MUS three-four time; *moteur m à deux ~* two-stroke engine; *à ~* in time; *de ~ à autre, de ~ en ~* from time to time, occasionally; *avoir tout son ~* have plenty of time, have all the time in the world; *tout le ~* all the time; *dans le ~* in the old days; *de mon ~* in my time *ou* day; *en tout ~* at all times; *du ~ que* when; *il est ~ de partir* it's time to go; *il est ~ que tu t'en ailles* (*subj*) it's time you left; *il est grand ~* it's high time, it's about time; *en même ~* at the same time; *au bon vieux ~* in the good old days; *par beau ~* in good weather; *quel ~ fait-il?* what's the weather like?

tenace [tənas] tenacious

ténacité [tenasite] *f* tenacity

tenailles [tə(ə)naj] *fpl* pincers

tenancier, -ère [tənɑ̃sje, -ɛr] *m/f* manager

tendance [tɑ̃dɑ̃s] *f* trend; (*disposition*) tendency; *avoir ~ à faire qch* have a tendency to do sth, tend to do sth

tendon [tɑ̃dɔ̃] *m* ANAT tendon

tendre¹ [tɑ̃dr] ⟨4a⟩ **1** *v/t filet, ailes* spread; *piège* set; *bras, main* hold out, stretch out; *muscles* tense; *corde* tighten; *~ qch à qn* hold sth out to s.o.; *se ~ de rapports* become strained **2** *v/i*: *~ à qch* strive for sth; *~ à faire qch* tend to do sth

tendre² [tɑ̃dr] tender; *couleur* soft; *âge m ~ fig* childhood

tendresse [tɑ̃drɛs] *f* tenderness

tendu, ~e [tɑ̃dy] **1** *p/p → tendre* **2** *adj corde* tight; *fig* tense; *relations* strained

ténèbres [tenɛbr] *fpl* darkness *sg*; **ténébreux, -euse** [tenebrø, -z] dark

teneur [tənœr] *f d'une lettre* contents

pl; (*concentration*) content; *~ en alcool* alcohol content

tenir [t(ə)nir] ⟨2h⟩ **1** *v/t* hold; (*maintenir*) keep; *registre, comptes, promesse* keep; *caisse* be in charge of; *restaurant* run; *place* take up; *~ pour* regard as; *~ compte de qch* take sth into account, bear sth in mind; *~ (bien) la route* AUTO hold the road well; *~ qch de qn* get sth from s.o.; *~ (sa) parole* keep one's word; *~ au chaud* keep warm; *~ le coup* F hold out; *~ à qch / qn* (*donner de l'importance à*) value sth / s.o.; *à un objet* be attached to sth; *~ à faire qch* really want to do sth; *cela ne tient qu'à toi* (*dépend de*) it's entirely up to you; *~ de qn* take after s.o. **2** *v/i* hold; *~ bon* hang in there, not give up; *~ dans* fit into; *tiens! surprise* one's word!; *au chaud* really? **3**: *se ~ d'un spectacle* be held, take place; (*être, se trouver*) stand; *se ~ mal* misbehave, behave badly; *se ~ à qch* hold *ou* hang on to sth; *s'en ~ à* confine o.s. to

tennis [tenis] *m* tennis; *terrain* tennis court; *~ pl* sneakers, *Br* trainers; SP tennis shoes; *~ de table* table tennis

ténor [tenɔr] *m* MUS tenor

tension [tɑ̃sjɔ̃] *f* tension (*aussi fig*); ÉL voltage, tension; MÉD blood pressure; *haute ~* high voltage; *faire de la ~* F have high blood pressure

tentaculaire [tɑ̃takylɛr] sprawling; **tentacule** *m* tentacle

tentant, ~e [tɑ̃tɑ̃, -t] tempting; **tentation** *f* temptation

tentative [tɑ̃tativ] *f* attempt

tente [tɑ̃t] *f* tent; *dresser ou monter ou planter / démonter une ~* pitch / take down a tent

tenter [tɑ̃te] ⟨1a⟩ tempt; (*essayer*) attempt, try; *être tenté(e) de faire qch* be tempted to do sth; *~ de faire qch* attempt *ou* try to do sth

tenture [tɑ̃tyr] *f* wallhanging

tenu, ~e [t(ə)ny] **1** *p/p → tenir* **2** *adj*: *être ~ de faire qch* be obliged to do sth; *bien ~* well looked after; *mal ~* badly kept; *enfant* neglected

ténu, ~e [teny] fine; *espoir* slim

tenue [t(ə)ny] *f de comptes* keeping; *de ménage* running; (*conduite*) behavior, *Br* behaviour; *du corps* posture; (*vêtements*) clothes *pl*; **en grande ~** MIL in full dress uniform; **~ de route** AUTO roadholding; **~ de soirée** evening wear

térébenthine [terebɑ̃tin] *f* turpentine, turps *sg*

tergiverser [tɛrʒiverse] ⟨1a⟩ hum and haw

terme [tɛrm] *m* (*fin*) end; (*échéance*) time limit; (*expression*) term; **à court / moyen / long ~** in the short / medium / long term; *emprunt, projet* short- / medium- / long-term; **mener à ~** complete; *grossesse* see through, go through with; **être en bons ~s avec qn** be on good terms with s.o.

terminaison [tɛrminɛzõ] *f* GRAM ending; **terminal, ~e** (*mpl* -aux) **1** *adj* terminal **2** *m* terminal **3** *f* ÉDU twelfth grade, *Br* upper sixth form; **terminer** ⟨1a⟩ finish; *se ~* end; *se ~ par* end with; *d'un mot* end in; *se ~ en pointe* end in a point

terminologie [tɛrminɔlɔʒi] *f* terminology

terminus [tɛrminys] *m* terminus

terne [tɛrn] dull; **ternir** ⟨2a⟩ tarnish (*aussi fig*)

terrain [tɛrɛ̃] *m* ground; GÉOL, MIL terrain; SP field; **un ~** a piece of land; **sur le ~** terrace *atr*; **essayer in the field**; **~ d'atterrissage** landing field; **~ d'aviation** airfield; **~ à bâtir** building lot; **~ de camping** campground; **~ de jeu** play park; **un ~ vague** a piece of waste ground, a gap site; **véhicule** *m* **tout ~** 4x4, off-road vehicle

terrasse [tɛras] *f* terrace; **terrassement** *m* (*travaux mpl de*) ~ *travail* banking; *ouvrage* embankment; **terrasser** ⟨1a⟩ *adversaire* fell, deck F

terre [tɛr] *f* (*sol, surface*) ground; *matière* earth, soil; *opposé à mer, propriété* land; (*monde*) earth, world; *pays, région* land, country; ÉL ground, *Br* earth; **à ~** esprit, personne down to earth; **à ou par ~** on the ground;

tomber par ~ fall down; **sur ~** on earth; **sur la ~** on the ground; **de / en ~** clay *atr*; **~ cuite** terracotta; **~ ferme** dry land, terra firma; **la Terre Sainte** the Holy Land

terreau [tero] *m* (*pl* -x) compost

Terre-Neuve [tɛrnœv] Newfoundland

terre-plein [tɛrplɛ̃] *m* (*pl* terre-pleins): **~ central** median strip, *Br* central reservation

terrer [tɛre] ⟨1a⟩: **se ~** *d'un animal* go to earth

terrestre [tɛrɛstr] *animaux* land *atr*; REL earthly; TV terrestrial

terreur [tɛrœr] *f* terror

terrible [tɛribl] terrible; F (*extraordinaire*) terrific; **c'est pas ~** it's not that good; **terriblement** *adv* terribly, awfully

terrien, ~ne [tɛrjɛ̃, -ɛn] **1** *adj:* **propriétaire** *m* **~** landowner **2** *m/f* (*habitant de la Terre*) earthling

terrier [tɛrje] *m de renard* earth; **chien ~** terrier

terrifier [tɛrifje] ⟨1a⟩ terrify

territoire [tɛritwar] *m* territory; **territorial, ~e** (*mpl* -aux) territorial; **eaux** *fpl* **territoriales** territorial waters

terroir [tɛrwar] *m viticulture* soil; **du ~** (*régional*) local

terroriser [tɛrɔrize] ⟨1a⟩ terrorize; **terrorisme** *m* terrorism; **terroriste** *m/f & adj* terrorist

tertiaire [tɛrsjɛr] tertiary; **secteur** *m* **~** ÉCON tertiary sector

tertre [tɛrtr] *m* mound

tes [te] → **ton²**

test [tɛst] *m* test; **passer un ~** take a test; **~ d'aptitude** aptitude test; **~ de résistance** endurance test

testament [tɛstamɑ̃] *m* JUR will; **Ancien / Nouveau Testament** REL Old / New Testament

tester [tɛste] ⟨1a⟩ test

testicule [tɛstikyl] *m* ANAT testicle

tétanos [tetanos] *m* MÉD tetanus

têtard [tɛtar] *m* tadpole

tête [tɛt] *f* head; (*cheveux*) hair; (*visage*) face; SP header; **sur un coup de ~** on impulse; **j'en ai par-dessus**

la ~ I've had it up to here (*de* with); *la* ~ *basse* hangdog, sheepish; *la* ~ *haute* with (one's) head held high; *de* ~ *calculer* mentally, in one's head; *répondre* without looking anything up; *avoir la* ~ *dure* be pigheaded *ou* stubborn; *se casser la* ~ *fig* rack one's brains; *n'en faire qu'à sa* ~ do exactly as one likes, suit o.s.; *tenir* ~ *à qn* stand up to s.o.; *péj* defy s.o.; *par* ~ a head, each; *faire une sale* ~ look miserable; *faire la* ~ sulk; *il se paie ta* ~ *fig* he's making a fool of you; ~ *nucléaire* nuclear warhead; *en* ~ in the lead; *à la* ~ *de* at the head of; **tête-à-queue** *m* (*pl inv*) AUTO spin; **tête-à-tête** *m* (*pl inv*) tête-à-tête; *en* ~ in private

tétine [tetin] *f de biberon* teat; (*sucette*) pacifier, *Br* dummy

téton [tetɔ̃] *m* F boob F

têtu, ~e [tety] obstinate, pigheaded

texte [tɛkst] *m* text; ~*s choisis* selected passages

textile [tɛkstil] **1** *adj* textile **2** *m* textile; *le* ~ *industrie* the textile industry, textiles *pl*

texto [tɛksto] *m* text (message); *envoyer un* ~ *à qn* send s.o. a text, text s.o.

textuel, ~le [tɛkstɥɛl] *traduction* word-for-word

texture [tɛkstyr] *f* texture

T.G.V. [teʒeve] *m abr* (= *train à grande vitesse*) high-speed train

thaï [taj] *m* Thai; **thaïlandais, ~e 1** *adj* Thai **2** *m/f* **Thaïlandais, ~e** Thai; **Thaïlande** *f* Thailand

thé [te] *m* tea

théâtral, ~e [teatral] (*mpl* -aux) theatrical; **théâtre** *m* theater, *Br* theatre; *fig: cadre* scene; *pièce f de* ~ play; ~ *en plein air* open-air theater

théière [tejɛr] *f* teapot

thème [tɛm] *m* theme; ÉDU translation (*into a foreign language*)

théologie [teɔlɔʒi] *f* theology; **théologien** *m* theologian

théorème [teɔrɛm] *m* theorem

théoricien, ~ne [teɔrisjɛ̃, -ɛn] *m/f* theoretician; **théorie** *f* theory; **théori-**

que theoretical

thérapeute [terapøt] *m/f* therapist; **thérapeutique 1** *f* (*thérapie*) treatment, therapy **2** *adj* therapeutic; **thérapie** *f* therapy; ~ *de groupe* group therapy

thermal, ~e [tɛrmal] (*mpl* -aux) thermal; *station f* ~ spa

thermique [tɛrmik] PHYS thermal

thermomètre [tɛrmɔmɛtr] *m* thermometer

thermonucléaire [tɛrmɔnykleɛr] thermonuclear

thermos [tɛrmos] *f ou m* thermos®

thermostat [tɛrmɔsta] *m* thermostat

thèse [tɛz] *f* thesis

thon [tɔ̃] *m* tuna

thorax [tɔraks] *m* ANAT thorax

thrombose [trɔ̃boz] *f* thrombosis

thym [tɛ̃] *m* BOT thyme

thyroïde [tirɔid] *f* MÉD thyroid

tibia [tibja] *m* ANAT tibia

tic [tik] *m* tic, twitch; *fig* habit

ticket [tikɛ] *m* ticket; ~ *de caisse* receipt; **ticket-repas** *m* (*pl* tickets-repas) luncheon voucher

tic-tac *m* (*pl inv*) ticking

tiède [tjɛd] warm; *péj* tepid, lukewarm (*aussi fig*); **tiédeur** [tjedœr] *f du climat, du vent* warmth, mildness; *péj* tepidness; *fig: d'un accueil* half-heartedness; **tiédir** ⟨2a⟩ cool down; *devenir plus chaud* warm up

tien, ~ne [tjɛ̃, tjɛn]: *le tien, la tienne, les tiens, les tiennes* yours; *à la* ~*ne!* F cheers!

tiercé [tjɛrse] *m* bet in which money is placed on a combination of three horses

tiers, tierce [tjɛr, -s] **1** *adj* third; *le* ~ *monde* the Third World **2** *m* MATH third; JUR third party

tige [tiʒ] *f* BOT stalk; TECH stem; ~*s de forage* drill bits

tignasse [tiɲas] *f* mop of hair

tigre [tigr] *m* tiger; **tigré, ~e** striped; **tigresse** *f* tigress (*aussi fig*)

tilleul [tijœl] *m* BOT lime (tree); *boisson* lime-blossom tea

timbre [tɛ̃br] *m* (*sonnette*) bell; (*son*) timbre; (*timbre-poste*) stamp; (*tampon*) stamp; **timbré, ~e** *papier, lettre* stamped; **timbre-poste** m (pl timbres-poste) postage stamp

timide [timid] timid; en société shy; **timidité** f timidity; en société shyness

timon [timɔ̃] m d'un navire tiller

timoré, **~e** [timɔre] timid

tintamarre [tɛ̃tamar] m din, racket

tintement [tɛ̃tmɑ̃] m tinkle; de clochettes ringing; **tinter** ⟨1a⟩ de verres clink; de clochettes ring

tir [tir] m fire; action, SP shooting; **~ à l'arc** archery

tirade [tirad] f tirade

tirage [tiraʒ] m à la loterie draw; PHOT print; TYP printing; (exemplaires de journal) circulation; d'un livre print run; COMM d'un chèque drawing; F (difficultés) trouble; **par un ~ au sort** by drawing lots

tirailler [tiraje] ⟨1a⟩ pull; **tiraillé entre** fig torn between

tirant [tirɑ̃] m MAR: **~ d'eau** draft, Br draught

tire [tir] f P AUTO car, jeep P; **vol m à la ~** pickpocketing

tiré, **~e** [tire] traits drawn

tire-au-flanc [tiroflɑ̃] m (pl inv) F shirker

tire-bouchon [tirbuʃɔ̃] m (pl tire-bouchons) corkscrew

tire-fesses [tirfes] m F (pl inv) T-bar

tirelire [tirlir] f piggy bank

tirer [tire] ⟨1a⟩ 1 v/t pull; chèque, ligne, conclusions draw; rideaux pull, draw; coup de fusil fire; oiseau, cible shoot at, fire at; PHOT, TYP print; plaisir, satisfaction derive; **~ les cartes** read the cards; **~ avantage de la situation** take advantage of the situation; **~ la langue** stick out one's tongue 2 v/i pull (sur on); avec arme shoot, fire (sur at); SP shoot; d'une cheminée draw; **~ à sa fin** draw to a close; **~ sur le bleu** verge on blue 3: **se ~ de** situation difficile get out of; **se ~** F take off

tiret [tire] m dash; (trait d'union) hyphen

tireur [tirœr, -øz] m marksman; d'un chèque drawer; **~ d'élite** sharpshooter; **tireuse** f: **~ de cartes** fortune-teller

tiroir [tirwar] m drawer; **tiroir-caisse** m (pl tiroirs-caisses) cash register

tisane [tizan] f herbal tea, infusion

tisonnier [tizɔnje] m poker

tissage [tisaʒ] m weaving; **tisser** ⟨1a⟩ weave; d'une araignée spin; fig hatch; **tisserand** m weaver

tissu [tisy] m fabric, material; BIOL tissue; **tissu-éponge** m (pl tissus-éponges) toweling, Br towelling

titre [titr] m title; d'un journal headline; FIN security; **à ce ~** therefore; **à juste ~** rightly; **à ~ d'essai** on a trial basis; **à ~ d'information** for your information; **à ~ officiel** in an official capacity; **à ~ d'ami** as a friend; **au même ~** on the same basis; **en ~** official

tituber [titybe] ⟨1a⟩ stagger

titulaire [tityler] **1** adj professeur tenured **2** m/f d'un document, d'une charge holder

toast [tost] m (pain grillé) piece ou slice of toast; de bienvenue toast

toboggan [tɔbɔgɑ̃] m slide; rue flyover; **~ de secours** escape chute

tocsin [tɔksɛ̃] m alarm bell

toge [tɔʒ] f de professeur, juge robe

tohu-bohu [tɔybɔy] m commotion

toi [twa] pron personnel you; **avec ~** with you; **c'est ~ qui l'as fait** you did it, it was you that did it

toile [twal] f de lin linen; (peinture) canvas; **~ d'araignée** spiderweb, Br spider's web; **~ cirée** oilcloth; **~ de fond** backcloth; fig backdrop

toilette [twalet] f (lavage) washing; (mise) outfit; (vêtements) clothes pl; **~s** toilet sg; **aller aux ~s** go to the toilet; **faire sa ~** get washed

toi-même [twamɛm] yourself

toiser [twaze] ⟨1a⟩ fig: **~ qn** look s.o. up and down

toison [twazɔ̃] f de laine fleece; (cheveux) mane of hair

toit [twa] m roof; **~ ouvrant** AUTO sun roof; **toiture** f roof

tôle [tol] f sheet metal; **~ ondulée** corrugated iron

tolérable [tɔlerabl] tolerable, bearable; **tolérance** *f aussi* TECH tolerance; **tolérant, ~e** tolerant; **tolérer** ⟨1f⟩ tolerate

tollé [tɔle] *m* outcry

tomate [tɔmat] *f* tomato

tombe [tɔ̃b] *f* grave; **tombeau** *m* (*pl* -x) tomb

tombée [tɔ̃be] *f*: **à la ~ de la nuit** at nightfall; **tomber** ⟨1a⟩ (*aux être*) fall; *de cheveux* fall out; *d'une colère* die down; *d'une fièvre, d'un prix, d'une demande* drop, fall; *d'un intérêt, enthousiasme* wane; **~ en ruine** go to rack and ruin; **~ malade** fall sick; **~ amoureux** fall in love; **~ en panne** have a breakdown; **faire ~** knock down; **laisser ~** drop (*aussi fig*); **laisse ~!** never mind!, forget it!; **~ sur** MIL attack; (*rencontrer*) bump into; **~ juste** get it right; **je suis bien tombé** I was lucky; **ça tombe bien** it's perfect timing; **~ d'accord** reach agreement

tombeur [tɔ̃bœr] *m* F womanizer

tome [tɔm] *m* volume

ton[1] [tɔ̃] *m* tone; MUS key; **il est de bon ~** it's the done thing

ton[2] *m*, **ta** *f*, **tes** *pl* [tɔ̃, ta, te] your

tonalité [tɔnalite] *f* MUS key; *d'une voix, radio* tone; TÉL dial tone, *Br aussi* dialling tone

tondeuse [tɔ̃døz] *f* lawnmower; *de coiffeur* clippers *pl*; AGR shears *pl*; **tondre** ⟨4a⟩ *mouton* shear; *haie* clip; *herbe* mow, cut; *cheveux* shave off

tonifier [tɔnifje] ⟨1a⟩ tone up

tonique [tɔnik] **1** *m* tonic **2** *adj climat* bracing

tonitruant, ~e [tɔnitryɑ̃, -t] thunderous

tonnage [tɔnaʒ] *m* tonnage

tonne [tɔn] *f* (metric) ton; **tonneau** *m* (*pl* -x) barrel; MAR ton; **tonnelet** *m* keg

tonner [tɔne] ⟨1a⟩ thunder; *fig* rage

tonnerre [tɔnɛr] *m* thunder

tonton [tɔ̃tɔ̃] *m* F uncle

tonus [tɔnys] *m d'un muscle* tone; (*dynamisme*) dynamism

top [tɔp] *m* pip

topaze [tɔpaz] *f* topaz

tope! [tɔp] done!

topo [tɔpo] *m* F report

topographie [tɔpɔgrafi] *f* topography

toqué, ~e [tɔke] F mad; **~ de** mad about; **toquer** ⟨1m⟩ F: **se ~ de** be madly in love with

torche [tɔrʃ] *f* flashlight, *Br* torch

torchon [tɔrʃɔ̃] *m* dishtowel

tordre [tɔrdr] ⟨4a⟩ twist; *linge* wring; **se ~** twist; **se ~ (de rire)** be hysterical with laughter; **se ~ le pied** twist one's ankle; **tordu, ~e** twisted; *fig: esprit* warped, twisted

tornade [tɔrnad] *f* tornado

torpille [tɔrpij] *f* MIL torpedo; **torpiller** ⟨1a⟩ torpedo (*aussi fig*); **torpilleur** *m* MIL motor torpedo boat

torrent [tɔrɑ̃] *m* torrent; *fig: de larmes* flood; *d'injures* torrent; **torrentiel, ~le** torrential

torse [tɔrs] *m* chest, torso; *sculpture* torso

tort [tɔr] *m* fault; (*préjudice*) harm; **à ~** wrongly; **à ~ et à travers** wildly; **être en ~ ou dans son ~** be in the wrong, be at fault; **avoir ~** be wrong (*de faire qch* to do sth); **il a eu le ~ de …** it was wrong of him to …; **donner ~ à qn** prove s.o. wrong; (*désapprouver*) blame s.o.; **faire du ~ à qn** hurt *ou* harm s.o.

torticolis [tɔrtikɔli] *m* MÉD stiff neck

tortiller [tɔrtije] ⟨1a⟩ twist; **se ~** wriggle

tortionnaire [tɔrsjɔnɛr] *m* torturer

tortue [tɔrty] *f* tortoise; **~ de mer** turtle

tortueux, -euse [tɔrtɥø, -z] winding; *fig* tortuous; *esprit, manœuvres* devious

torture [tɔrtyr] *f* torture (*aussi fig*); **torturer** ⟨1a⟩ torture (*aussi fig*)

tôt [to] *adv* early; (*bientôt*) soon; **plus ~** sooner, earlier; **le plus ~ possible** as soon as possible; **au plus ~** at the soonest *ou* earliest; **il ne reviendra pas de si ~** he won't be back in a hurry; **~ ou tard** sooner or later; **~ le matin** early in the morning

total, ~e [tɔtal] (*mpl* -aux) **1** *adj* total **2** *m* total; **au ~** in all; *fig* on the whole; **faire le ~** work out the total;

T

totalement *adv* totally; **totaliser** ⟨1a⟩ *dépenses* add up, total; **totalité** *f*: **la ~ de** all of; **en ~** in full

totalitaire [tɔtalitɛr] POL totalitarian; **totalitarisme** *m* POL totalitarianism

touchant, ~e [tuʃɑ̃, -t] touching

touche [tuʃ] *f* TECH *de clavier* key; SP touchline; *(remise en jeu)* throw-in; *pêche* bite; **ligne** *f* **de ~** SP touchline; **être mis sur la ~** *fig* F be sidelined; **faire une ~** make a hit; **~ entrée** INFORM enter (key)

touche-à-tout [tuʃatu] *m (pl inv)* qui fait plusieurs choses à la fois jack-of-all-trades

toucher¹ [tuʃe] ⟨1a⟩ touch; *but* hit; *(émouvoir)* touch, move; *(concerner)* affect, concern; *(contacter)* contact, get in touch with; *argent* get; **je vais lui en ~ un mot** I'll mention it to him; **~ à** touch; *réserves* break into; *d'une maison* adjoin; *(concerner)* concern; **~ au but** near one's goal; **~ à tout** *fig* be a jack-of-all-trades; **se ~** touch; *de maisons, terrains* adjoin

toucher² [tuʃe] *m* touch

touffe [tuf] *f* tuft; **touffu, ~e** dense, thick

toujours [tuʒur] always; *(encore)* still; **pour ~** for ever; **~ est-il que** the fact remains that

toupet [tupɛ] *m* F nerve; **avoir le ~ de faire qch** have the nerve to do sth

tour¹ [tur] *f* tower; *(immeuble)* high-rise; **~ de forage** drilling rig

tour² [tur] *m* turn; *(circonférence)* circumference; *(circuit)* lap; *(promenade)* stroll, walk; *(excursion, voyage)* tour; *(ruse)* trick; TECH lathe; *de potier* wheel; **à mon ~, c'est mon ~** it's my turn; **à ~ de rôle** turn and turn about; **en un ~ de main** in no time at all; **avoir le ~ de main** have the knack; **faire le ~ de** go round; *fig* review; **faire le ~ du monde** go around the world; **fermer à double ~** double-lock; **jouer un ~ à qn** play a trick on s.o.; **~ d'horizon** overview; **~ de scrutin** POL ballot **33** / **45 ~s** LP / single

tourbe [turb] *f matière* peat; **tourbière** *f* peat bog

tourbillon [turbijɔ̃] *m de vent* whirlwind; *d'eau* whirlpool; **~ de neige** flurry of snow; **tourbillonner** ⟨1a⟩ whirl

tourelle [turɛl] *f* turret

tourisme [turism] *m* tourism; **agence** *f* **de ~** travel *ou* tourist agency; **~ écologique** ecotourism; **touriste** *m/f* tourist; **classe** *f* **~** tourist class; **touristique** *guide, informations* tourist *atr*, **renseignements** *mpl* **~s** tourist information *sg*

tourment [turmɑ̃] *m litt* torture, torment; **tourmente** *f litt* storm; **tourmenter** ⟨1a⟩ torment; **se ~** worry, torment o.s.

tournage [turnaʒ] *m d'un film* shooting

tournant, ~e [turnɑ̃, -t] **1** *adj* revolving **2** *m* turn; *fig* turning point

tourne-disque [turnədisk] *m (pl tourne-disques)* record player

tournée [turne] *f* round; *d'un artiste* tour; **payer une ~** F buy a round (of drinks)

tourner [turne] ⟨1a⟩ **1** *v/t* turn; *sauce* stir; *salade* toss; *film* shoot; **bien tourné(e)** well-put; *phrase* well-turned; **~ la tête** turn one's head; **pour ne pas voir** turn (one's head) away; **~ en ridicule** make fun of **2** *v/i* turn; *du lait* turn, go bad *ou* Br off; **~ à droite** turn right; **j'ai la tête qui tourne** my head is spinning; **le temps tourne au beau** the weather is taking a turn for the better; **~ de l'œil** *fig* F faint; **~ en rond** *fig* go around in circles; **faire ~** *clé* turn; *entreprise* run; **~ autour de** ASTR revolve around; *fig*: *d'une discussion* center *ou* Br centre on **3**: **se ~** turn; **se ~ vers** *fig* turn to

tournesol [turnəsɔl] *m* BOT sunflower

tournevis [turnəvis] *m* screwdriver

tourniquet [turnikɛ] *m* turnstile; *(présentoir)* (revolving) stand

tournoi [turnwa] *m* tournament

tournoyer [turnwaje] ⟨1h⟩ *d'oiseaux* wheel; *de feuilles, flocons* swirl

tournure [turnyr] *f* (*expression*) turn of phrase; *des événements* turn; **sa ~ d'esprit** the way his mind works, his mindset

tourte [turt] *f* CUIS pie

tourterelle [turtərɛl] *f* turtledove

tous *ou* tus → **tout**

Toussaint [tusɛ̃]: *la ~* All Saints' Day

tousser [tuse] ⟨1a⟩ cough; **toussoter** ⟨1a⟩ have a slight cough

tout [tu, tut] *m*, **toute** [tut] *f*; **tous** [tu, tus] *mpl*, **toutes** [tut] *fpl* **1** *adj* all; (*n'importe lequel*) any; **~e la ville** all the city, the whole city, **~es les villes** all cities; **~es les villes que ...** all the cities that ...; **~ Français** every Frenchman, all Frenchmen; **tous les deux jours** every two days, every other day; **tous les ans** every year; **tous / ~es les trois, nous ...** all three of us ...; **~ Paris** all Paris; **il pourrait arriver à ~ moment** he could arrive at any moment

2 *pron sg* **tout** everything, *pl* **tous, toutes** all of us / them; **c'est ~, merci** that's everything thanks, that's all thanks; **après~** after all; **avant~** first of all; (*surtout*) above all; **facile comme ~** F as easy as anything; **nous tous** all of us; **c'est ~ ce que je sais** that's everything *ou* all I know; **elle ferait ~ pour ...** she would do anything to ...; **il a ~ oublié** he has forgotten it all, he has forgotten the lot

3 *adv* **tout** very, quite; **c'est ~ comme un ...** it's just like a ...; **~ nu** completely naked; **il est ~ mignon!** he's so cute!; **~ doux!** gently now!; **c'est ~ près d'ici** it's just nearby, it's very near; **je suis ~e seule** I'm all alone; **~ à fait** altogether; **oui, ~ à fait** yes, absolutely; **~ autant que** just as much as; **~ de suite** immediately, straight away

◇ *avec gérondif*: **il prenait sa douche ~ en chantant** he sang as he showered; **~ en acceptant ... je me permets de ...** while I accept that ... I would like to ...

◊: **tout ... que: tout pauvres qu'ils**

sont (*ou* **soient** (*subj*)) however poor they are, poor though they may be

4 *m*: **le tout** the whole lot, the lot, everything; (*le principal*) the main thing; **pas du ~** not at all; **plus du ~** no more; **du ~ au ~** totally; **en ~** in all

tout-à-l'égout [tutalegu] *m* mains drainage

toutefois [tutfwa] *adv* however

toute-puissance [tutpɥisɑ̃s] *f* omnipotence

toux [tu] *f* cough *m*

toxicomane [tɔksikɔman] *m/f* drug addict; **toxicomanie** *f* drug addiction

toxine [tɔksin] *f* toxin

toxique [tɔksik] **1** *adj* toxic **2** *m* poison

trac [trak] *m* nervousness; *pour un acteur* stage fright

traçabilité [trasabilite] *f* traceablility

tracas [traka] *m*: *des ~* worries; **tracasser** ⟨1a⟩: **~ qn** *d'une chose* worry s.o.; *d'une personne* pester s.o.; **se ~** worry; **tracasserie** *f*: **~s** hassle *sg*

trace [tras] *f* (*piste*) track, trail; (*marque*) mark; *fig* impression; **~s de sang, poison** traces; **des ~s de pas** footprints; **suivre les ~s de qn** *fig* follow in s.o.'s footsteps

tracé [trase] *m* (*plan*) layout; (*ligne*) line; *d'un dessin* drawing; **tracer** ⟨1k⟩ *plan, ligne* draw; **traceur** *m* INFORM plotter

trachée [traʃe] *f* windpipe, trachea

tractation [traktasjɔ̃] *f péj*: **~s** horse-trading *sg*

tracteur [traktœr] *m* tractor; **~ à chenilles** caterpillar tractor

traction [traksjɔ̃] *f* TECH traction; SP, *suspendu* pull-up; SP, *par terre* push-up; **~ avant** AUTO front wheel drive

tradition [tradisjɔ̃] *f* tradition; **traditionaliste** *m/f* & *adj* traditionalist; **traditionnel, ~le** traditional

traducteur, -trice [tradyktœr, -tris] *m/f* translator; **traduction** *f* translation; **~ automatique** machine translation; **traduire** ⟨4c⟩ translate (**en**

into); *fig* be indicative of; **~ qn en justice** JUR take s.o. to court, prosecute s.o.; **se ~ par** result in

trafic [trafik] *m* traffic; **~ aérien** air traffic; **~ de drogues** drugs traffic; **trafiquant** *m* trafficker; **~ de drogue(s)** drug trafficker; **trafiquer** ⟨1m⟩ traffic in; *moteur* tinker with

tragédie [traʒedi] *f* tragedy (*aussi fig*); **tragique** 1 *adj* tragic 2 *m* tragedy

trahir [trair] ⟨2a⟩ betray; **trahison** *f* betrayal; *crime* treason

train [trɛ̃] *m* train; *fig: de lois, décrets* series *sg*; **le ~ de Paris** the Paris train; **être en ~ de faire qch** be doing sth; **aller bon ~** go at a good speed; **mener grand ~** live it up; **mettre en ~** set in motion; **aller son petit ~** jog along; **au ~ où vont les choses** at the rate things are going; **~ d'atterrissage** undercarriage, landing gear; **~ express** express; **~ à grande vitesse** high-speed train; **~ de vie** lifestyle

traînard [trenar] *m* dawdler; **traîne** *f*: **à la ~** in tow

traîneau [-o] *m* (*pl* -x) sledge; *pêche* seine net

traînée [trene] *f* trail

traîner [trene] ⟨1b⟩ 1 *v/t* drag; *d'un bateau, d'une voiture* pull, tow; **laisser ~ ses affaires** leave one's things lying around 2 *v/i* de *vêtements, livres* lie around; *d'un procès* drag on; **~ dans les rues** hang around street corners 3: **se ~** drag o.s. along

train-train [trɛ̃trɛ̃] *m* F: **le ~ quotidien** the daily routine

traire [trer] ⟨4s⟩ milk

trait [tre] *m* (*ligne*) line; *du visage* feature; *de caractère* trait; *d'une œuvre, époque* feature, characteristic; **avoir ~ à** be about, concern; **boire d'un seul ~** drink in a single gulp, F knock back; **~ d'esprit** witticism; **~ d'union** hyphen

traite [tret] *f* COMM draft, bill of exchange; *d'une vache* milking; **~ des noirs** slave trade; **d'une seule ~** in one go

traité [trete] *m* treaty

traitement [trɛtmɑ̃] *m* treatment (*aussi* MÉD); (*salaire*) pay; TECH, INFORM processing; **~ électronique des données** INFORM electronic data processing; **~ de l'information** data processing; **~ de texte** word processing; **traiter** ⟨1b⟩ *v/t* treat (*aussi* MÉD); TECH, INFORM process; **~ qn de menteur** call s.o. a liar 2 *v/i* (*négocier*) negotiate; **~ de qch** deal with sth

traiteur [tretœr] *m* caterer

traître, ~sse [trɛtrə, -ɛs] 1 *m/f* traitor 2 *adj* treacherous; **traîtrise** *f* treachery

trajectoire [traʒɛktwar] *f* path, trajectory

trajet [traʒɛ] *m* (*voyage*) journey; (*chemin*) way; **une heure de ~ à pied / en voiture** one hour on foot / by car

tram [tram] *m abr → **tramway**

trame [tram] *f fig: d'une histoire* background; *de la vie* fabric; *d'un tissu* weft; TV raster

trampoline [trɑ̃pɔlin] *m* trampoline

tramway [tramwe] *m* streetcar, *Br* tram

tranchant, ~e [trɑ̃ʃɑ̃, -t] 1 *adj* cutting 2 *m d'un couteau* cutting edge, sharp edge

tranche [trɑ̃ʃ] *f* (*morceau*) slice; (*bord*) edge; **~ d'âge** age bracket

tranché, ~e [trɑ̃ʃe] *fig* clear-cut; *couleur* definite

tranchée [trɑ̃ʃe] *f* trench

trancher [trɑ̃ʃe] ⟨1a⟩ 1 *v/t* cut; *fig* settle 2 *v/i*: **~ sur** stand out against

tranquille [trɑ̃kil] *adj* quiet; (*sans inquiétude*) easy in one's mind; **laisse-moi ~!** leave me alone!; **avoir la conscience ~** have a clear conscience; **tranquillement** *adv* quietly; **tranquillisant** *m* tranquillizer; **tranquilliser** ⟨1a⟩: **~ qn** set s.o.'s mind at rest; **tranquillité** *f* quietness, tranquillity; *du sommeil* peacefulness; (*stabilité morale*) peace of mind

transaction [trɑ̃zaksjɔ] *f* JUR compromise; COMM transaction

transatlantique [trɑ̃zatlɑ̃tik] 1 *adj* transatlantic 2 *m bateau* transatlantic liner; *chaise* deck chair

transcription [trãskripsjõ] *f* transcription; **transcrire** ⟨4f⟩ transcribe

transférer [trãsfere] ⟨1f⟩ transfer; **transfert** *m* transfer; PSYCH transference; **~ de données** data transfer

transfigurer [trãsfigyre] ⟨1a⟩ transfigure

transformateur [trãsfɔrmatœr] *m* ÉL transformer; **transformation** *f* transformation, change; TECH processing; *en rugby* conversion; **transformer** ⟨1a⟩ change, transform; TECH process; *maison, appartement* convert; *en rugby* convert; **~ en** turn *ou* change into

transfuge [trãsfyʒ] *m* defector

transfusion [trãsfyzjõ] *f*: **~ (sanguine)** (blood) transfusion

transgénique [trãsʒenik] genetically modified, transgenic

transgresser [trãsgrese] ⟨1b⟩ *loi* break, transgress

transi, ~e [trãzi] ~ **(de froid)** frozen

transiger [trãziʒe] ⟨1l⟩ come to a compromise (**avec** with)

transistor [trãzistɔr] *m* transistor

transit [trãzit] *m* transit; **en ~** in transit

transitif, -ive [trãzitif, -iv] GRAM transitive

transition [trãzisjõ] *f* transition; **transitoire** transitional; *(fugitif)* transitory

translucide [trãslysid] translucent

transmettre [trãsmetr] ⟨4p⟩ transmit; *message, talent* pass on; *maladie* pass on, transmit; *tradition, titre, héritage* hand down; **~ en direct** RAD, TV broadcast live; **transmissible: sexuellement ~** sexually transmitted; **transmission** *f* transmission; *d'un message* passing on; *d'une tradition, d'un titre* handing down; RAD, TV broadcast; **~ en direct / en différé** RAD, TV live / recorded broadcast

transparaître [trãsparetr] ⟨4z⟩ show through

transparence [trãsparãs] *f* transparency; **transparent, ~e** transparent *(aussi fig)*

transpercer [trãsperse] ⟨1k⟩ pierce; *de l'eau, de la pluie* go right through; **~ le cœur à qn** *fig* break s.o.'s heart

transpiration [trãspirasjõ] *f* perspiration; **transpirer** ⟨1a⟩ perspire

transplant [trãsplã] *m* transplant; **transplantation** *f* transplanting; MÉD transplant; **transplanter** ⟨1a⟩ transplant

transport [trãspɔr] *m* transport; **~s publics** mass transit, *Br* public transport *sg*

transportable [trãspɔrtabl] transportable; **transporté, ~e: ~ de joie** beside o.s. with joy; **transporter** ⟨1a⟩ transport, carry; **transporteur** *m* carrier

transposer [trãspoze] ⟨1a⟩ transpose; **transposition** *f* transposition

transvaser [trãsvaze] ⟨1a⟩ decant

transversal, ~e [trãsversal] *(mpl -aux)* cross *atr*

trapèze [trapez] *m* trapeze

trappe [trap] *f (ouverture)* trapdoor

trapu, ~e [trapy] stocky

traquenard [traknar] *m* trap

traquer [trake] ⟨1m⟩ hunt

traumatiser [tromatize] ⟨1a⟩ PSYCH traumatize; **traumatisme** *m* MÉD, PSYCH trauma

travail [travaj] *m (pl travaux)* work; **être sans ~** be out of work, be unemployed; **travaux pratiques** practical work *sg*; **travaux (construction)** construction work *sg*; **travaux ménagers** housework *sg*; **travailler** ⟨1a⟩ 1 *v/i* work; **~ à qch** work on sth 2 *v/t* work on; *d'une pensée, d'un problème* trouble; **travailleur, -euse** 1 *adj* hard-working 2 *m/f* worker; **travailliste** *m/f* member of the Labour Party

travers [traver] 1 *adv*: **de ~** squint, crooked; *marcher* not in a straight line, not straight; **en ~** across; **prendre qch de ~** *fig* take sth the wrong way 2 *prép*: **à ~ qch, au ~ de qch** through sth; **à ~ champs** cross country 3 *m* shortcoming

traversée [traverse] *f* crossing; **traverser** ⟨1a⟩ *rue, mer* cross; *forêt, crise* go through; (*percer*) go right through

travesti, **~e** [travesti] **1** adj pour fête fancy-dress **2** m (*déguisement*) fancy dress; (*homosexuel*) transvestite; **travestir** [travestir] ⟨2a⟩ *vérité* distort; **se ~** dress up (**en** as a)

trébucher [trebyʃe] ⟨1a⟩ trip, stumble (**sur** over)

trèfle [trefl] m BOT clover; *aux cartes* clubs *pl*

treillage [treja3] m trellis; **~ métallique** wire mesh

treize [trez] thirteen; → **trois**; **treizième** thirteenth

tremblant, **~e** [trɑ̃blɑ̃, -t] trembling, quivering; **tremblement** m trembling; **~ de terre** earthquake; **trembler** ⟨1a⟩ tremble, shake (**de** with); *de la terre* shake

trémousser [tremuse] ⟨1a⟩: **se ~** wriggle

trempe [trɑ̃p] f *fig* caliber, *Br* calibre; **trempé**, **~e** soaked; *sol* saturated; **tremper** ⟨1a⟩ soak; *pain dans café etc* dunk; *pied dans l'eau* dip; *acier* harden; **~ dans** *fig* be involved in

tremplin [trɑ̃plɛ̃] m springboard; *pour ski* ski jump; *fig* stepping stone, launchpad

trentaine [trɑ̃ten] f: **une ~ de personnes** about thirty people *pl*, thirty or so people *pl*; **trente** thirty; → **trois**; **trentième** thirtieth

trépied [trepje] m tripod

trépigner [trepiɲe] ⟨1a⟩ stamp (one's feet)

très [tre] adv very; **~ lu / visité** much read / visited; **avoir ~ envie de qch** really feel like sth

trésor [trezɔr] m treasure; **des ~s de ...** endless ...; **Trésor** Treasury; **trésorerie** f treasury; *service* accounts *sg ou pl*; (*fonds*) finances *pl*; **des problèmes de ~** cashflow problems; **trésorier**, **-ère** m/f treasurer

tressaillement [tresajmɑ̃] m jump; **tressaillir** ⟨2c, *futur* 2a⟩ jump

tresse [tres] f de *cheveux* braid, *Br* plait; **tresser** ⟨1b⟩ *cheveux* braid, *Br* plait; *corbeille, câbles* weave

tréteau [treto] m (*pl* -x) TECH trestle

treuil [trœj] m TECH winch

trêve [trev] f truce; **~ de ...** that's enough ...; **sans ~** without respite

tri [tri] m *aussi* de *données* sort; **faire un ~ dans qch** sort sth out; **le ~ des déchets** waste separation

triangle [trijɑ̃gl] m triangle; **triangulaire** triangular

tribal, **~e** [tribal] (*mpl* -aux) tribal

tribord [tribɔr] m MAR starboard

tribu [triby] f tribe

tribulations [tribylasjɔ̃] *fpl* tribulations

tribunal [tribynal] m (*pl* -aux) court

tribune [tribyn] f platform (*aussi fig*); (*débat*) discussion; **à la ~ aujourd'hui ...** today's topic for discussion ...; **~s dans stade** bleachers, *Br* stands

tributaire [tribyter]: **être ~ de** be dependent on; **cours d'eau ~** tributary

tricher [triʃe] cheat; **tricherie** f cheating; **tricheur**, **-euse** m/f cheat

tricolore [trikɔlɔr]: **drapeau** m **~** tricolor *ou Br* tricolour (flag)

tricot [triko] m knitting; *vêtement* sweater; **de** *ou* **en ~** knitted; **tricotage** m knitting; **tricoter** ⟨1a⟩ knit

tricycle [trisikl] m tricycle

triennal, **~e** [trijenal] (*mpl* -aux) *qui a lieu tous les trois ans* three-yearly; *qui dure trois ans* three-year

trier [trije] ⟨1a⟩ (*choisir*) pick through; (*classer*) sort

trilingue [trilɛ̃g] trilingual

trille [trij] m MUS trill

trimballer [trɛ̃bale] ⟨1a⟩ F hump F, lug

trimer [trime] ⟨1a⟩ F work like a dog F

trimestre [trimestr] m quarter; ÉDU trimester, *Br* term; **trimestriel**, **~le** quarterly; ÉDU term *atr*

trinquer [trɛ̃ke] ⟨1m⟩ (*porter un toast*) clink glasses (**avec qn** with s.o.); **~ à** *fig* F toast, drink to

triomphe [trijɔ̃f] m triumph; **triompher** ⟨1a⟩ triumph (**de** over)

tripartite [tripartit] tripartite

tripes [trip] *fpl* guts; CUIS tripe *sg*

triple [tripl] triple; **tripler** ⟨1a⟩ triple; **triplés**, **-ées** *mpl, fpl* triplets

tripoter [tripɔte] ⟨1a⟩ F **1** v/t objet play around with; femme grope, feel up **2** v/i: **~ dans** (prendre part à) be involved in; (toucher) play around with

triste [trist] sad; temps, paysage dreary; **dans un ~ état** in a sorry state; **tristesse** f sadness

trivial, **~e** [trivjal] (mpl -aux) vulgar; litt (banal) trite; **trivialité** f vulgarity; litt triteness; expression vulgarism

troc [trɔk] m barter

trognon [trɔɲõ] m d'un fruit core; d'un chou stump

trois [trwa] **1** adj three; **le ~ mai** May third, Br the third of May **2** m three; **troisième** third; **troisièmement** thirdly

trombe [trɔ̃b] f: **des ~s d'eau** sheets of water; **en ~** fig at top speed

trombone [trɔ̃bɔn] m MUS trombone; pour papiers paper clip

trompe [trɔ̃p] f MUS horn; d'un éléphant trunk

tromper [trɔ̃pe] ⟨1a⟩ deceive; époux, épouse be unfaithful to; confiance abuse; **se ~** be mistaken, make a mistake; **se ~ de numéro / jour** get the wrong number / day; **tromperie** f deception

trompette [trɔ̃pɛt] **1** f trumpet **2** m trumpet player, trumpeter

trompeur, **-euse** [trɔ̃pœr, -øz] deceptive; (traître) deceitful

tronc [trɔ̃] m BOT, ANAT trunk; à l'église collection box

tronçon [trɔ̃sõ] m section

trône [tron] m throne

trop [tro, liaison: trop ou trɔp] adv avec verbe too much; devant adjectif ou adverbe too; **~ de lait / gens** too much milk / too many people; **un verre de ou en ~** one glass too many; **être de ~** be in the way, be de trop

trophée [trɔfe] m trophy

tropical, **~e** [trɔpikal] (mpl -aux) tropical; **tropique** m GÉOGR tropic; **les Tropiques** the Tropics

trop-plein [troplɛ̃] m (pl trop-pleins) overflow

troquer [trɔke] ⟨1m⟩ exchange, swap (contre for)

trot [tro] m trot; **aller au ~** trot; **trotter** ⟨1a⟩ d'un cheval trot; d'une personne run around; **trotteuse** f second hand; **trottiner** ⟨1a⟩ scamper; **trottinette** f scooter

trottoir [trɔtwar] m sidewalk, Br pavement; **faire le ~** F be on the streets, be a streetwalker

trou [tru] m (pl -s) hole; **j'ai un ~** my mind's a blank; **~ de mémoire** lapse of memory

troublant, **~e** [trublɑ̃, -t] disturbing; **trouble 1** adj eau, liquide cloudy; fig: explication unclear; situation murky **2** m (désarroi) trouble; (émoi) excitement; MÉD disorder; silence, sommeil unrest sg; **trouble-fête** m (pl inv) spoilsport, party-pooper F; **troubler** ⟨1a⟩ liquide make cloudy; silence, sommeil disturb; réunion disrupt; (inquiéter) bother, trouble; **~ l'ordre public** cause a disturbance; **se ~** d'un liquide become cloudy; d'une personne get flustered

troué, **~e** [true]: **avoir des semelles ~es** have holes in one's shoes; **trouée** f gap; **trouer** ⟨1a⟩ make a hole in

trouille [truj] f F: **avoir la ~** be scared witless

troupe [trup] f troop; de comédiens troupe

troupeau [trupo] m (pl -x) de vaches herd; de moutons flock (aussi fig)

trousse [trus] f kit; **être aux ~s de qn** fig be on s.o.'s heels; **~ d'écolier** pencil case; **~ de toilette** toilet bag

trousseau [truso] m (pl -x) d'une mariée trousseau; **~ de clés** bunch of keys

trouvaille [truvaj] f (découverte) find; (idée) bright idea; **trouver** ⟨1a⟩ find; plan come up with; (rencontrer) meet; aller **~ qn** go and see s.o.; **~ que** think that; **je la trouve sympathique** I think she's nice; **se ~** (être) be; **se ~ bien** be well; **il se trouve que** it turns out that

truand [tryɑ̃] m crook

truc [tryk] m F (chose) thing, thingamajig F; (astuce) trick

trucage → **truquage**

truchement [tryʃmɑ̃] m: **par le ~ de** through

truelle [tryɛl] f trowel

truffe [tryf] f BOT truffle; d'un chien nose; **truffé, ~e** with truffles; **~ de** fig: citations peppered with

truie [tryi] f sow

truite [tryit] f trout

truquage [tryka3] m dans film special effect; d'une photographie faking; **truquer** ⟨1m⟩ élections, cartes rig

T.S.V.P. abr (= **tournez s'il-vous-plaît**) PTO (= please turn over)

tu [ty] you

tuant, ~e [tyɑ̃, -t] F exhausting, Br knackering F

tuba [tyba] m snorkel; MUS tuba

tube [tyb] m tube; F (chanson) hit; **~ digestif** ANAT digestive tract

tuberculose [tyberkyloz] f MÉD tuberculosis, TB

tubulaire [tybyler] tubular

tuer [tye] ⟨1n⟩ kill; fig (épuiser) exhaust; (peiner) bother; **se ~** (se suicider) kill o.s.; (trouver la mort) be killed; **tuerie** f killing, slaughter

tue-tête [tytɛt]: **à ~** at the top of one's voice

tueur [tyœr] m killer; **~ à gages** hired assassin, hitman

tuile [tyil] f tile; fig F bit of bad luck

tulipe [tylip] f tulip

tuméfié, ~e [tymefje] swollen

tumeur [tymœr] f MÉD tumor, Br tumour

tumulte [tymylt] m uproar; fig (activité excessive) hustle and bustle; **tumultueux, -euse** noisy; passion tumultuous, stormy

tungstène [tɛ̃ksten, tœ̃-] m tungsten

tunique [tynik] f tunic

Tunisie [tynizi]: **la ~** Tunisia; **tuni-**sien, **~ne 1** adj Tunisian **2** m/f Tunisien, **~ne** Tunisian

tunnel [tynɛl] m tunnel

turbine [tyrbin] f TECH turbine; **turbiner** ⟨1a⟩ P slave away

turbo-moteur [tyrbɔmɔtœr] m turbomotor

turbo-réacteur [tyrbɔreaktœr] m AVIAT turbojet

turbulence [tyrbylɑ̃s] f turbulence; d'un élève unruliness; **turbulent, ~e** turbulent; élève unruly

turc, turque [tyrk] **1** adj Turkish **2** langue Turkish **3** m/f Turc, Turque Turk

turf [tœrf, tyrf] m SP horseracing; terrain racecourse

Turquie [tyrki]: **la ~** Turkey

turquoise [tyrkwaz] f turquoise

tutelle [tytɛl] f JUR guardianship; d'un état, d'une société supervision, control; fig protection; **tuteur, -trice 1** m/f JUR guardian **2** m BOT stake

tutoyer [tytwaje] ⟨1h⟩ address as 'tu'

tuyau [tɥijo] m (pl -x) pipe; flexible hose; F (information) tip; **~ d'arrosage** garden hose; **~ d'échappement** exhaust pipe; **tuyauter** ⟨1a⟩ F: **~ qn** tip s.o. off

T.V.A. [tevea] f abr (= **taxe sur ou à la valeur ajoutée**) sales tax, Br VAT (= value added tax)

tympan [tɛ̃pɑ̃] m ANAT eardrum

type [tip] m type; F (gars) guy F; **un chic ~** a great guy; **contrat** m **~** standard contract

typhoïde [tifɔid] f typhoid

typhon [tifɔ̃] m typhoon

typique [tipik] typical (**de** of); **typiquement** adv typically

tyran [tirɑ̃] m tyrant (aussi fig); **tyrannie** f tyranny (aussi fig); **tyrannique** tyrannical; **tyranniser** ⟨1a⟩ tyrannize; petit frère etc bully

U

U.E. [yə] *f abr* (= ***Union européenne***) EU (= European Union)

ulcère [ylsɛr] *m* MÉD ulcer; **ulcérer** ⟨1f⟩ *fig* aggrieve

ultérieur, ~e [ylterjœr] later, subsequent; **ultérieurement** *adv* later, subsequently

ultimatum [yltimatɔm] *m* ultimatum

ultime [yltim] last

ultra-conservateur, -trice [yltrakõsɛrvatœr, -tris] ultra-conservative

ultrason [yltrasõ] *m* PHYS ultrasound

ultraviolet, ~te [yltravjɔlɛ, -t] **1** *adj* ultraviolet **2** *m* ultraviolet

un, une [ɛ̃ *ou* œ̃, yn] *article* ◇ a; *devant voyelle* an; **un tigre / un éléphant** a tiger / an elephant; **un utilisateur** a user; **pas un seul ...** not a single ..., not one single ...

◇ *pron* one; **le un** one; **un à un** one by one; **un sur trois** one in three; **à la une** *dans journal* on the front page; **faire la une** make the headlines; **l'un / l'une des touristes** one of the tourists; **les uns avaient ...** some (of them) had ...; **elles s'aident les unes les autres** they help each other *ou* one another; **l'un et l'autre** both of them; **l'un après l'autre** one after the other, in turn

◇ *chiffre* one; **à une heure** at one o'clock

unanime [ynanim] unanimous; **unanimité** *f* unanimity; **à l'~** unanimously

uni, ~e [yni] *pays* united; *surface* even, smooth; *tissu* solid(-colored), *Br* self-coloured; *famille* close-knit

unification [ynifikasjõ] *f* unification; **unifier** ⟨1a⟩ unite, unify

uniforme [ynifɔrm] **1** *adj* uniform; *existence* unchanging **2** *m* uniform; **uniformiser** ⟨1a⟩ standardize; **uniformité** *f* uniformity

unilatéral, ~e [ynilateral] (*mpl* -aux) unilateral

union [ynjõ] *f* union; (*cohésion*) unity; **Union européenne** European Union; **l'Union soviétique** HIST the Soviet Union; **~ (conjugale)** marriage

unique [ynik] (*seul*) single; *fils* only; (*extraordinaire*) unique; **uniquement** *adv* only

unir [ynir] ⟨2a⟩ POL unite; *par moyen de communication* link; *couple* join in marriage, marry; **~ la beauté à l'intelligence** combine beauty with intelligence; **s'~** unite; (*se marier*) marry

unitaire [yniter] unitary; *prix* unit *atr*

unité [ynite] *f* unit; **~ centrale** INFORM central processing unit, CPU; **~ de commande** control unit

univers [yniver] *m* universe; *fig* world; **universel, ~le** universal

universitaire [yniversiter] **1** *adj* university *atr* **2** *m/f* academic; **université** *f* university

Untel [ɛ̃tɛl, œ̃-]: **monsieur ~** Mr So-and-So

uranium [yranjɔm] *m* CHIM uranium

urbain, ~e [yrbɛ̃, -ɛn] urban; **urbaniser** ⟨1a⟩ urbanize; **urbanisme** *m* town planning; **urbaniste** *m* town planner

urgence [yrʒɑ̃s] *f* urgency; **une ~** an emergency; **d'~** emergency *atr*; **état** *m* **d'~** state of emergency; **urgent, ~e** urgent

urine [yrin] *f* urine; **uriner** ⟨1a⟩ urinate

urne [yrn] *f*: **aller aux ~s** go to the polls

usage [yzaʒ] *m* use; (*coutume*) custom, practice; *linguistique* usage; **hors d'~** out of use; **à l'~** with use; **à l'~ de qn** for use by s.o.; **faire ~**

U

de use; *d'~* customary; usagé, *~e vêtements* worn; usager *m* user
usé, *~e* [yze] worn; *vêtement* worn-
out; *pneu* worn, threadbare; *personne*
worn-out, exhausted; *eaux ~es*
waste water *sg*; user ⟨1a⟩ *du gaz,
de l'eau* consume; *vêtement* wear
out; *yeux* ruin; ~ *qn* wear s.o. out, exhaust s.o.; *s'~* wear out; *personne*
wear o.s. out, exhaust o.s.; ~ *de
qch* use sth
usine [yzin] *f* plant, factory; ~ *d'automobiles* car plant; ~ *de retraite-
ment* reprocessing plant; usiner
⟨1a⟩ machine
usité, *~e* [yzite] *mot* common

ustensile [ystɑ̃sil] *m* tool; ~ *de cuisine* kitchen utensil
usuel, *~le* [yzɥɛl] usual; *expression*
common
usure [yzyr] *f* (*détérioration*) wear; *du
sol* erosion
utérus [yterys] *m* ANAT womb, uterus
utile [ytil] useful; *en temps* ~ in due
course
utilisable [ytilizabl] usable; utilisateur, -trice *m/f* user; ~ *final* end user;
utilisation *f* use; utiliser ⟨1a⟩ use
utilitaire [ytiliter] utilitarian
utilité [ytilite] *f* usefulness, utility; *ça
n'a aucune* ~ it's (of) no use whatever

V

v. *abr* (= *voir*) see
vacance [vakɑ̃s] *f poste* opening, *Br*
vacancy; *~s* vacation *sg*, *Br* holi-
day(s); *prendre des ~s* take a vacation; *en ~s* on vacation; vacancier,
-ère *m/f* vacationer, *Br* holiday-
maker; vacant, *~e* vacant
vacarme [vakarm] *m* din, racket
vaccin [vaksɛ̃] *m* MÉD vaccine; vaccination *f* MÉD vaccination; vacciner
⟨1a⟩ vaccinate (*contre* against)
vache [vaʃ] 1 *f* cow; *cuir* cowhide; ~ *à
lait fig* milch cow; *la ~!* F Christ! F
2 *adj* F mean, rotten F; vachement
adv F *bon, content* damn F, *Br aussi*
bloody F; *changer, vieillir* one helluva
lot F
vaciller [vasije] ⟨1a⟩ *sur ses jambes*
sway; *d'une flamme, de la lumière*
flicker; (*hésiter*) vacillate
vadrouiller [vadruje] ⟨1a⟩ F roam
about
va-et-vient [vaevjɛ̃] *m* (*pl inv*) *d'une
pièce mobile* backward and forward
motion; *d'une personne* toing-and-
-froing

vagabond, *~e* [vagabɔ̃, -d] 1 *adj* wandering 2 *m/f* hobo, *Br* tramp; vaga-
bondage *m* wandering; JUR va-
grancy; vagabonder ⟨1a⟩ wander
(*aussi fig*)
vagin [vaʒɛ̃] *m* vagina
vague¹ [vag] *f* wave (*aussi fig*); ~ *de
chaleur* heatwave; ~ *de froid* cold
snap
vague² [vag] 1 *adj* vague; *regard* far-
away; *un* ~ *magazine péj* some magazine or other; *terrain m* ~ waste
ground 2 *m* vagueness; *regarder
dans le* ~ stare into the middle distance; *laisser qch dans le* ~ leave
sth vague; vaguement *adv* vaguely
vaillant, *~e* [vajɑ̃, -t] brave, valiant; *se
sentir* ~ feel fit and well
vaille [vaj] *subj de valoir*, ~ *que* ~
come what may
vain, *~e* [vɛ̃, vɛn] vain; *mots* empty; *en*
~ in vain
vaincre [vɛ̃kr] ⟨4i⟩ conquer; SP defeat;
fig: angoisse overcome, conquer; *obstacle* overcome; vaincu, *~e* 1 *p/p* →
vaincre 2 *adj* conquered; SP de-

veau

feated; **s'avouer** ~ admit defeat **3** *m* loser; **l'armée des ~s** the defeated army

vainement [vɛnmɑ̃] *adv* in vain, vainly

vainqueur [vɛ̃kœr] *m* winner, victor

vaisseau [vɛso] *m* (*pl* -x) ANAT, *litt* (*bateau*) vessel; ~ **sanguin** blood vessel; ~ **spatial** spaceship

vaisselle [vɛsɛl] *f* dishes *pl*; **laver** *ou* **faire la** ~ do *ou* wash the dishes, *Br aussi* do the washing-up

val [val] *m* (*pl* vaux [vo] *ou* vals) *litt* valley

valable [valabl] valid

valet [valɛ] *m* cartes jack, knave

valeur [valœr] *f* value, worth; *d'une personne* worth; ~**s** COMM securities; ~ **ajoutée** added value; **sans** ~ worthless; **mettre en** ~ emphasize, highlight; **avoir de la** ~ be valuable

validation [validasjɔ̃] *f* validation; **valide** (*sain*) fit; *passeport, ticket* valid; **valider** ⟨1a⟩ validate; *ticket* stamp; **validité** *f* validity

valise [valiz] *f* bag, suitcase; **faire sa** ~ pack one's bags

vallée [vale] *f* valley

vallon [valɔ̃] *m* (small) valley; **vallonné, ~e** hilly

valoir [valwar] ⟨3h⟩ **1** *v/i* be worth; (*coûter*) cost; **ça ne vaut rien** (*c'est médiocre*) it's no good, it's worthless; ~ **pour** apply to; ~ **mieux** be better (*que* than); **il vaut mieux attendre** it's better to wait (*que de faire qch* than to do sth); **il vaut mieux que je ...** (+ *subj*) it's better for me to...; **ça vaut le coup** F it's worth it; **faire** ~ *droits* assert; *capital* make work; (*mettre en valeur*) emphasize **2** *v/t*: ~ **qch à qn** earn s.o. sth; **à** ~ **sur** *d'un montant* to be offset against **3**: **se** ~ be alike

valoriser [valɔrize] ⟨1a⟩ enhance the value of; *personne* enhance the image of

valse [vals] *f* waltz; **valser** ⟨1a⟩ waltz

valve [valv] *f* TECH valve

vampire [vɑ̃pir] *m* vampire; *fig* bloodsucker

vandale [vɑ̃dal] *m/f* vandal; **vandali-**

ser ⟨1a⟩ vandalize; **vandalisme** *m* vandalism

vanille [vanij] *f* vanilla

vanité [vanite] *f* (*fatuité*) vanity, conceit; (*inutilité*) futility; **vaniteux, -euse** vain, conceited

vanne [van] *f* sluice gate; F dig F

vannerie [vanri] *f* wickerwork

vantard, ~e [vɑ̃tar, -d] **1** *adj* bragging, boastful **2** *m/f* bragger, boaster; **vantardise** *f* bragging, boasting

vanter [vɑ̃te] ⟨1a⟩ praise; **se** ~ brag, boast; **se** ~ **de qch** pride o.s. on sth

vapeur [vapœr] *f* vapor, *Br* vapour; ~ (*d'eau*) steam; **cuire à la** ~ steam; **à** ~ *locomotive* steam *atr*

vaporeux, -euse [vapɔrø, -z] *paysage* misty; *tissu* filmy; **vaporisateur** *m* spray; **vaporiser** ⟨1a⟩ spray

varappe [varap] *f* rock-climbing; **mur de** ~ climbing wall; **varappeur, -euse** *m/f* rock-climber

variabilité [varjabilite] *f* variability; *du temps, d'humeur* changeability; **variable** variable; *temps, humeur* changeable; **variante** *f* variant; **variation** *f* (*changement*) change; (*écart*) variation

varice [varis] *f* ANAT varicose vein

varicelle [varisɛl] *f* MÉD chickenpox

varié, ~e [varje] varied; **varier** ⟨1a⟩ vary; **variété** *f* variety; ~**s** spectacle vaudeville *sg*, *Br* variety show *sg*

variole [varjɔl] *f* MÉD smallpox

Varsovie [varsɔvi] Warsaw

vase[1] [vaz] *m* vase

vase[2] [vaz] *f* mud

vasectomie [vazɛktɔmi] *f* vasectomy

vaseux, -euse [vazø, -z] muddy; F (*nauséeux*) under the weather; F *explication, raisonnement* muddled

vasistas [vazistas] *m* fanlight

vau-l'eau [volo]: (**s'en**) **aller à** ~ go to rack and ruin

vaurien, ~ne [vorjɛ̃, -ɛn] *m/f* good-for-nothing

vautour [votur] *m* vulture (*aussi fig*)

vautrer [votre] ⟨1a⟩: **se** ~ sprawl (out); *dans la boue* wallow

veau [vo] *m* (*pl* -x) calf; *viande* veal; *cuir* calfskin

V

vedette [vədɛt] *f au théâtre, d'un film* star; (*bateau*) launch; **en ~** in the headlines; **mettre en ~** highlight; **match** *m* ~ big game

végétal, ~e [veʒetal] (*mpl* -aux) **1** *adj* plant *atr; huile* vegetable **2** *m* plant; **végétalien, ~ne** *m/f & adj* vegan

végétarien, ~ne [veʒetarjɛ̃, -ɛn] *m/f & adj* vegetarian

végétation [veʒetasjɔ̃] *f* vegetation; **végéter** ⟨1f⟩ vegetate

véhémence [veemɑ̃s] *f* vehemence; **véhément, ~e** vehement

véhicule [veikyl] *m* vehicle (*aussi fig*)

veille [vɛj] *f* previous day; *absence de sommeil* wakefulness; **la ~ au soir** the previous evening; **la ~ de Noël** Christmas Eve; **à la ~ de** on the eve of; **veillée** *f d'un malade* night nursing; (*soirée*) evening; *vigil*; **veiller** ⟨1b⟩ stay up late; **~ à qch** see to sth; **~ à ce que tout soit** (*subj*) **prêt** see to it that everything is ready; **~ à faire qch** see to it that sth is done; **~ sur qn** watch over s.o.; **veilleuse** *f* (*flamme*) pilot light; AUTO sidelight; **mettre en ~ flamme** turn down low; *fig*: *affaire* put on the back burner; **en ~** IN-FORM on standby

veinard, ~e [vɛnar, -d] *m/f* F lucky devil F; **veine** *f* vein; F luck; **avoir de la ~** be lucky

véliplanchiste [veliplɑ̃ʃist] *m/f* windsurfer

vélo [velo] *m* bike; **faire du ~** go cycling; **~ tout-terrain** mountain bike

vélocité [velɔsite] *f* speed; TECH velocity

vélodrome [velɔdrom] *m* velodrome

vélomoteur [velɔmɔtœr] *m* moped

velours [v(ə)lur] *m* velvet; **~ côtelé** corduroy

velouté, ~e [vəlute] velvety; (*soupe*) smooth, creamy

velu, ~e [vəly] hairy

venaison [vənɛzɔ̃] *f* venison

vendable [vɑ̃dabl] saleable

vendange [vɑ̃dɑ̃ʒ] *f* grape harvest; **vendanger** ⟨1l⟩ bring in the grape harvest

vendeur [vɑ̃dœr] *m* sales clerk, *Br* shop assistant; **vendeuse** *f* sales clerk, *Br* shop assistant; **vendre** ⟨4a⟩ sell; *fig* betray; **à ~** for sale; **se ~** sell out

vendredi [vɑ̃drədi] *m* Friday; **Vendredi saint** Good Friday

vendu, ~e [vɑ̃dy] **1** *p/p* → **vendre 2** *adj* sold **3** *m/f péj* traitor

vénéneux, -euse [venenø, -z] *plantes* poisonous

vénérable [venerabl] venerable; **vénération** *f* veneration; **vénérer** ⟨1f⟩ revere

vénérien, ~ne [venerjɛ̃, -ɛn]: **maladie** *f* **~ne** venereal disease

vengeance [vɑ̃ʒɑ̃s] *f* vengeance; **venger** [vɑ̃ʒe] ⟨1l⟩ avenge (*qn de qch* s.o. for sth); **se ~ de qn** get one's revenge on s.o.; **se ~ de qch sur qn** get one's revenge for sth on s.o.; **ne te venge pas de son erreur sur moi** don't take his mistake out on me; **vengeur, -eresse 1** *adj* vengeful **2** *m/f* avenger

venimeux, -euse [vənimø, -z] *serpent* poisonous; *fig aussi* full of venom

venin [v(ə)nɛ̃] *m* venom (*aussi fig*)

venir [v(ə)nir] ⟨2h⟩ (*aux être*) come; **à ~** to come; **j'y viens** I'm coming to that; **en ~ à croire que** come to believe that; **en ~ aux mains** come to blows; **où veut-il en ~?** what's he getting at?; **~ de** come from; **je viens / je venais de faire la vaisselle** I have / I had just washed the dishes; **~ chercher**, **~ prendre** come for; **faire ~** *médecin* send for

Venise [vəniz] Venice

vent [vɑ̃] *m* wind; **être dans le ~** *fig* be modern; **c'est du ~** *fig* it's all hot air; **coup** *m* **de ~** gust of wind; **il y a du ~** it's windy; **avoir ~ de qch** *fig* get wind of sth

vente [vɑ̃t] *f* sale; *activité* selling; **être dans la ~** be in sales; **~ à crédit** installment plan, *Br* hire purchase

venteux, -euse [vɑ̃tø, -z] windy

ventilateur [vɑ̃tilatœr] *m* ventilator; *électrique* fan; **ventilation** *f* ventilation; **ventiler** ⟨1a⟩ *pièce* air; *montant* break down

ventre [vãtr] *m* stomach, belly F; *à plat* ~ flat on one's stomach; ~ *à bière* beer belly, beer gut

ventriloque [vãtrilɔk] *m* ventriloquist

venu, ~e [v(ə)ny] **1** *adj*: *bien / mal ~ action* appropriate / inappropriate **2** *m/f*: *le premier ~, la première ~e* the first to arrive; (*n'importe qui*) anybody; *nouveau ~, nouvelle ~e* newcomer

venue [v(ə)ny] *f* arrival, advent

ver [vɛr] *m* worm; ~ *de terre* earthworm; ~ *à soie* silkworm

véracité [verasite] *f* truthfulness, veracity

verbal, ~e [vɛrbal] (*mpl* -aux) verbal; **verbaliser** ⟨1a⟩ **1** *v/i* JUR bring a charge **2** *v/t* (*exprimer*) verbalize

verbe [vɛrb] *m* LING verb

verdâtre [vɛrdɑtr] greenish

verdict [vɛrdikt] *m* verdict

verdir [vɛrdir] ⟨2a⟩ turn green

verdure [vɛrdyr] *f* (*feuillages*) greenery; (*salade*) greens *pl*

verge [vɛrʒ] *f* ANAT penis; (*baguette*) rod

verger [vɛrʒe] *m* orchard

verglacé, ~e [vɛrglase] icy; **verglas** *m* black ice

vergogne [vɛrgɔɲ] *f*: *sans* ~ shameless; *avec verbe* shamelessly

véridique [veridik] truthful

vérifiable [verifjabl] verifiable, which can be checked; **vérification** *f* check; **vérifier** ⟨1a⟩ check; *se* ~ turn out to be true

vérin [verɛ̃] *m* jack

véritable [veritabl] real; *amour* true; **véritablement** *adv* really

vérité [verite] *f* truth; *en* ~ actually; *à la* ~ to tell the truth

vermeil, ~le [vɛrmɛj] bright red, vermillion

vermine [vɛrmin] *f* vermin

vermoulu, ~e [vɛrmuly] worm-eaten

vermouth [vɛrmut] *m* vermouth

verni, ~e [vɛrni] varnished; F lucky; **vernir** ⟨2a⟩ varnish; *céramique* glaze; **vernis** *m* varnish; *de céramique* glaze; ~ *à ongle* nail polish, Br *aussi* nail

varnish; **vernissage** *m du bois* varnishing; *de la céramique* glazing; (*exposition*) private view

vérole [verɔl] *f* MÉD F syphilis; *petite* ~ smallpox

verre [vɛr] *m* glass; *prendre un* ~ have a drink; *~s de contact* contact lenses, contacts F; ~ *dépoli* frosted glass; ~ *à eau* tumbler, water glass; ~ *à vin* wine glass; **verrerie** *f* glass-making; *fabrique* glassworks *sg*; *objets* glassware; **verrière** *f* (*vitrail*) stained--glass window; *toit* glass roof; **verroterie** *f* glass jewelry *ou* Br jewellery

verrou [veru] *m* (*pl* -s) bolt; *sous les* ~s F behind bars; **verrouillage** *m*: ~ *central* AUTO central locking; **verrouiller** ⟨1a⟩ bolt; F lock up, put behind bars

verrue [very] *f* wart

vers[1] [vɛr] *m* verse

vers[2] [vɛr] *prép* toward, Br towards; (*environ*) around, about

versant [vɛrsã] *m* slope

versatile [vɛrsatil] changeable; **versatilité** *f* changeability

verse [vɛrs]: *il pleut à* ~ it's pouring down, it's bucketing down

Verseau [vɛrso] *m* ASTROL Aquarius

versement [vɛrsəmã] *m* payment

verser [vɛrse] **1** *v/t* pour (out); *sang, larmes* shed; *argent à un compte* pay in, deposit; *intérêts, pension* pay; ~ *à boire à qn* pour s.o. a drink **2** *v/i* (*basculer*) overturn; ~ *dans qch fig* succumb to sth

verset [vɛrsɛ] *m* verse

version [vɛrsjõ] *f* version; (*traduction*) translation; (*film m en*) ~ *originale* original language version

verso [vɛrso] *m d'une feuille* back; *au* ~ on the back, on the other side

vert, ~e [vɛr, -t] **1** *adj* green; *fruit* unripe; *vin* too young; *fig: personne âgée* spry; *propos* risqué; *l'Europe f ~e* AGR European agriculture **2** *m* green; *les ~s* POL *mpl* the Greens

vertébral, ~e [vertebral] (*mpl* -aux) ANAT vertebral; *colonne f ~e* spine, spinal column; **vertèbre** *f* ANAT vertebra; **vertébrés** *mpl* vertebrates

vertement [vɛrtəmɑ̃] *adv* severely

vertical, **~e** [vɛrtikal] (*mpl* -aux) **1** *adj* vertical **2** *f* vertical (line); **verticalement** *adv* vertically

vertige [vɛrtiʒ] *m* vertigo, dizziness; *fig* giddiness; **un ~** a dizzy spell; *j'ai le ~* I feel dizzy; *des sommes qui donnent le ~* mind-blowing sums of money; **vertigineux**, **-euse** *hauteurs* dizzy; *vitesse* breathtaking

vertu [vɛrty] *f* virtue; (*pouvoir*) property; *en ~ de* in accordance with; **vertueux**, **-euse** virtuous

verve [vɛrv] *f* wit; *plein de ~* witty

vésicule [vezikyl] *f* ANAT: *~ biliaire* gall bladder

vessie [vesi] *f* ANAT bladder

veste [vɛst] *f* jacket; *retourner sa ~* F be a turncoat; *ramasser une ~* F suffer a defeat

vestiaire [vɛstjɛr] *m de théâtre* checkroom, *Br* cloakroom; *d'un stade* locker room

vestibule [vɛstibyl] *m* hall

vestige [vɛstiʒ] *m le plus souvent au pl*: *~s* traces, remnants

veston [vɛstɔ̃] *m* jacket, coat

vêtement [vɛtmɑ̃] *m* item of clothing, garment; *~s* clothes; (*industrie f du*) *~* clothing industry, rag trade F

vétéran [veterɑ̃] *m* veteran

vétérinaire [veteriner] **1** *adj* veterinary **2** *m/f* veterinarian, vet

vétille [vetij] *f* (*souvent au pl ~s*) trifle, triviality

vêtir [vetir] ⟨2g⟩ *litt* dress

veto [veto] *m* veto; *droit m de ~* right of veto; *opposer son ~ à* veto

vêtu, **~e** [vety] dressed

vexant, **~e** [vɛksɑ̃, -t] humiliating, mortifying; *c'est ~ contrariant* that's really annoying; **vexation** *f* humiliation, mortification; **vexer** ⟨1a⟩ *~ qn* hurt s.o.'s feelings; *se ~* get upset

viabilité [vjabilite] *f d'un projet*, BIOL viability; **viable** *projet*, BIOL viable

viaduc [vjadyk] *m* viaduct

viager, **-ère** [vjaʒe, -ɛr]: *rente f viagère* life annuity

viande [vjɑ̃d] *f* meat

vibrant, **~e** [vibrɑ̃, -t] vibrating; *fig* vibrant; *discours* stirring; **vibration** *f* vibration; **vibrer** ⟨1a⟩ vibrate; *faire ~ fig* give a buzz

vice [vis] *m* (*défaut*) defect; (*péché*) vice

vice-président [visprezidɑ̃] *m* COMM, POL vice-president; *Br* COMM vice-chairman

vicié, **~e** [visje]: *air m ~* stale air

vicieux, **-euse** [visjø, -z] *homme*, *regard* lecherous; *cercle* vicious

victime [viktim] *f* victim; *~ de guerre* war victim

victoire [viktwar] *f* victory; SP win, victory; *remporter la ~* be victorious, win; **victorieux**, **-euse** victorious

vidange [vidɑ̃ʒ] *f* emptying, draining; AUTO oil change; *faire une ~* change the oil; **vidanger** ⟨1l⟩ empty, drain; AUTO *huile* empty out, drain off

vide [vid] **1** *adj* empty (*aussi fig*); *~ de sens* devoid of meaning **2** *m* (*néant*) emptiness; *physique* vacuum; (*espace non occupé*) (empty) space; *à ~* empty; *regarder dans le ~* gaze into space; *avoir peur du ~* suffer from vertigo, be afraid of heights

vidéo [video] **1** *f* video **2** *adj inv* video; *bande f ~* video tape; *~ amateur* home movie

vidéocassette [videokasɛt] *f* video cassette

vidéoclip [videoklip] *m* video

vidéoconférence [videokɔ̃ferɑ̃s] *f* videoconference

vide-ordures [vidɔrdyr] *m* (*pl inv*) rubbish chute

vidéothèque [videotɛk] *f* video library

vider [vide] ⟨1a⟩ empty (out); F *personne d'une boîte de nuit* throw out; CUIS *volaille* draw; *salle* vacate, leave; *~ qn* F drain *ou* exhaust s.o.; *se ~* empty; **videur** *m* F bouncer

vie [vi] *f* life; (*vivacité*) life, liveliness;

moyens matériels living; **à ~** for life; **de ma ~** in all my life *ou* days; **sans ~** lifeless; **être en ~** be alive; **coût de la ~** cost of living; **gagner sa ~** earn one's living; **~ conjugale** married life; **~ sentimentale** love life

vieil [vjɛj] → **vieux**

vieillard [vjɛjar] *m* old man; **les ~s** old people *pl*, the elderly *pl*

vieille [vjɛj] → **vieux**

vieillesse [vjɛjɛs] *f* old age; **vieillir** ⟨2a⟩ **1** *v/t*: **~ qn** de soucis, d'une maladie age s.o.; *de vêtements, d'une coiffure* make s.o. look older **2** *v/i d'une personne* get old, age; *d'un visage* age; *d'une théorie, d'un livre* become dated; *d'un vin* age, mature; **vieillissement** *m* ageing

Vienne [vjɛn] Vienna; **viennoiseries** *fpl* croissants and similar types of bread

vierge [vjɛrʒ] **1** *f* virgin; **la Vierge (Marie)** REL the Virgin (Mary); **Vierge** ASTROL Virgo **2** *adj* virgin; *feuille* blank; **forêt** *f* **~** virgin forest; **laine** *f* **~** pure new wool

Viêt-nam [vjɛtnam]: **le ~** Vietnam; **vietnamien, ~ne 1** *adj* Vietnamese **2** *m langue* Vietnamese **3** *m/f* **Vietnamien, ~ne** Vietnamese

vieux, (*m* **vieil** *before a vowel or silent h*), **vieille** (*f*) [vjø, vjɛj] **1** *adj* old; **~** *jeu* old-fashioned **2** *m/f* old man / old woman; **les ~** old people *pl*, the aged *pl*; **mon ~ / ma vieille** F (*mon père / ma mère*) my old man / woman F; **prendre un coup de ~** age, look older

vif, **vive** [vif, viv] **1** *adj* lively; (*en vie*) alive; *plaisir, satisfaction, intérêt* great, keen; *critique, douleur* sharp; *air* bracing; *froid* biting; *couleur* bright; **de vive voix** in person **2** *m* **à ~** *plaie* open; **piqué au ~** cut to the quick; **entrer dans le ~ du sujet** get to the heart of the matter, get down to the nitty gritty F; **prendre sur le ~** catch in the act; **avoir les nerfs à ~** be on edge

vigie [viʒi] *f* MAR lookout man

vigilance [viʒilɑ̃s] *f* vigilance; **endormir la ~ de qn** lull s.o. into a false

sense of security; **vigilant, ~e** vigilant

vigile [viʒil] *m* (*gardien*) security man, guard

vigne [viɲ] *f* (*arbrisseau*) vine; (*plantation*) vineyard; **vigneron, ~ne** *m/f* wine grower

vignette [viɲɛt] *f de Sécurité Sociale*: label from medication which has to accompany an application for a refund; AUTO license tab, *Br* tax disc

vignoble [viɲɔbl] *m plantation* vineyard; *région* wine-growing area

vigoureux, -euse [vigurø, -z] *personne, animal, plante* robust, vigorous

vigueur [vigœr] *f* vigor, *Br* vigour, robustness; **plein de ~** full of energy *ou* vitality; **en ~** in force *ou* effect; **entrer en ~** come into force *ou* effect

V.I.H. [veiaʃ] *m abr* (= **Virus de l'Immunodéficience Humaine**) HIV (= human immunodeficiency virus)

vil, ~e [vil] *litt* vile; **à ~ prix** for next to nothing

vilain, ~e [vilɛ̃, -ɛn] nasty; *enfant* naughty; (*laid*) ugly

villa [vila] *f* villa

village [vilaʒ] *m* village; **villageois, ~e 1** *adj* village *atr* **2** *m/f* villager

ville [vil] *f* town; *grande city*; **~ d'eau** spa town; **la ~ de Paris** the city of Paris; **aller en ~** go into town

villégiature [vileʒjatyr] *f* holiday

vin [vɛ̃] *m* wine; **~ blanc** white wine; **~ d'honneur** reception; **~ de pays** regional wine; **~ rouge** red wine; **~ de table** table wine

vinaigre [vinɛgr] *m* vinegar

vinaigrette [vinɛgrɛt] *f* salad dressing

vindicatif, -ive [vɛ̃dikatif, -iv] vindictive

vingt [vɛ̃] twenty; → **trois**; **vingtaine**: **une ~ de personnes** about twenty people *pl*, twenty or so people *pl*; **vingtième** twentieth

vinicole [vinikɔl] wine *atr*

vinyle [vinil] *m* vinyl; **un ~** a record

viol [vjɔl] *m* rape; *d'un lieu saint* violation; **~ collectif** gang rape

violacé, ~e [vjɔlase] purplish

violation [vjɔlasjɔ̃] *f d'un traité* violation; *d'une église* desecration; **~ de domicile** JUR illegal entry

violemment [vjɔlamɑ̃] *adv* violently; *fig* intensely; **violence** *f* violence; *fig* intensity; **violent, ~e** [vjɔlɑ̃, -t] violent; *fig* intense

violer [vjɔle] ⟨1a⟩ *loi* break, violate; *promesse, serment* break; *sexuellement* rape; (*profaner*) desecrate; **violeur** *m* rapist

violet, ~te [vjɔlɛ, -t] violet

violette [vjɔlɛt] *f* BOT violet

violon [vjɔlɔ̃] *m* violin; *musicien* violinist; F *prison* slammer F

violoncelle [vjɔlɔ̃sɛl] *m* cello; **violoncelliste** *m/f* cellist

violoniste [vjɔlɔnist] *m/f* violinist

V.I.P. [veipe *ou* viajpi] *m* (*pl inv*) F VIP (= very important person)

vipère [vipɛr] *f* adder, viper; *fig* viper

virage [viraʒ] *m de la route* curve, corner; *d'un véhicule* turn; *fig* change of direction; **prendre le ~** corner, take the corner; **~ en épingle à cheveux** hairpin curve

viral, ~e [viral] (*mpl* -aux) viral

virée [vire] *f* F trip; (*tournée*) tour; (*balade*) stroll

virement [virmɑ̃] *m* COMM transfer

virer [vire] ⟨1a⟩ *v/i* (*changer de couleur*) change color *ou* Br colour; *d'un véhicule* corner; **~ de bord** MAR tack; *fig* change direction; *sexuellement* go gay **2** *v/t argent* transfer; **~ qn** F throw *ou* kick s.o. out

virevolte [virvɔlt] *f* spin

virginal, ~e [virʒinal] (*mpl* -aux) virginal; **virginité** *f* virginity; **se refaire une ~** *fig* get one's good reputation back

virgule [virgyl] *f* comma

viril, ~e [viril] male; (*courageux*) manly; **virilité** *f* manhood; (*vigueur sexuelle*) virility

virtuel, ~le [virtɥɛl] virtual; (*possible*) potential

virtuose [virtɥoz] *m/f* virtuoso; **virtuosité** *f* virtuosity

virulent, ~e [virylɑ̃, -t] virulent

virus [virys] *m* MÉD, INFORM virus

vis [vis] *f* screw; **escalier** *m* **à ~** spiral staircase; **serrer la ~ à qn** *fig* tighten the screws on s.o.

visa [viza] *m* visa

visage [vizaʒ] *m* face; **visagiste** *m/f* beautician

vis-à-vis [vizavi] **1** *prép*: **~ de** opposite; (*envers*) toward, Br towards; (*en comparaison de*) compared with **2** *m* person sitting opposite; (*rencontre*) face-to-face meeting

viscéral, ~e [viseral] (*mpl* -aux) *fig*: *peur, haine* deep-rooted

visée [vize] *f*: **~s** (*intentions*) designs

viser [vize] ⟨1a⟩ *v/t* aim at; (*s'adresser à*) be aimed at **2** *v/i* aim (*à* at); **~ à faire qch** aim to do sth; **~ haut** *fig* aim high

viseur [vizœr] *m d'une arme* sights *pl*; PHOT viewfinder

visibilité [vizibilite] *f* visibility; **visible** visible; (*évident*) clear

visière [vizjɛr] *f de casquette* peak

visioconférence [vizjɔkɔ̃ferɑ̃s] *f* video conference

vision [vizjɔ̃] *f* sight; (*conception, apparition*) vision; **visionnaire** *m/f & adj* visionary; **visionneuse** *f* PHOT viewer

visiophone [vizjɔfɔn] *m* videophone

visite [vizit] *f* visit; *d'une ville* tour; **être en ~ chez qn** be visiting s.o.; **rendre ~ à qn** visit s.o.; **avoir droit de ~** *d'un parent divorcé* have access; **~ de contrôle** follow-up visit; **~s à domicile** MÉD house calls; **~ de douane** customs inspection; **~ guidée** guided tour; **~ médicale** medical (examination); **visiter** ⟨1a⟩ visit; (*faire le tour de*) tour; *bagages* inspect; **visiteur, -euse** *m/f* visitor

vison [vizɔ̃] *m* mink

visqueux, -euse [viskø, -z] viscous; *péj* slimy

visser [vise] ⟨1a⟩ screw

visuel, ~le [vizɥɛl] visual; **champ** *m* **~** field of vision

vital, ~e [vital] (*mpl* -aux) vital; **vitalité** *f* vitality

vitamine [vitamin] *f* vitamin

vite [vit] *adv* fast, quickly; (*sous peu, bientôt*) soon; **~!** hurry up!, quick!; **vi-**

tesse *f* speed; AUTO gear; *à toute ~* at top speed; *en ~* F quickly

viticole [vitikɔl] wine *atr*

viticulteur [vitikyltœr] *m* wine-grower; **viticulture** *f* wine-growing

vitrage [vitraʒ] *m cloison* glass partition; *action* glazing; *ensemble de vitres* windows *pl*; *double ~* double glazing

vitrail [vitraj] *m* (*pl* -aux) stained-glass window

vitre [vitr] *f* window (pane); *de voiture* window; **vitrer** ⟨1a⟩ glaze; **vitreux, -euse** *regard* glazed; **vitrier** *m* glazier

vitrine [vitrin] *f* (*étalage*) (store) window; *meuble* display cabinet

vivace [vivas] *f* hardy; *haine, amour* strong, lasting; **vivacité** *f d'une personne* liveliness, vivacity

vivant, ~e [vivɑ̃, -t] **1** *adj* (*en vie*) alive; (*plein de vie*) lively; (*doué de vie*) living; *langue* modern **2** *m* living person; *de son ~* in his lifetime; *c'est un bon ~* he enjoys life; **vivement** *adv* (*d'un ton vif*) sharply; (*vite*) briskly; *ému, touché* deeply; *~ dimanche!* roll on Sunday!, Sunday can't come soon enough!

vivier [vivje] *m* fishpond; *dans un restaurant* fish tank

vivifier [vivifje] ⟨1a⟩ invigorate

vivoter [vivɔte] ⟨1a⟩ just get by

vivre [vivr] **1** *v/i* ⟨4e⟩ live **2** *v/t* experience; *vive …!* long live …! **3** *mpl*: *~s* supplies

vocabulaire [vɔkabylɛr] *m* vocabulary

vocal, ~e [vɔkal] (*mpl* -aux) vocal

vocation [vɔkasjɔ̃] *f* vocation, calling; *une entreprise à ~ philanthropique* a philanthropic organization

vociférer [vɔsifere] ⟨1f⟩ shout

vodka [vɔdka] *f* vodka

vœu [vø] *m* (*pl* -x) REL vow; (*souhait*) wish; *faire ~ de faire qch* vow to do sth; *tous mes ~x!* best wishes!

vogue [vɔg] *f*: *être en ~* be in fashion

voici [vwasi] here is *sg*, here are *pl*; *me ~!* here I am!; *le livre que ~* this book

voie [vwa] *f* way (*aussi fig*); *de chemin de fer* track; *d'autoroute* lane; *être en ~ de formation* be being formed;

être en ~ de guérison be on the road to recovery, be on the mend; *par (la) ~ de* by means of; *par ~ aérienne* by air; *par la ~ hiérarchique* through channels; *~ d'eau* leak; *~ express* expressway; *Voie lactée* Milky Way; *~ navigable* waterway; *~s de fait* JUR assault *sg*

voilà [vwala] there is *sg*, there are *pl*; (*et) ~!* there you are!; *en ~ assez!* that's enough!; *~ tout* that's all; *~ pourquoi* that's why; *me ~* here I am; *~ deux ans qu'il ne nous a pas écrit* he hasn't written to us in two years

voile [vwal] **1** *m* veil (*aussi fig*) **2** *f* MAR sail; SP sailing; *mettre les ~s* F take off

voiler[1] [vwale] ⟨1a⟩ veil; *se ~ d'une femme* wear the veil; *du ciel* cloud over

voiler[2] [vwale] ⟨1a⟩: *se ~ du bois* warp; *d'une roue* buckle

voilier [vwalje] *m* sailboat

voilure [vwalyr] *f* MAR sails *pl*

voir [vwar] ⟨3b⟩ see; *faire ~* show; *être bien vu* be acceptable; *cela n'a rien à ~* that has nothing to do with it; *~ à qch* see to sth; *se ~* see each other; *se ~ décerner un prix* be given a prize; *cela se voit* that's obvious; *voyons!* let's see!; *reproche* come now!; *je ne peux pas le ~* I can't stand him

voire [vwar] *adv* even

voirie [vwari] *f* (*voies*) roads *pl*; *administration* roads department

voisin, ~e [vwazɛ̃, -in] **1** *adj* neighboring, *Br* neighbouring; (*similaire*) similar **2** *m/f* neighbor; *Br* neighbour; **voisinage** *m* (*ensemble de gens*) neighborhood, *Br* neighbourhood; (*proximité*) vicinity; **voisiner** ⟨1a⟩: *~ avec* adjoin

voiture [vwatyr] *f* car; *d'un train* car, *Br* carriage; *~ de tourisme* touring car; *en ~* by car, in the car; *~ de fonction* company car; *~-piégée* car bomb

voix [vwa] *f* voice (*aussi* GRAM); POL vote; *avoir ~ au chapitre* *fig* have a say in the matter; **à haute ~** in a loud voice, aloud; **à ~ basse** in a low voice, quietly

vol[1] [vɔl] *m* theft; **c'est du ~!** that's daylight robbery!; **~ à main armée** armed robbery

vol[2] [vɔl] *m* flight; **à ~ d'oiseau** as the crow flies; **au ~** in flight; **saisir l'occasion au ~** jump at the chance; **attraper un bus au ~** jump on a bus; **~ à voile** gliding

volage [vɔlaʒ] flighty

volaille [vɔlaj] *f* poultry; (*poulet etc*) bird

volant [vɔlɑ̃] *m* AUTO (steering) wheel; SP shuttlecock; *d'un vêtement* flounce

volatil, **~e** [vɔlatil] CHIM volatile

volcan [vɔlkɑ̃] *m* GÉOGR volcano; **volcanique** volcanic

volée [vɔle] *f groupe d'oiseaux* flock; *tennis, de coups de feu* volley; **~ de coups** shower of blows; **attraper un ballon à la ~** catch a ball in mid-air

voler[1] [vɔle] ⟨1a⟩ steal; **~ qch à qn** steal sth from s.o., rob s.o. of sth; **~ qn** rob s.o.

voler[2] [vɔle] ⟨1a⟩ fly (*aussi fig*)

volet [vɔle] *m de fenêtre* shutter; *fig* part; **trier sur le ~** *fig* handpick

voleter [vɔlte] ⟨1c⟩ flutter

voleur, **-euse** [vɔlœr, -øz] **1** *adj* thieving **2** *m/f* thief; **~ à la tire** pickpocket; **~ à l'étalage** shoplifter

volley(-ball) [vɔlɛbol] *m* volleyball

volière [vɔljɛr] *f* aviary

volontaire [vɔlɔ̃tɛr] **1** *adj* voluntary; (*délibéré*) deliberate; (*décidé*) headstrong **2** *m/f* volunteer; **volonté** *f* faculté de vouloir (*souhait*) wish; (*fermeté*) willpower; **de l'eau / du pain à ~** as much water / bread as you like; **faire preuve de bonne ~** show willing; **tirer à ~** fire at will

volontiers [vɔlɔ̃tje] *adv* willingly, with pleasure

volt [vɔlt] *m* ÉL volt; **voltage** *m* ÉL voltage

volte-face [vɔltəfas] *f* (*pl inv*) about-turn (*aussi fig*)

voltmètre [vɔltmɛtr] *m* ÉL voltmeter

volubilité [vɔlybilite] *f* volubility

volume [vɔlym] *m* volume; **volumineux**, **-euse** bulky

voluptueux, **-euse** [vɔlyptɥø, -z] voluptuous

volute [vɔlyt] *f* curl

vomi [vɔmi] *m* vomit; **vomir** ⟨2a⟩ **1** *v/i* vomit, throw up **2** *v/t* bring up; *fig* spew out; **vomissement** *m* vomiting

vorace [vɔras] voracious

vos [vo] → **votre**

votant, **~e** [vɔtɑ̃, -t] *m/f* voter; **vote** *m* vote; *action* voting; **voter** ⟨1a⟩ **1** *v/i* vote **2** *v/t loi* pass

votre [vɔtr], *pl* **vos** [vo] your

vôtre [votr] **le / la ~, les ~s** yours

vouer [vwe] ⟨1a⟩ dedicate (**à** to); **~ sa vie à** dedicate *ou* devote one's life to; **se ~ à** dedicate *ou* devote o.s. to

vouloir [vulwar] ⟨3i⟩ want; **il veut partir** he wants to leave; **il veut que tu partes** (*subj*) he wants you to leave; **je voudrais** I would like, I'd like; **je veux bien** I'd like to; **je veux bien que tu prennes ...** (*subj*) I'd like you to take ...; **il veut bien** he'd like to; (*il est d'accord*) it's fine with him, it's ok by him; **veuillez ne pas fumer** please do not smoke; **on ne veut pas de moi** I'm not wanted

◊: **~ dire** mean

◊: **en ~ à qn** have something against s.o., bear s.o. a grudge; **je m'en veux de ne pas avoir ...** I feel bad about not having ...

◊: **veux-tu te taire!** will you shut up!

voulu, **~e** [vuly] **1** *p/p* → **vouloir 2** *adj* requisite; *délibéré* deliberate

vous [vu] *pron personnel* ◊ *sujet, sg et pl* you

◊ *complément d'objet direct, sg et pl* you; **il ne ~ a pas vu** he didn't see you

◊ *complément d'objet indirect, sg et pl* (to) you; **elle ~ en a parlé** she spoke to you about it; **je vais ~ chercher ...** I'll go and get you ...

◊ *avec verbe pronominal* yourself; *pl*

yourselves; **~ ~ êtes coupé** you've cut yourself; **~ ~ êtes coupés** you've cut yourselves; **si ~ ~ levez à …** if you get up at …

vous-même [vumɛm], *pl* **vous--mêmes** [vumɛm] yourself; *pl* yourselves

voûte [vut] *f* ARCH vault; **voûté**, **~e** *personne* hunched; *dos* bent; ARCH vaulted; **voûter** ⟨1a⟩ ARCH vault; *se* **~** have a stoop

vouvoyer [vuvwaje] ⟨1h⟩ address as 'vous'

voyage [vwajaʒ] *m* trip, journey; *en paquebot* voyage; **être en ~** be traveling *ou Br* travelling; **bon ~!** have a good trip!; **~ d'affaires** business trip; **~ de noces** honeymoon; **~ organisé** package holiday; **voyager** ⟨1l⟩ travel; **voyageur, -euse** *m/f* traveler, *Br* traveller; *par train, avion* passenger; **~ de commerce** traveling salesman, *Br* travelling salesman; **voyagiste** *m* (*tour*) operator

voyant, **~e** [vwajɑ̃, -t] **1** *adj couleur* garish **2** *m* (*signal*) light; **3** *m/f* (*devin*) clairvoyant

voyelle [vwajɛl] *f* GRAM vowel

voyou [vwaju] *m* (*pl* -s) *jeune* lout

vrac [vrak] *m*: **en ~** COMM loose; *fig* jumbled together

vrai, **~e** [vre] **1** *adj* (*après le subst*) true; (*devant le subst*) real, genuine; *ami* true, genuine; *il est ~ que* it is true that **2** *m*: **à ~ dire**, **à dire ~** to tell the truth; **vraiment** [vremɑ̃] *adv* really

vraisemblable [vresɑ̃blabl] likely, probable; **vraisemblance** *f* likelihood, probability

vrille [vrij] *f* BOT tendril; TECH gimlet; **descendre en ~** AVIAT go into a spin dive

vrombir [vrɔ̃bir] ⟨2a⟩ throb

VTT [vetete] *m abr* (= **vélo tout terrain**) mountain bike

vu¹ [vy] *prép* in view of; **~ que** seeing that; **au ~ et au su de tout le monde** openly, in front of everybody

vu², **~e** [vy] *p/p →* **voir**

vue [vy] *f* view; *sens, faculté* sight; **à ~ d'œil** visibly; **à première ~** at first sight; **à perte de ~** as far as the eye can see; **perdre qn de ~** lose sight of s.o.; (*perdre le contact*) lose touch with s.o.; **connaître qn de ~** know s.o. by sight; **avoir la ~ basse** be shortsighted; **point m de ~** viewpoint, point of view; **en ~** (*visible*) in view; **en ~ de faire qch** with a view to doing sth

vulgaire [vylɡɛr] (*banal*) common; (*grossier*) common, vulgar

vulgariser [vylɡarize] ⟨1a⟩ popularize; **vulgarité** *f péj* vulgarity

vulnérabilité [vylnerabilite] *f* vulnerability; **vulnérable** vulnerable

W

wagon [vaɡɔ̃] *m* car, *Br* carriage; *de marchandises* car, *Br* wagon; **wagon-lit** *m* (*pl* wagons-lits) sleeping car, *Br aussi* sleeper; **wagon-restaurant** *m* (*pl* wagons-restaurants) dining car

waters [water] *mpl* toilet *sg*

watt [wat] *m* ÉL watt

W.-C. [vese] *mpl* WC *sg*

week-end [wikɛnd] *m* (*pl* week-ends) weekend; **ce ~** on *ou Br* at the weekend

western [wɛstɛrn] *m* western

whisky [wiski] *m* whiskey, *Br* whisky

W

X

xénophobe [gzenɔfɔb] xenophobic;
xénophobie f xenophobia

xérès [gzerɛs, ks-] m sherry
xylophone [gzilɔfɔn] m xylophone

Y

y [i] there; **on ~ va!** let's go!; **je ne m'~
fie pas** I don't trust it; **ça ~ est!**
that's it!; **j'~ suis** (*je comprends*)
now I see, now I get it; **~ compris**
including; **n'~ compte pas** don't
count on it; **je m'~ attendais** I

thought as much; **j'~ travaille** I'm
working on it
yacht [jɔt] m yacht
yaourt [jaurt] m yoghurt
yeux [jø] *pl* → **œil**
yoga [jɔga] m yoga

Z

zapper [zape] channel-hop, *Br aussi*
zap
zèbre [zɛbr] m zebra
zèle [zɛl] m zeal; **faire du ~** be over-
zealous; **zélé, ~e** zealous
zéro [zero] **1** m zero, *Br aussi* nought;
SP *Br* nil; *fig* nonentity; **au-dessous
de ~** below zero; **partir de ~** start
from nothing **2** *adj*: **~ faute** no mistakes
zeste [zɛst] m peel, zest
zézaiement [zezemã] m lisp; **zézayer**
⟨1i⟩ lisp
zigouiller [ziguje] ⟨1a⟩ F bump off F
zigzag [zigzag] m zigzag; **zigzaguer**
⟨1m⟩ zigzag
zinc [zɛ̃g] m zinc
zizanie [zizani] f: **semer la ~** cause

trouble
zodiaque [zɔdjak] m zodiac
zombie [zõbi] m/f zombie
zona [zona] m shingles *sg*
zone [zon] f area, zone; *péj* slums *pl*; **~
de basse pression** low-pressure
area, low; **~ bleue** restricted parking
area; **~ euro** euro zone; **~ industrielle** industrial park, *Br* industrial
estate; **~ interdite** prohibited area,
no-go area; **~ de libre-échange** free
trade area; **~ résidentielle** residential area
zoo [zo] m zoo
zoologie [zɔɔlɔʒi] f zoology; **zoologiste** m/f zoologist
zoom [zum] m zoom lens
zut! [zyt] F blast!

A

a [ə], *stressed* [eɪ] *art* un(e); **$5 ~ ride** 5 $ le tour; **she's ~ dentist / an actress** elle est dentiste / actrice; **have ~ broken arm** avoir le bras cassé

a·back [ə'bæk] *adv:* **taken ~** décontenancé

a·ban·don [ə'bændən] *v/t* abandonner

a·bashed [ə'bæʃt] *adj* honteux*

a·bate [ə'beɪt] *v/i of storm* se calmer; *of flood waters* baisser

ab·at·toir ['æbətwɑːr] abattoir *m*

ab·bey ['æbɪ] abbaye *f*

ab·bre·vi·ate [ə'briːvieɪt] *v/t* abréger

ab·bre·vi·a·tion [əbriːvɪ'eɪʃn] abréviation *f*

ab·do·men ['æbdəmən] abdomen *m*

ab·dom·i·nal [æb'dɑːmɪnl] *adj* abdominal

ab·duct [əb'dʌkt] *v/t* enlever

ab·duc·tion [əb'dʌkʃn] enlèvement *m*

♦ a·bide by [ə'baɪd] *v/t* respecter

a·bil·i·ty [ə'bɪlətɪ] capacité *f*; *skill* faculté *f*

a·blaze [ə'bleɪz] *adj:* **be ~** être en feu

a·ble ['eɪbl] *adj* (*skillful*) compétent; **be ~ to do sth** pouvoir faire qch; **I wasn't ~ to hear** je ne pouvais pas entendre

a·ble-bod·ied ['eɪblbɑːdiːd] *adj* en bonne condition physique

ab·nor·mal [æb'nɔːrml] *adj* anormal

ab·nor·mal·ly [æb'nɔːrməlɪ] *adv* anormalement

a·board [ə'bɔːrd] **1** *prep* à bord **2** *adv:* **be ~** être à bord; **go ~** monter à bord

a·bol·ish [ə'bɑːlɪʃ] *v/t* abolir

ab·o·li·tion [æbə'lɪʃn] abolition *f*

a·bort [ə'bɔːrt] *v/t mission etc* suspendre; COMPUT: *program* suspendre l'exécution de

a·bor·tion [ə'bɔːrʃn] MED avortement *m*; **have an ~** se faire avorter

a·bor·tive [ə'bɔːrtɪv] *adj* avorté

a·bout [ə'baʊt] **1** *prep* (*concerning*) à propos de; **a book ~** un livre sur; **talk ~** parler de; **what's it ~?** *of book, movie* de quoi ça parle? **2** *adv* (*roughly*) à peu près; **~ noon** aux alentours de midi; **be ~ to do sth** (*be going to*) être sur le point de faire qch; (*have intention*) avoir l'intention de faire qch; **be ~** (*somewhere near*) être dans les parages

a·bove [ə'bʌv] **1** *prep* au-dessus de; **~ all** surtout **2** *adv* au-dessus; **on the floor ~** à l'étage du dessus

a·bove-men·tioned [əbʌv'menʃnd] *adj* ci-dessus, susmentionné

a·bra·sion [ə'breɪʒn] écorchure *f*

a·bra·sive [ə'breɪsɪv] *adj personality* abrupt

a·breast [ə'brest] *adv:* **three ~** les trois l'un à côté de l'autre; **keep ~ of** se tenir au courant de

a·bridge [ə'brɪdʒ] *v/t* abréger

a·broad [ə'brɔːd] *adv* à l'étranger

a·brupt [ə'brʌpt] *adj* brusque

a·brupt·ly [ə'brʌptlɪ] *adv* brusquement; *say* d'un ton brusque

ab·scess ['æbsɪs] abcès *m*

ab·sence ['æbsəns] absence *f*

ab·sent ['æbsənt] *adj* absent

ab·sen·tee [æbsən'tiː] absent(e) *m(f)*

ab·sen·tee·ism [æbsən'tiːɪzm] absentéisme *m*

ab·sent-mind·ed [æbsənt'maɪndɪd] *adj* distrait

ab·sent-mind·ed·ly [æbsənt'maɪndɪdlɪ] *adv* distraitement

ab·so·lute ['æbsəluːt] *adj* absolu

ab·so·lute·ly ['æbsəluːtlɪ] *adv* (*completely*) absolument; *mad* complètement; **~ not!** absolument pas!; **do you agree? – ~** tu es d'accord? - tout à fait

ab·so·lu·tion [æbsə'luːʃn] REL absolution *f*

ab·solve [əb'zɑːlv] *v/t* absoudre

ab·sorb [əbˈsɔːrb] *v/t* absorber; **~ed in ...** absorbé dans

ab·sorb·en·cy [əbˈsɔːrbənsɪ] capacité *f* d'absorption

ab·sorb·ent [əbˈsɔːrbənt] *adj* absorbant

ab·sorb·ent 'cot·ton coton *m* hydrophile

ab·sorb·ing [əbˈsɔːrbɪŋ] *adj* absorbant

ab·stain [əbˈsteɪn] *v/i from voting* s'abstenir

ab·sten·tion [əbˈstenʃn] *in voting* abstention *f*

ab·stract [ˈæbstrækt] *adj* abstrait

ab·struse [əbˈstruːs] *adj* abstrus

ab·surd [əbˈsɜːrd] *adj* absurde

ab·surd·i·ty [əbˈsɜːrdətɪ] absurdité *f*

ab·surd·ly [əbˈsɜːrdlɪ] *adv* absurdement

a·bun·dance [əˈbʌndəns] abondance *f*

a·bun·dant [əˈbʌndənt] *adj* abondant

a·buse¹ [əˈbjuːs] *n verbal* insultes *fpl*; *physical* violences *fpl* physiques; *sexual* sévices *mpl* sexuels; *of power etc* abus *m*

a·buse² [əˈbjuːz] *v/t verbally* insulter; *physically* maltraiter; *sexually* faire subir des sévices sexuels à; *power etc* abuser de

a·bu·sive [əˈbjuːsɪv] *adj language* insultant; **become ~** devenir insultant

a·bys·mal [əˈbɪzml] *adj* F (*very bad*) lamentable

a·byss [əˈbɪs] abîme *m*

AC [ˈeɪsɪ] *abbr* (*= alternating current*) CA (*= courant m alternatif*)

ac·a·dem·ic [ækəˈdemɪk] **1** *n* universitaire *m/f* **2** *adj year: at school* scolaire; *at university* universitaire; *person, interests, studies* intellectuel*

a·cad·e·my [əˈkædəmɪ] académie *f*

ac·cel·e·rate [əkˈseləreɪt] *v/i & v/t* accélérer

ac·cel·e·ra·tion [əkseləˈreɪʃn] accélération *f*

ac·cel·e·ra·tor [əkˈseləreɪtər] accélérateur *m*

ac·cent [ˈæksənt] *when speaking*, (*emphasis*) accent *m*

ac·cen·tu·ate [əkˈsentʊeɪt] *v/t* accentuer

ac·cept [əkˈsept] *v/t & v/i* accepter

ac·cept·a·ble [əkˈseptəbl] *adj* acceptable

ac·cept·ance [əkˈseptəns] acceptation *f*

ac·cess [ˈækses] **1** *n* accès *m*; **have ~ to** avoir accès à **2** *v/t also* COMPUT accéder à

ac·ces·si·ble [əkˈsesəbl] *adj* accessible

ac·ces·so·ry [əkˈsesərɪ] *for wearing* accessoire *m*; LAW complice *m/f*

'ac·cess road route *f* d'accès

'ac·cess time COMPUT temps *m* d'accès

ac·ci·dent [ˈæksɪdənt] accident *m*; **by ~** par hasard

ac·ci·den·tal [æksɪˈdentl] *adj* accidentel*

ac·ci·den·tal·ly [æksɪˈdentlɪ] *adv* accidentellement

ac·claim [əˈkleɪm] **1** *n: meet with ~* recevoir des louanges **2** *v/t* saluer (*as* comme)

ac·cla·ma·tion [ækləˈmeɪʃn] acclamation *f*

ac·cli·mate, ac·cli·ma·tize [əˈklaɪmət, əˈklaɪmətaɪz] *v/t of plant* s'acclimater

ac·com·mo·date [əˈkɑːmədeɪt] *v/t* loger; *special requirements* s'adapter à

ac·com·mo·da·tions [əkɑːməˈdeɪʃnz] *npl* logement *m*

ac·com·pa·ni·ment [əˈkʌmpənɪmənt] MUS accompagnement *m*

ac·com·pa·nist [əˈkʌmpənɪst] MUS accompagnateur(-trice) *m(f)*

ac·com·pa·ny [əˈkʌmpənɪ] *v/t* (*pret & pp -ied*) *also* MUS accompagner

ac·com·plice [əˈkʌmplɪs] complice *m/f*

ac·com·plish [əˈkʌmplɪʃ] *v/t* (*achieve*), *task, mission* accomplir

ac·com·plished [əˈkʌmplɪʃt] *adj pianist, cook etc* accompli

ac·com·plish·ment [əˈkʌmplɪʃmənt] *of task, mission* accomplissement *m*; (*achievement*) réussite *f*; (*talent*) talent *m*

ac·cord [əˈkɔːrd] accord *m*; *of one's own ~* de son plein gré

ac·cord·ance [əˈkɔːrdəns]: *in ~ with*

conformément à

ac·cord·ing [əˈkɔːrdɪŋ] *adv*: **~ to** selon

ac·cord·ing·ly [əˈkɔːrdɪŋlɪ] *adv* (*consequently*) par conséquent; (*appropriately*) en conséquence

ac·cor·di·on [əˈkɔːrdɪən] accordéon *m*

ac·cor·di·on·ist [əˈkɔːrdɪənɪst] accordéoniste *m/f*

ac·count [əˈkaʊnt] *financial* compte *m*; (*report, description*) récit *m*; **give an ~ of** faire le récit de; **on no ~** en aucun cas; **on ~ of** en raison de; **take ... into ~, take ~ of ...** tenir compte de ...

♦ **account for** *v/t* (*explain*) expliquer; (*make up, constitute*) représenter

ac·count·a·ble [əˈkaʊntəbl] *adj*: **be ~ to** devoir rendre des comptes à; **be held ~** être tenu responsable

ac·count·ant [əˈkaʊntənt] comptable *m/f*

ac'count hold·er titulaire *m/f* de compte

ac'count num·ber numéro *m* de compte

ac·counts [əˈkaʊnts] comptabilité *f*

ac·cu·mu·late [əˈkjuːmjʊleɪt] **1** *v/t* accumuler **2** *v/i* s'accumuler

ac·cu·mu·la·tion [əkjuːmjʊˈleɪʃn] accumulation *f*

ac·cu·ra·cy [ˈækjʊrəsɪ] justesse *f*

ac·cu·rate [ˈækjʊrət] *adj* juste

ac·cu·rate·ly [ˈækjʊrətlɪ] *adv* avec justesse

ac·cu·sa·tion [ækjuːˈzeɪʃn] accusation *f*

ac·cuse [əˈkjuːz] *v/t* accuser; **~ s.o. of doing sth** accuser qn de faire qch; **be ~d of** LAW être accusé de

ac·cused [əˈkjuːzd] LAW: **the ~** l'accusé(e) *m(f)*

ac·cus·ing [əˈkjuːzɪŋ] *adj* accusateur*

ac·cus·ing·ly [əˈkjuːzɪŋlɪ] *adv say* d'un ton accusateur; *look* d'un air accusateur

ac·cus·tom [əˈkʌstəm] *v/t*: **get ~ed to** s'accoutumer à; **be ~ed to doing sth** avoir l'habitude de faire qch, être accoutumé à faire qch

ace [eɪs] *in cards* as *m*; *tennis shot* ace *m*

ache [eɪk] **1** *n* douleur *f* **2** *v/i*: **my**

arm / head ~s j'ai mal au bras / à la tête

a·chieve [əˈtʃiːv] *v/t* accomplir

a·chieve·ment [əˈtʃiːvmənt] (*thing achieved*) accomplissement *m*; *of ambition* réalisation *f*

ac·id [ˈæsɪd] *n* acide *m*

a·cid·i·ty [əˈsɪdətɪ] acidité *f*

ac·id 'rain pluies *fpl* acides

'ac·id test *fig* test *m* décisif

ac·knowl·edge [əkˈnɑːlɪdʒ] *v/t* reconnaître; **~ receipt of a letter** accuser réception d'une lettre

ac·knowl·edg(e)·ment [əkˈnɑːlɪdʒmənt] reconnaissance *f*; *of a letter* accusé *m* de réception

ac·ne [ˈæknɪ] MED acné *m*

a·corn [ˈeɪkɔːrn] BOT gland *m* (de chêne)

a·cous·tics [əˈkuːstɪks] acoustique *f*

ac·quaint [əˈkweɪnt] *v/t fml*: **be ~ed with** connaître

ac·quaint·ance [əˈkweɪntəns] *person* connaissance *f*

ac·qui·esce [ækwiˈes] *v/i fml* acquiescer

ac·quire [əˈkwaɪr] *v/t* acquérir

ac·qui·si·tion [ækwɪˈzɪʃn] acquisition *f*

ac·quis·i·tive [æˈkwɪzətɪv] *adj* avide

ac·quit [əˈkwɪt] *v/t* LAW acquitter

ac·quit·tal [əˈkwɪtl] LAW acquittement *m*

a·cre [ˈeɪkər] acre *m*

a·cre·age [ˈeɪkrɪdʒ] acres *mpl*

ac·rid [ˈækrɪd] *adj smell* âcre

ac·ri·mo·ni·ous [ækrɪˈmoʊnɪəs] *adj* acrimonieux*

ac·ro·bat [ˈækrəbæt] acrobate *m/f*

ac·ro·bat·ic [ækrəˈbætɪk] *adj* acrobatique

ac·ro·bat·ics [ækrəˈbætɪks] *npl* acrobaties *fpl*

ac·ro·nym [ˈækrənɪm] acronyme *m*

a·cross [əˈkrɔːs] **1** *prep* de l'autre côté de; **sail ~ the Atlantic** traverser l'Atlantique en bateau; **walk ~ the street** traverser la rue; **~ Europe** *all over* dans toute l'Europe; **~ from ...** en face de ... **2** *adv*: **swim ~** traverser à la nage; **jump ~** sauter

par-dessus; *10m* ~ 10 m de large
a·cryl·ic [əˈkrɪlɪk] acrylique *m*
act [ækt] **1** *v/i* (*take action*) agir; THEA faire du théâtre; (*pretend*) faire semblant; ~ *as* faire office de **2** *n* (*deed*) fait *m*; *of play* acte *m*; *in variety show* numéro *m*; (*law*) loi *f*; *it's an* ~ (*pretense*) c'est du cinéma; ~ *of God* catastrophe *f* naturelle
act·ing [ˈæktɪŋ] **1** *adj* (*temporary*) intérimaire **2** *n* *performance* jeu *m*; *go into* ~ devenir acteur
ac·tion [ˈækʃn] action *f*; *out of* ~ (*not functioning*) hors service; *take* ~ prendre des mesures; *bring an* ~ *against* LAW intenter une action en justice contre
action ˈre·play TV reprise *f*
ac·tive [ˈæktɪv] *adj also* GRAM actif*
ac·tiv·ist [ˈæktɪvɪst] POL activiste *m/f*
ac·tiv·i·ty [ækˈtɪvətɪ] activité *f*
ac·tor [ˈæktər] acteur *m*
ac·tress [ˈæktrɪs] actrice *f*
ac·tu·al [ˈæktʃʊəl] *adj* véritable
ac·tu·al·ly [ˈæktʃʊəlɪ] *adv* (*in fact, to tell the truth*) en fait; *expressing surprise* vraiment; ~ *I do know him* *stressing converse* à vrai dire, je le connais
ac·u·punc·ture [ˈækjəpʌŋktʃər] acupuncture *f*, acuponcture *f*
a·cute [əˈkjuːt] *adj* *pain, embarrassment* intense; *sense of smell* très développé
a·cute·ly [əˈkjuːtlɪ] *adv* (*extremely*) extrêmement
AD [eɪˈdiː] *abbr* (= *anno domini*) av. J.-C. (= avant Jésus Christ)
ad [æd] → *advertisement*
ad·a·mant [ˈædəmənt] *adj*: *be* ~ *that* ... soutenir catégoriquement que ...
Ad·am's ap·ple [ædəmzˈæpl] pomme *f* d'Adam
a·dapt [əˈdæpt] **1** *v/t* adapter **2** *v/i* *of person* s'adapter
a·dapt·a·bil·i·ty [ədæptəˈbɪlətɪ] faculté *f* d'adaptation
a·dapt·a·ble [əˈdæptəbl] *adj* *person, plant* adaptable; *vehicle etc* multifonction *inv*
a·dap·ta·tion [ædæpˈteɪʃn] *of play etc* adaptation *f*

a·dapt·er [əˈdæptər] *electrical* adaptateur *m*
add [æd] **1** *v/t* ajouter; MATH additionner **2** *v/i of person* faire des additions
♦ add on *v/t* 15% *etc* ajouter
♦ add up **1** *v/t* additionner **2** *v/i fig* avoir du sens
ad·der [ˈædər] vipère *f*
ad·dict [ˈædɪkt] (*drug* ~) drogué(e) *m(f)*; *of TV program etc* accro *m/f* F
ad·dict·ed [əˈdɪktɪd] *adj* *to drugs* drogué; *to TV program etc* accro F; *be* ~ *to* être accro à
ad·dic·tion [əˈdɪkʃn] *to drugs* dépendance *f* (*to* de)
ad·dic·tive [əˈdɪktɪv] *adj*: *be* ~ entraîner une dépendance
ad·di·tion [əˈdɪʃn] MATH addition *f*; *to list* ajout *m*; *to company* recrue *f*; *in* ~ de plus; *in* ~ *to* en plus de; *the latest* ~ *to the family* le petit dernier / la petite dernière
ad·di·tion·al [əˈdɪʃnl] *adj* supplémentaire
ad·di·tive [ˈædɪtɪv] additif *m*
add-on [ˈædɑːn] accessoire *m*
ad·dress [əˈdres] **1** *n of person* adresse *f*; *form of* ~ titre *m* **2** *v/t letter* adresser; *audience, person* s'adresser à
ad·dress book carnet *m* d'adresses
ad·dress·ee [ædreˈsiː] destinataire *m/f*
ad·ept [ˈædept] *adj* expert; *be* ~ *at doing sth* être expert dans l'art de faire qch
ad·e·quate [ˈædɪkwət] *adj* (*sufficient*) suffisant; (*satisfactory*) satisfaisant
ad·e·quate·ly [ˈædɪkwətlɪ] *adv* suffisamment
ad·here [ədˈhɪr] *v/i* adhérer
♦ adhere to *v/t* adhérer à
ad·he·sive [ədˈhiːsɪv] *n* adhésif *m*
ad·he·sive ˈtape (ruban *m*) adhésif *m*
ad·ja·cent [əˈdʒeɪsnt] *adj* adjacent
ad·jec·tive [ˈædʒɪktɪv] adjectif *m*
ad·join [əˈdʒɔɪn] *v/t* être à côté de
ad·join·ing [əˈdʒɔɪnɪŋ] *adj* attenant
ad·journ [əˈdʒɜːrn] *v/i* ajourner
ad·journ·ment [əˈdʒɜːrnmənt] ajournement *m*
ad·just [əˈdʒʌst] *v/t* ajuster

ad·just·a·ble [ə'dʒʌstəbl] *adj* ajustable

ad·just·ment [ə'dʒʌstmənt] ajustement *m*

ad lib [æd'lɪb] **1** *adj* improvisé **2** *adv* en improvisant **3** *v/i* (*pret & pp* **-bed**) improviser

ad·min·is·ter [əd'mɪnɪstər] *v/t medicine* donner; *company, country* administrer

ad·min·is·tra·tion [ədmɪnɪ'streɪʃn] *of company, institution* administration *f*; (*administrative work*) tâches *fpl* administratives; (*government*) gouvernement *m*

ad·min·is·tra·tive [ədmɪnɪ'strətɪv] *adj* administratif*

ad·min·is·tra·tor [əd'mɪnɪstreɪtər] administrateur(-trice) *m(f)*

ad·mi·ra·ble ['ædmərəbl] *adj* admirable

ad·mi·ra·bly ['ædmərəblɪ] *adv* admirablement

ad·mi·ral ['ædmərəl] amiral *m*

ad·mi·ra·tion [ædmə'reɪʃn] admiration *f*

ad·mire [əd'maɪr] *v/t* admirer

ad·mir·er [əd'maɪrər] admirateur (-trice) *m(f)*

ad·mir·ing [əd'maɪrɪŋ] *adj* admiratif*

ad·mir·ing·ly [əd'maɪrɪŋlɪ] *adv* admirativement

ad·mis·si·ble [əd'mɪsəbl] *adj evidence* admis

ad·mis·sion [əd'mɪʃn] (*confession*) aveu *m*; **~ free** entrée *f* gratuite

ad·mit [əd'mɪt] *v/t* (*pret & pp* **-ted**) *into a place, accept* admettre; (*confess*) avouer

ad·mit·tance [əd'mɪtəns]: **no ~** entrée *f* interdite

ad·mit·ted·ly [əd'mɪtedlɪ] *adv* il faut l'admettre

ad·mon·ish [əd'mɑːnɪʃ] *v/t fml* réprimander

a·do [ə'duː]: **without further ~** sans plus parler

ad·o·les·cence [ædə'lesns] adolescence *f*

ad·o·les·cent [ædə'lesnt] **1** *adj* adolescent **2** *n* adolescent(e) *m(f)*

a·dopt [ə'dɑːpt] *v/t* adopter

a·dop·tion [ə'dɑːpʃn] adoption *f*

a·dop·tive [ə'dɑːptɪv] *adj*: **~ parents** parents *mpl* adoptifs

a·dor·a·ble [ə'dɔːrəbl] *adj* adorable

ad·o·ra·tion [ædə'reɪʃn] adoration *f*

a·dore [ə'dɔːr] *v/t* adorer

a·dor·ing [ə'dɔːrɪŋ] *adj expression* d'adoration; *fans* plein d'adoration

ad·ren·al·in [ə'drenəlɪn] adrénaline *f*

a·drift [ə'drɪft] *adj also fig* à la dérive

ad·u·la·tion [ædjuː'leɪʃn] adulation *f*

a·dult ['ædʌlt] **1** *adj* adulte **2** *n* adulte *m/f*

a·dult ed·u·ca·tion enseignement *m* pour adultes

a·dul·ter·ous [ə'dʌltərəs] *adj* adultère

a·dul·ter·y [ə'dʌltərɪ] adultère *m*

'a·dult film *euph* film *m* pour adultes

ad·vance [əd'væns] **1** *n money* avance *f*; *in science etc* avancée *f*; MIL progression *f*; **in ~** à l'avance; **payment in ~** paiement *m* anticipé; **make ~s** (*progress*) faire des progrès; *sexually* faire des avances **2** *v/i* MIL, (*make progress*) avancer **3** *v/t theory, sum of money* avancer; *human knowledge, cause* faire avancer

ad·vance 'book·ing: **~ advised** il est conseillé de réserver à l'avance

ad·vanced [əd'vænst] *adj* avancé

ad·vance 'no·tice préavis *m*

ad·vance 'pay·ment acompte *m*

ad·van·tage [əd'væntɪdʒ] avantage *m*; **it's to your ~** c'est dans ton intérêt; **take ~ of** *opportunity* profiter de

ad·van·ta·geous [ædvən'teɪdʒəs] *adj* avantageux*

ad·vent ['ædvent] *fig* arrivée *f*

'ad·vent cal·en·dar calendrier *m* de l'avent

ad·ven·ture [əd'ventʃər] aventure *f*

ad·ven·tur·ous [əd'ventʃərəs] *adj* aventureux*

ad·verb ['ædvɜːrb] adverbe *m*

ad·ver·sa·ry ['ædvərsərɪ] adversaire *m/f*

ad·verse ['ædvɜːrs] *adj* adverse

ad·vert ['ædvɜːrt] *Br* → **advertisement**

ad·ver·tise ['ædvərtaɪz] **1** *v/t product* faire de la publicité pour; *job* mettre

une annonce pour **2** v/i *for a product*
faire de la publicité; *to fill job* mettre
une annonce

ad·ver·tise·ment [ədvɜːr'taɪsmənt]
for a product publicité *f*, pub *f* F;
for job annonce *f*

ad·ver·tis·er ['ædvərtaɪzər] annon-
ceur(-euse) *m(f)*

ad·ver·tis·ing ['ædvərtaɪzɪŋ] publicité
f

'ad·ver·tis·ing a·gen·cy agence *f* de
publicité; 'ad·ver·tis·ing budg·et
budget *m* de publicité; 'ad·ver·tis-
ing cam·paign campagne *f* de publicité; 'ad·ver·tis·ing rev·e·nue recettes *fpl* publicitaires

ad·vice [əd'vaɪs] conseils *mpl*; *a bit of
~* un conseil; *take s.o.'s ~* suivre le
conseil de qn

ad·vis·a·ble [əd'vaɪzəbl] *adj* conseillé

ad·vise [əd'vaɪz] v/t conseiller; *~ s.o.
to do sth* conseiller à qn de faire qch

ad·vis·er [əd'vaɪzər] conseiller(-ère)
m(f)

ad·vo·cate ['ædvəkeɪt] v/t recommander

aer·i·al ['erɪəl] *n Br* antenne *f*

aer·i·al 'pho·to·graph photographie *f*
aérienne

aer·o·bics [e'roʊbɪks] *nsg* aérobic *m*

aer·o·dy·nam·ic [eroʊdaɪ'næmɪk] *adj*
aérodynamique

aer·o·nau·ti·cal [eroʊ'nɒːtɪkl] *adj* aéronautique

aer·o·plane ['eroʊpleɪn] *Br* avion *m*

aer·o·sol ['erəsɑːl] aérosol *m*

aer·o·space in·dus·try ['erəspeɪs] industrie *f* aérospatiale

aes·thet·ic *etc Br* → esthetic *etc*

af·fa·ble ['æfəbl] *adj* affable

af·fair [ə'fer] *(matter, business)* affaire *f*;
(love ~) liaison *f*; *foreign ~s* affaires
fpl étrangères; *have an ~ with* avoir
une liaison avec

af·fect [ə'fekt] v/t MED endommager;
decision influer sur; *person emotionally, (concern)* toucher

af·fec·tion [ə'fekʃn] affection *f*

af·fec·tion·ate [ə'fekʃnət] *adj* affectueux*

af·fec·tion·ate·ly [ə'fekʃnətlɪ] *adv* af-

fectueusement

af·fin·i·ty [ə'fɪnətɪ] affinité *f*

af·fir·ma·tive [ə'fɜːrmətɪv] **1** *adj* affirmatif* **2** *n*: *answer in the ~* répondre
affirmativement

af·flu·ence ['æfluəns] richesse *f*

af·flu·ent ['æfluənt] *adj* riche; *the ~
society* la société de consommation

af·ford [ə'fɔːrd] v/t: *be able to ~ sth
financially* pouvoir se permettre
d'acheter qch; *I can't ~ the time* je
n'ai pas assez de temps; *it's a risk
we can't ~ to take* c'est un risque
qu'on ne peut pas se permettre de
prendre

af·ford·a·ble [ə'fɔːrdəbl] *adj* abordable

a·float [ə'floʊt] *adj boat* sur l'eau;
keep the company ~ maintenir l'entreprise à flot

a·fraid [ə'freɪd] *adj*: *be ~* avoir peur *(of*
de); *I'm ~ of upsetting him* j'ai peur
de le contrarier; *I'm ~ expressing regret* je crains; *I'm ~ so / not* je crains
que oui / non

a·fresh [ə'freʃ] *adv*: *start ~* recommencer

Af·ri·ca ['æfrɪkə] Afrique *f*

Af·ri·can ['æfrɪkən] **1** *adj* africain **2** *n*
Africain(e) *m(f)*

af·ter ['æftər] **1** *prep* après; *~ doing
sth* après avoir fait qch; *~ all* après
tout; *it's ten ~ two* il est deux heures
dix; *that's what I'm ~* c'est ça que je
cherche **2** *adv (afterward)* après; *the
day ~* le lendemain

af·ter·math ['æftərmæθ] suite *f*

af·ter·noon [æftər'nuːn] après-midi
m; *in the ~* l'après-midi; *this ~* cet
après-midi

'af·ter sales serv·ice service *m* après-
-vente; 'af·ter·shave lotion *f* après-
-rasage; 'af·ter·taste arrière-goût *m*

af·ter·ward ['æftərwərd] *adv* ensuite

a·gain [ə'geɪn] *adv* encore; *I never
saw him ~* je ne l'ai jamais revu;
start ~ recommencer

a·gainst [ə'genst] *prep* contre; *I'm ~
the idea* je suis contre cette idée

age [eɪdʒ] **1** *n* âge *m*; *at the ~ of ten* à
l'âge de dix ans; *she's five years of*

~ elle a cinq ans; **under** ~ mineur; **I've been waiting for** ~**s** F ça fait une éternité que j'attends **2** v/i vieillir

aged[1] [eɪʒd] adj: ~ **16** âgé de 16 ans

a·ged[2] ['eɪʒɪd] **1** adj: **her** ~ **parents** ses vieux parents **2** npl: **the** ~ les personnes fpl âgées

'**age group** catégorie f d'âge

'**age lim·it** limite f d'âge

a·gen·cy ['eɪdʒənsɪ] agence f

a·gen·da [ə'dʒendə] of meeting ordre m du jour; **on the** ~ à l'ordre du jour

a·gent ['eɪdʒənt] COMM agent m

ag·gra·vate ['ægrəveɪt] v/t rash faire empirer; situation aggraver, faire empirer; (annoy) agacer

ag·gre·gate ['ægrɪgət] SP: **win on** ~ totaliser le plus de points

ag·gres·sion [ə'greʃn] agression f

ag·gres·sive [ə'gresɪv] adj agressif*; (dynamic) dynamique

ag·gres·sive·ly [ə'gresɪvlɪ] adv agressivement

a·ghast [ə'gæst] adj horrifié

a·gile ['ædʒəl] adj agile

a·gil·i·ty [ə'dʒɪlətɪ] agilité f

ag·i·tate ['ædʒɪteɪt] v/i: ~ **for** militer pour

ag·i·tat·ed ['ædʒɪteɪtɪd] adj agité

ag·i·ta·tion [ædʒɪ'teɪʃn] agitation f

ag·i·ta·tor [ædʒɪ'teɪtər] agitateur (-trice) m(f)

ag·nos·tic [æg'nɑːstɪk] n agnostique m/f

a·go [ə'gou] adv: **two days** ~ il y a deux jours; **long** ~ il y a longtemps; **how long** ~? il y a combien de temps?

ag·o·nize ['ægənaɪz] v/i se tourmenter (over sur)

ag·o·niz·ing ['ægənaɪzɪŋ] adj terrible

ag·o·ny ['ægənɪ] mental tourment m; physical grande douleur f; **be in** ~ être à l'agonie

a·gree [ə'griː]: **1** v/i être d'accord (of figures, accounts s'accorder; (reach agreement) s'entendre; **I** ~ je suis d'accord; **it doesn't** ~ **with me** of food je ne le digère pas **2** v/t price s'entendre sur; **I** ~ **that** ... je conviens que ...

a·gree·a·ble [ə'griːəbl] adj (pleasant) agréable; **be** ~ (in agreement) être d'accord

a·gree·ment [ə'griːmənt] (consent, contract) accord m; **reach** ~ **on** parvenir à un accord sur

ag·ri·cul·tur·al [ægrɪ'kʌltʃərəl] adj agricole

ag·ri·cul·ture ['ægrɪkʌltʃər] agriculture f

a·head [ə'hed] adv devant; **be** ~ **of s.o.** être devant qn; **plan / think** ~ prévoir / penser à l'avance

aid [eɪd] **1** n aide f **2** v/t aider

aide [eɪd] aide m/f

Aids [eɪdz] nsg sida m

ail·ing ['eɪlɪŋ] adj economy mal en point

ail·ment ['eɪlmənt] mal m

aim [eɪm] **1** n in shooting visée f; (objective) but m **2** v/i in shooting viser; ~ **at doing sth,** ~ **to do sth** essayer de faire qch **3** v/t: **be** ~**ed at** of remark etc viser qn; **be** ~**ed at** of gun être pointé sur qn

aim·less ['eɪmlɪs] adj sans but

air [er] **1** n air m; **by** ~ par avion; **in the open** ~ en plein air; **on the** ~ RAD, TV à l'antenne **2** v/t room aérer; fig: views exprimer

'**air·bag** airbag m; '**air·base** base f aérienne f; '**air·con·di·tioned** adj climatisé; '**air·con·di·tion·ing** climatisation f; '**air·craft** avion m; '**air·craft car·ri·er** porte-avions m inv; '**air fare** tarif m aérien; '**air·field** aérodrome m; '**air force** armée f de l'air; '**air host·ess** hôtesse f de l'air; '**air let·ter** aérogramme m; '**air·lift 1** n pont m aérien **2** v/t transporter par avion; '**air·line** compagnie f aérienne; '**air·lin·er** avion m de ligne; '**air·mail**: **by** ~ par avion; '**air·plane** avion m; '**air·pock·et** trou m d'air; '**air pol·lu·tion** pollution f atmosphérique; '**air·port** aéroport m; '**air·sick**: **get** ~ avoir le mal de l'air; '**air·space** espace m aérien; '**air ter·mi·nal** aérogare f; '**air·tight** adj container étanche; '**air traf·fic** trafic m aérien; **air-traf·fic con'trol** contrôle m aérien; **air-traf·fic con'trol·ler** contrô-leur(-euse) aérien(ne) *m(f)*

air·y [ˈeri] *adj room* aéré; *attitude* désinvolte

aisle [aɪl] *in airplane* couloir *m*; *in theater* allée *f*

'aisle seat *in airplane* place *f* couloir

a·jar [əˈdʒɑːr] *adj*: **be ~** être entrouvert

a·lac·ri·ty [əˈlækrəti] empressement *m*

a·larm [əˈlɑːrm] **1** *n (fear)* inquiétude *f*; *device* alarme *f*; **(~ clock)** réveil *m*; **raise the ~** donner l'alarme **2** *v/t* alarmer

a'larm clock réveil *m*

a·larm·ing [əˈlɑːrmɪŋ] *adj* alarmant

a·larm·ing·ly [əˈlɑːrmɪŋlɪ] *adv* de manière alarmante; **~ quickly** à une vitesse alarmante

al·bum [ˈælbəm] *for photographs, (record)* album *m*

al·co·hol [ˈælkəhɑːl] alcool *m*

al·co·hol·ic [ælkəˈhɑːlɪk] **1** *adj drink* alcoolisé **2** *n* alcoolique *m/f*

a·lert [əˈlɜːrt] **1** *adj* vigilant **2** *n signal* alerte *f*; **be on the ~** *of troops* être en état d'alerte; *of person* être sur le qui-vive **3** *v/t* alerter

al·ge·bra [ˈældʒɪbrə] algèbre *f*

al·i·bi [ˈælɪbaɪ] *n* alibi *m*

a·lien [ˈeɪliən] **1** *adj* étranger* **(to** à) **2** *n (foreigner)* étranger(-ère) *m(f)*; *from space* extra-terrestre *m/f*

a·lien·ate [ˈeɪliəneɪt] *v/t* s'aliéner

a·light [əˈlaɪt] *adj*: **be ~** *on fire* être en feu

a·lign [əˈlaɪn] *v/t* aligner

a·like [əˈlaɪk] **1** *adj*: **be ~** se ressembler **2** *adv*: **old and young ~** les vieux comme les jeunes

al·i·mo·ny [ˈælɪmənɪ] pension *f* alimentaire

a·live [əˈlaɪv] *adj*: **be ~** être en vie

all [ɔːl] **1** *adj* tout **2** *pron* tout; **~ of us / them** nous / eux tous; **he ate ~ of it** il l'a mangé en entier; **that's ~, thanks** ce sera tout, merci; **for ~ I care** pour ce que j'en ai à faire; **for ~ I know** pour autant que je sache; **~ but him** *(except)* tous sauf lui **3** *adv*: **~ at once** *(suddenly)* tout d'un coup; *(at the same time)* tous ensemble; **~**

but *(nearly)* presque; **~ the better** encore mieux; **~ the time** tout le temps; **they're not at ~ alike** ils ne se ressemblent pas du tout; **not at ~!** *(please do)* pas du tout!; **two ~** SP deux à deux; **thirty ~** *in tennis* trente à; **~ right → alright**

al·lay [əˈleɪ] *v/t* apaiser

al·le·ga·tion [ælɪˈgeɪʃn] allégation *f*

al·lege [əˈledʒ] *v/t* alléguer

al·leged [əˈledʒd] *adj* supposé

al·leg·ed·ly [əˈledʒɪdlɪ] *adv*: **he killed two women** il aurait assassiné deux femmes

al·le·giance [əˈliːdʒəns] loyauté *f* **(to** à)

al·ler·gic [əˈlɜːrdʒɪk] *adj* allergique **(to** à)

al·ler·gy [ˈælərdʒɪ] allergie *f*

al·le·vi·ate [əˈliːvieɪt] *v/t* soulager

al·ley [ˈælɪ] ruelle *f*

al·li·ance [əˈlaɪəns] alliance *f*

al·lied [ˈælaɪd] *adj* MIL allié

al·lo·cate [ˈæləkeɪt] *v/t* assigner

al·lo·ca·tion [æləˈkeɪʃn] *action* assignation *f*; *amount allocated* part *f*

al·lot [əˈlɑːt] *v/t (pret & pp -ted)* assigner

al·low [əˈlaʊ] *v/t (permit)* permettre; *period of time, amount* compter; **it's not ~ed** ce n'est pas permis; **~ s.o. to do sth** permettre à qn de faire qch

◆ **allow for** *v/t* prendre en compte

al·low·ance [əˈlaʊəns] *money* allocation *f*; *(pocket money)* argent *m* de poche; **make ~s** *for fact* prendre en considération; *person* faire preuve de tolérance envers

al·loy [ˈælɔɪ] alliage *m*

'all-pur·pose *adj device* universel*; *vehicle* tous usages; **'all-round** *adj improvement* d'ensemble; *athlete* complet; **'all-time**: **be at an ~ low** être à son point le plus bas

◆ **al·lude to** [əˈluːd] *v/t* faire allusion à

al·lur·ing [əˈluːrɪŋ] *adj* alléchant

all-wheel 'drive quatre roues motrices *fpl*; *vehicle* 4x4 *m*

al·ly [ˈælaɪ] *n* allié(e) *m(f)*

Al·might·y [ɔːlˈmaɪtɪ]: **the ~** le Tout-Puissant

al·mond ['ɑːmənd] amande f

al·most ['ɔːlmoust] adv presque; **I ~ came to see you** j'ai failli venir te voir

a·lone [ə'loun] adj seul

a·long [ə'lɒŋ] 1 prep le long de; **walk ~ this path** prenez ce chemin 2 adv: **she always brings the dog ~** elle amène toujours le chien avec elle; **~ with** in addition to ainsi que; **if you knew all ~** si tu le savais

a·long·side [əlɒŋ'saɪd] prep parallel to à côté de; in cooperation with aux côtés de

a·loof [ə'luːf] adj distant

a·loud [ə'laud] adv à haute voix

al·pha·bet ['ælfəbet] alphabet m

al·pha·bet·i·cal [ælfə'betɪkl] adj alphabétique

al·pine ['ælpaɪn] adj alpin

Alps [ælps] npl Alpes fpl

al·read·y [ɒːl'redɪ] adv déjà

al·right [ɒːl'raɪt] adj (permitted) permis; (acceptable) convenable; **be ~** (in working order) fonctionner; **she's ~ not hurt** elle n'est pas blessée; **would $50 be ~?** est-ce que 50 $ vous iraient?; **is it ~ with you if I ...?** est-ce que ça vous dérange si je ...?; **~, you can have one!** d'accord, tu peux en prendre un!; **~, I heard you!** c'est bon, je vous ai entendu!; **everything is ~ now between them** tout va bien maintenant entre eux; **that's ~** (don't mention it) c'est rien

al·so ['ɒːlsou] adv aussi

al·tar ['ɒːltər] autel m

al·ter ['ɒːltər] v/t plans, schedule modifier, faire des modifications à; person changer, transformer; garment retoucher, faire une retouche à

al·ter·a·tion [ɒːltə'reɪʃn] to plans etc modification f; to clothes retouche f

al·ter·nate 1 ['ɒːltərneɪt] v/i alterner (**between** entre) **2** ['ɒːltərnət] adj: **on ~ Mondays** un lundi sur deux

al·ter·nat·ing cur·rent ['ɒːltərneɪtɪŋ] courant m alternatif

al·ter·na·tive [ɒːl'tɜːrnətɪv] **1** adj alternatif* **2** n alternative f

al·ter·na·tive·ly [ɒːl'tɜːrnətɪvlɪ] adv sinon; **or ~** ou bien

al·though [ɒːl'ðou] conj bien que (+subj), quoique (+subj)

al·ti·tude ['æltɪtuːd] altitude f

al·to·geth·er [ɒːltə'geðər] adv (completely) totalement; (in all) en tout

al·tru·ism ['æltruːɪzm] altruisme m

al·tru·is·tic [æltruː'ɪstɪk] adj altruiste

a·lu·min·um [ə'luːmɪnəm], Br **a·lu·min·i·um** [æljuː'mɪnɪəm] aluminium m

al·ways ['ɒːlweɪz] adv toujours

a.m. ['eɪem] abbr (= **ante meridiem**) du matin

a·mal·gam·ate [ə'mælgəmeɪt] v/i of companies fusionner

a·mass [ə'mæs] v/t amasser

am·a·teur ['æmətʃur] n also pej, SP amateur m/f

am·a·teur·ish ['æmətʃurɪʃ] adj pej: attempt d'amateur; painter sans talent

a·maze [ə'meɪz] v/t étonner

a·mazed [ə'meɪzd] adj étonné

a·maze·ment [ə'meɪzmənt] étonnement m

a·maz·ing [ə'meɪzɪŋ] adj étonnant; F (very good) impressionnant

a·maz·ing·ly [ə'meɪzɪŋlɪ] adv étonnamment

am·bas·sa·dor [æm'bæsədər] ambassadeur(-drice) m(f)

am·ber ['æmbər] n: **at ~** à l'orange

am·bi·dex·trous [æmbɪ'dekstrəs] adj ambidextre

am·bi·ence ['æmbɪəns] ambiance f

am·bi·gu·i·ty [æmbɪ'gjuːətɪ] ambiguïté f

am·big·u·ous [æm'bɪgjuəs] adj ambigu*

am·bi·tion [æm'bɪʃn] ambition f

am·bi·tious [æm'bɪʃəs] adj ambitieux*

am·biv·a·lent [æm'bɪvələnt] adj ambivalent

am·ble ['æmbl] v/i déambuler

am·bu·lance ['æmbjuləns] ambulance f

am·bush ['æmbuʃ] **1** n embuscade f **2** v/t tendre une embuscade à; **be ~ed** tomber dans une embuscade a·mend [əˈmend] v/t modifier

a·mend·ment [əˈmendmənt] modification f

a·mends [əˈmendz]: **make ~** se racheter

a·men·i·ties [əˈmiːnətɪz] npl facilités fpl

A·mer·i·ca [əˈmerɪkə] (United States) États-Unis mpl; continent Amérique f

A·mer·i·can [əˈmerɪkən] 1 adj américain 2 n Américain(e) m(f)

A·mer·i·can plan pension f complète

a·mi·a·ble [ˈeɪmɪəbl] adj aimable

a·mi·ca·ble [ˈæmɪkəbl] adj à l'amiable

a·mi·ca·bly [ˈæmɪkəblɪ] adv à l'amiable

am·mu·ni·tion [æmjʊˈnɪʃn] munitions fpl

am·ne·si·a [æmˈniːzɪə] amnésie f

am·nes·ty [ˈæmnəstɪ] amnistie f

a·mong(st) [əˈmʌŋ(st)] prep parmi

a·mor·al [eɪˈmɔːrəl] adj amoral

a·mount [əˈmaʊnt] quantité f; (sum of money) somme f

♦ amount to v/t s'élever à; (be equivalent to) revenir à

am·phib·i·an [æmˈfɪbɪən] amphibien m

am·phib·i·ous [æmˈfɪbɪəs] adj amphibie

am·phi·the·a·ter, Br am·phi·the·a·tre [ˈæmfɪθɪətər] amphithéâtre m

am·ple [ˈæmpl] adj beaucoup de; **$4 will be ~** 4 $ sera amplement suffisant

am·pli·fi·er [ˈæmplɪfaɪr] amplificateur m

am·pli·fy [ˈæmplɪfaɪ] v/t (pret & pp **-ied**) sound amplifier

am·pu·tate [ˈæmpjʊteɪt] v/t amputer

am·pu·ta·tion [æmpjʊˈteɪʃn] amputation f

a·muse [əˈmjuːz] v/t (make laugh) amuser; (entertain) distraire

a·muse·ment [əˈmjuːzmənt] (merriment) amusement m; (entertainment) divertissement m; **to our great ~** à notre grand amusement

a·muse·ment park parc m d'attractions

a·mus·ing [əˈmjuːzɪŋ] adj amusant

an [æn], unstressed [ən] → **a**

an·a·bol·ic ster·oid [ænəˈbɑːlɪk] stéroïde m anabolisant

a·nae·mi·a etc Br → **anemia** etc

an·aes·thet·ic etc Br → **anesthetic** etc

an·a·log [ˈænəlɑːg] adj COMPUT analogique

a·nal·o·gy [əˈnælədʒɪ] analogie f

an·a·lyse v/t Br → **analyze**

a·nal·y·sis [əˈnæləsɪs] (pl **analyses** [əˈnæləsiːz]) analyse f

an·a·lyst [ˈænəlɪst] also PSYCH analyste m/f

an·a·lyt·i·cal [ænəˈlɪtɪkl] adj analytique

an·a·lyze [ˈænəlaɪz] v/t also PSYCH analyser

an·arch·y [ˈænərkɪ] anarchie f

a·nat·o·my [əˈnætəmɪ] anatomie f

an·ces·tor [ˈænsestər] ancêtre m/f

an·chor [ˈæŋkər] 1 n NAUT ancre f; TV présentateur(-trice) principal(e) m(f) 2 v/i NAUT ancrer

an·cient [ˈeɪnʃənt] adj Rome, Greece antique; object, buildings, tradition ancien

an·cil·lar·y [ænˈsɪlərɪ] adj staff auxiliaire

and [ənd], stressed [ænd] conj et; **bigger ~ bigger** de plus en plus grand; **go ~ look it** vas le chercher

An·dor·ra [ænˈdɔːrə] Andorre f

An·dor·ran [ænˈdɔːrən] 1 adj andorran 2 n Andorran(e) m(f)

an·ec·dote [ˈænɪkdoʊt] anecdote f

a·ne·mi·a [əˈniːmɪə] anémie f

a·ne·mic [əˈniːmɪk] adj anémique

an·es·the·si·ol·o·gist [ænəsθiːziːˈɑːlədʒɪst] anesthésiste m/f

an·es·thet·ic [ænəsˈθetɪk] n anesthésiant m

anesthetic: **local / general ~** anesthésie f locale / générale

an·es·the·tist [əˈniːsθətɪst] Br anesthésiste m/f

an·gel [ˈeɪndʒl] REL, fig ange m

an·ger [ˈæŋgər] 1 n colère f 2 v/t mettre en colère

an·gi·na [ænˈdʒaɪnə] angine f de poitrine

an·gle [ˈæŋgl] n angle m

an·gry ['æŋgrɪ] *adj person* en colère; *mood, voice, look* fâché; *be ~ with s.o.* être en colère contre qn

an·guish ['æŋgwɪʃ] angoisse *f*

an·gu·lar ['æŋgjʊlər] *adj* anguleux*

an·i·mal ['ænɪml] animal *m*

an·i·mat·ed ['ænɪmeɪtɪd] *adj* animé

an·i·mat·ed car'toon dessin *m* animé

an·i·ma·tion [ænɪ'meɪʃn] (*liveliness*), *technique* animation *f*

an·i·mos·i·ty [ænɪ'mɑːsətɪ] animosité *f*

an·kle ['æŋkl] cheville *f*

an·nex ['æneks] **1** *n building, to document* annexe *f* **2** *v/t state* annexer

an·nexe *n Br* → **annex**

an·ni·hi·late [ə'naɪəleɪt] *v/t* anéantir

an·ni·hi·la·tion [ənaɪə'leɪʃn] anéantissement *m*

an·ni·ver·sa·ry [ænɪ'vɜːrsərɪ] anniversaire *m*

an·no·tate ['ænəteɪt] *v/t report* annoter

an·nounce [ə'naʊns] *v/t* annoncer

an·nounce·ment [ə'naʊnsmənt] annonce *f*

an·nounc·er [ə'naʊnsər] TV, RAD speaker *m*, speakrine *f*

an·noy [ə'nɔɪ] *v/t* agacer; *be ~ed* être agacé

an·noy·ance [ə'nɔɪəns] (*anger*) agacement *m*; (*nuisance*) désagrément *m*

an·noy·ing [ə'nɔɪɪŋ] *adj* agaçant

an·nu·al ['ænʊəl] *adj* annuel*

an·nu·i·ty [ə'nuːətɪ] rente *f* (annuelle)

an·nul [ə'nʌl] *v/t* (*pret & pp* **-led**) *marriage* annuler

an·nul·ment [ə'nʌlmənt] annulation *f*

a·non·y·mous [ə'nɑːnɪməs] *adj* anonyme

an·o·rex·i·a [ænə'reksɪə] anorexie *f*

an·o·rex·ic [ænə'reksɪk] *adj* anorexique

an·oth·er [ə'nʌðər] **1** *adj* (*different, additional*) autre **2** *pron* un(e) autre *m(f)*; *help one ~* s'entraider; *they know one ~* ils se connaissent

an·swer ['ænsər] **1** *n* réponse *f*; (*solution*) solution *f* (**to** à) **2** *v/t* répondre à; *~ the door* ouvrir la porte; *~ the telephone* répondre au téléphone **3** *v/i* répondre

♦ **answer back 1** *v/t* répondre à **2** *v/i* répondre

♦ **answer for** *v/t one's actions, person* répondre de

'an·swer·phone répondeur *m*

an·tag·o·nism [æn'tægənɪzm] antagonisme *m*

an·tag·o·nis·tic [æntægə'nɪstɪk] *adj* hostile

an·tag·o·nize [æn'tægənaɪz] *v/t* provoquer

Ant·arc·tic [ænt'ɑːrktɪk] *n*: *the ~* l'Antarctique *m*

an·te·na·tal [æntɪ'neɪtl] *adj* prénatal; *~ class* cours *m* de préparation à l'accouchement

an·ten·na [æn'tenə] antenne *f*

an·thol·o·gy [æn'θɑːlədʒɪ] anthologie *f*

an·thro·pol·o·gy [ænθrə'pɑːlədʒɪ] anthropologie *f*

an·ti·bi·ot·ic [æntaɪbaɪ'ɑːtɪk] *n* antibiotique *m*

an·ti·bod·y ['æntaɪbɑːdɪ] anticorps *m*

an·tic·i·pate [æn'tɪsɪpeɪt] *v/t* prévoir

an·tic·i·pa·tion [æntɪsɪ'peɪʃn] prévision *f*

an·ti·clock·wise ['æntɪklɑː'kwaɪz] *adv Br* dans le sens inverse des aiguilles d'une montre

an·tics ['æntɪks] *npl* singeries *fpl*

an·ti·dote ['æntɪdoʊt] antidote *m*

an·ti·freeze ['æntɪfriːz] antigel *m*

an·tip·a·thy [æn'tɪpəθɪ] antipathie *f*

an·ti·quat·ed ['æntɪkweɪtɪd] *adj* antique

an·tique [æn'tiːk] *n* antiquité *f*

an'tique deal·er antiquaire *m/f*

an·tiq·ui·ty [æn'tɪkwətɪ] antiquité *f*

an·ti·sep·tic [æntər'septɪk] **1** *adj* antiseptique **2** *n* antiseptique *m*

an·ti·so·cial [æntaɪ'soʊʃl] *adj* asocial, antisocial

an·ti·vi·rus pro·gram [æntaɪ'vaɪrəs] COMPUT programme *m* antivirus

anx·i·e·ty [æŋ'zaɪətɪ] (*worry*) inquiétude *f*

anx·ious ['æŋkʃəs] *adj* (*worried*) inquiet*; (*eager*) soucieux*; *be ~ for for news etc* désirer vivement

an·y ['enɪ] **1** adj: **are there ~ diskettes / glasses?** est-ce qu'il y a des disquettes / des verres?; **is there ~ bread / improvement?** est-ce qu'il y a du pain / une amélioration; **there aren't ~ diskettes / glasses** il n'y a pas de disquettes / de verres; **there isn't ~ bread / improvement** il n'y a pas de pain / d'amélioration; **have you ~ idea at all?** est-ce que vous avez une idée?; **take ~ one you like** prends celui / celle que tu veux; **at ~ moment** à tout moment **2** pron: **do you have ~?** est-ce que vous en avez?; **there aren't / isn't ~ left** il n'y en a plus; **~ of them could be guilty** ils pourraient tous être coupables **3** adv: **is that ~ better / easier?** est-ce que c'est mieux / plus facile?; **I don't like it ~ more** je ne l'aime plus

an·y·bod·y ['enɪbɑːdɪ] pron ◊ quelqu'un ◊ with negatives personne; **there wasn't ~ there** il n'y avait personne ◊ no matter who n'importe qui; **~ can see that ...** tout le monde peut voir que ...

an·y·how ['enɪhaʊ] adv (anyway) enfin; (in any way) de quelque façon que ce soit

an·y·one ['enɪwʌn] → **anybody**

an·y·thing ['enɪθɪŋ] pron ◊ quelque chose; **~ else?** quelque chose d'autre?; **absolutely ~** n'importe quoi ◊ with negatives rien; **I didn't hear ~ but ...** tout sauf ...; **no, ~ but** non, pas du tout; **~ but** je n'ai rien entendu ~

an·y·way ['enɪweɪ] → **anyhow**

an·y·where ['enɪwer] adv quelque part; with negative nulle part; **I can't find it ~** je ne le trouve nulle part; **did you go ~ else?** est-ce que tu es allé ailleurs or autre part?

a·part [ə'pɑːrt] adv séparé; **the two cities are 250 miles ~** les deux villes sont à 250 miles l'une de l'autre; **live ~** vivre séparés; **~ from** (except) à l'exception de; **~ from** (in addition to) en plus de

a·part·ment [ə'pɑːrtmənt] appartement m

a·part·ment block immeuble m

ap·a·thet·ic [æpə'θetɪk] adj apathique

ap·a·thy ['æpəθɪ] apathie f

ape [eɪp] n singe m

a·pe·ri·tif [ə'perɪtiːf] apéritif m

ap·er·ture ['æpərtʃər] PHOTouverture f

a·piece [ə'piːs] adv chacun

a·pol·o·get·ic [əpɑːlə'dʒetɪk] adj person, expression désolé; letter d'excuse; **he was very ~** il s'est confondu en excuses

a·pol·o·gize [ə'pɑːlədʒaɪz] v/i s'excuser (**to s.o.** auprès de qn; **for sth** pour qch); **~ for doing sth** s'excuser de faire qch

a·pol·o·gy [ə'pɑːlədʒɪ] excuses fpl

a·pos·tle [ə'pɑːsl] REL apôtre m

a·pos·tro·phe [ə'pɑːstrəfɪ] GRAM apostrophe f

ap·pall [ə'pɒːl] v/t scandaliser

ap·pal·ling [ə'pɒːlɪŋ] adj scandaleux*

ap·pa·ra·tus [æpə'reɪtəs] appareils mpl

ap·par·ent [ə'pærənt] adj (obvious) évident; (seeming) apparent; **become ~ that ...** devenir évident que ...

ap·par·ent·ly [ə'pærəntlɪ] adv apparemment

ap·pa·ri·tion [æpə'rɪʃn] ghost apparition f

ap·peal [ə'piːl] **1** n (charm) charme m; for funds etc, LAW appel m

appeal 2 v/i LAW faire appel

◆ **appeal for** v/t calm etc appeler à; funds demander

◆ **appeal to** v/t (be attractive to) plaire à

ap·peal·ing [ə'piːlɪŋ] adj idea, offer séduisant

ap·pear [ə'pɪr] v/i of person, new product apparaître; in court comparaître; in movie jouer; (look, seem) paraître; **~ to be ...** avoir l'air d'être ...; **it ~s that ...** il semble que ...

ap·pear·ance [ə'pɪrəns] apparition f; in court comparution f; (look) apparence f; **put in an ~** faire acte de présence

ap·pease [ə'piːz] v/t apaiser

ap·pen·di·ci·tis [əpendɪ'saɪtɪs] appendicite f

ap·pen·dix [ə'pendɪks] MED, *of book etc* appendice *m*

ap·pe·tite ['æpɪtaɪt] appétit *m*

ap·pe·tiz·er ['æpɪtaɪzər] *to drink* apéritif *m*; *to eat* amuse-gueule *m*; (*starter*) entrée *f*

ap·pe·tiz·ing ['æpɪtaɪzɪŋ] *adj* appétissant

ap·plaud [ə'plɔːd] **1** *v/i* applaudir **2** *v/t performer* applaudir; *fig* saluer

ap·plause [ə'plɔːz] *for performer* applaudissements *mpl*; *fig* louanges *fpl*

ap·ple ['æpl] pomme *f*

ap·ple 'pie tarte *f* aux pommes

ap·ple 'sauce compote *f* de pommes

ap·pli·ance [ə'plaɪəns] appareil *m*

ap·plic·a·ble [ə'plɪkəbl] *adj* applicable

ap·pli·cant ['æplɪkənt] *for job* candidat(e) *m(f)*

ap·pli·ca·tion [æplɪ'keɪʃn] *for job* candidature *f*; *for passport etc* demande *f*

ap·pli·ca·tion form *for job* formulaire *m* de candidature; *for passport etc* demande *f*

ap·ply [ə'plaɪ] **1** *v/t* (*pret & pp* **-ied**) appliquer **2** *v/i of rule, law* s'appliquer

♦ **apply for** *v/t job* poser sa candidature pour; *passport etc* faire une demande de

♦ **apply to** *v/t* (*contact*) s'adresser à; *of rules etc* s'appliquer à

ap·point [ə'pɔɪnt] *v/t to position* nommer

ap·point·ment [ə'pɔɪntmənt] *to position* nomination *f*; (*meeting*) rendezvous *m*; **make an ~** prendre (un) rendez-vous

ap'point·ments di·a·ry carnet *m* de rendez-vous

ap·prais·al [ə'preɪzl] évaluation *f*

ap·pre·ci·a·ble [ə'priːʃəbl] *adj* considérable

ap·pre·ci·ate [ə'priːʃɪeɪt] **1** *v/t* (*be grateful for*), *wine, music* apprécier; (*acknowledge*) reconnaître; **thanks, I ~ it** merci, c'est très gentil **2** *v/i* FIN s'apprécier

ap·pre·ci·a·tion [əpriːʃɪ'eɪʃn] *of kindness etc* gratitude *f* (**of** pour), reconnaissance *f* (**of** de)

ap·pre·ci·a·tive [ə'priːʃətɪv] *adj* showing gratitude reconnaissant; *showing understanding* approbateur*; *audience* réceptif*

ap·pre·hen·sive [æprɪ'hensɪv] *adj* appréhensif*

ap·pren·tice [ə'prentɪs] apprenti(e) *m(f)*

ap·proach [ə'proʊtʃ] **1** *n to problem, place* approche *f*; (*proposal*) proposition *f* **2** *v/t* (*get near to*) approcher; (*contact*) faire des propositions à; *problem* aborder

ap·proach·a·ble [ə'proʊtʃəbl] *adj person* accessible, d'un abord facile

ap·pro·pri·ate¹ [ə'proʊprɪət] *adj* approprié

ap·pro·pri·ate² [ə'proʊprɪeɪt] *v/t* s'approprier

ap·prov·al [ə'pruːvl] approbation *f*

ap·prove [ə'pruːv] **1** *v/i* être d'accord **2** *v/t plan, suggestion* approuver; *application* accepter

♦ **approve of** *v/t plan, suggestion* approuver; *person* aimer

ap·prox·i·mate [ə'prɑːksɪmət] *adj* approximatif*

ap·prox·i·mate·ly [ə'prɑːksɪmətlɪ] *adv* approximativement

ap·prox·i·ma·tion [əprɑːksɪ'meɪʃn] approximation *f*

APR [eɪpiː'ɑːr] *abbr* (= **annual percentage rate**) TEG (= taux *m* effectif global)

a·pri·cot ['eɪprɪkɑːt] abricot *m*

A·pril ['eɪprəl] avril *m*

apt [æpt] *adj student* intelligent; *remark* pertinent; **be ~ to ...** avoir tendance à

ap·ti·tude ['æptɪtuːd] aptitude *f*

'ap·ti·tude test test *m* d'aptitude

a·quar·i·um [ə'kwerɪəm] aquarium *m*

A·quar·i·us [ə'kwerɪəs] ASTROL Verseau *m*

a·quat·ic [ə'kwætɪk] *adj* aquatique

Ar·ab ['ærəb] **1** *adj* arabe **2** *n* Arabe *m/f*

Ar·a·bic ['ærəbɪk] **1** *adj* arabe **2** *n* arabe *m*

ar·a·ble ['ærəbl] *adj* arable

ar·bi·tra·ry ['ɑːrbɪtrərɪ] *adj* arbitraire

ar·bi·trate ['ɑːrbɪtreɪt] *v/i* arbitrer

ar·bi·tra·tion [ɑːrbɪ'treɪʃn] arbitrage *m*

ar·bi·tra·tor ['ɑːrbɪ'treɪtər] arbitre *m*

arch [ɑːrtʃ] *n* voûte *f*

ar·chae·ol·o·gy *etc Br* → **archeology** *etc*

ar·cha·ic [ɑːr'keɪɪk] *adj* archaïque

arch·bish·op [ɑːrtʃ'bɪʃəp] archevêque *m*

ar·che·o·log·i·cal [ɑːrkɪə'lɑːdʒɪkl] *adj* archéologique

ar·che·ol·o·gist [ɑːrkɪ'ɑːlədʒɪst] archéologue *m/f*

ar·che·ol·o·gy [ɑːrkɪ'ɑːlədʒɪ] archéologie *f*

arch·er ['ɑːrtʃər] archer *m*

ar·chi·tect ['ɑːrkɪtekt] architecte *m/f*

ar·chi·tec·tur·al [ɑːrkɪ'tektʃərəl] *adj* architectural

ar·chi·tec·ture ['ɑːrkɪtektʃər] architecture *f*

ar·chives ['ɑːrkaɪvz] *npl* archives *fpl*

'arch·way arche *f*; *entrance* porche *m*

Arc·tic ['ɑːrktɪk] *n*: **the ~** l'Arctique *m*

ar·dent ['ɑːrdənt] *adj* fervent

ar·du·ous ['ɑːrdjuəs] *adj* ardu

ar·e·a ['erɪə] *of city* quartier *m*; *of country* région *f*; *of research, study etc* domaine *m*; *of room* surface *f*; *of land, figure* superficie *f*; **in the Boston ~** dans la région de Boston

'ar·e·a code TELEC indicatif *m* régional

a·re·na [ə'riːnə] SP arène *f*

Ar·gen·ti·na [ɑːrdʒən'tiːnə] Argentine *f*

Ar·gen·tin·i·an [ɑːrdʒən'tɪnɪən] **1** *adj* argentin **2** *n* Argentin(e) *m(f)*

ar·gu·a·bly ['ɑːrgjuəblɪ] *adv*: **it was ~ the best book of the year** on peut dire que c'était le meilleur livre de l'année

ar·gue ['ɑːrgjuː] **1** *v/i (quarrel)* se disputer; *(reason)* argumenter; **~ with s.o.** *discuss* se disputer avec qn **2** *v/t*: **~ that …** soutenir que …

ar·gu·ment ['ɑːrgjəmənt] *(quarrel)* dispute *f*; *(discussion)* discussion *f*; *(reasoning)* argument *m*

ar·gu·men·ta·tive [ɑːrgjuˈmentətɪv] *adj*: **stop being so ~ and …** arrête de discuter et …

a·ri·a ['ɑːrɪə] MUS aria *f*

ar·id ['ærɪd] *adj land* aride

Ar·ies ['eriːz] ASTROL Bélier *m*

a·rise [ə'raɪz] *v/i (pret* **arose**, *pp* **arisen)** *of situation, problem* survenir

a·ris·en [ə'rɪzn] *pp* → **arise**

ar·is·toc·ra·cy [ærɪ'stɑːkrəsɪ] aristocratie *f*

a·ris·to·crat ['ærɪstəkræt] aristocrate *m/f*

a·ris·to·crat·ic [ærɪstə'krætɪk] *adj* aristocratique

a·rith·me·tic [ə'rɪθmətɪk] arithmétique *f*

arm¹ [ɑːrm] *n* bras *m*

arm² [ɑːrm] *v/t* armer

ar·ma·ments ['ɑːrməmənts] *npl* armes *fpl*

'arm·chair fauteuil *m*

armed [ɑːrmd] *adj* armé

armed 'forc·es *npl* forces *fpl* armées

armed 'rob·ber·y vol *m* à main armée

ar·mor ['ɑːrmər] *on tank, armored vehicle* blindage *m*; *of knight* armure *f*

ar·mored 've·hi·cle ['ɑːrmərd] véhicule *m* blindé

ar·mour *etc Br* → **armor** *etc*

'arm·pit aisselle *f*

arms [ɑːrmz] *npl (weapons)* armes *fpl*

a·my ['ɑːrmɪ] armée *f*

a·ro·ma [ə'roumə] arôme *m*

a·rose [ə'rouz] *pret* → **arise**

a·round [ə'raund] **1** *prep (encircling)* autour de; **it's ~ the corner** c'est juste à côté **2** *adv (in the area)* dans les parages; *(encircling)* autour; *(roughly)* à peu près; *with expressions of time* à environ; **he lives ~ here** il habite dans ce quartier; **she's been ~ F** *(has traveled, is experienced)* elle n'est pas née de la dernière pluie; **he's still ~ F** *(alive)* il est toujours là

a·rouse [ə'rauz] *v/t* susciter; *sexually* exciter

ar·range [ə'reɪndʒ] *v/t flowers, music, room* arranger; *furniture* disposer; *meeting, party etc* organiser; *time* fixer; *appointment with doctor, dentist* prendre; **I've ~d to meet her** j'ai prévu de la voir

♦ arrange for *v/t*: **arrange for s.o. to do sth** s'arranger pour que qn fasse (subj) qch

ar·range·ment [əˈreɪndʒmənt] (agreement), music arrangement m; of furniture disposition f, flowers composition f

ar·rears [əˈrɪərz] npl arriéré m; **be in ~** of person être en retard

ar·rest [əˈrest] **1** n arrestation f; **be under ~** être en état d'arrestation **2** v/t arrêter

ar·riv·al [əˈraɪvl] arrivée f; **~s** at airport arrivées fpl

ar·rive [əˈraɪv] v/i arriver
♦ **arrive at** v/t place, decision arriver à

ar·ro·gance [ˈærəgəns] arrogance f

ar·ro·gant [ˈærəgənt] adj arrogant

ar·ro·gant·ly [ˈærəgəntlɪ] adv avec arrogance

ar·row [ˈærəʊ] flèche f

'ar·row key COMPUT touche f fléchée

ar·se·nic [ˈɑːrsənɪk] arsenic m

ar·son [ˈɑːrsn] incendie m criminel

ar·son·ist [ˈɑːrsənɪst] incendiaire m/f

art [ɑːrt] art m; **the ~s** les arts et les lettres mpl

ar·te·ry [ˈɑːrtərɪ] ANAT artère f

'art gal·ler·y galerie f d'art

ar·thri·tis [ɑːrˈθraɪtɪs] arthrite f

ar·ti·choke [ˈɑːrtɪtʃoʊk] artichaut m

ar·ti·cle [ˈɑːrtɪkl] article m; **~ of clothing** vêtement m

ar·tic·u·late [ɑːrˈtɪkjʊlət] adj person qui s'exprime bien

ar·ti·fi·cial [ɑːrtɪˈfɪʃl] adj artificiel*

ar·ti·fi·cial in·tel·li·gence intelligence f artificielle

ar·til·le·ry [ɑːrˈtɪlərɪ] artillerie f

ar·ti·san [ˈɑːrtɪzæn] artisan m

art·ist [ˈɑːrtɪst] artiste m/f

ar·tis·tic [ɑːrˈtɪstɪk] adj artistique

'arts de·gree licence f de lettres

as [æz] **1** conj (while, when) alors que; (because) comme; (like) comme; **~ it got darker** au fur et à mesure que la nuit tombait; **~ if** comme si; **~ usual** comme d'habitude; **~ necessary** quand c'est nécessaire **2** adv: **~ high / pretty / ...** aussi haut / jolie que ...; **~ much ~ that?** autant que ça?; **~ soon ~ possible** aussi vite que possible **3** prep comme; **work ~**

a team travailler en équipe; **~ a child / schoolgirl, I ...** quand j'étais enfant / écolière, je ...; **work ~ a teacher / translator** travailler comme professeur / traducteur; **~ for** quant à; **~ Hamlet** dans le rôle de Hamlet; **~ from** or **of Monday** à partir de lundi

asap [ˈeɪzæp] abbr (= **as soon as possible**) dans les plus brefs délais

as·bes·tos [æzˈbestɑːs] amiante m

As·cen·sion [əˈsenʃn] REL Ascension f

as·cent [əˈsent] ascension f

ash [æʃ] from cigarette etc cendres fpl; **~es** cendres fpl

a·shamed [əˈʃeɪmd] adj honteux*; **be ~ of** avoir honte de; **you should be ~ of yourself** tu devrais avoir honte

'ash can poubelle f

a·shore [əˈʃɔːr] adv à terre; **go ~** débarquer

'ash·tray cendrier m

A·sia [ˈeɪʃə] Asie f

A·sian [ˈeɪʃən] **1** adj asiatique **2** n Asiatique m/f

a·side [əˈsaɪd] adv de côté; **move ~ please** poussez-vous, s'il vous plaît; **take s.o. ~** prendre qn à part; **~ from** à part

ask [æsk] **1** v/t favor demander; question poser; (invite) inviter; **can I ~ you something?** est-ce que je peux vous demander quelque chose?; **I ~ed him about his holidays** je lui ai demandé comment ses vacances s'étaient passées; **~ s.o. for sth** demander qch à qn; **~ s.o. to do sth** demander à qn de faire qch **2** v/i demander

♦ **ask after** v/t person demander des nouvelles de

♦ **ask for** v/t demander; person demander à parler à; **you asked for that!** tu l'as cherché!

♦ **ask out** v/t: **he's asked me out** il m'a demandé de sortir avec lui

ask·ing price [ˈæskɪŋ] prix m demandé

a·sleep [əˈsliːp] adj: **be (fast) ~** être (bien) endormi; **fall ~** s'endormir

as·par·a·gus [əˈspærəgəs] *nsg* asper- ges *fpl*

as·pect [ˈæspekt] aspect *m*

as·phalt [ˈæsfælt] *n* bitume *m*

as·phyx·i·ate [æˈsfɪksɪeɪt] *v/t* asphyxi- er

as·phyx·i·a·tion [əsfɪksɪˈeɪʃn] asphy- xie *f*

as·pi·ra·tions [æspəˈreɪʃnz] *npl* aspi- rations *fpl*

as·pi·rin [ˈæsprɪn] aspirine *f*

ass¹ [æs] P *(backside, sex)* cul *m* P

ass² [æs] F *(idiot)* idiot(e) *m(f)*

as·sai·lant [əˈseɪlənt] assaillant(e) *m(f)*

as·sas·sin [əˈsæsɪn] assassin *m*

as·sas·sin·ate [əˈsæsɪneɪt] *v/t* assassi- ner

as·sas·sin·a·tion [əsæsɪˈneɪʃn] assas- sinat *m*

as·sault [əˈsɔːlt] **1** *n* agression *f* **(on** contre); MIL attaque *f* **(on** contre) **2** *v/t* agresser

as·sem·ble [əˈsembl] **1** *v/t parts* assem- bler **2** *v/i of people* se rassembler

as·sem·bly [əˈsembli] POL assemblée *f*; *of parts* assemblage *m*

as'sem·bly line chaîne *f* de montage

as'sem·bly plant usine *f* de montage

as·sent [əˈsent] *v/i* consentir

as·sert [əˈsɜːrt] *v/t (maintain)*, *right* af- firmer; **~ o.s.** s'affirmer

as·ser·tive [əˈsɜːrtɪv] *adj person* assuré

as·sess [əˈses] *v/t situation* évaluer; *value* estimer

as·sess·ment [əˈsesmənt] *of situation* évaluation *f*; *of value* estimation *f*

as·set [ˈæset] FIN actif *m*; *fig* atout *m*

'ass·hole P trou *m* du cul V; *(idiot)* abruti(e) *m(f)*

as·sign [əˈsaɪn] *v/t* assigner

as·sign·ment [əˈsaɪnmənt] mission *f*; EDU devoir *m*

as·sim·i·late [əˈsɪmɪleɪt] *v/t* assimiler

as·sist [əˈsɪst] *v/t* aider

as·sis·tance [əˈsɪstəns] aide *f*

as·sis·tant [əˈsɪstənt] assistant(e) *m(f)*

as·sis·tant di'rec·tor *of movie* assis- tant(e) réalisateur(-trice) *m(f)*; *of or- ganization* sous-directeur(-trice) *m(f)*

as·sis·tant 'man·ag·er sous-directeur *m*, sous-directrice *f*; *of department* as- sistant(e) *m(f)* du / de la responsable

as·so·ci·ate 1 *v/t* [əˈsoʊʃieɪt] associer **2** *n* [əˈsoʊʃiət] *(colleague)* collègue *m/f*

♦ **associate with** *v/t* fréquenter

as·so·ci·ate pro'fes·sor maître *m* de conférences

as·so·ci·a·tion [əsoʊsiˈeɪʃn] *(organiza- tion)* association *f*; **in ~ with** en asso- ciation avec

as·sort·ed [əˈsɔːrtɪd] *adj* assorti

as·sort·ment [əˈsɔːrtmənt] assorti- ment *m*

as·sume [əˈsuːm] *v/t (suppose)* suppo- ser

as·sump·tion [əˈsʌmpʃn] supposition *f*

as·sur·ance [əˈʃʊrəns] *(reassurance, confidence)* assurance *f*

as·sure [əˈʃʊr] *v/t (reassure)* assurer

as·sured [əˈʃʊrd] *adj (confident)* as- suré

as·ter·isk [ˈæstərɪsk] astérisque *m*

asth·ma [ˈæsmə] asthme *m*

asth·mat·ic [æsˈmætɪk] *adj* asthma- tique

as·ton·ish [əˈstɑːnɪʃ] *v/t* étonner; **be ~ed that ...** être étonné que ... *(+subj)*

as·ton·ish·ing [əˈstɑːnɪʃɪŋ] *adj* éton- nant

as·ton·ish·ing·ly [əˈstɑːnɪʃɪŋli] *adv* étonnamment

as·ton·ish·ment [əˈstɑːnɪʃmənt] éton- nement *m*

as·tound [əˈstaʊnd] *v/t* stupéfier

as·tound·ing [əˈstaʊndɪŋ] *adj* stupé- fiant

a·stray [əˈstreɪ] *adv:* **go ~** se perdre; **go ~ morally** se détourner du droit chemin

a·stride [əˈstraɪd] **1** *adv* à califourchon **2** *prep* à califourchon sur

as·trol·o·ger [əˈstrɑːlədʒər] astrolo- gue *m/f*

as·trol·o·gy [əˈstrɑːlədʒi] astrologie *f*

as·tro·naut [ˈæstrənɔːt] astronaute *m/f*

as·tron·o·mer [əˈstrɑːnəmər] astro- nome *m/f*

as·tro·nom·i·cal [æstrə'nɑ:mɪkl] *adj price etc* F astronomique F

as·tron·o·my [ə'strɑ:nəmɪ] astronomie *f*

as·tute [ə'stu:t] *adj mind, person* fin

a·sy·lum [ə'saɪləm] *political, (mental ~)* asile *m*

at [ət], *stressed* [æt] *prep with places* à; **~ Joe's** chez Joe; **~ the door** à la porte; **~ 10 dollars** au prix de 10 dollars; **~ the age of 18** à l'âge de 18 ans; **~ 5 o'clock** à 5 heures; **~ 100 mph** à 100 miles à l'heure; **be good / bad ~ …** être bon / mauvais en …; **his suggestion** sur sa suggestion

ate [eɪt] *pret* → **eat**

a·the·ism ['eɪθɪɪzm] athéisme *m*

a·the·ist ['eɪθɪɪst] athée *m/f*

ath·lete ['æθli:t] athlète *m/f*

ath·let·ic [æθ'letɪk] *adj* d'athlétisme; *(strong, sporting)* sportif*

ath·let·ics [æθ'letɪks] *nsg* athlétisme *m*

At·lan·tic [ət'læntɪk] *n*: **the ~** l'Atlantique *m*

at·las ['ætləs] atlas *m*

at·mos·phere ['ætməsfɪr] *of earth* atmosphère *f*; *(ambience)* atmosphère *f*, ambiance *f*

at·mos·pher·ic [ætməs'ferɪk] atmosphérique *lighting, music* d'ambiance; **~ pollution** pollution *f* atmosphérique

at·om ['ætəm] atome *m*

'at·om bomb bombe *f* atomique

a·tom·ic [ə'tɑ:mɪk] *adj* atomique

a·tom·ic 'en·er·gy énergie *f* atomique

a·tom·ic 'waste déchets *mpl* nucléaires

a·tom·iz·er ['ætəmaɪzər] atomiseur *m*

♦ **a·tone for** [ə'toʊn] *v/t sins, mistake* racheter

a·tro·cious [ə'troʊʃəs] *adj* F *(very bad)* atroce

a·troc·i·ty [ə'trɑ:sətɪ] atrocité *f*

at·tach [ə'tætʃ] *v/t* attacher; **be ~ed to** *emotionally* être attaché à

at·tach·ment [ə'tætʃmənt] *fondness* attachement *m*; *to e-mail* fichier *m* joint

at·tack [ə'tæk] **1** *n* attaque *f* **2** *v/t* attaquer

at·tempt [ə'tempt] **1** *n* tentative *f* **2** *v/t* essayer; **~ to do sth** essayer de faire qch

at·tend [ə'tend] *v/t* assister à; *school* aller à

♦ **attend to** *v/t* s'occuper de

at·tend·ance [ə'tendəns] *at meeting, wedding etc* présence *f*

at·tend·ant [ə'tendənt] *in museum etc* gardien(ne) *m(f)*

at·ten·tion [ə'tenʃn] attention *f*; **bring sth to s.o.'s ~** attirer l'attention de qn sur qch; **your ~ please** votre attention s'il vous plaît; **pay ~** faire attention

at·ten·tive [ə'tentɪv] *adj* attentif*

at·tic ['ætɪk] grenier *m*

at·ti·tude ['ætɪtu:d] attitude *f*

attn *abbr* (= *for the attention of*) à l'attention de

at·tor·ney [ə'tɜ:rnɪ] avocat *m*; **power of ~** procuration *f*

at·tract [ə'trækt] *v/t* attirer; **be ~ed to s.o.** être attiré par qn

at·trac·tion [ə'trækʃn] *of job, doing sth* attrait *m*; *romantic* attirance *f*; *in city, touristic* attraction *f*

at·trac·tive [ə'træktɪv] *adj person* attirant; *idea, proposal, city* attrayant

at·trib·ute[1] [ə'trɪbju:t] *v/t* attribuer (**to** à)

at·trib·ute[2] ['ætrɪbju:t] *n* attribut *m*

au·ber·gine ['oʊbərʒi:n] *Br* aubergine *f*

auc·tion ['ɔ:kʃn] **1** *n* vente *f* aux enchères **2** *v/t* vendre aux enchères

♦ **auction off** *v/t* mettre aux enchères

auc·tion·eer [ɔ:kʃə'nɪr] commissaire-priseur *m*

au·da·cious [ɔ:'deɪʃəs] *adj* audacieux*

au·dac·i·ty [ɔ:'dæsətɪ] audace *f*

au·di·ble ['ɔ:dəbl] *adj* audible

au·di·ence ['ɔ:dɪəns] public *m*

au·di·o ['ɔ:dɪoʊ] *adj* audio

au·di·o·vi·su·al *adj* audiovisuel*

au·dit ['ɔ:dɪt] **1** *n* FIN audit *m* **2** *v/t* FIN contrôler, vérifier; *course* suivre en auditeur libre

au·di·tion [ɔ:'dɪʃn] **1** *n* audition *f* **2** *v/i* passer une audition

au·di·tor ['ɔːdɪtər] auditeur(-trice) *m(f)*; *at course* auditeur(-trice) *m(f)* libre

au·di·to·ri·um [ɔːdɪ'tɔːriəm] *of theater etc* auditorium *m*

Au·gust ['ɔːgəst] août

aunt [ænt] tante *f*

au pair [ou'peɪ] jeune fille *f* au pair

au·ra ['ɔːrə] aura *f*

aus·pic·es ['ɔːspɪsɪz]: *under the ~ of* sous les auspices de

aus·pi·cious [ɔː'spɪʃəs] *adj* favorable

aus·tere [ɔː'stɪr] *adj* austère

aus·ter·i·ty [ɔːs'terətɪ] *economic* austérité *f*

Aus·tra·li·a [ɔː'streɪlɪə] Australie *f*

Aus·tra·li·an [ɔː'streɪlɪən] **1** *adj* australien* **2** *n* Australien(ne) *m(f)*

Aus·tri·a ['ɔːstrɪə] Autriche *f*

Aus·tri·an ['ɔːstrɪən] **1** *adj* autrichien* **2** *n* Autrichien(ne) *m(f)*

au·then·tic [ɔː'θentɪk] *adj* authentique

au·then·tic·i·ty [ɔːθen'tɪsətɪ] authenticité *f*

au·thor ['ɔːθər] auteur *m*

au·thor·i·tar·i·an [əθɑːrɪ'terɪən] *adj* autoritaire

au·thor·i·ta·tive [ə'θɑːrɪtətɪv] *adj* source qui fait autorité; *person, manner* autoritaire

au·thor·i·ty [ə'θɑːrətɪ] autorité *f*; (*permission*) autorisation *f*; *be an ~ on* être une autorité en matière de; *the authorities* les autorités *fpl*

au·thor·i·za·tion [ɔːθəraɪ'zeɪʃn] autorisation *f*

au·thor·ize ['ɔːθəraɪz] *v/t* autoriser; *be ~d to do sth* avoir l'autorisation officielle de faire qch

au·tis·tic [ɔː'tɪstɪk] *adj* autiste

au·to·bi·og·ra·phy [ɔːtəbaɪ'ɑːgrəfɪ] autobiographie *f*

au·to·crat·ic [ɔːtə'krætɪk] *adj* autocratique

au·to·graph ['ɔːtəgræf] *n* autographe *m*

au·to·mate ['ɔːtəmeɪt] *v/t* automatiser

au·to·mat·ic [ɔːtə'mætɪk] **1** *adj* automatique **2** *n car* automatique *f*; *gun* automatique *m*

au·to·mat·i·cal·ly [ɔːtə'mætɪklɪ] *adv* automatiquement

au·to·ma·tion [ɔːtə'meɪʃn] automatisation *f*

au·to·mo·bile ['ɔːtəmoubiːl] automobile *f*

'au·to·mo·bile in·dus·try industrie *f* automobile

au·ton·o·mous [ɔː'tɑːnəməs] *adj* autonome

au·ton·o·my [ɔː'tɑːnəmɪ] autonomie *f*

au·to·pi·lot ['ɔːtoupaɪlət] pilotage *m* automatique

au·top·sy ['ɔːtɑːpsɪ] autopsie *f*

au·tumn ['ɔːtəm] *Br* automne *m*

aux·il·ia·ry [ɔːg'zɪljərɪ] *adj* auxiliaire

a·vail [ə'veɪl] **1** *n*: *to no ~* en vain **2** *v/t*: *~ o.s. of* offer, opportunity saisir

a·vai·la·ble [ə'veɪləbl] *adj* disponible; *make sth ~ for s.o.* mettre qch à la disposition de qn

av·a·lanche ['ævəlænʃ] avalanche *f*

av·a·rice ['ævərɪs] avarice *m*

a·venge [ə'vendʒ] *v/t* venger

av·e·nue ['ævənuː] avenue *f*; *explore all ~s* *fig* explorer toutes les possibilités

av·e·rage ['ævərɪdʒ] **1** *adj* (*also mediocre*) moyen* **2** *n* moyenne *f*; *above / below ~* au-dessus / au-dessous de la moyenne; *on ~* en moyenne **3** *v/t*: *I ~ six hours of sleep a night* je dors en moyenne six heures par nuit

♦ **average out** *v/t* faire la moyenne de

♦ **average out at** *v/t* faire une moyenne de

a·verse [ə'vɜːrs] *adj*: *not be ~ to* ne rien avoir contre

a·ver·sion [ə'vɜːrʃn] aversion *f* (*to* pour)

a·vert [ə'vɜːrt] *v/t one's eyes* détourner; *crisis* empêcher

a·vi·a·tion [eɪvɪ'eɪʃn] aviation *f*

av·id ['ævɪd] *adj* avide

av·o·ca·do [ɑːvə'kɑːdou] *fruit* avocat *m*

a·void [ə'vɔɪd] *v/t* éviter

a·void·a·ble [ə'vɔɪdəbl] *adj* évitable

a·wait [ə'weɪt] *v/t* attendre

a·wake [ə'weɪk] *adj* éveillé; *it's keep-*

ing me ~ ça m'empêche de dormir

a·ward [əˈwɔːrd] **1** *n* (*prize*) prix *m* **2** *v/t* décerner; *as damages* attribuer

a·wards ce·re·mo·ny cérémonie *f* de remise des prix; EDU cérémonie *f* de remise des diplômes

a·ware [əˈwer] *adj*: *be* ~ *of sth* avoir conscience de qch; *become* ~ *of sth* prendre conscience de qch

a·ware·ness [əˈwernɪs] conscience *f*

a·way [əˈweɪ] *adv*: *be* ~ être absent, ne pas être là; *walk* ~ s'en aller; *look* ~ tourner la tête; *it's 2 miles* ~ c'est à 2 miles d'ici; *Christmas is still six weeks* ~ il reste encore six semaines avant Noël; *take sth* ~ *from s.o.* enlever qch à qn; *put sth* ~ ranger qch

a'way game SP match *m* à l'extérieur

awe [ɒː] émerveillement *m*; *worshipful* révérence *f*

awe·some [ˈɒːsəm] *adj* F (*terrific*) super F *inv*

aw·ful [ˈɒːfəl] *adj* affreux*

aw·ful·ly [ˈɒːfəlɪ] *adv* F *windy, expensive* terriblement; *pretty, nice, rich* drôlement

awn·ing [ˈɒːnɪŋ] store *m*

ax, *Br* **axe** [æks] **1** *n* hache *f* **2** *v/t project* abandonner; *budget* faire des coupures dans; *job* supprimer

ax·le [ˈæksl] essieu *m*

B

BA [biːˈeɪ] *abbr* (= *Bachelor of Arts*) licence d'arts et lettres

ba·by [ˈbeɪbɪ] *n* bébé *m*

'ba·by boom baby-boom *m*

ba·by car·riage [ˈbeɪbɪkærɪdʒ] landau *m*

ba·by·ish [ˈbeɪbɪʃ] *adj* de bébé

'ba·by·sit *v/i* (*pret & pp* **-sat**) faire du baby-sitting

ba·by·sit·ter [ˈbeɪbɪsɪtər] baby-sitter *m/f*

bach·e·lor [ˈbætʃələr] célibataire *m*

back [bæk] **1** *n of person, animal, hand, sweater, dress* dos *m*; *of chair* dossier *m*; *of wardrobe, drawer* fond *m*; *of house* arrière *m*; SP arrière *m*; *in* ~ (*of the car*) à l'arrière (de la voiture); *at the* ~ *of the bus* à l'arrière du bus; *at the* ~ *of the book* à la fin du livre; ~ *to front* à l'envers; *at the* ~ *of beyond* en pleine cambrousse F **2** *adj door, steps* de derrière; *wheels, legs, seat* arrière *inv*; ~ *road* petite route *f* **3** *adv*: *please move / stand* ~ recu-

lez / écartez-vous s'il vous plaît; *2 metres* ~ *from the edge* à 2 mètres du bord; ~ *in 1935* en 1935; *give sth* ~ *to s.o.* rendre qch à qn; *she'll be* ~ *tomorrow* elle sera de retour demain; *when are you coming* ~? quand est-ce que tu reviens?; *take sth* ~ *to the shop because unsatisfactory* ramener qch au magasin; *they wrote / phoned* ~ ils ont répondu à la lettre / ont rappelé; *he hit me* ~ il m'a rendu mon coup **4** *v/t* (*support*) soutenir; *car* faire reculer; *horse in race* miser sur **5** *v/i of driver* faire marche arrière

♦ **back away** *v/i* s'éloigner à reculons

♦ **back down** *v/i* faire marche arrière

♦ **back off** *v/i* reculer

♦ **back onto** *v/t* donner à l'arrière sur

♦ **back out** *v/i of commitment* se dégager

♦ **back up 1** *v/t* (*support*) soutenir; *file* sauvegarder; *be backed up of traffic* être ralenti **2** *v/i in car* reculer

'back·ache mal *m* de dos; **'back·bit·ing** médisances *fpl*; **'back·bone** ANAT colonne *f* vertébrale; *fig (courage)* caractère *m*; *fig (mainstay)* pilier *m*; **'back·break·ing** *adj* éreintant; **back 'burn·er**: *put sth on the* ~ mettre qch en veilleuse; **'back·date** *v/t* antidater; **'back·door** porte *f* arrière

back·er ['bækər] producteur(-trice) *m(f)*

'back·fire *v/i fig* se retourner (**on** contre); **'back·ground** *of picture* arrière-plan *m*; *social* milieu *m*; *of crime* contexte *m*; *her educational* ~ sa formation; *his work* ~ son expérience professionnelle; **'back·hand** *in tennis* revers *m*

'back·ing ['bækɪŋ] *(support)* soutien *m*; MUS accompagnement *m*

'back·ing group MUS groupe *m* d'accompagnement

'back·lash répercussion(s) *f(pl)*; **'back·log** retard *m* (**of** dans); **'back·pack 1** *n* sac *m* à dos **2** *v/i* faire de la randonnée; **'back·pack·er** randonneur(-euse) *m(f)*; **'back·pack·ing** randonnée *f*; **'back·ped·al** *v/i fig* faire marche arrière; **'back seat** *of car* siège *m* arrière; **'back·space (key)** touche *f* d'espacement arrière; **'back·stairs** *npl* escalier *m* de service; **'back streets** *npl* petites rues *fpl*; *poor area* bas-fonds *mpl*, quartiers *mpl* pauvres; **'back·stroke** SP dos *m* crawlé; **'back·track** *v/i* retourner sur ses pas; **'back·up** *(support)* renfort *m*; COMPUT copie *f* de sauvegarde; *take a* ~ COMPUT faire une copie de sauvegarde; **'back·up disk** COMPUT disquette *f* de sauvegarde

back·ward ['bækwərd] **1** *adj child* attardé; *society* arriéré; *glance* en arrière **2** *adv* en arrière

back·yard arrière-cour *f*; *Mexico is the United States'* ~ Mexico est à la porte des États-Unis

ba·con ['beɪkn] bacon *m*

bac·te·ri·a [bæk'tɪrɪə] *npl* bactéries *fpl*

bad [bæd] *adj* mauvais; *person* méchant; *(rotten)* avarié; *go* ~ s'avarier;

it's not ~ c'est pas mal; *that's really too* ~ *(a shame)* c'est vraiment dommage; *feel* ~ *about sth (guilty)* s'en vouloir de qch; *I feel* ~ *about it* je m'en veux; *be* ~ *at sth* être mauvais en qch; *be* ~ *at doing sth* avoir du mal à faire qch; *Friday's* ~*, how about Thursday?* vendredi ne va pas, et jeudi?

bad 'debt mauvaise créance *f*

badge [bædʒ] insigne *f*

bad·ger ['bædʒər] *v/t* harceler

bad 'lan·guage grossièretés *fpl*

bad·ly ['bædlɪ] *adv* mal; *injured* grièvement; *damaged* sérieusement; ~ *behaved* mal élevé; *do* ~ mal réussir; *he* ~ *needs a haircut / rest* il a grand besoin d'une coupe de cheveux / de repos; *he is* ~ *off (poor)* il n'est pas fortuné

bad-man·nered [bæd'mænərd] *adj* mal élevé

bad·min·ton ['bædmɪntən] badminton *m*

bad-tem·pered [bæd'tempərd] *adj* de mauvaise humeur

baf·fle ['bæfl] *v/t* déconcerter; *be* ~*d* être perplexe

baf·fling ['bæflɪŋ] *adj* déconcertant

bag [bæg] *of plastic, leather, woman's* sac *m*; *(piece of baggage)* bagage *m*

bag·gage ['bægɪdʒ] bagages *mpl*

'bag·gage car RAIL fourgon *m* (à bagages); **'bag·gage cart** chariot *m* à bagages; **'bag·gage check** contrôle *m* des bagages; **'bag·gage re·claim** ['ri:kleɪm] remise *f* des bagages

bag·gy ['bægɪ] *adj too big* flottant; *fashionably* large

bail [beɪl] *n* LAW caution *f*; *be out on* ~ être en liberté provisoire sous caution

♦ **bail out 1** *v/t* LAW se porter caution pour; *fig: company etc* tirer d'affaire **2** *v/i from airplane* sauter en parachute

bait [beɪt] *n* appât *m*

bake [beɪk] *v/t* cuire au four

baked 'beans [beɪkt] *npl* haricots *mpl* blancs à la sauce tomate

baked po'ta·to pomme *f* de terre au four

bankroll

bak·er ['beɪkər] boulanger(-ère) *m(f)*

bak·er·y ['beɪkərɪ] boulangerie *f*

bak·ing pow·der ['beɪkɪŋ] levure *f* (chimique)

bal·ance ['bæləns] **1** *n* équilibre *m*; (*remainder*) reste *m*; *of bank account* solde *m* **2** *v/t* mettre en équilibre; *~ the books* balancer les livres **3** *v/i* rester en équilibre; *of accounts* équilibrer

bal·anced ['bælənst] *adj* (*fair*) objectif*; *diet, personality* équilibré

bal·ance of 'pay·ments balance *f* des paiements; **bal·ance of 'trade** balance *f* commerciale; **'bal·ance sheet** bilan *m*

bal·co·ny ['bælkənɪ] balcon *m*

bald [bɔːld] *adj* chauve

bald·ing ['bɔːldɪŋ] *adj* qui commence à devenir chauve

Bal·kan ['bɔːlkən] *adj* balkanique

Bal·kans ['bɔːlkənz] *npl*: *the ~* les Balkans *mpl*

ball¹ [bɔːl] *for soccer, baseball, basketball etc* ballon *m*; *for tennis, golf* balle *f*; *be on the ~ fig* F : *know one's stuff* connaître son affaire; *I'm not on the ~ today* je ne suis pas dans mon assiette aujourd'hui F; *play ~ fig* coopérer; *the ~'s in his court* la balle est dans son camp

ball² [bɔːl] *dance* bal *m*

bal·lad ['bæləd] ballade *f*

ball 'bear·ing roulement *m* à billes

bal·le·ri·na [bælə'riːnə] ballerine *f*

bal·let ['bæleɪ] ballet *m*

bal·let danc·er danseur(-euse) *m(f)* de ballet

'ball game match *m* de baseball; *that's a different ~* F c'est une tout autre histoire F

bal·lis·tic mis·sile [bə'lɪstɪk] missile *m* balistique

bal·loon [bə'luːn] *child's* ballon *m*; *for flight* montgolfière *f*

bal·loon·ist [bə'luːnɪst] aéronaute *m/f*

bal·lot ['bælət] **1** *n* vote *m* **2** *v/t* *members* faire voter

'bal·lot box urne *f*

'bal·lot pa·per bulletin *m* de vote

'ball·park terrain *m* de baseball; *be in*

the right ~ F ne pas être loin; *we're not in the same ~* F on n'est pas du même monde; **'ball·park fig·ure** F chiffre *m* en gros; **'ball·point (pen)** stylo *m* bille

balls [bɔːlz] *npl* V (*also: courage*) couilles *fpl* V

bam·boo [bæm'buː] *n* bambou *m*

ban [bæn] **1** *n* interdiction *f* **2** *v/t* (*pret & pp -ned*) interdire

ba·nal [bə'næl] *adj* banal

ba·na·na [bə'nænə] banane *f*

band [bænd] MUS *brass* orchestre *m*; *pop* groupe *m*; *of material* bande *f*

ban·dage ['bændɪdʒ] **1** *n* bandage *m* **2** *v/t* faire un bandage à

'Band-Aid® sparadrap *m*

B&B [biːn'biː] *abbr* (*= bed and breakfast*) bed and breakfast *m*

ban·dit ['bændɪt] bandit *m*

'band·wag·on: *jump on the ~* prendre le train en marche

ban·dy ['bændɪ] *adj legs* arqué

bang [bæŋ] **1** *n noise* boum *m*; (*blow*) coup *m* **2** *v/t door* claquer; (*hit*) cogner **3** *v/i* claquer; *the shutter ~ed shut* le volet s'est fermé en claquant

ban·gle ['bæŋgl] bracelet *m*

bangs [bæŋz] *npl* frange *f*

ban·is·ters ['bænɪstərz] *npl* rampe *f*

ban·jo ['bændʒoʊ] banjo *m*

bank¹ [bæŋk] *of river* bord *m*, rive *f*

bank² [bæŋk] **1** *n* FIN banque *f* **2** *v/i*: *~ with* être à **3** *v/t money* mettre à la banque

♦ **bank on** *v/t* compter avoir; *don't bank on it* ne compte pas trop là-dessus; *bank on s.o. doing sth* compter sur qn pour faire qch

'bank ac·count compte *m* en banque; **'bank bal·ance** solde *m* bancaire; **'bank bill** billet *m* de banque

bank·er ['bæŋkər] banquier(-ière) *m(f)*

'bank·er's card carte *f* d'identité bancaire

bank·ing ['bæŋkɪŋ] banque *f*

'bank loan emprunt *m* bancaire; **'bank man·ag·er** directeur(-trice) *m(f)* de banque; **'bank rate** taux *m* bancaire; **'bank·roll** *v/t* F financer

B

bank·rupt [ˈbæŋkrʌpt] **1** *adj* en faillite; ***go ~*** faire faillite **2** *v/t* faire faire faillite à

bank·rupt·cy [ˈbæŋkrʌpsɪ] faillite *f*

'bank state·ment relevé *m* bancaire

ban·ner [ˈbænər] bannière *f*

banns [bænz] *npl Br* bans *mpl*

ban·quet [ˈbæŋkwɪt] *n* banquet *m*

ban·ter [ˈbæntər] *n* plaisanteries *fpl*

bap·tism [ˈbæptɪzm] baptême *m*

bap·tize [bæpˈtaɪz] *v/t* baptiser

bar¹ [bɑːr] *n of iron, chocolate* barre *f*; *for drinks, counter* bar *m*; ***a ~ of soap*** une savonnette; ***be behind ~s*** être derrière les barreaux

bar² [bɑːr] *v/t* (*pret & pp* -**red**) exclure

bar³ [bɑːr] *prep* (*except*) sauf

bar·bar·i·an [bɑːrˈberɪən] *also fig* barbare *m/f*

bar·ba·ric [bɑːrˈbærɪk] *adj* barbare

bar·be·cue [ˈbɑːrbɪkjuː] **1** *n* barbecue *m* **2** *v/t* cuire au barbecue

barbed 'wire [bɑːrbd] fil *m* barbelé

bar·ber [ˈbɑːrbər] coiffeur *m*

bar·bi·tu·rate [bɑːrˈbɪtjərət] barbiturique *m*

'bar code code *m* barre

bare [ber] *adj* (*naked*), *mountainside, floor tu; room, shelves* vide; ***in your / their ~ feet*** pieds nus

'bare·foot *adj*: ***be ~*** être pieds nus

bare·head·ed [berˈhedɪd] *adj* tête nue

bare·ly [ˈberlɪ] *adv* à peine

bar·gain [ˈbɑːrgɪn] **1** *n* (*deal*) marché *m*; (*good buy*) bonne affaire *f*; ***it's a ~!*** (*deal*) entendu!; ***into the ~*** par-dessus le marché **2** *v/i* marchander

♦ **bargain for** *v/t* (*expect*) s'attendre à; ***you might get more than you bargained for*** tu pourrais avoir une mauvaise surprise

barge [bɑːrdʒ] *n NAUT* péniche *f*

♦ **barge into** *v/t* se heurter contre; (*enter quickly and noisily*) faire irruption dans

bar·i·tone [ˈbærɪtoʊn] *n* baryton *m*

bark¹ [bɑːrk] **1** *n of dog* aboiement *m* **2** *v/i* aboyer

bark² [bɑːrk] *of tree* écorce *f*

bar·ley [ˈbɑːrlɪ] orge *f*

barn [bɑːrn] grange *f*

ba·rom·e·ter [bəˈrɑːmɪtər] *also fig* baromètre *m*

Ba·roque [bəˈrɑːk] *adj* baroque

bar·racks [ˈbærəks] *npl MIL* caserne *f*

bar·rage [bəˈrɑːʒ] *MIL* barrage *m*; *fig* flot *m*

bar·rel [ˈbærəl] *container* tonneau *m*

bar·ren [ˈbærən] *adj land* stérile

bar·rette [bɑːˈret] barrette *f*

bar·ri·cade [bærɪˈkeɪd] *n* barricade *f*

bar·ri·er [ˈbærɪər] *also fig* barrière *f*; ***language ~*** barrière linguistique

bar·ring [ˈbɑːrɪŋ] *prep*: ***~ accidents*** sauf accident

bar·row [ˈbæroʊ] brouette *f*

'bar tend·er barman *m*, barmaid *f*

bar·ter [ˈbɑːrtər] **1** *n* troc *m* **2** *v/t* troquer (*for* contre)

base [beɪs] **1** *n* (*bottom: of spine; center*, MIL) base *f*; *of vase* dessous *m* **2** *v/t* baser (*on* sur); ***be ~d in France / Paris*** *of employee etc* être basé en France / à Paris

'base·ball *game* baseball *m*; *ball* balle *f* de baseball

'base·ball bat batte *f* de baseball; **'base·ball cap** casquette *f* de baseball; **'base·ball play·er** joueur (-euse) *m(f)* de baseball

'base·board plinthe *f*

base·less [ˈbeɪslɪs] *adj* sans fondement

base·ment [ˈbeɪsmənt] sous-sol *m*

'base rate FIN taux *m* de base

bash [bæʃ] **1** *n* F coup *m* **2** *v/t* F cogner

ba·sic [ˈbeɪsɪk] *adj* (*rudimentary: idea*) rudimentaire; *knowledge, hotel* rudimentaire; (*fundamental: beliefs*) de base, fondamental; *salary* de base

ba·sic·al·ly [ˈbeɪsɪklɪ] *adv* au fond, en gros

ba·sics [ˈbeɪsɪks] *npl*: ***the ~*** les bases *fpl*; ***get down to ~*** en venir au principal

bas·il [ˈbæzɪl] basilic *m*

ba·sin [ˈbeɪsn] *for washing dishes* bassine *f*; *in bathroom* lavabo *m*

ba·sis [ˈbeɪsɪs] (*pl* ***bases*** [ˈbeɪsiːz]) base *f*; *of argument* fondement *m*

bask [bæsk] *v/i* se dorer

bas·ket ['bæskɪt] *for shopping, in basketball* panier *m*

'bas·ket·ball *game* basket(ball) *m*; **~ player** joueur(euse) *m(f)* de basket (-ball)

bass [beɪs] **1** *adj part, accompaniment* de basse; **~ clef** clef *f* de fa **2** *n part, singer, instrument* basse *f*; **double ~** contrebasse *f*; **~ guitar** basse *f*

bas·tard ['bæstərd] F salaud(e) *m(f)* F; **poor / stupid ~** pauvre couillon *m* F

bat[1] [bæt] **1** *n for baseball* batte *f*; *for table tennis* raquette *f* **2** *v/i (pret & pp -ted)* in baseball batter

bat[2] [bæt] *v/t (pret & pp -ted)*: **he didn't ~ an eyelid** il n'a pas sourcillé

bat[3] [bæt] *animal* chauve-souris *f*

batch [bætʃ] *n of students, data, goods* T lot *m*; *of bread* fournée *f*

ba·ted ['beɪtɪd] *adj*: **with ~ breath** en retenant son souffle

bath [bɑːθ] *(~tub)* baignoire *f*; **have a ~, take a ~** prendre un bain

bathe [beɪð] **1** *v/i (have a bath)* se baigner **2** *v/t child* faire prendre un bain à

'bath mat tapis *m* de bain; **'bath·robe** peignoir *m*; **'bath·room** salle *f* de bains; *toilet* toilettes *fpl*

'bath tow·el serviette *f* de bain

'bath·tub baignoire *f*

bat·on ['bətɑːn] *of conductor* baguette *f*

bat·tal·i·on [bə'tæljən] MIL bataillon *m*

bat·ter[1] ['bætər] *n for making cakes, pancakes etc* pâte *f* lisse; *for deepfrying* pâte *f* à frire

bat·ter[2] ['bætər] *n in baseball* batteur *m*

bat·tered ['bætərd] *adj wife, children* battu

bat·ter·y ['bætərɪ] *in watch, toy etc* pile *f*; MOT batterie *f*

bat·ter·y charg·er ['tʃɑːrdʒər] chargeur *m* (de batterie)

bat·ter·y-op·er·at·ed ['bætərɪ:pəreɪtɪd] *adj* à piles

bat·tle ['bætl] **1** *n* bataille *f*; *fig* lutte *f*, combat *m* **2** *v/i against illness etc* se battre, lutter

'bat·tle·field, 'bat·tle·ground champ *m* de bataille

'bat·tle·ship cuirassé *m*

bawd·y ['bɔːdɪ] *adj* paillard

bawl [bɔːl] *v/i* brailler

♦ **bawl out** *v/t* F engueuler F

bay [beɪ] *(inlet)* baie *f*

Bay of Bis·cay ['bɪskeɪ] Golfe *m* de Gascogne

bay·o·net ['beɪənet] *n* baïonnette *f*

bay 'win·dow fenêtre *f* en saillie

BC [biː'siː] *abbr (= before Christ)* av. J.-C.

be [biː] *v/i (pret was / were, pp been)*
◇ être; **~ 15** avoir 15 ans; **it's me** c'est moi; **was she there?** est-ce qu'elle était là?; **how much is ...?** combien coûte ...?; **there is / are** il y a; **~ careful** sois prudent; *(polite or plural)* soyez prudent; **don't ~ sad** ne sois / soyez pas triste; **he's very well** il va très bien; **how are you?** comment ça va?
◇: **has the mailman been?** est-ce que le facteur est passé?; **I've never been to Japan** je ne suis jamais allé au Japon; **I've been here for hours** je suis ici depuis des heures
◇ *tags*: **that's right, isn't it?** c'est juste, n'est-ce pas?; **she's American, isn't she?** elle est américaine, n'est-ce pas?
◇ *v/aux*: **I am thinking** je pense; **he was running** il courait; **stop ~ing stupid** arrête de faire l'imbécile; **he was just ~ing sarcastic** il faisait juste de l'ironie; **I have been looking at your file** j'ai jeté un œil à votre fichier
◇ *obligation*: **you are to do what I tell you** vous devez faire ce que je vous dis; **I was to tell you this** je devais vous dire ceci; **you were not to tell anyone** vous ne deviez rien dire à personne
◇ *passive*: **he was killed** il a été tué; **they have been sold** ils ont été vendus; **it hasn't been decided** on n'a encore rien décidé

♦ **be in for** *v/t* aller avoir; **he's in for it!** F il va se faire engueuler F

beach [biːtʃ] *n* plage *f*

'**beach ball** ballon *m* de plage

'**beach·wear** vêtements *mpl* de plage

beads [biːdz] *npl necklace* collier *m* de perles

beak [biːk] bec *m*

'**be-all**: *the ~ and end-all aim* le but suprême; *she thinks he's the ~ and end-all* pour elle c'est le centre du monde

beam [biːm] **1** *n in ceiling etc* poutre *f* **2** *v/i* (*smile*) rayonner **3** *v/t* (*transmit*) transmettre

bean [biːn] haricot *m*; *of coffee* grain *m*; *be full of ~s* F péter la forme F

'**bean-bag** *seat* fauteuil *m* poire

bear[1] [ber] *n animal* ours *m*

bear[2] [ber] **1** *v/t* (*pret* **bore**, *pp* **borne**) *weight* porter; *costs* prendre en charge; (*tolerate*) supporter; *child* donner naissance à; *she bore him six children* elle lui a donné six enfants **2** *v/i* (*pret* **bore**, *pp* **borne**) (*weigh*) peser; *bring pressure to ~ on* exercer une pression sur; *~ left / right* prendre à gauche / droite

♦ **bear out** *v/t* (*confirm*) confirmer; *bear s.o. out* confirmer ce que qn a dit

bear·a·ble ['berəbl] *adj* supportable

beard [bɪrd] barbe *f*

beard·ed ['bɪrdɪd] *adj* barbu

bear·ing ['berɪŋ] *in machine* roulement *m*; *that has no ~ on the situation* cela n'a aucun rapport avec la situation

'**bear mar·ket** FIN baissier *m*

beast [biːst] bête *f*; (*fig: nasty person*) peau *f* de vache

beat [biːt] **1** *n of heart* battement *m*, pulsation *f*; *of music* mesure *f* **2** *v/i* (*pret* **beat**, *pp* **beaten**) *of heart* battre; *of rain* s'abattre; *~ about the bush* tourner autour du pot **3** *v/t* (*pret* **beat**, *pp* **beaten**) *in competition* battre; (*hit*) battre; (*pound*) frapper; *~ it!* filez! F; *it ~s me* F je ne pige pas F

♦ **beat up** *v/t* tabasser

beat·en ['biːtən] **1** *pp* → **beat 2** *adj: off the ~ track* à l'écart; *off the ~ track*: *go somewhere off the ~ track* sortir

des sentiers battus

beat·ing ['biːtɪŋ] *physical* raclée *f*

'**beat-up** *adj* F déglingué F

beau·ti·cian [bjuː'tɪʃn] esthéticien (ne) *m(f)*

beau·ti·ful ['bjuːtəfəl] *adj* beau*; *thanks, that's just ~!* merci, c'est magnifique!

beau·ti·ful·ly ['bjuːtɪfəlɪ] *adv* admirablement

beau·ty ['bjuːtɪ] beauté *f*

'**beau·ty par·lor** ['paːrlər] institut *m* de beauté

bea·ver ['biːvər] castor *m*

♦ **beaver away** *v/i* F bosser dur F

be·came [bɪ'keɪm] *pret* → **become**

be·cause [bɪ'kɑːz] *conj* parce que; *~ of* à cause de

beck·on ['bekn] *v/i* faire signe (*to s.o.* à qn)

be·come [bɪ'kʌm] *v/i* (*pret* **became**, *pp* **become**) devenir; *what's ~ of her?* qu'est-elle devenue?

be·com·ing [bɪ'kʌmɪŋ] *adj hat etc* seyant; *it looks very ~ on you* ça te va très bien

bed [bed] *n also of sea, river* lit *m*; *of flowers* parterre *m*; *he's still in ~* il est toujours au lit; *go to ~* aller se coucher; *go to ~ with s.o.* coucher avec qn

'**bed·clothes** *npl* draps *mpl* de lit

bed·ding ['bedɪŋ] literie *f*

bed·lam ['bedləm] bazar *m*

bed·rid·den ['bedrɪdn] *adj* cloué au lit; '**bed·room** chambre *f* (à coucher); '**bed·side**: *be at the ~ of* être au chevet de qn; '**bed·spread** couvre-lit *m*, dessus-de-lit *m*; '**bed·time** heure *f* du coucher

bee [biː] abeille *f*

beech [biːtʃ] hêtre *m*

beef [biːf] **1** *n* bœuf *m*; F (*complaint*) plainte *f* **2** *v/i* F (*complain*) grommeler

♦ **beef up** *v/t* F étoffer

'**beef·bur·ger** steak *m* haché

'**bee-line**: *make a ~ for* aller droit vers

been [bɪn] *pp* → **be**

beep [biːp] **1** *n* bip *m* **2** *v/i* faire bip **3** *v/t*

B

(call on pager) appeler sur son récepteur d'appels

beep·er ['bi:pər] récepteur *m* d'appels

beer [bɪr] bière *f*

beet [bi:t] betterave *f*

bee·tle ['bi:tl] coléoptère *m*, cafard *m*

be·fore [bɪ'fɔ:r] **1** *prep* avant; **~** *sign·ing it* avant de le signer; **~** *a vowel* devant une voyelle **2** *adv* auparavant; *(already)* déjà; *the week / day* **~** la semaine / le jour d'avant **3** *conj* avant que (+ *subj*); **~** *I could stop him* avant que je (ne) puisse l'arrêter; **~** *it's too late* avant qu'il ne soit trop tard

◊ *with same subject:* *I had a coffee* **~** *I left* j'ai pris un café avant de partir

be·fore·hand *adv* à l'avance

be·friend [bɪ'frend] *v/t* se lier d'amitié avec; *(assist)* prendre sous son aile

beg [beg] **1** *v/i* *(pret & pp* **-ged***)* mendier **2** *v/t* *(pret & pp* **-ged***):* prier; **~** *s.o. to do sth* prier qn de faire qch

be·gan [bɪ'gæn] *pret* → *begin*

beg·gar ['begər] *n* mendiant(e) *m(f)*

be·gin [bɪ'gɪn] **1** *v/i* *(pret* **began,** *pp* **begun***)* commencer; *to* **~** *with (at first)* au début; *(in the first place)* d'abord **2** *v/t* *(pret* **began,** *pp* **begun***)* commencer

be·gin·ner [bɪ'gɪnər] débutant(e) *m(f)*

be·gin·ning [bɪ'gɪnɪŋ] début *m*

be·grudge [bɪ'grʌdʒ] *v/t* *(envy)* envier *(s.o. sth* qch à qn); *(give reluctantly)* donner à contre-cœur

be·gun [bɪ'gʌn] *pp* → *begin*

be·half [bɪ'hɑ:f]: *in or on* **~** *of* au nom de, de la part de; *on my / his* **~** de ma / sa part

be·have [bɪ'heɪv] *v/i* se comporter; **~** *(yourself)!* sois sage!

be·hav·ior, *Br* **be·hav·iour** [bɪ'heɪv-ɪər] comportement *m*

be·hind [bɪ'haɪnd] **1** *prep* derrière; *be* **~** *sth (responsible for, support)* être derrière qch; *be* **~** *s.o. (support)* être derrière qn **2** *adv (at the back)* à l'arrière; *leave, stay* derrière; *be* **~** *in match* être derrière; *be* **~** *with sth* être en retard dans qch

beige [beɪʒ] *adj* beige

be·ing ['bi:ɪŋ] *(creature)* être *m*; *(existence)* existence *f*

be·lat·ed [bɪ'leɪtɪd] *adj* tardif

belch [beltʃ] **1** *n* éructation *f*, rot *m* F **2** *v/i* éructer, roter F

Bel·gian ['beldʒən] **1** *adj* belge **2** *n* Belge *m/f*

Bel·gium ['beldʒəm] Belgique *f*

be·lief [bɪ'li:f] conviction *f*; REL *also* croyance *f*; *in person* foi *f* (*in* en); *it's my* **~** *that ...* je crois que ...

be·lieve [bɪ'li:v] *v/t* croire

♦ **believe in** *v/t God, person* croire en; *sth* croire à; *I don't believe in hiding the truth from people* je ne pense pas qu'il faille cacher la vérité aux gens

be·liev·er [bɪ'li:vər] *in God* croyant(e) *m(f)*; *fig: in sth* partisan(e) *m(f)* (*in* de)

be·lit·tle [bɪ'lɪtl] *v/t* déprécier, rapetisser

bell [bel] *on bike, door* sonnette *f*; *in church* cloche *f*; *in school: electric* sonnerie *f*

'bell·hop groom *m*

bel·lig·er·ent [bɪ'lɪdʒərənt] *adj* belligérant

bel·low ['beloʊ] **1** *n* braillement *m*; *of bull* beuglement *m* **2** *v/i* brailler; *of bull* beugler

bel·ly ['belɪ] *of person* ventre *m*; *(fat stomach)* bedaine *f*; *of animal* panse *f*

'bel·ly·ache *v/i* F rouspéter F

be·long [bɪ'lɔ:ŋ] *v/i: where does this* **~***?* où cela se place-t-il?; *I don't* **~** *here* je n'ai pas ma place ici

♦ **belong to** *v/t of object* appartenir à; *club, organization* faire partie de

be·long·ings [bɪ'lɔ:ŋɪŋz] *npl* affaires *fpl*

be·loved [bɪ'lʌvd] *adj* bien-aimé

be·low [bɪ'loʊ] **1** *prep* au-dessous de; **~** *freezing* au-dessous de zéro **2** *adv* en bas, au-dessous; *see* **~** voir en bas; *10 degrees* **~** moins dix

belt [belt] *n* ceinture *f*; *tighten one's* **~** *fig* se serrer la ceinture

bench [bentʃ] *seat* banc *m*; *in lecture hall* gradin *m*

bench *(work~)* établi *m*

B

'bench·mark référence *f*

bend [bend] **1** *n* tournant *m* **2** *v/t* (*pret & pp* bent) *head* baisser; *arm, knees* plier; *metal, plastic* tordre **3** *v/i* (*pret & pp* bent) *of road, river* tourner; *of person* se pencher; *of rubber etc* se plier
♦ bend down *v/i* se pencher

bend·er ['bendər] F soûlerie *f* F

be·neath [bɪ'niːθ] **1** *prep* sous; *in status* en dessous de **2** *adv* (au-)dessous

ben·e·fac·tor ['benɪfæktər] bienfaiteur(-trice) *m(f)*

ben·e·fi·cial [benɪ'fɪʃl] *adj* bénéfique

ben·e·fit ['benɪfɪt] **1** *n* bénéfice *m* **2** *v/t* bénéficier à **3** *v/i* bénéficier (*from* de)

be·nev·o·lence [bɪ'nevələns] bienveillance *f*

be·nev·o·lent [bɪ'nevələnt] *adj* bienveillant

be·nign [bɪ'naɪn] *adj* doux; MED bénin

bent [bent] *pret & pp* → bend

be·queath [bɪ'kwiːð] *v/t* léguer

be·quest [bɪ'kwest] legs *m*

be·reaved [bɪ'riːvd] **1** *adj* endeuillé **2** *npl*: bereaved; the ~ la famille du défunt / la défunte

be·ret [ber'eɪ] béret *m*

ber·ry ['berɪ] baie *f*

ber·serk [bər'zɜːrk] *adv*: go ~ F devenir fou* furieux*

berth [bɜːrθ] couchette *f*; *for ship* mouillage *m*; give s.o. a wide ~ éviter qn

be·seech [bɪ'siːtʃ] *v/t*: ~ s.o. to do sth implorer qn de faire qch

be·side [bɪ'saɪd] *prep* à côté de; *work* aux côtés de; be ~ o.s. être hors de soi; that's ~ the point c'est hors de propos

be·sides [bɪ'saɪdz] **1** *adv* en plus, d'ailleurs **2** *prep* (*apart from*) à part, en dehors de

be·siege [bɪ'siːdʒ] *v/t fig* assiéger

best [best] **1** *adj* meilleur **2** *adv* le mieux; *it would be* ~ *if ...* ce serait mieux si ...; I like her ~ c'est elle que j'aime le plus **3** *n*: do one's ~ faire de son mieux; the ~ le mieux; (*outstanding thing or person*) le (la) meilleur(e) *m(f)*; make the ~ of it s'y accommoder; all the ~! meilleurs

vœux!; (*good luck*) bonne chance!

best be'fore date *for food* date *f* limite de consommation; best 'man *at wedding* garçon *m* d'honneur; 'best-sell·er *book* best-seller *m*

bet [bet] **1** *n* pari *m* **2** *v/i* parier; you ~! évidemment! **3** *v/t* parier

be·tray [bɪ'treɪ] *v/t* trahir

be·tray·al [bɪ'treɪəl] trahison *f*

bet·ter ['betər] **1** *adj* meilleur; get ~ s'améliorer; he's getting ~ *in health* il va de mieux en mieux; he's ~ *in health* il va mieux **2** *adv* meilleur; you'd ~ ask permission tu devrais demander la permission; I'd really ~ not je ne devrais vraiment pas; all the ~ for us tant mieux pour nous; I like her ~ je l'aime plus, je la préfère

bet·ter-'off *adj* (*richer*) plus aisé; you're ~ without them tu es bien mieux sans eux

be·tween [bɪ'twiːn] *prep* entre; ~ you and me entre toi et moi

bev·er·age ['bevərɪdʒ] *fml* boisson *f*

be·ware [bɪ'wer]: ~ of méfiez-vous de, attention à; ~ of the dog (*attention*) chien méchant!

be·wil·der [bɪ'wɪldər] *v/t* confondre, ahurir

be·wil·der·ment [bɪ'wɪldərmənt] confusion *f*, ahurissement *m*

be·yond [bɪ'jɑːnd] **1** *prep* au-delà de; it's ~ me (*I don't understand*) cela me dépasse; (*I can't do it*) c'est trop difficile pour moi; for reasons ~ my control pour des raisons indépendantes de ma volonté **2** *adv* au-delà

bi·as ['baɪəs] *n* parti *m* pris, préjugé *m*

bi·as(s)ed ['baɪəst] *adj* partial, subjectif*

bib [bɪb] *for baby* bavette *f*

Bi·ble ['baɪbl] Bible *f*

bib·li·cal ['bɪblɪkl] *adj* biblique

bib·li·og·ra·phy [bɪblɪ'ɑːgrəfɪ] bibliographie *f*

bi·car·bon·ate of so·da [baɪ'kɑːrbəneɪt] bicarbonate *m* de soude

bi·cen·ten·ni·al [baɪsen'tenɪəl] bicentennial bicentenaire *m*

bi·ceps ['baɪseps] *npl* biceps *m*

bick·er ['bɪkər] *v/i* se chamailler

bi·cy·cle ['baɪsɪkl] *n* bicyclette *f*

bid [bɪd] **1** *n at auction* enchère *m*; *(attempt)* tentative *f*; *in takeover* offre *f* **2** *v/i (pret & pp* **bid)** *at auction* faire une enchère, faire une offre

bid·der ['bɪdər] enchérisseur(-euse) *m(f)*

bi·en·ni·al [baɪ'enɪəl] *adj* biennal

bi·fo·cals [baɪ'foʊkəlz] *npl* verres *mpl* à double foyer

big [bɪg] **1** *adj* grand; *sum of money, mistake* gros; *a great ~ helping* une grosse portion; *my ~ brother / sister* mon grand frère / ma grande sœur; *~ name* grand nom *m* **2** *adv*: *talk ~* se vanter

big·a·mist ['bɪgəmɪst] bigame *m/f*

big·a·mous ['bɪgəməs] *adj* bigame

big·a·my ['bɪgəmɪ] bigamie *f*

'big·head F crâneur(-euse) *m(f)* F

big·head·ed [bɪg'hedɪd] *adj* F crâneur* F

big·ot ['bɪgət] fanatique *m/f*, sectaire *m/f*

bike [baɪk] **1** *n* F vélo *m*; *(motorbike)* moto *f* **2** *v/i* F faire du vélo; *with motorbike* faire de la moto; *~ to work* aller au travail en vélo / moto

bik·er ['baɪkər] motard(e) *m(f)*

bi·ki·ni [bɪ'ki:nɪ] bikini *m*

bi·lat·er·al [baɪ'lætərəl] *adj* bilatéral

bi·lin·gual [baɪ'lɪŋgwəl] *adj* bilingue

bill [bɪl] **1** *n* facture *f*; *money* billet *m* (de banque); POL projet *m* de loi; *(poster)* affiche *f* **2** *v/t (invoice)* facturer

'bill·board panneau *m* d'affichage

'bill·fold portefeuille *m*

bil·liards ['bɪljərdz] *nsg* billard *m*

bil·lion ['bɪljən] milliard *m*

bill of ex'change FIN traite *f*, lettre *f* de change

bill of 'sale acte *m* de vente

bin [bɪn] *n for storage* boîte *f*

bi·na·ry ['baɪnərɪ] *adj* binaire

bind [baɪnd] *v/t (pret & pp* **bound)** *(connect)* unir; *(tie)* attacher; LAW *(oblige)* obliger, engager

bind·ing ['baɪndɪŋ] **1** *adj agreement, promise* obligatoire **2** *n of book* reliure *f*

bi·noc·u·lars [bɪ'nɑ:kjʊlərz] *npl* jumelles *fpl*

bi·o·chem·ist ['baɪoʊkemɪst] biochimiste *m/f*

bi·o·chem·is·try [baɪoʊ'kemɪstrɪ] biochimie *f*

bi·o·de·grad·able [baɪoʊdɪ'greɪdəbl] *adj* biodégradable

bi·og·ra·pher [baɪ'ɑ:grəfər] biographe *m/f*

bi·og·ra·phy [baɪ'ɑ:grəfɪ] biographie *f*

bi·o·log·i·cal [baɪoʊ'lɑ:dʒɪkl] *adj* biologique

bi·ol·o·gist [baɪ'ɑ:lədʒɪst] biologiste *m/f*

bi·ol·o·gy [baɪ'ɑ:lədʒɪ] biologie *f*

bi·o·tech·nol·o·gy [baɪoʊtek'nɑ:lədʒɪ] biotechnologie *f*

birch [bɜ:rtʃ] bouleau *m*

bird [bɜ:rd] oiseau *m*

'bird·cage cage *f* à oiseaux; **bird of 'prey** oiseau *m* de proie; **'bird sanc·tu·a·ry** refuge *m* d'oiseaux; **bird's eye 'view** vue *f* aérienne

birth [bɜ:rθ] naissance *f*; *(labor)* accouchement *m*; *give ~ to child* donner naissance à, mettre au monde; *date of ~* date *f* de naissance

'birth cer·tif·i·cate acte *m* de naissance; **'birth con·trol** contrôle *m* des naissances; **'birth·day** anniversaire *m*

'birth·day; *happy ~!* bon anniversaire!; **'birth·mark** tache *f* de naissance; **'birth·place** lieu *m* de naissance; **'birth·rate** natalité *f*

bis·cuit ['bɪskɪt] biscuit *m*

bi·sex·u·al ['baɪseksjʊəl] **1** *adj* bisexuel **2** *n* bisexuel(le) *m(f)*

bish·op ['bɪʃəp] REL évêque *m*

bit¹ [bɪt] *n (piece)* morceau *m*; *(part: of book)* passage *m*; *(part: of garden, road)* partie *f*; COMPUT bit *m*; *a ~ (a little)* un peu; *a ~ of (a little)* un peu de; *you haven't changed a ~* tu n'as pas du tout changé; *a ~ of a problem* un petit problème; *a ~ of news* une nouvelle; *~ by ~* peu à peu; *I'll be there in a ~ (in a little while)* je serai là dans peu de temps

bit² [bɪt] *pret → **bite***

B

bitch [bɪtʃ] **1** n dog chienne f; F: woman garce f F **2** v/i F (complain) rouspéter F

bitch·y ['bɪtʃɪ] adj F vache F

bite [baɪt] **1** n of dog, snake morsure f; of spider, mosquito, flea piqûre f; of food morceau m; **let's have a ~ (to eat)** et si on mangeait quelque chose **2** v/t (pret **bit**, pp **bitten**) of dog, snake, person mordre; of spider, flea, mosquito piquer; **~ one's nails** se ronger les ongles **3** v/i (pret **bit**, pp **bitten**) of dog, snake, person, fish mordre; of spider, flea, mosquito piquer

bit·ten ['bɪtn] pp → **bite**

bit·ter ['bɪtər] adj taste, person amer; weather glacial; argument violent

bit·ter·ly ['bɪtərlɪ] adv resent amèrement; **it's ~ cold** il fait un froid de canard

bi·zarre [bɪ'zɑːr] adj bizarre

blab [blæb] v/i (pret & pp **-bed**) F vendre la mèche

blab·ber·mouth ['blæbərmaʊθ] F bavard(e) m(f)

black [blæk] **1** adj noir; tea nature; future sombre **2** n color noir m; person Noir(e) m(f); **in the ~** FIN créditeur; **in ~ and white** fig noir sur blanc
♦ **black out** v/i s'évanouir

'**black·ber·ry** mûre f; '**black·bird** merle m; '**black·board** tableau m noir; **black 'box** boîte f noire; **black e'con·o·my** économie f souterraine

black·en ['blækn] v/t fig: person's name noircir

black 'eye œil m poché; '**black·head** point m noir; **black 'ice** verglas m; '**black·list 1** n liste f noire **2** v/t mettre à l'index, mettre sur la liste noire; '**black·mail 1** n chantage m; **emotional ~** chantage m psychologique **2** v/t faire chanter; **black·mail·er** ['blækmeɪlər] maître m chanteur; **black 'mar·ket** marché m noir

black·ness ['blæknɪs] noirceur f

'**black·out** ELEC panne f d'électricité; MED évanouissement m

black·smith ['blæksmɪθ] forgeron m

blad·der ['blædər] ANAT vessie f

blade [bleɪd] of knife, sword lame f; of helicopter ailette f; of grass brin m

blame [bleɪm] **1** n responsabilité f; **I got the ~** c'est moi qu'on a accusé **2** v/t: **~ s.o. for sth** reprocher qch à qn; **I ~ her parents** c'est la faute de ses parents

bland [blænd] adj fade

blank [blæŋk] **1** adj paper, tape vierge; look vide **2** n (empty space) espace m vide; **my mind's a ~** j'ai un trou (de mémoire)

blank 'check, Br **blank 'cheque** chèque m en blanc

blan·ket ['blæŋkɪt] n couverture f; **a ~ of snow** un manteau de neige

blare [bler] v/i beugler
♦ **blare out 1** v/i retentir **2** v/t: **the speakers were blaring out military music** des musiques militaires retentissaient dans les haut-parleurs

blas·pheme [blæs'fiːm] v/i blasphémer

blas·phe·my ['blæsfəmɪ] blasphème m

blast [blæst] **1** n (explosion) explosion f; (gust) rafale f **2** v/t tunnel etc percer (à l'aide d'explosifs); **~!** F mince!
♦ **blast off** v/i of rocket décoller

'**blast fur·nace** haut-fourneau m

'**blast-off** lancement m

bla·tant ['bleɪtənt] adj flagrant, évident; person éhonté

blaze [bleɪz] **1** n (fire) incendie m; **be a ~ of color** être resplendissant de couleur(s) **2** v/i of fire flamber
♦ **blaze away** v/i with gun tirer en rafales

blaz·er ['bleɪzər] blazer m

bleach [bliːtʃ] **1** n for clothes eau f de Javel; for hair décolorant m **2** v/t hair décolorer

bleak [bliːk] adj countryside désolé; weather morne; future sombre

blear·y-eyed ['blɪrɪaɪd] adj aux yeux troubles

bleat [bliːt] v/i of sheep bêler

bled [bled] pret & pp → **bleed**

bleed [bliːd] **1** v/i (pret & pp **bled**) saigner **2** v/t (pret & pp **bled**) fig saigner; radiator purger

bleed·ing ['bliːdɪŋ] n saignement m

bleep [bli:p] **1** *n* bip *m* **2** *v/i* faire bip **3** *v/t* (*call on pager*) appeler sur bip, biper

bleep·er ['bli:pər] (*pager*) bip *m*

blem·ish ['blemɪʃ] *n* tache *f*

blend [blend] **1** *n* mélange *m* **2** *v/t* mélanger

♦ **blend in 1** *v/i of person* s'intégrer; *of furniture* se marier **2** *v/t in cooking* mélanger

blend·er ['blendər] *machine* mixeur *m*

bless [bles] *v/t* bénir; (**God**) ~ **you!** Dieu vous bénisse!; ~ **you!** *in response to sneeze* à vos souhaits!; **be ~ed with** *disposition* être doté de; *children* avoir

bless·ing ['blesɪŋ] REL, *fig* bénédiction *f*

blew [blu:] *pret* → **blow**

blind [blaɪnd] **1** *adj person* aveugle; ~ **corner** virage *m* masqué; **be ~ to sth** *fig* ne pas voir qch **2** *npl*: **the ~** les aveugles *mpl* **3** *v/t* (*make blind*) rendre aveugle; *of sun* aveugler, éblouir; ~ **s.o. to sth** *fig* empêcher qn de voir qch

blind 'al·ley impasse *f*; **blind 'date** rendez-vous *m* arrangé; **'blind·fold 1** *n* bandeau *m* sur les yeux **2** *v/t* bander les yeux à **3** *adv* les yeux bandés

blind·ing ['blaɪndɪŋ] *adj light* aveuglant; *headache* terrible

blind·ly ['blaɪndlɪ] *adv* sans rien voir; *fig: obey, follow* aveuglément

'blind spot *in road* angle *m* mort; (*ability that is lacking*) faiblesse *f*

blink [blɪŋk] *v/i of person* cligner des yeux; *of light* clignoter

blink·ered ['blɪŋkərd] *adj fig* à œillères

blip [blɪp] *on radar screen* spot *m*; *fig* anomalie *f* passagère

bliss [blɪs] bonheur *m* (suprême)

blis·ter ['blɪstər] **1** *n* ampoule *f* **2** *v/i of skin, paint* cloquer

bliz·zard ['blɪzərd] tempête *f* de neige

bloat·ed ['bloʊtɪd] *adj* gonflé, boursouflé

blob [blɑːb] *of cream, paint etc* goutte *f*

bloc [blɑːk] POL bloc *m*

block [blɑːk] **1** *n* bloc *m*; *buildings* pâté *m* de maisons; *of shares* paquet *m*; (*blockage*) obstruction *f*, embouteillage *m*; **it's three ~s away** c'est à trois rues d'ici **2** *v/t* bloquer

♦ **block in** *v/t with vehicle* bloquer le passage de

♦ **block out** *v/t light* empêcher de passer; *memory* refouler

♦ **block up** *v/t sink etc* boucher

block·ade [blɑːˈkeɪd] **1** *n* blocus *m* **2** *v/t* faire le blocus de

block·age ['blɑːkɪdʒ] obstruction *f*

block·bust·er ['blɑːkbʌstər] *movie* film *m* à grand succès; *novel* roman *m* à succès

block 'let·ters *npl* capitales *fpl*

blond [blɑːnd] *adj* blond

blonde [blɑːnd] *n woman* blonde *f*

blood [blʌd] sang *m*; **in cold ~** de sang-froid

'blood al·co·hol lev·el alcoolémie *f*; **'blood bank** banque *f* du sang; **'blood bath** bain *m* de sang; **'blood do·nor** donneur(-euse) *m(f)* de sang; **'blood group** groupe *m* sanguin

blood·less ['blʌdlɪs] *adj coup* sans effusion de sang

blood poi·son·ing ['blʌdpɔɪznɪŋ] empoisonnement *m* du sang; **'blood pres·sure** tension *f* (artérielle); **'blood re·la·tion, 'blood rel·a·tive** parent *m* par le sang; **'blood sam·ple** prélèvement *m* sanguin; **'blood·shed** carnage *m*; **without ~** sans effusion de sang; **'blood·shot** *adj* injecté de sang; **'blood·stain** tache *f* de sang; **'blood·stained** *adj* taché de sang; **'blood·stream** sang *m*; **'blood test** test *m* sanguin; **'blood·thirst·y** *adj* sanguinaire; **'blood trans·fu·sion** transfusion *f* sanguine; **'blood ves·sel** vaisseau *m* sanguin

bloody ['blʌdɪ] *adj hands etc* ensanglanté; *battle* sanguinaire; *esp Br* F sacré

bloom [blu:m] **1** *n* fleur *f*; **in full ~** en fleurs **2** *v/i also fig* fleurir

bloop·er ['blu:pər] F gaffe *f*

blos·som ['blɑːsəm] **1** *n* fleur *f* **2** *v/i* fleurir; *fig* s'épanouir

blot [blɑːt] **1** *n* tache *f*; **be a ~ on the**

B

landscape fig faire tache dans le paysage **2** *v/t* (*pret & pp* **-ted**) (*dry*) sécher

♦ **blot out** *v/t* effacer

blotch [blɑːtʃ] *on skin* tache *f*

blotch·y ['blɑːtʃɪ] *adj* taché

blouse [blauz] chemisier *m*

blow¹ [bləu] *n also* fig coup *m*

blow² [bləu] **1** *v/t* (*pret* **blew**, *pp* **blown**) souffler; F (*spend*) claquer F; F *opportunity* rater; **~ one's whistle** donner un coup de sifflet; **~ one's nose** se moucher **2** *v/i* (*pret* **blew**, *pp* **blown**) *of wind, person* souffler; *of whistle* retentir; *of fuse* sauter; *of tire* éclater

♦ **blow off 1** *v/t* arracher **2** *v/i of hat etc* s'envoler

♦ **blow out 1** *v/t candle* souffler **2** *v/i of candle* s'éteindre

♦ **blow over 1** *v/t* renverser **2** *v/i* se renverser; (*pass*) passer

♦ **blow up 1** *v/t with explosives* faire sauter, faire exploser; *balloon* gonfler; *photograph* agrandir **2** *v/i of car, boiler etc* sauter, exploser; F (*get angry*) devenir furieux*

♦ **blow-dry** *v/t* (*pret & pp* **-ied**) sécher (au sèche-cheveux)

'blow job V pipe *f* V

blown [bləun] *pp* → **blow**

'blow-out *of tire* éclatement *m*; F (*big meal*) gueuleton *m* F

'blow-up *of photo* agrandissement *m*

blue [bluː] **1** *adj* bleu; F *movie* porno F **2** *n* bleu *m*

'blue·ber·ry myrtille *f*; **blue 'chip** *adj company* de premier ordre; **blue-'col·lar work·er** travailleur(-euse) *m(f)* manuel(le); **'blue·print** plan *m*; fig projet *m*

blues [bluːz] *npl* MUS blues *m*; **have the ~** avoir le cafard F

'blues sing·er chanteur(-euse) *m(f)* de blues

bluff [blʌf] **1** *n* (*deception*) bluff *m* **2** *v/i* bluffer

blun·der ['blʌndər] **1** *n* bévue *f*, gaffe *f* **2** *v/i* faire une bévue *or* gaffe

blunt [blʌnt] *adj* émoussé; *person* franc*

blunt·ly ['blʌntlɪ] *adv speak* franchement

blur [blɜːr] **1** *n* masse *f* confuse **2** *v/t* (*pret & pp* **-red**) brouiller

blurb [blɜːrb] *on book* promotion *f*

♦ **blurt out** [blɜːrt] *v/t* lâcher

blush [blʌʃ] **1** *n* rougissement *m* **2** *v/i* rougir

blush·er ['blʌʃər] *cosmetic* rouge *m*

blus·ter ['blʌstər] *v/i* faire le fanfaron

blus·ter·y ['blʌstərɪ] *adj weather* à bourrasques

BO [biː'əu] *abbr* (= *body odor*) odeur *f* corporelle

board [bɔːrd] **1** *n of wood* planche *f*; *cardboard* carton *m*; *for game* plateau *m de jeu*; *for notices* panneau *m*; **~ (of directors)** conseil *m* d'administration; **on ~** à bord; **take on ~** *comments etc* prendre en compte; (*fully realize truth of*) réaliser; **across the ~** d'une manière générale **2** *v/t plane, ship* monter à bord de; *train, bus* monter dans **3** *v/i of passengers* embarquer; *on train, bus* monter (à bord)

♦ **board up** *v/t windows* condamner

♦ **board with** *v/t* être en pension chez

board and 'lodg·ing ['lɑːdʒɪŋ] pension *f* complète

board·er ['bɔːrdər] pensionnaire *m/f*; EDU interne *m/f*

'board game jeu *m* de société

'board·ing card ['bɔːrdɪŋ] carte *f* d'embarquement; **'board·ing house** pension *f* (de famille); **'board·ing pass** carte *f* d'embarquement; **'board·ing school** internat *m*, pensionnat *m*

'board meet·ing réunion *f* du conseil d'administration; **'board room** salle *f* du conseil; **'board·walk** promenade *f* (en planches) *fpl*

boast [bəust] *v/i* se vanter (*about* de)

boast·ing ['bəustɪŋ] vantardise *f*

boat [bəut] (*ship*) bateau *m*; *small, for leisure* canot *m*; **go by ~** aller en bateau

bob¹ [bɑːb] *n haircut* coupe *f* au carré

bob² [bɑːb] *v/i* (*pret & pp* **-bed**) *of boat etc* se balancer, danser

♦ **bob up** *v/i* se lever subitement

'bob·sled, 'bob·sleigh bobsleigh *m*

bod·i·ly ['bɑːdɪlɪ] **1** *adj* corporel **2** *adv*: **they ~ ejected him** ils l'ont saisi à bras-le-corps et l'ont mis dehors

bod·y ['bɑːdɪ] corps *m*; *dead* cadavre *m*; ~ **(suit)** *undergarment* body *m*; ~ **of water** étendue *f* d'eau

'bod·y·guard garde *m* du corps; 'bod·y lan·guage langage *m* du corps; **I could tell by her ~ that …** je pouvais voir à ses gestes que …; 'bod·y o·dor odeur *f* corporelle; 'bod·y pierc·ing piercing *m*; 'bod·y shop MOT atelier *m* de carrosserie; 'bod·y stock·ing body *m*; 'bod·y suit body *m*; 'bod·y·work MOT carrosserie *f*

bog·gle ['bɑːgl] *v/t*: **it ~s the mind!** j'ai du mal à le croire!

bo·gus ['boʊgəs] *adj* faux

boil¹ [bɔɪl] *n* (*swelling*) furoncle *m*

boil² [bɔɪl] **1** *v/t* faire bouillir **2** *v/i* bouillir

◆ boil down to *v/t* se ramener à

◆ boil over *v/i* *of milk etc* déborder

boil·er ['bɔɪlər] chaudière *f*

'boil·ing point ['bɔɪlɪŋ] *of liquid point m* d'ébullition; **reach ~** *fig* éclater

bois·ter·ous ['bɔɪstərəs] *adj* bruyant

bold [boʊld] **1** *adj* (*brave*) courageux*; *text* en caractères gras **2** *n print* caractères *mpl* gras; **in ~** en caractères gras

bol·ster ['boʊlstər] *v/t* *confidence* soutenir

bolt [boʊlt] **1** *n* (*metal pin*) boulon *m*; *on door* verrou *m*; *of lightning* coup *m*; **come like a ~ from the blue** faire l'effet d'une bombe **2** *adv*: ~ **upright** tout droit **3** *v/t* (*fix with bolts*) boulonner; *close* verrouiller **4** *v/i* (*run off*) décamper; *of horse* s'emballer

bomb [bɑːm] **1** *n* bombe *f* **2** *v/t* *from airplane* bombarder; *of terrorist* faire sauter

bom·bard [bɑːm'bɑːrd] *v/t* (*attack*) bombarder; ~ **with questions** bombarder de questions

'bomb at·tack attaque *f* à la bombe

bomb·er ['bɑːmər] *airplane* bombardier *m*; *terrorist* poseur *m(f)* de bombes

'bomb·er jack·et blouson *m* d'aviateur

'bomb·proof *adj* bunker blindé; *building* protégé contre les bombes; 'bomb scare alerte *f* à la bombe; 'bomb·shell *fig* bombe *f*; **come as a ~** faire l'effet d'une bombe

bond [bɑːnd] **1** *n* (*tie*) lien *m*; FIN obligation *f* **2** *v/i* *of glue* se coller

bone [boʊn] **1** *n* os *m*; *in fish* arête *f* **2** *v/t meat, fish* désosser

bon·er ['boʊnər] F gaffe *f*

bon·fire ['bɑːnfaɪr] feu *m* (de jardin)

bo·nus ['boʊnəs] *money* prime *f*; (*something extra*) plus *m*

boo [buː] **1** *n* huée *f* **2** *v/t actor, speaker* huer **3** *v/i* pousser des huées

boob [buːb] *n* P (*breast*) nichon *m* P

boo·boo ['buːbuː] F bêtise *f*

book [bʊk] **1** *n* livre *m*; ~ **of matches** pochette *f* d'allumettes **2** *v/t table, seat* réserver; *ticket* prendre; *pop group, artiste* retenir; *of policeman* donner un P.V. à F; ~ **s.o. on a flight** réserver une place à qn sur un vol **3** *v/i* (*reserve*) réserver

'book·case bibliothèque *f*

booked up [bʊkt'ʌp] *adj* complet*; *person* complètement pris

book·ie ['bʊkɪ] F bookmaker *m*

book·ing ['bʊkɪŋ] (*reservation*) réservation *f*

'book·ing clerk employé(e) *m(f)* du guichet

book·keep·er ['bʊkkiːpər] comptable *m*

'book·keep·ing comptabilité *f*

book·let ['bʊklɪt] livret *m*

'book·mak·er bookmaker *m*

books [bʊks] *npl* (*accounts*) comptes *mpl*; **do the ~** faire la comptabilité

'book·sell·er libraire *m/f*; 'book·shelf étagère *f*; 'book·stall kiosque *m* à journaux; 'book·store librairie *f*; 'book to·ken chèque-livre *m*

boom¹ [buːm] **1** *n* boum *m* **2** *v/i of business* aller très fort

boom² [buːm] *n noise* boum *m*

boon·ies ['buːnɪz] *npl* F en pleine cambrousse F

boor [bʊr] rustre *m*

B

boor·ish ['bʊrɪʃ] *adj* rustre
boost [buːst] **1** *n*: **give sth a ~** stimuler qch **2** *v/t* stimuler
boot [buːt] *n* botte *f*; *for climbing, football* chaussure *f*
♦ **boot out** *v/t* F virer F
♦ **boot up** COMPUT **1** *v/i* démarrer **2** *v/t* faire démarrer
booth [buːð] *at market* tente *f* (de marché); *at fair* baraque *f*; *at trade fair* stand *m*; *in restaurant* alcôve *f*
booze [buːz] *n* F boisson *f* (alcoolique)
bor·der ['bɔːrdər] **1** *n* between countries frontière *f*; *(edge)* bordure *f* **2** *v/t* country avoir une frontière avec; *river* longer
♦ **border on** *v/t* country avoir une frontière avec; *(be almost)* friser
'bor·der·line *adj*: **a ~ case** un cas limite
bore[1] [bɔːr] *v/t* hole percer
bore[2] [bɔːr] **1** *n* person raseur(-euse) *m(f)* F **2** *v/t* ennuyer
bore[3] [bɔːr] *pret* → **bear**[2]
bored [bɔːrd] *adj* ennuyé; **be ~** s'ennuyer; **I'm ~** je m'ennuie
bore·dom ['bɔːrdəm] ennui *m*
bor·ing ['bɔːrɪŋ] *adj* ennuyeux*, chiant F
born [bɔːrn] *adj*: **be ~** être né; **be a ~ ...** être un(e) ... né(e)
borne [bɔːrn] *pp* → **bear**[2]
bor·row ['baːroʊ] *v/t* emprunter
bos·om ['bʊzm] *of woman* poitrine *f*
boss [baːs] *patron(ne) m(f)*
♦ **boss around** *v/t* donner des ordres à
boss·y ['baːsɪ] *adj* autoritaire
bo·tan·i·cal [bə'tænɪkl] *adj* botanique
bo·tan·i·cal gar·dens *npl* jardin *m* botanique
bot·a·nist ['baːtənɪst] botaniste *m/f*
bot·a·ny ['baːtənɪ] botanique *f*
botch [baːtʃ] *v/t* bâcler
both [boʊθ] **1** *adj* les deux; **I know ~ brothers** je connais les deux frères **2** *pron* les deux; **I know ~ of the brothers** je connais les deux frères; **~ of them** tous(-tes) *m(f)* les deux **3** *adv*: **~ ... and ...** à la fois ... et ...; **is it sweet or sour? – ~** c'est sucré ou

amer? – les deux (à la fois)
both·er ['baːðər] **1** *n* problèmes *mpl*; **it's no ~** ça ne pose pas de problème **2** *v/t (disturb)* déranger; *(worry)* ennuyer **3** *v/i* s'inquiéter (**with** de); **don't ~!** *(you needn't do it)* ce n'est pas la peine!; **you needn't have ~ed** ce n'était pas la peine
bot·tle ['baːtl] **1** *n* bouteille *f*; *for medicines* flacon *m*; *for baby* biberon *m* **2** *v/t* mettre en bouteille
♦ **bottle up** *v/t* feelings réprimer
'bot·tle bank conteneur *m* à verre
bot·tled wa·ter ['baːtld] eau *f* en bouteille
'bot·tle·neck *in road* rétrécissement *m*; *in production* goulet *m* d'étranglement
bot·tle-o·pen·er ['baːtloʊpnər] ouvre-bouteilles *m inv*
bot·tom ['baːtəm] **1** *adj* du bas **2** *n of drawer, pan, garden* fond *m*; *(underside)* dessous *m*; *(lowest part)* bas *m*; *of street* bout *m*; *(buttocks)* derrière *m*; **at the ~ of the screen** au bas de l'écran
♦ **bottom out** *v/i* se stabiliser
bot·tom 'line *fig (financial outcome)* résultat *m*; *(the real issue)* la question principale
bought [bɔːt] *pret & pp* → **buy**
boul·der ['boʊldər] rocher *m*
bounce [baʊns] **1** *v/t* ball faire rebondir **2** *v/i of ball* rebondir; *on sofa etc* sauter; *of check* être refusé
bounc·er ['baʊnsər] videur *m*
bounc·y ['baʊnsɪ] *adj* ball, cushion, chair qui rebondit
bound[1] [baʊnd] *adj*: **be ~ to do sth** *(sure to)* aller forcément faire qch; *(obliged to)* être tenu de faire qch
bound[2] [baʊnd] *adj*: **be ~ for** of ship être à destination de
bound[3] [baʊnd] **1** *n (jump)* bond *m* **2** *v/i* bondir
bound[4] [baʊnd] *pret & pp* → **bind**
bound·a·ry ['baʊndərɪ] frontière *f*
bound·less ['baʊndlɪs] *adj* sans bornes, illimité
bou·quet [buˈkeɪ] *flowers, of wine* bouquet *m*

bour·bon ['bɜːrbən] bourbon *m*

bout [baʊt] MED accès *m*; *in boxing match* *m*

bou·tique [buːˈtiːk] boutique *f*

bow[1] [baʊ] **1** *n as greeting* révérence *f* **2** *v/i* faire une révérence **3** *v/t head* baisser

bow[2] [boʊ] (*knot*) nœud *m*; MUS archet *m*

bow[3] [baʊ] *of ship* avant *m*

bow·els ['baʊəlz] *npl* intestins *mpl*

bowl[1] [boʊl] bol *m*; *for soup etc* assiette *f* creuse; *for serving salad etc* saladier *m*; *for washing dishes* cuvette *f*

bowl[2] [boʊl] *v/i* jouer au bowling

♦ **bowl over** *v/t fig* (*astonish*) renverser

bowl·ing ['boʊlɪŋ] bowling *m*

'bowl·ing al·ley bowling *m*

bow 'tie [boʊ] (nœud *m*) papillon *m*

box[1] [bɑːks] *n container* boîte *f*; *on form* case *f*

box[2] [bɑːks] *v/i* boxer

box·er ['bɑːksər] *sp* boxeur *m*

'box·er shorts *npl* caleçon *m*

box·ing ['bɑːksɪŋ] boxe *f*

'box·ing glove gant *m* de boxe; **'box·ing match** match *m* de boxe; **'box·ing ring** ring *m* (de boxe)

'box num·ber boîte *f* postale

'box of·fice bureau *m* de location

boy [bɔɪ] garçon *m*; (*son*) fils *m*

boy·cott ['bɔɪkɑːt] **1** *n* boycott *m* **2** *v/t* boycotter

'boy·friend petit ami *m*; *younger also* copain *m*

boy·ish ['bɔɪɪʃ] *adj* de garçon

boy'scout scout *m*

brace [breɪs] *on teeth* appareil *m* (dentaire)

brace·let ['breɪslɪt] bracelet *m*

brack·et ['brækɪt] *for shelf* support *m* (d'étagère); *in text* crochet *m*; *Br: round* parenthèse *f*

brag [bræg] *v/i* (*pret & pp* **-ged**) se vanter (*about* de)

braid [breɪd] *n in hair* tresse *f*; (*trimming*) galon *m*

braille [breɪl] braille *m*

brain [breɪn] ANAT cerveau *m*; **use your ~** fais travailler votre cerveau

'brain dead *adj* MED en coma dépassé

brain·less ['breɪnlɪs] *adj F* écervelé

brains [breɪnz] *npl* (*intelligence*), *also person* cerveau *m*; **it doesn't take much ~** il n'y a pas besoin d'être très intelligent

'brain·storm idée *f* de génie; **brain·storm·ing** ['breɪnstɔːrmɪŋ] brainstorming *m*; **'brain sur·geon** neurochirurgien(ne) *m(f)*; **'brain sur·ger·y** neurochirurgie *f*; **'brain tu·mor** tumeur *f* au cerveau; **'brain·wash** *v/t by media etc* conditionner; **'brain·wave** *Br* → **brainstorm**

brain·y ['breɪnɪ] *adj F* intelligent

brake [breɪk] **1** *n* frein *m* **2** *v/i* freiner

'brake flu·id liquide *m* de freins; **'brake light** feu *m* de stop; **'brake ped·al** pédale *f* de frein

branch [bræntʃ] *of tree, bank, company* branche *f*

♦ **branch off** *v/i of road* bifurquer

♦ **branch out** *v/i* (*diversify*) se diversifier

brand [brænd] **1** *n* marque *f* **2** *v/t*: **be ~ed a liar** être étiqueté comme voleur

brand 'im·age image *f* de marque

bran·dish ['brændɪʃ] *v/t* brandir

brand 'lead·er marque *f* dominante; **brand 'loy·al·ty** fidélité *f* à la marque; **'brand name** nom *m* de marque

brand-'new *adj* flambant neuf*

bran·dy ['brændɪ] brandy *m*

brass [bræs] cuivre *m* jaune, laiton *m*; **the ~** MUS les cuivres *mpl*

brass 'band fanfare *f*

bras·sière [brəˈzɪ(r)] soutien-gorge *m*

brat [bræt] *pej* garnement *m*

bra·va·do [brəˈvɑːdoʊ] bravade *f*

brave [breɪv] *adj* courageux*

brave·ly ['breɪvlɪ] *adv* courageusement

brav·er·y ['breɪvərɪ] courage *m*

brawl [brɔːl] **1** *n* bagarre *f* **2** *v/i* se bagarrer

brawn·y ['brɔːnɪ] *adj* costaud

Bra·zil [brəˈzɪl] Brésil *m*

Bra·zil·ian [brəˈzɪlɪən] **1** *adj* brésilien* **2** *n* Brésilien(ne) *m(f)*

breach [briːtʃ] *n* (*violation*) violation *f*;

in party désaccord *m*, différend *m*; (*split*) scission *f*

breach of 'con·tract LAW rupture *f* de contrat

bread [bred] pain *m*

'bread·crumbs *npl* miettes *fpl* de pain

'bread knife couteau *m* à pain

breadth [bredθ] largeur *f*; *of knowledge* étendue *f*

'bread·win·ner soutien *m* de famille

break [breɪk] **1** *n in bone* fracture *f*; (*rest*) repos *m*; *in relationship* séparation *f*; *give s.o. a ~* F (*opportunity*) donner une chance à qn; *take a ~* s'arrêter; *without a ~ work, travel* sans interruption **2** *v/t* (*pret* **broke**, *pp* **broken**) casser; *rules, law, promise* violer; *news* annoncer; *record* battre; *~ one's arm / leg* se casser le bras / la jambe **3** *v/i* (*pret* **broke**, *pp* **broken**) se casser; *of news, storm* éclater; *of boy's voice* muer; *the news has just broken that ...* on vient d'apprendre que ...

♦ **break away** *v/i* (*escape*) s'échapper; *from family, organization, tradition* rompre (*from* avec)

♦ **break down 1** *v/i of vehicle, machine* tomber en panne; *of talks* échouer; *in tears* s'effondrer; *mentally* faire une dépression **2** *v/t door* défoncer; *figures* détailler

♦ **break even** *v/i* COMM rentrer dans ses frais

♦ **break in** *v/i* (*interrupt*) interrompre qn; *of burglar* s'introduire par effraction

♦ **break off 1** *v/t* casser; *relationship* rompre; *they've broken it off* *engagement* ils ont rompu leurs fiançailles; *relationship* ils ont rompu **2** *v/i* (*stop talking*) s'interrompre

♦ **break out** *v/i* (*start up*) éclater; *of prisoners* s'échapper; *he broke out in a rash* il a eu une éruption (cutanée)

♦ **break up 1** *v/t into component parts* décomposer; *fight* interrompre **2** *v/i of ice* se briser; *of couple, band* se séparer; *of meeting* se dissoudre

break·a·ble ['breɪkəbl] *adj* cassable

break·age ['breɪkɪdʒ] casse *f*

'break·down *of vehicle, machine* panne *f*

breakdown *of talks* échec *m*; (*nervous ~*) dépression *f* (nerveuse); *of figures* détail *m*

break-'e·ven point seuil *m* de rentabilité

break·fast ['brekfəst] *n* petit-déjeuner *m*; *have ~* prendre son petit-déjeuner

'break·fast tel·e·vi·sion programmes *mpl* du petit-déjeuner

'break-in cambriolage *m*

break·ing ['breɪkɪŋ] *adj*: *~ news* information *f* de dernière minute

'break·through percée *f*

'break-up *of marriage, partnership* échec *m*

breast [brest] *of woman* sein *m*

'breast-feed *v/t* (*pret & pp* **breastfed**) allaiter

'breast·stroke brasse *f*

breath [breθ] souffle *m*; *be out of ~* être essoufflé; *take a deep ~* inspirer rofondément

Breath·a·lyz·er® ['breθəlaɪzər] alcootest *m*

breathe [briːð] **1** *v/i* respirer **2** *v/t* (*inhale*) respirer; (*exhale*) exhaler

♦ **breathe in 1** *v/i* inspirer **2** *v/t* respirer

♦ **breathe out** *v/i* expirer

breath·ing ['briːðɪŋ] *n* respiration *f*

breath·less ['breθlɪs] *adj* essoufflé

breath·less·ness ['breθlɪsnɪs] essoufflement *m*

breath·tak·ing ['breθteɪkɪŋ] *adj* à vous couper le souffle

bred [bred] *pret & pp* → **breed**

breed [briːd] **1** *n* race *f* **2** *v/t* (*pret & pp* **bred**) *racehorses, dogs* élever; *plants, also fig* cultiver **3** *v/i* (*pret & pp* **bred**) *of animals* se reproduire

breed·er ['briːdər] *of animals* éleveur (-euse) *m(f)*

breed·ing ['briːdɪŋ] *of animals* élevage *m*; *of person* éducation *f*

'breed·ing ground *fig* terrain *m* propice (*for* à)

breeze [briːz] brise *f*

breez·i·ly ['briːzɪlɪ] *adv fig* jovialement

breez·y ['bri:zɪ] *adj* venteux*; *fig* jovial
brew [bru:] **1** *v/t beer* brasser **2** *v/i* couver
brew·er ['bru:ər] brasseur(-euse) *m(f)*
brew·er·y ['bru:ərɪ] brasserie *f*
bribe [braɪb] **1** *n* pot-de-vin *m* **2** *v/t* soudoyer
brib·er·y ['braɪbərɪ] corruption *f*
brick [brɪk] brique *f*
'brick·lay·er maçon *m*
brid·al suite ['braɪdl] suite *f* nuptiale
bride [braɪd] *about to be married* (future) mariée *f*; *married* jeune mariée *f*
'bride·groom *about to be married* (futur) marié *m*; *married* jeune marié *m*
'brides·maid demoiselle *f* d'honneur
bridge[1] [brɪdʒ] **1** *n* pont *m*; *of nose* arête *f*; *of ship* passerelle *f* **2** *v/t gap* combler
bridge[2] [brɪdʒ] *card game* bridge *m*
bri·dle ['braɪdl] bride *f*
brief[1] [bri:f] *adj* bref, court
brief[2] [bri:f] **1** *n* (*mission*) instructions *fpl* **2** *v/t*: **~ s.o. on sth** (*give information*) informer qn de qch; (*instruct*) donner à qn des instructions sur qch
'brief·case serviette *f*
brief·ing ['bri:fɪŋ] *session* séance *f* d'information; *instructions* instructions *fpl*
brief·ly ['bri:flɪ] *adv* (*for short time, in a few words*) brièvement; (*to sum up*) en bref
briefs [bri:fs] *npl underwear* slip *m*
bright [braɪt] *adj color* vif*; *smile* radieux*; *future* brillant; (*sunny*) clair; (*intelligent*) intelligent
◆ **bright·en up** ['braɪtn] **1** *v/t room* donner de la couleur à; *emotionally* donner de l'animation à **2** *v/i of weather* s'éclaircir; *of face, person* s'animer
bright·ly ['braɪtlɪ] *adv smile* d'un air radieux; *colored* vivement; **shine ~** resplendir
bright·ness ['braɪtnɪs] *of weather* clarté *f*; *of smile* rayonnement *m*; (*intelligence*) intelligence *f*
bril·liance ['brɪljəns] *of person* esprit *m* lumineux; *of color* vivacité *f*
bril·liant ['brɪljənt] *adj sunshine etc* res-

plendissant; (*very good*) génial; (*very intelligent*) brillant
brim [brɪm] *of container, hat* bord *m*
brim·ful ['brɪmfəl] *adj* rempli à ras bord
bring [brɪŋ] *v/t* (*pret & pp* **brought**) *object* apporter; *person, peace* amener; *hope, happiness etc* donner; **~ shame on** déshonorer; **~ it here, will you?** tu veux bien l'apporter ici?; **can I ~ a friend?** puis-je amener un ami?
◆ **bring about** *v/t* amener, causer
◆ **bring around** *v/t from a faint* ranimer; (*persuade*) faire changer d'avis
◆ **bring back** *v/t* (*return*) ramener; (*reintroduce*) réintroduire; **it brought back memories of my childhood** ça m'a rappelé mon enfance
◆ **bring down** *v/t also fig: government* faire tomber; *bird, airplane* abattre; *inflation, prices etc* faire baisser
◆ **bring in** *v/t interest, income* rapporter; *legislation* introduire; *verdict* rendre; (*involve*) faire intervenir
◆ **bring on** *v/t illness* donner; **it brings on my asthma** ça me donne des crises d'asthme
◆ **bring out** *v/t* (*produce*) sortir
◆ **bring to** *v/t from a faint* ranimer
◆ **bring up** *v/t child* élever; *subject* soulever; (*vomit*) vomir
brink [brɪŋk] bord *m*; **be on the ~ of doing sth** être sur le point de faire qch
brisk [brɪsk] *adj* vif*; (*businesslike*) énergique; *trade* florissant
bris·tle ['brɪsl] *v/i*: **be bristling with** *spines, weapons* être hérissé de; *police etc* grouiller de
bris·tles ['brɪslz] *npl on chin* poils *mpl* raides; *of brush* poils *mpl*
Brit [brɪt] F Britannique *m/f*
Brit·ain ['brɪtn] Grande-Bretagne *f*
Brit·ish ['brɪtɪʃ] **1** *adj* britannique **2** *npl*: **the ~** les Britanniques
Brit·ish·er ['brɪtɪʃər] Britannique *m/f*
Brit·on ['brɪtn] Britannique *m/f*
Brit·ta·ny ['brɪtənɪ] Bretagne *f*
brit·tle ['brɪtl] *adj* fragile, cassant
broach [broʊtʃ] *v/t subject* soulever

B

broad [brɔːd] **1** *adj* street; shoulders, hips large; smile grand; (general) général; **in ~ daylight** en plein jour **2** *n* F gonzesse *f*

'**broad·cast 1** *n* émission *f* **2** *v/t* (pret & pp **-cast**) transmettre

'**broad·cast·er** on radio / TV présentateur(-trice) *m(f)* (radio / télé)

'**broad·cast·ing** ['brɔːdkæstɪŋ] radio *f*; télévision *f*

broad·en ['brɔːdn] **1** *v/i* s'élargir **2** *v/t* élargir

'**broad jump** *n* saut *m* en longueur

broad·ly ['brɔːdlɪ] *adv*: **~ speaking** en gros

broad-mind·ed [brɔːd'maɪndɪd] *adj* large d'esprit

broad-mind·ed·ness [brɔːd'maɪndɪd-nɪs] largeur *f* d'esprit

broc·co·li ['brɑːkəlɪ] brocoli(s) *m(pl)*

bro·chure ['brouʃər] brochure *f*

broil [brɔɪl] *v/t* griller

broil·er ['brɔɪlər] on stove grill *m*; chicken poulet *m* à rôtir

broke [brouk] **1** *adj* F fauché F; **go ~** (go bankrupt) faire faillite **2** *pret* → **break**

bro·ken ['broukn] **1** *adj* cassé; home brisé; English haché **2** *pp* → **break**

bro·ken-heart·ed [broukn'hɑːrtɪd] *adj* au cœur brisé

bro·ker ['broukər] courtier *m*

bron·chi·tis [brɑːŋ'kaɪtɪs] bronchite *f*

bronze [brɑːnz] *n* metal bronze *m*; medal médaille *f* de bronze

brooch [broutʃ] broche *f*

brood [bruːd] *v/i* of person ruminer

broom [bruːm] balai *m*

broth [brɑːθ] bouillon *m*

broth·el ['brɑːθl] bordel *m*

broth·er ['brʌðər] frère *m*

'**broth·er-in-law** (*pl* **brothers-in-law**) beau-frère *m*

broth·er·ly ['brʌðərlɪ] *adj* fraternel*

brought [brɔːt] *pret & pp* → **bring**

brow [brau] (forehead) front *m*; of hill sommet *m*

brown [braun] **1** *adj* marron *inv*; (tanned) bronzé **2** *n* marron *m* **3** *v/t* in cooking faire dorer **4** *v/i* in cooking dorer

'**brown·bag** *v/t* (pret & pp **-ged**); **~ it** F apporter son repas

Brown·ie ['braunɪ] jeannette *f*

brown·ie ['braunɪ] brownie *m*

'**Brownie points** *npl*: **earn ~** se faire bien voir

'**brown-nose** *v/t* P lécher le cul à P; **brown 'pa·per** papier *m* d'emballage, papier *m* kraft; **brown pa·per 'bag** sac *m* en papier kraft; **brown 'sug·ar** sucre *m* roux

browse [brauz] *v/i* in store flâner; COMPUT surfer; **~ through a book** feuilleter un livre

brows·er ['brauzər] COMPUT navigateur *m*

bruise [bruːz] **1** *n* bleu *m*; on fruit meurtrissure *f* **2** *v/t* fruit abîmer; leg se faire un bleu sur **3** *v/i* of fruit s'abîmer; of person se faire des bleus

bruis·ing ['bruːzɪŋ] *adj fig* douloureux

brunch [brʌntʃ] brunch *m*

bru·nette [bruː'net] brune *f*

brunt [brʌnt]: **bear the ~ of ...** subir le pire de ...

brush [brʌʃ] **1** *n* brosse *f*; (conflict) accrochage *m* **2** *v/t* jacket, floor brosser; (touch lightly) effleurer; **~ one's teeth / hair** se brosser les dents / les cheveux

♦ **brush against** *v/t* effleurer

♦ **brush aside** *v/t* person mépriser; remark, criticism écarter

♦ **brush off** *v/t* dust etc enlever; criticism ignorer

♦ **brush up** *v/t fig* réviser

'**brush-off**; **give s.o. the ~** F repousser qn; **get the ~** F se faire repousser

'**brush·work** in art touche *f* (de pinceau)

brusque [brusk] *adj* brusque

Brus·sels ['brʌslz] Bruxelles

Brus·sels 'sprouts *npl* choux *mpl* de Bruxelles

bru·tal ['bruːtl] *adj* brutal

bru·tal·i·ty [bruː'tælɪtɪ] brutalité *f*

bru·tal·ly ['bruːtəlɪ] *adv* brutalement; **be ~ frank** dire les choses carrément

brute [bruːt] brute *f*

'**brute force** force *f*

BSc [biːes 'siː] *abbr* (= **Bachelor of**

Science) licence scientifique

bub·ble ['bʌbl] bulle *f*

'**bub·ble bath** bain *m* moussant; '**bub·ble gum** bubble-gum *m*; '**bub·ble wrap** *n* film *m* de protection à bulles

bub·bly ['bʌblɪ] *n* F (*champagne*) champagne *m*

buck[1] [bʌk] *n* F (*dollar*) dollar *m*

buck[2] [bʌk] *v/i of horse* ruer

buck[3] [bʌk] *n*: **pass the ~** renvoyer la balle

buck·et ['bʌkɪt] *n* seau *m*

buck·le[1] ['bʌkl] **1** *n* boucle *f* **2** *v/t belt* boucler

buck·le[2] ['bʌkl] *v/i of wood, metal* déformer

◆ **buck·le down** *v/i* s'y mettre

bud [bʌd] *n* BOT bourgeon *m*

bud·dy ['bʌdɪ] F copain *m*, copine *f*; *form of address* mec F

budge [bʌdʒ] **1** *v/t* (*move*) déplacer; (*make reconsider*) faire changer d'avis **2** *v/i* (*move*) bouger; (*change one's mind*) changer d'avis

bud·ger·i·gar ['bʌdʒərɪgɑːr] perruche *f*

bud·get ['bʌdʒɪt] **1** *n* budget *m*; **be on a ~** faire des économies **2** *v/i* prévoir ses dépenses

◆ **budget for** *v/t* prévoir

bud·gie ['bʌdʒɪ] F perruche *f*

buff[1] [bʌf] *adj color* couleur chamois

buff[2] [bʌf] *n* passionné(e) *m(f)*; **a movie / jazz ~** un(e) passionné(e) *m(f)* de cinéma / de jazz

buf·fa·lo ['bʌfəloʊ] buffle *m*

buff·er ['bʌfər] RAIL, COMPUT, *fig* tampon *m*

buf·fet[1] ['bʊfeɪ] *n meal* buffet *m*

buf·fet[2] ['bʌfɪt] *v/t of wind* battre

bug [bʌg] **1** *n* (*insect*) insecte *m*; (*virus*) virus *m*; COMPUT bogue *f*; (*spying device*) micro *m* **2** *v/t* (*pret & pp -ged*) *room, telephone* mettre sur écoute; F (*annoy*) énerver

bug·gy ['bʌgɪ] *for baby* poussette *f*

build [bɪld] **1** *n of person* carrure *f* **2** *v/t* (*pret & pp* **built**) construire

◆ **build up 1** *v/t strength* développer; *relationship* construire; **build up a**

collection faire collection (**of** de) **2** *v/i* s'accumuler; *fig* s'intensifier

build·er ['bɪldər] constructeur(-trice) *m(f)*

build·ing ['bɪldɪŋ] *structure* bâtiment *m*; *activity* construction *f*

'**build·ing blocks** *npl for child* cube *m*; '**build·ing site** chantier *m*; '**build·ing trade** (industrie *f* du) bâtiment *m*

'**build-up** (*accumulation*) accumulation *f*, augmentation *f*; (*publicity*) publicité *f*; **give s.o. / sth a big ~** faire beaucoup de battage autour de qn / qch

built [bɪlt] *pret & pp* → **build**

'**built-in** *adj* encastré; *flash* incorporé

built-up 'ar·e·a agglomération *f* (urbaine)

bulb [bʌlb] BOT bulbe *m*; (*light ~*) ampoule *f*

bulge [bʌldʒ] **1** *n* gonflement *m*, saillie *f* **2** *v/i* être gonflé, faire saillie

bu·lim·i·a [buˈlɪmɪə] boulimie *f*

bulk [bʌlk]: **the ~ of** la plus grande partie de; **in ~** en bloc

'**bulk·y** ['bʌlkɪ] *adj* encombrant; *sweater* gros*

bull [bʊl] *animal* taureau *m*

bull·doze ['bʊldoʊz] *v/t* (*demolish*) passer au bulldozer; **~ s.o. into sth / doing sth** amener qn de force à qch / forcer qn à faire qch

bull·doz·er ['bʊldoʊzər] bulldozer *m*

bul·let ['bʊlɪt] balle *f*

bul·le·tin ['bʊlɪtɪn] bulletin *m*

'**bul·le·tin board** *on wall* tableau *m* d'affichage; COMPUT serveur *m* télématique

'**bul·let·proof** *adj* protégé contre les balles; *vest* pare-balles

'**bull horn** mégaphone *m*; '**bull market** FIN marché *m* orienté à la hausse; '**bull's-eye** mille *m*; **hit the ~** *also fig* mettre dans le mille; '**bull·shit 1** *n* V merde *f* V, conneries *fpl* P **2** *v/i* (*pret & pp -ted*) V raconter des conneries P

bul·ly ['bʊlɪ] **1** *n* brute *f* **2** *v/t* (*pret & pp -ied*) brimer

bul·ly·ing ['bʊlɪɪŋ] *n* brimades *fpl*

bum [bʌm] **1** n F (*worthless person*) bon à rien m; (*tramp*) clochard m **2** v/t (*pret & pp* **-med**): **can I ~ a cigarette?** est-ce que je peux vous taper une cigarette?

◆ **bum around** v/i F (*travel*) vagabonder; (*be lazy*) traînasser F

bum·ble·bee ['bʌmblbiː] bourdon m

bump [bʌmp] **1** n bosse f; **get a ~ on the head** recevoir un coup sur la tête **2** v/t se cogner

◆ **bump into** v/t se cogner contre; (*meet*) rencontrer (par hasard)

◆ **bump off** v/t F (*murder*) zigouiller F

◆ **bump up** v/t F prices gonfler

bump·er ['bʌmpər] **1** n MOT pare-chocs m inv; **the traffic was ~ to ~** les voitures étaient pare-chocs contre pare-chocs **2** adj (*extremely good*) exceptionnel*

'**bump-start** v/t: **~ a car** pousser une voiture pour la faire démarrer; **the economy** donner un coup de pouce à l'économie

bump·y ['bʌmpɪ] adj road cahoteux*; **we had a ~ flight** nous avons été secoués pendant le vol

bun [bʌn] hairstyle chignon m; for eating petit pain m au lait

bunch [bʌntʃ] of people groupe m; of keys trousseau m; of grapes grappe f; of flowers bouquet m; **thanks a ~** merci beaucoup; **a whole ~ of things to do** F tout un tas de choses à faire F

bun·dle ['bʌndl] n paquet m

◆ **bundle up** v/t mettre en paquet; (*dress warmly*) emmitoufler

bun·gee jump·ing ['bʌndʒɪdʒʌmpɪŋ] saut m à l'élastique

bun·gle ['bʌŋgl] v/t bousiller F

bunk [bʌŋk] couchette f

'**bunk beds** npl lits mpl superposés

buoy [bɔɪ] n NAUT bouée f

buoy·ant ['bɔɪənt] adj mood jovial; economy prospère

bur·den ['bɜːrdn] **1** n fardeau m **2** v/t: **~ s.o. with sth** fig accabler qn de qch

bu·reau ['bjʊroʊ] (*office, chest of drawers*) bureau m

bu·reauc·ra·cy [bjʊˈrɑːkrəsɪ] bureau-

cratie f

bu·reau·crat ['bjʊrəkræt] bureaucrate m/f

bu·reau·crat·ic [bjʊrəˈkrætɪk] adj bureaucratique

bur·ger ['bɜːrgər] steak m haché; in roll hamburger m

bur·glar ['bɜːrglər] cambrioleur (-euse) m(f)

'**bur·glar a·larm** alarme f antivol

bur·glar·ize ['bɜːrgləraɪz] v/t cambrioler

bur·glar·y ['bɜːrglərɪ] cambriolage m

bur·i·al ['berɪəl] enterrement m

bur·ly ['bɜːrlɪ] adj robuste

burn [bɜːrn] **1** n brûlure f **2** v/t (*pret & pp* **burnt**) brûler; **he ~t his hand** il s'est brûlé la main **3** v/i (*pret & pp* **burnt**) brûler

◆ **burn down 1** v/t incendier **2** v/i être réduit en cendres

◆ **burn out** v/t: **burn o.s. out** s'épuiser; **a burned-out car** incendié

burn·er ['bɜːrnər] on cooker brûleur m

'**burn·out** F (*exhaustion*) épuisement m

burnt [bɜːrnt] pret & pp → **burn**

burp [bɜːrp] **1** n rot m **2** v/i roter **3** v/t baby faire son rot à

burst [bɜːrst] **1** n in water pipe trou m; act éclatement m; of gunfire explosion f; **in a ~ of energy** dans un accès d'énergie **2** adj tire crevé **3** v/t (*pret & pp* **burst**) balloon crever **4** v/i (*pret & pp* **burst**) of balloon, tire crever; of pipe éclater; **~ into a room** se précipiter dans une pièce; **~ into tears** fondre en larmes; **~ out laughing** éclater de rire

bur·y ['berɪ] v/t (*pret & pp* **-ied**) person, animal enterrer; (*conceal*) cacher; **be buried under** (*covered by*) être caché sous; **~ o.s. in work** s'absorber dans son travail

bus [bʌs] **1** n local (auto)bus m; long distance (auto)car m **2** v/t (*pret & pp* **-sed**) amener en (auto)bus

'**bus·boy** aide-serveur(-euse) m(f)

'**bus driv·er** local conducteur(-trice) m(f) d'autobus; long-distance conducteur(-trice) m(f) d'autocar

bush [bʊʃ] *plant* buisson *m*; *land* brousse *f*

bushed [bʊʃt] *adj* F (*tired*) crevé F

bush·y [ˈbʊʃɪ] *adj beard* touffu

busi·ness [ˈbɪznɪs] (*trade*), *as subject of study* commerce *m*; (*company*) entreprise *f*; (*work*) travail *m*; (*sector*) secteur *m*; (*affair, matter*) affaire *f*; *how's ~? - ~ is good* comment vont les affaires? - les affaires vont bien; *on ~* en déplacement (professionnel); *that's none of your ~!* ça ne vous regarde pas!; *you have no ~ being in my office* vous n'avez rien à faire dans mon bureau!; *mind your own ~!* occupe-toi de tes affaires!

'**busi·ness card** carte *f* de visite;
'**busi·ness class** classe *f* affaires;
'**busi·ness hours** *npl* heures *fpl* d'ouverture; **busi·ness·like** *adj* sérieux*; '**busi·ness lunch** déjeuner *m* d'affaires; '**busi·ness·man** homme *m* d'affaires; '**busi·ness meet·ing** réunion *f* d'affaires; '**busi·ness school** école *f* de commerce; '**busi·ness stud·ies** *nsg course* études *fpl* de commerce; '**busi·ness trip** voyage *m* d'affaires; '**busi·ness·wom·an** femme *f* d'affaires

'**bus lane** couloir *m* d'autobus; '**bus shel·ter** abribus *m*; '**bus sta·tion** gare *f* routière; '**bus stop** arrêt *m* d'autobus

bust[1] [bʌst] *n of woman* poitrine *f*; *measurement* tour *m* de poitrine

bust[2] [bʌst] **1** *adj* F (*broken*) cassé; *go ~* faire faillite **2** *v/t* F casser

'**bus tick·et** ticket *m* d'autobus

♦ **bus·tle a·round** [ˈbʌsl] *v/i* s'affairer

'**bust-up** F brouille *f*

bust·y [ˈbʌstɪ] *adj* à la poitrine plantureuse

bus·y [ˈbɪzɪ] **1** *adj person*, TELEC occupé; *day, life* bien rempli; *street, shop, restaurant* plein de monde; *be ~ doing sth* être occupé à faire qch **2** *v/t* (*pret & pp -ied*): *~ o.s. with* s'occuper à

'**bus·y·bod·y** curieux(-se) *m(f)*; *he's a real ~* il se mêle toujours de ce qui ne le regarde pas

'**bus·y sig·nal** TELEC tonalité *f* occupé

but [bʌt], *unstressed* [bət] **1** *conj* mais; *~ that's not fair!* mais ce n'est pas juste!; *~ then* (*again*) mais après tout **2** *prep*: *all ~ him* tous sauf lui; *the last ~ one* l'avant-dernier; *the next ~ one* le deuxième; *~ for you* si tu n'avais pas été là; *nothing ~ the best* rien que le meilleur

butch·er [ˈbʊtʃər] *n* boucher(-ère) *m(f)*

butt [bʌt] **1** *n of cigarette* mégot *m*; *of joke* cible *f*; P (*backside*) cul *m* P **2** *v/t* donner un coup de tête à

♦ **butt in** *v/i* intervenir

but·ter [ˈbʌtər] **1** *n* beurre *m* **2** *v/t* beurrer

♦ **butter up** *v/t* F lécher les bottes à F

'**but·ter·fly** *also swimming* papillon *m*

but·tocks [ˈbʌtəks] *npl* fesses *fpl*

but·ton [ˈbʌtn] **1** *n* bouton *m*; (*badge*) badge *m* **2** *v/t* boutonner

♦ **button up** → **button 2**

'**but·ton-down col·lar** col *m* boutons

'**but·ton·hole 1** *n in suit* boutonnière *f* **2** *v/t* coincer

bux·om [ˈbʌksəm] *adj* bien en chair

buy [baɪ] **1** *n* achat *m* **2** *v/t* (*pret & pp bought*) acheter; *can I ~ you a drink?* est-ce que je peux vous offrir quelque chose à boire?; *$5 doesn't ~ much* on n'a pas grand chose pour 5 \$

♦ **buy off** *v/t* (*bribe*) acheter

♦ **buy out** *v/t* COMM racheter la part de

♦ **buy up** *v/t* acheter

buy·er [ˈbaɪr] acheteur(-euse) *m(f)*

buzz [bʌz] **1** *n* bourdonnement *m*; F (*thrill*) grand plaisir *m* **2** *v/i of insect* bourdonner; *with buzzer* appeler à l'interphone **3** *v/t with buzzer* appeler à l'interphone

♦ **buzz off** *v/i* F ficher le camp F

buzz·er [ˈbʌzər] sonnerie *f*

by [baɪ] **1** *prep* ◇ *agency* par; *a play ~ ...* une pièce de ...; *hit ~ a truck* renversé par un camion
◇ (*near, next to*) près de; *sea, lake* au bord de; *side ~ side* côte à côte

C

◇ (*no later than*) pour; **can you fix it ~ Tuesday?** est-ce que vous pouvez le réparer pour mardi?; **~ this time tomorrow** demain à cette heure ◇ (*past*) à côté de ◇ *mode of transport* en; **~ bus / train** en bus / train ◇ *measurement:* **2 ~ 4** 2 sur 4 ◇ *phrases:* **~ day / night** le jour / la nuit; **~ the hour / ton** à l'heure / la tonne; **~ my watch** selon ma montre; **~ o.s.** tout seul; **he won ~ a couple of minutes** il a gagné à quelques minutes près

2 *adv:* **~ and ~** (*soon*) sous peu
bye(-bye) [baɪ] au revoir
by·gones ['baɪgɑːnz]: **let ~ be ~** passons l'éponge; **'by·pass 1** *n road* déviation *f*; MED pontage *m* (coronarien) **2** *v/t* contourner; **'by-prod·uct** sous-produit *m*; **by·stand·er** ['baɪstændər] spectateur(-trice) *m(f)*
byte [baɪt] octet *m*
'by·word: **be a ~ for** être synonyme de

C

cab [kæb] (*taxi*) taxi *m*; *of truck* cabine *f*
'cab driv·er chauffeur *m* de taxi
cab·a·ret ['kæbəreɪ] spectacle *m* de cabaret
cab·bage ['kæbɪdʒ] chou *m*
cab·in ['kæbɪn] *of plane, ship* cabine *f*
'cab·in at·tend·ant *male* steward *m*; *female* hôtesse *f* (de l'air)
'cab·in crew équipage *m*
cab·i·net ['kæbɪnɪt] *furniture* meuble *m* (de rangement); POL cabinet *m*; **display ~** vitrine *f*; **medicine ~** armoire *f* à pharmacie
'cab·i·net mak·er ébéniste *m/f*
ca·ble ['keɪbl] câble *m*; **~ (TV)** câble *m*
'ca·ble car téléphérique *m*; *on rail* funiculaire *m*
'ca·ble tel·e·vi·sion (télévision *f* par) câble *m*
'cab stand, *Br* **'cab rank** station *f* de taxis
cac·tus ['kæktəs] cactus *m*
ca·dav·er [kə'dævər] cadavre *m*
cad·die ['kædɪ] **1** *n in golf* caddie *m* **2** *v/i:* **~ for s.o.** être le caddie de qn
ca·det [kə'det] élève *m* (officier)
cadge [kædʒ] *v/t:* **~ sth from s.o.** taxer qch à qn F
caf·é ['kæfeɪ] café *m*

caf·e·te·ri·a [kæfɪ'tɪrɪə] cafétéria *f*
caf·feine ['kæfiːn] caféine *f*
cage [keɪdʒ] cage *f*
ca·gey ['keɪdʒɪ] *adj* évasif*
ca·hoots [kə'huːts] *npl* F: **be in ~ with** être de mèche avec F
ca·jole [kə'dʒoʊl] *v/t* enjôler
cake [keɪk] **1** *n* gâteau *m*; **be a piece of ~** F être du gâteau F **2** *v/i of mud, blood* sécher, se solidifier
ca·lam·i·ty [kə'læmətɪ] calamité *f*
cal·ci·um ['kælsɪəm] calcium *m*
cal·cu·late ['kælkjuleɪt] *v/t* (*work out*) évaluer; *in arithmetic* calculer
cal·cu·lat·ing ['kælkjuleɪtɪŋ] *adj* calculateur*
cal·cu·la·tion [kælkju'leɪʃn] calcul *m*
cal·cu·la·tor ['kælkjuleɪtər] calculatrice *f*
cal·en·dar ['kælɪndər] calendrier *m*
calf[1] [kæf] (*pl* **calves** [kævz]) (*young cow*) veau *m*
calf[2] [kæf] (*pl* **calves** [kævz]) *of leg* mollet *m*
'calf-skin *n* veau *m*, vachette *f*
cal·i·ber ['kælɪbər] *of gun* calibre *m*; **a man of his ~** un homme de ce calibre
call [kɒːl] **1** *n* (*phone ~*) appel *m*, coup *m* de téléphone; (*shout*) appel, cri *m*;

(*demand*) appel *m*, demande *f*;
there's a ~ for you on te demande
au téléphone, il y a un appel pour
toi; ***be on ~*** être de garde **2** *v/t also
on phone* appeler; ***be ~ed …*** s'appeler …; ***~ s.o. a liar*** traiter qn de menteur; ***and you ~ yourself a Socialist!*** et tu te dis socialiste!; ***~ s.o.
names*** injurier qn; insulter qn **3** *v/i
also on phone* appeler; (*visit*) passer

♦ **call at** *v/t* (*stop at*) s'arrêter à; *of train
also* s'arrêter à, desservir

♦ **call back 1** *v/t on phone*, (*summon*)
rappeler **2** *v/i on phone* rappeler;
(*make another visit*) repasser

♦ **call for** *v/t* (*collect*) passer prendre,
venir chercher; (*demand, require*) demander

♦ **call in 1** *v/t* (*summon*) appeler, faire
venir **2** *v/i* (*phone*) appeler, téléphoner

♦ **call off** *v/t* (*cancel*) annuler

♦ **call on** *v/t* (*urge*) demander à; (*visit*)
rendre visite à, passer voir

♦ **call out** *v/t* (*shout*) crier; (*summon*)
appeler

♦ **call up** *v/t on phone* appeler, téléphoner à; COMPUT ouvrir

'call cen·ter centre *m* d'appel
call·er ['kɒːlər] *on phone* personne *f*
qui appelle; (*visitor*) visiteur *m*
'call girl call-girl *f*
cal·lous ['kæləs] *adj person* dur
cal·lous·ly ['kæləslɪ] *adv* durement
cal·lous·ness ['kæləsnəs] dureté *f*
calm [kɑːm] **1** *adj* calme, tranquille **2** *n*
calme *m*

♦ **calm down 1** *v/t* **2** *v/i of sea,
weather, person* se calmer

calm·ly ['kɑːmlɪ] *adv* calmement
cal·o·rie ['kælərɪ] calorie *f*
cam·cor·der ['kæmkɔːrdər] camé-
scope *m*
came [keɪm] *pret* → **come**
cam·e·ra ['kæmərə] appareil *m* photo;
TV caméra *f*
'cam·e·ra·man cadreur *m*, caméra-
man *m*
cam·i·sole ['kæmɪsool] caraco *m*
cam·ou·flage ['kæməflɑːʒ] **1** *n* camouflage *m* **2** *v/t* camoufler

camp [kæmp] **1** *n* camp *m* **2** *v/i* camper
cam·paign [kæm'peɪn] **1** *n* campagne
f **2** *v/i* faire campagne
cam·paign·er [kæm'peɪnər] militant
m
camp·er ['kæmpər] *person* campeur
m; *vehicle* camping-car *m*
camp·ing ['kæmpɪŋ] camping *m*; ***go ~***
faire du camping
'camp·site (terrain *m* de) camping *m*
cam·pus ['kæmpəs] campus *m*
can[1] [kæn], *unstressed* [kən] *v/aux*
◊ (*pret* **could**) *ability* pouvoir; ***~
you hear me?*** tu m'entends?; ***I can't
see*** je ne vois pas; ***~ you speak
French?*** parlez-vous français?; ***~
she swim?*** sait-elle nager?; ***~ he
call me back?*** peut-il me rappeler?;
as fast / well as you ~ aussi vite /
bien que possible; ***that can't be
right*** ça ne peut pas être vrai ◊ *permission* pouvoir; ***~ I help you?*** est-ce
que je peux t'aider?
can[2] [kæn] **1** *n for food* boîte *f*; *for
drinks* canette *f*; *of paint* bidon *m* **2**
v/t (*pret & pp* **-ned**) mettre en
conserve
Can·a·da ['kænədə] Canada *m*
Ca·na·di·an [kə'neɪdɪən] **1** *adj* canadien* **2** *n* Canadien *m*
ca·nal [kə'næl] canal *m*
ca·nar·y [kə'nerɪ] canari *m*
can·cel ['kænsl] *v/t* (*pret & pp* **-ed**, *Br*
-led) annuler
can·cel·la·tion [kænsə'leɪʃn] annulation *f*
can·cel·la·tion fee frais *mpl* d'annulation
can·cer ['kænsər] cancer *m*
Can·cer ['kænsər] ASTROL Cancer *m*
can·cer·ous ['kænsərəs] *adj* cancéreux*
c & f *abbr* (= *cost and freight*) C&F
(coût et fret)
can·did ['kændɪd] *adj* franc*
can·di·da·cy ['kændɪdəsɪ] candidature *f*
can·di·date ['kændɪdət] candidat *m*
can·did·ly ['kændɪdlɪ] *adv* franchement
can·died ['kændiːd] *adj* confit

can·dle ['kændl] bougie *f*; *in church* cierge *m*

'can·dle·stick bougeoir *m*; *long, thin* chandelier *m*

can·dor ['kændər] franchise *f*

can·dy ['kændɪ] (*sweet*) bonbon *m*; (*sweets*) bonbons *mpl*

cane [keɪn] (*tige f de*) bambou *m*

can·is·ter ['kænɪstər] boîte *f* (métallique); *for gas, spray* bombe *f*

can·na·bis ['kænəbɪs] cannabis *m*

canned [kænd] *adj fruit, tomatoes* en conserve, en boîte; F (*recorded*) enregistré

can·ni·bal·ize ['kænɪbəlaɪz] *v/t* cannibaliser

can·not ['kænɑːt] → **can¹**

can·ny ['kænɪ] *adj* (*astute*) rusé

ca·noe [kə'nuː] canoë *m*

'can o·pen·er ouvre-boîte *m*

can't [kænt] → **can**

can·teen [kæn'tiːn] *in factory* cantine *f*

can·vas ['kænvəs] toile *f*

can·vass ['kænvəs] **1** *v/t* (*seek opinion of*) sonder, interroger **2** *v/i* POL faire campagne

can·yon ['kænjən] canyon *m*

cap [kæp] *hat* bonnet *m*; *with peak* casquette *f*; *of soldier, policeman* képi *m*; *of bottle, jar* bouchon *m*; *of pen, lens* capuchon *m*

ca·pa·bil·i·ty [keɪpə'bɪlətɪ] capacité *f*

ca·pa·ble ['keɪpəbl] *adj* (*efficient*) capable, compétent; **be ~ of** être capable de

ca·pac·i·ty [kə'pæsətɪ] capacité *f*; *of factory* capacité *f* de production; aptitude *f*; **in my ~ as ...** en ma qualité de ...

cap·i·tal ['kæpɪtl] *n of country* capitale *f*; *letter* majuscule *f*; *money* capital *m*

cap·i·tal ex·'pend·i·ture dépenses *fpl* d'investissement; **cap·i·tal 'gains tax** impôt *m* sur la plus-value; **cap·i·tal 'growth** augmentation *f* de capital

cap·i·tal·ism ['kæpɪtəlɪzm] capitalisme *m*

cap·i·tal·ist ['kæpɪtəlɪst] **1** *adj* capitaliste **2** *n* capitaliste *m/f*

♦ **cap·i·tal·ize on** ['kæpɪtəlaɪz] *v/t* tirer

parti de, exploiter

cap·i·tal 'let·ter majuscule *f*

cap·i·tal 'pun·ish·ment peine *f* capitale

ca·pit·u·late [kə'pɪtʃʊleɪt] *v/i* capituler

ca·pit·u·la·tion [kæpɪtʃʊ'leɪʃn] capitulation *f*

Cap·ri·corn ['kæprɪkɔːrn] ASTROL Capricorne *m*

cap·size [kæp'saɪz] **1** *v/i* chavirer **2** *v/t* faire chavirer

cap·sule ['kæpsʊl] *of medicine* gélule *f*; (*space ~*) capsule *f* spatiale

cap·tain ['kæptɪn] *n of ship, team* capitaine *m*; *of aircraft* commandant *m* de bord

cap·tion ['kæpʃn] *n* légende *f*

cap·ti·vate ['kæptɪveɪt] *v/t* captiver, fasciner

cap·tive ['kæptɪv] *adj* captif*; **be held ~** être en captivité

cap·tive 'mar·ket marché *m* captif

cap·tiv·i·ty [kæp'tɪvətɪ] captivité *f*

cap·ture ['kæptʃər] **1** *n of city* prise *f*; *of person, animal* capture *f* **2** *v/t person, animal* capturer; *city, building* prendre; *market share* conquérir; (*portray*) reproduire; *moment* saisir

car [kɑːr] voiture *f*, automobile *f*; *of train* wagon *m*, voiture *f*; **by ~** en voiture

ca·rafe [kə'ræf] carafe *f*

car·at ['kærət] carat *m*

car·bo·hy·drate [kɑːrbou'haɪdreɪt] glucide *m*

'car bomb voiture *f* piégée

car·bon mon·ox·ide [kɑːrbənmən-'ɑːksaɪd] monoxyde *m* de carbone

car·bu·ret·er, car·bu·ret·or [kɑːrbʊ-'retər] carburateur *m*

car·cass ['kɑːrkəs] carcasse *f*

car·cin·o·gen [kɑːr'sɪnədʒen] substance *f* cancérigène

car·cin·o·gen·ic [kɑːrsɪnə'dʒenɪk] *adj* cancérigène, cancérogène

card [kɑːrd] carte *f*

'card·board carton *m*

card·board 'box carton *m*

car·di·ac ['kɑːrdɪæk] *adj* cardiaque

car·di·ac ar·'rest arrêt *m* cardiaque

car·di·gan ['kɑːrdɪgən] cardigan *m*, gilet m

car·di·nal ['kɑːrdɪnl] n REL cardinal m

'**card in·dex** fichier m; '**card key** carte f magnétique; '**card phone** téléphone m à carte

care [ker] **1** n of baby, pet garde f; of the elderly, sick soins mpl; MED soins mpl médicaux; (worry) souci m; ~ **of** chez; **take ~** (be cautious) faire attention; **goodbye, take ~** (of yourself!) au revoir, fais bien attention à toi!; **take ~ of** s'occuper de; (handle) **with ~!** on label fragile **2** v/i se soucier; **I don't ~!** ça m'est égal!; **I couldn't ~ less**, Br **I couldn't ~ less** ça m'est complètement égal, je m'en fous complètement F

♦ **care about** v/t s'intéresser à; **they don't care about the environment** ils ne se soucient pas de l'environnement

♦ **care for** v/t (look after) s'occuper de, prendre soin de; (like, be fond of) aimer; **would you care for ...?** aimeriez-vous ...?

ca·reer [kə'rɪr] (profession) carrière f

ca·reers of·fi·cer conseiller m d'orientation

'**care·free** adj insouciant, sans souci

care·ful ['kerfəl] adj (cautious) prudent; (thorough) méticuleux*; (be) **~!** (fais) attention!

care·ful·ly ['kerfəlɪ] adv (with caution) prudemment; worded etc soigneusement, avec soin

care·less ['kerlɪs] adj négligent; work négligé; **you are so ~!** tu es tellement tête en l'air!

care·less·ly ['kerlɪslɪ] adv négligemment

car·er ['kerər] accompagnateur(-trice) m(f)

ca·ress [kə'res] **1** n caresse f **2** v/t caresser

care·tak·er ['kerteɪkər] gardien m

'**care·worn** adj rongé par les soucis

'**car fer·ry** (car-)ferry m, transbordeur m

car·go ['kɑːrgoʊ] cargaison f, chargement m

car·i·ca·ture ['kærɪkətʃər] n caricature f

car·ing ['kerɪŋ] adj attentionné; **a more ~ society** une société plus humaine

'**car me·chan·ic** mécanicien m (dans un garage)

car·nage ['kɑːrnɪdʒ] n carnage m

car·na·tion [kɑːr'neɪʃn] œillet m

car·ni·val ['kɑːrnɪvl] fête f foraine; with processions etc carnaval m

car·ol ['kærəl] n chant m (de Noël)

car·ou·sel [kærə'sel] at airport tapis m roulant (à bagages); for slide projector carrousel m; (merry-go-round) manège m

'**car park** Br parking m

car·pen·ter ['kɑːrpɪntər] charpentier m; for smaller objects menuisier m

car·pet ['kɑːrpɪt] tapis m; fitted moquette f

'**car phone** téléphone m de voiture; '**car·pool 1** n voyage m groupé, covoiturage m **2** v/i voyager en groupes, faire du co-voiturage; '**car port** auvent m pour voiture(s); '**car ra·di·o** autoradio m; '**car rent·al** location f de voitures; '**car rent·al com·pa·ny** société f de location de voitures

car·riage ['kærɪdʒ] Br. of train wagon m

car·ri·er ['kærɪər] company entreprise f de transport; of disease porteur (-euse) m(f)

car·rot ['kærət] carotte f

car·ry ['kærɪ] **1** v/t (pret & pp -ied) porter; (from a place to another), of ship, plane, bus etc transporter; (have on one's person) avoir sur soi; disease être porteur de; proposal adopter; **get carried away** se laisser entraîner **2** v/i of sound porter

♦ **carry on 1** v/i (continue) continuer (**with sth** qch); F (make a fuss) faire une scène; F (have an affair) avoir une liaison avec **2** v/t business exercer; conversation tenir

♦ **carry out** v/t survey etc faire; orders etc exécuter

cart [kɑːrt] charrette f

car·tel [kɑːr'tel] cartel m

car·ton ['kɑːrtn] carton m; of cigarettes cartouche f

car·toon [kɑːrˈtuːn] dessin *m* humoristique; *on TV, movie* dessin *m* animé; *(strip ~)* BD *f*, bande *f* dessinée

car·toon·ist [kɑːrˈtuːnɪst] dessinateur(-trice) *m(f)* humoristique

car·tridge [ˈkɑːrtrɪdʒ] *for gun, printer etc* cartouche *f*

carve [kɑːrv] *v/t meat* découper; *wood* sculpter

carv·ing [ˈkɑːrvɪŋ] *figure* sculpture *f*

'car wash lave-auto *m*

case¹ [keɪs] *n for eyeglasses, camera* étui *m*; *for gadget* pochette *f*; *in museum* vitrine *f*; *of Scotch, wine* caisse *f*; *Br (suitcase)* valise *f*

case² [keɪs] *n (instance)* cas *m*; *(argument)* arguments *mpl* (**for sth / s.o.** en faveur de qch / qn); *for police, mystery* affaire *f*; MED cas *m*; LAW procès *m*; **in ~ it rains / you have forgotten** au cas où il pleuvrait / tu aurais oublié; **just in ~** au cas où; **in any ~** en tout cas; **in that ~** dans ce cas-là

'case his·to·ry MED antécédents *mpl*

'case·load dossiers *mpl*

cash [kæʃ] **1** *n (money)* argent *m*; *(coins and notes)* espèces *fpl*, *(argent m)* liquide *m*; **~ down** argent *m* comptant; **pay (in) ~** payer en espèces *or* en liquide; **~ in advance** paiement *m* par avance **2** *v/t check* toucher

♦ **cash in** *v/i* tirer profit de

'cash cow vache *f* à lait; **'cash desk** caisse *f*; **cash 'dis·count** escompte *m* au comptant; **'cash di·spens·er** distributeur *m* automatique (de billets); **'cash flow** COMM trésorerie *f*; **I've got ~ problems** j'ai des problèmes d'argent

cash·ier [kæˈʃɪr] *n in store etc* caissier (-ère) *m(f)*

'cash ma·chine distributeur *m* automatique (de billets)

cash·mere [ˈkæʃmɪr] *adj* en cashmere

'cash reg·is·ter caisse *f* enregistreuse

ca·si·no [kəˈsiːnoʊ] casino *m*

cas·ket [ˈkæskɪt] *(coffin)* cercueil *m*

cas·se·role [ˈkæsəroʊl] *meal* ragoût *m*;

container cocotte *f*

cas·sette [kəˈset] cassette *f*

cas·sette play·er lecteur *m* de cassettes

cas·sette re·cord·er magnétophone *m* à cassettes

cast [kæst] **1** *n of play* distribution *f*; *(mold)* moule *m*; *object cast* moulage *m* **2** *v/t (pret & pp cast)* doubt, suspicion jeter; *metal* couler; *play* distribuer les rôles de; **~ s.o. as** donner à qn le rôle de

♦ **cast off** *v/i of ship* larguer les amarres

caste [kæst] caste *f*

cast·er [ˈkæstər] *on chair etc* roulette *f*

cast iron *n* fonte *f*

cast-'iron *adj* en fonte

cas·tle [ˈkæsl] château *m*

'cast·or [ˈkæstər] → **caster**

cas·trate [kæˈstreɪt] *v/t* castrer

cas·tra·tion [kæˈstreɪʃn] castration *f*

cas·u·al [ˈkæʒʊəl] *adj (chance)* fait au hasard; *(offhand)* désinvolte; *(not formal)* décontracté; *(not permanent)* temporaire; **~ sex** relations *fpl* sexuelles sans engagement

cas·u·al·ly [ˈkæʒʊəlɪ] *adv dressed* de manière décontractée; *say* de manière désinvolte

cas·u·al wear vêtements *mpl* sport

cat [kæt] chat(te) *m(f)*

cat·a·log [ˈkætəlɔːg] *n* catalogue *m*

cat·a·lyst [ˈkætəlɪst] *fig* catalyseur *m*

cat·a·lyt·ic con·vert·er [kætəlɪtɪkənˈvɜːrtər] pot *m* catalytique

cat·a·pult [ˈkætəpʌlt] **1** *v/t fig: to fame, stardom* catapulter **2** *n Br* catapulte *f*

cat·a·ract [ˈkætərækt] MED cataracte *f*

ca·tas·tro·phe [kəˈtæstrəfɪ] catastrophe *f*

cat·a·stroph·ic [kætəˈstrɑːfɪk] *adj* catastrophique

catch [kætʃ] **1** *n* prise *f* (au vol); *of fish* pêche *f*; *(lock: on door)* loquet *m*; *on window* loqueteau *m*; *(problem)* entourloupette *f* F; **good ~!** bien joué! **2** *v/t (pret & pp caught)* ball, escaped prisoner attraper; *(get on: bus, train)* prendre; (*not miss: bus, train*) attraper; *fish* attraper; *in order to speak to* trouver; (*hear*) entendre; *illness attraper*; ~ *(a) cold* attraper un rhume; ~ *s.o.'s eye of person, object* attirer l'attention de qn; ~ *sight of*, ~ *a glimpse of* apercevoir; ~ *s.o. doing sth* surprendre qn en train de faire qch

◆ **catch on** *v/i* (*become popular*) avoir du succès; (*understand*) piger

◆ **catch up 1** *v/i of runner, in work etc* rattraper son retard **2** *v/t:* **I'll catch you up** je vous rejoins plus tard

◆ **catch up on** *v/t* rattraper

◆ **catch up with** *v/t* rattraper

catch-22 [kætʃtwentiˈtuː]: *it's a ~ situation* c'est un cercle vicieux

catch·er [ˈkætʃər] *in baseball* attrapeur *m*

catch·ing [ˈkætʃɪŋ] *adj also fig* contagieux*

catch·y [ˈkætʃɪ] *adj tune* facile à retenir

cat·e·gor·ic [kætəˈgɑːrɪk] *adj* catégorique

cat·e·gor·i·cal·ly [kætəˈgɑːrɪklɪ] *adv* catégoriquement

cat·e·go·ry [ˈkætəgɔːrɪ] catégorie *f*

◆ **ca·ter for** [ˈkeɪtər] *v/t* (*meet the needs of*) s'adresser à; (*provide food for*) fournir les repas pour

ca·ter·er [ˈkeɪtərər] traiteur *m*

ca·ter·pil·lar [ˈkætərpɪlər] chenille *f*

ca·the·dral [kəˈθiːdrl] cathédrale *f*

Cath·o·lic [ˈkæθəlɪk] **1** *adj* catholique **2** *n* catholique *m/f*

Ca·thol·i·cism [kəˈθɑːlɪsɪzm] catholicisme *m*

'cat·nap *n* (petit) somme *m*

'cat's eyes *npl on road* catadioptres *mpl*

cat·sup [ˈkætsʌp] ketchup *m*

cat·tle [ˈkætl] *npl* bétail *m*

cat·ty [ˈkætɪ] *adj* méchant

'cat·walk passerelle *f*

caught [kɔːt] *pret & pp* → **catch**

cau·li·flow·er [ˈkɒːlɪflaʊər] chou-fleur *m*

cause [kɒːz] **1** *n* cause *f*; (*grounds*) raison *f* **2** *v/t* causer; ~ *s.o. to do sth* pousser qn à faire qch

caus·tic [ˈkɒːstɪk] *adj fig* caustique

cau·tion [ˈkɒːʃn] **1** *n* (*carefulness*) prudence *f* **2** *v/t* (*warn*) avertir; ~ *s.o. against sth* mettre qn en garde contre qch

cau·tious [ˈkɒːʃəs] *adj* prudent

cau·tious·ly [ˈkɒːʃəslɪ] *adv* prudemment

cave [keɪv] caverne *f*, grotte *f*

◆ **cave in** *v/i of roof* s'effondrer

cav·i·ar [ˈkævɪɑːr] caviar *m*

cav·i·ty [ˈkævətɪ] cavité *f*

cc 1 *n* copie *f*, (*cubic centimeters*) cm^3 (centimètre *m* cube) **2** *v/t* envoyer une copie à

CD [siːˈdiː] *abbr* (= *compact disc*) CD *m* (= compact-disc *m*, disque *m* compact)

C'D play·er lecteur *m* de CD; **CD-'ROM** [siːdiːˈrɑːm] CD-ROM *m*; **CD-'ROM drive** lecteur *m* de CD-ROM

cease [siːs] **1** *v/i* cesser **2** *v/t* cesser; ~ *doing sth* cesser de faire qch

'cease-fire cessez-le-feu *m*

ceil·ing [ˈsiːlɪŋ] *also fig* plafond *m*

cel·e·brate [ˈselɪbreɪt] **1** *v/i* faire la fête **2** *v/t* fêter; *Christmas, public event* célébrer

cel·e·brat·ed [ˈselɪbreɪtɪd] *adj* célèbre

cel·e·bra·tion [selɪˈbreɪʃn] fête *f*; *of public event, wedding* célébration *f*

ce·leb·ri·ty [sɪˈlebrɪtɪ] célébrité *f*

cel·e·ry [ˈselərɪ] céleri *m*

cel·i·ba·cy [ˈselɪbəsɪ] célibat *m*

cel·i·bate [ˈselɪbət] *adj* chaste

cell [sel] *for prisoner, of spreadsheet*, BIOL cellule *f*; *phone* portable *m*

cel·lar [ˈselər] cave *f*

cel·list [ˈtʃelɪst] violoncelliste *m/f*

cel·lo [ˈtʃeloʊ] violoncelle *m*

cel·lo·phane [ˈseləfən] cellophane *f*

'cell phone, cel·lu·lar phone [ˈseljuːlər] (*téléphone m*) portable *m*

cel·lu·lite [ˈseljuːlaɪt] cellulite *f*

ce·ment [sɪˈment] **1** *n* ciment *m* **2** *v/t also fig* cimenter

cem·e·ter·y [ˈsemətərɪ] cimetière *m*

cen·sor [ˈsensər] *v/t* censurer

cen·sor·ship [ˈsensərʃɪp] censure *f*

cen·sus [ˈsensəs] recensement *m*

cent [sent] cent *m*

cen·te·na·ry [sen'ti:nəri] centenaire *m*

cen·ter ['sentər] **1** *n* centre *m*; **in the ~ of** au centre de **2** *v/t* centrer
  ♦ **center on** *v/t* tourner autour de

cen·ter of 'grav·i·ty centre *m* de gravité

cen·ti·grade ['sentigreid] centigrade *m*; **10 degrees ~** 10 degrés centigrades

cen·ti·me·ter ['sentimi:tər] centimètre *m*

cen·tral ['sentrəl] *adj* central; **~ Washington / France** le centre de Washington / de la France; **be ~ to sth** être au cœur de qch

cen·tral 'heat·ing chauffage *m* central

cen·tral·ize ['sentrəlaiz] *v/t* decision making centraliser

cen·tral 'lock·ing MOT verrouillage *m* centralisé

centre *Br* → **center**

cen·tu·ry ['sentʃəri] siècle *m*; **in the last ~** au siècle dernier

CEO [si:i:'ou] *abbr* (= **Chief Executive Officer**) directeur *m* général

ce·ram·ic [sɪ'ræmɪk] *adj* en céramique

ce·ram·ics [sɪ'ræmɪks] (*pl: objects*) objets *mpl* en céramique; (*sg: art*) céramique *f*

ce·re·al ['sɪrɪəl] (*grain*) céréale *f*; (*breakfast ~*) céréales *fpl*

cer·e·mo·ni·al [serɪ'mounɪəl] **1** *adj* de cérémonie **2** *n* cérémonial *m*

cer·e·mo·ny ['serɪmənɪ] cérémonie *f*

cer·tain ['sɜːrtn] *adj* (*sure*) certain, sûr; (*particular*) certain; **it's ~ that ...** il est sûr *or* certain que ...; **a ~ Mr Stein** un certain M. Stein; **make ~ that** s'assurer que; **know for ~ that ...** avoir la certitude que ...; **say for ~** dire de façon sûre *or* certaine

cer·tain·ly ['sɜːrtnlɪ] *adv* certainement; **~ not!** certainement pas!

cer·tain·ty ['sɜːrtntɪ] certitude *f*; **he's a ~ to be elected** il est sûr d'être élu

cer·tif·i·cate [sər'tɪfɪkət] certificat *m*

cer·ti·fied 'pub·lic ac·coun·tant ['sɜːrtɪfaɪd] expert *m* comptable

cer·ti·fy ['sɜːrtɪfaɪ] *v/t* (*pret & pp -ied*)

certifier

Ce·sar·e·an [sɪ'zerɪən] césarienne *f*

ces·sa·tion [se'seɪʃn] cessation *f*

c/f *abbr* (= **cost and freight**) C&F (coût et fret)

CFC [si:ef'si:] *abbr* (= **chlorofluorocarbon**) C.F.C. *m* (= chlorofluorocarbone *m*)

chain [tʃeɪn] **1** *n also of stores etc* chaîne *f* **2** *v/t*: **~ sth / s.o. to sth** enchaîner qch / qn à qch

chain re'ac·tion réaction *f* en chaîne; **'chain smoke** *v/i* fumer cigarette sur cigarette; **'chain smok·er** gros fumeur *m*, grosse fumeuse *f*; **'chain store** magasin *m* à succursales multiples

chair [tʃer] **1** *n* chaise *f*; (*arm~*) fauteuil *m*; *at university* chaire *f*; **the ~** (*electric ~*) la chaise électrique; *at meeting* la (le) président(e) *m(f)*; **go to the ~** passer à la chaise électrique; **take the ~** prendre la présidence **2** *v/t meeting* présider

'chair lift télésiège *m*

'chair·man président *m*

chair·man·ship ['tʃermənʃɪp] présidence *f*

'chair·per·son président(e) *m(f)*

'chair·wom·an présidente *f*

cha·let [ʃæ'leɪ] chalet *m*

chal·ice ['tʃælɪs] REL calice *m*

chalk [tʃɔːk] craie *f*

chal·lenge ['tʃælɪndʒ] **1** *n* défi *m*, challenge *m*; **I enjoy a ~** j'aime les défis; **his ~ for the presidency** sa candidature à la présidence **2** *v/t* (*defy*) défier; (*call into question*) mettre en doute; **~ s.o. to a debate / game** proposer à qn de faire un débat / une partie

chal·len·ger ['tʃælɪndʒər] challenger *m*

chal·len·ging ['tʃælɪndʒɪŋ] *adj job, undertaking* stimulant

cham·ber·maid ['tʃeɪmbərmeɪd] femme *f* de chambre; **'cham·ber mu·sic** musique *f* de chambre; **Cham·ber of 'Com·merce** Chambre *f* de commerce

cham·ois (leath·er) ['ʃæmɪ] (peau *f* de) chamois *m*

cham·pagne [ʃæm'peɪn] champagne *m*

cham·pi·on ['tʃæmpɪən] **1** *n* SP, *of cause* champion(ne) *m(f)* **2** *v/t cause* être le (la) champion(ne) *m(f)* de

cham·pi·on·ship ['tʃæmpɪənʃɪp] *event* championnat *m*; *title* titre *m* de champion(ne)

chance [tʃæns] *(possibility)* chances *fpl*; *(opportunity)* occasion *f*; *(risk)* risque *m*; *(luck)* hasard *m*; **by ~** par hasard; **take a ~** prendre un risque; **give s.o. a ~** donner une chance à qn; **no ~!** pas question!

Chan·cel·lor ['tʃænsələr] *in Germany* chancelier *m*; **~ (of the Exchequer)** *in Britain* Chancelier *m* de l'Échiquier

chan·de·lier [ʃændə'lɪr] lustre *m*

change [tʃeɪndʒ] **1** *n* changement *m*; *(money)* monnaie *f*; **for a ~** pour changer un peu; **a ~ of clothes** des vêtements *mpl* de rechange **2** *v/t* changer; *bankbill* faire la monnaie sur; **~ trains / planes / one's clothes** changer de train / d'avion / de vêtements **3** *v/i* changer; *(put on different clothes)* se changer

change·a·ble ['tʃeɪndʒəbl] *adj* changeant

'change·o·ver changement *m*; *in relay race* relève *f*; **the ~ to** le passage à

chang·ing room ['tʃeɪndʒɪŋ] SP vestiaire *m*; *in shop* cabine *f* d'essayage

chan·nel ['tʃænl] *on TV, radio* chaîne *f*; *(waterway)* chenal *m*

'Chan·nel Is·lands Îles *fpl* Anglo--Normandes

chant [tʃænt] **1** *n slogans mpl* scandés; REL chant *m* **2** *v/i if crowds etc* scander des slogans; REL psalmodier

cha·os ['keɪɑːs] chaos *m*

cha·ot·ic [keɪ'ɑːtɪk] *adj* chaotique

chap [tʃæp] *n Br* F type *m* F

chap·el ['tʃæpl] chapelle *f*

chapped [tʃæpt] *adj* gercé

chap·ter ['tʃæptər] *of book* chapitre *m*; *of organization* filiale *f*

char·ac·ter ['kærɪktər] *also in writing* caractère *m*; *(person)* personne *f*; *in book, play* personnage *m*; **he's a real**

~ c'est un personnage

char·ac·ter·is·tic [kærɪktə'rɪstɪk] **1** *n* caractéristique *f* **2** *adj* caractéristique

char·ac·ter·is·ti·cal·ly [kærɪktə'rɪstɪk-lɪ] *adv* de manière caractéristique

char·ac·ter·ize ['kærɪktəraɪz] *v/t* caractériser

cha·rade [ʃə'rɑːd] *fig* mascarade *f*

char·broiled ['tʃɑːrbrɔɪld] *adj* grillé au charbon de bois

char·coal ['tʃɑːrkoʊl] *for barbecue* charbon *m* de bois; *for drawing* fusain *m*

charge [tʃɑːrdʒ] **1** *n (fee)* frais *mpl*; LAW accusation *f*; **will there be a ~?** est-ce qu'il y aura quelque chose à payer?; **free of ~** *enter* gratuitement; **free of ~** *be* gratuit; **will that be cash or ~?** est-ce que vous payez comptant ou le mets sur votre compte?; **be in ~** être responsable; **take ~ (of things)** prendre les choses en charge **2** *v/t sum of money* faire payer; LAW inculper *(with* de); *battery* charger; **can you ~ it?** *(put on account)* pouvez-vous le mettre sur mon compte? **3** *v/i (attack)* charger

'charge ac·count compte *m*

'charge card carte *f* de paiement

cha·ris·ma [kə'rɪzmə] charisme *m*

char·is·mat·ic [kærɪz'mætɪk] *adj* charismatique

char·i·ta·ble ['tʃærɪtəbl] *adj* charitable

char·i·ty ['tʃærətɪ] *(assistance)* charité *f*; *(organization)* organisation *f* caritative

char·la·tan ['ʃɑːrlətən] charlatan *m*

charm [tʃɑːrm] **1** *n also on bracelet* charme *m* **2** *v/t (delight)* charmer

charm·ing ['tʃɑːrmɪŋ] *adj* charmant

charred [tʃɑːrd] *adj* carbonisé

chart [tʃɑːrt] *(diagram)* diagramme *m*; *(map)* carte *f*; **the ~s** MUS le hit-parade

char·ter ['tʃɑːrtər] *v/t* affréter

'char·ter flight (vol *m*) charter *m*

chase [tʃeɪs] **1** *n* poursuite *f*; **car ~** course-poursuite *f* (en voiture) **2** *v/t* poursuivre; **I ~d it out of the house** je l'ai chassé de la maison

♦ **chase away** *v/t* chasser

chas·er ['tʃeɪsər]: *with a whiskey ~* suivi par un verre de whisky

chas·sis ['ʃæsɪ] *of car* châssis *m*

chat [tʃæt] **1** *n* causette *f* **2** *v/i (pret & pp -ted)* causer

'chat room chat *m*; **'chat show** *Br* talk-show *m*

chat·ter ['tʃætər] **1** *n* bavardage *m* **2** *v/i (talk)* bavarder; *my teeth were ~ing* je claquais des dents

chat·ter·box moulin *m* à paroles F

chat·ty ['tʃætɪ] *adj person* bavard; *letter* plein de bavardages

chauf·feur ['ʃoufər] *n* chauffeur *m*

'chauf·feur-driv·en *adj* avec chauffeur

chau·vin·ist ['ʃouvɪnɪst] *n (male ~)* machiste *m*

chau·vin·ist·ic [ʃouvɪ'nɪstɪk] *adj* chauvin; *(sexist)* machiste

cheap [tʃiːp] *adj* bon marché, pas cher; *(nasty)* méchant; *(mean)* pingre

cheat [tʃiːt] **1** *n person* tricheur(-euse) *m(f)* **2** *v/t* tromper; *~ s.o. out of sth* escroquer qch à qn **3** *v/i* tricher; *~ on one's wife* tromper sa femme

check[1] [tʃek] **1** *adj shirt* à carreaux **2** *n* carreaux *m*

check[2] [tʃek] FIN chèque *m*; *in restaurant etc addition f*; *the ~ please* l'addition, s'il vous plaît

check[3] [tʃek] **1** *n to verify sth* contrôle *m*, vérification *f*; *keep a ~ on* contrôler; *keep in ~, hold in ~* maîtriser; contenir **2** *v/t* vérifier; *(restrain)* réfréner, contenir; *(stop)* arrêter; *with a ~mark* cocher; *coat, package etc* mettre au vestiaire **3** *v/i* vérifier; *~ for sth* vérifier qu'il n'y a pas qch

♦ **check in** *v/i at airport* se faire enregistrer; *at hotel* s'inscrire

♦ **check off** *v/t* cocher

♦ **check on** *v/t get information about* se renseigner sur; *workforce etc* surveiller; *check on the children* jeter un coup d'œil sur les enfants

♦ **check out 1** *v/i of hotel* régler sa note; *of alibi etc: make sense* tenir debout **2** *v/t (look into)* enquêter sur; *club, restaurant etc* essayer

♦ **check up on** *v/t* se renseigner sur

♦ **check with** *v/t of person* demander à; *(tally: of information)* correspondre à

'check·book carnet *m* de chèques

checked [tʃekt] *adj material* à carreaux

check·er·board ['tʃekərbɔːrd] damier *m*

check·ered ['tʃekərd] *adj pattern* à carreaux; *career* varié

check·ers ['tʃekərz] jeu *m* de dames; *play ~* jouer aux dames

'check-in (coun·ter) enregistrement *m*

check·ing ac·count ['tʃekɪŋ] compte *m* courant

'check-in time heure *f* d'enregistrement; **'check·list** liste *f* (de contrôle); **'check mark: put a ~ against sth** cocher qch; **'check·mate** *n* échec et mat *m*; **'check·out** *in supermarket* caisse *f*; **'check·out time** *from hotel* heure *f* de départ; **'check·point** contrôle *m*; **'check·room** *for coats* vestiaire *m*; *for baggage* consigne *f*; **'check·up** *medical* examen *m* médical; *dental* examen *m* dentaire

cheek [tʃiːk] *on face* joue *f*

'cheek·bone pommette *f*

cheek·i·ly ['tʃiːkɪlɪ] *adv Br* de manière insolente

cheer [tʃɪr] **1** *n* hourra *m*, cri *m* d'acclamation; *give a ~* pousser des hourras; *~s! (toast)* (à votre) santé!; *Br F (thanks)* merci! **2** *v/t* acclamer **3** *v/i* pousser des hourras

♦ **cheer on** *v/t* encourager

♦ **cheer up 1** *v/i* reprendre courage, s'égayer; *cheer up!* courage! **2** *v/t* remonter le moral à

cheer·ful ['tʃɪrfəl] *adj* gai, joyeux*

cheer·ing ['tʃɪrɪŋ] acclamations *fpl*

cheer·i·o [tʃɪrɪ'ou] *Br F* salut F

'cheer·lead·er meneuse *f* de ban

cheer·y ['tʃɪrɪ] *adj* → **cheerful**

cheese [tʃiːz] fromage *m*

'cheese·burg·er cheeseburger *m*

'cheese·cake gâteau *m* au fromage blanc

chef [ʃef] chef *m* (de cuisine)

chem·i·cal ['kemɪkl] **1** *adj* chimique **2**

n produit *m* chimique

chem·i·cal 'war·fare guerre *f* chimique

chemist ['kemɪst] *in laboratory* chimiste *m/f*

chem·is·try ['kemɪstrɪ] chimie *f*; ***the ~ was right fig* le courant passait**

chem·o·ther·a·py [ki:mouˈθerəpɪ] chimiothérapie *f*

cheque [tʃek] *Br* → **check²**

cher·ish ['tʃerɪʃ] *v/t memory* chérir; *hope* entretenir

cher·ry ['tʃerɪ] *fruit* cerise *f*; *tree* cerisier *m*

cher·ub ['tʃerəb] chérubin *m*

chess [tʃes] (jeu *m* d')échecs *mpl*; ***play ~** jouer aux échecs**

'chess·board échiquier *m*

'chess·man, 'chess·piece pièce *f* (d'échecs)

chest [tʃest] *of person* poitrine *f*; *(box)* coffre *m*, caisse *f*; ***get sth off one's ~** déballer ce qu'on a sur le cœur F**

chest·nut ['tʃesnʌt] châtaigne *f*, marron *m*; *tree* châtaignier *m*, marronnier *m*

chest of 'draw·ers commode *f*

chew [tʃu:] *v/t* mâcher; *of rats* ronger
♦ **chew on** *v/t* F enqueuler F

'chew·ing gum ['tʃu:ɪŋ] chewing-gum *m*

chic [ʃi:k] *adj* chic *inv*

chick [tʃɪk] poussin *m*; F: *girl* nana F

chick·en ['tʃɪkɪn] **1** *n* poulet *m*; F froussard(e) *m(f)* **2** *adj* F *(cowardly)* lâche
♦ **chicken out** *v/i* F se dégonfler F

'chick·en·feed F bagatelle *f*

'chick·en pox varicelle *f*

chief [tʃi:f] **1** *n* chef *m* **2** *adj* principal

chief·ly ['tʃi:flɪ] *adv* principalement

chil·blain ['tʃɪlbleɪn] engelure *f*

child [tʃaɪld] *(pl: **children** ['tʃɪldrən])* enfant *m/f*; *pej* gamin(e) *m(f)* F

'child a·buse mauvais traitements *mpl* infligés à un enfant; *sexual* abus *m* sexuel sur enfant; **'child·birth** accouchement *m*; **'child-friend·ly** *adj* aménagé pour les enfants

child·hood ['tʃaɪldhʊd] enfance *f*

child·ish ['tʃaɪldɪʃ] *adj pej* puéril

child·ish·ness ['tʃaɪldɪʃnɪs] *pej* puérilité *f*

child·ish·ly ['tʃaɪldɪʃlɪ] *adv pej* de manière puérile

child·less ['tʃaɪldlɪs] *adj* sans enfant

child·like ['tʃaɪldlaɪk] *adj* enfantin

'child·mind·er gardienne *f* d'enfants

child·ren ['tʃɪldrən] *pl* → **child**

Chil·e ['tʃɪlɪ] *n* Chili *m*

Chil·e·an ['tʃɪlɪən] **1** *adj* chilien* **2** *n* Chilien(ne) *m(f)*

chill [tʃɪl] **1** *n in air* froideur *f*, froid *m*; *illness* coup *m* de froid; ***there's a ~ in the air* l'air est frais *or* un peu froid **2** *v/t wine* mettre au frais
♦ **chill out** *v/i* P se détendre

chil·(l)i (pep·per) ['tʃɪlɪ] piment *m* (rouge)

chil·ly ['tʃɪlɪ] *adj weather* frais*, froid; *welcome* froid; ***I'm ~** j'ai un peu froid**

chime [tʃaɪm] *v/i* carillonner

chim·ney ['tʃɪmnɪ] cheminée *f*

chim·pan·zee [tʃɪmˈpænzɪ] chimpanzé *m*

chin [tʃɪn] menton *m*

Chi·na ['tʃaɪnə] Chine *f*

chi·na ['tʃaɪnə] **1** *n* porcelaine *f* **2** *adj* en porcelaine

Chi·nese [tʃaɪˈni:z] **1** *adj* chinois **2** *n language* chinois *m*; *person* Chinois(e) *m(f)*

chink [tʃɪŋk] *(gap)* fente *f*; *sound* tintement *m*

chip [tʃɪp] **1** *n fragment* copeau *m*; *damage* brèche *f*; *in gambling* jeton *m*; COMPUT puce *f*; ***~s** (potato ~s) chips *mpl* **2** *v/t (pret & pp* **-ped)** *damage* ébrécher
♦ **chip in** *v/i (interrupt)* intervenir

chi·ro·prac·tor ['kaɪroʊpræktər] chiropracteur *m*

chirp [tʃ3:rp] *v/i* gazouiller

chis·el ['tʃɪzl] *n* ciseau *m*, burin *m*

chit·chat ['tʃɪttʃæt] bavardages *mpl*

chiv·al·rous ['ʃɪvlrəs] *adj* chevaleresque, courtois

chive [tʃaɪv] ciboulette *f*

chlo·rine ['klɔ:ri:n] chlore *m*

chlor·o·form ['klɔ:rəfɔ:rm] chloroforme *m*

choc·a·hol·ic [tʃɑ:kəˈhɑ:lɪk] F accro *m/f* du chocolat F

chock-full [ʧɑːkˈfʊl] *adj* F plein à craquer

choc·o·late [ˈʧɑːkələt] chocolat *m*; **hot ~** chocolat *m* chaud

'**choc·o·late cake** gâteau *m* au chocolat

choice [ʧɔɪs] **1** *n* choix *m*; **I had no ~** je n'avais pas le choix **2** *adj* (*top quality*) de choix

choir [ˈkwaɪr] chœur *m*

'**choir·boy** enfant *m* de chœur

choke [ʧoʊk] **1** *n* MOT starter *m* **2** *v/i* s'étouffer, s'étrangler; **he ~d on a bone** il s'est étranglé avec un os **3** *v/t* étouffer; (*strangle*) étrangler

cho·les·te·rol [kəˈlestəroʊl] cholestérol *m*

choose [ʧuːz] *v/t & v/i* (*pret* **chose**, *pp* **chosen**) choisir

choos·ey [ˈʧuːzɪ] *adj* F difficile

chop [ʧɑːp] **1** *n of meat* côtelette *f* **2** *v/t* (*pret & pp* **-ped**) *wood* couper, fendre; *meat, vegetables* couper en morceaux

♦ **chop down** *v/t tree* abattre

chop·per [ˈʧɑːpər] *tool* hachoir *m*; F (*helicopter*) hélico *m*

chop·ping board [ˈʧɑːpɪŋ] planche *f* à découper

'**chop·sticks** *npl* baguettes *fpl*

cho·ral [ˈkɔːrəl] *adj* choral

chord [kɔːrd] MUS accord *m*

chore [ʧɔːr] **~s** travaux *mpl* domestiques

cho·re·o·graph [ˈkɔːrɪəgræf] *v/t* chorégraphier

chor·e·og·ra·pher [kɔːrɪˈɑːgrəfər] chorégraphe *m/f*

chor·e·og·ra·phy [kɔːrɪˈɑːgrəfɪ] chorégraphie *f*

cho·rus [ˈkɔːrəs] *singers* chœur *m*; *of song* refrain *m*

chose [ʧoʊz] *pret* → **choose**

cho·sen [ˈʧoʊzn] *pp* → **choose**

Christ [kraɪst] Christ *m*; **~!** mon Dieu!

chris·ten [ˈkrɪsn] *v/t* baptiser

chris·ten·ing [ˈkrɪsnɪŋ] baptême *m*

Chris·tian [ˈkrɪsʧən] **1** *n* chrétien(ne) *m(f)* **2** *adj* chrétien*

Chris·ti·an·i·ty [krɪstɪˈænətɪ] christianisme *m*

'**Chris·tian name** prénom *m*

Christ·mas [ˈkrɪsməs] Noël *m*; **at ~** à Noël; **Merry ~!** Joyeux Noël!

'**Christ·mas card** carte *f* de Noël; **Christ·mas 'Day** jour *m* de Noël; **Christ·mas 'Eve** veille *f* de Noël; '**Christ·mas pres·ent** cadeau *m* de Noël; '**Christ·mas tree** arbre *m* de Noël

chrome, chro·mi·um [kroʊm, ˈkroʊmɪəm] chrome *m*

chro·mo·some [ˈkroʊməsoʊm] chromosome *m*

chron·ic [ˈkrɑːnɪk] *adj* chronique

chron·o·log·i·cal [krɑːnəˈlɑːdʒɪkl] *adj* chronologique; **in ~ order** dans l'ordre chronologique

chrys·an·the·mum [krɪˈsænθəməm] chrysanthème *m*

chub·by [ˈʧʌbɪ] *adj* potelé

chuck [ʧʌk] *v/t* F lancer

♦ **chuck out** *v/t* F *object* jeter; *person* flanquer dehors *m*

chuck·le [ˈʧʌkl] **1** *n* petit rire *m* **2** *v/i* rire tout bas

chum [ʧʌm] copain *m*, copine *f*

chum·my [ˈʧʌmɪ] *adj* F copain*

chunk [ʧʌŋk] gros morceau *m*

chunk·y [ˈʧʌŋkɪ] *adj sweater, tumbler* gros*; *person, build* trapu

church [ʧɜːrʧ] église *f*

church 'hall salle *f* paroissiale; **church 'serv·ice** office *m*; '**church·yard** cimetière *m* (autour d'une église)

churl·ish [ˈʧɜːrlɪʃ] *adj* mal élevé

chute [ʃuːt] *for coal etc* glissière *f*; *for garbage* vide-ordures *m*; *for escape* toboggan *m*

CIA [siːaɪˈeɪ] *abbr* (= **Central Intelligence Agency**) C.I.A. *f* (= Central Intelligence Agency)

ci·der [ˈsaɪdər] cidre *m*

CIF [siːaɪˈef] *abbr* (= **cost insurance freight**) CAF (= Coût Assurance Fret)

ci·gar [sɪˈgɑːr] cigare *m*

cig·a·rette [sɪgəˈret] cigarette *f*

cig·a·rette end mégot *m*; **cig·a·rette light·er** briquet *m*; **cig·a·rette pa·pers** *npl* papier *m* à cigarettes

clarify

cin·e·ma ['sɪnɪmə] (*Br if building*) cinéma *m*

cin·na·mon ['sɪnəmən] cannelle *f*

cir·cle ['sɜːrkl] **1** *n* cercle *m* **2** *v/t* (*draw circle around*) entourer **3** *v/i of plane, bird* tournoyer

cir·cuit ['sɜːrkɪt] circuit *m*; (*lap*) tour *m* (de circuit)

'cir·cuit board COMPUT plaquette *f*; **'cir·cuit break·er** ELEC disjoncteur *m*; **'cir·cuit train·ing** SP programme *m* d'entraînement général

cir·cu·lar ['sɜːrkjʊlər] **1** *n giving information* circulaire *f* **2** *adj* circulaire

cir·cu·late ['sɜːrkjuleɪt] **1** *v/i* circuler **2** *v/t memo* faire circuler

cir·cu·la·tion [sɜːrkjʊ'leɪʃn] BIOL circulation *f*; *of newspaper, magazine* tirage *m*

cir·cum·fer·ence [sər'kʌmfərəns] circonférence *f*

cir·cum·flex ['sɜːrkəmfleks] accent *m* circonflexe

cir·cum·stances ['sɜːrkəmstænsɪs] *npl* circonstances *fpl*; *financial situation* finances *fpl*; *under no ~* en aucun cas; *under the ~* en de telles circonstances

cir·cus ['sɜːrkəs] cirque *m*

cir·rho·sis (of the liv·er) [sɪ'roʊsɪs] cirrhose *f* (du foie)

cis·tern ['sɪstərn] réservoir *m*; *of WC* réservoir *m* de chasse d'eau

cite [saɪt] *v/t also* LAW citer

cit·i·zen ['sɪtɪzn] citoyen(ne) *m(f)*

cit·i·zen·ship ['sɪtɪznʃɪp] citoyenneté *f*

cit·y ['sɪtɪ] (grande) ville *f*

cit·y 'cen·ter, *Br* **cit·y 'cen·tre** centre-ville *m*

cit·y 'hall hôtel *m* de ville

civ·ic ['sɪvɪk] *adj* municipal; *pride, responsibilities* civique

civ·il ['sɪvl] *adj* civil; (*polite*) poli

civ·il en·gi·neer ingénieur *m* des travaux publics

ci·vil·ian [sɪ'vɪljən] **1** *n* civil(e) *m(f)* **2** *adj clothes* civil

ci·vil·i·ty [sɪ'vɪlɪtɪ] politesse *f*

civ·i·li·za·tion [sɪvəlaɪ'zeɪʃn] civilisation *f*

civ·i·lize ['sɪvəlaɪz] *v/t* civiliser

civ·il 'rights *npl* droits *mpl* civils; **civ·il 'ser·vant** fonctionnaire *m/f*; **civ·il 'ser·vice** fonction *f* publique, administration *f*; **civ·il 'war** guerre *f* civile

claim [kleɪm] **1** *n for compensation etc* demande *f*; (*right*) droit *m* (*to sth* à qch); (*assertion*) affirmation *f* **2** *v/t* (*ask for as a right*) demander, réclamer; (*assert*) affirmer; *lost property* réclamer; *they have ~ed responsibility for the attack* ils ont revendiqué l'attentat

claim·ant ['kleɪmənt] demandeur (-euse) *m(f)*

clair·voy·ant [kler'vɔɪənt] *n* voyant(e) *m(f)*

clam [klæm] palourde *f*, clam *m*

◆ **clam up** *v/i* (*pret & pp -med*) F se taire (brusquement)

clam·ber ['klæmbər] *v/i* grimper

clam·my ['klæmɪ] *adj hands, weather* moite

clam·or ['klæmər] *noise* clameur *f*; *outcry* vociférations *fpl*

◆ **clamor for** *v/t* demander à grands cris

clamp [klæmp] **1** *n fastener* pince *f*, crampon *m* **2** *v/t fasten* cramponner; *car* mettre un sabot à

◆ **clamp down** *v/i* sévir

◆ **clamp down on** *v/t* sévir contre

clan [klæn] clan *m*

clan·des·tine [klæn'destɪn] *adj* clandestin

clang [klæŋ] **1** *n* bruit *m* métallique *or* retentissant **2** *v/i* retentir; *the metal door ~ed shut* la porte de métal s'est refermée avec un bruit retentissant

clap [klæp] **1** *v/i* (*pret & pp -ped*) (*applaud*) applaudir **2** *v/t* (*pret & pp -ped*) (*applaud*) applaudir; *~ one's hands* battre des mains; *~ s.o. on the back* donner à qn une tape dans le dos

clar·et ['klærɪt] *wine* bordeaux *m* (rouge)

clar·i·fi·ca·tion [klærɪfɪ'keɪʃn] clarification *f*

clar·i·fy ['klærɪfaɪ] *v/t* (*pret & pp -ied*)

clarifier
clar·i·net [klærɪˈnet] clarinette *f*
clar·i·ty [ˈklærətɪ] clarté *f*
clash [klæʃ] **1** *n between people* affrontement *m*, heurt *m*; **~ of personalities** incompatibilité *f* de caractères **2** *v/i* s'affronter; *of opinions* s'opposer; *of colors* détonner; *of events* tomber en même temps
clasp [klæsp] **1** *n of medal* agrafe *f* **2** *v/t in hand, to self* serrer
class [klæs] **1** *n* (*lesson*) cours *m*; (*group of people, category*) classe *f*; **social ~** classe *f* sociale; **the ~ of 2002** la promo(tion) 2002 **2** *v/t* classer
clas·sic [ˈklæsɪk] **1** *adj* classique **2** *n* classique *m*
clas·si·cal [ˈklæsɪkl] *adj music* classique
clas·si·fi·ca·tion [klæsɪfɪˈkeɪʃn] classification *f*
clas·si·fied [ˈklæsɪfaɪd] *adj information* secret*
'clas·si·fied ad(ver·tise·ment) petite annonce *f*
clas·si·fy [ˈklæsɪfaɪ] *v/t* (*pret & pp -ied*) (*categorize*) classifier
'class·mate camarade *m/f* de classe; **'class·room** salle *f* de classe; **'class war·fare** lutte *f* des classes
class·y [ˈklæsɪ] *adj* F: *restaurant etc* chic *inv*; *person* classe F
clat·ter [ˈklætər] **1** *n* fracas *m*
clat·ter 2 *v/i* faire du bruit
clause [klɔːz] (*in agreement*) clause *f*; GRAM proposition *f*
claus·tro·pho·bi·a [klɔːstrəˈfoʊbɪə] claustrophobie *f*
claw [klɔː] **1** *n of cat* griffe *f*; *of lobster, crab* pince *f* **2** *v/t* (*scratch*) griffer
clay [kleɪ] argile *f*, glaise *f*
clean [kliːn] **1** *adj* propre **2** *adv* F (*completely*) complètement **3** *v/t* nettoyer; **~ one's teeth** se laver les dents; **have sth ~ed** donner qch à nettoyer
◆ **clean out** *v/t room, closet* nettoyer à fond; *fig* dévaliser
◆ **clean up 1** *v/t also fig* nettoyer **2** *v/i in house* faire le ménage; (*wash*) se débarbouiller; *on stock market etc*

faire fortune
clean·er [ˈkliːnər] *male* agent *m* de propreté; *female* femme *f* de ménage; (*dry~*) teinturier(-ère) *m(f)*
clean·ing wom·an [ˈkliːnɪŋ] femme *f* de ménage
cleanse [klenz] *v/t skin* nettoyer
cleans·er [ˈklenzər] *for skin* démaquillant *m*
cleans·ing cream [ˈklenzɪŋ] crème *f* démaquillante
clear [klɪr] **1** *adj voice, photograph, vision, skin* net*; *to understand, weather, sky, water, eyes* clair; *conscience* tranquille; **I'm not ~ about it** je ne comprends pas; **I didn't make myself ~** je ne me suis pas fait comprendre **2** *adv:* **stand ~ of** s'écarter de; **steer ~ of** éviter **3** *v/t roads etc* dégager; *people out of a place, place* (faire) évacuer; *table* débarrasser; *ball* dégager; (*acquit*) innocenter; (*authorize*) autoriser; (*earn*) toucher net; **~ one's throat** s'éclaircir la voix **4** *v/i of sky* se dégager; *of mist* se dissiper; *of face* s'éclaircir
◆ **clear away** *v/t* ranger
◆ **clear off** *v/i* F ficher le camp F
◆ **clear out 1** *v/t closet* vider **2** *v/i* ficher le camp F
◆ **clear up 1** *v/i in room etc* ranger; *of weather* s'éclaircir; *of illness, rash* disparaître **2** *v/t* (*tidy*) ranger; *mystery* éclaircir; *problem* résoudre
clear·ance [ˈklɪrəns] (*space*) espace *m* (libre); (*authorization*) autorisation *f*
'clear·ance sale liquidation *f*
clear·ing [ˈklɪrɪŋ] clairière *f*
clear·ly [ˈklɪrlɪ] *adv speak, see* clairement; *hear* distinctement; (*evidently*) manifestement
cleav·age [ˈkliːvɪdʒ] décolleté *m*
cleav·er [ˈkliːvər] couperet *m*
clem·en·cy [ˈklemənsɪ] clémence *f*
clench [klentʃ] *v/t teeth, fist* serrer
cler·gy [ˈklɜːrdʒɪ] clergé *m*
cler·gy·man [ˈklɜːrdʒɪmæn] ecclésiastique *m*; *Protestant* pasteur *m*
clerk [klɜːrk] *administrative* employé(e) *m(f)* de bureau; *in store* vendeur(-euse) *m(f)*

clev·er ['klevər] adj intelligent; gadget, device ingénieux*; (skillful) habile

clev·er·ly ['klevərlɪ] adv intelligemment

cli·ché ['kli:ʃeɪ] cliché m

cli·chéd ['kli:ʃeɪd] adj rebattu

click [klɪk] 1 n COMPUT clic m 2 v/i cliquer; of camera faire un déclic
♦ **click on** v/t COMPUT cliquer sur

cli·ent ['klaɪənt] client(e) m(f)

cli·en·tele [kli:ɔn'tel] clientèle f

cliff [klɪf] falaise f

cli·mate ['klaɪmət] also fig climat m

'**cli·mate change** changement m climatique

cli·mat·ic [klaɪ'mætɪk] adj climatique

cli·max ['klaɪmæks] n point m culminant

climb [klaɪm] 1 n up mountain ascension f; up stairs montée f 2 v/t monter sur, grimper sur; mountain escalader 3 v/i into tree grimper; in mountains faire de l'escalade; of road, inflation monter
♦ **climb down** v/i descendre; fig reculer

climb·er ['klaɪmər] alpiniste m/f

climb·ing ['klaɪmɪŋ] escalade f

'**climb·ing wall** mur m d'escalade

clinch [klɪntʃ] v/t deal conclure; that **~es it** ça règle la question

cling [klɪŋ] v/i (pret & pp **clung**) of clothes coller
♦ **cling to** v/t also fig s'accrocher à

'**cling·film** film m transparent

cling·y ['klɪŋɪ] adj child, boyfriend collant

clin·ic ['klɪnɪk] clinique f

clin·i·cal ['klɪnɪkl] adj clinique; fig: decision etc froid

clink [klɪŋk] 1 n noise tintement m 2 v/i tinter

clip[1] [klɪp] 1 n fastener pince f; for hair barrette f 2 v/t (pret & pp **-ped**): ~ **sth to sth** attacher qch à qch

clip[2] [klɪp] 1 n (extract) extrait m 2 v/t (pret & pp **-ped**) hair, grass couper; hedge tailler

'**clip·board** planche f à papiers; COMPUT bloc-notes m

clip·pers ['klɪpərz] npl for hair tondeuse f; for nails pince f à ongles; for gardening sécateur m

clip·ping ['klɪpɪŋ] from newspaper coupure f (de presse)

clique [kli:k] coterie f

cloak [kloʊk] n grande cape f; fig voile m

'**cloak·room** Br: for coats vestiaire m

clock [klɑːk] horloge f; F (odometer) compteur m

'**clock ra·di·o** radio-réveil m; '**clock-wise** adv dans le sens des aiguilles d'une montre; '**clock·work** of toy mécanisme m; **it went like ~** tout est allé comme sur des roulettes
♦ **clog up** [klɑːg] (pret & pp **-ged**) 1 v/i se boucher 2 v/t boucher

clone [kloʊn] 1 n clone m 2 v/t cloner

close[1] [kloʊs] 1 adj family, friend proche; resemblance étroit 2 adv près; ~ **at hand**, ~ **by** tout près

close[2] [kloʊz] v/t & v/i fermer
♦ **close down** v/t & v/i fermer
♦ **close in** v/i of troops se rapprocher (**on** de); of fog descendre
♦ **close up** v/i building fermer 2 v/t (move closer) se rapprocher

closed [kloʊzd] adj fermé

closed-cir·cuit 'tel·e·vi·sion télévision f en circuit fermé; '**close-knit** adj très uni

close·ly ['kloʊslɪ] adv listen attentivement; watch also de près; cooperate étroitement

clos·et ['klɑːzɪt] armoire f, placard m

close-up ['kloʊsʌp] gros plan m

clos·ing date ['kloʊzɪŋ] date f limite

'**clos·ing time** heure f de fermeture

clo·sure ['kloʊʒər] fermeture f

clot [klɑːt] 1 n of blood caillot m 2 v/i (pret & pp **-ted**) of blood coaguler

cloth [klɑːθ] (fabric) tissu m; for drying torchon m; for washing lavette f

clothes [kloʊðz] npl vêtements mpl

'**clothes brush** brosse f à vêtements; '**clothes hang·er** cintre m; '**clothes·horse** séchoir m (à linge); '**clothes·line** corde f à linge; '**clothes peg**, '**clothes·pin** pince f à linge

cloth·ing ['kloʊðɪŋ] vêtements mpl

C

cloud [klaʊd] *n also of dust etc* nuage *m*
♦ **cloud over** *v/i of sky* se couvrir (de nuages)

'**cloud·burst** rafale *f* de pluie

'**cloud·less** ['klaʊdlɪs] *adj sky* sans nuages

cloud·y ['klaʊdɪ] *adj* nuageux*

clout [klaʊt] *(fig: influence)* influence *f*

clove of 'gar·lic [kloʊv] gousse *f* d'ail

clown [klaʊn] *also pej* clown *m*

club [klʌb] *n weapon* massue *f*; *in golf* club *m*; *organization* club *m*

'**club class** classe *f* affaires

clue [kluː] indice *m*; **I haven't a ~** F je n'en ai pas la moindre idée; **he hasn't a ~** *(is useless)* il n'y comprend rien

clued-up [kluːd'ʌp] *adj* F calé F

clump [klʌmp] *n of earth* motte *f*; *(group)* touffe *f*

clum·si·ness ['klʌmzɪnɪs] maladresse *f*

clum·sy ['klʌmzɪ] *adj person* maladroit

clung [klʌŋ] *pret & pp* → **cling**

clus·ter ['klʌstər] **1** *n of people, houses* groupe *m* **2** *v/i of people* se grouper; *of houses* être groupé

clutch [klʌtʃ] **1** *n* MOT embrayage *m* **2** *v/t* étreindre
♦ **clutch at** *v/t* s'agripper à

clut·ter ['klʌtər] **1** *n* fouillis *m* **2** *v/t* *(also: ~ up)* mettre le fouillis dans

Co. *abbr (= Company)* Cie (= Compagnie)

c/o *abbr* **care of** chez

coach [koʊtʃ] **1** *n (trainer)* entraîneur (-euse) *m(f)*; *on train* voiture *f*; *Br (bus) (auto)*car *m* **2** *v/t* SP entraîner

coach·ing ['koʊtʃɪŋ] SP entraînement *m*

co·ag·u·late [koʊ'ægjʊleɪt] *v/i of blood* coaguler

coal [koʊl] charbon *m*

co·a·li·tion [koʊə'lɪʃn] coalition *f*

'**coal·mine** mine *f* de charbon

coarse [kɔːrs] *adj skin, fabric* rugueux*; *hair* épais*; *(vulgar)* grossier*

coarse·ly ['kɔːrslɪ] *adv (vulgarly)*, *ground* grossièrement

coast [koʊst] *n* côte *f*; **at the ~** sur la côte

coast·al ['koʊstl] *adj* côtier*

coast·er ['koʊstər] dessous *m* de verre

'**coast·guard** *organization* gendarmerie *f* maritime; *person* gendarme *m* maritime

'**coast·line** littoral *m*

coat [koʊt] **1** *n* veston *m*; *(over~)* pardessus *m*; *of animal* pelage *m*; *of paint etc* couche *f* **2** *v/t (cover)* couvrir (**with** de)

'**coat·hang·er** cintre *m*

coat·ing ['koʊtɪŋ] couche *f*

co·au·thor ['koʊ:θər] **1** *n* coauteur *m* **2** *v/t* écrire en collaboration

coax [koʊks] *v/t* cajoler; **~ s.o. into doing sth** encourager qn à faire qch en le cajolant; **~ sth out of s.o.** *truth etc* obtenir qch de qn en le cajolant

cob·bled ['kɑːbld] *adj* pavé

cob·ble·stone ['kɑːblstoʊn] pavé *m*

cob·web ['kɑːbweb] toile *f* d'araignée

co·caine [kə'keɪn] cocaïne *f*

cock [kɑːk] *n chicken* coq *m*; *any male bird* (oiseau *m*) mâle *m*

cock·eyed [kɑːk'aɪd] *adj* F *idea etc* absurde

'**cock·pit** *of plane* poste *m* de pilotage, cockpit *m*

cock·roach ['kɑːkroʊtʃ] cafard *m*

'**cock·tail** cocktail *m*

'**cock·tail par·ty** cocktail *m*

'**cock·tail shak·er** shaker *m*

cock·y ['kɑːkɪ] *adj* F trop sûr de soi

co·coa ['koʊkoʊ] *drink* cacao *m*

co·co·nut ['koʊkənʌt] *to eat* noix *m* de coco

'**co·co·nut palm** cocotier *m*

COD [siːoʊ'diː] *abbr (= collect ou Br cash on delivery)* livraison contre remboursement

code [koʊd] *n* code *m*; **in ~** codé

co·ed·u·ca·tion·al [koʊedu'keɪʃnl] *adj school* mixte

co·erce [koʊ'ɜːrs] *v/t* contraindre, forcer

co·ex·ist [koʊɪg'zɪst] *v/i* coexister

co·ex·ist·ence [koʊɪg'zɪstəns] coexistence *f*

cof·fee ['kɑ:fɪ] café *m*; **'cof·fee bean** grain *m* de café; **'cof·fee break** pause-café *f*; **'cof·fee cup** tasse *f* à café; **'cof·fee grind·er** [graɪndər] moulin *m* à café; **'cof·fee mak·er** machine *f* à café; **'cof·fee pot** cafetière *f*; **'cof·fee shop** café *m*; **'cof·fee ta·ble** petite table basse *f*

cof·fin ['kɑ:fɪn] cercueil *m*

cog [kɑ:g] dent *f*; *fig*

co·gnac ['kɑ:njæk] cognac *m*

'cog·wheel roue *f* dentée

co·hab·it [kou'hæbɪt] *v/i* cohabiter

co·her·ent [kou'hɪrənt] *adj* cohérent

coil [kɔɪl] **1** *n of rope, wire* rouleau *m*; *of smoke, snake* anneau *m*

coil 2 *v/t*: ~ (**up**) enrouler

coin [kɔɪn] *n* pièce *f* (de monnaie)

co·in·cide [kouɪn'saɪd] *v/i* coïncider

co·in·ci·dence [kou'ɪnsɪdəns] coïncidence *f*

coke [kouk] P (*cocaine*) coke *f* F

Coke® [kouk] coca® *m* F

cold [kould] **1** *adj* froid; *I'm (feeling)* ~ j'ai froid; *it's* ~ *of weather* il fait froid; *in* ~ *blood* de sang-froid; *get* ~ *feet* F avoir la trouille F **2** *n* froid *m*; MED rhume *m*; *I have a* ~ j'ai un rhume, je suis enrhumé

cold-blood·ed [kould'blʌdɪd] *adj animal* à sang froid; *fig* insensible; *murder* commis de sang-froid

cold call·ing ['kɒ:lɪŋ] COMM appels *mpl* à froid; *visits* visites *fpl* à froid

'cold cuts *npl* assiette *f* anglaise

cold·ly ['kouldlɪ] *adv* froidement

'cold·ness ['kouldnɪs] *fig* froideur *f*

'cold sore bouton *m* de fièvre

cole·slaw ['koulslɔ:] salade *f* de choux

col·ic ['kɑ:lɪk] colique *f*

col·lab·o·rate [kə'læbəreɪt] *v/i* collaborer

col·lab·o·ra·tion [kəlæbə'reɪʃn] collaboration *f*

col·lab·o·ra·tor [kə'læbəreɪtər] collaborateur(-trice) *m(f)*

col·lapse [kə'læps] *v/i* s'effondrer; *of building* etc also s'écrouler

col·lap·si·ble [kə'læpsəbl] *adj* pliant

col·lar ['kɑ:lər] col *m*; *for dog* collier *m*

'col·lar·bone clavicule *f*

col·lat·er·al [kə'lætərəl] *n* nantissement *m*; ~ *damage* MIL dommage *m* collatéral

col·league ['kɑ:li:g] collègue *m/f*

col·lect [kə'lekt] **1** *v/t person, cleaning etc* aller / venir chercher; *as hobby* collectionner; (*gather: clothes etc*) recueillir; *wood* ramasser **2** *v/i* (*gather together*) s'assembler **3** *adv*: *call* ~ appeler en PCV

col·lect call communication *f* en PCV

col·lect·ed [kə'lektɪd] *adj works, poems etc* complet*; *person* serein

col·lec·tion [kə'lekʃn] collection *f*; *in church* collecte *f*

col·lec·tive [kə'lektɪv] *adj* collectif*

col·lec·tive 'bar·gain·ing convention *f* collective

col·lec·tor [kə'lektər] collectionneur(-euse) *m(f)*

col·lege ['kɑ:lɪdʒ] université *f*

col·lide [kə'laɪd] *v/i* se heurter; ~ *with sth / s.o.* heurter qch / qn

col·li·sion [kə'lɪʒn] collision *f*

col·lo·qui·al [kə'loukwɪəl] *adj* familier*

co·lon ['koulən] *punctuation* deux-points *mpl*; ANAT côlon *m*

colo·nel ['kɜ:rnl] colonel *m*

co·lo·ni·al [kə'lounɪəl] *adj* colonial

co·lo·nize ['kɑ:lənaɪz] *v/t country* coloniser

co·lo·ny ['kɑ:lənɪ] colonie *f*

col·or ['kʌlər] **1** *n* couleur *f*; *in cheeks* couleurs *fpl*; *in* ~ en couleur; ~*s* MIL couleurs *fpl*, drapeau *m* **2** *v/t one's hair* teindre **3** *v/i* (*blush*) rougir

'col·or-blind *adj* daltonien*

col·ored ['kʌlərd] *adj person* de couleur

'col·or fast *adj* bon teint *inv*

col·or·ful ['kʌlərfəl] *adj also fig* coloré

'col·or·ing ['kʌlərɪŋ] teint *m*

'col·or pho·to·graph photographie *f* (en) couleur; **'col·or scheme** combinaison *f* de couleurs; **'col·or TV** télé *f* (en) couleur

co·los·sal [kə'lɑ:sl] *adj* colossal

col·our etc *Br* → **color** etc

colt [koult] poulain *m*

col·umn ['kɑ:ləm] *architectural, of text*

colonne f; *in newspaper* chronique f

col·umn·ist ['kɑːləmɪst] chroniqueur(-euse) m(f)

co·ma ['koumə] coma m; **be in a ~** être dans le coma

comb [koum] **1** n peigne m **2** v/t peigner; *area* ratisser, passer au peigne fin

com·bat ['kɑːmbæt] **1** n combat m **2** v/t combattre

com·bi·na·tion [kɑːmbɪ'neɪʃn] *also of safe* combinaison f

com·bine [kəm'baɪn] **1** v/t allier, combiner; *ingredients* mélanger; (*associate*) associer; **~ business with pleasure** joindre l'utile à l'agréable **2** v/i *of sauce etc* se marier; *of chemical elements* se combiner

com·bine har·vest·er [kɑːmbaɪn-'hɑːrvɪstər] moissonneuse-batteuse f

com·bus·ti·ble [kəm'bʌstɪbl] *adj* combustible

com·bus·tion [kəm'bʌstʃn] combustion f

come [kʌm] v/i (pret **came**, pp **come**) venir; *of train, bus* venir; **you'll ~ to like it** tu finiras par l'aimer; **how ~?** F comment ça se fait? F

◆ **come about** v/i (*happen*) arriver

◆ **come across 1** v/t (*find*) tomber sur **2** v/i *of humor etc* passer; **she comes across as being ...** elle donne l'impression d'être ...

◆ **come along** v/i (*come too*) venir (aussi); (*turn up*) arriver; (*progress*) avancer

◆ **come apart** v/i tomber en morceaux; (*break*) se briser

◆ **come around** v/i *to s.o.'s home* passer; (*regain consciousness*) revenir à soi

◆ **come away** v/i (*leave*), *of button etc* partir

◆ **come back** v/i revenir; **it came back to me** ça m'est revenu

◆ **come by 1** v/i passer **2** v/t (*acquire*) obtenir; *bruise* avoir; (*find*) trouver

◆ **come down** v/i descendre; *in price, amount etc* baisser; *of rain, snow* tomber

◆ **come for** v/t (*attack*) attaquer; (*to collect*) venir chercher

◆ **come forward** v/i (*present o.s.*) se présenter

◆ **come in** v/i entrer; *of train, in race* arriver; *of tide* monter; **come in!** entrez!

◆ **come in for** v/t recevoir; **come in for criticism** recevoir des critiques

◆ **come in on** v/t prendre part à; **come in on a deal** prendre part à un marché

◆ **come off** v/i *of handle etc* se détacher

◆ **come on** v/i (*progress*) avancer; **come on!** (*hurry*) dépêche-toi!; *in disbelief* allons!

◆ **come out** v/i *of person* sortir; *of results* être communiqué; *of sun, product* apparaître; *of stain* partir; *of gay* révéler son homosexualité

◆ **come to 1** v/t (*reach*) arriver à; **that comes to $70** ça fait 70 $ **2** v/i (*regain consciousness*) revenir à soi, reprendre conscience

◆ **come up** v/i monter; *of sun* se lever; **something has come up** quelque chose est arrivé

◆ **come up with** v/t *new idea etc* trouver

'**come·back** *of singer, actor* retour m, come-back m; *of fashion* retour m; **make a ~** *of singer, actor* revenir en scène, faire un comeback; *of fashion* revenir à la mode

co·me·di·an [kə'miːdɪən] (*comic*) comique m/f; *pej* pitre m/f

'**come·down** déchéance f

com·e·dy ['kɑːmədɪ] comédie f

'**com·e·dy act·or** acteur(-trice) m(f) comique

com·et ['kɑːmɪt] comète f

come·up·pance [kʌm'ʌpəns] F: **he'll get his ~** il aura ce qu'il mérite

com·fort ['kʌmfərt] **1** n confort m; (*consolation*) consolation f, réconfort m **2** v/t consoler, réconforter

com·for·ta·ble ['kʌmfərtəbl] *adj chair, house, room* confortable; **be ~** *of person* être à l'aise; *financially* être aisé

com·ic ['kɑːmɪk] **1** n *to read* bande f dessinée; (*comedian*) comique m/f **2** *adj* comique

com·i·cal ['kɑːmɪkl] *adj* comique

'**com·ic book** bande *f* dessinée, BD *f*

com·ics ['kɑːmɪks] *npl* bandes *fpl* dessinées

'**com·ic strip** bande *f* dessinée

com·ma ['kɑːmə] virgule *f*

com·mand [kə'mænd] **1** *n* (*order*) ordre *m*; (*control: of situation, language*) maîtrise *f*; COMPUT commande *m* 2 MIL commandement *m* **2** *v/t* commander; ~ *s.o. to do sth* ordonner à qn de faire qch

com·man·deer [kɑːmən'dɪr] *v/t* réquisitionner

com·man·der [kə'mændər] commandant(e) *m(f)*

com·man·der-in-'chief commandant(e) *m(f)* en chef

com·mand·ing of·fi·cer [kə'mændɪŋ] commandant(e) *m(f)*

com·mand·ment [kə'mændmənt]: *the Ten Commandments* REL les dix commandements *mpl*

com·mem·o·rate [kə'meməreɪt] *v/t* commémorer

com·mem·o·ra·tion [kəmemə'reɪʃn]: *in ~ of* en commémoration de

com·mence [kə'mens] *v/t & v/i* commencer

com·mend [kə'mend] *v/t* louer

com·mend·a·ble [kə'mendəbl] *adj* louable

com·men·da·tion [kəmen'deɪʃn] *for bravery* éloge *m*

com·men·su·rate [kə'menʃərət] *adj*: ~ *with* proportionné à

com·ment ['kɑːment] **1** *n* commentaire *m*; *no ~!* sans commentaire! **2** *v/i*: ~ *on* commenter

com·men·ta·ry ['kɑːmənterɪ] commentaire *m*

com·men·tate ['kɑːmənteɪt] *v/i* faire le commentaire (*on* de)

com·men·ta·tor [kɑːmənteɪtər] commentateur(-trice) *m(f)*

com·merce ['kɑːmɜːrs] commerce *m*

com·mer·cial [kə'mɜːrʃl] **1** *adj* commercial **2** *n* (*advert*) publicité *f*

com·mer·cial 'break page *f* de publicité

com·mer·cial·ize [kə'mɜːrʃlaɪz] *v/t Christmas etc* commercialiser

com·mer·cial tel·e·vi·sion télévision *f* commerciale

com·mer·cial 'trav·el·er, *Br* **com·mer·cial 'trav·el·ler** représentant(e) *m(f)* de commerce

com·mis·e·rate [kə'mɪzəreɪt] *v/i* compatir; ~ *with s.o.* témoigner de la sympathie à qn

com·mis·sion [kə'mɪʃn] **1** *n* (*payment*) commission *f*; (*job*) commande *f*; (*committee*) commission *f* **2** *v/t for a job* charger (*to do sth* de faire qch)

Com·mis·sion·er [kə'mɪʃənər] *in European Union* commissaire *m/f*

com·mit [kə'mɪt] *v/t* (*pret & pp* **-ted**) *crime* commettre; *money* engager; ~ *o.s.* s'engager

com·mit·ment [kə'mɪtmənt] *to job, in relationship* engagement *m*; (*responsibility*) responsabilité *f*

com·mit·tee [kə'mɪtɪ] comité *m*

com·mod·i·ty [kə'mɑːdətɪ] marchandise *f*

com·mon ['kɑːmən] *adj* courant; *species etc* commun; (*shared*) commun; *in ~* en commun; *have sth in ~* avoir qch en commun

com·mon·er ['kɑːmənər] roturier (-ère) *m(f)*

com·mon 'law hus·band concubin *m*

com·mon 'law wife concubine *f*

com·mon·ly ['kɑːmənlɪ] *adv* communément

Com·mon 'Mar·ket Marché *m* commun

'**com·mon·place** *adj* banal

com·mon 'sense bon sens *m*

com·mo·tion [kə'mouʃn] agitation *f*

com·mu·nal [kəm'juːnl] *adj* en commun

com·mu·nal·ly [kəm'juːnəlɪ] *adv* en commun

com·mu·ni·cate [kə'mjuːnɪkeɪt] *v/t & v/i* communiquer

com·mu·ni·ca·tion [kəmjuːnɪ'keɪʃn] communication *f*

com·mu·ni·ca·tions *npl* communications *fpl*

com·mu·ni·ca·tions sat·el·lite satel-

C

lite *m* de communication
com·mu·ni·ca·tive [kə'mjuːnɪkətɪv]
adj person communicatif*
Com·mu·nion [kə'mjuːnjən] REL
communion *f*
com·mu·ni·qué [kə'mjuːnɪkeɪ] communiqué *m*
Com·mu·nism ['kɑːmjʊnɪzəm] communisme *m*
Com·mu·nist ['kɑːmjʊnɪst] **1** *adj* communiste **2** *n* communiste *m/f*
com·mu·ni·ty [kə'mjuːnətɪ] communauté *f*
com·mu·ni·ty cen·ter, Br **com·mu·ni·ty cen·tre** centre *m* social
com·mu·ni·ty serv·ice travail *m* d'intérêt général
com·mute [kə'mjuːt] **1** *v/i* faire la navette (pour aller travailler) **2** *v/t* LAW commuer
com·mut·er [kə'mjuːtər] banlieusard *m*
com·mut·er traf·fic circulation *f* aux heures de pointe
com·mut·er train train *m* de banlieue
com·pact 1 *adj* [kəm'pækt] compact **2** *n* ['kɑːmpækt] *for face powder* poudrier *m*; MOT petite voiture *f*
com·pact 'disc → **CD**
com·pan·ion [kəm'pænjən] compagnon *m*
com·pan·ion·ship [kəm'pænjənʃɪp] compagnie *f*
com·pa·ny ['kʌmpənɪ] COMM société *f*; *ballet* troupe *f*; (*companionship*) compagnie *f*; (*guests*) invités *mpl*; **keep s.o. ~** tenir compagnie à qn
com·pa·ny 'car voiture *f* de fonction
com·pa·ny 'law droit *m* des entreprises
com·pa·ra·ble ['kɑːmpərəbl] *adj* comparable
com·par·a·tive [kəm'pærətɪv] **1** *adj* (*relative*) relatif*; *study*, GRAM comparatif **2** *n* GRAM comparatif *m*
com·par·a·tive·ly [kəm'pærətɪvlɪ] *adv* comparativement
com·pare [kəm'per] **1** *v/t* comparer; **~ X with Y** comparer X à *or* avec Y; **~d with ...** par rapport à ... **2** *v/i* soutenir la comparaison

com·pa·ri·son [kəm'pærɪsn] comparaison *f*; **there's no ~** ce n'est pas comparable
com·part·ment [kəm'pɑːrtmənt] compartiment *m*
com·pass ['kʌmpəs] compas *m*
com·pas·sion [kəm'pæʃn] compassion *f*
com·pas·sion·ate [kəm'pæʃənət] *adj* compatissant
com·pas·sion·ate 'leave congé *m* exceptionnel (pour cas de force majeure)
com·pat·i·bil·i·ty [kəmpætə'bɪlɪtɪ] compatibilité *f*
com·pat·i·ble [kəm'pætəbl] *adj* compatible; **we're not ~** nous ne nous entendons pas
com·pel [kəm'pel] *v/t* (*pret & pp* **-led**) obliger
com·pel·ling [kəm'pelɪŋ] *adj argument* irréfutable; *reason* impératif*; *movie, book* captivant
com·pen·sate ['kɑːmpənseɪt] **1** *v/t with money* dédommager **2** *v/i*: **~ for** compenser
com·pen·sa·tion [kɑːmpən'seɪʃn] (*money*) dédommagement *m*; (*reward*) compensation *f*; (*comfort*) consolation *f*
com·pete [kəm'piːt] *v/i* être en compétition; (*take part*) participer (*in* à); **~ for sth** se disputer qch
com·pe·tence ['kɑːmpɪtəns] compétence *f*; **her ~ as an accountant** ses compétences de comptable
com·pe·tent ['kɑːmpɪtənt] *adj person* compétent, capable; *piece of work* (très) satisfaisant; **I'm not ~ to judge** je ne suis pas apte à juger
com·pe·tent·ly ['kɑːmpɪtəntlɪ] *adv* de façon compétente
com·pe·ti·tion [kɑːmpə'tɪʃn] (*contest*) concours *m*; SP compétition *f*; (*competing, competitors*) concurrence *f*; **they want to encourage ~** on veut encourager la concurrence
com·pet·i·tive [kəm'petɪtɪv] *adj* compétitif*; *price, offer also* concurrentiel*
com·pet·i·tive·ly [kəm'petɪtɪvlɪ] *adv*

de façon compétitive; **~ priced** à prix compétitif

com·pet·i·tive·ness COMM compétitivité *f*; *of person* esprit *m* de compétition

com·pet·i·tor [kəm'petɪtər] *in contest*, COMM concurrent *m*

com·pile [kəm'paɪl] *v/t anthology* compiler; *dictionary, list* rédiger

com·pla·cen·cy [kəm'pleɪsənsɪ] complaisance *f*

com·pla·cent [kəm'pleɪsənt] *adj* complaisant, suffisant

com·plain [kəm'pleɪn] *v/i* se plaindre; *to shop, manager also* faire une réclamation; **~ of** MED se plaindre de

com·plaint [kəm'pleɪnt] plainte *f*; *in shop* réclamation *f*; MED maladie *f*

com·ple·ment ['kɑːmplɪmənt] 1 *v/t* compléter; *of food* accompagner; **they ~ each other** ils se complètent 2 *n* complément *m*

com·ple·men·ta·ry [kɑːmplɪ'mentərɪ] *adj* complémentaire

com·plete [kəm'pliːt] 1 *adj* complet*; *(finished)* terminé 2 *v/t task, building etc* terminer, achever; *form* remplir

com·plete·ly [kəm'pliːtlɪ] *adv* complètement

com·ple·tion [kəm'pliːʃn] achèvement *m*

com·plex ['kɑːmpleks] 1 *adj* complexe 2 *n building*, PSYCH complexe *m*

com·plex·ion [kəm'plekʃn] *facial* teint *m*

com·plex·i·ty [kəm'pleksɪtɪ] complexité *f*

com·pli·ance [kəm'plaɪəns] conformité *f*, respect *m*

com·pli·cate ['kɑːmplɪkeɪt] *v/t* compliquer

com·pli·cat·ed ['kɑːmplɪkeɪtɪd] *adj* compliqué

com·pli·ca·tion [kɑːmplɪ'keɪʃn] complication *f*

com·pli·ment ['kɑːmplɪmənt] 1 *n* compliment *m* 2 *v/t* complimenter (**on** sur)

com·pli·men·ta·ry [kɑːmplɪ'mentərɪ] *adj* élogieux*, flatteur*; *(free)* gratuit

com·pli·ments slip ['kɑːmplɪmənts]

carte *f* avec les compliments de l'expéditeur

com·ply [kəm'plaɪ] *v/i* (*pret & pp* **-ied**) obéir; **~ with ...** se conformer à

com·po·nent [kəm'poʊnənt] composant *m*

com·pose [kəm'poʊz] *v/t* composer; **be ~d of** se composer de, être composé de; **~ o.s.** se calmer

com·posed [kəm'poʊzd] *adj* (*calm*) calme

com·pos·er [kəm'poʊzər] MUS compositeur *m*

com·po·si·tion [kɑːmpə'zɪʃn] composition *f*

com·po·sure [kəm'poʊʒər] calme *m*, sang-froid *m*

com·pound ['kɑːmpaʊnd] *n chemical* composé *m*

'com·pound in·ter·est intérêts *mpl* composés

com·pre·hend [kɑːmprɪ'hend] *v/t* (*understand*) comprendre

com·pre·hen·sion [kɑːmprɪ'henʃn] compréhension *f*

com·pre·hen·sive [kɑːmprɪ'hensɪv] *adj* complet*

com·pre·hen·sive in·sur·ance assurance *f* tous risques

com·pre·hen·sive·ly [kɑːmprɪ'hensɪvlɪ] *adv* de façon complète; *beaten* à plates coutures

com·press ['kɑːmpres] 1 *n* MED compresse *f* 2 *v/t* [kəm'pres] *air, gas* comprimer; *information* condenser

com·prise [kəm'praɪz] *v/t* comprendre, être composé de; (*make up*) constituer; **be ~d of** se composer de

com·pro·mise ['kɑːmprəmaɪz] 1 *n* compromis *m* 2 *v/i* trouver un compromis 3 *v/t* compromettre; **~ o.s.** se compromettre

com·pul·sion [kəm'pʌlʃn] PSYCH compulsion *f*

com·pul·sive [kəm'pʌlsɪv] *adj behavior* compulsif*; *reading* captivant

com·pul·so·ry [kəm'pʌlsərɪ] *adj* obligatoire; **~ ed·u·ca·tion** scolarité *f* obligatoire

com·put·er [kəm'pjuːtər] ordinateur *m*; **have sth on ~** avoir qch sur ordinateur

com·put·er-aid·ed de'sign conception *f* assistée par ordinateur; **comput·er-aid·ed man·u'fac·ture** production *f* assistée par ordinateur; **com·put·er-con'trolled** *adj* contrôlé par ordinateur; **com'put·er game** jeu *m* informatique; **play ~s** jouer à la console

com·put·er·ize [kəm'pjuːtəraɪz] *v/t* informatiser

com·put·er 'lit·er·ate *adj* qui a des connaissances en informatique; **com·put·er 'sci·ence** informatique *f*; **com·put·er 'sci·en·tist** informaticien(ne) *m(f)*

com·put·ing [kəm'pjuːtɪŋ] informatique *f*

com·rade ['kɑːmreɪd] camarade *m/f*

com·rade·ship ['kɑːmreɪdʃɪp] camaraderie *f*

con [kɑːn] **1** *n* F arnaque *f* F **2** *v/t* (*pret & pp -ned*) F arnaquer F; **he conned her out of her money** il lui a volé son argent

con·ceal [kən'siːl] *v/t* cacher, dissimuler

con·ceal·ment [kən'siːlmənt] dissimulation *f*; **live in ~** vivre caché

con·cede [kən'siːd] *v/t* (*admit*), *goal* concéder

con·ceit [kən'siːt] vanité *f*

con·ceit·ed [kən'siːtɪd] *adj* vaniteux*, prétentieux*

con·cei·va·ble [kən'siːvəbl] *adj* concevable

con·ceive [kən'siːv] *v/i of woman* concevoir; **~ of** (*imagine*) concevoir, imaginer

con·cen·trate ['kɑːnsəntreɪt] **1** *v/i* se concentrer **2** *v/t attention, energies* concentrer

con·cen·trat·ed ['kɑːnsəntreɪtɪd] *adj juice etc* concentré

con·cen·tra·tion [kɑːnsən'treɪʃn] concentration *f*

con·cept ['kɑːnsept] concept *m*

con·cep·tion [kən'sepʃn] *of child* conception *f*

con·cern [kən'sɜːrn] **1** *n* (*anxiety, care*) inquiétude *f*, souci *m*; (*intent, aim*)

préoccupation *f*; (*business*) affaire *f*; (*company*) entreprise *f*; **it's no ~ of yours** cela ne vous regarde pas **2** *v/t* (*involve*) concerner; (*worry*) inquiéter, préoccuper; **~ o.s. with** s'occuper de qch

con·cerned [kən'sɜːrnd] *adj* (*anxious*) inquiet*; (*caring, involved*) concerné; **as far as I'm ~** en ce qui me concerne

con·cern·ing [kən'sɜːrnɪŋ] *prep* concernant, au sujet de

con·cert ['kɑːnsərt] concert *m*

con·cert·ed [kən'sɜːrtɪd] *adj* (*joint*) concerté

'con·cert·mas·ter premier violon *m*

con·cer·to [kən'tʃertoʊ] concerto *m*

con·ces·sion [kən'seʃn] (*compromise*) concession *f*

con·cil·i·a·to·ry [kənsɪlɪ'eɪtərɪ] *adj* conciliant

con·cise [kən'saɪs] *adj* concis

con·clude [kən'kluːd] **1** *v/t* conclure; **~ sth from sth** déduire qch de qch **2** *v/i* conclure

con·clu·sion [kən'kluːʒn] conclusion *f*; **in ~** pour conclure

con·clu·sive [kən'kluːsɪv] *adj* concluant

con·coct [kən'kɑːkt] *v/t meal, drink* préparer, concocter; *excuse, story* inventer

con·coc·tion [kən'kɑːkʃn] (*food, drink*) mixture *f*

con·crete ['kɑːnkriːt] **1** *n* béton *m* **2** *adj* concret*

con·cur [kən'kɜːr] *v/i* (*pret & pp -red*) être d'accord

con·cus·sion [kən'kʌʃn] commotion *f* cérébrale

con·demn [kən'dem] *v/t* condamner

con·dem·na·tion [kɑːndəm'neɪʃn] *of action* condamnation *f*

con·den·sa·tion [kɑːnden'seɪʃn] *on walls, windows* condensation *f*

con·dense [kən'dens] **1** *v/t* (*make shorter*) condenser **2** *v/i of steam* se condenser

con·densed milk [kən'densd] lait *m* concentré

con·de·scend [kɑːndɪ'send] *v/i* daigner (*to do* faire); **he ~ed to speak**

to me il a daigné me parler

con·de·scend·ing [kɑːndɪ'sendɪŋ] *adj* (*patronizing*) condescendant

con·di·tion [kən'dɪʃn] **1** *n* (*state*) condition *f*, état *m*; (*requirement, term*) condition *f*; MED maladie *f*; **~s** (*circumstances*) conditions *fpl*; **on ~ that ...** à condition que ... **2** *v/t* PSYCH conditionner

con·di·tion·al [kən'dɪʃnl] **1** *adj acceptance* conditionnel* **2** *n* GRAM conditionnel *m*

con·di·tion·er [kən'dɪʃnər] *for hair* après-shampoing *m*; *for fabric* adoucissant *m*

con·di·tion·ing [kən'dɪʃnɪŋ] PSYCH conditionnement *m*

con·do ['kɑːndoʊ] F *building* immeuble *m* (en copropriété); *apartment* appart *m* F

con·do·len·ces [kən'doʊlənsɪz] *npl* condoléances *fpl*

con·dom ['kɑːndəm] préservatif *m*

con·do·min·i·um [kɑːndə'mɪniəm] → **condo**

con·done [kən'doʊn] *v/t actions* excuser

con·du·cive [kən'duːsɪv] *adj*: **~ to** favorable à

con·duct ['kɑːndʌkt] **1** *n* (*behavior*) conduite *f* **2** *v/t* [kən'dʌkt] (*carry out*) mener; ELEC conduire; MUS diriger; **~ o.s.** se conduire

con·duct·ed tour [kəndʌktɪd'tʊr] visite *f* guidée

con·duc·tor [kən'dʌktər] MUS chef *m* d'orchestre; *on train* chef *m* de train; PHYS conducteur *m*

cone [koʊn] *figure* cône *m*; *for ice cream* cornet *m*; *of pine tree* pomme *f* de pin; *on highway* cône *m* de signalisation

con·fec·tion·er [kən'fekʃənər] confiseur *m*

con·fec·tion·ers' 'sug·ar sucre *m* glace

con·fec·tion·e·ry [kən'fekʃəneri] (*candy*) confiserie *f*

con·fed·e·ra·tion [kənfedə'reɪʃn] confédération *f*

con·fer [kən'fɜːr] **1** *v/t* (*bestow*) confé-

rer (**on** à) **2** *v/i* (*pret & pp* **-red**) (*discuss*) s'entretenir

con·fe·rence ['kɑːnfərəns] conférence *f*; *discussion* réunion *f*

'con·fe·rence room salle *f* de conférences

con·fess [kən'fes] **1** *v/t* confesser, avouer; REL confesser; *I ~ I don't know* j'avoue que je ne sais pas **2** *v/i also to police* avouer; REL se confesser; **~ to a weakness for sth** avouer avoir un faible pour qch

con·fes·sion [kən'feʃn] confession *f*, aveu *m*; REL confession *f*

con·fes·sion·al [kən'feʃnl] REL confessionnal *m*

con·fes·sor [kən'fesər] REL confesseur *m*

con·fide [kən'faɪd] **1** *v/t* confier **2** *v/i*: **~ in s.o.** (*trust*) faire confiance à qn; (*tell secrets*) se confier à qn

con·fi·dence ['kɑːnfɪdəns] (*assurance*) assurance *f*, confiance *f* en soi; (*trust*) confiance *f*; (*secret*) confidence *f*; **in ~** confidentiellement

con·fi·dent ['kɑːnfɪdənt] *adj* (*self-assured*) sûr de soi; (*convinced*) confiant

con·fi·den·tial [kɑːnfɪ'denʃl] *adj* confidentiel*; *adviser, secretary* particulier*

con·fi·den·tial·ly [kɑːnfɪ'denʃlɪ] *adv* confidentiellement

con·fi·dent·ly ['kɑːnfɪdəntlɪ] *adv* avec assurance

con·fine [kən'faɪn] *v/t* (*imprison*) enfermer; *in institution* interner; (*restrict*) limiter; **be ~d to one's bed** être alité

con·fined [kən'faɪnd] *adj space* restreint

con·fine·ment [kən'faɪnmənt] (*imprisonment*) emprisonnement *m*; *in institution* internement *m*; MED accouchement *m*

con·firm [kən'fɜːrm] *v/t* confirmer

con·fir·ma·tion [kɑːnfər'meɪʃn] confirmation *f*

con·firmed [kən'fɜːrmd] *adj* (*inveterate*) convaincu; **a ~ bachelor** un célibataire endurci

con·fis·cate ['kɑːnfɪskeɪt] *v/t* confisquer

con·flict ['kɑːnflɪkt] **1** n (disagreement) conflit m **2** v/i [kən'flɪkt] (clash) s'opposer, être en conflit; of dates coïncider

con·form [kən'fɔːrm] v/i se conformer; of product être conforme (**to** à)

con·form·ist [kən'fɔːrmɪst] n conformiste m/f

con·front [kən'frʌnt] v/t (face) affronter; (tackle) confronter

con·fron·ta·tion [kɑːnfrən'teɪʃn] confrontation f; (clash, dispute) affrontement m

con·fuse [kən'fjuːz] v/t (muddle) compliquer; person embrouiller; (mix up) confondre; **~ s.o. with s.o.** confondre qn avec qn

con·fused [kən'fjuːzd] adj person perdu, désorienté; ideas, situation confus

con·fus·ing [kən'fjuːzɪŋ] adj déroutant

con·fu·sion [kən'fjuːʒn] (muddle, chaos) confusion f

con·geal [kən'dʒiːl] v/i of blood se coaguler; of fat se figer

con·gen·ial [kən'dʒiːnɪəl] adj (pleasant) agréable, sympathique

con·gen·i·tal [kən'dʒenɪtl] adj MED congénital

con·gest·ed [kən'dʒestɪd] adj roads encombré

con·ges·tion [kən'dʒestʃn] on roads encombrement m; in chest congestion f; **traffic ~** embouteillage m

con·grat·u·late [kən'grætʊleɪt] v/t féliciter (**on** pour)

con·grat·u·la·tions [kəngrætʊ'leɪʃnz] npl félicitations fpl; **~ on ...** félicitations pour ...

con·grat·u·la·to·ry [kəngrætʊ'leɪtərɪ] adj de félicitations

con·gre·gate ['kɑːngrɪgeɪt] v/i (gather) se rassembler

con·gre·ga·tion [kɑːngrɪ'geɪʃn] people in a church assemblée f

con·gress ['kɑːngres] (conference) congrès m; **Congress** in US le Congrès

Con·gres·sion·al [kən'greʃnl] adj du Congrès

Con·gress·man ['kɑːngresmən] membre m du Congrès

'Con·gress·wom·an membre m du Congrès

co·ni·fer ['kɑːnɪfər] conifère m

con·jec·ture [kən'dʒektʃər] n (speculation) conjecture f, hypothèse f

con·ju·gate ['kɑːndʒʊgeɪt] v/t GRAM conjuguer

con·junc·tion [kən'dʒʌŋkʃn] GRAM conjonction f; **in ~ with** conjointement avec

con·junc·ti·vi·tis [kəndʒʌŋktɪ'vaɪtɪs] conjonctivite f

♦ **con·jure up** ['kʌndʒər] v/t (produce) faire apparaître (comme par magie); (evoke) évoquer

con·jur·er, con·jur·or ['kʌndʒərər] (magician) prestidigitateur m

con·jur·ing tricks ['kʌndʒərɪŋ] npl tours mpl de prestidigitation

con man ['kɑːnmæn] F escroc m, arnaqueur m F

con·nect [kə'nekt] v/t (join) raccorder, relier; TELEC passer; (link) associer; to power supply brancher; **I'll ~ you with ...** TELEC je vous passe ...; **the two events are not ~ed** il n'y a aucun rapport entre les deux événements

con·nect·ed [kə'nektɪd] adj: **be well-~** avoir des relations; **be ~ with** être lié à; in family être apparenté à

con·nect·ing flight [kə'nektɪŋ] (vol m de) correspondance f

con·nec·tion [kə'nekʃn] in wiring branchement m, connexion f; causal etc rapport m; when traveling correspondance f; (personal contact) relation f; **in ~ with** à propos de

con·nois·seur [kɑːnə's3ːr] connaisseur m, connaisseuse f

con·quer ['kɑːŋkər] v/t conquérir; fig: fear etc vaincre

con·quer·or ['kɑːŋkərər] conquérant m

con·quest ['kɑːŋkwest] conquête f

con·science ['kɑːnʃəns] conscience f; **have a guilty ~** avoir mauvaise conscience; **have sth on one's ~** avoir qch sur la conscience

con·sci·en·tious [kɑːnʃɪˈenʃəs] *adj* consciencieux*

con·sci·en·tious·ness [kɑːnʃɪˈenʃəsnəs] conscience *f*

con·sci·en·tious ob'jec·tor objecteur *m* de conscience

con·scious [ˈkɑːnʃəs] *adj* (*aware*), MED conscient; (*deliberate*) délibéré; **be ~ of ...** être conscient de ...; **be·come ~ of ...** se rendre compte de ...

con·scious·ly [ˈkɑːnʃəslɪ] *adv* (*knowingly*) consciemment; (*deliberately*) délibérément

con·scious·ness [ˈkɑːnʃəsnɪs] conscience *f*; **lose / regain ~** perdre / reprendre connaissance

con·sec·u·tive [kənˈsekjʊtɪv] *adj* consécutif*

con·sen·sus [kənˈsensəs] consensus *m*

con·sent [kənˈsent] **1** *n* consentement *m*, accord *m* **2** *v/i* consentir (**to** à); **~ to do sth** consentir à faire qch, accepter de faire qch

con·se·quence [ˈkɑːnsɪkwəns] (*result*) conséquence *f*

con·se·quent·ly [ˈkɑːnsɪkwəntlɪ] *adv* (*therefore*) par conséquent

con·ser·va·tion [kɑːnsərˈveɪʃn] (*preservation*) protection *f*

con·ser·va·tion·ist [kɑːnsərˈveɪʃnɪst] écologiste *m/f*

con·ser·va·tive [kənˈsɜːrvətɪv] **1** *adj* (*conventional*) conservateur*, conventionnel*; *clothes* classique; *estimate* prudent; **Conservative** *Br* POL conservateur* **2** *n Br* POL: **~ Conservative** conservateur(-trice) *m(f)*

con·ser·va·to·ry [kənˈsɜːrvətɔːrɪ] *for plants* véranda *f*, serre *f*; MUS conservatoire *m*

con·serve [ˈkɑːnsɜːrv] **1** *n* (*jam*) confiture *f* **2** *v/t* [kənˈsɜːrv] *energy* économiser; *strength* ménager

con·sid·er [kənˈsɪdər] *v/t* (*regard*) considérer; (*show regard for*) prendre en compte; (*think about*) penser à; **~ yourself lucky** estime-toi heureux; **it is ~ed to be ...** c'est censé être ...

con·sid·e·ra·ble [kənˈsɪdrəbl] *adj* considérable

con·sid·e·ra·bly [kənˈsɪdrəblɪ] *adv* considérablement, beaucoup

con·sid·er·ate [kənˈsɪdərət] *adj* attentionné

con·sid·er·ate·ly [kənˈsɪdərətlɪ] *adv* gentiment

con·sid·e·ra·tion [kənsɪdəˈreɪʃn] (*thought*) réflexion *f*; (*factor*) facteur *m*; (*thoughtfulness, concern*) attention *f*; **under ~** à l'étude; **take sth into ~** prendre qch en considération

con·sign·ment [kənˈsaɪnmənt] COMM cargaison *f*

♦ **con·sist of** [kənˈsɪst] *v/t* consister en, se composer de

con·sis·ten·cy [kənˈsɪstənsɪ] (*texture*) consistance *f*; (*unchangingness*) constance *f*; (*logic*) cohérence *f*

con·sis·tent [kənˈsɪstənt] *adj* (*unchanging*) constant; *logically etc* cohérent

con·sis·tent·ly [kənˈsɪstəntlɪ] *adv* constamment, invariablement; *logically etc* de façon cohérente

con·so·la·tion [kɑːnsəˈleɪʃn] consolation *f*

con·sole [kənˈsoul] *v/t* consoler

con·sol·i·date [kənˈsɑːlɪdeɪt] *v/t* consolider

con·so·nant [ˈkɑːnsənənt] *n* GRAM consonne *f*

con·sor·ti·um [kənˈsɔːrtɪəm] consortium *m*

con·spic·u·ous [kənˈspɪkjʊəs] *adj* voyant; **look ~** se faire remarquer

con·spi·ra·cy [kənˈspɪrəsɪ] conspiration *f*, complot *m*

con·spi·ra·tor [kənˈspɪrətər] conspirateur(-trice) *m(f)*

con·spire [kənˈspaɪr] *v/i* conspirer, comploter

con·stant [ˈkɑːnstənt] *adj* (*continuous*) constant, continuel*

con·stant·ly [ˈkɑːnstəntlɪ] *adv* constamment, continuellement

con·ster·na·tion [kɑːnstərˈneɪʃn] consternation *f*

con·sti·pat·ed [ˈkɑːnstɪpeɪtɪd] *adj* constipé

con·sti·pa·tion [kɑːnstɪˈpeɪʃn] constipation *f*

con·sti·tu·en·cy [kən'stɪtʊənsɪ] *Br* POL circonscription *f* (électorale)

con·sti·tu·ent [kən'stɪtʊənt] *n* (*component*) composant *m*; *Br* POL électeur *m* (*d'une circonscription*)

con·sti·tute ['kɑːnstɪtuːt] *v/t* constituer

con·sti·tu·tion [kɑːnstɪ'tuːʃn] POL, *of person* constitution *f*

con·sti·tu·tion·al [kɑːnstɪ'tuːʃnl] *adj* POL constitutionnel*

con·straint [kən'streɪnt] (*restriction*) contrainte *f*

con·struct [kən'strʌkt] *v/t building etc* construire

con·struc·tion [kən'strʌkʃn] construction *f*; (*trade*) bâtiment *m*; *under* ~ en construction

con·struc·tion in·dus·try industrie *f* du bâtiment; **con'struc·tion site** chantier *m* (de construction); **con'struc·tion work·er** ouvrier *m* du bâtiment

con·struc·tive [kən'strʌktɪv] *adj* constructif*

con·sul ['kɑːnsl] consul *m*

con·su·late ['kɑːnsʊlət] consulat *m*

con·sult [kən'sʌlt] *v/t* (*seek the advice of*) consulter

con·sul·tan·cy [kən'sʌltənsɪ] *company* cabinet-conseil *m*; (*advice*) conseil

con·sul·tant [kən'sʌltənt] *n* (*adviser*) consultant *m*

con·sul·ta·tion [kɑːnsl'teɪʃn] consultation *f*

con·sume [kən'suːm] *v/t* consommer

con·sum·er [kən'suːmər] consommateur *m*

con·sum·er con·fi·dence confiance *f* des consommateurs; **con'sum·er goods** *npl* biens *mpl* de consommation; **con'sum·er so·ci·e·ty** société *f* de consommation

con·sump·tion [kən'sʌmpʃn] consommation *f*

con·tact ['kɑːntækt] **1** *n* contact *m*; *person also* relation *f*; *keep in* ~ *with s.o.* rester en contact avec qn **2** *v/t* contacter

'con·tact lens lentille *f* de contact

'con·tact num·ber numéro *m* de téléphone

con·ta·gious [kən'teɪdʒəs] *adj* contagieux*; *fig also* communicatif*

con·tain [kən'teɪn] *v/t* (*hold*), *also laughter etc* contenir; ~ *o.s.* se contenir

con·tain·er [kən'teɪnər] récipient *m*; COMM conteneur *m*, conteneur *m*

con'tain·er ship porte-conteneurs *m inv*

con'tain·er ter·min·al terminal *m* (de conteneurs)

con·tam·i·nate [kən'tæmɪneɪt] *v/t* contaminer

con·tam·i·na·tion [kəntæmɪ'neɪʃn] contamination *f*

con·tem·plate ['kɑːntəmpleɪt] *v/t* (*look at*) contempler; (*think about*) envisager

con·tem·po·ra·ry [kən'tempərerɪ] **1** *adj* contemporain **2** *n* contemporain *m*; *I was a* ~ *of his at university* il était à l'université en même temps que moi

con·tempt [kən'tempt] mépris *m*; *be beneath* ~ être tout ce qu'il y a de plus méprisable

con·temp·ti·ble [kən'temptəbl] *adj* méprisable

con·temp·tu·ous [kən'temptʊəs] *adj* méprisant

con·tend [kən'tend] *v/i*: ~ *for ...* se disputer ...; ~ *with ...* affronter

con·tend·er [kən'tendər] *in sport* prétendant *m*; *in competition* concurrent *m*; POL candidat *m*

con·tent[1] ['kɑːntent] *n* contenu *m*

con·tent[2] [kən'tent] **1** *adj* content, satisfait **2** *v/t*: ~ *o.s. with ...* se contenter de ...

con·tent·ed [kən'tentɪd] *adj* satisfait

con·ten·tion [kən'tenʃn] (*assertion*) affirmation *f*; *be in* ~ *for ...* être en compétition pour ...

con·ten·tious [kən'tenʃəs] *adj* controversé

con·tent·ment [kən'tentmənt] contentement *m*

con·tents ['kɑːntents] *npl of house, letter, bag etc* contenu *m*

con·test[1] ['kɑːntest] n (*competition*) concours m; *in sport* compétition f; (*struggle for power*) lutte f

con·test[2] [kən'test] v/t *leadership etc* disputer; (*oppose*) contester; **~ an election** se présenter à une élection

con·tes·tant [kən'testənt] concurrent m

con·text ['kɑːntekst] contexte m; **look at sth in ~ / out of ~** regarder qch dans son contexte / hors contexte

con·ti·nent ['kɑːntɪnənt] n continent m; **the ~** Br l'Europe f continentale

con·ti·nen·tal [kɑːntɪ'nentl] adj continental

con·ti·nen·tal 'break·fast Br petit-déjeuner m continental

con·tin·gen·cy [kən'tɪndʒənsɪ] éventualité f

con'tin·gen·cy plan plan m d'urgence

con·tin·u·al [kən'tɪnʊəl] adj continuel*

con·tin·u·al·ly [kən'tɪnʊəlɪ] adv continuellement

con·tin·u·a·tion [kəntɪnʊ'eɪʃn] continuation f; *of story, book* suite f

con·tin·ue [kən'tɪnjuː] 1 v/t continuer; **~ to do sth, ~ doing sth** continuer à faire qch; **to be ~d** à suivre 2 v/i continuer

con·ti·nu·i·ty [kɑːntɪ'nuːətɪ] continuité f

con·tin·u·ous [kən'tɪnjuːəs] adj continu, continuel*

con·tin·u·ous·ly [kən'tɪnjuːəslɪ] adv continuellement, sans interruption

con·tort [kən'tɔːrt] v/t *face* tordre; **~ one's body** se contorsionner

con·tour ['kɑːntʊr] contour m

con·tra·cep·tion [kɑːntrə'sepʃn] contraception f

con·tra·cep·tive [kɑːntrə'septɪv] n contraceptif m

con·tract[1] ['kɑːntrækt] n contrat m

con·tract[2] [kən'trækt] 1 v/i (*shrink*) se contracter 2 v/t *illness* contracter

con·trac·tor [kən'træktər] entrepreneur m

con·trac·tu·al [kən'træktʊəl] adj contractuel*

con·tra·dict [kɑːntrə'dɪkt] v/t contredire

con·tra·dic·tion [kɑːntrə'dɪkʃn] contradiction f

con·tra·dic·to·ry [kɑːntrə'dɪktərɪ] adj *account* contradictoire

con·trap·tion [kən'træpʃn] F truc m F, machin m F

con·tra·ry[1] ['kɑːntrərɪ] 1 adj contraire; **~ to ...** contrairement à ... 2 n : **on the ~** au contraire

con·tra·ry[2] [kən'trerɪ] adj (*perverse*) contrariant

con·trast ['kɑːntræst] 1 n contraste m 2 v/t [kən'træst] mettre en contraste 3 v/i opposer, contraster

con·trast·ing [kən'træstɪŋ] adj contrastant; *personalities, views* opposé

con·tra·vene [kɑːntrə'viːn] v/t enfreindre

con·trib·ute [kən'trɪbjuːt] 1 v/i *with money, material* contribuer (**to** à); *to magazine, paper* collaborer (**to** à) 2 v/t *money, suggestion* donner, apporter

con·tri·bu·tion [kɑːntrɪ'bjuːʃn] *money, to debate* contribution f, participation f; *to political party, church* don m; *to magazine* article m; poème m

con·trib·u·tor [kən'trɪbjʊtər] *of money* donateur m; *to magazine* collaborateur(-trice) m(f)

con·trive [kən'traɪv] v/t : **~ to do sth** réussir à faire qch

con·trol [kən'troʊl] 1 n contrôle m; **lose ~ of ...** perdre le contrôle de ...; **lose ~ of o.s.** perdre son sang-froid; *circumstances beyond our* **~** circonstances fpl indépendantes de notre volonté; **be in ~ of sth** contrôler qch; **get out of ~** devenir incontrôlable; **the situation is under ~** nous avons la situation bien en main; **bring a blaze under ~** maîtriser un incendie; **~s** *of aircraft, vehicle* commandes fpl; (*restrictions*) contrôle m 2 v/t contrôler; *company* diriger; **~ o.s.** se contrôler

con'trol cen·ter, Br **con'trol cen·tre**

centre *m* de contrôle

con·trol freak F *personne qui veut tout contrôler*

con·trolled 'sub·stance [kən'trould] substance *f* illégale

con·trol·ling 'in·ter·est [kən'troulɪŋ] FIN participation *f* majoritaire

con·trol pan·el tableau *m* de contrôle

con·trol tow·er tour *f* de contrôle

con·tro·ver·sial [kɑːntrə'vɜːrʃl] *adj* controversé

con·tro·ver·sy ['kɑːntrəvɜːrsɪ] controverse *f*

con·va·lesce [kɑːnvə'les] *v/i* être en convalescence

con·va·les·cence [kɑːnvə'lesns] convalescence *f*

con·vene [kən'viːn] *v/t* convoquer, organiser

con·ve·ni·ence [kən'viːnɪəns] *of having sth, location* commodité *f*; **at your / my ~** à votre / ma convenance; **(with) all (modern) ~s** tout confort

con·ve·ni·ence food plats *mpl* cuisinés

con·ve·ni·ence store magasin *m* de proximité

con·ve·ni·ent [kən'viːnɪənt] *adj* commode, pratique

con·ve·ni·ent·ly [kən'viːnɪəntlɪ] *adv* de façon pratique; **~ located** bien situé

con·vent ['kɑːnvənt] couvent *m*

con·ven·tion [kən'venʃn] *(tradition)* conventions *fpl*; *(conference)* convention *f*, congrès *m*; **it's a ~ that ...** traditionnellement ...

con·ven·tion·al [kən'venʃnl] *adj* conventionnel*; *person* conformiste

con·ven·tion cen·ter palais *m* des congrès

con·ven·tion·eer [kənvenʃ'nɪr] congressiste *m/f*

♦ **con·verge on** [kən'vɜːrdʒ] *v/t* converger vers / sur

con·ver·sant [kən'vɜːrsənt] *adj*: **be ~ with sth** connaître qch, s'y connaître en qch

con·ver·sa·tion [kɑːnvər'seɪʃn] conversation *f*

con·ver·sa·tion·al [kɑːnvər'seɪʃnl] *adj* de conversation; **a course in ~ Japanese** un cours de conversation japonaise

con·verse ['kɑːnvɜːrs] *n (opposite)* contraire *m*, opposé *m*

con·verse·ly [kən'vɜːrslɪ] *adv* inversement

con·ver·sion [kən'vɜːrʃn] conversion *f*; *of building* aménagement *m*, transformation *f*

con·ver·sion ta·ble table *f* de conversion

con·vert 1 *n* ['kɑːnvɜːrt] converti *m* **2** *v/t* [kən'vɜːrt] convertir; *building* aménager, transformer **3** *v/i* [kən'vɜːrt]: **~ to** se convertir à

con·ver·ti·ble [kən'vɜːrtəbl] *n car (voiture f)* décapotable *f*

con·vey [kən'veɪ] *v/t (transmit)* transmettre, communiquer; *(carry)* transporter

con·vey·or belt [kən'veɪər] convoyeur *m*, tapis *m* roulant

con·vict 1 *n* ['kɑːnvɪkt] détenu *m* **2** *v/t* [kən'vɪkt] LAW déclarer coupable; **~ s.o. of sth** déclarer *or* reconnaître qn coupable de qch

con·vic·tion [kən'vɪkʃn] LAW condamnation *f*; *(belief)* conviction *f*

con·vince [kən'vɪns] *v/t* convaincre, persuader

con·vinc·ing [kən'vɪnsɪŋ] *adj* convaincant

con·viv·i·al [kən'vɪvɪəl] *adj (friendly)* convivial

con·voy ['kɑːnvɔɪ] *of ships, vehicles* convoi *m*

con·vul·sion [kən'vʌlʃn] MED convulsion *f*

cook [kʊk] **1** *n* cuisinier(-ière) *m(f)* **2** *v/t meal* préparer; *food* faire cuire; **a ~ed meal** un repas chaud; **~ the books** F truquer les comptes **3** *v/i* faire la cuisine, cuisiner; *of food* cuire

'cook·book livre *m* de cuisine

cook·e·ry ['kʊkərɪ] cuisine *f*

cook·ie ['kʊkɪ] cookie *m*; **she's a smart ~** F c'est une petite maline F

cook·ing ['kʊkɪŋ] *(food)* cuisine *f*

cool [kuːl] **1** *n* F: **keep one's ~** garder

son sang-froid; **lose one's ~** F perdre
son sang-froid **2** *adj weather, breeze,*
drink frais*; *dress* léger*; *(calm)*
calme; *(unfriendly)* froid **3** *v/i of food*
refroidir; *of tempers* se calmer; *of in-*
terest diminuer **4** *v/t* F: **~ it** on se
calme F

♦ **cool down 1** *v/i* refroidir; *of weather*
se rafraîchir; *fig: of tempers* se calmer
2 *v/t food (cool)* refroidir; *fig* calmer

cool·ing 'off pe·ri·od délai *m* de réflexion

co·op·e·rate [kouˈɑːpəreɪt] *v/i* coopérer, collaborer

co·op·e·ra·tion [kouɑːpəˈreɪʃn] coopération *f*

co·op·e·ra·tive [kouˈɑːpərətɪv] **1** *n*
COMM coopérative *f* **2** *adj* coopératif*

co·or·di·nate [kouˈɔːrdɪneɪt] *v/t* coordonner

co·or·di·na·tion [kouɔːrdɪˈneɪʃn] coordination *f*

cop [kɑːp] *n* F flic *m* F

cope [koup] *v/i* se débrouiller; **~ with**
... faire face à ...; *(deal with)* s'occuper de ...

cop·i·er [ˈkɑːpɪər] *machine* photocopieuse *f*

co·pi·lot [ˈkoupaɪlət] copilote *m*

co·pi·ous [ˈkoupɪəs] *adj* copieux*;
notes abondant

cop·per [ˈkɑːpər] *n metal* cuivre *m*

cop·y [ˈkɑːpɪ] **1** *n* copie *f*; *(duplicate,*
imitation also) reproduction *f*; *of*
key double *m*; *of book* exemplaire
m; **advertising ~** texte *m* publicitaire; **make a ~ of a file** COMPUT
faire une copie d'un fichier **2** *v/t (pret*
& pp **-ied)** copier; *(imitate also)* imiter; *(photocopy)* photocopier

'cop·y cat F copieur(-euse) *m(f)*;
cop·y·cat 'crime crime inspiré par
un autre; **'cop·y·right** *n* copyright
m, droit *m* d'auteur; **'cop·y·writ·er**
in advertising rédacteur(-trice) *m(f)*
publicitaire

cor·al [ˈkɑːrəl] corail *m*

cord [kɔːrd] *(string)* corde *f*; *(cable)* fil
m, cordon *m*

cor·di·al [ˈkɔːrdʒəl] *adj* cordial

cord·less phone [ˈkɔːrdlɪs] téléphone *m* sans fil

cor·don [ˈkɔːrdn] cordon *m*

♦ **cordon off** *v/t* boucler; *street* barrer

cords [kɔːrdz] *npl pants* pantalon *m* en
velours (côtelé)

cor·du·roy [ˈkɔːrdərɔɪ] velours *m* côtelé

core [kɔːr] **1** *n of fruit* trognon *m*, cœur
m; *of problem* cœur *m*; *of organiza-*
tion, party noyau *m* **2** *v/t fruit* évider
3 *adj issue, meaning* fondamental,
principal

cork [kɔːrk] *in bottle* bouchon *m*; *ma-*
terial liège *m*

'cork·screw *n* tire-bouchon *m*

corn [kɔːrn] *grain* maïs *m*

cor·ner [ˈkɔːrnər] **1** *n* coin *m*; *of room,*
street also angle *m*; *(bend: in road)* virage *m*, tournant *m*; *in soccer* corner
m; **in the ~** dans le coin; **on the ~** *of*
street au coin, à l'angle **2** *v/t person* coincer F; **~ the market** accaparer le
marché **3** *v/i of driver, car* prendre
le / les virage(s)

'cor·ner kick *in soccer* corner *m*

'corn·flakes *npl* corn-flakes *mpl*, pé-
tales *fpl* de maïs

'corn·starch fécule *f* de maïs, maïzena *f*

corn·y [ˈkɔːrnɪ] *adj* F *(trite)* éculé, banal *(à mourir)*; *(sentimental)* à l'eau
de rose

cor·o·na·ry [ˈkɑːrənerɪ] **1** *adj* coronaire **2** *n* infarctus *m* (du myocarde)

cor·o·ner [ˈkɑːrənər] coroner *m*

cor·po·ral [ˈkɔːrpərəl] *n* caporal *m*

cor·po·ral 'pun·ish·ment châtiment
m corporel

cor·po·rate [ˈkɔːrpərət] *adj* COMM
d'entreprise, des sociétés; **~ image**
image *f* de marque de l'entreprise

cor·po·ra·tion [kɔːrpəˈreɪʃn] *(busi-*
ness) société *f*, entreprise *f*

corps [kɔːr] corps *m*

corpse [kɔːrps] cadavre *m*, corps *m*

cor·pu·lent [ˈkɔːrpjulənt] *adj* corpulent

cor·pus·cle [ˈkɔːrpʌsl] globule *m*

cor·ral [kəˈræl] *n* corral *m*

cor·rect [kəˈrekt] **1** *adj* correct; **the ~**

answer la bonne réponse; *that's ~* c'est exact **2** *v/t* corriger

cor·rec·tion [kəˈrekʃn] correction *f*

cor·rect·ly [kəˈrektlɪ] *adv* correctement

cor·re·spond [kɑːrɪˈspɑːnd] *v/i* correspondre (*to* à)

cor·re·spon·dence [kɑːrɪˈspɑːndəns] correspondance *f*

cor·re·spon·dent [kɑːrɪˈspɑːndənt] correspondant(e) *m(f)*

cor·re·spon·ding [kɑːrɪˈspɑːndɪŋ] *adj* (*equivalent*) correspondant; *in the ~ period last year* à la même période l'année dernière

cor·ri·dor [ˈkɔːrɪdər] *in building* couloir *m*

cor·rob·o·rate [kəˈrɑːbəreɪt] *v/t* corroborer

cor·rode [kəˈroud] **1** *v/t* corroder **2** *v/i* se désagréger; *of battery* couler

cor·ro·sion [kəˈrouʒn] corrosion *f*

cor·ru·gat·ed card·board [ˈkɑːrəgeɪtɪd] carton *m* ondulé

cor·ru·gat·ed 'i·ron tôle *f* ondulée

cor·rupt [kəˈrʌpt] **1** *adj also* COMPUT corrompu; *morals, youth* dépravé **2** *v/t* corrompre

cor·rup·tion [kəˈrʌpʃn] corruption *f*

Cor·si·ca [ˈkɔːrsɪkə] Corse *f*

Cor·si·can [ˈkɔːrsɪkən] **1** *adj* corse **2** *n* Corse *m/f*

cos·met·ic [kɑːzˈmetɪk] *adj* cosmétique; *fig* esthétique

cos·met·ics [kɑːzˈmetɪks] *npl* cosmétiques *mpl*, produits *mpl* de beauté

cos·met·ic 'sur·geon chirurgien(ne) *m(f)* esthétique

cos·met·ic 'sur·ger·y chirurgie *f* esthétique

cos·mo·naut [ˈkɑːzmənɒːt] cosmonaute *m/f*

cos·mo·pol·i·tan [kɑːzməˈpɑːlɪtən] *adj city* cosmopolite

cost¹ [kɑːst] **1** *n also fig* coût *m*; *at all ~s* à tout prix; *to my ~* à mes dépens **2** *v/t* (*pret & pp cost*) coûter; *how much does it ~?* combien est-ce que cela coûte?, combien ça coûte?; *it ~ me my health* j'en ai perdu la santé; *it ~ him his life* cela lui a coûté

la vie

cost² [kɑːst] *v/t* (*pret & pp* **-ed**) FIN *proposal, project* évaluer le coût de

cost and 'freight COMM coût et fret; **'cost-con·scious** économe; **'cost-ef·fec·tive** *adj* rentable; **'cost, in·sur·ance and freight** COMM CAF, coût, assurance, fret

cost·ly [ˈkɑːstlɪ] *mistake* coûteux

cost of 'liv·ing coût *m* de la vie

'cost price prix *m* coûtant

cos·tume [ˈkɑːstuːm] *for actor* costume *m*

cos·tume 'jew·el·ry bijoux *mpl* fantaisie

cot [kɑːt] (*camp-bed*) lit *m* de camp; *Br. for child* lit *m* d'enfant

cot·tage [ˈkɑːtɪdʒ] cottage *m*

'cot·tage cheese cottage *m*

cot·ton [ˈkɑːtn] **1** *n* coton *m* **2** *adj* en coton

♦ **cotton on** *v/i* F piger F

♦ **cotton on to** *v/t* F piger F

♦ **cotton to** *v/t* F accrocher avec

cot·ton 'can·dy barbe *f* à papa

cot·ton 'wool *Br* coton *m* hydrophile, ouate *f*

couch [kautʃ] *n* canapé *m*

cou·chette [kuːˈʃet] couchette *f*

'couch po·ta·to F téléphage *m/f*

cough [kɑːf] **1** *n* toux *f* **2** *v/i* tousser

♦ **cough up 1** *v/t also money* cracher **2** *v/i* F (*pay*) banquer F

'cough med·i·cine, 'cough syr·up sirop *m* contre la toux

could [kʊd] *pret* → *can*; *~ I have my key?* pourrais-je avoir ma clef (s'il vous plaît)?; *~ you help me?* pourrais-tu m'aider?; *this ~ be our bus* ça pourrait être notre bus; *you ~ be right* vous avez peut-être raison; *he ~ have got lost* il s'est peut-être perdu; *you ~ have warned me!* tu aurais pu me prévenir!

coun·cil [ˈkaunsl] (*assembly*) conseil *m*, assemblée *f*

'coun·cil·man conseiller *m* municipal

coun·cil·or [ˈkaunslər] conseiller *m*

coun·sel [ˈkaunsl] **1** *n* (*advice*) conseil *m*; (*lawyer*) avocat *m* **2** *v/t* conseiller

coun·sel·ing [ˈkaunslɪŋ] aide *f* (psychologique)

coun·sel·or, *Br* **coun·sel·lor** ['kaʊnslər] (*adviser*) conseiller *m*; LAW maître *m*

count[1] [kaʊnt] **1** *n* compte *m*; **keep ~ of** compter; **lose ~ of** ne plus compter; **I've lost ~ of the number we've sold** je ne sais plus combien nous en avons vendu; **at the last ~** au dernier décompte **2** *v/i* (*also: matter*) compter; **that doesn't ~** ça ne compte pas **3** *v/t* compter

♦ **count on** *v/t* compter sur

count[2] [kaʊnt] *nobleman* comte *m*

'count·down compte *m* à rebours

coun·te·nance ['kaʊntənəns] *v/t* approuver

coun·ter[1] ['kaʊntər] *in shop, café* comptoir *m*; *in game* pion *m*

coun·ter[2] ['kaʊntər] **1** *v/t* contrer **2** *v/i* (*retaliate*) riposter, contre-attaquer

coun·ter[3] ['kaʊntər] *adv*: **run ~ to** aller à l'encontre de

'coun·ter·act *v/t* neutraliser, contrecarrer

'coun·ter·at·tack 1 *n* contre-attaque *f* **2** *v/i* contre-attaquer

'coun·ter·bal·ance 1 *n* contrepoids *m* **2** *v/t* contrebalancer, compenser

coun·ter'clock·wise *adv* dans le sens inverse des aiguilles d'une montre

coun·ter·es·pi·o·nage contre-espionnage *m*

coun·ter·feit ['kaʊntərfɪt] **1** *v/t* contrefaire **2** *adj* faux*

'coun·ter·part *person* homologue *m/f*

coun·ter·pro'duc·tive *adj* contre-productif*

'coun·ter·sign *v/t* contresigner

coun·tess ['kaʊntes] comtesse *f*

count·less ['kaʊntlɪs] *adj* innombrable

coun·try ['kʌntrɪ] *n* nation pays *m*; *as opposed to town* campagne *f*; **in the ~** à la campagne

coun·try and 'west·ern MUS (musique *f*) country *f*; **'coun·try·man** (*fellow ~*) compatriote *m*; **'coun·try·side** campagne *f*

coun·ty ['kaʊntɪ] comté *m*

coup [kuː] POL coup *m* d'État; *fig*

beau coup *m*

cou·ple ['kʌpl] *n* (*two people*) couple *m*; **just a ~** juste deux ou trois; **a ~ of** (*a pair*) deux; (*a few*) quelques

cou·pon ['kuːpɑːn] (*form*) coupon-réponse *m*; (*voucher*) bon *m* (de réduction)

cour·age ['kʌrɪdʒ] courage *m*

cou·ra·geous [kə'reɪdʒəs] *adj* courageux*

cou·ri·er ['kʊrɪər] (*messenger*) coursier *m*; *with tourist party* guide *m/f*

course [kɔːrs] *n* (*of lessons*) cours *m*(*pl*); (*part of meal*) plat *m*; *of ship, plane* route *f*; *for sports event* piste *f*; *for golf* terrain *m*; *of action* ligne *f* de conduite; **~ of treatment** traitement *m*; **in the ~ of ...** au cours de ...

court [kɔːrt] *n* LAW tribunal *m*, cour *f*; SP *for tennis* court *m*; *for basketball* terrain *m*; **take s.o. to ~** faire un procès à qn

'court case affaire *f*, procès *m*

cour·te·ous ['kɜːrtɪəs] *adj* courtois

cour·te·sy ['kɜːrtəsɪ] courtoisie *f*

'court·house palais *m* de justice, tribunal *m*; **court 'mar·tial 1** *n* cour *m* martiale **2** *v/t* faire passer en cour martiale; **'court or·der** ordonnance *f* du tribunal; **'court·room** salle *f* d'audience; **'court·yard** cour *f*

cous·in ['kʌzn] cousin(e) *m(f)*

cove [koʊv] (*small bay*) crique *f*

cov·er ['kʌvər] **1** *n* protective housse *f*; *of book, magazine, bed* couverture *f*; *for bed* couverture *f*; (*shelter*) abri *m*; (*insurance*) couverture *f*, assurance *f* **2** *v/t* couvrir

♦ **cover up 1** *v/t* couvrir; *crime, scandal* dissimuler **2** *v/i fig* cacher la vérité; **cover up for s.o.** couvrir qn

cov·er·age ['kʌvərɪdʒ] *by media* couverture *f* (médiatique)

cov·er·ing let·ter ['kʌvrɪŋ] lettre *f* d'accompagnement

cov·ert ['koʊvərt] *adj* secret*, clandestin

'cov·er-up black-out *m inv*; **there has been a police ~** la police a étouffé l'affaire

cow [kaʊ] vache *f*

cow·ard ['kaʊərd] lâche *m/f*

cow·ard·ice ['kaʊərdɪs] lâcheté *f*

cow·ard·ly ['kaʊərdlɪ] *adj* lâche

'**cow·boy** cow-boy *m*

cow·er ['kaʊər] *v/i* se recroqueviller

coy [kɔɪ] *adj* (*evasive*) évasif*; (*flirtatious*) coquin

co·zy ['kəʊzɪ] *adj* confortable, douillet*

CPU [siːpiːˈjuː] *abbr* (= **central pro·cessing unit**) CPU *m*, unité *f* centrale

crab [kræb] *n* crabe *m*

crack [kræk] **1** *n* fissure *f*; *in cup, glass* fêlure *f*; (*joke*) vanne *f* F, (*mauvaise*) blague *f* F **2** *v/t cup, glass* fêler; *nut* casser; (*solve*) résoudre; *code* décrypter; ~ *a joke* sortir une blague F **3** *v/i* se fêler; *get ~ing Br* F s'y mettre

♦ **crack down on** *v/t* sévir contre

♦ **crack up** *v/i* (*have breakdown*) craquer; F (*laugh*) exploser de rire F

crack·brained ['krækbreɪnd] *adj* F (*complètement*) dingue F

'**crack·down** mesures *fpl* de répression (**on** contre)

cracked [krækt] *adj cup, glass* fêlé; dingue F

crack·er ['krækər] *to eat* cracker *m*, biscuit *m* salé

crack·le ['krækl] *v/i of fire* crépiter

cra·dle ['kreɪdl] *n for baby* berceau *m*

craft[1] [kræft] NAUT embarcation *f*

craft[2] (*trade*) métier *m*; *weaving, pottery etc* artisanat *m*; (*craftsmanship*) art *m*; ~**s** *at school* travaux *mpl* manuels

crafts·man ['kræftsmən] (*artisan*) artisan *m*; (*artist*) artiste *m/f*

craft·y ['kræftɪ] *adj* malin*, rusé

crag [kræg] (*rock*) rocher *m* escarpé

cram [kræm] *v/t* fourrer F; *food* enfourner; *people* entasser

cramp [kræmp] *n* crampe *f*

cramped [kræmpt] *adj apartment* exigu*

cramps [kræmps] *npl* crampe *f*

cran·ber·ry ['krænberɪ] canneberge *f*

crane [kreɪn] **1** *n* (*machine*) grue *f* **2** *v/t*:

~ **one's neck** tendre le cou

crank [kræŋk] *n* (*strange person*) allumé *m*

'**crank·shaft** vilebrequin *m*

crank·y ['kræŋkɪ] *adj* (*bad-tempered*) grognon*

crash [kræʃ] **1** *n* (*noise*) fracas *m*, grand bruit *m*; *accident* accident *m*; COMM faillite *f*; *of stock exchange* krach *m*; COMPUT plantage *m* F **2** *v/i* s'écraser; *of car* avoir un accident; COMM: *of market* s'effondrer; COMPUT se planter F; (*sleep*) pioncer F; *the car ~ed into a wall* la voiture a percuté un mur **3** *v/t car* avoir un accident avec

♦ **crash out** *v/i* (*fall asleep*) pioncer F

'**crash bar·ri·er** glissière *f* de sécurité;

'**crash course** cours *m* intensif;

'**crash di·et** régime *m* intensif;

'**crash hel·met** casque *m*; '**crash-land** *v/i* atterrir en catastrophe;

'**crash land·ing** atterrissage *m* forcé

crate [kreɪt] (*packing case*) caisse; *for fruit* cageot *m*

cra·ter ['kreɪtər] *of volcano* cratère *m*

crave [kreɪv] *v/t* avoir très envie de; *this child ~s attention* cet enfant a grand besoin d'affection

crav·ing ['kreɪvɪŋ] envie *f* (irrépressible); *a ~ for attention* un (grand) besoin d'attention; *a ~ for fame* la soif de gloire

crawl [krɒːl] **1** *n in swimming* crawl *m*; *at a ~* (*very slowly*) au pas **2** *v/i on belly* ramper; *on hands and knees* marcher à quatre pattes; (*move slowly*) se traîner

♦ **crawl with** *v/t* grouiller de

cray·on ['kreɪɑːn] *n* crayon *m* de couleur

craze [kreɪz] engouement *m*; *the latest ~* la dernière mode

cra·zy ['kreɪzɪ] *adj* fou*; *be ~ about* être fou de

creak [kriːk] **1** *n* craquement *m*, grincement *m* **2** *v/i* craquer, grincer

creak·y ['kriːkɪ] *adj* qui craque, grinçant

cream [kriːm] **1** *n for skin, coffee, cake* crème *f*; *color* crème *m* **2** *adj* crème *inv*

cream 'cheese fromage *m* à tartiner

cream·er ['kri:mər] (*pitcher*) pot *m* à crème; *for coffee* crème *f* en poudre

cream·y ['kri:mɪ] *adj with lots of cream* crémeux*

crease [kri:s] **1** *n* pli *m* **2** *v/t accidentally* froisser

cre·ate [kri:'eɪt] **1** *v/t* créer; (*cause*) provoquer **2** *v/i* (*be creative*) créer

cre·a·tion [kri:'eɪʃn] création *f*

cre·a·tive [kri:'eɪtɪv] *adj* créatif*

cre·a·tor [kri:'eɪtər] créateur(-trice) *m(f)*; **the Creator** REL le Créateur

crea·ture ['kri:tʃər] (*animal*) animal *m*; (*person*) créature *f*

crèche [kreʃ] *for kids*, REL crèche *f*

cred·i·bil·i·ty [kredə'bɪlətɪ] *of person* crédibilité *f*

cred·i·ble ['kredəbl] *adj* crédible

cred·it ['kredɪt] **1** *n* crédit *m*; (*honor*) honneur *m*, mérite *m*; **be in ~** être créditeur; **get the ~ for sth** se voir attribuer le mérite de qch **2** *v/t* (*believe*) croire; ~ *an amount to an account* créditer un compte d'une somme

cred·it·a·ble ['kredɪtəbl] *adj* honorable

'cred·it card carte *f* de crédit

'cred·it lim·it limite *f* de crédit

cred·i·tor ['kredɪtər] créancier *m*

'cred·it·wor·thy *adj* solvable

cred·u·lous ['kredʊləs] *adj* crédule

creed [kri:d] (*beliefs*) credo *m inv*

creek [kri:k] (*stream*) ruisseau *m*

creep [kri:p] **1** *n pej* sale type *m* **F 2** *v/i* (*pret & pp* **crept**) se glisser (*in silence*); (*move slowly*) avancer lentement; ~ *into a room* entrer dans une pièce sans faire de bruit

creep·er ['kri:pər] BOT *creeping* plante *f* rampante; *climbing* plante *f* grimpante

creeps [kri:ps] *npl* F: *the house* / *he gives me the ~* la maison / il me donne la chair de poule

creep·y ['kri:pɪ] *adj* F flippant F

cre·mate [krɪ'meɪt] *v/t* incinérer

cre·ma·tion [krɪ'meɪʃn] incinération *f*, crémation *f*

cre·ma·to·ri·um [kremə'tɔ:rɪəm] crématorium *m*

crept [krept] *pret & pp* → **creep**

cres·cent ['kresənt] *shape* croissant *m*

crest [krest] crête *f*

'crest·fal·len *adj* dépité

crev·ice ['krevɪs] fissure *f*

crew [kru:] *n of ship, airplane* équipage *m*; *of repairmen etc* équipe *f*; (*crowd, group*) bande *f*

'crew cut cheveux *mpl* en brosse

'crew neck col *m* rond

crib [krɪb] *n for baby* lit *m* d'enfant

crick [krɪk]: ~ *in the neck* torticolis *m*

crick·et ['krɪkɪt] *insect* grillon *m*

crime [kraɪm] *also fig* crime *m*; ~ *rate* taux *m* de criminalité

crim·i·nal ['krɪmɪnl] **1** *n* criminel *m* **2** *adj* criminel*; (*shameful*) honteux*

crim·son ['krɪmzn] *adj* cramoisi

cringe [krɪndʒ] *v/i* tressaillir, frémir

crip·ple ['krɪpl] **1** *n* (*disabled person*) handicapé(e) *m(f)* **2** *v/t person* estropier; *fig* paralyser

cri·sis ['kraɪsɪs] (*pl* **crises** ['kraɪsi:z]) crise *f*

crisp [krɪsp] *adj air, weather* vivifiant; *lettuce, apple* croquant; *bacon, toast* croustillant; *new shirt, bills* raide

crisps [krɪsps] *Br* chips *fpl*

cri·te·ri·on [kraɪ'tɪrɪən] (*pl* **criteria** [kraɪ'tɪrɪə]) critère *m*

crit·ic ['krɪtɪk] critique *m*

crit·i·cal ['krɪtɪkl] *adj* critique

crit·i·cal·ly ['krɪtɪklɪ] *adv speak etc* en critiquant, sévèrement; ~ *ill* gravement malade

crit·i·cism ['krɪtɪsɪzm] critique *f*

crit·i·cize ['krɪtɪsaɪz] *v/t* critiquer

croak [krouk] **1** *n of frog* coassement *m*; *of person* voix *f* rauque **2** *v/i of frog* coasser; *of person* parler d'une voix rauque

crock·e·ry ['krɑ:kərɪ] vaisselle *f*

croc·o·dile ['krɑ:kədaɪl] crocodile *m*

cro·cus ['kroukəs] crocus *m*

cro·ny ['krounɪ] F pote *m* F, copain *m*

crook [krʊk] *n* escroc *m*

crook·ed ['krʊkɪd] *adj* (*not straight*) de travers; *streets* tortueux*; (*dishonest*) malhonnête

crop [krɑ:p] **1** *n* culture *f*; (*harvest*) récolte f; fig fournée f **2** v/t (pret & pp **-ped**) hair, photo couper

♦ **crop up** v/i surgir; **something has cropped up** il y a un contretemps

cross [krɑs] **1** adj (angry) fâché, en colère **2** n croix f **3** v/t (go across) traverser; **~ o.s.** REL se signer; **~ one's legs** croiser les jambes; **keep one's fingers ~ed** croiser les doigts; **it never ~ed my mind** ça ne m'est jamais venu à l'esprit **4** v/i (go across) traverser; of lines se croiser

♦ **cross off, cross out** v/t rayer

'**cross·bar** of goal barre f transversale; of bicycle, in high jump barre f; '**cross-check 1** n recoupement m **2** v/t vérifier par recoupement

cross-coun·try '**ski·ing** ski m de fond

cross-ex·am·i'na·tion LAW contre-interrogatoire m

cross-ex·am·ine v/t LAW faire subir un contre-interrogatoire à

cross-eyed ['krɑsaɪd] adj qui louche

cross·ing ['krɑsɪŋ] NAUT traversée f

'**cross·roads** nsg or npl also fig carrefour m; '**cross-sec·tion** of people échantillon m; '**cross·walk** passage m (zle) piétons; '**cross·word** (**puz·zle**) mots mpl croisés

crotch [krɑtʃ] entrejambe m

crouch [kraʊtʃ] v/i s'accroupir

crow [kroʊ] n bird corbeau m; **as the ~ flies** à vol d'oiseau

'**crow·bar** pied-de-biche m

crowd [kraʊd] n foule f; at sports event public m

crowd·ed ['kraʊdɪd] adj bondé, plein (de monde)

crown [kraʊn] n also on tooth couronne f

cru·cial ['kruːʃl] adj crucial

cru·ci·fix ['kruːsɪfɪks] crucifix m

cru·ci·fix·ion [kruːsɪ'fɪkʃn] crucifiement m; of Christ crucifixion f

cru·ci·fy ['kruːsɪfaɪ] v/t (pret & pp **-ied**) REL crucifier; fig assassiner

crude [kruːd] **1** adj (vulgar) grossier*; (unsophisticated) rudimentaire **2** n: **~ (oil)** pétrole m brut

crude·ly ['kruːdlɪ] adv speak, made grossièrement

cru·el ['kruːəl] adj cruel*

cru·el·ty ['kruːəltɪ] cruauté f

cruise [kruːz] **1** n croisière f **2** v/i of people faire une croisière; of car rouler (à une vitesse de croisière); of plane voler (à une vitesse de croisière)

'**cruise lin·er** paquebot m (de croisière)

'**cruise mis·sile** missile m de croisière

cruis·ing speed ['kruːzɪŋ] also fig vitesse f de croisière

crumb [krʌm] miette f

crum·ble ['krʌmbl] **1** v/t émietter **2** v/i of bread s'émietter; of stonework s'effriter; fig: of opposition etc s'effondrer

crum·bly ['krʌmblɪ] adj friable

crum·ple ['krʌmpl] **1** v/t (crease) froisser **2** v/i (collapse) s'écrouler

crunch [krʌntʃ] **1** n F: **when it comes to the ~** au moment crucial **2** v/i of snow, gravel crisser

cru·sade [kruː'seɪd] n also fig croisade f

crush [krʌʃ] **1** n (crowd) foule f; **have a ~ on s.o.** craquer pour qn F **2** v/t écraser; (crease) froisser; **they were ~ed to death** ils se sont fait écraser **3** v/i (crease) se froisser

crust [krʌst] on bread croûte f

crust·y ['krʌstɪ] adj bread croustillant

crutch [krʌtʃ] for injured person béquille f

cry [kraɪ] **1** n (call) cri m; **have a ~** pleurer **2** v/t (pret & pp **-ied**) (call) crier **3** v/i (weep) pleurer

♦ **cry out** v/t crier, s'écrier **2** v/i crier, pousser un cri

♦ **cry out for** v/t (need) avoir grand besoin de

cryp·tic ['krɪptɪk] adj énigmatique

crys·tal ['krɪstl] cristal m

crys·tal·lize ['krɪstlaɪz] **1** v/t cristalliser, concrétiser **2** v/i of thoughts etc se concrétiser

cub [kʌb] petit m

Cu·ba ['kjuːbə] Cuba f

Cu·ban ['kjuːbən] **1** adj cubain **2** n Cubain(e) m(f)

cube [kjuːb] (shape) cube m

cu·bic ['kjuːbɪk] adj cubique; **~ me-**

ter / centimeter mètre *m* / centimètre *m* cube

cu·bic ca'pac·i·ty TECH cylindrée *f*

cu·bi·cle ['kju:bɪkl] (*changing room*) cabine *f*

cuck·oo ['kuku:] coucou *m*

cu·cum·ber ['kju:kʌmbər] concombre *m*

cud·dle ['kʌdl] **1** *n* câlin *m* **2** *v/t* câliner

cud·dly ['kʌdlɪ] *adj* kitten etc adorable; (*liking cuddles*) câlin

cue [kju:] *n* for actor etc signal *m*; for pool queue *f*

cuff [kʌf] **1** *n* of shirt poignet *m*; of pants revers *m*; (*blow*) gifle *f*; **off the ~** au pied levé **2** *v/t* (*hit*) gifler

'cuff link bouton *m* de manchette

'cul-de-sac ['kʌldəsæk] cul-de-sac *m*, impasse *f*

cu·li·nar·y ['kʌlɪnerɪ] *adj* culinaire

cul·mi·nate ['kʌlmɪneɪt] *v/i* aboutir; **~ in** ... se terminer par ...

cul·mi·na·tion [kʌlmɪ'neɪʃn] apogée *f*

cul·prit ['kʌlprɪt] coupable *m/f*

cult [kʌlt] (*sect*) secte *f*

cul·ti·vate ['kʌltɪveɪt] *v/t* land, person cultiver

cul·ti·vat·ed ['kʌltɪveɪtɪd] *adj* person cultivé

cul·ti·va·tion [kʌltɪ'veɪʃn] of land culture *f*

cul·tu·ral ['kʌltʃərəl] *adj* culturel*

cul·ture ['kʌltʃər] *n* culture *f*

cul·tured ['kʌltʃərd] *adj* (*cultivated*) cultivé

'cul·ture shock choc *m* culturel

cum·ber·some ['kʌmbərsəm] *adj* big encombrant; heavy, also fig lourd

cu·mu·la·tive ['kju:mjʊlətɪv] *adj* cumulatif*; **the ~ effect of** ... l'accumulation *f* de ...

cun·ning ['kʌnɪŋ] **1** *n* ruse *f* **2** *adj* rusé

cup [kʌp] *n* tasse *f*; (*trophy*) coupe *f*; **a ~ of tea** une tasse de thé

cup·board ['kʌbərd] placard *m*

'cup fi·nal finale *f* de (la) coupe

cu·po·la ['kju:pələ] coupole *f*

cu·ra·ble ['kjʊrəbl] *adj* guérissable

cu·ra·tor [kjʊ'reɪtər] conservateur (-trice) *m(f)*

curb [kɜ:rb] **1** *n* of street bord *m* du trottoir; on powers etc frein *m* **2** *v/t* réfréner; inflation juguler

cur·dle ['kɜ:rdl] *v/i* of milk (se) cailler

cure [kjʊr] **1** *n* MED remède *m* **2** *v/t* MED guérir; meat, fish saurer

cur·few ['kɜ:rfju:] couvre-feu *m*

cu·ri·os·i·ty [kjʊrɪ'ɑ:sətɪ] (*inquisitiveness*) curiosité *f*

cu·ri·ous ['kjʊrɪəs] *adj* (*inquisitive, strange*) curieux*

cu·ri·ous·ly ['kjʊrɪəslɪ] *adv* (*inquisitively*) avec curiosité; (*strangely*) curieusement; **~ enough** chose curieuse

curl [kɜ:rl] **1** *n* in hair boucle *f*, of smoke volute *f* **2** *v/t* hair boucler; (*wind*) enrouler **3** *v/i* of hair boucler; of leaf, paper etc se gondoler

◆ **curl up** *v/i* se pelotonner; **curl up into a ball** se rouler en boule

curl·y ['kɜ:rlɪ] *adj* hair bouclé; tail en tire-bouchon

cur·rant ['kʌrənt] raisin *m* sec

cur·ren·cy ['kʌrənsɪ] (*money*) monnaie *f*; **foreign ~** devise *f* étrangère

cur·rent ['kʌrənt] **1** *n* in sea, ELEC courant *m* **2** *adj* (*present*) actuel*

cur·rent af'fairs, cur·rent e'vents actualité *f*

cur·rent af'fairs pro·gram émission *f* d'actualité

cur·rent·ly ['kʌrəntlɪ] *adv* actuellement

cur·ric·u·lum [kə'rɪkjʊləm] programme *m*

cur·ry ['kʌrɪ] (*spice*) curry *m*; **a lamb ~** un curry d'agneau

curse [kɜ:rs] **1** *n* (*spell*) malédiction *f*; (*swearword*) juron *m* **2** *v/t* maudire; (*swear at*) injurier **3** *v/i* (*swear*) jurer

cur·sor ['kɜ:rsər] COMPUT curseur *m*

cur·so·ry ['kɜ:rsərɪ] *adj* superficiel*

curt [kɜ:rt] *adj* abrupt

cur·tail [kɜ:r'teɪl] *v/t* écourter

cur·tain ['kɜ:rtn] also THEA rideau *m*

curve [kɜ:rv] **1** *n* courbe *f*; **~s of woman** formes *fpl* **2** *v/i* (*bend*) s'incurver; of road faire ou décrire une courbe

cush·ion ['kʊʃn] **1** *n* for couch etc coussin *m* **2** *v/t* blow, fall amortir

cus·tard ['kʌstərd] crème *f* anglaise

cus·to·dy ['kʌstədɪ] *of children* garde *f*; **in ~** LAW en détention

cus·tom ['kʌstəm] *(tradition)* coutume *f*; COMM clientèle *f*; **as was his ~** comme à l'accoutumée

cus·tom·a·ry ['kʌstəmerɪ] *adj* habituel*; **it is ~ to ...** il est d'usage de ...

cus·tom·er ['kʌstəmər] client *m*

cus·tom·er re·la·tions relations *fpl* avec les clients

cus·tom·er 'serv·ice service *m* clientèle

cus·toms ['kʌstəmz] douane *f*

Customs and Excise *Br* administration *f* des douanes et des impôts indirects

'cus·toms clear·ance dédouanement *m*; **'cus·toms in·spec·tion** contrôle *m* douanier; **'cus·toms of·fi·cer** douanier *m*

cut [kʌt] **1** *n with knife, scissors* entaille *f*; *(injury)* coupure *f*; *of garment, hair* coupe *f*; *(reduction)* réduction *f*; **my hair needs a ~** mes cheveux ont besoin d'être coupés **2** *v/t (pret & pp **cut**)* couper; *into several pieces* découper; *(reduce)* réduire; **get one's hair ~** se faire couper les cheveux

♦ **cut back 1** *v/i in costs* faire des économies **2** *v/t employees* réduire

♦ **cut down 1** *v/t tree* abattre **2** *v/i in smoking etc* réduire (sa consommation)

♦ **cut down on** *v/t smoking etc* réduire (sa consommation de); **cut down on the cigarettes** fumer moins

♦ **cut off** *v/t with knife, scissors etc* couper; *(isolate)* isoler; **we were cut off** TELEC nous avons été coupés

♦ **cut out** *v/t with scissors* découper; *(eliminate)* éliminer; *alcohol, food* supprimer; **cut that out!** F ça suffit (maintenant)!; **be cut out for sth** être fait pour qch

♦ **cut up** *v/t meat etc* découper

cut·back réduction *f*

cute [kju:t] *adj in appearance* mignon*; *(clever)* malin*

cu·ti·cle ['kju:tɪkl] cuticule *f*

'cutoff date date *f* limite

cut-'price *adj* à prix *m* réduit

'cut-throat *adj competition* acharné

cut·ting ['kʌtɪŋ] **1** *n from newspaper* coupure *f* **2** *adj remark* blessant

cy·ber·space ['saɪbərspeɪs] cyberespace *m*

cy·cle ['saɪkl] **1** *n (bicycle)* vélo *m*; *(series of events)* cycle *m* **2** *v/i* aller en vélo

'cy·cle path piste *f* cyclable

cy·cling ['saɪklɪŋ] cyclisme *m*

cy·clist ['saɪklɪst] cycliste *m/f*

cyl·in·der ['sɪlɪndər] *in engine* cylindre *m*

cy·lin·dri·cal [sɪ'lɪndrɪkl] *adj* cylindrique

cyn·ic ['sɪnɪk] cynique *m/f*

cyn·i·cal ['sɪnɪkl] *adj* cynique

cyn·i·cal·ly ['sɪnɪklɪ] *adv* cyniquement

cyn·i·cism ['sɪnɪsɪzm] cynisme *m*

cy·press ['saɪprəs] cyprès *m*

cyst [sɪst] kyste *m*

Czech [tʃek] **1** *adj* tchèque; **the ~ Republic** la République tchèque **2** *n person* Tchèque *m/f*; *language* tchèque *m*

D

DA *abbr (= **district attorney**)* procureur *m*

dab [dæb] **1** *n (small amount)*: **a ~ of** un

peu de **2** *v/t (pret & pp **-bed**)* *with cloth etc* tamponner

♦ **dab off** *v/t* enlever (en tamponnant)

♦ **dab on** v/t appliquer

♦ **dabble in** v/t toucher à

dad [dæd] papa m

dad·dy ['dædɪ] papa m

dad·dy 'long·legs Br cousin m

daf·fo·dil ['dæfədɪl] jonquille f

dag·ger ['dægər] poignard m

dai·ly ['deɪlɪ] **1** n paper quotidien m

daily 2 adj quotidien*

dain·ty ['deɪntɪ] adj délicat

dair·y ['derɪ] on farm laiterie f

'**dair·y prod·ucts** npl produits mpl laitiers

dais [deɪs] estrade f

dai·sy ['deɪzɪ] pâquerette f; bigger marguerite f

dam [dæm] n for water barrage m

dam·age ['dæmɪdʒ] **1** n dégâts mpl, dommage(s) m(pl); fig: to reputation préjudice m

damage 2 v/t endommager; abîmer; fig: reputation nuire à; chances compromettre

dam·a·ges ['dæmɪdʒɪz] npl LAW dommages-intérêts mpl

dam·ag·ing ['dæmɪdʒɪŋ] adj to reputation préjudiciable

dame [deɪm] F (woman) gonzesse f F, nana f F

damn [dæm] **1** interj F merde F, zut F **2** n: F; **I don't give a ~!** je m'en fous F **damn 3** adj F sacré **4** adv F vachement F **5** v/t (condemn) condamner; **~ it!** merde! F, zut! F; **I'm ~ed if ...** F (I won't) il est hors de question que ...

damned [dæmd] → **damn** adj, adv

damn·ing ['dæmɪŋ] adj evidence, report accablant

damp [dæmp] adj humide

damp·en ['dæmpən] v/t humecter, humidifier

dance [dæns] **1** n danse f; social event bal m, soirée f (dansante) **2** v/i danser; **would you like to ~?** vous dansez?

danc·er ['dænsər] danseur(-euse) m(f)

danc·ing ['dænsɪŋ] danse f

dan·de·li·on ['dændɪlaɪən] pissenlit m

dan·druff ['dændrʌf] pellicules fpl

dan·druff sham'poo shampoing m antipelliculaire

Dane [deɪn] Danois(e) m(f)

dan·ger ['deɪndʒər] danger m; **be in ~** être en danger; **be out of ~** patient être hors de danger

dan·ger·ous ['deɪndʒərəs] adj dangereux*; assumption risqué

dan·ger·ous 'driv·ing conduite f dangereuse

dan·ger·ous·ly ['deɪndʒərəslɪ] adv drive dangereusement; **~ ill** gravement malade

dan·gle ['dæŋgl] **1** v/t balancer; **~ sth in front of s.o.** mettre qch sous le nez de qn; fig faire miroiter qch à qn **2** v/i pendre

Da·nish ['deɪnɪʃ] **1** adj danois **2** n language danois m; to eat feuilleté m (sucré)

dare [der] **1** v/i oser; **~ to do sth** faire qch; **how ~ you!** comment oses-tu? **2** v/t: **~ s.o. to do sth** défier qn de faire qch

'**dare·dev·il** casse-cou m/f F, tête f brûlée

dar·ing ['derɪŋ] adj audacieux*

dark [dɑːrk] **1** n noir m, obscurité f; **after ~** après la tombée de la nuit; **keep s.o. in the ~** fig laisser qn dans l'ignorance; ne rien dire à qn **2** adj room, night sombre, noir; hair brun; eyes foncé; color, clothes foncé, sombre; **~ green / blue** vert / bleu foncé

dark·en ['dɑːrkn] v/i of sky s'assombrir

dark 'glass·es npl lunettes fpl noires

dark·ness ['dɑːrknɪs] obscurité f

'**dark·room** PHOT chambre f noire

dar·ling ['dɑːrlɪŋ] **1** n chéri(e) m(f); **be a ~ and ...** tu serais un amour or un ange si ... **2** adj adorable; **~ Margaret ...** ma chère Margaret ...

darn¹ [dɑːrn] **1** n (mend) reprise f **2** v/t repriser

darn², **darned** [dɑːrn, dɑːrnd] → **damn** adj, adv

dart [dɑːrt] **1** n weapon flèche f; for game fléchette f **2** v/i se précipiter, foncer

darts [dɑːrts] nsg fléchettes fpl

'**dart(s)·board** cible f (de jeu de fléchettes)

dash [dæʃ] **1** n punctuation tiret m;

MOT (*dashboard*) tableau *m* de bord; **a ~ of** un peu de; **a ~ of brandy** une goutte de cognac; **a ~ of salt** une pincée de sel; **make a ~ for** se précipiter sur **2** *v/i* se précipiter; **I must ~** il faut que je file F **3** *v/t hopes* anéantir

♦ **dash off 1** *v/i* partir précipitamment **2** *v/t* (*write quickly*) griffonner

'**dash·board** MOT tableau *m* de bord; **data** ['deɪtə] données *fpl*, informations *fpl*

'**da·ta·base** base *f* de données; **da·ta 'cap·ture** saisie *f* de données; **da·ta 'pro·cess·ing** traitement *m* de données; **da·ta pro'tec·tion** protection *f* de l'information; **da·ta 'stor·age** stockage *m* de données

date¹ [deɪt] *fruit* datte *f*

date² [deɪt] **1** *n date f; meeting* rendez--vous *m; person* ami(e) *m(f)*, rendez--vous *m* F; **what's the ~ today?** quelle est la date aujourd'hui?, on est le combien? F; **out of ~** *clothes* démodé; *passport* périmé; **up to ~** *information* à jour; *style* à la mode, branché F **2** *v/t letter, check* dater; (*go out with*) sortir avec; **that ~s you** cela ne te rajeunit pas F

dat·ed ['deɪtɪd] *adj* démodé

daub [dɔːb] *v/t* barbouiller; **~ paint on a wall** barbouiller un mur (de peinture)

daugh·ter ['dɔːtər] fille *f*

'**daugh·ter-in-law** (*pl* **daughters-in--law**) belle-fille *f*

daunt [dɔːnt] *v/t* décourager

daw·dle ['dɔːdl] *v/i* traîner

dawn [dɔːn] **1** *n also fig* aube *f* **2** *v/i: it ~ed on me that …* je me suis rendu compte que …

day [deɪ] *n* jour *m; stressing duration* journée *f; what ~ is it today?* quel jour sommes-nous (aujourd'hui)?; **~ off** jour *m* de congé; **by ~** le jour; **travel by ~** voyager de jour; **~ by ~** jour après jour; **the ~ after** le lendemain; **the ~ after tomorrow** après-demain; **the ~ before** la veille; **the ~ before yesterday** avant-hier; **~ in ~ out** jour après jour; **in those ~s** en ce temps--là, à l'époque; **one ~** un jour; **the**

other ~ (*recently*) l'autre jour; **let's call it a ~!** ça suffit pour aujourd'hui!; **have a nice ~!** bonne journée!

'**day·break** aube *f*, point *m* du jour; '**day care** *for kids* garde *f* des enfants; '**day-dream 1** *n* rêverie *f* **2** *v/i* rêvasser; '**day dream·er** rêveur *m*; '**day·time**: *in the ~* pendant la journée; '**day-trip** excursion *f* d'une journée

daze [deɪz] *n: in a ~* dans un état de stupeur

dazed [deɪzd] *adj by news* hébété, sous le choc; *by blow* étourdi

daz·zle ['dæzl] *v/t also fig* éblouir

DC *abbr* (= **direct current**) CC (= courant *m* continu); (= **District of Columbia**) DC (= district *m* de Columbia)

dead [ded] **1** *adj* mort; *battery* à plat; *the phone's ~* il n'y a pas de tonalité **2** *adv* F (*very*) très; **~ beat, ~ tired** crevé F; *that's ~ right* c'est tout à fait vrai **3** *n: the ~* les morts *mpl*; *in the ~ of night* en pleine nuit

dead·en [dedn] *v/t pain* calmer; *sound* amortir

dead 'end *street* impasse *f*; **dead-'end job** emploi *m* sans avenir; **dead 'heat** arrivée *f* ex æquo; '**dead-line** date *f* limite; heure *f* limite, délai *m; for newspaper, magazine* heure *f* de clôture; **meet the ~** respecter le(s) délai(s); '**dead·lock** impasse *f*

dead·ly ['dedlɪ] *adj* (*fatal*) mortel*; *weapon* meurtrier*; F (*boring*) mortel* F

deaf [def] *adj* sourd

deaf-and-'dumb *adj* sourd-muet*

deaf·en ['defn] *v/t* assourdir

deaf·en·ing ['defnɪŋ] *adj* assourdissant

deaf·ness ['defnɪs] surdité *f*

deal [diːl] **1** *n* accord *m*, marché *m; it's a ~!* d'accord!, marché conclu!; **a good ~** (*bargain*) une bonne affaire; (*a lot*) beaucoup; **a great ~ of** (*lots of*) beaucoup de **2** *v/t* (*pret & pp* **dealt**) *cards* distribuer; **~ a blow to** porter un coup à

♦ **deal in** *v/t* (*trade in*) être dans le

commerce de; **deal in drugs** faire du trafic de drogue, dealer F

♦ **deal out** v/t cards distribuer

♦ **deal with** v/t (handle) s'occuper de; (do business with) traiter avec; (be about) traiter de

deal·er ['di:lər] (merchant) marchand m; (drug ~) dealer m, dealeuse f; large-scale trafiquant m de drogue; in card game donneur m

deal·ing ['di:lɪŋ] (drug ~) trafic m de drogue

deal·ings ['di:lɪŋz] npl (business) relations fpl

dealt [delt] pret & pp → **deal**

dean [di:n] of college doyen m

dear [dɪr] adj cher*; **Dear Sir** Monsieur; **Dear Richard / Margaret** Cher Richard / Chère Margaret; (oh) ~!, ~ **me!** oh là là!

dear·ly ['dɪrlɪ] adv love de tout son cœur

death [deθ] mort f

'**death cer·tif·i·cate** acte m de décès; '**death pen·al·ty** peine f de mort; '**death toll** nombre m de morts, bilan m

de·ba·ta·ble [dɪ'beɪtəbl] adj discutable

de·bate [dɪ'beɪt] **1** n débat m; **a lot of** ~ beaucoup de discussions; POL débat m **2** v/i débattre, discuter; ~ **with o.s.** se demander **3** v/t débattre de, discuter de

de·bauch·er·y [dɪ'bɔ:tʃərɪ] débauche f

deb·it ['debɪt] **1** n débit m **2** v/t account débiter; amount porter au débit

'**deb·it card** carte f bancaire

deb·ris [də'bri:] débris mpl

debt [det] dette f; **be in** ~ financially être endetté, avoir des dettes

debt·or ['detər] débiteur m

de·bug [di:'bʌg] v/t (pret & pp **-ged**) room enlever les micros cachés dans; COMPUT déboguer

dé·but ['deɪbju:] n débuts mpl

dec·ade ['dekeɪd] décennie f

dec·a·dence ['dekədəns] décadence f

dec·a·dent ['dekədənt] adj décadent

de·caf·fein·at·ed [dɪ'kæfɪneɪtɪd] adj décaféiné

de·cant·er [dɪ'kæntər] carafe f

de·cap·i·tate [dɪ'kæpɪteɪt] v/t décapiter

de·cay [dɪ'keɪ] **1** n (process) détérioration f, déclin m; of building délabrement m; in wood, plant pourriture f; in teeth carie f **2** v/i of wood, plant pourrir; of civilization tomber en décadence; of teeth se carier

de·ceased [dɪ'si:st]: **the** ~ le défunt

de·ceit [dɪ'si:t] duplicité f

de·ceit·ful [dɪ'si:tful] adj fourbe

de·ceive [dɪ'si:v] v/t tromper, duper; ~ **s.o. about sth** mentir à qn sur qch

De·cem·ber [dɪ'sembər] décembre m

de·cen·cy ['di:sənsɪ] décence f

de·cent ['di:sənt] adj person correct, honnête; salary, price correct, décent; meal, sleep bon*; (adequately dressed) présentable, visible F

de·cen·tral·ize [di:'sentrəlaɪz] v/t décentraliser

de·cep·tion [dɪ'sepʃn] tromperie f

de·cep·tive [dɪ'septɪv] adj trompeur*

de·cep·tive·ly [dɪ'septɪvlɪ] adv: **it looks** ~ **simple** c'est plus compliqué qu'il n'y paraît

dec·i·bel ['desɪbel] décibel m

de·cide [dɪ'saɪd] **1** v/t décider; (settle) régler **2** v/i décider, se décider; **you** ~ c'est toi qui décides

de·cid·ed [dɪ'saɪdɪd] adj (definite) décidé; views arrêté; improvement net*

de·cid·er [dɪ'saɪdər]: **be the** ~ être décisif*

de·cid·u·ous [dɪ'sɪdʊəs] adj à feuilles caduques

dec·i·mal ['desɪml] n décimale f

dec·i·mal 'point virgule f

dec·i·mate ['desɪmeɪt] v/t décimer

de·ci·pher [dɪ'saɪfər] v/t déchiffrer

de·ci·sion [dɪ'sɪʒn] décision f; **come to a** ~ arriver à une décision

de·ci·sion-mak·er décideur m, décideuse f

de·ci·sive [dɪ'saɪsɪv] adj décidé; (crucial) décisif*

deck [dek] of ship pont m; of cards jeu m (de cartes)

'**deck·chair** transat m, chaise f longue

dec·la·ra·tion [deklə'reɪʃn] déclaration f

de·clare [dɪ'kler] v/t déclarer

de·cline [dɪ'klaɪn] **1** n baisse f; of civilization, health déclin m **2** v/t invitation décliner; ~ **to comment** refuser de commenter **3** v/i (refuse) refuser; (decrease) baisser; of health décliner

de·clutch [di:'klʌtʃ] v/i débrayer

de·code [di:'koʊd] v/t décoder

de·com·pose [di:kəm'poʊz] v/i se décomposer

dé·cor ['deɪkɔːr] décor m

dec·o·rate ['dekəreɪt] v/t room refaire; with paint peindre; with paper tapisser; (adorn), soldier décorer

dec·o·ra·tion [dekə'reɪʃn] paint, paper décoration f (intérieure); (ornament, medal) décoration f

dec·o·ra·tive ['dekərətɪv] adj décoratif*

dec·o·ra·tor ['dekəreɪtər] (interior ~) décorateur m (d'intérieur)

de·co·rum [dɪ'kɔːrəm] bienséance f

de·coy ['di:kɔɪ] n appât m, leurre m

de·crease ['di:kri:s] **1** n baisse f, diminution f; in size réduction f **2** v/t & v/i diminuer

de·crep·it [dɪ'krepɪt] adj décrépit; car, building délabré; coat, shoes usé

ded·i·cate ['dedɪkeɪt] v/t book etc dédicacer, dédier; ~ **o.s. to ...** se consacrer à ...

ded·i·ca·ted ['dedɪkeɪtɪd] adj dévoué

ded·i·ca·tion [dedɪ'keɪʃn] in book dédicace f; to cause, work dévouement m

de·duce [dɪ'du:s] v/t déduire

de·duct [dɪ'dʌkt] v/t déduire (from de)

de·duc·tion [dɪ'dʌkʃn] from salary prélèvement m, retenue f; (conclusion) déduction f

deed [di:d] n (act) acte m; LAW acte m (notarié)

dee·jay ['di:dʒeɪ] F DJ inv

deem [di:m] v/t considérer, juger

deep [di:p] adj profond; voice grave; color intense, sombre; **be in ~ trouble** avoir de gros problèmes

deep·en ['di:pn] **1** v/t creuser **2** v/i devenir plus profond; of crisis s'aggraver; of mystery s'épaissir

'deep freeze n congélateur m; **'deep-froz·en food** aliments mpl surgelés; **'deep-fry** v/t (pret & pp -ied) faire frire; **deep 'fry·er** [di:p'fraɪər] friteuse f

deer [dɪr] (pl **deer**) cerf m; female biche f

de·face [dɪ'feɪs] v/t abîmer, dégrader

def·a·ma·tion [defə'meɪʃn] diffamation f

de·fam·a·to·ry [dɪ'fæmətɔːrɪ] adj diffamatoire

de·fault ['di:fɔːlt] **1** adj COMPUT par défaut **2** v/i: ~ **on payments** ne pas payer

de·feat [dɪ'fi:t] **1** n défaite f **2** v/t battre, vaincre; of task, problem dépasser

de·feat·ist [dɪ'fi:tɪst] adj attitude défaitiste

de·fect ['di:fekt] n défaut m

de·fec·tive [dɪ'fektɪv] adj défectueux*

defence etc Br → **defense** etc

de·fend [dɪ'fend] v/t défendre; action, decision justifier

de·fend·ant [dɪ'fendənt] défendeur m, défenderesse f; in criminal case accusé(e) m(f)

de·fense [dɪ'fens] défense f; **come to s.o.'s ~** prendre la défense de qn

de·fense budg·et POL budget m de la Défense

de·fense law·yer avocat m de la défense

de·fense·less [dɪ'fenslɪs] adj sans défense

de·fense play·er SP défenseur m; **De·'fense Se·cre·ta·ry** POL ministre de la Défense; **de·'fense wit·ness** LAW témoin m à décharge

de·fen·sive [dɪ'fensɪv] **1** n: **on the ~** sur la défensive; **go on(to) the ~** se mettre sur la défensive **2** adj défensif*; **be ~** être sur la défensive

de·fen·sive·ly [dɪ'fensɪvlɪ] adv say d'un ton défensif; play d'une manière défensive

de·fer [dɪ'fɜːr] v/t (pret & pp -red) reporter, repousser

def·er·ence ['defərəns] déférence f

def·er·en·tial [defə'renʃl] adj déférent

de·fi·ance [dɪ'faɪəns] défi m; **in ~ of** au mépris de

de·fi·ant [dɪˈfaɪənt] *adj* provocant; *look also de* défi

de·fi·cien·cy [dɪˈfɪʃənsɪ] (*lack*) manque *m*, insuffisance *f*; MED carence *f*

de·fi·cient [dɪˈfɪʃənt] *adj* insuffisant; *be ~ in ...* être pauvre en ..., manquer de ...

def·i·cit [ˈdefɪsɪt] déficit *m*

de·fine [dɪˈfaɪn] *v/t* définir

def·i·nite [ˈdefɪnɪt] *adj date, time* précis, définitif*; *answer* définitif*; *improvement* net*; (*certain*) catégorique; *are you ~ about that?* es-tu sûr de cela?; *nothing ~ has been arranged* rien n'a été fixé

def·i·nite 'ar·ti·cle GRAM article *m* défini

def·i·nite·ly [ˈdefɪnɪtlɪ] *adv* sans aucun doute; *I ~ want to go* je veux vraiment y aller; *~ not* certainement pas!

def·i·ni·tion [defɪˈnɪʃn] définition *f*

de·fin·i·tive [dɪˈfɪnɪtɪv] *adj* magistral, qui fait autorité

de·flect [dɪˈflekt] *v/t ball, blow* faire dévier; *criticism, from course of action* détourner; *be ~ed from* se laisser détourner de

de·for·es·ta·tion [dɪfɑːrɪsˈteɪʃn] déboisement *m*

de·form [dɪˈfɔːrm] *v/t* déformer

de·for·mi·ty [dɪˈfɔːrmətɪ] difformité *f*, malformation *f*

de·fraud [dɪˈfrɔːd] *v/t tax authority* frauder; *person, company* escroquer

de·frost [diːˈfrɒst] *v/t food* décongeler; *fridge* dégivrer

deft [deft] *adj* adroit

de·fuse [diːˈfjuːz] *v/t bomb, situation* désamorcer

de·fy [dɪˈfaɪ] *v/t* (*pret & pp -ied*) défier; *superiors, orders* braver

de·gen·e·rate [dɪˈdʒenəreɪt] *v/i* dégénérer (*into* en)

de·grade [dɪˈɡreɪd] *v/t* avilir, être dégradant pour

de·grad·ing [dɪˈɡreɪdɪŋ] *adj position, work* dégradant, avilissant

de·gree [dɪˈɡriː] *from university* diplôme *m*

de·gree *of temperature, angle, latitude,* (*amount*) degré *m*; *by ~s* petit à petit;

get one's ~ avoir son diplôme

de·hy·drat·ed [diːhaɪˈdreɪtɪd] *adj* déshydraté

de·ice [diːˈaɪs] *v/t* dégivrer

de·ic·er [diːˈaɪsər] *spray* dégivrant *m*

deign [deɪn] *v/i: ~ to ...* daigner ...

de·i·ty [ˈdiːɪtɪ] divinité *f*

de·ject·ed [dɪˈdʒektɪd] *adj* déprimé

de·lay [dɪˈleɪ] **1** *n* retard *m*

delay 2 *v/t* retarder; *~ doing sth* attendre pour faire qch, remettre qch à plus tard; *be ~ed* être en retard, être retardé **3** *v/i* attendre, tarder

del·e·gate [ˈdelɪɡət] **1** *n* délégué(e) *m(f)* **2** [ˈdelɪɡeɪt] *v/t* déléguer

del·e·ga·tion [delɪˈɡeɪʃn] délégation *f*

de·lete [dɪˈliːt] *v/t* effacer; (*cross out*) rayer; *~ where not applicable* rayer les mentions inutiles

de'lete key COMPUT touche *f* de suppression

de·le·tion [dɪˈliːʃn] *act* effacement *m*; *that deleted* rature *f*, suppression *f*

deli [ˈdelɪ] → *delicatessen*

de·lib·e·rate [dɪˈlɪbərət] **1** *adj* délibéré **2** [dɪˈlɪbəreɪt] *v/i* délibérer; (*reflect*) réfléchir

de·lib·e·rate·ly [dɪˈlɪbərətlɪ] *adv* délibérément, exprès

del·i·ca·cy [ˈdelɪkəsɪ] délicatesse *f*; (*food*) mets *m* délicat; *a matter of some ~* une affaire assez délicate

del·i·cate [ˈdelɪkət] *adj* délicat

del·i·ca·tes·sen [delɪkəˈtesn] traiteur *m*, épicerie *f* fine

de·li·cious [dɪˈlɪʃəs] *adj* délicieux*

de·light [dɪˈlaɪt] *n* joie *f*, plaisir *m*; *take great ~ in sth* être ravi de qch; *take great ~ in doing sth* prendre grand plaisir à faire qch

de·light·ed [dɪˈlaɪtɪd] *adj* ravi, enchanté

de·light·ful [dɪˈlaɪtfʊl] *adj* charmant

de·lim·it [dɪˈlɪmɪt] *v/t* délimiter

de·lin·quen·cy [dɪˈlɪŋkwənsɪ] délinquance *f*

de·lin·quent [dɪˈlɪŋkwənt] *n* délinquant(e) *m(f)*

de·lir·i·ous [dɪˈlɪrɪəs] *adj* MED délirant; (*ecstatic*) extatique, fou* de joie; *be ~* délirer

de·liv·er [dɪ'lɪvər] **1** v/t goods livrer; *letters* distribuer; *parcel etc* remettre; *message* transmettre; *baby* mettre au monde; *speech* faire **2** v/i tenir ses promesses

de·liv·er·y [dɪ'lɪvərɪ] *of goods* livraison f; *of mail* distribution f; *of baby* accouchement m; *of speech* débit m

de·liv·ery charge frais mpl de livraison; **de·liv·er·y date** date f de livraison; **de·liv·er·y man** livreur m; **de·liv·er·y note** bon m de livraison; **de·liv·er·y serv·ice** service m de livraison; **de·liv·er·y van** camion m de livraison

de·lude [dɪ'luːd] v/t tromper; **you're deluding yourself** tu te fais des illusions

del·uge ['deljuːdʒ] **1** n also fig déluge m **2** v/t fig submerger, inonder

de·lu·sion [dɪ'luːʒn] illusion f

de luxe [də'lʌks] adj de luxe; *model* haut de gamme inv

◆ **delve into** [delv] v/t subject approfondir; *person's past* fouiller dans

de·mand [dɪ'mænd] **1** n also COMM demande f; *of terrorist, unions etc* revendication f; **in ~** demandé, recherché **2** v/t exiger; *pay rise etc* réclamer

de·mand·ing [dɪ'mændɪŋ] adj job éprouvant; *person* exigeant

de·mean·ing [dɪ'miːnɪŋ] adj dégradant

de·ment·ed [dɪ'mentɪd] adj fou*

de·mise [dɪ'maɪz] décès m, mort f; fig mort f

dem·i·tasse ['demɪtæs] tasse f à café

dem·o ['demou] (*protest*) manif f F; *of video etc* démo f F

de·moc·ra·cy [dɪ'mɑːkrəsɪ] démocratie f

dem·o·crat ['deməkræt] démocrate m/f; **Democrat** POL démocrate m/f

dem·o·crat·ic [demə'krætɪk] adj démocratique

dem·o·crat·ic·al·ly [demə'krætɪklɪ] adv démocratiquement

'dem·o disk disquette f de démonstration

de·mo·graph·ic [demou'græfɪk] adj démographique

de·mol·ish [dɪ'mɑːlɪʃ] v/t building, argument démolir

dem·o·li·tion [demə'lɪʃn] of building, argument démolition f

de·mon ['diːmən] démon m

dem·on·strate ['demənstreɪt] **1** v/t (prove) démontrer; *machine etc* faire une démonstration de **2** v/i politically manifester

dem·on·stra·tion [demən'streɪʃn] démonstration f; (protest) manifestation f, of machine démonstration f

de·mon·stra·tive [dɪ'mɑːnstrətɪv] adj démonstratif*

de·mon·stra·tor ['demənstreɪtər] (protester) manifestant(e) m(f)

de·mor·al·ized [dɪ'mɔːrəlaɪzd] adj démoralisé

de·mor·al·iz·ing [dɪ'mɔːrəlaɪzɪŋ] adj démoralisant

de·mote [diː'mout] v/t rétrograder

de·mure [dɪ'mjuər] adj sage

den [den] room antre f

de·ni·al [dɪ'naɪəl] of rumor, accusation démenti m, dénégation f; of request refus m

den·im ['denɪm] jean m; **~ jacket** veste m en jean

den·ims ['denɪmz] npl (jeans) jean m

Den·mark ['denmɑːrk] le Danemark

de·nom·i·na·tion [dɪnɑːmɪ'neɪʃn] of money coupure f; religious confession f

de·nounce [dɪ'naʊns] v/t dénoncer

dense [dens] adj (thick) dense; (stupid) stupide, bête

dense·ly ['denslɪ] adv: **~ populated** densément peuplé

den·si·ty ['densɪtɪ] densité f

dent [dent] **1** n bosse f **2** v/t bosseler

den·tal ['dentl] adj treatment, hospital dentaire; **~ surgeon** chirurgien(ne) m(f) dentiste

den·ted ['dentɪd] adj bosselé

den·tist ['dentɪst] dentiste m/f

den·tist·ry ['dentɪstrɪ] dentisterie f

den·tures ['dentʃərz] npl dentier m

Den·ver boot ['denvər] sabot m de Denver

de·ny [dɪ'naɪ] v/t (pret & pp **-ied**) charge, rumor nier; right, request refuser

de·o·do·rant [diː'oʊdərənt] déodorant *m*

de·part [dɪ'pɑːrt] *v/i* partir; **~ *from*** *normal procedure etc* ne pas suivre

de·part·ment [dɪ'pɑːrtmənt] *of company* service *m*; *of university* département *m*; *of government* ministère *m*; *of store* rayon *m*

De·part·ment of 'De·fense ministère *m* de la Défense; **De·part·ment of the In·te·ri·or** ministère *m* de l'Intérieur; **De·part·ment of 'State** ministère *m* des Affaires étrangères; **de·'part·ment store** grand magasin *m*

de·par·ture [dɪ'pɑːrtʃər] départ *m*; *from standard procedure etc* entorse *f* (**from** à); ***a new* ~** un nouveau départ

de·par·ture lounge salle *f* d'embarquement

de·par·ture time heure *f* de départ

de·pend [dɪ'pend] *v/i* dépendre; ***that* ~*s*** cela dépend; ***it* ~*s on the weather*** ça dépend du temps; ***I'm* ~*ing on you*** je compte sur toi

de·pen·da·ble [dɪ'pendəbl] *adj* digne de confiance, fiable

de·pen·dence, de·pen·den·cy [dɪ'pendəns, dɪ'pendənsɪ] dépendance *f*

de·pen·dent [dɪ'pendənt] **1** *n* personne *f* à charge **2** *adj* dépendant; **~ *children*** enfants *mpl* à charge

de·pict [dɪ'pɪkt] *v/t in painting, writing* représenter

de·plete [dɪ'pliːt] *v/t* épuiser

de·plor·a·ble [dɪ'plɔːrəbl] *adj* déplorable

de·plore [dɪ'plɔːr] *v/t* déplorer

de·ploy [dɪ'plɔɪ] *v/t* (*use*) faire usage de; (*position*) déployer

de·pop·u·la·tion [diːpɑːpjə'leɪʃn] dépeuplement *m*

de·port [dɪ'pɔːrt] *v/t from a country* expulser

de·por·ta·tion [diːpɔːr'teɪʃn] expulsion *f*

de·por·ta·tion or·der arrêté *m* d'expulsion

de·pose [dɪ'pɔʊz] *v/t* déposer

de·pos·it [dɪ'pɑːzɪt] **1** *n in bank* dépôt

m; *on purchase* acompte *m*; *security* caution *f*; *of mineral* gisement *m*

deposit 2 *v/t money, object* déposer

dep·o·si·tion [diːpoʊ'zɪʃn] LAW déposition *f*

de·pot ['depoʊ] (*train station*) gare *f*; (*bus station*) gare *f* routière; *for storage* dépôt *m*, entrepôt *m*

de·praved [dɪ'preɪvd] *adj* dépravé

de·pre·ci·ate [dɪ'priːʃɪeɪt] *v/i* FIN se déprécier

de·pre·ci·a·tion [dɪpriːʃɪ'eɪʃn] FIN dépréciation *f*

de·press [dɪ'pres] *v/t person* déprimer

de·pressed [dɪ'prest] *adj* déprimé

de·press·ing [dɪ'presɪŋ] *adj* déprimant

de·pres·sion [dɪ'preʃn] MED, *meteorological* dépression *f*; *economic* crise *f*, récession *f*

dep·ri·va·tion [deprɪ'veɪʃn] privation(s) *f(pl)*

de·prive [dɪ'praɪv] *v/t*: **~ *s.o. of sth*** priver qn de qch

de·prived [dɪ'praɪvd] *adj* défavorisé

depth [depθ] profondeur *f*; *of voice* gravité *f*; *of color* intensité *f*; ***in* ~** (*thoroughly*) en profondeur; ***in the* ~*s of winter*** au plus fort de l'hiver, en plein hiver; ***be out of one's* ~** *in water* ne pas avoir pied; *fig: in discussion etc* être dépassé

dep·u·ta·tion [depjʊ'teɪʃn] députation *f*

♦ **dep·u·tize for** ['depjʊtaɪz] *v/t* remplacer, suppléer

dep·u·ty ['depjʊtɪ] adjoint(e) *m(f)*; *of sheriff* shérif *m* adjoint

de·rail [dɪ'reɪl] *v/t*: **be ~*ed*** *of train* dérailler

de·ranged [dɪ'reɪndʒd] *adj* dérangé

de·reg·u·late [diː'regjʊleɪt] *v/t* déréglementer

de·reg·u·la·tion [diːregjʊ'leɪʃn] déréglementation *f*

der·e·lict ['derəlɪkt] *adj* délabré

de·ride [dɪ'raɪd] *v/t* se moquer de

de·ri·sion [dɪ'rɪʒn] dérision *f*

de·ri·sive [dɪ'raɪsɪv] *adj remarks, laughter* moqueur*

de·ri·sive·ly [dɪ'raɪsɪvlɪ] *adv* avec dérision

de·ri·so·ry [dɪˈraɪsəri] *adj amount, salary* dérisoire

de·riv·a·tive [dɪˈrɪvətɪv] *adj (not original)* dérivé

de·rive [dɪˈraɪv] *v/t* tirer (**from** de); **be ~d from** *of word* dériver de

der·ma·tol·o·gist [dɜːrməˈtɑːlədʒɪst] dermatologue *m/f*

de·rog·a·to·ry [dɪˈrɑːgətɔːri] *adj* désobligeant; *term* péjoratif*

de·scend [dɪˈsend] **1** *v/t* descendre; **be ~ed from** descendre de **2** *v/i* descendre; *of darkness* tomber; *of mood* se répandre

◆ **descend on** *v/t of mood, darkness* envahir

de·scen·dant [dɪˈsendənt] descendant(e) *m(f)*

de·scent [dɪˈsent] descente *f*; *(ancestry)* descendance *f*, origine *f*; **of Chinese ~** d'origine chinoise

de·scribe [dɪˈskraɪb] *v/t* décrire; **~ X as Y** décrire X comme (étant) Y

de·scrip·tion [dɪˈskrɪpʃn] description *f*; *of criminal* signalement *m*

des·e·crate [ˈdesɪkreɪt] *v/t* profaner

des·e·cra·tion [desɪˈkreɪʃn] profanation *f*

de·seg·re·gate [diːˈsegrəgeɪt] supprimer la ségrégation *f*

des·ert[1] [ˈdezərt] *n also fig* désert *m*

des·ert[2] [dɪˈzɜːrt] **1** *v/t (abandon)* abandonner

desert 2 *v/i of soldier* déserter

de·sert·ed [dɪˈzɜːrtɪd] *adj* désert

de·sert·er [dɪˈzɜːrtər] MIL déserteur *m*

de·ser·ti·fi·ca·tion [dɪzɜːrtɪfɪˈkeɪʃn] désertification *f*

de·ser·tion [dɪˈzɜːrʃn] *(abandonment)* abandon *m*; MIL désertion *f*

desert 'is·land île *f* déserte

de·serve [dɪˈzɜːrv] *v/t* mériter

de·sign [dɪˈzaɪn] **1** *n (subject)* design *m*; *(style)* style *m*, conception *f*; *(drawing, pattern)* dessin *m* **2** *v/t (draw)* dessiner; *building, car, ship, machine* concevoir

des·ig·nate [ˈdezɪgneɪt] *v/t person* désigner

de·sign·er [dɪˈzaɪnər] designer *m/f*, dessinateur(-trice) *m(f)*; *of car, ship* concepteur(-trice) *m(f)*; *of clothes* styliste *m/f*

de'sign·er clothes *npl* vêtements *mpl* de marque

de'sign fault défaut *m* de conception

de'sign school école *f* de design

de·sir·a·ble [dɪˈzaɪrəbl] *adj* souhaitable; *sexually, change* désirable; *offer, job* séduisant; **a very ~ residence** une très belle propriété

de·sire [dɪˈzaɪr] *n* désir *m*; **have no ~ to ...** n'avoir aucune envie de ...

desk [desk] bureau *m*; *in hotel* réception *f*

'desk clerk réceptionniste *m/f*; **'desk di·a·ry** agenda *m* de bureau; **'desk·top** bureau *m*; *computer* ordinateur *m* de bureau; **desk·top 'pub·lish·ing** publication *f* assistée par ordinateur, microédition *f*

des·o·late [ˈdesələt] *adj place* désolé

de·spair [dɪˈsper] **1** *n* désespoir *m*; **in ~** désespéré; **be in ~** être au désespoir **2** *v/i* désespérer (**of** de); **~ of s.o.** ne se faire aucune illusion sur qn

des·per·ate [ˈdespərət] *adj* désespéré; **be ~ for a whiskey / cigarette** avoir très envie d'un whisky / d'une cigarette; **be ~ for news** attendre désespérément des nouvelles

des·per·a·tion [despəˈreɪʃn] désespoir *m*; **in ~** en désespoir de cause; **an act of ~** un acte désespéré

des·pic·a·ble [dɪsˈpɪkəbl] *adj* méprisable

de·spise [dɪˈspaɪz] *v/t* mépriser

de·spite [dɪˈspaɪt] *prep* malgré, en dépit de

de·spon·dent [dɪˈspɑːndənt] *adj* abattu, découragé

des·pot [ˈdespɑːt] despote *m*

des·sert [dɪˈzɜːrt] dessert *m*

des·ti·na·tion [destɪˈneɪʃn] destination *f*

des·tined [ˈdestɪnd] *adj*: **be ~ for** *fig* être destiné à

des·ti·ny [ˈdestɪni] destin *m*, destinée *f*

des·ti·tute [ˈdestɪtuːt] *adj* démuni

de·stroy [dɪˈstrɔɪ] *v/t* détruire

de·stroy·er [dɪˈstrɔɪr] NAUT destroyer *m*, contre-torpilleur *m*

de·struc·tion [dɪˈstrʌkʃn] destruction *f*

de·struc·tive [dɪˈstrʌktɪv] *adj power* destructeur*; *criticism* négatif*, non constructif*; **a ~ child** un enfant qui casse tout

de·tach [dɪˈtætʃ] *v/t* détacher

de·tach·a·ble [dɪˈtætʃəbl] *adj* détachable

de·tached [dɪˈtætʃt] *adj (objective)* neutre, objectif*

de·tach·ment [dɪˈtætʃmənt] *(objectivity)* neutralité *f*, objectivité *f*

de·tail [ˈdiːteɪl] *n* détail *m*; **in ~** en détail; **for more ~s** pour plus de renseignements

de·tailed [ˈdiːteɪld] *adj* détaillé

de·tain [dɪˈteɪn] *v/t (hold back)* retenir; *as prisoner* détenir

de·tain·ee [dɪteɪmˈiː] détenu(e) *m(f)*; *political ~* prisonnier *m* politique

de·tect [dɪˈtekt] *v/t* déceler; *of device* détecter

de·tec·tion [dɪˈtekʃn] *of crime* découverte *f*; *of smoke etc* détection *f*

de·tec·tive [dɪˈtektɪv] inspecteur *m* de police

de·tec·tive nov·el roman *m* policier

de·tec·tor [dɪˈtektər] détecteur *m*

dé·tente [ˈdeɪtɑːnt] POL détente *f*

de·ten·tion [dɪˈtenʃn] *(imprisonment)* détention *f*

de·ter [dɪˈtɜːr] *v/t (pret & pp -red)* décourager, dissuader; **~ s.o. from doing sth** dissuader qn de faire qch

de·ter·gent [dɪˈtɜːrdʒənt] détergent *m*

de·te·ri·o·rate [dɪˈtɪriəreɪt] *v/i* se détériorer, se dégrader

de·te·ri·o·ra·tion [dɪtɪriəˈreɪʃn] détérioration *f*

de·ter·mi·na·tion [dɪtɜːrmɪˈneɪʃn] *(resolution)* détermination *f*

de·ter·mine [dɪˈtɜːrmɪn] *v/t (establish)* déterminer

de·ter·mined [dɪˈtɜːrmɪnd] *adj* déterminé, résolu; *effort* délibéré

de·ter·rent [dɪˈterənt] *n* moyen *m* de dissuasion

de·test [dɪˈtest] *v/t* détester

de·test·a·ble [dɪˈtestəbl] *adj* détestable

de·to·nate [ˈdetəneɪt] **1** *v/t* faire exploser **2** *v/i* détoner

de·to·na·tion [detəˈneɪʃn] détonation *f*

de·tour [ˈdiːtʊr] *n* détour *m*; *(diversion)* déviation *f*

♦ **de·tract from** [dɪˈtrækt] *v/t* diminuer

de·tri·ment [ˈdetrɪmənt]: **to the ~ of** au détriment de

de·tri·men·tal [detrɪˈmentl] *adj* néfaste, nuisible

deuce [duːs] *in tennis* égalité *f*

de·val·u·a·tion [diːvæljuˈeɪʃn] *of currency* dévaluation *f*

de·val·ue [diːˈvælju] *v/t currency* dévaluer

dev·a·state [ˈdevəsteɪt] *v/t crops, countryside, city* dévaster, ravager; *fig: person* anéantir

dev·a·stat·ing [ˈdevəsteɪtɪŋ] *adj* désastreux*; *news* accablant

de·vel·op [dɪˈveləp] **1** *v/t film, business* développer; *land, site* aménager; *technique, vaccine* mettre au point; *illness, cold* attraper **2** *v/i (grow)* se développer; grandir; **~ into** devenir, se transformer en

de·vel·op·er [dɪˈveləpər] *of property* promoteur(-trice) *m(f)*; **be a late ~** *of student etc* se développer tard

de·vel·op·ing coun·try [dɪˈveləpɪŋ] pays *m* en voie de développement

de·vel·op·ment [dɪˈveləpmənt] *of film, business* développement *m*; *of land, site* aménagement *m*; *(event)* événement *m*; *of technique, vaccine* mise *f* au point

de·vice [dɪˈvaɪs] *(tool)* appareil *m*

dev·il [ˈdevl] diable *m*; **a little ~** un petit monstre

de·vi·ous [ˈdiːviəs] *person* sournois; *method* détourné

de·vise [dɪˈvaɪz] *v/t* concevoir

de·void [dɪˈvɔɪd] *adj*: **be ~ of** être dénué de, être dépourvu de

dev·o·lu·tion [diːvəˈluːʃn] POL décentralisation *f*

de·vote [dɪˈvoʊt] *v/t* consacrer

de·vot·ed [dɪˈvoʊtɪd] *adj son etc* dévoué (*to* à)

dev·o·tee [dɪvou'tiː] passionné(e) *m(f)*

de·vo·tion [dɪ'vouʃn] dévouement *m*

de·vour [dɪ'vauər] *v/t also fig* dévorer

de·vout [dɪ'vaut] *adj* fervent, pieux*

dew [duː] rosée *f*

dex·ter·i·ty [dek'sterətɪ] dextérité *f*

di·a·be·tes [daɪə'biːtiːz] *nsg* diabète *m*

di·a·bet·ic [daɪə'betɪk] **1** *n* diabétique *m/f* **2** *adj* pour diabétiques

di·ag·nose ['daɪəgnouz] *v/t* diagnostiquer

di·ag·no·sis [daɪəg'nousɪs] (*pl* **diagnoses** [daɪəg'nousiːz]) diagnostic *m*

di·ag·o·nal [daɪ'ægənl] *adj* diagonal

di·ag·o·nal·ly [daɪ'ægənlɪ] *adv* en diagonale

di·a·gram ['daɪəgræm] diagramme *m*, schéma *m*

di·al ['daɪl] **1** *n* cadran *m* **2** *v/i* (*pret & pp* **-ed**, *Br* **-led**) TELEC faire le numéro **3** *v/t* (*pret & pp* **-ed**, *Br* **-led**) TELEC *number* composer, faire

di·a·lect ['daɪəlekt] dialecte *m*

di·a·log, *Br* **di·a·logue** ['daɪəlɔːg] dialogue *m*

'di·a·log box COMPUT boîte *f* de dialogue

'di·al tone tonalité *f*

di·am·e·ter [daɪ'æmɪtər] diamètre *m*; **6 inches in ~** 6 pouces de diamètre

di·a·met·ri·cal·ly [daɪə'metrɪklɪ] *adv*: **~ opposed** diamétralement opposé

di·a·mond ['daɪəmənd] *jewel* diamant *m*; *in cards* carreau *m*; *shape* losange *m*

di·a·per ['daɪpər] couche *f*

di·a·phragm ['daɪəfræm] diaphragme *m*

di·ar·rhe·a, *Br* **di·ar·rhoe·a** [daɪə'riːə] diarrhée *f*

di·a·ry ['daɪrɪ] *for thoughts* journal *m* (intime); *for appointments* agenda *m*

dice [daɪs] **1** *n* dé *m*; *pl* dés *mpl* **2** *v/t* (*cut*) couper en dés

di·chot·o·my [daɪ'kɑːtəmɪ] dichotomie *f*

dic·tate [dɪk'teɪt] *v/t letter, course of action* dicter

dic·ta·tion [dɪk'teɪʃn] dictée *f*

dic·ta·tor [dɪk'teɪtər] POL, *fig* dictateur *m*

dic·ta·to·ri·al [dɪktə'tɔːrɪəl] *adj tone, person* autoritaire; *powers* dictatorial

dic·ta·tor·ship [dɪk'teɪtərʃɪp] dictature *f*

dic·tion·a·ry ['dɪkʃənrɪ] dictionnaire *m*

did [dɪd] *pret* → **do**

die [daɪ] *v/i* mourir; **~ of cancer / Aids** mourir d'un cancer / du sida; **I'm dying to know** je meurs d'envie de savoir; **I'm dying for a beer** je meurs d'envie de boire une bière

♦ **die away** *v/i of noise* diminuer, mourir

♦ **die down** *v/i of noise* diminuer; *of storm* se calmer; *of fire* mourir, s'éteindre; *of excitement* s'apaiser

♦ **die out** *v/i* disparaître

die·sel ['diːzl] *fuel* diesel *m*, gazole *m*

di·et ['daɪət] **1** *n* (*regular food*) alimentation *f*; *to lose weight, for health* régime *m*; **be on a ~** être au régime **2** *v/i to lose weight* faire un régime

di·e·ti·tian [daɪə'tɪʃn] diététicien(ne) *m(f)*

dif·fer ['dɪfər] *v/i* différer; (*disagree*) différer

dif·fe·rence ['dɪfrəns] différence *f*; (*disagreement*) différend *m*, désaccord *m*; **it doesn't make any ~** (*doesn't change anything*) cela ne fait pas de différence; (*doesn't matter*) peu importe

dif·fe·rent ['dɪfrənt] *adj* différent

dif·fe·ren·ti·ate [dɪfə'renʃɪeɪt] *v/i*: **~ between** *things* faire la différence entre; *people* faire des différences entre

dif·fe·rent·ly ['dɪfrəntlɪ] *adv* différemment

dif·fi·cult ['dɪfɪkəlt] *adj* difficile

dif·fi·cul·ty ['dɪfɪkəltɪ] difficulté *f*; **with ~** avec difficulté, difficilement

dif·fi·dent ['dɪfɪdənt] *adj* hésitant

dig [dɪg] **1** *v/t* (*pret & pp* **dug**) creuser **2** *v/i* (*pret & pp* **dug**): **it was ~ging into my back** cela me rentrait dans le dos

♦ **dig out** *v/t* (*find*) retrouver, dénicher

♦ **dig up** *v/t* (*find*) déterrer; *garden,*

earth fouiller, retourner

di·gest [daɪˈdʒest] *v/t* digérer; *information* assimiler

di·gest·i·ble [daɪˈdʒestəbl] *adj food* digestible, digeste

di·ges·tion [daɪˈdʒestʃn] digestion *f*

di·ges·tive [daɪˈdʒestɪv] *adj* digestif*

dig·ger [ˈdɪgər] *machine* excavateur *m*, excavatrice *f*

dig·it [ˈdɪdʒɪt] *(number)* chiffre *m*; *a 4 ~ number* un nombre à 4 chiffres

dig·i·tal [ˈdɪdʒɪtl] *adj* digital, numérique

dig·ni·fied [ˈdɪgnɪfaɪd] *adj* digne

dig·ni·ta·ry [ˈdɪgnəteri] dignitaire *m*

dig·ni·ty [ˈdɪgnɪti] *fml* dignité *f*

di·gress [daɪˈgres] *v/i* faire une parenthèse

di·gres·sion [daɪˈgreʃn] digression *f*

dike [daɪk] *wall* digue *f*

di·lap·i·dat·ed [dɪˈlæpɪdeɪtɪd] *adj* délabré

di·late [daɪˈleɪt] *v/i of pupils* se dilater

di·lem·ma [dɪˈlemə] dilemme *m*; *be in a ~* être devant un dilemme

dil·et·tante [dɪleˈtæntɪ] dilettante *m/f*

dil·i·gent [ˈdɪlɪdʒənt] *adj* consciencieux*

di·lute [daɪˈluːt] *v/t* diluer

dim [dɪm] **1** *adj room, prospects* sombre; *light* faible; *outline* flou, vague; *(stupid)* bête **2** *v/t (pret & pp -med)*: *~ the headlights* se mettre en code(s) **3** *v/i (pret & pp -med) of lights* baisser

dime [daɪm] *(pièce f de)* dix cents *mpl*

di·men·sion [daɪˈmenʃn] dimension *f*

di·min·ish [dɪˈmɪnɪʃ] *v/t & v/i* diminuer

di·min·u·tive [dɪˈmɪnʊtɪv] **1** *n* diminutif *m* **2** *adj* tout petit, minuscule

dim·ple [ˈdɪmpl] *in cheeks* fossette *f*

din [dɪn] *n* brouhaha *m*, vacarme *m*

dine [daɪn] *v/i fml* dîner

din·er [ˈdaɪnər] *person* dîneur(-euse) *m(f)*; *restaurant* petit restaurant *m*

din·ghy [ˈdɪŋgɪ] *small yacht* dériveur *m*; *rubber boat* canot *m* pneumatique

din·gy [ˈdɪndʒɪ] *adj atmosphere* glauque; *(dirty)* défraîchi

din·ing car [ˈdaɪnɪŋ] RAIL wagon-restaurant *m*; **'din·ing room** salle *f* à manger; *in hotel* salle *f* de restaurant; **'din·ing ta·ble** table *f* de salle à manger

din·ner [ˈdɪnər] dîner *m*; *at midday* déjeuner *m*; *gathering* repas *m*

'din·ner guest invité(e) *m(f)*; **'din·ner jack·et** smoking *m*; **'din·ner par·ty** dîner *m*, repas *m*; **'din·ner serv·ice** service *m* de table

di·no·saur [ˈdaɪnəsɔːr] dinosaure *m*

dip [dɪp] **1** *n (swim)* baignade *f*; *for food* sauce *f* (dans laquelle on trempe des aliments); *in road* inclinaison *f* **2** *v/t (pret & pp -ped)* plonger, tremper; *~ the headlights* se mettre en code **3** *v/i (pret & pp -ped) of road* s'incliner

di·plo·ma [dɪˈploʊmə] diplôme *m*

di·plo·ma·cy [dɪˈploʊməsɪ] *also (tact)* diplomatie *f*

di·plo·mat [ˈdɪpləmæt] diplomate *m/f*

di·plo·mat·ic [dɪpləˈmætɪk] *adj* diplomatique; *(tactful)* diplomate

dip·lo·mat·i·cal·ly [dɪpləˈmætɪklɪ] *adv* diplomatiquement

dip·lo·mat·ic im·mu·ni·ty immunité *f* diplomatique

dire [ˈdaɪr] *adj situation* désespérée; *consequences* terrible; *need* extrême

di·rect [daɪˈrekt] **1** *adj* direct **2** *v/t to a place* indiquer *(to sth* qch); *play* mettre en scène; *movie* réaliser; *attention* diriger

di·rect 'cur·rent ELEC courant *m* continu

di·rec·tion [dɪˈrekʃn] direction *f*; *of movie* réalisation *f*; *of play* mise *f* en scène; *~s (instructions)* indications *fpl*; *for use* mode *m* d'emploi; *for medicine* instructions *fpl*; *ask for ~s to a place* demander son chemin

di·rec·tion 'in·di·ca·tor *Br* MOT clignotant *m*

di·rec·tive [dɪˈrektɪv] *of UN etc* directive *f*

di·rect·ly [dɪˈrektlɪ] **1** *adv (straight)* directement; *(soon)* dans très peu de temps; *(immediately)* immédiatement **2** *conj* aussitôt que

di·rec·tor [dɪˈrektər] *of company* directeur(-trice) *m(f)*; *of movie* réalisateur(-trice) *m(f)*; *of play* metteur (-euse) *m(f)* en scène

di·rec·to·ry [dɪ'rektərɪ] répertoire *m* (d'adresses); TELEC annuaire *m* (des téléphones); COMPUT répertoire *m*

dirt [dɜːrt] saleté *f*, crasse *f*

'dirt cheap *adj* F très bon marché

dirt·y ['dɜːrtɪ] **1** *adj* sale; (*pornographic*) cochon* F **2** *v/t* (*pret & pp* **-ied**) salir

dirt·y 'trick sale tour *m*

dis·a·bil·i·ty [dɪsə'bɪlətɪ] infirmité *f*, handicap *m*

dis·a·bled [dɪs'eɪbld] **1** *npl*: **the ~** les handicapés *mpl* **2** *adj* handicapé

dis·ad·van·tage [dɪsəd'væntɪdʒ] désavantage *m*, inconvénient *m*; **be at a ~** être désavantagé

dis·ad·van·taged [dɪsəd'væntɪdʒd] *adj* défavorisé

dis·ad·van·ta·geous [dɪsədvæn-'teɪdʒəs] *adj* désavantageux*, défavorable

dis·a·gree [dɪsə'griː] *v/i of person* ne pas être d'accord

◆ **disagree with** *v/t of person* être contre; **lobster disagrees with me** je ne digère pas le homard

dis·a·gree·a·ble [dɪsə'griːəbl] *adj* désagréable

dis·a·gree·ment [dɪsə'griːmənt] désaccord *m*; (*argument*) dispute *f*

dis·ap·pear [dɪsə'pɪr] *v/i* disparaître

dis·ap·pear·ance [dɪsə'pɪrəns] disparition *f*

dis·ap·point [dɪsə'pɔɪnt] *v/t* décevoir

dis·ap·point·ed [dɪsə'pɔɪntɪd] *adj* déçu

dis·ap·point·ing [dɪsə'pɔɪntɪŋ] *adj* décevant

dis·ap·point·ment [dɪsə'pɔɪntmənt] déception *f*

dis·ap·prov·al [dɪsə'pruːvl] désapprobation *f*

dis·ap·prove [dɪsə'pruːv] *v/i* désapprouver; **~ of actions** désapprouver; *s.o.* ne pas aimer

dis·ap·prov·ing [dɪsə'pruːvɪŋ] *adj* désapprobateur*

dis·ap·prov·ing·ly [dɪsə'pruːvɪŋlɪ] *adv* avec désapprobation

dis·arm [dɪs'ɑːrm] **1** *v/t* désarmer **2** *v/i* désarmer

dis·ar·ma·ment [dɪs'ɑːrməmənt] désarmement *m*

dis·arm·ing [dɪs'ɑːrmɪŋ] *adj* désarmant

dis·as·ter [dɪ'zæstər] désastre *m*

di·sas·ter a·re·a région *f* sinistrée; *fig*: *person* catastrophe *f* (ambulante)

di·sas·trous [dɪ'zæstrəs] *adj* désastreux*

dis·band [dɪs'bænd] **1** *v/t* disperser **2** *v/i* se disperser

dis·be·lief [dɪsbə'liːf] incrédulité *f*; **in ~** avec incrédulité

disc [dɪsk] disque *m*; *CD* CD *m*

dis·card [dɪ'skɑːrd] *v/t old clothes etc* se débarrasser de; *boyfriend, theory* abandonner

dis·cern [dɪ'sɜːrn] *v/t* discerner

dis·cern·i·ble [dɪ'sɜːrnəbl] *adj* visible; *improvement* perceptible

dis·cern·ing [dɪ'sɜːrnɪŋ] *adj* judicieux*

dis·charge ['dɪstʃɑːrdʒ] **1** *n from hospital* sortie *f*, MIL *for disciplinary reasons* révocation *f*, MIL *for health reasons* réforme *f* **2** *v/t* [dɪs'tʃɑːrdʒ] *from hospital* faire sortir; MIL *for disciplinary reasons* révoquer; MIL *for health reasons* réformer; *from job* renvoyer; **~ o.s.** *from hospital* décider de sortir

di·sci·ple [dɪ'saɪpl] *religious* disciple *m/f*

dis·ci·pli·nar·y [dɪsɪ'plɪnərɪ] *adj* disciplinaire

dis·ci·pline ['dɪsɪplɪn] **1** *n* discipline *f* **2** *v/t child, dog* discipliner; *employee* punir

'disc jock·ey disc-jockey *m*

dis·claim [dɪs'kleɪm] *v/t* nier

dis·close [dɪs'kloʊz] *v/t* révéler, divulguer

dis·clo·sure [dɪs'kloʊʒər] *of information, name* révélation *f*, divulgation *f*; *about scandal etc* révélation *f*

dis·co ['dɪskoʊ] discothèque *f*; *type of dance, music* disco *m*; **school ~** soirée *f* (de l'école)

dis·col·or, Br **dis·col·our** [dɪs'kʌlər] v/i décolorer

dis·com·fort [dɪs'kʌmfərt] n gêne f; **be in ~** être incommodé

dis·con·cert [dɪskən'sɜːrt] v/t déconcerter

dis·con·cert·ed [dɪskən'sɜːrtɪd] adj déconcerté

dis·con·nect [dɪskə'nekt] v/t hose etc détacher; electrical appliance etc débrancher; supply, telephones couper; **I was ~ed** TELEC j'ai été coupé

dis·con·so·late [dɪs'kɑːnsələt] adj inconsolable

dis·con·tent [dɪskən'tent] mécontentement m

dis·con·tent·ed [dɪskən'tentɪd] adj mécontent

dis·con·tin·ue [dɪskən'tɪnuː] v/t product, magazine arrêter; bus, train service supprimer

dis·cord ['dɪskɔːrd] MUS dissonance f; in relations discorde f

dis·co·theque ['dɪskətek] discothèque f

dis·count ['dɪskaʊnt] 1 n remise f 2 v/t [dɪs'kaʊnt] goods escompter; theory ne pas tenir compte de

dis·cour·age [dɪs'kʌrɪdʒ] v/t décourager

dis·cour·age·ment [dɪs'kʌrɪdʒmənt] découragement m

dis·cov·er [dɪs'kʌvər] v/t découvrir

dis·cov·er·er [dɪs'kʌvərər] découvreur(-euse) m(f)

dis·cov·er·y [dɪs'kʌvərɪ] découverte f

dis·cred·it [dɪs'kredɪt] v/t discréditer

dis·creet [dɪs'kriːt] adj discret*

dis·creet·ly [dɪs'kriːtlɪ] adv discrètement

dis·crep·an·cy [dɪs'krepənsɪ] divergence f

dis·cre·tion [dɪs'kreʃn] discrétion f; **at your ~** à votre discrétion

dis·crim·i·nate [dɪs'krɪmɪneɪt] v/i: **~ against** pratiquer une discrimination contre; **be ~d against** être victime de discrimination; **~ between sth and sth** distinguer qch de qch

dis·crim·i·nat·ing [dɪs'krɪmɪneɪtɪŋ] adj avisé

dis·crim·i·na·tion [dɪˈskrɪmɪneɪʃn] sexual, racial etc discrimination f

dis·cus ['dɪskəs] SP object disque m; event (lancer m du) disque m

dis·cuss [dɪˈskʌs] v/t discuter de; of article traiter de

dis·cus·sion [dɪˈskʌʃn] discussion f

'**dis·cus throw·er** [ˈθroʊər] lanceur (-euse) m(f) de disque

dis·dain [dɪsˈdeɪn] n dédain m

dis·ease [dɪˈziːz] maladie f

dis·em·bark [dɪsəmˈbɑːrk] v/i débarquer

dis·en·chant·ed [dɪsənˈtʃæntɪd] adj désenchanté (**with** par)

dis·en·gage [dɪsənˈgeɪdʒ] v/t dégager

dis·en·tan·gle [dɪsənˈtæŋgl] v/t démêler

dis·fig·ure [dɪsˈfɪgər] v/t défigurer

dis·grace [dɪsˈgreɪs] 1 n honte f; **be a ~ to** faire honte à; **it's a ~** c'est une honte or un scandale; **in ~** en disgrâce 2 v/t faire honte à

dis·grace·ful [dɪsˈgreɪsful] adj behavior, situation honteux*, scandaleux*

dis·grun·tled [dɪsˈgrʌntld] adj mécontent

dis·guise [dɪsˈgaɪz] 1 n déguisement m; **in ~** déguisé 2 v/t voice, handwriting déguiser; fear, anxiety dissimuler; **~ o.s. as** se déguiser en; **he was ~d as** il était déguisé en

dis·gust [dɪsˈgʌst] 1 n dégoût m; **in ~** dégoûté 2 v/t dégoûter

dis·gust·ing [dɪsˈgʌstɪŋ] adj dégoûtant

dish [dɪʃ] plat m; **~es** vaisselle f

'**dish·cloth** for washing lavette f; Br for drying torchon m

dis·heart·ened [dɪsˈhɑːrtnd] adj découragé

dis·heart·en·ing [dɪsˈhɑːrtnɪŋ] adj décourageant

di·shev·eled, Br **di·shev·el·led** [dɪˈʃevld] adj hair ébouriffé; clothes en désordre; person débraillé

dis·hon·est [dɪsˈɑːnɪst] adj malhonnête

dis·hon·est·y [dɪsˈɑːnɪstɪ] malhonnêteté f

dis·hon·or [dɪsˈɑːnər] n déshonneur

m; **bring ~ on** déshonorer

dis·hon·o·ra·ble [dɪs'ɑːnərəbl] *adj* déshonorant

dis·hon·our *etc Br* → **dishonor** *etc*

'dish·wash·er *person* plongeur(-euse) *m(f)*; *machine* lave-vaisselle *m*; **'dish·wash·ing liq·uid** produit *m* à vaisselle; **'dish·wa·ter** eau *f* de vaisselle

dis·il·lu·sion [dɪsɪ'luːʒn] *v/t* désillusionner

dis·il·lu·sion·ment [dɪsɪ'luːʒnmənt] désillusion *f*

dis·in·clined [dɪsɪn'klaɪnd] *adj* peu disposé *or* enclin (**to** à)

dis·in·fect [dɪsɪn'fekt] *v/t* désinfecter

dis·in·fec·tant [dɪsɪn'fektənt] désinfectant *m*

dis·in·her·it [dɪsɪn'herɪt] *v/t* déshériter

dis·in·te·grate [dɪs'ɪntəgreɪt] *v/i* se désintégrer; *of marriage* se désagréger

dis·in·ter·est·ed [dɪs'ɪntərestɪd] *adj* (*unbiased*) désintéressé

dis·joint·ed [dɪs'dʒɔɪntɪd] *adj* incohérent, décousu

disk [dɪsk] *also* COMPUT disque *m*; *floppy* disquette *f*; **on ~** sur disque / disquette

'disk drive COMPUT lecteur *m* de disque / disquette

disk·ette [dɪs'ket] disquette *f*

dis·like [dɪs'laɪk] **1** *n* aversion *f*; **take a ~ to s.o.** prendre qn en grippe; **her likes and ~s** ce qu'elle aime et ce qu'elle n'aime pas **2** *v/t* ne pas aimer

dis·lo·cate ['dɪsləkeɪt] *v/t shoulder* disloquer

dis·lodge [dɪs'lɑːdʒ] *v/t* déplacer

dis·loy·al [dɪs'lɔɪəl] *adj* déloyal

dis·loy·al·ty [dɪs'lɔɪəltɪ] déloyauté *f*

dis·mal ['dɪzməl] *adj weather* morne; *news, prospect* sombre; *person* (*sad*) triste; *person* (*negative*) lugubre; *failure* lamentable

dis·man·tle [dɪs'mæntl] *v/t object* démonter; *organization* démanteler

dis·may [dɪs'meɪ] **1** *n* consternation *f* **2** *v/t* consterner

dis·miss [dɪs'mɪs] *v/t employee* renvoyer; *suggestion* rejeter; *idea, thought*

écarter; *possibility* exclure

dis·miss·al [dɪs'mɪsl] *of employee* renvoi *m*

dis·mount [dɪs'maunt] *v/i* descendre

dis·o·be·di·ence [dɪsə'biːdɪəns] désobéissance *f*

dis·o·be·di·ent [dɪsə'biːdɪənt] *adj* désobéissant

dis·o·bey [dɪsə'beɪ] *v/t* désobéir à

dis·or·der [dɪs'ɔːrdər] (*untidiness*) désordre *m*; (*unrest*) désordre(s) *m(pl)*; MED troubles *mpl*

dis·or·der·ly [dɪs'ɔːrdərlɪ] *adj room, desk* en désordre; (*unruly*) indiscipliné; **~ conduct** trouble *m* à l'ordre public

dis·or·gan·ized [dɪs'ɔːrgənaɪzd] *adj* désorganisé

dis·o·ri·ent·ed [dɪs'ɔːriəntɪd] *adj* désorienté

dis·own [dɪs'oun] *v/t* désavouer, renier

dis·par·ag·ing [dɪ'spærɪdʒɪŋ] *adj* désobligeant

dis·par·i·ty [dɪ'spærətɪ] disparité *f*

dis·pas·sion·ate [dɪ'spæʃənət] *adj* (*objective*) impartial, objectif*

dis·patch [dɪ'spætʃ] *v/t* (*send*) envoyer

dis·pen·sa·ry [dɪ'spensərɪ] *in pharmacy* officine *f*

♦ **dis·pense with** [dɪ'spens] *v/t* se passer de

dis·perse [dɪ'spɜːrs] **1** *v/t* disperser **2** *v/i* se disperser

dis·pir·it·ed [dɪ'spɪrɪtɪd] *adj* abattu

dis·place [dɪs'pleɪs] *v/t* (*supplant*) supplanter

dis·play [dɪ'spleɪ] **1** *n of paintings etc* exposition *f*; *of emotion, in store window* étalage *m*; COMPUT affichage *m*; **be on ~** *at exhibition, for sale* être exposé **2** *v/t emotion* montrer; *at exhibition, for sale* exposer; COMPUT afficher

dis·play cab·i·net *in museum, store* vitrine *f*

dis·please [dɪs'pliːz] *v/t* déplaire à

dis·plea·sure [dɪs'pleʒər] mécontentement *m*

dis·po·sa·ble [dɪ'spouzəbl] *adj* jetable

dis·po·sa·ble 'in·come salaire *m* disponible

dis·pos·al [dɪ'spəuzl] *of waste* élimination *f*; *(sale)* cession *f*; *I am at your ~* je suis à votre disposition; *put sth at s.o.'s ~* mettre qch à la disposition de qn

♦ **dis·pose of** [dɪ'spəuz] *v/t (get rid of)* se débarrasser de; *rubbish* jeter; *(sell)* céder

dis·posed [dɪ'spəuzd] *adj*: *be ~ to do sth (willing)* être disposé à faire qch; *be well ~ toward* être bien disposé à l'égard de

dis·po·si·tion [dɪspə'zɪʃn] *(nature)* disposition *f*

dis·pro·por·tion·ate [dɪsprə'pɔːr-ʃənət] *adj* disproportionné

dis·prove [dɪs'pruːv] *v/t* réfuter

di·spute [dɪ'spjuːt] **1** *n* contestation *f*; *between two countries* conflit *m*; *industrial ~* conflit *m* social; *that's not in ~* cela n'est pas remis en cause **2** *v/t* contester; *(fight over)* se disputer

dis·qual·i·fi·ca·tion [dɪskwɑːlɪfɪ'keɪʃn] disqualification *f*

dis·qual·i·fy [dɪs'kwɑːlɪfaɪ] *v/t (pret & pp -ied)* disqualifier

dis·re·gard [dɪsrə'gɑːrd] **1** *n* indifférence *f (for* à l'égard de) **2** *v/t* ne tenir aucun compte de

dis·re·pair [dɪsrə'per]: *in a state of ~* délabré

dis·rep·u·ta·ble [dɪs'repjʊtəbl] *adj* peu recommandable

dis·re·spect [dɪsrə'spekt] manque *m* de respect, irrespect *m*

dis·re·spect·ful [dɪsrə'spektfʊl] *adj* irrespectueux*

dis·rupt [dɪs'rʌpt] *v/t* perturber

dis·rup·tion [dɪs'rʌpʃn] perturbation *f*

dis·rup·tive [dɪs'rʌptɪv] *adj* perturbateur*; *be a ~influence* être un élément perturbateur

dis·sat·is·fac·tion [dɪssætɪs'fækʃn] mécontentement *m*

dis·sat·is·fied [dɪs'sætɪsfaɪd] *adj* mécontent

dis·sen·sion [dɪ'senʃn] dissension *f*

dis·sent [dɪ'sent] **1** *n* dissensions *fpl* **2** *v/i*: *~ from* s'opposer à

dis·si·dent ['dɪsɪdənt] *n* dissident(e) *m(f)*

dis·sim·i·lar [dɪ'sɪmɪlər] *adj* différent

dis·so·ci·ate [dɪ'səuʃɪeɪt] *v/t*: *~ o.s. from* se démarquer de

dis·so·lute ['dɪsəluːt] *adj* dissolu

dis·so·lu·tion ['dɪsəluːʃn] POL dissolution *f*

dis·solve [dɪ'zɑːlv] **1** *v/t in liquid* dissoudre **2** *v/i of substance* se dissoudre

dis·suade [dɪ'sweɪd] *v/t* dissuader *(from doing sth* de faire qch)

dis·tance ['dɪstəns] **1** *n* distance *f*; *in the ~* au loin **2** *v/t*: *~ o.s. from* se distancier de

dis·tant ['dɪstənt] *adj place, time, relative* éloigné; *fig (aloof)* distant

dis·taste [dɪs'teɪst] dégoût *m*

dis·taste·ful [dɪs'teɪstfʊl] *adj* désagréable

dis·till·er·y [dɪs'tɪlərɪ] distillerie *f*

dis·tinct [dɪ'stɪŋkt] *adj (clear)* net*; *(different)* distinct; *as ~ from* par opposition à

dis·tinc·tion [dɪ'stɪŋkʃn] *(differentiation)* distinction *f*; *hotel / product of ~* hôtel / produit réputé

dis·tinc·tive [dɪ'stɪŋktɪv] *adj* distinctif*

dis·tinct·ly [dɪ'stɪŋktlɪ] *adv* distinctement; *(decidedly)* vraiment

dis·tin·guish [dɪ'stɪŋgwɪʃ] *v/t (see)* distinguer; *~ between X and Y* distinguer X de Y

dis·tin·guished [dɪ'stɪŋgwɪʃt] *adj* distingué

dis·tort [dɪ'stɔːrt] *v/t* déformer

dis·tract [dɪ'strækt] *v/t person* distraire; *attention* détourner

dis·tract·ed [dɪ'stræktɪd] *adj (worried)* préoccupé

dis·trac·tion [dɪ'strækʃn] distraction *f*; *of attention* détournement *m*; *drive s.o. to ~* rendre qn fou

dis·traught [dɪ'strɔːt] *adj* angoissé; *~ with grief* fou* de chagrin

dis·tress [dɪ'stres] **1** *n* douleur *f*; *in ~ ship, aircraft* en détresse **2** *v/t (upset)* affliger

dis·tress·ing [dɪ'stresɪŋ] *adj* pénible

dis·tress sig·nal signal *m* de détresse

dis·trib·ute [dɪ'strɪbjuːt] *v/t also* COMM distribuer; *wealth* répartir

dis·tri·bu·tion [dɪstrɪˈbjuːʃn] *also*
COMM distribution *f*; *of wealth* répartition *f*
dis·trib·u·tor [dɪˈstrɪbjuːtər] COMM
distributeur *m*
dis·trict [ˈdɪstrɪkt] *of town* quartier *m*;
of country région *f*
dis·trict at·tor·ney procureur *m*
dis·trust [dɪsˈtrʌst] **1** *n* méfiance *f* **2** *v/t*
se méfier de
dis·turb [dɪˈstɜːrb] (*interrupt*) déranger; (*upset*) inquiéter; **do not ~** ne
pas déranger
dis·turb·ance [dɪˈstɜːrbəns] (*interruption*) dérangement *m*; **~s** (*civil unrest*)
troubles *mpl*
dis·turbed [dɪˈstɜːrbd] *adj* (*concerned, worried*) perturbé; (*mentally*) dérangé
dis·turb·ing [dɪˈstɜːrbɪŋ] *adj* perturbant
dis·used [dɪsˈjuːzd] *adj* désaffecté
ditch [dɪtʃ] **1** *n* fossé *m* **2** *v/t* F (*get rid of*) se débarrasser de; *boyfriend, plan* laisser tomber
dith·er [ˈdɪðər] *v/i* hésiter
dive [daɪv] **1** *n* plongeon *m*; *underwater* plongée *f*; *of plane* (vol *m*) piqué *m*; F *bar etc* bouge *m*, boui-boui *m* F; **take a ~** F *of dollar etc* dégringoler **2** *v/i* (*pret also* **dove** [doʊv]) plonger; *underwater* faire de la plongée sous-marine; *of plane* descendre en piqué
div·er [ˈdaɪvər] plongeur(-euse) *m(f)*
di·verge [daɪˈvɜːrdʒ] *v/i* diverger
di·verse [daɪˈvɜːrs] *adj* divers
di·ver·si·fi·ca·tion [daɪvɜːrsɪfɪˈkeɪʃn]
COMM diversification *f*
di·ver·si·fy [daɪˈvɜːrsɪfaɪ] *v/i* (*pret & pp* **-ied**) COMM se diversifier
di·ver·sion [daɪˈvɜːrʃn] *for traffic* déviation *f*; *to distract attention* diversion *f*
di·ver·si·ty [daɪˈvɜːrsətɪ] diversité *f*
di·vert [daɪˈvɜːrt] *v/t traffic* dévier; *attention* détourner
di·vest [daɪˈvest] *v/t*: **~ s.o. of sth** dépouiller qn de qch
di·vide [dɪˈvaɪd] *v/t* (*share*) partager; MATH, *fig: country, family* diviser
div·i·dend [ˈdɪvɪdend] FIN dividende *m*; **pay ~s** *fig* porter ses fruits

di·vine [dɪˈvaɪn] *adj also* F divin
div·ing [ˈdaɪvɪŋ] *from board* plongeon *m*; *underwater* plongée *f* (sous-marine)
'div·ing board plongeoir *m*
di·vis·i·ble [dɪˈvɪzəbl] *adj* divisible
di·vi·sion [dɪˈvɪʒn] division *f*
di·vorce [dɪˈvɔːrs] **1** *n* divorce *m*; **get a ~** divorcer **2** *v/t* divorcer de; **get ~d** divorcer **3** *v/i* divorcer
di·vorced [dɪˈvɔːrst] *adj* divorcé
di·vor·cee [dɪvɔːrˈsiː] divorcé(e) *m(f)*
di·vulge [daɪˈvʌldʒ] *v/t* divulguer
DIY [diːaɪˈwaɪ] *abbr* (= **do it yourself**)
bricolage *m*
DI'Y store magasin *m* de bricolage
diz·zi·ness [ˈdɪzɪnɪs] vertige *m*
diz·zy [ˈdɪzɪ] *adj*: **feel ~** avoir un vertige *or* des vertiges, avoir la tête qui tourne
DJ [ˈdiːdʒeɪ] *abbr* (= **disc jockey**) D.J.
m/f (= disc-jockey); (= **dinner jacket**) smoking *m*
DNA [diːenˈeɪ] *abbr* (= **deoxyribonucleic acid**) AND *m* (= acide *m* désoxyribonucléique)
do [duː] **1** *v/t* (*pret* **did**, *pp* **done**) faire;
~ one's hair se coiffer; **~ French / chemistry** faire du français / de la chimie; **~ 100mph** faire du 100 miles à l'heure; **what are you going to~ to-night?** que faites-vous ce soir?; **I don't know what to ~** je ne sais pas quoi faire; **have one's hair done** se faire coiffer
2 *v/i* (*be suitable, enough*) aller; **that will ~!** ça va!; **~ well** *in health, of business* aller bien; (*be successful*) réussir; **~ well at school** être bon à l'école; **well done!** (*congratulations!*) bien!; **how ~ you ~?** enchanté
3 *v/aux* ◇ : **~ you know him?** est-ce que vous le connaissez?; **I don't know** je ne sais pas; **~ be quick** surtout dépêche-toi; **~ you like Cherbourg? - yes I ~** est-ce que vous aimez Cherbourg? - oui; **don't you know the answer? - ~ you? - no I don't** vous ne connaissez pas la réponse, n'est-ce pas? - non
◇ *tags*: **he works hard, doesn't he?**

il travaille beaucoup, non?; **you don't believe me, ~ you?** tu ne me crois pas, hein?; **you ~ believe me, don't you?** vous me croyez, n'est-ce pas?

♦ **do away with** *v/t* (*abolish*) supprimer

♦ **do in** *v/t* F (*exhaust*) épuiser; **I'm done in** je suis mort (de fatigue) F

♦ **do out of** *v/t*: **do s.o. out of sth** by *cheating* escroquer qn de qch

♦ **do up** *v/t* building rénover; *street* refaire; (*fasten*), *coat etc* fermer; *laces* faire

♦ **do with** *v/t*: **I could do with a cup of coffee** j'aurais bien besoin d'un café; **this room could do with new drapes** cette pièce aurait besoin de nouveaux rideaux; **he won't have anything to do with it** (*won't get involved*) il ne veut pas y être impliqué

♦ **do without 1** *v/i* s'en passer **2** *v/t* se passer de

do·cile ['dousail] *adj* docile

dock[1] [dɑːk] **1** *n* NAUT bassin *m* **2** *v/i of ship* entrer au bassin; *of spaceship* s'arrimer

dock[2] [dɑːk] *n* LAW banc *m* des accusés

'**dock·yard** *Br* chantier *m* naval

doc·tor ['dɑːktər] *n* MED docteur *m*, médecin *m*; *form of address* docteur

doc·tor·ate ['dɑːktərət] doctorat *m*

doc·trine ['dɑːktrɪn] doctrine *f*

doc·u·dra·ma ['dɑːkjudrɑːmə] docudrame *m*

doc·u·ment ['dɑːkjumənt] *n* document *m*

doc·u·men·ta·ry [dɑːkju'mentərɪ] *n program* documentaire *m*

doc·u·men·ta·tion [dɑːkjumen'teɪʃn] documentation *f*

dodge [dɑːdʒ] *v/t blow, person, issue* éviter; *question* éluder

dodg·ems ['dɑːdʒəms] *npl Br* auto *f* tamponneuse

doe [dou] *deer* biche *f*

dog [dɒːg] **1** *n* chien *m* **2** *v/t* (*pret & pp -ged*) *of bad luck* poursuivre

'**dog catch·er** employé(e) municipal(e) qui recueille les chiens errants

dog-eared ['dɒːgɪrd] *adj book* écorné

dog·ged ['dɒːgɪd] *adj* tenace

dog·gie ['dɒːgɪ] *in children's language* toutou *m* F

dog·gy bag ['dɒːgɪbæg] sac pour emporter les restes

'**dog·house**: **be in the ~** F être en disgrâce

dog·ma ['dɒːgmə] dogme *m*

dog·mat·ic [dɒːg'mætɪk] *adj* dogmatique

do-good·er ['duːgudər] *pej* âme *f* charitable

dogs·bod·y ['dɒːgzbɑːdɪ] F bon(ne) *m(f)* à tout faire

'**dog tag** MIL plaque *f* d'identification

'**dog-tired** *adj* F crevé F

do-it-your·self [duːɪtjər'self] bricolage *m*

dol·drums ['douldrəmz]: **be in the ~** *of economy* être dans le marasme; *of person* avoir le cafard

♦ **dole out** *v/t* distribuer

doll [dɑːl] *also* F *woman* poupée *f*

♦ **doll up** *v/t*: **get dolled up** se bichonner

dol·lar ['dɑːlər] dollar *m*

dol·lop ['dɑːləp] *n* F *of cream etc* bonne cuillérée *f*

dol·phin ['dɑːlfɪn] dauphin *m*

dome [doum] *of building* dôme *m*

do·mes·tic [də'mestɪk] *adj chores* domestique; *news* national; *policy* intérieur

do·mes·tic 'an·i·mal animal *m* domestique

do·mes·ti·cate [də'mestɪkeɪt] *v/t animal* domestiquer; **be ~d** *of person* aimer les travaux ménagers

do·mes·tic flight vol *m* intérieur

dom·i·nant ['dɑːmɪnənt] *adj* dominant

dom·i·nate ['dɑːmɪneɪt] *v/t* dominer

dom·i·na·tion [dɑːmɪ'neɪʃn] domination *f*

dom·i·neer·ing [dɑːmɪ'nɪrɪŋ] *adj* dominateur*

do·nate [dou'neɪt] *v/t* faire don de

do·na·tion [dou'neɪʃn] don *m*

done [dʌn] *pp* → **do**

don·key ['dɑːŋkɪ] âne *m*

do·nor ['dounər] *of money* donateur

(-trice) *m(f)*; MED donneur(-euse) *m(f)*

do·nut ['dəʊnʌt] beignet *m*

doo·dle ['duːdl] *v/i* griffonner

doom [duːm] *n (fate)* destin *m*; *(ruin)* ruine *f*

doomed [duːmd] *adj* project voué à l'échec; *we are ~* nous sommes condamnés; *the ~ ship* le navire qui allait couler; *the ~ plane* l'avion qui allait s'écraser

door [dɔːr] porte *f*; *of car* portière *f*; *(entrance)* entrée *f*; *there's someone at the ~* il y a quelqu'un à la porte

'door·bell sonnette *f*; **'door·knob** poignée *f* de porte *or* de portière; **'door·man** portier *m*; **'door·mat** paillasson *m*; **'door·step** pas *m* de porte; **'door·way** embrasure *f* de porte

dope [dəʊp] **1** *n (drugs)* drogue *f*; *(idiot)* idiot(e) *m(f)*; *(information)* tuyaux *mpl* **F 2** *v/t* doper

dor·mant ['dɔːrmənt] *adj* plant dormant; *~ volcano* volcan *m* en repos

dor·mi·to·ry ['dɔːrmɪtɔːrɪ] résidence *f* universitaire; Br dortoir *m*

dos·age ['dəʊsɪdʒ] dose *f*

dose [dəʊs] *n* dose *f*

dot [dɒt] *n* also in e-mail address point *m*; *at six o'clock on the ~* à six heures pile

dot.com (com·pa·ny) [dɒt'kɑːm] société *f* dot.com

♦ **dote on** [dəʊt] *v/t* raffoler de

dot·ing ['dəʊtɪŋ] *adj*: *his ~ parents* ses parents qui raffolent de lui

dot·ted line ['dɒtɪd] pointillés *mpl*

dot·ty ['dɑːtɪ] *adj* **F** toqué **F**

dou·ble ['dʌbl] **1** *n* double *m*; *of film star* doublure *f*; *room* chambre *f* pour deux personnes **2** *adj* double; *doors* à deux battants; *sink* à deux bacs; *her salary is ~ his* son salaire est le double du sien; *in ~ figures* à deux chiffres **3** *adv* deux fois (plus); *~ the size* deux fois plus grand **4** *v/t* doubler **5** *v/i* doubler

♦ **double back** *v/i (go back)* revenir sur ses pas

♦ **double up** *v/i in pain* se plier en

deux; *sharing room* partager une chambre

dou·ble·'bass contrebasse *f*; **dou·ble· 'bed** grand lit *m*; **dou·ble·breast·ed** [dʌbl'brestɪd] *adj* croisé; **dou·ble· -'check** *v/t & v/i* revérifier; **dou·ble· 'chin** double menton *m*; **dou·ble· -'cross** *v/t* trahir; **dou·ble 'glaz·ing** double vitrage *m*; **dou·ble·park** *v/i* stationner en double file; **'dou·ble· -quick** *adj*: *in ~ time* en un rien de temps; **'dou·ble room** chambre *f* pour deux personnes

dou·bles ['dʌblz] *in tennis* double *m*

doubt [daʊt] **1** *n (uncertainty)* doute *m*; *be in ~* être incertain; *no ~ (probably)* sans doute **2** *v/t*: *~ s.o. / sth* douter de qn / qch; *~ that ...* douter que ... (+subj)

doubt·ful ['daʊtfʊl] *adj remark, look* douteux*; *be ~ of person* avoir des doutes; *it is ~ whether ...* il est douteux que ... (+subj)

doubt·ful·ly ['daʊtflɪ] *adv* dubitativement

doubt·less ['daʊtlɪs] *adv* sans aucun doute

dough [dəʊ] pâte *f*; **F** *(money)* fric *m* **F**

dough·nut ['dəʊnʌt] Br beignet *m*

dove[1] [dʌv] *also fig* colombe *f*

dove[2] [dəʊv] *pret* → **dive**

Dov·er ['dəʊvər] Douvres

dow·dy ['daʊdɪ] *adj* peu élégant

Dow Jones Av·er·age [daʊ'dʒəʊnz] indice *m* Dow-Jones

down[1] [daʊn] *n (feathers)* duvet *m*

down[2] **1** *adv (downward)* en bas, vers le bas; *(onto the ground)* par terre; *~ there* là-bas; *take the plates ~* descendre les assiettes; *put sth ~* poser qch; *pull the shade ~* baisser le store; *come ~ of leaves etc* tomber; *shoot a plane ~* abattre un avion; *cut ~ a tree* abattre *or* couper un arbre; *fall ~* tomber; *die ~* se calmer; *$200 ~ (as deposit)* 200 dollars d'acompte; *~ south* dans le sud; *be ~ of price, rate, numbers, amount* être en baisse; *(not working)* être en panne; **F** *(depressed)* être déprimé **2** *prep (along)* le long de; *run ~ the stairs* descendre les escaliers en courant; *look ~ a list* parcourir une liste; *it's halfway ~ Baker Street* c'est au milieu de Baker Street; *it's just ~ the street* c'est à deux pas **3** *v/t* (*swallow*) avaler; (*destroy*) abattre

'**down-and-out** *n* clochard(e) *m(f)*; '**down-cast** *adj* abattu; '**down-fall** chute *f*; *alcohol etc* ruine *f*; '**down-grade** *v/t employee* rétrograder; **down-heart-ed** [daʊnˈhɑːrtɪd] *adj* déprimé; **down'hill** *adv*: *the road goes ~* la route descend; *go ~ fig* être sur le déclin; '**down-hill ski-ing** ski *m* alpin; '**down-load** *v/t* COMPUT télécharger; '**down-mark-et** *adj* bas de gamme; '**down pay-ment** paiement *m* au comptant; '**down-play** *v/t* minimiser; '**down-pour** averse *f*; '**down-right 1** *adj idiot, nuisance etc* parfait; *lie* éhonté **2** *adv dangerous, stupid etc* franchement; '**down-side** (*disadvantage*) inconvénient *m*; '**down-size 1** *v/t car etc* réduire la taille de; *company* réduire les effectifs de **2** *v/i of company* réduire ses effectifs; '**down-stairs 1** *adj neighbors etc* d'en bas **2** *adv* en bas; **down-to-'earth** *adj approach, person* terre-à-terre; '**down-town 1** *adj* du centre-ville **2** *adv* en ville; '**down-turn** *in economy* baisse *f*

'**down-ward 1** *adj glance* vers le bas; *trend* à la baisse **2** *adv look* vers le bas; *revise figures* à la baisse

doze [doʊz] **1** *n* petit somme *m* **2** *v/i* sommeiller

♦ **doze off** *v/i* s'assoupir

doz-en [ˈdʌzn] douzaine *f*; *a ~ eggs* une douzaine d'œufs; *~s of* F des tas *mpl* de

drab [dræb] *adj* terne

draft [dræft] **1** *n of air* courant *m* d'air; *of document* brouillon *m*; MIL conscription *f*; *~ (beer), beer on ~* bière *f* à la pression **2** *v/t document* faire le brouillon de; (*write*) rédiger; MIL appeler

draft dodg-er [ˈdræftdɑːdʒər] MIL réfractaire *m*

draft-ee [dræftˈiː] MIL appelé *m*

drafts-man [ˈdræftsmən] dessina-

teur(-trice) *m(f)*

draft-y [ˈdræftɪ] *adj* plein de courants d'air

drag [dræg] **1** *n*: *it's a ~ having to ...* F c'est barbant de devoir ... F; *he's a ~* F il est mortel F; *the main ~* P la rue principale; *in ~* en travesti **2** *v/t* (*pret & pp -ged*) traîner, tirer; (*search*) draguer; ♦ *o.s. into work* se traîner jusqu'au boulot **3** *v/i of time* se traîner; *of show, movie* traîner en longueur; ♦ *s.o. into sth* (*involve*) mêler qn à qch; ♦ *sth out of s.o.* (*get information from*) arracher qch à qn

♦ **drag away** *v/t*: *drag o.s. away from the TV* s'arracher de la télé

♦ **drag in** *v/t into conversation* placer

♦ **drag on** *v/i* (*last long time*) s'éterniser

♦ **drag out** *v/t* (*prolong*) faire durer

♦ **drag up** *v/t* F (*mention*) remettre sur le tapis

drag-on [ˈdrægn] *also fig* dragon *m*

drain [dreɪn] **1** *n pipe* tuyau *m* d'écoulement; *under street* égout *m*; *be a ~ on resources* épuiser les ressources **2** *v/t oil* vidanger; *vegetables* égoutter; *land* drainer; *glass, tank* vider; (*exhaust: person*) épuiser **3** *v/i of dishes* égoutter

♦ **drain away** *v/i of liquid* s'écouler

♦ **drain off** *v/t water* évacuer

drain-age [ˈdreɪnɪdʒ] (*drains*) système *m* d'écoulement des eaux usées; *of water from soil* drainage *m*

'**drain-pipe** tuyau *m* d'écoulement

dra-ma [ˈdrɑːmə] *art form* art *m* dramatique; (*excitement*) action *f*, drame *m*; (*play*) drame *m*

dra-mat-ic [drəˈmætɪk] *adj* dramatique; *events, scenery, decision* spectaculaire; *gesture* théâtral

dra-mat-i-cal-ly [drəˈmætɪklɪ] *adv say* d'un ton théâtral; *decline, rise, change etc* radicalement

dram-a-tist [ˈdræmətɪst] dramaturge *m/f*

dram-a-ti-za-tion [dræmətaɪˈzeɪʃn] *of novel etc* adaptation *f*

dram-a-tize [ˈdræmətaɪz] *v/t story* adapter (*for* pour); *fig* dramatiser

drank [dræŋk] *pret* → **drink**

drape [dreɪp] *v/t cloth, coat* draper, poser; **~d in** (*covered with*) recouvert de, enveloppé dans

drap·er·y ['dreɪpərɪ] draperie *f*

drapes [dreɪps] *npl* rideaux *mpl*

dras·tic ['dræstɪk] *adj* radical; *measures also* drastique

draw [drɔː] **1** *n in competition* match *m* nul; *in lottery* tirage *m* (au sort); (*attraction*) attraction *f* **2** *v/t* (*pret* **drew**, *pp* **drawn**) *picture, map* dessiner; (*pull*), *in lottery, gun, knife* tirer; (*attract*) attirer; (*lead*) emmener; *from bank account* retirer **3** *v/i of artist* dessiner; *in competition* faire match nul; **~ near** *of person* s'approcher; *of date* approcher

◆ **draw back 1** *v/i* (*recoil*) reculer **2** *v/t* (*pull back*) retirer; *drapes* ouvrir

◆ **draw on 1** *v/i* (*approach*) approcher **2** *v/t* (*make use of*) puiser dans, s'inspirer de

◆ **draw out** *v/t wallet, money from bank* retirer

◆ **draw up 1** *v/t document* rédiger; *chair* approcher **2** *v/i of vehicle* s'arrêter

'draw·back désavantage *m*, inconvénient *m*

draw·er[^1] [drɔːr] *of desk etc* tiroir *m*

draw·er[^2] [drɔːr] *artist* dessinateur (-trice) *m(f)*

draw·ing ['drɔːɪŋ] dessin *m*

'draw·ing board planche *f* à dessin; **go back to the ~** retourner à la case départ

drawl [drɔːl] *n* voix *f* traînante

drawn [drɔːn] *pp* → **draw**

dread [dred] *v/t*: **~ doing sth** redouter de faire qch; **~ s.o. doing sth** redouter que qn fasse (*subj*) qch

dread·ful ['dredfʊl] *adj* épouvantable

dread·ful·ly ['dredflɪ] *adv* F (*extremely*) terriblement; *behave* de manière épouvantable

dream [driːm] **1** *n* rêve *m* **2** *adj* F *house etc* de ses / vos rêves **3** *v/t & v/i* rêver (*about, of* de)

◆ **dream up** *v/t* inventer

dream·er ['driːmər] (*daydreamer*) rêveur(-euse) *m(f)*

dream·y ['driːmɪ] *adj voice, look* rêveur*

drear·y ['drɪrɪ] *adj* morne

dredge [dredʒ] *v/t harbor, canal* draguer

◆ **dredge up** *v/t fig* déterrer

dregs [dregz] *npl* lie *f*; *of coffee* marc *m*; **the ~ of society** la lie de la société

drench [drentʃ] *v/t* tremper; **get ~ed** se faire tremper

dress [dres] **1** *n for woman* robe *f*; (*clothing*) tenue *f*; **~ code** code *m* vestimentaire **2** *v/t person* habiller; *wound* panser; **get ~ed** s'habiller **3** *v/i* s'habiller

◆ **dress up** *v/i* s'habiller chic, se mettre sur son trente et un; (*wear a disguise*) se déguiser; **dress up as** se déguiser en

'dress cir·cle premier balcon *m*

dress·er ['dresər] (*dressing table*) coiffeuse *f*; *in kitchen* buffet *m*; **be a snazzy ~** s'habiller classe F

dress·ing ['dresɪŋ] *for salad* assaisonnement *m*; *for wound* pansement *m*

dress·ing 'down savon *m* F; **give s.o. a ~** passer un savon à qn F; **'dress·ing gown** *Br* robe *f* de chambre; **'dress·ing room** *in theater* loge *f*; **'dress·ing ta·ble** coiffeuse *f*

'dress·mak·er couturière *f*

'dress re·hears·al (répétition *f*) générale *f*

dress·y ['dresɪ] *adj* F habillé

drew [druː] *pret* → **draw**

drib·ble ['drɪbl] *v/i of person* baver; *of water* dégouliner; SP dribbler

dried [draɪd] *adj fruit etc* sec*

dri·er → **dryer**

drift [drɪft] **1** *n of snow* amas *m* **2** *v/i of snow* s'amonceler; *of ship* être à la dérive; (*go off course*) dériver; *of person* aller à la dérive; **~ from town to town** aller de ville en ville

◆ **drift apart** *v/i of couple* s'éloigner l'un de l'autre

drift·er ['drɪftər] personne qui vit au jour le jour; **be a bit of a ~** être un peu bohème

drill [drɪl] **1** *n tool* perceuse *f*; *exercise*

[^1]:
[^2]:

exercice(s) *m(pl)*; MIL exercice *m* **2** *v/t hole* percer **3** *v/i for oil* forer; MIL faire l'exercice

dril·ling rig ['drɪlɪŋrɪg] *platform* plateforme *f* de forage; *on land* tour *f* de forage

dri·ly ['draɪlɪ] *adv remark* d'un ton pince-sans-rire

drink [drɪŋk] **1** *n* boisson *f*; *can I have a ~ of water* est-ce que je peux avoir de l'eau?; *go for a ~* aller boire un verre **2** *v/t & v/i* (*pret* **drank**, *pp* **drunk**) boire; *I don't ~* je ne bois pas

◆ **drink up 1** *v/i* (*finish drink*) finir son verre **2** *v/t* (*drink completely*) finir

drink·a·ble ['drɪŋkəbl] *adj* buvable; *water* potable

drink·er ['drɪŋkər] buveur(-euse) *m(f)*

drink·ing ['drɪŋkɪŋ] *of alcohol* boisson *f*

'drink·ing wa·ter eau *f* potable

'drinks ma·chine distributeur *m* de boissons

drip [drɪp] **1** *n liquid* goutte *f*; MED goutte-à-goutte *m*, perfusion *f* **2** *v/i* (*pret & pp* **-ped**) goutter

drip·ping ['drɪpɪŋ] *adv*: *~ wet* trempé

drive [draɪv] **1** *n* trajet *m* (en voiture); *outing* promenade *f* (en voiture); (*energy*) dynamisme *m*; COMPUT unité *f*, lecteur *m*; (*campaign*) campagne *f*; *it's a short ~ from the station* c'est à quelques minutes de la gare en voiture; *left- / right-hand ~* MOT conduite *f* à gauche / droite **2** *v/t* (*pret* **drove**, *pp* **driven**) *vehicle* conduire; (*be owner of*) avoir; (*take in car*) amener; TECH faire marcher, actionner; *that noise is driving me mad* ce bruit me rend fou; *~n by a desire to ...* poussé par le désir de ... **3** *v/i* (*pret* **drove**, *pp* **driven**) conduire; *~ to work* aller au travail en voiture

◆ **drive at** *v/t*: *what are you driving at?* où voulez-vous en venir?

◆ **drive away 1** *v/t* emmener; (*chase off*) chasser **2** *v/i* partir

◆ **drive in** *v/t nail* enfoncer

◆ **drive off** → *drive away*

'drive-in *n movie theater* drive-in *m*

driv·el ['drɪvl] *n* bêtises *fpl*

driv·en ['drɪvn] *pp* → *drive*

driv·er ['draɪvər] conducteur(-trice) *m(f)*; *of truck* camionneur(-euse) *m(f)*; COMPUT pilote *m*

'driv·er's li·cense permis *m* de conduire

'drive-thru *restaurant / banque où l'on sert le client sans qu'il doive sortir de sa voiture*; Mc-Drive® *m*

'drive·way allée *f*

driv·ing ['draɪvɪŋ] **1** *n* conduite *f* **2** *adj rain* battant

driv·ing 'force force *f* motrice; **'driv·ing in·struct·or** moniteur(-trice) *m(f)* de conduite; **'driv·ing les·son** leçon *f* de conduite; **'driv·ing li·cence** *Br* permis *m* de conduire; **'driv·ing school** auto-école *f*; **'driv·ing test** (examen *m* du) permis *m* de conduire

driz·zle ['drɪzl] **1** *n* bruine *f* **2** *v/i* bruiner

drone [droʊn] *n of engine* ronronnement *m*

droop [druːp] *v/i* s'affaisser; *of shoulders* tomber; *of plant* baisser la tête

drop [drɑːp] **1** *n* goutte *f*; *in price, temperature, number* chute *f* **2** *v/t* (*pret & pp* **-ped**) *object* faire tomber; *bomb* lancer; *person from car* déposer; *person from team* écarter; (*stop seeing*), *charges, demand, subject* laisser tomber; (*give up*) arrêter; *~ a line to* envoyer un mot à **3** *v/i* (*pret & pp* **-ped**) tomber

◆ **drop in** *v/i* (*visit*) passer

◆ **drop off 1** *v/t person, goods* déposer; (*deliver*) **2** *v/i* (*fall asleep*) s'endormir; (*decline*) diminuer

◆ **drop out** *v/i* (*withdraw*) se retirer (*of* de); *of school* abandonner (*of sth* qch)

'drop·out *from school* personne qui abandonne l'école; *from society* marginal(e) *m(f)*

drops [drɑːps] *npl for eyes* gouttes *fpl*

drought [draʊt] sécheresse *f*

drove [droʊv] *pret* → *drive*

drown [draʊn] **1** *v/i* se noyer **2** *v/t per-*

son noyer; *sound* étouffer; ***be ~ed*** se noyer

drow·sy ['drauzɪ] *adj* somnolent

drudg·er·y ['drʌdʒərɪ] corvée *f*

drug [drʌg] **1** *n* MED médicament *m*; *illegal* drogue *f*; ***be on ~s*** se droguer **2** *v/t* (*pret & pp* **-ged**) droguer

'**drug ad·dict** toxicomane *m/f*

'**drug deal·er** dealer *m*, dealeuse *f*; *large-scale* trafiquant(e) *m(f)* de drogue

drug·gist ['drʌgɪst] pharmacien(ne) *m(f)*

'**drug·store** drugstore *m*

drug traf·fick·ing ['drʌgtræfɪkɪŋ] trafic *m* de drogue

drum [drʌm] *n* MUS tambour *m*; *container* tonneau *m*; ***~s*** batterie *f*

♦ **drum into** *v/t* (*pret & pp* **-med**): ***drum sth into s.o.*** enfoncer qch dans la tête de qn

♦ **drum up** *v/t*: ***drum up support*** obtenir du soutien

drum·mer ['drʌmər] joueur(-euse) *m(f)* de tambour; *in pop band* batteur *m*

'**drum·stick** MUS baguette *f* de tambour; *of poultry* pilon *m*

drunk [drʌŋk] **1** *n* ivrogne *m/f*, *habitually* alcoolique *m/f* **2** *adj* ivre, soûl; ***get ~*** se soûler **3** *pp* → **drink**

drunk·en ['drʌŋkn] *voices, laughter* d'ivrogne; *party* bien arrosé

drunk 'driv·ing conduite *f* en état d'ivresse

dry [draɪ] **1** *adj* sec*; (*ironic*) pince-sans-rire; ***~ humor*** humour *m* à froid **2** *v/t* (*pret & pp* **-ied**) *clothes* faire sécher; *dishes, eyes* essuyer **3** *v/i* (*pret & pp* **-ied**) sécher

♦ **dry out** *v/i* sécher; *of alcoholic* subir une cure de désintoxication

♦ **dry up** *v/i* *of river* s'assécher; F (*be quiet*) se taire

'**dry-clean** *v/t* nettoyer à sec; '**dry clean·er** pressing *m*; '**dry-clean·ing** *clothes* vêtements *mpl* laissés au pressing

dry·er ['draɪr] *machine* sèche-linge *m*

DTP [di:ti:'pi:] *abbr* (= **desk-top publishing**) PAO *f* (= publication assis-

tée par ordinateur)

du·al ['du:əl] *adj* double

du·al car·riage·way *Br* route *f* à deux chaussées, quatre voies *f*

dub [dʌb] *v/t* (*pret & pp* **-bed**) *movie* doubler

du·bi·ous ['du:bɪəs] *adj* douteux*; ***I'm still ~ about the idea*** j'ai encore des doutes quant à cette idée

duch·ess ['dʌtʃɪs] duchesse *f*

duck [dʌk] **1** *n* canard *m*; *female* cane *f* **2** *v/i* se baisser **3** *v/t* *one's head* baisser (subitement); *question* éviter

dud [dʌd] *n* F (*false bill*) faux *m*

due [du:] *adj* (*owed*) dû; (*proper*) qui convient; ***the rent is ~ tomorrow*** il faut payer le loyer demain; ***be ~ to do sth*** devoir faire qch; ***be ~*** (*to arrive*) devoir arriver; ***when is the baby ~?*** quand est-ce que le bébé doit naître?; ***~ to*** (*because of*) à cause de; ***be ~ to*** (*be caused by*) être dû à; ***in ~ course*** en temps voulu

dues [du:z] *npl* cotisation *f*

du·et [du:'et] MUS duo *m*

dug [dʌg] *pret & pp* → **dig**

duke [du:k] duc *m*

dull [dʌl] *adj* *weather* sombre; *sound, pain* sourd; (*boring*) ennuyeux*

du·ly ['du:lɪ] *adv* (*as expected*) comme prévu; (*properly*) dûment, comme il se doit

dumb [dʌm] *adj* (*mute*) muet*; F (*stupid*) bête

♦ **dumb down** *v/t* TV *programs etc* abaisser le niveau (intellectuel) de

dumb·found·ed [dʌm'faundɪd] *adj* abasourdi

dum·my ['dʌmɪ] *in store window* mannequin *m*; *Br. for baby* tétine *f*

dump [dʌmp] **1** *n for garbage* décharge *f*, (*unpleasant place*) trou *m* F; *house, hotel* taudis *m* **2** *v/t* (*deposit*) déposer; (*throw away*) jeter; (*leave*) laisser; *waste* déverser

dump·ling ['dʌmplɪŋ] boulette *f*

dune [du:n] dune *f*

dung [dʌŋ] fumier *m*, engrais *m*

dun·ga·rees [dʌŋgə'ri:z] *npl for workman* bleu(s) *m(pl)* de travail; *for child* salopette *f*

dunk [dʌŋk] *v/t in coffee etc* tremper

Dun·kirk [dʌn'kɜːrk] Dunkerque

du·o ['duːoʊ] MUS duo *m*

du·plex (a·part·ment) ['duːpleks] duplex *m*

du·pli·cate ['duːplɪkət] **1** *n* double *m*; **in** ~ en double **2** *v/t* ['duːplɪkeɪt] *(copy)* copier; *(repeat)* reproduire

du·pli·cate 'key MUS double *m* de clef

du·ra·ble ['dʊrəbl] *adj material* résistant, solide; *relationship* durable

du·ra·tion [dʊ'reɪʃn] durée *f*

du·ress [dʊ'res]: **under** ~ sous la contrainte

dur·ing ['dʊrɪŋ] *prep* pendant

dusk [dʌsk] crépuscule *m*

dust [dʌst] **1** *n* poussière *f* **2** *v/t* épousseter; ~ **sth with sth** *(sprinkle)* saupoudrer qch de qch

'dust·bin *Br* poubelle *f*

'dust cov·er *for book* jaquette *f*

dust·er ['dʌstər] *cloth* chiffon *m* (à poussière)

'dust jack·et *of book* jaquette *f*; **'dust·man** *Br* éboueur *m*; **'dust·pan** pelle *f* à poussière

dust·y ['dʌstɪ] *adj* poussiéreux*

Dutch [dʌtʃ] **1** *adj* hollandais; **go** ~ **F** partager les frais **2** *n language* néer-

landais *m*, hollandais *m*; **the** ~ les Hollandais *mpl*, les Néerlandais *mpl*

du·ty ['duːtɪ] devoir *m*; *(task)* fonction *f*; *on goods* droit(s) *m(pl)*; **be on** ~ être de service; **be off** ~ ne pas être de service

du·ty-free *adj* hors taxe

du·ty-free shop magasin *m* hors taxe

DVD [diːviː'diː] *abbr (= digital versa-tile disk)* DVD *m*

dwarf [dwɔːrf] **1** *n* nain(e) *m(f)* **2** *v/t* rapetisser

♦ **dwell on** [dwel] *v/t* s'étendre sur

dwin·dle ['dwɪndl] *v/i* diminuer

dye [daɪ] **1** *n* teinture *f* **2** *v/t* teindre; ~ **one's hair** se teindre les cheveux

dy·ing ['daɪɪŋ] *adj person* mourant; *in-dustry* moribond; *tradition* qui se perd

dy·nam·ic [daɪ'næmɪk] *adj* dynamique

dy·na·mism ['daɪnəmɪzm] dynamis-me *m*

dy·na·mite ['daɪnəmaɪt] *n* dynamite *f*

dy·na·mo ['daɪnəmoʊ] TECH dynamo *f*

dy·nas·ty ['daɪnəstɪ] dynastie *f*

dys·lex·i·a [dɪs'leksɪə] dyxlexie *f*

dys·lex·ic [dɪs'leksɪk] **1** *adj* dyslexique **2** *n* dyslexique *m/f*

E

E

each [iːtʃ] **1** *adj* chaque; ~ **one** chacun(e) **2** *adv* chacun; **they're $1.50** ~ ils coûtent 1,50 $ chacun, ils sont 1,50 $ pièce **3** *pron* chacun(e) *m(f)*; ~ **of them** chacun(e) d'entre eux (elles) *m(f)*; **we know** ~ **other** nous nous connaissons; **do you know** ~ **other?** est-ce que vous vous connaissez?; **they drive** ~ **other's cars** ils (elles) conduisent la voiture l'un(e) de l'autre

ea·ger ['iːgər] *adj* désireux*; *look* avide; **be** ~ **to do sth** désirer vive-

ment faire qch

ea·ger·ly ['iːgərlɪ] *adv* avec empresse-ment; *wait* impatiemment

ea·ger·ness ['iːgərnɪs] ardeur *f*, em-pressement *m*

ea·gle ['iːgl] aigle *m*

ea·gle-eyed [iːgl'aɪd] *adj*: **be** ~ avoir des yeux d'aigle

ear¹ [ɪr] oreille *f*

ear² [ɪr] *of corn* épi *m*

'ear·ache mal *m* d'oreilles

'ear·drum tympan *m*

earl [ɜːrl] comte *m*

'ear·lobe lobe *m* de l'oreille

ear·ly ['ɜːrlɪ] **1** *adv (not late)* tôt; *(ahead of time)* en avance; *it's too ~ to say* c'est trop tôt pour le dire **2** *adj hours, stages, Romans* premier*; *potato* précoce; *arrival* en avance; *retirement* anticipé; *music* ancien; *(in the near future)* prochain; *~ vegetables* primeurs *fpl*; *(in) ~ October* début octobre; *an ~ Picasso* une des premières œuvres de Picasso; *have an ~ supper* dîner tôt *or* de bonne heure; *be an ~ riser* se lever tôt *or* de bonne heure

'ear·ly bird: *be an ~ (early riser)* être matinal; *(ahead of the others)* arriver avant les autres

ear·mark ['ɪrmɑːrk] *v/t*: *~ sth for sth* réserver qch à qch

earn [ɜːrn] *v/t money, holiday, respect* gagner; *interest* rapporter

ear·nest ['ɜːrnɪst] *adj* sérieux*; *be in ~* être sérieux

earn·ings ['ɜːrnɪŋz] *npl* salaire *m*; *of company* profits *mpl*

'ear·phones *npl* écouteurs *mpl*; 'ear-pierc·ing *adj* strident; 'ear·ring boucle *f* d'oreille; 'ear·shot: *within ~* à portée de la voix;; *out of ~* hors de portée de la voix

earth [ɜːrθ] terre *f*; *where on ~ ...?* F où diable ...? F

earth·en·ware ['ɜːrθnwer] *n* poterie *f*

earth·ly ['ɜːrθlɪ] *adj* terrestre; *it's no ~ use doing that* F ça ne sert strictement à rien de faire cela

earth·quake ['ɜːrθkweɪk] tremblement *m* de terre

earth-shat·ter·ing ['ɜːrθʃætərɪŋ] *adj* stupéfiant

ease [iːz] **1** *n* facilité *f*; *be or feel at (one's) ~* être *or* se sentir à l'aise; *be or feel ill at ~* être *or* se sentir mal à l'aise **2** *v/t pain, mind* soulager; *suffering, shortage* diminuer **3** *v/i of pain* diminuer

♦ ease off **1** *v/t (remove)* enlever doucement **2** *v/i of pain, rain* se calmer

ea·sel ['iːzl] chevalet *m*

eas·i·ly ['iːzəlɪ] *adv (with ease)* facilement; *(by far)* de loin

east [iːst] **1** *n* est *m*; *to the ~ of* à l'est de **2** *adj* est *inv*; *wind* d'est; *~ San Francisco* l'est de San Francisco **3** *adv travel* vers l'est; *~ of* à l'est de

Eas·ter ['iːstər] Pâques *fpl*

'Eas·ter 'Day (jour *m* de) Pâques *m*

'Eas·ter egg œuf *m* de Pâques

eas·ter·ly ['iːstərlɪ] *adj wind* de l'est; *direction* vers l'est

Eas·ter 'Mon·day lundi *m* de Pâques

east·ern ['iːstərn] *adj* de l'est; *(oriental)* oriental

east·er·ner ['iːstərnər] habitant(e) *m(f)* de l'Est des États-Unis

east·ward ['iːstwərd] *adv* vers l'est

eas·y ['iːzɪ] *adj* facile; *(relaxed)* tranquille; *take things ~ (slow down)* ne pas se fatiguer; *take it ~! (calm down)* calme-toi!

'eas·y chair fauteuil *m*

eas·y-go·ing ['iːzɪgoʊɪŋ] *adj* accommodant

eat [iːt] *v/t & v/i (pret ate, pp eaten)* manger

♦ eat out *v/i* manger au restaurant

♦ eat up *v/t food* finir; *fig* consumer

eat·a·ble ['iːtəbl] *adj* mangeable

eat·en ['iːtn] *pp → eat*

eaves [iːvz] *npl* avant-toit *m*

eaves·drop ['iːvzdrɑːp] *v/i (pret & pp -ped)* écouter de façon indiscrète (*on s.o.* qn)

ebb [eb] *v/i of tide* descendre

♦ ebb away *v/i of courage, strength* baisser, diminuer

'ebb tide marée *f* descendante

ec·cen·tric [ɪk'sentrɪk] **1** *adj* excentrique **2** *n* original(e) *m(f)*

ec·cen·tric·i·ty [ɪksen'trɪsɪtɪ] excentricité *f*

ech·o ['ekoʊ] **1** *n* écho *m* **2** *v/i* faire écho, retentir (*with* de) **3** *v/t words* répéter; *views* se faire l'écho de

e·clipse [ɪ'klɪps] **1** *n* éclipse *f* **2** *v/t fig* éclipser

e·co·lo·gi·cal [iːkə'lɑːdʒɪkl] *adj* écologique; *~ balance* équilibre *m* écologique

e·co·lo·gi·cal·ly [iːkə'lɑːdʒɪklɪ] *adv* écologiquement

e·co·lo·gi·cal·ly friend·ly *adj* écologique

e·col·o·gist [iːˈkɑːlədʒɪst] écologiste *m/f*

e·col·o·gy [iːˈkɑːlədʒɪ] écologie *f*

ec·o·nom·ic [iːkəˈnɑːmɪk] *adj* économique

ec·o·nom·i·cal [iːkəˈnɑːmɪkl] *adj* (*cheap*) économique; (*thrifty*) économe

ec·o·nom·i·cal·ly [iːkəˈnɑːmɪklɪ] *adv* économiquement

ec·o·nom·ics [iːkəˈnɑːmɪks] (*verb in sg*) science économie *f*, (*verb in pl*) *financial aspects* aspects *mpl* économiques

e·con·o·mist [ɪˈkɑːnəmɪst] économiste *m/f*

e·con·o·mize [ɪˈkɑːnəmaɪz] *v/i* économiser

♦ **economize on** *v/t* économiser

e·con·o·my [ɪˈkɑːnəmɪ] économie *f*; **e'con·o·my class** classe *f* économique; **e'con·o·my drive** plan *m* d'économies; **e'con·o·my size** taille *f* économique

e·co·sys·tem [ˈiːkoʊsɪstm] écosystème *m*

e·co·tour·ism [ˈiːkoʊtʊrɪzm] tourisme *m* écologique

ec·sta·sy [ˈekstəsɪ] extase *f*

ec·stat·ic [ɪkˈstætɪk] *adj* extatique

ec·ze·ma [ˈeksmə] eczéma *m*

edge [edʒ] **1** *n of table, seat, road, cliff* bord *m*; *of knife, in voice* tranchant *m*; **on ~ 2** *v/t* énervé **3** *v/i* (*move slowly*) se faufiler

edge·wise [ˈedʒwaɪz] *adv*: **I couldn't get a word in ~** je n'ai pas pu en placer une F

edg·y [ˈedʒɪ] *adj* énervé

ed·i·ble [ˈedɪbl] *adj* comestible

Ed·in·burgh [ˈedɪnbrə] Édimbourg

ed·it [ˈedɪt] *v/t text* mettre au point; *book* préparer pour la publication; *newspaper* diriger; *TV program* réaliser; *film* monter

e·di·tion [ɪˈdɪʃn] édition *f*

ed·i·tor [ˈedɪtər] *of text, book* rédacteur(-trice) *m(f)*; *of newspaper* rédacteur(-trice) *m(f)* en chef; *of TV program* réalisateur(-trice) *m(f)*; *of film*

monteur(-euse) *m(f)*; **sports / political ~** rédacteur(-trice) sportif (-ive) / politique *m(f)*

ed·i·to·ri·al [edɪˈtɔːrɪəl] **1** *adj* de la rédaction **2** *n* éditorial *m*

EDP [iːdiːˈpiː] *abbr* (= **electronic data processing**) traitement *m* électronique des données

ed·u·cate [ˈedʊkeɪt] *v/t* instruire (**about** sur); **she was ~d in France** elle a fait sa scolarité en France

ed·u·cat·ed [ˈedʊkeɪtɪd] *adj person* instruit

ed·u·ca·tion [edʊˈkeɪʃn] éducation *f*; *as subject* pédagogie *f*; **he got a good ~** il a reçu une bonne instruction; **continue one's ~** continuer ses études

ed·u·ca·tion·al [edʊˈkeɪʃnl] *adj* scolaire; (*informative*) instructif*

eel [iːl] anguille *f*

ee·rie [ˈɪrɪ] *adj* inquiétant

ef·fect [ɪˈfekt] effet *m*; **take ~** *of drug* faire son effet; **come into ~** *of law* prendre effet, entrer en vigueur

ef·fec·tive [ɪˈfektɪv] *adj* (*efficient*) efficace; (*striking*) frappant; **~ May 1** à compter du 1er mai

ef·fem·i·nate [ɪˈfemɪnət] *adj* efféminé

ef·fer·ves·cent [efərˈvesnt] *adj* gazeux*; *fig* pétillant

ef·fi·cien·cy [ɪˈfɪʃənsɪ] efficacité *f*

ef·fi·cient [ɪˈfɪʃənt] *adj* efficace

ef·fi·cient·ly [ɪˈfɪʃəntlɪ] *adv* efficacement

ef·flu·ent [ˈefluənt] effluent *m*

ef·fort [ˈefərt] effort *m*; **make an ~ to do sth** faire un effort pour faire qch

ef·fort·less [ˈefərtlɪs] *adj* aisé, facile

ef·fort·less·ly [ˈefərtlɪslɪ] *adv* sans effort

ef·fron·te·ry [ɪˈfrʌntərɪ] effronterie *f*, toupet *m* F

ef·fu·sive [ɪˈfjuːsɪv] *adj* démonstratif*

e.g. [iːdʒiː] ex; *spoken* par example

e·gal·i·tar·i·an [ɪɡælɪˈterɪən] *adj* égalitariste

egg [eg] œuf *m*; *of woman* ovule *m*

♦ **egg on** *v/t* inciter, pousser (**to do sth** à faire qch)

'**egg·cup** coquetier *m*; '**egg·head** F

intello *m/f* F; **'egg·plant** aubergine *f*;
'egg·shell coquille *f* (d'œuf); **'egg
tim·er** sablier *m*

e·go ['i:gou] PSYCH ego *m*, moi *m*;
(self-esteem) ego *m*

e·go·cen·tric [i:gou'sentrɪk] *adj* égocentrique

e·go·ism ['i:gouɪzm] égoïsme *m*

e·go·ist ['i:gouɪst] égoïste *m/f*

E·gypt ['i:dʒɪpt] Égypte *f*

E·gyp·tian [ɪ'dʒɪpʃn] **1** *adj* égyptien* **2**
n Égyptien(ne) *m(f)*

ei·der·down ['aɪdərdaun] *(quilt)* édredon *m*

eight [eɪt] huit

eigh·teen [eɪ'ti:n] dix-huit

eigh·teenth [eɪ'ti:nθ] dix-huitième; →
fifth

eighth [eɪtθ] huitième; → *fifth*

eigh·ti·eth ['eɪtɪɪθ] quatre-vingtième

eigh·ty ['eɪtɪ] quatre-vingts; **~-two /
four etc** quatre-vingt-deux / -quatre
etc

ei·ther ['i:ðər] **1** *adj* l'un ou l'autre;
(both) chaque **2** *pron* l'un(e) ou l'autre, n'importe lequel (laquelle) **3** *adv*:
I won't go ~ je n'irai pas non plus **4**
conj: **~ ... or** soit ... soit ...; *with negative* ni ... ni ...

e·ject [ɪ'dʒekt] **1** *v/t* éjecter; *person* expulser **2** *v/i from plane* s'éjecter

◆ **eke out** [i:k] *v/t* suppléer à l'insuffisance de; *eke out a living* vivoter,
gagner juste de quoi vivre

el [el] métro *m* aérien

e·lab·o·rate [ɪ'læbərət] **1** *adj (complex)*
compliqué; *preparations* soigné; *embroidery* minutieux* **2** *v/i* [ɪ'læbəreɪt]
donner des détails *(on* sur)

e·lab·o·rate·ly [ɪ'læbəreɪtlɪ] *adv* minutieusement

e·lapse [ɪ'læps] *v/i* (se) passer, s'écouler

e·las·tic [ɪ'læstɪk] **1** *adj* élastique **2** *n*
élastique *m*

e·las·ti·ca·ted [ɪ'læstɪkeɪtɪd] *adj* élastique

e·las·ti·ci·ty [ɪlæs'tɪsətɪ] élasticité *f*

e·las·ti·cized [ɪ'læstɪsaɪzd] *adj* élastique

e·lat·ed [ɪ'leɪtɪd] *adj* transporté (de

joie)

el·a·tion [ɪ'leɪʃn] exultation *f*

el·bow ['elbou] **1** *n* coude *m* **2** *v/t*: **~ out
of the way** écarter à coups de coude

el·der ['eldər] **1** *adj* aîné **2** *n* plus âgé(e)
m(f), aîné(e) *m(f)*; *of tribe* ancien *m*

el·der·ly ['eldərlɪ] *adj* âgé

el·dest ['eldəst] **1** *adj* aîné **2** *n*: **the ~**
l'aîné(e) *m(f)*

e·lect [ɪ'lekt] *v/t* élire; **~ to ...** choisir
de ...

e·lect·ed [ɪ'lektɪd] *adj* élu

e·lec·tion [ɪ'lekʃn] élection *f*

e'lec·tion cam·paign campagne *f*
électorale

e'lec·tion day jour *m* des élections

e·lec·tive [ɪ'lektɪv] *adj* facultatif*

e·lec·tor [ɪ'lektər] électeur(-trice)
m(f)

e·lec·to·ral sys·tem [ɪ'lektərəl] système *m* électoral

e·lec·to·rate [ɪ'lektərət] électorat *m*

e·lec·tric [ɪ'lektrɪk] *adj also fig* électrique

e·lec·tri·cal [ɪ'lektrɪkl] *adj* électrique

e·lec·tri·cal en·gi'neer électrotechnicien(ne) *m(f)*, ingénieur *m/f* électricien(ne)

e·lec·tri·cal en·gi·neer·ing électrotechnique *f*

e·lec·tric 'blan·ket couverture *f*
chauffante

e·lec·tric 'chair chaise *f* électrique

e·lec·tri·cian [ɪlek'trɪʃn] électricien(ne) *m(f)*

e·lec·tri·ci·ty [ɪlek'trɪsətɪ] électricité *f*

e·lec·tric 'ra·zor rasoir *m* électrique

e·lec·tri·fy [ɪ'lektrɪfaɪ] *v/t (pret & pp
-ied)* électrifier; *fig* électriser

e·lec·tro·cute [ɪ'lektrəkju:t] *v/t* électrocuter

e·lec·trode [ɪ'lektroud] électrode *f*

e·lec·tron [ɪ'lektrɑ:n] électron *m*

e·lec·tron·ic [ɪlek'trɑ:nɪk] *adj* électronique; **~ engineer** ingénieur *m/f*
électronicien(ne), électronicien(ne)
m(f); **~ engineering** électronique *f*

e·lec·tron·ic da·ta 'pro·ces·sing traitement *m* électronique de l'information

e·lec·tron·ic 'mail courrier *m* électro-

embrace

nique

e·lec·tron·ics [ɪlek'trɑːnɪks] électronique *f*

el·e·gance ['elɪɡəns] élégance *f*

el·e·gant ['elɪɡənt] *adj* élégant

el·e·gant·ly ['elɪɡəntlɪ] *adv* élégamment

el·e·ment ['elɪmənt] élément *m*

el·e·men·ta·ry [elɪ'mentərɪ] *adj* élémentaire

el·e·phant ['elɪfənt] éléphant *m*

el·e·vate ['elɪveɪt] *v/t* élever

el·e·vat·ed rail·road ['elɪveɪtɪd] métro *m* aérien

el·e·va·tion [elɪ'veɪʃn] *(altitude)* altitude *f*, hauteur *f*

el·e·va·tor ['elɪveɪtər] ascenseur *m*

e·lev·en [ɪ'levn] onze

e·lev·enth [ɪ'levnθ] onzième; → **fifth**; **at the ~ hour** à la dernière minute

el·i·gi·ble ['elɪdʒəbl] *adj*: **be ~ to do sth** avoir le droit de faire qch; **be ~ for sth** avoir droit à qch

el·i·gi·ble 'bach·e·lor bon parti *m*

e·lim·i·nate [ɪ'lɪmɪneɪt] *v/t* éliminer; *(kill)* supprimer; **be ~d from competition** être éliminé

e·lim·i·na·tion [ɪ'lɪmɪneɪʃn] élimination *f*, *(murder)* suppression *f*; **by a process of ~** par élimination

e·lite [eɪ'liːt] **1** *n* élite *f* **2** *adj* d'élite

elk [elk] élan *m*

el·lipse [ɪ'lɪps] ellipse *f*

elm [elm] orme *m*

e·lope [ɪ'loʊp] *v/i* s'enfuir (avec un amant)

el·o·quence ['eləkwəns] éloquence *f*

el·o·quent ['eləkwənt] *adj* éloquent

el·o·quent·ly ['eləkwəntlɪ] *adv* éloquemment

else [els] *adv*: **anything ~?** autre chose?; *in store* vous désirez autre chose?; **if you've got nothing ~ to do** si tu n'as rien d'autre à faire; **no one ~** personne d'autre; **everyone ~ is going** tous les autres y vont; **who ~ was there?** qui d'autre y était?; **someone ~** quelqu'un d'autre; **something ~** autre chose; **let's go somewhere ~** allons autre part; **or ~** sinon

else·where ['elswer] *adv* ailleurs

e·lude [ɪ'luːd] *v/t (escape from)* échapper à; *(avoid)* éviter

e·lu·sive [ɪ'luːsɪv] *adj* insaisissable

e·ma·ci·at·ed [ɪ'meɪsɪeɪtɪd] *adj* émacié

e-mail ['iːmeɪl] **1** *n* e-mail *m*, courrier *m* électronique **2** *v/t person* envoyer un e-mail à; *text* envoyer par e-mail

'e-mail ad·dress adresse *f* e-mail, adresse *f* électronique

e·man·ci·pat·ed [ɪ'mænsɪpeɪtɪd] *adj woman* émancipé

e·man·ci·pa·tion [ɪmænsɪ'peɪʃn] émancipation *f*

em·balm [ɪm'bɑːm] *v/t* embaumer

em·bank·ment [ɪm'bæŋkmənt] *of river* berge *f*, quai *m*; RAIL remblai *m*, talus *m*

em·bar·go [em'bɑːrɡoʊ] embargo *m*

em·bark [ɪm'bɑːrk] *v/i* (s')embarquer

♦ **embark on** *v/t adventure etc* s'embarquer dans

em·bar·rass [ɪm'bærəs] *v/t* gêner, embarrasser; *government* mettre dans l'embarras

em·bar·rassed [ɪm'bærəst] *adj* gêné, embarrassé

em·bar·rass·ing [ɪm'bærəsɪŋ] *adj* gênant, embarrassant

em·bar·rass·ment [ɪm'bærəsmənt] gêne *f*, embarras *m*

em·bas·sy ['embəsɪ] ambassade *f*

em·bel·lish [ɪm'belɪʃ] *v/t* embellir; *story* enjoliver

em·bers ['embərz] *npl* braise *f*

em·bez·zle [ɪm'bezl] *v/t* détourner *(from* de)

em·bez·zle·ment [ɪm'bezlmənt] détournement *m* de fonds

em·bez·zler [ɪm'bezlər] détourneur (-euse) *m(f)* de fonds

em·bit·ter [ɪm'bɪtər] *v/t* aigrir

em·blem ['embləm] emblème *m*

em·bod·i·ment [ɪm'bɑːdɪmənt] incarnation *f*, personnification *f*

em·bod·y [ɪm'bɑːdɪ] *v/t (pret & pp -ied)* incarner, personnifier

em·bo·lism ['embəlɪzm] embolie *f*

em·boss [ɪm'bɑːs] *v/t metal* travailler en relief; *paper, fabric* gaufrer

em·brace [ɪm'breɪs] **1** *n* étreinte *f* **2** *v/t*

(*hug*) serrer dans ses bras, étreindre; (*take in*) embrasser **3** *v/i of two people* se serrer dans les bras, s'étreindre

em·broi·der [ɪmˈbrɔɪdər] *v/t* broder; *fig* enjoliver

em·broi·der·y [ɪmˈbrɔɪdərɪ] broderie *f*

em·bry·o [ˈembrɪəʊ] embryon *m*

em·bry·on·ic [embrɪˈɑːnɪk] *adj fig* embryonnaire

em·e·rald [ˈemərəld] *precious stone* émeraude *f*; *color* (vert *m*) émeraude *m*

e·merge [ɪˈmɜːrdʒ] *v/i* sortir; *from mist, of truth* émerger; *it has ~d that …* il est apparu que …

e·mer·gen·cy [ɪˈmɜːrdʒənsɪ] urgence *f*; *in an ~* en cas d'urgence

eˈmer·gen·cy exˈit sortie *f* de secours; **eˈmer·gen·cy ˈland·ing** atterrissage *m* forcé; **eˈmer·gen·cy ˈserv·ices** *npl* services *mpl* d'urgence

em·er·y board [ˈemərɪbɔːrd] lime *f* à ongles

em·i·grant [ˈemɪgrənt] émigrant(e) *m(f)*

em·i·grate [ˈemɪgreɪt] *v/i* émigrer

em·i·gra·tion [emɪˈgreɪʃn] émigration *f*

Em·i·nence [ˈemɪnəns] REL: *His ~* son Éminence

em·i·nent [ˈemɪnənt] *adj* éminent

em·i·nent·ly [ˈemɪnəntlɪ] *adv* éminemment

e·mis·sion [ɪˈmɪʃn] *of gases* émission *f*

e·mit [ɪˈmɪt] *v/t* (*pret & pp* -**ted**) émettre

e·mo·tion [ɪˈməʊʃn] émotion *f*

e·mo·tion·al [ɪˈməʊʃnl] *adj problems, development* émotionnel*; affectif*; (*full of emotion: person*) ému; *reunion, moment* émouvant

em·pa·thize [ˈempəθaɪz] *v/i* compatir; *~ with sth* compatir à; *s.o.* avoir de la compassion pour

em·pe·ror [ˈempərər] empereur *m*

em·pha·sis [ˈemfəsɪs] accent *m*

em·pha·size [ˈemfəsaɪz] *v/t syllable* accentuer; *fig* souligner

em·phat·ic [ɪmˈfætɪk] *adj* énergique, catégorique; *be very ~ about sth* être catégorique à propos de qch

em·pire [ˈempaɪr] *also fig* empire *m*

em·ploy [ɪmˈplɔɪ] *v/t* employer

em·ploy·ee [emplɔɪˈiː] employé(e) *m(f)*

em·ploy·er [emˈplɔɪər] employeur (-euse) *m(f)*

em·ploy·ment [emˈplɔɪmənt] (*jobs*) emplois *mpl*; (*work*) emploi *m*; *be seeking ~* être à la recherche d'un emploi

emˈploy·ment aˌgen·cy agence *f* de placement

em·press [ˈemprɪs] impératrice *f*

emp·ti·ness [ˈemptɪnɪs] vide *m*

emp·ty [ˈemptɪ] **1** *adj* vide; *promises* vain **2** *v/t* (*pret & pp* -**ied**) vider **3** *v/i of room, street* se vider

em·u·late [ˈemjʊleɪt] *v/t* imiter

e·mul·sion [ɪˈmʌlʃn] *paint* peinture *f* mate

en·a·ble [ɪˈneɪbl] *v/t* permettre; *~ s.o. to do sth* permettre à qn de faire qch

en·act [ɪˈnækt] *v/t law* décréter; THEA représenter

e·nam·el [ɪˈnæml] émail *m*

enc *abbr* (*= enclosure(s)*) PJ (= pièce(s) jointe(s))

en·chant [ɪnˈtʃænt] *v/t* (*delight*) enchanter

en·chant·ing [ɪnˈtʃæntɪŋ] *adj* ravissant

en·cir·cle [ɪnˈsɜːrkl] *v/t* encercler, entourer

encl *abbr* (*= enclosure(s)*) PJ (= pièce(s) jointe(s))

en·close [ɪnˈkləʊz] *v/t in letter* joindre; *area* entourer; *please find ~d …* veuillez trouver ci-joint …

en·clo·sure [ɪnˈkləʊʒər] *with letter* pièce *f* jointe

en·core [ˈɑːŋkɔːr] bis *m*

en·coun·ter [ɪnˈkaʊntər] **1** *n* rencontre *f* **2** *v/t person* rencontrer; *problem, resistance* affronter

en·cour·age [ɪnˈkʌrɪdʒ] *v/t* encourager

en·cour·age·ment [ɪnˈkʌrɪdʒmənt] encouragement *m*

en·cour·ag·ing [ɪnˈkʌrɪdʒɪŋ] *adj* encourageant

♦ **encroach on** [ɪnˈkrəʊtʃ] *v/t land, rights, time* empiéter sur

en·cy·clo·pe·di·a [ɪnsaɪklə'piːdɪə] encyclopédie *f*

end [end] **1** *n (extremity)* bout *m*; *(conclusion, purpose)* fin *f*; ***in the* ~** à la fin; ***for hours on* ~** pendant des heures; ***stand sth on* ~** mettre qch debout; ***at the* ~ *of July*** à la fin du mois de juillet; ***put an* ~ *to*** mettre fin à **2** *v/t* terminer, finir **3** *v/i* se terminer, finir

♦ **end up** *v/i* finir; ***I ended up* (*by*) *doing it myself*** j'ai fini par le faire moi-même

en·dan·ger [ɪn'deɪndʒər] *v/t* mettre en danger

en·dan·gered spe·cies *nsg* espèce *f* en voie de disparition

en·dear·ing [ɪn'dɪrɪŋ] *adj* attachant

en·deav·or [ɪn'devər] **1** *n* effort *m*, tentative *f* **2** *v/t* essayer (***to do sth*** de faire qch), chercher (***to do sth*** à faire qch)

en·dem·ic [ɪn'demɪk] *adj* endémique

end·ing ['endɪŋ] fin *f*; GRAM terminaison *f*

end·less ['endlɪs] *adj* sans fin

en·dorse [ɪn'dɔːrs] *v/t check* endosser; *candidacy* appuyer; *product* associer son image à

en·dorse·ment [ɪn'dɔːrsmənt] *of check* endos(sement) *m*; *of candidacy* appui *m*; *of product* association *f* de son image à

end 'prod·uct produit *m* fini

end re'sult résultat *m* final

en·dur·ance [ɪn'dʊrəns] *of person* endurance *f*; *of car* résistance *f*

en'dur·ance test *for machine* test *m* de résistance; *for person* test *m* d'endurance

en·dure [ɪn'dʊər] **1** *v/t* endurer **2** *v/i (last)* durer

en·dur·ing [ɪn'dʊrɪŋ] *adj* durable

end·'us·er utilisateur(-trice) *m(f)* final(e)

en·e·my ['enəmɪ] ennemi(e) *m(f)*; *in war* ennemi *m*

en·er·get·ic [enərdʒetɪk] *adj also fig* énergique

en·er·get·i·cal·ly [enərdʒetɪklɪ] *adv* énergiquement

en·er·gy ['enərʒɪ] énergie *f*

'en·er·gy-sav·ing *adj device* à faible consommation d'énergie

'en·er·gy sup·ply alimentation *f* en énergie

en·force [ɪn'fɔːrs] *v/t* appliquer, mettre en vigueur

en·gage [ɪn'geɪdʒ] **1** *v/t (hire)* engager **2** *v/i of machine part* s'engrener; *of clutch* s'embrayer

♦ **engage in** *v/t* s'engager dans

en·gaged [ɪn'geɪdʒd] *adj* to be married fiancé; *Br* TELEC occupé; ***get* ~** se fiancer

en·gage·ment [ɪn'geɪdʒmənt] *(appointment)* rendez-vous *m*; *to be married* fiançailles *fpl*; MIL engagement *m*

en·gage·ment ring bague *f* de fiançailles

en·gag·ing [ɪn'geɪdʒɪŋ] *adj smile, person* engageant

en·gine ['endʒɪn] moteur *m*; *of train* locomotive *f*

en·gi·neer [endʒɪ'nɪr] **1** *n* ingénieur *m/f*; NAUT, RAIL mécanicien(ne) *m(f)* **2** *v/t fig: meeting etc* combiner

en·gi·neer·ing [endʒɪ'nɪrɪŋ] ingénierie *f*, engineering *m*

Eng·land ['ɪŋglənd] Angleterre *f*

Eng·lish ['ɪŋglɪʃ] **1** *adj* anglais **2** *n language* anglais *m*; ***the* ~** les Anglais *mpl*

Eng·lish 'Chan·nel Manche *f*

Eng·lish·man ['ɪŋglɪʃmən] Anglais *m*

Eng·lish·wom·an ['ɪŋglɪʃwʊmən] Anglaise *f*

en·grave [ɪn'greɪv] *v/t* graver

en·grav·ing [ɪn'greɪvɪŋ] gravure *f*

en·grossed [ɪn'groʊst] *adj*: ~ **in** absorbé dans

en·gulf [ɪn'gʌlf] *v/t* engloutir

en·hance [ɪn'hæns] *v/t beauty, flavor* rehausser; *reputation* accroître; *performance* améliorer; *enjoyment* augmenter

e·nig·ma [ɪ'nɪgmə] énigme *f*

e·nig·mat·ic [enɪg'mætɪk] *adj* énigmatique

en·joy [ɪn'dʒɔɪ] *v/t* aimer; ~ **o.s.** s'amuser; ~ **!** *said to s.o. eating* bon appétit!

en·joy·a·ble [ɪn'dʒɔɪəbl] *adj* agréable

en·joy·ment [ɪn'dʒɔɪmənt] plaisir *m*
en·large [ɪn'lɑːrdʒ] *v/t* agrandir
en·large·ment [ɪn'lɑːrdʒmənt] agrandissement *m*
en·light·en [ɪn'laɪtn] *v/t* éclairer
en·list [ɪn'lɪst] **1** *v/i* MIL enrôler **2** *v/t*: ~ *the help of* se procurer l'aide de
en·liv·en [ɪn'laɪvn] *v/t* animer
en·mi·ty ['enmətɪ] inimitié *f*
e·nor·mi·ty [ɪ'nɔːrmətɪ] énormité *f*
e·nor·mous [ɪ'nɔːrməs] *adj* énorme
e·nor·mous·ly [ɪ'nɔːrməslɪ] *adv* énormément
e·nough [ɪ'nʌf] **1** *adj* assez de **2** *pron* assez; *will $50 be ~?* est-ce que 50 $ suffiront?; *I've had ~!* j'en ai assez!; *that's ~, calm down!* ça suffit, calme-toi! **3** *adv* assez; *big / strong* ~ assez grand / fort; *strangely* ~ chose curieuse, curieusement
en·quire *etc* → *inquire etc*
en·raged [ɪn'reɪdʒd] *adj* furieux*
en·rich [ɪn'rɪtʃ] *v/t* enrichir
en·roll [ɪn'roʊl] *v/i* s'inscrire
en·roll·ment [ɪn'roʊlmənt] inscriptions *fpl*
en·sue [ɪn'suː] *v/i* s'ensuivre; *the ensuing months* les mois qui ont suivi
en suite (bath·room) ['ɑːnswiːt] salle *f* de bains attenante
en·sure [ɪn'ʃʊər] *v/t* assurer; ~ *that ...* s'assurer que ...
en·tail [ɪn'teɪl] *v/t* entraîner
en·tan·gle [ɪn'tæŋgl] *v/t* in rope empêtrer; *become ~d in* also fig s'empêtrer dans
en·ter ['entər] **1** *v/t* room, house entrer dans; *competition* entrer en; *person, horse in race* inscrire; *write down* inscrire (*in* sur); COMPUT entrer **2** *v/i* entrer; *in competition* s'inscrire **3** *n* COMPUT touche *f* entrée
en·ter·prise ['entərpraɪz] (*initiative*) (esprit *m* d')initiative *f*; (*venture*) entreprise *f*
en·ter·pris·ing ['entərpraɪzɪŋ] *adj* entreprenant
en·ter·tain [entər'teɪn] **1** *v/t* (*amuse*) amuser, divertir; (*consider: idea*) envisager **2** *v/i* (*have guests*) recevoir
en·ter·tain·er [entər'teɪnər] artiste *m/f*

de variété
en·ter·tain·ing [entər'teɪnɪŋ] *adj* amusant, divertissant
en·ter·tain·ment [entər'teɪnmənt] *adj* divertissement *m*
en·thrall [ɪn'θrɔːl] *v/t* captiver
en·thu·si·asm [ɪn'θuːzɪæzəm] enthousiasme *m*
en·thu·si·ast [ɪn'θuːzɪæst] enthousiaste *m/f*
en·thu·si·as·tic [ɪnθuːzɪ'æstɪk] *adj* enthousiaste
en·thu·si·as·ti·cal·ly [ɪnθuːzɪ'æstɪklɪ] *adv* avec enthousiasme
en·tice [ɪn'taɪs] *v/t* attirer
en·tire [ɪn'taɪr] *adj* entier*
en·tire·ly [ɪn'taɪrlɪ] *adv* entièrement
en·ti·tle [ɪn'taɪtl] *v/t*: ~ *s.o. to sth / to do sth* donner à qn droit à qch / le droit de faire qch; *be ~d to sth / to do sth* avoir droit à qch / le droit de faire qch
en·ti·tled [ɪn'taɪtld] *adj book* intitulé
en·trance ['entrəns] entrée *f*
'en·trance ex·am(·i·na·tion) examen *m* d'entrée
en·tranced [ɪn'trænst] *adj* enchanté
'en·trance fee droit *m* d'entrée
en·trant ['entrənt] inscrit(e) *m(f)*
en·treat [ɪn'triːt] *v/t*: ~ *s.o. to do sth* supplier qn de faire qch
en·trenched [ɪn'trentʃt] *adj attitudes* enraciné
en·tre·pre·neur [ɑːntrəprə'nɜːr] entrepreneur(-euse) *m(f)*
en·tre·pre·neur·i·al [ɑːntrəprə'nɜːrɪəl] *adj skills* d'entrepreneur
en·trust [ɪn'trʌst] *v/t*: ~ *X with Y, ~ Y to X* confier Y à X
en·try ['entrɪ] (*way in, admission*) entrée *f*; *for competition: person* participant(e) *m(f)*; *in diary, accounts* inscription *f*; *in reference book* article *m*; *no* ~ défense d'entrer
'en·try form feuille *f* d'inscription; **'en·try·phone** interphone *m*; **'en·try vi·sa** visa *m* d'entrée
e·nu·me·rate [ɪ'nuːmərəɪt] *v/t* énumérer
en·vel·op [ɪn'veləp] *v/t* envelopper
en·ve·lope ['envəloʊp] enveloppe *f*

en·vi·a·ble ['envɪəbl] *adj* enviable

en·vi·ous ['envɪəs] *adj* envieux*; **be ~ of s.o.** envier qn

en·vi·ron·ment [ɪn'vaɪrənmənt] environnement *m*

en·vi·ron·men·tal [ɪnvaɪrən'mentl] *adj* écologique

en·vi·ron·men·tal·ist [ɪnvaɪrən'mentəlɪst] écologiste *m/f*

en·vi·ron·men·tal·ly friend·ly [ɪnvaɪrənmentəlɪ'frendlɪ] *adj* écologique

en·vi·ron·men·tal pol·lu·tion pollution *f* de l'environnement

en·vi·ron·men·tal pro·tec·tion protection *f* de l'environnement

en·vi·rons [ɪn'vaɪrənz] *npl* environs *mpl*

en·vis·age [ɪn'vɪzɪdʒ] *v/t* envisager; *I can't ~ doing that* je ne peux pas l'imaginer faire cela

en·voy ['envɔɪ] envoyé(e) *m(f)*

en·vy ['envɪ] **1** *n* envie *f*; **be the ~ of** être envié par **2** *v/t* (*pret & pp -ied*): *~ s.o. sth* envier qch à qn

e·phem·er·al [ɪ'femərəl] *adj* éphémère

ep·ic ['epɪk] **1** *n* épopée *f*; *movie* film *m* à grand spectacle **2** *adj* *journey, scale* épique

ep·i·cen·ter ['epɪsentər] épicentre *m*

ep·i·dem·ic [epɪ'demɪk] *also fig* épidémie *f*

ep·i·lep·sy ['epɪlepsɪ] épilepsie *f*

ep·i·lep·tic [epɪ'leptɪk] épileptique *m/f*

ep·i·lep·tic 'fit crise *f* d'épilepsie

ep·i·log ['epɪlɔg] épilogue *m*

ep·i·sode ['epɪsoʊd] épisode *m*

ep·i·taph ['epɪtæf] épitaphe *f*

e·poch ['iːpɑːk] époque *f*

e·poch-mak·ing ['iːpɑːkmeɪkɪŋ] *adj* qui fait époque

e·qual ['iːkwl] **1** *adj* égal; **be ~ to task** être à la hauteur de **2** *n* égal *m* **3** *v/t* (*pret & pp -ed*, *Br -led*) égaler

e·qual·i·ty [ɪ'kwɑːlətɪ] égalité *f*

e·qual·ize ['iːkwəlaɪz] **1** *v/t* égaliser **2** *v/i Br* SP égaliser

e·qual·iz·er ['iːkwəlaɪzər] *Br* SP but *m* égalisateur

e·qual·ly ['iːkwəlɪ] *adv* *divide* de manière égale; *qualified, intelligent* tout aussi; *~, ...* pareillement, ...

e·qual 'rights *npl* égalité *f* des droits

e·quate [ɪ'kweɪt] *v/t* mettre sur le même pied; *~ X with Y* mettre X et Y sur le même pied

e·qua·tion [ɪ'kweɪʒn] MATH équation *f*

e·qua·tor [ɪ'kweɪtər] équateur *m*

e·qui·lib·ri·um [iːkwɪ'lɪbrɪəm] équilibre *m*

e·qui·nox ['iːkwɪnɑːks] équinoxe *m*

e·quip [ɪ'kwɪp] *v/t* (*pret & pp -ped*) équiper; *he's not ~ped to handle it fig* il n'est pas préparé pour gérer cela

e·quip·ment [ɪ'kwɪpmənt] équipement *m*

eq·ui·ty ['ekwətɪ] FIN capitaux *mpl* propres

e·quiv·a·lent [ɪ'kwɪvələnt] **1** *adj* équivalent **2** *n* équivalent *m*

e·ra ['ɪrə] ère *f*

e·rad·i·cate [ɪ'rædɪkeɪt] *v/t* éradiquer

e·rase [ɪ'reɪz] *v/t* effacer

e·ras·er [ɪ'reɪzər] gomme *f*

e·rect [ɪ'rekt] **1** *adj* droit

e·rect 2 *v/t* ériger, élever

e·rec·tion [ɪ'rekʃn] *of building, penis* érection *f*

er·go·nom·ic [ɜːrgoʊ'nɑːmɪk] *adj* ergonomique

e·rode [ɪ'roʊd] *v/t* éroder; *fig: power* miner; *rights* supprimer progressivement

e·ro·sion [ɪ'roʊʒn] érosion *f*; *fig: of rights* suppression *f* progressive

e·rot·ic [ɪ'rɑːtɪk] *adj* érotique

e·rot·i·cism [ɪ'rɑːtɪsɪzm] érotisme *m*

er·rand ['erənd] commission *f*; *run ~s* faire des commissions

er·rat·ic [ɪ'rætɪk] *adj* *performance, course* irrégulier*; *driving* capricieux*; *behavior* changeant

er·ror ['erər] erreur *f*

'er·ror mes·sage COMPUT message *m* d'erreur

e·rupt [ɪ'rʌpt] *v/i* *of volcano* entrer en éruption; *of violence* éclater; *of person* exploser F

e·rup·tion [ɪ'rʌpʃn] *of volcano* éruption *f*; *of violence* explosion *f*

es·ca·late ['eskəleɪt] *v/i* s'intensifier

E

es·ca·la·tion [eskə'leɪʃn] intensification *f*

es·ca·la·tor ['eskəleɪtər] escalier *m* mécanique, escalator *m*

es·cape [ɪ'skeɪp] **1** *n of prisoner* évasion *f*; *of animal, gas* fuite *f*; **have a narrow ~** l'échapper belle **2** *v/i of prisoner* s'échapper, s'évader; *of animal* s'échapper, s'enfuir; *of gas* s'échapper **3** *v/t*: **the word ~s me** le mot m'échappe

es·cape chute AVIAT toboggan *m* de secours

es·cort ['eskɔːrt] **1** *n (companion)* cavalier(-ière) *m(f)*; *(guard)* escorte *f* **2** *v/t* [ɪ'skɔːrt] *socially* accompagner; *(act as guard to)* escorter

es·pe·cial [ɪ'speʃl] → **special**

es·pe·cial·ly [ɪ'speʃlɪ] *adv* particulièrement, surtout

es·pi·o·nage ['espɪɒnɑːʒ] espionnage *m*

es·pres·so (cof·fee) [es'presəʊ] expresso *m*

es·say ['eseɪ] *n at school* rédaction *f; at university* dissertation *f; by writer* essai *m*

es·sen·tial [ɪ'senʃl] *adj* essentiel*

es·sen·tial·ly [ɪ'senʃlɪ] *adv* essentiellement

es·tab·lish [ɪ'stæblɪʃ] *v/t company* fonder, créer; *(create, determine)* établir; **~ o.s. as** s'établir comme

es·tab·lish·ment [ɪ'stæblɪʃmənt] *firm, shop etc* établissement *m*; **the Establishment** l'establishment *m*

es·tate [ɪ'steɪt] *(area of land)* propriété *f*, domaine *m*; *(possessions of dead person)* biens *mpl*

es·tate a·gen·cy *Br* agence *f* immobilière

es·thet·ic [ɪs'θetɪk] *adj* esthétique

es·ti·mate ['estɪmət] **1** *n* estimation *f*; *from builder etc* devis *m* **2** *v/t* estimer

es·ti·ma·tion [estɪ'meɪʃn] estime *f*; **he has gone up / down in my ~** il a monté / baissé dans mon estime; **in my ~** *(opinion)* à mon avis *m*

es·tu·a·ry ['estʃəwerɪ] estuaire *m*

ETA [iːtiː'eɪ] *abbr (= estimated time of arrival)* heure *f* prévue d'arrivée

etc [et'setrə] *abbr (= et cetera)* etc.

etch·ing ['etʃɪŋ] *(gravure f à l')eau-forte f*

e·ter·nal [ɪ'tɜːrnl] *adj* éternel*

e·ter·ni·ty [ɪ'tɜːrnətɪ] éternité *f*

eth·i·cal ['eθɪkl] *adj problem* éthique; *(morally right), behavior* moral

eth·ics ['eθɪks] éthique *f*

eth·nic ['eθnɪk] *adj* ethnique

eth·nic 'cleans·ing purification *f* ethnique

eth·nic 'group ethnie *f*

eth·nic mi'nor·i·ty minorité *f* ethnique

EU [iː'juː] *abbr (= European Union)* U.E. *f (= Union f européenne)*

eu·phe·mism ['juːfəmɪzm] euphémisme *m*

eu·pho·ri·a [juː'fɔːrɪə] euphorie *f*

eu·ro ['jʊərəʊ] FIN euro *m*; **'Eu·ro MP** député(e) européen(ne) *m(f)*

Eu·rope ['jʊərəp] Europe *f*

Eu·ro·pe·an [jʊərə'pɪən] **1** *adj* européen* **2** *n* Européen(ne) *m(f)*; **Eu·ro·pe·an Com'mis·sion** Commission *f* européenne; **Eu·ro·pe·an Com'mis·sion·er** Commissaire européen(ne) *m(f)*; **Eu·ro·pe·an 'Par·lia·ment** Parlement *m* européen; **Eu·ro·pe·an 'Un·ion** Union *f* européenne

eu·tha·na·si·a [juːθə'neɪzɪə] euthanasie *f*

e·vac·u·ate [ɪ'vækjueɪt] *v/t (clear people from)* faire évacuer; *(leave)* évacuer

e·vade [ɪ'veɪd] *v/t* éviter; *question* éluder

e·val·u·ate [ɪ'væljueɪt] *v/t* évaluer

e·val·u·a·tion [ɪvæljʊ'eɪʃn] évaluation *f*

e·van·gel·ist [ɪ'vændʒəlɪst] évangélisateur(-trice) *m(f)*

e·vap·o·rate [ɪ'væpəreɪt] *v/i also fig* s'évaporer

e·vap·o·ra·tion [ɪvæpə'reɪʃn] *of water* évaporation *f*

e·va·sion [ɪ'veɪʒn] fuite *f*; **~ of re·spon·si·bil·i·ties** fuite *f* devant ses responsabilités; **tax ~** fraude *f* fiscale

e·va·sive [ɪ'veɪsɪv] *adj* évasif*

eve [i:v] veille *f*; **on the ~ of** à la veille de

e·ven ['i:vn] **1** *adj breathing* régulier*; *distribution* égal, uniforme; (*level*) plat; *surface* plan; *number* pair; **get ~ with ...** prendre sa revanche sur ... **2** *adv* même; **~** *bigger* / *smaller* encore plus grand / petit; **not ~** pas même; **~** *so* quand même; **~** *if* même si **3** *v/t:* **~** *the score* égaliser

eve·ning ['i:vnɪŋ] soir *m*; **in the ~** le soir; **at 7 in the ~** à 7 heures du soir; **this ~** ce soir; **good ~** bonsoir

'eve·ning class cours *m* du soir; **'eve·ning dress** *for woman* robe *f* du soir; *for man* tenue *f* de soirée; **eve·ning 'pa·per** journal *m* du soir

e·ven·ly ['i:vnlɪ] *adv* (*regularly*) de manière égale; *breathe* régulièrement

e·vent [ɪ'vent] événement *m*; SP épreuve *f*; **at all ~s** en tout cas

e·vent·ful [ɪ'ventfl] *adj* mouvementé

e·ven·tu·al [ɪ'ventʃʊəl] *adj* final

e·ven·tu·al·ly [ɪ'ventʃʊəlɪ] *adv* finalement

ev·er ['evər] *adv* jamais; **have you ~ been to Japan?** est-ce que tu es déjà allé au Japon?; **for ~** pour toujours; **~ since** depuis lors; **~ since we ...** depuis le jour où nous ...; **the fastest ~** le / la plus rapide qui ait jamais existé

ev·er·green ['evərgri:n] *n* arbre *m* à feuilles persistantes

ev·er·last·ing [evər'læstɪŋ] *adj* éternel*

ev·ery ['evrɪ] *adj*: **~** *day* tous les jours, chaque jour; **~** *one of his fans* chacun de ses fans, tous ses fans; **one in ~ ten houses** une maison sur dix; **~** *now and then* de temps en temps

ev·ery·bod·y ['evrɪbɑ:dɪ] → **everyone**

ev·ery·day ['evrɪdeɪ] *adj* de tous les jours

ev·ery·one ['evrɪwʌn] *pron* tout le monde; **~** *who knew him* tous ceux qui l'ont connu

ev·ery·thing ['evrɪθɪŋ] *pron* tout; **~** *I say* tout ce que je dis

ev·ery·where ['evrɪwer] *adv* partout; **~** *you go* (*wherever*) partout où tu vas,

où que tu ailles (*subj*)

e·vict [ɪ'vɪkt] *v/t* expulser

ev·i·dence ['evɪdəns] preuve(s) *f(pl)*; LAW témoignage *m*; **give ~** témoigner

ev·i·dent ['evɪdənt] *adj* évident

ev·i·dent·ly ['evɪdəntlɪ] *adv* (*clearly*) à l'évidence; (*apparently*) de toute évidence

e·vil ['i:vl] **1** *adj* mauvais, méchant **2** *n* mal *m*

e·voke [ɪ'voʊk] *v/t image* évoquer

ev·o·lu·tion [i:və'lu:ʃn] évolution *f*

e·volve [ɪ'vɑ:lv] *v/i* évoluer

ewe [ju:] brebis *f*

ex- [eks] ex-

ex [eks] F *wife, husband* ex *m/f* F

ex·act [ɪg'zækt] *adj* exact

ex·act·ing [ɪg'zæktɪŋ] *adj* exigeant

ex·act·ly [ɪg'zæktlɪ] *adv* exactement

ex·ag·ge·rate [ɪg'zædʒəreɪt] *v/t & v/i* exagérer

ex·ag·ge·ra·tion [ɪgzædʒə'reɪʃn] exagération *f*

ex·am [ɪg'zæm] examen *m*; **take an ~** passer un examen; **pass / fail an ~** réussir à / échouer à un examen

ex·am·i·na·tion [ɪgzæmɪ'neɪʃn] examen *m*

ex·am·ine [ɪg'zæmɪn] *v/t* examiner

ex·am·in·er [ɪg'zæmɪnər] EDU examinateur(-trice) *m(f)*

ex·am·ple [ɪg'zæmpl] exemple *m*; **for ~** par exemple; **set a good / bad ~** donner / ne pas donner l'exemple

ex·as·pe·rat·ed [ɪg'zæspəreɪtɪd] *adj* exaspéré

ex·as·pe·rat·ing [ɪg'zæspəreɪtɪŋ] *adj* exaspérant

ex·ca·vate ['ekskəveɪt] *v/t* (*dig*) excaver; *of archeologist* fouiller

ex·ca·va·tion [ekskə'veɪʃn] excavation *f*; *archeological* fouille(s) *f(pl)*

ex·ceed [ɪk'si:d] *v/t* dépasser; *authority* outrepasser

ex·ceed·ing·ly [ɪk'si:dɪŋlɪ] *adv* extrêmement

ex·cel [ɪk'sel] **1** *v/i* (*pret & pp -led*) exceller; **~** *at* exceller en **2** *v/t*: **~** *o.s.* se surpasser

ex·cel·lence ['eksələns] excellence *f*

ex·cel·lent ['eksələnt] *adj* excellent

ex·cept [ɪk'sept] *prep* sauf; **~ for** à l'exception de

ex·cep·tion [ɪk'sepʃn] exception *f*; **with the ~ of** à l'exception de; **take ~ to** s'offenser de

ex·cep·tion·al [ɪk'sepʃnl] *adj* exceptionnel*

ex·cep·tion·al·ly [ɪk'sepʃnlɪ] *adv* (*extremely*) exceptionnellement

ex·cerpt ['eksɜːrpt] extrait *m*

ex·cess [ɪk'ses] **1** *n* excès *m*; **drink to ~** boire à l'excès; **in ~ of** au-dessus de **2** *adj*: **~ water** excédent *m* d'eau

ex·cess 'bag·gage excédent *m* de bagages

ex·cess 'fare supplément *m*

ex·ces·sive [ɪk'sesɪv] *adj* excessif*

ex·change [ɪks'tʃeɪndʒ] **1** *n* échange *m*; **in ~ for** en échange de **2** *v/t* échanger; **~ X for Y** échanger X contre Y

ex'change rate FIN cours *m* du change, taux *m* du change

ex·cit·a·ble [ɪk'saɪtəbl] *adj* excitable

ex·cite [ɪk'saɪt] *v/t* (*make enthusiastic*) enthousiasmer

ex·cit·ed [ɪk'saɪtɪd] *adj* excité; **get ~** s'exciter; **get ~ about sth** *trip etc* être excité à l'idée de qch; *changes etc* être enthousiaste à l'idée de qch

ex·cite·ment [ɪk'saɪtmənt] excitation *f*

ex·cit·ing [ɪk'saɪtɪŋ] *adj* passionnant

ex·claim [ɪk'skleɪm] *v/t* s'exclamer

ex·cla·ma·tion [eksklə'meɪʃn] exclamation *f*

ex·cla·ma·tion point point *m* d'exclamation

ex·clude [ɪk'skluːd] *v/t* exclure

ex·clud·ing [ɪk'skluːdɪŋ] *prep* sauf; **six ~ the children** six sans compter les enfants; **open year-round ~ ...** ouvert toute l'année à l'exclusion de ....

ex·clu·sive [ɪk'skluːsɪv] *adj hotel, restaurant* huppé; *rights, interview* exclusif*

ex·com·mu·ni·cate [ekskə'mjuːnɪkeɪt] *v/t* REL excommunier

ex·cru·ci·at·ing [ɪk'skruːʃieɪtɪŋ] *adj pain* atroce

ex·cur·sion [ɪk'skɜːrʃn] excursion *f*

ex·cuse [ɪk'skjuːs] **1** *n* excuse *f* **2** *v/t* [ɪk'skjuːz] excuser; (*forgive*) pardonner; **~ X from Y** dispenser X de Y; **~ me** excusez-moi

ex·di'rec·to·ry *Br*: **be ~** être sur liste rouge

e·x·e·cute ['eksɪkjuːt] *v/t criminal, plan* exécuter

ex·e·cu·tion [eksɪ'kjuːʃn] *of criminal, plan* exécution *f*

ex·e·cu·tion·er [eksɪ'kjuːʃnər] bourreau *m*

ex·ec·u·tive [ɪg'zekjutɪv] **1** *n* cadre *m* **2** *adj* de luxe

ex·ec·u·tive 'brief·case attaché-case *m*

ex·em·pla·ry [ɪg'zemplərɪ] *adj* exemplaire *m*

ex·empt [ɪg'zempt] *adj* exempt; **be ~ from** être exempté de

ex·er·cise ['eksərsaɪz] **1** *n* exercice *m*; **take ~** prendre de l'exercice **2** *v/t muscle* exercer; *dog* promener; *caution, restraint* user de **3** *v/i* prendre de l'exercice

'ex·er·cise bike vélo *m* d'appartement; **'ex·er·cise book** EDU cahier *m* (d'exercices); **'ex·er·cise class** cours *m* de gymnastique

ex·ert [ɪg'zɜːrt] *v/t authority* exercer; **~ o.s.** se dépenser

ex·er·tion [ɪg'zɜːrʃn] effort *m*

ex·hale [eks'heɪl] *v/t* exhaler

ex·haust [ɪg'zɔːst] **1** *n fumes* gaz *m* d'échappement; *pipe* tuyau *m* d'échappement **2** *v/t* (*tire, use up*) épuiser

ex·haust·ed [ɪg'zɔːstɪd] *adj* (*tired*) épuisé

ex·haust fumes *npl* gaz *mpl* d'échappement

ex·haust·ing [ɪg'zɔːstɪŋ] *adj* épuisant

ex·haus·tion [ɪg'zɔːstʃn] épuisement *m*

ex·haus·tive [ɪg'zɔːstɪv] *adj* exhaustif*

ex'haust pipe tuyau *m* d'échappement

ex·hib·it [ɪg'zɪbɪt] **1** *n in exhibition* objet *m* exposé **2** *v/t of artist* exposer; (*give evidence of*) montrer

ex·hi·bi·tion [eksɪ'bɪʃn] exposition *f*;

E

of bad behavior étalage m; of skill démonstration f

ex·hi·bi·tion·ist [eksɪ'bɪʃnɪst] exhibitionniste m/f

ex·hil·a·rat·ing [ɪg'zɪləreɪtɪŋ] adj weather vivifiant; sensation grisant

ex·ile ['eksaɪl] **1** n exil m; person exilé(e) m(f) **2** v/t exiler

ex·ist [ɪg'zɪst] v/i exister; ~ on subsister avec

ex·ist·ence [ɪg'zɪstəns] existence f; be in ~ exister; come into ~ être créé, naître

ex·ist·ing [ɪg'zɪstɪŋ] adj existant

ex·it ['eksɪt] **1** n sortie f **2** v/i COMPUT sortir

ex·on·e·rate [ɪg'zɑ:nəreɪt] v/t (clear) disculper

ex·or·bi·tant [ɪg'zɔ:rbɪtənt] adj exorbitant

ex·ot·ic [ɪg'zɑ:tɪk] adj exotique

ex·pand [ɪk'spænd] **1** v/t étendre, développer **2** v/i of population s'accroître, augmenter; of business, city se développer, s'étendre; of metal, gas se dilater

♦ **expand on** v/t s'étendre sur

ex·panse [ɪk'spæns] étendue f

ex·pan·sion [ɪk'spænʃn] of business, city développement m, extension f; of population accroissement m, augmentation f; of metal, gas dilatation f

ex·pat·ri·ate [eks'pætrɪət] **1** adj expatrié **2** n expatrié(e) m(f)

ex·pect [ɪk'spekt] **1** v/t also baby attendre; (suppose) penser, croire; (demand) exiger, attendre (from sth de qch) **2** v/i: be ~ing attendre un bébé; I ~ so je pense que oui

ex·pec·tant [ɪk'spektənt] adj crowd, spectators impatient; silence d'expectative

ex·pec·tant 'moth·er future maman f

ex·pec·ta·tion [ekspek'teɪʃn] attente f, espérance f; ~s (demands) exigence f

ex·pe·di·ent [ɪk'spi:dɪənt] adj opportun, pratique

ex·pe·di·tion [ekspɪ'dɪʃn] expédition f

ex·pel [ɪk'spel] v/t (pret & pp -led) person expulser

ex·pend [ɪk'spend] v/t energy dépenser

ex·pend·a·ble [ɪk'spendəbl] adj person pas indispensable, pas irremplaçable

ex·pen·di·ture [ɪk'spendɪtʃər] dépenses fpl (on de)

ex·pense [ɪk'spens] dépense f; at vast ~ à grands frais; at the company's ~ aux frais mpl de la compagnie; a joke at my ~ une plaisanterie à mes dépens; at the ~ of his health aux dépens de sa santé

ex·pense ac·count note f de frais

ex·pen·ses [ɪk'spensɪz] npl frais mpl

ex·pen·sive [ɪk'spensɪv] adj cher*

ex·pe·ri·ence [ɪk'spɪrɪəns] **1** n expérience f **2** v/t pain, pleasure éprouver; problem, difficulty connaître

ex·pe·ri·enced [ɪk'spɪrɪənst] adj expérimenté

ex·per·i·ment [ɪk'sperɪmənt] **1** n expérience f **2** v/i faire des expériences; ~ on animals faire des expériences sur; ~ with (try out) faire l'expérience de

ex·per·i·men·tal [ɪksperɪ'mentl] adj expérimental

ex·pert ['ekspɜ:rt] **1** adj expert **2** n expert(e) m(f)

ex·pert ad·vice conseil m d'expert

ex·per·tise [ekspɜ:r'ti:z] savoir-faire m

ex·pi·ra·tion date date f d'expiration

ex·pire [ɪk'spaɪr] v/i expirer

ex·pi·ry [ɪk'spaɪrɪ] expiration f

ex·plain [ɪk'spleɪn] v/t & v/i expliquer

ex·pla·na·tion [eksplə'neɪʃn] explication f

ex·plan·a·to·ry [eksplænətɔ:rɪ] adj explicatif*

ex·plic·it [ɪk'splɪsɪt] adj instructions explicite

ex·plic·it·ly [ɪk'splɪsɪtlɪ] adv state, forbid explicitement

ex·plode [ɪk'sploud] **1** v/i of bomb, fig exploser **2** v/t bomb faire exploser

ex·ploit¹ ['eksplɔɪt] n exploit m

ex·ploit² [ɪk'splɔɪt] v/t person, resources exploiter

ex·ploi·ta·tion [eksplɔɪ'teɪʃn] of person exploitation f

ex·plo·ra·tion [eksplə'reɪʃn] exploration f

ex·plor·a·to·ry [ɪk'splɔːrətərɪ] *adj surgery* exploratoire

ex·plore [ɪk'splɔːr] *v/t country, possibility* explorer

ex·plo·rer [ɪk'splɔːrər] explorateur (-trice) *m(f)*

ex·plo·sion [ɪk'sploʊʒn] *also in population* explosion *f*

ex·plo·sive [ɪk'sploʊsɪv] *n* explosif *m*

ex·port ['ekspɔːrt] **1** *n* exportation *f* **2** *v/t also* COMPUT exporter

'**ex·port cam·paign** campagne *f* export

ex·port·er [eks'pɔːrtər] exportateur (-trice) *m(f)*

ex·pose [ɪk'spoʊz] *v/t (uncover)* mettre à nu; *scandal* dévoiler; *person* démasquer; **~ X to Y** exposer X à Y

ex·po·sure [ɪk'spoʊʒər] exposition *f*; MED effets *mpl* du froid; *of dishonest behaviour* dénonciation *f*; PHOT pose *f*; *in media* couverture *f*

ex·press [ɪk'spres] **1** *adj (fast)* express; *(explicit)* formel*, explicite **2** *n train, bus* express *m* **3** *v/t* exprimer; **~ o.s. well / clearly** s'exprimer bien / clairement; **~ o.s.** *(emotionally)* s'exprimer

ex'press el·e·va·tor ascenseur *m* sans arrêt

ex·pres·sion [ɪk'spreʃn] expression *f*

ex·pres·sive [ɪk'spresɪv] *adj* expressif*

ex·press·ly [ɪk'spreslɪ] *adv (explicitly)* formellement, expressément; *(deliberately)* exprès

ex·press·way [ɪk'spresweɪ] voie *f* express

ex·pul·sion [ɪk'spʌlʃn] expulsion *f*

ex·qui·site [ek'skwɪzɪt] *adj (beautiful)* exquis

ex·tend [ɪk'stend] **1** *v/t house, garden* agrandir; *search* étendre (**to** à); *runway, contract, visa* prolonger; *thanks, congratulations* présenter **2** *v/i of garden etc* s'étendre

ex·ten·sion [ɪk'stenʃn] *to house* agrandissement *m*; *of contract, visa* prolongation *f*; TELEC poste *m*

ex'ten·sion ca·ble rallonge *f*

ex·ten·sive [ɪk'stensɪv] *adj search,*

knowledge vaste, étendu; *damage, work* considérable

ex·tent [ɪk'stent] étendue *f*, ampleur *f*; **to such an ~ that** à tel point que; **to a certain ~** jusqu'à un certain point

ex·ten·u·at·ing cir·cum·stan·ces [ɪk'stenveɪtɪŋ] *npl* circonstances *fpl* atténuantes

ex·te·ri·or [ɪk'stɪrɪər] **1** *adj* extérieur **2** *n of building* extérieur *m*; *of person* dehors *mpl*

ex·ter·mi·nate [ɪk'stɜːrmɪneɪt] *v/t* exterminer

ex·ter·nal [ɪk'stɜːrnl] *adj (outside)* extérieur

ex·tinct [ɪk'stɪŋkt] *adj species* disparu

ex·tinc·tion [ɪk'stɪŋkʃn] *of species* extinction *f*

ex·tin·guish [ɪk'stɪŋgwɪʃ] *v/t fire, cigarette* éteindre

ex·tin·guish·er [ɪk'stɪŋgwɪʃər] extincteur *m*

ex·tort [ɪk'stɔːrt] *v/t* extorquer; **~ money from s.o.** extorquer de l'argent à qn

ex·tor·tion [ɪk'stɔːrʃn] extortion *f*

ex·tor·tion·ate [ɪk'stɔːrʃənət] *adj prices* exorbitant

ex·tra ['ekstrə] **1** *n* extra *m* **2** *adj (spare)* de rechange; *(additional)* en plus, supplémentaire; **be ~** *(cost more)* être en supplément **3** *adv* ultra-

ex·tra 'charge supplément *m*

ex·tract[1] ['ekstrækt] *n* extrait *m*

ex·tract[2] [ɪk'strækt] *v/t* extraire; *tooth also* arracher; *information* arracher

ex·trac·tion [ɪk'strækʃn] extraction *f*

ex·tra·dite ['ekstrədaɪt] *v/t* extrader

ex·tra·di·tion [ekstrə'dɪʃn] extradition *f*

ex·tra·di·tion trea·ty accord *m* d'extradition

ex·tra·mar·i·tal [ekstrə'mærɪtl] *adj* extraconjugal

ex·tra·or·di·nar·i·ly [ɪkstrə'ɔːrdn'erɪlɪ] *adv* extraordinairement

ex·tra·or·di·na·ry [ɪkstrə'ɔːrdnerɪ] *adj* extraordinaire

ex·tra 'time *Br* SP prolongation(s) *f(pl)*

ex·trav·a·gance [ɪk'strævəgəns] dépenses *fpl* extravagantes; *single act* dépense *f* extravagante

ex·trav·a·gant [ɪkˈstrævəgənt] *adj person* dépensier*; *price* exorbitant; *claim* excessif*

ex·treme [ɪkˈstriːm] **1** *n* extrême *m* **2** *adj* extrême

ex·treme·ly [ɪkˈstriːmlɪ] *adv* extrêmement

ex·trem·ist [ɪkˈstriːmɪst] extrémiste *m/f*

ex·tri·cate [ˈekstrɪkeɪt] *v/t* dégager, libérer (*from* de)

ex·tro·vert [ˈekstrəvɜːrt] **1** *n* extraverti(e) *m(f)* **2** *adj* extraverti

ex·u·be·rant [ɪgˈzuːbərənt] *adj* exubérant

eye [aɪ] **1** *n* œil *m*; *of needle* trou *m*; *have blue ~s* avoir les yeux bleus; *keep an ~ on* surveiller; *in my ~s* à mes yeux **2** *v/t* regarder

'eye·ball globe *m* oculaire; **'eye·brow** sourcil *m*

'eye-catch·ing *adj* accrocheur*; **'eye·glasses** lunettes *fpl*; **'eye·lash** cil *m*; **'eye·lid** paupière *f*; **'eye·lin·er** eye-liner *m*; **'eye·sha·dow** ombre *f* à paupières; **'eye·sight** vue *f*; **'eye·sore** horreur *f*; **'eye strain** fatigue *f* des yeux; **'eye·wit·ness** témoin *m* oculaire

F

F *abbr* (*= Fahrenheit*) F (= Fahrenheit)

fab·ric [ˈfæbrɪk] (*material*) tissu *m*

fab·u·lous [ˈfæbjʊləs] *adj* fabuleux*

fab·u·lous·ly [ˈfæbjʊləslɪ] *adv* fabuleusement

fa·çade [fəˈsɑːd] *of building, person* façade *f*

face [feɪs] **1** *n* visage *m*, figure *f*; *of mountain* face *f*; *~ to ~* en personne; *lose ~* perdre la face **2** *v/t person, sea* faire face à

♦ **face up to** *v/t bully* affronter; *responsibilities* faire face à

'face·cloth gant *m* de toilette; **'face·lift** lifting *m*; *the building / area has been given a ~* le bâtiment / quartier a été complètement refait; **'face pack** masque *m* de beauté; **face 'val·ue**: *take sth at ~* juger qch sur les apparences

fa·cial [ˈfeɪʃl] *n* soin *m* du visage

fa·cil·i·tate [fəˈsɪlɪteɪt] *v/t* faciliter

fa·cil·i·ties [fəˈsɪlətiz] *npl of school, town etc* installations *fpl*; (*equipment*) équipements *mpl*

rant

ex·ult [ɪgˈzʌlt] *v/i* exulter

fact [fækt] fait *m*; *in ~, as a matter of ~* en fait

fac·tion [ˈfækʃn] faction *f*

fac·tor [ˈfæktər] facteur *m*

fac·to·ry [ˈfæktərɪ] usine *f*

fac·tu·al [ˈfæktʊəl] *adj* factuel*

fac·ul·ty [ˈfækltɪ] (*hearing etc*), *at university* faculté *f*

fad [fæd] lubie *f*

fade [feɪd] *v/i of colors* passer

fad·ed [ˈfeɪdɪd] *adj color, jeans* passé

fag [fæg] *pej* F (*homosexual*) pédé *m* F

Fahr·en·heit [ˈfærənhaɪt] *adj* Fahrenheit

fail [feɪl] **1** *v/i* échouer **2** *n*: *without ~* sans faute

fail·ing [ˈfeɪlɪŋ] *n* défaut *m*, faiblesse *f*

fail·ure [ˈfeɪljər] échec *m*; *feel a ~* avoir l'impression de ne rien valoir

faint [feɪnt] **1** *adj* faible, léger* **2** *v/i* s'évanouir

faint·ly [ˈfeɪntlɪ] *adv* légèrement

fair¹ [fer] *n* (*fun~*), COMM foire *f*

fair² [fer] *adj hair* blond; *complexion* blanc*

fair³ [fer] *adj* (*just*) juste, équitable; *it's*

not ~ ce n'est pas juste

fair·ly ['feɪrlɪ] *adv treat* équitablement; (*quite*) assez

fair·ness ['fernɪs] *of treatment* équité *f*

fai·ry ['ferɪ] fée *f*

'fai·ry tale conte *m* de fées

faith [feɪθ] *also* REL foi *f*; **the Catholic ~** la religion catholique

faith·ful ['feɪθfl] *adj* fidèle

faith·ful·ly ['feɪθflɪ] *adv* fidèlement; **Yours ~** *Br* veuillez agréer l'expression de mes salutations distinguées

fake [feɪk] **1** *n* (*article m*) faux *m* **2** *adj* faux*; *suicide attempt* simulé **3** *v/t* (*forge*) falsifier; (*feign*) feindre; *suicide, kidnap* simuler

fall¹ [fɔːl] *n season* automne *m*

fall² [fɔːl] **1** *v/i* (*pret* **fell**, *pp* **fallen**) *of person, government, night* tomber; *of prices, temperature* baisser; **it ~s on a Tuesday** ça tombe un mardi; **~ ill** tomber malade **2** *n of person, government, minister* chute *f*; *in price, temperature* baisse *f*

♦ **fall back on** *v/t* se rabattre sur

♦ **fall behind** *v/i with work, studies* prendre du retard

♦ **fall down** *v/i of person* tomber (par terre); *of wall, building* s'effondrer

♦ **fall for** *v/t person* tomber amoureux de; (*be deceived by*) se laisser prendre à

♦ **fall out** *v/i of hair* tomber; (*argue*) se brouiller

♦ **fall over** *v/i of person, tree* tomber (par terre)

♦ **fall through** *v/i of plans* tomber à l'eau

fal·len ['fɔːlən] *pp* → **fall**

fal·li·ble ['fæləbl] *adj* faillible

'fallout retombées *fpl* (*radioactives*)

false [fɔːls] *adj* faux*

false a'larm fausse alarme *f*

false·ly ['fɔːlslɪ] *adv*: **be ~ accused of sth** être accusé à tort de qch

false 'start *in race* faux départ *m*

false 'teeth *npl* fausses dents *fpl*

fal·si·fy ['fɔːlsɪfaɪ] *v/t* (*pret & pp* **-ied**) falsifier

fame [feɪm] célébrité *f*

fa·mil·i·ar [fə'mɪljər] *adj* familier*; **be**

~ with sth bien connaître qch; **that looks / sounds ~** ça me dit quelque chose

fa·mil·i·ar·i·ty [fəmɪlɪ'erɪtɪ] *with subject etc* (bonne) connaissance *f* (*with* de)

fa·mil·i·ar·ize [fə'mɪljəraɪz] *v/t* familiariser; **~ o.s. with** se familiariser avec

fam·i·ly ['fæməlɪ] famille *f*

fam·i·ly 'doc·tor médecin *m* de famille; **fam·i·ly 'name** nom *m* de famille; **fam·i·ly 'plan·ning** planning *m* familial; **fam·i·ly 'plan·ning clin·ic** centre *m* de planning familial; **fam·i·ly 'tree** arbre *m* généalogique

fam·ine ['fæmɪn] famine *f*

fam·ished ['fæmɪʃt] *adj* F affamé

fa·mous ['feɪməs] *adj* célèbre

fan¹ [fæn] *n in sport* fana *m/f* F; *of singer, band* fan *m/f*

fan² [fæn] **1** *n for cooling: electric* ventilateur *m*; *handheld* éventail *m* **2** *v/t* (*pret & pp* **-ned**): **~ o.s.** s'éventer

fa·nat·ic [fə'nætɪk] *n* fanatique *m/f*

fa·nat·i·cal [fə'nætɪkl] *adj* fanatique

fa·nat·i·cism [fə'nætɪsɪzm] fanatisme *m*

'fan belt MOT courroie *f* de ventilateur

'fan club fan-club *m*

fan·cy ['fænsɪ] *adj restaurant* huppé

fan·cy 'dress déguisement *m*

fan·cy-'dress par·ty fête *f* déguisée

fang [fæŋ] *of dog* croc *m*; *of snake* crochet *m*

'fan mail courrier *m* des fans

fan·ta·size ['fæntəsaɪz] *v/i* fantasmer (*about* sur)

fan·tas·tic [fæn'tæstɪk] *adj* fantastique

fan·tas·tic·al·ly [fæn'tæstɪklɪ] *adv* (*extremely*) fantastiquement

fan·ta·sy ['fæntəsɪ] *hopeful* rêve *m*; *unrealistic, sexual* fantasme *m*; **the realm of ~** le domaine de l'imaginaire

fan·zine ['fænziːn] fanzine *m*

far [fɑːr] *adv* loin; (*much*) bien; **~ away** très loin; **how ~ is it?** c'est loin?, c'est à quelle distance?; **how ~ have you got in …?** où en êtes-vous dans …?; **as ~ as the corner / hotel** jusqu'au coin / jusqu'à l'hôtel; **as ~ as I**

favor

know pour autant que je sache; **you've gone too ~** *in behavior* tu vas trop loin; **so ~ so good** tout va bien pour le moment

farce [fɑːrs] farce *f*

fare [fer] *n for ticket* prix *m* du billet; *for taxi* prix *m*

Far 'East Extrême-Orient *m*

fare·well [fer'wel] *n* adieu *m*

fare'well par·ty fête *f* d'adieu

far·fetched [fɑːr'fetʃt] *adj* tiré par les cheveux

farm [fɑːrm] *n* ferme *f*

farm·er ['fɑːrmər] fermier(-ière) *m(f)*

'farm·house (maison *f* de) ferme *f*

farm·ing ['fɑːrmɪŋ] *n* agriculture *f*

'farm·work·er ouvrier(-ière) *m(f)* agricole

'farm·yard cour *f* de ferme

far-'off *adj* lointain, éloigné

far·sight·ed [fɑːr'saɪtɪd] *adj* prévoyant; *visually* hypermétrope

fart [fɑːrt] **1** *n* F pet *m* **2** *v/i* F péter

far·ther ['fɑːrðər] *adv* plus loin

far·thest ['fɑːrðəst] *adv travel etc* le plus loin

fas·ci·nate ['fæsɪneɪt] *v/t* fasciner

fas·ci·nat·ing ['fæsɪneɪtɪŋ] *adj* fascinant

fas·ci·na·tion [fæsɪ'neɪʃn] fascination *f*

fas·cism ['fæʃɪzm] fascisme *m*

fas·cist ['fæʃɪst] **1** *n* fasciste *m/f* **2** *adj* fasciste

fash·ion ['fæʃn] *n* mode *f*; *(manner)* manière *f*, façon *f*; **in ~** à la mode; **out of ~** démodé

fash·ion·a·ble ['fæʃnəbl] *adj* à la mode

fash·ion·a·bly ['fæʃnəblɪ] *adv* à la mode

'fash·ion-con·scious *adj* au courant de la mode; **'fash·ion de·sign·er** créateur(-trice) *m(f)* de mode; **'fash·ion mag·a·zine** magazine *m* de mode; **'fash·ion show** défilé *m* de mode

fast¹ [fæst] **1** *adj* rapide; **be ~** *of clock* avancer **2** *adv* vite; **stuck ~** coincé; **be ~ asleep** dormir à poings fermés

fast² [fæst] *n (not eating)* jeûne *m*

fas·ten ['fæsn] **1** *v/t* attacher; *lid, window* fermer; **~ sth onto sth** attacher qch à qch **2** *v/i of dress etc* s'attacher

fas·ten·er ['fæsnər] *for dress* agrafe *f*; *for lid* fermeture *f*

fast 'food fast-food *m*; **fast-food 'res·tau·rant** fast-food *m*; **fast 'for·ward 1** *n on video etc* avance *f* rapide **2** *v/i* avancer; **'fast lane** *on road* voie *f* rapide; **live in the ~** *fig: of life* vivre à cent à l'heure; **'fast train** train *m* rapide

fat [fæt] **1** *adj* gros* **2** *n on meat* gras *m*; *for baking* graisse *f*; *food category* lipide *m*; **95% ~ free** allégé à 5% de matières grasses

fa·tal ['feɪtl] *adj also error* fatal

fa·tal·i·ty [fə'tælətɪ] *accident m* mortel; **there were no fatalities** il n'y a pas eu de morts

fa·tal·ly ['feɪtəlɪ] *adv*: fatalement; **~ in·jured** mortellement blessé

fate [feɪt] destin *m*

fat·ed ['feɪtɪd] *adj*: **be ~ to do sth** être destiné à faire qch

fa·ther ['fɑːðər] *n* père *m*; *Father Martin* REL le père Martin

Fa·ther 'Christ·mas *Br* le père *m* Noël

fa·ther·hood ['fɑːðərhʊd] paternité *f*

'fa·ther-in-law *(pl fathers-in-law)* beau-père *m*

fa·ther·ly ['fɑːðərlɪ] *adj* paternel*

fath·om ['fæðəm] *n* NAUT brasse *f*

♦ **fathom** *v/t fig* comprendre

fa·tigue [fə'tiːɡ] *n* fatigue *f*

fat·so ['fætsoʊ] *n* F gros(se) *m(f)*; *hey, ~!* hé, gros lard!

fat·ten ['fætn] *v/t animal* engraisser

fat·ty ['fætɪ] **1** *adj* adipeux* **2** *n* F *person* gros(se) *m(f)*

fau·cet ['fɔːsɪt] robinet *m*

fault [fɔːlt] *n (defect)* défaut *m*; *it's your / my ~* c'est de ta / ma faute; *find ~ with* trouver à redire à

fault·less ['fɔːltlɪs] *adj* impeccable

fault·y ['fɔːltɪ] *adj goods* défectueux*

fa·vor ['feɪvər] **1** *n* faveur *f*; *do s.o. a ~* rendre (un) service à qn; *do me a ~!* *(don't be stupid)* tu plaisantes!; *in ~ of resign, withdraw* en faveur de; *be in ~*

of être en faveur de **2** *v/t* (*prefer*) préférer

fa·vo·ra·ble ['feɪvərəbl] *adj reply etc* favorable (**to** à)

fa·vo·rite ['feɪvərɪt] **1** *n person* préféré(e) *m(f)*; *food* plat *m* préféré; *in race, competition* favori(te) *m(f)*; **that's my ~** c'est ce que je préfère **2** *adj* préféré

fa·vor·it·ism ['feɪvrɪtɪzm] favoritisme *m*

fax [fæks] **1** *n* fax *m*; **by ~** par fax **2** *v/t* faxer; **~ sth to s.o.** faxer qch à qn

FBI [efbiː'aɪ] *abbr* (= *Federal Bureau of Investigation*) F.B.I. *m*

fear [fɪr] **1** *n* peur *f* **2** *v/t* avoir peur de

fear·less ['fɪrlɪs] *adj* sans peur

fear·less·ly ['fɪrlɪslɪ] *adv* sans peur

fea·si·bil·i·ty stud·y [fiːzə'bɪlətɪ] étude *f* de faisabilité

fea·si·ble ['fiːzəbl] *adj* faisable

feast [fiːst] *n* festin *m*

'feast day REL fête *f*

feat [fiːt] exploit *m*

feath·er ['feðər] plume *f*

fea·ture ['fiːtʃər] **1** *n on face* trait *m*; *of city, building, style* caractéristique *f*; *article in paper* chronique *f*; *movie* long métrage *m*; **make a ~ of** mettre en valeur **2** *v/t of movie* mettre en vedette

'fea·ture film long métrage *m*

Feb·ru·a·ry ['februərɪ] février *m*

fed [fed] *pret & pp* → **feed**

fed·e·ral ['fedərəl] *adj* fédéral

fed·e·ra·tion [fedə'reɪʃn] fédération *f*

fed 'up *adj* F: **be ~ with** en avoir ras-le-bol de F

fee [fiː] *of lawyer, doctor etc* honoraires *mpl*; *for entrance, membership* frais *mpl*

fee·ble ['fiːbl] *adj* faible

feed [fiːd] *v/t* (*pret & pp* **fed**) nourrir

'feed·back réactions *fpl*; **we need more customer ~** nous devons connaître mieux l'avis de nos clients

feel [fiːl] **1** *v/t* (*pret & pp* **felt**) (*touch*) toucher; (*sense*) sentir; *pain, pleasure, sensation* ressentir; (*think*) penser **2** *v/i*: **it ~s like silk / cotton** on dirait de la soie / du coton; **your hand**

~s hot / cold vos mains sont chaudes / froides; **I ~ hungry / tired** j'ai faim / je suis fatigué; **how are you ~ing today?** comment vous sentez-vous aujourd'hui?; **how does it ~ to be rich?** qu'est-ce que ça fait d'être riche?; **do you ~ like a drink / meal?** est-ce que tu as envie de boire / manger quelque chose?; **I ~ like leaving / staying** j'ai envie de m'en aller / rester; **I don't ~ like it** je n'en ai pas envie

♦ **feel up to** *v/t* se sentir capable de (*doing sth* faire qch); **I don't feel up to it** je ne m'en sens pas capable

feel·er ['fiːlər] *of insect* antenne *f*

'feel-good fac·tor sentiment *m* de bien-être

feel·ing ['fiːlɪŋ] (*emotional, mental*) sentiment *m*; (*sensation*) sensation *f*; **what are your ~s about it?** quels sont tes sentiments là-dessus?; **I have mixed ~s about him** je ne sais pas quoi penser de lui

feet [fiːt] *pl* → **foot**

fe·line ['fiːlaɪn] *adj* félin

fell [fel] *pret* → **fall**

fel·la ['felə] F mec *m* F; **listen, ~** écoute mon vieux

fel·low ['felou] *n* (*man*) type *m*

fel·low 'cit·i·zen *n* concitoyen(ne) *m(f)*; **fel·low 'coun·try·man** *n* compatriote *m/f*; **fel·low 'man** prochain *m*

fel·o·ny ['felənɪ] crime *m*

felt[1] [felt] *pret & pp* → **feel**

felt[2] [felt] *n* feutre *m*

felt 'tip, felt tip 'pen stylo *m* feutre

fe·male ['fiːmeɪl] **1** *adj animal, plant* femelle; *relating to people* féminin **2** *n of animals, plants* femelle *f*; *person* femme *f*; F (*woman*) nana *f* F

fem·i·nine ['femɪnɪn] **1** *adj* féminin **2** *n* GRAM féminin *m*

fem·i·nism ['femɪnɪzm] féminisme *m*

fem·i·nist ['femɪnɪst] **1** *n* féministe *m/f* **2** *adj* féministe

fence [fens] *n around garden etc* barrière *f*, clôture *f*; F *criminal* receleur(-euse) *m(f)*; **sit on the ~** *fig* ne pas se prononcer, attendre de voir

fifteenth

d'où vient le vent

◆ **fence in** v/t land clôturer

fenc·ing ['fensɪŋ] SP escrime f

fend [fend] v/i: **~ for o.s.** se débrouiller tout seul

fend·er ['fendər] MOT aile f

fer·ment[1] [fər'ment] v/i of liquid fermenter

fer·ment[2] ['fɜːrment] n (unrest) effervescence f; agitation f

fer·men·ta·tion [fɜːrmen'teɪʃn] fermentation f

fern [fɜːrn] fougère f

fe·ro·cious [fə'rouʃəs] adj féroce

fer·ry ['feri] n ferry m

fer·tile ['fɜːrtl] adj fertile

fer·til·i·ty [fɜːr'tɪlətɪ] fertilité f

fer·til·i·ty drug médicament m contre la stérilité

fer·ti·lize ['fɜːrtəlaɪz] v/t ovum féconder

fer·ti·liz·er ['fɜːrtəlaɪzər] for soil engrais m

fer·vent ['fɜːrvənt] adj admirer fervent

fer·vent·ly ['fɜːrvəntlɪ] adv avec ferveur

fes·ter ['festər] v/i of wound suppurer; fig: of ill will etc s'envenimer

fes·ti·val ['festɪvl] festival m

fes·tive ['festɪv] adj de fête; **the ~ season** la saison des fêtes

fes·tiv·i·ties [fe'stɪvətɪz] npl festivités fpl

fe·tal ['fiːtl] adj fœtal

fetch [fetʃ] v/t (go and ~) aller chercher (from à); (come and ~) venir chercher (from à); price atteindre

fetch·ing ['fetʃɪŋ] adj séduisant

fe·tus ['fiːtəs] fœtus m

feud [fjuːd] **1** n querelle f **2** v/i se quereller

fe·ver ['fiːvər] fièvre f

fe·ver·ish ['fiːvərɪʃ] adj also fig fiévreux*

few [fjuː] **1** adj ◇ (not many) peu de; **he has so ~ friends** il a tellement peu d'amis

◇: **a ~ ...** quelques; **quite a ~, a good ~** (a lot) beaucoup de **2** pron ◇ (not many) peu; **~ of them** peu d'entre eux

◇: **a ~** quelques-un(e)s m(f); **quite a ~, a good ~** beaucoup **3** npl: **the ~ who ...** les quelques or rares personnes qui ...

few·er ['fjuːər] adj moins de; **~ than ...** moins de

few·est ['fjuːəst] adj le moins de

fi·an·cé [fɪ'ɑːnseɪ] fiancé m

fi·an·cée [fɪ'ɑːnseɪ] fiancée f

fi·as·co [fɪ'æskou] fiasco m

fib [fɪb] n petit mensonge m

fi·ber ['faɪbər] fibre f

'fi·ber·glass n fibre f de verre; **fi·ber 'op·tic** adj en fibres optiques; **fi·ber 'op·tics** npl fibres fpl optiques; nsg technology technologie f des fibres optiques

fi·bre Br → **fiber**

fick·le ['fɪkl] adj inconstant, volage

fic·tion ['fɪkʃn] (novels) romans mpl; (made-up story) fiction f

fic·tion·al ['fɪkʃnl] adj character de roman

fic·ti·tious [fɪk'tɪʃəs] adj fictif*

fid·dle ['fɪdl] **1** n F (violin) violon m; **it's a ~** (cheat) c'est une magouille F **2** v/i: **~ with** tripoter; **~ around with** tripoter **3** v/t accounts, results truquer

fi·del·i·ty [fɪ'delətɪ] fidélité f

fid·get ['fɪdʒɪt] v/i remuer, gigoter F

fid·get·y ['fɪdʒɪtɪ] adj remuant

field [fiːld] champ m; for sport terrain m; (competitors in race) concurrent(e)s m(f)pl; of research, knowledge etc domaine m; **there's a strong ~ for the 1500m** il y a une forte concurrence pour le 1500 mètres; **that's not my ~** ce n'est pas de mon domaine

field·er ['fiːldər] in baseball joueur m de champ, défenseur m

'field e·vents npl concours mpl

'field work recherche(s) f(pl) de terrain

fierce [fɪrs] adj animal féroce; wind, storm violent

fierce·ly ['fɪrslɪ] adv avec férocité

fi·er·y ['faɪrɪ] adj ardent, fougueux*

fif·teen [fɪf'tiːn] quinze

fif·teenth [fɪf'tiːnθ] quinzième; → **fifth**

fifth [fɪfθ] cinquième; *May ~*, *Br the ~ of May* le cinq mai

fifth·ly ['fɪfθlɪ] *adv* cinquièmement

fif·ti·eth ['fɪftɪɪθ] cinquantième

fif·ty ['fɪftɪ] cinquante

fif·ty-'fif·ty *adv* moitié-moitié

fig [fɪg] figue *f*

fight [faɪt] **1** *n* MIL, *in boxing* combat *m*; *(argument)* dispute *f*, *fig*: *for survival, championship etc* lutte *f* (*for* pour) **2** *v/t* (*pret & pp* **fought**) *enemy, person* combattre; *in boxing* se battre contre; *disease, injustice* lutter contre **3** *v/i* se battre; *(argue)* se disputer

♦ **fight for** *v/t rights, cause* se battre pour

fight·er ['faɪtər] combattant(e) *m(f)*; *(airplane)* avion *m* de chasse; *(boxer)* boxeur *m*; *she's a ~* c'est une battante

fight·ing ['faɪtɪŋ] *n physical* combat *m*; *verbal* dispute *f*

fig·ment ['fɪgmənt]: *it's just a ~ of your imagination* ce n'est qu'un produit de ton imagination

fig·u·ra·tive ['fɪgjərətɪv] *adj use of word* figuré; *art* figuratif*

fig·ure ['fɪgjər] **1** *n* (*digit*) chiffre *m*; *of person* ligne *f*; *(form, shape)* figure *f*; *(human form)* silhouette *f*; *bad for your ~* mauvais pour la ligne **2** *v/t* F (*think*) penser

♦ **figure on** *v/t* F (*plan*) compter; *be figuring on doing sth* compter faire qch

♦ **figure out** *v/t* (*understand*) comprendre; *calculation* calculer

'fig·ure skat·er patineur(-euse) *m(f)* artistique

'fig·ure skat·ing patinage *m* artistique

file[1] [faɪl] **1** *n of documents* dossier *m*, classeur *m*; COMPUT fichier *m* **2** *v/t documents* classer

♦ **file away** *v/t documents* classer

♦ **file for** *v/t divorce* demander

file[2] [faɪl] *n for wood, fingernails* lime *f*

'file cab·i·net classeur *m*

'file man·ag·er COMPUT gestionnaire *m* de fichiers

fi·li·al ['fɪlɪəl] *adj* filial

fill [fɪl] **1** *v/t* remplir; *tooth* plomber; *prescription* préparer **2** *n*: *eat one's ~* manger à sa faim

♦ **fill in** *v/t form* remplir; *hole* boucher; *fill s.o. in* mettre qn au courant (*on sth* de qch)

♦ **fill in for** *v/t* remplacer

♦ **fill out 1** *v/t form* remplir **2** *v/i* (*get fatter*) grossir

♦ **fill up 1** *v/t* remplir (jusqu'au bord) **2** *v/i of stadium, theater* se remplir

fil·let ['fɪlɪt] *n* filet *m*

fil·let 'steak filet *m* de bœuf

fill·ing ['fɪlɪŋ] **1** *n in sandwich* garniture *f*; *in tooth* plombage *m* **2** *adj food* nourrissant

'fill·ing sta·tion station-service *f*

film [fɪlm] **1** *n for camera* pellicule *f*; *(movie)* film *m* **2** *v/t person, event* filmer

'film-mak·er réalisateur(-trice) *m(f)* de films; **'film star** star *f* de cinéma; **'film stu·di·o** studio *m* de cinéma

fil·ter ['fɪltər] **1** *n* filtre *m* **2** *v/t coffee, liquid* filtrer

♦ **filter through** *v/i of news reports* filtrer

'fil·ter pa·per papier-filtre *m*

'fil·ter tip (*cigarette*) filtre *m*

filth [fɪlθ] saleté *f*

filth·y ['fɪlθɪ] *adj* sale; *language etc* obscène

fin [fɪn] *of fish* nageoire *f*

fi·nal ['faɪnl] **1** *adj* (*last*) dernier*; *decision* définitif*, irrévocable **2** *n* SP finale *f*

fi·na·le [fɪ'nælɪ] apothéose *f*

fi·nal·ist ['faɪnəlɪst] finaliste *m/f*

fi·nal·ize ['faɪnəlaɪz] *v/t plans, design* finaliser, mettre au point

fi·nal·ly ['faɪnəlɪ] *adv* finalement, enfin; *~, I would like to …* pour finir, j'aimerais …

fi·nance ['faɪnæns] **1** *n* finance *f*; *(funds)* financement *m* **2** *v/t* financer

fi·nan·ces ['faɪnænsɪz] *npl* finances *fpl*

fi·nan·cial [faɪ'nænʃl] *adj* financier

fi·nan·cial·ly [faɪ'nænʃəlɪ] *adv* financièrement

fi·nan·cier [faɪ'nænsɪr] financier

(-ière) *m(f)*

find [faɪnd] *v/t (pret & pp* **found**) trouver; *if you ~ it too difficult* si vous trouvez ça trop difficile; *~ a person innocent / guilty* LAW déclarer une personne innocente / coupable

♦ **find out 1** *v/t* découvrir; *(enquire about)* se renseigner sur **2** *v/i (enquire)* se renseigner; *(discover)* découvrir; *you'll find out* tu verras

find·ings ['faɪndɪŋz] *npl of report* constatations *fpl,* conclusions *fpl*

fine¹ [faɪn] *adj* day, weather beau*; *(good)* bon*, excellent; *distinction* subtil; *line* fin; *how's that? - that's ~* que dites-vous de ça? - c'est bien; *that's ~ by me* ça me va; *how are you? - ~* comment vas-tu? - bien

fine² [faɪn] **1** *n* amende *f* **2** *v/t* condamner à une amende; *~ s.o. $5,000* condamner qn à une amende de 5.000 \$

fine-'tooth comb: *go through sth with a ~* passer qch au peigne fin

fine-'tune *v/t engine* régler avec précision; *fig* peaufiner

fin·ger ['fɪŋɡər] **1** *n* doigt *m* **2** *v/t* toucher, tripoter

'fin·ger·nail ongle *m;* **'fin·ger·print 1** *n* empreinte *f* digitale **2** *v/t* prendre les empreintes digitales de; **'fin·ger·tip** bout *m* du doigt; *have sth at one's ~s* connaître qch sur le bout des doigts

fin·ick·y ['fɪnɪkɪ] *adj person* tatillon*; *design, pattern* alambiqué

fin·ish ['fɪnɪʃ] **1** *v/t* finir, terminer; *~ doing sth* finir de faire qch **2** *v/i* finir **3** *n of product* finition *f; of race* arrivée *f*

♦ **finish off** *v/t* finir

♦ **finish up** *v/t food* finir; *he finished up living there* il a fini par habiter là

♦ **finish with** *v/t boyfriend etc* en finir avec

'fin·ish line, *Br* **fin·ish·ing line** ['fɪnɪʃɪŋ] ligne *f* d'arrivée

Fin·land ['fɪnlənd] Finlande *f*

Finn [fɪn] Finlandais(e) *m(f)*

Finn·ish ['fɪnɪʃ] **1** *adj* finlandais, finnois **2** *n (language)* finnois *m*

fir [fɜːr] sapin *m*

fire ['faɪr] **1** *n* feu *m; (blaze)* incendie *m; (electric, gas)* radiateur *m; be on ~* être en feu; *catch ~* prendre feu; *set sth on ~, set ~ to sth* mettre le feu à qch **2** *v/i (shoot)* tirer **3** *v/t F (dismiss)* virer F

'fire a·larm signal *m* d'incendie; **'fire·arm** arme *f* à feu; **'fire bri·gade** *Br* sapeurs-pompiers *mpl;* **'fire·crack·er** pétard *m;* **'fire de·part·ment** sapeurs-pompiers *mpl;* **'fire door** porte *f* coupe-feu; **'fire drill** exercice *m* d'évacuation; **'fire en·gine** *esp Br* voiture *f* de pompiers; **'fire es·cape** *ladder* échelle *f* de secours; *stairs* escalier *m* de secours; **'fire ex·tin·guish·er** extincteur *m* (d'incendie); **'fire fight·er** pompier *m;* **'fire·guard** garde-feu *m;* **'fire·man** pompier *m;* **'fire·place** cheminée *f;* **'fire sta·tion** caserne *f* de pompiers; **'fire truck** voiture *f* de pompiers; **'fire·wood** bois *m* à brûler; **'fire·works** *npl* pièce *f* d'artifice; *(display)* feu *m* d'artifice

firm¹ [fɜːrm] *adj* ferme; *a ~ deal* un marché ferme

firm² [fɜːrm] *n* COMM firme *f*

first [fɜːrst] **1** *adj* premier*; *who's please?* à qui est-ce? **2** *n* premier(-ière) *m(f)* **3** *adv* arrive, finish le / la premier(-ière) *m(f); (beforehand)* d'abord; *~ of all (for one reason)* d'abord; *at ~* au début

first 'aid premiers secours *mpl;* **first-'aid box, first-'aid kit** trousse *f* de premier secours; **'first-born** *adj* premier-né; **'first class 1** *adj ticket, seat* de première classe **2** *adv travel* en première classe

first-class *adj (very good)* de première qualité; **'first floor** rez-de-chaussée *m; Br* premier étage *m;* **first'hand** *adj* de première main; **First 'La·dy** *of US* première dame *f*

first·ly ['fɜːrstlɪ] *adv* premièrement

first 'name prénom *m;* **first 'night** première *f;* **first of'fend·er** délinquant(e) *m(f)* primaire; **first-'rate** *adj* de premier ordre

fis·cal ['fɪskl] *adj* fiscal

fis·cal 'year année *f* fiscale

fish [fɪʃ] **1** *n* (*pl* **fish**) poisson *m*; ***drink like a ~*** F boire comme un trou F; ***feel like a ~ out of water*** ne pas se sentir dans son élément **2** *v/i* pêcher

'fish·bone arête *f*

fish·er·man ['fɪʃərmən] pêcheur *m*

fish 'fin·ger *Br* bâtonnet *m* de poisson

fish·ing ['fɪʃɪŋ] pêche *f*

'fish·ing boat bateau *m* de pêche; **'fish·ing line** ligne *f* (de pêche); **'fish·ing rod** canne *f* à pêche

'fish stick bâtonnet *m* de poisson

fish·y ['fɪʃɪ] *adj* F (*suspicious*) louche

fist [fɪst] poing *m*

fit[1] [fɪt] *n* MED crise *f*, attaque *f*; ***a ~ of rage / jealousy*** une crise de rage / jalousie

fit[2] [fɪt] *adj physically* en forme; *morally* digne; ***keep ~*** garder la forme

fit[3] [fɪt] **1** *v/t* (*pret & pp* **-ted**) *of clothes* aller à; (*install, attach*) poser; ***it doesn't ~ me any more*** je ne rentre plus dedans **2** *v/i of clothes* aller; *of piece of furniture etc* (r)entrer; ***it doesn't ~*** *of clothing* ce n'est pas la bonne taille **3** *n*: ***it's a tight ~*** c'est juste

♦ **fit in 1** *v/i of person in group* s'intégrer; ***it fits in with our plans*** ça cadre avec nos projets **2** *v/t*: ***fit s.o. in*** *in schedule* trouver un moment pour qn

fit·ful ['fɪtfl] *adj sleep* agité

fit·ness ['fɪtnɪs] *physical* (bonne) forme *f*

'fit·ness cen·ter, *Br* **'fit·ness cen·tre** centre *m* sportif

fit·ted 'car·pet ['fɪtɪd] *Br* moquette *f*; **fit·ted 'kitch·en** cuisine *f* aménagée; **fit·ted 'sheet** drap *m* housse

fit·ter ['fɪtər] *n* monteur(-euse) *m(f)*

fit·ting ['fɪtɪŋ] *adj* approprié

fit·tings ['fɪtɪŋz] *npl* installations *fpl*

five [faɪv] cinq

fix [fɪks] **1** *n* (*solution*) solution *f*; ***be in a ~*** F être dans le pétrin F **2** *v/t* (*attach*) attacher; (*repair*) réparer; (*arrange*: *meeting etc*) arranger; *lunch* préparer; *dishonestly*: *match etc* truquer; ***~ sth onto sth*** attacher qch

à qch; ***I'll ~ you a drink*** je vous offre un verre

♦ **fix up** *v/t meeting* arranger

fixed [fɪkst] *adj* fixe

fix·ings ['fɪksɪŋz] *npl* garniture *f*

fix·ture ['fɪkstʃər] *device* appareil *m* fixe; *piece of furniture* meuble *m* fixe

♦ **fizzle out** ['fɪzl] *v/i* F tomber à l'eau

fiz·zy ['fɪzɪ] *adj Br*: *drink* pétillant

flab [flæb] *on body* graisse *f*

flab·ber·gast ['flæbərgæst] *v/t* F: ***be ~ed*** être abasourdi

flab·by ['flæbɪ] *adj muscles, stomach* mou*

flag[1] [flæg] *n* drapeau *m*; NAUT pavillon *m*

flag[2] [flæg] *v/i* (*pret & pp* **-ged**) (*tire*) faiblir

♦ **flag up** *v/t* signaler

'flag·pole mât *m* (de drapeau)

fla·grant ['fleɪgrənt] *adj* flagrant

'flag·ship *fig*: *store* magasin *m* le plus important; *product* produit *m* phare; **'flag·staff** mât *m* (de drapeau); **'flag·stone** dalle *f*

flair [fler] (*talent*) flair *m*; ***have a natural ~ for*** avoir un don pour

flake [fleɪk] *n of snow* flocon *m*; *of plaster* écaille *f*; ***~ of skin*** petit bout *m* de peau morte

♦ **flake off** *v/i of plaster, paint* s'écailler; *of skin* peler

flak·y ['fleɪkɪ] *adj skin* qui pèle; *paint* qui s'écaille

flak·y 'pas·try pâte *f* feuilletée

flam·boy·ant [flæm'bɔɪənt] *adj personality* extravagant

flam·boy·ant·ly [flæm'bɔɪəntlɪ] *adv dressed* avec extravagance

flame [fleɪm] *n* flamme *f*; ***go up in ~s*** être détruit par le feu

flam·ma·ble ['flæməbl] *adj* inflammable

flan [flæn] tarte *f*

flank [flæŋk] **1** *n* flanc *m* **2** *v/t*: ***be ~ed by*** être flanqué de

flap [flæp] **1** *n of envelope, pocket, table* rabat *m*; ***be in a ~*** F être dans tous ses états **2** *v/t* (*pret & pp* **-ped**) *wings* battre **3** *v/i of flag etc* battre

flare [fler] **1** *n* (*distress signal*) signal *m*

lumineux; *in dress* godet *m* **2** *v/t* nostrils dilater

♦ **flare up** *v/i of violence, rash* éclater; *of fire* s'enflammer; *(get very angry)* s'emporter

flash [flæʃ] **1** *n of light* éclair *m*; PHOT flash *m*; *in a* ∼ F en un rien de temps; *have a* ∼ *of inspiration* avoir un éclair de génie; ∼ *of lightning* éclair *m* **2** *v/i of light* clignoter **3** *v/t*: ∼ *one's headlights* faire des appels de phares

'flash-back *n in movie* flash-back *m*

'flash-light lampe *f* de poche; PHOT flash *m*

flash-y ['flæʃɪ] *adj pej* voyant

flask [flæsk] *(hip* ∼*)* fiole *f*

flat [flæt] **1** *adj* plat; *beer* éventé; *battery, tire* à plat; *sound, tone* monotone; *and that's* ∼ F un point c'est tout; *A / B* ∼ MUS la / si bémol **2** *adv* MUS trop bas; ∼ *out work* le plus possible; *run, drive* le plus vite possible **3** *n* pneu *m* crevé

flat² [flæt] *n Br (apartment)* appartement *m*

flat-chest-ed [flæt'tʃestɪd] *adj* plat

flat-ly ['flætlɪ] *adv refuse, deny* catégoriquement

'flat rate tarif *m* unique

flat-ten ['flætn] *v/t land, road* aplanir; *by bombing, demolition* raser

flat-ter ['flætər] *v/t* flatter

flat-ter-er ['flætərər] flatteur(-euse) *m(f)*

flat-ter-ing ['flætərɪŋ] *adj comments* flatteur*; *color, clothes* avantageux*

flat-ter-y ['flætərɪ] flatterie *f*

flat-u-lence ['flætjʊləns] flatulence *f*

'flat-ware couverts *mpl*

flaunt [flɔːnt] *v/t wealth, car, jewelery* étaler; *girlfriend* afficher

flau-tist ['flɔːtɪst] flûtiste *m/f*

fla-vor ['fleɪvər] **1** *n* goût *m*; *of ice cream* parfum *m*; *of food* assaisonner

fla-vor-ing ['fleɪvərɪŋ] arôme *m*

flaw [flɔː] *n* défaut *m*, imperfection *f*; *in system, plan* défaut *m*, inconvénient *m*

flaw-less ['flɔːlɪs] *adj* parfait

flea [fliː] puce *f*

fleck [flek] petite tache *f*

fled [fled] *pret & pp* → **flee**

flee [fliː] *v/i (pret & pp fled)* s'enfuir

fleece [fliːs] **1** *v/t* F arnaquer F **2** *n jacket (veste f)* polaire *f*

fleet [fliːt] *n* NAUT flotte *f*; *of taxis, trucks* parc *m*

fleet-ing ['fliːtɪŋ] *adj visit etc* très court; *catch a* ∼ *glimpse of ...* apercevoir ... l'espace d'un instant

flesh [fleʃ] *also of fruit* chair *f*; *meet a person in the* ∼ rencontrer une personne en chair et en os

flew [fluː] *pret* → **fly**

flex [fleks] *v/t muscles* fléchir

flex-i-bil-i-ty [fleksə'bɪlətɪ] flexibilité *f*

flex-i-ble ['fleksəbl] *adj* flexible

'flex-time horaire *m* à la carte

flick [flɪk] *v/t tail* donner un petit coup de; *she* ∼*ed her hair out of her eyes* elle a repoussé les cheveux qui lui tombaient devant les yeux

♦ **flick through** *v/t magazine* feuilleter

flick-er ['flɪkər] *v/i of light, screen* vaciller

fli-er ['flaɪr] *(circular)* prospectus *m*

flies [flaɪz] *npl Br. on pants* braguette *f*

flight [flaɪt] *n in airplane* vol *m*; *(fleeing)* fuite *f*; *capable of* ∼ capable de voler; ∼ *(of stairs)* escalier *m*

'flight at-ten-dant *male* steward *m*; *female* hôtesse *f* de l'air; **'flight crew** équipage *m*; **'flight deck** AVIAT poste *m* de pilotage; *of aircraft carrier* pont *m* d'envol; **'flight num-ber** numéro *m* de vol; **'flight path** trajectoire *f* de vol; **'flight re-cord-er** enregistreur *m* de vol; **'flight time** *departure* heure *f* de vol; *duration* durée *f* de vol

flight-y ['flaɪtɪ] *adj* frivole

flim-sy ['flɪmzɪ] *adj structure, furniture* fragile; *dress, material* léger*; *excuse* faible

flinch [flɪntʃ] *v/i* tressaillir

fling [flɪŋ] **1** *v/t (pret & pp flung)* jeter; ∼ *o.s. into a chair* se jeter dans un fauteuil **2** *n* F *(affair)* aventure *f*

♦ **flip through** [flɪp] *v/t (pret & pp -ped)* *book, magazine* feuilleter

flip·per ['flɪpər] *for swimming* nageoire *f*

flirt [flɜːrt] **1** *v/i* flirter **2** *n* flirteur (-euse) *m(f)*

flir·ta·tious [flɜːr'teɪʃəs] *adj* flirteur(-euse)*

float [floʊt] *v/i also* FIN flotter

float·ing vot·er ['floʊtɪŋ] indécis(e) *m(f)*

flock [flɑːk] **1** *n of sheep* troupeau *m* **2** *v/i* venir en masse

flog [flɑːg] *v/t (pret & pp* -**ged**) *(whip)* fouetter

flood [flʌd] *n* inondation *f* **2** *v/t of river* inonder; ~ *its banks* déborder
♦ **flood in** *v/i* arriver en masse

flood·ing ['flʌdɪŋ] inondation(s) *f(pl)*

flood·light *n* projecteur *m*; **'flood-lit** *adj match* illuminé (aux projecteurs); **'flood wa·ters** *npl* inondations *fpl*

floor [flɔːr] **1** *n* sol *m*; *wooden* plancher *m*; *(story)* étage *m* **2** *v/t of problem, question* déconcentrer; *(astound)* sidérer

'floor·board planche *f*; **'floor cloth** serpillière *f*; **'floor lamp** lampadaire *m*

flop [flɑːp] **1** *v/i (pret & pp* -**ped**) s'écrouler; F *(fail)* faire un bide F **2** *n* F *(failure)* bide *m* F

flop·py ['flɑːpɪ] **1** *adj (not stiff)* souple; *(weak)* mou* **2** *n (also* ~ *disk)* disquette *f*

flor·ist ['flɔːrɪst] fleuriste *m/f*

floss [flɑːs] *for teeth* fil *m* dentaire; ~ *one's teeth* se passer du fil dentaire entre les dents

flour ['flaʊr] farine *f*

flour·ish ['flʌrɪʃ] *v/i of plants* fleurir; *of business, civilization* prospérer

flour·ish·ing ['flʌrɪʃɪŋ] *adj business, trade* florissant, prospère

flow [floʊ] *v/i of river* couler; *of electric current* passer; *of traffic* circuler; *of work* se dérouler **2** *n of river* cours *m*; *of information, ideas* circulation *f*

'flow·chart organigramme *m*

flow·er ['flaʊr] **1** *n* fleur *f* **2** *v/i* fleurir **'flow·er·bed** platebande *f*; **'flow·er-pot** pot *m* de fleurs; **'flow·er show** exposition *f* florale

flow·er·y ['flaʊrɪ] *adj pattern, style* fleu-

ri

flown [floʊn] *pp* → **fly³**

flu [fluː] grippe *f*

fluc·tu·ate ['flʌktʃueɪt] *v/i* fluctuer

fluc·tu·a·tion [flʌktʃu'eɪʃn] fluctuation *f*

flu·en·cy ['fluːənsɪ] *in a language* maîtrise *f (in* de); ~ *in French is a requirement* il est nécessaire de maîtriser parfaitement le français

flu·ent ['fluːənt] *adj person* qui s'exprime avec aisance; *he speaks* ~ *Spanish* il parle couramment l'espagnol

flu·ent·ly ['fluːəntlɪ] *adv* couramment; *in own language* avec aisance

fluff [flʌf] *material* peluche *f*; *a bit of* ~ une peluche

fluff·y ['flʌfɪ] *adj material, clouds* duveteux*; *hair* flou; ~ *toy* peluche *f*

fluid ['fluːɪd] *n* fluide *m*

flung [flʌŋ] *pret & pp* → **fling**

flunk [flʌŋk] *v/t* F: *subject* rater

flu·o·res·cent [flʊ'resnt] *adj light* fluorescent

flur·ry ['flʌrɪ] *of snow* rafale *f*

flush [flʌʃ] **1** *v/t:* ~ *the toilet* tirer la chasse d'eau; ~ *sth down the toilet* jeter qch dans les W.-C. **2** *v/i (go red in the face)* rougir; *the toilet won't* ~ la chasse d'eau ne marche pas **3** *adj (level)* de même niveau; *be* ~ *with ...* être au même niveau que ...
♦ **flush away** *v/t down toilet* jeter dans les W.-C.
♦ **flush out** *v/t rebels etc* faire sortir

flus·ter ['flʌstər] *v/t* faire perdre la tête à; *get* ~*ed* s'énerver

flute [fluːt] MUS, *glass* flûte *f*

flut·ist ['fluːtɪst] flûtiste *m/f*

flut·ter ['flʌtər] *v/i of bird* voleter; *of wings* battre; *of flag* s'agiter; *of heart* palpiter

fly¹ [flaɪ] *n (insect)* mouche *f*

fly² [flaɪ] *n on pants* braguette *f*

fly³ [flaɪ] **1** *v/i (pret flew, pp flown)* of bird, airplane voler; *in airplane* voyager en avion, prendre l'avion; *of flag* flotter; *(rush)* se précipiter; ~ *into a rage* s'emporter **2** *v/t (pret flew, pp flown)* airplane prendre; *of pilot* piloter, voler; *airline* voyager par; *(transport by air)* envoyer par avion

◆ **fly away** *v/i of bird, airplane* s'envoler

◆ **fly back** *v/i (travel back)* revenir en avion

◆ **fly in 1** *v/i of airplane, passengers* arriver **2** *v/t supplies etc* amener en avion

◆ **fly off** *v/i of hat etc* s'envoler

◆ **fly out** *v/i* partir (en avion)

◆ **fly past** *v/i in formation* faire un défilé aérien; *of time* filer

fly·ing ['flaɪɪŋ]: *I hate ~* je déteste prendre l'avion

fly·ing 'sau·cer soucoupe *f* volante

foal [fəul] poulain *m*

foam [fəum] *n on sea* écume *f*; *on drink* mousse *f*

foam 'rub·ber caoutchouc *m* mousse

FOB [efəu'biː] *abbr* (= *free on board*) F.A.B. (franco à bord)

fo·cus ['fəukəs] **1** *n of attention* centre *m*; PHOT mise *f* au point; *be in ~ / out of ~* PHOT être / ne pas être au point **2** *v/t*: *~ one's attention on* concentrer son attention sur **3** *v/i* fixer (son regard)

◆ **focus on** *v/t problem, issue* se concentrer sur; PHOT mettre au point sur

fod·der ['fɑːdər] fourrage *m*

fog [fɑːg] brouillard *m*

◆ **fog up** *v/i* (*pret & pp* -**ged**) se couvrir de buée

'fog·bound *adj* bloqué par le brouillard

fog·gy ['fɑːgɪ] *adj* brumeux*; *I haven't the foggiest idea* je n'en ai pas la moindre idée

foi·ble ['fɔɪbl] manie *f*

foil[1] [fɔɪl] *n silver* feuille *f* d'aluminium; *kitchen ~* papier *m* d'aluminium

foil[2] *v/t* (*thwart*) faire échouer

fold[1] [fəuld] **1** *v/t paper etc* plier; *~ one's arms* croiser les bras **2** *v/i of business* fermer (ses portes) **3** *n in cloth etc* pli *m*

◆ **fold up 1** *v/t* plier **2** *v/i of chair, table* se (re)plier

fold[2] *n for sheep etc* enclos *m*

fold·er ['fəuldər] *for documents* chemise *f*, pochette *f*; COMPUT dossier *m*

fold·ing ['fəuldɪŋ] *adj* pliant; *~ chair* chaise *f* pliante

fo·li·age ['fəulɪdʒ] feuillage *m*

folk [fəuk] (*people*) gens *mpl*; *my ~s* (*family*) ma famille; *hi there ~s* F salut tout le monde

'folk dance danse *f* folklorique; **'folk mu·sic** folk *m*; **'folk sing·er** chanteur(-euse) *m(f)* de folk; **'folk song** chanson *f* folk

fol·low ['fɑːləu] **1** *v/t also TV progam*, (*understand*) suivre **2** *v/i logically* s'ensuivre; *you go first and I'll ~* passez devant, je vous suis; *it ~s from this that …* il s'ensuit que …; *as ~s: the items we need are as ~s: …* les articles dont nous avons besoin sont les suivants: …

◆ **follow up** *v/t letter, inquiry* donner suite à

fol·low·er ['fɑːləuər] *of politician etc* partisan(e) *m(f)*; *of football team* supporteur(-trice) *m(f)*

fol·low·ing ['fɑːləuɪŋ] **1** *adj* suivant **2** *n people* partisans *mpl*; *the ~* la chose suivante

'fol·low-up meet·ing réunion *f* complémentaire

'fol·low-up vis·it *to doctor etc* visite *f* de contrôle

fol·ly ['fɑːlɪ] (*madness*) folie *f*

fond [fɑːnd] *adj* (*loving*) aimant, tendre; *memory* agréable; *be ~ of* beaucoup aimer

fon·dle ['fɑːndl] *v/t* caresser

fond·ness ['fɑːndnɪs] *for s.o.* tendresse *f* (*for* pour); *for sth* penchant *m* (*for* pour)

font [fɑːnt] *for printing* police *f*; *in church* fonts *mpl* baptismaux

food [fuːd] nourriture *f*; *French ~* la cuisine française; *there's no ~* il n'y a rien à manger

'food chain chaîne *f* alimentaire

food·ie ['fuːdɪ] F fana *m/f* de cuisine F

'food mix·er mixeur *m*

food poi·son·ing ['fuːdpɔɪznɪŋ] intoxication *f* alimentaire

fool [fuːl] **1** *n* idiot(e) *m(f)*; *make a ~*

of o.s. se ridiculiser **2** *v/t* berner; *he ~ed them into thinking …* il leur a fait croire que …
♦ **fool around** *v/i* faire l'imbécile (les imbéciles); *sexually* avoir des liaisons
♦ **fool around with** *v/t* knife, drill etc jouer avec; *sexually* coucher avec
'**fool·har·dy** *adj* téméraire
fool·ish ['fuːlɪʃ] *adj* idiot, bête
fool·ish·ly ['fuːlɪʃlɪ] *adv* bêtement
'**fool·proof** *adj* à toute épreuve
foot [fʊt] (*pl*: **feet**) *also measurement* pied *m*; *of animal* patte *f*; *on ~* à pied; *I've been on my feet all day* j'ai été debout toute la journée; *be back on one's feet* être remis sur pied; *at the ~ of page* au bas de; *hill* au pied de; *put one's ~ in it* F mettre les pieds dans le plat F
foot·age ['fʊtɪdʒ] séquences *fpl*
'**foot·ball** football *m* américain; (*soccer*) football *m*, foot *m* F; (*ball*) ballon *m* de football
foot·bal·ler ['fʊtbɔːlər] joueur(-euse) *m(f)* de football américain; *soccer* footballeur(-euse) *m(f)*
'**foot·ball play·er** joueur(-euse) *m(f)* de football américain; *soccer* joueur(-euse) *m(f)* de football; '**foot·bridge** passerelle *f*; **foot·hills** ['fʊthɪlz] *npl* contreforts *mpl*
'**foot·hold** *in climbing* prise *f* de pied; *gain a ~* *fig* prendre pied
foot·ing ['fʊtɪŋ] (*basis*) position *f*; *lose one's ~* perdre pied; *be on the same / a different ~* être / ne pas être au même niveau; *be on a friendly ~ with* entretenir des rapports amicaux avec
foot·lights ['fʊtlaɪts] *npl* rampe *f*; '**foot·mark** trace *f* de pas; '**foot·note** note *f* (de bas de page); '**foot·path** sentier *m*; *of PC etc* (surface *f* d')encombrement *m*; '**foot·print** trace *f* de pas; '**foot·step** pas *m*; *follow in s.o.'s ~s* marcher sur les pas de qn, suivre les traces de; '**foot·stool** tabouret *m* (pour les pieds); '**foot·wear** chaussures *fpl*
for [fər], [fɔːr] *prep* ◊ *purpose, destination etc* pour; *a train ~ …* un train à

destination de …; *clothes ~ children* vêtements *mpl* pour enfants; *what's ~ lunch?* qu'est-ce qu'il y a pour le déjeuner?; *a check ~ $500* un chèque de 500 \$; *what is this ~?* pour quoi est-ce que c'est fait?; *what ~?* pourquoi?
◊ *time* pendant; *~ three days / two hours* pendant trois jours / deux heures; *it lasted ~ three days* ça a duré trois jours; *it will last ~ three days* ça va durer trois jours; *I've been waiting ~ an hour* j'attends depuis une heure; *I waited ~ an hour* j'ai attendu (pendant) une heure; *please get it done ~ Monday* faites-le pour lundi s'il vous plaît
◊ *distance*: *I walked ~ a mile* j'ai marché un mile; *it stretches ~ 100 miles* ça s'étend sur 100 miles
◊ (*in favor of*) pour; *I am ~ the idea* je suis pour cette idée
◊ (*instead of, in behalf of*) pour; *let me do that ~ you* laissez-moi le faire pour vous
◊ (*in exchange for*) pour; *I bought it ~ $25* je l'ai acheté pour 25 \$; *how much did you sell it ~?* pour combien l'as-tu vendu?
for·bade [fər'bæd] *pret* → **forbid**
for·bid [fər'bɪd] *v/t* (*pret* **forbade**, *pp* **forbidden**) interdire; *~ s.o. to do sth* interdire à qn de faire qch
for·bid·den [fər'bɪdn] **1** *adj* interdit; *smoking ~ sign* défense de fumer; *parking ~ sign* stationnement interdit **2** *pp* → **forbid**
for·bid·ding [fər'bɪdɪŋ] *adj* menaçant
force [fɔːrs] **1** *n* force *f*; *come into ~ of law etc* entrer en vigueur; *the ~s* MIL les forces *fpl* armées **2** *v/t* door, lock forcer; *~ s.o. to do sth* forcer qn à faire qch; *~ sth open* ouvrir qch de force
♦ **force back** *v/t* réprimer
forced [fɔːrst] *adj* laugh, confession forcé
forced 'land·ing atterrissage *m* forcé
force·ful ['fɔːrsfl] *adj* argument, speaker puissant; *character* énergique
force·ful·ly ['fɔːrsflɪ] *adv* énergique-

ment

for·ceps ['fɔːrseps] *npl* MED forceps *m*

for·ci·ble ['fɔːrsəbl] *adj entry* de force; *argument* puissant

for·ci·bly ['fɔːrsəblɪ] *adv restrain* par force

ford [fɔːrd] *n* gué *m*

fore [fɔːr] *n*: **come to the ~** *person* se faire remarquer; *theory* être mis en évidence

'fore·arm avant-bras *m*; **fore-bears** ['fɔːrberz] *npl* aïeux *mpl*; **fore·bod·ing** [fərˈboʊdɪŋ] pressentiment *m*; **'fore·cast 1** *n of results* pronostic *m*; *of weather* prévisions *fpl* **2** *v/t (pret & pp* **forecast***) result* pronostiquer; *future, weather* prévoir; **'fore·court** *of garage* devant *m*; **fore·fa·thers** ['fɔːrfɑːðərz] *npl* ancêtres *mpl*; **'fore·fin·ger** index *m*

'fore·front: be in the ~ of être au premier rang de

'fore·gone *adj*: **that's a ~ conclusion** c'est prévu d'avance; **'fore·ground** premier plan *m*; **'fore·hand** *in tennis* coup *m* droit; **'fore·head** front *m*

for·eign ['fɑːrən] *adj* étranger*; *travel, correspondent* à l'étranger

for·eign af'fairs *npl* affaires *fpl* étrangères; **for·eign 'aid** aide *f* aux pays étrangers; **for·eign 'bod·y** corps *m* étranger; **for·eign 'cur·ren·cy** devises *fpl* étrangères

for·eign·er ['fɑːrənər] étranger(-ère) *m(f)*

for·eign ex'change change *m*; *currency* devises *fpl* étrangères; **for·eign 'le·gion** Légion *f* (étrangère); **'For·eign Of·fice** *in UK* ministère *m* des Affaires étrangères; **for·eign 'pol·i·cy** politique *f* étrangère; **For·eign 'Sec·re·ta·ry** *in UK* ministre *m/f* des Affaires étrangères

'fore·man chef *m* d'équipe

'fore·most *adv (uppermost)* le plus important; *(leading)* premier*

fo·ren·sic 'med·i·cine [fəˈrensɪk] médecine *f* légale

fo·ren·sic 'scien·tist expert *m* légiste; **'fore·run·ner** *person* prédécesseur *m*; *thing* ancêtre *m/f*; **fore'saw** *pret*

→ **foresee**; **fore'see** *v/t (pret* **fore·saw**, *pp* **foreseen***)* prévoir; **fore·see·a·ble** [fərˈsiːəbl] *adj* prévisible; **in the ~ future** dans un avenir prévisible; **fore'seen** *pp* → **foresee**; **'fore·sight** prévoyance *f*

for·est ['fɑːrɪst] forêt *f*

for·est·ry ['fɑːrɪstrɪ] sylviculture *f*

'fore·taste avant-goût *m*

fore'tell *v/t (pret & pp* **foretold***)* prédire

fore'told *pret & pp* → **foretell**

for·ev·er [fərˈevər] *adv* toujours; **it's ~ raining here** il n'arrête pas de pleuvoir ici

'fore·word avant-propos *m*

for·feit ['fɔːrfət] *v/t right, privilege etc* perdre; *(give up)* renoncer à

for·gave [fərˈgeɪv] *pret* → **forgive**

forge [fɔːrdʒ] *v/t (counterfeit)* contrefaire

♦ **forge ahead** *v/i* avancer

forg·er ['fɔːrdʒər] faussaire *m/f*

forg·er·y ['fɔːrdʒərɪ] *bank bill* faux billet *m*; *document* faux *m*; *signature* contrefaçon *f*

for·get [fərˈget] *v/t & v/i (pret* **forgot**, *pp* **forgotten***)* oublier

for·get·ful [fərˈgetfl] *adj*: **you're so ~** tu es vraiment mauvaise mémoire

for'get-me-not *flower* myosotis *m*

for·give [fərˈgɪv] **1** *v/t (pret* **forgave**, *pp* **forgiven***)*: **~ s.o. sth** pardonner qch à qn **2** *v/i (pret* **forgave**, *pp* **forgiven***)* pardonner

for·gi·ven [fərˈgɪvn] *pp* → **forgive**

for·give·ness [fərˈgɪvnɪs] pardon *m*

for·got [fərˈgɑːt] *pret* → **forget**

for·got·ten [fərˈgɑːtn] **1** *adj* oublié; *author* tombé dans l'oubli *pp* → **forget**

fork [fɔːrk] *n* fourchette *f*; *for gardening* fourche *f*; *in road* embranchement *m*

♦ **fork out** *v/i* F *(pay)* casquer F

fork·lift 'truck chariot *m* élévateur (à fourches)

form [fɔːrm] **1** *n (shape)* forme *f*; *document* formulaire *m*; **be on / off ~** être / ne pas être en forme **2** *v/t* former; *friendship* développer; *opinion* se faire **3** *v/i (take shape, develop)* se

F

former
form·al ['fɔːrml] *adj language* soutenu; *word* du langage soutenu; *dress* de soirée; *manner, reception* cérémonieux*; *recognition etc* officiel*
for·mal·i·ty [fər'mælətɪ] *of language* caractère *m* soutenu; *of occasion* cérémonie *f*; *it's just a* ~ c'est juste une formalité; *the formalities* les formalités *fpl*
for·mal·ly ['fɔːrmlɪ] *adv speak, behave* cérémonieusement; *accepted, recognized* officiellement
for·mat ['fɔːrmæt] **1** *v/t* (*pret & pp -ted*) *diskette, document* formater **2** *n* format *m*
for·ma·tion [fɔːr'meɪʃn] formation *f*
for·ma·tive ['fɔːrmətɪv] *adj* formateur*; *in his* ~ *years* dans sa période formatrice
for·mer ['fɔːrmər] *adj* ancien*, précédent; *the* ~ le premier, la première
for·mer·ly ['fɔːrmərlɪ] *adv* autrefois
for·mi·da·ble ['fɔːrmɪdəbl] *adj* redoutable
for·mu·la ['fɔːrmjʊlə] MATH, *chemical* formule *f*; *fig* recette *f*
for·mu·late ['fɔːrmjʊleɪt] *v/t* (*express*) formuler
for·ni·cate ['fɔːrnɪkeɪt] *v/i fml* forniquer
for·ni·ca·tion [fɔːrnɪ'keɪʃn] *fml* fornication *f*
fort [fɔːrt] MIL fort *m*
forth [fɔːrθ] *adv*: *travel back and* ~ faire la navette; *and so* ~ et ainsi de suite; *from that day* ~ à partir de ce jour-là
forth·com·ing [fɔːrθ'kʌmɪŋ] *adj* (*future*) futur; *personality* ouvert
'forth·right *adj* franc*
for·ti·eth ['fɔːrtɪɪθ] quarantième
fort·night ['fɔːrtnaɪt] *Br* quinze jours *mpl*, quinzaine *f*
for·tress ['fɔːrtrɪs] MIL forteresse *f*
for·tu·nate ['fɔːrtʃnət] *adj decision etc* heureux*; *be* ~ avoir de la chance; *be* ~ *enough to* ... avoir la chance de ...
for·tu·nate·ly ['fɔːrtʃnətlɪ] *adv* heureusement

for·tune ['fɔːrtʃən] (*fate*) destin *m*; (*luck*) chance *f*; (*lot of money*) fortune *f*; *tell s.o.'s* ~ dire la bonne aventure à qn
'for·tune-tell·er diseur(-euse) *m(f)* de bonne aventure
for·ty ['fɔːrtɪ] quarante; *have* ~ *winks* F faire une petite sieste
fo·rum ['fɔːrəm] *fig* tribune *f*
for·ward ['fɔːrwərd] **1** *adv push, nudge* en avant; *walk / move / drive* ~ avancer; *from that day* ~ à partir de ce jour-là **2** *adj pej: person* effronté **3** *n* SP avant *m* **4** *v/t letter* faire suivre
for·ward·ing ad·dress ['fɔːrwərdɪŋ] nouvelle adresse *f*
'for·ward·ing a·gent COMM transitaire *m/f*
for·ward-look·ing ['fɔːrwərdlʊkɪŋ] *adj* moderne, tourné vers l'avenir
fos·sil ['fɑːsl] fossile *m*
fos·sil·ized ['fɑːsəlaɪzd] *adj* fossilisé
fos·ter ['fɑːstər] *v/t child* servir de famille d'accueil à; *attitude, belief* encourager
'fos·ter child enfant placé(e) *m(f)*;
'fos·ter home foyer *m* d'accueil;
'fos·ter par·ents *npl* parents *mpl* d'accueil
fought [fɔːt] *pret & pp* → **fight**
foul [faʊl] **1** *n* SP faute *f* **2** *adj smell, taste* infect; *weather* sale **3** *v/t* SP commettre une faute contre
found¹ [faʊnd] *v/t institution, school etc* fonder
found² [faʊnd] *pret & pp* → **find**
foun·da·tion [faʊn'deɪʃn] *of theory etc* fondement *m*; (*organization*) fondation *f*
foun·da·tions [faʊn'deɪʃnz] *npl of building* fondations *fpl*
found·er ['faʊndər] *n* fondateur (-trice) *m(f)*
found·ing ['faʊndɪŋ] *n* fondation *f*
foun·dry ['faʊndrɪ] fonderie *f*
foun·tain ['faʊntɪn] fontaine *f*; *with vertical spout* jet *m* d'eau
'foun·tain pen stylo *m* plume
four [fɔːr] **1** *adj* quatre **2** *n*: *on all* ~*s* à quatre pattes
four-let·ter 'word gros mot *m*; **four-**

post·er ('bed) lit m à baldaquin;
'four-star adj hotel etc quatre étoiles
four·teen ['fɔːrtiːn] quatorze
four·teenth ['fɔːrtiːnθ] quatorzième
→ **fifth**
fourth [fɔːrθ] quatrième; → **fifth**
four-wheel 'drive MOT quatre-quatre
m
fowl [faʊl] volaille f
fox [fɑːks] **1** n renard m **2** v/t (puzzle)
mystifier
foy·er ['fɔɪər] hall m d'entrée
frac·tion ['frækʃn] also MATH fraction
f
frac·tion·al·ly ['frækʃnəlɪ] adv très légèrement
frac·ture ['fræktʃər] **1** n fracture f **2** v/t
fracturer; **he ~d his arm** il s'est frac-
turé le bras
fra·gile ['frædʒəl] adj fragile
frag·ment ['frægmənt] n fragment m;
bribe f
frag·men·tar·y [fræg'mentərɪ] adj
fragmentaire
fra·grance ['freɪgrəns] parfum m
fra·grant ['freɪgrənt] adj parfumé,
odorant
frail [freɪl] adj frêle, fragile
frame [freɪm] **1** n of picture, bicycle cadre m; of window châssis m; of eyeglasses monture f; **~ of mind** état m
d'esprit **2** v/t picture encadrer; F person monter un coup contre
'frame-up F coup m monté
'frame·work structure f; **within the ~
of** dans le cadre de
France [fræns] France f
fran·chise ['fræntʃaɪz] n for business
franchise f
frank [fræŋk] adj franc*
frank·furt·er ['fræŋkfɜːrtər] saucisse f
de Francfort
frank·ly ['fræŋklɪ] adv franchement
frank·ness ['fræŋknɪs] franchise f
fran·tic ['fræntɪk] adj frénétique, fou*
fran·ti·cal·ly ['fræntɪklɪ] adv frénétiquement; busy terriblement
fra·ter·nal [frə'tɜːrnl] adj fraternel*
fraud [frɔːd] fraude f; person imposteur m
fraud·u·lent ['frɔːdjʊlənt] adj fraudu-

leux*
fraud·u·lent·ly ['frɔːdjʊləntlɪ] adv
frauduleusement
frayed [freɪd] adj cuffs usé
freak [friːk] **1** n (unusual event) phénomène m étrange; (two-headed person,
animal etc) monstre m; F (strange person) taré(e) m(f) F; **movie / jazz ~** F
mordu(e) m(f) de cinéma / jazz F **2**
adj wind, storm etc anormalement
violent
freck·le ['frekl] tache f de rousseur
free [friː] **1** adj libre; no cost gratuit; **~
and easy** sans gêne; **for ~** travel, get
sth gratuitement **2** v/t prisoners libérer
free·bie ['friːbɪ] Br F cadeau m
free·dom ['friːdəm] liberté f
free·dom of 'speech liberté f d'expression
free·dom of the 'press liberté f de la
presse
free 'en·ter·prise libre entreprise f;
free 'kick in soccer coup m franc;
free·lance ['friːlæns] **1** adj indépendant, free-lance inv **2** adv work en indépendant, en free-lance; **free·lanc-
er** ['friːlænsər] travailleur(-euse) in-
dépendant(e) m(f); **free·load·er**
['friːloʊdər] F parasite m, pique-assiette m/f
free·ly ['friːlɪ] adv admit volontiers
free mar·ket e'con·o·my économie f
de marché; **free-range 'chick·en**
poulet m fermier; **free-range 'eggs**
npl œufs mpl fermiers; **free 'sam·ple**
échantillon m gratuit; **free 'speech**
libre parole f; **'free·way** autoroute
f; **free'wheel** v/i on bicycle être en
roue libre; **free 'will** libre arbitre
m; **he did it of his own ~** il l'a fait
de son plein gré
freeze [friːz] **1** v/t (pret froze, pp frozen) food, river congeler; wages geler;
bank account bloquer; **~ a video** faire
un arrêt sur image **2** v/i of water geler
♦ **freeze over** v/i of river geler
'freeze-dried adj lyophilisé
freez·er ['friːzər] congélateur m
freez·ing ['friːzɪŋ] **1** adj glacial; **it's ~
(cold)** of weather, in room il fait un

froid glacial; *of sea* elle est glaciale;
I'm ~ (*cold*) je gèle **2** n: *10 below ~*
10 degrés au-dessous de zéro, moins
10

'freez·ing com·part·ment freezer m

'freez·ing point point m de congélation

freight [freɪt] n fret m

'freight car *on train* wagon m de marchandises

freight·er ['freɪtər] *ship* cargo m; *airplane* avion-cargo m

'freight train train m de marchandises

French [frentʃ] **1** adj français **2** n *language* français m; *the ~* les Français
mpl

French 'bread baguette f; French
'doors npl porte-fenêtre f; 'French
fries npl frites fpl; 'French kiss patin m F; 'French·man Français m;
French Ri·vi·er·a Côte f d'Azur;
'French-speak·ing adj francophone;
'French·wom·an Française f

fren·zied ['frenzɪd] adj attack, activity
forcené; mob déchaîné

fren·zy ['frenzɪ] frénésie f

fre·quen·cy ['fri:kwənsɪ] also of radio
fréquence f

fre·quent¹ ['fri:kwənt] adj fréquent;
how ~ are the trains? il y a des
trains tous les combien? F

fre·quent² [frɪ'kwent] v/t bar etc fréquenter

fre·quent·ly ['fri:kwəntlɪ] adv fréquemment

fres·co ['freskoʊ] fresque f

fresh [freʃ] adj fruit, meat etc, (cold)
frais*; (new: start) nouveau*; sheets
propre; (impertinent) insolent; *don't
you get ~ with me!* ne me parle
pas comme ça

fresh 'air air m

fresh·en ['freʃn] v/i of wind se rafraîchir

♦ freshen up **1** v/i se rafraîchir **2** v/t
room, paintwork rafraîchir

fresh·ly ['freʃlɪ] adv fraîchement

'fresh·man étudiant m(f) de première année

fresh·ness ['freʃnɪs] of fruit, meat,
style, weather fraîcheur f; of approach

nouveauté f

fresh 'or·ange Br orange f pressée

'fresh·wa·ter adj fish d'eau douce;
fishing en eau douce

fret¹ [fret] v/i (pret & pp -ted) s'inquiéter

fret² n of guitar touche f

Freud·i·an ['frɔɪdɪən] adj freudien*

fric·tion ['frɪkʃn] friction f

'friction tape chatterton m

Fri·day ['fraɪdeɪ] vendredi m

fridge [frɪdʒ] frigo m F

friend [frend] ami(e) m(f); *make ~s of
one person* se faire des amis; *of two
people* devenir amis; *make ~s with
s.o.* devenir ami(e) avec qn

friend·li·ness ['frendlɪnɪs] amabilité f

friend·ly ['frendlɪ] adj smile, meeting,
match, relations amical; restaurant, hotel, city sympathique; person amical,
sympathique; (easy to use) convivial;
argument entre amis; *be ~ with
s.o.* (be friends) être ami(e) avec qn

friend·ship ['frendʃɪp] amitié f

fries [fraɪz] npl frites fpl

fright [fraɪt] peur f; *give s.o. a ~* faire
peur à qn

fright·en ['fraɪtn] v/t faire peur à, effrayer; *be ~ed* avoir peur (*of* de);
don't be ~ed n'aie pas peur

♦ frighten away v/t faire fuir

fright·en·ing ['fraɪtnɪŋ] adj noise, person, prospect effrayant

frig·id ['frɪdʒɪd] adj sexually frigide

frill [frɪl] on dress etc, (extra) falbala m

frill·y ['frɪlɪ] adj à falbalas

fringe [frɪndʒ] frange f; of city périphérie f; of society marge f

'fringe ben·e·fits npl avantages mpl
sociaux

frisk [frɪsk] v/t fouiller

frisk·y ['frɪskɪ] adj puppy etc vif*

♦ frit·ter away ['frɪtər] v/t time, fortune
gaspiller

friv·ol·i·ty [frɪ'vɑːlətɪ] frivolité f

friv·o·lous ['frɪvələs] adj frivole

frizz·y ['frɪzɪ] adj hair crépu

frog [frɑːg] grenouille f

'frog·man homme-grenouille m

from [frɑːm] prep ◊ in time de; *~ 9 to 5
(o'clock)* de 9 heures à 5 heures; *~*

the 18th century à partir du XVIIIe siècle; **~ today on** à partir d'aujourd'hui ◇ *in space* de; **~ here to there** d'ici à là(-bas) ◇ *origin* de; *a letter ~ Joe* une lettre de Joe; *it doesn't say who it's ~* ça ne dit pas de qui c'est; *I am ~ New Jersey* je viens du New Jersey; *made ~ bananas* fait avec des bananes ◇ (*because of*) à cause de; *tired ~ the journey* fatigué par le voyage; *it's ~ overeating* c'est d'avoir trop mangé

front [frʌnt] **1** *n of building* façade *f*, devant *m*; *of book* devant *m*; (*cover organization*) façade *f*; MIL, *of weather* front *m*; *in ~* devant; *in a race* en tête; *in ~ of* devant; *at the ~ of* à l'avant de **2** *adj* wheel, seat avant **3** *v/t* TV *program* présenter

front 'cov·er couverture *f*; **front 'door** porte *f* d'entrée; **front 'entrance** entrée *f* principale

fron·tier ['frʌntɪr] *also fig* frontière *f*

'**front line** MIL front *m*; **front 'page** *of newspaper* une *f*; **front page 'news**: *be ~* faire la une des journaux; **front 'row** premier rang *m*; **front seat 'pas·sen·ger** *in car* passager(-ère) *m(f)* avant; **front-wheel 'drive** traction *f* avant

frost [frɑːst] *n* gel *m*, gelée *f*

'**frost·bite** gelure *f*

'**frost·bit·ten** *adj* gelé

frosted glass ['frɑːstɪd] verre *m* dépoli

frost·ing ['frɑːstɪŋ] *on cake* glaçage *m*

frost·y ['frɑːstɪ] *adj also fig* glacial

froth [frɑːθ] *n* écume *f*, mousse *f*

froth·y ['frɑːθɪ] *adj cream etc* écumeux*, mousseux*

frown [fraʊn] **1** *n* froncement *m* de sourcils **2** *v/i* froncer les sourcils

froze [froʊz] *pret* → *freeze*

fro·zen [froʊzn] **1** *adj* gelé; *wastes* glacé; *food* surgelé; *I'm ~* je suis gelé **2** *pp* → *freeze*

fro·zen 'food surgelés *mpl*

fruit [fruːt] fruit *m*; *collective* fruits *mpl*

'**fruit cake** cake *m*

fruit·ful ['fruːtfl] *adj* discussions etc fructueux*

'**fruit juice** jus *m* de fruit

fruit 'sal·ad salade *f* de fruits

frus·trate ['frʌstreɪt] *v/t person* frustrer; *plans* contrarier

frus·trat·ed ['frʌstreɪtɪd] *adj* look, sigh frustré

frus·trat·ing ['frʌstreɪtɪŋ] *adj* frustrant

frus·trat·ing·ly [frʌ'streɪtɪŋlɪ] *adv*: *~ slow / hard* d'une lenteur / difficulté frustrante

frus·tra·tion [frʌ'streɪʃn] frustration *f*

fry [fraɪ] *v/t* (*pret & pp* *-ied*) (faire) frire

fried 'egg [fraɪd] œuf *m* sur le plat

fried po'ta·toes *npl* pommes *fpl* de terre sautées

'**fry·pan** poêle *f* (à frire)

fuck [fʌk] *v/t* V baiser V; *~!* putain! V; *~ you!* va te faire enculer! V; *~ that!* j'en ai rien à foutre! F

♦ **fuck off** *v/i* V se casser P; *fuck off!* va te faire enculer! V

fuck·ing ['fʌkɪŋ] V **1** *adj*: *this ~ rain / computer* cette putain de pluie / ce putain d'ordinateur V **2** *adv*: *don't be ~ stupid* putain, sois pas stupide V

fu·el ['fjuːəl] **1** *n* carburant *m* **2** *v/t fig* entretenir

fu·gi·tive ['fjuːdʒətɪv] *n* fugitif(-ive) *m(f)*

ful·fil *Br* → **fulfill**

ful·fill [fʊl'fɪl] *v/t dreams* réaliser; *task* accomplir; *contract, responsibilities* remplir; *feel ~ed in job, life* avoir un sentiment d'accomplissement

ful·fill·ing [fʊl'fɪlɪŋ] *adj job* qui donne un sentiment d'accomplissement

ful·fil·ment *Br* → **fulfillment**

ful·fill·ment [fʊl'fɪlmənt] *of contract etc* exécution *f*; *moral, spiritual* accomplissement *m*

full [fʊl] *adj* plein (*of* de); *hotel, account* complet*; *~ up* hotel etc complet; *~ up*: *be ~ with food* avoir trop mangé; *pay in ~* tout payer

'**full back** arrière *m*; **full 'board** *Br* pension *f* complète; '**full-grown** *adj* adulte; '**full-length** *adj dress* long*; *~ movie* long métrage *m*; **full 'moon** pleine lune *f*; **full 'stop** *Br* point *m*; **full-'time** *adj & adv* à plein temps

ful·ly ['fʊlɪ] *adv* trained, recovered complètement; *understand* parfaitement; *describe, explain* en détail; **be ~ booked** hotel être complet*

fum·ble ['fʌmbl] *v/t catch* mal attraper
♦ **fumble about** *v/i* fouiller

fume [fjuːm] *v/i*: **be fuming** F être furieux*

fumes [fjuːmz] *npl from vehicles, machines* fumée *f*; *from chemicals* vapeurs *fpl*

fun [fʌn] **1** *n* amusement *m*; *it was great ~* on s'est bien amusé; *bye, have ~!* au revoir, amuse-toi bien!; *for ~* pour s'amuser; *make ~ of* se moquer de **2** *adj* F marrant F

func·tion ['fʌŋkʃn] **1** *n* (*purpose*) fonction *f*; (*reception etc*) réception *f* **2** *v/i* fonctionner; *~ as* faire fonction de

func·tion·al ['fʌŋkʃnl] *adj* fonctionnel*

fund [fʌnd] **1** *n* fonds *m* **2** *v/t project etc* financer

fun·da·men·tal [fʌndə'mentl] *adj* fondamental

fun·da·men·tal·ist [fʌndə'mentlɪst] *n* fondamentaliste *m/f*

fun·da·men·tal·ly [fʌndə'mentlɪ] *adv* fondamentalement

fund·ing ['fʌndɪŋ] (*money*) financement *m*

funds [fʌndz] *npl* fonds *mpl*

fu·ne·ral ['fjuːnərəl] enterrement *m*, obsèques *fpl*

'fu·ne·ral di·rec·tor entrepreneur (-euse) *m(f)* de pompes funèbres

'fu·ne·ral home établissement *m* de pompes funèbres

fun·gus ['fʌŋgəs] champignon *m*; *mold* moisissure *f*

fu·nel·ar ['fʌnl] *n of ship* cheminée *f*

fun·nel ['fʌnl] *n of ship* cheminée *f*

fun·nies ['fʌnɪz] *npl* F pages *fpl* drôles

fun·ni·ly ['fʌnɪlɪ] *adv* (*oddly*) bizarrement; (*comically*) comiquement; *~ enough* chose curieuse

fun·ny ['fʌnɪ] *adj* (*comical*) drôle; (*odd*) bizarre, curieux*

'fun·ny bone petit juif *m*

fur [fɜːr] fourrure *f*

fu·ri·ous ['fjʊrɪəs] *adj* furieux*; *at a ~ pace* à une vitesse folle

fur·nace ['fɜːrnɪs] four(neau) *m*

fur·nish ['fɜːrnɪʃ] *v/t room* meubler; (*supply*) fournir

fur·ni·ture ['fɜːrnɪtʃər] meubles *mpl*; *a piece of ~* un meuble

fur·ry ['fɜːrɪ] *adj animal* à poil

fur·ther ['fɜːrðər] **1** *adj* (*additional*) supplémentaire; (*more distant*) plus éloigné; *at the ~ side of the field* de l'autre côté du champ; *until ~ notice* jusqu'à nouvel ordre; *have you anything ~ to say?* avez-vous quelque chose d'autre à dire; **2** *adv walk, drive* plus loin; *~, I want to say ...* de plus, je voudrais dire ...; *two miles ~* (on) deux miles plus loin **3** *v/t cause etc* faire avancer, promouvoir

fur·ther·more *adv* de plus, en outre

fur·thest ['fɜːrðɪst] **1** *adj* le plus lointain; *the ~ point north* le point le plus au nord **2** *adv* le plus loin; *the ~ north* le plus au nord

fur·tive ['fɜːrtɪv] *adj glance* furtif*

fur·tive·ly ['fɜːrtɪvlɪ] *adv* furtivement

fu·ry ['fjʊrɪ] (*anger*) fureur *f*

fuse [fjuːz] **1** *n* ELEC fusible *m*, plomb *m* F **2** *v/i* ELEC: *the lights have ~d* les plombs ont sauté **3** *v/t* ELEC faire sauter

'fuse·box boîte *f* à fusibles

fu·se·lage ['fjuːzəlɑːʒ] fuselage *m*

'fuse wire fil *m* à fusible

fu·sion ['fjuːʒn] fusion *f*

fuss [fʌs] *n* agitation *f*; *make a ~* (*complain*) faire des histoires; (*behave in exaggerated way*) faire du cinéma; *make a ~ of s.o.* (*be very attentive to*) être aux petits soins pour qn

fuss·y ['fʌsɪ] *adj person* difficile; *design etc* trop compliqué; *be a ~ eater* être difficile (sur la nourriture)

fu·tile ['fjuːtl] *adj* futile

fu·til·i·ty [fjuː'tɪlətɪ] futilité *f*

fu·ton ['fuːtɑːn] futon *m*

fu·ture ['fjuːtʃər] **1** *n* avenir *f*; GRAM futur *m*; *in ~* à l'avenir **2** *adj* futur

fu·tures ['fjuːtʃərz] *npl* FIN opérations

gargoyle

fpl à terme

'fu·tures mar·ket FIN marché *m* à terme

fu·tur·is·tic [fjuːtʃəˈrɪstɪk] *adj design*

futuriste

fuzz·y ['fʌzɪ] *adj hair* duveteux*, crépu; *(out of focus)* flou; **~ logic** logique *f* floue

G

gab [gæb] *n*: **have the gift of the ~** F avoir du bagout F

gab·ble ['gæbl] *v/i* bredouiller

gad·get ['gædʒɪt] gadget *m*

gaffe [gæf] gaffe *f*

gag [gæg] **1** *n* bâillon *m*; *(joke)* gag *m* **2** *v/t (pret & pp -ged) also fig* bâillonner

gai·ly ['geɪlɪ] *adv (blithely)* gaiement

gain [geɪn] *v/t respect, knowledge* acquérir; *victory* remporter; *advantage, sympathy* gagner; **~ 10 pounds / speed** prendre 10 livres / de la vitesse

ga·la ['gɑːlə] gala *m*

gal·ax·y ['gæləksɪ] ASTR galaxie *f*

gale [geɪl] coup *m* de vent, tempête *f*

gal·lant ['gælənt] *adj* galant

gall blad·der ['gɒːlblædər] vésicule *f* biliaire

gal·le·ry ['gælərɪ] *for art, in theater* galerie *f*

gal·ley ['gælɪ] *on ship* cuisine *f*

♦ **gal·li·vant around** ['gælɪvænt] *v/i* vadrouiller

gal·lon ['gælən] gallon *m*; **~s of tea** F des litres de thé F

gal·lop ['gæləp] *v/i* galoper

gal·lows ['gæloʊz] *npl* gibet *m*

gall·stone ['gɒːlstoʊn] calcul *m* biliaire

ga·lore [gəˈlɔːr] *adj*: **apples / novels ~** des pommes / romans à gogo

gal·va·nize ['gælvənaɪz] *v/t also fig* galvaniser

gam·ble ['gæmbl] *v/i* jouer

gam·bler ['gæmblər] joueur(-euse) *m(f)*

gam·bling ['gæmblɪŋ] jeu *m*

game [geɪm] *n also in tennis* jeu *m*; **have a ~ of tennis / chess** faire une partie de tennis / d'échecs

'game re·serve réserve *f* naturelle

gam·mon ['gæmən] *Br* jambon *m* fumé

gang [gæŋ] gang *m*

♦ **gang up on** *v/t* se liguer contre

'gang rape 1 *n* viol *m* collectif **2** *v/t* commettre un viol collectif sur

gan·grene ['gæŋgriːn] MED gangrène *f*

gang·ster ['gæŋstər] gangster *m*

'gang war·fare guerre *m* des gangs

'gang·way passerelle *f*

gaol [dʒeɪl] → **jail**

gap [gæp] trou *m*; *in time* intervalle *m*; *between two personalities* fossé *m*

gape [geɪp] *v/i of person* rester bouche bée; *of hole* être béant

♦ **gape at** *v/t* rester bouche bée devant

gap·ing ['geɪpɪŋ] *adj hole* béant

gar·age [gəˈrɑːʒ] *n* garage *m*

ga·rage sale vide-grenier *m* (chez un particulier)

gar·bage ['gɑːrbɪdʒ] ordures *fpl*; *(fig: nonsense)* bêtises *fpl*

'garbage bag sac-poubelle *m*; **'garbage can** poubelle *f*; **'garbage truck** benne *f* à ordures

gar·bled ['gɑːrbld] *adj message* confus

gar·den ['gɑːrdn] jardin *m*

'gar·den cen·ter jardinerie *f*

gar·den·er ['gɑːrdnər] jardinier(-ière) *m(f)*

gar·den·ing ['gɑːrdnɪŋ] jardinage *m*

gar·gle ['gɑːrgl] *v/i* se gargariser

gar·goyle ['gɑːrgɔɪl] gargouille *f*

gar·ish ['geriʃ] *adj* criard

gar·land ['gɑ:rlənd] *n* guirlande *f*, couronne *f*

gar·lic ['gɑ:rlɪk] ail *m*

gar·lic 'bread pain chaud à l'ail

gar·ment ['gɑ:rmənt] vêtement *m*

gar·nish ['gɑ:rnɪʃ] *v/t* garnir (*with* de)

gar·ri·son ['gærɪsn] *n* garnison *f*

gar·ter ['gɑ:rtər] jarretière *f*

gas [gæs] *n* gaz *m*; (*gasoline*) essence *f*

gash [gæʃ] *n* entaille *f*

gas·ket ['gæskɪt] joint *m* d'étanchéité

gas·o·line ['gæsəli:n] essence *f*

gasp [gæsp] **1** *n in surprise* hoquet *m*; *with exhaustion* halètement *m* **2** *v/i with exhaustion* haleter; *~ for breath* haleter; *~ with surprise* pousser une exclamation de surprise

'gas ped·al accélérateur *m*; **'gas pipe·line** gazoduc *m*; **'gas pump** pompe *f* (à essence); **'gas sta·tion** station-service *f*; **'gas stove** cuisinière *f* à gaz

gas·tric ['gæstrɪk] *adj* MED gastrique

gas·tric 'flu MED grippe *f* gastro-intestinale; **gas·tric 'juices** *npl* sucs *mpl* gastriques; **gas·tric 'ul·cer** MED ulcère *m* à l'estomac

gate [geɪt] *also at airport* porte *f*

'gate·crash *v/t* s'inviter à

'gate·way entrée *f*; *also fig* porte *f*

gath·er ['gæðər] **1** *v/t facts, information* recueillir; *am I to ~ that ...?* dois-je comprendre que ...?; *~ speed* prendre de la vitesse **2** *v/i* (*understand*) comprendre

♦ **gather up** *v/t possessions* ramasser

gath·er·ing ['gæðərɪŋ] *n* (*group of people*) assemblée *f*

gau·dy ['gɒ:dɪ] *adj* voyant, criard

gauge [geɪdʒ] **1** *n* jauge *f* **2** *v/t oil pressure* jauger; *opinion* mesurer

gaunt [gɒ:nt] *adj* émacié

gauze [gɒ:z] gaze *f*

gave [geɪv] *pret* → *give*

gaw·ky ['gɒ:kɪ] *adj* gauche

gawp [gɒ:p] *v/i* F rester bouche bée (at devant)

gay [geɪ] **1** *n* (*homosexual*) homosexuel(le) *m(f)*, gay *m* **2** *adj* homosexuel*, gay *inv*

gaze [geɪz] **1** *n* regard *m* (fixe) **2** *v/i* regarder fixement

♦ **gaze at** *v/t* regarder fixement

GB [dʒi:'bi:] *abbr* (= *Great Britain*) Grande Bretagne *f*

GDP [dʒi:di:'pi:] *abbr* (= *gross domestic product*) P.I.B. *m* (= Produit *m* Intérieur Brut)

gear [gɪr] *n* (*equipment*) équipement *m*; *in vehicles* vitesse *f*

'gear·box MOT boîte *f* de vitesses

'gear le·ver, 'gear shift MOT levier *m* de vitesse

geese [gi:s] *pl* → *goose*

gel [dʒel] *for hair, shower* gel *m*

gel·a·tine ['dʒeləti:n] gélatine *f*

gel·ig·nite ['dʒelɪgnaɪt] gélignite *f*

gem [dʒem] pierre *f* précieuse; *fig* perle *f*

Gem·i·ni ['dʒemɪnaɪ] ASTROL les Gémeaux

gen·der ['dʒendər] genre *m*

gene [dʒi:n] gène *m*; *it's in his ~s* c'est dans ses gènes

gen·er·al ['dʒenrəl] **1** *n* MIL général(e) *m(f)*; *in ~* en général **2** *adj* général

gen·er·al e'lec·tion *Br* élections *fpl* générales

gen·er·al·i·za·tion [dʒenrəlaɪ'zeɪʃn] généralisation *f*

gen·er·al·ize ['dʒenrəlaɪz] *v/i* généraliser

gen·er·al·ly ['dʒenrəlɪ] *adv* généralement; *~ speaking* de manière générale

gen·er·ate ['dʒenəreɪt] *v/t* (*create*) engendrer, produire; *electricity* produire; *in linguistics* générer

gen·er·a·tion [dʒenə'reɪʃn] génération *f*

gen·e'ra·tion gap conflit *m* des générations

gen·er·a·tor ['dʒenəreɪtər] générateur *m*

ge·ner·ic drug [dʒə'nerɪk] MED médicament *m* générique

gen·er·os·i·ty [dʒenə'rɑ:sətɪ] générosité *f*

gen·er·ous ['dʒenərəs] *adj* généreux*

ge·net·ic [dʒɪ'netɪk] *adj* génétique

ge·net·i·cal·ly [dʒɪ'netɪklɪ] *adv* généti-

get by

quement; ~ **modified** génétiquement modifié, transgénique

ge·net·ic 'code code *m* génétique; **ge·net·ic en·gi'neer·ing** génie *m* génétique; **ge·net·ic 'fin·ger·print** empreinte *f* génétique

ge·net·i·cist [dʒɪ'netɪsɪst] généticien(ne) *m(f)*

ge·net·ics [dʒɪ'netɪks] *nsg* génétique *f*

ge·ni·al ['dʒiːnjəl] *adj person* cordial, agréable; *company* agréable

gen·i·tals ['dʒenɪtlz] *npl* organes *mpl* génitaux

ge·ni·us ['dʒiːnjəs] génie *m*

gen·o·cide ['dʒenəsaɪd] génocide *m*

gen·tle ['dʒentl] *adj* doux*; *breeze* léger*

gen·tle·man ['dʒentlmən] monsieur *m*; **he's a real** ~ c'est un vrai gentleman

gen·tle·ness ['dʒentlnɪs] douceur *f*

gen·tly ['dʒentlɪ] *adv* doucement; *blow* légèrement

gents [dʒents] *nsg Br: toilet* toilettes *fpl* (pour hommes)

gen·u·ine ['dʒenuɪn] *adj* authentique

gen·u·ine·ly ['dʒenuɪnlɪ] *adv* vraiment, sincèrement

ge·o·graph·i·cal [dʒɪə'græfɪkl] *adj* géographique

ge·og·ra·phy [dʒɪ'ɑːgrəfɪ] géographie *f*

ge·o·log·i·cal [dʒɪə'lɑːdʒɪkl] *adj* géologique

ge·ol·o·gist [dʒɪ'ɑːlədʒɪst] géologue *m/f*

ge·ol·o·gy [dʒɪ'ɑːlədʒɪ] géologie *f*

ge·o·me·tric, ge·o·met·ri·cal [dʒɪə'metrɪk(l)] *adj* géométrique

ge·om·e·try [dʒɪ'ɑːmətrɪ] géométrie *f*

ge·ra·ni·um [dʒɪ'reɪnɪəm] géranium *m*

ger·i·at·ric [dʒerɪ'ætrɪk] **1** *adj* gériatrique **2** *n* patient(e) *m(f)* gériatrique

germ [dʒɜːrm] *also of idea etc* germe *m*

Ger·man ['dʒɜːrmən] **1** *adj* allemand **2** *n person* Allemand(e) *m(f)*; *language* allemand *m*

Ger·man 'mea·sles *nsg* rubéole *f*

Ger·man 'shep·herd berger *m* allemand

Ger·ma·ny ['dʒɜːrmənɪ] Allemagne *f*

ger·mi·nate ['dʒɜːrmɪneɪt] *v/i of seed* germer

germ 'war·fare guerre *f* bactériologique

ges·tic·u·late [dʒe'stɪkjuleɪt] *v/i* gesticuler

ges·ture ['dʒestʃər] *n also fig* geste *m*

get [get] *v/t* (*pret & pp* **got**, *pp also* **gotten**) ◊ (*obtain*) obtenir; (*buy*) acheter; (*fetch*) aller chercher (**s.o. sth** qch pour qn); (*receive: letter*) recevoir; (*receive: knowledge, respect etc*) acquérir; (*catch: bus, train etc*) prendre; (*understand*) comprendre

◊ : **when we ~ home** quand nous arrivons chez nous

◊ (*become*) devenir; ~ **old** / **tired** vieillir / se fatiguer

◊ (*causative*): ~ **sth done** (*by s.o. else*) faire faire qch; ~ **s.o. to do sth** faire faire qch à qn; **I got her to change her mind** je lui ai fait changer d'avis; ~ **one's hair cut** se faire couper les cheveux; ~ **sth ready** préparer qch

◊ (*have opportunity*): ~ **to do sth** pouvoir faire qch

◊ : **have got** avoir

◊ : **have got to** devoir; **I have got to study** je dois étudier, il faut que j'étudie (*subj*)

◊ : ~ **going** (*leave*) s'en aller; (*start*) s'y mettre; ~ **to know** commencer à bien connaître

♦ **get along** *v/i* (*progress*) faire des progrès; (*come to party etc*) venir; **with s.o.** s'entendre

♦ **get around** *v/i* (*travel*) voyager; (*be mobile*) se déplacer

♦ **get at** *v/t* (*criticize*) s'en prendre à; (*imply, mean*) vouloir dire

♦ **get away 1** *v/i* (*leave*) partir **2** *v/t*: **get sth away from s.o.** retirer qch à qn

♦ **get away with** *v/t*: **let s.o. get away with sth** tolérer qch à qn

♦ **get back 1** *v/i* (*return*) revenir; **I'll get back to you on that** je vous recontacterai à ce sujet **2** *v/t health, breath, girlfriend etc* retrouver; *possession* récupérer

♦ **get by** *v/i* (*pass*) passer; *financially* s'en sortir

♦ **get down 1** v/i *from ladder etc* descendre; (*duck*) se baisser; (*be informal*) se détendre, se laisser aller **2** v/t (*depress*) déprimer

♦ **get down to** v/t (*start: work*) se mettre à; (*reach: real facts*) en venir à

♦ **get in 1** v/i (*of train, plane*) arriver; (*come home*) rentrer; *to car* entrer; *how did they ~ in?* *of thieves, mice etc* comment sont-ils entrés? **2** v/t *to suitcase etc* rentrer

♦ **get off 1** v/i *from bus etc* descendre; (*finish work*) finir; (*not be punished*) s'en tirer **2** v/t (*remove*) enlever; *get off the grass!* va-t-en de la pelouse!

♦ **get off with** v/t *Br F* (*sexually*) coucher avec F; *get off with a small fine* s'en tirer avec une petite amende

♦ **get on 1** v/i *to bike, bus, train* monter; (*be friendly*) s'entendre; (*advance: of time*) se faire tard; (*become old*) prendre de l'âge; (*progress: of book*) avancer; *how is she getting on at school?* comment ça se passe pour elle à l'école?; *it's getting on* (*getting late*) il se fait tard; *he's getting on* il prend de l'âge; *he's getting on for 50* il approche la cinquantaine **2** v/t: *get on the bus / one's bike* monter dans le bus / sur son vélo; *get one's hat on* mettre son chapeau; *I can't get these pants on* je n'arrive pas à enfiler ce pantalon

♦ **get on with** v/t *one's work* continuer; (*figure out*) se débrouiller

♦ **get out 1** v/i *of car, prison etc* sortir; *get out!* va-t-en!; *let's get out of here* allons-nous-en; *I don't get out much these days* je ne sors pas beaucoup ces temps-ci **2** v/t *nail, sth jammed, stain* enlever; *gun, pen* sortir; *what do you get out of it?* qu'est-ce que ça t'apporte?

♦ **get over** v/t *fence* franchir; *disappointment, lover* se remettre de

♦ **get over with** v/t en finir avec; *let's get it over with* finissons-en avec ça

♦ **get through** v/i *on telephone* obtenir la communication; (*make self understood*) se faire comprendre; *get through to s.o.* se faire comprendre

♦ **get up 1** v/i *in morning, from chair, of wind* se lever **2** v/t (*climb: hill*) monter

'**get·a·way** *from robbery* fuite f

'**get·a·way car** voiture utilisée pour s'enfuir

'**get-to·geth·er** n réunion f

ghast·ly ['gæstlɪ] adj horrible, affreux*

gher·kin ['gɜːkɪn] cornichon m

ghet·to ['getou] ghetto m

ghost [goust] fantôme m, spectre m

ghost·ly ['goustlɪ] adj spectral

'**ghost town** ville f fantôme

'**ghost·writ·er** nègre m

ghoul [guːl] personne f morbide; *he's a ~* il est morbide

ghoul·ish ['guːlɪʃ] adj macabre

gi·ant ['dʒaɪənt] **1** n géant(e) m(f) **2** adj géant

gib·ber·ish ['dʒɪbərɪʃ] F charabia m

gibe [dʒaɪb] n raillerie f, moquerie f

gib·lets ['dʒɪblɪts] npl abats mpl

gid·di·ness ['gɪdɪnɪs] vertige m

gid·dy ['gɪdɪ] adj: *feel ~* avoir le vertige

gift [gɪft] cadeau m; *talent* don m

gift·ed ['gɪftɪd] adj doué

'**gift-wrap 1** n papier m cadeau **2** v/t (*pret & pp -ped*): *~ sth* faire un paquet-cadeau

gig [gɪg] F concert m

gi·ga·byte ['gɪgəbaɪt] COMPUT gigaoctet m

gi·gan·tic [dʒaɪ'gæntɪk] adj gigantesque

gig·gle ['gɪgl] **1** v/i glousser **2** n gloussement m; *a fit of the ~s* une crise de fou rire

gig·gly ['gɪglɪ] adj qui rit bêtement

gill [gɪl] *of fish* ouïe f

gilt [gɪlt] n dorure f; *~s* FIN fonds mpl d'Etat

gim·mick ['gɪmɪk] truc f

gim·mick·y ['gɪmɪkɪ] adj à trucs

gin [dʒɪn] gin m; *~ and tonic* gin m tonic

gin·ger ['dʒɪndʒər] **1** n spice gingembre m **2** adj hair, cat roux*

gin·ger 'beer limonade f au gingembre

'**gin·ger·bread** pain *m* d'épice

gin·ger·ly ['dʒɪndʒərlɪ] *adv* avec précaution

gip·sy ['dʒɪpsɪ] gitan(e) *m(f)*

gi·raffe [dʒɪ'ræf] girafe *f*

gir·der ['gɜːrdər] *n* poutre *f*

girl [gɜːrl] (jeune) fille *f*

'**girl·friend** *of boy* petite amie *f*; *younger also* copine *f*; *of girl* amie *f*, *younger
also* copine *f*

girl·ie mag·a·zine ['gɜːrlɪ] magazine
m de cul F

girl·ish ['gɜːrlɪʃ] *adj* de jeune fille

girl 'scout éclaireuse *f*

gist [dʒɪst] point *m* essentiel, essence *f*

give [gɪv] *v/t* (*pret* **gave**, *pp* **given**)
donner; *present* offrir; (*supply: electricity etc*) fournir; *talk, lecture* faire; *cry,
groan* pousser; **~ her my love** faites-
lui mes amitiés

♦ **give away** *v/t as present* donner; (*betray*) trahir; **give o.s. away** se trahir

♦ **give back** *v/t* rendre

♦ **give in 1** *v/i* (*surrender*) céder, se rendre **2** *v/t* (*hand in*) remettre

♦ **give off** *v/t smell*, fumes émettre

♦ **give onto** *v/t open onto* donner sur

♦ **give out 1** *v/t leaflets etc* distribuer **2**
v/i of supplies, strength s'épuiser

♦ **give up 1** *v/t smoking etc* arrêter;
give up smoking arrêter de fumer;
give o.s. up to the police se rendre
à la police **2** *v/i* (*cease habit*) arrêter;
(*stop making effort*) abandonner, renoncer; **I give up** (*can't guess*) je
donne ma langue au chat

♦ **give way** *v/i of bridge etc* s'écrouler

give-and-'take concessions *fpl* mu-
tuelles

giv·en ['gɪvn] **1** *adj* donné **2** *pp* → **give**

'**giv·en name** prénom *m*

giz·mo ['gɪzmoʊ] F truc *m*, bidule *m* F

gla·ci·er ['gleɪʃər] glacier *m*

glad [glæd] *adj* heureux*

glad·ly ['glædlɪ] *adv* volontiers, avec
plaisir

glam·or ['glæmər] éclat *m*, fascination
f

glam·or·ize ['glæməraɪz] *v/t* donner
un aspect séduisant à

glam·or·ous ['glæmərəs] *adj* sédui-

sant, fascinant; *job* prestigieux*

glamour *Br* → **glamour**

glance [glæns] **1** *n* regard *m*, coup *m*
d'œil **2** *v/i* jeter un regard, lancer un
coup d'œil

♦ **glance at** *v/t* jeter un regard sur, lancer un coup d'œil à

gland [glænd] glande *f*

glan·du·lar fe·ver ['glændʒələr] mononucléose *f* infectieuse

glare [gler] **1** *n of sun, headlights* éclat
m (éblouissant) **2** *v/i of sun, headlights*
briller d'un éclat éblouissant

♦ **glare at** *v/t* lancer un regard furieux
à

glar·ing ['glerɪŋ] *adj mistake* flagrant

glar·ing·ly ['glerɪŋlɪ] *adv*: **be ~ obvious** sauter aux yeux

glass [glæs] *material, for drink* verre *m*

glass 'case vitrine *f*

glass·es *npl* lunettes *fpl*

'**glass·house** serre *f*

glaze [gleɪz] *n* vernis *m*

♦ **glaze over** *v/i of eyes* devenir vitreux

glazed [gleɪzd] *adj expression* vitreux*

gla·zi·er ['gleɪzɪr] vitrier *m*

glaz·ing ['gleɪzɪŋ] vitrerie *f*

gleam [gliːm] **1** *n* lueur *f* **2** *v/i* luire

glee [gliː] joie *f*

glee·ful ['gliːful] *adj* joyeux*

glib [glɪb] *adj* désinvolte

glib·ly ['glɪblɪ] *adv* avec désinvolture

glide [glaɪd] *v/i* glisser; *of bird, plane*
planer

glid·er ['glaɪdər] planeur *m*

glid·ing ['glaɪdɪŋ] *n sport* vol *m* à voile

glim·mer ['glɪmər] **1** *n of light* faible
lueur *f*; **a ~ of hope** *n* une lueur d'espoir **2** *v/i* jeter une faible lueur

glimpse [glɪmps] **1** *n*: **catch a ~ of ...**
entrevoir **2** *v/t* entrevoir

glint [glɪnt] **1** *n* lueur *f*, reflet *m* **2** *v/i of
light* luire, briller; *of eyes* luire

glis·ten ['glɪsn] *v/i of light* luire; *of
water* miroiter; *of silk* chatoyer

glit·ter ['glɪtər] *v/i of light, jewels* briller, scintiller

glit·ter·a·ti *npl* le beau monde

gloat [gloʊt] *v/i* jubiler

♦ **gloat over** *v/t* se réjouir de

glo·bal ['gloʊbl] *adj* (*worldwide*) mondial; (*without exceptions*) global

glo·bal e'con·o·my économie *f* mondiale

glo·bal·i·za·tion ['gloubəlaizeiʃn] *of markets etc* mondialisation *f*

glo·bal·ly ['gloubəli] *adv* (*on worldwide basis*) mondialement; (*without exceptions*) globalement

glo·bal 'mar·ket marché *m* international

glo·bal war·ming ['wɔːrmiŋ] réchauffement *m* de la planète

globe [gloub] globe *m*

gloom [gluːm] (*darkness*) obscurité *f*; *mood* tristesse *f*, mélancolie *f*

gloom·i·ly ['gluːmili] *adv* tristement, mélancoliquement

gloom·y ['gluːmi] *adj* sombre

glo·ri·ous ['glɔːriəs] *adj weather, day* magnifique; *victory* glorieux*

glo·ry ['glɔːri] *n* gloire *f*

gloss [glɑs] *n* (*shine*) brillant *m*, éclat *m*; (*general explanation*) glose *f*, commentaire *m*

♦ **gloss over** *v/t* passer sur

glos·sa·ry ['glɑsəri] glossaire *m*

'gloss paint peinture *f* brillante

gloss·y ['glɑsi] **1** *adj paper* glacé **2** *n magazine* magazine *m* de luxe

glove [glʌv] gant *m*

'glove com·part·ment *in car* boîte *f* à gants

'glove pup·pet marionnette *f* (à gaine)

glow [glou] **1** *n of light* lueur *f*; *of fire* rougeoiement *m*; *in cheeks* couleurs *fpl* **2** *v/i of light* luire; *of fire* rougeoyer; *of cheeks* être rouge

glow·er ['glauər] *v/i* lancer un regard noir (*at* à)

glow·ing ['glouiŋ] *adj description* élogieux*

glu·cose ['gluːkous] glucose *m*

glue [gluː] **1** *n* colle *f* **2** *v/t*: ~ *sth to sth* coller qch à qch; *be* ~*d to the TV* F être collé devant la télé F

glum [glʌm] *adj* morose

glum·ly ['glʌmli] *adv* d'un air morose

glut [glʌt] *n* surplus *m*

glut·ton ['glʌtən] glouton(ne) *m(f)*

glut·ton·y ['glʌtəni] gloutonnerie *f*

GM [dʒiː'em] *abbr* (= **genetically modified**) génétiquement modifié

GMT [dʒiːem'tiː] *abbr* (= **Greenwich Mean Time**) G.M.T. *m* (= Temps *m* moyen de Greenwich)

gnarled [nɑːrld] *adj branch, hands* noueux*

gnat [næt] moucheron *m*

gnaw [nɒ] *v/t bone* ronger

GNP [dʒiːen'piː] *abbr* (= **gross national product**) P.N.B. *m* (= Produit *m* national brut)

go [gou] **1** *n*: *on the* ~ actif **2** *v/i* (*pret went, pp gone*) ◊ aller; (*leave: of train, plane*) partir; (*leave: of people*) s'en aller, partir; (*work, function*) marcher, fonctionner; (*come out: of stain etc*) s'en aller; (*cease: of pain etc*) partir, disparaître; (*match: of colors etc*) aller ensemble; ~ *shopping / jogging* aller faire les courses / faire du jogging; *I must be* ~*ing* je dois partir, je dois m'en aller; *let's* ~*!* allons-y!; ~ *for a walk* aller se promener; ~ *to bed* aller se coucher; ~ *to school* aller à l'école; *how's the work* ~*ing?* comment va le travail?; *they're* ~*ing for $50* (*being sold at*) ils sont à 50 $; *hamburger to* ~ hamburger à emporter; *the milk is all gone* il n'y a plus du tout de lait ◊ (*become*) devenir; *she went all red* elle est devenue toute rouge ◊ *to express the future, intention*: *be* ~*ing to do sth* aller faire qch; *I'm not going to*

♦ **go ahead** *v/i*: *she just went ahead* elle l'a fait quand même; *go ahead!* (*on you go*) allez-y!

♦ **go ahead with** *v/t plans etc* commencer

♦ **go along with** *v/t suggestion* accepter

♦ **go at** *v/t* (*attack*) attaquer

♦ **go away** *v/i of person* s'en aller, partir; *of rain* cesser; *of pain, clouds* partir, disparaître

♦ **go back** *v/i* (*return*) retourner; (*date back*) remonter (*to* à); *we go back a long way* on se connaît depuis longtemps; *go back to sleep* se rendormir

- ◆ **go by** *v/i of car, people, time* passer
- ◆ **go down** *v/i* descendre; *of sun* se coucher; *of ship* couler; *of swelling* diminuer; **go down well / badly** *of suggestion etc* être bien / mal reçu
- ◆ **go for** *v/t (attack)* attaquer; *(like)* beaucoup aimer
- ◆ **go in** *v/i to room, house* entrer; *of sun* se cacher; *(fit: of part etc)* s'insérer; **it won't go in** ça ne va pas rentrer
- ◆ **go in for** *v/t competition, race* prendre part à; *(like)* aimer; *sport* jouer à
- ◆ **go off 1** *v/i (leave)* partir; *of bomb* exploser; *of gun* partir; *of light* s'éteindre; *of alarm* se déclencher **2** *v/t (stop liking)* se lasser de; **I've gone off the idea** l'idée ne me plaît plus
- ◆ **go on** *v/i (continue)* continuer; *(happen)* se passer; **can I? - yes, go on** est-ce que je peux? - oui, vas-y; **go on, do it!** *(encouraging)* allez, fais-le!; **what's going on?** qu'est-ce qui se passe?; **don't go on about it** arrête de parler de cela
- ◆ **go on at** *v/t (nag)* s'en prendre à
- ◆ **go out** *v/i of person* sortir; *of light, fire* s'éteindre
- ◆ **go out with** *v/t romantically* sortir avec
- ◆ **go over** *v/t (check)* revoir
- ◆ **go through** *v/t hard times* traverser; *illness* subir; *(check)* revoir; *(read through)* lire en entier
- ◆ **go through with** *v/t* aller jusqu'au bout de; **go through with it** aller jusqu'au bout
- ◆ **go under** *v/i (sink)* couler; *of company* faire faillite
- ◆ **go up** *v/i (climb)* monter; *of prices* augmenter
- ◆ **go without 1** *v/t food etc* se passer de **2** *v/i* s'en passer

goad [gəʊd] *v/t:* **~ s.o. into doing sth** talonner qn jusqu'à ce qu'il fasse *(subj)* qch

'**go-a-head 1** *n* feu vert **m 2** *adj (enterprising, dynamic)* entreprenant, dynamique

goal [gəʊl] *in sport, (objective)* but *m*

goal-ie ['gəʊlɪ] F goal *m* F

'**goal-keep-er** gardien *m* de but; '**goal kick** remise *f* en jeu; '**goal-mouth** entrée *f* des buts; '**goal-post** poteau *m* de but; '**goal-scor-er** buteur *m*; **their top ~** leur meilleur buteur

goat [gəʊt] chèvre *m*

gob-ble ['gɑ:bl] *v/t* dévorer

- ◆ **gobble up** *v/t* engloutir

gob-ble-dy-gook ['gɑ:bldɪguːk] F charabia *m* F

'**go-be-tween** intermédiaire *m/f*

god [gɑːd] dieu *m*; **thank God!** Dieu merci!; **oh God!** mon Dieu!

'**god-child** filleul(e) *m(f)*

'**god-daugh-ter** filleule *f*

'**god-dess** ['gɑːdɪs] déesse *f*

'**god-fa-ther** *also in mafia* parrain *m*; **god-for-sak-en** ['gɑːdfərseɪkn] *adj place, town* perdu; '**god-moth-er** marraine *m*; '**god-par-ents** *npl* parrains *mpl*; '**god-send** don *m* du ciel; '**god-son** filleul *m*

go-fer ['gəʊfər] F coursier(-ière) *m(f)*

gog-gles ['gɑːglz] *npl* lunettes *fpl*

go-ing ['gəʊɪŋ] *adj price etc* actuel*; **~ concern** affaire *f* qui marche

go-ings-on [gəʊɪŋz'ɑːn] *npl* activités *fpl*; **there were some strange ~** il se passait de drôles de choses

gold [gəʊld] **1** *n or m; medal* médaille *f* d'or **2** *adj watch, necklace etc* en or; *ingot* d'or

gold-en ['gəʊldn] *adj sky* doré; *hair also* n'or

gold-en 'hand-shake (grosse) prime *f* de départ

gold-en 'wed-ding (an-ni-ver-sa-ry) noces *fpl* d'or

'**gold-fish** poisson *m* rouge; '**gold mine** *fig* mine *f* d'or; '**gold-smith** orfèvre *m*

golf [gɑːlf] golf *m*

'**golf ball** balle *f* de golf; '**golf club** *organization, stick* club *m* de golf; '**golf course** terrain *m* de golf

golf-er ['gɑːlfər] golfeur(-euse) *m(f)*

gone [gɑːn] *pp* → **go**

gong [gɑːŋ] gong *m*

good [gʊd] *adj* bon*; *weather* beau*; *child* sage; **a ~ many** beaucoup; **a ~**

many ... beaucoup de ...; *be ~ at ...* être bon en ...; *it's ~ for you* for *health* c'est bon pour la santé

good-bye [gʊd'baɪ] au revoir

'**good-for-noth-ing** *n* bon(ne) *m(f)* à rien; **Good 'Fri-day** Vendredi *m* saint; **good-hu-mored** [gʊd'hjuː-mərd] *adj* jovial; **good-look-ing** [gʊd'lʊkɪŋ] *adj woman* beau*; **good-na-tured** [gʊd'neɪtʃərd] bon*, au bon naturel

good-ness ['gʊdnɪs] *moral* bonté *f*; *of fruit etc* bonnes choses *fpl*; *thank ~!* Dieu merci!

goods [gʊdz] *npl* COMM marchandises *fpl*

good-will bonne volonté *f*, bienveillance *f*

good-y-good-y ['gʊdɪgʊdɪ] *n* F petit(e) saint(e) *m(f)*; *child* enfant *m/f* modèle

goo-ey ['guːɪ] *adj* gluant

goof [guːf] *v/i* F gaffer F

goose [guːs] *(pl geese)* oie *f*

goose-ber-ry ['gʊzberɪ] groseille *f* (à maquereau)

'**goose bumps** *npl* chair *f* de poule

'**goose pim-ples** *npl* chair *f* de poule

gorge [gɔːrdʒ] **1** *n in mountains* gorge *f* **2** *v/t*: *~ o.s. on sth* se gorger de qch

gor-geous ['gɔːrdʒəs] *adj* magnifique, superbe

go-ril-la [gə'rɪlə] gorille *m*

gosh [gɑːʃ] *int* ça alors!

go-'slow grève *f* perlée

gos-pel ['gɑːspl] *in Bible* évangile *m*

'**gos-pel truth** parole *f* d'évangile

gos-sip ['gɑːsɪp] **1** *n* potins *mpl*; *malicious* commérages *mpl*; *person* commère *f* **2** *v/i* bavarder; *maliciously* faire des commérages

'**gos-sip col-umn** échos *mpl*

'**gos-sip col-um-nist** échotier(-ière) *m(f)*

gos-sip-y ['gɑːsɪpɪ] *adj letter* plein de potins

got [gɑːt] *pret & pp → get*

got-ten ['gɑːtn] *pp → get*

gour-met ['gʊrmeɪ] *n* gourmet *m*, gastronome *m/f*

gov-ern ['gʌvərn] *v/t country* gouver-

ner

gov-ern-ment ['gʌvərnmənt] gouvernement *m*; *~ spending* dépenses *fpl* publiques; *~ loan* emprunt *m* d'État

gov-er-nor ['gʌvərnər] gouverneur *m*

gown [gaʊn] robe *f*; *(wedding dress)* robe *f* de mariée; *of academic, judge* toge *f*; *of surgeon* blouse *f*

grab [græb] *v/t (pret & pp -bed)* saisir; *food* avaler; *~ some sleep* dormir un peu

grace [greɪs] *of dancer etc* grâce *f*; *before meals* bénédicité *m*

grace-ful ['greɪsfʊl] *adj* gracieux*

grace-ful-ly ['greɪsfʊlɪ] *adv move* gracieusement

gra-cious ['greɪʃəs] *adj person* bienveillant; *style, living* élégant; *good ~!* mon Dieu!

grade [greɪd] **1** *n (quality)* qualité *f*; EDU classe *f*; *(mark)* note *f* **2** *v/t* classer; *school work* noter

grade 'cross-ing passage *m* à niveau

'**grade school** école *f* primaire

gra-di-ent ['greɪdɪənt] pente *f*, inclinaison *f*

grad-u-al ['grædʒʊəl] *adj* graduel*, progressif*

grad-u-al-ly ['grædʒʊəlɪ] *adv* peu à peu, progressivement

grad-u-ate ['grædʒʊət] **1** *n* diplômé(e) *m(f)* **2** *v/i* ['grædʒʊeɪt] obtenir son diplôme *(from* de)

grad-u-a-tion [grædʒʊ'eɪʃn] obtention *f* du diplôme

grad-u-a-tion cer-e-mon-y cérémonie *f* de remise de diplômes

graf-fi-ti [grə'fiːtiː] graffitis *mpl*; *single* graffiti *m*

graft [græft] **1** *n* BOT, MED greffe *f*; F *(corruption)* corruption *f*; Br F *(hard work)* corvée *f* **2** *v/t* BOT, MED greffer

grain [greɪn] blé *m*; *of rice etc, in wood* grain *m*; *it goes against the ~ for me to do this* c'est contre ma nature de faire ceci

gram [græm] gramme *m*

gram-mar ['græmər] grammaire *f*

'**gram-mar school** Br lycée *m*

gram-mat-i-cal [grə'mætɪkl] *adj* gram-

greasy

matical

gram·mat·i·cal·ly adv grammaticalement

grand [grænd] **1** adj grandiose; F (very good) génial F **2** n F ($1000) mille dollars mpl

gran·dad ['grændæd] grand-père m

'grand·child petit-fils m, petite-fille f; **'grand·child·ren** npl petits-enfants mpl; **'grand·daugh·ter** petite-fille f

gran·deur ['grændʒər] grandeur f, splendeur f

'grand·fa·ther grand-père m

'grand·fa·ther clock horloge f de parquet

gran·di·ose ['grændɪoʊs] adj grandiose, pompeux*

grand 'ju·ry grand jury m; **'grand·ma** F mamie f F; **'grand·moth·er** grand-mère f; **'grand·pa** F papi m F; **'grand·par·ents** npl grands-parents mpl; **grand pi·an·o** piano m à queue; **grand 'slam** in tennis grand chelem m; **'grand·son** petit-fils m; **'grand·stand** tribune f

gran·ite ['grænɪt] granit m

gran·ny ['grænɪ] F mamie f F

grant [grænt] **1** n money subvention f **2** v/t wish, visa, request accorder; **take s.o. / sth for ~ed** considérer qn / qch comme acquis

gran·u·lat·ed sug·ar ['grænuleɪtɪd] sucre m en poudre

gran·ule ['grænuːl] grain m

grape [greɪp] grain m (de) raisin m; **some ~s** du raisin

'grape·fruit pamplemousse m; **'grape·fruit juice** jus m de pamplemousse; **'grape·vine**: **hear sth on the ~** apprendre qch par le téléphone arabe

graph [græf] graphique m, courbe f

graph·ic ['græfɪk] **1** adj (vivid) très réaliste **2** n COMPUT graphique m; **~s** graphiques mpl

graph·i·cal·ly ['græfɪklɪ] adv describe de manière réaliste

graph·ic de·sign·er graphiste m/f

♦ **grap·ple with** ['græpl] v/t attacker en venir aux prises avec; problem etc s'attaquer à

grasp [græsp] **1** n physical prise f; mental compréhension f **2** v/t physically saisir; (understand) comprendre

grass [græs] n herbe f

'grass·hop·per sauterelle f; **grass 'roots** npl people base f; **grass 'wid·ow**: I'm a ~ this week je suis célibataire cette semaine

gras·sy ['græsɪ] adj herbeux*, herbu

grate[1] [greɪt] n metal grill grille f

grate[2] [greɪt] **1** v/t in cooking râper **2** v/i: **~ on the ear** faire mal aux oreilles

grate·ful ['greɪtful] adj reconnaissant; **be ~ to s.o.** être reconnaissant envers qn

grate·ful·ly ['greɪtfulɪ] adv avec reconnaissance

grat·er ['greɪtər] râpe f

grat·i·fy ['grætɪfaɪ] v/t (pret & pp **-ied**) satisfaire, faire plaisir à

grat·ing ['greɪtɪŋ] **1** n grille f **2** adj sound, voice grinçant

grat·i·tude ['grætɪtuːd] gratitude f, reconnaissance f

gra·tu·i·tous [grə'tuːɪtəs] adj gratuit

gra·tu·i·ty [grə'tuːətɪ] gratification f, pourboire m

grave[1] [greɪv] n tombe f

grave[2] [greɪv] adj error, face, voice grave

grav·el ['grævl] gravier m

'grave·stone pierre f tombale

'grave·yard cimetière m

♦ **grav·i·tate toward** ['grævɪteɪt] v/t être attiré par

grav·i·ty ['grævətɪ] PHYS, of situation gravité f

gra·vy ['greɪvɪ] jus m de viande

gray [greɪ] adj gris; **be going ~** grisonner

gray-haired [greɪ'herd] adj aux cheveux gris

graze[1] [greɪz] v/i of cow, horse paître

graze[2] [greɪz] **1** v/t arm etc écorcher; **~ one's arm** s'écorcher le bras **2** n écorchure f

grease [griːs] for cooking graisse f; for car lubrifiant m

grease·proof 'pa·per papier m sulfurisé

greas·y ['griːsɪ] adj gras*; (covered in

grease) graisseux*

great [greɪt] *adj* grand; *mistake, sum of money* gros*; *composer, writer* grand; F (*very good*) super F; ~ **to see you!** ravi de te voir!

Great 'Brit·ain Grande-Bretagne *f*

great-'grand·daugh·ter arrière-petite-fille *f*; **great-'grand·fa·ther** arrière-grand-père *m*; **great-'grand·moth·er** arrière-grand-mère *f*; **great-'grand·par·ents** *npl* arrière--grands-parents *mpl*; **great-'grand·son** arrière-petit-fils *m*

great·ly ['greɪtlɪ] *adv* beaucoup; **not ~ different** pas très différent

great·ness ['greɪtnɪs] grandeur *f*, importance *f*

Greece [griːs] Grèce *f*

greed [griːd] *for money* avidité *f*; *for food also* gourmandise *f*

greed·i·ly ['griːdɪlɪ] *adv* avec avidité

greed·y ['griːdɪ] *adj for money* avide; *for food also* gourmand

Greek [griːk] **1** *n* Grec(que) *m(f)*; *language* grec *m* **2** *adj* grec*

green [griːn] *adj* vert; *environmentally* écologique

green 'beans *npl* haricots *mpl* verts; **'green belt** ceinture *f* verte; **'green card** (*work permit*) permis *m* de travail; **'green·field site** terrain *m* non construit; **'green·horn** F blanc-bec *m*; **'green·house** serre *f*; **'green·house ef·fect** effet *m* de serre; **'green·house gas** gaz *m* à effet de serre

greens [griːnz] *npl* légumes *mpl* verts

green 'thumb: have a ~ avoir la main verte

greet [griːt] *v/t* saluer; (*welcome*) accueillir

greet·ing ['griːtɪŋ] salut *m*

'greet·ing card carte *f* de vœux

gre·gar·i·ous [grɪˈgeriəs] *adj person* sociable

gre·nade [grɪˈneɪd] grenade *f*

grew [gruː] *pret* → **grow**

grey [greɪ] *adj Br* → **gray**

'grey·hound lévrier *m*, levrette *f*

grid [grɪd] grille *f*; **'grid·iron** SP terrain *m* de football; **'grid·lock** *in traffic*

embouteillage *m*

grief [griːf] chagrin *m*, douleur *f*

grief-strick·en ['griːfstrɪkn] *adj* affligé

griev·ance ['griːvəns] grief *m*

grieve [griːv] *v/i* être affligé; **~ for s.o.** pleurer qn

grill [grɪl] **1** *n on window* grille *f* **2** *v/t* (*interrogate*) mettre sur la sellette

grille [grɪl] grille *f*

grim [grɪm] *adj* sinistre, sombre

gri·mace ['grɪməs] *n* grimace *f*

grime [graɪm] saleté *f*, crasse *f*

grim·ly ['grɪmlɪ] *adv determined etc* fermement; *say, warn* sinistrement

grim·y ['graɪmɪ] *adj* sale, crasseux*

grin [grɪn] **1** *n* (*large*) sourire *m* **2** *v/i* (*pret & pp* **-ned**) sourire

grind [graɪnd] *v/t* (*pret & pp* **ground**) *coffee* moudre; *meat* hacher; **~ one's teeth** grincer des dents

grip [grɪp] **1** *n on rope etc* prise *f*; **be losing one's ~** (*losing one's skills*) baisser **2** *v/t* (*pret & pp* **-ped**) saisir, serrer

gripe [graɪp] **1** *n* plainte *f* **2** *v/i* rouspéter F

grip·ping ['grɪpɪŋ] *adj* prenant, captivant

gris·tle ['grɪsl] cartilage *m*

grit [grɪt] **1** *n for roads* gravillon *m*; **a bit of ~ in eye** une poussière **2** *v/t* (*pret & pp* **-ted**): **~ one's teeth** grincer des dents

grit·ty ['grɪtɪ] *adj* F *book, movie etc* réaliste

groan [groʊn] **1** *n* gémissement *m* **2** *v/i* gémir

gro·cer ['groʊsər] épicier(-ère) *m(f)*

gro·cer·ies ['groʊsərɪz] *npl* (*articles mpl d'*)épicerie *f*, provisions *fpl*

gro·cer·y store ['groʊsərɪ] épicerie *f*; **at the ~** chez l'épicier, à l'épicerie

grog·gy ['grɑːgɪ] *adj* F groggy F

groin [grɔɪn] ANAT aine *f*

groom [gruːm] **1** *n for bride* marié *m*; *for horse* palefrenier(-ère) *m(f)* **2** *v/t horse* panser; (*train, prepare*) préparer, former; **well ~ed in appearance** très soigné

groove [gruːv] rainure *f*; *on record* sillon *m*

grope [groʊp] **1** *v/i in the dark* tâtonner **2** *v/t sexually* peloter F

♦ **grope for** *v/t door handle* chercher à tâtons; *right word* chercher

gross [groʊs] *adj* (*coarse, vulgar*) grossier*; *exaggeration* gros*; FIN brut

gross 'do·mes·tic prod·uct produit *m* intérieur brut

gross 'na·tion·al prod·uct produit *m* national brut

ground[1] [graʊnd] **1** *n* sol *m*, terre *f*; *area of land, for football, fig* terrain; (*reason*) raison *f*, motif *m*; ELEC terre *f*; **on the ~** par terre **2** *v/t* ELEC mettre une prise de terre à

'ground con·trol contrôle *m* au sol; **'ground crew** personnel *m* au sol; **'ground floor** *Br* rez-de-chaussée *m*

ground[2] *pret & pp* → **grind**

ground·ing ['graʊndɪŋ] *in subject* bases *fpl*

ground·less ['graʊndlɪs] *adj* sans fondement

'ground meat viande *f* hachée; **'ground·nut** arachide *f*; **'ground plan** projection *f* horizontale; **'ground staff** SP personnel *m* d'entretien; *at airport* personnel *m* au sol; **'ground·work** travail *m* préparatoire; **Ground 'Ze·ro** Ground Zero *m*

group [gruːp] **1** *n* groupe *m* **2** *v/t* grouper

group·ie ['gruːpɪ] groupie *f* F

group 'ther·a·py thérapie *f* de groupe

grouse [graʊs] **1** *n* F rouspéter F **2** *v/i* F plainte *f*

grov·el ['grɑːvl] *v/i fig* ramper (**to** devant)

grow [groʊ] **1** *v/i* (*pret* **grew**, *pp* **grown**) *of child, animal, anxiety* grandir; *of plants, hair, beard* pousser; *of number, amount* augmenter; *of business* se développer; (*become*) devenir **2** *v/t flowers* faire pousser

♦ **grow up** *of person* devenir adulte; *of city* se développer; **grow up!** sois adulte!

growl [graʊl] **1** *n* grognement *m* **2** *v/i* grogner

grown [groʊn] *pp* → **grow**

'grown-up 1 *n* adulte *m/f* **2** *adj* adulte

growth [groʊθ] *of person, company* croissance *f*; (*increase*) augmentation *f*; MED tumeur *f*

grub [grʌb] *of insect* larve *f*, ver *m*

grub·by ['grʌbɪ] *adj* sale

grudge [grʌdʒ] **1** *n* rancune *f*; **bear a ~** avoir de la rancune **2** *v/t* (*give unwillingly*) accorder à contrecœur; **~ s.o. sth** (*resent*) en vouloir à qn de qch

grudg·ing ['grʌdʒɪŋ] *adj* accordé à contrecœur; *person* plein de ressentiment

grudg·ing·ly ['grʌdʒɪŋlɪ] *adv* à contre-cœur

gru·el·ing, *Br* **gruel·ling** ['gruːəlɪŋ] *adj climb, task* épuisant, éreintant

gruff [grʌf] *adj* bourru, revêche

grum·ble ['grʌmbl] *v/i* ronchonner

grum·bler ['grʌmblər] grognon(ne) *m(f)*

grump·y ['grʌmpɪ] *adj* grincheux*

grunt [grʌnt] **1** *n* grognement *m* **2** *v/i* grogner

guar·an·tee [gærən'tiː] **1** *n* garantie *f*; **~ period** période *f* de garantie **2** *v/t* garantir

guar·an·tor [gærən'tɔːr] garant(e) *m(f)*

guard [gɑːrd] **1** *n* (*security guard*), *in prison* gardien(ne) *m(f)*; MIL garde *f*; **be on one's ~** être sur ses gardes; **be on one's ~ against** faire attention à **2** *v/t* garder

♦ **guard against** *v/t* se garder de

'guard dog chien *m* de garde

guard·ed ['gɑːrdɪd] *adj reply* prudent, réservé

guard·i·an ['gɑːrdɪən] LAW tuteur (-trice) *m(f)*

guard·i·an 'an·gel ange-gardien *m*

guer·ril·la [gə'rɪlə] guérillero *m*

guer·ril·la 'war·fare guérilla *f*

guess [ges] **1** *n* conjecture *f* **2** *v/t answer* deviner **2** *v/i* deviner; **I ~ so** je crois; **I ~ not** je ne crois pas

'guess·work conjecture(s) *f(pl)*

guest [gest] invité(e) *m(f)*; *in hotel* hôte *m/f*

'guest·house pension *f* de famille

'guest·room chambre f d'amis

guf·faw [gʌ'fɔː] **1** n gros rire m **2** v/i s'esclaffer

guid·ance ['gaɪdəns] conseils mpl

guide [gaɪd] **1** n person guide m/f; book guide m **2** v/t guider

'guide-book guide m

guid·ed mis·sile ['gaɪdɪd] missile m téléguidé

'guide dog chien m d'aveugle

guid·ed 'tour visite f guidée

guide·lines ['gaɪdlaɪnz] npl directives fpl

guilt [gɪlt] culpabilité f

guilt·y ['gɪltɪ] adj coupable; **have a ~ conscience** avoir mauvaise conscience

guin·ea pig ['gɪnɪpɪg] cochon m d'Inde, cobaye m; fig cobaye m

guise [gaɪz]: **under the ~ of** sous l'apparence de

gui·tar [gɪ'tɑːr] guitare f

gui·tar case étui m à guitare

gui·tar·ist [gɪ'tɑːrɪst] guitariste m/f

gui·tar play·er guitariste m/f

gulf [gʌlf] golfe m; fig gouffre m, abîme m; **the Gulf** le Golfe

gull [gʌl] mouette f; bigger goéland m

gul·let ['gʌlɪt] ANAT gosier m

gul·li·ble ['gʌlɪbl] adj crédule

gulp [gʌlp] **1** n of drink gorgée f; of food bouchée f **2** v/i in surprise dire en s'étranglant

♦ gulp down v/t drink avaler à grosses gorgées; food avaler à grosses bouchées

gum¹ [gʌm] n in mouth gencive f

gum² [gʌm] n (glue) colle f; (chewing gum) chewing-gum m

gump·tion ['gʌmpʃn] jugeote f F

gun [gʌn] arme f à feu; pistol pistolet m; revolver revolver m; rifle fusil m; cannon canon m

♦ gun down v/t (pret & pp -ned) abattre

'gun·fire coups mpl de feu; 'gun·man homme m armé; 'gun·point: **at ~** sous la menace d'une arme; 'gun·shot coup m de feu; 'gun·shot wound blessure f par balle

gur·gle ['gɜːrgl] v/i of baby gazouiller; of drain gargouiller

gu·ru ['guːruː] fig gourou m

gush [gʌʃ] v/i of liquid jaillir

gush·y ['gʌʃɪ] adj F (enthusiastic) excessif*

gust [gʌst] rafale f, coup m de vent

gus·to ['gʌstoʊ]: **with ~** avec enthousiasme

gust·y ['gʌstɪ] adj weather très venteux*; **~ wind** vent soufflant en rafales

gut [gʌt] **1** n intestin m; F (stomach) bide m F **2** v/t (pret & pp -ted) (destroy) ravager; (strip down) casser

gut 'feel·ing F intuition f

guts [gʌts] npl entrailles fpl; F (courage) cran m F; **hate s.o.'s ~** ne pas pouvoir saquer qn F

guts·y ['gʌtsɪ] adj F (brave) qui a du cran F

gut·ter ['gʌtər] on sidewalk caniveau m; on roof gouttière f

'gut·ter·press Br presse f de bas-étage

guy [gaɪ] F type m F; **hey, you ~s** salut, vous

guz·zle ['gʌzl] v/t food engloutir; drink avaler

gym [dʒɪm] sports club club m de gym; in school gymnase m; activity gym f, gymnastique f

gym·na·si·um [dʒɪm'neɪzɪəm] gymnase m

gym·nast ['dʒɪmnæst] gymnaste m/f

gym·nas·tics [dʒɪm'næstɪks] gymnastique f

gy·ne·col·o·gy, Br gy·nae·col·o·gy [gaɪnɪ'kɑːlədʒɪ] gynécologie f

gy·ne·col·o·gist, Br gy·nae·col·o·gist [gaɪnɪ'kɑːlədʒɪst] gynécologue m/f

gyp·sy ['dʒɪpsɪ] gitan(e) m(f)

H

hab·it ['hæbɪt] habitude f; **get into the ~ of doing sth** prendre l'habitude de faire qch
hab·it·a·ble ['hæbɪtəbl] adj habitable
hab·i·tat ['hæbɪtæt] habitat m
ha·bit·u·al [hə'bɪtʃuəl] adj habituel*; *smoker, drinker* invétéré
hack [hæk] n (*poor writer*) écrivaillon(ne) m(f)
hack·er ['hækər] COMPUT pirate m informatique
hack·neyed ['hæknɪd] adj rebattu
had [hæd] pret & pp → **have**
had·dock ['hædək] aiglefin m; **smoked ~** haddock m
haem·or·rhage Br → **hemorrhage**
hag·gard ['hægərd] adj hagard, égaré
hag·gle ['hægl] v/i chipoter (*for, over* sur)
hail [heɪl] n grêle f
'hail·stone grêlon m
'hail·storm averse f de grêle
hair [her] n cheveux mpl; *single* cheveu m; *on body* poils mpl; *single* poil m
'hair·brush brosse f à cheveux; 'hair·cut coupe f de cheveux; 'hair·do coiffure f; 'hair·dress·er coiffeur (-euse) m(f); **at the ~** chez le coiffeur; 'hair·dri·er, 'hair·dry·er sèche-cheveux m
hair·less ['herlɪs] adj person sans cheveux, chauve; *chin* imberbe; *animal* sans poils
'hair·pin épingle f à cheveux; hair·pin 'curve virage m en épingle à cheveux; hair·rais·ing ['herreɪzɪŋ] adj horrifique, à faire dresser les cheveux sur la tête; hair re·mov·er ['herrɪmuːvər] crème f épilatoire
'hair's breadth *fig*: **by a ~** de justesse
hair·split·ting ['hersplɪtɪŋ] n ergotage m; 'hair spray laque f; 'hair·style coiffure f; 'hair·styl·ist coiffeur (-euse) m(f)

hair·y ['herɪ] adj arm, animal poilu; F (*frightening*) effrayant
half [hæf] 1 n (pl halves [hævz]) moitié f; **~ past ten** dix heures et demie; **~ an hour** une demi-heure; **~ a pound** une demi-livre; **go halves with s.o. on sth.** se mettre de moitié avec qn pour qch, partager avec qn pour qch 2 adj demi; **at ~ price** à moitié prix; **~ size** demi-taille f 3 adv à moitié
half-heart·ed [hæf'hɑːrtɪd] adj tiède, hésitant; half 'time n SP mi-temps f; half-time adj à mi-temps; **~ score** score m à la mi-temps; half'way 1 adj: **reach the ~ point** être à la moitié 2 adv in space, distance à mi-chemin; finished à moitié
hall [hɔːl] (*large room*) salle f; (*hallway in house*) vestibule m
Hal·low·e'en [hælou'wiːn] halloween f
halo ['heɪlou] auréole f; ASTR halo m
halt [hɔːlt] 1 v/i faire halte, s'arrêter 2 v/t arrêter 3 n: **come to a ~** of traffic, production être interrompu; of person faire halte, s'arrêter
halve [hæv] v/t couper en deux; input, costs réduire de moitié
ham [hæm] jambon m
ham·burg·er ['hæmbɜːrgər] hamburger m
ham·mer ['hæmər] 1 n marteau m 2 v/i marteler, battre au marteau; **~ at the door** frapper à la porte à coups redoublés
ham·mock ['hæmək] hamac m
ham·per¹ ['hæmpər] n for food panier m
ham·per² ['hæmpər] v/t (obstruct) entraver, gêner
ham·ster ['hæmstər] hamster m
hand [hænd] 1 n main f; of clock aiguille f; (worker) ouvrier(-ère) m(f); **at ~, to ~** thing sous la main; **at ~ per-**

son à disposition; **at first ~** de première main; **by ~** à la main; **on the one ~ ..., on the other ~** d'une part ..., d'autre part; **in ~** (*being done*) en cours; **on your right ~** sur votre droite; **~s off!** n'y touchez pas!; **~s up!** haut les mains!; **change ~s** changer de propriétaire *or* de mains; **give s.o. a ~** donner un coup de main à qn

♦ **hand down** *v/t* transmettre
♦ **hand in** *v/t* remettre
♦ **hand on** *v/t* transmettre
♦ **hand out** *v/t* distribuer
♦ **hand over** *v/t* donner; *to authorities* livrer

'**hand·bag** *Br* sac *m* à main; '**hand bag·gage** bagages *mpl* à main; '**hand·book** livret *m*, guide *m*; '**hand·cuff** *v/t* menotter; **hand·cuffs** ['hæn(d)kʌfs] *npl* menottes *fpl*

hand·i·cap ['hændɪkæp] handicap *m*

hand·i·capped ['hændɪkæpt] *adj* handicapé

hand·i·craft ['hændɪkræft] artisanat *m*

hand·i·work ['hændɪwɜːrk] *object* ouvrage *m*

hand·ker·chief ['hæŋkərtʃɪf] mouchoir *m*

han·dle ['hændl] **1** *n* of door, suitcase, bucket poignée *f*, of knife, pan manche *m* **2** *v/t* goods manier, manipuler; case, deal s'occuper de; difficult person gérer; **let me ~ this** laissez-moi m'en occuper

han·dle·bars ['hændlbɑːrz] *npl* guidon *m*

'**hand lug·gage** bagages *m* à main; **hand·made** [hæn(d)meɪd] *adj* fait (à la) main; '**hand·rail** of stairs balustrade *f*, main *f* courante; of bridge garde-fou *m*, balustrade *f*; '**hand·shake** poignée *f* de main

hands-off [hændz'ɑːf] *adj approach* théorique; *manager* non-interventionniste

hand·some ['hænsəm] *adj* beau*

hands-on [hændz'ɑːn] *adj* pratique; *manager* impliqué; **he has a ~ style** il s'implique (dans ce qu'il fait)

'**hand·writ·ing** écriture *f*
'**hand·writ·ten** *adj* écrit à la main
hand·y ['hændɪ] *adj tool, device* pratique; **it might come in ~** ça pourrait servir, ça pourrait être utile

hang [hæŋ] **1** *v/t* (pret & pp **hung**) picture accrocher; person pendre **2** *v/i* of dress, hair tomber; of washing pendre **3** *n*: **get the ~ of sth** F piger qch F

♦ **hang around** *v/i* F traîner; **who does he hang around with?** avec qui traîne-t-il?
♦ **hang on** *v/i* (*wait*) attendre
♦ **hang on to** *v/t* (*keep*) garder
♦ **hang up** *v/i* TELEC raccrocher

han·gar ['hæŋər] hangar *m*
hang·er ['hæŋər] for clothes cintre *m*
'**hang glid·er** person libériste *m/f*; device deltaplane *m*
'**hang glid·ing** deltaplane *m*
'**hang·o·ver** F gueule *f* de bois
'**hang-up** F complexe *m*
♦ **han·ker after** ['hæŋkər] *v/t* rêver de
han·kie, han·ky ['hæŋkɪ] F mouchoir *m*

hap·haz·ard [hæp'hæzərd] *adj* au hasard, au petit bonheur
hap·pen ['hæpn] *v/i* se passer, arriver; **if you ~ to see him** si par hasard vous le rencontrez; **what has ~ed to you?** qu'est-ce qui t'est arrivé?
♦ **happen across** *v/t* tomber sur
hap·pen·ing ['hæpnɪŋ] événement *m*
hap·pi·ly ['hæpɪlɪ] *adv* gaiement; spend volontiers; (*luckily*) heureusement
hap·pi·ness ['hæpɪnɪs] bonheur *m*
hap·py ['hæpɪ] *adj* heureux*
'**hap·py-go-'luck·y** *adj* insouciant
'**hap·py hour** happy hour *f*
har·ass ['hərᴂs] *v/t* harceler, tracasser
har·assed ['hərᴂst] *adj* surmené
har·ass·ment [hə'ræsmənt] harcèlement *m*; **sexual ~** harcèlement *m* sexuel
har·bor ['hɑːrbər] **1** *n* port *m* **2** *v/t criminal* héberger; grudge entretenir
hard [hɑːrd] **1** *adj* dur; (*difficult*) dur, difficile; facts brut; evidence concret*; **be ~ of hearing** être dur d'oreille **2** *adv* work dur; rain, pull, push fort; **try**

~ to do sth faire tout son possible pour faire qch

'**hard·back** n livre m cartonné; **hard-boiled** [haːrdˈbɔɪld] adj egg dur; '**hard cop·y** copie f sur papier; '**hard core** n pornography (pornographie f) hard m; '**hard cur·ren·cy** monnaie f forte; '**hard disk** disque m dur

hard·en [ˈhaːrdn] **1** v/t durcir **2** v/i of glue, attitude se durcir

'**hard hat** casque m; (construction worker) ouvrier m du bâtiment; **hard-head·ed** [haːrdˈhedɪd] adj réaliste, qui garde la tête froide; **hard-heart·ed** [haːrdˈhaːrtɪd] adj au cœur dur; **hard 'line** ligne f dure; **take a ~ on** adopter une ligne dure sur; **hard'lin·er** dur(e) m(f)

hard·ly [ˈhaːrdlɪ] adv à peine; see s.o. etc presque pas; expect sûrement pas; **~ ever** presque jamais

hard·ness [ˈhaːrdnɪs] dureté f; (difficulty) difficulté f

hard'sell techniques fpl de vente agressives

hard·ship [ˈhaːrdʃɪp] privation f, gêne f

hard 'up adj fauché F; '**hard·ware** quincaillerie f; COMPUT hardware m, matériel m; '**hard·ware store** quincaillerie f; **hard-'work·ing** adj travailleur*

har·dy [ˈhaːrdɪ] adj robuste

hare [her] n lièvre m

hare·brained [ˈherbreɪnd] adj écervelé

harm [haːrm] **1** n mal m; **it wouldn't do any ~ to …** ça ne ferait pas de mal de … **2** v/t physically faire du mal à; non-physically nuire à; economy, relationship endommager, nuire à

harm·ful [ˈhaːrmfl] adj substance nocif*; influence nuisible

harm·less [ˈhaːrmlɪs] adj inoffensif*

har·mo·ni·ous [haːrˈmoʊnɪəs] adj harmonieux*

har·mo·nize [ˈhaːrmənaɪz] v/i s'harmoniser

har·mo·ny [ˈhaːrmənɪ] harmonie f

harp [haːrp] n harpe f

♦ **harp on about** v/t F rabâcher

har·poon [haːrˈpuːn] harpon m

harsh [haːrʃ] adj criticism, words rude, dur; color criard; light cru

harsh·ly [ˈhaːrʃlɪ] adv durement, rudement

har·vest [ˈhaːrvɪst] n moisson f

hash [hæʃ] F pagaille f, gâchis m; **make a ~ of** faire un beau gâchis de

hash·ish [ˈhæʃiːʃ] ha(s)chisch m

'**hash mark** caractère m #, dièse f

haste [heɪst] n hâte f

has·ten [ˈheɪsn] v/i: **~ to do sth** se hâter de faire qch

hast·i·ly [ˈheɪstɪlɪ] adv à la hâte, précipitamment

hast·y [ˈheɪstɪ] adj hâtif*, précipité

hat [hæt] chapeau m

hatch [hætʃ] n for serving food guichet m; on ship écoutille f

♦ **hatch out** v/i of eggs éclore

hatch·et [ˈhætʃɪt] hachette f; **bury the ~** enterrer la hache de guerre

hate [heɪt] **1** n haine f **2** v/t détester, haïr

ha·tred [ˈheɪtrɪd] haine f

haugh·ty [ˈhɔːtɪ] adj hautain, arrogant

haul [hɔːl] **1** n of fish coup m de filet **2** v/t (pull) tirer, traîner

haul·age [ˈhɔːlɪdʒ] transports mpl (routiers)

'**haul·age com·pa·ny** entreprise f de transports (routiers)

haunch [hɔːntʃ] of person hanche f; of animal arrière-train m; **squatting on their ~es** accroupis

haunt [hɔːnt] **1** v/t hanter; **this place is ~ed** ce lieu est hanté **2** n lieu m fréquenté, repaire m

haunt·ing [ˈhɔːntɪŋ] adj tune lancinant

have [hæv] **1** v/t (pret & pp **had**) (own) avoir

◇ breakfast, lunch prendre

◇ : **you've been had** F tu t'es fait avoir F

◇ : **can I ~ …?** est-ce que je peux or puis-je avoir …?; **do you ~ …?** est-ce que vous avez …?

◇ (must): **~ (got) to** devoir; **you don't ~ to do it** tu n'es pas obligé de le faire; **do I ~ to pay?** est-ce qu'il faut payer?

◇ (*causative*): ~ *sth done* faire faire qch; *I'll* ~ *it sent to you* je vous le ferai envoyer; *I had my hair cut* je me suis fait couper les cheveux; *will you* ~ *him come in?* faites-le entrer 2 *v/aux* ◇ (*past tense*): ~ *you seen her?* l'as-tu vue?; *they* ~ *arrived* ils sont arrivés; *I hadn't expected that* je ne m'attendais pas à cela ◇ *tags*: *you haven't seen him,* ~ *you?* tu ne l'as pas vu, n'est-ce pas?; *he had signed it, hadn't he?* il l'avait bien signé, n'est-ce pas?

♦ **have back** *v/t*: *when can I have it back?* quand est-ce que je peux le récupérer?

♦ **have on** *v/t* (*wear*) porter; *do you have anything on tonight?* (*have planned*) est-ce que vous avez quelque chose de prévu ce soir?

ha·ven ['heɪvn] *fig* havre *m*

hav·oc ['hævək] ravages *mpl*; *play* ~ *with* mettre sens dessus dessous

hawk [hɒːk] *also fig* faucon *m*

hay [heɪ] foin *m*

'hay fe·ver rhume *m* des foins

haz·ard ['hæzərd] *n* danger *m*, risque *m*

'haz·ard lights *npl* MOT feux *mpl* de détresse

haz·ard·ous ['hæzərdəs] *adj* dangereux*, risqué; ~ *waste* déchets *mpl* dangereux

haze [heɪz] brume *f*

ha·zel ['heɪzl] *n tree* noisetier *m*

'ha·zel·nut noisette *f*

haz·y ['heɪzɪ] *adj view* brumeux*; *image* flou; *memories* vague; *I'm a bit* ~ *about it don't remember* je ne m'en souviens que vaguement; *don't understand* je ne comprends que vaguement

he [hiː] *pron* il; *stressed* lui; ~ *was the one who …* c'est lui qui …; *there* ~ *is* le voilà; ~ *who …* celui qui

head [hed] **1** *n* tête *f*; (*boss, leader*) chef *m/f*; *of delegation* chef *m/f*; *Br. of school* directeur(-trice) *m(f)*; *on beer* mousse *f*; *of nail* bout *m*; *of line* tête *f*; *$15 a* ~ 15 $ par personne; ~*s or tails?* pile ou face?; *at the* ~ *of*

the list en tête de liste; *fall* ~ *over heels* faire la culbute; *fall* ~ *over heels in love with* tomber éperdument amoureux* de; *lose one's* ~ (*go crazy*) perdre la tête **2** *v/t* (*lead*) être à la tête de; *ball* jouer de la tête

♦ **head for** *v/t* se diriger vers

'head·ache mal *m* de tête

'head·band bandeau *m*

head·er ['hedər] *in soccer* (coup *m* de) tête *f*; *in document* en-tête *m*

'head·hunt *v/t*: *be* ~*ed* COMM être recruté (par un chasseur de têtes)

'head·hunt·er COMM chasseur *m* de têtes

head·ing ['hedɪŋ] titre *m*

'head·lamp phare *m*; **'head·light** phare *m*; **'head·line** *in newspaper* (gros) titre *m*, manchette *f*; *make the* ~*s* faire les gros titres; **'head·long** *adv fall* de tout son long; **'head·mas·ter** *Br. of school* directeur *m*; *of high school* proviseur *m*; **'head·mis·tress** *Br. of school* directrice *f*; *of high school* proviseur *f*; **head 'of·fice** *of company* bureau *m* central; **head-'on 1** *adv crash* de front **2** *adj* frontal; **'head·phones** *npl* écouteurs *mpl*; **'head·quar·ters** *npl* quartier *m* général; **'head·rest** appui-tête *m*; **'head·room** *under bridge* hauteur *f* limite; *in car* hauteur *f* au plafond; **'head·scarf** foulard *m*; **'head·strong** *adj* entêté, obstiné; **head 'wait·er** maître d'hôtel; **'head·wind** vent *m* contraire

head·y ['hedɪ] *adj drink, wine etc* capiteux*

heal [hiːl] *v/t* guérir

♦ **heal up** *v/i* se guérir

health [helθ] santé *f*; *your* ~*!* à votre santé!

'health care soins *mpl* médicaux; **'health club** club *m* de gym; **'health food** aliments *mpl* diététiques; **'health food store** magasin *m* d'aliments diététiques; **'health in·su·rance** assurance *f* maladie; **'health re·sort** station *f* thermale

health·y ['helθɪ] *adj person* en bonne santé; *food, lifestyle, economy* sain

helper

heap [hi:p] *n* tas *m*
♦ **heap up** *v/t* entasser
hear [hɪr] *v/t & v/i* (*pret & pp* **heard**) entendre
♦ **hear about** *v/t* entendre parler de; **have you heard about Mike?** as-tu entendu ce qui est arrivé à Mike?
♦ **hear from** *v/t* (*have news from*) avoir des nouvelles de
heard [hɜːrd] *pret & pp* → **hear**
hear·ing ['hɪrɪŋ] ouïe *f*; LAW audience *f*; **within ~** à portée de voix; **out of ~** hors de portée de voix
'hear·ing aid appareil *m* acoustique, audiophone *m*
'hear·say: **by ~** par ouï-dire
hearse [hɜːrs] corbillard *m*
heart [hɑːrt] *also fig* cœur *m*; **know sth by ~** connaître qch par cœur
'heart at·tack crise *f* cardiaque; **'heart·beat** battement *m* de cœur; **heart-break·ing** *adj* navrant; **'heart-brok·en** *adj*: **be ~** avoir le cœur brisé; **'heart·burn** brûlures *fpl* d'estomac; **'heart fail·ure** arrêt *m* cardiaque; **'heart·felt** *adj sympathy* sincère, profond
hearth [hɑːrθ] foyer *m*, âtre *f*
heart·less ['hɑːrtlɪs] *adj* insensible, cruel*
heart-rend·ing ['hɑːrtrendɪŋ] *adj plea, sight* déchirant, navrant
hearts [hɑːrts] *npl in cards* cœur *m*
'heart throb F idole *f*, coqueluche *f*
'heart trans·plant greffe *f* du cœur
heart·y ['hɑːrtɪ] *adj appetite* gros*; *meal* copieux*; *person* jovial, chaleureux*
heat [hi:t] chaleur *f*; *in contest* (épreuve *f*) éliminatoire *f*
♦ **heat up** *v/t* réchauffer
heat·ed ['hi:tɪd] *adj swimming pool* chauffé; *discussion* passionné
heat·er ['hi:tər] radiateur *m*; *in car* chauffage *m*
hea·then ['hi:ðn] *n* païen(ne) *m(f)*
heath·er ['heðər] bruyère *f*
heat·ing ['hi:tɪŋ] chauffage *m*
'heat·proof, 'heat-re·sis·tant *adj* résistant à la chaleur; **'heat·stroke** coup *m* de chaleur; **'heat·wave** va-

gue *f* de chaleur
heave [hi:v] *v/t* (*lift*) soulever
heav·en ['hevn] ciel *m*; **good ~s!** mon Dieu!
heav·en·ly ['hevnlɪ] *adj* F divin
heav·y ['hevɪ] *adj also food, loss* lourd; *cold* grand; *rain, accent* fort; *traffic, smoker, drinker, bleeding* gros*
heav·y·du·ty *adj* très résistant
'heav·y·weight *adj* SP poids lourd
heck·le ['hekl] *v/t* interpeller, chahuter
hec·tic ['hektɪk] *adj* agité, bousculé
hedge [hedʒ] *n* haie *f*
hedge·hog ['hedʒhɑːg] hérisson *m*
hedge·row ['hedʒrou] haie *f*
heed [hi:d] **1** *v/t* faire attention à, tenir compte de **2** *n*: **pay ~ to** faire attention à, tenir compte de
heel [hi:l] *of foot* talon *m*
'heel bar talon-minute *m*
hef·ty ['heftɪ] *adj* gros*; *person also* costaud
height [haɪt] *of person* taille *f*; *of building* hauteur *f*; *of airplane* altitude *f*; **at the ~ of the season** en pleine saison
height·en ['haɪtn] *v/t effect, tension* accroître
heir [er] héritier *m*
heir·ess ['erɪs] héritière *f*
held [held] *pret & pp* → **hold**
hel·i·cop·ter ['helɪkɑːptər] hélicoptère *m*
hell [hel] enfer *m*; **what the ~ are you doing?** F mais enfin qu'est-ce que tu fais?; **go to ~!** F va te faire foutre!; P; **a ~ of a lot of** F tout un tas de F; **one ~ of a nice guy** F un type vachement bien F; **it hurts like ~** ça fait vachement mal F
hel·lo [hə'lou] bonjour; TELEC allô; **say ~ to s.o.** dire bonjour à qn
helm [helm] NAUT barre *f*
hel·met ['helmɪt] casque *m*
help [help] **1** *n* aide *f*; ~! à l'aide!, au secours! **2** *v/t* aider; ~ **o.s.** *to food* se servir; **I can't ~ it** je ne peux pas m'en empêcher; **I couldn't ~ laughing** je n'ai pas pu m'empêcher de rire; **it can't be ~ed** on n'y peut rien
help·er ['helpər] aide *m/f*, assistant(e) *m(f)*

H

help·ful ['helpfl] *adj advice* utile; *person* serviable

help·ing ['helpɪŋ] *of food* portion *f*

help·less ['helplɪs] *adj (unable to cope)* sans défense; *(powerless)* sans ressource, impuissant

help·less·ness ['helplɪsnɪs] impuissance *f*

'help screen COMPUT écran *m* d'aide

hem [hem] *n of dress etc* ourlet *m*

hem·i·sphere ['hemɪsfɪr] hémisphère *m*

'hem·line ourlet *m*; **~s are going up** les jupes raccourcissent

hem·or·rhage ['heməridʒ] **1** *n* hémorragie *f* **2** *v/i* faire une hémorragie

hen [hen] poule *f*

hench·man ['hentʃmən] *pej* acolyte *m*

'hen par·ty soirée *f* entre femmes; *before wedding* soirée entre femmes avant un mariage

hen-pecked ['henpekt] *adj* dominé par sa femme

hep·a·ti·tis [hepə'taɪtɪs] hépatite *f*

her [hɜːr] **1** *adj* son, sa; *pl* ses **2** *pron object* la; *before vowel* l'; *indirect object* lui, à elle; *with preps* elle; *I know ~* je la connais; *I gave ~ a dollar* je lui ai donné un dollar; *this is for ~* c'est pour elle; *who? - ~* qui? - elle

herb [ɜːrb] herbe *f*

herb(al) tea ['ɜːrb(əl)] tisane *f*

herd [hɜːrd] *n* troupeau *m*

here [hɪr] *adv* ici; *in ~, over ~* ici; *~'s to you!* as toast à votre santé!; *~ you are giving sth* voilà; *~ we are! finding sth* le / la voilà!

he·red·i·ta·ry [hə'redɪterɪ] *adj disease* héréditaire

he·red·i·ty [hə'redɪtɪ] hérédité *f*

her·i·tage ['herɪtɪdʒ] héritage *m*

her·mit ['hɜːrmɪt] ermite *m*

her·ni·a ['hɜːrnɪə] MED hernie *f*

he·ro ['hɪrou] héros *m*

he·ro·ic [hɪ'rouɪk] *adj* héroïque

he·ro·i·cal·ly [hɪ'rouɪklɪ] *adv* héroïquement

her·o·in ['herouɪn] héroïne *f*

'her·o·in ad·dict héroïnomane *m/f*

her·o·ine ['herouɪn] héroïne *f*

her·o·ism ['herouɪzm] héroïsme *f*

her·on ['herən] héron *m*

her·pes ['hɜːrpiːz] MED herpès *m*

her·ring ['herɪŋ] hareng *m*

hers [hɜːrz] *pron* le sien, la sienne; *pl* les siens, les siennes; *it's ~* c'est à elle

her·self [hɜːr'self] *pron* elle-même; *reflexive* se; *after prep* elle; *she hurt ~* elle s'est blessée; *by ~* toute seule

hes·i·tant ['hezɪtənt] *adj* hésitant

hes·i·tant·ly ['hezɪtəntlɪ] *adv* avec hésitation

hes·i·tate ['hezɪteɪt] *v/i* hésiter

hes·i·ta·tion [hezɪ'teɪʃn] hésitation *f*

het·er·o·sex·u·al [hetərou'sekʃuəl] *adj* hétérosexuel*

hey·day ['heɪdeɪ] apogée *m*, âge *m* d'or

hi [haɪ] *int* salut

hi·ber·nate ['haɪbərneɪt] *v/i* hiberner

hic·cup ['hɪkʌp] *n* hoquet *m*; *(minor problem)* hic *m* F; *have the ~s* avoir le hoquet

hick [hɪk] *pej* F paysan *m*

'hick town *pej* F bled *m* F

hid [hɪd] *pret* → *hide*

hid·den ['hɪdn] **1** *adj* caché **2** *pp* → *hide*

hid·den a'gen·da *fig* motifs *mpl* secrets

hide¹ [haɪd] **1** *v/t (pret hid, pp hidden)* cacher **2** *v/i* se cacher

hide² [haɪd] *n of animal* peau *f*; *as product* cuir *m*

hide-and-'seek cache-cache *m*

'hide·a·way cachette *f*

hid·e·ous ['hɪdɪəs] *adj* affreux*, horrible

hid·ing¹ ['haɪdɪŋ] *(beating)* rossée *f*

hid·ing² ['haɪdɪŋ]: *be in ~* être caché; *go into ~* prendre le maquis

'hid·ing place cachette *f*

hi·er·ar·chy ['haɪərɑːrkɪ] hiérarchie *f*

hi-fi ['haɪfaɪ] chaîne *f* hi-fi

high [haɪ] **1** *adj building, quality, society, opinion* haut; *salary, price, rent, temperature* élevé; *wind* fort; *speed* grand; *on drugs* défoncé F; *it's ~ time he came* il est grand temps qu'il vienne *(subj)* **2** *n* MOT quatrième *f*; cinquième *f*; *in statistics* pointe *f*, plafond *m*; EDU collège *m*, lycée *m* **3** *adv* haut; *that's as ~ as we can go* on ne peut pas monter plus

'**high-brow** *adj* intellectuel*; '**high-chair** chaise *f* haute; '**high-class** *adj* de première classe, de première qualité; **high 'div-ing** plongeon *m* de haut vol; **high-'fre-quen-cy** *adj* de haute fréquence; **high-'grade** *adj ore* à haute teneur; ~ *gasoline* supercarburant *m*; **high-hand-ed** [haɪˈhændɪd] *adj* arbitraire; **high--heeled** [haɪˈhiːld] *adj* à hauts talons; '**high jump** saut *m* en hauteur; **high-'lev-el** *adj* à haut niveau; '**high life** grande vie *f*; '**high-light 1** *n* (*main event*) point *m* marquant, point *m* culminant; *in hair* reflets *mpl*, mèches *fpl* **2** *v/t with pen* surligner; COMPUT mettre en relief; '**high-light-er** *pen* surligneur *m*

high-ly [ˈhaɪlɪ] *adv desirable, likely* fort(ement), très; *be ~ paid* être très bien payé; *think ~ of s.o.* penser beaucoup de bien de qn; très sensible

high per'form-ance *adj drill, battery* haute performance; **high-pitched** [haɪˈpɪtʃt] *adj* aigu*; '**high point** *of life, career* point *m* marquant, point *m* culminant; **high-pow-ered** [haɪˈpaʊərd] *adj engine* très puissant; *intellectual, salesman* très compétent; **high 'pres-sure** *n weather* anticyclone *m*

high-'pressure *adj* TECH à haute pression; *salesman* de choc; *job, lifestyle* dynamique; **high 'priest** grand prêtre *m*; '**high school** collège *m*, lycée *m*; **high so'ci-e-ty** haute société *f*; **high-speed 'train** train *m* à grande vitesse, T.G.V. *m*; **high--'strung** *adj* nerveux*, très sensible; **high-'tech 1** *n* technologie *f* de pointe, high-tech *m* **2** *adj* de pointe, high-tech; **high-'ten-sion** *adj cable* haute tension; **high 'tide** marée *f* haute; **high 'volt-age** haute tension *f*; **high 'wa-ter** marée *f* haute; '**high-way** grande route *f*; '**high wire** *in circus* corde *f* raide

hi-jack [ˈhaɪdʒæk] **1** *v/t plane, bus* dé-

tourner **2** *n of plane, bus* détournement *m*

hi-jack-er [ˈhaɪdʒækər] *of plane* pirate *m* de l'air; *of bus* pirate *m* de la route

hike[1] [haɪk] **1** *n* randonnée *f* à pied **2** *v/i* marcher à pied, faire une randonnée à pied

hike[2] [haɪk] *n in prices* hausse *f*

hik-er [ˈhaɪkər] randonneur(-euse) *m(f)*

hik-ing [ˈhaɪkɪŋ] randonnée *f* (pédestre)

'**hik-ing boots** *npl* chaussures *fpl* de rmarche

hi-lar-i-ous [hɪˈlerɪəs] *adj* hilarant, désopilant

hill [hɪl] colline *f*; (*slope*) côte *f*

hill-bil-ly [ˈhɪlbɪlɪ] F habitant *m* des montagnes du sud-est des États-Unis; '**hill-side** (flanc *m*) de coteau *m*; '**hill-top** sommet *m* de la colline

hill-y [ˈhɪlɪ] *adj* montagneux*; *road* vallonné

hilt [hɪlt] poignée *f*

him [hɪm] *pron object* le; *before vowel* l'; *indirect object, with preps* lui; *I know ~* je le connais; *I gave ~ a dollar* je lui ai donné un dollar; *this is for ~* c'est pour lui; *who? - him* qui? - lui

him-self [hɪmˈself] *pron* lui-même; *reflexive; after prep* lui; *he hurt ~* il s'est blessé; *by ~* tout seul

hind [haɪnd] *adj* de derrière, postérieur

hin-der [ˈhɪndər] *v/t* gêner, entraver; ~ *s.o. from doing sth* empêcher qn de faire qch

hin-drance [ˈhɪndrəns] obstacle *m*; *be a ~ to s.o. / sth* gêner qn / qch

hind-sight [ˈhaɪndsaɪt]: *with ~* avec du recul

hinge [hɪndʒ] charnière *f*; *on door also* gond *m*

♦ **hinge on** *v/t* dépendre de

hint [hɪnt] *n* (*clue*) indice *m*; (*piece of advice*) conseil *m*; (*implied suggestion*) allusion *f*, signe *m*; *of red, sadness etc* soupçon *m*

hip [hɪp] *n* hanche *f*

hip 'pock-et poche *f* revolver

H

hip·po·pot·a·mus [hɪpəˈpɑːtəməs] hippopotame *m*

hire [ˈhaɪr] *v/t* louer; *workers* engager, embaucher

his [hɪz] **1** *adj* son, sa; *pl* ses **2** *pron* le sien, la sienne; *pl* les siens, les siennes; *it's* ~ c'est à lui

His·pan·ic [hɪˈspænɪk] **1** *n* Latino--Américain(e) *m(f)*, Hispano-Américain(e) *m(f)* **2** *adj* latino-américain, hispano-américain

hiss [hɪs] *v/i of snake, audience* siffler

his·to·ri·an [hɪˈstɔːrɪən] historien(ne) *m(f)*

his·tor·ic [hɪˈstɑːrɪk] *adj* historique

his·tor·i·cal [hɪˈstɑːrɪkl] *adj* historique

his·to·ry [ˈhɪstərɪ] histoire *f*

hit [hɪt] **1** *v/t* (*pret & pp* **hit**) *also ball* frapper; (*collide with*) heurter; *he was* ~ *by a bullet* il a été touché par une balle; *it suddenly* ~ *me* (*I realized*) j'ai réalisé tout d'un coup; ~ *town* arriver en ville **2** *n* (*blow*) coup *m*; MUS, (*success*) succès *m*; *on website* visiteur *m*; *be a big* ~ *with* of *idea* avoir un grand succès auprès de

♦ **hit back** *v/i physically* rendre son coup à; *verbally, with actions* riposter

♦ **hit on** *v/t idea* trouver

♦ **hit out at** *v/t* (*criticize*) attaquer

hit-and-run *adj:* ~ *accident* accident *m* avec délit de fuite; ~ *driver* conducteur(-trice) *m(f)* en délit de fuite

hitch [hɪtʃ] **1** *n* (*problem*) anicroche *f*, accroc *m*; *without a* ~ sans accroc **2** *v/t* attacher; ~ *a ride* faire de l'auto-stop

hitch 3 *v/i* (*hitchhike*) faire du stop

♦ **hitch up** *v/t wagon, trailer* remonter

ˈhitch·hike *v/i* faire du stop

ˈhitch·hik·er auto-stoppeur(-euse) *m(f)*

ˈhitch·hik·ing auto-stop *m*, stop *m*

hi-tech 1 *n* technologie *f* de pointe, high-tech *m* **2** *adj* de pointe, high-tech

ˈhit-list liste *f* noire; ˈhit-man tueur *m* à gages; **hit-or-ˈmiss** *adj* aléatoire; ˈhit squad commando *m*

HIV [eɪtʃaɪˈviː] *abbr* (= *human immunodeficiency virus*) V.I.H. *m* (= Virus de l'Immunodéficience Humaine); *people with* ~ les séropositifs

hive [haɪv] *for bees* ruche *f*

♦ **hive off** *v/t* COMM (*separate off*) séparer

HIV-ˈpos·i·tive *adj* séropositif*

hoard [hɔːrd] **1** *n* réserves *fpl* **2** *v/t money* amasser; *in times of shortage* faire des réserves de

hoard·er [ˈhɔːrdər]: *be a* ~ ne jamais rien jeter

hoarse [hɔːrs] *adj* rauque

hoax [hoʊks] *n* canular *m*; *bomb* ~ fausse alerte *f* à la bombe

hob [hɑːb] *on cooker* plaque *f* chauffante

hob·ble [ˈhɑːbl] *v/i* boitiller

hob·by [ˈhɑːbɪ] passe-temps *m* (favori), hobby *m*

ho·bo [ˈhoʊboʊ] F vagabond *m*

hock·ey [ˈhɑːkɪ] (*ice hockey*) hockey *m* (sur glace)

hog [hɑːg] *n* (*pig*) cochon *m*

hoist [hɔɪst] **1** *n* palan *m* **2** *v/t* hisser

ho·kum [ˈhoʊkəm] *n* (*nonsense*) balivernes *fpl*; (*sentimental stuff*) niaiseries *fpl*

hold [hoʊld] **1** *v/t* (*pret & pp* **held**) *in hand* tenir; (*support, keep in place*) soutenir, maintenir en place; *passport, license* détenir; *prisoner, suspect* garder, détenir; (*contain*) contenir; *job, post* avoir, occuper; *course* tenir; ~ *one's breath* retenir son souffle; *he can* ~ *his drink* il tient bien l'alcool; ~ *s.o. responsible* tenir qn responsable; ~ *that …* (*believe, maintain*) estimer que …, maintenir que …; ~ *the line* TELEC ne quittez pas! **2** *n in ship* cale *f*; *in plane* soute *f*; *take* ~ *of sth* saisir qch; *lose one's* ~ *on sth on rope etc* lâcher qch; *lose one's* ~ *on reality* perdre le sens des réalités

♦ **hold against** *v/t:* *hold sth against s.o.* en vouloir à qn de qch

♦ **hold back 1** *v/t crowds* contenir; *facts, information* retenir **2** *v/i* (*not tell* *all*) se retenir

♦ **hold on** *v/i* (*wait*) attendre; TELEC ne pas quitter; ***now hold on a minute!*** pas si vite!

♦ **hold on to** *v/t* (*keep*) garder; *belief* se cramponner à, s'accrocher à

♦ **hold out 1** *v/t hand* tendre; *prospect* offrir, promettre **2** *v/i of supplies* durer; *of trapped miners etc* tenir (bon)

♦ **hold up 1** *v/t hand* lever; *bank etc* attaquer; (*make late*) retenir; ***hold sth up as an example*** citer qch en exemple

♦ **hold with** *v/t* (*approve of*) approuver

hold·er ['hoʊldər] (*container*) boîtier *m*; *of passport, ticket, record* détenteur(-trice) *m(f)*

hold·ing com·pa·ny ['hoʊldɪŋ] holding *m*

'**hold·up** (*robbery*) hold-up *m*; (*delay*) retard *m*

hole [hoʊl] trou *m*

hol·i·day ['hɑːlədeɪ] *single day* jour *m* de congé; *Br. period* vacances *fpl*; ***take a ~*** prendre un jour de congé / des vacances

Hol·land ['hɑːlənd] Hollande *f*

hol·low ['hɑːloʊ] *adj* creux*; *promise* faux*

hol·ly ['hɑːlɪ] houx *m*

hol·o·caust ['hɑːləkɔːst] holocauste *m*

hol·o·gram ['hɑːləgræm] hologramme *m*

hol·ster ['hoʊlstər] holster *m*

ho·ly ['hoʊlɪ] *adj* saint

Ho·ly 'Spir·it Saint-Esprit *m*

'**Ho·ly Week** semaine *f* sainte

home [hoʊm] **1** *n* maison *f*; (*native country, town*) patrie *f*; *for old people* maison *f* de retraite; (*in my country*) dans mon pays; SP à domicile; ***make o.s. at ~*** faire comme chez moi; ***at ~ and abroad*** dans son pays et à l'étranger; ***work from ~*** travailler chez soi *or* à domicile **2** *adv* à la maison, chez soi; (*in own country*) dans son pays; (*in own town*) dans sa ville; ***go ~*** rentrer (chez soi *or* à la maison); (*to country*) rentrer dans son pays; *to town* rentrer

dans sa ville

home ad·dress adress *f* personnelle; **home 'bank·ing** services *mpl* télématiques (bancaires); **home·com·ing** ['hoʊmkʌmɪŋ] retour *m* (à la maison); **home com'put·er** ordinateur *m* familial; '**home game** match *m* à domicile

home·less ['hoʊmlɪs] **1** *adj* sans abri, sans domicile fixe **2** *npl*: **the ~** les sans-abri *mpl*, les S.D.F. *mpl* (sans domicile fixe)

'**home·lov·ing** *adj* casanier*

home·ly ['hoʊmlɪ] *adj* (*homelike*) simple, comme à la maison; (*not good-looking*) sans beauté

home'made *adj* fait (à la) maison

home 'mov·ie vidéo *f* amateur

ho·me·op·a·thy [hoʊmɪ'ɑːpəθɪ] homéopathie *f*

'**home page** COMPUT page *f* d'accueil; '**home·sick** *adj*: **be ~** avoir le mal du pays; '**home town** ville *f* natale

home·ward ['hoʊmwərd] **1** *adv to own house* vers la maison; *to own country* vers son pays **2** *adj*: ***the ~ journey*** le retour

'**home·work** EDU devoirs *mpl*

'**home·work·ing** COMM travail *m* à domicile

hom·i·cide ['hɑːmɪsaɪd] *crime* homicide *m*; *police department* homicides *mpl*

hom·o·graph ['hɑːməgræf] homographe *m*

ho·mo·pho·bi·a [hoʊmə'foʊbɪə] homophobie *f*

ho·mo·sex·u·al [hoʊmə'sekʃʊəl] **1** *adj* homosexuel* **2** *n* homosexuel(le) *m(f)*

hon·est ['ɑːnɪst] *adj* honnête, sincère

hon·est·ly ['ɑːnɪstlɪ] *adv* honnêtement; **~!** vraiment!

hon·es·ty ['ɑːnɪstɪ] honnêteté *f*

hon·ey ['hʌnɪ] miel *m*; F (*darling*) chéri(e) *m(f)*

'**hon·ey·comb** rayon *m* de miel

'**hon·ey·moon** *n* lune *f* de miel

honk [hɑːŋk] *v/t horn* klaxonner

honk·y ['hɑːŋkɪ] *pej* P blanc(he) *m(f)*

H

hon·or ['ɑːnər] **1** *n* honneur *f* **2** *v/t* honorer

hon·or·a·ble ['ɑːnrəbl] *adj* honorable

hon·our *Br* → **honor**

hood [hʊd] *over head* capuche *f*; *over cooker* hotte *f*; MOT capot *m*; F (*gangster*) truand *m*

hood·lum ['huːdləm] voyou *m*

hoof [huːf] sabot *m*

hook [hʊk] *to hang clothes on* patère *f*; *for fishing* hameçon *m*; **off the ~** TELEC décroché

hooked [hʊkt] *adj* accro F; **be ~ on sth** être accro de qch

hook·er ['hʊkər] F putain *f* P; *in rugby* talonneur *m*

hoo·li·gan ['huːlɪgən] voyou *m*, hooligan *m*

hoo·li·gan·ism ['huːlɪgənɪzm] hooliganisme *m*

hoop [huːp] cerceau *m*

hoot [huːt] **1** *v/t horn* donner un coup de 2 *v/i of car* klaxonner; *of owl* huer

hoo·ver® ['huːvər] *Br* **1** *n* aspirateur *m* **2** *v/t carpets* passer l'aspirateur sur; *room* passer l'aspirateur dans

hop¹ [hɑːp] *n plant* houblon *m*

hop² [hɑːp] *v/i* (*pret & pp* **-ped**) sauter, sautiller

hope [hoʊp] **1** *n* espoir *m*; **there's no ~ of that** ça ne risque pas d'arriver **2** *v/i* espérer; **~ for sth** espérer qch; *I* **~ so** je l'espère, j'espère que oui; *I* **~ not** j'espère que non **2** *v/t*: **~ that ...** espérer que ...

hope·ful ['hoʊpfl] *adj* plein d'espoir; (*promising*) prometteur*

hope·ful·ly ['hoʊpfli] *adv say, wait* avec espoir; (*I / we hope*) avec un peu de chance

hope·less ['hoʊplɪs] *adj position, prospect* sans espoir, désespéré; (*useless: person*) nul*

ho·ri·zon [hə'raɪzn] horizon *m*

hor·i·zon·tal [hɑːrɪ'zɑːntl] *adj* horizontal

hor·mone ['hɔːrmoʊn] hormone *f*

horn [hɔːrn] *of animal* corne *f*; MOT klaxon *m*

hor·net ['hɔːrnɪt] frelon *m*

horn-rimmed spec·ta·cles [hɔːrn-rɪmd'spektəklz] lunettes *fpl* à monture d'écaille

horn·y ['hɔːrnɪ] *adj* F *sexually* excité; **he's one ~ guy** c'est un chaud lapin F

hor·o·scope ['hɑːrəskoʊp] horoscope *m*

hor·ri·ble ['hɑːrɪbl] *adj* horrible, affreux*

hor·ri·fy ['hɑːrɪfaɪ] *v/t* (*pret & pp* **-ied**) horrifier

hor·ri·fy·ing ['hɑːrɪfaɪɪŋ] *adj* horrifiant

hor·ror ['hɑːrər] horreur *f*

'hor·ror mov·ie film *m* d'horreur

hors d'oeu·vre [ɔːr'dɜːrv] hors d'œuvre *m*

horse [hɔːrs] cheval *m*

'horse·back: on ~ à cheval, sur un cheval; **horse 'chest·nut** marron *m* d'Inde; **'horse·pow·er** cheval-vapeur *m*; **'horse race** course *f* de chevaux; **'horse·shoe** fer *m* à cheval

hor·ti·cul·ture ['hɔːrtɪkʌlʧər] horticulture *f*

hose [hoʊz] *n* tuyau *m*; (*garden ~*) tuyau *m* d'arrosage

hos·pice ['hɑːspɪs] hospice *m*

hos·pi·ta·ble ['hɑːspɪtəbl] *adj* hospitalier*

hos·pi·tal ['hɑːspɪtl] hôpital *m*; **go into the ~** aller à l'hôpital

hos·pi·tal·i·ty [hɑːspɪ'tælətɪ] hospitalité *f*

host [hoʊst] *n at party, reception* hôte *m/f*; *of TV program* présentateur (-trice) *m(f)*

hos·tage ['hɑːstɪdʒ] otage *m*; **be taken ~** être pris en otage

'hos·tage tak·er ['teɪkər] preneur (-euse) *m(f)* d'otages

hos·tel ['hɑːstl] *for students* foyer *m*; (*youth ~*) auberge *f* de jeunesse

hos·tess ['hoʊstɪs] hôtesse *f*

hos·tile ['hɑːstl] *adj* hostile

hos·til·i·ty [hɑː'stɪlətɪ] *of attitude* hostilité *f*; **hostilities** hostilités *fpl*

hot [hɑːt] *adj* chaud; (*spicy*) épicé, fort; F (*good*) bon*; *I'm* **~** j'ai chaud; *it's* **~** *weather* il fait chaud; *food etc* c'est chaud

'hot dog hot-dog *m*

hundredth

ho·tel [hoʊ'tel] hôtel *m*
'hot·plate plaque *f* chauffante
'hot spot *military, political* point *m* chaud
hour ['aʊr] heure *f*
hour·ly ['aʊrlɪ] *adj* de toutes les heures; **at ~ intervals** toutes les heures
house [haʊs] *n* maison *f*; **at your ~** chez vous
'house·boat house-boat *m*, péniche *f* (aménagée); **'house·break·ing** cambriolage *m*; **'house·hold** ménage *m*, famille *f*; **house·hold 'name** nom *m* connu de tous; **'house hus·band** homme *m* au foyer; **house·keep·er** ['haʊskiːpər] femme *f* de ménage; **'house·keep·ing** *activity* ménage *m*; *money* argent *m* du ménage; **House of Rep·re'sent·a·tives** Chambre *f* des Représentants; **house·warm·ing (par·ty)** ['haʊswɔːrmɪŋ] pendaison *f* de crémaillère; **'house·wife** femme *f* au foyer; **'house·work** travaux *mpl* domestiques
hous·ing ['haʊzɪŋ] logement *m*; TECH boîtier *m*
'hous·ing con·di·tions *npl* conditions *fpl* de logement
hov·el ['haːvl] taudis *m*, masure *f*
hov·er ['haːvər] *v/i* planer
'hov·er·craft aéroglisseur *m*
how [haʊ] *adv* comment; **~ are you?** comment allez-vous?, comment ça va?; **~ about a drink?** et si on allait prendre un pot?; **~ much?** combien?; **~ much is it?** *cost* combien ça coûte?; **~ many?** combien?; **~ often?** tous les combien?; **~ funny / sad!** comme c'est drôle / triste!
how·ev·er *adv* cependant; **~ big / rich they are** qu'ils soient (*subj*) grands / riches ou non
howl [haʊl] *v/i* hurler
hub [hʌb] *of wheel* moyeu *m*
'hub·cap enjoliveur *m*
◆ **hud·dle together** ['hʌdl] *v/i* se blottir les uns contre les autres
Hud·son Bay ['hʌdsn] Baie *f* d'Hudson

hue [hjuː] teinte *f*
huff [hʌf]: **be in a ~** être froissé, être fâché
hug [hʌg] *v/t* (*pret & pp* **-ged**) serrer dans ses bras, étreindre
huge [hjuːdʒ] *adj* énorme, immense
hull [hʌl] coque *f*
hul·la·ba·loo [hʌləbə'luː] vacarme *m*, brouhaha *m*
hum [hʌm] **1** *v/t* (*pret & pp* **-med**) *song, tune* fredonner **2** *v/i of person* fredonner; *of machine* ronfler
hu·man ['hjuːmən] **1** *n* être *m* humain **2** *adj* humain
hu·man 'be·ing être *m* humain
hu·mane [hjuː'meɪn] *adj* humain, plein d'humanité
hu·man·i·tar·i·an [hjuːmænɪ'terɪən] *adj* humanitaire
hu·man·i·ty [hjuː'mænətɪ] humanité *f*
hu·man 'race race *f* humaine
hu·man re'sources *npl department* ressources *fpl* humaines
hum·ble ['hʌmbl] *adj attitude, person* humble, modeste; *origins, meal, house* modeste
hum·drum ['hʌmdrʌm] *adj* monotone, banal
hu·mid ['hjuːmɪd] *adj* humide
hu·mid·i·fi·er [hjuː'mɪdɪfaɪr] humidificateur *m*
hu·mid·i·ty [hjuː'mɪdətɪ] humidité *f*
hu·mil·i·ate [hjuː'mɪlɪeɪt] *v/t* humilier
hu·mil·i·at·ing [hjuː'mɪlɪeɪtɪŋ] *adj* humiliant
hu·mil·i·a·tion [hjuːmɪlɪ'eɪʃn] humiliation *f*
hu·mil·i·ty [hjuː'mɪlətɪ] humilité *f*
hu·mor ['hjuːmər] humour *m*; (*mood*) humeur *f*; **sense of ~** sens *m* de l'humour
hu·mor·ous ['hjuːmərəs] *adj movie etc* drôle; *movie etc* comique
hu·mour *Br* → **humor**
hump [hʌmp] **1** *n* bosse *f* **2** *v/t* F (*carry*) trimballer F
hunch [hʌntʃ] (*idea*) intuition *f*, pressentiment *m*
hun·dred ['hʌndrəd] cent *m*
hun·dredth ['hʌndrədθ] centième

H

'hun·dred·weight quintal *m*

hung [hʌŋ] *pret & pp* → **hang**

Hun·gar·i·an [hʌŋ'geriən] **1** *adj* hongrois **2** *n person* Hongrois(e) *m(f)*; *language* hongrois *m*

Hun·ga·ry ['hʌŋgəri] Hongrie *f*

hun·ger ['hʌŋgər] faim *f*

hung·'o·ver *adj*: **be ~** avoir la gueule de bois *F*

hun·gry ['hʌŋgri] *adj* affamé; **I'm ~** j'ai faim

hunk [hʌŋk] *n* gros morceau *m*; *F man* beau mec *F*

hun·ky-do·rey [hʌŋki'dɔːri] *adj F* au poil *F*

hunt [hʌnt] **1** *n* chasse *f* (**for** à); *for new leader, missing child etc* recherche *f* (**for** de) **2** *v/t animal* chasser

♦ hunt for *v/t* chercher

hunt·er ['hʌntər] chasseur(-euse) *m(f)*

hunt·ing ['hʌntɪŋ] chasse *f*

hur·dle ['hɜːrdl] SP haie *f*; (*fig: obstacle*) obstacle *m*

hur·dler ['hɜːrdlər] SP sauteur(-euse) *m(f)* de haies

hur·dles *npl* SP haies *fpl*

hurl [hɜːrl] *v/t* lancer, jeter

hur·ray [hʊ'reɪ] *int* hourra

hur·ri·cane ['hʌrɪkən] ouragan *m*

hur·ried ['hʌrɪd] *adj* précipité; *meal also* pris à la hâte; *piece of work also* fait à la hâte

hur·ry ['hʌri] **1** *n* hâte *f*, précipitation *f*; **be in a ~** être pressé **2** *v/i* (*pret & pp -ied*) se dépêcher, se presser

♦ hurry up **1** *v/i* se dépêcher, se presser; **hurry up!** dépêchez-vous! **2** *v/t* presser

hurt [hɜːrt] **1** *v/i* (*pret & pp hurt*) faire mal; **does it ~?** est-ce que ça vous fait mal? **2** *v/t* (*pret & pp hurt*) *physically* faire mal à, blesser; *emotionally* blesser

hus·band ['hʌzbənd] mari *m*

hush [hʌʃ] *n* silence *m*; **~!** silence!, chut!

♦ hush up *v/t scandal etc* étouffer

husk [hʌsk] *of peanuts etc* écale *f*

hus·ky ['hʌski] *adj voice* rauque

hus·tle ['hʌsl] **1** *n* agitation *f*; **~ and bustle** tourbillon *m* **2** *v/t person* bousculer

hus·tler ['hʌslər] F *conman etc* arnaqueur(-euse) *m(f)* F; *dynamic person* battant(e) *m(f)*; *prostitute* prostitué(e) *m(f)*

hut [hʌt] cabane *f*, hutte *f*

hy·a·cinth ['haɪəsɪnθ] jacinthe *f*

hy·brid ['haɪbrɪd] *n* hybride *m*

hy·drant ['haɪdrənt] prise *f* d'eau; (*fire ~*) bouche *f* d'incendie

hy·drau·lic [haɪ'drɔːlɪk] *adj* hydraulique

hy·dro·e·lec·tric [haɪdroʊɪ'lektrɪk] *adj* hydroélectrique

hy·dro·foil ['haɪdrəfɔɪl] hydrofoil *m*

hy·dro·gen ['haɪdrədʒən] hydrogène *m*

'hy·dro·gen bomb bombe *f* à hydrogène

hy·giene ['haɪdʒiːn] hygiène *f*

hy·gien·ic [haɪ'dʒiːnɪk] *adj* hygiénique

hymn [hɪm] hymne *m*

hype [haɪp] *n* battage *m* publicitaire

hy·per·ac·tive [haɪpər'æktɪv] *adj* hyperactif*

hy·per·mar·ket ['haɪpərmɑːrkɪt] *Br* hypermarché *m*

hy·per·sen·si·tive [haɪpər'sensɪtɪv] *adj* hypersensible

hy·per·ten·sion [haɪpər'tenʃn] hypertension *f*

hy·per·text ['haɪpərtekst] COMPUT hypertexte *m*

hy·phen ['haɪfn] trait *m* d'union

hyp·no·sis [hɪp'noʊsɪs] hypnose *f*

hyp·no·ther·a·py [hɪpnoʊ'θerəpi] hypnothérapie *f*

hyp·no·tize ['hɪpnətaɪz] *v/t* hypnotiser

hy·po·chon·dri·ac [haɪpə'kɑːndriæk] *n* hypocondriaque *m/f*

hy·poc·ri·sy [hɪ'pɑːkrəsi] hypocrisie *f*

hyp·o·crite ['hɪpəkrɪt] hypocrite *m/f*

hyp·o·crit·i·cal [hɪpə'krɪtɪkl] *adj* hypocrite

hy·po·ther·mi·a [haɪpoʊ'θɜːrmiə] hypothermie *f*

hy·poth·e·sis [haɪ'pɑːθəsɪs] (*pl hypotheses* [haɪ'pɑːθəsiːz]) hypothèse *f*

hy·po·thet·i·cal [haɪpə'θetɪkl] *adj* hypothétique

hys·ter·ec·to·my [hɪstəˈrektəmɪ] hystérectomie *f*

hys·te·ri·a [hɪˈstɪrɪə] hystérie *f*

hys·ter·i·cal [hɪˈsterɪkl] *adj person, laugh* hystérique; *F (very funny)* à mourir de rire F

hys·ter·ics [hɪˈsterɪks] *npl* crise *f* de nerfs; *laughter* fou rire *m*

I

I [aɪ] *pron* je; *before vowels* j'; *stressed* moi; *you and ~ are going to talk* toi et moi, nous allons parler

ice [aɪs] glace *f*; *on road* verglas *m*; *break the ~ fig* briser la glace
◆ **ice up** *v/i of engine, wings* se givrer

ice·berg ['aɪsbɜːrg] iceberg *m*; **'ice·box** glacière *f*; **ice-break·er** ['aɪsbreɪkər] *ship* brise-glace *m*; **'ice cream** glace *f*; **'ice cream par·lor,** *Br* **'ice cream par·lour** salon *m* de dégustation de glaces; **'ice cube** glaçon *m*

iced [aɪst] *adj drink* glacé

iced 'cof·fee café *m* frappé

'ice hock·ey hockey *m* sur glace; **'ice rink** patinoire *f*; **'ice skate** patin *m* (à glace); **'ice skat·ing** patinage *m* (sur glace)

i·ci·cle ['aɪsɪkl] stalactite *f*

i·con ['aɪkɑːn] *cultural* symbole *m*; COMPUT icône *f*

i·cy ['aɪsɪ] *adj road, surface* gelé; *welcome* glacial

ID [aɪˈdiː] *abbr (= identity)* identité *f*; *do you have any ~ on you?* est-ce que vous avez des papiers *mpl* d'identité *or* une preuve d'identité sur vous?

i·dea [aɪˈdiːə] idée *f*; *good ~!* bonne idée!; *I have no ~* je n'en ai aucune idée; *it's not a good ~ to …* ce n'est pas une bonne idée de …

i·deal [aɪˈdiːəl] *adj (perfect)* idéal

i·deal·is·tic [aɪdiːəˈlɪstɪk] *adj* idéaliste

i·deal·ly [aɪˈdiːəlɪ] *adv situated etc* idéalement; *~, we would do it like this* dans l'idéal, on le ferait comme ça

i·den·ti·cal [aɪˈdentɪkl] *adj* identique; *~ twins boys* vrais jumeaux *mpl*; *girls* vraies jumelles *fpl*

i·den·ti·fi·ca·tion [aɪdentɪfɪˈkeɪʃn] identification *f*; *(papers etc)* papiers *mpl* d'identité, preuve *f* d'identité

i·den·ti·fy [aɪˈdentɪfaɪ] *v/t (pret & pp -ied)* identifier

i·den·ti·ty [aɪˈdentətɪ] identité *f*; *~ card* carte *f* d'identité

i·de·o·log·i·cal [aɪdɪəˈlɑːdʒɪkl] *adj* idéologique

i·de·ol·o·gy [aɪdɪˈɑːlədʒɪ] idéologie *f*

id·i·om ['ɪdɪəm] *(saying)* idiome *m*

id·i·o·mat·ic [ɪdɪəˈmætɪk] *adj (natural)* idiomatique

id·i·o·syn·cra·sy [ɪdɪəˈsɪŋkrəsɪ] particularité *f*

id·i·ot ['ɪdɪət] idiot(e) *m(e)*

id·i·ot·ic [ɪdɪˈɑːtɪk] *adj* idiot, bête

i·dle ['aɪdl] **1** *adj (not working)* inoccupé; *(lazy)* paresseux*; *threat* oiseux*; *machinery* non utilisé; *in an ~ moment* dans un moment d'oisiveté **2** *v/i of engine* tourner au ralenti
◆ **idle away** *v/t the time etc* passer à ne rien faire

i·dol ['aɪdl] idole *f*

i·dol·ize ['aɪdəlaɪz] *v/t* idolâtrer, adorer (à l'excès)

i·dyl·lic [ɪˈdɪlɪk] *adj* idyllique

if [ɪf] *conj* si; *what ~ he …?* et s'il …?; *~ not* sinon

ig·nite [ɪgˈnaɪt] *v/t* mettre le feu à, enflammer

ig·ni·tion [ɪgˈnɪʃn] *in car* allumage *m*; *~ key* clef *f* de contact

ig·no·rance ['ɪgnərəns] ignorance *f*

ig·no·rant ['ɪgnərənt] *adj* ignorant; (*rude*) grossier*

ig·nore [ɪg'nɔːr] *v/t* ignorer

ill [ɪl] *adj* malade; **fall ~**, **be taken ~** tomber malade; **feel ~ at ease** se sentir mal à l'aise

il·le·gal [ɪ'liːgl] *adj* illégal

il·le·gi·ble [ɪ'ledʒəbl] *adj* illisible

il·le·git·i·mate [ɪlɪ'dʒɪtɪmət] *adj child* illégitime

ill-fat·ed [ɪl'feɪtɪd] *adj* néfaste

il·li·cit [ɪ'lɪsɪt] *adj* illicite

il·lit·e·rate [ɪ'lɪtərət] *adj* illettré

ill-man·nered [ɪl'mænərd] *adj* mal élevé

ill-na·tured [ɪl'neɪtʃərd] *adj* méchant, désagréable

ill·ness ['ɪlnɪs] maladie *f*

il·log·i·cal [ɪ'lɑːdʒɪkl] *adj* illogique

ill-tem·pered [ɪl'tempərd] *adj* de méchant caractère; *temporarily* de mauvaise humeur

ill'treat *v/t* maltraiter

il·lu·mi·nate [ɪ'luːmɪneɪt] *v/t building etc* illuminer

il·lu·mi·nat·ing [ɪ'luːmɪneɪtɪŋ] *adj remarks etc* éclairant

il·lu·sion [ɪ'luːʒn] illusion *f*

il·lus·trate ['ɪləstreɪt] *v/t* illustrer

il·lus·tra·tion [ɪlə'streɪʃn] illustration *f*

il·lus·tra·tor [ɪlə'streɪtər] illustrateur (-trice) *m(f)*

ill 'will rancune *f*

im·age ['ɪmɪdʒ] (*picture*), *of politician, company* image *f*, (*exact likeness*) portrait *m*

'im·age-con·scious *adj* soucieux* de son image

i·ma·gi·na·ble [ɪ'mædʒɪnəbl] *adj* imaginable; **the smallest size ~** la plus petite taille qu'on puisse imaginer

i·ma·gi·na·ry [ɪ'mædʒɪnəri] *adj* imaginaire

i·ma·gi·na·tion [ɪmædʒɪ'neɪʃn] imagination *f*; **it's all in your ~** tout est dans votre tête

i·ma·gi·na·tive [ɪ'mædʒɪnətɪv] *adj* imaginatif*

i·ma·gine [ɪ'mædʒɪn] *v/t* imaginer; **I can just ~ it** je peux l'imaginer; **you're imagining things** tu te fais

des idées

im·be·cile ['ɪmbəsiːl] imbécile *m/f*

IMF [aɪem'ef] *abbr* (= **International Monetary Fund**) F.M.I. *m* (= Fonds *m* Monétaire International)

im·i·tate ['ɪmɪteɪt] *v/t* imiter

im·i·ta·tion [ɪmɪ'teɪʃn] imitation *f*

im·mac·u·late [ɪ'mækjʊlət] *adj* impeccable; (*spotless*) immaculé

im·ma·te·ri·al [ɪmə'tɪriəl] *adj* (*not relevant*) peu important

im·ma·ture [ɪmə'tʊr] *adj* immature

im·me·di·ate [ɪ'miːdɪət] *adj* immédiat

im·me·di·ate·ly [ɪ'miːdɪətli] *adv* immédiatement; **~ after the bank** juste après la banque

im·mense [ɪ'mens] *adj* immense

im·merse [ɪ'mɜːrs] *v/t* immerger, plonger; **~ o.s. in** se plonger dans

im·mi·grant ['ɪmɪgrənt] *n* immigrant(e) *m(f)*, immigré(e) *m(f)*

im·mi·grate ['ɪmɪgreɪt] *v/i* immigrer

im·mi·gra·tion [ɪmɪ'greɪʃn] immigration *f*; **Immigration** *government department* l'immigration *f*

im·mi·nent ['ɪmɪnənt] *adj* imminent

im·mo·bi·lize [ɪ'moʊbɪlaɪz] *v/t factory, person* immobiliser; *car* immobiliser

im·mo·bi·liz·er [ɪ'moʊbɪlaɪzər] *on car* système *m* antidémarrage

im·mod·e·rate [ɪ'mɑːdərət] *adj* immodéré

im·mor·al [ɪ'mɔːrəl] *adj* immoral

im·mor·al·i·ty [ɪmɔːˈrælɪti] immoralité *f*

im·mor·tal [ɪ'mɔːrtl] *adj* immortel*

im·mor·tal·i·ty [ɪmɔːr'tælɪti] immortalité *f*

im·mune [ɪ'mjuːn] *adj to illness, infection* immunisé (**to** contre); *from ruling* exempt (**from** de)

im'mune sys·tem MED système *m* immunitaire

im·mu·ni·ty [ɪ'mjuːnəti] *to infection* immunité *f*; *from ruling* exemption *f*; **diplomatic ~** immunité *f* diplomatique

im·pact ['ɪmpækt] *n* impact *m*; **on ~** au moment de l'impact

♦ **impact on** *v/t* avoir un impact sur, affecter

im·pair [ɪmˈper] v/t affaiblir, abîmer

im·paired [ɪmˈperd] adj affaibli, abîmé

im·par·tial [ɪmˈpɑːrʃl] adj impartial

im·pass·a·ble [ɪmˈpæsəbl] adj road impraticable

im·passe [ˈɪmpæs] in negotations etc impasse f

im·pas·sioned [ɪmˈpæʃnd] adj speech, plea passionné

im·pas·sive [ɪmˈpæsɪv] adj impassible

im·pa·tience [ɪmˈpeɪʃəns] impatience f

im·pa·tient [ɪmˈpeɪʃənt] adj impatient

im·pa·tient·ly [ɪmˈpeɪʃəntlɪ] adv impatiemment

im·peach [ɪmˈpiːtʃ] v/t President mettre en accusation

im·pec·ca·ble [ɪmˈpekəbl] adj impeccable

im·pec·ca·bly [ɪmˈpekəblɪ] adv impeccablement

im·pede [ɪmˈpiːd] v/t gêner, empêcher

im·ped·i·ment [ɪmˈpedɪmənt] obstacle obstacle m; **speech~** défaut m d'élocution

im·pend·ing [ɪmˈpendɪŋ] adj imminent

im·pen·e·tra·ble [ɪmˈpenɪtrəbl] adj impénétrable

im·per·a·tive [ɪmˈperətɪv] 1 adj impératif*; **it is ~ that ...** il est impératif que ... (+subj) 2 n GRAM impératif m

im·per·cep·ti·ble [ɪmpɜːrˈseptɪbl] adj imperceptible

im·per·fect [ɪmˈpɜːrfekt] 1 adj imparfait 2 n GRAM imparfait m

im·pe·ri·al [ɪmˈpɪrɪəl] adj impérial

im·per·son·al [ɪmˈpɜːrsənl] adj impersonnel*

im·per·so·nate [ɪmˈpɜːrsəneɪt] v/t as a joke imiter; illegally se faire passer pour

im·per·son·a·tor [ɪmˈpɜːrsəneɪtər] imitateur(-trice) m(f); **female ~** travesti m

im·per·ti·nence [ɪmˈpɜːrtɪnəns] impertinence f

im·per·ti·nent [ɪmˈpɜːrtɪnənt] adj impertinent

im·per·tur·ba·ble [ɪmpərˈtɜːrbəbl] adj imperturbable

im·per·vi·ous [ɪmˈpɜːrvɪəs] adj: **~ to** insensible à

im·pe·tu·ous [ɪmˈpetʃʊəs] adj impétueux*

im·pe·tus [ˈɪmpətəs] of campaign etc force f, élan m

im·ple·ment [ˈɪmplɪmənt] 1 n instrument m, outil m 2 v/t [ˈɪmplɪment] measures etc appliquer

im·pli·cate [ˈɪmplɪkeɪt] v/t impliquer (**in** dans)

im·pli·ca·tion [ɪmplɪˈkeɪʃn] implication f

im·pli·cit [ɪmˈplɪsɪt] adj implicite; trust absolu

im·plore [ɪmˈplɔːr] v/t implorer (s.o. to do sth qn de faire qch)

im·ply [ɪmˈplaɪ] v/t (pret & pp **-ied**) impliquer; (suggest) suggérer

im·po·lite [ɪmpəˈlaɪt] adj impoli

im·port [ˈɪmpɔːrt] 1 n importation f 2 v/t importer

im·por·tance [ɪmˈpɔːrtəns] importance f

im·por·tant [ɪmˈpɔːrtənt] adj important

im·por·ter [ɪmˈpɔːrtər] importateur (-trice) m(f)

im·pose [ɪmˈpoʊz] v/t tax imposer; **~ o.s. on s.o.** s'imposer à qn

im·pos·ing [ɪmˈpoʊzɪŋ] adj imposant

im·pos·si·bil·i·ty [ɪmpɑːsɪˈbɪlɪtɪ] impossibilité f

im·pos·si·ble [ɪmˈpɑːsɪbəl] adj impossible

im·pos·tor [ɪmˈpɑːstər] imposteur m

im·po·tence [ˈɪmpətəns] impuissance f

im·po·tent [ˈɪmpətənt] adj impuissant

im·pov·e·rished [ɪmˈpɑːvərɪʃt] adj appauvri

im·prac·ti·cal [ɪmˈpræktɪkəl] adj person dénué de sens pratique; suggestion peu réaliste

im·press [ɪmˈpres] v/t impressionner; **I'm not ~ed** ça ne m'impressionne pas

im·pres·sion [ɪmˈpreʃn] impression f; (impersonation) imitation f; **make a good / bad ~ on s.o.** faire une bonne / mauvaise impression sur qn; **I get the ~ that …** j'ai l'impression que …

im·pres·sion·a·ble [ɪmˈpreʃənəbl] *adj* influençable

im·pres·sive [ɪmˈpresɪv] *adj* impressionnant

im·print [ˈɪmprɪnt] *n of credit card* empreinte *f*

im·pris·on [ɪmˈprɪzn] *v/t* emprisonner

im·pris·on·ment [ɪmˈprɪznmənt] emprisonnement *m*

im·prob·a·ble [ɪmˈprɑːbəbl] *adj* improbable

im·prop·er [ɪmˈprɑːpər] *adj behavior* indécent, déplacé; *use etc* incorrecte

im·prove [ɪmˈpruːv] **1** *v/t* améliorer **2** *v/i* s'améliorer

im·prove·ment [ɪmˈpruːvmənt] amélioration *f*

im·pro·vize [ˈɪmprəvaɪz] *v/i* improviser

im·pu·dent [ˈɪmpjʊdənt] *adj* impudent

im·pulse [ˈɪmpʌls] impulsion *f*; **do sth on (an) ~** faire qch sous le coup d'une impulsion *or* sur un coup de tête

ˈim·pulse buy achat *m* impulsif

im·pul·sive [ɪmˈpʌlsɪv] *adj* impulsif*

im·pu·ni·ty [ɪmˈpjuːnətɪ] impunité *f*; **with ~** impunément

im·pure [ɪmˈpjʊr] *adj* impur

in [ɪn] **1** *prep* dans; **~ Washington / Rouen** à Washington / Rouen; **~ the street** dans la rue; **~ the box** dans la boîte; **wounded ~ the leg / arm** blessé à la jambe / au bras ◊ *with time* en; **~ 1999** en 1999; **~ the morning** le matin; **~ the mornings** le matin; **~ the summer** l'été; **~ August** en août, au mois d'août; **~ two hours** *from now* dans deux heures; *over period of* en deux heures; **I haven't been to France ~ years** il y a des années que je n'ai pas été en France ◊ *manner:* **~ English / French** en anglais / français; **~ a loud voice** d'une voix forte; **~ his style** à sa manière; **~ yellow** en jaune ◊ : **~ crossing the road** (*while*) en traversant la route; **~ agreeing to this** (*by virtue of*) en acceptant ceci ◊ : **~ his novel** dans son roman; **~ Faulkner** chez Faulkner ◊ : **~ three ~ all** trois en tout (*et pour tout*); **one ~ ten** un sur dix **2** *adv* (*at home, in the building etc*) là; (*arrived: train*) arrivé; (*in its position*) dedans; **~ here** ici; **when the diskette is ~** quand la disquette est à l'intérieur **3** *adj* (*fashionable, popular*) à la mode

in·a·bil·i·ty [ɪnəˈbɪlɪtɪ] incapacité *f*

in·ac·ces·si·ble [ɪnəkˈsesɪbl] *adj* inaccessible

in·ac·cu·rate [ɪnˈækjʊrət] *adj* inexact, incorrect

in·ac·tive [ɪnˈæktɪv] *adj* inactif*; *volcano* qui n'est pas en activité

in·ad·e·quate [ɪnˈædɪkwət] *adj* insuffisant, inadéquat

in·ad·vis·a·ble [ɪnədˈvaɪzəbl] *adj* peu recommandé

in·an·i·mate [ɪnˈænɪmət] *adj* inanimé

in·ap·pro·pri·ate [ɪnəˈproʊprɪət] *adj* peu approprié

in·ar·tic·u·late [ɪnɑːrˈtɪkjʊlət] *adj person* qui s'exprime mal

in·au·di·ble [ɪnˈɔːdəbl] *adj* inaudible

in·au·gu·ral [ɪˈnɔːgjʊrəl] *adj speech* inaugural

in·au·gu·rate [ɪˈnɔːgjʊreɪt] *v/t* inaugurer

in·born [ˈɪnbɔːrn] *adj* inné

in·bred [ˈɪnbred] *adj* inné

in·breed·ing [ˈɪnbriːdɪŋ] *unions fpl* consanguines

inc. *abbr* (= **incorporated**) S.A. *f* (= Société *f* Anonyme)

in·cal·cu·la·ble [ɪnˈkælkjʊləbl] *adj damage* incalculable

in·ca·pa·ble [ɪnˈkeɪpəbl] *adj* incapable; **be ~ of doing sth** être incapable de faire qch

in·cen·di·a·ry de·vice [ɪnˈsendərɪ] bombe *f* incendiaire

in·cense¹ [ˈɪnsens] *n* encens *m*

in·cense² [ɪnˈsens] *v/t* rendre furieux*

in·cen·tive [ɪnˈsentɪv] encouragement *m*, stimulation *f*

in·ces·sant [ɪnˈsesnt] *adj* incessant

in·ces·sant·ly [ɪnˈsesntlɪ] *adv* sans arrêt

in-cest ['ınsest] inceste *m*

inch [ıntʃ] pouce *m*

in-ci-dent ['ınsıdənt] incident *m*

in-ci-den-tal [ınsı'dentl] *adj* fortuit; **~ expenses** frais *mpl* accessoires

in-ci-den-tal-ly [ınsı'dentlı] *adv* soit dit en passant

in-cin-e-ra-tor [ın'sınəreıtər] incinérateur *m*

in-ci-sion [ın'sıʒn] incision *f*

in-ci-sive [ın'saısıv] *adj mind, analysis* incisif*

in-cite [ın'saıt] *v/t* inciter; **~ s.o. to do sth** inciter qn à faire qch

in-clem-ent [ın'klemənt] *adj weather* inclément

in-cli-na-tion [ınklı'neıʃn] *(liking)* penchant *m*; *(tendency)* tendance *f*

in-cline [ın'klaın] *v/t*: **be ~d to do sth** avoir tendance à faire qch

in-close, in-clos-ure → enclose, enclosure

in-clude [ın'kluːd] *v/t* inclure, comprendre

in-clud-ing [ın'kluːdıŋ] *prep* y compris; **~ service** service compris

in-clu-sive [ın'kluːsıv] **1** *adj price* tout compris **2** *prep*: **~ of** en incluant **3** *adv* tout compris; **from Monday to Thursday ~** du lundi au jeudi inclus

in-co-her-ent [ınkou'hırənt] *adj* incohérent

in-come ['ınkəm] revenu *m*

'in-come tax impôt *m* sur le revenu

in-com-ing ['ınkʌmıŋ] *adj tide* montant; *flight, mail* qui arrive; *phonecall* de l'extérieur; *president* nouveau*

in-com-pa-ra-ble [ın'kɑːmpərəbl] *adj* incomparable

in-com-pat-i-bil-i-ty [ınkəmpætɪ'bɪlɪtɪ] incompatibilité *f*

in-com-pat-i-ble [ınkəm'pætɪbl] *adj* incompatible

in-com-pe-tence [ın'kɑːmpɪtəns] incompétence *f*

in-com-pe-tent [ın'kɑːmpɪtənt] *adj* incompétent

in-com-plete [ınkəm'pliːt] *adj* incomplet*

in-com-pre-hen-si-ble [ınkɑːmprı-

'hensɪbl] *adj* incompréhensible

in-con-cei-va-ble [ınkən'siːvəbl] *adj* inconcevable

in-con-clu-sive [ınkən'kluːsıv] *adj* peu concluant

in-con-gru-ous [ın'kɑːngruəs] *adj* incongru

in-con-sid-er-ate [ınkən'sıdərət] *adj action* inconsidéré; **be ~ of** *person* manquer d'égards

in-con-sis-tent [ınkən'sıstənt] *adj* incohérent; *person* inconstant; **~ with** incompatible avec

in-con-so-la-ble [ınkən'soʊləbl] *adj* inconsolable

in-con-spic-u-ous [ınkən'spıkjuəs] *adj* discret*

in-con-ve-ni-ence [ınkən'viːnıəns] *n* inconvénient *m*

in-con-ve-ni-ent [ınkən'viːnıənt] *adj time* inopportun; *place, arrangement* peu commode

in-cor-po-rate [ın'kɔːrpəreıt] *v/t* incorporer

in-cor-rect [ınkə'rekt] *adj* incorrect

in-cor-rect-ly [ınkə'rektlı] *adv* incorrectement, mal

in-cor-ri-gi-ble [ın'kɑːrıdʒəbl] *adj* incorrigible

in-crease 1 *v/t & v/i* [ın'kriːs] augmenter **2** *n* ['ınkriːs] augmentation *f*

in-creas-ing [ın'kriːsıŋ] *adj* croissant

in-creas-ing-ly [ın'kriːsıŋlı] *adv* de plus en plus

in-cred-i-ble [ın'kredıbl] *adj (amazing, very good)* incroyable

in-crim-i-nate [ın'krımıneıt] *v/t* incriminer; **~ o.s.** s'incriminer

in-cu-ba-tor ['ıŋkjubeıtər] *for chicks* incubateur *m*; *for babies* couveuse *f*

in-cur [ın'kɜːr] *v/t (pret & pp -red) costs* encourir; *debts* contracter; *s.o.'s anger* s'attirer

in-cu-ra-ble [ın'kjʊrəbl] *adj also fig* incurable

in-debt-ed [ın'detıd] *adj*: **be ~ to s.o.** être redevable à qn **(for sth** de qch)

in-de-cent [ın'diːsnt] *adj* indécent

in-de-ci-sive [ındı'saısıv] *adj argument* peu concluant; *person* indécis

in-de-ci-sive-ness [ındı'saısıvnıs] indécision *f*

in·deed [ɪn'diːd] *adv* (*in fact*) vraiment; (*yes, agreeing*) en effet; **very much ~** beaucoup

in·de·fi·na·ble [ɪndɪ'faɪnəbl] *adj* indéfinissable

in·def·i·nite [ɪn'defɪnɪt] *adj* indéfini; **~ article** GRAM article *m* indéfini

in·def·i·nite·ly [ɪn'defɪnɪtlɪ] *adv* indéfiniment

in·del·i·cate [ɪn'delɪkət] *adj* indélicat

in·dent ['ɪndent] **1** *n in text* alinéa *m* **2** *v/t* [ɪn'dent] *line* renfoncer

in·de·pen·dence [ɪndɪ'pendəns] indépendance *f*

In·de·pen·dence Day fête *f* de l'Indépendance

in·de·pen·dent [ɪndɪ'pendənt] *adj* indépendant

in·de·pen·dent·ly [ɪndɪ'pendəntlɪ] *adv deal with* indépendamment; **~ of** indépendamment de

in·de·scri·ba·ble [ɪndɪ'skraɪbəbl] *adj* indescriptible; (*very bad*) inqualifiable

in·de·scri·ba·bly [ɪndɪ'skraɪbəblɪ] *adv:* **~ beautiful** d'une beauté indescriptible; **~ bad** *book, movie* inqualifiable

in·de·struc·ti·ble [ɪndɪ'strʌktəbl] *adj* indestructible

in·de·ter·mi·nate [ɪndɪ'tɜːrmɪnət] *adj* indéterminé

in·dex ['ɪndeks] *for book* index *m*

'in·dex card fiche *f*; **'in·dex fin·ger** index *m*

In·di·a ['ɪndɪə] Inde *f*

In·di·an ['ɪndɪən] **1** *adj* indien **2** *n also American* Indien(ne) *m(f)*

In·di·an 'sum·mer été *m* indien

in·di·cate ['ɪndɪkeɪt] **1** *v/t* indiquer **2** *v/i Br. when driving* mettre ses clignotants

in·di·ca·tion [ɪndɪ'keɪʃn] indication *f*, signe *m*

in·di·ca·tor ['ɪndɪkeɪtər] *Br. on car* clignotant *m*

in·dict [ɪn'daɪt] *v/t* accuser

in·dif·fer·ence [ɪn'dɪfrəns] indifférence *f*

in·dif·fer·ent [ɪn'dɪfrənt] *adj* indifférent; (*mediocre*) médiocre

in·di·ges·ti·ble [ɪndɪ'dʒestɪbl] *adj* indigeste

in·di·ges·tion [ɪndɪ'dʒestʃn] indigestion *f*

in·dig·nant [ɪn'dɪgnənt] *adj* indigné

in·dig·na·tion [ɪndɪg'neɪʃn] indignation *f*

in·di·rect [ɪndɪ'rekt] *adj* indirect

in·di·rect·ly [ɪndɪ'rektlɪ] *adv* indirectement

in·dis·creet [ɪndɪ'skriːt] *adj* indiscret*

in·dis·cre·tion [ɪndɪ'skreʃn] *act* indiscrétion *f*, faux pas *m* F

in·dis·crim·i·nate [ɪndɪ'skrɪmɪnət] *adj* aveugle; *accusations* à tort et à travers

in·dis·pen·sa·ble [ɪndɪ'spensəbl] *adj* indispensable

in·dis·posed [ɪndɪ'spouzd] *adj* (*not well*) indisposé

in·dis·pu·ta·ble [ɪndɪ'spjuːtəbl] *adj* incontestable

in·dis·pu·ta·bly [ɪndɪ'spjuːtəblɪ] *adv* incontestablement

in·dis·tinct [ɪndɪ'stɪŋkt] *adj* indistinct

in·dis·tin·guish·a·ble [ɪndɪ'stɪŋgwɪʃəbl] *adj* indifférenciable

in·di·vid·u·al [ɪndɪ'vɪdʒʊəl] **1** *n* individu *m* **2** *adj* (*separate*) particulier*; (*personal*) individuel*

in·di·vid·u·a·list·ic [ɪndɪ'vɪdʒʊəlɪstɪk] *adj* individualiste

in·di·vid·u·al·i·ty [ɪndɪvɪdʒʊ'ælɪtɪ] individualité *f*

in·di·vid·u·al·ly [ɪndɪ'vɪdʒʊəlɪ] *adv* individuellement

in·di·vis·i·ble [ɪndɪ'vɪzɪbl] *adj* indivisible

in·doc·tri·nate [ɪn'dɑːktrɪneɪt] *v/t* endoctriner

in·do·lence ['ɪndələns] indolence *f*

in·do·lent ['ɪndələnt] *adj* indolent

In·do·ne·sia [ɪndə'niːʒə] Indonésie *f*

In·do·ne·sian [ɪndə'niːʒən] **1** *adj* indonésien* **2** *n person* Indonésien(ne) *m(f)*

in·door ['ɪndɔːr] *adj activities, games* d'intérieur; *sport* en salle; *arena* couvert

in·doors [ɪn'dɔːrz] *adv* à l'intérieur; (*at home*) à la maison

in·dorse → **endorse**

in·dulge [ɪn'dʌldʒ] **1** v/t tastes satisfaire; **~ o.s.** se faire plaisir **2** v/i: **~ in sth** se permettre qch

in·dul·gence [ɪn'dʌldʒəns] of tastes, appetite etc satisfaction f; (laxity) indulgence f

in·dul·gent [ɪn'dʌldʒənt] adj (not strict enough) indulgent

in·dus·tri·al [ɪn'dʌstrɪəl] adj industriel*; **~ action** action f revendicative

in·dus·tri·al dis·pute conflit m social

in·dus·tri·al·ist [ɪn'dʌstrɪəlɪst] industriel(le) m(f)

in·dus·tri·al·ize [ɪn'dʌstrɪəlaɪz] **1** v/t industrialiser **2** v/i s'industrialiser

in·dus·tri·al 'waste déchets mpl industriels

in·dus·tri·ous [ɪn'dʌstrɪəs] adj travailleur*

in·dus·try ['ɪndəstrɪ] industrie f

in·ef·fec·tive [ɪnɪ'fektɪv] adj inefficace

in·ef·fec·tu·al [ɪnɪ'fektʃuəl] adj person inefficace

in·ef·fi·cient [ɪnɪ'fɪʃənt] adj inefficace

in·el·i·gi·ble [ɪn'elɪdʒɪbl] adj inéligible

in·ept [ɪ'nept] adj inepte

in·e·qual·i·ty [ɪnɪ'kwɑ:lɪtɪ] inégalité f

in·es·ca·pa·ble [ɪnɪ'skeɪpəbl] adj inévitable

in·es·ti·ma·ble [ɪn'estɪməbl] adj inestimable

in·ev·i·ta·ble [ɪn'evɪtəbl] adj inévitable

in·ev·i·ta·bly [ɪn'evɪtəblɪ] adv inévitablement

in·ex·cu·sa·ble [ɪnɪk'skju:zəbl] adj inexcusable

in·ex·haus·ti·ble [ɪnɪg'zɔ:stəbl] adj supply inépuisable

in·ex·pen·sive [ɪnɪk'spensɪv] adj bon marché, pas cher*

in·ex·pe·ri·enced [ɪnɪk'spɪrɪənst] adj inexpérimenté

in·ex·plic·a·ble [ɪnɪk'splɪkəbl] adj inexplicable

in·ex·pres·si·ble [ɪnɪk'spresɪbl] adj joy inexprimable

in·fal·li·ble [ɪn'fælɪbl] adj infaillible

in·fa·mous ['ɪnfəməs] adj infâme

in·fan·cy ['ɪnfənsɪ] of person petite enfance f; of state, institution débuts mpl

in·fant ['ɪnfənt] petit(e) enfant m(f)

in·fan·tile ['ɪnfəntaɪl] adj pej infantile

in·fant mor·tal·i·ty rate taux m de mortalité infantile

in·fan·try ['ɪnfəntrɪ] infanterie f

'in·fan·try sol·dier soldat m d'infanterie, fantassin m

'in·fant school Br école f maternelle

in·fat·u·at·ed [ɪn'fætʃueɪtɪd] adj: **be ~ with s.o.** être enticher de qn

in·fect [ɪn'fekt] v/t contaminer; **become ~ed** of person être contaminé; of wound s'infecter

in·fec·tion [ɪn'fekʃn] contamination f; (disease), of wound infection f

in·fec·tious [ɪn'fekʃəs] adj disease infectieux*; fig: laughter contagieux*

in·fer [ɪn'fɜ:r] v/t (pret & pp **-red**): **~ X from Y** déduire X de Y

in·fe·ri·or [ɪn'fɪrɪər] adj inférieur

in·fe·ri·or·i·ty [ɪnfɪrɪ'ɑ:rətɪ] in quality infériorité f

in·fe·ri·or·i·ty com·plex complexe m d'infériorité

in·fer·tile [ɪn'fɜ:rtl] adj stérile

in·fer·til·i·ty [ɪnfər'tɪlɪtɪ] stérilité f

in·fi·del·i·ty [ɪnfɪ'delɪtɪ] infidélité f

in·fil·trate ['ɪnfɪltreɪt] v/t infiltrer

in·fi·nite ['ɪnfɪnət] adj infini

in·fin·i·tive [ɪn'fɪnətɪv] infinitif m

in·fin·i·ty [ɪn'fɪnətɪ] infinité f; MATH infini m

in·firm [ɪn'fɜ:rm] adj infirme

in·fir·ma·ry [ɪn'fɜ:rmərɪ] infirmerie f

in·fir·mi·ty [ɪn'fɜ:rmətɪ] infirmité f

in·flame [ɪn'fleɪm] v/t enflammer

in·flam·ma·ble [ɪn'flæməbl] adj inflammable

in·flam·ma·tion [ɪnflə'meɪʃn] MED inflammation f

in·flat·a·ble [ɪn'fleɪtəbl] adj dinghy gonflable

in·flate [ɪn'fleɪt] v/t tire, dinghy gonfler

in·fla·tion [ɪn'fleɪʃn] inflation f

in·fla·tion·a·ry [ɪn'fleɪʃənərɪ] adj inflationniste

in·flec·tion [ɪn'flekʃn] of voice inflexion f

in·flex·i·ble [ɪn'fleksɪbl] adj attitude, person inflexible

in·flict [ɪn'flɪkt] v/t: **~ sth on s.o.** infliger qch à qn

'in-flight adj en vol; **~ entertainment** divertissements mpl en vol

in-flu-ence ['ɪnfluəns] **1** n influence f; **be a good / bad ~ on s.o.** avoir une bonne / mauvaise influence sur qn **2** v/t influencer

in-flu-en-tial [ɪnflu'enʃl] adj influent

in-flu-en-za [ɪnflu'enzə] grippe f

in-form [ɪn'fɔ:rm] **1** v/t: **~ s.o. about sth** informer qn de qch; **please keep me ~ed** veuillez me tenir informé **2** v/i: **~ on s.o.** dénoncer qn

in-for-mal [ɪn'fɔ:rml] adj meeting, agreement non-officiel*; form of address familier*; conversation, dress simple

in-for-mal-i-ty [ɪnfɔ:r'mælɪtɪ] of meeting, agreement caractère m non officiel; of form of address familiarité f; of conversation, dress simplicité f

in-form-ant [ɪn'fɔ:rmənt] informateur(-trice) m(f)

in-for-ma-tion [ɪnfər'meɪʃn] renseignements mpl

in-for-ma-tion 'sci-ence informatique f; **in-for-ma-tion 'sci-en-tist** informaticien(ne) m(f); **in-for-ma-tion tech'nol-o-gy** informatique f

in-form-a-tive [ɪn'fɔ:rmətɪv] adj instructif*

in-form-er [ɪn'fɔ:rmər] dénonciateur (-trice) m(f)

in-fra-red [ɪnfrə'red] adj infrarouge

in-fra-struc-ture ['ɪnfrəstrʌktʃər] infrastructure f

in-fre-quent [ɪn'fri:kwənt] adj rare

in-fu-ri-ate [ɪn'fjurɪeɪt] v/t rendre furieux*

in-fu-ri-at-ing [ɪn'fjurɪeɪtɪŋ] adj exaspérant

in-fuse [ɪn'fju:z] v/i of tea infuser

in-fu-sion [ɪn'fju:ʒn] (herb tea) infusion f

in-ge-ni-ous [ɪn'dʒi:nɪəs] adj ingénieux*

in-ge-nu-i-ty [ɪndʒɪ'nu:ətɪ] ingéniosité f

in-got ['ɪŋgət] lingot m

in-gra-ti-ate [ɪn'greɪʃɪeɪt] v/t: **~ o.s. with s.o.** s'insinuer dans les bonnes grâces de qn

in-grat-i-tude [ɪn'grætɪtu:d] ingratitude f

in-gre-di-ent [ɪn'gri:dɪənt] for cooking ingrédient m; **~s** fig: for success recette f (for pour)

in-hab-it [ɪn'hæbɪt] v/t habiter

in-hab-it-a-ble [ɪn'hæbɪtəbl] adj habitable

in-hab-i-tant [ɪn'hæbɪtənt] habitant(e) m(f)

in-hale [ɪn'heɪl] **1** v/t inhaler, respirer **2** v/i when smoking avaler la fumée

in-ha-ler [ɪn'heɪlər] inhalateur m

in-her-it [ɪn'herɪt] v/t hériter

in-her-i-tance [ɪn'herɪtəns] héritage m

in-hib-it [ɪn'hɪbɪt] v/t conversation etc empêcher; growth, entraver

in-hib-it-ed [ɪn'hɪbɪtɪd] adj inhibé

in-hi-bi-tion [ɪnhɪ'bɪʃn] inhibition f

in-hos-pi-ta-ble [ɪnhɑː'spɪtəbl] adj inhospitalier*

'in-house adj & adv sur place

in-hu-man [ɪn'hju:mən] adj inhumain

i-ni-tial [ɪ'nɪʃl] **1** adj initial **2** n initiale f **3** v/t (write initials on) parapher

i-ni-tial-ly [ɪ'nɪʃlɪ] adv au début

i-ni-ti-ate [ɪ'nɪʃɪeɪt] v/t procedure lancer; person initier

i-ni-ti-a-tion [ɪnɪʃɪ'eɪʃn] lancement m; of person initiation f

i-ni-ti-a-tive [ɪ'nɪʃətɪv] initiative f; **do sth on one's own ~** faire qch de sa propre initiative

in-ject [ɪn'dʒekt] v/t injecter

in-jec-tion [ɪn'dʒekʃn] injection f

'in-joke: it's an ~ c'est une plaisanterie entre nous / eux

in-jure [ɪn'dʒʊr] v/t blesser

in-jured ['ɪndʒərd] **1** adj leg, feelings blessé **2** npl: **the ~** les blessés mpl

in-ju-ry ['ɪndʒərɪ] blessure f

'in-ju-ry time SP arrêt(s) m(pl) de jeu

in-jus-tice [ɪn'dʒʌstɪs] injustice f

ink [ɪŋk] encre f

'ink-jet printer imprimante f à jet d'encre

in-land ['ɪnlənd] adj intérieur

in-laws ['ɪnlɔːz] npl belle-famille f

in-lay ['ɪnleɪ] n incrustation f

in-let ['ɪnlet] of sea bras m de mer; in machine arrivée f

in·mate ['ɪnmeɪt] *of prison* détenu(e) *m(f)*; *of mental hospital* interné(e) *m(f)*

inn [ɪn] auberge *f*

in·nate [ɪ'neɪt] *adj* inné

in·ner ['ɪnər] *adj courtyard* intérieur; *thoughts* intime; *ear* interne

in·ner 'cit·y quartiers défavorisés situés au milieu d'une grande ville

'in·ner·most *adj* le plus profond

'in·ner tube chambre *f* à air

in·no·cence ['ɪnəsəns] innocence *f*

in·no·cent ['ɪnəsənt] *adj* innocent

in·no·cu·ous [ɪ'nɑːkjʊəs] *adj* inoffensif*

in·no·va·tion [ɪnə'veɪʃn] innovation *f*

in·no·va·tive ['ɪnəvətɪv] *adj* innovant

in·no·va·tor ['ɪnəveɪtər] innovateur (-trice) *m(f)*

in·nu·me·ra·ble [ɪ'nuːmərəbl] *adj* innombrable

i·noc·u·late [ɪ'nɑːkjʊleɪt] *v/t* inoculer

i·noc·u·la·tion [ɪnɑːkjʊ'leɪʃn] inoculation *f*

in·of·fen·sive [ɪnə'fensɪv] *adj* inoffensif*

in·or·gan·ic [ɪnɔːr'ɡænɪk] *adj* inorganique

'in·pa·tient patient(e) hospitalisé(e) *m(f)*

in·put ['ɪnpʊt] **1** *n into project etc* apport *m*, contribution *f*; COMPUT entrée *f* **2** *v/t* (*pret & pp* **-ted** *or* **input**) *into project* apporter; COMPUT entrer

in·quest ['ɪnkwest] enquête *f* (**on** sur)

in·quire [ɪn'kwaɪr] *v/i* se renseigner; ~ **into** *causes of disease etc* faire des recherches sur; *cause of an accident etc* enquêter sur

in·quir·y [ɪn'kwaɪrɪ] demande *f* de renseignements; **government** ~ enquête *f* officielle

in·quis·i·tive [ɪn'kwɪzətɪv] *adj* curieux*

in·sane [ɪn'seɪn] *adj* fou*

in·san·i·ta·ry [ɪn'sænɪterɪ] *adj* insalubre

in·san·i·ty [ɪn'sænɪtɪ] folie *f*

in·sa·ti·a·ble [ɪn'seɪʃəbl] *adj* insatiable

in·scrip·tion [ɪn'skrɪpʃn] inscription *f*

in·scru·ta·ble [ɪn'skruːtəbl] *adj* impénétrable

in·sect ['ɪnsekt] insecte *m*

in·sec·ti·cide [ɪn'sektɪsaɪd] insecticide *m*

in·se·cure [ɪnsɪ'kjʊr] *adj*: **feel / be** ~ *not safe* ne pas se sentir en sécurité; *not sure of self* manquer d'assurance

in·se·cu·ri·ty [ɪnsɪ'kjʊrɪtɪ] *psychological* manque *m* d'assurance

in·sen·si·tive [ɪn'sensɪtɪv] *adj* insensible (**to** à)

in·sen·si·tiv·i·ty [ɪnsensɪ'tɪvɪtɪ] insensibilité *f*

in·sep·a·ra·ble [ɪn'seprəbl] *adj* inséparable

in·sert 1 ['ɪnsɜːrt] *n in magazine etc* encart *m* **2** [ɪn'sɜːrt] *v/t*: ~ **sth into sth** insérer qch dans qch

in·ser·tion [ɪn'sɜːrʃn] insertion *f*

in·side [ɪn'saɪd] **1** *n of house, box* intérieur *m*; **somebody on the** ~ quelqu'un qui connaît la maison; ~ **out** à l'envers; **turn sth** ~ **out** retourner qch; **know sth** ~ **out** connaître qch à fond **2** *prep* à l'intérieur de; **they went** ~ **the house** ils sont entrés dans la maison; ~ **of 2 hours** en moins de 2 heures **3** *adv* à l'intérieur; **we went** ~ nous sommes entrés (à l'intérieur); **we looked** ~ nous avons regardé à l'intérieur **4** *adj*: ~ **information** informations *fpl* internes; ~ **lane** SP couloir *m* intérieur; *Br: on road: in UK* voie *f* de gauche; *in France* voie *f* de droite; ~ **pocket** poche *f* intérieure

in·sid·er [ɪn'saɪdər] initié(e) *m(f)*

in·sid·er 'deal·ing FIN délit *m* d'initié

in·sides [ɪn'saɪdz] *npl* (*stomach*) ventre *m*

in·sid·i·ous [ɪn'sɪdɪəs] *adj* insidieux*

in·sight ['ɪnsaɪt] aperçu *m* (**into** de); (*insightfulness*) perspicacité *f*

in·sig·nif·i·cant [ɪnsɪɡ'nɪfɪkənt] *adj* insignifiant

in·sin·cere [ɪnsɪn'sɪr] *adj* peu sincère

in·sin·cer·i·ty [ɪnsɪn'serɪtɪ] manque *f* de sincérité

in·sin·u·ate [ɪn'sɪnjʊeɪt] *v/t* (*imply*) insinuer

in·sist [ɪn'sɪst] *v/i* insister

♦ **in·sist on** v/t insister sur

in·sis·tent [ɪnˈsɪstənt] adj insistant

in·so·lent [ˈɪnsələnt] adj insolent

in·sol·u·ble [ɪnˈsɑːljʊbl] adj problem, substance insoluble

in·sol·vent [ɪnˈsɑːlvənt] adj insolvable

in·som·ni·a [ɪnˈsɑːmnɪə] insomnie f

in·spect [ɪnˈspekt] v/t work, tickets, baggage contrôler; building, factory, school inspecter

in·spec·tion [ɪnˈspekʃn] of work, tickets, baggage contrôle m; of building, factory, school inspection f

in·spec·tor [ɪnˈspektər] in factory, police inspecteur(-trice) m(f)

in·spi·ra·tion [ɪnspəˈreɪʃn] inspiration f

in·spire [ɪnˈspaɪr] v/t inspirer

in·sta·bil·i·ty [ɪnstəˈbɪlɪtɪ] instabilité f

in·stall [ɪnˈstɔːl] v/t installer

in·stal·la·tion [ɪnstəˈleɪʃn] installation f; military ~ installation f militaire

in·stall·ment, Br **in·stal·ment** [ɪnˈstɔːlmənt] of story, TV drama etc épisode m; (payment) versement m

in·stall·ment plan vente f à crédit

in·stance [ˈɪnstəns] (example) exemple m; **for ~** par exemple

in·stant [ˈɪnstənt] **1** adj instantané **2** n instant m; **in an ~** dans un instant

in·stan·ta·ne·ous [ɪnstənˈteɪnɪəs] adj instantané

in·stant 'cof·fee café m soluble

in·stant·ly [ˈɪnstəntlɪ] adv immédiatement

in·stead [ɪnˈsted] adv à la place; **~ of me** à ma place; **~ of going home** au lieu de rentrer à la maison

in·step [ˈɪnstep] cou-de-pied m; of shoe cambrure f

in·stinct [ˈɪnstɪŋkt] instinct m

in·stinc·tive [ɪnˈstɪŋktɪv] adj instinctif*

in·sti·tute [ˈɪnstɪtuːt] **1** n institut m; (special home) établissement m **2** v/t new law, inquiry instituer

in·sti·tu·tion [ɪnstɪˈtuːʃn] institution f

in·struct [ɪnˈstrʌkt] v/t (order) ordonner; (teach) instruire; **~ s.o. to do sth** (order) ordonner à qn de faire qch

in·struc·tion [ɪnˈstrʌkʃn] instruction f; **~s for use** mode m d'emploi

in'struc·tion man·u·al manuel m d'utilisation

in·struc·tive [ɪnˈstrʌktɪv] adj instructif*

in·struc·tor [ɪnˈstrʌktər] moniteur (-trice) m(f)

in·stru·ment [ˈɪnstrʊmənt] instrument m

in·sub·or·di·nate [ɪnsəˈbɔːrdɪneɪt] adj insubordonné

in·suf·fi·cient [ɪnsəˈfɪʃnt] adj insuffisant

in·su·late [ˈɪnsəleɪt] v/t ELEC, against cold isoler (against de)

in·su·la·tion [ɪnsəˈleɪʃn] isolation f; material isolement m

in·su·lin [ˈɪnsəlɪn] insuline f

in·sult 1 [ˈɪnsʌlt] n insulte f **2** [ɪnˈsʌlt] v/t insulter

in·sur·ance [ɪnˈʃʊrəns] assurance f

in'sur·ance com·pa·ny compagnie f d'assurance; **in'sur·ance pol·i·cy** police f d'assurance; **in'sur·ance pre·mi·um** prime f d'assurance

in·sure [ɪnˈʃʊr] v/t assurer

in·sured [ɪnˈʃʊrd] **1** adj assuré **2** n: **the ~** les assurés mpl

in·sur·moun·ta·ble [ɪnsərˈmaʊntəbl] adj insurmontable

in·tact [ɪnˈtækt] adj (not damaged) intact

in·take [ˈɪnteɪk] of college etc admission f

in·te·grate [ˈɪntɪgreɪt] v/t intégrer

in·te·grat·ed cir·cuit [ˈɪntɪgreɪtɪd] circuit m intégré

in·teg·ri·ty [ɪnˈtegrətɪ] (honesty) intégrité f

in·tel·lect [ˈɪntəlekt] intellect m

in·tel·lec·tual [ɪntəˈlektʊəl] **1** adj intellectuel* **2** n intellectuel(le) m(f)

in·tel·li·gence [ɪnˈtelɪdʒəns] intelligence f; (information) renseignements mpl

in'tel·li·gence of·fi·cer officier m de renseignements

in'tel·li·gence ser·vice service m des renseignements

in·tel·li·gent [ɪnˈtelɪdʒənt] adj intelligent

in·tel·li·gi·ble [ɪn'telɪdʒəbl] *adj* intelligible

in·tend [ɪn'tend] *v/i:* **~ to do sth** avoir l'intention de; **that's not what I ~ed** ce n'était pas ce que je voulais

in·tense [ɪn'tens] *adj* intense; *personality* passionné

in·ten·si·fy [ɪn'tensɪfaɪ] **1** *v/t* (*pret & pp -ied*) *effect, pressure* intensifier **2** *v/i of pain, fighting* s'intensifier

in·ten·si·ty [ɪn'tensətɪ] intensité *f*

in·ten·sive [ɪn'tensɪv] *adj* intensif*

in·ten·sive 'care (u·nit) MED service *m* de soins intensifs

in·ten·sive course *of language study* cours *mpl* intensifs

in·tent [ɪn'tent] *adj:* **be ~ on doing sth** (*determined to do*) être (bien) décidé à faire qch

in·ten·tion [ɪn'tenʃn] intention *f*; **I have no ~ of ...** (*refuse to*) je n'ai pas l'intention de ...

in·ten·tion·al [ɪn'tenʃnl] *adj* intentionnel*

in·ten·tion·al·ly [ɪn'tenʃnlɪ] *adv* délibérément

in·ter·ac·tion [ɪntər'ækʃn] interaction *f*

in·ter·ac·tive [ɪntər'æktɪv] *adj* interactif*

in·ter·cede [ɪntər'siːd] *v/i* intercéder

in·ter·cept [ɪntər'sept] *v/t* intercepter

in·ter·change ['ɪntərtʃeɪndʒ] *n of highways* échangeur *m*

in·ter·change·a·ble [ɪntər'tʃeɪndʒəbl] *adj* interchangeable

in·ter·com ['ɪntərkɑːm] interphone *m*

in·ter·course ['ɪntərkɔːrs] *sexual* rapports *mpl*

in·ter·de·pen·dent [ɪntərdɪ'pendənt] *adj* interdépendant

in·ter·est ['ɪntrɪst] **1** *n* intérêt *m*; *financial* intérêt(s) *m(pl)*; **take an ~ in sth** s'intéresser à qch **2** *v/t* intéresser

in·ter·est·ed ['ɪntrɪstɪd] *adj* intéressé; **be ~ in sth** être intéressé par qch; **thanks, but I'm not ~** merci, mais ça ne m'intéresse pas

in·ter·est-free 'loan prêt *m* sans intérêt

in·ter·est·ing ['ɪntrəstɪŋ] *adj* intéressant

'in·ter·est rate FIN taux *m* d'intérêt

in·ter·face ['ɪntərfeɪs] **1** *n* interface *f* **2** *v/i* avoir une interface (**with** avec)

in·ter·fere [ɪntər'fɪr] *v/i* se mêler (**with** de)

♦ **interfere with** *v/t controls* toucher à; *plans* contrecarrer

in·ter·fer·ence [ɪntər'fɪrəns] ingérence *f*; *on radio* interférence *f*

in·te·ri·or [ɪn'tɪrɪər] **1** *adj* intérieur **2** *n* intérieur *m*; *Department of the Interior* ministère *m* de l'Intérieur

in·te·ri·or 'dec·o·ra·tor décorateur (-trice) *m(f)* d'intérieur; **in·te·ri·or de'sign** design *m* d'intérieurs; **in·te·ri·or de'sign·er** designer *m/f* d'intérieurs

in·ter·lude ['ɪntərluːd] intermède *m*

in·ter·mar·ry [ɪntər'mærɪ] *v/i* (*pret & pp -ied*) se marier entre eux

in·ter·me·di·a·ry [ɪntər'miːdɪərɪ] *n* intermédiaire *m/f*

in·ter·me·di·ate [ɪntər'miːdɪət] *adj stage, level* intermédiaire; *course* (de niveau) moyen

in·ter·mis·sion [ɪntər'mɪʃn] *in theater* entracte *m*

in·tern[1] [ɪn'tɜːrn] *v/t* interner

in·tern[2] ['ɪntɜːrn] *n* MED interne *m/f*

in·ter·nal [ɪn'tɜːrnl] *adj* interne; *trade* intérieur

in·ter·nal com'bus·tion en·gine moteur *m* à combustion interne

In·ter·nal 'Rev·e·nue (Ser·vice) (direction *f* générale des) impôts *mpl*

in·ter·nal·ly [ɪn'tɜːrnəlɪ] *adv in organization* en interne; **bleed ~** avoir des saignements internes; **not to be taken ~** à usage externe

in·ter·na·tion·al [ɪntər'næʃnl] **1** *adj* international **2** *n match* match *m* international; *player* international(e) *m(f)*

In·ter·na·tion·al Court of 'Jus·tice Cour *f* internationale de justice

in·ter·na·tion·al·ly [ɪntər'næʃnəlɪ] *adv* internationalement

In·ter·na·tion·al 'Mon·e·ta·ry Fund Fonds *m* monétaire international, F.M.I. *m*

In·ter·net ['ıntərnet] Internet *m*; *on the* ~ sur Internet

in·ter·nist [ın'tɜːrnıst] spécialiste *m(f)* des maladies organiques

in·ter·pret [ın'tɜːrprıt] *v/t & v/i* interpréter

in·ter·pre·ta·tion [ıntɜːrprı'teıʃn] interprétation *f*

in·ter·pret·er [ın'tɜːrprıtər] interprète *m/f*

in·ter·re·lat·ed [ıntərı'leıtıd] *adj* facts en corrélation

in·ter·ro·gate [ın'terəgeıt] *v/t* interroger

in·ter·ro·ga·tion [ıntərə'geıʃn] interrogatoire *m*

in·ter·rog·a·tive [ıntə'rɑːgətıv] *n* GRAM interrogatif*

in·ter·ro·ga·tor [ın'terə'geıtər] interrogateur(-trice) *m(f)*

in·ter·rupt [ıntə'rʌpt] *v/t & v/i* interrompre

in·ter·rup·tion [ıntə'rʌpʃn] interruption *f*

in·ter·sect [ıntər'sekt] **1** *v/t* couper, croiser **2** *v/i* s'entrecouper, s'entrecroiser

in·ter·sec·tion ['ıntərsekʃn] *of roads* carrefour *m*

in·ter·state ['ıntərsteıt] *n* autoroute *f*

in·ter·val ['ıntərvl] intervalle *m*; *in theater, at concert* entracte *m*; *sunny ~s* éclaircies *fpl*

in·ter·vene [ıntər'viːn] *v/i of person, police etc* intervenir

in·ter·ven·tion [ıntər'venʃn] intervention *f*

in·ter·view ['ıntərvjuː] **1** *n on TV, in paper* interview *f*, *for job* entretien *m* **2** *v/t on TV, for paper* interviewer; *for job* faire passer un entretien à

in·ter·view·ee [ıntərvjuː'iː] *on TV* personne *f* interviewée; *for job* candidat(e) *m(f)* (qui passe un entretien)

in·ter·view·er ['ıntərvjuːər] *on TV, for paper* intervieweur(-euse) *m(f)*; *for job* personne *f* responsable d'un entretien

in·tes·tine [ın'testın] intestin *m*

in·ti·ma·cy ['ıntıməsı] *of friendship* intimité *f*; *sexual* rapports *mpl* intimes

in·ti·mate ['ıntımət] *adj friend, thoughts* intime; *be ~ with s.o. sexually* avoir des rapports intimes avec qn

in·tim·i·date [ın'tımıdeıt] *v/t* intimider

in·tim·i·da·tion [ıntımı'deıʃn] intimidation *f*

in·to ['ıntə] *prep*: *he put it ~ his suitcase* il l'a mis dans sa valise; *translate ~ English* traduire en anglais; *2 ~ 12 is ...* 12 divisé par 2 égale ...; *be ~ sth* F (*like*) aimer qch; *politics etc* être engagé dans qch; *he's really ~ ...* (*likes*) ..., c'est son truc F; *once you're ~ the job* une fois que tu t'es habitué au métier

in·tol·er·a·ble [ın'tɑːlərəbl] *adj* intolérable

in·tol·er·ant [ın'tɑːlərənt] *adj* intolérant

in·tox·i·cat·ed [ın'tɑːksıkeıtıd] *adj* ivre

in·tran·si·tive [ın'trænsıtıv] *adj* intransitif*

in·tra·ve·nous [ıntrə'viːnəs] *adj* intraveineux*

in·trep·id [ın'trepıd] *adj* intrépide

in·tri·cate ['ıntrıkət] *adj* compliqué, complexe

in·trigue 1 ['ıntriːg] *n* intrigue *f* **2** [ın-'triːg] *v/t* intriguer

in·tri·guing [ın'triːgıŋ] *adj* intrigant

in·tro·duce [ıntrə'duːs] *v/t new technique etc* introduire; *~ s.o. to s.o.* présenter qn à qn; *~ s.o. to sth new sport, activity* initier qn à qch; *type of food etc* faire connaître qch à qn; *may I ~ ...?* puis-je vous présenter ...?

in·tro·duc·tion [ıntrə'dʌkʃn] *to person* présentations *fpl*; *in book, of new techniques* introduction *f*; *to a new sport* initiation *f* (*to* à)

in·tro·vert ['ıntrəvɜːrt] *n* introverti(e) *m(f)*

in·trude [ın'truːd] *v/i* déranger, s'immiscer

in·trud·er [ın'truːdər] intrus(e) *m(f)*

in·tru·sion [ın'truːʒn] intrusion *f*

in·tu·i·tion [ıntuː'ıʃn] intuition *f*

in·vade [ın'veıd] *v/t* envahir

in·val·id¹ [ɪn'vælɪd] adj non valable

in·va·lid² ['ɪnvəlɪd] n MED invalide m/f

in·val·i·date [ɪn'vælɪdeɪt] v/t claim, theory invalider

in·val·u·able [ɪn'væljubl] adj help, contributor inestimable

in·var·i·a·bly [ɪn'veɪriəblɪ] adv (always) invariablement

in·va·sion [ɪn'veɪʒn] invasion f

in·vent [ɪn'vent] v/t inventer

in·ven·tion [ɪn'venʃn] invention f

in·ven·tive [ɪn'ventɪv] adj inventif*

in·ven·tor [ɪn'ventər] inventeur(-trice) m(f)

in·ven·to·ry ['ɪnvəntɔːrɪ] inventaire m

in·verse [ɪn'vɜːrs] adj order inverse

in·vert [ɪn'vɜːrt] v/t inverser

in·vert·ed com·mas [ɪn'vɜːrtɪd] Br guillemets mpl

in·ver·te·brate [ɪn'vɜːrtɪbrət] n invertébré m

in·vest [ɪn'vest] v/t & v/i investir

in·ves·ti·gate [ɪn'vestɪgeɪt] v/t crime enquêter sur; scientific phenomenon étudier

in·ves·ti·ga·tion [ɪnvestɪ'geɪʃn] of crime enquête f; in science étude f

in·ves·ti·ga·tive jour·nal·ism [ɪn-'vestɪgətɪv] journalisme m d'investigation

in·vest·ment [ɪn'vestmənt] investissement m

in·ves·tor [ɪn'vestər] investisseur m

in·vig·or·at·ing [ɪn'vɪgəreɪtɪŋ] adj climate vivifiant

in·vin·ci·ble [ɪn'vɪnsəbl] adj invincible

in·vis·i·ble [ɪn'vɪzɪbl] adj invisible

in·vi·ta·tion [ɪnvɪ'teɪʃn] invitation f

in·vite [ɪn'vaɪt] v/t inviter

♦ invite in v/t inviter à entrer

in·voice ['ɪnvɔɪs] 1 n facture f 2 v/t customer facturer

in·vol·un·ta·ry [ɪn'vɑːləntərɪ] adj involontaire

in·volve [ɪn'vɑːlv] v/t hard work nécessiter; expense entraîner; (concern) concerner; what does it ~? qu'est-ce que cela implique?; get ~d with sth with company s'engager avec qch; with project s'impliquer dans

qch; of police intervenir dans qch; get ~d with s.o. romantically avoir une liaison avec qn; you're far too ~d with him emotionally tu t'investis trop (dans ta relation) avec lui

in·volved [ɪn'vɑːlvd] adj (complex) compliqué

in·volve·ment [ɪn'vɑːlvmənt] in project etc, crime, accident participation f; in politics engagement m; (implicating) implication f (in dans)

in·vul·ne·ra·ble [ɪn'vʌlnərəbl] adj invulnérable

in·ward ['ɪnwərd] 1 adj intérieur 2 adv vers l'intérieur

in·ward·ly ['ɪnwərdlɪ] adv intérieurement, dans son / mon etc for intérieur

i·o·dine ['aɪoʊdiːn] iode m

IOU [aɪoʊ'juː] abbr (= I owe you) reconnaissance f de dette

IQ [aɪ'kjuː] abbr (= intelligence quotient) Q.I. m (= Quotient m intellectuel)

I·ran [ɪ'rɑːn] Iran m

I·ra·ni·an [ɪ'reɪnɪən] 1 adj iranien* 2 n Iranien(ne) m(f)

I·raq [ɪ'ræk] Iraq m

I·ra·qi [ɪ'ræːkɪ] 1 adj irakien* 2 n Irakien(ne) m(f)

Ire·land ['aɪrlənd] Irlande f

i·ris ['aɪrɪs] of eye, flower iris m

I·rish ['aɪrɪʃ] 1 adj irlandais 2 npl: the ~ les Irlandais

I·rish·man Irlandais m

I·rish·wom·an Irlandaise f

i·ron ['aɪərn] 1 n substance fer m; for clothes fer m à repasser 2 v/t shirts etc repasser

i·ron·ic(·al) [aɪ'rɑːnɪk(l)] adj ironique

i·ron·ing ['aɪərnɪŋ] repassage m; do the ~ repasser, faire le repassage

i·ron·ing board planche f à repasser

i·ron·works usine f de sidérurgie

i·ron·y ['aɪrənɪ] ironie f

ir·ra·tion·al [ɪ'ræʃnl] adj irrationnel*

ir·rec·on·ci·la·ble [ɪrekən'saɪləbl] adj people irréconciliable; positions inconciliable

ir·re·cov·e·ra·ble [ɪrɪ'kʌvərəbl] adj data irrécupérable; loss irrémédiable

ir·re·gu·lar [ɪˈregjʊlər] *adj* irrégulier*

ir·rel·e·vant [ɪˈreləvənt] *adj* hors de propos; **that's completely ~** ça n'a absolument aucun rapport

ir·rep·a·ra·ble [ɪˈrepərəbl] *adj* irréparable

ir·re·place·a·ble [ɪrɪˈpleɪsəbl] *adj object, person* irremplaçable

ir·re·pres·si·ble [ɪrɪˈpresəbl] *adj sense of humor* à toute épreuve; *person* qui ne se laisse pas abattre

ir·re·proach·a·ble [ɪrɪˈprəʊtʃəbl] *adj* irréprochable

ir·re·sis·ti·ble [ɪrɪˈzɪstəbl] *adj* irrésistible

ir·re·spec·tive [ɪrɪˈspektɪv] *adv:* **~ of** sans tenir compte de

ir·re·spon·si·ble [ɪrɪˈspɑːnsəbl] *adj* irresponsable

ir·re·trie·va·ble [ɪrɪˈtriːvəbl] *adj data* irrécupérable; *loss* irréparable

ir·rev·e·rent [ɪˈrevərənt] *adj* irrévérencieux*

ir·rev·o·ca·ble [ɪˈrevəkəbl] *adj* irrévocable

ir·ri·gate [ˈɪrɪgeɪt] *v/t* irriguer

ir·ri·ga·tion [ɪrɪˈgeɪʃn] irrigation *f*

ir·ri·ga·tion ca'nal canal *m* d'irrigation

ir·ri·ta·ble [ˈɪrɪtəbl] *adj* irritable

ir·ri·tate [ˈɪrɪteɪt] *v/t* irriter

ir·ri·ta·ting [ˈɪrɪteɪtɪŋ] *adj* irritant

ir·ri·ta·tion [ɪrɪˈteɪʃn] irritation *f*

IRS [aɪɑːrˈes] *abbr* (= **Internal Revenue Service**) (direction *f* générale des) impôts *mpl*

Is·lam [ˈɪzlɑːm] *religion* islam *m*; *peoples, civilization* Islam *m*

Is·lam·ic [ɪzˈlæmɪk] *adj* islamique

is·land [ˈaɪlənd] île *f*; **(traffic) ~** refuge *m*

is·land·er [ˈaɪləndər] insulaire *m/f*

i·so·late [ˈaɪsəleɪt] *v/t* isoler

i·so·lat·ed [ˈaɪsəleɪtɪd] *adj house, occurence* isolé

i·so·la·tion [aɪsəˈleɪʃn] *of a region* isolement *m*; **in ~** isolément

i·so'la·tion ward salle *f* des contagieux

ISP [aɪesˈpiː] *abbr* (= **Internet service**

provider) fournisseur *m* Internet

Is·rael [ˈɪzreɪl] Israël *m*

Is·rae·li [ɪzˈreɪli] **1** *adj* israélien* **2** *n person* Israélien(ne) *m(f)*

is·sue [ˈɪʃuː] **1** *n* (*matter*) question *f*, problème *m*; (*result*) résultat *m*; *of magazine* numéro *m*; **the point at ~** le point en question; **take ~ with** s.o. ne pas être d'accord avec; *sth* contester **2** *v/t supplies* distribuer; *coins, warning* émettre; *passport* délivrer

it [ɪt] *pron* ◊ *as subject* il, elle; **what color's your car?** - **~'s black** de quelle couleur est ta voiture? - elle est noire; **where's your bathroom?** -**~'s through there** où est la salle de bains - c'est par là
◊ *as object* le, la; **give ~ to him** donne-le-lui
◊ *with prepositions:* **on top of ~** dessus; **it's just behind ~** c'est juste derrière; **let's talk about ~** parlons-en; **we went to ~** nous y sommes allés
◊ *impersonal:* **~'s raining** il pleut; **~'s me / him** c'est moi / lui; **~'s your turn** c'est ton tour; **that's ~!** (*that's right*) c'est ça!; (*finished*) c'est fini!

IT [aɪˈtiː] *abbr* (= **information technology**) informatique *f*

I·tal·i·an [ɪˈtæljən] **1** *adj* italien* **2** *n person* Italien(ne) *m(f)*; *language* italien *m*

I·ta·ly [ˈɪtəli] Italie *f*

itch [ɪtʃ] **1** *n* démangeaison *f* **2** *v/i:* **it ~es** ça me démange

i·tem [ˈaɪtəm] *on shopping list, in accounts* article *m*; *on agenda* point *m*; **~ of news** nouvelle *f*

i·tem·ize [ˈaɪtəmaɪz] *v/t invoice* détailler

i·tin·e·ra·ry [aɪˈtɪnərerɪ] itinéraire *m*

its [ɪts] *adj* son, sa; *pl* ses

it's [ɪts] → **it is, it has**

it·self [ɪtˈself] *pron reflexive* se; *stressed* lui-même; elle-même; **by ~** (*alone*) tout(e) seul(e) *m(f)*; (*automatically*) tout(e) seul(e)

i·vo·ry [ˈaɪvərɪ] ivoire *m*

i·vy [ˈaɪvɪ] lierre *m*

J

jab [dʒæb] **1** v/t (pret & pp **-bed**) planter (*into* dans); **~ one's elbow / a stick into s.o.** donner un coup de coude / bâton à qn **2** n in boxing coup m droit

jab·ber ['dʒæbər] v/i baragouiner

jack [dʒæk] MOT cric m; in cards valet m

♦ **jack up** v/t MOT soulever (avec un cric)

jack·et ['dʒækɪt] (*coat*) veste f; of book couverture f

jack·et po·ta·to pomme f de terre en robe des champs

'**jack-knife** v/i of truck se mettre en travers

'**jack·pot** jackpot m; **hit the ~** gagner le jackpot

jade [dʒeɪd] n jade m

jad·ed ['dʒeɪdɪd] adj blasé

jag·ged ['dʒægɪd] adj découpé, dentelé

jail [dʒeɪl] prison f

jam¹ [dʒæm] n for bread confiture f

jam² [dʒæm] **1** n MOT embouteillage m; F (*difficulty*) pétrin m F; **be in a ~** être dans le pétrin **2** v/t (pret & pp **-med**) (*ram*) fourrer; (*cause to stick*) bloquer; *broadcast* brouiller; **be ~med** of roads être engorgé; of door, window être bloqué **3** v/i (*stick*) se bloquer; (*squeeze*) s'entasser

♦ **jam in** v/t into suitcase etc entasser

♦ **jam on** v/t: **jam on the brakes** freiner brutalement

jam-'packed adj F plein à craquer F (*with* de)

jan·i·tor ['dʒænɪtər] concierge m/f

Jan·u·a·ry ['dʒænjʊerɪ] janvier m

Ja·pan [dʒə'pæn] Japon m

Jap·a·nese [dʒæpə'niːz] **1** adj japonais **2** n person Japonais(e) m(f); *language* japonais m; **the ~** les Japonais mpl

jar¹ [dʒɑːr] n container pot m

jar² [dʒɑːr] v/i (pret & pp **-red**) of noise irriter; of colors détonner; **~ on s.o.'s ears** écorcher les oreilles de qn

jar·gon ['dʒɑːrgən] jargon m

jaun·dice ['dʒɒndɪs] n jaunisse f

jaun·diced ['dʒɒndɪst] adj fig cynique

jaunt [dʒɒnt] n excursion f

jaunt·y ['dʒɒntɪ] adj enjoué

jav·e·lin ['dʒævlɪn] (*spear*) javelot m; *event* (lancer m du) javelot m

jaw [dʒɒː] n mâchoire f

jay·walk·er ['dʒeɪwɒːkər] piéton(ne) m(f) imprudent(e)

'jay·walk·ing traversement m imprudent d'une route

jazz [dʒæz] n jazz m

♦ **jazz up** v/t F égayer

jeal·ous ['dʒeləs] adj jaloux*

jeal·ous·ly ['dʒeləslɪ] adv jalousement

jeal·ous·y ['dʒeləsɪ] jalousie f

jeans [dʒiːnz] npl jean m

jeep [dʒiːp] jeep f

jeer [dʒɪr] **1** n raillerie f; of crowd huée f **2** v/i of crowd huer; **~ at** railler, se moquer de

Jel·lo® ['dʒelou] gelée f

jel·ly ['dʒelɪ] jam confiture f

'jel·ly bean bonbon m mou

'jel·ly·fish méduse f

jeop·ar·dize ['dʒepərdaɪz] v/t mettre en danger

jeop·ar·dy ['dʒepərdɪ]: **be in ~** être en danger

jerk¹ [dʒɜːrk] **1** n secousse f, saccade f **2** v/t tirer d'un coup sec

jerk² [dʒɜːrk] n F couillon m F

jerk·y ['dʒɜːrkɪ] adj movement saccadé

jer·sey ['dʒɜːrzɪ] (*sweater*) tricot m; *fabric* jersey m

jest [dʒest] **1** n plaisanterie f; **in ~** en plaisantant **2** v/i plaisanter

Je·sus ['dʒiːzəs] Jésus

jet [dʒet] **1** n (*airplane*) avion m à réaction, jet m; of water jet m; (*nozzle*) bec *m* 2 *v/i* (*pret* & *pp* **-ted**) (*travel*) voyager en jet

jet-'black *adj* (noir) de jais; **'jet engine** moteur *m* à réaction, réacteur *m*; **'jet-lag** (troubles *mpl* dus au) décalage *m* horaire; **jet-lagged** ['dʒetlægd] *adj*: **I'm still ~** je souffre encore du décalage horaire

jet·ti·son ['dʒetɪsn] *v/t* jeter par-dessus bord; *fig* abandonner

jet·ty ['dʒetɪ] jetée *f*

Jew [dʒuː] Juif(-ive) *m(f)*

jew·el ['dʒuːəl] bijou *m*; *fig: person* perle *f*

jew·el·er, *Br* **jew·el·ler** ['dʒuːlər] bijoutier(-ère) *m(f)*

jew·el·ry, *Br* **jew·el·lery** ['dʒuːlrɪ] bijoux *mpl*

Jew·ish ['dʒuːɪʃ] *adj* juif*

jif·fy ['dʒɪfɪ] F: **in a ~** en un clin *m* d'œil

jig·saw (puz·zle) ['dʒɪgsɔː] puzzle *m*

jilt [dʒɪlt] *v/t* laisser tomber

jin·gle ['dʒɪŋgl] 1 *n song* jingle *m* 2 *v/i of keys, coins* cliqueter

jinx [dʒɪŋks] *n person* porte-malheur *m/f*; **there's a ~ on this project** ce projet porte malheur *or* porte la guigne

jit·ters ['dʒɪtərz] F: **get the ~** avoir la frousse

jit·ter·y ['dʒɪtərɪ] *adj* F nerveux*

job [dʒɑːb] (*employment*) travail *m*, emploi *m*, boulot *m* F; (*task*) travail *m*; **~s** *newspaper section* emplois *mpl*; **out of a ~** sans travail, sans emploi; **it's a good ~ you remembered** heureusement que tu t'en es souvenu; **you'll have a ~** (*it'll be difficult*) tu vas avoir du mal

'job de·scrip·tion description *f* d'emploi

'job hunt: **be ~ing** être à la recherche d'un emploi

job·less ['dʒɑːblɪs] *adj* sans travail, sans emploi

job sat·is·fac·tion satisfaction *f* dans le travail

jock·ey ['dʒɑːkɪ] *n* jockey *m*

jog [dʒɑːg] 1 *n* footing *m*, jogging; *pace* petit trot *m*; **go for a ~** aller faire du footing *or* jogging 2 *v/i* (*pret* & *pp* **-ged**) *as exercise* faire du footing *or* jogging; **he just ~ged the last lap** il a fait le dernier tour de piste en trottinant 3 *v/t*: **~ s.o.'s elbow** donner à qn un coup léger dans le coude; **~ s.o.'s memory** rafraîchir la mémoire de qn

♦ **jog along** *v/i* F aller son petit bonhomme de chemin F; *of business* aller tant bien que mal

jog·ger ['dʒɑːgər] *person* joggeur (-euse) *m(f)*; *shoe* chaussure *f* de jogging

jog·ging ['dʒɑːgɪŋ] jogging *m*; **go ~** faire du jogging *or* du footing

'jog·ging suit survêtement *m*, jogging *m*

john [dʒɑːn] F (*toilet*) petit coin *m* F

join [dʒɔɪn] 1 *n* joint *m* 2 *v/i of roads, rivers* se rejoindre; (*become a member*) devenir membre 3 *v/t* (*connect*) relier; *person, of road* rejoindre; *club* devenir membre de; (*go to work for*) entrer dans

♦ **join in** *v/i* participer; **we joined in (with them) and sang ...** nous nous sommes joints à eux pour chanter ...

♦ **join up** *v/i Br* MIL s'engager dans l'armée

join·er ['dʒɔɪnər] menuisier(-ère) *m(f)*

joint [dʒɔɪnt] 1 *n* ANAT articulation *f*; *in woodwork* joint *m*; *of meat* rôti *m*; F (*place*) boîte *f* F; *of cannabis* joint *m* 2 *adj* (*shared*) joint

joint ac'count compte *m* joint

joint 'ven·ture entreprise *f* commune

joke [dʒouk] 1 *n story* plaisanterie *f*, blague *f* F; (*practical ~*) tour *m*; **play a ~ on** jouer un tour à; **it's no ~** ce n'est pas drôle 2 *v/i* plaisanter

jok·er ['dʒoukər] *person* farceur(-euse) *m(f)*, blagueur(-euse) *m(f)* F; *pej* plaisantin *m*; *in cards* joker *m*

jok·ing ['dʒoukɪŋ]: **~ apart** plaisanterie mise à part

jok·ing·ly ['dʒoukɪŋlɪ] *adv* en plaisantant

jol·ly ['dʒɑːlɪ] *adj* joyeux*

jolt [dʒoult] 1 *n* (*jerk*) cahot *m*, secousse *f* 2 *v/t* (*push*) pousser

jos·tle ['dʒɑːsl] *v/t* bousculer

♦ **jot down** [dʒɒt] *v/t (pret & pp* **-ted)**
noter
jour·nal ['dʒɜːrnl] *(magazine)* revue *f*;
(diary) journal *m*
jour·nal·ism ['dʒɜːrnəlɪzm] journalisme *m*
jour·nal·ist ['dʒɜːrnəlɪst] journaliste
m/f
jour·ney ['dʒɜːrnɪ] *n* voyage *m*; **the
daily ~ to the office** le trajet quotidien jusqu'au bureau
jo·vi·al ['dʒoʊvɪəl] *adj* jovial
joy [dʒɔɪ] joie *f*
'joy·stick COMPUT manette *f* (de
jeux)
ju·bi·lant ['dʒuːbɪlənt] *adj* débordant
de joie
ju·bi·la·tion [dʒuːbɪ'leɪʃn] jubilation *f*
judge [dʒʌdʒ] **1** *n* juge *m/f* **2** *v/t juger;
measurement, age* estimer **3** *v/i* juger
judg(e)·ment ['dʒʌdʒmənt] jugement
m; *(opinion)* avis *m*; **the Last
Judg(e)ment** REL le Jugement dernier
'Judg(e)·ment Day le Jugement dernier
ju·di·cial [dʒuː'dɪʃl] *adj* judiciaire
ju·di·cious [dʒuː'dɪʃəs] *adj* judicieux*
ju·do ['dʒuːdoʊ] judo *m*
jug [dʒʌɡ] *Br* pot *m*
jug·gle ['dʒʌɡl] *v/t also fig* jongler avec
jug·gler ['dʒʌɡlər] jongleur(-euse)
m(f)
juice [dʒuːs] *n* jus *m*
juic·y ['dʒuːsɪ] *adj* juteux*; *news, gossip* croustillant
juke·box ['dʒuːkbɑːks] juke-box *m*
Ju·ly [dʒu'laɪ] juillet *m*
jum·ble ['dʒʌmbl] *n* méli-mélo *m*
♦ **jumble up** *v/t* mélanger
jum·bo (jet) ['dʒʌmboʊ] jumbo-jet *m*,
gros-porteur *m*
jum·bo-sized ['dʒʌmboʊsaɪzd] *adj* F
géant
jump [dʒʌmp] **1** *n* saut *m*; *(increase)*
bond *m*; **with one ~** d'un seul bond;
give a ~ of *surprise* sursauter **2** *v/i*
sauter; *in surprise* sursauter; *(increase)*
faire un bond; **~ to one's feet** se lever d'un bond; **~ to conclusions** tirer des conclusions hâtives **3** *v/t fence*

etc sauter; F *(attack)* attaquer; **~ the
lights** griller un feu (rouge)
♦ **jump at** *v/t* **opportunity** sauter sur
jump·er¹ ['dʒʌmpər] *dress* robe-cha-
suble *f*; *Br* pull *m*
jump·er² ['dʒʌmpər] SP sauteur(-euse)
m(f)
jump·y ['dʒʌmpɪ] *adj* nerveux*
junc·tion ['dʒʌŋkʃn] *of roads* jonction
f
junc·ture ['dʒʌŋktʃər] *fml*: **at this ~** à
ce moment
June [dʒuːn] juin *m*
jun·gle ['dʒʌŋɡl] jungle *f*
ju·ni·or ['dʒuːnjər] **1** *adj (subordinate)*
subalterne; *(younger)* plus jeune;
William Smith Junior William
Smith fils **2** *n in rank* subalterne
m/f; **she is ten years my ~** elle est
ma cadette de dix ans
ju·ni·or 'high collège *m*
junk [dʒʌŋk] camelote *f* F
'junk food cochonneries *fpl*
junk·ie ['dʒʌŋkɪ] F drogué(e) *m(f)*, ca-
mé(e) *m(f)* F
'junk mail prospectus *mpl*; **'junk
shop** brocante *f*; **'junk·yard** dépotoir *m*
jur·is·dic·tion [dʒʊrɪs'dɪkʃn] LAW juridiction *f*
ju·ror ['dʒʊrər] juré(e) *m(f)*
ju·ry ['dʒʊrɪ] jury *m*
just [dʒʌst] **1** *adj law, war, cause* juste **2**
adv (barely, only) juste; **~ as intelligent** tout aussi intelligent; **I've ~
seen her** je viens de la voir; **~ about**
(almost) presque; **I was ~ about to
leave when …** j'étais sur le point
de partir quand …; **~ as he …** at
the very time au moment même où
il …; **~ like that** *(abruptly)*
comme le vôtre; **~ like that** *(abruptly)*
tout d'un coup, sans prévenir; **~ now**
(a few moments ago) à l'instant, tout à
l'heure; *(at this moment)* en ce moment; **~ be quiet!** veux-tu te taire!
jus·tice ['dʒʌstɪs] justice *f*
jus·ti·fi·a·ble [dʒʌstɪ'faɪəbl] *adj* justifiable
jus·ti·fi·a·bly [dʒʌstɪ'faɪəblɪ] *adv* à
juste titre

J

jus·ti·fi·ca·tion [dʒʌstɪfɪ'keɪʃn] justification f

jus·ti·fy ['dʒʌstɪfaɪ] v/t (pret & pp **-ied**) also text justifier

just·ly ['dʒʌstlɪ] adv (fairly) de manière juste; (rightly) à juste titre

◆ **jut out** [dʒʌt] v/i (pret & pp **-ted**) être en saillie

ju·ve·nile ['dʒuːvənəl] **1** adj crime juvénile; court pour enfants; pej: attitude puéril **2** n fml jeune m/f, adolescent(e) m(f)

ju·ve·nile de·lin·quen·cy délinquance f juvénile

ju·ve·nile de·lin·quent délinquant(e) juvénile m(f)

K

k [keɪ] abbr (= **kilobyte**) Ko m (= kilo-octet m); (= **thousand**) mille

kan·ga·roo ['kæŋgəruː] kangourou m

ka·ra·te [kə'rɑːtɪ] karaté m

ka'ra·te chop coup m de karaté

ke·bab [kɪ'bæb] kébab m

keel [kiːl] NAUT quille f

◆ **keel over** v/i of structure se renverser; of person s'écrouler

keen [kiːn] adj (intense) vif*; esp Br. person enthousiaste; **be ~ to do sth** esp Br tenir à faire qch

keep [kiːp] **1** n (maintenance) pension f; **for ~s** F pour de bon **2** v/t (pret & pp **kept**) also (not give back, not lose) garder; (detain) retenir; in specific place mettre; family entretenir; dog etc avoir; bees, cattle élever; promise tenir; **~ s.o. company** tenir compagnie à qn; **~ s.o. waiting** faire attendre qn; **~ sth to o.s.** (not tell) garder qch pour soi; **~ sth from s.o.** cacher qch à qn; **~ s.o. from doing sth** empêcher qn de faire qch; **~ trying!** essaie encore!; **don't ~ interrupting!** arrête de m'interrompre tout le temps! **3** v/i (remain) rester; of food, milk se conserver

◆ **keep away 1** v/i se tenir à l'écart (from de); **keep away from** tienstoi à l'écart de; **keep away from drugs** ne pas toucher à la drogue **2** v/t tenir à l'écart; **keep s.o. away from sth** tenir qn à l'écart de qch;

it's keeping the tourists away cela dissuade les touristes de venir

◆ **keep back** v/t (hold in check) retenir; information cacher (**from** de)

◆ **keep down** v/t costs, inflation etc réduire; food garder; **keep one's voice down** parler à voix basse; **keep the noise down** ne pas faire de bruit

◆ **keep in** v/t in hospital garder; in school mettre en retenue

◆ **keep off 1** v/t (avoid) éviter; **keep off the grass!** ne marchez pas sur la pelouse! **2** v/i: **if the rain keeps off** s'il ne pleut pas

◆ **keep on 1** v/i continuer; **keep on doing sth** continuer de faire qch **2** v/t in job, jacket etc garder

◆ **keep on at** v/t (nag) harceler

◆ **keep out 1** v/t the cold protéger de; person empêcher d'entrer **2** v/i rester à l'écart; **keep out!** as sign défense d'entrer; **you keep out of this!** ne te mêle pas de ça!

◆ **keep to** v/t path rester sur; rules s'en tenir à; **keep to the point** rester dans le sujet

◆ **keep up 1** v/i when walking, running etc suivre; **keep up with** aller au même rythme que; (stay in touch with) rester en contact avec **2** v/t pace, payments continuer; bridge, pants soutenir

keep·ing ['kiːpɪŋ] n: **be in ~ with** être en accord avec '**keep·sake** souvenir *m*

keg [keg] tonnelet *m*, barillet *m*

ken·nel ['kenl] niche *f*

ken·nels ['kenlz] *npl* chenil *m*

kept [kept] *pret & pp* → **keep**

ker·nel ['kɜːrnl] *of nut* intérieur *m*

ker·o·sene ['kerəsiːn] AVIAT kérosène *m*; *for lamps* pétrole *m* (lampant)

ketch·up ['ketʃʌp] ketchup *m*

ket·tle ['ketl] bouilloire *f*

key [kiː] **1** *n* clef *f*, clé *f*; COMPUT, MUS touche *f* **2** *adj* (*vital*) clef *inv*, clé *inv* **3** *v/t & v/i* COMPUT taper

♦ **key in** *v/t data* taper

'**key·board** COMPUT, MUS clavier *m*; '**key·board·er** COMPUT claviste *m/f*; '**key·card** carte-clé *f*, carte-clef *f*

keyed-up [kiːd'ʌp] *adj* tendu

'**key·hole** trou *m* de serrure; **key·note** '**speech** discours *m* programme; '**key·ring** porte-clefs *m*

kha·ki ['kækɪ] *adj color* kaki *inv*

kick [kɪk] **1** *n* coup *m* de pied; F (*thrill*): **get a ~ out of sth** éprouver du plaisir à qch; (*just*) **for ~s** F (juste) pour le plaisir **2** *v/t ball, shins* donner un coup de pied dans; *person* donner un coup de pied à; **~ the habit** F *of smoker* arrêter de fumer; F *of drug-addict* décrocher F **3** *v/i of person* donner un coup de pied / des coups de pied; *of horse* ruer

♦ **kick around** *v/t ball* taper dans; (*treat harshly*) maltraiter; F (*discuss*) débattre

♦ **kick in 1** *v/t* P *money* cracher **2** *v/i* (*start to operate*) se mettre en marche

♦ **kick off** *v/i* SP donner le coup d'envoi; F (*start*) démarrer F

♦ **kick out** *v/t* mettre à la porte; **be kicked out of the company / army** être mis à la porte de la société / l'armée

♦ **kick up** *v/t*: **kick up a fuss** piquer une crise F

'**kick·back** F (*bribe*) dessous-de-table *m* F

'**kick·off** SP coup *m* d'envoi

kid [kɪd] **1** *n* F (*child*) gamin(e) *m(f)*; **~ brother / sister** petit frère *m* / petite sœur *f* **2** *v/t* (*pret & pp* **-ded**) F ta-

quiner **3** *v/i* F plaisanter; **I was only ~ding** je plaisantais; **no ~ding!** sans blague! F

kid·der ['kɪdər] F farceur(-euse) *m(f)*

kid·nap ['kɪdnæp] *v/t* (*pret & pp* **-ped**) kidnapper

kid·nap·(p)er ['kɪdnæpər] kidnappeur(-euse) *m(f)*

'**kid·nap·(p)ing** ['kɪdnæpɪŋ] kidnapping *m*

kid·ney ['kɪdnɪ] ANAT rein *m*; *in cooking* rognon *m*

'**kid·ney bean** haricot *m* nain

'**kid·ney ma·chine** MED rein *m* artificiel

kill [kɪl] *v/t also time* tuer; **~ o.s.** se suicider; **~ o.s. laughing** F être mort de rire F

kil·ler ['kɪlər] (*murderer*) tueur(-euse) *m(f)*; **be a ~** *of disease etc* tuer

kil·ling ['kɪlɪŋ] *n* meurtre *m*; **make a ~** F (*lots of money*) réaliser un profit énorme

kiln [kɪln] four *m*

ki·lo ['kiːloʊ] kilo *m*

ki·lo·byte ['kɪloʊbaɪt] kilo-octet *m*

ki·lo·gram ['kɪloʊɡræm] kilogramme *m*

ki·lo·me·ter, *Br* **ki·lo·me·tre** [kɪ'lɑːmɪtər] kilomètre *m*

kind[1] [kaɪnd] *adj* gentil; **that's very ~ of you** c'est très aimable à vous

kind[2] [kaɪnd] *n* (*sort*) sorte *f*, genre *m*; (*make, brand*) marque *f*; **what ~ of ...?** quelle sorte de ...?; **all ~s of people** toutes sortes de gens; **you'll do nothing of the ~!** tu n'en feras rien!; **~ of sad / strange** F plutôt *or* un peu triste / bizarre; **~ of green** F dans les tons verts

kin·der·gar·ten ['kɪndərɡɑːrtn] jardin *m* d'enfants

kind-heart·ed [kaɪnd'hɑːrtɪd] *adj* bienveillant, bon*

kind·ly ['kaɪndlɪ] **1** *adj* gentil, bon* **2** *adv* aimablement; **~ don't interrupt** voulez-vous bien ne pas m'interrompre

kind·ness ['kaɪndnɪs] bonté *f*, gentillesse *f*

king [kɪŋ] roi *m*

king·dom ['kɪŋdəm] royaume *m*

'king-size *adj* F *bed* géant; *cigarettes* long*

kink [kɪŋk] *in hose etc* entortillement *m*

kink·y ['kɪŋkɪ] *adj* F bizarre

ki·osk ['kiːɑːsk] kiosque *m*

kiss [kɪs] **1** *n* baiser *m*, bisou *m* F **2** *v/t* embrasser **3** *v/i* s'embrasser

kiss of 'life *Br* bouche-à-bouche *m*

kit [kɪt] *(equipment)* trousse *f*, *for assembly* kit *m*

kitch·en ['kɪtʃɪn] cuisine *f*

kitch·en·ette [kɪtʃɪ'net] kitchenette *f*

kitch·en 'sink: everything but the ~ F tout sauf les murs

kite [kaɪt] cerf-volant *m*

kit·ten ['kɪtn] chaton(ne) *m(f)*

kit·ty ['kɪtɪ] *money* cagnotte *f*

klutz [klʌts] F *(clumsy person)* empoté(e) *m(f)* F

knack [næk]: **have the ~ of doing sth** avoir le chic pour faire qch; **there's a ~ to it** il y a un truc F

knead [niːd] *v/t dough* pétrir

knee [niː] *n* genou *m*

'knee-cap *n* rotule *f*

kneel [niːl] *v/i (pret & pp knelt)* s'agenouiller

'knee-length *adj* à la hauteur du genou

knelt [nelt] *pret & pp → kneel*

knew [nuː] *pret → know*

knick-knacks ['nɪknæks] *npl* F bibelots *mpl*, babioles *fpl*

knife [naɪf] **1** *n (pl: knives* [naɪfvz]) couteau *m* **2** *v/t* poignarder

knight [naɪt] chevalier *m*

knit [nɪt] *v/t & v/i (pret & pp -ted)* tricoter

♦ **knit together** *v/i of broken bone* se souder

knit·ting ['nɪtɪŋ] tricot *m*

'knit·ting nee·dle aiguille *f* à tricoter

'knit-wear tricot *m*

knob [nɑːb] *on door* bouton *m*; *of butter* noix *f*

knock [nɑːk] **1** *n on door*, *(blow)* coup *m* **2** *v/t (hit)* frapper; *knee etc* se co-

gner; F *(criticize)* débiner F; **~ s.o. to the ground** jeter qn à terre **3** *v/i on door* frapper

♦ **knock around 1** *v/t (beat)* maltraiter **2** *v/i* F *(travel)* vadrouiller F

♦ **knock down** *v/t* renverser; *wall, building* abattre; F *(reduce the price of)* solder (**to** à)

♦ **knock off 1** *v/t* F *(steal)* piquer F; **knock it off!** arrête ça! **2** *v/i* F *(stop work)* s'arrêter (de travailler)

♦ **knock out** *v/t* assommer; *boxer* mettre knock-out; *power lines etc* détruire; *(eliminate)* éliminer

♦ **knock over** *v/t* renverser

'knock·down *adj*: **a ~ price** un prix très bas; **knock-kneed** [nɑːk'niːd] *adj* cagneux*; **'knock-out** *n in boxing* knock-out *m*

knot [nɑːt] **1** *n* nœud *m* **2** *v/t (pret & pp -ted)* nouer

knot·ty ['nɑːtɪ] *adj problem* épineux*

know [nou] **1** *v/t (pret knew, pp known)* savoir; *person, place, language* connaître; *(recognize)* reconnaître; **how to do sth** savoir faire qch; **will you let her ~ that ...?** pouvez-vous lui faire savoir que ...? **2** *v/i* savoir; **~ about sth** être au courant de qch **3** *n*: **be in the ~** F être au courant (de l'affaire)

'know-how F savoir-faire *m*

know·ing ['nouɪŋ] *adj smile* entendu

know·ing·ly ['nouɪŋlɪ] *adv (wittingly)* sciemment, en connaissance de cause; *smile etc* d'un air entendu

'know-it-all F je-sais-tout *m/f*

knowl·edge ['nɑːlɪdʒ] savoir *m*; *of a subject* connaissance(s) *f(pl)*; **to the best of my ~** autant que je sache, à ma connaissance; **have a good ~ of ...** avoir de bonnes connaissances en ...

knowl·edge·a·ble ['nɑːlɪdʒəbl] *adj* bien informé

known [noun] *pp → know*

knuck·le ['nʌkl] articulation *f* du doigt

♦ **knuckle down** *v/i* F s'y mettre

♦ **knuckle under** *v/i* F céder

KO [keɪ'ou] *(knockout)* K.-O. *m*

Ko·ran [kə'ræn] Coran *m*

Ko·re·a [kə'riːə] Corée f

Ko·re·an [kə'riːən] **1** adj coréen* **2** n Coréen(ne) m(f); language coréen m

ko·sher ['kəʊʃər] adj REL casher inv; F réglo inv F; **there's something not quite ~ about ...** il y a quelque chose de pas très catholique dans ...

kow·tow ['kaʊtaʊ] v/i F faire des courbettes (**to** à)

ku·dos ['kjuːdɑːs] prestige m

L

lab [læb] labo m

la·bel ['leɪbl] **1** n étiquette f **2** v/t (pret & pp **-ed**, Br **-led**) also fig étiqueter; **~ s.o. a liar** traiter qn de menteur

la·bor ['leɪbər] **1** n also in pregnancy travail m; **be in ~** être en train d'accoucher **2** v/i travailler

la·bor·a·to·ry ['læbrətɔːrɪ] laboratoire m

la·bor·a·to·ry tech·ni·cian laborantin(e) m(f)

la·bored ['leɪbərd] adj style, speech laborieux*

la·bor·er ['leɪbərər] travailleur m manuel

la·bo·ri·ous [lə'bɔːrɪəs] adj style, task laborieux*

'la·bor u·ni·on syndicat m

'la·bor ward MED salle f d'accouchement

la·bour Br → **labor**

'La·bour Par·ty Br POL parti m travailliste

lace [leɪs] n material dentelle f; for shoe lacet m

♦ **lace up** v/t shoes lacer

lack [læk] **1** n manque m **2** v/t manquer de **3** v/i: **be ~ing** manquer

lac·quer ['lækər] n laque f

lad [læd] garçon m, jeune homme m

lad·der ['lædər] échelle f

la·den ['leɪdn] adj chargé (**with** de)

la·dies room ['leɪdiːz] toilettes fpl (pour dames)

la·dle ['leɪdl] n louche f

la·dy ['leɪdɪ] dame f

la·dy·bug ['leɪdɪbʌg] coccinelle f

'la·dy·like adj distingué

lag [læg] v/t (pret & pp **-ged**) pipes isoler

♦ **lag behind** v/i être en retard, être à la traîne

la·ger ['lɑːgər] Br bière f blonde

la·goon [lə'guːn] lagune f; small lagon m

laid [leɪd] pret & pp → **lay**

laid'back adj relax F, décontracté

lain [leɪn] pp → **lie**

lake [leɪk] lac m

lamb [læm] agneau m

lame [leɪm] adj person boîteux*; excuse mauvais

la·ment [lə'ment] **1** n lamentation f **2** v/t pleurer

lam·en·ta·ble ['læməntəbl] adj lamentable

lam·i·nat·ed ['læmɪneɪtɪd] adj flooring, paper stratifié; wood contreplaqué; with plastic plastifié; **~ glass** verre m feuilleté

lamp [læmp] lampe f

'lamp·post réverbère m

'lamp·shade abat-jour m inv

land [lænd] **1** n terre f; (country) pays m; **by ~** par (voie de) terre; **on ~** à terre; **work on the ~** as farmer travailler la terre **2** v/t airplane faire atterrir; job décrocher F **3** v/i of airplane atterrir; of ball, sth thrown tomber; of jumper retomber

land·ing ['lændɪŋ] n of airplane atterrissage m; (top of staircase) palier m

'land·ing field terrain m d'atterrissage; **'land·ing gear** train m d'atterrissage; **'land·ing strip** piste *f* d'atterrissage

'land·la·dy propriétaire *f*; *of rented room* logeuse *f*; *Br of bar* patronne *f*; **'land·lord** propriétaire *m*; *of rented room* logeur *m*; *Br of bar* patron *m*; **'land·mark** point *m* de repère; *be a ~ in fig* faire date dans; **'land own·er** propriétaire *m* foncier, propriétaire *m* terrien; **land·scape** ['lændskeɪp] **1** *n* paysage *m* **2** *adv print* en format paysage; **'land·slide** glissement *m* de terrain; **land·slide 'vic·to·ry** victoire *f* écrasante

lane [leɪn] *in country* petite route *f* (de campagne); *(alley)* ruelle *f*; MOT voie *f*

lan·guage ['læŋgwɪdʒ] langue *f*, *(style, code etc)* langage *m*

'lan·guage lab laboratoire *m* de langues

lank [læŋk] *adj hair* plat

lank·y ['læŋkɪ] *adj person* dégingandé

lan·tern ['læntərn] lanterne *f*

lap[1] [læp] *n of track* tour *m*

lap[2] [læp] *n of water* clapotis *m*

♦ **lap up** *v/t (pret & pp -ped) milk etc* laper; *flattery* se délecter de

lap[3] [læp] *n of person* genoux *mpl*

la·pel [lə'pel] revers *m*

lapse [læps] **1** *n (mistake, slip)* erreur *f*; *in behavior* écart *m* (de conduite); *of attention* baisse *f*; *of time* intervalle *m*; *~ of memory* trou *m* de mémoire **2** *v/i* expirer

♦ **lapse into** *v/t silence, despair* sombrer dans; *language* revenir à

lap·top ['læptɑːp] COMPUT portable *m*

lar·ce·ny ['lɑːrsənɪ] vol *m*

lard [lɑːrd] lard *m*

lar·der ['lɑːrdər] garde-manger *m inv*

large [lɑːrdʒ] *adj building, country, hands* grand; *sum of money, head* gros*; *at ~ criminal, animal* en liberté

large·ly ['lɑːrdʒlɪ] *adv (mainly)* en grande partie

lark [lɑːrk] *bird* alouette *f*

lar·va ['lɑːrvə] larve *f*

lar·yn·gi·tis [lærɪn'dʒaɪtɪs] laryngite *f*

lar·ynx ['lærɪŋks] larynx *m*

la·ser ['leɪzər] laser *m*

'la·ser beam rayon *m* laser

'la·ser print·er imprimante *f* laser

lash[1] [læʃ] *v/t with whip* fouetter

♦ **lash down** *v/t with rope* attacher

♦ **lash out** *v/i with fists* donner des coups (*at* à); *with words* se répandre en invectives (*at* contre)

lash[2] [læʃ] *n (eyelash)* cil *m*

lass [læs] jeune fille *f*

last[1] [læst] **1** *adj* dernier*; *~ but one* avant-dernier *m*; *~ night* hier soir **2** *adv* arrive, leave en dernier; *he finished ~ in race* il est arrivé dernier; *when I ~ spoke to her* la dernière fois que je lui ai parlé; *at ~* enfin; *~ but not least* enfin et surtout

last[2] [læst] *v/i* durer

last·ing ['læstɪŋ] *adj* durable

last·ly ['læstlɪ] *adv* pour finir

latch [lætʃ] verrou *m*

late [leɪt] **1** *adj (behind time)* en retard; *in day* tard; *it's getting ~* il se fait tard; *of ~* récemment; *in the ~ 20th century* vers la fin du XXᵉ siècle **2** *adv* arrive, leave tard

late·ly ['leɪtlɪ] *adv* récemment

lat·er ['leɪtər] *adv* plus tard; *see you ~!* à plus tard!; *~ on* plus tard

lat·est ['leɪtɪst] *adj* dernier*

lathe [leɪð] *n* tour *m*

la·ther ['læðər] *from soap* mousse *f*; *the horse was in a ~* le cheval était couvert d'écume

Lat·in ['lætɪn] **1** *adj* latin **2** *n* latin *m*

Lat·in A'mer·i·ca Amérique *f* latine

Lat·in A'mer·i·can 1 *n* Latino-Américain *m* **2** *adj* latino-américain

lat·i·tude ['lætɪtuːd] *also (freedom)* latitude *f*

lat·ter ['lætər] **1** *adj* dernier* **2** *n: the ~* ce dernier, cette dernière

laugh [læf] **1** *n* rire *m*; *it was a ~ F* on s'est bien amusés **2** *v/i* rire

♦ **laugh at** *v/t* rire de; *(mock)* se moquer de

laugh·ing stock ['læfɪŋ]: *make o.s. a ~* se couvrir de ridicule; *be a ~* être la risée de tous

laugh·ter ['læftər] rires *mpl*

launch [lɒːntʃ] **1** *n* boat vedette *f*; *of rocket, product* lancement *m*; *of ship* mise *f* à l'eau **2** *v/t* rocket, product lancer; *ship* mettre à l'eau

'launch cer·e·mo·ny cérémonie *f* de lancement

'launch pad plate-forme *f* de lancement

laun·der ['lɔːndər] *v/t clothes, money* blanchir

laun·dro·mat ['lɔːndrəmæt] laverie *f* automatique

laun·dry ['lɔːndrɪ] *place* blanchisserie *f*; *clothes* lessive *f*; **get one's ~ done** faire sa lessive

lau·rel ['lɔːrəl] laurier *m*

lav·a·to·ry ['lævətərɪ] W.-C. *mpl*

lav·en·der ['lævəndər] lavande *f*

lav·ish ['lævɪʃ] *adj* somptueux*

law [lɔː] loi *f*; *as subject* droit *m*; **be against the ~** être contraire à la loi; **forbidden by ~** interdit par la loi

law-a·bid·ing ['lɔːəbaɪdɪŋ] *adj* respectueux* des lois

'law court tribunal *m*

law·ful ['lɔːfʊl] *adj activity* légal; *wife, child* légitime

law·less ['lɔːlɪs] *adj* anarchique

lawn [lɔːn] pelouse *f*

'lawn mow·er tondeuse *f* (à gazon)

'law·suit procès *m*

law·yer ['lɔːjər] avocat *m*

lax [læks] *adj* laxiste; *security* relâché

lax·a·tive ['læksətɪv] *n* laxatif *m*

lay¹ [leɪ] *pret* → **lie**

lay² [leɪ] *v/t* (*pret & pp* **laid**) (*put down*) poser; *eggs* pondre; V *sexually* s'envoyer V

♦ **lay into** *v/t* (*attack*) attaquer

♦ **lay off** *v/t workers* licencier; *temporarily* mettre au chômage technique

♦ **lay on** *v/t* (*provide*) organiser

♦ **lay out** *v/t objects* disposer; *page* faire la mise en page de

'lay·a·bout *Br* F glandeur *m* F

'lay-by *Br*: *on road* bande *f* d'arrêt d'urgence

lay·er ['leɪr] couche *f*

'lay·man REL laïc *m*; *fig* profane *m*

'lay-off *from employment* licenciement *m*

♦ **laze around** [leɪz] *v/i* paresser

la·zy ['leɪzɪ] *adj person* paresseux*; *day* tranquille, peinard F

lb *abbr* (= *pound*) livre *f*

LCD [elsiː'diː] *abbr* (= *liquid crystal display*) affichage *m* à cristaux liquides

lead¹ [liːd] **1** *v/t* (*pret & pp* **led**) *procession, race* mener; *company, team* être à la tête de; (*guide, take*) mener, conduire **2** *v/i in race, competition* mener; (*provide leadership*) diriger; *a street ~ing off the square* une rue partant de la place; *a street ~ing into the square* une rue menant à la place; *where is this ~ing?* à quoi ceci va nous mener? **3** *n in race* tête *f*; *be in the ~* mener; *take the ~* prendre l'avantage; *lose the ~* perdre l'avantage

♦ **lead on** *v/i* (*go in front*) passer devant

♦ **lead up to** *v/t* amener; *what is she leading up to?* où veut-elle en venir?

lead² [liːd] *n for dog* laisse *f*

lead³ [led] *n substance* plomb *m*

lead·ed ['ledɪd] *adj gas* au plomb

lead·er ['liːdər] *of state* dirigeant *m*; *in race* leader *m*; *of group* chef *m*

lead·er·ship ['liːdərʃɪp] *of party etc* direction *f*; *~ skills* qualités *fpl* de chef

'lead·er·ship con·test POL bataille *f* pour la direction du parti

lead-free ['ledfriː] *adj gas* sans plomb

lead·ing ['liːdɪŋ] *adj runner* en tête (de la course); *company, product* premier*

'lead·ing-edge *adj company, technology* de pointe

leaf [liːf] (*pl* **leaves** [liːvz]) feuille *f*

♦ **leaf through** *v/t* feuilleter

leaf·let ['liːflət] dépliant *m*; *instruction ~* mode *m* d'emploi

league [liːg] ligue *f*

leak [liːk] **1** *n also of information* fuite *f* **2** *v/i of pipe* fuir; *of boat* faire eau **3** *v/t information* divulguer

♦ **leak out** *v/i of air, gas* fuir; *of news* transpirer

leak·y ['liːkɪ] *adj pipe* qui fuit; *boat* qui fait eau

lean¹ [liːn] **1** *v/i* (*be at an angle*) pencher; *~ against sth* s'appuyer contre qch **2** *v/t* appuyer

lean² [liːn] *adj meat* maigre; *style, prose* sobre

leap [liːp] **1** *n* saut *m*; **a great ~ forward** un grand bond en avant **2** *v/i* sauter

leap year année *f* bissextile

learn [lɜːrn] *v/t & v/i* apprendre; **~ how to do sth** apprendre à faire qch

learn·er ['lɜːrnər] apprenant(e) *m(f)*

'learn·er driv·er apprenti *m* conducteur

learn·ing ['lɜːrnɪŋ] *n* (*knowledge*) savoir *m*; *act* apprentissage *m*

'learn·ing curve courbe *f* d'apprentissage

lease [liːs] **1** *n for apartment* bail *m*; *for equipment* location *f* **2** *v/t apartment, equipment* louer

♦ **lease out** *v/t apartment, equipment* louer

lease 'pur·chase crédit-bail *m*

leash [liːʃ] *for dog* laisse *f*

least [liːst] **1** *adj* (*slightest*) (le ou la) moindre, (le ou la) plus petit(e); *smallest quantity of* le moins de **2** *adv* (le) moins **3** *n* le moins; **not in the ~ suprised** absolument pas surpris; **at ~** au moins

leath·er ['leðər] **1** *n* cuir *m* **2** *adj* de cuir

leave [liːv] **1** *n* (*vacation*) congé *m*; (*permission*) permission *f*; **on ~** en congé **2** *v/t* (*pret & pp* **left**) *city, place also* partir de; *food, scar, memory* laisser; (*forget, leave behind*) oublier; **let's ~ things as they are** laissons faire les choses; **how did you ~ things with him?** où en es-tu avec lui?; **~ sth alone** ne pas toucher à qch; **~ s.o. alone** laisser qn tranquille; **be left** rester **2** *v/i* (*pret & pp* **left**) *of person, plane etc* quitter

♦ **leave behind** *v/t intentionally* laisser; (*forget*) oublier

♦ **leave on** *v/t hat, coat* garder; *TV, computer* laisser allumé

♦ **leave out** *v/t word, figure* omettre; (*not put away*) ne pas ranger; **leave me out of this** laissez-moi en dehors de ça

leav·ing par·ty ['liːvɪŋ] soirée *f* d'adieu

lec·ture ['lektʃər] **1** *n* conférence *f*; *at university* cours *m* **2** *v/i at university* donner des cours

'lec·ture hall amphithéâtre *m*

lec·tur·er ['lektʃərər] conférencier *m*; *at university* maître *m* de conférences

led [led] *pret & pp* → **lead1**

LED [eliː'diː] *abbr* (= **light-emitting diode**) DEL *f* (= diode électroluminescente)

ledge [ledʒ] *of window* rebord *m*; *on rock face* saillie *f*

ledg·er ['ledʒər] COMM registre *m* de comptes

leek [liːk] poireau *m*

leer [lɪr] *n sexual* regard *m* vicieux; *evil* regard *m* malveillant

left¹ [left] **1** *adj* gauche **2** *n* gauche *f*; **on the ~** (**of sth**) à gauche (de qch); **to the ~** à gauche **3** *adv turn, look* à gauche

left² [left] *pret & pp* → **leave**

'left-hand *adj* gauche; *curve* à gauche; **left-hand 'drive** conduite *f* à gauche; **left-hand·ed** [left'hændɪd] gaucher; **left 'lug·gage (of·fice)** *Br* consigne *f*; **'left-overs** *npl of food* restes *mpl*; **left 'wing** POL gauche *f*; SP ailier *m* gauche;**'left-wing** *adj* POL de gauche

leg [leg] jambe *f*; *of animal* patte *f*; *of table etc* pied *m*; **pull s.o.'s ~** faire marcher qn

leg·a·cy ['legəsɪ] héritage *m*, legs *m*

le·gal ['liːgl] *adj* (*allowed*) légal; *relating to the law* juridique

le·gal ad'vis·er conseiller(-ère) *m(f)* juridique

le·gal·i·ty [lɪ'gælətɪ] légalité *f*

le·gal·ize ['liːgəlaɪz] *v/t* légaliser

le·gend ['ledʒənd] légende *f*

le·gen·da·ry ['ledʒəndrɪ] *adj* légendaire

le·gi·ble ['ledʒəbl] *adj* lisible

le·gion·naire [liːdʒə'ner] légionnaire *m*

le·gis·late ['ledʒɪslet] *v/i* légiférer

le·gis·la·tion [ledʒɪs'leɪʃn] (*laws*) législation *f*; (*passing of laws*) élaboration *f* des lois

le·gis·la·tive ['ledʒɪslətɪv] *adj* législatif*

le·gis·la·ture ['ledʒɪslətʃər] POL corps *m* législatif

le·git·i·mate [lɪ'dʒɪtɪmət] *adj* légitime

'leg room place *f* pour les jambes

lei·sure ['liːʒər] loisir *m*; *(free time)* temps *m* libre; **at your** ~ à loisir

'lei·sure cen·ter, *Br* 'lei·sure cen·tre centre *m* de loisirs

lei·sure·ly ['liːʒərlɪ] *adj pace, lifestyle* tranquille

'lei·sure time temps *m* libre

le·mon ['lemən] citron *m*

le·mon·ade [lemə'neɪd] citronnade *f*; *carbonated* limonade *f*

'le·mon juice jus *m* de citron

'le·mon tea thé *m* au citron

lend [lend] *v/t (pret & pp* **lent***)* prêter; ~ **s.o. sth** prêter qch à qn

length [leŋθ] longueur *f*; *(piece: of material)* pièce *f*; *of piping, road* tronçon *m*; **at** ~ *describe, explain* en détail; *(eventually)* finalement

length·en ['leŋθən] *v/t sleeve etc* allonger; *contract* prolonger

length·y ['leŋθɪ] *adj speech, stay* long*

le·ni·ent ['liːnɪənt] *adj* indulgent

lens [lenz] *of microscope etc* lentille *f*; *of eyeglasses* verre *m*; *of camera* objectif *m*; *of eye* cristallin *m*

'lens cov·er *of camera* capuchon *m* d'objectif

Lent [lent] REL Carême *m*

lent [lent] *pret & pp* → **lend**

len·til ['lentl] lentille *f*

'len·til soup soupe *f* aux lentilles

Leo ['liːou] ASTROL Lion *m*

leop·ard ['lepərd] léopard *m*

le·o·tard ['liːoutɑːrd] justaucorps *m*

les·bi·an ['lezbɪən] **1** *n* lesbienne *f* **2** *adj* lesbien*

less [les] **1** *adv* moins; *eat* ~ manger moins; ~ *interesting* moins intéressant; *it cost* ~ c'était moins cher; ~ *than $200* moins de 200 dollars **2** *adj money, salt* moins de

less·en ['lesn] **1** *v/t* réduire **2** *v/i* diminuer

les·son ['lesn] leçon *f*; *at school* cours *m*

let [let] *v/t (pret & pp* **let***) (allow)* lais-

ser; *Br house* louer; ~ **s.o. do sth** laisser qn faire qch; ~ **him come in!** laissez-le entrer!; ~ **him stay if he wants to** laissez-le rester s'il le souhaite, qu'il reste s'il le souhaite; ~**'s stay here** restons ici; ~**'s not argue** ne nous disputons pas; ~ **alone** encore moins; ~ **me go!** lâchez-moi!; ~ **go of sth** *of rope, handle* lâcher qch

♦ **let down** *v/t hair* détacher; *blinds* baisser; *(disappoint)* décevoir; *dress, pants* allonger

♦ **let in** *v/t to house* laisser entrer

♦ **let off** *v/t (not punish)* pardonner; *from car* laisser descendre; **he was let off with a small fine** il s'en est tiré avec une petite amende

♦ **let out** *v/t from room, building* laisser sortir; *jacket etc* agrandir; *groan, yell* laisser échapper; *Br (rent)* louer

♦ **let up** *v/i (stop)* s'arrêter

le·thal ['liːθl] mortel

le·thar·gic [lɪ'θɑːrdʒɪk] *adj* léthargique

leth·ar·gy ['leθərdʒɪ] léthargie *f*

let·ter ['letər] *of alphabet, in mail* lettre *f*

'let·ter·box *Br* boîte *f* aux lettres; 'let·ter·head *(heading)* en-tête *m*; *(headed paper)* papier *m* à en-tête; let·ter of 'cred·it COMM lettre *f* de crédit

let·tuce ['letɪs] laitue *f*

'let-up: *without (a)* ~ sans répit

leu·ke·mia [luː'kiːmɪə] leucémie *f*

lev·el ['levl] **1** *adj field, surface* plat; *in competition, scores* à égalité; *draw* ~ *with s.o.* rattraper qn **2** *n (amount, quantity)* niveau *m*; *on scale, in hierarchy* échelon *m*; *on the* ~ sur un terrain plat; F *(honest)* réglo F

lev·el·head·ed [levl'hedɪd] *adj* pondéré

le·ver ['levər] **1** *n* levier *m* **2** *v/t*: ~ *sth open* ouvrir qch à l'aide d'un levier

lev·er·age ['levrɪdʒ] effet *m* de levier; *(influence)* poids *m*

lev·y ['levɪ] *v/t (pret & pp* **-ied***) taxes* lever

lewd [luːd] *adj* obscène

li·a·bil·i·ty [laɪə'bɪlətɪ] *(responsibility)*

responsabilité *f*; (*likeliness*) disposition *f* (**to** à)

li·a·ble ['laɪəbl] *adj* (*answerable*) responsable (*for* de); **be ~ to** (*likely*) être susceptible de

◆ **li·ai·se with** [lɪ'eɪz] *v/t* assurer la liaison avec

li·ai·son [lɪ'eɪzɑːn] (*contacts*) communication(s) *f*

li·ar [laɪr] menteur(-euse) *m(f)*

li·bel ['laɪbl] **1** *n* diffamation *f* **2** *v/t* diffamer

lib·er·al ['lɪbərəl] *adj* (*broad-minded*) large d'esprit; (*generous: portion etc*) généreux*; POL libéral

lib·e·rate ['lɪbəreɪt] *v/t* libérer

lib·er·at·ed ['lɪbəreɪtɪd] *adj* woman libéré

lib·e·ra·tion [lɪbə'reɪʃn] libération *f*

lib·er·ty ['lɪbərtɪ] liberté *f*; **at ~** prisoner etc en liberté; **be at ~ to do sth** être libre de faire qch

Li·bra ['liːbrə] ASTROL Balance *f*

li·brar·i·an [laɪ'brerɪən] bibliothécaire *m/f*

li·bra·ry ['laɪbrərɪ] bibliothèque *f*

Lib·y·a ['lɪbɪə] Libye *f*

Lib·y·an ['lɪbɪən] **1** *adj* libyen* **2** *n* Libyen(ne) *m(f)*

lice [laɪs] *pl* → **louse**

li·cence ['laɪsns] *Br* → **license** 1 *n*

li·cense ['laɪsns] **1** *n* permis *m*; *Br: for TV* redevance *f* **2** *v/t* company accorder une licence à (**to do** pour faire); **be ~d** equipment être autorisé; *gun* être déclaré

'li·cense num·ber numéro *m* d'immatriculation

'li·cense plate *of car* plaque *f* d'immatriculation

lick [lɪk] *v/t* lécher; **~ one's lips** fig se frotter les mains

lick·ing ['lɪkɪŋ] F (*defeat*) raclée *f* F; **get a ~** prendre une raclée

lid [lɪd] couvercle *m*

lie¹ [laɪ] **1** *n* (*untruth*) mensonge *m* **2** *v/i* mentir

lie² [laɪ] *v/i* (*pret* lay, *pp* lain) of person (*lie down*) s'allonger; (*be lying down*) être allongé; *of object* être; (*be situated*) être, se trouver

◆ **lie down** *v/i* se coucher, s'allonger

lieu [luː]: **in ~ of** au lieu de; **in ~ of payment** en guise de paiement

lieu·ten·ant [luː'tenənt] lieutenant *m*

life [laɪf] (*pl* lives [laɪvz]) vie *f*; *of machine* durée *f* de vie; **all her ~** toute sa vie; **that's ~!** c'est la vie!

'life belt bouée *f* de sauvetage; **'lifeboat** canot *m* de sauvetage; **life ex·pect·an·cy** ['laɪfekspektənsɪ] espérance *f* de vie; **'life·guard** maître nageur *m*; **'life his·to·ry** vie *f*; **life im'pris·on·ment** emprisonnement *m* à vie; **'life in·sur·ance** assurance-vie *f*; **'life jack·et** gilet *m* de sauvetage

life·less ['laɪflɪs] *adj* body inanimé; *personality* mou*; *town* mort

life·like ['laɪflaɪk] *adj* réaliste

'life·long *adj* de toute une vie; **'life mem·ber** membre *m* à vie; **life pre·serv·er** ['laɪfprɪzɜːrvər] *for swimmer* bouée *f* de sauvetage; **'life-sav·ing** *adj* medical equipment de sauvetage; *drugs d'importance vitale*; **life-sized** ['laɪfsaɪzd] *adj* grandeur nature; **'life-style** mode *m* de vie; **life sup·port sys·tem** respirateur *m* (artificiel); **'life-threat·en·ing** *adj* illness extrêmement grave; **'life·time** vie *f*; **in my ~** de mon vivant

lift [lɪft] **1** *v/t* soulever **2** *v/i* of fog se lever **3** *n* Br (*elevator*) ascenseur *m*; **give s.o. a ~ in car** emmener qn en voiture

◆ **lift off** *v/i* of rocket décoller

'lift-off of rocket décollage *m*

lig·a·ment ['lɪgəmənt] ligament *m*

light¹ [laɪt] **1** *n* lumière *f*; **in the ~ of** à la lumière de; **do you have a ~?** vous avez du feu? **2** *v/t* (*pret & pp* lit) fire, cigarette allumer; (*illuminate*) éclairer **3** *adj* (*not dark*) clair

light² [laɪt] **1** *adj* (*not heavy*) léger* **2** *adv*: *travel ~* voyager léger

◆ **light up 1** *v/t* (*illuminate*) éclairer **2** *v/i* (*start to smoke*) s'allumer une cigarette

'light bulb ampoule *f*

light·en¹ ['laɪtn] *v/t* color éclaircir

light·en² ['laɪtn] v/t load alléger
♦ **lighten up** v/i of person se détendre
light·er ['laɪtər] for cigarettes briquet m
light-head·ed [laɪt'hedɪd] (dizzy) étourdi; **light-heart·ed** [laɪt'hɑːrtɪd] adj mood enjoué; criticism, movie léger*; **'light·house** phare m
light·ing ['laɪtɪŋ] éclairage m
light·ly ['laɪtlɪ] adv touch légèrement; **get off** ~ s'en tirer à bon compte
light·ness¹ ['laɪtnɪs] of room, color clarté f
light·ness² ['laɪtnɪs] in weight légèreté f
light·ning ['laɪtnɪŋ] éclair m, foudre f
'light·ning rod paratonnerre m
'light·weight in boxing poids m léger
'light year année-lumière f
like¹ [laɪk] **1** prep comme; **be** ~ **s.o. / sth** ressembler à qn / qch; **what is she** ~? in looks, character comment est-elle?; **it's not** ~ **him** not his character ça ne lui ressemble pas **2** conj F (as) comme; ~ **I said** comme je l'ai dit
like² [laɪk] v/t aimer; **I** ~ **it** ça me plaît (bien); **I** ~ **Susie** j'aime bien Susie; romantically Susie me plaît (bien); **I would** ~ ... je voudrais, j'aimerais ...; **I would** ~ **to leave** je voudrais or j'aimerais partir; **would you** ~ ...? voulez-vous ...?; **would you** ~ **to** ...? as-tu envie de ...?; ~ **to do sth** aimer faire qch; **if you** ~ si vous voulez
like·a·ble ['laɪkəbl] agréable, plaisant
like·li·hood ['laɪklɪhʊd] probabilité f; **in all** ~ selon toute probabilité
like·ly ['laɪklɪ] **1** adj probable **2** adv probablement
like·ness ['laɪknɪs] ressemblance f
like·wise ['laɪkwaɪz] adv de même, aussi
lik·ing ['laɪkɪŋ] for person affection f; for sth penchant m; **to your** ~ à votre goût; **take a** ~ **to s.o.** se prendre d'affection pour qn; **take a** ~ **to sth** se mettre à aimer qch
li·lac ['laɪlək] flower, color lilas m
li·ly ['lɪlɪ] lis m
li·ly of the 'val·ley muguet m
limb [lɪm] membre m

lime¹ [laɪm] fruit citron m vert; tree limettier m
lime² [laɪm] substance chaux f
lime³ [laɪm] (linden tree) tilleul m
lime'green adj jaune-vert
'lime·light: be in the ~ être sous les projecteurs
lim·it ['lɪmɪt] **1** n limite f; **within** ~s dans une certaine mesure; **off** ~s interdit d'accès; **that's the** ~! ça dépasse les bornes!, c'est le comble! **2** v/t limiter
lim·i·ta·tion [lɪmɪ'teɪʃn] limitation f; **know one's** ~s connaître ses limites
lim·it·ed com·pa·ny ['lɪmɪtɪd] société f à responsabilité limitée
li·mo ['lɪmoʊ] F limousine f
lim·ou·sine ['lɪməziːn] limousine f
limp¹ [lɪmp] adj mou*
limp² [lɪmp] **1** n claudication f; **he has a** ~ il boite **2** v/i boiter
line¹ [laɪn] n on paper, road, of text, TELEC ligne f; RAIL voie f; of people file f; of trees rangée f; of poem vers m; of business domaine m, branche f; **hold the** ~ ne quittez pas; **draw the** ~ **at sth** refuse to do se refuser à faire qch, not tolerate ne pas tolérer qch; ~ **of inquiry** piste f; ~ **of reasoning** raisonnement m; **stand in** ~ faire la queue; **in** ~ **with** conformément à, en accord avec
line² [laɪn] v/t with material recouvrir, garnir; clothes doubler
♦ **line up** v/i se mettre en rang(s)
lin·e·ar ['lɪnɪər] adj linéaire
lin·en ['lɪnɪn] material lin m; (sheets etc) linge m
lin·er ['laɪnər] ship paquebot m de grande ligne
lines·man ['laɪnzmən] SP juge m de touche; tennis juge m de ligne
'line-up for sports event sélection f
lin·ger ['lɪŋgər] v/i of person s'attarder, traîner; of pain persister
lin·ge·rie ['lænʒəriː] lingerie f
lin·guist ['lɪŋgwɪst] linguiste m; **she's a good** ~ elle est douée pour les langues
lin·guis·tic [lɪŋ'gwɪstɪk] adj linguistique

L

lin·ing ['laɪnɪŋ] *of clothes* doublure *f*; *of brakes, pipes* garniture *f*

link [lɪŋk] **1** *n* (*connection*) lien *m*; *in chain* maillon *m* **2** *v/t* lier, relier; **her name has been ~ed with …** son nom a été associé à …
♦ **link up** *v/i* se rejoindre; TV se connecter

li·on ['laɪən] lion *m*

li·on·ess ['laɪənes] lionne *f*

lip [lɪp] lèvre *f*

'lip-read *v/i* (*pret & pp* **-read** [-red]) lire sur les lèvres

'lip·stick rouge *m* à lèvres

li·queur [lɪ'kjʊr] liqueur *f*

liq·uid ['lɪkwɪd] **1** *n* liquide *m* **2** *adj* liquide

liq·ui·date ['lɪkwɪdeɪt] *v/t* liquider

liq·ui·da·tion [lɪkwɪ'deɪʃn] liquidation *f*; **go into ~** entrer en liquidation

li·quid·i·ty [lɪ'kwɪdɪtɪ] FIN liquidité *f*

liq·uid·ize ['lɪkwɪdaɪz] *v/t* passer au mixeur, rendre liquide

liq·uid·iz·er ['lɪkwɪdaɪzər] mixeur *m*

liq·uor ['lɪkər] alcool *m*

'liq·uor store magasin *m* de vins et spiritueux

lisp [lɪsp] **1** *n* zézaiement *m* **2** *v/i* zézayer

list [lɪst] **1** *n* liste *f* **2** *v/t* faire la liste de; (*enumerate*) énumérer; COMPUT lister

lis·ten ['lɪsn] *v/i* écouter
♦ **listen in** *v/i* écouter
♦ **listen to** *v/t radio, person* écouter

lis·ten·er ['lɪsnər] *to radio* auditeur (-trice) *m(f)*; **he's a good ~** il sait écouter

list·ings mag·a·zine ['lɪstɪŋz] programme *m* télé / cinéma

list·less ['lɪstlɪs] *adj* amorphe

lit [lɪt] *pret & pp* → **light**

li·ter ['liːtər] litre *m*

lit·e·ral ['lɪtərəl] *adj* littéral

lit·e·ral·ly ['lɪtərəlɪ] *adv* littéralement

lit·e·ra·ry ['lɪtərerɪ] *adj* littéraire

lit·e·rate ['lɪtərət] *adj* lettré; **be ~** savoir lire et écrire

lit·e·ra·ture ['lɪtrətʃər] littérature *f*; *about a product* documentation *f*

li·tre ['liːtər] *Br* → **liter**

lit·ter ['lɪtər] détritus *mpl*, ordures *fpl*; *of animal* portée *f*

'lit·ter bin *Br* poubelle *f*

lit·tle ['lɪtl] **1** *adj* petit; **the ~ ones** les petits **2** *n* peu *m*; **the ~ I know** le peu que je sais; **a ~** un peu; **a ~ bread / wine** un peu de pain / vin **3** *adv* peu; **~ by ~** peu à peu; **a ~ bigger** un peu plus gros; **a ~ before 6** un peu avant 6h00

live[1] [lɪv] *v/i* (*reside*) vivre, habiter; (*be alive*) vivre
♦ **live on 1** *v/t rice, bread* vivre de **2** *v/i* (*continue living*) survivre
♦ **live up** *v/t*: **live it up** faire la fête
♦ **live up to** *v/t* être à la hauteur de; **live up to expectations** *person* être à la hauteur; *vacation, product* tenir ses promesses
♦ **live with** *v/t* vivre avec; (*accept*) se faire à; **I can live with it** je peux m'y faire

live[2] [laɪv] *adj broadcast* en direct; *bomb* non désamorcé

live·li·hood ['laɪvlɪhʊd] gagne-pain *m inv*; **earn one's ~ from …** gagner sa vie grâce à …

live·li·ness ['laɪvlɪnɪs] vivacité *f*

live·ly ['laɪvlɪ] *adj person, city* plein de vie, vivant; *party* animé; *music* entraînant

liv·er ['lɪvər] foie *m*

live·stock ['laɪvstɑːk] bétail *m*

liv·id ['lɪvɪd] *adj* (*angry*) furieux*

liv·ing ['lɪvɪŋ] **1** *adj* vivant **2** *n* vie *f*; **earn one's ~** gagner sa vie; **standard of ~** niveau *m* de vie

'liv·ing room salle *f* de séjour

liz·ard ['lɪzərd] lézard *m*

load [loʊd] **1** *n* charge *f*, chargement *m*; ELEC charge *f*; **~s of** F plein de **2** *v/t truck, camera, gun, software* charger

load·ed ['loʊdɪd] *adj* F (*very rich*) plein aux as F; (*drunk*) bourré F

loaf [loʊf] (*pl* **loaves** [loʊvz]): **a ~ of bread** un pain
♦ **loaf around** *v/i* F traîner

loaf·er ['loʊfər] *shoe* mocassin *m*

loan [loʊn] **1** *n* prêt *m*; **I've got it on ~** on me l'a prêté **2** *v/t*: **~ s.o. sth** prêter qch à qn

loathe [louð] *v/t* détester

loath·ing ['louðɪŋ] dégoût *m*

lob·by ['lɑːbɪ] **1** *n in hotel* hall *m*; *in theater* entrée *f*, vestibule *m*; POL lobby *m* **2** *v/t politician* faire pression sur
♦ **lobby for** *v/t* faire pression pour obtenir

lobe [loub] *of ear* lobe *m*

lob·ster ['lɑːbstər] homard *m*

lo·cal ['loukl] **1** *adj* local; **I'm not ~** je ne suis pas de la région / du quartier **2** *n* habitant *m* de la région / du quartier

'lo·cal call TELEC appel *m* local; **lo·cal e'lec·tions** élections *fpl* locales; **lo·cal 'gov·ern·ment** autorités *f* locales

lo·cal·i·ty [lou'kælətɪ] endroit *m*

lo·cal·ize ['loukəlaɪz] *v/t* localiser

lo·cal·ly ['loukəlɪ] *adv live, work* dans le quartier, dans la région

lo·cal 'pro·duce produits *mpl* locaux

'lo·cal time heure *f* locale

lo·cate [lou'keɪt] *v/t new factory etc* établir; (*identify position of*) localiser; **be ~d** se trouver

lo·ca·tion [lou'keɪʃn] (*siting*) emplacement *m*; (*identifying position of*) localisation *f*; **on ~** *movie* en extérieur

lock[1] [lɑːk] *of hair* mèche *f*

lock[2] [lɑːk] **1** *n on door* serrure *f* **2** *v/t door* fermer à clef; **~ sth in position** verrouiller qch, bloquer qch
♦ **lock away** *v/t* mettre sous clef
♦ **lock in** *v/t person* enfermer à clef
♦ **lock out** *v/t of house* enfermer dehors; **I locked myself out** je me suis enfermé dehors
♦ **lock up** *v/t in prison* mettre sous les verrous, enfermer

lock·er ['lɑːkər] casier *m*

'lock·er room vestiaire *m*

lock·et ['lɑːkɪt] médaillon *m*

lock·smith ['lɑːksmɪθ] serrurier *m*

lo·cust ['loukəst] locuste *f*, sauterelle *f*

lodge [lɑːdʒ] **1** *v/t complaint* déposer **2** *v/i of bullet, ball* se loger, rester coincé

lodg·er ['lɑːdʒər] *Br* locataire *m/f*; *with meals* pensionnaire *m/f*

loft [lɑːft] grenier *m*; *apartment* loft *m*; *raised bed area* mezzanine *f*

'loft con·ver·sion *Br* grenier *m* aménagé

loft·y ['lɑːftɪ] *adj heights* haut; *ideals* élevé

log [lɑːg] bûche *f*; (*written record*) journal *m* de bord
♦ **log off** *v/i* (*pret & pp* **-ged**) se déconnecter
♦ **log on** *v/i* se connecter
♦ **log on to** *v/t* se connecter à

'log·book journal *m* de bord

log 'cab·in cabane *f* en rondins

log·ger·heads ['lɑːgərhedz]: **be at ~** être en désaccord

lo·gic ['lɑːdʒɪk] logique *f*

lo·gic·al ['lɑːdʒɪkl] *adj* logique

lo·gic·al·ly ['lɑːdʒɪklɪ] *adv* logiquement

lo·gis·tics [lə'dʒɪstɪks] logistique *f*

lo·go ['lougou] logo *m*, sigle *m*

loi·ter ['lɔɪtər] *v/i* traîner

lol·li·pop ['lɑːlɪpɑːp] sucette *f*

Lon·don ['lʌndn] Londres

lone·li·ness ['lounlɪnɪs] *of person* solitude *f*, *of place* isolement *m*

lone·ly ['lounlɪ] *adj person* seul, solitaire; *place* isolé

lon·er ['lounər] solitaire *m/f*

long[1] [lɑːŋ] **1** *adj* long*; **it's a ~ way** c'est loin **2** *adv* longtemps; **don't be ~** dépêche-toi; **how ~ will it take?** combien de temps cela va-t-il prendre?; **5 weeks is too ~** 5 semaines, c'est trop long; **will it take ~?** est-ce que cela va prendre longtemps?; **that was ~ ago** c'était il y a longtemps; **~ before then** bien avant cela; **before ~** *in the past* peu après; *in the future* dans peu de temps; **we can't wait any ~er** nous ne pouvons pas attendre plus longtemps; **he no ~er works here** il ne travaille plus ici; **so ~ as** (*provided*) pourvu que; **so ~!** à bientôt!

long[2] [lɑːŋ] *v/i*: **~ for sth** avoir très envie de qch, désirer (ardemment) qch; **be ~ing to do sth** avoir très envie de faire qch

long-'dis·tance *adj phonecall* longue distance; *race* de fond; *flight* long-courrier

lon·gev·i·ty [lɑːnˈdʒevɪtɪ] longévité f
long·ing [ˈlɑːŋɪŋ] n désir m, envie f
lon·gi·tude [ˈlɑːndʒɪtuːd] longitude f
'long jump saut m en longueur;
'long-range adj missile à longue portée; forecast à long terme; **long-
-sight·ed** [lɑːŋˈsaɪtɪd] adj hypermétrope; due to old age presbyte;
long-sleeved [lɑːŋˈsliːvd] adj à
manches longues; **long-'stand·ing**
adj de longue date; **'long-term** adj
à long terme; unemployment de longue durée; **'long wave** RAD grandes
ondes fpl
long·wind·ed [lɑːŋˈwɪndɪd] adj story,
explanation interminable; person intarissable
loo [luː] Br F toilettes fpl
look [lʊk] **1** n (appearance) air m, apparence f; (glance) coup m d'œil, regard
m; **give s.o. / sth a ~** regarder qn /
qch; **have a ~ at sth** (examine) examiner qch, regarder qch; **can I have a
~?** je peux regarder?, fais voir; **can
I have a ~ around?** in shop etc
puis-je jeter un coup d'œil?; **~s**
(beauty) beauté f; **she still has her
~s** elle est toujours aussi belle **2** v/i
regarder; (search) chercher, regarder;
(seem) avoir l'air; **you ~ tired** tu as
l'air fatigué
♦ **look after** v/t s'occuper de
♦ **look ahead** v/i fig regarder en avant
♦ **look around** v/i jeter un coup d'œil
♦ **look at** v/t regarder; (examine) examiner; (consider) voir, envisager
♦ **look back** v/i regarder derrière soi
♦ **look down on** v/t mépriser
♦ **look for** v/t chercher
♦ **look forward to** v/t attendre avec
impatience, se réjouir de; **I'm not
looking forward to it** je ne suis
pas pressé que ça arrive
♦ **look in on** v/t (visit) passer voir
♦ **look into** v/t (investigate) examiner
♦ **look on 1** v/i (watch) regarder **2** v/t:
look on s.o. / sth as considérer
qn / qch comme
♦ **look onto** v/t garden, street donner
sur
♦ **look out** v/i of window etc regarder

dehors; (pay attention) faire attention;
look out! attention!
♦ **look out for** v/t essayer de repérer;
(be on guard against) se méfier de;
(take care of) prendre soin de
♦ **look out of** v/t window regarder par
♦ **look over** v/t house, translation examiner
♦ **look through** v/t magazine, notes
parcourir, feuilleter
♦ **look to** v/t (rely on) compter sur
♦ **look up 1** v/i from paper etc lever les
yeux; (improve) s'améliorer; **things
are looking up** ça va mieux **2** v/t
word, phone number chercher; (visit)
passer voir
♦ **look up to** v/t (respect) respecter
'look·out person sentinelle f; **be on
the ~ for** être à l'affût de
♦ **loom up** [luːm] v/i out of mist etc surgir
loon·y [ˈluːnɪ] **1** n F dingue m/f F **2** adj
F dingue F
loop [luːp] n boucle f
'loop·hole in law etc lacune f
loose [luːs] adj knot lâche; connection,
screw desserré; clothes ample; morals
relâché; wording vague; **~ change**
petite monnaie f; **~ ends** of problem,
discussion derniers détails mpl
loose·ly [ˈluːslɪ] adv tied sans serrer;
worded de manière approximative
loos·en [ˈluːsn] v/t collar, knot desserrer
loot [luːt] **1** n butin m **2** v/i se livrer au
pillage
loot·er [ˈluːtər] pilleur(-euse) m(f)
♦ **lop off** [lɑːp] v/t (pret & pp -ped)
couper, tailler
lop-sid·ed [lɑːpˈsaɪdɪd] adj déséquilibré, disproportionné
Lord [lɔːrd] (god) Seigneur m
Lord's 'Prayer Pater m
lor·ry [ˈlɑːrɪ] Br camion m
lose [luːz] **1** v/t (pret & pp lost) perdre;
I'm lost je suis perdu; **get lost!** F va
te faire voir! **2** v/i SP perdre; of clock
retarder
♦ **lose out** v/i être perdant
los·er [ˈluːzər] perdant(e) m(f)
loss [lɑːs] perte f; **make a ~** subir une

perte; **be at a ~** ne pas savoir quoi faire

lost [lɑːst] **1** adj perdu **2** pret & pp → **lose**

lost-and-'found (of·fice) (bureau m des) objets mpl trouvés

lot [lɑːt]: **the ~** tout, le tout; **a ~, ~s** beaucoup; **a ~ of, ~s of** beaucoup de; **a ~ better** beaucoup mieux; **quite a ~ of people / snow** pas mal de gens / neige

lo·tion ['louʃn] lotion f

lot·te·ry ['lɑːtərɪ] loterie f

loud [laud] adj music, voice fort; noise grand; color criard; **say it out ~** dites-le à voix haute

loud·speak·er haut-parleur m

lounge [laundʒ] salon m

♦ **lounge around** v/i paresser

'lounge suit Br complet m

louse [laus] (pl lice [laɪs]) pou m

lous·y ['lauzɪ] adj F minable F, mauvais; **I feel ~** je suis mal fichu F

lout [laut] rustre m

lov·a·ble ['lʌvəbl] adj sympathique, adorable

love [lʌv] **1** n amour m; in tennis zéro m; **be in ~** être amoureux (**with** de); **fall in ~** tomber amoureux (**with** de); **make ~** faire l'amour (**to** avec); **yes, my ~** oui mon amour **2** v/t aimer; wine, music adorer; **~ to do sth** aimer faire qch

'love af·fair aventure f; **'love let·ter** billet m doux; **'love life** vie f sentimentale; **how's your ~?** comment vont tes amours?

love·ly ['lʌvlɪ] adj beau*; house, wife ravissant; character charmant; meal délicieux*; **we had a ~ time** nous nous sommes bien amusés; **it's ~ to be here again** c'est formidable d'être à nouveau ici

lov·er ['lʌvər] man amant m; woman maîtresse f; person in love amoureux(-euse) m(f); of good food etc amateur m

lov·ing ['lʌvɪŋ] adj affectueux*

lov·ing·ly ['lʌvɪŋlɪ] adv avec amour

low [lou] **1** adj bas*; quality mauvais; **be feeling ~** être déprimé; **be ~ on**

gas / tea être à court d'essence / de thé **2** n in weather dépression f; in sales, statistics niveau m bas

'low·brow adj peu intellectuel*; **'low-cal·o·rie** adj (à) basses calories; **'low-cut** adj dress décolleté

low·er ['louər] v/t baisser; to the ground faire descendre; boat mettre à la mer

'low-fat adj allégé; **'low-key** adj discret*, mesuré; **'low·lands** npl plaines fpl; **low-'pres·sure ar·e·a** zone f de basse pression; **'low sea·son** basse saison f; **'low tide** marée f basse

loy·al ['lɔɪəl] adj fidèle, loyal

loy·al·ly ['lɔɪəlɪ] adv fidèlement

loy·al·ty ['lɔɪəltɪ] loyauté f

loz·enge ['lɑːzɪndʒ] shape losange m; tablet pastille f

LP [el'piː] abbr (= **long-playing rec·ord**) 33 tours m

Ltd abbr (= **limited**) company à responsabilité limitée

lu·bri·cant ['luːbrɪkənt] lubrifiant m

lu·bri·cate ['luːbrɪkeɪt] v/t lubrifier

lu·bri·ca·tion [luːbrɪ'keɪʃn] lubrification f

lu·cid ['luːsɪd] adj (clear) clair; (sane) lucide

luck [lʌk] chance f, hasard m; **bad ~** malchance f; **hard ~!** pas de chance!; **good ~** (bonne) chance f; **good ~!** bonne chance!

♦ **luck out** v/i F avoir du bol F

luck·i·ly ['lʌkɪlɪ] adv heureusement

luck·y ['lʌkɪ] adj person chanceux*; number porte-bonheur inv; coincidence heureux*; **it's her ~ day!** c'est son jour de chance!; **you were ~ to be alive** il a de la chance d'être encore en vie; **that's ~!** c'est un coup de chance!

lu·cra·tive ['luːkrətɪv] adj lucratif*

lu·di·crous ['luːdɪkrəs] adj ridicule

lug [lʌg] v/t (pret & pp -ged) F traîner

lug·gage ['lʌgɪdʒ] bagages mpl

luke·warm ['luːkwɔːrm] adj also fig tiède

lull [lʌl] **1** n in storm, fighting accalmie f; in conversation pause f **2** v/t: **~ s.o. into a false sense of security** en-

dormir la vigilance de qn
lul·la·by ['lʌləbaɪ] berceuse *f*
lum·ba·go [lʌmbeɪgoʊ] lumbago *m*
lum·ber ['lʌmbər] (*timber*) bois *m* de
construction
lu·mi·nous ['lu:mɪnəs] *adj* lumineux*
lump [lʌmp] *of sugar* morceau *m*;
(*swelling*) grosseur *f*
♦ **lump together** *v/t* mettre dans le
même panier
lump 'sum forfait *m*
lump·y ['lʌmpɪ] *adj liquid, sauce* grumeleux*; *mattress* défoncé
lu·na·cy ['lu:nəsɪ] folie *f*
lu·nar ['lu:nər] *adj* lunaire
lu·na·tic ['lu:nətɪk] *n* fou *m*, folle *f*
lunch [lʌntʃ] déjeuner *m*; *have ~* déjeuner
'lunch box panier-repas *m*; **'lunch
break** pause-déjeuner *f*; **'lunch
hour** heure *f* du déjeuner; **'lunch-
time** heure *f* du déjeuner, midi *m*
lung [lʌŋ] poumon *m*
'lung can·cer cancer *m* du poumon
♦ **lunge at** [lʌndʒ] *v/t* se jeter sur
lurch [lɜ:rtʃ] *v/i of person* tituber; *of*

ship tanguer
lure [lʊr] **1** *n* attrait *m*, appât *m* **2** *v/t*
attirer, entraîner
lu·rid ['lʊrɪd] *adj color* cru; *details* choquant
lurk [lɜ:rk] *v/i of person* se cacher; *of
doubt* persister
lus·cious ['lʌʃəs] *adj fruit, dessert* succulent; F *woman, man* appétissant
lush [lʌʃ] *adj vegetation* luxuriant
lust [lʌst] *n* désir *m*; *rel* luxure *f*
Lux·em·bourg ['lʌksmbɜ:rg] **1** *n* Luxembourg *m* **2** *adj* luxembourgeois
Lux·em·bourg·er ['lʌksmbɜ:rgər] Lu-
xembourgeois(e) *m(f)*
lux·u·ri·ous [lʌg'ʒʊrɪəs] *adj* luxueux*
lux·u·ri·ous·ly [lʌg'ʒʊrɪəslɪ] *adv* luxueusement
lux·u·ry ['lʌkʃərɪ] **1** *n* luxe *m* **2** *adj* de
luxe
lymph gland ['lɪmfglænd] ganglion *m*
lymphatique
lynch [lɪntʃ] *v/t* lyncher
Ly·ons ['liː(ə)n] Lyon
lyr·i·cist ['lɪrɪsɪst] parolier(-ière) *m(f)*
lyr·ics ['lɪrɪks] *npl* paroles *fpl*

M

M

M [em] *abbr* (= *medium*) M
MA [em'eɪ] *abbr* (= *Master of Arts*)
maîtrise *f* de lettres
ma'am [mæm] madame
ma·chine [mə'ʃiːn] **1** *n* machine *f* **2** *v/t
with sewing machine* coudre à la ma-
chine; TECH usiner
ma'chine gun *n* mitrailleuse *f*
ma·chine-'read·a·ble *adj* lisible par
ordinateur
ma·chin·e·ry [mə'ʃiːnərɪ] (*machines*)
machines *fpl*
ma·chine trans·la·tion traduction *f*
automatique
ma·chis·mo [mə'kɪzmoʊ] machisme
m

mach·o ['mætʃoʊ] *adj* macho *inv*; *~
type* macho *m*
mack·in·tosh ['mækɪntɑːʃ] imperméable *m*
mac·ro ['mækroʊ] COMPUT macro *f*
mad [mæd] *adj* (*insane*) fou*; F (*angry*)
furieux*; *be ~ about* F (*keen on*) être
fou de; *drive s.o. ~* rendre qn fou; *go
~ also with enthusiasm* devenir fou;
like ~ F *run, work* comme un fou
mad·den ['mædən] *v/t* (*infuriate*) exaspérer
mad·den·ing ['mædnɪŋ] *adj* exaspérant
made [meɪd] *pret & pp* → **make**
'mad·house *fig* maison *f* de fous

mad·ly ['mædlɪ] *adv* follement, comme un fou; **~ in love** éperdument amoureux*

'mad·man fou *m*

mad·ness ['mædnɪs] folie *f*

Ma·don·na [mə'dɑːnə] Madone *f*

Ma·fi·a ['mɑːfɪə]: **the ~** la Mafia

mag·a·zine [mægə'ziːn] *printed* magazine *m*

mag·got ['mægət] ver *m*

Ma·gi ['meɪdʒaɪ] REL: **the ~** les Rois *mpl* mages

mag·ic ['mædʒɪk] **1** *adj* magique **2** *n* magie *f*; **like ~** comme par enchantement

mag·i·cal ['mædʒɪkl] *adj* magique

ma·gi·cian [mə'dʒɪʃn] magicien(ne) *m(f)*; *performer* prestidigitateur(-trice) *m(f)*

ma·gic 'spell sort *m*; *formula* formule *f* magique; **ma·gic 'trick** tour *m* de magie; **mag·ic 'wand** baguette *f* magique

mag·nan·i·mous [mæg'nænɪməs] *adj* magnanime

mag·net ['mægnɪt] aimant *m*

mag·net·ic [mæg'netɪk] *adj also fig* magnétique

mag·net·ic 'stripe piste *f* magnétique

mag·net·ism ['mægnɪtɪzm] *also fig* magnétisme *m*

mag·nif·i·cence [mæg'nɪfɪsəns] magnificence *f*

mag·nif·i·cent [mæg'nɪfɪsənt] *adj* magnifique

mag·ni·fy ['mægnɪfaɪ] *v/t* (*pret & pp -ied*) grossir; *difficulties* exagérer

mag·ni·fy·ing glass ['mægnɪfaɪɪŋ] loupe *f*

mag·ni·tude ['mægnɪtuːd] ampleur *f*

ma·hog·a·ny [mə'hɑːgənɪ] acajou *m*

maid [meɪd] *servant* domestique *f*; *in hotel* femme *f* de chambre

maid·en name ['meɪdn] nom *m* de jeune fille

maid·en 'voy·age premier voyage *m*

mail [meɪl] **1** *n* courrier *m*, poste *f*; **put sth in the ~** poster qch **2** *v/t letter* poster

'mail·box boîte *f* aux lettres

mail·ing list ['meɪlɪŋ] fichier *m* d'adresses

'mail·man facteur *m*; **mail·'or·der cat·a·log**, *Br* **mail·'or·der cat·a·logue** catalogue *m* de vente par correspondance; **mail·'or·der firm** société *f* de vente par correspondance; **'mail·shot** mailing *m*, publipostage *m*

maim [meɪm] *v/t* estropier, mutiler

main [meɪn] *adj* principal

'main course plat *m* principal; **main 'en·trance** entrée *f* principale; **'main·frame** ordinateur *m* central; **'main·land** continent *m*

main·ly ['meɪnlɪ] *adv* principalement, surtout

main 'road route *f* principale; **'main·stream** *n* courant *m* dominant; **'main street** rue *f* principale

main·tain [meɪn'teɪn] *v/t peace, law and order* maintenir; *pace, speed* soutenir; *relationship, machine, building* entretenir; *family* subvenir aux besoins de; *innocence, guilt* affirmer; **~ that** soutenir que

main·te·nance ['meɪntənəns] *of machine, building* entretien *m*; *Br money* pension *f* alimentaire; *of law and order* maintien *m*

'main·te·nance costs *npl* frais *mpl* d'entretien

'main·te·nance staff personnel *m* d'entretien

ma·jes·tic [mə'dʒestɪk] *adj* majestueux*

maj·es·ty ['mædʒəstɪ] majesté *f*; **Her Majesty** Sa Majesté

ma·jor ['meɪdʒər] **1** *adj* (*significant*) important, majeur; **in C ~** MUS en do majeur **2** *n* MIL commandant *m*

♦ **major in** *v/t* se spécialiser en

ma·jor·i·ty [mə'dʒɑːrətɪ] majorité *f*, plupart *f*; POL majorité *f*; **be in the ~** être majoritaire

make [meɪk] **1** *n* (*brand*) marque *f* **2** *v/t* (*pret & pp made*) ◊ faire; (*manufacture*) fabriquer; (*earn*) gagner; **~ a decision** prendre une décision; **~ a telephone call** téléphoner, passer un coup de fil; **made in Japan** fabriqué au Japon; **3 and 3 ~ 6** 3 et

M

3 font 6; **~ it** (*catch bus, train*) arriver à temps; (*come*) venir; (*succeed*) réussir; (*survive*) s'en sortir; **what time do you ~ it?** quelle heure as-tu?; **~ believe** prétendre; **~ do with** se contenter de, faire avec; **what do you ~ of it?** qu'en dis-tu?
◇ : **~ s.o. do sth** (*force to*) forcer qn à faire qch; (*cause to*) faire faire qch à qn; **you can't ~ me do it!** tu ne m'obligeras pas à faire ça!; **what made you think that?** qu'est-ce qui t'a fait penser ça?; **~ s.o. happy / angry** rendre qn heureux / furieux;

♦ **make for** v/t (*go toward*) se diriger vers

♦ **make off** v/i s'enfuir

♦ **make off with** v/t (*steal*) s'enfuir avec

♦ **make out 1** v/t *list, check* faire; (*see*) voir, distinguer; (*imply*) prétendre **2** v/i F *kiss etc* se peloter; *have sex* s'envoyer en l'air F

♦ **make over** v/t: **make sth over to s.o** céder qch à qn

♦ **make up 1** v/i *of woman, actor* se maquiller; *after quarrel* se réconcilier **2** v/t *story, excuse* inventer; *face* maquiller; (*constitute*) constituer; **be made up of** être constitué de; **make up one's mind** se décider; **make it up** *after quarrel* se réconcilier

♦ **make up for** v/t compenser; **I'll try to make up for it** j'essaierai de me rattraper; **make up for lost time** rattraper son retard

'make-be·lieve: **it's just ~** c'est juste pour faire semblant

mak·er ['meɪkər] (*manufacturer*) fabricant *m*

make·shift ['meɪkʃɪft] *adj* de fortune

'make-up (*cosmetics*) maquillage *m*

'make-up bag trousse *f* de maquillage

mal·ad·just·ed [mælə'dʒʌstɪd] *adj* inadapté

male [meɪl] **1** *adj* masculin; BIOL, TECH mâle; **~ bosses / teachers** patrons / enseignants hommes **2** *n* (*man*) homme *m*; *animal, bird, fish* mâle *m*

male chau·vin·ism ['ʃoʊvɪnɪzm] machisme *m*; **male chau·vin·ist 'pig** macho *m*; **male 'nurse** infirmier *m*

ma·lev·o·lent [mə'levələnt] *adj* malveillant

mal·func·tion [mæl'fʌŋkʃn] **1** *n* mauvais fonctionnement *m*, défaillance *f* **2** v/i mal fonctionner

mal·ice ['mælɪs] méchanceté *f*, malveillance *f*

ma·li·cious [mə'lɪʃəs] *adj* méchant, malveillant

ma·lig·nant [mə'lɪgnənt] *adj tumor* malin*

mall [mɔːl] (*shopping ~*) centre *m* commercial

mal·nu·tri·tion [mælnuː'trɪʃn] malnutrition *f*

mal·treat [mæl'triːt] v/t maltraiter

mal·treat·ment [mæl'triːtmənt] mauvais traitement *m*

mam·mal ['mæml] mammifère *m*

mam·moth ['mæməθ] *adj* (*enormous*) colossal, géant

man [mæn] **1** *n* (*pl* **men** [men]) homme *m*; (*humanity*) l'homme *m*; *in checkers* pion *m* **2** v/t (*pret & pp* **-ned**) *telephones* être de permanence à; *front desk* être de service à; **~ned by a crew of three** avec un équipage de trois personnes

man·age ['mænɪdʒ] **1** v/t *business* diriger; *money* gérer; *bags* porter; **~ to ...** réussir à ...; **I couldn't ~ another thing** *to eat* je ne peux plus rien avaler **2** v/i (*cope*) se débrouiller; **can you ~?** tu vas y arriver?

man·age·a·ble ['mænɪdʒəbl] *adj* gérable; *vehicle* maniable; *task* faisable

man·age·ment ['mænɪdʒmənt] (*managing*) gestion *f*, direction *f*; (*managers*) direction *f*; **under his ~** sous sa direction

man·age·ment 'buy-out rachat *m* d'entreprise par la direction; **man·age·ment con'sult·ant** conseiller (-ère) *m(f)* en gestion; **'man·age·ment stud·ies** études *fpl* de gestion; **'man·age·ment team** équipe *f* dirigeante

man·ag·er ['mænɪdʒər] directeur

(-trice) *m(f)*; *of store, restaurant, hotel* gérant(e) *m(f)*; *of department* responsable *m/f*; *of singer, band, team* manageur(-euse) *m(f)*; *can I talk to the ~?* est-ce que je peux parler au directeur?

man·a·ge·ri·al [mænɪˈdʒɪrɪəl] *adj* de directeur, de gestionnaire; *a ~ post* un poste d'encadrement

man·ag·ing di·rec·tor [ˈmænɪdʒɪŋ] directeur(-trice) *m(f)* général(e)

man·da·rin or·ange [mændərɪn-ˈɔːrɪndʒ] mandarine *f*

man·date [ˈmændeɪt] mandat *m*

man·da·to·ry [ˈmændətɔːrɪ] *adj* obligatoire

mane [meɪn] *of horse* crinière *f*

ma·neu·ver [məˈnuːvər] **1** *n* manœuvre *f* **2** *v/t* manœuvrer

man·gle [ˈmæŋgl] *v/t* (*crush*) broyer, déchiqueter

man·han·dle [ˈmænhændl] *v/t person* malmener; *object* déplacer manuellement

man·hood [ˈmænhʊd] (*maturity*) âge *m* d'homme; (*virility*) virilité *f*

'man·hour heure *f* de travail

'man·hunt chasse *f* à l'homme

ma·ni·a [ˈmeɪnɪə] (*craze*) manie *f*

ma·ni·ac [ˈmeɪnɪæk] F fou *m*, folle *f*

man·i·cure [ˈmænɪkjʊr] manucure *f*

man·i·fest [ˈmænɪfest] **1** *adj* manifeste **2** *v/t* manifester; *~ itself* se manifester

ma·nip·u·late [məˈnɪpjəleɪt] *v/t* manipuler

ma·nip·u·la·tion [mənɪpjəˈleɪʃn] manipulation *f*

ma·nip·u·la·tive [mənɪpjəˈlətɪv] *adj* manipulateur*

man'kind humanité *f*

man·ly [ˈmænlɪ] *adj* viril

'man-made *adj* synthétique

man·ner [ˈmænər] *of doing sth* manière *f*, façon *f*; (*attitude*) comportement *m*

man·ners [ˈmænərz] *npl* manières *fpl*; *good / bad ~* bonnes / mauvaises manières *fpl*; *have no ~* n'avoir aucun savoir-vivre

ma·noeu·vre [məˈnuːvər] *Br* → **ma-neuver**

'man·pow·er main-d'œuvre *f*

man·sion [ˈmænʃn] (grande) demeure *f*

'man·slaugh·ter *Br* homicide *m* involontaire

man·tel·piece [ˈmæntlpiːs] manteau *m* de cheminée

man·u·al [ˈmænjʊəl] **1** *adj* manuel* **2** *n* manuel *m*

man·u·al·ly [ˈmænjʊəlɪ] *adv* manuellement

man·u·fac·ture [mænjʊˈfæktʃər] **1** *n* fabrication *f* **2** *v/t equipment* fabriquer

man·u·fac·tur·er [mænjʊˈfæktʃərər] fabricant *m*

man·u·fac·tur·ing [mænjʊˈfæktʃərɪŋ] *n industry* industrie *f*

ma·nure [məˈnʊr] fumier *m*

man·u·script [ˈmænjʊskrɪpt] manuscrit *m*

man·y [ˈmenɪ] **1** *adj* beaucoup de; *~ times* bien des fois; *not ~ people* pas beaucoup de gens; *too ~ problems* trop de problèmes; *as ~ as possible* autant que possible **2** *pron* beaucoup; *a great ~, a good ~* un bon nombre; *how ~ do you need?* combien en veux-tu?

'man-year année de travail moyenne par personne

map [mæp] *n* carte *f*; *of town* plan *m*

♦ **map out** *v/t* (*pret & pp -ped*) planifier

ma·ple [ˈmeɪpl] érable *m*

ma·ple 'syr·up sirop *m* d'érable

mar [mɑːr] *v/t* (*pret & pp -red*) gâcher

mar·a·thon [ˈmærəθɑːn] *race* marathon *m*

mar·ble [ˈmɑːrbl] *material* marbre *m*

March [mɑːrtʃ] mars *m*

march [mɑːrtʃ] **1** *n also* (*demonstration*) marche *f* **2** *v/i* marcher au pas; *in protest* défiler

march·er [ˈmɑːrtʃər] manifestant(e) *m(f)*

mare [mer] jument *f*

mar·ga·rine [mɑːrdʒəˈriːn] margarine *f*

mar·gin [ˈmɑːrdʒɪn] *of page*, COMM

M

marge f; **by a narrow ~** de justesse

mar‑gin‑al ['mɑːrdʒɪnl] adj (slight) léger*

mar‑gin‑al‑ly ['mɑːrdʒɪnlɪ] adv (slightly) légèrement

mar‑i‑hua‑na, mar‑i‑jua‑na [mærɪ'hwɑːnə] marijuana f

ma‑ri‑na [mə'riːnə] port m de plaisance

mar‑i‑nade [mærɪ'neɪd] n marinade f

mar‑i‑nate ['mærɪneɪt] v/t mariner

ma‑rine [mə'riːn] **1** adj marin **2** n MIL marine m

mar‑i‑tal ['mærɪtl] adj conjugal

mar‑i‑tal 'sta‑tus situation f de famille

mar‑i‑time ['mærɪtaɪm] adj maritime

mark [mɑːrk] **1** n marque f; (stain) tache f; (sign, token) signe m; (trace) trace f; Br EDU note f; **leave one's ~** marquer de son influence **2** v/t marquer; (stain) tacher; Br EDU noter; (indicate) indiquer, marquer **3** v/i of fabric se tacher

♦ **mark down** v/t goods démarquer; price baisser

♦ **mark out** v/t with a line etc délimiter; fig (set apart) distinguer

♦ **mark up** v/t price majorer; goods augmenter le prix de

marked [mɑːrkt] adj (definite) marqué

mark‑er ['mɑːrkər] (highlighter) marqueur m

mar‑ket ['mɑːrkɪt] **1** n marché m; **on the ~** sur le marché **2** v/t commercialiser

mar‑ket‑a‑ble ['mɑːrkɪtəbl] adj commercialisable

mar‑ket e‑con‑o‑my économie f de marché

'mar‑ket for‑ces npl forces fpl du marché

mar‑ket‑ing ['mɑːrkɪtɪŋ] marketing m

'mar‑ket‑ing cam‑paign campagne f de marketing; **'mar‑ket‑ing de‑part‑ment** service m marketing; **'mar‑ket‑ing mix** marchéage m; **'mar‑ket‑ing strat‑e‑gy** stratégie f marketing

mar‑ket 'lead‑er product produit m vedette; company leader m du marché; **'mar‑ket place** in town place f

du marché; for commodities marché m; **mar‑ket 're‑search** étude f de marché; **mar‑ket 'share** part f du marché

mark‑up ['mɑːrkʌp] majoration f

mar‑ma‑lade ['mɑːrməleɪd] marmelade f (d'oranges)

mar‑riage ['mærɪdʒ] mariage m

'mar‑riage cer‑tif‑i‑cate acte m de mariage

mar‑riage 'guid‑ance coun‑se‑lor or Br **coun‑sel‑lor** conseiller m conjugal, conseillère f conjugal

mar‑ried ['mærɪd] adj marié; **be ~ to** être marié à

'mar‑ried life vie f conjugale

mar‑ry ['mærɪ] v/t (pret & pp **-ied**) épouser, se marier avec; of priest marier; **get married** se marier

Mar‑seilles [mɑːr'seɪ] Marseille

marsh [mɑːrʃ] Br marais m

mar‑shal ['mɑːrʃl] n in police chef m de la police; in security service membre m du service d'ordre

marsh‑mal‑low ['mɑːrʃmæloʊ] guimauve f

marsh‑y ['mɑːrʃɪ] adj Br marécageux*

mar‑tial arts [mɑːrʃl'ɑːrtz] npl arts mpl martiaux

mar‑tial 'law loi f martiale

mar‑tyr ['mɑːrtər] also fig martyr(e) m(f)

mar‑vel ['mɑːrvl] n (wonder) merveille f

♦ **marvel at** v/t s'émerveiller devant

mar‑vel‑ous, Br **mar‑vel‑lous** ['mɑːrvələs] adj merveilleux*

Marx‑ism ['mɑːrksɪzm] marxisme m

Marx‑ist ['mɑːrksɪst] **1** adj marxiste **2** n marxiste m/f

mar‑zi‑pan ['mɑːrzɪpæn] pâte f d'amandes

mas‑ca‑ra [mæ'skærə] mascara m

mas‑cot ['mæskət] mascotte f

mas‑cu‑line ['mæskjʊlɪn] adj also GRAM masculin

mas‑cu‑lin‑i‑ty [mæskjʊ'lɪnɪtɪ] (virility) masculinité f

mash [mæʃ] v/t réduire en purée

mashed po'ta‑toes [mæʃt] npl purée f (de pommes de terre)

matter

mask [mæsk] **1** *n* masque *m* **2** *v/t feelings* masquer

mask·ing tape ['mæskɪŋ] ruban *m* de masquage

mas·och·ism ['mæsəkɪzm] masochisme *m*

mas·och·ist ['mæsəkɪst] masochiste *m/f*

ma·son ['meɪsn] maçon *m*

ma·son·ry ['meɪsnrɪ] maçonnerie *f*

mas·que·rade [mæskə'reɪd] **1** *n fig* mascarade *f* **2** *v/i*: ~ **as** se faire passer pour

mass¹ [mæs] **1** *n (great amount)* masse *f*; *the ~es* les masses *fpl*; ~*es of* F des tas de F **2** *adj* de masse

mass² [mæs] REL messe *f*

mas·sa·cre ['mæsəkər] **1** *n also fig* F massacre *m* **2** *v/t also fig* F massacrer

mas·sage ['mæsɑːʒ] **1** *n* massage *m* **2** *v/t* masser; *figures* manipuler

'mas·sage par·lor, *Br* 'mas·sage par·lour salon *m* de massage

mas·seur [mæ'sɜːr] masseur *m*

mas·seuse [mæ'sɜːz] masseuse *f*

mas·sive ['mæsɪv] *adj* énorme; *heart attack* grave

mass 'me·di·a *npl* médias *mpl*; mass-·pro'duce *v/t* fabriquer en série; mass pro'duc·tion fabrication *f* en série; 'mass trans·it transports *mpl* publics

mast [mæst] *of ship* mât *m*; *for radio signal* pylône *m*

mas·ter ['mæstər] **1** *n of dog* maître *m*; *of ship* capitaine *m*; *be a ~ of* être maître dans l'art de **2** *v/t* maîtriser

'mas·ter bed·room chambre *f* principale

'mas·ter key passe-partout *m inv*

mas·ter·ly ['mæstərlɪ] *adj* magistral

'mas·ter·mind **1** *n* cerveau *m* **2** *v/t* organiser; Mas·ter of 'Arts maîtrise *f* de lettres; mas·ter of 'cer·e·mo·nies maître de cérémonie, animateur *m*; 'mas·ter·piece chef-d'œuvre *m*; 'mas·ter's (de·gree) maîtrise *f*

mas·ter·y ['mæstərɪ] maîtrise *f*

mas·tur·bate ['mæstərbeɪt] *v/i* se masturber

mat [mæt] *for floor* tapis *m*; *for table* napperon *m*

match¹ [mætʃ] *n for cigarette* allumette *f*

match² [mætʃ] **1** *n (competition)* match *m*, partie *f*; *be no ~ for s.o.* ne pas être à la hauteur de qn; *meet one's ~* trouver un adversaire à sa mesure **2** *v/t (be the same as)* être assorti à; *(equal)* égaler **3** *v/i of colors, patterns* aller ensemble

'match·box boîte *f* d'allumettes

match·ing ['mætʃɪŋ] *adj* assorti

'match point *in tennis* balle *f* de match

'match stick allumette *f*

mate [meɪt] **1** *n of animal* mâle *m*, femelle *f*; NAUT second *m* **2** *v/i* s'accoupler

ma·te·ri·al [mə'tɪrɪəl] **1** *n (fabric)* tissu *m*; *(substance)* matériau *m*, matière *f*; ~*s* matériel *m* **2** *adj* matériel*

ma·te·ri·al·ism [mə'tɪrɪəlɪzm] matérialisme *m*

ma·te·ri·al·ist [mətɪrɪə'lɪst] matérialiste *m/f*

ma·te·ri·al·is·tic [mətɪrɪə'lɪstɪk] *adj* matérialiste

ma·te·ri·al·ize [mə'tɪrɪəlaɪz] *v/i (appear)* apparaître; *(happen)* se concrétiser

ma·ter·nal [mə'tɜːrnl] *adj* maternel*

ma·ter·ni·ty [mə'tɜːrnətɪ] maternité *f*

ma'ter·ni·ty dress robe *f* de grossesse; ma'ter·ni·ty leave congé *m* de maternité; ma'ter·ni·ty ward maternité *f*

math [mæθ] maths *fpl*

math·e·mat·i·cal [mæθə'mætɪkl] *adj* mathématique

math·e·ma·ti·cian [mæθmə'tɪʃn] mathématicien(ne) *m(f)*

math·e·mat·ics [mæθ'mætɪks] *nsg* mathématiques *fpl*

maths [mæθs] *Br* → **math**

mat·i·née ['mætɪneɪ] matinée *f*

ma·tri·arch ['meɪtrɪɑːrk] femme *f* chef de famille

mat·ri·mo·ny ['mætrəmoʊnɪ] mariage *m*

matt [mæt] *adj* mat

mat·ter ['mætər] **1** *n (affair)* affaire *f*, question *f*; PHYS matière *f*; *as a ~*

of course systématiquement; *as a ~ of fact* en fait; *what's the ~?* qu'est-ce qu'il y a?; *no ~ what she says* quoi qu'elle dise **2** *v/i* importer; *it doesn't ~* cela ne fait rien

mat·ter-of-'fact impassible

mat·tress ['mætrɪs] matelas *m*

ma·ture [mə'tjʊr] **1** *adj* mûr **2** *v/i of person* mûrir; *of insurance policy etc* arriver à échéance

ma·tu·ri·ty [mə'tjʊrətɪ] maturité *f*

maul [mɒːl] *v/t of animal* déchiqueter; *of critics* démolir

max·i·mize ['mæksɪmaɪz] *v/t* maximiser

max·i·mum ['mæksɪməm] **1** *adj* maximal, maximum **2** *n* maximum *m*

May [meɪ] mai *m*

may [meɪ] ◇ *possibility*: *it ~ rain* il va peut-être pleuvoir, il risque de pleuvoir; *you ~ be right* tu as peut-être raison, il est possible que tu aies raison; *it ~ not happen* cela n'arrivera peut-être pas ◇ *permission* pouvoir; *~ I help?* puis-je aider?; *you ~ go if you like* tu peux partir si tu veux ◇ *wishing*: *~ your dreams come true* que vos rêves se réalisent (*subj*)

may·be ['meɪbɪ] *adv* peut-être

'May Day le premier mai

may·o, may·on·naise ['meɪoʊ, meɪə-'neɪz] mayonnaise *f*

may·or ['meɪər] maire *m*

maze [meɪz] labyrinthe *m*

MB *abbr* (= *megabyte*) Mo (= méga-octet)

MBA [embiː'eɪ] *abbr* (= *master of business administration*) MBA *m*

MBO [embiː'oʊ] *abbr* (= *management buyout*) rachat *m* d'entreprise par la direction

MC [em'siː] *abbr* (= *master of cere-monies*) maître *m* de cérémonie

MD [em'diː] *abbr* (= *Doctor of Medi-cine*) docteur *m* en médecine; (= *managing director*) DG *m* (= direc-teur général)

me [miː] *pron* me; *before vowel* m'; *after prep* moi; *he knows ~* il me connaît; *she gave ~ a dollar* elle m'a donné un dollar; *it's for ~* c'est pour moi;

it's ~ c'est moi

mead·ow ['medoʊ] pré *m*

mea·ger, *Br* **mea·gre** ['miːgər] *adj* maigre

meal [miːl] repas *m*; *enjoy your ~!* bon appétit!

'meal·time heure *f* du repas

mean[1] [miːn] *adj with money* avare; (*nasty*) mesquin

mean[2] [miːn] **1** *v/t* (*pret & pp* **meant**) (*signify*) signifier, vouloir dire; *do you ~ it?* vous êtes sérieux*?; *you weren't ~t to hear that* tu n'étais pas supposé entendre cela; *~ to do sth* avoir l'intention de faire qch; *be ~t for* être destiné à; *of remark* être adressé à; *doesn't it ~ anything to you?* (*doesn't it matter?*) est-ce que cela ne compte pas pour toi? **2** *v/i* (*pret & pp* **meant**): *~ well* avoir de bonnes intentions

mean·ing ['miːnɪŋ] *of word* sens *m*

mean·ing·ful ['miːnɪŋfʊl] *adj* (*compre-hensible*) compréhensible; (*construc-tive*) significatif*; *glance* éloquent

mean·ing·less ['miːnɪŋlɪs] *adj* sen-tence etc dénué de sens; *gesture* insi-gnifiant

means [miːnz] *npl financial* moyens *mpl*; *nsg* (*way*) moyen *m*; *a ~ of trans-port* un moyen de transport; *by all ~* (*certainly*) bien sûr; *by no ~ rich / poor* loin d'être riche / pauvre; *by ~ of* au moyen de

meant *pret & pp* → **mean**[2]

mean·time ['miːntaɪm] *adv* pendant ce temps, entre-temps

mean·while ['miːnwaɪl] *adv* pendant ce temps, entre-temps

mea·sles ['miːzlz] *nsg* rougeole *f*

mea·sure ['meʒər] **1** *n* (*step*) mesure *f*; *we've had a ~ of success* nous avons eu un certain succès **2** *v/t & v/i* mesurer

♦ **measure out** *v/t* doser, mesurer

♦ **measure up to** *v/t* être à la hauteur de

mea·sure·ment ['meʒərmənt] *action* mesure *f*; (*dimension*) dimension *f*; *take s.o.'s ~s* prendre les mensura-tions de qn; *system of ~* système *m* de mesures

mea·sur·ing tape ['meʒərɪŋ] mètre *m* ruban

meat [mi:t] viande *f*

'meat·ball boulette *f* de viande

'meat·loaf pain *m* de viande

me·chan·ic [mɪ'kænɪk] mécanicien(ne) *m(f)*

me·chan·i·cal [mɪ'kænɪkl] *adj device* mécanique; *gesture etc also* machinal

me·chan·i·cal en·gi'neer ingénieur *m* mécanicien

me·chan·i·cal en·gi'neer·ing génie *m* mécanique

me·chan·i·cal·ly [mɪ'kænɪklɪ] *adv* mécaniquement; *do sth* machinalement

mech·a·nism ['mekənɪzm] mécanisme *m*

mech·a·nize ['mekənaɪz] *v/t* mécaniser

med·al ['medl] médaille *f*

med·al·list, *Br* **med·al·list** ['medəlɪst] médaillé *m*

med·dle ['medl] *v/i in affairs* se mêler (**in** de); *with object* toucher (**with** à)

me·di·a ['mi:dɪə] *npl:* **the ~** les médias *mpl*

'me·di·a cov·er·age couverture *f* médiatique; **'me·di·a e·vent** événement *m* médiatique; **'me·di·a 'hype** battage *m* médiatique

'me·di·an strip [mi:dɪən'strɪp] terre-plein *m* central

'me·d·ia stud·ies études *fpl* de communication

me·di·ate ['mi:dɪeɪt] *v/i* arbitrer

me·di·a·tion [mi:dɪ'eɪʃn] médiation *f*

me·di·a·tor ['mi:dɪeɪtər] médiateur (-trice) *m(f)*

med·i·cal ['medɪkl] **1** *adj* médical **2** *n* visite *f* médicale

'med·i·cal cer·tif·i·cate certificat *m* médical; **'med·i·cal ex·am·i·na·tion** visite *f* médicale; **'med·i·cal his·to·ry** dossier *m* médical; **'med·i·cal pro·fes·sion** médecine *f*; *(doctors)* corps *m* médical; **'med·i·cal re·cord** dossier *m* médical

Med·i·care ['medɪker] assistance médicale pour les personnes âgées

med·i·cat·ed ['medɪkeɪtɪd] *adj* phar-maceutique, traitant

med·i·ca·tion [medɪ'keɪʃn] médicaments *mpl*

me·dic·i·nal [mɪ'dɪsɪnl] *adj* médicinal

med·i·cine ['medsən] *science* médecine *f*; *(medication)* médicament *m*

'med·i·cine cab·i·net armoire *f* à pharmacie

med·i·e·val [medɪ'i:vl] *adj* médiéval; *fig* moyenâgeux*

me·di·o·cre [mi:dɪ'oukər] *adj* médiocre

me·di·oc·ri·ty [mi:dɪ'ɑ:krətɪ] *of work etc* médiocrité *f*; *person* médiocre *m/f*

med·i·tate ['medɪteɪt] *v/i* méditer

med·i·ta·tion [medɪ'teɪʃn] méditation *f*

Med·i·ter·ra·ne·an [medɪtə'reɪnɪən] **1** *adj* méditerranéen **2** *n:* **the ~** la Méditerranée

me·di·um ['mi:dɪəm] **1** *adj (average)* moyen*; *steak* à point **2** *n in size* taille *f* moyenne; *(vehicle)* moyen *m*; *(spiritualist)* médium *m*

me·di·um-sized ['mi:dɪəmsaɪzd] *adj* de taille moyenne; **me·di·um 'term:** **in the ~** à moyen terme; **'me·di·um wave** RAD ondes *fpl* moyennes

med·ley ['medlɪ] *(assortment)* mélange *m*; *of music* pot-pourri *m*

meek [mi:k] *adj* docile, doux*

meet [mi:t] **1** *v/t (pret & pp* **met***)* rencontrer; *(be introduced to)* faire la connaissance de; *(collect)* (aller / venir) chercher; *in competition* affronter; *of eyes* croiser; *(satisfy)* satisfaire **2** *v/i (pret & pp* **met***)* se rencontrer; *by appointment* se retrouver; *of eyes* se croiser; *of committee etc* se réunir; **have you two met?** est-ce que vous vous connaissez? **3** *n* SP rencontre *f*

♦ **meet with** *v/t person, opposition etc* rencontrer

meet·ing ['mi:tɪŋ] *by accident* rencontre *f*; *in business, of committee* réunion *f*; **he's in a ~** il est en réunion

'meet·ing place lieu *m* de rendez-vous

meg·a·byte ['megəbaɪt] COMPUT méga-octet *m*

M

mel·an·chol·y ['melənkəlɪ] *adj* mélancolique

mel·low ['melou] **1** *adj* doux* **2** *v/i of person* s'adoucir

me·lo·di·ous [mɪ'loudɪəs] *adj* mélodieux*

mel·o·dra·mat·ic [melədrə'mætɪk] *adj* mélodramatique

mel·o·dy ['melədɪ] mélodie *f*

mel·on ['melən] melon *m*

melt [melt] **1** *v/i* fondre **2** *v/t* faire fondre

♦ **melt away** *v/i fig* disparaître

♦ **melt down** *v/t metal* fondre

melt·ing pot ['meltɪŋpɑːt] *fig* creuset *m*

mem·ber ['membər] membre *m*

Mem·ber of 'Con·gress membre *m* du Congrès

Mem·ber of 'Par·lia·ment *Br* député *m*

mem·ber·ship ['membərʃɪp] adhésion *f, number of members* membres *mpl*

'mem·ber·ship card carte *f* de membre

mem·brane ['membreɪn] membrane *f*

me·men·to [me'mentou] souvenir *m*

mem·o ['memou] note *f* (de service)

mem·oirs ['memwɑːrz] *npl* mémoires *fpl*

'mem·o pad bloc-notes *m*

mem·o·ra·ble ['memərəbl] *adj* mémorable

me·mo·ri·al [mɪ'mɔːrɪəl] **1** *adj* commémoratif* **2** *n* mémorial *m;* **be a ~ to s.o.** *also fig* célébrer la mémoire de qn

Me'mo·ri·al Day jour *m* commémoration des soldats américains morts à la guerre

mem·o·rize ['meməraɪz] *v/t* apprendre par cœur

mem·o·ry ['memərɪ] mémoire *f; sth remembered* souvenir *m;* **have a good / bad ~** avoir une bonne / mauvaise mémoire; **in ~ of** à la mémoire de

men [men] *pl* → **man**

men·ace ['menɪs] **1** *n* menace *f; person* danger *m* **2** *v/t* menacer

men·ac·ing ['menɪsɪŋ] *adj* menaçant

mend [mend] **1** *v/t* réparer; *clothes* raccommoder **2** *n:* **be on the ~** *after illness* être en voie de guérison

me·ni·al ['miːnɪəl] *adj* subalterne

men·in·gi·tis [menɪn'dʒaɪtɪs] méningite *f*

men·o·pause ['menoupɔːz] ménopause *f*

'men's room toilettes *fpl* pour hommes

men·stru·ate ['menstrʊeɪt] *v/i* avoir ses règles

men·stru·a·tion [menstru'eɪʃn] menstruation *f*

men·tal ['mentl] *adj* mental; *ability, powers* intellectuel*; *health, suffering* moral; F (*crazy*) malade F

men·tal a'rith·me·tic calcul *m* mental; **men·tal 'cru·el·ty** cruauté *f* mentale; **'men·tal hos·pi·tal** hôpital *m* psychiatrique; **men·tal 'ill·ness** maladie *f* mentale

men·tal·i·ty [men'tælətɪ] mentalité *f*

men·tal·ly ['mentəlɪ] *adv* (*inwardly*) intérieurement; *calculate etc* mentalement

men·tal·ly 'hand·i·capped *adj* handicapé mental

men·tal·ly 'ill *adj* malade mental

men·tion ['menʃn] **1** *n* mention *f* **2** *v/t* mentionner; **don't ~ it** (*you're welcome*) il n'y a pas de quoi!

men·tor ['mentɔːr] mentor *m*

men·u ['menjuː] *also* COMPUT menu *m*

mer·ce·na·ry ['mɜːrsɪnerɪ] **1** *adj* intéressé **2** *n* MIL mercenaire *m*

mer·chan·dise ['mɜːrʃəndaɪz] marchandises *fpl*

mer·chant ['mɜːrʃənt] négociant *m*, commerçant *m*

mer·chant 'bank *Br* banque *f* d'affaires

mer·ci·ful ['mɜːrsɪfl] *adj* clément; *God* miséricordieux*

mer·ci·ful·ly ['mɜːrsɪflɪ] *adv* (*thankfully*) heureusement

mer·ci·less ['mɜːrsɪlɪs] *adj* impitoyable

mer·cu·ry ['mɜːrkjʊrɪ] mercure *m*

mer·cy ['mɜːrsɪ] clémence *f*, pitié *f;* **be**

M

at s.o.'s ~ être à la merci de qn
mere [mɪr] *adj* simple
mere·ly ['mɪrlɪ] *adv* simplement, seulement
merge [mɜːrdʒ] *v/i of two lines etc* se rejoindre; *of companies* fusionner
merg·er ['mɜːrdʒər] COMM fusion *f*
mer·it ['merɪt] **1** *n* mérite *m* **2** *v/t* mériter
mer·ry ['merɪ] *adj* gai, joyeux*; *Merry Christmas!* Joyeux Noël!
'mer·ry-go-round manège *m*
mesh [meʃ] *of net* maille(s) *f(pl)*; *of grid* grillage *m*
mess [mes] *(untidiness)* désordre *m*, pagaille *f*; *(trouble)* gâchis *m*; *be a* ~ *of room, desk, hair* être en désordre; *of situation, life* être un désastre
♦ **mess around 1** *v/i* perdre son temps **2** *v/t person* se moquer de
♦ **mess around with** *v/t* jouer avec; *s.o.'s wife* s'amuser avec
♦ **mess up** *v/t room, papers* mettre en désordre; *task* bâcler; *plans, marriage* gâcher
mes·sage ['mesɪdʒ] *also of movie etc* message *m*
mes·sen·ger ['mesɪndʒər] *(courier)* messager *m*
mess·y ['mesɪ] *adj room* en désordre; *person* désordonné; *job* salissant; *divorce, situation* pénible
met [met] *pret & pp* → *meet*
me·tab·o·lism [mə'tæbəlɪzm] métabolisme *m*
met·al ['metl] **1** *adj* en métal **2** *n* métal *m*
me·tal·lic [mɪ'tælɪk] *adj* métallique; *paint* métallisé; *taste* de métal
met·a·phor ['metəfər] métaphore *f*
me·te·or ['miːtɪɔːr] météore *m*
me·te·or·ic [miːtɪ'ɒrɪk] *adj fig* fulgurant
me·te·or·ite ['miːtɪərait] météorite *m* or *f*
me·te·or·o·log·i·cal [miːtɪərə'lɒdʒɪkl] *adj* météorologique
me·te·o·rol·o·gist [miːtɪə'rɒlədʒɪst] météorologiste *m/f*
me·te·o·rol·o·gy [miːtɪə'rɒlədʒɪ] météorologie *f*

me·ter[1] ['miːtər] *for gas, electricity* compteur *m*; *(parking* ~*)* parcmètre *m*
me·ter[2] ['miːtər] *unit of length* mètre *m*
'me·ter read·ing relevé *m* (de compteur)
meth·od ['meθəd] méthode *f*
me·thod·i·cal [mə'θɒdɪkl] *adj* méthodique
me·thod·i·cal·ly [mə'θɒdɪklɪ] *adv* méthodiquement
me·tic·u·lous [mə'tɪkjʊləs] *adj* méticuleux*
me·tre ['miːtə(r)] *Br* → *meter*
met·ric ['metrɪk] *adj* métrique
me·trop·o·lis [mə'trɒpəlɪs] métropole *f*
met·ro·pol·i·tan [metrə'pɒlɪtən] *adj* citadin; *area* urbain
mew [mjuː] → *miaow*
Mex·i·can ['meksɪkən] **1** *adj* mexicain **2** *n* Mexicain(e) *m(f)*
Mex·i·co ['meksɪkəʊ] Mexique *m*
mez·za·nine (floor) ['mezəniːn] mezzanine *f*
mi·aow [miau] **1** *n* miaou *m* **2** *v/i* miauler
mice [mais] *pl* → *mouse*
mick·ey mouse [mɪkɪ'maʊs] *adj* F *course, qualification* bidon F
mi·cro·bi·ol·o·gy [maɪkrəʊbaɪ'ɒlədʒɪ] microbiologie *f*; **'mi·cro·chip** puce *f*; **'mi·cro·cli·mate** microclimat *m*; **mi·cro·cosm** ['maɪkrəkɒzm] microcosme *m*; **'mi·cro·e·lec·tron·ics** microélectronique *f*; **'mi·cro·film** microfilm *m*; **'mi·cro·or·gan·ism** micro-organisme *m*; **'mi·cro·phone** microphone *m*; **'mi·cro·pro·ces·sor** microprocesseur *m*; **'mi·cro·scope** microscope *m*; **mi·cro·scop·ic** [maɪkrə'skɒpɪk] *adj* microscopique; **'mi·cro·wave** *oven* micro-ondes *m inv*
mid [mɪd] *adj*: *in the* ~ *nineties* au milieu des années 90; *she's in her* ~ *thirties* elle a dans les trente-cinq ans
mid-air [mɪd'er]: *in* ~ en vol
mid·day [mɪd'deɪ] midi *m*
mid·dle ['mɪdl] **1** *adj* du milieu **2** *n* mi-

M

lieu *m*; *in the ~ of* au milieu de; *in the ~ of winter* en plein hiver; *in the ~ of September* à la mi-septembre; *be in the ~ of doing sth* être en train de faire qch

'mid·dle-aged *adj* entre deux âges; **Mid·dle A·ges** *npl* Moyen Âge *m*; **mid·dle-'class** *adj* bourgeois

'mid·dle class(·es) classe(s) moyenne(s) *f(pl)*; **Mid·dle 'East** Moyen-Orient *m*; **'mid·dle·man** intermédiaire *m*; **mid·dle 'man·age·ment** cadres *mpl* moyens; **mid·dle 'name** deuxième prénom *m*; **'mid·dle·weight** *boxer* poids moyen *m*

mid·dling ['mɪdlɪŋ] *adj* médiocre, moyen*

mid·field·er [mɪd'fiːldər] *in soccer* milieu *m* de terrain

midg·et ['mɪdʒɪt] *adj* miniature

'mid·night minuit *m*; *at ~* à minuit; **'mid·sum·mer** milieu *m* de l'été; **'mid·way** *adv* à mi-chemin; *~ through* au milieu de; **'mid·week** *adv* en milieu de semaine; **'Mid·west** Middle West *m*; **'mid·wife** sage-femme *f*; **'mid·win·ter** milieu *m* de l'hiver

might¹ [maɪt] *v/aux*: *I ~ be late* je serai peut-être en retard; *it ~ rain* il va peut-être pleuvoir; *it ~ never happen* cela n'arrivera peut-être jamais; *I ~ have lost it but I'm not sure* je l'ai peut-être perdu; *that would have been possible* j'aurais pu l'avoir perdu; *he ~ have left* il est peut-être parti; *you ~ as well spend the night here* tu ferais aussi bien de passer la nuit ici; *you ~ have told me!* vous auriez pu m'avertir!

might² [maɪt] *n* (*power*) puissance *f*

might·y ['maɪtɪ] **1** *adj* puissant **2** *adv* F (*extremely*) vachement F, très

mi·graine ['miːɡreɪn] migraine *f*

mi·grant work·er ['maɪɡrənt] travailleur *m* itinérant

mi·grate [maɪ'ɡreɪt] *v/i* migrer

mi·gra·tion [maɪ'ɡreɪʃn] migration *f*

mike [maɪk] F micro *m*

mild [maɪld] *adj* doux*; *taste* léger*

mil·dew ['mɪldjuː] mildiou *m*

mild·ly ['maɪldlɪ] *adv* doucement; *spicy* légèrement; *to put it ~* pour ne pas dire plus

mild·ness ['maɪldnɪs] douceur *f*; *of taste* légèreté *f*

mile [maɪl] mile *m*; *~s easier* F bien plus facile; *it's ~s away!* c'est vachement loin! F

mile·age ['maɪlɪdʒ] kilométrage *m*; *distance* nombre *m* de miles

'mile·stone *fig* événement *m* marquant, jalon *m*

mil·i·tant ['mɪlɪtənt] **1** *adj* militant **2** *n* militant(e) *m(f)*

mil·i·ta·ry ['mɪlɪterɪ] **1** *adj* militaire **2** *n*: *the ~* l'armée *f*

mil·i·ta·ry a'cad·e·my école *f* militaire; **mil·i·ta·ry po'lice** police *f* militaire; **mil·i·tar·y 'serv·ice** service *m* militaire

mi·li·tia [mɪ'lɪʃə] milice *f*

milk [mɪlk] **1** *n* lait *m* **2** *v/t* traire

milk 'choc·o·late chocolat *m* au lait; **'milk·shake** milk-shake *m*

milk·y ['mɪlkɪ] *adj* au lait; (*made with milk*) lacté

Milk·y 'Way Voie *f* lactée

mill [mɪl] *for grain* moulin *m*; *for textiles* usine *f*

♦ mill around *v/i* grouiller

mil·len·ni·um [mɪ'lenɪəm] millénaire *m*

mil·li·gram ['mɪlɪɡræm] milligramme *m*

mil·li·me·ter, *Br* mil·li·me·tre ['mɪlɪmiːtər] millimètre *m*

mil·lion ['mɪljən] million *m*

mil·lion·aire [mɪljə'ner] millionnaire *m/f*

mime [maɪm] *v/t* mimer

mim·ic ['mɪmɪk] **1** *n* imitateur(-trice) *m(f)* **2** *v/t* (*pret & pp* **-ked**) imiter

mince [mɪns] *v/t* hacher

'mince·meat préparation de fruits secs et d'épices servant à fourrer des tartelettes

mind [maɪnd] **1** *n* esprit *m*; *it's all in your ~* tu te fais des idées; *be out of one's ~* avoir perdu la tête; *bear or keep sth in ~* ne pas oublier qch; *I've a good ~ to …* j'ai bien envie de

...; *change one's ~* changer d'avis; *it didn't enter my ~* cela ne m'est pas venu à l'esprit; *give s.o. a piece of one's ~* dire son fait à qn; *make up one's ~* se décider; *have sth on one's ~* être préoccupé par qch; *keep one's ~ on sth* se concentrer sur qch **2** *v/t* (*look after*) surveiller; (*heed*) faire attention à; *would you ~ answering a few questions?* est-ce que cela vous dérangerait de répondre à quelques questions?; *I don't ~ herbal tea* je n'ai rien contre une tisane; *I don't ~ what he thinks* il peut penser ce qu'il veut, cela m'est égal; *do you ~ if I smoke?, do you ~ my smoking?* cela ne vous dérange pas si je fume?; *would you ~ opening the window?* pourriez-vous ouvrir la fenêtre?; *~ the step!* attention à la marche!; *~ your own business!* occupe-toi de tes affaires! **3** *v/i: ~! (be careful)* fais attention!; *never ~!* peu importe!; *I don't ~* cela m'est égal

mind-bog·gling ['maɪndbɒːɡlɪŋ] *adj* ahurissant

mind·less ['maɪndlɪs] *adj violence* gratuit

mine[1] [maɪn] *pron* le mien *m*, la mienne *f*; *pl* les miens, les miennes; *it's ~* c'est à moi

mine[2] [maɪn] **1** *n for coal etc* mine *f* **2** *v/i: ~ for coal etc* extraire

mine[3] [maɪn] **1** *n explosive* mine *f* **2** *v/t* miner

'mine·field MIL champ *m* de mines; *fig* poudrière *f*

min·er ['maɪnər] mineur *m*

min·e·ral ['mɪnərəl] *n* minéral *m*

'min·e·ral wa·ter eau *f* minérale

mine·sweep·er ['maɪnswiːpər] NAUT dragueur *m* de mines

min·gle ['mɪŋɡl] *v/i of sounds, smells* se mélanger; *at party* se mêler (aux gens)

min·i ['mɪnɪ] *skirt* minijupe *f*

min·i·a·ture ['mɪnɪtʃər] *adj* miniature

'min·i·bus minibus *m*

min·i·mal ['mɪnɪməl] *adj* minime

min·i·mal·ism ['mɪnɪməlɪzm] minima-

lisme *m*

min·i·mize ['mɪnɪmaɪz] *v/t* réduire au minimum; (*downplay*) minimiser

min·i·mum ['mɪnɪməm] **1** *adj* minimal, minimum **2** *n* minimum *m*

min·i·mum 'wage salaire *m* minimum

min·ing ['maɪnɪŋ] exploitation *f* minière

'min·i·se·ries *nsg* TV mini-feuilleton *m*

'min·i·skirt minijupe *f*

min·is·ter ['mɪnɪstər] POL, REL ministre *m*

min·is·te·ri·al [mɪnɪ'stɪrɪəl] *adj* ministériel*

min·is·try ['mɪnɪstrɪ] POL ministère *m*

mink [mɪŋk] vison *m*

mi·nor ['maɪnər] **1** *adj* mineur, de peu d'importance; *pain* léger*; *in D ~* MUS en ré mineur **2** *n* LAW mineur(e) *m(f)*

mi·nor·i·ty [maɪ'nɑːrətɪ] minorité *f*; *be in the ~* être en minorité

mint [mɪnt] *n herb* menthe *f*; *chocolate* chocolat *m* à la menthe; *hard candy* bonbon *m* à la menthe

mi·nus ['maɪnəs] **1** *n* (*~ sign*) moins *m* **2** *prep* moins

mi·nus·cule ['mɪnəskjuːl] *adj* minuscule

min·ute[1] ['mɪnɪt] *of time* minute *f*; *in a ~* (*soon*) dans une minute; *just a ~* une minute *f*, un instant *m*

mi·nute[2] [maɪ'nuːt] *adj* (*tiny*) minuscule; (*detailed*) minutieux*; *in ~ detail* dans les moindres détails

'min·ute hand grande aiguille *f*

mi·nute·ly [maɪ'nuːtlɪ] *adv* (*in detail*) minutieusement; (*very slightly*) très légèrement

min·utes ['mɪnɪts] *npl of meeting* procès-verbal *m*

mir·a·cle ['mɪrəkl] miracle *m*

mi·rac·u·lous [mɪ'rækjʊləs] *adj* miraculeux*

mi·rac·u·lous·ly [mɪ'rækjʊləslɪ] *adv* par miracle

mi·rage [mɪ'rɑːʒ] mirage *m*

mir·ror ['mɪrər] **1** *n* miroir *m*; MOT rétroviseur *m* **2** *v/t* refléter

mis·an·thro·pist [mɪ'zænθrəpɪst] mis-

M

anthrope *m/f*

mis·ap·pre·hen·sion [mɪsæprɪ-'henʃn]: *be under a ~* se tromper

mis·be·have [mɪsbə'heɪv] *v/i* se conduire mal

mis·be·hav·ior, *Br* mis·be·hav·iour [mɪsbə'heɪvɪər] mauvaise conduite *f*

mis·cal·cu·late [mɪs'kælkjʊleɪt] **1** *v/t* mal calculer **2** *v/i* se tromper dans ses calculs

mis·cal·cu·la·tion [mɪs'kælkjʊleɪʃn] erreur *f* de calcul; *fig* mauvais calcul *m*

mis·car·riage ['mɪskærɪdʒ] MED fausse couche *f*; *~ of justice* erreur *f* judiciaire

mis·car·ry [mɪs'kærɪ] *v/i* (*pret & pp -ied*) *of plan* échouer

mis·cel·la·ne·ous [mɪsə'leɪnɪəs] *adj* divers; *collection* varié

mis·chief ['mɪstʃɪf] (*naughtiness*) bêtises *fpl*

mis·chie·vous ['mɪstʃɪvəs] *adj* (*naughty*) espiègle; (*malicious*) malveillant

mis·con·cep·tion [mɪskən'sepʃn] idée *f* fausse

mis·con·duct [mɪs'kɑ:ndʌkt] mauvaise conduite *f*; *professional ~* faute *f* professionnelle

mis·con·strue [mɪskən'stru:] *v/t* mal interpréter

mis·de·mea·nor, *Br* mis·de·mea·nour [mɪsdə'mi:nər] délit *m*

mi·ser ['maɪzər] avare *m/f*

mis·e·ra·ble ['mɪzrəbl] *adj* (*unhappy*) malheureux*; *weather, performance* épouvantable

mi·ser·ly ['maɪzərlɪ] *adj* avare; *sum* dérisoire

mis·e·ry ['mɪzərɪ] (*unhappiness*) tristesse *f*; (*wretchedness*) misère *f*

mis·fire [mɪs'faɪr] *v/i of scheme* rater; *of joke* tomber à plat

mis·fit ['mɪsfɪt] *in society* marginal(e) *m(f)*

mis·for·tune [mɪs'fɔ:rtʃən] malheur *m*, malchance *f*

mis·giv·ings [mɪs'gɪvɪŋz] *npl* doutes *mpl*

mis·guid·ed [mɪs'gaɪdɪd] *adj* mal avisé, imprudent

mis·han·dle [mɪs'hændl] *v/t situation* mal gérer

mis·hap ['mɪshæp] incident *m*

mis·in·form [mɪsɪn'fɔ:rm] *v/t* mal informer

mis·in·ter·pret [mɪsɪn'tɜ:rprɪt] *v/t* mal interpréter

mis·in·ter·pre·ta·tion [mɪsɪntɜ:rprɪ-'teɪʃn] mauvaise interprétation *f*

mis·judge [mɪs'dʒʌdʒ] *v/t* mal juger

mis·lay [mɪs'leɪ] *v/t* (*pret & pp -laid*) égarer

mis·lead [mɪs'li:d] *v/t* (*pret & pp -led*) induire en erreur, tromper

mis·lead·ing [mɪs'li:dɪŋ] *adj* trompeur*

mis·man·age [mɪs'mænɪdʒ] *v/t* mal gérer

mis·man·age·ment [mɪs'mænɪdʒmənt] mauvaise gestion *f*

mis·match ['mɪsmætʃ] divergence *f*

mis·placed ['mɪspleɪst] *adj enthusiasm* déplacé; *loyalty* mal placé

mis·print ['mɪsprɪnt] *n* faute *f* typographique

mis·pro·nounce [mɪsprə'naʊns] *v/t* mal prononcer

mis·pro·nun·ci·a·tion [mɪsprənʌn-sɪ'eɪʃn] mauvaise prononciation *f*

mis·read [mɪs'ri:d] *v/t* (*pret & pp -read* [red]) *word, figures* mal lire; *situation* mal interpréter; *I must have misread the 6 as 8* j'ai dû confondre le 6 avec un 8

mis·rep·re·sent [mɪsreprɪ'zent] *v/t* présenter sous un faux jour

miss¹ [mɪs]: *Miss Smith* mademoiselle Smith; *~!* mademoiselle!

miss² [mɪs] **1** *n* SP coup *m* manqué **2** *v/t* manquer, rater; *bus, train* etc rater; (*not notice*) rater, ne pas remarquer; *~ you* tu me manques; *I ~ New York* New York me manque; *I ~ having a garden* je regrette de ne pas avoir de jardin **3** *v/i* rater son coup

mis·shap·en [mɪs'ʃeɪpən] *adj* déformé; *person, limb* difforme

mis·sile ['mɪsəl] *mil* missile *m*; *stone etc* projectile *m*

miss·ing ['mɪsɪŋ] *adj*: *be ~* have disap-

peared avoir disparu; *member of school party, one of a set etc* ne pas être là; *the ~ child* l'enfant qui a disparu; *one of them is ~* il en manque un(e)

mis·sion ['mɪʃn] mission *f*

mis·sion·a·ry ['mɪʃənrɪ] REL missionaire *m/f*

mis·spell [mɪs'spel] *v/t* mal orthographier

mist [mɪst] brume *f*

♦ **mist over** *v/i of eyes* s'embuer

♦ **mist up** *v/i of mirror, window* s'embuer

mis·take [mɪ'steɪk] **1** *n* erreur *f*, faute *f*; *make a ~* faire une erreur, se tromper; *by ~* par erreur **2** *v/t* (*pret mistook, pp mistaken*) se tromper de; *~ s.o. / sth for s.o. / sth* prendre qn / qch pour qn / qch d'autre

mis·tak·en [mɪ'steɪkən] **1** *adj* erroné, faux*; *be ~* faire erreur, se tromper **2** *pp* → **mistake**

mis·ter ['mɪstər] → **Mr**

mis·took [mɪ'stʊk] *pret* → **mistake**

mis·tress ['mɪstrɪs] maîtresse *f*

mis·trust [mɪs'trʌst] **1** *n* méfiance *f* **2** *v/t* se méfier de

mist·y ['mɪstɪ] *adj weather* brumeux*; *eyes* embué; ~ **blue** color bleuâtre

mis·un·der·stand [mɪsʌndər'stænd] *v/t* (*pret & pp* **-stood**) mal comprendre

mis·un·der·stand·ing [mɪsʌndər'stændɪŋ] malentendu *m*

mis·use 1 [mɪs'juːs] *n* mauvais usage *m* **2** [mɪs'juːz] *v/t* faire mauvais usage de; *word* employer à tort

mit·i·gat·ing cir·cum·stan·ces ['mɪtɪgeɪtɪŋ] *npl* circonstances *fpl* atténuantes

mitt [mɪt] *in baseball* gant *m*

mit·ten ['mɪtən] moufle *f*

mix [mɪks] **1** *n* mélange *m*; *in cooking: ready to use* préparation *f* **2** *v/t* mélanger; *cement* malaxer **3** *v/i socially* aller vers les gens, être sociable

♦ **mix up** *v/t* confondre; *get out of order* mélanger; **mix s.o. up with s.o.** confondre qn avec qn; **be mixed up emotionally** être perdu; *of figures, papers* être en désordre; **be mixed**

up in être mêlé à; **get mixed up with** (se mettre à) fréquenter

♦ **mix with** *v/t (associate with)* fréquenter

mixed [mɪkst] *adj economy, school, races* mixte; *reactions, reviews* mitigé

mixed 'mar·riage mariage *m* mixte

mix·er ['mɪksər] *for food* mixeur *m*; *drink* boisson non-alcoolisée que l'on mélange avec certains alcools; **she's a good ~** elle est très sociable

mix·ture ['mɪkstʃər] mélange *m*; *medicine* mixture *f*

mix-up ['mɪksʌp] confusion *f*

moan [moʊn] **1** *n of pain* gémissement *m* **2** *v/i in pain* gémir

mob [mɑːb] **1** *n* foule *f* **2** *v/t* (*pret & pp* **-bed**) assaillir

mo·bile ['moʊbəl] **1** *adj* mobile; *be ~ have car* être motorisé; *willing to travel* être mobile; *after breaking leg etc* pouvoir marcher **2** *n for decoration* mobile *m*; *Br: phone* portable *m*

mo·bile 'home mobile home *m*

mo·bile 'phone *Br* téléphone *m* portable

mo·bil·i·ty [məˈbɪlɪtɪ] mobilité *f*

mob·ster ['mɑːbstər] gangster *m*

mock [mɑːk] **1** *adj* faux*, feint; ~ *exam* examen *m* blanc **2** *v/t* se moquer de, ridiculiser

mock·e·ry ['mɑːkərɪ] *(derision)* moquerie *f*; *(travesty)* parodie *f*

mock-up ['mɑːkʌp] *(model)* maquette *f*

mode [moʊd] mode *m*

mod·el ['mɑːdl] **1** *adj employee, husband* modèle; *boat, plane* modèle réduit *inv* **2** *n (miniature)* maquette *f*; *(pattern)* modèle *m*; *(fashion ~)* mannequin *m*; **male ~** mannequin *m* homme **3** *v/t* présenter **4** *v/i for designer* être mannequin; *for artist, photographer* poser

mo·dem ['moʊdem] modem *m*

mod·e·rate 1 ['mɑːdərət] *adj also* POL modéré **2** *n* POL modéré *m* **3** *v/t* ['mɑːdəreɪt] modérer

mod·e·rate·ly ['mɑːdərətlɪ] *adv* modérément

mod·e·ra·tion [mɑːdəˈreɪʃn] *(restraint)*

M

modération f; **in ~** avec modération

mod·ern ['mɑːdərn] *adj* moderne

mod·ern·i·za·tion [mɑːdərnaɪˈzeɪʃn] modernisation f

mod·ern·ize ['mɑːdərnaɪz] **1** *v/t* moderniser **2** *v/i* se moderniser

mod·ern 'lan·gua·ges *npl* langues *fpl* vivantes

mod·est ['mɑːdɪst] *adj* modeste; *wage, amount* modique

mod·es·ty ['mɑːdɪsti] *of house, apartment* simplicité f; *of wage* modicité f; *(lack of conceit)* modestie f

mod·i·fi·ca·tion [mɑːdɪfɪˈkeɪʃn] modification f

mod·i·fy ['mɑːdɪfaɪ] *v/t (pret & pp* **-ied)** modifier

mod·u·lar ['mɑːdʒələr] *adj* modulaire

mod·ule ['mɑːdʒuːl] module m

moist [mɔɪst] *adj* humide

moist·en ['mɔɪsn] *v/t* humidifier, mouiller légèrement

mois·ture ['mɔɪstʃər] humidité f

mois·tur·iz·er ['mɔɪstʃəraɪzər] *for skin* produit m hydratant

mo·lar ['moʊlər] molaire f

mo·las·ses [məˈlæsɪz] *nsg* mélasse f

mold[1] [mould] *on food* moisi m, moisissure f *f(pl)*

mold[2] [mould] **1** *n* moule m **2** *v/t clay etc* modeler; *character, person* façonner

mold·y ['mouldɪ] *adj food* moisi

mole [moul] *on skin* grain m de beauté; *animal* taupe f

mo·lec·u·lar [məˈlekjulər] *adj* moléculaire

mol·e·cule ['mɑːlɪkjuːl] molécule f

mo·lest [məˈlest] *v/t child, woman* agresser (sexuellement)

mol·ly·cod·dle ['mɑːlɪkɑːdl] *v/t* F dorloter

mol·ten ['moultən] *adj* en fusion

mom [mɑːm] F maman f

mo·ment ['moumənt] instant m, moment m; **at the ~** en ce moment; **for the ~** pour l'instant

mo·men·tar·i·ly [moumənˈterɪlɪ] *adv (for a moment)* momentanément; *(in a moment)* dans un instant

mo·men·ta·ry ['moumənterɪ] *adj* momentané

mo·men·tous [məˈmentəs] *adj* capital

mo·men·tum [məˈmentəm] élan m

mon·arch ['mɑːnərk] monarque m

mon·as·ter·y ['mɑːnəstrɪ] monastère m

mo·nas·tic [məˈnæstɪk] *adj* monastique

Mon·day ['mʌndeɪ] lundi m

mon·e·ta·ry ['mʌnəterɪ] *adj* monétaire

mon·ey ['mʌnɪ] argent m; **I'm not made of ~** je ne suis pas cousu d'or

'mon·ey belt sac m banane; **mon·ey·lend·er** ['mʌnɪlendər] prêteur m; **'mon·ey mar·ket** marché m monétaire; **'mon·ey or·der** mandat m postal

mon·grel ['mʌŋgrəl] bâtard m

mon·i·tor ['mɑːnɪtər] **1** *n* COMPUT moniteur m **2** *v/t* surveiller, contrôler

monk [mʌŋk] moine m

mon·key ['mʌŋkɪ] singe m; F *child* polisson m

♦ **monkey around with** *v/t* F jouer avec; *stronger* trafiquer F

'mon·key wrench clef f anglaise

mon·o·gram ['mɑːnəgræm] monogramme m

mon·o·grammed ['mɑːnəgræmd] *adj* orné d'un monogramme

mon·o·log, *Br* **mon·o·logue** ['mɑːnəlɑːg] monologue m

mo·nop·o·lize [məˈnɑːpəlaɪz] *v/t* exercer un monopole sur; *fig* monopoliser

mo·nop·o·ly [məˈnɑːpəlɪ] monopole m

mo·not·o·nous [məˈnɑːtənəs] *adj* monotone

mo·not·o·ny [məˈnɑːtənɪ] monotonie f

mon·soon [mɑːnˈsuːn] mousson f

mon·ster ['mɑːnstər] *n* monstre m

mon·stros·i·ty [mɑːnˈstrɑːsətɪ] horreur f

mon·strous ['mɑːnstrəs] *adj* monstrueux*

month [mʌnθ] mois m

month·ly ['mʌnθlɪ] **1** *adj* mensuel* **2** *adv* mensuellement; **I'm paid ~** je

527

motherhood

suis payé au mois **3** n *magazine* mensuel m

Mon·tre·al [mɑːntrɪˈɒːl] Montréal

mon·u·ment [ˈmɑːnjəmənt] monument m

mon·u·ment·al [mɑːnjuˈmentl] *adj fig* monumental

mood [muːd] (*frame of mind*) humeur f; (*bad ~*) mauvaise humeur f; *of meeting, country* état m d'esprit; **be in a good / bad ~** être de bonne / mauvaise humeur; **be in the ~ for** avoir envie de

mood·y [ˈmuːdɪ] *adj changing moods* lunatique; (*bad-tempered*) maussade

moon [muːn] n lune f

'moon·light 1 n clair m de lune **2** v/i travailler au noir; **'moon·lit** *adj* éclairé par la lune

moor [mʊr] v/t *boat* amarrer

moor·ings [ˈmʊrɪŋz] npl mouillage m

moose [muːs] original m

mop [mɑːp] **1** n *for floor* balai-éponge; *for dishes* éponge f à manche **2** v/t (*pret & pp -ped*) *floor* laver; *eyes, face* éponger, essuyer

◆ **mop up** v/t éponger; MIL balayer

mope [moʊp] v/i se morfondre

mo·ped [ˈmoʊped] *Br* mobylette f

mor·al [ˈmɔːrəl] **1** *adj* moral **2** n *of story* morale f; **~s** moralité f

mo·rale [məˈræl] moral m

mo·ral·i·ty [məˈrælətɪ] moralité f

mor·bid [ˈmɔːrbɪd] *adj* morbide

more [mɔːr] **1** *adj* plus de; **could you make a few ~ sandwiches?** pourriez-vous faire quelques sandwichs de plus?; **some ~ tea?** encore un peu de thé?; **there's no ~ coffee** il n'y a plus de café; **~ and ~ students / time** de plus en plus d'étudiants / de temps **2** *adv* plus; **~ important** plus important; **~ and ~** de plus en plus; **~ or less** plus ou moins; **once ~** une fois de plus; **~ than** plus de; **I don't live there any ~** je n'habite plus là-bas **3** *pron* plus; **do you want some ~?** est-ce que tu en veux encore *or* davantage?; **a little ~** un peu plus

more·o·ver [mɔːˈroʊvər] *adv* de plus

morgue [mɔːrg] morgue f

morn·ing [ˈmɔːrnɪŋ] matin m; **in the ~** le matin; (*tomorrow*) demain matin; **this ~** ce matin; **tomorrow ~** demain matin; **good ~** bonjour

'morn·ing sick·ness nausées fpl du matin

mo·ron [ˈmɔːrɑːn] F crétin m

mo·rose [məˈroʊs] *adj* morose

mor·phine [ˈmɔːrfiːn] morphine f

mor·sel [ˈmɔːrsl] morceau m

mor·tal [ˈmɔːrtl] **1** *adj* mortel* **2** n mortel m

mor·tal·i·ty [mɔːrˈtælətɪ] condition f mortelle; (*death rate*) mortalité f

mor·tar[1] [ˈmɔːrtər] MIL mortier m

mor·tar[2] [ˈmɔːrtər] (*cement*) mortier m

mort·gage [ˈmɔːrgɪdʒ] **1** n prêt m immobilier; *on own property* hypothèque f **2** v/t hypothéquer

mor·ti·cian [mɔːrˈtɪʃn] entrepreneur m de pompes funèbres

mor·tu·a·ry [ˈmɔːrtʃʊerɪ] morgue f

mo·sa·ic [moʊˈzeɪk] mosaïque f

Mos·cow [ˈmɑːskaʊ] Moscou

Mos·lem [ˈmʊzlm] **1** *adj* musulman **2** n Musulman(e) m(f)

mosque [mɑːsk] mosquée f

mos·qui·to [mɑːsˈkiːtoʊ] moustique m

moss [mɑːs] mousse f

moss·y [ˈmɑːsɪ] *adj* couvert de mousse

most [moʊst] **1** *adj* la plupart de; **~ people** la plupart des gens **2** *adv* (*very*) extrêmement, très; *play, swim, eat etc* le plus; **the ~ beautiful / interesting** le plus beau / intéressant; **~ of all** surtout **3** *pron*: **~ of** la plupart de; **at (the) ~** au maximum; **that's the ~ I can offer** c'est le maximum que je peux proposer; **make the ~ of** profiter au maximum de

most·ly [ˈmoʊstlɪ] *adv* surtout

mo·tel [moʊˈtel] motel m

moth [mɑːθ] papillon m de nuit

'moth·ball boule f de naphtaline

moth·er [ˈmʌðər] **1** n mère f **2** v/t materner

'moth·er·board COMPUT carte f mère

'moth·er·hood maternité f

'Moth·er·ing Sun·day → **Mother's Day**

'moth·er-in-law (pl **mothers-in-law**) belle-mère f

moth·er·ly ['mʌðərlɪ] adj maternel*

moth·er-of-'pearl nacre f; '**Mother's Day** la fête des Mères; '**mother tongue** langue f maternelle

mo·tif [mou'ti:f] motif m

mo·tion ['mouʃn] **1** n (movement) mouvement m; (proposal) motion f; **set things in** ~ mettre les choses en route **2** v/t: **he ~ed me forward** il m'a fait signe d'avancer

mo·tion·less ['mouʃnlɪs] adj immobile

mo·ti·vate ['moutɪveɪt] v/t motiver

mo·ti·va·tion [moutɪ'veɪʃn] motivation f

mo·tive ['moutɪv] for crime mobile m

mo·tor ['moutər] moteur m

'mo·tor·bike moto f

'mo·tor·boat bateau m à moteur

mo·tor·cade ['moutərkeɪd] cortège m (de voitures)

'mo·tor·cy·cle moto f; '**mo·tor·cy·clist** motocycliste m/f; '**mo·tor home** camping-car m

mo·tor·ist ['moutərɪst] automobiliste m/f

'mo·tor me·chan·ic mécanicien(ne) m(f); '**mo·tor rac·ing** course f automobile; '**mo·tor-scoot·er** scooter m; '**mo·tor ve·hi·cle** véhicule m à moteur; '**mo·tor·way** Br autoroute f

mot·to ['mɑːtou] devise f

mould etc [mould] Br → **mold** etc

mound [maund] (hillock) monticule m; (pile) tas m

mount [maunt] **1** n (mountain) mont m; (horse) monture f **2** v/t steps, photo monter; horse, bicycle monter sur; campaign organiser **3** v/i monter

♦ mount up v/i s'accumuler, s'additionner

moun·tain ['mauntɪn] montagne f

'moun·tain bike vélo m tout-terrain, V.T.T. m

moun·tain·eer [mauntɪ'nɪr] alpiniste m/f

moun·tain·eer·ing [mauntɪ'nɪrɪŋ] al-

pinisme m

moun·tain·ous ['mauntɪnəs] adj montagneux*

mount·ed po·lice ['mauntɪd] police f montée

mourn [mɔːrn] **1** v/t pleurer **2** v/i: ~ **for** pleurer

mourn·er ['mɔːrnər] parent / ami m du défunt

mourn·ful ['mɔːrnfl] adj triste, mélancolique

mourn·ing ['mɔːrnɪŋ] deuil m; **be in** ~ être en deuil; **wear** ~ porter le deuil

mouse [maus] (pl **mice** [maɪs]) also COMPUT souris f

'mouse mat COMPUT tapis m de souris

mous·tache Br → **mustache**

mouth [mauθ] of person bouche f; of animal gueule f; of river embouchure f

mouth·ful ['mauθful] of food bouchée f; of drink gorgée f

'mouth·or·gan harmonica m; '**mouth·piece** of instrument embouchure f; (spokesperson) porte-parole m inv; **mouth-to-'mouth** bouche-à-bouche m; '**mouth·wash** bain m de bouche; '**mouth·wa·ter·ing** adj alléchant, appétissant

move [muːv] **1** n mouvement m; in chess etc coup m; (step, action) action f; (change of house) déménagement m; **it's up to you to make the first** ~ c'est à toi de faire le premier pas; **get a** ~ **on!** F grouille-toi! F; **don't make a** ~! ne bouge pas!, pas un geste! **2** v/t object déplacer; limbs bouger; (transfer) transférer; emotionally émouvoir; ~ **house** déménager **3** v/i bouger; (transfer) être transféré

♦ move around v/i bouger, remuer; from place to place bouger, déménager

♦ move away v/i s'éloigner, s'en aller; (move house) déménager

♦ move in v/i emménager

♦ move on v/i to another town partir; **move on to another subject** passer à un autre sujet; **I want to move on**

(to another job) je veux changer de travail

♦ **move out** v/i *of house* déménager; *of area* partir

♦ **move up** v/i *in league* monter; *(make room)* se pousser

move-ment ['mu:vmənt] *also organization*, MUS mouvement *m*

mov-ers ['mu:vərz] *npl* déménageurs *mpl*

mov-ie ['mu:vɪ] film *m*; **go to a / the ~s** aller au cinéma

mov-ie-go-er ['mu:vɪɡouər] amateur *m* de cinéma, cinéphile *m/f*

'mov-ie thea-ter cinéma *m*

mov-ing ['mu:vɪŋ] *adj parts of machine* mobile; *emotionally* émouvant

mow [mou] v/t *grass* tondre

♦ **move down** v/t faucher

mow-er ['mouər] tondeuse *f* (à gazon)

MP [em'pi:] *abbr Br* POL (= ***Member of Parliament***) député *m*; (= ***Military Policeman***) membre *m* de la police militaire

mph [empi:'eɪtʃ] *abbr* (= ***miles per hour***) miles à l'heure

Mr ['mɪstər] Monsieur, M.

Mrs ['mɪsɪz] Madame, Mme

Ms [mɪz] Madame, Mme

Mt *abbr* (= ***Mount***) Mt (= mont)

much [mʌtʃ] **1** *adj* beaucoup de; **so ~ money** tant d'argent; **as ~ ... as ...** autant (de) ... que ... **2** *adv* beaucoup; **very ~** beaucoup; **too ~** trop **3** *pron* beaucoup; **nothing ~** pas grand-chose; **as ~ as ...** autant que ...; **I thought as ~** c'est bien ce qu'il me semblait

muck [mʌk] *(dirt)* saleté *f*

mu-cus ['mju:kəs] mucus *m*

mud [mʌd] boue *f*

mud-dle ['mʌdl] **1** *n (mess)* désordre *m*; *(confusion)* confusion *f* **2** v/t embrouiller

♦ **muddle up** v/t mettre en désordre; *(confuse)* mélanger

mud-dy ['mʌdɪ] *adj* boueux*

mues-li ['mju:zlɪ] muesli *m*

muf-fin ['mʌfɪn] muffin *m*

muf-fle ['mʌfl] v/t étouffer

♦ **muffle up** v/i se couvrir, s'emmitou-

fler

muf-fler ['mʌflər] MOT silencieux *m*

mug[1] [mʌɡ] *for tea, coffee* chope *f*; F *(face)* gueule *f* F; F fool poire *f* F

mug[2] v/t *(pret & pp **-ged**) (attack)* agresser, attaquer

mug-ger ['mʌɡər] agresseur *m*

mug-ging ['mʌɡɪŋ] agression *f*

mug-gy ['mʌɡɪ] *adj* lourd, moite

mule [mju:l] *animal* mulet *m*, mule *f*; *slipper* mule *f*

♦ **mull over** [mʌl] v/t bien réfléchir à

mul-ti-lat-e-ral [mʌltɪ'lætərəl] *adj* POL multilatéral

mul-ti-lin-gual [mʌltɪ'lɪŋɡwəl] *adj* multilingue

mul-ti-me-di-a [mʌltɪ'mi:dɪə] **1** *adj* multimédia **2** *n* multimédia *m*

mul-ti-na-tion-al [mʌltɪ'næʃnl] **1** *adj* multinational **2** *n* COMM multinationale *f*

mul-ti-ple ['mʌltɪpl] *adj* multiple

mul-ti-ple 'choice ques-tion question *f* à choix multiple

mul-ti-ple scle-ro-sis [sklɛ'rousɪs] sclérose *f* en plaques

mul-ti-ply ['mʌltɪplaɪ] **1** v/t *(pret & pp **-ied**)* multiplier **2** v/i se multiplier

mum [mʌm] *Br* maman *f*

mum-ble ['mʌmbl] **1** *n* marmonnement *m* **2** v/t & v/i marmonner

mum-my ['mʌmɪ] *Br* F maman *f*

mumps [mʌmps] *nsg* oreillons *mpl*

munch [mʌntʃ] v/t mâcher

mu-ni-ci-pal [mju:'nɪsɪpl] *adj* municipal

mu-ral ['mjurəl] peinture *f* murale

mur-der ['mɜ:rdər] **1** *n* meurtre *m* **2** v/t *person* assassiner; *song* massacrer

mur-der-er ['mɜ:rdərər] meurtrier (-ière) *m(f)*

mur-der-ous ['mɜ:rdrəs] *adj rage, look* meurtrier*

murk-y ['mɜ:rkɪ] *adj also fig* trouble

mur-mur ['mɜ:rmər] **1** *n* murmure *m* **2** v/t murmurer

mus-cle ['mʌsl] muscle *m*

mus-cu-lar ['mʌskjulər] *adj pain, strain* musculaire; *person* musclé

M

muse [mjuːz] v/i songer

mu·se·um [mjuːˈzɪəm] musée m

mush·room [ˈmʌʃrʊm] 1 n champignon m 2 v/i fig proliférer

mu·sic [ˈmjuːzɪk] musique f; in written form partition f

mu·si·cal [ˈmjuːzɪkl] 1 adj musical; person musicien*; voice mélodieux*, musical 2 n comédie f musicale

'mu·sic·al box boîte f à musique

mu·si·cal 'in·stru·ment instrument m de musique

mu·si·cian [mjuːˈzɪʃn] musicien(ne) m(f)

mus·sel [ˈmʌsl] moule f

must [mʌst] 1 v/aux ◇ necessity devoir; I ~ be on time je dois être à l'heure, il faut que je sois (subj) à l'heure; I ~ not be late; I ~n't be late je ne dois pas être en retard, il ne faut pas que je sois en retard ◇ probability devoir; it ~ be about 6 o'clock il doit être environ six heures; they ~ have arrived by now ils doivent être arrivés maintenant 2 n: insurance is a ~ l'assurance est obligatoire

mus·tache [məˈstæʃ] moustache f

mus·tard [ˈmʌstərd] moutarde f

'must-have F 1 adj incontournable 2 n must m

must·y [ˈmʌstɪ] adj room qui sent le renfermé; smell de moisi, de renfermé

mute [mjuːt] adj muet*

mut·ed [ˈmjuːtɪd] adj sourd; criticism voilé

mu·ti·late [ˈmjuːtɪleɪt] v/t mutiler

mu·ti·ny [ˈmjuːtɪnɪ] 1 n mutinerie f 2 v/i (pret & pp -ied) se mutiner

mut·ter [ˈmʌtər] 1 v/i marmonner 2 v/t marmonner; curse, insult grommeler

mut·ton [ˈmʌtn] mouton m

mu·tu·al [ˈmjuːtʃuəl] adj (reciprocal) mutuel*, réciproque; (common) commun

muz·zle [ˈmʌzl] 1 n of animal museau m; for dog muselière f 2 v/t: ~ the press bâillonner la presse

my [maɪ] adj mon m, ma f; pl mes

my·op·ic [maɪˈɑːpɪk] adj myope

my·self [maɪˈself] pron moi-même; reflexive me; before vowel m'; after prep moi; I hurt ~ je me suis blessé; by ~ tout seul

mys·te·ri·ous [mɪˈstɪrɪəs] adj mystérieux*

mys·te·ri·ous·ly [mɪˈstɪrɪəslɪ] adv mystérieusement

mys·te·ry [ˈmɪstərɪ] mystère m; (~ story) roman m à suspense

mys·ti·fy [ˈmɪstɪfaɪ] v/t (pret & pp -ied) rendre perplexe; of tricks mystifier; be mystified être perplexe

myth [mɪθ] also fig mythe m

myth·i·cal [ˈmɪθɪkl] adj mythique

my·thol·o·gy [mɪˈθɑːlədʒɪ] mythologie f

N

nab [næb] v/t (pret & pp -bed) F (take for o.s.) s'approprier

nag [næg] 1 v/i (pret & pp -ged) of person faire des remarques continuelles 2 v/t (pret & pp -ged) harceler; ~ s.o. to do sth harceler qn pour qu'il fasse (subj) qch

nag·ging [ˈnægɪŋ] adj pain obsédant; I

have this ~ doubt that ... je n'arrive pas à m'empêcher de penser que ...

nail [neɪl] for wood clou m; on finger, toe ongle m

'nail clip·pers npl coupe-ongles m inv; 'nail file lime f à ongles; 'nail pol·ish vernis m à ongles; 'nail pol·ish re·mov·er [rɪˈmuːvər] dissolvant *m*; **'nail scis·sors** *npl* ciseaux *mpl* à ongles; **'nail var·nish** *Br* vernis *m* à ongles

na·ive [naɪˈiːv] *adj* naïf*

na·ked [ˈneɪkɪd] *adj* nu; **to the ~ eye** à l'œil nu

name [neɪm] **1** *n* nom *m*; **what's your ~?** comment vous appelez-vous?; **call s.o. ~s** insulter qn, traiter qn de tous les noms; **make a ~ for o.s.** se faire un nom **2** *v/t* appeler
♦ **name for** *v/t*: **name s.o. for s.o.** appeler qn comme qn

name·ly [ˈneɪmlɪ] *adv* à savoir

'name·sake homonyme *m/f*

'name·tag *on clothing etc* étiquette *f* (portant le nom du propriétaire)

nan·ny [ˈnænɪ] nurse *f*

nap [næp] *n* sieste *f*; **have a ~** faire une sieste

nape [neɪp]: **~ (of the neck)** nuque *f*

nap·kin [ˈnæpkɪn] (*table ~*) serviette *f* (de table); (*sanitary ~*) serviette *f* hygiénique

nar·cot·ic [nɑːrˈkɑːtɪk] *n* stupéfiant *m*

nar·cot·ics a·gent agent *m* de la brigade des stupéfiants

nar·rate [ˈnæreɪt] *v/t* sound track raconter

nar·ra·tion [næˈreɪʃn] (*telling*) narration *f*; *for documentary* commentaire *m*

nar·ra·tive [ˈnærətɪv] **1** *adj* poem, style narratif* **2** *n* (*story*) récit *m*

nar·ra·tor [næˈreɪtər] narrateur(-trice) *m/f*

nar·row [ˈnæroʊ] *adj* étroit; *victory* serré

nar·row·ly [ˈnæroʊlɪ] *adv* win de justesse; **~ escape sth** échapper de peu à qch

nar·row-mind·ed [næroʊˈmaɪndɪd] *adj* étroit d'esprit

na·sal [ˈneɪzl] *adj* voice nasillard

nas·ty [ˈnæstɪ] *adj* person, thing to say méchant; smell nauséabond; weather, cut, wound, disease mauvais

na·tion [ˈneɪʃn] nation *f*

na·tion·al [ˈnæʃənl] **1** *adj* national **2** *n* national *m*, ressortissant *m*; **a French ~** un(e) ressortissant(e) *m/f* fran-

çais(e)

na·tion·al 'an·them hymne *m* national

na·tion·al 'debt dette *f* publique

na·tion·al·ism [ˈnæʃənlɪzm] nationalisme *m*

na·tion·al·i·ty [næʃəˈnælətɪ] nationalité *f*

na·tion·al·ize [ˈnæʃənəlaɪz] *v/t* industry etc nationaliser

na·tion·al 'park parc *m* national

na·tive [ˈneɪtɪv] **1** *adj* natal; wit etc inné; population indigène; **~ tongue** langue *f* maternelle **2** *n* natif(-ive) *m(f)*; (tribesman) indigène *m*

na·tive 'coun·try pays *m* natal

na·tive 'speak·er locuteur *m* natif; **an English ~** un / une anglophone

NATO [ˈneɪtoʊ] *abbr* (= **North Atlantic Treaty Organization**) OTAN *f* (= Organisation du traité de l'Atlantique Nord)

nat·u·ral [ˈnætʃrəl] *adj* naturel*; **a ~ blonde** une vraie blonde

nat·u·ral 'gas gaz *m* naturel

nat·u·ral·ist [ˈnætʃrəlɪst] naturaliste *m/f*

nat·u·ral·ize [ˈnætʃrəlaɪz] *v/t*: **become ~d** se faire naturaliser

nat·u·ral·ly [ˈnætʃərəlɪ] *adv* (of course) bien entendu; behave, speak naturellement, avec naturel; (by nature) de nature

nat·u·ral 'sci·ence sciences *fpl* naturelles

na·ture [ˈneɪtʃər] nature *f*

'na·ture re·serve réserve *f* naturelle

naugh·ty [ˈnɔːtɪ] *adj* vilain; photograph, word etc coquin

nau·se·a [ˈnɔːzɪə] nausée *f*

nau·se·ate [ˈnɔːzɪeɪt] *v/t* fig écœurer

nau·se·at·ing [ˈnɔːzɪeɪtɪŋ] *adj* écœurant

nau·seous [ˈnɔːʃəs] *adj*: **feel ~** avoir la nausée

nau·ti·cal [ˈnɔːtɪkl] *adj* nautique, marin

'nau·ti·cal mile mille *m* marin

na·val [ˈneɪvl] *adj* naval, maritime; history de la marine

'na·val base base *f* navale**

na·vel ['neɪvl] nombril *m*

nav·i·ga·ble ['nævɪgəbl] *adj river* navigable

nav·i·gate ['nævɪgeɪt] *v/i also* COMPUT naviguer; *in car* diriger

nav·i·ga·tion [nævɪ'geɪʃn] navigation *f*; *in car* indications *fpl*

nav·i·ga·tor ['nævɪgeɪtər] navigateur *m*

na·vy ['neɪvɪ] marine *f*

na·vy 'blue 1 *adj* bleu marine *inv* **2** *n* bleu *m* marine

near [nɪr] **1** *adv* près; *come ~er* approche-toi **2** *prep* près de; *~ the bank* près de la banque **3** *adj* proche; *the ~est bus stop* l'arrêt de bus le plus proche; *in the ~ future* dans un proche avenir

near·by [nɪr'baɪ] *adv live* à proximité, tout près

near·ly ['nɪrlɪ] *adv* presque; *I ~ lost / broke it* j'ai failli le perdre / casser; *he was ~ crying* il était au bord des larmes

near-sight·ed [nɪr'saɪtɪd] *adj* myope

neat [niːt] *adj room, desk* bien rangé; *person* ordonné; *in appearance* soigné; *whiskey etc* sec*; *solution* ingénieux*; F (*terrific*) super *inv* F

ne·ces·sar·i·ly ['nesəserɪlɪ] *adv* nécessairement, forcément

ne·ces·sa·ry ['nesəserɪ] *adj* nécessaire; *it is ~ to ...* il faut ...

ne·ces·si·tate [nɪ'sesɪteɪt] *v/t* nécessiter

ne·ces·si·ty [nɪ'sesɪtɪ] nécessité *f*

neck [nek] *n* cou *m*; *of dress, sweater* col *m*

neck·lace ['neklɪs] collier *m*; **'neck·line** *of dress* encolure *f*; **'neck·tie** cravate *f*

née [neɪ] *adj* née

need [niːd] **1** *n* besoin *m*; *if ~ be* si besoin est; *in ~* dans le besoin; *be in ~ of sth* avoir besoin de qch; *there's no ~ to be rude / upset* ce n'est pas la peine d'être impoli / triste **2** *v/t* avoir besoin de; *you'll ~ to buy one* il faudra que tu en achètes un; *you don't ~ to wait* vous n'êtes pas obligés d'attendre; *I ~ to talk*

to you il faut que je te parle; *~ I say more?* dois-je en dire plus?

nee·dle ['niːdl] aiguille *f*

'nee·dle·work travaux *mpl* d'aiguille

need·y ['niːdɪ] *adj* nécessiteux*

neg·a·tive ['negətɪv] **1** *adj* négatif* **2** *n* PHOT négatif *m*; *answer in the ~* répondre par la négative

ne·glect [nɪ'glekt] **1** *n* négligence *f*; *state* abandon *m* **2** *v/t* négliger; *~ to do sth* omettre de faire qch

ne·glect·ed [nɪ'glektɪd] *adj* négligé, à l'abandon; *feel ~* se sentir négligé *or* délaissé

neg·li·gence ['neglɪdʒəns] négligence *f*

neg·li·gent ['neglɪdʒənt] *adj* négligent

neg·li·gi·ble ['neglɪdʒəbl] *adj quantity* négligeable

ne·go·ti·a·ble [nɪ'gouʃəbl] *adj salary, contract* négociable

ne·go·ti·ate [nɪ'gouʃɪeɪt] **1** *v/i* négocier **2** *v/t deal* négocier; *obstacles* franchir; *bend in road* négocier, prendre

ne·go·ti·a·tion [nɪgouʃɪ'eɪʃn] négociation *f*

ne·go·ti·a·tor [nɪ'gouʃɪeɪtər] négociateur(-trice) *m(f)*

Ne·gro ['niːgrou] Noir(e) *m(f)*

neigh [neɪ] *v/i* hennir

neigh·bor ['neɪbər] voisin(e) *m(f)*

neigh·bor·hood ['neɪbərhʊd] *in town* quartier *m*; *in the ~ of fig* environ

neigh·bor·ing ['neɪbərɪŋ] *adj* voisin

neigh·bor·ly ['neɪbərlɪ] *adj* aimable

neigh·bour *etc Br* → **neighbor** *etc*

nei·ther ['niːðər] **1** *adj*: *~ player* aucun(e) des deux joueurs **2** *pron* ni l'un ni l'autre **3** *adv*: *~ ... nor ...* ni ... ni ... **4** *conj*: *~ do / can I* moi non plus

ne·on light ['niːɑːn] néon *m*

neph·ew ['nefjuː] neveu *m*

nerd [nɜːrd] F barjo *m* F

nerve [nɜːrv] ANAT nerf *m*; (*courage*) courage *m*; (*impudence*) culot *m* F; *it's bad for my ~s* ça me porte sur les nerfs; *she gets on my ~s* elle me tape sur les nerfs

nerve-rack·ing ['nɜːrvrækɪŋ] *adj* angoissant, éprouvant

ner·vous ['nɜːrvəs] *adj* nerveux*; ***be ~ about doing sth*** avoir peur de faire qch

ner·vous 'break·down dépression *f* nerveuse

ner·vous 'en·er·gy vitalité *f*; ***be full of ~*** avoir de l'énergie à revendre

ner·vous·ness ['nɜːrvəsnɪs] nervosité *f*

ner·vous 'wreck paquet *m* de nerfs

nerv·y ['nɜːrvɪ] *adj* (*fresh*) effronté, culotté F

nest [nest] *n* nid *m*

nes·tle ['nesl] *v/i* se blottir

Net [net] *n* COMPUT Internet *m*; ***on the ~*** sur Internet

net[1] [net] *n for fishing, tennis etc* filet *m*

net[2] [net] *adj price etc* net*

net 'pro·fit bénéfice *m* net

net·tle ['netl] *n* ortie *f*

'net·work *also* COMPUT réseau *m*

neu·rol·o·gist [nʊ'rɑːlədʒɪst] neurologue *m/f*

neu·ro·sis [nʊ'roʊsɪs] névrose *f*

neu·rot·ic [nʊ'rɑːtɪk] *adj* névrosé

neu·ter ['nuːtər] *v/t animal* castrer

neu·tral ['nuːtrl] **1** *adj* neutre **2** *n gear* point *m* mort; ***in ~*** au point mort

neu·tral·i·ty [nuː'trælətɪ] neutralité *f*

neu·tral·ize ['nuːtrəlaɪz] *v/t* neutraliser

nev·er ['nevər] *adv* jamais; ***I've ~ been to New York*** je ne suis jamais allé à New York; ***you're ~ going to believe this*** tu ne vas jamais me croire; ***he ~ said that, did he?*** il n'a pas pu dire cela!; ***you ~ promised, did you?*** tu n'as rien promis?; ***~! in disbelief:*** non!

nev·er·'end·ing *adj* continuel*, interminable

nev·er·the·less [nevərðə'les] *adv* néanmoins

new [nuː] *adj* nouveau*; (*not used*) neuf*; ***this system is still ~ to me*** je ne suis pas encore habitué à ce système; ***I'm ~ to the job*** je suis nouveau dans le métier?; ***that's nothing ~*** vous ne m'apprenez rien

'new·born *adj* nouveau-né; **new·com·er** ['nuːkʌmər] nouveau venu *m*, nouvelle venue *f*; **New·found-**

land ['nuːfʌndlʌnd] Terre-Neuve *f*

new·ly ['nuːlɪ] *adv* (*recently*) récemment, nouvellement

'new·ly·weds [wedz] *npl* jeunes mariés *mpl*

new 'moon nouvelle lune *f*

news [nuːz] *nsg* nouvelle(s) *f(pl)*; *on TV, radio* informations *fpl*; ***that's ~ to me!*** on en apprend tous les jours!

'news a·gen·cy agence *f* de presse; **'news·cast** TV journal *m* télévisé; **'news·cast·er** TV présentateur (-trice) *m(f)*; **'news·deal·er** marchand(e) *m(f)* de journaux; **'news flash** flash *m* d'information; **'news·pa·per** journal *m*; **'news·read·er** TV *etc* présentateur(-trice) *m(f)*; **'news re·port** reportage *m*; **'news·stand** kiosque *m* à journaux; **'news·ven·dor** vendeur(-euse) *m(f)* de journaux

'New Year nouvel an *m*; ***Happy ~!*** Bonne année!; **New Year's 'Day** jour *m* de l'an; **New Year's 'Eve** la Saint-Sylvestre; **New Zea·land** ['ziːlənd] la Nouvelle-Zélande *f*; **New Zea·land·er** ['ziːləndər] Néo-Zélandais(e) *m(f)*

next [nekst] **1** *adj* prochain; ***the ~ house / door*** la maison / porte d'à côté; ***the ~ week / month he came back again*** il est revenu la semaine suivante / le mois suivant; ***who's ~?*** *to be served, interviewed etc* c'est à qui (le tour)? **2** *adv* (*after*) ensuite, après; ***~ to*** (*beside, in comparison with*) à côté de

next-'door 1 *adj neighbor* d'à côté **2** *adv live* à côté

next of 'kin parent *m* le plus proche; ***have the ~ been informed?*** est-ce qu'on a prévenu la famille?

nib·ble ['nɪbl] *v/t cheese* grignoter; *ear* mordiller

nice [naɪs] *adj* agréable; *person also* sympathique; *house, hair* beau*; ***be ~ to your sister!*** sois gentil* avec ta sœur!; ***that's very ~ of you*** c'est très gentil de votre part

nice·ly ['naɪslɪ] *adv written, presented, welcome, treat* bien; (*pleasantly*) agréablement, joliment

ni·ce·ties ['naisətiz] *npl*: **social ~** mondanités *fpl*

niche [ni:ʃ] *in market* créneau *m*; (*special position*) place *f*

nick [nɪk] *n on face, hand* coupure *f*; **in the ~ of time** juste à temps

nick·el ['nɪkl] nickel *m*; *coin* pièce *f* de cinq cents

'nick·name *n* surnom *m*

niece [ni:s] nièce *f*

nig·gard·ly ['nɪgərdlɪ] *adj amount* maigre; *person* avare

night [naɪt] nuit *f*; (*evening*) soir *m*; **to-morrow ~** demain soir; **11 o'clock at ~** onze heures du soir; **travel by ~** voyager de nuit; **during the ~** pendant la nuit; **stay the ~** passer la nuit; **work ~s** travailler de nuit; **good ~** *going to bed* bonne nuit; *leaving office, friends' house etc* bonsoir; **in the middle of the ~** en pleine nuit

'night·cap *drink* boisson *f* du soir; **'night·club** boîte *f* de nuit; **'night-dress** chemise *f* de nuit; **'night-fall**: **at ~** à la tombée de la nuit; **'night flight** vol *m* de nuit; **'night-gown** chemise *f* de nuit

night·in·gale ['naɪtɪŋgeɪl] rossignol *m*

'night-life vie *f* nocturne

night·ly ['naɪtlɪ] **1** *adj* de toutes les nuits; *in evening* de tous les soirs **2** *adv* toutes les nuits; *in evening* tous les soirs

'night·mare *also fig* cauchemar *m*; **'night por·ter** gardien *m* de nuit; **'night school** cours *mpl* du soir; **'night shift** équipe *f* de nuit; **'night-shirt** chemise *f* de nuit (d'homme); **'night·spot** boîte *f* (de nuit); **'night-time**: **at ~, in the ~** la nuit

nil [nɪl] *Br* zéro

nim·ble ['nɪmbl] *adj* agile; *mind* vif*

nine [naɪn] neuf

nine·teen [naɪn'tiːn] dix-neuf

nine·teenth ['naɪn'tiːnθ] dix-neuvième; → **fifth**

nine·ti·eth ['naɪntɪɪθ] quatre-vingt-dixième

nine·ty ['naɪntɪ] quatre-vingt-dix

ninth [naɪnθ] neuvième; → **fifth**

nip [nɪp] *n* (*pinch*) pincement *m*; (*bite*) morsure *f*

nip·ple ['nɪpl] mamelon *m*

ni·tro·gen ['naɪtrədʒn] azote *m*

no [nou] **1** *adv* non **2** *adj* aucun, pas de; **there's ~ coffee left** il ne reste plus de café; **I have ~ family / money** je n'ai pas de famille / d'argent; **I have ~ idea** je n'en ai aucune idée; **I'm ~ linguist / expert** je n'ai rien d'un linguiste / expert; **~ smoking / parking** défense de fumer / de stationner

no·bil·i·ty [nou'bɪlətɪ] noblesse *f*

no·ble ['noubl] *adj* noble

no·bod·y ['noubɑdɪ] **1** *pron* personne; **~ knows** personne ne le sait; **there was ~ at home** il n'y avait personne **2** *n*: **he's a ~** c'est un rien

nod [nɑːd] **1** *n* signe *m* de tête **2** *v/i* (*pret & pp* **-ded**) faire un signe de tête

♦ **nod off** *v/i* (*fall asleep*) s'endormir

no-hop·er [nou'houpər] F raté(e) *m(f)* F

noise [nɔɪz] bruit *m*

nois·y ['nɔɪzɪ] *adj* bruyant; **be ~** *of person* faire du bruit

nom·i·nal ['nɑːmɪnl] *adj* nominal; (*token*) symbolique

nom·i·nate ['nɑːmɪneɪt] *v/t* (*appoint*) nommer; **~ s.o. for a post** (*propose*) proposer qn pour un poste

nom·i·na·tion [nɑːmɪ'neɪʃn] (*appointment*) nomination *f*; (*person proposed*) candidat *m*; **who was your ~?** qui aviez-vous proposé pour le poste?

nom·i·nee [nɑːmɪ'niː] candidat *m*

non … [nɑːn] non …

non-al·co·hol·ic [nɑːn] non alcoolisé

non-a·ligned ['nɑːnəlaɪnd] *adj* non-aligné

non-cha·lant ['nɑːnʃələnt] *adj* nonchalant

non-com·mis·sioned 'of·fi·cer ['nɑːnkəmɪʃnd] sous-officier *m*

non-com·mit·tal [nɑːn'mɪtl] *adj person, response* évasif*

non-de·script ['nɑːndɪskrɪpt] *adj* quelconque; *color* indéfinissable

nostalgic

none [nʌn] *pron* aucun(e); **~ of the students** aucun des étudiants; **there is / are ~ left** il n'en reste plus; **~ of the water was left** il ne restait pas une seule goutte d'eau

non·en·ti·ty [nɑːnˈentətɪ] être *m* insignifiant

none·the·less [nʌnðəˈles] *adv* néanmoins

non·ex·ist·ent *adj* inexistant

non·fic·tion ouvrages *mpl* non littéraires

non·(in)ˈflam·ma·ble *adj* ininflammable

non·in·terˈfer·ence non-ingérence *f*

non·in·terˈven·tion non-intervention *f*

non-ˈi·ron *adj shirt* infroissable

'no-no: *that's a ~* F c'est hors de question

no-ˈnon·sense *adj approach* pragmatique

nonˈpay·ment non-paiement *m*

non·polˈlut·ing *adj* non polluant

non·resˈi·dent non-résident *m*; *in hotel* client *m* de passage

non·reˈturn·a·ble *adj deposit* non remboursable

non·sense [ˈnɑːnsəns] absurdité(s) *f(pl)*; **don't talk ~** ne raconte pas n'importe quoi; **~, it's easy!** mais non, c'est facile!, n'importe quoi, c'est facile!

nonˈskid *adj tires* antidérapant

nonˈslip *adj surface* antidérapant

nonˈsmok·er *person* non-fumeur (-euse) *m(f)*

nonˈstand·ard *adj* non standard *inv*; *use of word* impropre

nonˈstick *adj pan* antiadhésif*

nonˈstop 1 *adj flight, train* direct; *chatter* incessant **2** *adv fly, travel* sans escale; *chatter, argue* sans arrêt

nonˈswim·mer: *be a ~* ne pas savoir nager

non·ˈu·nion *adj worker* non syndiqué

non·ˈvi·o·lence non-violence *f*

non·ˈvi·o·lent *adj* non-violent

noo·dles [ˈnuːdlz] *npl* nouilles *fpl*

nook [nʊk] coin *m*

noon [nuːn] midi *m*; *at ~* à midi

noose [nuːs] nœud *m* coulant

nor [nɔːr] *conj* ni; *I neither know ~ care what he's doing* je ne sais pas ce qu'il fait et ça ne m'intéresse pas non plus; *~ do I* moi non plus

norm [nɔːrm] norme *f*

nor·mal [ˈnɔːrml] *adj* normal

nor·malˈi·ty [nɔːrˈmælətɪ] normalité *f*

nor·mal·ize [ˈnɔːrməlaɪz] *v/t relationships* normaliser

nor·mal·ly [ˈnɔːrməlɪ] *adv* normalement

Norman 1 *adj* normand **2** *n* Normand(e) *m(f)*

north [nɔːrθ] **1** *n* nord *m*; **to the ~ of** au nord de **2** *adj* nord *inv*; *wind* du nord; **~ Chicago** le nord de Chicago **3** *adv travel* vers le nord; **~ of** au nord de

North A'mer·i·ca Amérique *f* du Nord; **North A'mer·i·can 1** *adj* nord-américain **2** *n* Nord-Américain(e) *m(f)*; **northˈeast 1** *n* nord-est *m* **2** *adj* nord-est *inv*; *wind* du nord-est **3** *adv travel* vers le nord-est; **~ of** au nord-est de

nor·ther·ly [ˈnɔːrðərlɪ] *adj wind* du nord; *direction* vers le nord

nor·thern [ˈnɔːrðərn] du nord

nor·thern·er [ˈnɔːrðərnər] habitant *m* du Nord

North Ko're·a Corée *f* du Nord; **North Ko're·an 1** *adj* nord-coréen* **2** *n* Nord-Coréen(ne) *m(f)*; **North 'Pole** pôle *m* Nord; **North 'Sea** Mer *f* du Nord

north·ward [ˈnɔːrθwərd] *adv travel* vers le nord

north·west [nɔːrθˈwest] **1** *n* nord-ouest *m* **2** *adj* nord-ouest *inv*; *wind* du nord-ouest **3** *adv travel* vers le nord-ouest; **~ of** au nord-ouest de

Nor·way [ˈnɔːrweɪ] Norvège *f*

Nor·we·gian [nɔːrˈwiːdʒn] **1** *adj* norvégien* **2** *n* Norvégien(ne) *m(f)*; *language* norvégien *m*

nose [nouz] nez *m*; *it was right under my ~!* c'était juste sous mon nez

♦ **nose around** *v/i* F fouiner, fureter

'nose·bleed: *have a ~* saigner du nez

nos·tal·gia [nɑːˈstældʒə] nostalgie *f*

nos·tal·gic [nɑːˈstældʒɪk] *adj* nostalgique

nos·tril ['nɑːstrəl] narine *f*

nos·y ['nouzi] *adj* F curieux*, indiscret*

not [nɑːt] *adv* ◊ *with verbs* ne … pas; *it's ~ allowed* ce n'est pas permis; *he didn't help* il n'a pas aidé ◊ pas; ~ *now* pas maintenant; ~ *there* pas là; ~ *a lot* pas beaucoup

no·ta·ble ['noutəbl] *adj* notable

no·ta·ry ['noutəri] notaire *m*

notch [nɑːtʃ] *n* entaille *f*

note [nout] *n* MUS, (*memo to self, comment on text*) note *f*; (*short letter*) mot *m*; *take ~s* prendre des notes; *take ~ of sth* noter qch, prendre note de qch

♦ **note down** *v/t* noter

'note·book carnet *m*; COMPUT ordinateur *m* bloc-notes

not·ed ['noutid] *adj* célèbre

'note·pad bloc-notes *m*

'note·pa·per papier *m* à lettres

noth·ing ['nʌθɪŋ] *pron* rien; *she said ~* elle n'a rien dit; ~ *but* rien que; ~ *much* pas grand-chose; *for ~* (*for free*) gratuitement; (*for no reason*) pour un rien; *I'd like ~ better* je ne demande pas mieux; ~ *new* rien de neuf

no·tice ['noutis] **1** *n on bulletin board, in street* affiche *f*; (*advance warning*) avertissement *m*, préavis *m*; *in newspaper* avis *m*; *to leave job* démission *f*; *to leave house* préavis *m*; *at short ~* dans un délai très court; *until further ~* jusqu'à nouvel ordre; *give s.o. his / her ~ to quit job* congédier qn, renvoyer qn; ~ *s.o. to leave house* donner congé à qn; *hand in one's ~ to employer* donner sa démission; *four weeks' ~* un préavis de quatre semaines; *take ~ of s.o. / sth* faire attention à qn / qch; *take no ~ of s.o. / sth* ne pas faire attention à qn / qch **2** *v/t* remarquer

no·tice·a·ble ['noutisəbl] *adj* visible

no·ti·fy ['noutifai] *v/t* (*pret & pp -ied*): ~ *s.o. of sth* signaler qch à qn

no·tion ['noufn] idée *f*

no·tions ['noufnz] *npl* articles *mpl* de mercerie

no·to·ri·ous [nou'tɔːriəs] *adj* notoire; *be ~ for* être bien connu pour

nou·gat ['nuːgət] nougat *m*

noun [naun] substantif *m*, nom *m*

nour·ish·ing ['nʌrɪʃɪŋ] *adj* nourrissant

nour·ish·ment ['nʌrɪʃmənt] nourriture *f*

nov·el ['nɑːvl] *n* roman *m*

nov·el·ist ['nɑːvlɪst] romancier(-ière) *m(f)*

no·vel·ty ['nɑːvəlti] nouveauté *f*

No·vem·ber [nou'vembər] novembre *m*

nov·ice ['nɑːvɪs] (*beginner*) novice *m*, débutant *m*

now [nau] *adv* maintenant; ~ *and again*, ~ *and then* de temps à autre; *by ~* maintenant; *from ~ on* dorénavant, désormais; *right ~* (*immediately*) tout de suite; (*at this moment*) à l'instant même; *just ~* (*at this moment*) en ce moment, maintenant; (*a little while ago*) à l'instant; ~, ~! allez allez!; ~, *where did I put it?* où est-ce que j'ai bien pu le mettre?

now·a·days ['nauədeiz] *adv* aujourd'hui, de nos jours

no·where ['nouwer] *adv* nulle part; *it's ~ near finished* c'est loin d'être fini

noz·zle ['nɑːzl] *of hose* ajutage *m*; *of engine, gas pipe etc* gicleur *m*

nu·cle·ar ['nuːkliər] *adj* nucléaire

nu·cle·ar 'en·er·gy énergie *f* nucléaire; **nu·cle·ar fis·sion** ['fɪʃn] fission *f* nucléaire; **'nu·cle·ar-free** *adj* interdit au nucléaire; **nu·cle·ar 'phys·ics** physique *f* nucléaire; **nu·cle·ar 'pow·er** *energy* énergie *f* nucléaire; POL puissance *f* nucléaire; **nu·cle·ar 'pow·er sta·tion** centrale *f* nucléaire; **nu·cle·ar re'ac·tor** réacteur *m* nucléaire; **nu·cle·ar 'waste** déchets *mpl* nucléaires; **nu·cle·ar 'weap·on** arme *f* nucléaire

nude [nuːd] **1** *adj* nu **2** *n painting* nu *m*; *in the ~* tout nu

nudge [nʌdʒ] *v/t person* donner un coup de coude à; *parked car* pousser (un peu)

nud·ist ['nu:dɪst] *n* nudiste *m/f*

nui·sance ['nu:sns] *person, thing* peste *f*, plaie *f* F; *event, task* ennui *m*; **make a ~ of o.s.** être embêtant F; **what a ~!** que c'est agaçant!

nuke [nu:k] *v/t* F détruire à l'arme atomique

null and 'void [nʌl] *adj* nul* et non avenu

numb [nʌm] *adj* engourdi; *emotionally* insensible

num·ber ['nʌmbər] **1** *n* nombre *m*; *symbol* chiffre *m*; *of hotel room, house, phone ~ etc* numéro *m* **2** *v/t* (*put a ~ on*) numéroter

nu·mer·al ['nu:mərəl] chiffre *m*

nu·me·rate ['nu:mərət] *adj*: **be ~** savoir compter

nu·me·rous ['nu:mərəs] *adj* nombreux*

nun [nʌn] religieuse *f*

nurse [nɜ:rs] *n* infirmier(-ière) *m(f)*

nur·se·ry ['nɜ:rsərɪ] (*~ school*) maternelle *f*, *for plants* pépinière *f*

'nur·se·ry rhyme comptine *f*; **'nur-se·ry school** école *f* maternelle; **'nur·se·ry school teach·er** instituteur *m* de maternelle

nurs·ing ['nɜ:rsɪŋ] profession *f* d'infirmier; **she went into ~** elle est devenue infirmière

'nurs·ing home *for old people* maison *f* de retraite

nut [nʌt] (*walnut*) noix *f*, (*Brazil*) noix *f* du Brésil; (*hazelnut*) noisette *f*, (*peanut*) cacahuète *f*, *for bolt* écrou *m*; **~s** F (*testicles*) couilles *fpl* P

'nut·crack·ers *npl* casse-noisettes *m inv*

nu·tri·ent ['nu:trɪənt] élément *m* nutritif

nu·tri·tion [nu:'trɪʃn] nutrition *f*

nu·tri·tious [nu:'trɪʃəs] *adj* nutritif*

nuts [nʌts] *adj* F (*crazy*) fou*; **be ~ about s.o.** être fou de qn

'nut·shell: **in a ~** en un mot

nut·ty ['nʌtɪ] *adj taste* de noisettes; *chocolate* aux noisettes; F (*crazy*) fou*

ny·lon ['naɪlɑ:n] **1** *adj* en nylon **2** *n* nylon *m*

O

oak [ouk] chêne *m*

oar [ɔ:r] aviron *m*, rame *f*

o·a·sis [ou'eɪsɪs] (*pl* **oases** [ou'eɪsi:z]) *also fig* oasis *f*

oath [ouθ] LAW serment *m*; (*swearword*) juron *m*; **be on ~** être sous serment

oats [outs] *npl* avoine *f*

o·be·di·ence [ou'bi:dɪəns] obéissance *f*

o·be·di·ent [ou'bi:dɪənt] *adj* obéissant

o·be·di·ent·ly [ou'bi:dɪəntlɪ] *adv* docilement

o·bese [ou'bi:s] *adj* obèse

o·bes·i·ty [ou'bi:sɪtɪ] obésité *f*

o·bey [ou'beɪ] *v/t* obéir à

o·bit·u·a·ry [ou'bɪtʃuərɪ] nécrologie *f*

ob·ject[1] ['ɑ:bdʒɪkt] *n* (*thing*) objet *m*; (*aim*) objectif *m*, but *m*; GRAM complément *m* d'objet

ob·ject[2] [əb'dʒekt] *v/i* protester; **if nobody ~s** si personne n'y voit d'objection

♦ **object to** *v/t* s'opposer à; **I object to that** je ne suis pas d'accord avec ça

ob·jec·tion [əb'dʒekʃn] objection *f*

ob·jec·tio·na·ble [əb'dʒekʃnəbl] *adj* (*unpleasant*) désagréable

ob·jec·tive [əb'dʒektɪv] **1** *adj* objectif* **2** *n* objectif *m*

ob·jec·tive·ly [əb'dʒektɪvlɪ] *adv* objectivement

ob·jec·tiv·i·ty [ɑ:bdʒek'tɪvətɪ] objectivité *f*

O

ob·li·ga·tion [ɑːblɪˈɡeɪʃn] obligation f; **be under an ~ to s.o.** être redevable (de qch) à qn, avoir une dette envers qn

ob·lig·a·to·ry [əˈblɪɡətɔːrɪ] adj obligatoire

o·blige [əˈblaɪdʒ] v/t: **much ~d!** merci beaucoup!

o·blig·ing [əˈblaɪdʒɪŋ] adj serviable, obligeant

o·blique [əˈbliːk] **1** adj reference indirect; line oblique **2** n in punctuation barre f oblique

o·blit·er·ate [əˈblɪtəreɪt] v/t city détruire; memory effacer

o·bliv·i·on [əˈblɪvɪən] oubli m; **fall into ~** tomber dans l'oubli

o·bliv·i·ous [əˈblɪvɪəs] adj: **be ~ of to sth** ne pas être conscient de qch

ob·long [ˈɑːblɑːŋ] **1** adj oblong* **2** n rectangle m

ob·nox·ious [ɑːbˈnɑːkʃəs] adj person odieux*; smell abominable

ob·scene [ɑːbˈsiːn] adj obscène; salary, poverty scandaleux*

ob·scen·i·ty [ɑːbˈsenətɪ] obscénité f

ob·scure [əbˈskjʊr] adj obscur; village inconnu

ob·scu·ri·ty [əbˈskjʊrətɪ] (anonymity) obscurité f

ob·ser·vance [əbˈzɜːrvns] observance f

ob·ser·vant [əbˈzɜːrvnt] adj observateur*

ob·ser·va·tion [ɑːbzərˈveɪʃn] observation f

ob·ser·va·to·ry [əbˈzɜːrvətɔːrɪ] observatoire m

ob·serve [əbˈzɜːrv] v/t observer, remarquer

ob·serv·er [əbˈzɜːrvər] observateur (-trice) m(f)

ob·sess [ɑːbˈses] v/t: **be ~ed by or with** être obsédé par

ob·ses·sion [ɑːbˈseʃn] obsession f (**with** de)

ob·ses·sive [ɑːbˈsesɪv] adj person, behavior obsessionnel*

ob·so·lete [ˈɑːbsəliːt] adj obsolète

ob·sta·cle [ˈɑːbstəkl] also fig obstacle m

ob·ste·tri·cian [ɑːbstəˈtrɪʃn] obstétricien(ne) m(f)

ob·stet·rics [ɑːbˈstetrɪks] nsg obstétrique f

ob·sti·na·cy [ˈɑːbstɪnəsɪ] entêtement m, obstination f

ob·sti·nate [ˈɑːbstɪnət] adj obstiné

ob·sti·nate·ly [ˈɑːbstɪnətlɪ] adv avec obstination, obstinément

ob·struct [ɑːbˈstrʌkt] v/t road, passage bloquer, obstruer; investigation entraver; police gêner

ob·struc·tion [əbˈstrʌkʃn] on road etc obstacle m

ob·struc·tive [əbˈstrʌktɪv] adj behavior qui met des bâtons dans les roues; tactics obstructionniste

ob·tain [əbˈteɪn] v/t obtenir

ob·tain·a·ble [əbˈteɪnəbl] adj products disponible

ob·tru·sive [əbˈtruːsɪv] adj person, noise etc importun; object voyant

ob·tuse [əbˈtuːs] adj fig obtus

ob·vi·ous [ˈɑːbvɪəs] adj évident, manifeste; (not subtle) flagrant, lourd

ob·vi·ous·ly [ˈɑːbvɪəslɪ] adv manifestement; **~!** évidemment!

oc·ca·sion [əˈkeɪʒn] (time) occasion f

oc·ca·sion·al [əˈkeɪʒənl] adj occasionnel*; **I like the ~ whiskey** j'aime prendre un whisky de temps en temps

oc·ca·sion·al·ly [əˈkeɪʒənlɪ] adv de temps en temps, occasionnellement

oc·cult [əˈkʌlt] **1** adj occulte **2** n: **the ~** les sciences fpl occultes

oc·cu·pant [ˈɑːkjʊpənt] occupant(e) m(f)

oc·cu·pa·tion [ɑːkjʊˈpeɪʃn] (job) métier m, profession f; of country occupation f

oc·cu·pa·tion·al 'ther·a·pist [ɑːkjʊˈpeɪʃnl] ergothérapeute m/f

oc·cu·pa·tion·al 'ther·a·py ergothérapie f

oc·cu·py [ˈɑːkjʊpaɪ] v/t (pret & pp **-ied**) occuper; **~ one's mind** s'occuper l'esprit

oc·cur [əˈkɜːr] v/i (pret & pp **-red**) (happen) avoir lieu, se produire; **it ~red to me that ...** il m'est venu à l'esprit que …

oc·cur·rence [əˈkɔːrəns] (*event*) fait *m*

o·cean [ˈoʊʃn] océan *m*

o·cea·nog·ra·phy [oʊʃnˈɑːgrəfɪ] océanographie *f*

o'clock [əˈklɑːk]: *at five* ~ à cinq heures

Oc·to·ber [ɑːkˈtoʊbər] octobre *m*

oc·to·pus [ˈɑːktəpəs] pieuvre *f*

OD [oʊˈdiː] *v/i* F: ~ *on drug* faire une overdose de

odd [ɑːd] *adj* (*strange*) bizarre; (*not even*) impair; *the* ~ *one out* l'intrus; *50* ~ 50 et quelques, une cinquantaine

'odd·ball F original *m*

odds [ɑːdz] *npl*: *be at* ~ *with* être en désaccord avec; *the* ~ *are 10 to one betting* la cote est à 10 contre 1; *the* ~ *are that* … il y a de fortes chances que …; *against all the* ~ contre toute attente

odds and 'ends *npl* petites choses *fpl*, bricoles *fpl*

'odds-on *adj*: *the* ~ *favorite* le grand favori

o·di·ous [ˈoʊdɪəs] *adj* odieux*

o·dom·e·ter [oʊˈdɑːmətər] odomètre *m*

o·dor, *Br* **o·dour** [ˈoʊdər] odeur *f*

of [ɑːv], [əv] *prep possession* de; *the name* ~ *the street / hotel* le nom de la rue / de l'hôtel; *the color* ~ *the paper* la couleur du papier; *the works* ~ *Dickens* les œuvres de Dickens; *five minutes* ~ *ten* dix heures moins cinq; *die* ~ *cancer* mourir d'un cancer; *love* ~ *money / adventure* l'amour de l'argent / l'aventure; ~ *the three this is* … des trois, c'est …; *that's nice* ~ *him* c'est gentil de sa part

off [ɑːf] **1** *prep*: ~ *the main road away from* en retrait de la route principale; *near* près de la route principale; *$20* ~ *the price* 20 dollars de réduction; *he's* ~ *his food* il n'a pas d'appétit **2** *adv*: *be* ~ *of light, TV, machine* être éteint; *of brake* être desserré; *of lid, top* ne pas être mis; *not at work* ne pas être là; *canceled* être annulé;

we're ~ *tomorrow leaving* nous partons demain; *I'm* ~ *to New York* je m'en vais à New York; *I must be* ~ il faut que je m'en aille (*subj*); *with his pants / hat* ~ sans son pantalon / chapeau; *take a day* ~ prendre un jour de congé; *it's 3 miles* ~ c'est à 3 miles; *it's a long way* ~ c'est loin; *he got into his car and drove* ~ il est monté dans sa voiture et il est parti; ~ *and on* de temps en temps **3** *adj*: *the* ~ *switch* le bouton d'arrêt

of·fence *Br* → **offense**

of·fend [əˈfend] *v/t* (*insult*) offenser, blesser

of·fend·er [əˈfendər] LAW délinquant(e) *m(f)*

of·fense [əˈfens] LAW *minor* infraction *f*; *serious* délit *m*; *take* ~ *at sth* s'offenser de qch

of·fen·sive [əˈfensɪv] **1** *adj behavior, remark* offensant, insultant; *smell* repoussant **2** *n* MIL offensive *f*; *go on(to) the* ~ passer à l'offensive

of·fer [ˈɑːfər] **1** *n* offre *f* **2** *v/t* offrir; ~ *s.o. sth* offrir qch à qn

off'hand 1 *adj attitude* désinvolte **2** *adv* comme ça

of·fice [ˈɑːfɪs] bureau *m*; (*position*) fonction *f*

'of·fice block immeuble *m* de bureaux

'of·fice hours *npl* heures *fpl* de bureau

of·fi·cer [ˈɑːfɪsər] MIL officier *m*; *in police* agent *m* de police

of·fi·cial [əˈfɪʃl] **1** *adj* officiel* **2** *n civil servant* fonctionnaire *m/f*

of·fi·cial·ly [əˈfɪʃlɪ] *adv* officiellement; (*strictly speaking*) en théorie

of·fi·ci·ate [əˈfɪʃɪeɪt] *v/i* officier

of·fi·cious [əˈfɪʃəs] *adj* trop zélé

'off-line 1 *adj* hors connexion **2** *adv work* hors connexion; *go* ~ se déconnecter

'off-peak *adj rates* en période creuse

'off-sea·son 1 *adj rates, vacation* hors-saison **2** *n* basse saison *f*

'off·set *v/t* (*pret & pp* **-set**) *losses, disadvantage* compenser

'off·shore *adj* offshore

'off·side 1 adj Br wheel etc côté conducteur **2** adv SP hors jeu

'off·spring progéniture f

'off-the-rec·ord adj officieux*

'off-white adj blanc cassé inv

of·ten ['ɑːfn] adv souvent; **how ~ do you go there?** vous y allez les combien?; **how ~ have you been there?** combien de fois y êtes-vous allé?; **every so ~** de temps en temps

oil [ɔɪl] **1** n huile f; petroleum pétrole m **2** v/t lubrifier, huiler

'oil change vidange f; **'oil com·pa·ny** compagnie f pétrolière; **'oil·field** champ m pétrolifère; **'oil-fired** ['ɔɪlfaɪrd] adj central heating au mazout; **'oil paint·ing** peinture f à l'huile; **'oil-pro·duc·ing coun·try** pays m producteur de pétrole; **'oil re·fin·e·ry** raffinerie f de pétrole; **'oil rig** at sea plate-forme f de forage; on land tour f de forage; **'oil·skins** npl ciré m; **'oil slick** marée f noire; **'oil tank·er** ship pétrolier m; **'oil well** puits m de pétrole

oil·y ['ɔɪlɪ] adj graisseux*; skin, hair gras*

oint·ment ['ɔɪntmənt] pommade f

ok [ouˈkeɪ] adj & adv F: **can I? - ~** je peux? – d'accord; **is it ~ with you if ...?** ça te dérange si ...?; **does that look ~?** ça va?; **that's ~ by me** ça me va; **are you ~?** (well, not hurt) ça va?; **are you ~ for Friday?** tu es d'accord pour vendredi?; **he's ~** (is a good guy) il est bien; **is this bus ~ for ...?** est-ce que ce bus va à ...?

old [ould] adj vieux*; (previous) ancien*; **how ~ is he?** quel âge a-t-il?; **he's getting ~** il vieillit

old 'age vieillesse f

old-fash·ioned [ouldˈfæʃnd] adj démodé

ol·ive ['ɑːlɪv] olive f

'ol·ive oil huile f d'olive

O·lym·pic Games [əˈlɪmpɪk] npl Jeux mpl Olympiques

om·e·let, Br **om·e·lette** ['ɑːmlət] omelette f

om·i·nous ['ɑːmɪnəs] adj signs inquiétant

o·mis·sion [ouˈmɪʃn] omission f

o·mit [ouˈmɪt] v/t (pret & pp **-ted**) omettre; **~ to do sth** omettre de faire qch

om·nip·o·tent [ɑːmˈnɪpətənt] adj omnipotent

om·nis·ci·ent [ɑːmˈnɪsɪənt] adj omniscient

on [ɑːn] **1** prep sur; **~ the table** sur la table; **~ the bus / train** dans le bus / train; **~ the island / ~ Haiti** sur l'île / à Haïti; **~ the third floor** au deuxième étage; **~ TV / the radio** à la télé / radio; **hang sth ~ the wall** accrocher qch au mur; **don't put anything ~ it** ne pose rien dessus; **~ Sunday** dimanche; **~ Sundays** le dimanche; **~ the 1st of ...** le premier ...; **this is ~ me** (I'm paying) c'est moi qui paie; **have you any money ~ you?** as-tu de l'argent sur toi?; **~ his arrival** à son arrivée; **~ his departure** au moment de son départ; **~ hearing this** en entendant ceci **2** adv: **be ~** of light, TV, computer etc être allumé; of brake être serré; of lid, top être mis; of program: being broadcast passer; of meeting etc: be scheduled to happen avoir lieu; **what's ~ tonight?** on TV etc qu'est-ce qu'il y a ce soir?; (what's planned?) qu'est-ce qu'on fait ce soir?; **with his jacket / hat ~** sa veste sur le dos / son chapeau sur la tête; **you're ~** (I accept your offer etc) c'est d'accord; **that's not ~** (not allowed, not fair) cela ne se fait pas; **~ you go** (go ahead) vas-y; **walk / talk ~** continuer à marcher / parler; **and so ~** et ainsi de suite; **~ and ~** talk etc pendant des heures **3** adj: **the ~ switch** le bouton marche

once [wʌns] **1** adv (one time) une fois; (formerly) autrefois; **~ again, ~ more** encore une fois; **at ~** (immediately) tout de suite; **all at ~** (suddenly) tout à coup; (all) **at ~** (together) tous en même temps; **~ upon a time there was ...** il était une fois ...; **~ in a while** de temps en temps; **~ and for all** une fois pour toutes; **for ~**

pour une fois **2** *conj* une fois que; **~ you have finished** une fois que tu auras terminé

one [wʌn] **1** *n number* un *m* **2** *adj* un(e); **~ day** un jour; **that's ~ fierce dog** c'est un chien vraiment féroce **3** *pron* ◇ : **~ is bigger than the other** l'un(e) est plus grand(e) que l'autre; **which ~?** lequel / laquelle?; **~ by ~** un(e) à la fois; **the little ~s** les petits *mpl*; **I for ~** pour ma part ◇ *fml* on; **what can ~ say / do?** qu'est-ce qu'on peut dire / faire? ◇ : **~ another** l'un(e) l'autre; **we help ~ another** nous nous entraidons; **they respect ~ another** ils se respectent

one-'off *n*: **be a ~** être unique; *(exception)* être exceptionnel*

one-par-ent 'fam-i-ly famille *f* monoparentale

one'self *pron*: **hurt ~** se faire mal; **for ~** pour soi *or* soi-même; **do sth by ~** faire qch tout seul

one-sid-ed [wʌn'saɪdɪd] *adj discussion, fight* déséquilibré; **'one-track mind** *hum*: **have a ~** ne penser qu'à ça; **'one-way street** rue *f* à sens unique; **'one-way tick-et** aller *m* simple

on-ion ['ʌnjən] oignon *m*

'on-line *adj & adv* en ligne; **go ~ to** se connecter à

'on-line serv-ice COMPUT service *m* en ligne

on-look-er ['ɒnlʊkər] spectateur (-trice) *m(f)*

on-ly ['əʊnlɪ] **1** *adv* seulement; **he's ~ six** il n'a que six ans; **not ~ X but also Y** non seulement X mais aussi Y; **~ just** de justesse **2** *adj* seul, unique; **~ son / daughter** fils *m* / fille *f* unique

'on-set début *m*

'on-side: **be ~** *adv* SP ne pas être hors jeu

on-the-job 'train-ing formation *f* sur le tas

on-to ['ɒntuː] *prep* (*on top of*) sur; **the police are ~ him** la police est sur sa piste

on-ward ['ɒnwərd] *adv* en avant;

from ... ~ à partir de ...

ooze [uːz] **1** *v/i of liquid, mud* suinter **2** *v/t*: **he ~s charm** il déborde de charme

o-paque [əʊ'peɪk] *adj glass* opaque

OPEC ['əʊpek] *abbr* (= **Organization of Petroleum Exporting Countries**) OPEP *f* (= Organisation des pays exportateurs de pétrole)

o-pen ['əʊpən] **1** *adj overt; relationship* libre; *countryside* découvert, dégagé; **in the ~ air** en plein air; **be ~ to abuse** présenter des risques d'abus **2** *v/t* ouvrir **3** *v/i of door, shop, flower* s'ouvrir

♦ **open up** *v/i of person* s'ouvrir

o-pen-'air *adj meeting, concert* en plein air; *pool* découvert; **'o-pen day** journée *f* portes ouvertes; **o-pen-end-ed** [əʊpən'endɪd] *adj contract etc* flexible

o-pen-ing ['əʊpənɪŋ] *in wall etc* ouverture *f, of film, novel etc* début *m*; *(job)* poste *m* (vacant)

'o-pen-ing hours *npl* heures *fpl* d'ouverture

o-pen-ly ['əʊpənlɪ] *adv* (*honestly, frankly*) ouvertement

o-pen-mind-ed [əʊpən'maɪndɪd] *adj* à l'esprit ouvert, ouvert; **o-pen 'plan of-fice** bureau *m* paysagé; **'o-pen tick-et** billet *m* open

op-e-ra ['ɒːpərə] opéra *m*

'op-e-ra glass-es *npl* jumelles *fpl* de théâtre; **'op-e-ra house** opéra *m*; **'op-e-ra sing-er** chanteur(-euse) *m(f)* d'opéra

op-e-rate ['ɒːpəreɪt] **1** *v/i of company* opérer; *of airline, bus service* circuler; *of machine* fonctionner; MED opérer **2** *v/t machine* faire marcher

♦ **operate on** *v/t* MED opérer

op-e-rat-ing in-struc-tions ['ɒːpəreɪtɪŋ] *npl* mode *m* d'emploi; **'op-e-rat-ing room** MED salle *f* d'opération; **'op-e-rat-ing sys-tem** COMPUT système *m* d'exploitation

op-e-ra-tion [ɒːpə'reɪʃn] MED opération *f* (chirurgicale); *of machine* fonctionnement *m*; **~s** *of company* activités *fpl*; **have an ~** MED se faire opérer

op-e-ra-tor ['ɒːpəreɪtər] *of machine*

O

opérateur(-trice) *m(f)*; (*tour ~*) tour-opérateur *m*, voyagiste *m*; TELEC standardiste *m/f*

oph·thal·mol·o·gist [ɑːpθæl'mɑːlə-dʒɪst] ophtalmologue *m/f*

o·pin·ion [ə'pɪnjən] opinion *f*; **in my ~** à mon avis

o'pin·ion poll sondage *m* d'opinion

op·po·nent [ə'pounənt] adversaire *m/f*

op·por·tune ['ɑːpərtuːn] *adj fml* opportun

op·por·tun·ist [ɑːpər'tuːnɪst] opportuniste *m*

op·por·tu·ni·ty [ɑːpər'tuːnətɪ] occasion *f*

op·pose [ə'pouz] *v/t* s'opposer à; **be ~d to** être opposé à; **as ~d to** contrairement à

op·po·site ['ɑːpəzɪt] **1** *adj* opposé; *meaning* contraire; **the ~ sex** l'autre sexe **2** *adv* en face; **the house ~** la maison d'en face **3** *prep* en face de **4** *n* contraire *m*; **they're ~s** in *character* ils ont des caractères opposés

op·po·site 'num·ber homologue *m/f*

op·po·si·tion [ɑːpə'zɪʃn] opposition *f*

op·press [ə'pres] *v/t people* opprimer

op·pres·sive [ə'presɪv] *adj rule, dictator* oppressif*; *weather* oppressant

opt [ɑːpt] *v/t*: **~ to do sth** choisir de faire qch

op·ti·cal il·lu·sion ['ɑːptɪkl] illusion *f* d'optique

op·ti·cian [ɑːp'tɪʃn] opticien(ne) *m(f)*

op·ti·mism ['ɑːptɪmɪzəm] optimisme *m*

op·ti·mist ['ɑːptɪmɪst] optimiste *m/f*

op·ti·mist·ic [ɑːptɪ'mɪstɪk] *adj* optimiste

op·ti·mist·ic·ally [ɑːptɪ'mɪstɪklɪ] *adv* avec optimisme

op·ti·mum ['ɑːptɪməm] **1** *adj* optimum *inv in feminine*, optimal **2** *n* optimum *m*

op·tion ['ɑːpʃn] option *f*; **I had no ~ but to ...** je n'ai pas pu faire autrement que de ...

op·tion·al ['ɑːpʃnl] *adj* facultatif*

op·tion·al 'ex·tras *npl* options *fpl*

or [ɔːr] *conj* ou; **~ else!** sinon ...

o·ral ['ɔːrəl] *adj exam* oral; *hygiene* den-

taire; *sex* buccogénital

or·ange ['ɔːrɪndʒ] **1** *adj color* orange *inv* **2** *n fruit* orange *f*; *color* orange *m*

or·ange·ade ['ɔːrɪndʒeɪd] orangeade *f*; *carbonated* soda *m* à l'orange

'or·ange juice jus *m* d'orange

or·a·tor ['ɔːrətər] orateur(-trice) *m(f)*

or·bit ['ɔːrbɪt] **1** *n of earth* orbite *f*; **send into ~** *satellite* mettre sur orbite **2** *v/t the earth* décrire une orbite autour de

or·chard ['ɔːrtʃərd] verger *m*

or·ches·tra ['ɔːrkəstrə] orchestre *m*

or·chid ['ɔːrkɪd] orchidée *f*

or·dain [ɔːr'deɪn] *v/t priest* ordonner

or·deal [ɔːr'diːl] épreuve *f*

or·der ['ɔːrdər] **1** *n* ordre *m*; *for goods, in restaurant* commande *f*; **an ~ of fries** une portion de frites; **in ~ to** pour; **out of ~** (*not functioning*) hors service; (*not in sequence*) pas dans l'ordre **2** *v/t* (*put in sequence, proper layout*) ranger; *goods, meal* commander; **~ s.o. to do sth** ordonner à qn de faire qch **3** *v/i in restaurant* commander

or·der·ly ['ɔːrdərlɪ] **1** *adj lifestyle* bien réglé **2** *n in hospital* aide-soignant *m*

or·di·nal num·ber ['ɔːrdɪnl] ordinal *m*

or·di·nar·i·ly [ɔːrdɪ'nerɪlɪ] *adv* (*as a rule*) d'habitude

or·di·nar·y ['ɔːrdɪnerɪ] *adj* ordinaire

ore [ɔːr] minerai *m*

or·gan ['ɔːrgən] ANAT organe *m*; MUS orgue *m*

or·gan·ic [ɔːr'gænɪk] *adj food, fertilizer* biologique

or·gan·i·cal·ly [ɔːr'gænɪklɪ] *adv grown* biologiquement

or·gan·ism ['ɔːrgənɪzm] organisme *m*

or·gan·i·za·tion [ɔːrgənaɪ'zeɪʃn] organisation *f*

or·gan·ize ['ɔːrgənaɪz] *v/t* organiser

or·gan·iz·er ['ɔːrgənaɪzər] *person* organisateur(-trice) *m(f)*; *electronic* agenda *m* électronique

or·gasm ['ɔːrgæzm] orgasme *m*

O·ri·ent ['ɔːrɪənt] Orient *m*

o·ri·ent *v/t* (*direct*) orienter; **~ o.s.** (*get bearings*) s'orienter

O·ri·en·tal [ɔːrɪ'entl] **1** *adj* oriental **2** *n*

Oriental(e) *m(f)*

o·ri·gin ['ɑːrɪdʒɪn] origine *f*

o·rig·i·nal [ə'rɪdʒənl] **1** *adj (not copied)* original; *(first)* d'origine, initial **2** *n painting etc* original *m*

o·rig·i·nal·i·ty [ərɪdʒə'nælətɪ] originalité *f*

o·rig·i·nal·ly [ə'rɪdʒənəlɪ] *adv* à l'origine; *(at first)* au départ

o·rig·i·nate [ə'rɪdʒɪneɪt] **1** *v/t scheme, idea* être à l'origine de **2** *v/i of idea, belief* émaner (**from** de); *of family* être originaire (**from** de)

o·rig·i·na·tor [ə'rɪdʒɪneɪtər] *of scheme etc* auteur *m*, initiateur *m*; **he's not an ~** il n'a pas l'esprit d'initiative

or·na·ment ['ɔːrnəmənt] *n* ornement *m*

or·na·men·tal [ɔːrnə'mentl] *adj* décoratif*

or·nate [ɔːr'neɪt] *adj architecture* chargé; *prose style* fleuri

or·phan ['ɔːrfn] *n* orphelin(e) *m(f)*

or·phan·age ['ɔːrfənɪdʒ] orphelinat *m*

or·tho·dox ['ɔːrθədɑːks] *adj* REL, *fig* orthodoxe

or·tho·pe·dic, *Br also* **or·tho·pae·dic** [ɔːrθə'piːdɪk] *adj* orthopédique

os·ten·si·bly [ɑː'stensəblɪ] *adv* en apparence

os·ten·ta·tion [ɑːsten'teɪʃn] ostentation *f*

os·ten·ta·tious [ɑːsten'teɪʃəs] *adj* prétentieux*, tape-à-l'œil *inv*

os·ten·ta·tious·ly [ɑːsten'teɪʃəslɪ] *adv* avec ostentation

os·tra·cize ['ɑːstrəsaɪz] *v/t* frapper d'ostracisme

oth·er ['ʌðər] **1** *adj* autre; **the ~ day** *(recently)* l'autre jour; **every ~ day / person** un jour / une personne sur deux; **~ people** d'autres **2** *n*: **the ~** l'autre *m/f*

oth·er·wise ['ʌðərwaɪz] **1** *conj* sinon **2** *adv (differently)* autrement

ot·ter ['ɑːtər] loutre *f*

ought [ɔːt] *v/aux*: **I / you ~ to know** je / tu devrais le savoir; **you ~ to have done it** tu aurais dû le faire

ounce [aʊns] once *f*

our ['aʊər] *adj* notre; *pl* nos

ours ['aʊərz] *pron* le nôtre, la nôtre; *pl* les nôtres; **it's ~** c'est à nous

our·selves [aʊr'selvz] *pron* nous-mêmes; *reflexive* nous; *after prep* nous; **by ~** tout seuls, toutes seules

oust [aʊst] *v/t from office* évincer

out [aʊt] *adv*: **be ~** *of light, fire* être éteint; *of flower* être épanoui, être en fleur; *of sun* briller; *(not at home, not in building)* être sorti; *of calculations* être faux*; *(be published)* être sorti; *of secret* être connu; *(no longer in competition)* être éliminé; *(no longer in fashion)* être passé de mode; **~ here in Dallas** ici à Dallas; **he's in the garden** il est dans le jardin; **(get) ~!** dehors!; **(get) ~ of my room!** sors de ma chambre!; **that's ~!** *(~ of the question)* hors de question!; **he's ~ to win** *(fully intends to)* il est bien décidé à gagner

out·board 'mo·tor moteur *m* hors-bord

'out·break *of war* déclenchement *m*; *of violence* éruption *f*

'out·build·ing dépendance *f*

'out·burst *emotional* accès *m*, crise *f*

'out·cast exclu(e) *m(f)*

'out·come résultat *m*

'out·cry tollé *m*

out'dat·ed *adj* démodé, dépassé

out'do *v/t (pret -did, pp -done)* surpasser

out'door *adj activities* de plein air; *life* au grand air; *toilet* extérieur

out'doors *adv* dehors

out·er ['aʊtər] *adj wall etc* extérieur

out·er 'space espace *m* extra-atmosphérique

'out·fit *(clothes)* tenue *f*, ensemble *m*; *(company, organization)* boîte *f* F

'out·go·ing *adj flight* en partance; *personality* extraverti; *president* sortant

out'grow *v/t (pret -grew, pp -grown)* old ideas abandonner avec le temps; *clothes* devenir trop grand pour

out·ing ['aʊtɪŋ] *(trip)* sortie *f*

out'last *v/t* durer plus longtemps que; *person* survivre à

'out·let *of pipe* sortie *f*; *for sales* point *m* de vente

'out·line 1 n silhouette f; of plan, novel esquisse f **2** v/t plans etc ébaucher

out'live v/t survivre à

'out·look (prospects) perspective f

out·ly·ing ['aʊtlaɪɪŋ] adj areas périphérique, excentré

out'num·ber v/t être plus nombreux que

out of prep ◇ motion de, hors de; **run ~ the house** sortir de la maison en courant ◇ position: **20 miles ~ Detroit** à 32 kilomètres de Détroit ◇ cause par; **~ jealousy** par jalousie ◇ without: **we're ~ gas / beer** nous n'avons plus d'essence / de bière ◇ from a group sur; **5 ~ 10** 5 sur 10 ◇ : **made ~ wood** en bois

out-of-'date adj dépassé; (expired) périmé

out-of-the-'way adj à l'écart

'out·pa·tient malade m en consultation externe

'out·pa·tients' (clin·ic) service m de consultations externes

'out·per·form v/t l'emporter sur

'out·put 1 n of factory production f, rendement m; COMPUT sortie f **2** v/t (pret & pp **-ted** or **output**) (produce) produire

'out·rage 1 n feeling indignation f; act outrage m **2** v/t faire outrage à; **I was ~d to hear …** j'étais outré d'apprendre …

out·ra·geous [aʊt'reɪdʒəs] adj acts révoltant; prices scandaleux*

'out·right 1 adj winner incontesté; disaster, disgrace absolu **2** adv pay comptant; buy au comptant; kill sur le coup; refuse catégoriquement

out'run v/t (pret **-ran**, pp **-run**) distancer

'out·set début m; **from the ~** dès le début

out'shine v/t (pret & pp **-shone**) éclipser

'out·side 1 adj extérieur **2** adv dehors, à l'extérieur **3** prep à l'extérieur de; (in front of) devant; (apart from) en dehors de **4** n of building, case etc extérieur m; **at the ~** tout au plus

out·side 'broad·cast émission f en

extérieur

out'sid·er [aʊt'saɪdər] in election, race outsider m; in life étranger m

'out·size adj clothing grande taille

'out·skirts npl of town banlieue f

'out·smart → **outwit**

'out·source v/t externaliser

'out·spo·ken adj franc*

out'stand·ing adj exceptionnel*, remarquable; invoice, sums impayé

out·stretched ['aʊtstretʃt] adj hands tendu

'out·vote v/t mettre en minorité

out·ward ['aʊtwərd] adj appearance extérieur; **~ journey** voyage m aller

out·ward·ly ['aʊtwərdlɪ] adv en apparence

out'weigh v/t l'emporter sur

out'wit v/t (pret & pp **-ted**) se montrer plus malin* que

o·val ['oʊvl] adj ovale

o·va·ry ['oʊvərɪ] ovaire m

o·va·tion [oʊ'veɪʃn] ovation f; **give s.o. a standing ~** se lever pour ovationner qn

ov·en ['ʌvn] four m

'ov·en glove, 'ov·en mitt gant m de cuisine; **'ov·en·proof** adj qui va au four; **'ov·en-read·y** adj prêt à cuire

o·ver ['oʊvər] **1** prep (above) au-dessus de; (across) de l'autre côté de; (more than) plus de; (during) pendant; **she walked ~ the street** elle traversa la rue; **travel all ~ Brazil** voyager à travers le Brésil; **you find them all ~ Brazil** vous les trouvez partout au Brésil; **she's ~ 40** elle a plus de 40 ans; **let's talk ~ a drink** discutons-en autour d'un verre; **we're ~ the worst** le pire est passé; **~ and above** en plus de **2** adv: **be ~** (finished) être fini; (left) rester; **there were just 6 ~** il n'en restait que 6; **~ to you** (your turn) c'est à vous; **~ in Japan** au Japon; **~ here** ici; **~ there** là-bas; **it hurts all ~** ça fait mal partout; **painted white all ~** peint tout en blanc; **it's all ~** c'est fini; **~ and ~ again** maintes et maintes fois; **do sth ~** (again) refaire qch

o·ver·all ['oʊvərɔːl] **1** adj length total **2**

adv measure en tout; (*in general*) dans l'ensemble

o·ver·alls ['ouvərɔːlz] *npl* bleu *m* de travail

o·ver·awe [ouvər'ɔː] *v/t* impressionner, intimider

o·ver·bal·ance *v/i of person* perdre l'équilibre

o·ver·bear·ing *adj* dominateur*

'o·ver·board *adv* par-dessus bord; **man ~!** un homme à la mer!; **go ~ for s.o. / sth** s'emballer pour qn / qch

'o·ver·cast *adj sky* couvert

o·ver·charge *v/t* faire payer trop cher à

'o·ver·coat pardessus *m*

o·ver·come *v/t* (*pret* **-came**, *pp* **-come**) difficulties, shyness surmonter; **be ~ by emotion** être submergé par l'émotion

o·ver·crowd·ed *adj city* surpeuplé; *train* bondé

o·ver·do *v/t* (*pret* **-did**, *pp* **-done**) (*exaggerate*) exagérer; *in cooking* trop cuire; **you're ~ing things** tu en fais trop

o·ver·done *adj meat* trop cuit

'o·ver·dose *n* overdose *f*

'o·ver·draft découvert *m*; **have an ~** être à découvert

o·ver·draw *v/t* (*pret* **-drew**, *pp* **-drawn**) *account* mettre à découvert; **be \$800 ~n** avoir un découvert de 800 dollars, être à découvert de 800 dollars

o·ver·dressed [ouvər'drest] *adj* trop habillé

'o·ver·drive MOT overdrive *m*

o·ver·due *adj* en retard

o·ver·es·ti·mate *v/t abilities, value* surestimer

o·ver·ex·pose *v/t photograph* surexposer

'o·ver·flow[1] *n pipe* trop-plein *m inv*

o·ver·flow[2] *v/i of water* déborder

o·ver·grown *adj garden* envahi par les herbes; **he's an ~ baby** il est resté très bébé

o·ver·haul *v/t engine, brakes etc* remettre à neuf; *plans, voting system* remanier

'o·ver·head 1 *adj* au-dessus; **~ light** *in ceiling* plafonnier *m* **2** *n* FIN frais *mpl* généraux

o·ver·hear *v/t* (*pret & pp* **-heard**) entendre (par hasard)

o·ver·heat·ed *adj room* surchauffé; *engine* qui chauffe; *fig: economy* en surchauffe

o·ver·joyed [ouvər'dʒɔɪd] *adj* ravi, enchanté

'o·ver·kill: **that's ~** c'est exagéré

'o·ver·land 1 *adj transport* par terre; **~ route** voie *f* de terre **2** *adv travel* par voie de terre

o·ver·lap *v/i* (*pret & pp* **-ped**) *of tiles, periods etc* se chevaucher; *of theories* se recouper

o·ver·leaf: **see ~** voir au verso

o·ver·load *v/t vehicle, electric circuit* surcharger

o·ver·look *v/t of tall building etc* surplomber, dominer; *of window, room* donner sur; (*not see*) laisser passer

o·ver·ly ['ouvərlı] *adv* trop; **not ~ ...** pas trop ...

'o·ver·night *adv stay, travel* la nuit; *fig: change, learn etc* du jour au lendemain

o·ver·paid *adj* trop payé, surpayé

'o·ver·pass pont *m*

o·verpop·u·lat·ed [ouvər'pɑːpjəleɪtɪd] *adj* surpeuplé

o·ver·pow·er *v/t physically* maîtriser

o·ver·pow·er·ing [ouvər'paurɪŋ] *adj smell* suffocant; *sense of guilt* irrépressible

o·ver·priced [ouvər'praɪst] *adj* trop cher*

o·ver·rat·ed [ouvə'reɪtɪd] *adj* surfait

o·ver·re·act *v/i* réagir de manière excessive

o·ver·re·ac·tion réaction *f* disproportionnée

o·ver·ride *v/t* (*pret* **-rode**, *pp* **-ridden**) *decision etc* annuler; *technically* forcer

o·ver·rid·ing *adj concern* principal

o·ver·rule *v/t decision* annuler

o·ver·run *v/t* (*pret* **-ran**, *pp* **-run**) *country* envahir; *time* dépasser; **be ~ with** *tourists* être envahi par; *rats* être infesté de

O

o·ver'seas 1 *adj travel etc* à l'étranger
2 *adv* à l'étranger

o·ver'see *v/t (pret -saw, pp -seen)* superviser

o·ver'shad·ow *v/t fig* éclipser

'o·ver·sight omission *f*, oubli *m*

o·ver·sim·pli·fi·ca·tion [ouvərsɪmplɪ-
fɪ'keɪʃn] schématisation *f*

o·ver'sim·pli·fy *v/t (pret & pp -ied)*
schématiser

o·ver'sleep *v/i (pret & pp -slept)* se
réveiller en retard

o·ver'state *v/t* exagérer

o·ver'state·ment exagération *f*

o·ver'step *v/t (pret & pp -ped):* ~ *the
mark* dépasser les bornes

o·ver'take *v/t (pret -took, pp -taken)*
in work, development dépasser, devancer; *Br MOT* dépasser, doubler

o·ver'throw¹ *v/t (pret -threw, pp
-thrown) government* renverser

'o·ver·throw² *n of government* renversement *m*

'o·ver·time 1 *n SP* temps *m* supplémentaire, prolongation *f* **2** *adv:* **work**
~ faire des heures supplémentaires

o·ver·ture ['ouvərtʃur] *MUS* ouverture
f; **make ~s to** faire des ouvertures à

o·ver'turn¹ *v/t also government* renverser **2** *v/i of vehicle* se retourner

'o·ver·view vue *f* d'ensemble

o·ver'weight *adj* trop gros*

o·ver'whelm [ouvər'welm] *v/t with
work* accabler, surcharger; *with emotion* submerger; *be ~ed by* by response être bouleversé par

o·ver'whelm·ing [ouvər'welmɪŋ] *adj
guilt, fear* accablant, irrépressible; *relief* énorme; *majority* écrasant

o·ver'work 1 *n* surmenage *m* **2** *v/i* se
surmener **3** *v/t* surmener

owe [ou] *v/t* devoir (s.o. à qn); ~ *s.o. an
apology* devoir des excuses à qn;
how much do I ~ you? combien
est-ce que je te dois?

ow·ing to ['ouɪŋ] *prep* à cause de

owl [aul] hibou *m*, chouette *f*

own¹ [oun] *v/t* posséder

own² [oun] **1** *adj* propre

own 2 *pron:* **an apartment of my ~** un
appartement à moi; **on my / his ~**
tout seul

♦ own up *v/i* avouer

own·er ['ounər] propriétaire *m/f*

own·er·ship ['ounərʃɪp] possession *f*,
propriété *f*

ox·ide ['ɑːksaɪd] oxyde *m*

ox·y·gen ['ɑːksɪdʒən] oxygène *m*

oy·ster ['ɔɪstər] huître *f*

oz *abbr (= ounce(s))*

o·zone ['ouzoun] ozone *m*

'o·zone lay·er couche *f* d'ozone

P

PA [piː'eɪ] *abbr (= personal assistant)* secrétaire *m/f*

pace [peɪs] **1** *n (step)* pas *m*; *(speed)* allure *f* **2** *v/i:* ~ *up and down* faire les
cent pas

'pace·mak·er *MED* stimulateur *m* cardiaque, pacemaker *m; SP* lièvre *m*

Pa·cif·ic [pə'sɪfɪk]: *the ~ (Ocean)* le
Pacifique, l'océan *m* Pacifique

pac·i·fi·er ['pæsɪfaɪər] *for baby* sucette
f

pac·i·fism ['pæsɪfɪzm] pacifisme *m*

pac·i·fist ['pæsɪfɪst] *n* pacifiste *m/f*

pac·i·fy ['pæsɪfaɪ] *v/t (pret & pp -ied)*
calmer, apaiser

pack [pæk] **1** *n (back~)* sac *m* à dos; *of
cereal, cigarettes etc* paquet *m; of
cards* jeu *m* **2** *v/t item of clothing etc* mettre
dans ses bagages; *goods* emballer; ~
one's bag faire sa valise **3** *v/i* faire
ses bagages

pack·age ['pækɪdʒ] **1** *n (parcel)* paquet *m; of offers etc* forfait *m* **2** *v/t in packs* conditionner; *idea, project* présenter

'**pack·age deal** *for holiday* forfait *m*

'**pack·age tour** voyage *m* à forfait

pack·ag·ing ['pækɪdʒɪŋ] *of product* conditionnement *m; material* emballage *m; of idea, project* présentation *f; of rock star etc* image *f* (de marque)

packed [pækt] *adj (crowded)* bondé

pack·et ['pækɪt] paquet *m*

pact [pækt] pacte *m*

pad[1] [pæd] **1** *n protective* tampon *m* de protection; *over wound* tampon *m; for writing* bloc *m* **2** *v/t (pret & pp -ded) with material* rembourrer; *speech, report* délayer

pad[2] [pæd] *v/i (pret & pp -ded) (move quietly)* marcher à pas feutrés

pad·ded ['pædɪd] *adj jacket* matelassé, rembourré

pad·ding ['pædɪŋ] *material* rembourrage *m; in speech etc* remplissage *m*

pad·dle[1] ['pædl] **1** *n for canoe* pagaie *f* **2** *v/i in canoe* pagayer

pad·dle[2] ['pædl] *v/i in water* patauger

pad·dock ['pædək] paddock *m*

pad·lock ['pædlɑːk] **1** *n* cadenas *m* **2** *v/t:* cadenasser; **~ sth to sth** attacher qch à qch à l'aide d'un cadenas

page[1] [peɪdʒ] *n of book etc* page *f;* **~ number** numéro *m* de page

page[2] [peɪdʒ] *v/t (call)* (faire) appeler

pag·er ['peɪdʒər] pager *m*, radiomesageur *m; for doctor* bip *m*

paid [peɪd] *pret & pp →* **pay**

paid em'ploy·ment travail *m* rémunéré

pail [peɪl] seau *m*

pain [peɪn] *n* douleur *f;* **be in ~** souffrir; **take ~s to do sth** se donner de la peine pour faire qch; **a ~ in the neck** F un casse-pieds

pain·ful ['peɪnfʊl] *adj arm, leg etc* douloureux*; (distressing)* pénible; *(laborious)* difficile

pain·ful·ly ['peɪnflɪ] *adv (extremely, acutely)* terriblement

'**pain·kill·er** analgésique *m*

pain·less ['peɪnlɪs] *adj* indolore; *fig* F pas méchant F

pains·tak·ing ['peɪnzteɪkɪŋ] *adj* minutieux*

paint [peɪnt] **1** *n* peinture *f* **2** *v/t* peindre **3** *v/i as art form* faire de la peinture, peindre

'**paint·brush** pinceau *m*

paint·er ['peɪntər] peintre *m*

paint·ing ['peɪntɪŋ] *activity* peinture *f; picture* tableau *m*

'**paint·work** peinture *f*

pair [per] paire *f; of people, animals, birds* couple *m;* **a ~ of shoes / san·dals** une paire de chaussures / sandales; **a ~ of pants** un pantalon; **a ~ of scissors** des ciseaux *mpl*

pa·ja·ma 'jack·et veste *f* de pyjama

pa·ja·ma 'pants *npl* pantalon *m* de pyjama

pa·ja·mas [pə'dʒɑːməz] *npl* pyjama *m*

Pa·ki·stan [pækɪ'stɑːn] Pakistan *m*

Pa·ki·sta·ni [pækɪ'stɑːnɪ] **1** *adj* pakistanais **2** *n* Pakistanais(e) *m(f)*

pal [pæl] F *(friend)* copain *m*, copine *f*, pote *m* F; **hey ~, got a light?** eh toi, t'as du feu?

pal·ace ['pælɪs] palais *m*

pal·ate ['pælət] ANAT, *fig* palais *m*

pa·la·tial [pə'leɪʃl] *adj* sompteux*

pale [peɪl] *adj* pâle; **go ~** pâlir

Pal·e·stine ['pæləstaɪn] Palestine *f*

Pal·e·stin·i·an [pælə'stɪnɪən] **1** *adj* palestinien* **2** *n* Palestinien(ne) *m(f)*

pal·let ['pælɪt] palette *f*

pal·lor ['pælər] pâleur *f*

palm[1] [pɑːm] *of hand* paume *f*

palm[2] [pɑːm] *tree* palmier *m*

pal·pi·ta·tions [pælpɪ'teɪʃnz] *npl* MED palpitations *fpl*

pal·try ['pɔːltrɪ] *adj* dérisoire

pam·per ['pæmpər] *v/t* choyer, gâter

pam·phlet ['pæmflɪt] *for information* brochure *f; political tract* tract *m*

pan [pæn] **1** *n* casserole *f; for frying* poêle *f* **2** *v/t (pret & pp -ned)* F *(criticize)* démolir

♦ **pan out** *v/i (develop)* tourner

pan·cake ['pænkeɪk] crêpe *f*

pan·da ['pændə] panda *m*

pan·de·mo·ni·um [pændɪ'moʊnɪəm] désordre *m*

♦ **pan·der to** ['pændər] *v/t* céder à

P

pane [peɪn]: *a ~ of glass* un carreau, une vitre

pan·el ['pænl] panneau *m*; *people* comité *m*; *on TV program* invités *mpl*

pan·el·ing, *Br* **pan·el·ling** ['pænəlɪŋ] lambris *m*

pang [pæŋ] *of remorse* accès *m*; *~s of hunger* des crampes d'estomac

pan·han·dle *v/i* F faire la manche F

pan·ic ['pænɪk] **1** *n* panique *f* **2** *v/i* (*pret & pp* **-ked**) s'affoler, paniquer; *don't ~!* ne t'affole pas!

'pan·ic buy·ing achat *m* en catastrophe; 'pan·ic sel·ling FIN vente *f* en catastrophe; 'pan·ic-strick·en *adj* affolé, pris de panique

pan·o·ra·ma [pænə'rɑːmə] panorama *m*

pa·no·ram·ic [pænə'ræmɪk] *adj view* panoramique

pan·sy ['pænzi] *flower* pensée *f*

pant [pænt] *v/i of person* haleter

pan·ties ['pæntiz] *npl* culotte *f*

pan·ti·hose → **pantyhose**

pants [pænts] *npl* pantalon *m*; *a pair of ~* un pantalon

pan·ty·hose ['pæntɪhoʊz] *npl* collant *m*

pa·pal ['peɪpəl] *adj* papal

pa·per ['peɪpər] **1** *n material* papier *m*; (*news~*) journal *m*; (*wall~*) papier *m* peint; *academic* article *m*, exposé *m*; (*examination ~*) épreuve *f*; *~s* (*documents*) documents *mpl*; (*identity ~s*) papiers *mpl* **2** *adj* (*made of ~*) en papier **3** *v/t room, walls* tapisser

'pa·per·back livre *m* de poche; 'pa·per bag sac *m* en papier; 'pa·per boy livreur *m* de journaux; 'pa·per clip trombone *m*; 'pa·per cup gobelet *m* en carton; 'pa·per·work tâches *fpl* administratives

Pap test [pæp] MED frottis *m*

par [pɑːr] *in golf* par *m*; *be on a ~ with* être comparable à; *feel below ~* ne pas être dans son assiette

par·a·chute ['pærəʃuːt] **1** *n* parachute *m* **2** *v/i* sauter en parachute **3** *v/t troops, supplies* parachuter

par·a·chut·ist ['pærəʃuːtɪst] parachutiste *m/f*

pa·rade [pə'reɪd] **1** *n* (*procession*) défilé *m* **2** *v/i of soldiers* défiler; *showing off* parader, se pavaner **3** *v/t knowledge, new car* faire étalage de

par·a·dise ['pærədaɪs] REL, *fig* paradis *m*

par·a·dox ['pærədɑːks] paradoxe *m*

par·a·dox·i·cal [pærə'dɑːksɪkl] *adj* paradoxal

par·a·dox·i·cal·ly [pærə'dɑːksɪklɪ] *adv* paradoxalement

par·a·graph ['pærəgræf] paragraphe *m*

par·al·lel ['pærəlel] **1** *n* parallèle *f*; GEOG, *fig* parallèle *m*; *do two things in ~* faire deux choses en même temps **2** *adj also fig* parallèle **3** *v/t* (*match*) égaler

pa·ral·y·sis [pə'ræləsɪs] *also fig* paralysie *f*

par·a·lyze ['pærəlaɪz] *v/t* paralyser

par·a·med·ic [pærə'medɪk] auxiliaire *m/f* médical(e)

pa·ram·e·ter [pə'ræmɪtər] paramètre *m*

par·a·mil·i·tar·y [pærə'mɪlɪterɪ] **1** *adj* paramilitaire **2** *n* membre *m* d'une organisation paramilitaire

par·a·mount ['pærəmaʊnt] *adj* suprême, primordial; *be ~* être de la plus haute importance

par·a·noi·a [pærə'nɔɪə] paranoïa *f*

par·a·noid ['pærənɔɪd] *adj* paranoïaque

par·a·pher·na·li·a [pærəfər'neɪlɪə] attirail *m*, affaires *fpl*

par·a·phrase ['pærəfreɪz] *v/t* paraphraser

par·a·pleg·ic [pærə'pliːdʒɪk] *n* paraplégique *m/f*

par·a·site ['pærəsaɪt] *also fig* parasite *m*

par·a·sol ['pærəsɑːl] parasol *m*

par·a·troop·er ['pærətruːpər] parachutiste *m*, para *m* F

par·cel ['pɑːrsl] *n* colis *m*, paquet *m*
♦ **parcel up** *v/t* emballer

parch [pɑːrtʃ] *v/t* dessécher; *be ~ed* F *of person* mourir de soif

par·don ['pɑːrdn] **1** *n* LAW grâce *f*; *I beg your ~?* (*what did you say?*)

comment?; (*I'm sorry*) je vous demande pardon **2** *v/t* pardonner; LAW gracier; **~ me?** pardon?

pare [per] *v/t* (*peel*) éplucher

par·ent ['perənt] père *m*; mère *f*; *my* **~s** mes parents; *as a* **~** en tant que parent

pa·ren·tal [pə'rentl] *adj* parental

'par·ent com·pa·ny société *f* mère

par·en·the·sis [pə'renθəsɪz] (*pl* **par·entheses** [pə'renθəsiːz]) parenthèse *f*

par·ent-'tea·cher as·so·ci·a·tion association *f* de parents d'élèves

par·ish ['pærɪʃ] paroisse *f*

park[1] [pɑːrk] *n* parc *m*

park[2] [pɑːrk] **1** *v/t* MOT garer **2** *v/i* MOT stationner, se garer

par·ka ['pɑːrkə] parka *m* or *f*

park·ing ['pɑːrkɪŋ] MOT stationnement *m*; *no* **~** défense de stationner, stationnement interdit

'park·ing brake frein *m* à main; **'park·ing ga·rage** parking *m* couvert; **'par·king lot** parking *m*, parc *m* de stationnement; **'par·king me·ter** parcmètre *m*; **'par·king place** place *f* de stationnement; **'par·king tick·et** contravention *f*

par·lia·ment ['pɑːrləmənt] parlement *m*

par·lia·men·ta·ry [pɑːrlə'mentərɪ] *adj* parlementaire

pa·role [pə'roʊl] **1** *n* libération *f* conditionnelle; *be on* **~** être en liberté conditionnelle **2** *v/t* mettre en liberté conditionnelle

par·rot ['pærət] *n* perroquet *m*

pars·ley ['pɑːrslɪ] persil *m*

part [pɑːrt] **1** *n* partie *f*; (*episode*) épisode *m*; *of machine* pièce *f*; *in play, movie* rôle *m*; *in hair* raie *f*; *take ~ in* participer à, prendre part à **2** *adv* (*partly*) en partie **3** *v/i of two people* se quitter, se séparer; *I ~ed from her* je l'ai quittée **4** *v/t*: *~ one's hair* se faire une raie

♦ **part** *with v/t* se séparer de

'part ex·change: *take sth in* **~** reprendre qch

par·tial ['pɑːrʃl] *adj* (*incomplete*) partiel*; *be* **~** *to* avoir un faible pour, bien aimer

par·tial·ly ['pɑːrʃəlɪ] *adv* en partie, partiellement

par·ti·ci·pant [pɑːr'tɪsɪpənt] participant(e) *m(f)*

par·ti·ci·pate [pɑːr'tɪsɪpeɪt] *v/i* participer (*in* à), prendre part (*in* à)

par·ti·ci·pa·tion [pɑːrtɪsɪ'peɪʃn] participation *f*

par·ti·cle ['pɑːrtɪkl] PHYS particule *f*

par·tic·u·lar [pər'tɪkjələr] *adj* particulier*; (*fussy*) à cheval (*about* sur), exigeant; *this plant is a* **~** *favorite of mine* j'aime tout particulièrement cette plante; *in* **~** en particulier

par·tic·u·lar·ly [pər'tɪkjələrlɪ] *adv* particulièrement

part·ing ['pɑːrtɪŋ] *of people* séparation *f*; *Br. in hair* raie *f*

par·ti·tion [pɑːr'tɪʃn] **1** *n* (*screen*) cloison *f*; *of country* partage *m*, division *f* **2** *v/t country* partager, diviser

♦ **partition off** *v/t* cloisonner

part·ly ['pɑːrtlɪ] *adv* en partie

part·ner ['pɑːrtnər] *n* partenaire *m*; COMM associé *m*; *in relationship* compagnon(ne) *m(f)*

part·ner·ship ['pɑːrtnərʃɪp] COMM, *in relationship* association *f*; *in particular activity* partenariat *m*

part of 'speech classe *f* grammaticale; **'part own·er** copropriétaire *m/f*; **'part-time** *adj* & *adv* à temps partiel; **part-'tim·er** employé(e) *m(f)* à temps partiel

par·ty ['pɑːrtɪ] **1** *n* (*celebration*) fête *f*; *for adults in the evening also* soirée *f*; POL parti *m*; (*group of people*) groupe *m*; *be a* **~** *to* prendre part à **2** *v/i* (*pret & pp* **-ied**) F faire la fête

par·ty-pooper ['pɑːrtɪpuːpər] F trouble-fête *m inv*

pass [pæs] **1** *n for entry* laissez-passer *m inv*; SP passe *f*; *in mountains* col *m inv*; *make a* **~** *at* faire des avances à; **2** *v/t* (*go past*) passer devant; *another car* doubler, dépasser; *competitor* dépasser; (*go beyond*) dépasser; (*approve*) approuver; **~** *an exam* réussir un examen; **~** *sentence* LAW prononcer

le verdict; **~ the time** of person passer
le temps; of activity faire passer le
temps **3** v/i of time passer; **in exam**
être reçu; SP faire une passe; (**go
away**) passer

♦ **pass around** v/t faire passer
♦ **pass by 1** v/t (go past) passer devant / à côté de **2** v/i (go past) passer
♦ **pass on 1** v/t information, book passer; costs répercuter; savings faire
profiter de **2** v/i (euph: die) s'éteindre
♦ **pass out** v/i (faint) s'évanouir
♦ **pass through** v/t town traverser
♦ **pass up** v/t F chance laisser passer

pass·a·ble ['pæsəbl] adj road praticable; (acceptable) passable
pas·sage ['pæsɪdʒ] (corridor) couloir
m; from book, of time passage m; **with
the ~ of time** avec le temps
pas·sage·way ['pæsɪdʒweɪ] passage
m
pas·sen·ger ['pæsɪndʒər] passager
(-ère) m(f)
'**pas·sen·ger seat** siège m du passager
pas·ser·by [pæsər'baɪ] (pl **passers-
-by**) passant(e) m(f)
pas·sion ['pæʃn] passion f
pas·sion·ate ['pæʃnət] adj lover passionné; (fervent) fervent, véhément
pas·sive ['pæsɪv] **1** adj passif* **2** n
GRAM passif m; **in the ~** à la voix passive
'**pass mark** EDU moyenne f; '**Pass-
o·ver** REL la Pâque; '**pass·port** passeport m; '**pass·port con·trol**
contrôle m des passeports; '**password** mot m de passe
past [pæst] **1** adj (former) passé, ancien*; **the ~ few days** ces derniers
jours; **that's all ~ now** c'est du passé
F **2** n passé m; **in the ~** autrefois **3**
prep après; **it's ~ 7 o'clock** il est plus
de 7 heures; **it's half ~ two** il est deux
heures et demie **4** adv: **run ~** passer
en courant
pas·ta ['pæstə] pâtes fpl
paste [peɪst] **1** n (adhesive) colle f **2** v/t
(stick) coller
pas·tel ['pæstl] n pastel m; **~ blue** bleu

pastel
pas·time ['pæstaɪm] passe-temps m
inv
past·or pasteur m
past par·ti·ci·ple [pɑr'tɪsɪpl] GRAM
participe m passé
pas·tra·mi [pæ'strɑːmɪ] bœuf m fumé
et épicé
pas·try ['peɪstrɪ] for pie pâte f; small
cake pâtisserie f
'**past tense** GRAM passé m
pas·ty ['peɪstɪ] adj complexion blafard
pat [pæt] **1** n petite tape f; **give s.o. a
~ on the back** fig féliciter qn **2** v/t (pret
& pp **-ted**) tapoter
patch [pætʃ] **1** n on clothing pièce f;
(period of time) période f; (area) tache
f; of fog nappe f; **go through a bad ~**
traverser une mauvaise passe; **be not
a ~ on** F être loin de valoir **2** v/t clothing rapiécer
♦ **patch up** v/t (repair temporarily) rafistoler F; quarrel régler
patch·work ['pætʃwɜːrk] **1** adj quilt en
patchwork **2** n patchwork m
patch·y ['pætʃɪ] adj inégal
pâ·té [pɑː'teɪ] pâté m
pa·tent ['peɪtnt] **1** adj (obvious) manifeste **2** n for invention brevet m **3** v/t
invention breveter
pa·tent 'leath·er cuir m verni
pa·tent·ly ['peɪtntlɪ] adv (clearly) manifestement
pa·ter·nal [pə'tɜːrnl] adj paternel*
pa·ter·nal·ism [pə'tɜːrnlɪzm] paterna-
lisme m
pa·ter·nal·is·tic [pətɜːrnl'ɪstɪk] adj paternaliste
pa·ter·ni·ty [pə'tɜːrnɪtɪ] paternité f
path [pæθ] chemin m; surfaced walkway allée f; fig voie f
pa·thet·ic [pə'θetɪk] adj touchant; F
(very bad) pathétique
path·o·log·i·cal [pæθə'lɑːdʒɪkl] adj pathologique
pa·thol·o·gist [pə'θɑːlədʒɪst] pathologiste m/f
pa·thol·o·gy [pə'θɑːlədʒɪ] pathologie
f; department service m de pathologie
pa·tience ['peɪʃns] patience f
pa·tient ['peɪʃnt] **1** adj patient; **just be**

~! patience! **2** n patient m

pa·tient·ly ['peɪʃntlɪ] adv patiemment

pat·i·o ['pætɪoʊ] Br patio m

pat·ri·ot ['peɪtrɪət] patriote m/f

pat·ri·ot·ic [peɪtrɪ'ɑːtɪk] adj person patriote; song patriotique

pa·tri·ot·ism ['peɪtrɪətɪzm] patriotisme m

pa·trol [pə'troʊl] **1** n patrouille f; be on the ~ être de patrouille **2** v/t (pret & pp **-led**) streets, border patrouiller dans / à

pa·trol car voiture f de police; **pa·trol·man** agent m de police; **pa·trol wag·on** fourgon m cellulaire

pa·tron ['peɪtrən] of store, movie theater client(e) m(f); of artist, charity etc protecteur(-trice) m(f); be a ~ of sth parrainer qch

pa·tron·ize ['pætrənaɪz] v/t person traiter avec condescendance

pa·tron·iz·ing ['pætrənaɪzɪŋ] adj condescendant

pa·tron 'saint patron(ne) m(f)

pat·ter ['pætər] **1** n of rain etc bruit m, crépitement m; of feet, mice etc trottinement m; F of salesman boniment m **2** v/i crépiter, tambouriner

pat·tern ['pætərn] n on fabric motif m; for knitting, sewing patron m; (model) modèle m; in events scénario m; eating / sleeping ~s habitudes fpl alimentaires / de sommeil; there's a regular ~ to his behavior il y a une constante dans son comportement

pat·terned ['pætərnd] adj imprimé

paunch [pɔːntʃ] ventre m, brioche f F

pause [pɔːz] **1** n pause f, arrêt m **2** v/i faire une pause, s'arrêter **3** v/t tape mettre en mode pause

pave [peɪv] v/t paver; ~ the way for fig ouvrir la voie à

pave·ment ['peɪvmənt] (roadway) chaussée f; Br (sidewalk) trottoir m

pav·ing stone ['peɪvɪŋ] pavé m

paw [pɔː] **1** n patte f **2** F tripoter

pawn[1] [pɔːn] n in chess, fig pion m

pawn[2] [pɔːn] v/t mettre en gage

'pawn·bro·ker prêteur m sur gages

'pawn·shop mont-de-piété m

pay [peɪ] **1** n paye f, salaire m; in the ~ of à la solde de **2** v/t (pret & pp **paid**) payer; bill also régler; ~ attention faire attention; ~ s.o. a compliment faire un compliment à qn **3** v/i (pret & pp **paid**) payer; (be profitable) rapporter, être rentable; it doesn't ~ to ... on n'a pas intérêt à ...; ~ for purchase payer; you'll ~ for this! fig tu vas me le payer!

◆ **pay back** v/t rembourser; (get revenge on) faire payer à

◆ **pay in** v/t to bank déposer, verser

◆ **pay off 1** v/t debt rembourser; corrupt official acheter **2** v/i (be profitable) être payant, être rentable

◆ **pay up** v/i payer

pay·a·ble ['peɪəbl] adj payable

'pay check salaire m, chèque m de paie

'pay·day jour m de paie

pay·ee [peɪ'iː] bénéficiaire m/f

'pay en·ve·lope salary salaire m

pay·er ['peɪər] payeur(-euse) m(f)

pay·ment ['peɪmənt] of bill règlement m, paiement m; money paiement m, versement m

'pay phone téléphone m public; **'pay·roll** money argent m de la paye; employees personnel m; be on the ~ être employé; **'pay·slip** feuille f de paie, bulletin m de paie

PC [piː'siː] abbr (= **personal computer**) P.C. m; (= **politically correct**) politiquement correct

PDA [piːdiː'eɪ] abbr (= **personal digital assistant**) organiseur m électronique

pea [piː] petit pois m

peace [piːs] paix f

peace·a·ble ['piːsəbl] adj person pacifique

peace·ful ['piːsfʊl] adj paisible, tranquille; demonstration pacifique

peace·ful·ly ['piːsflɪ] adv paisiblement

peach [piːtʃ] pêche f

pea·cock ['piːkɑːk] paon m

peak [piːk] **1** n of mountain pic m; fig apogée f; reach a ~ of physical fitness être au meilleur de sa forme **2** v/i culminer

P

'peak con·sump·tion consommation f en heures pleines; **'peak hours** npl of electricity consumption heures fpl pleines; of traffic heures fpl de pointe

pea·nut ['piːnʌt] cacahuète f; **get paid ~s** F être payé trois fois rien; **that's ~s to him** F pour lui c'est une bagatelle

pea·nut 'but·ter beurre m de cacahuètes

pear [per] poire f

pearl [pɜːrl] perle f

peas·ant ['peznt] paysan(ne) m(f)

peb·ble ['pebl] caillou m, galet m

pe·can ['piːkən] pécan m

peck [pek] **1** n (bite) coup m de bec; (kiss) bise f (rapide) **2** v/t (bite) donner un coup de bec à; (kiss) embrasser rapidement

pe·cu·li·ar [pɪˈkjuːljər] adj (strange) bizarre; **~ to** (special) propre à

pe·cu·li·ar·i·ty [pɪkjuːliˈærətɪ] (strangeness) bizarrerie f; (special feature) particularité f

ped·al ['pedl] **1** n of bike pédale f **2** v/i (pret & pp **~ed**, Br **~led**) pédaler; **he ~ed off home** il est rentré chez lui à vélo

pe·dan·tic [pɪˈdæntɪk] adj pédant

ped·dle ['pedl] v/t drugs faire le trafic de

ped·es·tal ['pedəstl] for statue socle m, piédestal m

pe·des·tri·an [pɪˈdestrɪən] n piéton(ne) m(f)

pe·des·tri·an 'cros·sing Br passage m (pour) piétons

pe·di·at·ric [piːdɪˈætrɪk] adj pédiatrique

pe·di·a·tri·cian [piːdɪæˈtrɪʃn] pédiatre m/f

pe·di·at·rics [piːdɪˈætrɪks] nsg pédiatrie f

ped·i·cure ['pedɪkjʊr] soins mpl des pieds

ped·i·gree ['pedɪgriː] **1** adj avec pedigree **2** n of dog, racehorse pedigree m; of person arbre m généalogique

pee [piː] v/i F faire pipi F

peek [piːk] **1** n coup m d'œil (furtif) **2** v/i jeter un coup d'œil, regarder fur-

tivement

peel [piːl] **1** n peau f **2** v/t fruit, vegetables éplucher, peler **3** v/i of nose, shoulders peler; of paint s'écailler

♦ peel off **1** v/t enlever **2** v/i of wrapper se détacher, s'enlever

peep [piːp] → **peek**

'peep·hole judas m; in prison guichet m

peer¹ [pɪr] n (equal) pair m; of same age group personne f du même âge

peer² v/i regarder; **~ through the mist** of person essayer de regarder à travers la brume; **~ at** regarder (fixement), scruter

peeved [piːvd] adj F en rogne F

peg [peg] n for hat, coat patère f; for tent piquet m; **off the ~** de confection

pe·jo·ra·tive [pɪˈdʒɑːrətɪv] adj péjoratif*

pel·let ['pelɪt] boulette f; for gun plomb m

pelt [pelt] **1** v/t: **~ s.o. with sth** bombarder qn de qch **2** v/i F (race) aller à toute allure; **it's ~ing down** F il pleut à verse

pel·vis ['pelvɪs] bassin m

pen¹ [pen] n stylo m; (ballpoint) stylo m (à) bille

pen² [pen] (enclosure) enclos m

pen³ → **penitentiary**

pe·nal·ize ['piːnəlaɪz] v/t pénaliser

pen·al·ty ['penltɪ] sanction f; LAW peine f; fine amende f; SP pénalisation f; soccer penalty m; rugby coup m de pied de pénalité; **take the ~** soccer tirer le penalty; rugby tirer le coup de pied de pénalité

'pen·al·ty ar·e·a soccer surface f de réparation; **'pen·al·ty clause** LAW clause f pénale; **'pen·al·ty kick** soccer penalty m; rugby coup m de pied de pénalité; **pen·al·ty 'shoot-out** épreuve f des tirs au but; **'pen·al·ty spot** point m de réparation

pen·cil ['pensɪl] crayon m (de bois)

'pen·cil sharp·en·er ['ʃɑːrpnər] taille-crayon m inv

pen·dant ['pendənt] necklace pendentif m

pend·ing ['pendɪŋ] **1** prep en attendant **2** *adj*: **be ~** (*awaiting decision*) en suspens; (*about to happen*) imminent

pen·e·trate ['penɪtreɪt] *v/t* pénétrer

pen·e·trat·ing ['penɪtreɪtɪŋ] *adj* stare pénétrant; *scream* perçant; *analysis* perspicace

pen·e·tra·tion [penɪ'treɪʃn] pénétration *f*

'pen friend correspondant(e) *m(f)*

pen·guin ['peŋgwɪn] manchot *m*

pen·i·cil·lin [penɪ'sɪlɪn] pénicilline *f*

pe·nin·su·la [pə'nɪnsʊlə] presqu'île *f*

pe·nis ['piːnɪs] pénis *m*, verge *f*

pen·i·tence ['penɪtəns] pénitence *f*, repentir *m*

pen·i·tent ['penɪtənt] *adj* pénitent, repentant

pen·i·tent·ia·ry [penɪ'tenʃərɪ] pénitencier *m*

'pen name nom *m* de plume

pen·nant ['penənt] fanion *m*

pen·ni·less ['penɪlɪs] *adj* sans le sou

pen·ny ['penɪ] cent *m*

'pen pal correspondant(e) *m(f)*

pen·sion ['penʃn] retraite *f*, pension *f*
◆ pension off *v/t* mettre à la retraite

'pen·sion fund caisse *f* de retraite

'pen·sion scheme régime *m* de retraite

pen·sive ['pensɪv] *adj* pensif*

Pen·ta·gon ['pentəgɑːn]: **the ~** le Pentagone

pen·tath·lon [pen'tæθlən] pentathlon *m*

Pen·te·cost ['pentɪkɑːst] Pentecôte *f*

pent·house ['penthaʊs] penthouse *m*, appartement *m* luxueux (édifié sur le toit d'un immeuble)

pent-up ['pentʌp] *adj* refoulé

pe·nul·ti·mate [pe'nʌltɪmət] *adj* avant-dernier

peo·ple ['piːpl] *npl* gens *mpl nsg* (*race, tribe*) peuple *m*; **10 ~** 10 personnes; **the ~** le peuple; **the American ~** les Américains; **~ say ...** on dit ...

pep·per ['pepər] *spice* poivre *m*; *vegetable* poivron *m*

'pep·per·mint *candy* bonbon *m* à la menthe; *flavoring* menthe *f* poivrée

'pep talk discours *m* d'encourage-

ment

per [pɜːr] *prep* par; **~ annum** par an; **how much ~ kilo?** combien c'est le kilo?

per·ceive [pər'siːv] *v/t* percevoir

per·cent [pər'sent] *adv* pour cent

per·cent·age [pər'sentɪdʒ] pourcentage *m*

per·cep·ti·ble [pər'septəbl] *adj* perceptible

per·cep·ti·bly [pər'septəblɪ] *adv* sensiblement

per·cep·tion [pər'sepʃn] perception *f*; *of situation also* vision *f*; (*insight*) perspicacité *f*

per·cep·tive [pər'septɪv] *adj* person, remark perspicace

perch [pɜːrtʃ] **1** *n for bird* perchoir *m* **2** *v/i* se percher; *of person* s'asseoir

per·co·late ['pɜːrkəleɪt] *v/i of coffee* passer

per·co·la·tor ['pɜːrkəleɪtər] cafetière *f* à pression

per·cus·sion [pər'kʌʃn] percussions *fpl*

per·cus·sion in·stru·ment instrument *m* à percussion

pe·ren·ni·al [pə'renɪəl] *n* BOT plante *f* vivace

per·fect ['pɜːrfɪkt] **1** *adj* parfait **2** *n* GRAM passé *m* composé **3** *v/t* [pər'fekt] parfaire, perfectionner

per·fec·tion [pər'fekʃn] perfection *f*; **to ~** à la perfection

per·fec·tion·ist [pər'fekʃnɪst] *n* perfectionniste *m/f*

per·fect·ly ['pɜːrfɪktlɪ] *adv* parfaitement; (*totally*) tout à fait

per·fo·rat·ed ['pɜːrfəreɪtɪd] *adj* perforé; **~ line** pointillé *m*

per·fo·ra·tions [pɜːrfə'reɪʃnz] *npl* pointillés *mpl*

per·form [pər'fɔːrm] **1** *v/t* (*carry out*) accomplir, exécuter; *of actor, musician etc* jouer **2** *v/i of actor, musician, dancer* jouer; *of machine* fonctionner

per·form·ance [pər'fɔːrməns] *by actor, musician etc* interprétation *f*; (*event*) représentation *f*; *of employee, company etc* résultats *mpl*; *of machine* performances *fpl*, rendement *m*

per·form·ance car voiture *f* puissante

per·form·er [pərˈfɔːrmər] artiste *m/f*, interprète *m/f*

per·fume [ˈpɜːrfjuːm] parfum *m*

per·func·to·ry [pərˈfʌŋktərɪ] *adj* sommaire

per·haps [pərˈhæps] *adv* peut-être

per·il [ˈperəl] péril *m*

per·il·ous [ˈperələs] *adj* périlleux*

pe·rim·e·ter [pəˈrɪmɪtər] périmètre *m*

pe'rim·e·ter fence clôture *f*

pe·ri·od [ˈpɪrɪəd] période *f*; (*menstruation*) règles *fpl*; *punctuation mark* point *m*; **I don't want to, ~!** je ne veux pas, un point c'est tout!

pe·ri·od·ic [pɪrɪˈɑːdɪk] *adj* périodique

pe·ri·od·i·cal [pɪrɪˈɑːdɪkl] *n* périodique *m*

pe·ri·od·i·cal·ly [pɪrɪˈɑːdɪklɪ] *adv* périodiquement

pe·riph·e·ral [pəˈrɪfərəl] **1** *adj* (*not crucial*) secondaire **2** *n* COMPUT périphérique *m*

pe·riph·e·ry [pəˈrɪfərɪ] périphérie *f*

per·ish [ˈperɪʃ] *v/i* of rubber se détériorer; *of person* périr

per·ish·a·ble [ˈperɪʃəbl] *adj* food périssable

per·jure [ˈpɜːrdʒər] *v/t*: **~ o.s.** faire un faux témoignage

per·ju·ry [ˈpɜːrdʒərɪ] faux témoignage *m*

perk [pɜːrk] *n* of job avantage *m*

♦ **perk up 1** *v/t* F remonter le moral à **2** *v/i* F se ranimer

perk·y [ˈpɜːrkɪ] *adj* F (*cheerful*) guilleret

perm [pɜːrm] **1** *n* permanente *f* **2** *v/t*: **have one's hair ~ed** se faire faire une permanente

per·ma·nent [ˈpɜːrmənənt] *adj* permanent; *address* fixe

per·ma·nent·ly [ˈpɜːrmənəntlɪ] *adv* en permanence, définitivement

per·me·a·ble [ˈpɜːrmɪəbl] *adj* perméable

per·me·ate [ˈpɜːrmɪeɪt] *v/t also fig* imprégner

per·mis·si·ble [pərˈmɪsəbl] *adj* permis

per·mis·sion [pərˈmɪʃn] permission *f*

per·mis·sive [pərˈmɪsɪv] *adj* permissif*

per·mis·sive so'ci·e·ty société *f* permissive

per·mit [ˈpɜːrmɪt] **1** *n* permis *m* **2** *v/t* (*pret & pp* **-ted**) [pərˈmɪt] permettre, autoriser; **~ s.o. to do sth** permettre à qn de faire qch

per·pen·dic·u·lar [pɜːrpənˈdɪkjulər] *adj* perpendiculaire

per·pet·u·al [pərˈpetʃuəl] *adj* perpétuel*

per·pet·u·al·ly [pərˈpetʃuəlɪ] *adv* perpétuellement, sans cesse

per·pet·u·ate [pərˈpetʃueɪt] *v/t* perpétuer

per·plex [pərˈpleks] *v/t* laisser perplexe

per·plexed [pərˈplekst] *adj* perplexe

per·plex·i·ty [pərˈpleksɪtɪ] perplexité *f*

per·se·cute [ˈpɜːrsɪkjuːt] *v/t* persécuter

per·se·cu·tion [pɜːrsɪˈkjuːʃn] persécution *f*

per·se·cu·tor [pɜːrsɪˈkjuːtər] persécuteur(-trice) *m(f)*

per·se·ver·ance [pɜːrsɪˈvɪrəns] persévérance *f*

per·se·vere [pɜːrsɪˈvɪr] *v/i* persévérer

per·sist [pərˈsɪst] *v/i* persister; **~ in doing sth** persister à faire qch, s'obstiner à faire qch

per·sis·tence [pərˈsɪstəns] persistance

per·sis·tent [pərˈsɪstənt] *adj person* têtu; *questions* incessant; *rain, unemployment etc* persistant

per·sis·tent·ly [pərˈsɪstəntlɪ] *adv* (*continually*) continuellement

per·son [ˈpɜːrsn] personne *f*; **in ~** en personne

per·son·al [ˈpɜːrsənl] *adj* personnel*

per·son·al as'sis·tant secrétaire *m/f* particulier(-ère); assistant(e) *m(f)*; **'per·son·al col·umn** annonces *fpl* personnelles; **per·son·al com'put·er** ordinateur *m* individuel; **per·son·al 'hy·giene** hygiène *f* intime

per·son·al·i·ty [pɜːrsəˈnælətɪ] personnalité *f*

per·son·al·ly [ˈpɜːrsənəlɪ] *adv* (*for my part*) personnellement; *come, inter-*

vene en personne; *know* personnellement; **don't take it ~** n'y voyez rien de personnel

per·son·al 'or·gan·iz·er organiseur *m*, agenda *m* électronique; *in book form* agenda *m*; **per·son·al 'pro·noun** pronom *m* personnel; **per·son·al 'ster·e·o** baladeur *m*

per·son·i·fy [pɜːrˈsɑːnɪfaɪ] *v/t* (*pret & pp* **-ied**) *of person* personnifier

per·son·nel [pɜːrsəˈnel] (*employees*) personnel *m*; *department* service *m* du personnel

per·son·nel man·a·ger directeur (-trice) *m(f)* du personnel

per·spec·tive [pərˈspektɪv] *in art* perspective *f*; **get sth into ~** relativiser qch, replacer qch dans son contexte

per·spi·ra·tion [pɜːrspɪˈreɪʃn] transpiration *f*

per·spire [pɜːrˈspaɪr] *v/i* transpirer

per·suade [pərˈsweɪd] *v/t person* persuader, convaincre; **~ s.o. to do sth** persuader ou convaincre qn de faire qch

per·sua·sion [pərˈsweɪʒn] persuasion *f*

per·sua·sive [pərˈsweɪsɪv] *adj person* persuasif*; *argument* convaincant

per·ti·nent [ˈpɜːrtɪnənt] *adj fml* pertinent

per·turb [pərˈtɜːrb] *v/t* perturber

per·turb·ing [pərˈtɜːrbɪŋ] *adj* perturbant, inquiétant

pe·ruse [pəˈruːz] *v/t fml* lire

per·va·sive [pərˈveɪsɪv] *adj influence, ideas* envahissant

per·verse [pərˈvɜːrs] *adj* (*awkward*) contrariant; *sexually* pervers

per·ver·sion [pərˈvɜːrʃn] *sexual* perversion *f*

per·vert [ˈpɜːrvɜːrt] *n sexual* pervers(e) *m(f)*

pes·si·mism [ˈpesɪmɪzm] pessimisme *m*

pes·si·mist [ˈpesɪmɪst] pessimiste *m/f*

pes·si·mist·ic [pesɪˈmɪstɪk] *adj* pessimiste

pest [pest] parasite *m*; F *person* peste *f*, plaie *f*

pes·ter [ˈpestər] *v/t* harceler; **~ s.o. to do sth** harceler qn pour qu'il fasse (*subj*) qch

pes·ti·cide [ˈpestɪsaɪd] pesticide *m*

pet [pet] **1** *n animal* animal *m* domestique; (*favorite*) chouchou *m* F; **do you have any ~s?** as-tu des animaux? **2** *adj* préféré, favori; **~ subject** sujet *m* de prédilection; **my ~ rabbit** mon lapin (apprivoisé) **3** *v/t* (*pret & pp* **-ted**) *animal* caresser **4** *v/i* (*pret & pp* **-ted**) *of couple* se caresser, se peloter F

pet·al [ˈpetl] pétale *m*

♦ **pe·ter out** [ˈpiːtər] *v/i* cesser petit à petit

pe·tite [pəˈtiːt] *adj* menu

pe·ti·tion [pəˈtɪʃn] *n* pétition *f*

'pet name surnom *m*, petit nom *m*

pet·ri·fied [ˈpetrɪfaɪd] *adj* pétrifié

pet·ri·fy [ˈpetrɪfaɪ] *v/t* (*pret & pp* **-ied**) pétrifier

pet·ro·chem·i·cal [petrouˈkemɪkl] *adj* pétrochimique

pet·rol [ˈpetrl] *Br* essence *f*

pe·tro·le·um [pɪˈtrouliəm] pétrole *m*

pet·ting [ˈpetɪŋ] pelotage *m* F

pet·ty [ˈpetɪ] *adj person, behavior* mesquin; *details, problem* insignifiant

pet·ty 'cash petite caisse *f*

pet·u·lant [ˈpetʃələnt] *adj* irritable; *remark* irrité

pew [pjuː] banc *m* d'église

pew·ter [ˈpjuːtər] étain *m*

phar·ma·ceu·ti·cal [fɑːrməˈsuːtɪkl] *adj* pharmaceutique

phar·ma·ceu·ti·cals [fɑːrməˈsuːtɪklz] *npl* produits *mpl* pharmaceutiques

phar·ma·cist [ˈfɑːrməsɪst] pharmacien(ne) *m(f)*

phar·ma·cy [ˈfɑːrməsɪ] *store* pharmacie *f*

phase [feɪz] phase *f*

♦ **phase in** *v/t* introduire progressivement

♦ **phase out** *v/t* supprimer progressivement

PhD [piːeɪtʃˈdiː] *abbr* (= **Doctor of Philosophy**) doctorat *m*

phe·nom·e·nal [fəˈnɑːmɪnl] *adj* phénoménal

phe·nom·e·nal·ly [fəˈnɑːmɪnəlɪ] *adv*

prodigieusement

phe·nom·e·non [fə'nɑːmɪnən] phénomène *m*

phil·an·throp·ic [fɪlən'θrɑːpɪk] *adj
person* philanthrope; *action* philanthropique

phi·lan·thro·pist [fɪ'lænθrəpɪst] philanthrope *m/f*

phi·lan·thro·py [fɪ'lænθrəpɪ] philan-
thropie *f*

Phil·ip·pines ['fɪlɪpiːnz]: *the* ~ les Phi-
lippines *fpl*

phil·is·tine ['fɪlɪstaɪn] *n* inculte *m/f*

phi·los·o·pher [fɪ'lɑːsəfər] philosophe *m/f*

phil·o·soph·i·cal [fɪlə'sɑːfɪkl] *adj*
philosophique; *attitude etc* philosophe

phi·los·o·phy [fɪ'lɑːsəfɪ] philosophie *f*

pho·bi·a ['foʊbiə] phobie *f* (*about* de)

phone [foʊn] 1 *n* téléphone *m*; *be on
the* ~ (*have a* ~) avoir le téléphone; *be
talking* être au téléphone 2 *v/t* téléphoner à 3 *v/i* téléphoner

'phone book annuaire *m*; 'phone
booth cabine *f* téléphonique;
'phone-call coup *m* de fil *or* de téléphone; 'phone card télécarte *f*;
'phone num·ber numéro *m* de téléphone

pho·net·ics [fə'netɪks] phonétique *f*

pho·n(e)y ['foʊnɪ] *adj* F faux*

pho·to ['foʊtoʊ] photo *f*

'pho·to al·bum album *m* photos;
'pho·to·cop·i·er photocopieuse *f*,
photocopieur *m*; 'pho·to·cop·y 1 *n*
photocopie *f* 2 *v/t* (*pret & pp -ied*)
photocopier

pho·to·gen·ic [foʊtoʊ'dʒenɪk] *adj*
photogénique

pho·to·graph ['foʊtəgræf] 1 *n* photographie *f* 2 *v/t* photographier

pho·tog·ra·pher [fə'tɑːgrəfər] photographe *m/f*

pho·tog·ra·phy [fə'tɑːgrəfɪ] photographie *f*

phrase [freɪz] 1 *n* expression *f*; *in
grammar* syntagme *m* 2 *v/t* formuler,
exprimer

'phrase·book guide *m* de conversation

phys·i·cal ['fɪzɪkl] 1 *adj* physique 2 *n*
MED visite *f* médicale

phys·i·cal 'hand·i·cap handicap *m*
physique

phys·i·cal·ly ['fɪzɪklɪ] *adv* physiquement

phys·i·cal·ly 'hand·i·cap·ped *adj*: *be*
~ être handicapé physique

phy·si·cian [fɪ'zɪʃn] médecin *m*

phys·i·cist ['fɪzɪsɪst] physicien(ne)
m(f)

phys·ics ['fɪzɪks] physique *f*

phys·i·o·ther·a·pist [fɪzioʊ'θerəpɪst]
kinésithérapeute *m/f*

phys·i·o·ther·a·py [fɪzioʊ'θerəpɪ] kinésithérapie *f*

phy·sique [fɪ'ziːk] physique *m*

pi·a·nist ['pɪənɪst] pianiste *m/f*

pi·an·o [pɪ'ænoʊ] piano *m*

pick [pɪk] 1 *n*: *take your* ~ fais ton
choix 2 *v/t* (*choose*) choisir; *flowers,
fruit* cueillir; ~ *one's nose* se mettre
les doigts dans le nez 3 *v/i*: ~ *and
choose* faire la fine bouche

♦ pick at *v/t*: *pick at one's food* manger du bout des dents, chipoter

♦ pick on *v/t* (*treat unfairly*) s'en prendre à; (*select*) désigner, choisir

♦ pick out *v/t* (*identify*) reconnaître

♦ pick up 1 *v/t* prendre; *phone* décrocher; *from ground* ramasser; (*collect*)
passer prendre; *information* recueillir; *in car* prendre; *in sexual sense* lever
F; *language, skill* apprendre; *habit*
prendre; *illness* attraper; (*buy*) dénicher, acheter; *criminal* arrêter 2 *v/i
of business, economy* reprendre; *of
weather* s'améliorer

pick·et ['pɪkɪt] 1 *n of strikers* piquet *m*
de grève 2 *v/t*: ~ *a factory* faire le piquet de grève devant une usine

'pick·et line piquet *m* de grève

pick·le ['pɪkl] *v/t* conserver dans du vinaigre

pick·les ['pɪklz] *npl* pickles *mpl*

'pick·pock·et voleur *m* à la tire, pickpocket *m*

pick-up (truck) ['pɪkʌp] pick-up *m*,
camionnette *f*

pick·y ['pɪkɪ] *adj* F difficile

pic·nic ['pɪknɪk] 1 *n* pique-nique *m* 2

*v/i (pret & pp **-ked**)* pique-niquer

pic·ture ['pɪktʃər] **1** *n (photo)* photo *f*; *(painting)* tableau *m*; *(illustration)* image *f*; *(movie)* film *m*; **keep s.o. in the ~** tenir qn au courant **2** *v/t* imaginer

'pic·ture book livre *m* d'images

pic·ture 'post·card carte *f* postale

pic·tur·esque [pɪktʃə'resk] *adj* pittoresque

pie [paɪ] tarte *f*; *with top* tourte *f*

piece [piːs] morceau *m*; *(component)* pièce *f*; *in board game* pion *m*; **a ~ of bread** un morceau de pain; **a ~ of advice** un conseil; **go to ~s** s'effondrer; **take to ~s** démonter
♦ **piece together** *v/t broken plate* recoller; *evidence* regrouper

piece·meal ['piːsmiːl] *adv* petit à petit

piece·work ['piːswɜːrk] travail *m* à la tâche

pier [pɪr] *Br: at seaside* jetée *f*

pierce [pɪrs] *v/t (penetrate)* transpercer; *ears* percer; **have one's ears / navel ~d** se faire percer les oreilles / le nombril

pierc·ing ['pɪrsɪŋ] *adj noise, eyes* perçant; *wind* pénétrant

pig [pɪg] cochon *m*, porc *m*; *(unpleasant person)* porc *m*

pi·geon ['pɪdʒɪn] pigeon *m*

'pi·geon·hole 1 *n* casier *m* **2** *v/t person* cataloguer; *proposal* mettre de côté

pig·gy·bank ['pɪgɪbæŋk] tirelire *f*

pig·head·ed [pɪg'hedɪd] *adj* obstiné; **that ~ father of mine** mon père, cette tête de lard *F*

'pig·pen porcherie *f*, **'pig·skin** porc *m*; **'pig·tail** plaited natte *f*

pile [paɪl] *of books, plates etc* pile *f*; *of earth, sand etc* tas *m*; **a ~ of work** *F* un tas de boulot *F*
♦ **pile up 1** *v/i of work, bills* s'accumuler **2** *v/t* empiler

piles [paɪlz] *nsg MED* hémorroïdes *fpl*

'pile-up MOT carambolage *m*

pil·fer·ing ['pɪlfərɪŋ] chapardage *m F*

pil·grim ['pɪlgrɪm] pèlerin(e) *m(f)*

pil·grim·age ['pɪlgrɪmɪdʒ] pèlerinage *m*

pill [pɪl] pilule *f*; **be on the ~** prendre la pilule

pil·lar ['pɪlər] pilier *m*

pil·lion ['pɪljən] *of motorbike* siège *m* arrière

pil·low ['pɪlou] oreiller *m*

'pil·low·case taie *f* d'oreiller

pi·lot ['paɪlət] **1** *n* AVIAT, NAUT pilote *m* **2** *v/t airplane* piloter

'pi·lot light *on cooker* veilleuse *f*

'pi·lot plant usine-pilote *f*

'pi·lot scheme projet-pilote *m*

pimp [pɪmp] *n* maquereau *m*, proxénète *m*

pim·ple ['pɪmpl] bouton *m*

PIN [pɪn] *abbr (= **personal identification number**)* code *m* confidentiel

pin [pɪn] **1** *n for sewing* épingle *f*; *in bowling* quille *f*; *(badge)* badge *m*; fiche *f* **2** *v/t (pret & pp **-ned**) (hold down)* clouer; *(attach)* épingler
♦ **pin down** *v/t (identify)* identifier; **pin s.o. down to a date** obliger qn à s'engager sur une date
♦ **pin up** *v/t notice* accrocher, afficher

pin·cers ['pɪnsərz] *npl of crab* pinces *fpl*; **a pair of ~** *tool* des tenailles *fpl*

pinch [pɪntʃ] **1** *n* pincement *m*; *of salt, sugar etc* pincée *f*; **at a ~** à la rigueur **2** *v/t squeeze* pincer **3** *v/i of shoes* serrer

pine[1] [paɪn] *n tree, wood* pin *m*

pine[2] [paɪn] *v/i* se languir
♦ **pine for** *v/i* languir de

pine·ap·ple ['paɪnæpl] ananas *m*

ping [pɪŋ] **1** *n* tintement *m* **2** *v/i* tinter

ping-pong ['pɪŋpɑːŋ] ping-pong *m*

pink [pɪŋk] *adj* rose

pin·na·cle ['pɪnəkl] *fig* apogée *f*

'pin·point *v/t* indiquer précisément; *find* identifier; **pins and 'nee·dles** *npl* fourmillements *mpl*; **have ~ in one's feet** avoir des fourmis dans les pieds; **'pin·stripe** *adj* rayé

pint [paɪnt] pinte *f (0,473 litre aux États-Unis et 0,568 en Grande-Bretagne)*

'pin-up (girl) pin-up *f inv*

pi·o·neer [paɪə'nɪr] **1** *n fig* pionnier (-ière) *m(f)* **2** *v/t* lancer

pi·o·neer·ing [paɪə'nɪrɪŋ] *adj work* innovateur*

pi·ous ['paɪəs] *adj* pieux*

pip [pɪp] *n Br. of fruit* pépin *m*

pipe [paɪp] **1** *n for smoking* pipe *f; for water, gas, sewage* tuyau *m* **2** *v/t* transporter par tuyau

♦ **pipe down** *v/i* F se taire; *tell the kids to pipe down* dis aux enfants de la boucler F

piped mu·sic [paɪpt'mjuːzɪk] musique *f* de fond

'pipe-line *for oil* oléoduc *m; for gas* gazoduc *m; in the ~ fig* en perspective

pip·ing hot [paɪpɪŋ'hɑːt] *adj* très chaud

pi·rate ['paɪrət] **1** *n* pirate *m* **2** *v/t software* pirater

Pis·ces ['paɪsiːz] ASTROL Poissons *mpl*

piss [pɪs] **1** *n* P (*urine*) pisse *f* P **2** *v/i* P (*urinate*) pisser F

pissed [pɪst] *adj* P (*annoyed*) en rogne F; *Br* P (*drunk*) bourré

pis·tol ['pɪstl] pistolet *m*

pis·ton ['pɪstən] piston *m*

pit [pɪt] *n* (*hole*) fosse *f*; (*coalmine*) mine *f*

pitch¹ [pɪtʃ] *n* ton *m*

pitch² [pɪtʃ] **1** *v/i in baseball* lancer **2** *v/t tent* planter; *ball* lancer

'pitch-black *adj* noir comme jais; ~ *night* nuit *f* noire

pitch·er¹ ['pɪtʃər] *in baseball* lanceur *m*

pitch·er² ['pɪtʃər] *container* pichet *m*

pit·e·ous ['pɪtɪəs] *adj* pitoyable

pit·fall ['pɪtfɔːl] piège *m*

pith [pɪθ] *of citrus fruit* peau *f* blanche

pit·i·ful ['pɪtɪfl] *adj* pitoyable

pit·i·less ['pɪtɪləs] *adj* impitoyable

pits [pɪts] *npl in motor racing* stand *m* de ravitaillement

'pit stop *in motor racing* arrêt *m* au stand

pit·tance ['pɪtns] somme *f* dérisoire

pit·y ['pɪtɪ] **1** *n* pitié *f*; *take ~ on* avoir pitié de; *it's a ~ that ...* c'est dommage que ...; *what a ~!* quel dommage! **2** *v/t* (*pret & pp* **-ied**) *person* avoir pitié de

piv·ot ['pɪvət] *v/i* pivoter

piz·za ['piːtsə] pizza *f*

plac·ard ['plækɑːrd] pancarte *f*

place [pleɪs] **1** *n* endroit *m*; *in race,* competition place *f*; (*seat*) place *f*; *at my / his ~* chez moi / lui; *I've lost my ~ in book* j'ai perdu ma page; *in ~ of* à la place de; *feel out of ~* ne pas se sentir à sa place; *take ~* avoir lieu; *in the first ~* (*firstly*) premièrement; (*in the beginning*) au début **2** *v/t* (*put*) mettre, poser; (*identify*) situer; *~ an order* passer une commande

'place mat set *m* de table

place·ment ['pleɪsmənt] *of trainee* stage *m*

plac·id ['plæsɪd] *adj* placide

pla·gia·rism ['pleɪdʒərɪzm] plagiat *m*

pla·gia·rize ['pleɪdʒəraɪz] *v/t* plagier

plague [pleɪg] **1** *n* peste *f* **2** *v/t* (*bother*) harceler, tourmenter

plain¹ [pleɪn] *n* plaine *f*

plain² [pleɪn] **1** *adj* (*clear, obvious*) clair, évident; (*not ornate*) simple; (*not patterned*) uni; (*not pretty*) quelconque, ordinaire; (*blunt*) franc*; ~ *chocolate* chocolat *m* noir **2** *adv* tout simplement; *it's ~ crazy* c'est de la folie pure

'plain clothes: in ~ en civil

plain·ly ['pleɪnlɪ] *adv* (*clearly*) manifestement; (*bluntly*) franchement; (*simply*) simplement

'plain-spo·ken *adj* direct, franc*

plain·tiff ['pleɪntɪf] plaignant *m*

plain·tive ['pleɪntɪv] *adj* plaintif*

plan [plæn] **1** *n* plan *m*, projet *m*; (*drawing*) plan *m* **2** *v/t* (*pret & pp* **-ned**) (*prepare*) organiser, planifier; (*design*) concevoir; ~ *to do*, ~ *on doing* prévoir de faire, compter faire **3** *v/i* faire des projets

plane¹ [pleɪn] *n* AVIAT avion *m*

plane² [pleɪn] *tool* rabot *m*

plan·et ['plænɪt] planète *f*

plank [plæŋk] *of wood* planche *f; fig: of policy* point *m*

plan·ning ['plænɪŋ] organisation *f*, planification *f*; *at the ~ stage* à l'état de projet

plant¹ [plænt] **1** *n* BOT plante *f* **2** *v/t* planter

plant² [plænt] *n* (*factory*) usine *f*; (*equipment*) installation *f*, matériel *m*

plodder

plan·ta·tion [plæn'teɪʃn] plantation f

plaque[1] [plæk] on wall plaque f

plaque[2] [plæk] on teeth plaque f dentaire

plas·ter ['plɑːstər] **1** n on wall, ceiling plâtre m **2** v/t wall, ceiling plâtrer; **be ~ed with** être couvert de

'**plas·ter cast** plâtre m

plas·tic ['plæstɪk] **1** adj en plastique **2** n plastique m

plas·tic 'bag sac m plastique; '**plas·tic mon·ey** cartes fpl de crédit; **plas·tic 'sur·geon** spécialiste m en chirurgie esthétique; **plas·tic 'sur·ge·ry** chirurgie f esthétique

plate [pleɪt] n for food assiette f; (sheet of metal) plaque f

pla·teau ['plætou] plateau m

plat·form ['plætfɔːrm] (stage) estrade f; of railroad station quai m; fig: political plate-forme f

plat·i·num ['plætɪnəm] **1** adj en platine **2** n platine m

plat·i·tude ['plætɪtuːd] platitude f

pla·ton·ic [plə'tɑːnɪk] adj relationship platonique

pla·toon [plə'tuːn] of soldiers section f

plat·ter ['plætər] for food plat m

plau·si·ble ['plɔːzəbl] adj plausible

play [pleɪ] **1** n also TECH, SP jeu m; in theater, on TV pièce f **2** v/i jouer **3** v/t musical instrument jouer de; piece of music jouer; game jouer à; opponent jouer contre; (perform: Macbeth etc) jouer; **~ a joke on** jouer un tour à

♦ **play around** v/i F (be unfaithful) coucher à droite et à gauche; **play around with s.o.** coucher avec qn

♦ **play down** v/t minimiser

♦ **play up** v/i of machine, child faire des siennes; **my back is playing up** mon dos me fait souffrir

'**play·act** v/i (pretend) jouer la comédie, faire semblant; '**play·back** enregistrement m; '**play·boy** play-boy m

play·er ['pleɪr] SP joueur(-euse) m(f); (musician) musicien(ne) m(f); (actor) acteur(-trice) m(f); in business acteur m; **he's a guitar ~** il joue de la guitar

play·ful ['pleɪfl] adj enjoué

'**play·ground** aire f de jeu

'**play·group** garderie f

'**play·ing card** ['pleɪɪŋ] carte f à jouer

'**play·ing field** terrain m de sport

'**play·mate** camarade m de jeu

'**play·wright** ['pleɪraɪt] dramaturge m/f

pla·za ['plɑːzə] for shopping centre m commercial

plc [piːel'siː] abbr Br (= **public limited company**) S.A. f (= société anonyme)

plea [pliː] n appel

plead [pliːd] v/i: **~ for mercy etc** implorer; **~ guilty / not guilty** plaider coupable / non coupable; **~ with** implorer, supplier

pleas·ant ['pleznt] agréable

please [pliːz] **1** adv s'il vous plaît, s'il te plaît; **more tea? – yes, ~** encore un peu de thé? – oui, s'il vous plaît; **~ do** je vous en prie **2** v/t plaire à; **~ yourself** comme tu veux

pleased [pliːzd] adj content, heureux*; **~ to meet you** enchanté

pleas·ing ['pliːzɪŋ] adj agréable

pleas·ure ['pleʒər] plaisir m; **it's a ~** (you're welcome) je vous en prie; **with ~** avec plaisir

pleat [pliːt] n in skirt pli m

pleat·ed skirt ['pliːtɪd] jupe f plissée

pledge [pledʒ] **1** n (promise) promesse f, engagement m; as guarantee gage m; **Pledge of Allegiance** serment m d'allégeance **2** v/t (promise) promettre; money mettre en gage, engager

plen·ti·ful ['plentɪfl] adj abondant; **be ~** abonder

plen·ty ['plentɪ] (abundance) abondance f; **~ of** beaucoup de; **that's ~** c'est largement suffisant; **there's ~ for everyone** il y en a (assez) pour tout le monde

pli·a·ble adj flexible

pli·ers npl pinces fpl; **a pair of ~** des pinces

plight [plaɪt] détresse f

plod [plɑːd] v/i (pret & pp **-ded**) (walk) marcher d'un pas lourd

♦ **plod on** v/i with a job persévérer

plod·der ['plɑːdər] at work, school bûcheur(-euse) m(f) F

P

plot¹ [plɑːt] *n of land* parcelle *f*

plot² [plɑːt] **1** *n* (*conspiracy*) complot *m*; *of novel* intrigue *f* **2** *v/t* (*pret & pp* **-ted**) comploter; **~ s.o.'s death** comploter de tuer qn **3** *v/i* comploter

plot·ter ['plɑːtər] conspirateur(-trice) *m(f)*; COMPUT traceur *m*

plough [plaʊ] *Br* → **plow**

plow [plaʊ] **1** *n* charrue *f* **2** *v/t & v/i* labourer

♦ **plow back** *v/t profits* réinvestir

pluck [plʌk] *v/t chicken* plumer; **~ one's eyebrows** s'épiler les sourcils

♦ **pluck up** *v/t*: **pluck up courage** prendre son courage à deux mains

plug [plʌg] **1** *n for sink, bath* bouchon *m*; *electrical* prise *f*; (*spark* **~**) bougie *f*; *for new book etc* coup *m* de pub F; **give sth a ~** faire de la pub pour qch F **2** *v/t* (*pret & pp* **-ged**) *hole* boucher; *new book etc* faire de la pub pour F

♦ **plug away** *v/i* F s'acharner, bosser F

♦ **plug in** *v/t* brancher

plum [plʌm] **1** *n fruit* prune *f*; *tree* prunier *m* **2** *adj* F: **a ~ job** un boulot en or F

plum·age ['pluːmɪdʒ] plumage *m*

plumb [plʌm] *adj* d'aplomb

♦ **plumb in** *v/t washing machine* raccorder

plumb·er ['plʌmər] plombier *m*

plumb·ing ['plʌmɪŋ] plomberie *f*

plum·met ['plʌmɪt] *v/i of airplane* plonger, piquer; *of share prices* dégringoler, chuter

plump [plʌmp] *adj person, chicken* dodu; *hands, feet* potelé; *face, cheek* rond

♦ **plump for** *v/t* F se décider pour

plunge [plʌndʒ] **1** *n* plongeon *m*; *in prices* chute *f*; **take the ~** se jeter à l'eau **2** *v/i* tomber; *of prices* chuter **3** *v/t knife* enfoncer; **the city was ~d into darkness** la ville était plongée dans l'obscurité

plung·ing ['plʌndʒɪŋ] *adj neckline* plongeant

plu·per·fect ['pluːpɜːrfɪkt] GRAM plus-que-parfait *m*

plu·ral ['plʊrəl] **1** *adj* pluriel* **2** *n* pluriel *m*; **in the ~** au pluriel

plus [plʌs] **1** *prep* plus **2** *adj* plus de; **$500 ~** plus de 500 $ **3** *n sign* signe *m* plus; (*advantage*) plus *m* **4** *conj* (*moreover, in addition*) en plus

plush [plʌʃ] *adj* luxueux*

'plus sign signe *m* plus

ply·wood ['plaɪwʊd] contreplaqué *m*

PM [piː'em] *abbr Br* (= *Prime Minister*) Premier ministre

p.m. [piː'em] *abbr* (= *post meridiem*) *afternoon* de l'après-midi; *evening* du soir

pneu·mat·ic [nuː'mætɪk] *adj* pneumatique

pneu·mat·ic 'drill marteau-piqueur *m*

pneu·mo·ni·a [nuː'moʊnɪə] pneumonie *f*

poach¹ [poʊtʃ] *v/t cook* pocher

poach² [poʊtʃ] *v/t salmon etc* braconner

poached egg [poʊtʃt'eg] œuf *m* poché

poach·er ['poʊtʃər] *of salmon etc* braconnier *m*

P.O. Box [piː'oʊbɑːks] *abbr* (= *Post Office Box*) boîte *f* postale, B. P. *f*

pock·et ['pɑːkɪt] **1** *n* poche *f*; **line one's own ~s** se remplir les poches; **be out of ~** en être de sa poche F **2** *adj* (*miniature*) de poche **3** *v/t* empocher, mettre dans sa poche

'pock·et·book *purse* pochette *f*; (*billfold*) portefeuille *m*; *book* livre *m* de poche; **pock·et 'cal·cu·la·tor** calculatrice *f* de poche; **'pock·et·knife** couteau *m* de poche, canif *m*

po·di·um ['poʊdɪəm] estrade *f*; *for winner* podium *m*

po·em ['poʊɪm] poème *m*

po·et ['poʊɪt] poète *m*, poétesse *f*

po·et·ic [poʊ'etɪk] *adj* poétique

po·et·ic 'jus·tice justice *f* divine

po·et·ry ['poʊɪtrɪ] poésie *f*

poign·ant ['pɔɪnjənt] *adj* poignant

point [pɔɪnt] **1** *n of pencil, knife* pointe *f*; *in competition, exam* point *m*; (*purpose*) objet *m*; (*moment*) moment *m*; *in argument, discussion* point *m*; *in decimals* virgule *f*; **that's beside the ~** là n'est pas la question; **be**

on the ~ of doing sth être sur le
point de faire qch; *get to the ~* en
venir au fait; *the ~ is ...* le fait est
(que) ...; *there's no ~ in waiting*
ça ne sert à rien d'attendre **2** *v/i* montrer (du doigt) **3** *v/t gun* braquer,
pointer
♦ **point at** *v/t with finger* montrer du
doigt, désigner
♦ **point out** *v/t sights* montrer; *advantages etc* faire remarquer
♦ **point to** *v/t with finger* montrer du
doigt, désigner; *fig (indicate)* indiquer
'point-blank 1 *adj: at ~ range* à bout
portant **2** *adv refuse, deny* catégoriquement, de but en blanc
point·ed ['pɔɪntɪd] *adj remark* acerbe,
mordant
point·er ['pɔɪntər] *for teacher* baguette
f; *(hint)* conseil *m*; *(sign, indication)* indice *m*
point·less ['pɔɪntləs] *adj* inutile; *it's ~
trying* ça ne sert à rien d'essayer
point of *'sale place* point *m* de vente;
promotional material publicité *f* sur
les lieux de vente, P.L.V. *f*
point of 'view point *m* de vue
poise [pɔɪz] assurance *f*, aplomb *m*
poised [pɔɪzd] *adj person* posé
poi·son ['pɔɪzn] **1** *n* poison *m* **2** *v/t* empoisonner
poi·son·ous ['pɔɪznəs] *adj snake, spider* venimeux*; *plant* vénéneux*
poke [poʊk] **1** *n* coup *m* **2** *v/t (prod)*
pousser; *(stick)* enfoncer; *~ one's
head out of the window* passer la
tête par la fenêtre; *~ fun at* se moquer de; *~ one's nose into* mettre
son nez dans
♦ **poke around** *v/i* F fouiner F
pok·er ['poʊkər] *card game* poker *m*
pok·y ['poʊki] *adj (cramped)* exigu*
Po·land ['poʊlənd] la Pologne
po·lar ['poʊlər] *adj* polaire
'po·lar bear ours *m* polaire
po·lar·ize ['poʊləraɪz] *v/t* diviser
Pole [poʊl] Polonais(e) *m(f)*
pole[1] [poʊl] *of wood, metal* perche *f*
pole[2] [poʊl] *of earth* pôle *m*
'pole star étoile *f* Polaire; **'pole·vault**
n event saut *m* à la perche; **pole-**

-vault·er ['poʊlvɔːltər] perchiste *m/f*
po·lice [pə'liːs] *n* police *f*
po'lice car voiture *f* de police; **po'-
lice·man** gendarme *m*; *criminal* policier *m*; **po'lice state** État *m* policier;
po'lice sta·tion gendarmerie *f*; *for
criminal matters* commissariat *m*; **po'-
lice·wo·man** femme *f* gendarme;
criminal femme *f* policier
pol·i·cy[1] ['pɑːləsi] politique *f*
pol·i·cy[2] ['pɑːləsi] *(insurance ~)* police
f (d'assurance)
po·li·o ['poʊlioʊ] polio *f*
Pol·ish ['poʊlɪʃ] **1** *adj* polonais **2** *n* polonais *m*
pol·ish ['pɑːlɪʃ] **1** *n for furniture, floor*
cire *f*; *for shoes* cirage *m*; *for metal*
produit *m* lustrant; *(nail ~)* vernis
m (à ongles) **2** *v/t* faire briller, lustrer;
shoes cirer; *speech* parfaire
♦ **polish off** *v/t food* finir
♦ **polish up** *v/t skill* perfectionner
pol·ished ['pɑːlɪʃt] *adj performance*
impeccable
po·lite [pə'laɪt] *adj* poli
po·lite·ly [pə'laɪtli] *adv* poliment
po·lite·ness [pə'laɪtnɪs] politesse *f*
po·lit·i·cal [pə'lɪtɪkl] *adj* politique
po·lit·i·cal·ly cor·rect [pəlɪtɪkli
kə'rekt] *adj* politiquement correct
pol·i·ti·cian [pɑːlɪ'tɪʃn] politicien *m*,
homme *m* politique
pol·i·tics ['pɑːlɪtɪks] politique *f*; *what
are his ~?* quelles sont ses opinions
politiques?
poll [poʊl] **1** *n (survey)* sondage *m*; *the
~s (election)* les élections *fpl*, le scrutin; *go to the ~s (vote)* aller aux urnes **2** *v/t people* faire un sondage auprès de; *votes* obtenir
pol·len ['pɑːlən] pollen *m*
'pol·len count taux *m* de pollen
poll·ing booth ['poʊlɪŋ] isoloir *m*
'poll·ing day jour *m* des élections
poll·ster ['poʊlstər] sondeur *m*
pol·lu·tant [pə'luːtənt] polluant *m*
pol·lute [pə'luːt] *v/t* polluer
pol·lu·tion [pə'luːʃn] pollution *f*
po·lo ['poʊloʊ] SP polo *m*
'po·lo neck *sweater* pull *m* à col roulé
'po·lo shirt polo *m*

P

pol·y·es·ter [pɑːliˈestər] polyester *m*
pol·y·eth·yl·ene [pɑːlɪˈeθɪliːn] poly-éthylène *m*
pol·y·sty·rene [pɑːlɪˈstaɪriːn] polysty-rène *m*
pol·y·un·sat·u·rat·ed [pɑːliʌnˈsætʃə-reɪtɪd] *adj* polyinsaturé
pom·pous [ˈpɑːmpəs] *adj person* pré-tentieux*, suffisant; *speech* pomp-eux*
pond [pɑːnd] étang *m*; *artificial* bassin *m*
pon·der [ˈpɑːndər] *v/i* réfléchir
pon·tiff [ˈpɑːntɪf] pontife *m*
pon·y [ˈpoʊni] poney *m*
'pon·y·tail queue *f* de cheval
poo·dle [ˈpuːdl] caniche *m*
pool[1] [puːl] (*swimming* ~) piscine *f*; *of water, blood* flaque *f*
pool[2] [puːl] *game* billard *m* américain
pool[3] [puːl] **1** *n* (*common fund*) caisse *f* commune **2** *v/t resources* mettre en commun
'pool hall salle *f* de billard
'pool ta·ble table *f* de billard
poop [puːp] F caca *m* F
pooped [puːpt] *adj* F crevé F
poor [pʊr] **1** *adj* pauvre; *quality etc* mé-diocre, mauvais; **be in ~ health** être en mauvaise santé; ~ *old Tony!* ce pauvre Tony! **2** *npl:* **the** ~ les pauvres *mpl*
poor·ly [ˈpʊrli] **1** *adj* (*unwell*) malade **2** *adv* mal
pop[1] [pɑːp] **1** *n noise* bruit *m* sec **2** *v/i* (*pret & pp* **-ped**) *of balloon etc* éclater; *of cork* sauter **3** *v/t* (*pret & pp* **-ped**) *cork* faire sauter; *balloon* faire éclater
pop[2] [pɑːp] **1** *adj* MUS pop *inv* **2** *n* pop *f*
pop[3] [pɑːp] F (*father*) papa *m*
pop[4] [pɑːp] *v/t* (*pret & pp* **-ped**) F (*put*) mettre; ~ *one's head around the door* passer la tête par la porte
♦ **pop in** *v/i* F (*make brief visit*) passer
♦ **pop out** *v/i* F (*go out for a short time*) sortir
♦ **pop up** *v/i* F (*appear*) surgir; *of miss-ing person* réapparaître
'pop con·cert concert *m* de musique pop
'pop·corn pop-corn *m*

Pope [poʊp] pape *m*
'pop group groupe *m* pop
'pop·py [ˈpɑːpi] *flower* coquelicot *m*
Pop·si·cle® [ˈpɑːpsɪkl] glace *f* à l'eau
'pop song chanson *f* pop
pop·u·lar [ˈpɑːpjələr] *adj* populaire
pop·u·lar·i·ty [pɑːpjəˈlærətɪ] popula-rité *f*
pop·u·late [ˈpɑːpjəleɪt] *v/t* peupler
pop·u·la·tion [pɑːpjəˈleɪʃn] popula-tion *f*
por·ce·lain [ˈpɔːrsəlɪn] **1** *adj* en porce-laine **2** *n* porcelaine *f*
porch [pɔːrtʃ] porche *m*
por·cu·pine [ˈpɔːrkjʊpaɪn] porc-épic *m*
pore [pɔːr] *of skin* pore *m*
♦ **pore over** *v/t* étudier attentivement
pork [pɔːrk] porc *m*
porn [pɔːrn] *n* F porno M F
porn(o) [pɔːrn, ˈpɔːrnoʊ] *adj* F porno F
por·no·graph·ic [pɔːrnəˈɡræfɪk] *adj* pornographique
porn·og·ra·phy [pɔːrˈnɑːɡrəfɪ] porno-graphie *f*
po·rous [ˈpɔːrəs] *adj* poreux*
port[1] [pɔːrt] port *m*
port[2] [pɔːrt] *adj* (*left-hand*) de bâbord
por·ta·ble [ˈpɔːrtəbl] **1** *adj* portable, portatif* **2** *n* COMPUT portable *m*; *TV* téléviseur *m* portable *or* portatif
por·ter [ˈpɔːrtər] (*doorman*) portier *m*
port·hole [ˈpɔːrthoʊl] NAUT hublot *m*
por·tion [ˈpɔːrʃn] partie *f*, part *f*; *of food* portion *f*
por·trait [ˈpɔːrtreɪt] **1** *n* portrait *m* **2** *adv print* en mode portrait, à la fran-çaise
por·tray [pɔːrˈtreɪ] *v/t of artist* repré-senter; *of actor* interpréter, présenter; *of author* décrire
por·tray·al [pɔːrˈtreɪəl] *by actor* inter-prétation *f*; *by author* description *f*
Por·tu·gal [ˈpɔːrtʃəɡl] le Portugal
Por·tu·guese [pɔːrtʃəˈɡiːz] **1** *adj* por-tugais **2** *n person* Portugais(e) *m(f)*; *language* portugais *m*
pose [poʊz] **1** *n attitude f; it's all a* ~ c'est de la frime! **2** *v/i for artist* poser; ~ *as* se faire passer pour **3** *v/t problem* poser; ~ *a threat* constituer une me-

nace

posh [pɑːʃ] *adj Br* F chic *inv*, snob *inv*

po·si·tion [pəˈzɪʃn] **1** *n* position *f*; **what would you do in my ~?** que feriez-vous à ma place? **2** *v/t* placer

pos·i·tive [ˈpɑːzətɪv] *adj* positif*; GRAM affirmatif*; **be ~ (sure)** être sûr

pos·i·tive·ly [ˈpɑːzətɪvlɪ] *adv* vraiment

pos·sess [pəˈzes] *v/t* posséder

pos·ses·sion [pəˈzeʃn] possession *f*; **~s** possessions *fpl*, biens *mpl*

pos·ses·sive [pəˈzesɪv] *adj* person, GRAM possessif*

pos·si·bil·i·ty [pɑːsəˈbɪlətɪ] possibilité *f*

pos·si·ble [ˈpɑːsəbl] *adj* possible; **the fastest ~ route** l'itinéraire le plus rapide possible; **the best ~ solution** la meilleure solution possible

pos·si·bly [ˈpɑːsəblɪ] *adv* (*perhaps*) peut-être; **they're doing everything they ~ can** ils font vraiment tout leur possible; **how could I ~ have known that?** je ne vois vraiment pas comment j'aurais pu le savoir; **that can't ~ be right** ce n'est pas possible

post¹ [poʊst] **1** *n of wood, metal* poteau *m* **2** *v/t* notice afficher; profits enregistrer; **keep s.o. ~ed** tenir qn au courant

post² [poʊst] **1** *n* (*place of duty*) poste *m* **2** *v/t* soldier, employee affecter; guards poster

post³ [poʊst] **1** *n Br* (*mail*) courrier *m* **2** *v/t Br*: letter poster

post·age [ˈpoʊstɪdʒ] affranchissement *m*, frais *mpl* de port

post·age stamp *fml* timbre *m*

post·al [ˈpoʊstl] *adj* postal

post·card carte *f* postale; **post·code** *Br* code *m* postal; **post·date** *v/t* postdater

post·er [ˈpoʊstər] poster *m*, affiche *f*

pos·te·ri·or [pɑːˈstɪrɪər] *n hum* postérieur *m* F, popotin *m* F

pos·ter·i·ty [pɑːˈsterətɪ] postérité *f*

post·grad·u·ate [poʊstˈgrædʒʊət] **1** *adj* de troisième cycle **2** *n* étudiant(e) *m(f)* de troisième cycle

post·hu·mous [ˈpɑːstʃəməs] *adj* posthume

post·hu·mous·ly [ˈpɑːstʃəməslɪ] *adv* à titre posthume; **publish sth ~** publier qch après la mort de l'auteur

post·ing [ˈpoʊstɪŋ] (*assignment*) affectation *f*, nomination *f*

post·mark cachet *m* de la poste

post·mor·tem [poʊstˈmɔːrtəm] autopsie *f*

post of·fice poste *f*

post·pone [poʊstˈpoʊn] *v/t* remettre (à plus tard), reporter

post·pone·ment [poʊstˈpoʊnmənt] report *m*

pos·ture [ˈpɑːstʃər] *n* posture *f*

post·war *adj* d'après-guerre

pot¹ [pɑːt] *for cooking* casserole *f*; *for coffee* cafetière *f*; *for tea* théière *f*; *for plant* pot *m*

pot² [pɑːt] F (*marijuana*) herbe *f*, shit *m* F

po·ta·to [pəˈteɪtoʊ] pomme *f* de terre

po·ta·to chips, *Br* **po·ta·to crisps** *npl* chips *fpl*

pot·bel·ly brioche *f* F

po·tent [ˈpoʊtənt] *adj* puissant, fort

po·ten·tial [pəˈtenʃl] **1** *adj* potentiel* **2** *n* potentiel *m*

po·ten·tial·ly [pəˈtenʃəlɪ] *adv* potentiellement

pot·hole *in road* nid-de-poule *m*

pot·ter [ˈpɑːtər] *n* potier(-ière) *m(f)*

pot·ter·y [ˈpɑːtərɪ] poterie *f*; items poteries *fpl*

pot·ty [ˈpɑːtɪ] *n for baby* pot (de bébé) *m*

pouch [paʊtʃ] bag petit sac *m*; of kangaroo poche *f*

poul·try [ˈpoʊltrɪ] volaille *f*; meat volaille *f*

pounce [paʊns] *v/i of animal* bondir; fig sauter

pound¹ [paʊnd] *n* weight livre *f* (0,453 kg)

pound² *n for strays, cars* fourrière *f*

pound³ [paʊnd] *v/i of heart* battre (la chamade); **~ on** (hammer on) donner de grands coups sur; of rain battre contre

pound 'ster·ling livre *f* sterling

pour [pɔːr] **1** *v/t* liquid verser **2** *v/i*: **it's ~ing (with rain)** il pleut à verse

♦ **pour out** *v/t* liquid verser; troubles

déballer F

pout [paʊt] v/i faire la moue

pov·er·ty ['pɑːvərtɪ] pauvreté f

pov·er·ty-strick·en ['pɑːvərtɪstrɪkn] adj miséreux*

pow·der ['paʊdər] 1 n poudre f 2 v/t: ~ one's face se poudrer le visage

'pow·der room euph toilettes fpl pour dames

pow·er ['paʊər] 1 n (strength) puissance f, force f; (authority) pouvoir m / ; (energy) énergie f; (electricity) courant m; in ~ au pouvoir; fall from ~ POL perdre le pouvoir 2 v/t: be ~ed by fonctionner à

'pow·er-as·sist·ed adj assisté; 'pow·er drill perceuse f; 'pow·er fail·ure panne f d'électricité

pow·er·ful ['paʊərfl] adj puissant

pow·er·less ['paʊərlɪs] adj impuissant; be ~ to ... ne rien pouvoir faire pour ...

'pow·er line ligne f électrique; 'pow·er out·age panne f d'électricité; 'pow·er sta·tion centrale f électrique; 'pow·er steer·ing direction f assistée; 'pow·er u·nit bloc m d'alimentation

PR [piːˈɑːr] abbr (= public relations) relations fpl publiques

prac·ti·cal ['præktɪkl] adj pratique

prac·ti·cal 'joke farce f

prac·tic·al·ly ['præktɪklɪ] adv behave, think d'une manière pratique; (almost) pratiquement

prac·tice ['præktɪs] 1 n pratique f; training also entraînement m; (rehearsal) répétition f; (custom) coutume f; in ~ (in reality) en pratique; be out of ~ manquer d'entraînement; ~ makes perfect c'est en forgeant qu'on devient forgeron 2 v/i s'entraîner 3 v/t travailler; speech répéter; law, medicine exercer

prac·tise Br → practice v/i & v/t

prag·mat·ic [præɡˈmætɪk] adj pragmatique

prag·ma·tism ['præɡmətɪzm] pragmatisme m

prai·rie ['peɪrɪ] prairie f, plaine f

praise [preɪz] 1 n louange f, éloge m 2

v/t louer

'praise·wor·thy adj méritoire, louable

prank [præŋk] blague f, farce f

prat·tle ['prætl] v/i jacasser

prawn [prɔːn] crevette f

pray [preɪ] v/i prier

prayer [prer] prière f

preach [priːtʃ] v/t & v/i prêcher

preach·er ['priːtʃər] pasteur m

pre·am·ble [priːˈæmbl] préambule m

pre·car·i·ous [prɪˈkerɪəs] adj précaire

pre·car·i·ous·ly [prɪˈkerɪəslɪ] adv précairement

pre·cau·tion [prɪˈkɔːʃn] précaution f

pre·cau·tion·a·ry [prɪˈkɔːʃnrɪ] adj measure préventif*, de précaution

pre·cede [prɪˈsiːd] v/t précéder

pre·ce·dent ['presɪdənt] précédent m

pre·ced·ing [prɪˈsiːdɪŋ] adj précédent

pre·cinct ['priːsɪŋkt] (district) circonscription f (administrative)

pre·cious ['preʃəs] adj précieux*

pre·cip·i·tate [prɪˈsɪpɪteɪt] v/t crisis précipiter

pré·cis ['preɪsiː] n résumé m

pre·cise [prɪˈsaɪs] adj précis

pre·cise·ly [prɪˈsaɪslɪ] adv précisément

pre·ci·sion [prɪˈsɪʒn] précision f

pre·co·cious [prɪˈkoʊʃəs] adj child précoce

pre·con·ceived ['priːkənsiːvd] adj idea préconçu

pre·con·di·tion [priːkənˈdɪʃn] condition f requise

pred·a·tor ['predətər] prédateur m

pred·a·to·ry ['predətɔːrɪ] adj prédateur*

pre·de·ces·sor ['priːdɪsesər] prédécesseur m

pre·des·ti·na·tion [priːdestɪˈneɪʃn] prédestination f

pre·des·tined [priːˈdestɪnd] adj: be ~ to être prédestiné à

pre·dic·a·ment [prɪˈdɪkəmənt] situation f délicate

pre·dict [prɪˈdɪkt] v/t prédire, prévoir

pre·dict·a·ble [prɪˈdɪktəbl] adj prévisible

pre·dic·tion [prɪˈdɪkʃn] prédiction f

preserve

pre·dom·i·nant [prɪ'dɑːmɪnənt] *adj*
prédominant

pre·dom·i·nant·ly [prɪ'dɑːmɪnəntlɪ]
adv principalement

pre·dom·i·nate [prɪ'dɑːmɪneɪt] *v/i* prédominer

pref·ace ['prefɪs] *n* préface *f*

pre·fer [prɪ'fɜːr] *v/t (pret & pp -red)*
préférer; **~ X to Y** préférer X à Y, aimer mieux X que Y

pref·e·ra·ble ['prefərəbl] *adj* préférable

pref·e·ra·bly ['prefərəblɪ] *adv* de préférence

pref·e·rence ['prefərəns] préférence *f*

pref·er·en·tial [prefə'renʃl] *adj* préférentiel*

pre·fix ['priːfɪks] préfixe *m*

preg·nan·cy ['pregnənsɪ] grossesse *f*

preg·nant ['pregnənt] *adj* enceinte;
animal pleine

pre·heat ['priːhiːt] *v/t oven* préchauffer

pre·his·tor·ic [priːhɪs'tɑːrɪk] *adj also*
fig préhistorique

pre·judge [priː'dʒʌdʒ] *v/t situation*
préjuger de; *person* porter un jugement prématuré sur

prej·u·dice ['predʒudɪs] **1** *n (bias)* préjugé *m* **2** *v/t person* influencer;
chances compromettre; *reputation*
nuire à, porter préjudice à

prej·u·diced ['predʒudɪst] *adj* partial

pre·lim·i·na·ry [prɪ'lɪmɪnerɪ] *adj* préliminaire

pre·mar·i·tal [priː'mærɪtl] *adj sex* avant
le mariage

pre·ma·ture [priːmə'tʊr] *adj* prématuré

pre·med·i·tat·ed [priː'medɪteɪtɪd] *adj*
prémédité

prem·i·er ['premɪr] POL Premier ministre *m*

prem·i·ère ['premɪer] *n* première *f*

prem·is·es ['premɪsɪz] *npl* locaux *mpl*;
live on the ~ vivre sur place

pre·mi·um ['priːmɪəm] *in insurance*
prime *f*

pre·mo·ni·tion [premə'nɪʃn] prémonition *f*, pressentiment *m*

pre·na·tal [priː'neɪtl] *adj* prénatal

pre·oc·cu·pied [priː'ɑːkjʊpaɪd] *adj*
préoccupé

prep·a·ra·tion [prepə'reɪʃn] préparation *f*; **in ~ for** en prévision de; **~s**
préparatifs *mpl*

pre·pare [prɪ'per] **1** *v/t* préparer; **be ~d**
to do sth *willing, ready* être prêt à
faire qch; **be ~d for sth** *(be expecting)*
s'être préparé à qch, s'attendre à qch;
(be ready) s'être préparé pour qch,
être prêt pour qch **2** *v/i* se préparer

prep·o·si·tion [prepə'zɪʃn] préposition *f*

pre·pos·ter·ous [prɪ'pɑːstərəs] *adj* absurde, ridicule

pre·req·ui·site [priː'rekwɪzɪt] condition *f* préalable

pre·scribe [prɪ'skraɪb] *v/t of doctor*
prescrire

pre·scrip·tion [prɪ'skrɪpʃn] MED ordonnance *f*

pres·ence ['prezns] présence *f*; **in the**
~ of en présence de

pres·ence of 'mind présence *f* d'esprit

pres·ent¹ ['preznt] **1** *adj (current)* actuel*; **be ~** être présent **2** *n*: **the ~** *also*
GRAM le présent; **at ~** *(at this very mo-*
ment) en ce moment; *(for the time*
being) pour le moment

pres·ent² ['preznt] *n (gift)* cadeau *m*

pre·sent³ [prɪ'zent] *v/t award, bouquet*
remettre; *program* présenter; **~ s.o.**
with sth, ~ sth to s.o. remettre *or*
donner qch à qn

pre·sen·ta·tion [prezn'teɪʃn] présentation *f*

pres·ent-day [preznt'deɪ] *adj* actuel*

pre·sent·er [prɪ'zentər] présenta-
teur(-trice) *m(f)*

pres·ent·ly ['prezntlɪ] *adv (at the mo-*
ment) à présent; *(soon)* bientôt

'pres·ent tense présent *m*

pres·er·va·tion [prezər'veɪʃn] *of envi-*
ronment préservation *f*; *of building*
protection *f*; *of standards, peace* maintien *m*

pre·ser·va·tive [prɪ'zɜːrvətɪv] conservateur *m*

pre·serve [prɪ'zɜːrv] **1** *n (domain)* do-

P

maine *m* **2** *v/t standards, peace etc* maintenir; *wood etc* préserver; *food* conserver, mettre en conserve

pre·side [prɪˈzaɪd] *v/i at meeting* présider; ~ **over a meeting** présider une réunion

pres·i·den·cy [ˈprezɪdənsɪ] présidence *f*

pres·i·dent [ˈprezɪdnt] POL président(e) *m(f)*; *of company* président-directeur *m* général, PDG *m*

pres·i·den·tial [prezɪˈdenʃl] *adj* présidentiel*

press¹ [pres] *n*: **the** ~ la presse

press² [pres] **1** *v/t button* appuyer sur; *hand* serrer; *grapes, olives* presser; *clothes* repasser; ~ **s.o. to do sth** (*urge*) presser qn de faire qch **2** *v/i*: ~ **for** faire pression pour obtenir, exiger

press a·gen·cy agence *f* de presse

press con·fer·ence conférence *f* de presse

press·ing [ˈpresɪŋ] *adj* pressant

pres·sure [ˈpreʃər] **1** *n* pression *f*; **be under** ~ être sous pression; **he's under** ~ **to resign** on fait pression sur lui pour qu'il démissionne (*subj*) **2** *v/t* faire pression sur

pres·tige [preˈstiːʒ] prestige *m*

pres·ti·gious [preˈstɪdʒəs] *adj* prestigieux*

pre·su·ma·bly [prɪˈzuːməblɪ] *adv* sans doute, vraisemblablement

pre·sume [prɪˈzuːm] *v/t* présumer; ~ **to do** *fml* se permettre de faire

pre·sump·tion [prɪˈzʌmpʃn] *of innocence, guilt* présomption *f*

pre·sump·tu·ous [prɪˈzʌmptʊəs] *adj* présomptueux*

pre·sup·pose [priːsəˈpəʊz] *v/t* présupposer

pre·tax [ˈpriːtæks] *adj* avant impôts

pre·tence *Br* → **pretense**

pre·tend [prɪˈtend] **1** *v/t* prétendre; **the children are ~ing to be spacemen** les enfants se prennent pour des astronautes **2** *v/i* faire semblant

pre·tense [prɪˈtens] hypocrisie *f*, semblant *m*; **under the** ~ **of cooperation** sous prétexte de coopération

pre·ten·tious [prɪˈtenʃəs] *adj* prétentieux*

pre·text [ˈpriːtekst] prétexte *m*

pret·ty [ˈprɪtɪ] **1** *adj* joli **2** *adv* (*quite*) assez; ~ **much complete** presque complet; **are they the same? -** ~ **much** c'est la même chose? - à quelque chose près

pre·vail [prɪˈveɪl] *v/i* (*triumph*) prévaloir, l'emporter

pre·vail·ing [prɪˈveɪlɪŋ] *adj wind* dominant; *opinion* prédominant; (*current*) actuel*

pre·vent [prɪˈvent] *v/t* empêcher; *disease* prévenir; ~ **s.o. (from) doing sth** empêcher qn de faire qch

pre·ven·tion [prɪˈvenʃn] prévention *f*; ~ **is better than cure** mieux vaut prévenir que guérir

pre·ven·tive [prɪˈventɪv] *adj* préventif*

pre·view [ˈpriːvjuː] **1** *n* avant-première *f* **2** *v/t* voir en avant-première

pre·vi·ous [ˈpriːvɪəs] *adj* (*earlier*) antérieur; (*the one before*) précédent

pre·vi·ous·ly [ˈpriːvɪəslɪ] *adv* auparavant, avant

pre·war [ˈpriːwɔːr] *adj* d'avant-guerre

prey [preɪ] proie *f*

♦ **prey on** *v/t* chasser, se nourrir de; *fig*: *of con man etc* s'attaquer à

price [praɪs] **1** *n* prix *m* **2** *v/t* COMM fixer le prix de

price·less [ˈpraɪslɪs] *adj* inestimable, sans prix

price tag étiquette *f*, prix *m*

price war guerre *f* des prix

price·y [ˈpraɪsɪ] *adj* F cher*

prick¹ [prɪk] **1** *n pain* piqûre *f* **2** *v/t* (*jab*) piquer

prick² [prɪk] *n* V (*penis*) bite *f* V; *person* con *m* F

♦ **prick up** *v/t*: **prick up one's ears** *of dog* dresser les oreilles; *of person* dresser l'oreille

prick·le [ˈprɪkl] *on plant* épine *f*, piquant *m*

prick·ly [ˈprɪklɪ] *adj beard, plant* piquant; (*irritable*) irritable

pride [praɪd] **1** *n* fierté *f*; (*self-respect*) amour-propre *m*, orgueil *m* **2** *v/t*: ~

o.s. on être fier de

priest [priːst] prêtre *m*

pri·ma·ri·ly [praɪˈmerɪlɪ] *adv* essentiellement, principalement

pri·ma·ry [ˈpraɪmərɪ] **1** *adj* principal **2** *n* POL (élection *f*) primaire *f*

prime [praɪm] **1** *adj* fondamental; **of ~ importance** de la plus haute importance **2** *n*: **be in one's ~** être dans la fleur de l'âge

prime 'min·is·ter Premier ministre *m*

'prime time TV heures *fpl* de grande écoute

prim·i·tive [ˈprɪmɪtɪv] *adj* primitif*; *conditions* rudimentaires

prince [prɪns] prince *m*

prin·cess [prɪnˈses] princesse *f*

prin·ci·pal [ˈprɪnsəpl] **1** *adj* principal **2** *n of school* directeur(-trice) *m(f)*

prin·ci·pal·ly [ˈprɪnsəplɪ] *adv* principalement

prin·ci·ple [ˈprɪnsəpl] principe *m*; **on ~** par principe; **in ~** en principe

print [prɪnt] **1** *n in book, newspaper etc* texte *m*, caractères *mpl*; *(photograph)* épreuve *f*; **out of ~** épuisé **2** *v/t* imprimer; *(use block capitals)* écrire en majuscules

◆ **print out** *v/t* imprimer

print·ed mat·ter [ˈprɪntɪd] imprimés *mpl*

print·er [ˈprɪntər] *person* imprimeur *m*; *machine* imprimante *f*

'print·ing press [ˈprɪntɪŋ] presse *f*

'print·out impression *f*, sortie *f* (sur) imprimante

pri·or [ˈpraɪər] **1** *adj* préalable, antérieur **2** *prep*: **~ to** avant

pri·or·i·tize *v/t (put in order of priority)* donner un ordre de priorité à; *(give priority to)* donner la priorité à

pri·or·i·ty [praɪˈɑːrətɪ] priorité *f*; **have ~** être prioritaire, avoir la priorité

pris·on [ˈprɪzn] prison *f*

pris·on·er [ˈprɪznər] prisonnier(-ière) *m(f)*; **take s.o. ~** faire qn prisonnier

pris·on·er of 'war prisonnier(-ière) *m(f)* de guerre

priv·a·cy [ˈprɪvəsɪ] intimité *f*

pri·vate [ˈpraɪvət] **1** *adj* privé*; *letter* personnel*; *secretary* particulier* **2**

n MIL simple soldat *m*; **in ~** *talk to s.o.* en privé

pri·vate·ly [ˈpraɪvətlɪ] *adv talk to s.o.* en privé; *(inwardly)* intérieurement; **~ owned** privé; **~ funded** à financement privé

'pri·vate sec·tor secteur *m* privé

pri·va·tize [ˈpraɪvətaɪz] *v/t* privatiser

priv·i·lege [ˈprɪvəlɪdʒ] privilège *m*

priv·i·leged [ˈprɪvəlɪdʒd] *adj* privilégié; *(honored)* honoré

prize [praɪz] **1** *n* prix *m* **2** *v/t* priser, faire (grand) cas de

'prize·win·ner gagnant *m*

'prize·win·ning *adj* gagnant

pro[1] [proʊ] *n*: **the ~s and cons** le pour et le contre

pro[2] [proʊ] F *professional* pro *m/f inv* F

pro[3] [proʊ] *prep (in favor of)* pro-; **be ~ ...** être pour ...

prob·a·bil·i·ty [prɑːbəˈbɪlətɪ] probabilité *f*

prob·a·ble [ˈprɑːbəbl] *adj* probable

prob·a·bly [ˈprɑːbəblɪ] *adv* probablement

pro·ba·tion [prəˈbeɪʃn] *in job* période *f* d'essai; LAW probation *f*, mise *f* à l'épreuve; **be on ~** *in job* être à l'essai

pro·ba·tion of·fi·cer contrôleur (-euse) *m(f)* judiciaire

pro·ba·tion pe·ri·od *in job* période *f* d'essai

probe [proʊb] **1** *n (investigation)* enquête *f*; *scientific* sonde *f* **2** *v/t* sonder; *(investigate)* enquêter sur

prob·lem [ˈprɑːbləm] problème *m*; **no ~** pas de problème; **it doesn't worry me** c'est pas grave; **it's not a ~ with that** ça ne me pose pas de problème

pro·ce·dure [prəˈsiːdʒər] procédure *f*

pro·ceed [prəˈsiːd] *v/i (go: of people)* se rendre; *of work etc* avancer, se dérouler; **~ to do sth** se mettre à faire qch

pro·ceed·ings [prəˈsiːdɪŋz] *npl (events)* événements *mpl*

pro·ceeds [ˈproʊsiːdz] *npl* bénéfices *mpl*

pro·cess [ˈprɑːses] **1** *n* processus *m*; *industrial* procédé *m*, processus *m*; **in the ~** *(while doing it)* ce faisant;

by a ~ of elimination (en procédant) par élimination **2** v/t *food, raw materials* transformer; *data, application* traiter

pro·ces·sion [prəˈseʃn] procession f

pro·claim [prəˈkleɪm] v/t proclamer

prod [prɑːd] **1** n (petit) coup m **2** v/t (*pret & pp* **-ded**) donner un (petit) coup à, pousser

prod·i·gy [ˈprɑːdɪdʒɪ]: prodige m; (*child*) ~ enfant m/f prodige

prod·uce[1] [ˈprɑːduːs] n produits mpl (agricoles)

pro·duce[2] [prəˈduːs] v/t produire; (*bring about*) provoquer; (*bring out*) sortir

pro·duc·er [prəˈduːsər] producteur m

prod·uct [ˈprɑːdʌkt] produit m

pro·duc·tion [prəˈdʌkʃn] production f

pro·duc·tion ca·pac·i·ty capacité f de production

pro·duc·tion costs npl coûts mpl de production

pro·duc·tive [prəˈdʌktɪv] adj productif*

pro·duc·tiv·i·ty [prɑːdʌkˈtɪvətɪ] productivité f

pro·fane [prəˈfeɪn] adj *language* blasphématoire

pro·fess [prəˈfes] v/t (*claim*) prétendre

pro·fes·sion [prəˈfeʃn] profession f

pro·fes·sion·al [prəˈfeʃnl] **1** adj professionnel*; *piece of work* de haute qualité; **take ~ advice** consulter un professionnel; **do a very ~ job** faire un travail de professionnel; **turn ~** passer professionnel **2** n (*doctor, lawyer etc*) personne f qui exerce une profession libérale; *not amateur* professionnel(le) m(f)

pro·fes·sion·al·ly [prəˈfeʃnlɪ] adv *play sport* professionnellement; (*well, skillfully*) de manière professionnelle

pro·fes·sor [prəˈfesər] professeur m

pro·fi·cien·cy [prəˈfɪʃnsɪ] compétence f; *in a language* maîtrise f

pro·fi·cient [prəˈfɪʃnt] adj excellent, compétent; **must be ~ in French** doit bien maîtriser le français

pro·file [ˈprəʊfaɪl] profil m

prof·it [ˈprɑːfɪt] **1** n bénéfice m, profit

m **2** v/i: **~ by** *or* **~ from** profiter de

prof·it·a·bil·i·ty [prɑːfɪtəˈbɪlətɪ] rentabilité f

prof·it·a·ble [ˈprɑːfɪtəbl] adj rentable

ˈprof·it mar·gin marge f bénéficiaire

ˈprof·it shar·ing participation f aux bénéfices

pro·found [prəˈfaʊnd] adj profond

pro·found·ly [prəˈfaʊndlɪ] adv profondément

prog·no·sis [prɑːɡˈnəʊsɪs] MED pronostic m

pro·gram [ˈprəʊɡræm] **1** n programme m; *on radio, TV* émission f **2** v/t (*pret & pp* **-med**) programmer

pro·gramme Br → **program**

pro·gram·mer [ˈprəʊɡræmər] COMPUT programmeur(-euse) m(f)

pro·gress [ˈprɑːɡres] **1** n progrès m(pl); **make ~** faire des progrès; *of patient* aller mieux; *of building* progresser, avancer; **in ~** en cours **2** [prəˈɡres] v/i (*in time*) avancer, se dérouler; (*move on*) passer à; (*make ~*) faire des progrès, progresser; **how is the work ~ing?** ça avance bien?

pro·gres·sive [prəˈɡresɪv] adj (*enlightened*) progressiste; (*which progresses*) progressif*

pro·gres·sive·ly [prəˈɡresɪvlɪ] adv progressivement

pro·hib·it [prəˈhɪbɪt] v/t défendre, interdire

pro·hi·bi·tion [prəʊɪˈbɪʃn] interdiction f; **during Prohibition** pendant la prohibition

pro·hib·i·tive [prəˈhɪbɪtɪv] adj *prices* prohibitif*

proj·ect[1] [ˈprɑːdʒekt] n projet m; EDU étude f, dossier m; (*housing area*) cité f (H.L.M.)

pro·ject[2] [prəˈdʒekt] **1** v/t *figures, sales* prévoir; *movie* projeter **2** v/i (*stick out*) faire saillie

pro·jec·tion [prəˈdʒekʃn] (*forecast*) projection f, prévision f

pro·jec·tor [prəˈdʒektər] *for slides* projecteur m

pro·lif·ic [prəˈlɪfɪk] adj prolifique

pro·log, Br **pro·logue** [ˈprəʊlɑːɡ] prologue m

569   **prospect**

pro·long [prəˈlɒŋ] *v/t* prolonger

prom [prɑːm] (*school dance*) bal *m* de
fin d'année

prom·i·nent [ˈprɑːmɪnənt] *adj* nose,
chin proéminent; *visually* voyant; (*significant*) important

prom·is·cu·i·ty [prɑːmɪˈskjuːətɪ] promiscuité *f*

pro·mis·cu·ous [prəˈmɪskjʊəs] *adj*
dévergondé, dissolu

prom·ise [ˈprɑːmɪs] **1** *n* promesse *f* **2**
v/t promettre; **~ to do sth** promettre
de faire qch; **~ s.o. sth** promettre qch
à qn **3** *v/i* promettre

prom·is·ing [ˈprɑːmɪsɪŋ] *adj* prometteur*

pro·mote [prəˈmoʊt] *v/t* employee, *idea*
promouvoir; COMM *also* faire la promotion de

pro·mot·er [prəˈmoʊtər] *of sports event*
organisateur *m*

pro·mo·tion [prəˈmoʊʃn] promotion *f*

prompt [prɑːmpt] **1** *adj* (*on time*) ponctuel*; (*speedy*) prompt **2** *adv*: **at two
o'clock ~** à deux heures pile *or* précises **3** *v/t* (*cause*) provoquer; *actor*
souffler à; **something ~ed me to
turn back** quelque chose me poussa
à me retourner **4** *n* COMPUT invite *f*

prompt·ly [ˈprɑːmptlɪ] *adv* (*on time*)
ponctuellement; (*immediately*) immédiatement

prone [proʊn] *adj*: **be ~ to** être sujet à

pro·noun [ˈproʊnaʊn] pronom *m*

pro·nounce [prəˈnaʊns] *v/t* prononcer

pro·nounced [prəˈnaʊnst] *adj* accent
prononcé; *views* arrêté

pron·to [ˈprɑːntoʊ] *adv* F illico (presto) F

pro·nun·ci·a·tion [prənʌnsɪˈeɪʃn] prononciation *f*

proof [pruːf] *n* preuve *f*; *of book*
épreuve *f*

prop[1] [prɑːp] *n* THEA accessoire *m*

prop[2] [prɑːp] *v/t* (*pret & pp* **-ped**) appuyer (*against* contre)

♦ **prop up** *v/t also fig* soutenir

prop·a·gan·da [prɑːpəˈgændə] propagande *f*

pro·pel [prəˈpel] *v/t* (*pret & pp* **-led**)
propulser

pro·pel·lant [prəˈpelənt] *in aerosol* gaz
m propulseur

pro·pel·ler [prəˈpelər] hélice *f*

prop·er [ˈprɑːpər] *adj* (*real*) vrai; (*correct*) bon*, correct; (*fitting*) convenable, correct

prop·er·ly [ˈprɑːpərlɪ] *adv* (*correctly*)
correctement; (*fittingly also*) convenablement

prop·er·ty [ˈprɑːpərtɪ] propriété *f*;
(*possession also*) bien(s) *m(pl)*; **it's
his ~** c'est à lui

ˈprop·er·ty de·vel·op·er promoteur *m*
immobilier

ˈprop·er·ty mar·ket marché *m* immobilier; *for land* marché *m* foncier

proph·e·cy [ˈprɑːfəsɪ] prophétie *f*

proph·e·sy [ˈprɑːfəsaɪ] *v/t* (*pret & pp*
-ied) prophétiser, prédire

pro·por·tion [prəˈpɔːrʃn] proportion *f*;
a large ~ of Americans une grande
partie de la population américaine

pro·por·tion·al [prəˈpɔːrʃnl] *adj* proportionnel*

pro·por·tion·al   rep·re·sen·ta·tion
[reprəzenˈteɪʃn] POL représentation
f proportionnelle

pro·pos·al [prəˈpoʊzl] proposition *f*;
of marriage demande *f* en mariage

pro·pose [prəˈpoʊz] **1** *v/t* (*suggest*) proposer; **~ to do sth** (*plan*) se proposer
de faire qch **2** *v/i* (*make offer of marriage*) faire sa demande en mariage
(**to** à)

prop·o·si·tion [prɑːpəˈzɪʃn] **1** *n* proposition *f* **2** *v/t woman* faire des avances
à

pro·pri·e·tor [prəˈpraɪətər] propriétaire *m*

pro·pri·e·tress [prəˈpraɪətrɪs] propriétaire *f*

prose [proʊz] prose *f*

pros·e·cute [ˈprɑːsɪkjuːt] *v/t* LAW
poursuivre (en justice)

pros·e·cu·tion [prɑːsɪˈkjuːʃn] LAW
poursuites *fpl* (judiciaires); *lawyers*
accusation *f*, partie *f* plaignante

pros·e·cu·tor → **public prosecutor**

pros·pect [ˈprɑːspekt] **1** *n* (*chance,
likelihood*) chance(s) *f(pl)*; (*thought
of something in the future*) perspective

f; **~s** perspectives *fpl* (d'avenir) **2** *v/i:*
~ for *gold* chercher

pro·spec·tive [prə'spektɪv] *adj* potentiel*, éventuel*

pros·per ['prɑ:spər] *v/i* prospérer

pros·per·i·ty [prɑ:'sperətɪ] prospérité *f*

pros·per·ous ['prɑ:spərəs] *adj* prospère

pros·ti·tute ['prɑ:stɪtu:t] *n* prostituée *f*; **male ~** prostitué *m*

pros·ti·tu·tion [prɑ:stɪ'tu:ʃn] prostitution *f*

pros·trate ['prɑ:streɪt] *adj*: **be ~ with grief** être accablé de chagrin

pro·tect [prə'tekt] *v/t* protéger

pro·tec·tion [prə'tekʃn] protection *f*

pro·tec·tion mon·ey argent versé à un racketteur

pro·tec·tive [prə'tektɪv] *adj* protecteur*

pro·tec·tive 'cloth·ing vêtements *mpl* de protection

pro·tec·tor [prə'tektər] protecteur (-trice) *m(f)*

pro·tein [prouti:n] protéine *f*

pro·test ['proutest] **1** *n* protestation *f*; *(demonstration)* manifestation *f* **2** *v/t* [prə'test] *(object to)* protester contre **3** *v/i* [prə'test] protester; *(demonstrate)* manifester

Prot·es·tant ['prɑ:tɪstənt] **1** *adj* protestant **2** *n* protestant(e) *m(f)*

pro·test·er [prə'testər] manifestant(e) *m(f)*

pro·to·col ['proutəkɑ:l] protocole *m*

pro·to·type ['proutətaɪp] prototype *m*

pro·tract·ed [prə'træktɪd] *adj* prolongé, très long*

pro·trude [prə'tru:d] *v/i of eyes, ear* être saillant; *from pocket etc* sortir

pro·trud·ing [prə'tru:dɪŋ] *adj* saillant; *ears* décollé; *chin* avancé; *teeth* en avant

proud [praud] *adj* fier*; **be ~ of** être fier de

proud·ly ['praudlɪ] *adv* fièrement, avec fierté

prove [pru:v] *v/t* prouver

prov·erb ['prɑ:vɜ:rb] proverbe *m*

pro·vide [prə'vaɪd] *v/t* fournir; **~ sth to**

s.o., ~ s.o. with sth fournir qch à qn

♦ **provide for** *v/t family* pourvoir *or* subvenir aux besoins de; *of law etc* prévoir

pro·vi·ded [prə'vaɪdɪd] *conj:* **~ (that)** *(on condition that)* pourvu que (+*subj*), à condition que (+*subj*)

prov·ince ['prɑ:vɪns] province *f*

pro·vin·cial [prə'vɪnʃl] *adj also pej* provincial; *city* de province

pro·vi·sion [prə'vɪʒn] *(supply)* fourniture *f*; *of services* prestation *f*; *in a law, contract* disposition *f*

pro·vi·sion·al [prə'vɪʒnl] *adj* provisoire

pro·vi·so [prə'vaɪzou] condition *f*

prov·o·ca·tion [prɑ:və'keɪʃn] provocation *f*

pro·voc·a·tive [prə'vɑ:kətɪv] *adj* provocant

pro·voke [prə'vouk] *v/t* provoquer

prow [prau] NAUT proue *f*

prow·ess ['prauɪs] talent *m*, prouesses *fpl*

prowl [praul] *v/i of tiger etc* chasser; *of burglar* rôder

'prowl car voiture *f* de patrouille

prowl·er ['praulər] rôdeur(-euse) *m(f)*

prox·im·i·ty [prɑ:k'sɪmətɪ] proximité *f*

prox·y ['prɑ:ksɪ] *(authority)* procuration *f*; *person* mandataire *m/f*

prude [pru:d] puritain *m*

pru·dence ['pru:dns] prudence *f*

pru·dent ['pru:dnt] *adj* prudent

prud·ish ['pru:dɪʃ] *adj* prude

prune[1] [pru:n] *n* pruneau *m*

prune[2] [pru:n] *v/t plant* tailler; *fig: costs etc* réduire; *fig: essay* élaguer

pry [praɪ] *v/i (pret & pp* **-ied**) être indiscret, fouiner

♦ **pry into** *v/t* mettre son nez dans, s'immiscer dans

PS ['pi:es] *abbr (= postscript)* P.-S. *m*

pseu·do·nym ['su:dənɪm] pseudonyme *m*

psy·chi·at·ric [saɪkɪ'ætrɪk] *adj* psychiatrique

psy·chi·a·trist [saɪ'kaɪətrɪst] psychiatre *m/f*

psy·chi·a·try [saɪ'kaɪətrɪ] psychiatrie *f*

psy·chic ['saɪkɪk] *adj power* parapsychique; *phenomenon* paranormal; *I'm not ~!* je ne suis pas devin!

psy·cho ['saɪkoʊ] F psychopathe *m/f*

psy·cho·a·nal·y·sis [saɪkoʊən'æləsɪs] psychanalyse *f*

psy·cho·an·a·lyst [saɪkoʊ'ænəlɪst] psychanalyste *m/f*

psy·cho·an·a·lyze [saɪkoʊ'ænəlaɪz] *v/t* psychanalyser

psy·cho·log·i·cal [saɪkə'lɑːdʒɪkl] *adj* psychologique

psy·cho·log·i·cal·ly [saɪkə'lɑːdʒɪklɪ] *adv* psychologiquement

psy·chol·o·gist [saɪ'kɑːlədʒɪst] psychologue *m/f*

psy·chol·o·gy [saɪ'kɑːlədʒɪ] psychologie *f*

psy·cho·path ['saɪkoʊpæθ] psychopathe *m/f*

psy·cho·so·mat·ic [saɪkoʊsə'mætɪk] *adj* psychosomatique

PTO [piːtiː'oʊ] *abbr* (= *please turn over*) T.S.V.P. (= tournez s'il vous plaît)

pub [pʌb] *Br* pub *m*

pu·ber·ty ['pjuːbərtɪ] puberté *f*

pu·bic hair [pjuː'bɪk'her] poils *mpl* pubiens; *single* poil *m* pubien

pub·lic ['pʌblɪk] **1** *adj* public* **2** *n*: **the ~** le public; **in ~** en public

pub·li·ca·tion [pʌblɪ'keɪʃn] publication *f*

pub·lic 'hol·i·day jour *m* férié

pub·lic·i·ty [pʌb'lɪsətɪ] publicité *f*

pub·li·cize ['pʌblɪsaɪz] *v/t* (*make known*) faire connaître, rendre public; COMM faire de la publicité pour

pub·lic do·main [doʊ'meɪn]: **be ~** faire partie du domaine public

pub·lic 'li·bra·ry bibliothèque *f* municipale

pub·lic·ly ['pʌblɪklɪ] *adv* en public, publiquement

pub·lic 'pros·e·cu·tor procureur *m* général; **pub·lic re'la·tions** *npl* relations *fpl* publiques; **'pub·lic school** école *f* publique; *Br* école privée (du secondaire); **'pub·lic sec·tor** secteur *m* public

pub·lish ['pʌblɪʃ] *v/t* publier

pub·lish·er ['pʌblɪʃər] éditeur(-trice)

pub·lish·ing ['pʌblɪʃɪŋ] édition *f*

'pub·lish·ing com·pa·ny maison *f* d'édition

pud·dle ['pʌdl] flaque *f*

Puer·to Ri·can [pwertoʊ'riːkən] **1** *adj* portoricain **2** *n* Portoricain(e) *m(f)*

Puer·to Ri·co [pwertoʊ'riːkoʊ] Porto Rico

puff [pʌf] **1** *n* *of wind* bourrasque *f*; *of smoke* bouffée *f* **2** *v/i* (*pant*) souffler, haleter; **~ on a cigarette** tirer sur une cigarette

puff·y ['pʌfɪ] *adj eyes, face* bouffi, gonflé

puke [pjuːk] *v/i* P dégueuler F

pull [pʊl] **1** *n* *on rope* coup *m*; F (*appeal*) attrait *m*; F (*influence*) influence *f* **2** *v/t* tirer; *tooth* arracher; *muscle* se déchirer **3** *v/i* tirer

♦ **pull ahead** *v/i* *in race, competition* prendre la tête

♦ **pull apart** *v/t* (*separate*) séparer

♦ **pull away 1** *v/t* retirer **2** *v/i* *of car, train* s'éloigner

♦ **pull down** *v/t* (*lower*) baisser; (*demolish*) démolir

♦ **pull in** *v/i* *of bus, train* arriver

♦ **pull off** *v/t* *leaves etc* détacher; *clothes* enlever; F *deal etc* décrocher; *he pulled it off* il a réussi

♦ **pull out 1** *v/t* sortir; *troops* retirer **2** *v/i* *from agreement, competition, of troops* se retirer; *of ship* partir

♦ **pull over** *v/i* se garer

♦ **pull through** *v/i* *from illness* s'en sortir

♦ **pull together 1** *v/i* (*cooperate*) travailler ensemble **2** *v/t*: **pull o.s. together** se reprendre

♦ **pull up 1** *v/t* (*raise*) remonter; *plant* arracher **2** *v/i* *of car etc* s'arrêter

pul·ley ['pʊlɪ] poulie *f*

pull·o·ver ['pʊloʊvər] pull *m*

pulp [pʌlp] pulpe *f*; *for paper-making* pâte *f* à papier

pul·pit ['pʊlpɪt] chaire *f*

'pulp nov·el roman *m* de gare

pul·sate [pʌl'seɪt] *v/i* *of heart, blood* battre; *of rhythm* vibrer

pulse [pʌls] pouls *m*

pul·ver·ize ['pʌlvəraɪz] *v/t* pulvériser

pump [pʌmp] **1** *n* pompe *f* **2** *v/t* pomper

♦ **pump up** *v/t* gonfler

pump·kin ['pʌmpkɪn] potiron *m*

pun [pʌn] jeu *m* de mots

punch [pʌntʃ] **1** *n blow* coup *m* de poing; *implement* perforeuse *f* **2** *v/t with fist* donner un coup de poing à; *hole* percer; *ticket* composter

'**punch line** chute *f*

punc·tu·al ['pʌŋktʃʊəl] *adj* ponctuel*

punc·tu·al·i·ty [pʌŋktʃʊ'ælətɪ] ponctualité *f*

punc·tu·al·ly ['pʌŋktʃʊəlɪ] *adv* à l'heure, ponctuellement

punc·tu·ate ['pʌŋktʃʊeɪt] *v/t* GRAM ponctuer

punc·tu·a·tion [pʌŋktʃʊ'eɪʃn] ponctuation *f*

punc·tu·a·tion mark signe *m* de ponctuation

punc·ture ['pʌŋktʃər] **1** *n* piqûre *f* **2** *v/t* percer, perforer

pun·gent ['pʌndʒənt] *adj* âcre, piquant

pun·ish ['pʌnɪʃ] *v/t* punir

pun·ish·ing ['pʌnɪʃɪŋ] *adj schedule, pace* éprouvant, épuisant

pun·ish·ment ['pʌnɪʃmənt] punition *f*

punk [pʌŋk]: ~ (**rock**) MUS musique *f* punk

pu·ny ['pjuːnɪ] *adj person* chétif*

pup [pʌp] chiot *m*

pu·pil[1] ['pjuːpl] *of eye* pupille *f*

pu·pil[2] ['pjuːpl] (*student*) élève *m/f*

pup·pet ['pʌpɪt] *also fig* marionnette *f*

'**pup·pet gov·ern·ment** gouvernement *m* fantoche

pup·py ['pʌpɪ] chiot *m*

pur·chase[1] ['pɜːrtʃəs] **1** *n* achat *m* **2** *v/t* acheter

pur·chase[2] ['pɜːrtʃəs] (*grip*) prise *f*

pur·chas·er ['pɜːrtʃəsər] acheteur (-euse) *m(f)*

pure [pjur] *adj* pur; *white* immaculé; ~ **new wool** pure laine *f* vierge

pure·ly ['pjurlɪ] *adv* purement

pur·ga·to·ry ['pɜːrgətɔːrɪ] purgatoire *m*; *fig* enfer *m*

purge [pɜːrdʒ] **1** *n* POL purge *f* **2** *v/t* POL épurer

pu·ri·fy ['pjurɪfaɪ] *v/t* (*pret & pp* -*ied*) *water* épurer

pu·ri·tan ['pjurɪtən] *n* puritain(e) *m(f)*

pu·ri·tan·i·cal [pjurɪ'tænɪkl] *adj* puritain

pu·ri·ty ['pjurɪtɪ] pureté *f*

pur·ple ['pɜːrpl] *adj reddish* pourpre; *bluish* violet*

Pur·ple 'Heart MIL décoration remise aux blessés de guerre

pur·pose ['pɜːrpəs] (*aim, object*) but *m*; **on** ~ exprès

pur·pose·ful ['pɜːrpəsfʊl] *adj* résolu, déterminé

pur·pose·ly ['pɜːrpəslɪ] *adv* exprès

purr [pɜːr] *v/i of cat* ronronner

purse [pɜːrs] *n* (*pocketbook*) sac *m* à main; *Br; for money* porte-monnaie *m inv*

pur·sue [pərˈsuː] *v/t* poursuivre

pur·su·er [pərˈsuːər] poursuivant(e) *m(f)*

pur·suit [pərˈsuːt] poursuite *f*; (*activity*) activité *f*; **those in** ~ les poursuivants

pus [pʌs] pus *m*

push [pʊʃ] **1** *n* (*shove*) poussée *f*; **at the** ~ **of a button** en appuyant sur un bouton **2** *v/t* (*shove, pressure*) pousser; *button* appuyer sur; F *drugs* revendre, trafiquer; **be** ~**ed for** F être à court de, manquer de; **be** ~**ing 40** F friser la quarantaine **3** *v/i* pousser

♦ **push ahead** *v/i* continuer

♦ **push along** *v/t cart etc* pousser

♦ **push away** *v/t* repousser

♦ **push off** *v/t lid* soulever

♦ **push on** *v/i* (*continue*) continuer (sa route)

♦ **push up** *v/t prices* faire monter

push·er ['pʊʃər] F *of drugs* dealer (-euse) *m(f)*

'**push-up** *n*: **do** ~**s** faire des pompes

push·y ['pʊʃɪ] *adj* F qui se met en avant

puss [pʊs], **pus·sy** (**cat**) [pʊs, 'pʊsɪ (kæt)] F minou *m*

♦ **pus·sy·foot around** ['pʊsɪfʊt] *v/i* tourner autour du pot F

put [pʊt] *v/t* (*pret & pp* **put**) mettre;

question poser; **~ the cost at** estimer le prix à
♦ **put across** v/t *idea etc* faire comprendre
♦ **put aside** v/t *money* mettre de côté; *work* mettre de côté
♦ **put away** v/t *money etc* ranger; *in institution* enfermer; *in prison* emprisonner; (*consume*) consommer, s'enfiler F; *money* mettre de côté; *animal* faire piquer
♦ **put back** v/t (*replace*) remettre
♦ **put by** v/t *money* mettre de côté
♦ **put down** v/t poser; *deposit* verser; *rebellion* réprimer; (*belittle*) rabaisser; *in writing* mettre (par écrit); **put one's foot down** *in car* appuyer sur le champignon F; (*be firm*) se montrer ferme; **put sth down to sth** (*attribute*) mettre qch sur le compte de qch
♦ **put forward** v/t *idea etc* soumettre, suggérer
♦ **put in** v/t mettre; *time* passer; *request, claim* présenter, déposer
♦ **put in for** v/t (*apply for*) demander
♦ **put off** v/t *light, radio, TV* éteindre; (*postpone*) repousser; (*deter*) dissuader; (*repel*) dégoûter; **put s.o. off sth** dégoûter qn de qch; **you've put me off** (**the idea**) tu m'as coupé l'envie
♦ **put on** v/t *light, radio, TV* allumer;

music, jacket etc mettre; (*perform*) monter; *accent etc* prendre; **put on make-up** se mettre du maquillage; **put on the brake** freiner; **put on weight** prendre du poids; **she's just putting it on** (*pretending*) elle fait semblant
♦ **put out** v/t *hand* tendre; *fire, light* éteindre
♦ **put through** v/t *on phone* passer
♦ **put together** v/t (*assemble*) monter; (*organize*) organiser
♦ **put up** v/t *hand* lever; *person* héberger; (*erect*) ériger; *prices* augmenter; *poster* accrocher; *money* fournir; **put sth up for sale** mettre qch en vente; **put your hands up!** haut les mains!
♦ **put up with** v/t (*tolerate*) supporter, tolérer

putt [pʌt] v/i *in golf* putter
put·ty ['pʌtɪ] mastic m
puz·zle ['pʌzl] **1** n (*mystery*) énigme f, mystère m; *game* jeu m, casse-tête m; (*jigsaw ~*) puzzle m **2** v/t laisser perplexe
puz·zling ['pʌzlɪŋ] adj curieux*
PVC [piːviːˈsiː] abbr (= **polyvinyl chloride**) P.V.C. m (= polychlorure de vinyle)
py·ja·mas Br → **pajamas**
py·lon ['paɪlɒn] pylône m
Py·re·nees ['pɪrəniːz] npl Pyrénées fpl

Q

quack[1] [kwæk] **1** n *of duck* coin-coin m inv **2** v/i cancaner
quack[2] [kwæk] n F (*bad doctor*) charlatan m
quad·ran·gle ['kwɑːdræŋgl] *figure* quadrilatère m; *courtyard* cour f
quad·ru·ped ['kwɑːdrʊped] quadrupède m
quad·ru·ple ['kwɑːdrʊpl] v/i quadru-

pler
quad·ru·plets ['kwɑːdrʊplɪts] npl quadruplés mpl
quads [kwɑːdz] npl F quadruplés mpl
quag·mire ['kwɑːgmaɪr] bourbier m
quail [kweɪl] v/i flancher
quaint [kweɪnt] adj *cottage* pittoresque; (*eccentric: ideas etc*) curieux*
quake [kweɪk] **1** n (*earthquake*) trem-

blement *m* de terre **2** *v/i of earth, with fear* trembler

qual·i·fi·ca·tion [kwɑːlɪfɪ'keɪʃn] *from university etc* diplôme *m*; *of remark etc* restriction *f*; **have the right ~s for a job** avoir les qualifications requises pour un poste

qual·i·fied ['kwɑːlɪfaɪd] *adj doctor, engineer etc* qualifié; *(restricted)* restreint; *I am not ~ to judge* je ne suis pas à même de juger

qual·i·fy ['kwɑːlɪfaɪ] **1** *v/t (pret & pp -ied) of degree, course etc* qualifier; *remark etc* nuancer **2** *v/i (get degree etc)* obtenir son diplôme; *in competition* se qualifier; *that doesn't ~ as ...* on ne peut pas considérer cela comme ...

qual·i·ty ['kwɑːlətɪ] qualité *f*

qual·i·ty con'trol contrôle *m* de qualité

qualm [kwɑːm] scrupule *m*; **have no ~s about ...** n'avoir aucun scrupule à ...

quan·da·ry ['kwɑːndərɪ] dilemme *m*

quan·ti·fy ['kwɑːntɪfaɪ] *v/t (pret & pp -ied)* quantifier

quan·ti·ty ['kwɑːntətɪ] quantité *f*

quan·tum phys·ics ['kwɑːntəm] physique *f* quantique

quar·an·tine ['kwɑːrəntiːn] *n* quarantaine *f*

quar·rel ['kwɑːrəl] **1** *n* dispute *f*, querelle *f* **2** *v/i (pret & pp -ed, Br pp -led)* se disputer

quar·rel·some ['kwɑːrəlsʌm] *adj* agressif*, belliqueux*

quar·ry[1] ['kwɑːrɪ] *in hunt* gibier *m*

quar·ry[2] ['kwɑːrɪ] *for mining* carrière *f*

quart [kwɔːrt] quart *m* de gallon *(0,946 litre)*

quar·ter ['kwɔːrtər] **1** *n* quart *m*; *(25 cents)* vingt-cinq cents *mpl*; *(part of town)* quartier *m*; **divide the pie into ~s** couper la tarte en quatre (parts); *a ~ of an hour* un quart d'heure; *a ~ of 5* cinq heures moins le quart; *a ~ after 5* cinq heures et quart **2** *v/t* diviser en quatre

'quar·ter·back SP quarterback *m*, quart *m* arrière; **quar·ter·fi·nal** quart

m de finale; **quar·ter·fi·nal·ist** quart de finaliste *m*, quart-finaliste *m*

quar·ter·ly ['kwɔːrtərlɪ] **1** *adj* trimestriel* **2** *adv* trimestriellement, tous les trois mois

'quar·ter·note MUS noire *f*

quar·ters ['kwɔːrtərz] *npl* MIL quartiers *mpl*

quar·tet [kwɔːr'tet] MUS quatuor *m*

quartz [kwɑːrts] quartz *m*

quash [kwɑːʃ] *v/t rebellion* réprimer, écraser; *court decision* casser, annuler

qua·ver ['kweɪvər] **1** *n in voice* tremblement *m* **2** *v/i of voice* trembler

quay [kiː] quai *m*

'quay·side quai *m*

quea·sy ['kwiːzɪ] *adj* nauséeux*; **feel ~** avoir mal au cœur, avoir la nausée

Que·bec [kwəˈbek] Québec

queen [kwiːn] reine *f*

queen 'bee reine *f* des abeilles

queer [kwɪr] *adj (peculiar)* bizarre

queer·ly ['kwɪrlɪ] *adv* bizarrement

quell [kwel] *v/t* réprimer

quench [kwentʃ] *v/t thirst* étancher, assouvir; *flames* éteindre, étouffer

que·ry ['kwɪrɪ] **1** *n* question *f* **2** *v/t (pret & pp -ied) (express doubt about)* mettre en doute; *(check)* vérifier; **~ sth with s.o.** poser des questions sur qch à qn, vérifier qch auprès de qn

quest [kwest] quête *f*

ques·tion ['kwestʃn] **1** *n* question *f*; *in ~ (being talked about)* en question; *be in ~ (in doubt)* être mis en question; *it's a ~ of money* c'est une question d'argent; *that's out of the ~* c'est hors de question **2** *v/t person* questionner, interroger; *(doubt)* mettre en question

ques·tion·a·ble ['kwestʃnəbl] *adj* contestable, discutable

ques·tion·ing ['kwestʃnɪŋ] **1** *adj look, tone* interrogateur* **2** *n* interrogatoire *m*

'ques·tion mark point *m* d'interrogation

ques·tion·naire [kwestʃəˈner] questionnaire *m*

queue [kjuː] *Br* **1** *n* queue *f* **2** *v/i* faire la queue

quib·ble ['kwɪbl] v/i chipoter, chercher la petite bête

quick [kwɪk] adj rapide; **be ~!** fais vite!, dépêche-toi!; **let's go for a ~ drink** on va se prendre un petit verre?; **can I have a ~ look?** puis-je jeter un coup d'œil?; **that was ~!** c'était rapide!

quick·ly ['kwɪklɪ] adv vite, rapidement

'quick·sand sables mpl mouvants; **'quick·sil·ver** mercure m; **quick-wit·ted** [kwɪk'wɪtɪd] adj vif*, à l'esprit vif

qui·et ['kwaɪət] adj street, house, life calme, tranquille; music doux; engine silencieux*; voice bas*; **keep ~ about sth** ne pas parler de qch, garder qch secret; **~!** silence!

♦ **quieten down** ['kwaɪətn] **1** v/t class, children calmer, faire taire **2** v/i of children, situation se calmer

qui·et·ly ['kwaɪətlɪ] adv doucement, sans bruit; (unassumingly, peacefully) tranquillement

qui·et·ness ['kwaɪətnɪs] calme m, tranquillité f

quilt [kwɪlt] on bed couette f

quilt·ed ['kwɪltɪd] adj matelassé

quin·ine ['kwɪniːn] quinine f

quin·tet [kwɪn'tet] MUS quintette m

quip [kwɪp] **1** n trait m d'esprit **2** v/i (pret & pp **-ped**) plaisanter, railler

quirk [kwɜːrk] manie f, lubie f

quirk·y ['kwɜːrkɪ] adj bizarre, excentrique

quit [kwɪt] **1** v/t (pret & pp **quit**) job quitter; **~ doing sth** arrêter de faire qch **2** v/i (leave job) démissionner; COMPUT quitter; **get or be given one's notice to ~** from landlord recevoir son congé

quite [kwaɪt] adv (fairly) assez; (completely) tout à fait; **not ~ ready** pas tout à fait prêt; **I didn't ~ understand** je n'ai pas bien compris; **is that right? - not ~** c'est cela? - non, pas exactement; **~!** parfaitement!; **~ a lot** pas mal, beaucoup; **~ a few** plusieurs, un bon nombre; **it was ~ a surprise / change** c'était vraiment une surprise / un changement

quits [kwɪts] adj: **be ~ with s.o.** être quitte envers qn

quit·ter ['kwɪtər] F lâcheur m

quiv·er ['kwɪvər] v/i trembler

quiz [kwɪz] **1** n on TV jeu m télévisé; on radio jeu m radiophonique; at school interrogation f **2** v/t (pret & pp **-zed**) interroger, questionner

'quiz mas·ter animateur m de jeu

quo·ta ['kwoʊtə] quota m

quo·ta·tion [kwoʊ'teɪʃn] from author citation f; price devis m

quo·ta·tion marks npl guillemets mpl; **in ~** entre guillemets

quote [kwoʊt] **1** n from author citation f; price devis m; (quotation mark) guillemet m; **in ~s** entre guillemets **2** v/t text citer; price proposer **3** v/i: **~ from an author** citer un auteur; **~ for a job** faire un devis pour un travail

R

R

rab·bi ['ræbaɪ] rabbin m

rab·bit ['ræbɪt] lapin m

rab·ble ['ræbl] cohue f, foule f

rab·ble-rous·er ['ræblraʊzər] agitateur(-trice) m(f)

ra·bies ['reɪbiːz] nsg rage f

rac·coon [rə'kuːn] raton m laveur

race¹ [reɪs] n of people race f

race² [reɪs] **1** n SP course f; **the ~s** horses les courses **2** v/i (run fast) courir à toute vitesse; **he ~d through his work** il a fait son travail à toute vitesse **3** v/t: **I'll ~ you** le premier arrivé a gagné

'**race-course** champ m de courses, hippodrome m; '**race-horse** cheval m de course; '**race riot** émeute f raciale; '**race-track** for cars circuit m, piste f; for horses champ m de courses, hippodrome m

ra-cial ['reɪʃl] adj racial; **~ equality** égalité f des races

rac-ing ['reɪsɪŋ] course f

'**rac-ing bike** vélo m de course

rac-ism ['reɪsɪzm] racisme m

ra-cist ['reɪsɪst] **1** adj raciste **2** n raciste m/f

rack [ræk] **1** n for bikes: on car porte vélo m inv; at station etc râtelier m à vélos; for bags on train porte-bagages m inv; for CDs range-CD m inv **2** v/t: **~ one's brains** se creuser la tête

rack-et[1] ['rækɪt] SP raquette f

rack-et[2] ['rækɪt] (noise) vacarme m; criminal activity escroquerie f

ra-dar ['reɪdɑːr] radar m

'**ra-dar screen** écran m radar

'**ra-dar trap** contrôle-radar m

ra-di-ance ['reɪdɪəns] éclat m, rayonnement m

ra-di-ant ['reɪdɪənt] adj smile, appearance radieux*

ra-di-ate ['reɪdɪeɪt] v/i of heat, light irradier, rayonner

ra-di-a-tion [reɪdɪ'eɪʃn] nuclear radiation f

ra-di-a-tor ['reɪdɪeɪtər] in room, car radiateur m

rad-i-cal ['rædɪkl] **1** adj radical **2** n POL radical(e) m(f)

rad-i-cal-ism ['rædɪkəlɪzm] POL radicalisme m

rad-i-cal-ly ['rædɪklɪ] adv radicalement

ra-di-o ['reɪdɪoʊ] radio f; **on the ~** à la radio; **by ~** par radio

ra-di-o-ac-tive adj radioactif*; **ra-di-o-ac-tive 'waste** déchets mpl radioactifs; **ra-di-o-ac'tiv-i-ty** radioactivité f; **ra-di-o a'larm** radio-réveil m

ra-di-og-ra-pher [reɪdɪ'ɑːgrəfər] radiologue m/f

ra-di-og-ra-phy [reɪdɪ'ɑːgrəfɪ] radio-

graphie f

'**ra-di-o sta-tion** station f de radio; '**ra-di-o tax-i** radio-taxi m; **ra-di-o-'ther-a-py** radiothérapie f

rad-ish ['rædɪʃ] radis m

ra-di-us ['reɪdɪəs] rayon m

raf-fle ['ræfl] n tombola f

raft [ræft] radeau m; fig: of new measures etc paquet m

raf-ter ['ræftər] chevron m

rag [ræg] n for cleaning etc chiffon m; **in ~s** en haillons

rage [reɪdʒ] **1** n colère f, rage f; **be in a ~** être furieux*; **be all the ~** F faire fureur **2** v/i of person être furieux*, rager; of storm faire rage

rag-ged ['rægɪd] adj edge irrégulier*; appearance négligé; clothes en loques

raid [reɪd] **1** n by troops raid m; by police descente f, by robbers hold-up m; FIN raid m **2** v/t of troops attaquer; of police faire une descente dans; of robbers attaquer; fridge, orchard faire une razzia dans

raid-er ['reɪdər] (robber) voleur m

rail [reɪl] n on track rail m; (hand~) rampe f; for towel porte-serviettes m inv; **by ~** en train

rail-ings ['reɪlɪŋz] npl around park etc grille f

'**rail-road** system chemin m de fer; track voie f ferrée; '**rail-road sta-tion** gare f; '**rail-way** Br chemin m de fer; track voie f ferrée

rain [reɪn] **1** n pluie f; **in the ~** sous la pluie **2** v/i pleuvoir; **it's ~ing** il pleut

'**rain-bow** arc-en-ciel m; '**rain-check**: **can I take a ~ on that?** peut-on remettre cela à plus tard?; '**rain-coat** imperméable m; '**rain-drop** goutte f de pluie; '**rain-fall** précipitations fpl; '**rain for-est** forêt f tropicale (humide); '**rain-proof** adj fabric imperméable; '**rain-storm** pluie f torrentielle

rain-y ['reɪnɪ] adj pluvieux*; **it's ~** il pleut beaucoup

raise [reɪz] **1** n in salary augmentation f (de salaire) **2** v/t shelf etc surélever; offer augmenter; children élever; question soulever; money rassembler

rai·sin ['reɪzn] raisin *m* sec

rake [reɪk] *n for garden* râteau *m*

♦ **rake up** *v/t leaves* ratisser; *fig* révéler, mettre au grand jour

ral·ly ['rælɪ] *n (meeting, reunion)* rassemblement *m*; MOT rallye *m*; *in tennis* échange *m*

♦ **rally round 1** *v/i (pret & pp **-ied**)* se rallier **2** *v/t (pret & pp **-ied**)*: **rally round s.o.** venir en aide à qn

RAM [ræm] *abbr* COMPUT (= *random access memory*) RAM *f*, mémoire *f* vive

ram [ræm] **1** *n* bélier *m* **2** *v/t (pret & pp -med) ship, car* heurter, percuter

ram·ble ['ræmbl] **1** *n walk* randonnée *f* **2** *v/i walk* faire de la randonnée; *when speaking* discourir; *(talk incoherently)* divaguer

ram·bler ['ræmblər] *walker* randonneur(-euse) *m(f)*

ram·bling ['ræmblɪŋ] **1** *adj speech* décousu **2** *n walking* randonnée *f*; *in speech* digression *f*

ramp [ræmp] rampe *f* (d'accès), passerelle *f*; *for raising vehicle* pont *m* élévateur

ram·page ['ræmpeɪdʒ] **1** *v/i* se déchaîner; **~ through the streets** tout saccager dans les rues **2** *n*: **go on the ~** tout saccager

ram·pant ['ræmpənt] *adj inflation* galopant

ram·part ['ræmpɑːrt] rempart *m*

ram·shack·le ['ræmʃækl] *adj* délabré

ran [ræn] *pret* → **run**

ranch [rænʃ] *n* ranch *m*

ranch·er ['rænʃər] propriétaire *m/f* de ranch

'ranch·hand employé *m* de ranch

ran·cid ['rænsɪd] *adj* rance

ran·cor, *Br* **ran·cour** ['ræŋkər] rancœur *f*

R & D [ɑːrən'diː] (= *research and development*) R&D *f* (= recherche et développement)

ran·dom ['rændəm] **1** *adj* aléatoire, au hasard; **~ sample** échantillon *m* pris au hasard; **~ violence** violence *f* aveugle **2** *n*: **at ~** au hasard

ran·dy ['rændɪ] *adj Br F* en manque F, excité

rang [ræŋ] *pret* → **ring**

range [reɪndʒ] **1** *n of products* gamme *f*; *of gun* portée *f*; *of airplane* autonomie *f*; *of voice, instrument* registre *m*; *of mountains* chaîne *f*; **at close ~** de près **2** *v/i*: **~ from X to Y** aller de X à Y

rang·er ['reɪndʒər] garde *m* forestier

rank [ræŋk] *n* **1** MIL grade *m*; *in society* rang *m*; **the ~s** MIL les hommes *mpl* de troupe **2** *v/t* classer

♦ **rank among** *v/t* compter parmi

ran·kle ['ræŋkl] *v/i* rester sur le cœur

ran·sack ['rænsæk] *v/t searching* fouiller; *plundering* saccager

ran·som ['rænsəm] *n money* rançon *f*; **hold s.o. to ~** *also fig* tenir qn en otage (contre une rançon)

'ran·som mon·ey rançon *f*

rant [rænt] *v/i*: **~ and rave** pester, tempêter

rap [ræp] **1** *n at door etc* petit coup *m* sec; MUS rap *m* **2** *v/t (pret & pp -ped) table etc* taper sur

♦ **rap at** *v/t window etc* frapper à

rape[^1] [reɪp] **1** *n* viol *m* **2** *v/t* violer

rape[^2] *n* BOT colza *m*

'rape vic·tim victime *f* d'un viol

rap·id ['ræpɪd] *adj* rapide

ra·pid·i·ty [rə'pɪdətɪ] rapidité *f*

rap·id·ly ['ræpɪdlɪ] *adv* rapidement

rap·ids ['ræpɪdz] *npl* rapides *mpl*

rap·ist ['reɪpɪst] violeur *m*

rap·port [ræ'pɔːr] relation *f*, rapports *mpl*

rap·ture ['ræptʃər]: **go into ~s over** s'extasier sur

rap·tur·ous ['ræptʃərəs] *adj welcome* enthousiaste; *applause* frénétique

rare [rer] *adj* rare; *steak* saignant, bleu

rare·ly ['rerlɪ] *adv* rarement

rar·i·ty ['rerətɪ] rareté *f*

ras·cal ['ræskl] coquin *m*

rash[^1] [ræʃ] *n* MED éruption *f* (cutanée)

rash[^2] [ræʃ] *adj action, behavior* imprudent, impétueux*

rash·ly ['ræʃlɪ] *adv* sans réflexion, sur un coup de tête

rasp·ber·ry ['ræzberɪ] framboise *f*

R

rat [ræt] *n* rat *m*

rate [reɪt] **1** *n* taux *m*; (*price*) tarif *m*; (*speed*) rythme *m*; **~ of interest** FIN taux *m* d'intérêt; **at this** ... à ce rythme; (*carrying on like this*) si ça continue comme ça; **at any ~** que pense-vous de ce vin? **2** *v/t* (*rank*) classer (among parmi); (*consider*) considérer (as comme); **how do you ~ this wine?** que pensez-vous de ce vin?

rather ['rɑːðər] *adv* (*fairly, quite*) plutôt; **I would ~ stay here** je préférerais rester ici; **or would you ~ ...?** ou voulez-vous plutôt ...?

rat·i·fi·ca·tion [rætɪfɪ'keɪʃn] *of treaty* ratification *f*

rat·i·fy ['rætɪfaɪ] *v/t* (*pret & pp -ied*) ratifier

rat·ings ['reɪtɪŋz] *npl* indice *m* d'écoute

ra·tio ['reɪʃɪoʊ] rapport *m*, proportion *f*

ra·tion ['ræʃn] **1** *n* ration *f* **2** *v/t supplies* rationner

ra·tion·al ['ræʃənl] *adj* rationnel*

ra·tion·al·i·ty [ræʃə'nælɪtɪ] rationalité *f*

ra·tion·al·i·za·tion [ræʃənəlar'zeɪʃn] rationalisation *f*

ra·tion·al·ize ['ræʃənəlaɪz] **1** *v/t* rationaliser **2** *v/i* (se) chercher des excuses

ra·tion·al·ly ['ræʃənlɪ] *adv* rationnellement

'**rat race** jungle *f*; **get out of the ~** sortir du système

rat·tle ['rætl] **1** *n of bottles, chains* cliquetis *m*; *in engine* bruit *m* de ferraille; *of windows* vibration *f*; *toy* hochet *m* **2** *v/t chains etc* entrechoquer, faire du bruit avec **3** *v/i* faire du bruit; *of engine* faire un bruit de ferraille; *of crates, bottles* s'entrechoquer; *of chains* cliqueter

◆ **rattle off** *v/t poem, list of names* débiter à toute vitesse

◆ **rattle through** *v/t* expédier

'**rat·tle·snake** serpent *m* à sonnette

rau·cous ['rɔːkəs] *adj laughter, party* bruyant

rav·age ['rævɪdʒ] **1** *n:* **the ~s of time** les ravages *mpl* du temps **2** *v/t:* **~d by war** ravagé par la guerre

rave [reɪv] **1** *n party* rave *f*, rave-party *f* **2** *v/i* délirer; **~ about sth** (*be very enthusiastic*) s'emballer pour qch

ra·ven ['reɪvn] corbeau *m*

rav·e·nous ['rævənəs] *adj* affamé; *appetite* féroce, vorace

'**rave re·view** critique *f* élogieuse

ra·vine [rə'viːn] ravin *m*

rav·ing ['reɪvɪŋ] *adv:* **~ mad** fou à lier

rav·ish·ing ['rævɪʃɪŋ] *adj* ravissant

raw [rɔː] *adj meat, vegetable* cru; *sugar, iron* brut

raw ma·te·ri·als *npl* matières *fpl* premières

ray [reɪ] rayon *m*; **a ~ of hope** une lueur d'espoir

raze [reɪz] *v/t:* **~ to the ground** raser

ra·zor ['reɪzər] rasoir *m*

'**ra·zor blade** lame *f* de rasoir

re [riː] *prep* COMM en référence à; **~:** ... objet: ...

reach [riːtʃ] **1** *n:* **within ~** à portée; **out of ~** hors de portée **2** *v/t* atteindre; *destination* arriver à; (*go as far as*) arriver (jusqu')à; *decision, agreement* aboutir à, parvenir à

◆ **reach out** *v/i* tendre la main / le bras

re·act [rɪ'ækt] *v/i* réagir

re·ac·tion [rɪ'ækʃn] réaction *f*

re·ac·tion·ar·y [rɪ'ækʃnrɪ] **1** *adj* POL réactionnaire, réac F *inv in feminine* **2** *n* POL réactionnaire *m/f*, réac *m/f* F

re·ac·tor [rɪ'æktər] *nuclear* réacteur *m*

read [riːd] *v/t* (*pret & pp* **read** [red]) *also* COMPUT lire **2** *v/i* lire; **~ to s.o.** faire la lecture à qn

◆ **read out** *v/t aloud* lire à haute voix

◆ **read up on** *v/t* étudier

read·a·ble ['riːdəbl] *adj* lisible

read·er ['riːdər] *person* lecteur(-trice) *m(f)*

read·i·ly ['redɪlɪ] *adv admit, agree* volontiers, de bon cœur

read·i·ness ['redɪnɪs] *to agree, help* empressement *m*, bonne volonté *f*; **be in (a state of) ~** être prêt

read·ing ['riːdɪŋ] *activity* lecture *f*; *from meter etc* relevé *m*

'**read·ing mat·ter** lecture *f*

recap

re·ad·just [riːəˈdʒʌst] **1** *v/t equipment, controls* régler (de nouveau) **2** *v/i to conditions* se réadapter (**to** à)

read-'on·ly file COMPUT fichier *m* en lecture seule

read-'on·ly mem·o·ry COMPUT mémoire *f* morte

read·y [ˈredɪ] *adj (prepared, willing)* prêt; **get (o.s.) ~** se préparer; **get sth ~** préparer qch

read·y 'cash (argent *m*) liquide *m*; **'read·y-made** *adj stew etc* cuisiné; *solution* tout trouvé; **read·y-to-'wear** *adj* de confection; **~ clothing** prêt-à-porter *m*

real [riːl] *adj not imaginary* réel*; *not fake* vrai, véritable

'real es·tate immobilier *m*, biens *mpl* immobiliers

'real es·tate a·gent agent *m* immobilier

re·al·ism [ˈrɪəlɪzəm] réalisme *m*

re·al·ist [ˈrɪəlɪst] réaliste *m/f*

re·al·is·tic [rɪəˈlɪstɪk] *adj* réaliste

re·al·is·tic·al·ly [rɪəˈlɪstɪklɪ] *adv* de façon réaliste

re·al·i·ty [rɪˈælətɪ] réalité *f*

re'al·i·ty TV télé-réalité *f*

re·al·i·za·tion [rɪəlaɪˈzeɪʃn] *of hopes etc* réalisation *f*; *(awareness)* prise *f* de conscience; **come to the ~ that ...** se mettre à comprendre que ...

re·al·ize [ˈrɪəlaɪz] *v/t* se rendre compte de, prendre conscience de; FIN réaliser; **the sale ~d $50m** la vente a rapporté 50 millions de dollars; **I ~ now that ...** je me rends compte maintenant que ...

real·ly [ˈrɪəlɪ] *adv* vraiment; **not ~** pas vraiment

'real time COMPUT temps *m* réel

'real-time *adj* COMPUT en temps réel

re·al·tor [ˈriːltər] agent *m* immobilier

re·al·ty [ˈriːltɪ] immobilier *m*, biens *mpl* immobiliers

reap [riːp] *v/t* moissonner; *fig* récolter

re·ap·pear [riːəˈpɪr] *v/i* réapparaître

re·ap·pear·ance [riːəˈpɪrəns] réapparition *f*

rear [rɪr] **1** *adj* arrière *inv*, de derrière **2** *n* arrière *m*

rear 'end F *of person* derrière *m*

'rear-end *v/t* F: **be ~ed** se faire rentrer dedans (par derrière) F

'rear light *of car* feu *m* arrière

re·arm [riːˈɑːrm] *v/t & v/i* réarmer

'rear·most *adj* dernier*, du fond

re·ar·range [riːəˈreɪndʒ] *v/t flowers* réarranger; *furniture* déplacer, changer de place; *schedule, meetings* réorganiser

rear-view 'mir·ror rétroviseur *m*, rétro *m* F

rea·son [ˈriːzn] **1** *n (cause), faculty* raison *f*; **see / listen to ~** entendre raison, se rendre à la raison **2** *v/i*: **~ with s.o.** raisonner qn

rea·so·na·ble [ˈriːznəbl] *adj person, behavior, price* raisonnable; **a ~ number of people** un certain nombre de gens

rea·son·a·bly [ˈriːznəblɪ] *adv act, behave* raisonnablement; *(quite)* relativement

rea·son·ing [ˈriːznɪŋ] raisonnement *m*

re·as·sure [riːəˈʃur] *v/t* rassurer

re·as·sur·ing [riːəˈʃurɪŋ] *adj* rassurant

re·bate [ˈriːbeɪt] *(refund)* remboursement *m*

reb·el¹ [ˈrebl] *n* rebelle *m/f*; **~ troops** troupes *fpl* rebelles

re·bel² [rɪˈbel] *v/i (pret & pp -led)* se rebeller, se révolter

re·bel·lion [rɪˈbeljən] rébellion *f*

re·bel·lious [rɪˈbeljəs] *adj* rebelle

re·bel·lious·ly [rɪˈbeljəslɪ] *adv* de façon rebelle

re·bel·lious·ness [rɪˈbeljəsnɪs] esprit *m* de rébellion

re·bound [rɪˈbaund] *v/i of ball etc* rebondir

re·buff [rɪˈbʌf] *n* rebuffade *f*

re·build [riːˈbɪld] *v/t (pret & pp -built)* reconstruire

re·buke [rɪˈbjuːk] *v/t* blâmer

re·call [rɪˈkɔːl] *v/t goods, ambassador* rappeler; *(remember)* se souvenir de, se rappeler (**that** que); **I don't ~ saying that** je ne me rappelle pas avoir dit cela

re·cap [ˈriːkæp] *v/i (pret & pp -ped)* récapituler

R

re·cap·ture [riːˈkæptʃər] *v/t* reprendre

re·cede [rɪˈsiːd] *v/i of flood waters* baisser, descendre; *of sea* se retirer

re·ced·ing [rɪˈsiːdɪŋ] *adj forehead, chin* fuyant; **have a ~ hairline** se dégarnir

re·ceipt [rɪˈsiːt] *for purchase* reçu *m* (**for** de), ticket *m* de caisse; **acknowl·edge ~ of sth** accuser réception de qch; **~s** FIN recette(s) *f(pl)*

re·ceive [rɪˈsiːv] *v/t* recevoir

re·ceiv·er [rɪˈsiːvər] TELEC combiné *m*; *for radio* (poste *m*) récepteur *m*; **pick up / replace the ~** décrocher / raccrocher

re·ceiv·er·ship [rɪˈsiːvərʃɪp] *be in ~* être en liquidation judiciaire

re·cent [ˈriːsnt] *adj* récent

re·cent·ly [ˈriːsntlɪ] *adv* récemment

re·cep·tion [rɪˈsepʃn] réception *f*; *(welcome)* accueil *m*

re·cep·tion desk réception *f*

re·cep·tion·ist [rɪˈsepʃnɪst] réceptionniste *m/f*

re·cep·tive [rɪˈseptɪv] *adj*: **be ~ to sth** être réceptif à qch

re·cess [ˈriːses] *n in wall etc* renfoncement *m*, recoin *m*; EDU récréation *f*; *of legislature* vacances *fpl* judiciaires

re·ces·sion [rɪˈseʃn] *economic* récession *f*

re·charge [riːˈtʃɑːrdʒ] *v/t battery* recharger

re·ci·pe [ˈresəpɪ] recette *f*

're·ci·pe book livre *m* de recettes

re·cip·i·ent [rɪˈsɪpɪənt] *of parcel etc* destinataire *m/f*; *of payment* bénéficiaire *m/f*

re·cip·ro·cal [rɪˈsɪprəkl] *adj* réciproque

re·cit·al [rɪˈsaɪtl] MUS récital *m*

re·cite [rɪˈsaɪt] *v/t poem* réciter; *details, facts* énumérer

reck·less [ˈreklɪs] *adj* imprudent

reck·less·ly [ˈreklɪslɪ] *adv* imprudemment

reck·on [ˈrekən] *v/t* (*think, consider*) penser

♦ **reckon on** *v/t* compter sur

♦ **reckon with** *v/t*: **have s.o. / sth to reckon with** devoir compter avec qn / qch

reck·on·ing [ˈrekənɪŋ] calculs *mpl*; **by my ~** d'après mes calculs

re·claim [rɪˈkleɪm] *v/t land from sea* gagner sur la mer; *lost property* récupérer

re·cline [rɪˈklaɪn] *v/i* s'allonger

re·clin·er [rɪˈklaɪnər] *chair* chaise *f* longue, relax *m*

re·cluse [rɪˈkluːs] reclus *m*

rec·og·ni·tion [rekəɡˈnɪʃn] reconnaissance *f*; **changed beyond ~** méconnaissable

rec·og·niz·a·ble [rekəɡˈnaɪzəbl] *adj* reconnaissable

rec·og·nize [ˈrekəɡnaɪz] *v/t* reconnaître

re·coil [rɪˈkɔɪl] *v/i* reculer

rec·ol·lect [rekəˈlekt] *v/t* se souvenir de

rec·ol·lec·tion [rekəˈlekʃn] souvenir *m*

rec·om·mend [rekəˈmend] *v/t* recommander

rec·om·men·da·tion [rekəmenˈdeɪʃn] recommandation *f*

rec·om·pense [ˈrekəmpens] *n* compensation *f*, dédommagement *m*

rec·on·cile [ˈrekənsaɪl] *v/t* réconcilier; *differences* faire concorder; *facts* faire concorder; **~ o.s. to sth** se résigner à qch; **be ~d** *of two people* s'être réconcilié

rec·on·cil·i·a·tion [rekənsɪlɪˈeɪʃn] réconciliation *f*, *of differences, facts* conciliation *f*

re·con·di·tion [riːkənˈdɪʃn] *v/t* refaire, remettre à neuf

re·con·nais·sance [rɪˈkɑːnɪsəns] MIL reconnaissance *f*

re·con·sid·er [riːkənˈsɪdər] **1** *v/t* reconsidérer **2** *v/i* reconsidérer la question

re·con·struct [riːkənˈstrʌkt] *v/t* reconstruire; *crime* reconstituer

re·cord[1] [ˈrekərd] *n* MUS disque *m*; SP *etc* record *m*; *written document etc* rapport *m*; *in database* article *m*, enregistrement *m*; **~s** (*archives*) archives *fpl*, dossiers *mpl*; **keep a ~ of sth** garder une trace de qch; **say sth off the ~** dire qch officieusement; **have a criminal ~** avoir un casier judiciaire;

have a good ~ for avoir une bonne réputation en matière de

record² [rɪˈkɔːrd] *v/t electronically* enregistrer; *in writing* consigner

'rec·ord-break·ing *adj* record *inv*, qui bat tous les records

re·cor·der [rɪˈkɔːrdər] MUS flûte *f* à bec

'rec·ord hold·er recordman *m*, recordwoman *f*

re·cord·ing [rɪˈkɔːrdɪŋ] enregistrement *m*

re'cord·ing stu·di·o studio *m* d'enregistrement

'rec·ord play·er platine *f* (tourne-disque)

re·count [rɪˈkaunt] *v/t (tell)* raconter

re·count [ˈriːkaunt] **1** *n of votes* recompte *m* **2** *v/t* recompter

re·coup [rɪˈkuːp] *v/t financial losses* récupérer

re·cov·er [rɪˈkʌvər] **1** *v/t* retrouver **2** *v/i from illness* se remettre; *of economy, business* reprendre

re·cov·er·y [rɪˈkʌvərɪ] *of sth* récupération *f*; *from illness* rétablissement *m*; *he has made a good ~* il s'est bien remis

rec·re·a·tion [rekrɪˈeɪʃn] récréation *f*

rec·re·a·tion·al [rekrɪˈeɪʃnl] *adj done for pleasure* de loisirs; *~ drug* drogue *f* récréative

re·cruit [rɪˈkruːt] **1** *n* recrue *f* **2** *v/t* recruter

re·cruit·ment [rɪˈkruːtmənt] recrutement *m*

rec·tan·gle [ˈrektæŋgl] rectangle *m*

rec·tan·gu·lar [rekˈtæŋgjʊlər] *adj* rectangulaire

rec·ti·fy [ˈrektɪfaɪ] *v/t (pret & pp -ied)* rectifier

re·cu·pe·rate [rɪˈkuːpəreɪt] *v/i* récupérer

re·cur [rɪˈkɜːr] *v/i (pret & pp -red) of error, event* se reproduire, se répéter; *of symptoms* réapparaître

re·cur·rent [rɪˈkʌrənt] *adj* récurrent

re·cy·cla·ble [riːˈsaɪkləbl] *adj* recyclable

re·cy·cle [riːˈsaɪkl] *v/t* recycler

re·cy·cling [riːˈsaɪklɪŋ] recyclage *m*

---

red [red] **1** *adj* rouge **2** *n:* **in the ~** FIN dans le rouge

Red 'Cross Croix-Rouge *f*

re·dec·o·rate [riːˈdekəreɪt] *v/t* refaire

re·deem [rɪˈdiːm] *v/t debt* rembourser; *sinners* racheter

re·deem·ing [rɪˈdiːmɪŋ] *adj: his one ~ feature* sa seule qualité

re·demp·tion [rɪˈdempʃn] REL rédemption *f*

re·de·vel·op [riːdɪˈveləp] *v/t part of town* réaménager, réhabiliter

red-handed [redˈhændɪd] *adj: catch s.o. ~* prendre qn en flagrant délit; **'red·head** roux *m*, rousse *f*; **red-'hot** *adj* chauffé au rouge, brûlant; **red-'let·ter day** jour *m* mémorable, jour *m* à marquer d'une pierre blanche; **red 'light** *for traffic* feu *m* rouge; **red 'light dis·trict** quartier *m* chaud; **red 'meat** viande *f* rouge; **'red·neck** F plouc *m* F

re·dou·ble [riːˈdʌbl] *v/t: ~ one's efforts* redoubler ses efforts

red 'pep·per poivron *m* rouge

red 'tape F paperasserie *f*

re·duce [rɪˈduːs] *v/t* réduire; diminuer

re·duc·tion [rɪˈdʌkʃn] réduction *f*; diminution *f*

re·dun·dant [rɪˈdʌndənt] *adj (unnecessary)* redondant; *be made ~ Br. at work* être licencié

reed [riːd] BOT roseau *m*

reef [riːf] *in sea* récif *m*

'reef knot *Br* nœud *m* plat

reek [riːk] *v/i* empester (*of sth* qch), puer (*of sth* qch)

reel [riːl] *n of film, thread* bobine *f*

♦ **reel off** *v/t* débiter

re-e·lect *v/t* réélire

re-e·lec·tion réélection *f*

re-'en·try *of spacecraft* rentrée *f*

ref [ref] F arbitre *m*

re·fer [rɪˈfɜːr] **1** *v/t (pret & pp -red): ~ a decision / problem to s.o.* soumettre une décision / un problème à qn **2** *v/i (pret & pp -red): ~ to (allude to)* faire allusion à; *dictionary etc* se reporter à

ref·er·ee [refəˈriː] SP arbitre *m*; *for job:*

R

personne qui fournit des références

ref·er·ence ['refərəns] *(allusion)* allusion *f*; *for job* référence *f*; *(~ number)* (numéro *m* de) référence *f*; **with ~ to** en ce qui concerne

'**ref·er·ence book** ouvrage *m* de référence; '**ref·er·ence li·bra·ry** bibliothèque *f* d'ouvrages de référence; *in a library* salle *f* des références; '**ref·er·ence num·ber** numéro *m* de référence

ref·er·en·dum [refə'rendəm] référendum *m*

re·fill ['riːfɪl] *v/t tank, glass* remplir

re·fine [rɪ'faɪn] *v/t oil, sugar* raffiner; *technique* affiner

re·fined [rɪ'faɪnd] *adj manners, language* raffiné

re·fine·ment [rɪ'faɪnmənt] *to process, machine* perfectionnement *m*

re·fin·e·ry [rɪ'faɪnərɪ] raffinerie *f*

re·fla·tion [riː'fleɪʃn] relance *f*

re·flect [rɪ'flekt] **1** *v/t light* réfléchir, refléter; *fig* refléter; **be ~ed in** se réfléchir dans, se refléter dans **2** *v/i (think)* réfléchir

re·flec·tion [rɪ'flekʃn] *also fig* reflet *m*; *(consideration)* réflexion *f*; **on ~** après réflexion

re·flex ['riːfleks] *in body* réflexe *m*

'**re·flex re·ac·tion** réflexe *m*

re·form [rɪ'fɔːrm] **1** *n* réforme *f* **2** *v/t* réformer

re·form·er [rɪ'fɔːrmər] réformateur (-trice) *m(f)*

re·frain[1] [rɪ'freɪn] *v/i fml* s'abstenir *(from* de); *please ~ from smoking* prière de ne pas fumer

re·frain[2] [rɪ'freɪn] *n in song* refrain *m*

re·fresh [rɪ'freʃ] *v/t* rafraîchir; *of sleep, rest* reposer; *of meal* redonner des forces à; *feel ~ed* se sentir revigoré

re·fresh·er course [rɪ'freʃər] cours *m* de remise à niveau

re·fresh·ing [rɪ'freʃɪŋ] *adj drink* rafraîchissant; *experience* agréable

re·fresh·ments [rɪ'freʃmənts] *npl* rafraîchissements *mpl*

re·fri·ge·rate [rɪ'frɪdʒəreɪt] *v/t* réfrigérer; *keep ~d* conserver au réfrigérateur

re·fri·ge·ra·tor [rɪ'frɪdʒəreɪtər] réfrigérateur *m*

re·fu·el [riː'fjuəl] **1** *v/t airplane* ravitailler **2** *v/i of airplane* se ravitailler (en carburant)

ref·uge ['refjuːdʒ] refuge *m*; **take ~** *from storm etc* se réfugier

ref·u·gee [refjuˈdʒiː] réfugié(e) *m(f)*

ref·u·gee camp camp *m* de réfugiés

re·fund 1 *n* ['riːfʌnd] remboursement *m* **2** *v/t* [rɪ'fʌnd] rembourser

re·fus·al [rɪ'fjuːzl] refus *m*

re·fuse [rɪ'fjuːz] *v/t* refuser **2** *v/t* refuser; *~ s.o. sth* refuser qch à qn; *~ to do sth* refuser de faire qch

re·gain [rɪ'geɪn] *v/t control, territory, the lead* reprendre; *composure* retrouver

re·gal ['riːgl] *adj* royal

re·gard [rɪ'gɑːrd] **1** *n*: **have great ~ for s.o.** avoir beaucoup d'estime pour qn; *in this ~* à cet égard; **with ~ to** en ce qui concerne; *(kind)* **~s** cordialement; *give my ~s to Paula* transmettez mes amitiés à Paula; **with no ~ for** sans égard pour **2** *v/t*: *~ s.o. / sth as sth* considérer qn / qch comme qch; *as ~s* en ce qui concerne

re·gard·ing [rɪ'gɑːrdɪŋ] *prep* en ce qui concerne

re·gard·less [rɪ'gɑːrdlɪs] *adv* malgré tout, quand même; *~ of* sans se soucier de

re·gime [reɪ'ʒiːm] *(government)* régime *m*

re·gi·ment ['redʒɪmənt] *n* régiment *m*

re·gion ['riːdʒən] région *f*; *in the ~ of* environ

re·gion·al ['riːdʒənl] *adj* régional

re·gis·ter ['redʒɪstər] **1** *n* registre *m* 2 *v/t birth, death* déclarer; *vehicle* immatriculer; *letter* recommander; *emotion* exprimer; *send a letter ~ed* envoyer une lettre en recommandé **3** *v/i for a course* s'inscrire; *with police* se déclarer *(with* à)

re·gis·tered let·ter ['redʒɪstərd] lettre *f* recommandée

re·gis·tra·tion [redʒɪ'streɪʃn] *of birth, death* déclaration *f*; *of vehicle* immatriculation *f; for a course* inscription *f*

re·gis·tra·tion num·ber *Br* MOT numéro *m* d'immatriculation

re·gret [rɪ'gret] **1** *v/t (pret & pp -ted)* regretter **2** *n* regret *m*

re·gret·ful [rɪ'gretfəl] *adj* plein de regrets

re·gret·ful·ly [rɪ'gretfəlɪ] *adv* avec regret

re·gret·ta·ble [rɪ'gretəbl] *adj* regrettable

re·gret·ta·bly [rɪ'gretəblɪ] *adv* malheureusement

reg·u·lar ['regjʊlər] **1** *adj* régulier*; (*normal, ordinary*) normal **2** *n at bar etc* habitué(e) *m(f)*

reg·u·lar·i·ty [regjʊ'lærətɪ] régularité *f*

reg·u·lar·ly ['regjʊlərlɪ] *adv* régulièrement

reg·u·late ['regjʊleɪt] *v/t* régler; *expenditure* contrôler

reg·u·la·tion [regjʊ'leɪʃn] (*rule*) règlement *m*

re·hab ['riːhæb] F *of alcoholic etc* désintoxication *f*; *of criminal* réinsertion *f*; *of disabled or sick person* rééducation *f*

re·ha·bil·i·tate [riːhə'bɪlɪteɪt] *v/t ex-criminal* réinsérer; *disabled person* rééduquer

re·hears·al [rɪ'hɜːrsl] répétition *f*

re·hearse [rɪ'hɜːrs] *v/t & v/i* répéter

reign [reɪn] **1** *n* règne *m* **2** *v/i* régner

re·im·burse [riːɪm'bɜːrs] *v/t* rembourser

rein [reɪn] rêne *f*

re·in·car·na·tion [riːɪnkɑːr'neɪʃn] réincarnation *f*

re·in·force [riːɪn'fɔːrs] *v/t* renforcer; *argument* étayer

re·in·forced con·crete [riːɪn'fɔːrst] béton *m* armé

re·in·force·ments [riːɪn'fɔːrsmənts] *npl* MIL renforts *mpl*

re·in·state [riːɪn'steɪt] *v/t person in office* réintégrer, rétablir dans ses fonctions; *paragraph etc* réintroduire

re·it·e·rate [riː'ɪtəreɪt] *v/t* réitérer

re·ject [rɪ'dʒekt] *v/t* rejeter

re·jec·tion [rɪ'dʒekʃn] rejet *m*; *he felt a sense of ~* il s'est senti rejeté

re·lapse ['riːlæps] *n* MED rechute *f*; **have a ~** faire une rechute

re·late [rɪ'leɪt] **1** *v/t story* raconter; **~ X to Y** *connect* établir un rapport entre X et Y, associer X à Y **2** *v/i*: **~ to be connected with** se rapporter à; **he doesn't ~ to people** il a de la peine à communiquer avec les autres

re·lat·ed [rɪ'leɪtɪd] *adj by family* apparenté; *events, ideas etc* associé; **are you two ~?** êtes-vous de la même famille?

re·la·tion [rɪ'leɪʃn] *in family* parent(e) *m(f)*; (*connection*) rapport *m*, relation *f*; **business / diplomatic ~s** relations d'affaires / diplomatiques

re·la·tion·ship [rɪ'leɪʃnʃɪp] relation *f*; *sexual* liaison *f*, aventure *f*

rel·a·tive ['relətɪv] **1** *adj* relatif*; **X is ~ to Y** X dépend de Y **2** *n* parent(e) *m(f)*

rel·a·tive·ly ['relətɪvlɪ] *adv* relativement

re·lax [rɪ'læks] **1** *v/i* se détendre; **~!, don't get angry** du calme! ne t'énerve pas **2** *v/t muscle* relâcher, décontracter; *rules etc* assouplir

re·lax·a·tion [riːlæk'seɪʃn] détente *f*, relaxation *f*; *of rules etc* assouplissement *m*

re·laxed [rɪ'lækst] *adj* détendu, décontracté

re·lax·ing [rɪ'læksɪŋ] *adj* reposant, relaxant

re·lay[1] ['riːleɪ] *v/t message* transmettre; *radio, TV signals* relayer, retransmettre

re·lay[2] ['riːleɪ] *n*: **~ (race)** (course *f* de) relais *m*

re·lease [rɪ'liːs] **1** *n from prison* libération *f*; *of CD, movie etc* sortie *f*; *CD, record* album *m*, nouveauté *f*; *movie* film *m*, nouveauté *f* **2** *v/t prisoner* libérer; *CD, record, movie* sortir; *parking brake* desserrer; *information* communiquer

rel·e·gate ['relɪgeɪt] *v/t* reléguer

re·lent [rɪ'lent] *v/i* se calmer, se radoucir

re·lent·less [rɪ'lentlɪs] *adj* (*determined*) acharné; *rain etc* incessant

R

re·lent·less·ly [rɪ'lentlɪslɪ] adv (*tirelessly*) avec acharnement; *rain* sans cesse

rel·e·vance ['reləvəns] pertinence f, rapport m

rel·e·vant ['reləvənt] adj pertinent; *it's not ~ to our problem* ça n'a rien à voir avec notre problème

re·li·a·bil·i·ty [rɪlaɪə'bɪlɪtɪ] fiabilité f

re·li·a·ble [rɪ'laɪəbl] adj fiable

re·li·a·bly [rɪ'laɪəblɪ] adv: *I am ~ informed that …* je sais de source sûre que …

re·li·ance [rɪ'laɪəns] on person, information confiance f (on en); on equipment etc dépendance f (on vis-à-vis de)

re·li·ant [rɪ'laɪənt] adj: *be ~ on* dépendre de

rel·ic ['relɪk] relique f

re·lief [rɪ'liːf] soulagement m; *that's a ~* c'est un soulagement; *in ~ in art* en relief

re·lieve [rɪ'liːv] v/t pressure, pain soulager, alléger; (*take over from*) relayer, relever; *be ~d at news etc* être soulagé

re·li·gion [rɪ'lɪdʒən] religion f

re·li·gious [rɪ'lɪdʒəs] adj religieux*; person croyant, pieux*

re·li·gious·ly [rɪ'lɪdʒəslɪ] adv (*conscientiously*) religieusement

re·lin·quish [rɪ'lɪŋkwɪʃ] v/t abandonner

rel·ish ['relɪʃ] **1** n sauce relish f, (*enjoyment*) délectation f **2** v/t idea, prospect se réjouir de

re·live [riː'lɪv] v/t past, event revivre

re·lo·cate [riːlə'keɪt] v/i of business déménager, se réimplanter; of employee être muté

re·lo·ca·tion [riːlə'keɪʃn] of business délocalisation f, réimplantation f; of employee mutation f

re·luc·tance [rɪ'lʌktəns] réticence f, répugnance f

re·luc·tant [rɪ'lʌktənt] adj réticent, hésitant; *be ~ to do sth* hésiter à faire qch

re·luc·tant·ly [rɪ'lʌktəntlɪ] adv avec réticence, à contrecœur

♦ **re·ly on** [rɪ'laɪ] v/t (*pret & pp -ied*)

compter sur, faire confiance à; *rely on s.o. to do sth* compter sur qn pour faire qch

re·main [rɪ'meɪn] v/i rester; *~ silent* garder le silence

re·main·der [rɪ'meɪndər] **1** n also MATH reste m **2** v/t book solder

re·main·ing [rɪ'meɪnɪŋ] adj restant; *the ~ refugees* le reste des réfugiés

re·mains [rɪ'meɪnz] npl of body restes mpl

re·make ['riːmeɪk] n of movie remake m, nouvelle version f

re·mand [rɪ'mænd] **1** n: *be on ~ in prison* être en détention provisoire; *on bail* être en liberté provisoire **2** v/t: *~ s.o. in custody* placer qn en détention provisoire

re·mark [rɪ'mɑːrk] **1** n remarque f **2** v/t (*comment*) faire remarquer

re·mark·a·ble [rɪ'mɑːrkəbl] adj remarquable

re·mark·a·bly [rɪ'mɑːrkəblɪ] adv remarquablement

re·mar·ry [riː'mærɪ] v/i (*pret & pp -ied*) se remarier

rem·e·dy ['remədɪ] n MED, fig remède m

re·mem·ber [rɪ'membər] **1** v/t se souvenir de, se rappeler; *~ to lock the door!* n'oublie pas de fermer la porte à clef!; *~ me to her* transmettez-lui mon bon souvenir **2** v/i se souvenir; *I don't ~* je ne me souviens pas

re·mind [rɪ'maɪnd] v/t: *~ s.o. to do sth* rappeler à qn de faire qch; *~ X of Y* rappeler Y à X; *you ~ me of your father* tu me rappelles ton père; *~ s.o. of sth (bring to their attention)* rappeler qch à qn

re·mind·er [rɪ'maɪndər] rappel m

rem·i·nisce [remɪ'nɪs] v/i évoquer le passé

rem·i·nis·cent [remɪ'nɪsənt] adj: *be ~ of sth* rappeler qch, faire penser à qch

re·miss [rɪ'mɪs] adj fml négligent

re·mis·sion [rɪ'mɪʃn] MED rémission f; *go into ~ of patient* être en sursis

rem·nant ['remnənt] vestige m, reste m

repellent

re·morse [rɪ'mɔːrs] remords *m*

re·morse·less [rɪ'mɔːrslɪs] *adj* impitoyable; *demands* incessant

re·mote [rɪ'mout] *adj village* isolé; *possibility, connection* vague; *ancestor* lointain; *(aloof)* distant

re·mote 'ac·cess COMPUT accès *m* à distance

re·mote con'trol *also for TV* télécommande *f*

re·mote·ly [rɪ'moutlɪ] *adv related, connected* vaguement; **I'm not ~ interested** je ne suis pas du tout intéressé; **it's just ~ possible** c'est tout juste possible

re·mote·ness [rɪ'moutnəs] isolement *m*

re·mov·a·ble [rɪ'muːvəbl] *adj* amovible

re·mov·al [rɪ'muːvl] enlèvement *m*; *of unwanted hair* épilation *f*; *of demonstrators* expulsion *f*; *of doubt* dissipation *f*; **~ of stains** détachage *m*

re·move [rɪ'muːv] *v/t* enlever; *demonstrators* expulser; *doubt, suspicion* dissiper

re·mu·ner·a·tion [rɪmjuːnə'reɪʃn] rémunération *f*

re·mu·ner·a·tive [rɪ'mjuːnərətɪv] *adj* rémunérateur

Re·nais·sance [rɪ'neɪsəns] Renaissance *f*

re·name [riː'neɪm] *v/t* rebaptiser; *file* renommer

ren·der ['rendər] *v/t* rendre; **~ s.o. helpless** laisser qn sans défense; **~ s.o. unconscious** faire perdre connaissance à qn

ren·der·ing ['rendərɪŋ] *of piece of music* interprétation *f*

ren·dez·vous ['rɑːndeɪvuː] *n* rendez-vous *m*

re·new [rɪ'nuː] *v/t contract, license* renouveler; *discussion* reprendre

re·new·a·ble [rɪ'nuːəbl] *adj resource* renouvelable

re·new·al [rɪ'nuːəl] *of contract etc* renouvellement *m*; *of talks* reprise *f*

re·nounce [rɪ'nauns] *v/t title, rights* renoncer à

ren·o·vate ['renəveɪt] *v/t* rénover

ren·o·va·tion [renə'veɪʃn] rénovation *f*

re·nown [rɪ'naun] renommée *f*; renom *m*

re·nowned [rɪ'naund] *adj* renommé; réputé

rent [rent] **1** *n* loyer *m*; **for ~** à louer **2** *v/t* louer

rent·al ['rentl] *for apartment* loyer *m*; *for TV, car* location *f*

'rent·al a·gree·ment contrat *m* de location

'rent·al car voiture *f* de location

rent-'free *adv* sans payer de loyer

re·o·pen [riː'oupn] **1** *v/t business, store, case* rouvrir; *negotiations* reprendre **2** *v/i store etc* rouvrir

re·or·gan·i·za·tion [riːɔːrgənaɪ'zeɪʃn] réorganisation *f*

re·or·gan·ize [riː'ɔːrgənaɪz] *v/t* réorganiser

rep [rep] COMM représentant(e) *m(f)* (de commerce)

re·paint [riː'peɪnt] *v/t* repeindre

re·pair [rɪ'per] **1** *v/t* réparer **2** *n* réparation *f*; **in a good / bad state of ~** en bon / mauvais état

re'pair·man réparateur *m*

re·pa·tri·ate [riː'pætrieɪt] *v/t* rapatrier

re·pa·tri·a·tion [riːpætrɪ'eɪʃn] rapatriement *m*

re·pay [riː'peɪ] *v/t (pret & pp* **-paid**) rembourser

re·pay·ment [riː'peɪmənt] remboursement *m*

re·peal [rɪ'piːl] *v/t law* abroger

re·peat [rɪ'piːt] **1** *v/t* répéter; *performance, experiment* renouveler; **am I ~ing myself?** est-ce que je me répète? **2** *n TV program etc* rediffusion *f*

re·peat 'busi·ness COMM: **get ~** recevoir de nouvelles commandes (d'un client)

re·peat·ed [rɪ'piːtɪd] *adj* répété

re·peat·ed·ly [rɪ'piːtɪdlɪ] *adv* à plusieurs reprises

re·pel [rɪ'pel] *v/t (pret & pp* **-led**) repousser; *(disgust)* dégoûter

re·pel·lent [rɪ'pelənt] **1** *adj* repoussant, répugnant **2** *n (insect ~)* répulsif *m*

R

re·pent [rɪ'pent] *v/i* se repentir (*of* de)

re·per·cus·sions [ri:pər'kʌʃnz] *npl* répercussions *fpl*

rep·er·toire ['repərtwɑːr] répertoire *m*

rep·e·ti·tion [repɪ'tɪʃn] répétition *f*

re·pet·i·tive [rɪ'petɪtɪv] *adj* répétitif*

re·place [rɪ'pleɪs] *v/t* (*put back*) remettre; (*take the place of*) remplacer

re·place·ment [rɪ'pleɪsmənt] *person* remplaçant *m*; *product* produit *m* de remplacement

re·place·ment 'part pièce *f* de rechange

re·play ['riːpleɪ] **1** *n recording* relecture *f*, replay *m*; *match* nouvelle rencontre *f*, replay *m* **2** *v/t match* rejouer

re·plen·ish [rɪ'plenɪʃ] *v/t container* remplir (de nouveau); *supplies* refaire; **~ one's supplies of sth** se réapprovisionner en qch

rep·li·ca ['replɪkə] réplique *f*

re·ply [rɪ'plaɪ] **1** *n* réponse *f* **2** *v/t & v/i* (*pret & pp* **-ied**) répondre

re·port [rɪ'pɔːrt] **1** *n* (*account*) rapport *m*, compte-rendu *m*; *in newspaper* bulletin *m* **2** *v/t facts* rapporter; *to authorities* déclarer, signaler; **~ one's findings to s.o.** rendre compte des résultats de ses recherches à qn; **~ s.o. to the police** dénoncer qn à la police; **he is ~ed to be in Washington** il serait à Washington, on dit qu'il est à Washington **3** *v/i* (*present o.s.*) se présenter; **this is Joe Jordan ~ing from Moscow** de Moscou, Joe Jordan

♦ **report to** *v/t in business* être sous les ordres de; **who do you report to?** qui est votre supérieur (hiérarchique)?

re'port card bulletin *m* scolaire

re·port·er [rɪ'pɔːrtər] reporter *m/f*

re·pos·sess [riːpə'zes] *v/t* COMM reprendre possession de, saisir

rep·re·hen·si·ble [reprɪ'hensəbl] *adj* répréhensible

rep·re·sent [reprɪ'zent] *v/t* représenter

Rep·re·sen·ta·tive [reprɪ'zentətɪv] POL député *m*

rep·re·sen·ta·tive [reprɪ'zentətɪv] **1** *adj* (*typical*) représentatif* **2** *n* représentant(e) *m(f)*

re·press [rɪ'pres] *v/t* réprimer

re·pres·sion [rɪ'preʃn] POL répression *f*

re·pres·sive [rɪ'presɪv] *adj* POL répressif*

re·prieve [rɪ'priːv] **1** *n* LAW sursis *m*; *fig also* répit *m* **2** *v/t prisoner* accorder un sursis à

rep·ri·mand ['reprɪmænd] *v/t* réprimander

re·print ['riːprɪnt] **1** *n* réimpression *f* **2** *v/t* réimprimer

re·pri·sal [rɪ'praɪzl] représailles *fpl*; **take ~s** se venger, exercer des représailles; **in ~** en représailles à

re·proach [rɪ'proʊtʃ] **1** *n* reproche *m*; **be beyond ~** être irréprochable **2** *v/t* reprocher; **~ s.o. for sth** reprocher qch à qn

re·proach·ful [rɪ'proʊtfəl] *adj* réprobateur*, chargé de reproche

re·proach·ful·ly [rɪ'proʊtfəlɪ] *adv look* avec un air de reproche; *say* sur un ton de reproche

re·pro·duce [riːprə'duːs] **1** *v/t* reproduire **2** *v/i* BIOL se reproduire

re·pro·duc·tion [riːprə'dʌkʃn] reproduction *f*; *piece of furniture* copie *f*

re·pro·duc·tive [riprə'dʌktɪv] *adj* BIOL reproducteur*

rep·tile ['reptaɪl] reptile *m*

re·pub·lic [rɪ'pʌblɪk] république *f*

Re·pub·li·can [rɪ'pʌblɪkən] **1** *adj* républicain **2** *n* Républicain(e) *m(f)*

re·pu·di·ate [rɪ'pjuːdɪeɪt] *v/t* (*deny*) nier

re·pul·sive [rɪ'pʌlsɪv] *adj* repoussant, répugnant

rep·u·ta·ble ['repjʊtəbl] *adj* de bonne réputation, respectable

rep·u·ta·tion [repjʊ'teɪʃn] réputation *f*; **have a good / bad ~** avoir bonne / mauvaise réputation

re·put·ed [rɪ'pjuːtəd] *adj*: **be ~ to be** avoir la réputation d'être

re·put·ed·ly [rɪ'pjuːtədlɪ] *adv* à ce que l'on dit, apparemment

re·quest [rɪ'kwest] **1** *n* demande *f*; **on ~** sur demande **2** *v/t* demander

re·qui·em ['rekwɪəm] MUS requiem *m*

re·quire [rɪˈkwaɪr] v/t (need) avoir besoin de; *it ~s great care* cela demande beaucoup de soin; *as ~d by law* comme l'exige la loi; *guests are ~d to ...* les clients sont priés de ...

re·quired [rɪˈkwaɪrd] adj (necessary) requis; *~ reading* ouvrage(s) m(pl) au programme

re·quire·ment [rɪˈkwaɪrmənt] n (need) besoin m, exigence f, (condition) condition f (requise)

req·ui·si·tion [rekwɪˈzɪʃn] v/t réquisitionner

re·route [riːˈruːt] v/t airplane etc dérouter

re·run [ˈriːrʌn] 1 n of TV program rediffusion f 2 v/t (pret -ran, pp -run) tape repasser

re·sched·ule [riːˈskedjuːl] v/t changer l'heure / la date de

res·cue [ˈreskjuː] 1 n sauvetage m; *come to s.o.'s ~* venir au secours de qn 2 v/t sauver, secourir

'res·cue par·ty équipe f de secours

re·search [rɪˈsɜːrtʃ] n recherche f
♦ **research into** v/t faire des recherches sur

research and de·vel·op·ment recherche f et développement

re'search as·sis·tant assistant(e) m(f) de recherche

re·search·er [rɪˈsɜːrtʃər] chercheur (-euse) m(f)

're·search proj·ect projet m de recherche

re·sem·blance [rɪˈzembləns] ressemblance f

re·sem·ble [rɪˈzembl] v/t ressembler à

re·sent [rɪˈzent] v/t ne pas aimer; *person also* en vouloir à

re·sent·ful [rɪˈzentfəl] adj plein de ressentiment

re·sent·ful·ly [rɪˈzentfəlɪ] adv say avec ressentiment

re·sent·ment [rɪˈzentmənt] ressentiment m (of par rapport à)

res·er·va·tion [rezərˈveɪʃn] of room, table réservation f; mental, (special area) réserve f; *I have a ~* in hotel, restaurant j'ai réservé

re·serve [rɪˈzɜːrv] 1 n (store, aloofness) réserve f; SP remplaçant(e) m(f); *~s* FIN réserves fpl; *keep sth in ~* garder qch en réserve 2 v/t seat, judgment réserver

re·served [rɪˈzɜːrvd] adj table, manner réservé

res·er·voir [ˈrezərvwɑːr] for water réservoir m

re·shuf·fle [ˈriːʃʌfl] Br POL 1 n remaniement m 2 v/t remanier

re·side [rɪˈzaɪd] v/i fml résider

res·i·dence [ˈrezɪdəns] fml: house etc résidence f; (stay) séjour m

'res·i·dence per·mit permis m de séjour

res·i·dent [ˈrezɪdənt] 1 adj manager etc qui habite sur place 2 n résident(e) m(f), habitant(e) m(f); on street riverain(e) m(f); in hotel client(e) m(f); pensionnaire m/f

res·i·den·tial [rezɪˈdenʃl] adj résidentiel*

res·i·due [ˈrezɪduː] résidu m

re·sign [rɪˈzaɪn] 1 v/t position démissionner de; *~ o.s. to* se résigner à 2 v/i from job démissionner

res·ig·na·tion [rezɪgˈneɪʃn] from job démission f; mental résignation f

re·signed [rɪˈzaɪnd] adj résigné; *we have become ~ to the fact that ...* nous nous sommes résignés au fait que ...

re·sil·i·ent [rɪˈzɪliənt] adj personality fort; material résistant

res·in [ˈrezɪn] résine f

re·sist [rɪˈzɪst] 1 v/t résister à; new measures s'opposer à 2 v/i résister

re·sis·tance [rɪˈzɪstəns] résistance f

re·sis·tant [rɪˈzɪstənt] adj material résistant

res·o·lute [ˈrezəluːt] adj résolu

res·o·lu·tion [rezəˈluːʃn] résolution f

re·solve [rɪˈzɑːlv] v/t mystery résoudre; *~ to do sth* se résoudre à faire qch

re·sort [rɪˈzɔːrt] n place lieu m de vacances; at seaside station f balnéaire; for health cures station f thermale; *as a last ~* en dernier ressort or recours
♦ **resort to** v/t avoir recours à, recourir à

♦ **re-sound with** [rɪ'zaʊnd] v/t résonner de

re-sound-ing [rɪ'zaʊndɪŋ] adj success, victory retentissant

re-source [rɪ'sɔːrs] ressource f; **be left to one's own ~s** être livré à soi-même

re-source-ful [rɪ'sɔːrsfʊl] adj ingénieux*

re-spect [rɪ'spekt] **1** n respect m; **show ~ to** montrer du respect pour; **with / that ~ to** en ce qui concerne; **in this / that ~** à cet égard; **in many ~s** à bien des égards; **pay one's last ~s to s.o.** rendre un dernier hommage à qn **2** v/t respecter

re-spect-a-bil-i-ty [rɪspektə'bɪlətɪ] respectabilité f

re-spect-a-ble [rɪ'spektəbl] adj respectable

re-spec-ta-bly [rɪ'spektəblɪ] adv convenablement, comme il faut

re-spect-ful [rɪ'spektfəl] adj respectueux*

re-spect-ful-ly [rɪ'spektflɪ] adv respectueusement

re-spec-tive [rɪ'spektɪv] adj respectif*

re-spec-tive-ly [rɪ'spektɪvlɪ] adv respectivement

res-pi-ra-tion [respɪ'reɪʃn] respiration f

res-pi-ra-tor ['respɪreɪtər] MED respirateur m

re-spite ['respaɪt] répit m; **without ~** sans répit

re-spond [rɪ'spɑːnd] v/i répondre; (re-act also) réagir

re-sponse [rɪ'spɑːns] réponse f; (reaction also) réaction f

re-spon-si-bil-i-ty [rɪspɑːnsɪ'bɪlətɪ] responsabilité f; **accept ~ for** accepter la responsabilité de; **a job with more ~** un poste avec plus de responsabilités

re-spon-si-ble [rɪ'spɑːnsəbl] adj responsable (**for** de); **a ~ job** un poste à responsabilités

re-spon-sive [rɪ'spɑːnsɪv] adj audience réceptif*; TECH qui répond bien

rest[1] [rest] **1** n repos m; during walk, work pause f; **set s.o.'s mind at ~**

rassurer qn **2** v/i se reposer; **~ on** (be based on) reposer sur; (lean against) être appuyé contre; **it all ~s with him** tout dépend de lui **3** v/t (lean, balance) poser

rest[2] [rest]: **the ~** objects le reste; people les autres

res-tau-rant ['restərɑːnt] restaurant m

'res-tau-rant car wagon-restaurant m

'rest cure cure f de repos

rest-ful ['restfl] adj reposant

'rest home maison f de retraite

rest-less ['restlɪs] adj agité; **have a ~ night** passer une nuit agitée; **be ~ un-able to stay in one place** avoir la bougeotte F

rest-less-ly ['restlɪslɪ] adv nerveusement

res-to-ra-tion [restə'reɪʃn] of building restauration f

re-store [rɪ'stɔːr] v/t building etc restaurer; (bring back) rendre, restituer; confidence redonner

re-strain [rɪ'streɪn] v/t retenir; **~ o.s.** se retenir

re-straint [rɪ'streɪnt] (moderation) retenue f

re-strict [rɪ'strɪkt] v/t restreindre, limiter; **I'll ~ myself to ...** je me limiterai à ...

re-strict-ed [rɪ'strɪktɪd] adj restreint, limité

re-strict-ed 'ar-e-a MIL zone f interdite

re-stric-tion [rɪ'strɪkʃn] restriction f

'rest room toilettes fpl

re-sult [rɪ'zʌlt] n résultat m; **as a ~ of this** par conséquent

♦ **result from** v/t résulter de, découler de

♦ **result in** v/t entraîner, avoir pour résultat

re-sume [rɪ'zuːm] v/t & v/i reprendre

ré-su-mé ['rezumeɪ] of career curriculum vitæ m inv, C.V. m inv

re-sump-tion [rɪ'zʌmpʃn] reprise f

re-sur-face [riː'sɜːrfɪs] **1** v/t roads refaire (le revêtement de) **2** v/i (reappear) refaire surface

Res-ur-rec-tion [rezə'rekʃn] REL Résurrection f

re·sus·ci·tate [rɪ'sʌsɪteɪt] v/t réanimer

re·sus·ci·ta·tion [rɪsʌsɪ'teɪʃn] réanimation f

re·tail ['riːteɪl] **1** adv: **sell sth ~** vendre qch au détail **2** v/i: **~ at** se vendre à

re·tail·er ['riːteɪlər] détaillant(e) m(f)

're·tail out·let point m de vente, magasin m (de détail)

're·tail price prix m de détail

re·tain [rɪ'teɪn] v/t garder, conserver

re·tain·er [rɪ'teɪnər] FIN provision f

re·tal·i·ate [rɪ'tælieɪt] v/i riposter, se venger

re·tal·i·a·tion [rɪtælɪ'eɪʃn] riposte f; **in ~ for** pour se venger de

re·tard·ed [rɪ'tɑːrdɪd] adj mentally attardé, retardé

re·think [riː'θɪŋk] v/t (pret & pp **-thought**) repenser

re·ti·cence ['retɪsns] réserve f

re·ti·cent ['retɪsnt] adj réservé

re·tire [rɪ'taɪr] v/i from work prendre sa retraite; fml: go to bed aller se coucher

re·tired [rɪ'taɪrd] adj à la retraite

re·tire·ment [rɪ'taɪrmənt] retraite f; act départ m à la retraite

re'tire·ment age âge de la retraite

re·tir·ing [rɪ'taɪrɪŋ] adj réservé

re·tort [rɪ'tɔːrt] **1** n réplique f **2** v/t répliquer

re·trace [rɪ'treɪs] v/t: **~ one's footsteps** revenir sur ses pas

re·tract [rɪ'trækt] v/t claws, undercarriage rentrer; statement retirer

re·train [riː'treɪn] v/i se recycler

re·treat [rɪ'triːt] **1** v/i also MIL battre en retraite **2** n MIL, place retraite f

re·trieve [rɪ'triːv] v/t récupérer

re·triev·er [rɪ'triːvər] dog chien m d'arrêt, retriever m

ret·ro·ac·tive [retrou'æktɪv] adj law etc rétroactif*

ret·ro·ac·tive·ly [retrou'æktɪvlɪ] adv rétroactivement, par rétroaction

ret·ro·grade ['retrəgreɪd] adj move, decision rétrograde

ret·ro·spect ['retrəspekt]: **in ~** rétrospectivement

ret·ro·spec·tive [retrə'spektɪv] n rétrospective f

re·turn [rɪ'tɜːrn] **1** n retour m; (profit) bénéfice m; **~ (ticket)** Br aller m retour; **by ~ (mail)** par retour (du courrier); **many happy ~s (of the day)** bon anniversaire; **in ~ for** en échange de; contre **2** v/t (give back) rendre; (send back) renvoyer; (put back) remettre; **~ the favor** rendre la pareille **3** v/i (go back) retourner; (come back) revenir

re·turn 'flight vol m (de) retour

re·turn jour·ney retour m

re·u·ni·fi·ca·tion [riːjuːnɪfɪ'keɪʃn] réunification f

re·u·nion [riː'juːnjən] réunion f

re·u·nite [riːjuː'naɪt] v/t réunir; country réunifier

re·us·a·ble [riː'juːzəbl] adj réutilisable

re·use [riː'juːz] v/t réutiliser

rev [rev] n: **~s per minute** tours mpl par minute

♦ **rev up** v/t (pret & pp **-ved**) engine emballer

re·val·u·a·tion [riːvæljʊ'eɪʃn] réévaluation f

re·veal [rɪ'viːl] v/t révéler; (make visible) dévoiler

re·veal·ing [rɪ'viːlɪŋ] adj remark révélateur*; dress suggestif*

♦ **rev·el** ['revl] v/t (pret & pp **-ed**, Br **-led**) se délecter de; **revel in doing sth** se délecter à faire qch

rev·e·la·tion [revə'leɪʃn] révélation f

re·venge [rɪ'vendʒ] n vengeance f; **take one's ~** se venger; **in ~ for** pour se venger de

rev·e·nue ['revənuː] revenu m

re·ver·be·rate [rɪ'vɜːrbəreɪt] v/i of sound retentir, résonner

re·vere [rɪ'vɪr] v/t révérer

rev·e·rence ['revərəns] déférence f, respect m

Rev·e·rend ['revərənd] Protestant pasteur m; Catholic abbé m; Anglican révérend m

rev·e·rent ['revərənt] adj respectueux*

re·verse [rɪ'vɜːrs] **1** adj sequence inverse; **in ~ order** à l'envers **2** n (opposite) contraire m; (back) verso m; MOT gear marche f arrière **3** v/t sequence

R

inverser; *vehicle* faire marche arrière avec ◆ 4 *v/i* MOT faire marche arrière

re·vert [rɪ'vɜːrt] *v/i*: **~ to** revenir à; *habit* reprendre; **the land ~ed to ...** la terre est retournée à l'état de ...

re·view [rɪ'vjuː] **1** *n of book, movie* critique *f*; *of troops* revue *f*; *of situation etc* bilan *m* **2** *v/t book, movie* faire la critique de; *troops* passer en revue; *situation etc* faire le bilan de; EDU réviser

re·view·er [rɪ'vjuːər] *of book, movie* critique *m*

re·vise [rɪ'vaɪz] *v/t opinion* revenir sur; *text* réviser

re·vi·sion [rɪ'vɪʒn] *of text* révision *f*

re·viv·al [rɪ'vaɪvl] *of custom, old style etc* renouveau *m*; *of patient* rétablissement *m*; **a ~ of interest in** un regain d'intérêt pour

re·vive [rɪ'vaɪv] **1** *v/t custom, old style etc* faire renaître; *patient* ranimer **2** *v/i of business* reprendre

re·voke [rɪ'vouk] *v/t law* abroger; *license* retirer

re·volt [rɪ'voult] **1** *n* révolte *f* **2** *v/i* se révolter

re·volt·ing [rɪ'voultɪŋ] *adj* répugnant

rev·o·lu·tion [revə'luːʃn] révolution *f*

rev·o·lu·tion·ar·y [revə'luːʃnərɪ] **1** *adj* révolutionnaire **2** *n* révolutionnaire *m/f*

rev·o·lu·tion·ize [revə'luːʃnaɪz] *v/t* révolutionner

re·volve [rɪ'vɑːlv] *v/i* tourner (**around** autour de)

re·volv·er [rɪ'vɑːlvər] revolver *m*

re·volv·ing door [rɪ'vɑːlvɪŋ] tambour *m*

re·vue [rɪ'vjuː] THEA revue *f*

re·vul·sion [rɪ'vʌlʃn] dégoût *m*, répugnance *f*

re·ward [rɪ'wɔːrd] **1** *n financial* récompense *f*; *(benefit derived)* gratification *f* **2** *v/t financially* récompenser

re·ward·ing [rɪ'wɔːrdɪŋ] *adj experience* gratifiant, valorisant

re·wind [riː'waɪnd] *v/t (pret & pp -wound) film, tape* rembobiner

re·wire [riː'waɪr] *v/t* refaire l'installation électrique de

re·write [riː'raɪt] *v/t (pret -wrote, pp -written)* réécrire

rhet·o·ric ['retərɪk] rhétorique *f*

rhe·tor·i·cal 'ques·tion [rɪ'tɑːrɪkl] question *f* pour la forme, question *f* rhétorique

rheu·ma·tism ['ruːmətɪzm] rhumatisme *m*

rhi·no·ce·ros [raɪ'nɑːsərəs] rhinocéros *m*

rhu·barb ['ruːbɑːrb] rhubarbe *f*

rhyme [raɪm] **1** *n* rime *f* **2** *v/i* rimer (**with** avec)

rhythm ['rɪðm] rythme *m*

rib [rɪb] ANAT côte *f*

rib·bon ['rɪbən] ruban *m*

rice [raɪs] riz *m*

rich [rɪtʃ] **1** *adj person, food* riche **2** *npl*: **the ~** les riches *mpl*

rich·ly ['rɪtʃlɪ] *adv deserved* largement, bien

rick·et·y ['rɪkətɪ] *adj* bancal, branlant

ric·o·chet ['rɪkəʃeɪ] *v/i* ricocher (**off** sur)

rid [rɪd] *v/t (pret & pp rid)*: **get ~ of** se débarrasser de

rid·dance ['rɪdns]: **good ~!** bon débarras!

rid·den ['rɪdn] *pp* → **ride**

rid·dle¹ ['rɪdl] *n puzzle* devinette *f*

rid·dle² ['rɪdl] *v/t*: **be ~d with** être criblé de

ride [raɪd] **1** *n on horse* promenade *f* (à cheval); *excursion in vehicle* tour *m*; *(journey)* trajet *m*; **do you want a ~ into town?** est-ce que tu veux que je t'emmène en ville?; **you've been taken for a ~** *fig* F tu t'es fait avoir F **2** *v/t (pret rode, pp ridden) horse* monter; *bike* se déplacer en; **can you ~ a bike?** sais-tu faire du vélo?; **can I ~ your bike?** est-ce que je peux monter sur ton vélo? **3** *v/i (pret rode, pp ridden) on horse* monter à cheval; *on bike* rouler (à vélo); **~ on a bus / train** prendre le bus / train; **those riding at the back of the bus** ceux qui étaient à l'arrière du bus

rid·er ['raɪdər] *on horse* cavalier(-ière) *m(f)*; *on bike* cycliste *m/f*

ridge [rɪdʒ] (*raised strip*) arête *f* (saillante); *along edge* rebord *m*; *of mountain* crête *f*, *of roof* arête *f*

rid·i·cule ['rɪdɪkjuːl] **1** *n* ridicule *m* **2** *v/t* ridiculiser

ri·dic·u·lous [rɪ'dɪkjʊləs] *adj* ridicule

ri·dic·u·lous·ly [rɪ'dɪkjʊləslɪ] *adv* ridiculement

rid·ing ['raɪdɪŋ] *on horseback* équitation *f*

ri·fle ['raɪfl] *n* fusil *m*, carabine *f*

rift [rɪft] *in earth* fissure *f*; *in party etc* division *f*, scission *f*

rig [rɪg] **1** *n* (*oil ∼*) tour *f* de forage; *at sea* plateforme *f* de forage; (*truck*) semi-remorque *f* **2** *v/t* (*pret & pp* **-ged**) *elections* truquer

right [raɪt] **1** *adj* bon*; (*not left*) droit; *be ∼ of answer* être juste; *of person* avoir raison; *of clock* être à l'heure; *it's not ∼ to ...* ce n'est pas bien de ...; *the ∼ thing to do* la chose à faire; *put things ∼* arranger les choses; *that's ∼!* c'est ça!; *that's all ∼* (*doesn't matter*) ce n'est pas grave; *when s.o. says thank you* je vous en prie; *it's all ∼* (*is acceptable*) ça me va; *I'm all ∼ not hurt* je vais bien; *have enough* ça ira pour moi; (*all*) ∼, *that's enough!* bon, ça suffit! **2** *adv* (*directly*) directement, juste; (*correctly*) correctement, bien; (*completely*) tout, complètement; (*not left*) à droite; ∼ *now* (*immediately*) tout de suite; (*at the moment*) en ce moment; *it's ∼ here* c'est juste là **3** *n civil, legal* droit *m*; (*not left*), POL droite *f*; *on the ∼ also* POL à droite; *turn to the ∼*, *take a ∼* tourner à droite; *be in the ∼* avoir raison; *know ∼ from wrong* savoir discerner le bien du mal

'right-an·gle angle *m* droit; *at ∼s to* perpendiculaire à

right·ful ['raɪtfʊl] *adj heir, owner etc* légitime

'right-hand *adj*: *on the ∼ side* à droite; **right-hand 'drive** MOT (*voiture f avec*) conduite *f* à droite; **right-hand·ed** [raɪt'hændɪd] *adj person* droitier*; **right-hand 'man** bras *m* droit; **right of 'way** *in traffic* priorité

f; *across land* droit *m* de passage; **right 'wing** POL droite *f*; SP ailier *m* droit; **right-'wing** *adj* POL de droite; **right-wing ex'trem·ist** POL extrémiste *m/f* de droite

rig·id ['rɪdʒɪd] *adj also fig* rigide

rig·or ['rɪgər] *of discipline* rigueur *f*

rig·or·ous ['rɪgərəs] *adj* rigoureux*

rig·or·ous·ly ['rɪgərəslɪ] *adv check, examine* rigoureusement

rig·our *Br* → **rigor**

rile [raɪl] *v/t* F agacer

rim [rɪm] *of wheel* jante *f*; *of cup* bord *m*; *of eyeglasses* monture *f*

ring[1] [rɪŋ] *n* (*circle*) cercle *m*; *on finger* anneau *m*; *in boxing* ring *m*; *at circus* piste *f*

ring[2] [rɪŋ] **1** *n of bell* sonnerie *f*, *of voice* son *m*; *give s.o. a ∼ Br* TELEC passer un coup de fil à qn **2** *v/t* (*pret rang*, *pp rung*) *bell* (faire) sonner; *Br* TELEC téléphoner à **3** *v/i* (*pret rang*, *pp rung*) *of bell* sonner, retentir; *Br* TELEC téléphoner; *please ∼ for attention* prière de sonner

'ring-lead·er meneur(-euse) *m(f)*

'ring-pull anneau *m* (d'ouverture)

rink [rɪŋk] patinoire *f*

rinse [rɪns] **1** *n for hair color* rinçage *m* **2** *v/t clothes, dishes, hair* rincer

ri·ot ['raɪət] **1** *n* émeute *f* **2** *v/i* participer à une émeute; *start to ∼* créer une émeute

ri·ot·er ['raɪətər] émeutier(-ière) *m(f)*

ri·ot po·lice police *f* anti-émeute

rip [rɪp] **1** *n in cloth etc* accroc *m* **2** *v/t* (*pret & pp* **-ped**) *cloth etc* déchirer; ∼ *sth open letter* ouvrir qch à la hâte

♦ **rip off** *v/t* F *cheat* arnaquer F

♦ **rip up** *v/t letter, sheet* déchirer

ripe [raɪp] *adj fruit* mûr

rip·en ['raɪpn] *v/i of fruit* mûrir

rip·ness ['raɪpnɪs] *of fruit* maturité *f*

'rip-off F arnaque *f* F

rip·ple ['rɪpl] *on water* ride *f*, ondulation *f*

rise [raɪz] **1** *v/i* (*pret rose*, *pp risen*) *from chair, bed, of sun* se lever; *of rocket, price, temperature* monter **2** *n in price, temperature* hausse *f*, augmentation *f*; *in water level* élévation

R

f; *Br: in salary* augmentation f; **give ~ to** donner lieu à, engendrer

ris·en ['rɪzn] *pp* → **rise**

ris·er ['raɪzər]: **be an early ~** être matinal, être lève-tôt *inv* F; **be a late ~** être lève-tard *inv* F

risk [rɪsk] **1** n risque m; **take a ~** prendre un risque **2** v/t risquer; **let's ~ it** c'est un risque à courir, il faut tenter le coup F

risk·y ['rɪskɪ] *adj* risqué

ris·qué [rɪ'skeɪ] *adj* osé

rit·u·al ['rɪtʊəl] **1** *adj* rituel* **2** n rituel m

ri·val ['raɪvl] **1** n rival(e) m(f) **2** v/t (*match*) égaler; (*compete with*) rivaliser avec; **I can't ~ that** je ne peux pas faire mieux

ri·val·ry ['raɪvlrɪ] rivalité f

riv·er ['rɪvər] rivière f; *bigger* fleuve m

'riv·er·bank rive f; **'riv·er·bed** lit m de la rivière / du fleuve; **'riv·er·side 1** *adj* en bord de rivière **2** n berge f, bord m de l'eau

riv·et ['rɪvɪt] **1** n rivet m **2** v/t riveter, river

riv·et·ing ['rɪvɪtɪŋ] *adj story etc* fascinant

Ri·vi·er·a [rɪvɪ'erə] *French* Côte f d'Azur

road [roʊd] route f; *in city* rue f; **it's just down the ~** c'est à deux pas d'ici

'road·block barrage m routier; **'road hog** chauffard m; **'road-hold·ing** *of vehicle* tenue f de route; **'road map** carte f routière; **road 'safe·ty** sécurité f routière; **'road·side: at the ~** au bord de la route; **'road-sign** panneau m (de signalisation); **'road·way** chaussée f; **'road·wor·thy** *adj* en état de marche

roam [roʊm] v/i errer

roar [rɔːr] **1** n rugissement m; *of rapids, traffic* grondement m; *of engine* vrombissement m **2** v/i rugir; *of rapids, traffic* gronder; *of engine* vrombir; **~ with laughter** hurler de rire, rire à gorge déployée

roast [roʊst] **1** n *of beef etc* rôti m **2** v/t rôtir **3** v/i *of food* rôtir; **we're ~ing** on étouffe

roast 'beef rôti m de bœuf, rosbif m

roast 'pork rôti m de porc

rob [rɑːb] v/t (*pret & pp* **-bed**) *person* voler, dévaliser; *bank* cambrioler, dévaliser; **I've been ~bed** j'ai été dévalisé

rob·ber ['rɑːbər] voleur(-euse) m(f)

rob·ber·y ['rɑːbərɪ] vol m

robe [roʊb] *of judge, priest* robe f; (*bath~*) peignoir m; (*dressing gown*) robe f de chambre

rob·in ['rɑːbɪn] rouge-gorge m

ro·bot ['roʊbɑːt] robot m

ro·bust [roʊ'bʌst] *adj* robuste

rock [rɑːk] **1** n rocher m; MUS rock m; **on the ~s** *drink* avec des glaçons; *marriage* en pleine débâcle **2** v/t *baby* bercer; *cradle* balancer; (*surprise*) secouer, ébranler **3** v/i *on chair, of boat* se balancer

'rock band groupe m de rock; **rock 'bot·tom: reach ~** toucher le fond; *of levels of employment, currency* être au plus bas; **'rock-bot·tom** *adj price* le plus bas possible; **'rock climb·er** varappeur(-euse) m(f); **'rock climb·ing** varappe f

'rock·et ['rɑːkɪt] **1** n fusée f **2** v/i *of prices etc* monter en flèche

rock·ing chair ['rɑːkɪŋ] rocking-chair m

'rock·ing horse cheval m à bascule

rock 'n' roll [rɑːkn'roʊl] rock-and-roll m inv

'rock star rock-star f

rock·y ['rɑːkɪ] *adj* rocheux*; *path* rocailleux*; F *marriage* instable, précaire; **I'm feeling kind of ~** F je ne suis pas dans mon assiette F

Rock·y 'Moun·tains *npl* Montagnes *fpl* Rocheuses

rod [rɑːd] baguette f, tige f; *for fishing* canne f à pêche

rode [roʊd] *pret* → **ride**

ro·dent ['roʊdnt] rongeur m

rogue [roʊg] vaurien m, coquin m

role [roʊl] rôle m

'role mod·el modèle m

roll [roʊl] **1** n (*bread ~*) petit pain m; *of film* pellicule f; *of thunder* grondement m; (*list, register*) liste f **2** v/i *of*

ball, boat rouler **3** v/t: **~ sth into a ball** mettre qch en boule; **~ sth along the ground** faire rouler qch sur le sol
♦ **roll over 1** v/i se retourner **2** v/t *person, object* tourner; (*renew*) renouveler; (*extend*) prolonger
♦ **roll up 1** v/t *sleeves* retrousser **2** v/i F (*arrive*) se pointer F
'**roll call** appel *m*
roll·er ['roʊlər] *for hair* rouleau *m*, bigoudi *m*
'**roll·er blade®** *n* roller *m* (en ligne); **roll·er coast·er** ['roʊlərkoʊstər] montagnes *fpl* russes; '**roll·er skate** *n* patin *m* à roulettes
roll·ing pin ['roʊlɪŋ] rouleau *m* à pâtisserie
ROM [rɑːm] *abbr* COMPUT (= *read only memory*) ROM *f*, mémoire *f* morte
Ro·man ['roʊmən] **1** *adj* romain **2** *n* Romain(e) *m(f)*
Ro·man 'Cath·o·lic 1 *adj* REL catholique **2** *n* catholique *m/f*
ro·mance ['roʊmæns] (*affair*) idylle *f*; *novel, movie* histoire *f* d'amour
ro·man·tic [roʊˈmæntɪk] *adj* romantique
ro·man·tic·al·ly [roʊˈmæntɪklɪ] *adv* de façon romantique; **be ~ involved with s.o.** avoir une liaison avec qn
roof [ruːf] toit *m*; **have a ~ over one's head** avoir un toit
'**roof box** MOT coffre *m* de toit
'**roof·rack** MOT galerie *f*
rook·ie ['rʊkɪ] F bleu *m* F
room [ruːm] pièce *f*, salle *f*; (*bed~*) chambre *f*; (*space*) place *f*; **there's no ~ for** il n'y a pas de place pour
'**room clerk** réceptionniste *m/f*; '**roommate** *in apartment* colocataire *m/f*; *in room* camarade *m/f* de chambre; '**room ser·vice** service *m* en chambre; '**room tem·per·a·ture** température *f* ambiante
room·y ['ruːmɪ] *adj* spacieux*; *clothes* ample
root [ruːt] *n of plant, word* racine *f*; **~s** *of person* racines *fpl*
♦ **root for** v/t F encourager
♦ **root out** v/t (*get rid of*) éliminer;

(*find*) dénicher
rope [roʊp] corde *f*; **show s.o. the ~s** F montrer à qn comment ça marche
♦ **rope off** v/t fermer avec une corde
ro·sa·ry ['roʊzərɪ] REL rosaire *m*, chapelet *m*
rose[1] [roʊz] BOT rose *f*
rose[2] [roʊz] *pret* → **rise**
rose·ma·ry ['roʊzmerɪ] romarin *m*
ros·ter ['rɑːstər] tableau *m* de service
ros·trum ['rɑːstrəm] estrade *f*
ros·y ['roʊzɪ] *adj also fig* rose
rot [rɑːt] **1** *n* pourriture *f* **2** v/i (*pret & pp* **-ted**) pourrir
ro·tate [roʊˈteɪt] **1** v/i tourner **2** v/t (*turn*) (faire) tourner
ro·ta·tion [roʊˈteɪʃn] rotation *f*; **do sth in ~** faire qch à tour de rôle
rot·ten ['rɑːtn] *adj food, wood etc* pourri; F *trick, thing to do* dégueulasse F; *weather, luck* pourri F
rough [rʌf] **1** *adj surface* rugueux*; *hands, skin* rêche; *voice* rude; (*violent*) brutal; *crossing, seas* agité; (*approximate*) approximatif*; **~ draft** brouillon *m* **2** *adv*: **sleep ~** dormir à la dure **3** *n in golf* rough *m* **4** v/t: **~ it** F vivre à la dure
♦ **rough up** v/t F tabasser F
rough·age ['rʌfɪdʒ] *in food* fibres *fpl*
rough·ly ['rʌflɪ] *adv* (*approximately*) environ, à peu près; (*harshly*) brutalement; **~ speaking** en gros
rou·lette [ruːˈlet] roulette *f*
round [raʊnd] **1** *adj* rond, circulaire; **in ~ figures** en chiffres ronds **2** *n of mailman, doctor* tournée *f*; *of toast* tranche *f*; *of drinks* tournée *f*; *of competition* manche *f*, tour *m*; *in boxing match* round *m* **3** v/t *corner* tourner **4** *adv & prep* → **around**
♦ **round off** v/t *edges* arrondir; *meeting, night out* conclure
♦ **round up** v/t *figure* arrondir; *suspects* ramasser
round·a·bout ['raʊndəbaʊt] **1** *adj* détourné, indirect; **come by a ~ route** faire un détour *m in Br. on road* rond-point *m*; '**round-the-world** *adj* autour du monde; **round 'trip** aller-retour *m*; **round trip 'tick·et** billet *m*

aller-retour; **'round-up** *of cattle* rassemblement *m*; *of suspects* rafle *f*; *of news* résumé *m*

rouse [rauz] *v/t from sleep* réveiller; *interest, emotions* soulever

rous·ing ['rauzɪŋ] *adj speech, finale* exaltant

route [ruːt] *n* itinéraire *m*

rou·tine [ruː'tiːn] **1** *adj* de routine; *behavior* routinier **2** *n* routine *f*; *as a matter of* ~ systématiquement

row[1] [rou] *n* (*line*) rangée *f*; *of troops* rang *m*; *5 days in a* ~ 5 jours de suite

row[2] [rou] **1** *v/t*: *he* ~*ed them across the river* il leur a fait traverser la rivière en barque **2** *v/i* ramer

row[3] [rau] *n* (*quarrel*) dispute *f*; (*noise*) vacarme *m*

row·boat ['roubout] bateau *m* à rames

row·dy ['raudɪ] *adj* tapageur*, bruyant

roy·al ['rɔɪəl] *adj* royal

roy·al·ty ['rɔɪəltɪ] (*royal persons*) (membres *mpl* de) la famille royale; *on book, recording* droits *mpl* d'auteur

rub [rʌb] *v/t* (*pret & pp* **-bed**) frotter

♦ **rub down** *v/t paintwork* poncer; *with towel* se sécher

♦ **rub in** *v/t cream, ointment* faire pénétrer; *don't rub it in! fig* pas besoin d'en rajouter! F

♦ **rub off** **1** *v/t* enlever (en frottant) **2** *v/i*: *rub off on s.o.* déteindre sur qn

rub·ber ['rʌbər] **1** *n material* caoutchouc *m*; P (*condom*) capote *f* F **2** *adj* en caoutchouc

rub·ber 'band élastique *m*; **rub·ber 'gloves** gants *mpl* en caoutchouc; **'rub·ber·neck** F *at accident etc* badaud(e) *m(f)*

rub·ble ['rʌbl] *from building* gravats *mpl*, décombres *mpl*

ru·by ['ruːbɪ] *n jewel* rubis *m*

ruck·sack ['rʌksæk] sac *m* à dos

rud·der ['rʌdər] gouvernail *m*

rud·dy ['rʌdɪ] *adj complexion* coloré

rude [ruːd] *adj* impoli; *word, gesture* grossier*

rude·ly ['ruːdlɪ] *adv* (*impolitely*) impoliment

rude·ness ['ruːdnɪs] impolitesse *f*

ru·di·men·ta·ry [ruːdɪ'mentərɪ] *adj* rudimentaire

ru·di·ments ['ruːdɪmənts] *npl* rudiments *mpl*

rue·ful ['ruːfl] *adj* contrit, résigné

rue·ful·ly ['ruːfəlɪ] *adv* avec regret; *smile* d'un air contrit

ruf·fi·an ['rʌfɪən] voyou *m*, brute *f*

ruf·fle ['rʌfl] **1** *n on dress* ruche *f* **2** *v/t hair* ébouriffer; *person* énerver; *get* ~*d* s'énerver

rug [rʌg] tapis *m*; *blanket* couverture *f*; *travel* ~ plaid *m*, couverture *f* de voyage

rug·by ['rʌgbɪ] rugby *m*

'rug·by match match *m* de rugby

'rug·by play·er joueur *m* de rugby, rugbyman *m*

rug·ged ['rʌgɪd] *adj scenery, cliffs* découpé, escarpé; *face* aux traits rudes; *resistance* acharné

ru·in ['ruːɪn] **1** *n* ruine *f*; *in* ~*s* en ruine **2** *v/t* ruiner; *party, birthday, plans* gâcher; *be* ~*ed financially* être ruiné

rule [ruːl] **1** *n* règle *f*; *of monarch* règne *m*; *as a* ~ en règle générale **2** *v/t country* diriger, gouverner; *the judge* ~*d that ...* le juge a déclaré que ... **3** *v/i of monarch* régner

♦ **rule out** *v/t* exclure

rul·er ['ruːlər] *for measuring* règle *f*; *of state* dirigeant(e) *m(f)*

rul·ing ['ruːlɪŋ] **1** *n* décision *f* **2** *adj party* dirigeant, au pouvoir

rum [rʌm] *n drink* rhum *m*

rum·ble ['rʌmbl] *v/i of stomach* gargouiller; *of thunder* gronder

♦ **rum·mage around** ['rʌmɪdʒ] *v/i* fouiller

'rum·mage sale vente *f* de bric-à--brac

ru·mor, *Br* **ru·mour** ['ruːmər] **1** *n* bruit *m*, rumeur *f* **2** *v/t*: *it is* ~*ed that ...* il paraît que ..., le bruit court que ...

rump [rʌmp] *of animal* croupe *f*

rum·ple ['rʌmpl] *v/t clothes, paper* froisser

'rump·steak rumsteck *m*

run [rʌn] **1** *n on foot* course *f*; *in pantyhose* échelle *f*; *the play has had a three-year* ~ la pièce est restée trois ans à l'affiche; **go for a ~** *for exercise* aller courir; **make a ~ for it** s'enfuir; **a criminal on the ~** un criminel en cavale F; **in the short / long ~** à court / long terme; **a ~ on the dollar** une ruée sur le dollar **2** *v/i* (*pret ran, pp run*) *of person, animal* courir; *of river, paint, makeup, nose, faucet* couler; *of trains, buses* passer, circuler; *of eyes* pleurer; *of play* être à l'affiche, se jouer; *of engine, machine* marcher, tourner; *of software* fonctionner; *in election* se présenter; **~ for President** être candidat à la présidence **3** *v/t* (*pret ran, pp run*) *race, 3 miles* courir; *business, hotel, project etc* diriger; *software* exécuter, faire tourner; *car* entretenir; *risk* courir; **he ran his eye down the page** il lut la page en diagonale

♦ **run across** *v/t* (*meet, find*) tomber sur
♦ **run away** *v/i* s'enfuir; **run away (from home)** *for a while* faire une fugue; *for good* s'enfuir de chez soi; **run away with s.o. / sth** partir avec qn / qch
♦ **run down 1** *v/t* (*knock down*) renverser; (*criticize*) critiquer; *stocks* diminuer **2** *v/i of battery* se décharger
♦ **run into** *v/t* (*meet*) tomber sur; *difficulties* rencontrer
♦ **run off 1** *v/i* s'enfuir **2** *v/t* (*print*) imprimer, tirer
♦ **run out** *v/i of contract* expirer; *of time* s'écouler; *of supplies* s'épuiser
♦ **run out of** *v/t time, patience, supplies* ne plus avoir de; **I ran out of gas** je suis tombé en panne d'essence
♦ **run over 1** *v/t* (*knock down*) renverser; (*go through*) passer en revue, récapituler **2** *v/i of water etc* déborder
♦ **run through** *v/t* (*rehearse*) répéter; (*go over*) passer en revue, récapituler
♦ **run up** *v/t debts* accumuler; *clothes* faire

'run·a·way *n* fugueur(-euse) *m(f)*
run-'down *adj person* fatigué, épuisé; *area, building* délabré
rung[1] [rʌŋ] *of ladder* barreau *m*
rung[2] [rʌŋ] *pp* → **ring**

run·ner ['rʌnər] coureur(-euse) *m(f)*
run·ner 'beans *npl* haricots *mpl* d'Espagne
run·ner-'up second(e) *m(f)*
run·ning ['rʌnɪŋ] **1** *n* SP course *f*; *of business* direction *f*, gestion *f* **2** *adj*: **for two days ~** pendant deux jours de suite
'run·ning mate POL candidat *m* à la vice-présidence
run·ning 'wa·ter eau *f* courante
run·ny ['rʌnɪ] *adj substance* liquide; *nose* qui coule
'run-up SP élan *m*; **in the ~ to** pendant la période qui précède, juste avant
'run·way AVIAT piste *f*
rup·ture ['rʌptʃər] **1** *n also fig* rupture *f* **2** *v/i of pipe* éclater
ru·ral ['rʊrəl] *adj* rural
ruse [ruːz] ruse *f*
rush [rʌʃ] **1** *n* ruée *f*, course *f*; **do sth in a ~** faire qch en vitesse *or* à la hâte; **be in a ~** être pressé; **what's the big ~?** pourquoi se presser? **2** *v/t person* presser, bousculer; *meal* avaler (à toute vitesse); **~ s.o. to the hospital** emmener qn d'urgence à l'hôpital **3** *v/i* se presser, se dépêcher
'rush hour heures *fpl* de pointe
Rus·sia ['rʌʃə] Russie *f*
Rus·sian ['rʌʃən] **1** *adj* russe **2** *n* Russe *m/f*; *language* russe *m*
rust [rʌst] **1** *n* rouille *f* **2** *v/i* se rouiller
rus·tle[1] ['rʌsl] **1** *n of silk, leaves* bruissement *m* **2** *v/i of silk, leaves* bruisser
rus·tle[2] ['rʌsl] *v/t cattle* voler
'rust·proof *adj* antirouille *inv*
rust re·mov·er ['rʌstrɪmuːvər] antirouille *m*
rust·y ['rʌstɪ] *adj also fig* rouillé; **I'm a little ~** j'ai un peu perdu la main
rut [rʌt] *in road* ornière *f*; **be in a ~** *fig* être tombé dans la routine
ruth·less ['ruːθlɪs] *adj* impitoyable, sans pitié
ruth·less·ly ['ruːθlɪslɪ] *adv* impitoyablement
ruth·less·ness ['ruːθlɪsnɪs] dureté *f* (impitoyable)
rye [raɪ] seigle *m*
'rye bread pain *m* de seigle

S

sab·bat·i·cal [sə'bætɪkl] *n:* ***year's ~***
année *f* sabbatique

sab·o·tage ['sæbətɑːʒ] **1** *n* sabotage *m*
2 *v/t* saboter

sab·o·teur [sæbə'tɜːr] saboteur(-euse)
m(f)

sac·cha·rin ['sækərɪn] saccharine *f*

sa·chet ['sæʃeɪ] *of shampoo, cream etc*
sachet *m*

sack [sæk] **1** *n bag, for groceries* sac *m*;
get the ~ F se faire virer F **2** *v/t* F virer
F

sa·cred ['seɪkrɪd] *adj* sacré

sac·ri·fice ['sækrɪfaɪs] **1** *n* sacrifice *m*;
make ~s *fig* faire des sacrifices **2** *v/t*
also fig sacrifier

sac·ri·lege ['sækrɪlɪdʒ] REL, *fig* sacrilège *m*

sad [sæd] *adj* triste

sad·dle ['sædl] **1** *n* selle *f* **2** *v/t horse*
seller; ***~ s.o. with sth*** *fig* mettre
qch sur le dos de qn

sa·dism ['seɪdɪzm] sadisme *m*

sa·dist ['seɪdɪst] sadique *m/f*

sa·dis·tic [sə'dɪstɪk] *adj* sadique

sad·ly ['sædlɪ] *adv say, sing etc* tristement; (*regrettably*) malheureusement

sad·ness ['sædnɪs] tristesse *f*

safe [seɪf] **1** *adj* (*not dangerous*) pas
dangereux*; *driver* prudent; (*not in
danger*) en sécurité; *investment, prediction* sans risque **2** *n* coffre-fort *m*

'safe·guard 1 *n:* ***as a ~ against*** par
mesure de protection contre **2** *v/t*
protéger

'safe·keep·ing: ***give sth to s.o. for ~***
confier qch à qn

safe·ly ['seɪflɪ] *adv arrive,* (*successfully*)
bel et bien; *drive, assume* sans risque

safe·ty ['seɪftɪ] *of equipment, wiring,
person* sécurité *f; of investment, prediction* sûreté *f*

'safe·ty belt ceinture *f* de sécurité;
'safe·ty-con·scious *adj* sensible à

la sécurité; **safe·ty 'first:** ***learn ~*** apprendre à faire attention sur la route;
'safe·ty pin épingle *f* de nourrice

sag [sæg] **1** *n in ceiling etc* affaissement
m **2** *v/i* (*pret & pp* ***-ged***) *of ceiling* s'affaisser; *of rope* se détendre; *fig: of out-
put, production* fléchir

sa·ga ['sɑːgə] saga *f*

sage [seɪdʒ] *n herb* sauge *f*

Sa·git·tar·i·us [sædʒɪ'terɪəs] ASTROL
Sagittaire *m*

said [sed] *pret & pp →* ***say***

sail [seɪl] **1** *n of boat* voile *f; trip* voyage
m (en mer); ***go for a ~*** faire un tour
(en bateau) **2** *v/t yacht* piloter **3** *v/i*
faire de la voile; *depart* partir

'sail·board 1 *n* planche *f* à voile **2** *v/i*
faire de la planche à voile; **'sail-
board·ing** planche *f* à voile; **'sailboat** bateau *m* à voiles

sail·ing ['seɪlɪŋ] SP voile *f*

'sail·ing ship voilier *m*

sail·or ['seɪlər] marin *m; **be a good /
bad ~*** avoir / ne pas avoir le pied marin

'sailor's knot nœud *m* plat

saint [seɪnt] saint(e) *m(f)*

sake [seɪk]: ***for my / your ~*** pour
moi / toi; ***for the ~ of*** pour

sal·ad ['sæləd] salade *f*

'sal·ad dress·ing vinaigrette *f*

sal·a·ry ['sælərɪ] salaire *m*

'sal·a·ry scale échelle *f* des salaires

sale [seɪl] vente *f; reduced prices* soldes
*mpl; **for ~*** *sign* à vendre; ***be on ~*** être
en vente; *at reduced prices* être en
solde

sales [seɪlz] *npl department* vente *f*

'sales clerk *in store* vendeur(-euse)
m(f); **'sales fig·ures** *npl* chiffre *m*
d'affaires; **'sales·man** vendeur *m;
(*rep*) représentant *m*; **'sales
man·ag·er** directeur *m* commercial,
directrice *f* commerciale; **'sales**

meet·ing réunion *f* commerciale; **'sales team** équipe *f* de vente; **'sales·wom·an** vendeuse *f*

sa·lient ['seɪlɪənt] *adj* marquant

sa·li·va [sə'laɪvə] salive *f*

salm·on ['sæmən] (*pl* **salmon**) saumon *m*

sa·loon [sə'luːn] (*bar*) bar *m*

salt [sɒːlt] **1** *n* sel *m* **2** *v/t food* saler

'salt·cel·lar salière *f*; **salt 'wa·ter** eau *f* salée; **'salt-wa·ter fish** poisson *m* de mer

salt·y ['sɒːltɪ] *adj* salé

sal·u·tar·y ['sæljʊterɪ] *adj experience* salutaire

sa·lute [sə'luːt] **1** *n* MIL salut *m*; *take the* ~ passer les troupes en revue **2** *v/t* MIL, *fig* saluer **3** *v/i* MIL faire un salut

sal·vage ['sælvɪdʒ] *v/t from wreck* sauver

sal·va·tion [sæl'veɪʃn] *also fig* salut *m*

Sal·va·tion 'Ar·my Armée *f* du Salut

same [seɪm] **1** *adj* même **2** *pron: the* ~ le / la même; *pl* les mêmes; *Happy New Year - the* ~ *to you* Bonne année - à vous aussi; *he's not the* ~ *any more* il n'est plus celui qu'il était; *all the* ~ (*even so*) quand même; *men are all the* ~ les hommes sont tous les mêmes; *it's all the* ~ *to me* cela m'est égal **3** *adv: smell / look / sound the* ~ se ressembler, être pareil

sam·ple ['sæmpl] *n of work, cloth* échantillon *m*; *of urine* échantillon *m*, prélèvement *m*; *of blood* prélèvement *m*

sanc·ti·mo·ni·ous [sæŋktɪ'moʊnɪəs] *adj* moralisateur*

sanc·tion ['sæŋkʃn] **1** *n* (*approval*) approbation *f*; (*penalty*) sanction *f* **2** *v/t* (*approve*) approuver

sanc·ti·ty ['sæŋktətɪ] caractère *m* sacré

sanc·tu·a·ry ['sæŋktʃʊerɪ] REL sanctuaire *m*; *for wild animals* réserve *f*

sand [sænd] **1** *n* sable *m* **2** *v/t with ~pa-per* poncer au papier de verre

san·dal ['sændl] sandale *f*

'sand·bag sac *m* de sable; **'sand-blast** *v/t* décaper au jet de sable;

'sand dune dune *f*

sand·er ['sændər] *tool* ponceuse *f*

'sand·pa·per 1 *n* papier *m* de verre **2** *v/t* poncer au papier de verre

'sand·stone grès *m*

sand·wich ['sænwɪtʃ] **1** *n* sandwich *m* **2** *v/t: be ~ed between two ...* être coincé entre deux ...

sand·y ['sændɪ] *adj beach* de sable; *soil* sablonneux*; *feet, towel* plein de sable; *hair* blond roux

sane [seɪn] *adj* sain (d'esprit)

sang [sæŋ] *pret* → **sing**

san·i·tar·i·um [sænɪ'terɪəm] sanatorium *m*

san·i·ta·ry ['sænɪterɪ] *adj conditions, installations* sanitaire; (*clean*) hygiénique

'san·i·tary nap·kin serviette *f* hygiénique

san·i·ta·tion [sænɪ'teɪʃn] (*sanitary installations*) installations *fpl* sanitaires; (*removal of waste*) système *m* sanitaire

san·i'ta·tion de·part·ment voirie *f*

san·i·ty ['sænɪtɪ] santé *f* mentale

sank [sæŋk] *pret* → **sink**

San·ta Claus ['sæntəklɔːz] le Père Noël

sap [sæp] **1** *n in tree* sève *f* **2** *v/t* (*pret & pp* **-ped**) *s.o.'s energy* saper

sap·phire ['sæfaɪr] *n jewel* saphir *m*

sar·cas·m ['sɑːrkæzm] sarcasme *m*

sar·cas·tic [sɑːr'kæstɪk] *adj* sarcastique

sar·cas·tic·al·ly [sɑːr'kæstɪklɪ] *adv* sarcastiquement

sar·dine [sɑːr'diːn] *n* sardine *f*

sar·don·ic [sɑːr'dɑːnɪk] *adj* sardonique

sar·don·i·cal·ly [sɑːr'dɑːnɪklɪ] *adv* sardoniquement

sash [sæʃ] *on dress* large ceinture *f* à nœud; *on uniform* écharpe *f*

sat [sæt] *pret & pp* → **sit**

Sa·tan ['seɪtn] Satan *m*

satch·el ['sætʃl] *for schoolchild* cartable *m*

sat·el·lite ['sætəlaɪt] satellite *m*

'sat·el·lite dish antenne *f* parabolique

sat·el·lite T'V télévision *f* par satellite

sat·in ['sætɪn] *n* satin *m*

sat·ire ['sætaɪr] satire *f*

sa·tir·i·cal [sə'tɪrɪkl] *adj* satirique

sat·i·rist ['sætərɪst] satiriste *m/f*

sat·i·rize ['sætəraɪz] *v/t* satiriser

sat·is·fac·tion [sætɪs'fækʃn] satisfaction *f*; **get ~ out of doing sth** trouver de la satisfaction à faire qch; **I get a lot of ~ out of my job** mon travail me donne grande satisfaction; **is that to your ~?** êtes-vous satisfait?

sat·is·fac·to·ry [sætɪs'fæktərɪ] *adj* satisfaisant; *(just good enough)* convenable; **this is not ~** c'est insuffisant

satisfy ['sætɪsfaɪ] *v/t (pret & pp -ied)* satisfaire; *(convince)* convaincre; **I am satisfied** *had enough to eat* je n'ai plus faim; **I am satisfied that he …** *convinced* je suis convaincu qu'il …; **I hope you're satisfied!** te voilà satisfait!

Sat·ur·day ['sætərdeɪ] samedi *m*

sauce [sɔːs] sauce *f*

'sauce·pan casserole *f*

sau·cer ['sɔːsər] soucoupe *f*

saucy ['sɔːsɪ] *adj person, dress* déluré

Sa·u·di A·ra·bi·a [saudɪə'reɪbɪə] Arabie *f* saoudite

Sa·u·di A·ra·bi·an [saudɪə'reɪbɪən] **1** *adj* saoudien* **2** *n* Saoudien(ne) *m(f)*

sau·na ['sɔːnə] sauna *m*

saun·ter ['sɔːntər] *v/i* flâner

sau·sage ['sɔːsɪdʒ] saucisse *f*; *dried* saucisson *m*

sav·age ['sævɪdʒ] **1** *adj* féroce **2** *n* sauvage *m/f*

sav·age·ry ['sævɪdʒrɪ] férocité *f*

save [seɪv] **1** *v/t (rescue)*, SP sauver; *(economize, put aside)* économiser; *(collect)* faire collection de; COMPUT sauvegarder **2** *v/i (put money aside)* faire des économies; SP arrêter le ballon **3** *n* SP arrêt *m*

♦ **save up for** *v/t* économiser pour acheter

sav·er ['seɪvər] *person* épargneur (-euse) *m(f)*

sav·ing ['seɪvɪŋ] *(amount saved)* économie *f*; *activity* épargne *f*

sav·ings ['seɪvɪŋz] *npl* économies *fpl*

'sav·ings ac·count compte *m* d'épargne; **sav·ings and 'loan** caisse *f*

d'épargne-logement; **'sav·ings bank** caisse *f* d'épargne

sa·vior, *Br* **sa·viour** ['seɪvjər] REL sauveur *m*

sa·vor ['seɪvər] *v/t* savourer

sa·vor·y ['seɪvərɪ] *adj (not sweet)* salé

sa·vour *etc Br* → **savor** *etc*

saw[1] [sɔː] *pret* → **see**

saw[2] [sɔː] **1** *n tool* scie *f* **2** *v/t* scier

♦ **saw off** *v/t* enlever à la scie

'saw·dust sciure *f*

sax·o·phone ['sæksəfoun] saxophone *m*

say [seɪ] **1** *v/t (pret & pp said)* dire; **that is to ~** c'est-à-dire; **what do you ~ to that?** qu'est-ce que tu en penses?; **what does the note ~?** que dit le message? **2** *n*: **have one's ~** dire ce qu'on a à dire; **have a ~ in sth** avoir son mot à dire dans qch

say·ing ['seɪɪŋ] dicton *m*

scab [skæb] *on wound* croûte *f*

scaf·fold·ing ['skæfəldɪŋ] échafaudage *m*

scald [skɔːld] *v/t* ébouillanter

scale[1] [skeɪl] *on fish* écaille *f*

scale[2] [skeɪl] **1** *n of project, map etc, on thermometer* échelle *f*; MUS gamme *f*; **on a larger / smaller ~** à plus grande / petite échelle **2** *v/t cliffs etc* escalader

♦ **scale down** *v/t* réduire l'ampleur de

scale 'draw·ing dessin *m* à l'échelle

scales [skeɪlz] *npl for weighing* balance *f*

scal·lop ['skæləp] *n shellfish* coquille *f* Saint-Jacques

scalp [skælp] *n* cuir *m* chevelu

scal·pel ['skælpl] scalpel *m*

scam [skæm] F arnaque *m* F

scan [skæn] **1** *n* MED scanographie *f* **2** *v/t (pret & pp -ned) horizon, page* parcourir du regard; MED faire une scanographie de; COMPUT scanner

♦ **scan in** *v/t* COMPUT scanner

scan·dal ['skændl] scandale *m*

scan·dal·ize ['skændəlaɪz] *v/t* scandaliser

scan·dal·ous ['skændələs] *adj* scandaleux*

Scan·di·na·vi·a [skændɪ'neɪvɪə] Scandinavie f

Scan·di·na·vi·an [skændɪ'neɪvɪən] **1** adj scandinave **2** n Scandinave m/f

scan·ner ['skænər] MED, COMPUT scanneur m

scant [skænt] adj: **have ~ consideration for sth** attacher peu d'importance à qch

scant·i·ly ['skæntɪlɪ] adv: **~ clad** en tenue légère

scant·y ['skæntɪ] adj dress réduit au minimum

scape·goat ['skeɪpgoʊt] bouc m émissaire

scar [skɑːr] **1** n cicatrice f **2** v/t (pret & pp **-red**) marquer d'une cicatrice; **be ~red for life by sth** fig être marqué à vie par qch

scarce [skers] adj in short supply rare; **make o.s. ~** se sauver

scarce·ly ['skerslɪ] adv à peine

scar·ci·ty ['skersɪtɪ] manque m

scare [sker] **1** v/t faire peur à; **be ~d of** avoir peur de **2** n (panic, alarm) rumeurs fpl alarmantes; **give s.o. a ~** faire peur à qn

♦ **scare away** v/t faire fuir

'scare·crow épouvantail m

scare·mon·ger ['skermʌŋgər] alarmiste m/f

scarf [skɑːrf] around neck écharpe f; over head foulard m

scar·let ['skɑːrlət] adj écarlate

scar·let 'fe·ver scarlatine f

scar·y ['skerɪ] adj effrayant

scath·ing ['skeɪðɪŋ] adj cinglant

scat·ter ['skætər] **1** v/t leaflets, seed éparpiller **2** v/i of people se disperser

scat·ter·brained ['skætərbreɪnd] adj écervelé

scat·tered ['skætərd] adj showers intermittent; villages, family éparpillé

scav·enge ['skævɪndʒ] v/i: **~ for sth** fouiller pour trouver qch

scav·eng·er ['skævɪndʒər] animal, bird charognard m; person fouilleur(euse) m/f

sce·na·ri·o [sɪ'nɑːrɪoʊ] scénario m

scene [siːn] THEA, (view, sight, argument) scène f; of accident, crime, novel, movie lieu m; **make a ~** faire une

scène; **~s** THEA décor(s) m(pl); **the jazz / rock ~** le monde du jazz / rock; **behind the ~s** dans les coulisses

sce·ne·ry ['siːnərɪ] paysage m; THEA décor(s) m(pl)

scent [sent] n (smell) odeur f; (perfume) parfum m; of animal piste f

scep·tic etc Br → **skeptic** etc

sched·ule ['skedjuːl, Br; 'ʃedjuːl] **1** n of events calendrier m; for trains horaire m; of lessons, work programme m; **be on ~** of work, workers être dans les temps; of train être à l'heure; **be behind ~** être en retard **2** v/t (put on ~) prévoir

sched·uled flight ['ʃeduːld] vol m régulier

scheme [skiːm] **1** n plan m **2** v/i (plot) comploter

schem·ing ['skiːmɪŋ] adj intrigant

schiz·o·phre·ni·a [skɪtsə'friːnɪə] schizophrénie f

schiz·o·phren·ic [skɪtsə'frenɪk] **1** adj schizophrène **2** n schizophrène m/f

schol·ar ['skɑːlər] érudit(e) m(f)

schol·ar·ly ['skɑːlərlɪ] adj savant, érudit

schol·ar·ship ['skɑːlərʃɪp] (learning) érudition f; financial award bourse f

school [skuːl] n école f; (university) université f

'school bag (satchel) cartable m; **'school·boy** écolier m; **'school·child·ren** npl écoliers mpl; **'school days** npl années fpl d'école; **'school·girl** écolière f; **'school·teach·er → teacher**

sci·at·i·ca [saɪ'ætɪkə] sciatique f

sci·ence ['saɪəns] science f

sci·ence 'fic·tion science-fiction f

sci·en·tif·ic [saɪən'tɪfɪk] adj scientifique

sci·en·tist ['saɪəntɪst] scientifique m/f

scis·sors ['sɪzərz] npl ciseaux mpl

scoff¹ [skɑːf] v/t food engloutir

scoff² [skɑːf] v/i (mock) se moquer

♦ **scoff at** v/t se moquer de

scold [skoʊld] v/t réprimander

scoop [skuːp] **1** n for ice-cream cuiller f à glace; for grain, flour pelle f; on *dredger* benne *f* preneuse; *of ice cream* boule *f*; *story* scoop *m* **2** *v/t of machine* ramasser; *ice cream* prendre une boule de

♦ **scoop up** *v/t* ramasser

scoot·er ['sku:tər] *with motor* scooter *m*; *child's* trottinette *f*

scope [skəʊp] ampleur *f*; (*freedom, opportunity*) possibilités *fpl*; **he wants more ~** il voudrait plus de liberté

scorch [skɔ:rtʃ] *v/t* brûler

scorch·ing ['skɔ:rtʃɪŋ] *adj* très chaud

score [skɔ:r] **1** *n* SP score *m*; (*written music*) partition *f*; *of movie etc* musique *f*; **what's the ~?** SP quel est le score?; **have a ~ to settle with s.o.** avoir un compte à régler avec qn; **keep (the) ~** marquer les points **2** *v/t goal, point* marquer; (*cut: line*) rayer **3** *v/i* SP marquer; (*keep the ~*) marquer les points; **that's where he ~s** c'est son point fort

'**score·board** tableau *m* des scores

scor·er ['skɔ:rər] *of goal, point, (scorekeeper)* marqueur(-euse) *m(f)*

scorn [skɔ:rn] **1** *n* mépris *m*; **pour ~ on sth** traiter qch avec mépris **2** *v/t idea, suggestion* mépriser

scorn·ful ['skɔ:rnfʊl] *adj* méprisant

scorn·ful·ly ['skɔ:rnfʊlɪ] *adv* avec mépris

Scor·pi·o ['skɔ:rpɪəʊ] ASTROL Scorpion *m*

Scot [skɑ:t] Écossais(e) *m(f)*

Scotch [skɑ:tʃ] *whiskey* scotch *m*

Scotch 'tape® scotch *m*

scot-'free *adv*: **get off ~** se tirer d'affaire

Scot·land ['skɑ:tlənd] Écosse *f*

Scots·man ['skɑ:tsmən] Écossais *m*

Scots·wom·an ['skɑ:tswʊmən] Écossaise *f*

Scot·tish ['skɑ:tɪʃ] *adj* écossais

scoun·drel ['skaʊndrəl] gredin *m*

scour[1] ['skaʊər] *v/t* (*search*) fouiller

scour[2] ['skaʊər] *v/t pans* récurer

scout [skaʊt] *n* (*boy ~*) scout *m*

scowl [skaʊl] **1** *n* air *m* renfrogné **2** *v/i* se renfrogner

scram [skræm] *v/i* (*pret & pp* **-med**) F

ficher le camp F

scram·ble ['skræmbl] **1** *n* (*rush*) course *f* folle **2** *v/t message* brouiller **3** *v/i*: **~d to his feet** il se releva d'un bond

scram·bled eggs ['skræmbld] *npl* œufs *mpl* brouillés

scrap [skræp] **1** *n metal* ferraille *f*; (*fight*) bagarre *f*; *of food, paper* bout *m*; **there isn't a ~ of evidence** il n'y a pas la moindre preuve **2** *v/t* (*pret & pp* **-ped**) *idea, plan etc* abandonner

scrape [skreɪp] **1** *n on paint, skin* éraflure *f* **2** *v/t paintwork, arm etc* érafler; *vegetables* gratter; **~ a living** vivoter

♦ **scrape through** *v/i in exam* réussir de justesse

'**scrap heap** tas *m* de ferraille; **good for the ~** *also fig* bon pour la ferraille; **scrap 'met·al** ferraille *f*; **scrap 'pa·per** brouillon *m*

scrap·py ['skræpɪ] *adj work, essay* décousu; *person* bagarreur*

scratch [skrætʃ] **1** *n mark* égratignure *f*; **have a ~** *to stop itching* se gratter; **start from ~** partir de zéro; **not up to ~** pas à la hauteur **2** *v/t* (*mark: skin, paint*) égratigner; *of cat* griffer; *because of itch* se gratter; **he ~ed his head** il se gratta la tête **3** *v/i of cat* griffer

scrawl [skrɔ:l] **1** *n* gribouillis *m* **2** *v/t* gribouiller

scraw·ny ['skrɔ:nɪ] *adj* décharné

scream [skri:m] **1** *n cri m*; **~s of laughter** hurlements *mpl* de rire **2** *v/i* pousser un cri

screech [skri:tʃ] **1** *n of tires* crissement *m*; (*scream*) cri *m* strident **2** *v/i of tires* crisser; (*scream*) pousser un cri strident

screen [skri:n] **1** *n in room, hospital* paravent *m*; *in movie theater, of TV, computer* écran *m*; **on the ~** *in movie* à l'écran; **on (the) ~** COMPUT sur l'écran **2** *v/t* (*protect, hide*) cacher; *movie* projeter; *for security reasons* passer au crible

'**screen·play** scénario *m*; '**screen sav·er** COMPUT économiseur *m* d'écran; '**screen test** *for movie* bout *m* d'essai

screw [skruː] **1** *n* vis *m*; *I had a good ~* V j'ai bien baisé V **2** *v/t attach* visser (*to* à); F (*cheat*) rouler F; V (*have sex with*) baiser V

♦ **screw up 1** *v/t eyes* plisser; *paper* chiffonner; F (*make a mess of sth*) foutre en l'air **2** *v/i* F merder F

'**screw·driv·er** tournevis *m*

screwed up [skruːd'ʌp] *adj* F *psychologically* paumé F

'**screw top** *on bottle* couvercle *m* à pas de vis

screw·y ['skruːɪ] *adj* F déjanté F

scrib·ble ['skrɪbl] **1** *n* griffonnage *m* **2** *v/t* (*write quickly*) griffonner **3** *v/i* gribouiller

scrimp [skrɪmp] *v/i*: *~ and save* économiser par tous les moyens

script [skrɪpt] *for movie* scénario *m*; *for play* texte *m*; *form of writing* script *m*

Scrip·ture ['skrɪptʃər]: *the ~s* les Saintes Écritures *fpl*

'**script·writ·er** scénariste *m/f*

♦ **scroll down** [skroʊl] *v/i* COMPUT faire défiler vers le bas

♦ **scroll up** *v/i* COMPUT faire défiler vers le haut

scrounge [skraʊndʒ] *v/t* se faire offrir

scroung·er ['skraʊndʒər] profiteur (-euse) *m(f)*

scrub [skrʌb] *v/t* (*pret & pp* **-bed**) *floor* laver à la brosse; *~ one's hands* se brosser les mains

'**scrub·bing brush** ['skrʌbɪŋ] *for floor* brosse *f* dure

scruff·y ['skrʌfɪ] *adj* débraillé

scrum [skrʌm] *in rugby* mêlée *f*

'**scrum·half** demi *m* de mêlée

♦ **scrunch up** [skrʌntʃ] *v/t plastic cup etc* écraser

scru·ples ['skruːplz] *npl* scrupules *mpl*; *have no ~ about doing sth* n'avoir aucun scrupule à faire qch

scru·pu·lous ['skruːpjʊləs] *adj morally*, (*thorough*) scrupuleux*

scru·pu·lous·ly ['skruːpjʊləslɪ] *adv* (*meticulously*) scrupuleusement

scru·ti·nize ['skruːtɪnaɪz] *v/t* (*examine closely*) scruter

scru·ti·ny ['skruːtɪnɪ] examen *m* minutieux*; *come under ~* faire l'objet d'un examen minutieux

scu·ba div·ing ['skuːbə] plongée *f* sous-marine autonome

scuf·fle ['skʌfl] *n* bagarre *f*

sculp·tor ['skʌlptər] sculpteur(-trice) *m(f)*

sculp·ture ['skʌlptʃər] sculpture *f*

scum [skʌm] *on liquid* écume *f*; *pej: people* bande *f* d'ordures F; *he's ~* c'est une ordure, c'est un salaud

sea [siː] mer *f*; *by the ~* au bord de la mer

'**sea·bed** fond *m* de la mer; '**sea·bird** oiseau *m* de mer; **sea·far·ing** ['siːferɪŋ] *adj nation* de marins; '**sea·food** fruits *mpl* de mer; '**sea·front** bord *m* de mer; '**sea·go·ing** *adj vessel* de mer; '**sea·gull** mouette *f*

seal¹ [siːl] *n animal* phoque *m*

seal² [siːl] **1** *n on document* sceau *m*; TECH étanchéité *f*; *device* joint *m* (d'étanchéité) **2** *v/t container* sceller

♦ **seal off** *v/t area* boucler

'**sea lev·el**: *above / below ~* au-dessus / au-dessous du niveau de la mer

seam [siːm] *on garment* couture *f*; *of ore* veine *f*

'**sea·man** marin *m*

'**sea·port** port *m* maritime

'**sea pow·er** *nation* puissance *f* maritime

search [sɜːrtʃ] **1** *n* recherche *f* (*for* de); *be in ~ of* être à la recherche de **2** *v/t city*, *files* chercher dans

♦ **search for** *v/t* chercher

search·ing ['sɜːrtʃɪŋ] *adj look*, *question* pénétrant

'**search·light** projecteur *m*; '**search par·ty** groupe à la recherche d'un disparu ou de disparus; '**search war·rant** mandat *m* de perquisition

'**sea·shore** plage *f*; '**sea·sick** *adj*: *get ~* avoir le mal de mer; '**sea·side**: *at the ~* au bord de la mer; *go to the ~* aller au bord de la mer; '**sea·side re·sort** station *f* balnéaire

sea·son ['siːzn] *n also for tourism etc* saison *f*; *plums are / aren't in ~* c'est / ce n'est pas la saison des pru-

nes
sea·son·al ['siːznl] *adj vegetables, employment* saisonnier*
sea·soned ['siːznd] *adj wood* sec*; *traveler, campaigner* expérimenté
sea·son·ing ['siːznɪŋ] assaisonnement *m*
'**sea·son tick·et** carte *f* d'abonnement
seat [siːt] **1** *n* place *f*; *chair* siège *m*; *of pants* fond *m*; *please take a ~* veuillez vous asseoir **2** *v/t: the hall can ~ 200 people* la salle contient 200 places assises; *please remain ~ed* veuillez rester assis
'**seat belt** ceinture *f* de sécurité
'**sea ur·chin** oursin *m*
'**sea·weed** algues *fpl*
se·clud·ed [sɪ'kluːdɪd] *adj* retiré
se·clu·sion [sɪ'kluːʒn] isolement *m*
sec·ond[1] ['sekənd] **1** *n of time* seconde *f*; *just a ~* un instant; *the ~ of June* le deux juin **2** *adj* deuxième **3** *adv come in* deuxième; *he's the ~ tallest in the school* c'est le deuxième plus grand de l'école **4** *v/t motion* appuyer
se·cond[2] [sɪ'kɑːnd] *v/t: be ~ed to* être détaché à
sec·ond·a·ry ['sekəndrɪ] *adj* secondaire; *of ~ importance* secondaire
sec·ond·a·ry ed·u·ca·tion enseignement *m* secondaire
sec·ond-best *adj runner, time* deuxième; *(inferior)* de second ordre; **sec·ond 'big·gest** *adj* deuxième; **sec·ond 'class** *adj ticket* de seconde classe; **sec·ond 'floor** premier étage *m*, *Br* deuxième étage *m*; **sec·ond 'gear** MOT seconde *f*; '**sec·ond hand** *n on clock* trotteuse *f*; **sec·ond-'hand** *adj & adv* d'occasion
sec·ond·ly ['sekəndlɪ] *adv* deuxièmement
sec·ond-'rate *adj* de second ordre
sec·ond 'thoughts: *I've had ~* j'ai changé d'avis
se·cre·cy ['siːkrəsɪ] secret *m*
se·cret ['siːkrət] **1** *n* secret *m*; *do sth in ~* faire qch en secret **2** *adj* secret*
se·cret 'a·gent agent *m* secret
sec·re·tar·i·al [sekrə'terɪəl] *adj tasks, job* de secrétariat

sec·re·tar·y ['sekrətərɪ] secrétaire *m/f*; *pol* ministre *m/f*
Sec·re·tar·y of 'State *in USA* secrétaire *m/f* d'État
se·crete [sɪ'kriːt] *v/t (give off)* sécréter; *(hide)* cacher
se·cre·tion [sɪ'kriːʃn] sécrétion *f*
se·cre·tive ['siːkrətɪv] *adj* secret*
se·cret·ly ['siːkrətlɪ] *adv* en secret
se·cret po·lice police *f* secrète
se·cret 'ser·vice services *mpl* secrets
sect [sekt] secte *f*
sec·tion ['sekʃn] section *f*
sec·tor ['sektər] secteur *m*
sec·u·lar ['sekjʊlər] *adj* séculier*
se·cure [sɪ'kjʊr] **1** *adj shelf etc* bien fixé; *job, contract* sûr **2** *v/t shelf etc* fixer; *s.o.'s help, finances* se procurer
se·cu·ri·ties mar·ket [sɪ'kjʊrətɪz] fin marché *m* des valeurs, marché *m* des titres
se·cu·ri·ty [sɪ'kjʊrətɪ] sécurité *f*, *for investment* garantie *f*; *tackle ~ problems* POL combattre l'insécurité
se·cu·ri·ty a·lert alerte *f* de sécurité; **se'cu·ri·ty check** contrôle *m* de sécurité; **se'cu·ri·ty-con·scious** *adj* sensible à la sécurité; **se'cu·ri·ty for·ces** *npl* forces *fpl* de sécurité; **se'cu·ri·ty guard** garde *m* de sécurité; **se'cu·ri·ty risk** *person* menace potentielle à la sécurité de l'État ou d'une organisation
se·dan [sɪ'dæn] *mot* berline *f*
se·date [sɪ'deɪt] *v/t* donner un calmant à
se·da·tion [sɪ'deɪʃn]: *be under ~* être sous calmants
sed·a·tive ['sedətɪv] *n* calmant *m*
sed·en·ta·ry ['sedəntərɪ] *adj job* sédentaire
sed·i·ment ['sedɪmənt] sédiment *m*
se·duce [sɪ'duːs] *v/t* séduire
se·duc·tion [sɪ'dʌkʃn] séduction *f*
se·duc·tive [sɪ'dʌktɪv] *adj dress, offer* séduisant
see [siː] *v/t (pret saw, pp seen) with eyes, (understand)* voir; *romantically* sortir avec; *I ~* je vois; *oh, I ~* ah bon!; *can I ~ the manager?* puis-je voir le directeur?; *you should ~ a doctor* tu devrais aller voir un doc-

teur; **~ s.o. home** raccompagner qn chez lui; **I'll ~ you to the door** je vais vous raccompagner à la porte; **~ you!** F à plus! F

♦ **see about** v/t: **I'll see about it** je vais m'en occuper

♦ **see off** v/t at airport etc raccompagner; (chase away) chasser; **they came to see me off** ils sont venus me dire au revoir

♦ **see out** v/t: **see s.o. out** raccompagner qn

♦ **see to** v/t: **see to sth** s'occuper de qch; **see to it that sth gets done** veiller à ce que qch soit fait

seed [siːd] single graine f; collective graines fpl; of fruit pépin m; in tennis tête f de série; **go to ~** of person se laisser aller; of district se dégrader

seed·ling ['siːdlɪŋ] semis m

seed·y ['siːdɪ] adj miteux*

see·ing 'eye dog ['siːɪŋ] chien m d'aveugle

see·ing (that) ['siːɪŋ] conj étant donné que

seek [siːk] v/t (pret & pp **sought**) chercher

seem [siːm] v/i sembler; **it ~s that ...** il semble que ... (+subj)

seem·ing·ly ['siːmɪŋlɪ] adv apparemment

seen [siːn] pp → **see**

seep [siːp] v/i of liquid suinter

♦ **seep out** v/i of liquid suinter

see·saw ['siːsɔː] n bascule f

seethe [siːð] v/i fig: **~ (with rage)** être furieux

'see-through adj dress, material transparent

seg·ment ['segmənt] segment m; of orange morceau m

seg·ment·ed [seg'mentɪd] adj segmenté

seg·re·gate ['segrɪgeɪt] v/t séparer

seg·re·ga·tion [segrɪ'geɪʃn] of races ségrégation f; of sexes séparation f

seis·mol·o·gy [saɪz'mɒlədʒɪ] sismologie f

seize [siːz] v/t opportunity, arm, of police etc saisir; power s'emparer de

♦ **seize up** v/i of engine se gripper

sei·zure ['siːʒər] med crise f; of drugs etc saisie f

sel·dom ['seldəm] adv rarement

se·lect [sɪ'lekt] **1** v/t sélectionner **2** adj group of people choisi; hotel, restaurant etc chic inv

se·lec·tion [sɪ'lekʃn] sélection f

se·lec·tion pro·cess sélection f

se·lec·tive [sɪ'lektɪv] adj sélectif*

self [self] (pl **selves** [selvz]) moi m

self-ad·dressed en·ve·lope [selfə'drest]: **please send us a ~** veuillez nous envoyer une enveloppe à votre nom et adresse; **self-as·sur·ance** confiance f en soi; **self-as·sured** [selfə'ʃʊrd] adj sûr de soi; **self-cen·tered**, Br **self-cen·tred** [self'sentərd] adj égocentrique; **self-'clean·ing** adj oven autonettoyant; **self-con·fessed** [selfkən'fest] adj de son propre aveu; **self-'con·fi·dence** confiance en soi; **self-'con·fi·dent** adj sûr de soi; **self-'con·scious** adj intimidé; about sth gêné (about par); **self-'con·scious·ness** timidité f; about sth gêne f (about par rapport à); **self-con·tained** [selfkən'teɪnd] adj apartment indépendant; **self-con'trol** contrôle m de soi; **self-de'fense**, Br **self-de·fence** autodéfense f; LAW légitime défense f; **self-'dis·ci·pline** autodiscipline f; **self-'doubt** manque m de confiance en soi; **self-em·ployed** [selfɪm'plɔɪd] adj indépendant; **self-e'steem** amour-propre m; **self-'ev·i·dent** adj évident; **self-ex-'pres·sion** expression f; **self-'gov·ern·ment** autonomie f; **self-'in·terest** intérêt m

self·ish ['selfɪʃ] adj égoïste

self·less ['selflɪs] adj désintéressé

self-made 'man self-made man m; **self-'pit·y** apitoiement m sur soi-même; **self-'por·trait** autoportrait m; **self-pos·sessed** [selfpə'zest] adj assuré; **self-re'li·ant** adj autonome; **self-re'spect** respect m de soi; **self-right·eous** [self'raɪtʃəs] adj pej content de soi; **self-'sat·is·fied** [self'sætɪsfaɪd] adj pej suffisant;

self-'ser·vice adj libre-service; self-ser·vice 'res·tau·rant self m; self-'taught adj autodidacte

sell [sel] 1 v/t (pret & pp sold) vendre 2 v/i (pret & pp sold) of products se vendre

♦ sell out v/i: we've sold out nous avons tout vendu

♦ sell out of v/t vendre tout son stock de

♦ sell up v/i tout vendre

'sell-by date date f limite de vente; be past its ~ être périmé; he's past his ~ F il a fait son temps

sell·er ['selər] vendeur(-euse) m(f)

sell·ing ['selɪŋ] COMM vente f

'sell·ing point COMM point m fort

Sel·lo·tape® ['seləteɪp] Br scotch m

se·men ['siːmən] sperme m

se·mes·ter [sɪ'mestər] semestre m

sem·i ['semɪ] truck semi-remorque f

'sem·i·cir·cle demi-cercle m; sem·i·'cir·cu·lar adj demi-circulaire; sem·i·'co·lon point-virgule m; sem·i·con'duc·tor ELEC semi-conducteur m; sem·i'fi·nal demi-finale f

sem·i·nar ['semɪnɑːr] séminaire m

sem·i'skilled adj worker spécialisé

sen·ate ['senət] POL Sénat m

sen·a·tor ['senətər] sénateur(-trice) m(f)

send [send] v/t (pret & pp sent) envoyer (to a); ~ s.o. to s.o. envoyer qn chez qn; ~ her my best wishes envoyez-lui tous mes vœux

♦ send back v/t renvoyer

♦ send for v/t doctor faire venir; help envoyer chercher

♦ send in v/t troops, form envoyer; next interviewee faire entrer

♦ send off v/t letter, fax etc envoyer

send·er ['sendər] of letter expéditeur (-trice) m(f)

se·nile ['siːnaɪl] adj sénile

se·nil·i·ty [sɪ'nɪlətɪ] sénilité f

se·ni·or ['siːnjər] adj (older) plus âgé; in rank supérieur; be ~ to s.o. in rank être au-dessus de qn

se·ni·or 'cit·i·zen personne f âgée

se·ni·or·i·ty [siːnjɑː'rɑːtɪ] in job an-

cienneté f

sen·sa·tion [sen'seɪʃn] sensation f; cause a ~ faire sensation; be a ~ (s.o. / sth very good) être sensationnel*

sen·sa·tion·al [sen'seɪʃnl] adj sensationnel*

sense [sens] 1 n sens m; (common ~) bon sens m; (feeling) sentiment m; in a ~ dans un sens; talk ~, man! sois raisonnable!; come to one's ~s revenir à la raison; it doesn't make ~ cela n'a pas de sens; there's no ~ in waiting cela ne sert à rien d'attendre 2 v/t sentir

sense·less ['senslɪs] adj (pointless) stupide; accusation gratuit

sen·si·ble ['sensəbl] adj sensé; clothes, shoes pratique

sen·si·bly ['sensəblɪ] adv raisonnablement

sen·si·tive ['sensətɪv] adj skin, person sensible

sen·si·tiv·i·ty [sensə'tɪvətɪ] of skin, person sensibilité f

sen·sor ['sensər] détecteur m

sen·su·al ['senʃʊəl] adj sensuel*

sen·su·al·i·ty [senʃʊ'ælətɪ] sensualité f

sen·su·ous ['senʃʊəs] adj voluptueux*

sent [sent] pret & pp → send

sen·tence ['sentəns] 1 n GRAM phrase f; LAW peine f 2 v/t LAW condamner

sen·ti·ment ['sentɪmənt] (sentimentality) sentimentalité f; (opinion) sentiment m

sen·ti·men·tal [sentɪ'mentl] adj sentimental

sen·ti·men·tal·i·ty [sentɪmen'tælətɪ] sentimentalité f

sen·try ['sentrɪ] sentinelle f

sep·a·rate¹ ['sepərət] adj séparé; keep sth ~ from sth ne pas mélanger qch avec qch

sep·a·rate² ['sepəreɪt] 1 v/t séparer (from de) 2 v/i of couple se séparer

sep·a·rat·ed ['sepəreɪtɪd] adj couple séparé

sep·a·rate·ly ['sepərətlɪ] adv séparément

sep·a·ra·tion [sepəˈreɪʃn] séparation *f*
Sep·tem·ber [sepˈtembər] septembre *m*
sep·tic [ˈseptɪk] *adj* septique; **go ~ of** *wound* s'infecter
se·quel [ˈsiːkwəl] *n* suite *f*
se·quence [ˈsiːkwəns] ordre *m*; **in ~** l'un après l'autre; **out of ~** en désordre; **the ~ of events** le déroulement des événements
se·rene [sɪˈriːn] *adj* serein
ser·geant [ˈsɑːrdʒənt] sergent *m*
se·ri·al [ˈsɪrɪəl] *n* feuilleton *m*
se·ri·al·ize [ˈsɪrɪəlaɪz] *v/t* *novel on TV* adapter en feuilleton
se·ri·al kill·er tueur(-euse) *m(f)* en série; **se·ri·al num·ber** *of product* numéro *m* de série; **se·ri·al port** COMPUT port *m* série
se·ries [ˈsɪriːz] *nsg* série *f*
se·ri·ous [ˈsɪrɪəs] *adj* *person, company* sérieux*; *illness, situation, damage* grave; **I'm ~** je suis sérieux; **we'd bet·ter have a ~ think about it** nous ferions mieux d'y penser sérieusement
se·ri·ous·ly [ˈsɪrɪəslɪ] *adv* *injured* gravement; *understaffed* sérieusement; **~ intend to …** avoir sérieusement l'intention de …; **~?** vraiment?; **take s.o. ~** prendre qn au sérieux
se·ri·ous·ness [ˈsɪrɪəsnɪs] *of person, situation, illness etc* gravité *f*
ser·mon [ˈsɜːrmən] sermon *m*
ser·vant [ˈsɜːrvənt] domestique *m/f*
serve [sɜːrv] **1** *n* *in tennis* service *m* **2** *v/t* *food, customer, one's country etc* servir; **it ~s you / him right** c'est bien fait pour toi / lui **3** *v/i* (*give out food*), *in tennis* servir; **~ in a gov·ernment** *of politician* être membre d'un gouvernement
♦ **serve up** *v/t* *meal* servir
serv·er [ˈsɜːrvər] *in tennis* serveur (-euse) *m(f)*; COMPUT serveur *m*
ser·vice [ˈsɜːrvɪs] **1** *n* *also in tennis* service *m*; *for vehicle, machine* entretien *m*; **~s** *fpl* services *mpl*; **the ~s** MIL les forces *fpl* armées **2** *v/t* *vehicle, machine* entretenir
'ser·vice ar·e·a aire *f* de services; **'ser·vice charge** *in restaurant, club*

service *m*; **'ser·vice in·dus·try** industrie *f* de services; **'ser·vice·man** MIL militaire *m*; **'ser·vice pro·vid·er** COMPUT fournisseur *m* de service; **'ser·vice sec·tor** secteur *m* tertiaire; **'ser·vice sta·tion** station-service *f*
ser·vile [ˈsɜːrvaɪl] *adj pej* servile
serv·ing [ˈsɜːrvɪŋ] *of food* portion *f*
ses·sion [ˈseʃn] *of Congress, parliament* session *f*; *with psychiatrist, specialist etc* séance *f*; *meeting, talk* discussion *f*
set [set] **1** *n* (*collection*) série *f*; (*group of people*) groupe *m*; MATH ensemble *m*; THEA (*scenery*) décor *m*; *for movie* plateau *m*; *in tennis* set *m*; **television ~** poste *m* de télévision **2** *v/t* (*pret & pp set*) (*place*) poser; *movie, novel etc* situer; *date, time, limit* fixer; *mechanism, alarm clock* mettre; *broken limb* remettre en place; *jewel* sertir; (*type~*) composer; **~ the table** mettre la table; **~ s.o. a task** donner une tâche à qn **3** *v/i* (*pret & pp set*) *of sun* se coucher; *of glue* durcir **4** *adj* *views, ideas* arrêté; (*ready*) prêt; **be dead ~ on doing sth** être fermement résolu à faire qch; **be ~ in one's ways** être conservateur; **~ meal** table *f* d'hôte
♦ **set apart** *v/t* distinguer (**from** de)
♦ **set aside** *v/t* *for future use* mettre de côté
♦ **set back** *v/t* *in plans etc* retarder; **it set me back $400** F cela m'a coûté 400 $
♦ **set off** **1** *v/i* *on journey* partir **2** *v/t* *alarm etc* déclencher
♦ **set out** **1** *v/i* *on journey* partir **2** *v/t* *ideas, proposal, goods* exposer; **set out to do sth** (*intend*) chercher à faire qch
♦ **set to** *v/i* (*start on a task*) s'y mettre
♦ **set up** **1** *v/t* *company, equipment, machine* monter; *market stall* installer; *meeting* arranger; F (*frame*) faire un coup à **2** *v/i* *in business* s'établir
'set·back revers *m*
set·tee [seˈtiː] (*couch, sofa*) canapé *m*
set·ting [ˈsetɪŋ] *of novel, play, house* cadre *m*

set·tle ['setl] **1** *v/i* *of bird* se poser; *of sediment, dust* se déposer; *of building* se tasser; *to live* s'installer **2** *v/t dispute, issue, debts* régler; *nerves, stomach* calmer; ***that ~s it!*** ça règle la question!

♦ **settle down** *v/i* (*stop being noisy*) se calmer; (*stop wild living*) se ranger; *in an area* s'installer

♦ **settle for** *v/t* (*take, accept*) accepter

♦ **settle up** *v/i* *pay bill* payer, régler; ***settle up with s.o.*** payer qn

set·tled ['setld] *adj weather* stable

set·tle·ment ['setlmənt] *of claim, debt, dispute*, (*payment*) règlement *m*; *of building* tassement *m*

set·tler ['setlər] *in new country* colon *m*

'set-up (*structure*) organisation *f*; (*relationship*) relation *f*; F (*frameup*) coup *m* monté

sev·en ['sevn] sept

sev·en·teen [sevn'ti:n] dix-sept

sev·en·teenth [sevn'ti:nθ] dix-septième; → *fifth*

sev·enth ['sevnθ] septième; → *fifth*

sev·en·ti·eth ['sevntɪθ] soixante-dixième

sev·en·ty ['sevntɪ] soixante-dix

sev·er ['sevər] *v/t arm, cable etc* sectionner; *relations* rompre

sev·er·al ['sevrl] *adj & pron* plusieurs

se·vere [sɪ'vɪr] *adj illness* grave; *penalty* lourd; *winter, weather* rigoureux*; *disruption* gros*; *teacher, parents* sévère

se·vere·ly [sɪ'vɪrlɪ] *adv punish, speak* sévèrement; *injured* grièvement; *disrupted* fortement

se·ver·i·ty [sɪ'verətɪ] *of illness* gravité *f*; *of penalty* lourdeur *f*; *of winter* rigueur *f*; *of teacher, parents* sévérité *f*

sew [sou] *v/t & v/i* (*pret* **-ed**, *pp* **sewn**) coudre

♦ **sew on** *v/t button* coudre

sew·age ['su:dʒ] eaux *fpl* d'égouts

'sew·age plant usine *f* de traitement des eaux usées

sew·er ['su:ər] égout *m*

sew·ing ['souɪŋ] *skill* couture *f*; (*that being sewn*) ouvrage *m*

'sew·ing ma·chine machine *f* à cou-

dre

sewn [soun] *pp* → *sew*

sex [seks] sexe *m*; **have ~ with** coucher avec, avoir des rapports sexuels avec

sex·ist ['seksɪst] **1** *adj* sexiste **2** *n* sexiste *m/f*

sex·u·al ['sekʃʊəl] *adj* sexuel*

sex·u·al as'sault violences *fpl* sexuelles; **sex·u·al ha'rass·ment** harcèlement *m* sexuel; **sex·u·al 'in·ter·course** rapports *mpl* sexuels

sex·u·al·i·ty [sekʃʊ'ælətɪ] sexualité *f*

sex·u·al·ly ['sekʃʊlɪ] *adv* sexuellement

sex·u·al·ly trans·mit·ted dis'ease maladie *f* sexuellement transmissible

sex·y ['seksɪ] *adj* sexy *inv*

shab·bi·ly ['ʃæbɪlɪ] *adv dressed* pauvrement; *treat* mesquinement

shab·bi·ness ['ʃæbɪnɪs] *of coat, clothes* aspect *m* usé

shab·by ['ʃæbɪ] *adj coat etc* usé; *treatment* mesquin

shack [ʃæk] cabane *f*

shade [ʃeɪd] **1** *n for lamp* abat-jour *m*; *of color* nuance *f*; *on window* store *m*; **in the ~** à l'ombre **2** *v/t from sun* protéger du soleil; *from light* protéger de la lumière

shades [ʃeɪdz] *npl* F lunettes *fpl* de soleil

shad·ow ['ʃædou] *n* ombre *f*

shad·y ['ʃeɪdɪ] *adj spot* ombragé; *fig: character, dealings* louche

shaft [ʃæft] *of axle* arbre *m*; *of mine* puits *m*

shag·gy ['ʃægɪ] *adj hair* hirsute; *dog* à longs poils

shake [ʃeɪk] **1** *n:* **give sth a good ~** bien agiter qch **2** *v/t* (*pret* **shook**, *pp* **shaken**) *bottle* agiter; *emotionally* bouleverser; **~ one's head** *in refusal* dire non de la tête; **~ hands** *of two people* se serrer la main; **~ hands with s.o.** serrer la main à qn **3** *v/i* (*pret* **shook**, *pp* **shaken**) *of hands, voice, building* trembler

shak·en ['ʃeɪkn] **1** *adj emotionally* bouleversé **2** *pp* → *shake*

'shake-up remaniement *m*

shak·y ['ʃeɪkɪ] *adj table etc* branlant;

after illness, shock faible; *voice, hand* tremblant; *grasp of sth, grammar etc* incertain

shall [ʃæl] *v/aux* ◇ *future*: **I ~ do my best** je ferai de mon mieux; **I shan't see them** je ne les verrai pas ◇ *suggesting*: **~ we go now?** si nous y allions maintenant?

shal·low ['ʃælou] *adj water* peu profond; *person* superficiel*

sham·bles ['ʃæmblz] *nsg*: **be a ~ room etc** être en pagaille; *elections etc* être un vrai foutoir F

shame [ʃeɪm] **1** *n* honte *f*; **bring ~ on** déshonorer; **~ on you!** quelle honte!; **what a ~!** quel dommage! **2** *v/t* faire honte à; **~ s.o. into doing sth** faire honte à qn pour qu'il fasse (*subj*) qch

shame·ful ['ʃeɪmful] *adj* honteux*

shame·ful·ly ['ʃeɪmfulɪ] *adv* honteusement

shame·less ['ʃeɪmlɪs] *adj* effronté

sham·poo [ʃæm'puː] **1** *n* shampo(o)ing *m*; **a ~ and set** un shampo(o)ing et mise en plis **2** *v/t* faire un shampo(o)ing à; **~ one's hair** se faire un shampo(o)ing

shape [ʃeɪp] **1** *n* forme *f* **2** *v/t clay, character* façonner; *the future* influencer
♦ **shape up** *v/i of person* s'en sortir; *of plans etc* se présenter

shape·less ['ʃeɪplɪs] *adj dress etc* informe

shape·ly ['ʃeɪplɪ] *adv figure* bien fait

share [ʃer] **1** *n part f*; FIN action *f*; **do one's ~ of the work** fournir sa part de travail **2** *v/t food, room, feelings, opinions* partager **3** *v/i* partager
♦ **share out** *v/t* partager

'share·hold·er actionnaire *m/f*

shark [ʃɑːrk] *fish* requin *m*

sharp [ʃɑːrp] **1** *adj knife* tranchant; *fig: mind, pain* vif*; *taste* piquant; **C / G ~** MUS do / sol dièse **2** *adv* MUS trop haut; **at 3 o'clock ~** à 3 heures pile

sharp·en ['ʃɑːrpn] *v/t knife, skills* aiguiser

sharpen *pencil* tailler

sharp 'prac·tice procédés *mpl* malhonnêtes

shat [ʃæt] *pret & pp* → **shit**

shat·ter ['ʃætər] **1** *v/t glass, illusions* briser **2** *v/i of glass* se briser

shat·tered ['ʃætərd] *adj* F (*exhausted*) crevé F; F (*very upset*) bouleversé

shat·ter·ing ['ʃætərɪŋ] *adj news, experience* bouleversant

shave [ʃeɪv] **1** *v/t* raser **2** *v/i* se raser **3** *n*: **have a ~** se raser; **that was a close ~** on l'a échappé belle
♦ **shave off** *v/t beard* se raser; *piece of wood* enlever

shav·en ['ʃeɪvn] *adj head* rasé

shav·er ['ʃeɪvər] rasoir *m* électrique

shav·ing brush ['ʃeɪvɪŋ] blaireau *m*

'shav·ing soap savon *m* à barbe

shawl [ʃɔːl] châle *m*

she [ʃiː] *pron* elle; **~ was the one who ...** c'est elle qui ...; **there ~ is** la voilà; **~ who ...** celle qui ...

shears [ʃɪrz] *npl for gardening* cisailles *fpl*; *for sewing* grands ciseaux *mpl*

sheath [ʃiːθ] *for knife* étui *m*; *contraceptive* préservatif *m*

shed¹ [ʃed] *v/t (pret & pp shed) blood, tears* verser; *leaves* perdre; **~ light on** *fig* faire la lumière sur

shed² [ʃed] *n* abri *m*

sheep [ʃiːp] (*pl sheep*) mouton *m*

'sheep·dog chien *m* de berger

sheep·ish ['ʃiːpɪʃ] *adj* penaud

'sheep·skin *adj* en peau de mouton

sheer [ʃɪr] *adj madness, luxury etc* pur; *drop, cliffs* abrupt

sheet [ʃiːt] *for bed* drap *m*; *of paper, metal, glass* feuille *f*

shelf [ʃelf] étagère *f*; **shelves** *set of shelves* étagère(s) *f(pl)*

'shelf-life *of product* durée *f* de conservation avant vente

shell [ʃel] **1** *n of mussel, egg* coquille *f*; *of tortoise* carapace *f*; MIL obus *m*; **come out of one's ~** *fig* sortir de sa coquille **2** *v/t peas* écosser; MIL bombarder

'shell·fire bombardements *mpl*; **come under ~** être bombardé

'shell·fish *nsg or npl* fruits *mpl* de mer

shel·ter ['ʃeltər] **1** *n (refuge), at bus stop etc* abri *m* **2** *v/i from rain, bombing etc* s'abriter (*from* de) **3** *v/t (protect)* protéger

shel·tered ['ʃeltərd] *adj place* protégé; *lead a ~ life* mener une vie protégée

shelve [ʃelv] *v/t fig* mettre en suspens

shep·herd ['ʃepərd] *n* berger(-ère) *m(f)*

sher·iff ['ʃerɪf] *n* shérif *m*

sher·ry ['ʃerɪ] xérès *m*

shield [ʃiːld] **1** *n* MIL bouclier *m; sports trophy* plaque *f; badge: of policeman* plaque *f* **2** *v/t (protect)* protéger

shift [ʃɪft] **1** *n (change)* changement *m; (move, switchover)* passage *m (to* à); *period of work* poste *m; people* équipe *f* **2** *v/t (move)* déplacer, changer de place; *production, employee* transférer; *stains etc* faire partir; **~ the em·pha·sis on·to** reporter l'accent sur **3** *v/i (move)* se déplacer; *of foundations* bouger; *in attitude, opinion, of wind* virer

'shift key COMPUT touche *f* majuscule; **'shift work** travail *m* par roulement; **'shift work·er** ouvrier *m* posté

shift·y ['ʃɪftɪ] *adj pej: person* louche; *eyes* fuyant

shil·ly-shal·ly ['ʃɪlɪʃælɪ] *v/i (pret & pp -ied)* hésiter

shim·mer ['ʃɪmər] *v/i* miroiter

shin [ʃɪn] *n* tibia *m*

shine [ʃaɪn] **1** *v/i (pret & pp* **shone**) briller; *fig: of student etc* être brillant *(at, in* en) **2** *v/t (pret & pp* **shone**): *~ a flashlight in s.o.'s face* braquer une lampe sur le visage de qn **3** *n on shoes etc* brillant *m*

shin·gle ['ʃɪŋgl] *on beach* galets *mpl*

shin·gles ['ʃɪŋglz] *nsg* MED zona *m*

shin·y ['ʃaɪnɪ] *adj surface* brillant

ship [ʃɪp] **1** *n* bateau *m*, navire *m* **2** *v/t (pret & pp* **-ped**) *(send)* expédier, envoyer; *by sea* expédier par bateau **3** *v/i (pret & pp* **-ped**) *of new product* être lancé (sur le marché)

ship·ment ['ʃɪpmənt] *(consignment)* expédition *f*, envoi *m*

'ship-own·er armateur *m*

ship·ping ['ʃɪpɪŋ] *(sea traffic)* navigation *f; (sending)* expédition *f*, envoi *m; (sending by sea)* envoi par bateau

'ship·ping com·pa·ny compagnie *f* de navigation

'ship·ping costs *npl* frais *mpl* d'expédition; *by ship* frais *mpl* d'embarquement; **'ship-wreck 1** *n* naufrage *m* **2** *v/t: be ~ed* faire naufrage; **'ship-yard** chantier *m* naval

shirk [ʃɜːrk] *v/t* esquiver

shirk·er ['ʃɜːrkər] tire-au-flanc *m*

shirt [ʃɜːrt] chemise *f; in his ~ sleeves* en bras de chemise

shit [ʃɪt] **1** *n* P *(excrement, bad quality goods etc)* merde *f* P; *I need a ~* je dois aller chier P **2** *v/i (pret & pp* **shat**) P chier P **3** *int* P merde P

shit·ty ['ʃɪtɪ] *adj* F dégueulasse F

shiv·er ['ʃɪvər] *v/i* trembler

shock [ʃɑːk] **1** *n* choc *m;* ELEC décharge *f; be in ~* MED être en état de choc **2** *v/t* choquer

shock ab·sorb·er ['ʃɑːkəbzɔːrbər] MOT amortisseur *m*

shock·ing ['ʃɑːkɪŋ] *adj behavior, poverty* choquant; F *(very bad)* épouvantable

shock·ing·ly ['ʃɑːkɪŋlɪ] *adv behave* de manière choquante

shod·dy ['ʃɑːdɪ] *adj goods* de mauvaise qualité; *behavior* mesquin

shoe [ʃuː] chaussure *f*, soulier *m*

'shoe·horn chausse-pied *m;* **'shoe·lace** lacet *m;* **'shoe-mak·er** cordonnier(-ière) *m(f);* **shoe mend·er** ['ʃuːmendər] cordonnier(-ière) *m(f);* **'shoe·store** magasin *m* de chaussures; **'shoe·string:** *do sth on a ~* faire qch à peu de frais

shone [ʃɑːn] *pret & pp* → **shine**

♦ **shoo away** [ʃuː] *v/t children, chicken* chasser

shook [ʃuːk] *pret* → **shake**

shoot [ʃuːt] **1** *n* BOT pousse *f* **2** *v/t (pret & pp* **shot**) tirer sur; *and kill* tuer d'un coup de feu; *movie* tourner; *I've been shot* j'ai reçu un coup de feu; *~ s.o. in the leg* tirer une balle dans la jambe de qn **3** *v/i (pret & pp* **shot**) tirer

♦ **shoot down** *v/t airplane* abattre; *fig: suggestion* descendre

♦ **shoot off** *v/i (rush off)* partir comme une flèche

♦ **shoot up** *v/i of prices* monter en flèche; *of children, new buildings etc* pousser; F: *of drug addict* se shooter

shoot·ing star ['ʃuːtɪŋ] étoile *f* filante

shop [ʃɑːp] **1** *n* magasin *m*; **talk ~** parler affaires **2** *v/i (pret & pp -ped)* faire ses courses; **go ~ping** faire les courses

shop·keep·er ['ʃɑːpkiːpər] commerçant *m*,-ante *f*; **shop·lift·er** ['ʃɑːp-lɪftər] voleur(-euse) *m(f)* à l'étalage; **shop·lift·ing** ['ʃɑːplɪftɪŋ] *n* vol *m* à l'étalage

shop·ping ['ʃɑːpɪŋ] *items* courses *fpl*; *I hate ~* je déteste faire les courses; *do one's ~* faire ses courses

'**shop·ping bag** sac *m* à provisions; '**shop·ping cen·ter**, *Br* '**shop·ping cen·tre** centre *m* commercial; '**shop·ping list** liste *f* de comissions; '**shop·ping mall** centre *m* commercial

shop 'stew·ard délégué *m* syndical, déléguée *f* syndicale

shore [ʃɔːr] rivage *m*; **on ~** *not at sea* à terre

short [ʃɔːrt] **1** *adj* court; *in height* petit; *time is ~* il n'y a pas beaucoup de temps; **be ~ of** manquer de **2** *adv*: *cut a vacation / meeting ~* abréger des vacances / une réunion; **stop a person ~** couper la parole à une personne; **go ~ of** se priver de; **in ~** bref

short·age ['ʃɔːrtɪdʒ] manque *m*

short 'cir·cuit *n* court-circuit *m*; **short·com·ing** ['ʃɔːrtkʌmɪŋ] défaut *m*; **short·cut** raccourci *m*

short·en ['ʃɔːrtn] *v/t* raccourcir

short·en·ing ['ʃɔːrtnɪŋ] matière *f* grasse

'**short·fall** déficit *m*; '**short·hand** sténographie *f*; **short·handed** [ʃɔːrt-'hændɪd] *adj*: *be ~* manquer de personnel; **short·lived** ['ʃɔːrtlɪvd] *adj* de courte durée

short·ly ['ʃɔːrtlɪ] *adv (soon)* bientôt; *~ before / after that* peu avant / après

short·ness ['ʃɔːrtnɪs] *of visit* brièveté *f*; *in height* petite taille *f*

shorts [ʃɔːrts] *npl* short *m*; *underwear* caleçon *m*

short·sight·ed [ʃɔːrt'saɪtɪd] *adj* myope; *fig* peu perspicace; **short-sleeved** ['ʃɔːrtsliːvd] *adj* à manches courtes; **short·staffed** [ʃɔːrt'stæft] *adj*: *be ~* manquer de personnel; **short 'sto·ry** nouvelle *f*; **short-tem·pered** [ʃɔːrt'tempərd] *adj by nature* d'un caractère emporté; *at a particular time* de mauvaise humeur; '**short-term** *adj* à court terme; '**short wave** ondes *fpl* courtes

shot[1] [ʃɑːt] *from gun* coup *m* de feu; *(photograph)* photo *f*; *(injection)* piqûre *f*; *be a good / poor ~* être un bon / mauvais tireur; *(turn)* tour *m*; *like a ~ accept* sans hésiter; *run off* comme une flèche; *it's my ~* c'est mon tour

shot[2] [ʃɑːt] *pret & pp* → **shoot**

'**shot·gun** fusil *m* de chasse

'**shot put** lancer *m* du poids

should [ʃʊd] *v/aux*: *what ~ I do?* que dois-je faire?; *you ~n't do that* tu ne devrais pas faire ça; *that ~ be long enough* cela devrait être assez long; *you ~ have heard him* tu aurais dû l'entendre

shoul·der ['ʃoʊldər] *n* épaule *f*

'**shoul·der bag** sac *m* à bandoulière; '**shoul·der blade** omoplate *f*; '**shoul·der strap** *of brassière, dress* bretelle *f*; *of bag* bandoulière *f*

shout [ʃaʊt] **1** *n* cri *m* **2** *v/i* crier; *~ for help* appeler à l'aide **3** *v/t order* crier

♦ **shout at** *v/t* crier après

shout·ing ['ʃaʊtɪŋ] cris *mpl*

shove [ʃʌv] **1** *n*: *give s.o. a ~* pousser qn **2** *v/t & v/i* pousser

♦ **shove in** *v/i*: *this guy shoved in front of me* ce type m'est passé devant

♦ **shove off** *v/i* F *(go away)* ficher le camp F

shov·el ['ʃʌvl] **1** *n* pelle *f* **2** *v/t (pret & pp -ed, Br -led) snow* enlever à la pelle

show [ʃoʊ] **1** *n* THEA, TV spectacle *m*; *(display)* démonstration *f*; *on ~ at exhibition* exposé; *it's all done for ~ pej* c'est fait juste pour impressionner **2**

v/t (*pret* **-ed**, *pp* **shown**) *passport, interest, emotion etc* montrer; *at exhibition* présenter; *movie* projeter; *~ s.o. sth, ~ sth to s.o.* montrer qch à qn **3** *v/i* (*pret* **-ed**, *pp* **shown**) (*be visible*) se voir; *of movie* passer

♦ **show around** *v/t tourists, visitors* faire faire la visite à

♦ **show in** *v/t* faire entrer

♦ **show off 1** *v/t skills* faire étalage de **2** *v/i pej* crâner

♦ **show up 1** *v/t s.o.'s shortcomings etc* faire ressortir; *don't show me up in public* ne me fais pas honte en public **2** *v/i* F (*arrive, turn up*) se pointer F; (*be visible*) se voir

'**show busi·ness** monde *m* du spectacle; '**show·case** *n also fig* vitrine *f*; '**show·down** confrontation *f*

show·er ['ʃaʊər] **1** *n of rain* averse *f*; *to wash* douche *f*; *party*: petite fête avant un mariage ou un accouchement à laquelle tout le monde apporte un cadeau; *take a ~* prendre une douche **2** *v/i* prendre une douche **3** *v/t*: *~ s.o. with compliments / praise* couvrir de compliments / louanges

'**show·er cap** bonnet *m* de douche; '**show·er cur·tain** rideau *m* de douche; '**show·er·proof** *adj* imperméable

'**show-jump·er** *person* cavalier *m* d'obstacle, cavalière *f* d'obstacle

show-jump·ing ['ʃəʊdʒʌmpɪŋ] concours *m* hippique, jumping F

shown [ʃəʊn] *pp* → **show**

'**show-off** *pej* prétentieux(-euse) *m(f)*

'**show·room** salle *f* d'exposition; *in ~ condition* à l'état de neuf

show·y ['ʃəʊɪ] *adj* voyant

shrank [ʃræŋk] *pret* → **shrink**[1]

shred [ʃred] **1** *n of paper etc* lambeau *m*; *of meat etc* morceau *m*; *not a ~ of evidence* pas la moindre preuve **2** *v/t* (*pret & pp* **-ded**) *documents* déchiqueter; *in cooking* râper

shred·der ['ʃredər] *for documents* déchiqueteuse *f*

shrewd [ʃruːd] *adj* perspicace

shrewd·ly ['ʃruːdlɪ] *adv* avec perspicacité

shrewd·ness ['ʃruːdnɪs] perspicacité *f*

shriek [ʃriːk] **1** *n* cri *m* aigu **2** *v/i* pousser un cri aigu

shrill [ʃrɪl] *adj* perçant

shrimp [ʃrɪmp] crevette *f*

shrine [ʃraɪn] *holy place* lieu *m* saint

shrink[1] [ʃrɪŋk] *v/i* (*pret* **shrank**, *pp* **shrunk**) *of material* rétrécir; *of support* diminuer

shrink[2] [ʃrɪŋk] *n* F (*psychiatrist*) psy *m* F

'**shrink-wrap 1** *v/t* (*pret & pp* **-ped**) emballer sous pellicule plastique **2** *n material* pellicule *f* plastique

shriv·el ['ʃrɪvl] *v/i* (*pret & pp* **-ed**, *Br* **-led**) se flétrir

shrub [ʃrʌb] arbuste *m*

shrub·be·ry ['ʃrʌbərɪ] massif *m* d'arbustes

shrug [ʃrʌg] **1** *n* haussement *m* d'épaules **2** *v/i* (*pret & pp* **-ged**) hausser les épaules **3** *v/t* (*pret & pp* **-ged**): *~ one's shoulders* hausser les épaules

shrunk [ʃrʌŋk] *pp* → **shrink**[1]

shud·der ['ʃʌdər] **1** *n of fear, disgust* frisson *m*; *of earth, building* vibration *f* **2** *v/i with fear, disgust* frissonner; *of earth, building* vibrer; *I ~ to think* je n'ose y penser

shuf·fle ['ʃʌfl] **1** *v/t cards* battre **2** *v/i in walking* traîner les pieds

shun [ʃʌn] *v/t* (*pret & pp* **-ned**) fuir

shut [ʃʌt] **1** *v/t* (*pret & pp* **shut**) fermer **2** *v/i* (*pret & pp* **shut**) *of door, box* se fermer; *of store* fermer; *they were ~* c'était fermé

♦ **shut down 1** *v/t business* fermer; *computer* éteindre **2** *v/i of business* fermer ses portes; *of computer* s'éteindre

♦ **shut off** *v/t gas, water etc* couper

♦ **shut up** *v/i* F (*be quiet*) se taire; *shut up!* tais-toi!

shut·ter ['ʃʌtər] *on window* volet *m*; PHOT obturateur *m*

'**shut·ter speed** PHOT vitesse *f* d'obturation

shut·tle ['ʃʌtl] *v/i* faire la navette (*between* entre)

'shut·tle bus *at airport* navette *f*;
'shut·tle·cock SP volant *m*; 'shut·tle ser·vice navette *f*

shy [ʃaɪ] *adj* timide

shy·ness ['ʃaɪnɪs] timidité *f*

Si·a·mese twins [saɪəmi:z'twɪnz] *npl boys* frères *mpl* siamois; *girls* sœurs *fpl* siamoises

sick [sɪk] *adj* malade; *sense of humor* noir; *be ~ (vomit)* vomir; *be ~ of (fed up with)* en avoir marre de qch

sick·en ['sɪkn] 1 *v/t (disgust)* écœurer; *make ill* rendre malade 2 *v/i: be ~ing for* couver

sick·en·ing ['sɪknɪŋ] *adj* écœurant

'sick leave congé *m* de maladie; *be on ~* être en congé de maladie

sick·ly ['sɪklɪ] *adj person* maladif*; color* écœurant

sick·ness ['sɪknɪs] maladie *f*; *(vomiting)* vomissements *mpl*

side [saɪd] *n* côté *m*; SP équipe *f*; *take ~s (favor one ~)* prendre parti; *I'm on your ~* je suis de votre côté; *~ by ~* côte à côte; *at the ~ of the road* au bord de la route; *on the big / small ~* plutôt grand / petit

♦ side *with v/t* prendre parti pour

'side·board buffet *m*; 'side·burns *npl* pattes *fpl*; 'side dish plat *m* d'accompagnement; 'side ef·fect effet *m* secondaire; 'side·line 1 *n* activité *f* secondaire 2 *v/t: feel ~d* se sentir relégué à l'arrière-plan; 'side sal·ad salade *f*; 'side·step *v/t (pret & pp -ped)* éviter; *fig also* contourner; 'side street rue *f* transversale; 'side·track *v/t* distraire; *get ~ed* être pris par autre chose; 'side·walk trottoir *m*; 'side·walk 'caf·é café-terrasse *m*; 'side·ways ['saɪdweɪz] *adv* de côté

siege [si:dʒ] siège *m*; *lay ~ to* assiéger

sieve [sɪv] *n for flour* tamis *m*

sift [sɪft] *v/t flour* tamiser; *data* passer en revue

♦ sift through *v/t details, data* passer en revue

sigh [saɪ] 1 *n* soupir *m*; *heave a ~ of relief* pousser un soupir de soulagement 2 *v/i* soupirer

sight [saɪt] *n* spectacle *m*; *(power of seeing)* vue *f*; *~s of city* monuments *mpl*; *he can't stand the ~ of blood* il ne supporte pas la vue du sang; *catch ~ of* apercevoir; *know by ~* connaître de vue; *be within ~ of* se voir de; *out of ~* hors de vue; *what a ~ you look!* de quoi tu as l'air!; *lose ~ of objective etc* perdre de vue

sight·see·ing ['saɪtsi:ɪŋ] tourisme *m*; *go ~* faire du tourisme

'sight·see·ing tour visite *f* guidée

'sight·seer ['saɪtsi:ər] touriste *m/f*

sign [saɪn] 1 *n (indication)* signe *m*; *(road~)* panneau *m*; *outside shop, on building* enseigne *f*; *it's a ~ of the times* c'est un signe des temps 2 *v/t & v/i* signer

♦ sign in *v/i* signer le registre

sig·nal ['sɪɡnl] 1 *n* signal *m*; *be sending out all the right / wrong ~s fig* envoyer le bon / mauvais message 2 *v/i (pret & pp -ed, Br -led) of driver* mettre son clignotant

sig·na·to·ry ['sɪɡnətɔ:rɪ] *n* signataire *m/f*

sig·na·ture ['sɪɡnətʃər] signature *f*

'sig·na·ture tune indicatif *m*

'sig·net ring ['sɪɡnɪtrɪŋ] chevalière *f*

sig·nif·i·cance [sɪɡ'nɪfɪkəns] importance *f*

sig·nif·i·cant [sɪɡ'nɪfɪkənt] *adj event, sum of money, improvement etc* important

sig·nif·i·cant·ly [sɪɡ'nɪfɪkəntlɪ] *adv larger, more expensive* nettement

sig·ni·fy ['sɪɡnɪfaɪ] *v/t (pret & pp -ied)* signifier

'sign lan·guage langage *m* des signes

'sign·post poteau *m* indicateur

si·lence ['saɪləns] 1 *n* silence *m*; *in ~ work, march* en silence; *~!* silence! 2 *v/t* faire taire

si·lenc·er ['saɪlənsər] *on gun* silencieux *m*

si·lent ['saɪlənt] *adj* silencieux*; movie* muet*; stay ~ (not comment)* se taire

'si·lent part·ner COMM commanditaire *m*

sil·hou·ette [sɪlu:'et] *n* silhouette *f*

sil·i·con ['sɪlɪkən] silicium *m*

sil·i·con 'chip puce *f* électronique

S

sil·i·cone ['sɪlɪkoʊn] silicone *f*

silk [sɪlk] **1** *adj shirt etc* en soie **2** *n* soie *f*

silk·y ['sɪlkɪ] *adj hair, texture* soyeux*

sil·li·ness ['sɪlɪnɪs] stupidité *f*

sil·ly ['sɪlɪ] *adj* bête

si·lo ['saɪloʊ] AGR, MIL silo *m*

sil·ver ['sɪlvər] **1** *adj ring* en argent; *hair* argenté **2** *n metal* argent *m*; *medal* médaille *f* d'argent; (*~ objects*) argenterie *f*

'sil·ver med·al médaille *f* d'argent; **sil·ver-plat·ed** [sɪlvər'pleɪtɪd] *adj* argenté; **sil·ver·ware** ['sɪlvərwer] argenterie *f*; **sil·ver 'wed·ding** noces *fpl* d'argent

sim·i·lar ['sɪmɪlər] *adj* semblable (*to* à)

sim·i·lar·i·ty [sɪmɪ'lærətɪ] ressemblance *f*

sim·i·lar·ly ['sɪmɪlərlɪ] *adv*: *be ~ dressed* être habillé de la même façon; *~, you must ...* de même, tu dois ...

sim·mer ['sɪmər] *v/i in cooking* mijoter; *with rage* bouillir de rage

♦ **simmer down** *v/i* se calmer

sim·ple ['sɪmpl] *adj* simple

sim·ple-mind·ed [sɪmpl'maɪndɪd] *adj pej* simple, simplet*

sim·u·late ['sɪmjuleɪt] *v/t* simuler

sim·ul·ta·ne·ous [saɪməl'teɪnɪəs] *adj* simultané

sim·ul·ta·ne·ous·ly [saɪməl'teɪnɪəslɪ] *adv* simultanément

sin [sɪn] **1** *n* péché *m* **2** *v/i* (*pret* & *pp -ned*) pécher

since [sɪns] **1** *prep* depuis; *I've been here ~ last week* je suis là depuis la semaine dernière **2** *adv* depuis; *I haven't seen him ~* je ne l'ai pas revu depuis **3** *conj in expressions of time* depuis que; (*seeing that*) puisque; *~ you left* depuis que tu es parti; *~*

you don't like it puisque ça ne te plaît pas

sin·cere [sɪn'sɪr] *adj* sincère

sin·cere·ly [sɪn'sɪrlɪ] *adv* sincèrement; *hope* vivement; *Sincerely yours* Je vous prie d'agréer, Madame / Monsieur, l'expression de mes sentiments les meilleurs

sin·cer·i·ty [sɪn'serətɪ] sincérité *f*

sin·ful ['sɪnful] *adj deeds* honteux*; *~ person* pécheur *m*, pécheresse *f*; *it is ~ to ...* c'est un péché de ...

sing [sɪŋ] *v/t* & *v/i* (*pret sang*, *pp sung*) chanter

singe [sɪndʒ] *v/t* brûler légèrement

sing·er ['sɪŋər] chanteur(-euse) *m(f)*

sin·gle ['sɪŋgl] **1** *adj* (*sole*) seul; (*not double*) simple; *bed* à une place; (*not married*) célibataire; *there wasn't a ~ ...* il n'y avait pas un seul ...; *in ~ file* en file indienne **2** *n* MUS single *m*; (*~ room*) chambre *f* à un lit; *person* personne *f* seule; *~s in tennis* simple *m*

♦ **single out** *v/t* (*choose*) choisir; (*distinguish*) distinguer

sin·gle-breast·ed [sɪŋgl'brestɪd] *adj* droit; **sin·gle-hand·ed** [sɪŋgl'hændɪd] **1** *adj* fait tout seul **2** *adv* tout seul; **Sin·gle 'Mar·ket** *in Europe* Marché *m* unique; **sin·gle-mind·ed** [sɪŋgl'maɪndɪd] *adj* résolu; **sin·gle 'moth·er** mère *f* célibataire; **sin·gle 'pa·rent** mère / père qui élève ses enfants tout seul; **sin·gle pa·rent 'fam·i·ly** famille *f* monoparentale; **sin·gle 'room** chambre *f* à un lit

sin·gu·lar ['sɪŋgjulər] **1** *adj* GRAM au singulier **2** *n* GRAM singulier *m*; *in the ~* au singulier

sin·is·ter ['sɪnɪstər] *adj* sinistre

sink [sɪŋk] **1** *n* évier *m* **2** *v/i* (*pret sank*, *pp sunk*) *of ship, object* couler; *of sun* descendre; *of interest rates, pressure etc* baisser; *he sank onto the bed* il s'est effondré sur le lit **3** *v/t* (*pret sank*, *pp sunk*) *ship* couler; *money* investir

♦ **sink in** *v/i of liquid* pénétrer; *it still hasn't really sunk in* *of realization* je n'arrive pas encore très bien à m'en rendre compte

sin·ner ['sɪnər] pécheur *m*, pécheresse *f*

si·nus ['saɪnəs] sinus *m*

si·nus·i·tis [saɪnə'saɪtɪs] MED sinusite *f*

sip [sɪp] **1** *n* petite gorgée *f*; **try a ~** tu veux goûter? **2** *v/t* (*pret & pp* **-ped**) boire à petites gorgées

sir [sɜːr] monsieur *m*

si·ren ['saɪrən] *on police car* sirène *f*

sir·loin ['sɜːrlɔɪn] aloyau *m*

sis·ter ['sɪstər] sœur *f*

'sis·ter-in-law (*pl* **sisters-in-law**) belle-sœur *f*

sit [sɪt] *v/i* (*pret & pp* **sat**) (**~ down**) s'asseoir; **she was ~ting** elle était assise

♦ **sit down** *v/i* s'asseoir

♦ **sit up** *v/i in bed* se dresser; (*straighten back*) se tenir droit; (*wait up at night*) rester debout

sit·com ['sɪtkɑːm] sitcom *m*

site [saɪt] **1** *n* emplacement *m*; *of battle* site *m* **2** *v/t new offices etc* situer

sit·ting ['sɪtɪŋ] *n of committee, court, for artist* séance *f*; *for meals* service *m*

'sit·ting room salon *m*

sit·u·at·ed ['sɪtʃueɪtɪd] *adj*: **be ~** être situé

sit·u·a·tion [sɪtʃu'eɪʃn] situation *f*; *of building etc* emplacement *m*

six [sɪks] six

'six-pack *of beer* pack *m* de six

six·teen [sɪks'tiːn] seize

six·teenth [sɪks'tiːnθ] seizième; → *page 720*

sixth [sɪksθ] sixième; → **fifth**

six·ti·eth ['sɪkstɪɪθ] soixantième

six·ty ['sɪkstɪ] soixante

size [saɪz] *of room, jacket* taille *f*; *of project* envergure *f*; *of loan* montant *m*; *of shoes* pointure *f*

♦ **size up** *v/t* évaluer

size·a·ble ['saɪzəbl] *adj meal, house* assez grand; *order, amount of money* assez important

siz·zle ['sɪzl] *v/i* grésiller

skate [skeɪt] **1** *n* patin *m* **2** *v/i* patiner

'skate·board *n* skateboard *m*; **'skate-board·er** skateur(-euse) *m(f)*;

'skate·board·ing skateboard *m*

skat·er ['skeɪtər] patineur(-euse) *(m)f*

skat·ing ['skeɪtɪŋ] patinage *f*

'skat·ing rink patinoire *f*

skel·e·ton ['skelɪtn] squelette *m*

'skel·e·ton key passe-partout *m*

skep·tic ['skeptɪk] sceptique *m/f*

skep·ti·cal ['skeptɪkl] *adj* sceptique

skep·ti·cism ['skeptɪsɪzm] scepticisme *m*

sketch [sketʃ] **1** *n* croquis *m*; THEA sketch *m* **2** *v/t* esquisser

'sketch·book carnet *m* à croquis

sketch·y ['sketʃɪ] *adj knowledge etc* sommaire

skew·er ['skjuər] *n* brochette *f*

ski [skiː] **1** *n* ski *m* **2** *v/i* faire du ski; **we ~ed back** nous sommes revenus en skiant

'ski boots *npl* chaussures *fpl* de ski

skid [skɪd] **1** *n* dérapage *m* **2** *v/i* (*pret & pp* **-ded**) déraper

ski·er ['skiːər] skieur(-euse) *m(f)*

ski·ing ['skiːɪŋ] ski *m*

'ski in·struc·tor moniteur(-trice) *m(f)* de ski

'ski jump saut *m* à ski; *structure* tremplin *m*

skil·ful *etc* Br → **skillful** *etc*

'ski lift remonte-pente *m*, téléski *m*

skill [skɪl] technique *f*; **~s** connaissances *fpl*, compétences *fpl*; **with great ~** avec adresse

skilled [skɪld] *adj person* habile

skilled 'work·er ouvrier *m* qualifié, ouvrière *f* qualifiée

skill·ful ['skɪlful] *adj* habile

skill·ful·ly ['skɪlfulɪ] *adv* habilement

skim [skɪm] *v/t* (*pret & pp* **-med**) *surface* effleurer

♦ **skim off** *v/t the best* retenir

♦ **skim through** *v/t text* parcourir

'skimmed milk [skɪmd] lait *m* écrémé

skimp·y ['skɪmpɪ] *adj account etc* sommaire; *dress* étriqué

skin [skɪn] **1** *n* peau *f* **2** *v/t* (*pret & pp* **-ned**) *animal* écorcher; *tomato, peach* peler

'skin div·ing plongée *f* sous-marine autonome

skin·flint ['skɪnflɪnt] F radin(e) *m(f)* F

'skin graft greffe *f* de la peau

skin·ny ['skɪnɪ] *adj* maigre

'skin-tight *adj* moulant

skip [skɪp] **1** *n* (*little jump*) saut *m* **2** *v/i* (*pret & pp* **-ped**) sautiller **3** *v/t* (*pret & pp* **-ped**) (*omit*) sauter

'ski pole bâton *m* de ski

skip·per ['skɪpər] capitaine *m/f*

'ski re·sort station *f* de ski

skirt [skɜːrt] *n* jupe *f*

'ski run piste *f* de ski

'ski tow téléski *m*

skull [skʌl] crâne *m*

skunk [skʌŋk] mouffette *f*

sky [skaɪ] ciel *m*

'sky·light lucarne *f*; **'sky·line** of city silhouette *f*; **sky·scrap·er** ['skaɪskreɪpər] gratte-ciel *m inv*

slab [slæb] *of stone, butter* plaque *f*; *of cake* grosse tranche*

slack [slæk] *adj rope* mal tendu; *discipline* pas strict; *person* négligent; *work* négligé; *period* creux*

slack·en ['slækn] *v/t rope* détendre; *pace* ralentir

♦ **slacken off** *v/i of trading, pace* se ralentir

slacks [slæks] *npl* pantalon *m*

slain [sleɪn] *pp* → **slay**

slam [slæm] *v/t & v/i* (*pret & pp* **-med**) claquer

♦ **slam down** *v/t* poser brutalement

slan·der ['slændər] **1** *n* calomnie *f* **2** *v/t* calomnier

slan·der·ous ['slændərəs] *adj* calomnieux*

slang [slæŋ] *also of a specific group* argot *m*

slant [slænt] **1** *v/i* pencher **2** *n* inclinaison *f*; *given to a story* perspective *f*

slant·ing ['slæntɪŋ] *adj roof* en pente; *eyes* bridé

slap [slæp] **1** *n* (*blow*) claque *f* **2** *v/t* (*pret & pp* **-ped**) donner une claque à; **~ s.o. in the face** gifler qn

'slap·dash *adj work* sans soin; *person* négligent

slash [slæʃ] **1** *n cut* entaille *f*; *in punctuation* barre *f* oblique **2** *v/t painting, skin* entailler; *prices, costs* réduire radicalement; **~ one's wrists** s'ouvrir

les veines

slate [sleɪt] *n material* ardoise *f*

slaugh·ter ['slɔːtər] **1** *n of animals* abattage *m*; *of people, troops* massacre *m* **2** *v/t animals* abattre; *people, troops* massacrer

'slaugh·ter·house *for animals* abattoir *m*

Slav [slɑːv] *adj* slave

slave [sleɪv] *n* esclave *m/f*

'slave-driv·er F négrier(-ère) *m(f)* F

slay [sleɪ] *v/t* (*pret* **slew**, *pp* **slain**) tuer

slay·ing ['sleɪɪŋ] (*murder*) meurtre *m*

sleaze [sliːz] POL corruption *f*

slea·zy ['sliːzɪ] *adj bar, character* louche

sled, sledge [sled, sledʒ] traîneau *m*

'sledge ham·mer masse *f*

sleep [sliːp] **1** *n* sommeil *m*; **go to ~** s'endormir; **I need a good ~** j'ai besoin de dormir; **a good night's ~** une bonne nuit de sommeil; **I couldn't get to ~** je n'ai pas réussi à m'endormir **2** *v/i* (*pret & pp* **slept**) dormir; **~ late** faire la grasse matinée

♦ **sleep on** *v/t*: **sleep on it** attendre le lendemain pour décider; **sleep on it!** la nuit porte conseil!

♦ **sleep with** *v/t* (*have sex with*) coucher avec

sleep·i·ly ['sliːpɪlɪ] *adv say* d'un ton endormi; *look at s.o.* d'un air endormi

sleep·ing bag ['sliːpɪŋ] sac *m* de couchage; **'sleep·ing car** RAIL wagon-lit *m*; **'sleep·ing pill** somnifère *m*

sleep·less ['sliːplɪs] *adj*: **a ~ night** une nuit blanche

'sleep·walk·er somnambule *m/f*

'sleep·walk·ing somnambulisme *m*

sleep·y ['sliːpɪ] *adj person* qui a envie de dormir; *yawn*, *fig: town* endormi; **I'm ~** j'ai sommeil

sleet [sliːt] *n* neige *f* fondue

sleeve [sliːv] *of jacket etc* manche *f*

sleeve·less ['sliːvlɪs] *adj* sans manches

sleigh [sleɪ] traîneau *m*

sleight of 'hand [slaɪt] *trick* tour *m* de passe-passe

slen·der ['slendər] *adj* mince; *chance*,

income, margin faible

slept [slept] *pret & pp* → **sleep**

slew [sluː] *pret* → **slay**

slice [slaɪs] **1** *n of bread, pie* tranche *f*; *fig: of profits* part *f* **2** *v/t loaf etc* couper en tranches

sliced 'bread [slaɪst] pain *m* coupé en tranches

slick [slɪk] **1** *adj performance* habile; *pej (cunning)* rusé **2** *n of oil* marée *f* noire

slid [slɪd] *pret & pp* → **slide**

slide [slaɪd] **1** *n for kids* toboggan *m*; PHOT diapositive *f* **2** *v/i (pret & pp slid)* glisser; *of exchange rate etc* baisser **3** *v/t (pret & pp slid) item of furniture* faire glisser

slid·ing door ['slaɪdɪŋ] porte *f* coulissante

slight [slaɪt] **1** *adj person, figure* frêle; *(small)* léger*; **no, not in the ~est** non, pas le moins du monde **2** *n (insult)* affront *m*

slight·ly ['slaɪtlɪ] *adv* légèrement

slim [slɪm] **1** *adj person* mince; *chance* faible **2** *v/i (pret & pp -med)* être au régime

slime [slaɪm] *(mud)* vase *f*; *of slug, snail* bave *f*

slim·y ['slaɪmɪ] *adj liquid etc* vaseux*

sling [slɪŋ] **1** *n for arm* écharpe *f* **2** *v/t (pret & pp slung) F (throw)* lancer

'sling·shot catapulte *f*

slip [slɪp] **1** *n on ice etc* glissade *f*; *(mistake)* erreur *f*; **a ~ of paper** un bout de papier; **a ~ of the tongue** un lapsus; **give s.o. the ~** se dérober à qn **2** *v/i (pret & pp -ped) on ice etc* glisser; *in quality, quantity* baisser; **he ~ped out of the room** il se glissa hors de la pièce **3** *v/t (pret & pp -ped) (put)* glisser; **it ~ped my mind** cela m'est sorti de la tête

♦ **slip away** *v/i of time* passer; *of opportunity* se dérober; *(die quietly)* s'éteindre

♦ **slip off** *v/t jacket etc* enlever

♦ **slip on** *v/t jacket etc* enfiler

♦ **slip out** *v/i (go out)* sortir

♦ **slip up** *v/i (make a mistake)* faire une gaffe

slipped 'disc [slɪpt] hernie *f* discale

slip·per ['slɪpər] chausson *m*

slip·per·y ['slɪpərɪ] *adj* glissant

slip·shod ['slɪpʃɑːd] *adj* négligé

'slip-up *(mistake)* gaffe *f*

slit [slɪt] **1** *n (tear)* déchirure *f*; *(hole), in skirt* fente *f* **2** *v/t (pret & pp slit)* ouvrir, fendre; **~ s.o.'s throat** couper la gorge à qn

slith·er ['slɪðər] *v/i of person* déraper; *of snake* ramper

sliv·er ['slɪvər] *of wood, glass* éclat *m*; *of soap, cheese, garlic* petit morceau *m*

slob [slɑːb] *pej* rustaud(e) *m(f)*

slob·ber ['slɑːbər] *v/i* baver

slog [slɑːg] *n long walk* trajet *m* pénible; *hard work* corvée *f*

slo·gan ['slougən] slogan *m*

slop [slɑːp] *v/t (pret & pp -ped) (spill)* renverser

slope [sloup] **1** *n* inclinaison *f*; *of mountain* côté *m*; **built on a ~** construit sur une pente **2** *v/i* être incliné; **the road ~s down to the sea** la route descend vers la mer

slop·py ['slɑːpɪ] *adj* F *work, in dress* négligé; *(too sentimental)* gnangnan F

slot [slɑːt] *n* fente *f*; *in schedule* créneau *m*

♦ **slot in 1** *v/t (pret & pp -ted)* insérer **2** *v/i (pret & pp -ted)* s'insérer

'slot ma·chine *for vending* distributeur *m (automatique)*; *for gambling* machine *f* à sous

slouch [slautʃ] *v/i* être avachi; **don't ~!** tiens-toi droit!

slov·en·ly ['slʌvnlɪ] *adj* négligé

slow [slou] *adj* lent; **be ~ *of clock* retarder; **they were not ~ to ...** ils n'ont pas été longs à ...

♦ **slow down 1** *v/t* ralentir **2** *v/i* ralentir; *in life* faire moins de choses

'slow·down *in production* ralentissement *m*

slow·ly ['sloulɪ] *adv* lentement

slow 'mo·tion: in ~ au ralenti

slow·ness ['slounɪs] lenteur *f*

'slow·poke F lambin(e) *m(f)* F

slug [slʌg] *n animal* limace *f*

slug·gish ['slʌgɪʃ] *adj pace, start* lent; *river* à cours lent

slum [slʌm] *n area* quartier *m* pauvre; *house* taudis *m*

slum·ber par·ty ['slʌmbər] soirée où des enfants / adolescents se réunissent chez l'un d'entre eux et restent dormir là-bas

slump [slʌmp] **1** *n in trade* effondrement *m* **2** *v/i of economy* s'effondrer; *of person* s'affaisser

slung [slʌŋ] *pret & pp → sling*

slur [slɜːr] **1** *n on s.o.'s character* tache *f* **2** *v/t (pret & pp -red) words* mal articuler

slurp [slɜːrp] *v/t* faire du bruit en buvant

slurred [slɜːrd] *adj speech* mal articulé

slush [slʌʃ] neige *f* fondue; *pej (sentimental stuff)* sensiblerie *f*

'slush fund caisse *f* noire

slush·y ['slʌʃɪ] *adj snow* à moitié fondu; *movie, novel* fadement sentimental

slut [slʌt] *pej* pute *f* F

sly [slaɪ] *adj (furtive)* sournois; *(crafty)* rusé; *on the ~* en cachette

smack [smæk] **1** *n: a ~ on the bottom* une fessée; *a ~ in the face* une gifle **2** *v/t: ~ a child's bottom* donner une fessée à un enfant; *~ s.o.'s face* gifler qn

small [smɔːl] **1** *adj* petit **2** *n: the ~ of the back* la chute des reins

small 'change monnaie *f*; **'small hours** *npl* heures *fpl* matinales; **small-pox** ['smɔːlpɒks] variole *f*; **'small print** texte *m* en petits caractères; **'small talk** papotage *m*; *make ~* faire de la conversation

smart [smɑːrt] **1** *adj in appearance* élégant; *(intelligent)* intelligent; *pace* vif*; *get ~ with s.o.* faire le malin avec qn **2** *v/i (hurt)* brûler

'smart ass F frimeur(-euse) *m(f)* F

'smart bomb bombe *f* intelligente

'smart card carte *f* à puce, carte *f* à mémoire

♦ **smart·en up** ['smɑːrtn] *v/t* rendre plus élégant

smart·ly ['smɑːrtlɪ] *adv dressed* avec élégance

smash [smæʃ] **1** *n noise* fracas *m*; *(car*

crash) accident *m*; *in tennis* smash *m* **2** *v/t break* fracasser; *(hit hard)* frapper; *~ sth to pieces* briser qch en morceaux **3** *v/i break* se fracasser; *the driver ~ed into ...* le conducteur heurta violemment ...

♦ **smash up** *v/t place* tout casser dans

smash 'hit F: *be a ~* avoir un succès foudroyant

smat·ter·ing ['smætərɪŋ]: *have a ~ of Chinese* savoir un peu de chinois

smear [smɪr] **1** *n of ink etc* tache *f*; *Br MED* frottis *m*; *on character* diffamation *f* **2** *v/t smudge: paint* faire des traces sur; *character* entacher; *~ X with Y, ~ Y on X* cover, apply appliquer Y sur X; *stain, dirty* faire des taches de Y sur X

'smear cam·paign campagne *f* de diffamation

smell [smel] **1** *n* odeur *f*; *sense of ~* sens *m* de l'odorat **2** *v/t* sentir **3** *v/i unpleasantly* sentir mauvais; *(sniff)* renifler; *what does it ~ of?* qu'est-ce que ça sent?; *you~ of beer* tu sens la bière; *it ~s good* ça sent bon

smell·y ['smelɪ] *adj*: qui sent mauvais; *have ~ feet* puer des pieds; *it's ~ in here* ça sent mauvais ici

smile [smaɪl] **1** *n* sourire *m* **2** *v/i* sourire

♦ **smile at** *v/t* sourire à

smirk [smɜːrk] **1** *n* petit sourire *m* narquois **2** *v/i* sourire d'un air narquois

smog [smɑːg] smog *m*

smoke [smoʊk] **1** *n* fumée *f*; *have a ~* fumer (une cigarette) **2** *v/t also food* fumer **3** *v/i of person* fumer

smok·er ['smoʊkər] *person* fumeur(-euse) *m(f)*

smok·ing ['smoʊkɪŋ] tabagisme *m*; *~ is bad for you* c'est mauvais de fumer; *no ~* défense de fumer

'smok·ing car RAIL compartiment *m* fumeurs

smok·y ['smoʊkɪ] *adj room, air* enfumé

smol·der ['smoʊldər] *v/i of fire* couver; *fig: with anger, desire* se consumer (*with* de)

smooth [smuːð] **1** *adj surface, skin, sea*

lisse; *ride, flight, crossing* bon*; *pej: person* mielleux*² **2** *v/t hair* lisser

♦ **smooth down** *v/t with sandpaper etc* lisser

♦ **smooth out** *v/t paper, cloth* défroisser

♦ **smooth over** *v/t:* **smooth things over** arranger les choses

smooth·ly ['smuːðlɪ] *adv (without any problems)* sans problème

smooth·er ['smʌðər] *v/t person, flames* étouffer; **~ s.o. with kisses** couvrir qn de baisers; **~ the bread with jam** recouvrir le pain de confiture

smoul·der *Br* → **smolder**

smudge [smʌdʒ] **1** *n* tache *f* **2** *v/t ink, mascara, paint* faire des traces sur

smug [smʌg] *adj* suffisant

smug·gle ['smʌgl] *v/t* passer en contrebande

smug·gler ['smʌglər] contrebandier (-ière) *m(f)*

smug·gling ['smʌglɪŋ] contrebande *f*

smug·ly ['smʌglɪ] *adv say* d'un ton suffisant; *smile* d'un air suffisant

smut·ty ['smʌtɪ] *adj joke, sense of humor* grossier*

snack [snæk] *n* en-cas *m*

'**snack bar** snack *m*

snag [snæg] *n (problem)* hic *m* F

snail [sneɪl] *n* escargot *m*

snake [sneɪk] *n* serpent *m*

snap [snæp] **1** *n sound* bruit *m* sec; PHOT instantané *m* **2** *v/t (pret & pp -ped) break* casser; *(say sharply)* dire d'un ton cassant **3** *v/i (pret & pp -ped) break* se casser net **4** *adj decision, judgment* rapide, subit

♦ **snap up** *v/t bargains* sauter sur

snap fast·en·er ['snæpfæsnər] bouton-pression *m*

snap·py ['snæpɪ] *adj person, mood* cassant; *decision, response* prompt; **be a ~ dresser** s'habiller chic

'**snap·shot** photo *f*

snarl [snɑːrl] **1** *n of dog* grondement **2** *v/i of dog* gronder en montrant les dents

snatch [snætʃ] **1** *v/t (grab)* saisir; F *(steal)* voler; F *(kidnap)* enlever **2** *v/i:* **don't ~!** ne l'arrache pas!

snaz·zy ['snæzɪ] *adj* F *necktie etc* qui tape F

sneak [sniːk] **1** *v/t (remove, steal)* chiper F; **~ a glance at** regarder à la dérobée **2** *v/i (pret & pp ~ed or snuck):* **~ into the room** entrer furtivement dans la pièce; **~ out of the room** sortir furtivement de la pièce

sneak·ers ['sniːkərz] *npl* tennis *mpl*

sneak·ing ['sniːkɪŋ] *adj:* **have a ~ suspicion that ...** soupçonner que ..., avoir comme l'impression que ... F

sneak·y ['sniːkɪ] *adj* F *(underhanded)* sournois

sneer [snɪr] **1** *n* ricanement *m* **2** *v/i* ricaner

sneeze [sniːz] **1** *n* éternuement *m* **2** *v/i* éternuer

snick·er ['snɪkər] **1** *n* rire *m* en dessous **2** *v/i* pouffer de rire

sniff [snɪf] *v/t & v/i* renifler

snip [snɪp] *n Br* F *(bargain)* affaire *f*

snip·er ['snaɪpər] tireur *m* embusqué

snitch [snɪtʃ]] **1** *n (telltale)* mouchard(e) *m(f)* F **2** *v/i (tell tales)* vendre la mèche

sniv·el ['snɪvl] *v/i (pret & pp -ed, Br -led)* pleurnicher

snob [snɑːb] snob *m/f*

snob·ber·y ['snɑːbərɪ] snobisme *m*

snob·bish ['snɑːbɪʃ] *adj* snob *inv*

♦ **snoop around** *v/i* fourrer le nez partout

snoot·y ['snuːtɪ] *adj* arrogant

snooze [snuːz] **1** *n* petit somme *m*; **have a ~** faire un petit somme **2** *v/i* roupiller F

snore [snɔːr] *v/i* ronfler

snor·ing ['snɔːrɪŋ] ronflement *m*

snor·kel ['snɔːrkl] *n of swimmer* tuba *m*

snort [snɔːrt] *v/i of bull, horse* s'ébrouer; *of person* grogner

snout [snaʊt] *of pig, dog* museau *m*

snow [snoʊ] **1** *n* neige *f* **2** *v/i* neiger

♦ **snow under** *v/t:* **be snowed under with work** être submergé de travail

'**snow·ball** *n* boule *f* de neige; '**snow·bound** *adj* pris dans la neige; '**snow chains** *npl* MOT chaînes *fpl* à neige;

S

'**snow·drift** amoncellement *m* de neige; '**snow·drop** perce-neige *m*; '**snow·flake** flocon *m* de neige; '**snow·man** bonhomme *m* de neige; '**snow·plow** chasse-neige *m inv* '**snow·storm** tempête *f* de neige

snow·y ['snəʊɪ] *adj weather* neigeux*; *roads, hills* enneigé

snub [snʌb] **1** *n* rebuffade *f* **2** *v/t (pret & pp -bed)* snober

snub-nosed ['snʌbnəʊzd] *adj* au nez retroussé

snuck [snʌk] *pret & ptp* → **sneak**

snug [snʌg] *adj* bien au chaud; *(tight-fitting)* bien ajusté; *(too tight)* un peu trop serré

♦ **snug·gle down** ['snʌgl] *v/i* se blottir

♦ **snuggle up to** *v/t* se blottir contre

so [səʊ] **1** *adv* ◊ si, tellement; ~ *kind* tellement gentil; *not ~ much for me thanks* pas autant pour moi merci; ~ *much better / easier* tellement mieux / plus facile; *eat / drink ~ much* tellement manger / boire; *there were ~ many people* il y avait tellement de gens; *I miss you ~* tu me manques tellement

◊ : ~ *am I / do I* moi aussi; ~ *is / does she* elle aussi; *and~ on* et ainsi de suite; ~ *as to be able to …* afin de pouvoir …; *you didn't tell me – I did* tu ne me l'as pas dit - si, je te l'ai dit

2 *pron*: *I hope ~* je l'espère bien; *I think ~* je pense que oui; *50 or ~* une cinquantaine, à peu près cinquante

3 *conj (for that reason)* donc; *(in order that)* pour que (+*subj*); *and ~ I missed the train* et donc j'ai manqué le train; ~ *(that) I could come too* pour que je puisse moi aussi venir; ; ~ *what?* F et alors?

soak [səʊk] *v/t (steep)* faire tremper; *of water, rain* tremper

♦ **soak up** *v/t liquid* absorber; *soak up the sun* prendre un bain de soleil

soaked [səʊkt] *adj* trempé; *be ~ to the skin* être mouillé jusqu'aux os

soak·ing (wet) ['səʊkɪŋ] *adj* trempé

so-and-so ['səʊənsəʊ] F *unknown*

person un tel, une telle; *euph: annoying person* crétin(e) *m(f)*

soap [səʊp] *n for washing* savon *m*

soap, '**soap op·e·ra** feuilleton *m*

soap·y ['səʊpɪ] *adj water* savonneux*

soar [sɔːr] *v/i of rocket, prices etc* monter en flèche

sob [sɑːb] **1** *n* sanglot *m* **2** *v/i (pret & pp -bed)* sangloter

so·ber ['səʊbər] *adj (not drunk)* en état de sobriété; *(serious)* sérieux*

♦ **sober up** *v/i* dessoûler F

so-'called *adj referred to as* comme on le / la / les appelle; *incorrectly referred to as* soi-disant *inv*

soc·cer ['sɑːkər] football *m*

'**soc·cer hoo·li·gan** hooligans *mpl*

so·cia·ble ['səʊʃəbl] *adj* sociable

so·cial ['səʊʃl] *adj* social; *(recreational)* mondain

so·cial 'dem·o·crat social-démocrate *m/f (pl* sociaux-démocrates)

so·cial·ism ['səʊʃəlɪzm] socialisme *m*

so·cial·ist ['səʊʃəlɪst] **1** *adj* socialiste **2** *n* socialiste *m/f*

so·cial·ize ['səʊʃəlaɪz] *v/i* fréquenter des gens

'**so·cial life**: *I don't have much ~* je ne vois pas beaucoup de monde; **so·cial 'sci·ence** sciences *fpl* humaines; '**so·cial work** travail *m* social; '**so·cial work·er** assistante sociale *m*, assistante sociale *f*

so·ci·e·ty [sə'saɪətɪ] société *f*

so·ci·ol·o·gist [səʊsɪ'ɑːlədʒɪst] sociologue *m/f*

so·ci·ol·o·gy [səʊsɪ'ɑːlədʒɪ] sociologie *f*

sock[1] [sɑːk] *for wearing* chaussette *f*

sock[2] [sɑːk] **1** *n (punch)* coup *m* **2** *v/t (punch)* donner un coup de poing à

sock·et ['sɑːkɪt] ELEC *for light bulb* douille *f*; *(wall ~)* prise *f* de courant; *of bone* cavité *f* articulaire; *of eye* orbite *f*

so·da ['səʊdə] (~ *water)* eau *f* gazeuse; *(soft drink)* soda *m*; *(ice-cream ~)* soda *m* à la crème glacée; *whiskey and ~* un whisky soda

sod·den ['sɑːdn] *adj* trempé

so·fa ['səʊfə] canapé *m*

'so·fa bed canapé-lit *m*

soft [sɑ:ft] *adj* doux*; (*lenient*) gentil*; **have a ~ spot for** avoir un faible pour

'soft drink boisson *f* non alcoolisée

'soft ware ['sɑ:ftwer] logiciel *m*

sog·gy ['sɑ:gɪ] *adj soil* détrempé; *pastry* pâteux*

soil [sɔɪl] **1** *n* (*earth*) terre *f* **2** *v/t* salir

so·lar ['soʊlər] *adj* solaire; 'so·lar pan·el panneau *m* solaire; 'so·lar sys·tem système *m* solaire

sold [soʊld] *pret & pp* → **sell**

sol·dier ['soʊldʒər] soldat *m*

♦ soldier on *v/i* continuer coûte que coûte

sole¹ [soʊl] *n of foot* plante *f*; *of shoe* semelle *f*

sole² [soʊl] *adj* seul; *responsibility* exclusif*

sole³ [soʊl] *fish* sole *f*

sole·ly ['soʊlɪ] *adv* exclusivement; **she was not ~ to blame** elle n'était pas la seule responsable

sol·emn ['sɑ:ləm] *adj* solennel*

so·lem·ni·ty [sə'lemnətɪ] solennité *f*

sol·emn·ly ['sɑ:ləmlɪ] *adv* solennellement

so·li·cit [sə'lɪsɪt] *v/i of prostitute* racoler

so·lic·i·tor [sə'lɪsɪtər] *Br* avocat *m*; *for property, wills* notaire *m*

sol·id ['sɑ:lɪd] *adj* (*hard*) dur; (*without holes*) compact; *gold, silver etc, support* massif*; (*sturdy*) solide; *evidence* solide; **frozen ~** complètement gelé; **a ~ hour** toute une heure

sol·i·dar·i·ty [sɑ:lɪ'dærətɪ] solidarité *f*

so·lid·i·fy [sə'lɪdɪfaɪ] *v/i* (*pret & pp -ied*) se solidifier

sol·id·ly ['sɑ:lɪdlɪ] *adv built* solidement; *in favor of* massivement

so·lil·o·quy [sə'lɪləkwɪ] *on stage* monologue *m*

sol·i·taire [sɑ:lɪ'ter] *card game* réussite

f

sol·i·ta·ry ['sɑ:lɪterɪ] *adj life, activity* solitaire; (*single*) isolé

sol·i·ta·ry con'fine·ment régime *m* cellulaire

sol·i·tude ['sɑ:lɪtu:d] solitude *f*

so·lo ['soʊloʊ] **1** *adj* en solo **2** *n* MUS solo *m*

so·lo·ist ['soʊloʊɪst] soliste *m/f*

sol·u·ble ['sɑ:ljʊbl] *adj substance, problem* soluble

so·lu·tion [sə'lu:ʃn] *also mixture* solution *f*

solve [sɑ:lv] *v/t* résoudre

sol·vent ['sɑ:lvənt] *adj financially* solvable

som·ber ['sɑ:mbər] *adj* (*dark, serious*) sombre

som·bre ['sɑ:mbər] *Br* → **somber**

some [sʌm] **1** *adj* ◊ : **~ cream / chocolate / cookies** de la crème / du chocolat / des biscuits

◊ (*certain*): **~ people say that ...** certains disent que ...

◊ : **that was ~ party!** c'était une sacrée fête!, quelle fête!; **he's ~ lawyer!** quel avocat!

2 *pron* ◊ : **~ of the money** une partie de l'argent; **~ of the group** certaines personnes du groupe, certains du groupe

◊ : **would you like ~?** est-ce que vous en voulez?; **give me ~** donnez-m'en

3 *adv* ◊ (*a bit*) un peu; **we'll have to wait ~** on va devoir attendre un peu

◊ (*around*): **~ 500 letters** environ 500 lettres

some·bod·y ['sʌmbədɪ] *pron* quelqu'un

'some·day *adv* un jour

'some·how *adv* (*by one means or another*) d'une manière ou d'une autre; (*for some unknown reason*) sans savoir pourquoi

'some·one *pron* → **somebody**

'some·place *adv* → **somewhere**

som·er·sault ['sʌmərsɔ:lt] **1** *n* roulade *f*; *by vehicle* tonneau *m* **2** *v/i of vehicle* faire un tonneau

'some·thing *pron* quelque chose;

would you like ~ to drink / eat?
voulez-vous boire / manger quelque
chose?; *~ strange* quelque chose
de bizarre; *are you bored or ~?* tu
t'ennuies ou quoi?

'**some·time** *adv* un de ces jours; *~ last
year* dans le courant de l'année dernière

'**some·times** ['sʌmtaimz] *adv* parfois

'**some·what** *adv* quelque peu

'**some·where 1** *adv* quelque part **2**
pron: *let's go ~ quiet* allons dans
un endroit calme; *~ to park* un endroit où se garer

son [sʌn] fils *m*

so·na·ta [sə'nɑːtə] MUS sonate *f*

song [sɒŋ] chanson *f*

'**song·bird** oiseau *m* chanteur

'**song·writ·er** *of music* compositeur *m*,
compositrice *f*; *of words* auteur *m* de
chansons; *both* auteur-compositeur
m

'**son-in-law** (*pl **sons-in-law***) beau-
-fils *m*

son·net ['sɒnɪt] sonnet *m*

son of a 'bitch V fils *m* de pute V

soon [suːn] *adv* (*in a short while*) bientôt; (*quickly*) vite; (*early*) tôt; *come
back ~* reviens vite; *it's too ~* c'est
trop tôt; *~ after* peu (de temps) après;
how ~ dans combien de temps; *as ~
as this* dès que; *as ~ as possible* le plus
tôt possible; *~er or later* tôt ou tard;
the ~er the better le plus tôt sera le
mieux; *see you ~* à bientôt

soot [sut] suie *f*

soothe [suːð] *v/t* calmer

so·phis·ti·cat·ed [sə'fistikeitid] *adj*
sophistiqué

so·phis·ti·ca·tion [sə'fistikeɪʃn] sophistication *f*

soph·o·more ['sɑːfəmɔːr] étudiant(e)
m(f) de deuxième année

sop·py ['sɑːpɪ] *adj* F gnangnan F

so·pra·no [sə'prɑːnoʊ] *n* soprano *m/f*

sor·did ['sɔːrdɪd] *adj* *affair, business*
sordide

sore [sɔːr] **1** *adj* (*painful*): *is it ~?* ça
vous fait mal?; *have a ~ throat* avoir
mal à la gorge; *be ~* F (*angry*) être fâché; *get ~* se fâcher **2** *n* plaie *f*

sor·row ['sɑːroʊ] chagrin *m*

sor·ry ['sɑːrɪ] *adj* *day* triste; *sight* misérable; (*I'm*) *~!* (*apologizing*) pardon!;
be ~ être désolé; *I was ~ to hear of
your mother's death* j'ai été peiné
d'apprendre le décès de ta mère; *I
won't be ~ to leave here* je ne re-
gretterai pas de partir d'ici; *I feel ~
for her* elle me fait pitié

sort [sɔːrt] **1** *n* sorte *f*; *~ of ...* F plutôt;
it looks ~ of like a pineapple ça res-
semble un peu à un ananas; *is it finished? - ~ of* F c'est fini? - en
quelque sorte **2** *v/t* *also* COMPUT trier

♦ **sort out** *v/t* *papers* ranger; *problem*
résoudre

SOS [esoʊ'es] S.O.S. *m*; *fig*: *plea for
help* appel *m* à l'aide

so·'so *adv* F comme ci comme ça F

sought [sɔːt] *pret & pp* → **seek**

soul [soʊl] *also fig* âme *f*; *there wasn't
a ~* il n'y avait pas âme qui vive; *he's
a kind ~* c'est une bonne âme

sound¹ [saʊnd] **1** *adj* (*sensible*) judicieux*; *judgment* solide; (*healthy*) en
bonne santé; *business* qui se porte
bien; *walls* en bon état; *sleep* profond
2 *adv*: *be ~ asleep* être profonde-
ment endormi

sound² [saʊnd] **1** *n* son *m*; (*noise*)
bruit *m* **2** *v/t* (*pronounce*) prononcer;
MED *ausculter*; *s.o.'s chest* ausculter qn; *~ one's horn* klaxonner
3 *v/i*: *that ~s interesting* ça a l'air
intéressant; *that ~s like a good idea*
ça a l'air d'être une bonne idée; *she
~ed unhappy* elle avait l'air malheu-
reuse; *it ~s hollow* ça sonne creux

♦ **sound out** *v/t* sonder

'**sound ef·fects** *npl* effets *mpl* sonores

'**sound·ly** *adv* *sleep* profondément; *beaten* à plates coutures

'**sound·proof** *adj* *room* insonorisé

'**sound·track** bande *f* sonore

soup [suːp] soupe *f*

'**soup bowl** bol *m* de soupe

souped-up [suːpt'ʌp] *adj* F gonflé F

'**soup plate** assiette *f* à soupe

'**soup spoon** cuillère *f* à soupe

sour ['saʊər] *adj* *apple, milk* aigre; *expression* revêche; *comment* désobli-

geant

source[sɔːrs] *n of river, noise, information etc* source *f*

sour(ed) 'cream [sauərd] crème *f* aigre

south [sauθ] **1** *n* sud *m*; **the South of France** le Midi; **to the ~ of** au sud de **2** *adj* sud *inv*; *wind* du sud; **~ Des Moines** le sud de Des Moines **3** *adv travel* vers le sud; **~ of** au sud de

South 'Af·ri·ca Afrique *f* du sud; **South 'Af·ri·can 1** *adj* sud-africain **2** *n* Sud-Africain(e) *m(f)*; **South A'mer·i·ca** Amérique *f* du sud; **South A'mer·i·can 1** *adj* sud-américain **2** *n* Sud-Américain(e) *m(f)*; **south'east 1** *n* sud-est *m* **2** *adj* sud-est *inv*; *wind* du sud-est **3** *adv travel* vers le sud-est; **~ of** au sud-est de; **south'east·ern** *adj* sud-est *inv*

south·er·ly['sʌðərlɪ] *adj wind* du sud; *direction* vers le sud

south·ern ['sʌðərn] *adj* du Sud

south·ern·er ['sʌðərnər] habitant(e) *m(f)* du Sud; *US* HIST sudiste *m/f*

south·ern·most ['sʌðərnmoust] *adj* le plus au sud

South 'Pole pôle *m* Sud; **south·ward** ['sauθwərd] *adv* vers le sud; **south·'west 1** *n* sud-ouest *m* **2** *adj* sud-ouest *inv*; *wind* du sud-ouest **3** *adv* vers le sud-ouest; **~ of** au sud-ouest de; **south'west·ern** *adj part of a country etc* sud-ouest *inv*

sou·ve·nir [suːvə'nɪr] souvenir *m*

sove·reign ['sɑːvrɪn] *adj state* souverain

sove·reign·ty ['sɑːvrɪntɪ] *of state* souveraineté *f*

So·vi·et ['souvɪət] *adj* soviétique

So·vi·et 'U·nion Union *f* soviétique

sow[1] [sau] *n (female pig)* truie *f*

sow[2] [sou] *v/t (pret* **sowed**, *pp* **sown**) *seeds* semer

sown [soun] *pp* → **sow**[2]

soy bean ['sɔɪbiːn] soja *m*

soy 'sauce sauce *f* au soja

space [speɪs] *n (outer ~, area)* espace *m*; *(room)* place *f*

♦ **space out** *v/t* espacer

spaced out [speɪst'aut] *adj* F défoncé F

'space-bar COMPUT barre *f* d'espacement; **'space-craft** vaisseau *m* spatial; **'space-ship** vaisseau *m* spatial; **'space shut·tle** navette *f* spatiale; **'space sta·tion** station *f* spatiale; **'space-suit** scaphandre *m* de cosmonaute

spa·cious ['speɪʃəs] *adj* spacieux*

spade[speɪd] *for digging* bêche *f*; **~s** *in card game* pique *m*

spa·ghet·ti [spə'getɪ] *nsg* spaghetti *mpl*

Spain [speɪn] Espagne *f*

span[spæn] *v/t (pret & pp* **-ned**) *(cover)* recouvrir; *of bridge* traverser

Span·iard ['spænjərd] Espagnol *m*, Espagnole *f*

Span·ish['spænɪʃ] **1** *adj* espagnol **2** *n language* espagnol *m*; **the ~** les Espagnols

spank[spæŋk] *v/t* donner une fessée à

spank·ing ['spæŋkɪŋ] fessée *f*

span·ner ['spænər] *Br* clef *f*

spare [sper] *v/t time* accorder; *(lend: money)* prêter; *(do without)* se passer de; **money to ~** argent en trop; **time to ~** temps libre; **can you ~ the time?** est-ce que vous pouvez trouver un moment?; **there were five to ~** *(left over, in excess)* il y en avait cinq de trop **2** *adj (extra) cash* en trop; *eyeglasses, clothes* de rechange **3** *n:* **~s** *(~ parts)* pièces *fpl* de rechange

spare 'part pièce *f* de rechange; **spare 'ribs** *npl* côtelette *f* de porc dans l'échine; **spare 'room** chambre *f* d'ami; **spare 'time** temps *m* libre; **spare 'tire** MOT pneu *m* de rechange; **spare 'tyre** *Br* → **spare tire**

spar·ing ['sperɪŋ] *adj:* **be ~ with** économiser

spa·ring·ly ['sperɪŋlɪ] *adv* en petite quantité

spark [spɑːrk] *n* étincelle *f*

spar·kle ['spɑːrkl] *v/i* étinceler

spark·ling wine ['spɑːrklɪŋ] vin *m* mousseux

'spark plug bougie *f*

spar·row ['spæroʊ] moineau *m*

S

sparse [spɑːrs] *adj vegetation* épars

sparse·ly ['spɑːrslɪ] *adv:* **~ populated** faiblement peuplé

spar·tan ['spɑːrtn] *adj room* spartiate

spas·mod·ic [spæz'mɑːdɪk] *adj visits, attempts* intermittent; *conversation* saccadé

spat [spæt] *pret & pp →* **spit**

spate [speɪt] *fig* série *f*, avalanche *f*

spa·tial ['speɪʃl] *adj* spatial

spat·ter ['spætər] *v/t mud, paint* éclabousser

speak [spiːk] **1** *v/i (pret* **spoke***, pp* **spoken)** parler (*to, with* à); **we're not ~ing (to each other)** (*we've quarreled*) on ne se parle plus; **~ing** TELEC lui-même, elle-même **2** *v/t (pret* **spoke***, pp* **spoken)** *foreign language* parler; **~ one's mind** dire ce que l'on pense

♦ **speak for** *v/t* parler pour

♦ **speak out** *v/i* s'élever (*against* contre)

♦ **speak up** *v/i (speak louder)* parler plus fort

speak·er ['spiːkər] *at conference* intervenant(e) *m(f)*; (*orator*) orateur (-trice) *m(f)*; *of sound system* haut-parleur *m*; **French / Spanish~** francophone *m/f* / hispanophone *m/f*

spear·mint ['spɪrmɪnt] menthe *f* verte

spe·cial ['speʃl] *adj* spécial; *effort, day etc* exceptionnel*; **be on ~** être en réduction

special effects *npl* effets *mpl* spéciaux, trucages *mpl*

spe·cial·ist ['speʃlɪst] spécialiste *m/f*

spe·ci·al·i·ty [speʃɪ'ælətɪ] *Br →* **specialty**

spe·cial·ize ['speʃəlaɪz] *v/i* se spécialiser (*in* en, dans); **we ~ in ...** nous sommes spécialisés en ...

spe·cial·ly ['speʃlɪ] *adv →* **especially**

spe·cial·ty ['speʃəltɪ] spécialité *f*

spe·cies ['spiːʃiːz] *nsg* espèce *f*

spe·cif·ic [spə'sɪfɪk] *adj* spécifique

spe·cif·i·cal·ly [spə'sɪfɪklɪ] *adv* spécifiquement; **I ~ told you that ...** je vous avais bien dit que ...

spec·i·fi·ca·tions [spesɪfɪ'keɪʃnz] *npl of machine etc* spécifications *fpl*, ca-

ractéristiques *mpl*

spe·ci·fy ['spesɪfaɪ] *v/t (pret & pp* **-ied)** préciser

spe·ci·men ['spesɪmən] *of work* spécimen *m*; *of blood, urine* prélèvement *m*

speck [spek] *of dust, soot* grain *m*

spec·ta·cle ['spektəkl] (*impressive sight*) spectacle *m*

spec·tac·u·lar [spek'tækjʊlər] *adj* spectaculaire

spec·ta·tor [spek'teɪtər] spectateur (-trice) *m(f)*

spec·ta·tor sport *sport* que l'on regarde en spectateur

spec·trum ['spektrəm] *fig* éventail *m*

spec·u·late ['spekjʊleɪt] *v/i also* FIN spéculer (*about, on* sur)

spec·u·la·tion [spekjʊ'leɪʃn] spéculations *fpl*; FIN spéculation *f*

spec·u·la·tor ['spekjʊleɪtər] FIN spéculateur(-trice) *m(f)*

sped [sped] *pret & pp →* **speed**

speech [spiːtʃ] (*address*) discours *m*; (*ability to speak*) parole *f*; (*way of speaking*) élocution *f*

'speech de·fect trouble *m* d'élocution

speech·less ['spiːtʃlɪs] *adj with shock, surprise* sans voix

'speech ther·a·pist orthophoniste *m/f*; **'speech ther·a·py** orthophonie *f*; **'speech writ·er** personne qui écrit les discours d'une autre

speed [spiːd] **1** *n* vitesse *f*; **at a ~ of ...** à une vitesse de ... **2** *v/i (pret & pp* **sped)** (*go quickly*) se précipiter; *of vehicle* foncer; (*drive too quickly*) faire de la vitesse

♦ **speed by** *v/i* passer à toute vitesse

♦ **speed up 1** *v/i* aller plus vite **2** *v/t* accélérer

'speed·boat vedette *f*; *with outboard motor* hors-bord *m inv*

'speed bump dos d'âne *m*, ralentisseur *m*

speed·i·ly ['spiːdɪlɪ] *adv* rapidement

speed·ing ['spiːdɪŋ] *when driving* excès *m* de vitesse

'speed·ing fine contravention *f* pour excès de vitesse

'speed lim·it limitation *f* de vitesse

speed·om·e·ter [spi:'dɑːmɪtər] compteur *m* de vitesse

'speed trap contrôle *m* de vitesse

speed·y ['spi:dɪ] *adj* rapide

spell¹ [spel] 1 *v/t word* écrire, épeler; **how do you ~ it?** comment ça s'écrit? 2 *v/i*: **he can / can't ~** il a une bonne / mauvaise orthographe

spell² *n (period of time)* période *f*

spell³ *n magic* sort *m*

'spell·bound *adj* sous le charme; 'spell-check COMPUT correction *f* orthographique; **do a ~** effectuer une correction orthographique (**on** sur); 'spell-check·er COMPUT correcteur *m* d'orthographe, correcteur *m* orthographique

spell·ing ['spelɪŋ] orthographe *f*

spend [spend] *v/t (pret & pp* **spent**) *money* dépenser; *time* passer

'spend·thrift *n pej* dépensier(-ère) *m(f)*

spent [spent] *pret & pp* → **spend**

sperm [spɜːrm] spermatozoïde *m*; *(semen)* sperme *m*

'sperm bank banque *f* de sperme

'sperm count taux *m* de spermatozoïdes

sphere [sfɪr] *also fig* sphère *f*; **~ of influence** sphère d'influence

spice [spaɪs] *n (seasoning)* épice *f*

spic·y ['spaɪsɪ] *adj food* épicé

spi·der ['spaɪdər] araignée *f*

'spi·der-web toile *f* d'araignée

spike [spaɪk] *n* pointe *f*; *on plant, animal* piquant *m*

'spike heels *npl* talons *mpl* aiguille

spill [spɪl] 1 *v/t* renverser 2 *v/i* se répandre 3 *n* of oil, chemicals déversement *m* accidentel

spin¹ [spɪn] 1 *n (turn)* tour *m* 2 *v/t (pret & pp* **spun**) faire tourner 3 *v/i (pret & pp* **spun**) of wheel tourner; **my head is ~ning** j'ai la tête qui tourne

spin² *v/t (pret & pp* **spun**) *wool etc* filer; *web* tisser

♦ spin around *v/i of person* faire volte-face; *of car* faire un tête-à-queue; *of dancer, several times* tourner

♦ spin out *v/t* faire durer

spin·ach ['spɪnɪdʒ] épinards *mpl*

spin·al ['spaɪnl] *adj* de vertèbres

spin·al 'col·umn colonne *f* vertébrale

spin·al 'cord moelle *f* épinière

'spin doc·tor F conseiller(-ère) *m(f)* en communication; 'spin-dry *v/t* essorer; 'spin-dry·er essoreuse *f*

spine [spaɪn] *of person, animal* colonne *f* vertébrale; *of book* dos *m*; *on plant, hedgehog* épine *f*

spine·less ['spaɪnlɪs] *adj (cowardly)* lâche

'spin-off retombée *f*

spin·ster ['spɪnstər] célibataire *f*

spin·y ['spaɪnɪ] *adj* épineux*

spi·ral ['spaɪrəl] 1 *n* spirale *f* 2 *v/i (pret & pp* **-ed**, *Br* **-led**) *(rise quickly)* monter en spirale

spi·ral 'stair·case escalier *m* en colimaçon

spire ['spaɪr] *of church* flèche *f*

spir·it ['spɪrɪt] esprit *m*; *(courage)* courage *m*; **in a ~ of cooperation** dans un esprit de coopération

spir·it·ed ['spɪrɪtɪd] *adj (energetic)* énergique

'spir·it lev·el niveau *m* à bulle d'air

spir·its¹ ['spɪrɪts] *npl (alcohol)* spiritueux *mpl*

spir·its² *npl (morale)* moral *m*; **be in good / poor ~** avoir / ne pas avoir le moral

spir·i·tu·al ['spɪrɪtʊəl] *adj* spirituel*

spir·it·u·al·ism ['spɪrɪtʊəlɪzm] spiritisme *m*

spir·it·u·al·ist ['spɪrɪtʊəlɪst] *n* spirite *m/f*

spit [spɪt] *v/i (pret & pp* **spat**) *of person* cracher; **it's ~ting with rain** il bruine

♦ spit out *v/t food, liquid* recracher

spite [spaɪt] *n* malveillance *f*; **in ~ of** en dépit de

spite·ful ['spaɪtfl] *adj* malveillant

spite·ful·ly ['spaɪtflɪ] *adv* avec malveillance

spit·ting im·age ['spɪtɪŋ]: **be the ~ of s.o.** être qn tout craché F

splash [splæʃ] 1 *n noise* plouf *m*; *(small amount of liquid)* goutte *f*; *of color* tache *f* 2 *v/t person* éclabousser; *water, mud* asperger 3 *v/i of person* patauger; **~ against sth** *of waves* s'écraser contre qch

♦ **splash down** *v/i of spacecraft* amerrir

♦ **splash out** *v/i in spending* faire une folie

'**splash-down** amerrissage *m*

splen·did ['splendɪd] *adj* magnifique

splen·dor, *Br* **splen·dour** ['splendər] splendeur *f*

splint [splɪnt] *n* MED attelle *f*

splin·ter ['splɪntər] **1** *n of wood, glass* éclat *m*; *of bone* esquille *f*; *in finger* écharde *f* **2** *v/i* se briser

'**splin·ter group** groupe *m* dissident

split [splɪt] **1** *n damage: in wood* fente *f*; *in fabric* déchirure *f*; *(disagreement)* division *f*; *(of profits etc)* partage *m*; *(share)* part *f* **2** *v/t (pret & pp split)* *wood* fendre; *fabric* déchirer; *log* fendre en deux; *(cause disagreement in, divide)* diviser **3** *v/i (pret & pp split)* *of fabric* se déchirer; *of wood* se fendre; *(disagree)* se diviser (**on, over** au sujet de)

♦ **split up** *v/i of couple* se séparer

split per·son·al·i·ty PSYCH dédoublement *m* de personnalité

split·ting ['splɪtɪŋ] *adj*: **a ~ headache** un mal de tête terrible

splut·ter ['splʌtər] *v/i* bredouiller

spoil [spɔɪl] *v/t child* gâter; *surprise, party* gâcher

'**spoil-sport** F rabat-joie *m/f*

spoilt [spɔɪlt] *adj child* gâté; **be ~ for choice** avoir l'embarras du choix

spoke[^1] [spouk] *of wheel* rayon *m*

spoke[^2] [spouk] *pret → **speak***

spo·ken ['spoukən] *pp → **speak***

spokes·man ['spouksmən] porte-parole *m*

spokes·per·son ['spoukspɜːrsən] porte-parole *m/f*

spokes·wom·an ['spoukswumən] porte-parole *f*

sponge [spʌndʒ] *n* éponge *f*

♦ **sponge off, sponge on** *v/t* F vivre aux crochets de F

'**sponge cake** génoise *f*

spong·er ['spʌndʒər] F parasite *m/f*

spon·sor ['spɑːnsər] **1** *n (guarantor)* répondant(e) *m(f)*; *for club membership* parrain *m*, marraine *f*; RAD, TV, SP sponsor *m/f* **2** *v/t for immigration etc* se porter garant de; *for club membership* parrainer; RAD, TV, SP sponsoriser

spon·sor·ship ['spɑːnsərʃɪp] RAD, TV, SP, *of exhibition etc* sponsorisation *f*

spon·ta·ne·ous [spɑːn'teɪnɪəs] *adj* spontané

spon·ta·ne·ous·ly [spɑːn'teɪnɪəslɪ] *adv* spontanément

spook·y ['spuːkɪ] *adj* F qui fait froid dans le dos

spool [spuːl] *n* bobine *f*

spoon [spuːn] *n* cuillère *f*

'**spoon-feed** *v/t (pret & pp -fed) fig* mâcher tout à

spoon·ful ['spuːnful] cuillerée *f*

spo·rad·ic [spə'rædɪk] *adj* intermittent

sport [spɔːrt] *n* sport *m*

sport·ing ['spɔːrtɪŋ] *adj event* sportif*; *(fair, generous)* chic *inv*; **a ~ gesture** un geste élégant

'**sports car** [spɔːrts] voiture *f* de sport; '**sports-coat** veste *f* sport; '**sports jour·nal·ist** journaliste *m* sportif, journaliste *f* sportive; '**sports·man** sportif *m*; '**sports med·i·cine** médecine *f* du sport; '**sports news** *nsg* nouvelles *fpl* sportives; '**sports page** page *f* des sports; '**sportswear** vêtements *mpl* de sport; '**sports·wom·an** sportive *f*

sport·y ['spɔːrtɪ] *adj person* sportif*

spot[^1] [spɑːt] *n on skin* bouton *m*; *part of pattern* pois *m*; **a ~ of ...** *(a little)* un peu de ...

spot[^2] *n (place)* endroit *m*; **on the ~** sur place; *(immediately)* sur-le-champ; **put s.o. on the ~** mettre qn dans l'embarras

spot[^3] *v/t (pret & pp -ted) (notice, identify)* repérer

spot 'check *n* contrôle *m* au hasard; **carry out ~s** effectuer des contrôles au hasard

spot·less ['spɑːtlɪs] *adj* impeccable

'**spot·light** *beam* feu *m* de projecteur; *device* projecteur *m*

spot·ted ['spɒtɪd] *adj fabric* à pois

spot·ty ['spɒtɪ] *adj with pimples* boutonneux*

spouse [spaʊs] *fml* époux *m*, épouse *f*

spout [spaʊt] **1** *n* bec *m* **2** *v/i of liquid* jaillir **3** *v/t* F débiter

sprain [spreɪn] **1** *n* foulure *f*; *serious* entorse *f* **2** *v/t ankle, wrist* se fouler; *seriously* se faire une entorse à

sprang ['spræŋ] *pret* → **spring³**

sprawl [sprɔːl] *v/i* s'affaler; *of city* s'étendre (de tous les côtés); *send s.o. ~ing of punch* envoyer qn par terre

sprawl·ing ['sprɔːlɪŋ] *adj* tentaculaire

spray [spreɪ] **1** *n of sea water* embruns *mpl*; *from fountain* gouttes *fpl* d'eau; *for hair* laque *f*; *container* atomiseur *m* **2** *v/t perfume, hair lacquer, furniture polish* vaporiser; *paint, weed-killer etc* pulvériser; *~ s.o. with sth* asperger qn de qch; *~ graffiti on sth* peindre des graffitis à la bombe sur qch

'spray-gun pulvérisateur *m*

spread [spred] **1** *n of disease, religion etc* propagation *f*; F (*big meal*) festin *m* **2** *v/t* (*pret & pp* **spread**) (*lay*), *butter* étaler; *news, rumor, disease* répandre; *arms, legs* étendre **3** *v/i* (*pret & pp* **spread**) se répandre; *of butter* s'étaler

'spread-sheet COMPUT feuille *f* de calcul; *program* tableur *m*

spree [spriː] F: *go (out) on a ~* faire la bringue F; *go on a shopping ~* aller claquer son argent dans les magasins F

sprig [sprɪg] brin *m*

spright·ly ['spraɪtlɪ] *adj* alerte

spring¹ [sprɪŋ] *n season* printemps *m*

spring² [sprɪŋ] *n device* ressort *m*

spring³ [sprɪŋ] **1** *n* (*jump*) bond *m*; (*stream*) source *f* **2** *v/i* (*pret* **sprang**, *pp* **sprung**) bondir; *~ from* venir de, provenir de

'spring-board tremplin *m*; **spring 'chick·en** *hum*: *she's no ~* elle n'est plus toute jeune; **spring-'clean·ing** nettoyage *m* de printemps; **'spring·time** printemps *m*

spring·y ['sprɪŋɪ] *adj mattress, ground,* walk souple

sprin·kle ['sprɪŋkl] *v/t* saupoudrer; *~ sth with sth* saupoudrer qch de qch

sprin·kler ['sprɪŋklər] *for garden* arroseur *m*; *in ceiling* extincteur *m*

sprint [sprɪnt] **1** *n* sprint *m* **2** *v/i* SP sprinter; *fig* piquer un sprint F

sprint·er ['sprɪntər] SP sprinteur (-euse) *m(f)*

sprout [spraʊt] **1** *v/i of seed* pousser **2** *n*: (**Brussels**) *~s* choux *mpl* de Bruxelles

spruce [spruːs] *adj* pimpant

sprung [sprʌŋ] *pp* → **spring³**

spry [spraɪ] *adj* alerte

spun [spʌn] *pret & pp* → **spin**

spur [spɜːr] *n* éperon *m*; *fig* aiguillon *m*; *on the ~ of the moment* sous l'impulsion du moment

♦ **spur on** *v/t* (*pret & pp* **-red**) (*encourage*) encourager

spurt [spɜːrt] **1** *n in race* accélération *f*; *put on a ~ in race* sprinter; *fig: in work* donner un coup de collier **2** *v/i of liquid* jaillir

sput·ter ['spʌtər] *v/i of engine* tousser

spy [spaɪ] **1** *n* espion(ne) *m(f)* **2** *v/i* (*pret & pp* **-ied**) faire de l'espionnage **3** *v/t* (*pret & pp* **-ied**) (*see*) apercevoir

♦ **spy on** *v/t* espionner

squab·ble ['skwɑːbl] **1** *n* querelle *f* **2** *v/i* se quereller

squad [skwɑːd] escouade *f*, groupe *m*; SP équipe *f*

squal·id ['skwɑːlɪd] *adj* sordide

squal·or ['skwɑːlər] misère *f*

squan·der ['skwɑːndər] *v/t* gaspiller

square [skwer] **1** *adj in shape* carré; *~ mile / yard* mile / yard carré **2** *n shape*, MATH carré *m*; *in town* place *f*; *in board game* case *f*; *we're back to ~ one* nous sommes revenus à la case départ

♦ **square up** *v/i* (*settle accounts*) s'arranger; *square up with s.o.* régler ses comptes avec qn

square 'root racine *f* carrée

squash¹ [skwɑːʃ] *n vegetable* courge *f*

squash² [skwɑːʃ] *n game* squash *m*

squash³ [skwɑːʃ] *v/t* (*crush*) écraser

squat [skwɑːt] **1** *adj in shape* ramassé

S

2 v/i (pret & pp **-ted**) sit s'accroupir; illegally squatter

squat·ter ['skwɑːtər] squatteur(-euse) m(f)

squeak [skwiːk] **1** n of mouse couinement m; of hinge grincement m **2** v/i of mouse couiner; of hinge grincer; of shoes crisser

squeak·y ['skwiːkɪ] adj hinge grinçant; shoes qui crissent; **~ voice** petite voix aiguë

'squeak·y clean adj F blanc* comme neige

squeal [skwiːl] **1** n cri m aigu; of brakes grincement m **2** v/i pousser des cris aigus; of brakes grincer

squeam·ish ['skwiːmɪʃ] adj trop sensible

squeeze [skwiːz] **1** n: **with a ~ of her shoulder** en lui pressant l'épaule; **give s.o.'s hand a ~** serrer la main de qn **2** v/t hand serrer; shoulder, (remove juice from) presser; fruit, parcel palper; **~ sth out of s.o.** soutirer qch à qn

♦ **squeeze in 1** v/i to car etc rentrer en se serrant **2** v/t réussir à faire rentrer

♦ **squeeze up** v/i to make space se serrer

squid [skwɪd] calmar m

squint [skwɪnt] n: **have a ~** loucher

squirm [skwɜːrm] v/i (wriggle) se tortiller; in embarrassment être mal à l'aise

squir·rel ['skwɪrl] écureuil m

squirt [skwɜːrt] **1** v/t faire gicler **2** n F pej morveux(-euse) m(f)

St abbr (= **saint**) St(e) (= saint(e)); (= **street**) rue

stab [stæb] **1** n F: **have a ~** essayer (**at doing sth** de faire qch) **2** v/t (pret & pp **-bed**) person poignarder

sta·bil·i·ty [stə'bɪlətɪ] stabilité f

sta·bil·ize ['steɪbɪlaɪz] **1** v/t stabiliser **2** v/i se stabiliser

sta·ble[1] ['steɪbl] n for horses écurie f

sta·ble[2] ['steɪbl] adj stable

stack [stæk] **1** n (pile) pile f; (smoke~) cheminée f; **~s of** F énormément de **2** v/t empiler

sta·di·um ['steɪdɪəm] stade m

staff [stæf] npl (employees) personnel m; (teachers) personnel m enseignant

staf·fer ['stæfər] employé(e) m(f)

'staff-room Br: in school salle f des professeurs

stag [stæg] cerf m

stage[1] [steɪdʒ] n in life, project, journey étape f

stage[2] **1** n THEA scène f; **go on the ~** devenir acteur(-trice) **2** v/t play mettre en scène; demonstration organiser

'stage-coach diligence f

stage 'door entrée f des artistes; **'stage fright** trac m; **'stage hand** machiniste m/f

stag·ger ['stægər] **1** v/i tituber **2** v/t (amaze) ébahir; coffee breaks etc échelonner

stag·ger·ing ['stægərɪŋ] adj stupéfiant

stag·nant ['stægnənt] adj water, economy stagnant

stag·nate [stæg'neɪt] v/i fig: of person, mind stagner

stag·na·tion [stæg'neɪʃn] stagnation f

'stag par·ty enterrement m de vie de garçon

stain [steɪn] **1** n (dirty mark) tache f; for wood teinture f **2** v/t (dirty) tacher; wood teindre **3** v/i of wine etc tacher; of fabric se tacher

stained-glass 'win·dow [steɪnd] vitrail m

stain·less steel [steɪnlɪs'stiːl] **1** adj en acier inoxydable **2** n acier m inoxydable

stain re·mov·er ['steɪnrɪmuːvər] détachant m

stair [ster] marche f; **the ~s** l'escalier m

'stair·case escalier m

stake [steɪk] **1** n of wood pieu m; when gambling enjeu m; (investment) investissements mpl; **be at ~** être en jeu **2** v/t tree soutenir avec un pieu; money jouer; person financer

stale [steɪl] adj bread rassis; air empesté; fig: news plus très frais*

'stale·mate in chess pat m; fig impasse f; **reach ~** finir dans l'impasse

stalk[1] [stɔːk] n of fruit, plant tige f

stalk[2] [stɔːk] v/t animal, person traquer

stalk·er ['stɔ:kər] *of person* harceleur *m*, -euse *f*

stall¹ [stɔ:l] *n at market* étalage *m*; *for cow, horse* stalle *f*

stall² [stɔ:l] **1** *v/i of vehicle, engine* caler; (*play for time*) chercher à gagner du temps **2** *v/t engine* caler; *person* faire attendre

stal·li·on ['stæljən] étalon *m*

stalls [stɔ:lz] *npl* THEA orchestre *m*

stal·wart ['stɔ:lwərt] *adj supporter* fidèle

stam·i·na ['stæmɪnə] endurance *f*

stam·mer ['stæmər] **1** *n* bégaiement *m* **2** *v/i* bégayer

stamp¹ [stæmp] **1** *n for letter* timbre *m*; *device, mark* tampon *m* **2** *v/t letter* timbrer; *document, passport* tamponner; ***I sent them a self-addressed ~ed envelope*** je leur ai envoyé une enveloppe timbrée à mon adresse

stamp² [stæmp] *v/t:* ***one's feet*** taper du pied

♦ **stamp out** *v/t* (*eradicate*) éradiquer

'**stamp col·lect·ing** philatélie *f*; '**stamp col·lec·tion** collection *f* de timbres; '**stamp col·lec·tor** collectionneur(-euse) *m(f)* de timbres

stam·pede [stæm'pi:d] **1** *n of cattle etc* débandade *f*; *of people* ruée *f* **2** *v/i of cattle* s'enfuir à la débandade; *of people* se ruer

stance [stæns] position *f*

stand [stænd] **1** *n at exhibition* stand *m*; (*witness* **~**) barre *f* des témoins; (*support, base*) support *m*; ***take the ~*** LAW venir à la barre **2** *v/i* (*pret & pp* **stood**) (*be situated*) se trouver; *as opposed to sit* rester debout; (*rise*) se lever; ***~ still*** ne bouge pas; ***where do I ~ with you?*** quelle est ma position vis-à-vis de toi? **3** *v/t* (*pret & pp* **stood**) (*tolerate*) supporter; (*put*) mettre; ***you don't ~ a chance*** tu n'as aucune chance; ***~ s.o. a drink*** payer à boire à qn; ***~ one's ground*** tenir ferme

♦ **stand back** *v/i* reculer

♦ **stand by 1** *v/i* (*not take action*) rester là sans rien faire; (*be ready*) se tenir prêt **2** *v/t person* soutenir; *decision* s'en tenir à

♦ **stand down** *v/i* (*withdraw*) se retirer

♦ **stand for** *v/t* (*tolerate*) supporter; (*represent*) représenter

♦ **stand in for** *v/t* remplacer

♦ **stand out** *v/i be visible* ressortir

♦ **stand up 1** *v/i* se lever **2** *v/t* F: ***stand s.o. up*** poser un lapin à qn F

♦ **stand up for** *v/t* défendre

♦ **stand up to** *v/t* (*face*) tenir tête à

stan·dard ['stændərd] **1** *adj procedure etc* normal; ***~ practice*** pratique *f* courante **2** *n* (*level*) niveau *m*; *moral* critère *m*; TECH norme *f*; ***be up to ~ of work*** être à la hauteur; ***set high ~s*** être exigeant

stan·dard·ize ['stændərdaɪz] *v/t* normaliser

stan·dard of 'liv·ing niveau *m* de vie

'**stand·by 1** *n ticket* stand-by *m*; ***be on ~ at airport*** être en stand-by; ***be ready to act*** être prêt à intervenir **2** *adv fly* en stand-by

'**stand·by pas·sen·ger** stand-by *m/f inv*

stand·ing ['stændɪŋ] *n in society* position *f* sociale; (*repute*) réputation *f*; ***a musician / politician of some ~*** un musicien / un politicien réputé; ***a friendship of long ~*** une amitié de longue date

'**stand·ing room** *npl* fpl debout

stand-off·ish [stænd'ɔːfɪʃ] *adj* distant; '**stand·point** point *m* de vue; '**stand·still**: ***be at a ~*** être paralysé; *of traffic also* être immobilisé; ***bring to a ~*** paralyser; *traffic also* immobiliser

stank [stæŋk] *pret* → **stink**

stan·za ['stænzə] strophe *f*

sta·ple¹ ['steɪpl] *n foodstuff* aliment *m* de base

sta·ple² ['steɪpl] **1** *n fastener* agrafe *f* **2** *v/t* agrafer

sta·ple 'di·et alimentation *f* de base

'**sta·ple gun** agrafeuse *f*

sta·pler ['steɪplər] agrafeuse *f*

star [stɑːr] **1** *n in sky* étoile *f*; *fig also* vedette *f* **2** *v/t* (*pret & pp* **-red**) *of movie* avoir comme vedette(s) **3** *v/i* (*pret & pp* **-red**) *in movie* jouer le rôle

S

principal

'star·board *adj* de tribord

starch [stɑːtʃ] *in foodstuff* amidon *m*

stare [ster] **1** *n* regard *m* fixe **2** *v/i*: ~ *into space* regarder dans le vide; *it's rude to* ~ ce n'est pas poli de fixer les gens

♦ stare at *v/t* regarder fixement, fixer

'star·fish étoile *f* de mer

stark [stɑːrk] **1** *adj landscape, color* austère; *reminder, contrast etc* brutal **2** *adv*: ~ *naked* complètement nu

star·ling ['stɑːrlɪŋ] étourneau *m*

star·ry ['stɑːrɪ] *adj night* étoilé

star·ry-eyed ['stɑːrɪaɪd] *adj person* idéaliste

Stars and 'Stripes bannière *f* étoilée

start [stɑːrt] **1** *n* début *m*; *make a* ~ *on sth* commencer qch; *get off to a good / bad* ~ *in race* faire un bon / mauvais départ; *in marriage, career* bien / mal démarrer; *from the* ~ dès le début; *well, it's a* ~ c'est un début **2** *v/i* commencer; *of engine, car* démarrer; ~*ing from tomorrow* à partir de demain **3** *v/t* commencer; *engine, car* mettre en marche; *business* monter; ~ *to do sth*, ~ *doing sth* commencer à faire qch

start·er ['stɑːrtər] *part of meal* entrée *f*; *of car* démarreur *m*

'start·ing point point *m* de départ

'start·ing sal·a·ry salaire *m* de départ

start·le ['stɑːrtl] *v/t* effrayer

start·ling ['stɑːrtlɪŋ] *adj* surprenant

star·va·tion [stɑːr'veɪʃn] inanition *f*; *die of* ~ mourir de faim

starve [stɑːrv] *v/i* souffrir de la faim; ~ *to death* mourir de faim; *I'm starving* F je meurs de faim F

state¹ [steɪt] **1** *n* (*condition, country, part of country*) état *m*; *the States* les États-Unis *mpl* **2** *adj capital, police etc* d'état; *banquet, occasion etc* officiel*

state² [steɪt] *v/t* déclarer; *qualifications, name and address* décliner

'State De·part·ment Département *m* d'État (américain)

state·ment ['steɪtmənt] *to police* dé-

claration *f*; (*announcement*) communiqué *m*; (*bank* ~) relevé *m* de compte

state of e'mer·gen·cy état *m* d'urgence

state-of-the-'art *adj* de pointe

states·man ['steɪtsmən] homme *m* d'État

state troop·er ['truːpər] policier *m* d'état

state 'vis·it visite *f* officielle

stat·ic (e·lec·tric·i·ty) ['stætɪk] électricité *f* statique

sta·tion ['steɪʃn] **1** *n* RAIL gare *f*; *of subway*, RAD station *f*; TV chaîne *f* **2** *v/t guard etc* placer; *be ~ed at of soldier* être stationné à

sta·tion·a·ry ['steɪʃənrɪ] *adj* immobile

sta·tion·er·y ['steɪʃənərɪ] papeterie *f*

'sta·tion·er·y store papeterie *f*

sta·tion 'man·ag·er RAIL chef *m* de gare

'sta·tion wag·on break *m*

sta·tis·ti·cal [stə'tɪstɪkl] *adj* statistique

sta·tis·ti·cal·ly [stə'tɪstɪklɪ] *adv* statistiquement

sta·tis·ti·cian [stætɪs'tɪʃn] statisticien(ne) *m(f)*

sta·tis·tics [stə'tɪstɪks] *nsg science* statistique *f npl figures* statistiques *fpl*

stat·ue ['stætʃuː] statue *f*

Stat·ue of 'Lib·er·ty Statue *f* de la Liberté

sta·tus ['steɪtəs] (*position*) statut *m*; (*prestige*) prestige *m*

'sta·tus bar COMPUT barre *f* d'état

'sta·tus sym·bol signe *m* extérieur de richesse

stat·ute ['stætʃuːt] loi *f*

staunch [stɒntʃ] *adj* fervent

stay [steɪ] **1** *n* séjour *m* **2** *v/i* rester; *come to* ~ *for a week* venir passer une semaine; ~ *in a hotel* descendre dans un hôtel; *I am ~ing at Hotel ...* je suis descendu à l'Hôtel ...; ~ *right there!* tenez-vous là!; ~ *put* ne pas bouger

♦ stay away *v/i* ne pas s'approcher

♦ stay away from *v/t* éviter

♦ stay behind *v/i* rester; *in school* rester après la classe

♦ **stay up** v/i (*not go to bed*) rester debout

stead·i·ly ['stedɪlɪ] adv improve etc de façon régulière

stead·y ['stedɪ] **1** adj hand ferme; voice posé; (*regular*) régulier*; (*continuous*) continu; **be ~ on one's feet** être d'aplomb sur ses jambes **2** adv: **be going ~** of couple sortir ensemble; **be going ~ (with s.o.)** sortir avec qn; **~ on!** calme-toi! **3** v/t (pret & pp **-ied**) person soutenir; one's voice raffermir

steak [steɪk] bifteck m

steal [stiːl] **1** v/t (pret **stole**, pp **stolen**) money etc voler **2** v/i (pret **stole**, pp **stolen**) (*be a thief*) voler; **~ in / out** entrer / sortir à pas feutrés

'stealth bomb·er [stelθ] avion m furtif

stealth·y ['stelθɪ] adj furtif*

steam [stiːm] **1** n vapeur f **2** v/t food cuire à la vapeur

♦ **steam up 1** v/i of window s'embuer **2** v/t: **be steamed up** F être fou de rage

steam·er ['stiːmər] for cooking cuiseur m à vapeur

'steam i·ron fer m à vapeur

steel [stiːl] **1** adj (made of ~) en acier **2** n acier m

'steel·work·er ouvrier(-ière) m(f) de l'industrie sidérurgique

steep¹ [stiːp] adj hill etc raide; F prices excessif*

steep² [stiːp] v/t (soak) faire tremper

stee·ple ['stiːpl] of church flèche f

'stee·ple·chase in athletics steeplechase m

steep·ly ['stiːplɪ] adv: **climb ~** of path monter en pente raide; of prices monter en flèche

steer¹ [stɪr] n animal bœuf m

steer² [stɪr] v/t diriger

steer·ing ['stɪrɪŋ] n of motor vehicle direction f

'steer·ing wheel volant m

stem¹ [stem] n of plant tige f; of glass pied m; of pipe tuyau m; of word racine f

♦ **stem from** v/t (pret & pp **-med**) pro-

venir de

stem² v/t (block) enrayer

stem·ware ['stemwer] verres mpl

stench [stentʃ] odeur f nauséabonde

sten·cil ['stensɪl] **1** n tool pochoir m; pattern peinture f au pochoir **2** v/t (pret & pp **-ed**, Br **-led**) pattern peindre au pochoir

step [step] **1** n (pace) pas m; (stair) marche f; (measure) mesure f; **~ by ~** progressivement **2** v/i (pret & pp **-ped**) in puddle, on nail marcher; **~ forward / back** faire un pas en avant / en arrière

♦ **step down** v/i from post etc se retirer

♦ **step up** v/t (increase) augmenter

'step·broth·er demi-frère m; **'step·daugh·ter** belle-fille f; **'step·fa·ther** beau-père m; **'step·lad·der** escabeau m; **'step·moth·er** belle-mère f

step·ping stone ['stepɪŋ] pierre f de gué; fig tremplin m

'step·sis·ter demi-sœur f

'step·son beau-fils m

ster·e·o ['sterɪoʊ] n (sound system) chaîne f stéréo

ster·e·o·type ['sterɪoʊtaɪp] stéréotype m

ster·ile ['sterəl] adj stérile

ster·il·ize ['sterəlaɪz] v/t stériliser

ster·ling ['stɜːrlɪŋ] n FIN sterling m

stern¹ [stɜːrn] adj sévère

stern² [stɜːrn] n NAUT arrière m

stern·ly ['stɜːrnlɪ] adv sévèrement

ster·oids ['sterɔɪdz] npl stéroïdes mpl

steth·o·scope ['steθəskoʊp] stéthoscope m

Stet·son® ['stetsn] stetson m

stew [stuː] n ragoût m

stew·ard ['stuːərd] on plane, ship steward m; at demonstration, meeting membre m du service d'ordre

stew·ard·ess ['stuːərdes] on plane, ship hôtesse f

stewed [stuːd] adj: **~ apples** compote f de pommes

stick¹ [stɪk] n morceau m de bois; of policeman bâton m; (walking ~) canne f; **live in the ~s** F habiter dans un trou perdu F

stick² [stɪk] **1** v/t (pret & pp **stuck**)

with adhesive coller (*to* à); F (*put*)
mettre **2** v/i (*pret & pp* **stuck**) (*jam*)
se coincer; (*adhere*) adhérer

♦ **stick around** v/i F rester là

♦ **stick by** v/t F ne pas abandonner

♦ **stick out** v/i (*protrude*) dépasser; (*be noticeable*) ressortir; **his ears stick out** il a les oreilles décollées

♦ **stick to** v/t (*adhere to*) coller à; F (*keep to*) s'en tenir à; F (*follow*) suivre

♦ **stick together** v/i F rester ensemble

♦ **stick up** v/t *poster, leaflet* afficher; **stick 'em up** F les mains en l'air!

♦ **stick up for** v/t F défendre

stick·er ['stɪkər] autocollant *m*

'stick-in-the-mud F encroûté(e) *m(f)*

stick·y ['stɪkɪ] *adj hands, surface* gluant; *label* collant

stiff [stɪf] **1** *adj brush, cardboard, mixture etc* dur; *muscle, body* raide; *in manner* guindé; *drink* bien tassé; *competition* acharné; *fine* sévère **2** *adv*: **be scared ~** F être mort de peur; **be bored ~** F s'ennuyer à mourir

stiff·en ['stɪfn] v/i se raidir

♦ **stiffen up** v/i *of muscle* se raidir

stiff·ly ['stɪflɪ] *adv* avec raideur; *fig: smile, behave* de manière guindée

stiff·ness ['stɪfnɪs] *of muscles* raideur *f*; *fig: in manner* aspect *m* guindé

sti·fle ['staɪfl] v/t *yawn, laugh, criticism, debate* étouffer

sti·fling ['staɪflɪŋ] *adj* étouffant; **it's ~ in here** on étouffe ici

stig·ma ['stɪɡmə] honte *f*

sti·let·tos [stɪ'letəʊz] *npl Br: shoes* talons *mpl* aiguille

still¹ [stɪl] **1** *adj* calme **2** *adv*: **keep ~!** reste tranquille!; **stand ~!** ne bouge pas!

still² [stɪl] *adv* (*yet*) encore, toujours; (*nevertheless*) quand même; **do you ~ want it?** est-ce que tu le veux encore?; **she ~ hasn't finished** elle n'a toujours pas fini; **she might ~ come** il se peut encore qu'elle vienne; **they are ~ my parents** ce sont quand même mes parents; **~ more** (*even more*) encore plus

'still·born *adj* mort-né; **be ~** être mort à la naissance, être mort-né

still 'life nature *f* morte

stilt·ed ['stɪltɪd] *adj* guindé

stim·u·lant ['stɪmjʊlənt] stimulant *m*

stim·u·late ['stɪmjʊleɪt] v/t stimuler

stim·u·lat·ing ['stɪmjʊleɪtɪŋ] *adj* stimulant

stim·u·la·tion [stɪmjʊ'leɪʃn] stimulation *f*

stim·u·lus ['stɪmjʊləs] (*incentive*) stimulation *f*

sting [stɪŋ] **1** *n from bee, jellyfish* piqûre *f* **2** v/t & v/i (*pret & pp* **stung**) piquer

sting·ing ['stɪŋɪŋ] *adj remark, criticism* blessant

stin·gy ['stɪndʒɪ] *adj* F radin F

stink [stɪŋk] **1** *n* (*bad smell*) puanteur *f*; F (*fuss*) grabuge *m* F; **make a ~** F faire du grabuge **2** v/i (*pret* **stank**, *pp* **stunk**) (*smell bad*) puer; F (*be very bad*) être nul

stint [stɪnt] *n* période *f*; **do a six-month ~ in prison / in the army** faire six mois de prison / dans l'armée

♦ **stint on** v/t F lésiner sur

stip·u·late ['stɪpjʊleɪt] v/t stipuler

stip·u·la·tion [stɪpjʊ'leɪʃn] condition *f*; *of will, contract* stipulation *f*

stir [stɜːr] **1** *n*: **give the soup a ~** remuer la soupe; **cause a ~** faire du bruit **2** v/t (*pret & pp* **-red**) remuer **3** v/i (*pret & pp* **-red**) *of sleeping person* bouger

♦ **stir up** v/t *crowd* agiter; *bad memories* remuer; **stir things up** *cause problems* semer la zizanie

stir-'cra·zy *adj* F: **be ~** être devenu fou en raison d'un confinement prolongé

'stir-fry v/t (*pret & pp* **-ied**) faire sauter

stir·ring ['stɜːrɪŋ] *adj music, speech* émouvant

stir·rup ['stɪrəp] étrier *m*

stitch [stɪtʃ] **1** *n* *in sewing* point *m*; **~es** MED points *mpl* de suture; **be in ~es** *laughing* se tordre de rire; **have a ~** avoir un point de côté **2** v/t (*sew*) coudre

♦ **stitch up** v/t *wound* recoudre

stitch·ing ['stɪtʃɪŋ] (*stitches*) couture *f*

stock [stɑːk] **1** *n* (*reserve*) réserves *fpl*;

COMM *of store* stock *m*; *animals* bétail *m*; FIN actions *fpl*; *for soup etc* bouillon *m*; **be in / out of ~** être en stock / épuisé; **take ~** faire le bilan **2** *v/t* COMM avoir (en stock)

♦ **stock up on** *v/t* faire des réserves de

'stock·brok·er agent *m* de change; 'stock ex·change bourse *f*; 'stock·hold·er actionnaire *m/f*

stock·ing ['stɑːkɪŋ] bas *m*

stock·ist ['stɑːkɪst] revendeur *m*

'stock mar·ket marché *m* boursier; 'stock·mar·ket crash krach *m* boursier; 'stock·pile **1** *n of food, weapons* stocks *mpl* de réserve **2** *v/t* faire des stocks de; 'stock·room *of store* réserve *f*; stock-'still *adv*: **stand ~** rester immobile; 'stock·tak·ing inventaire *m*

stock·y ['stɑːkɪ] *adj* trapu

stodg·y ['stɑːdʒɪ] *adj food* bourratif*

sto·i·cal ['stəʊɪkl] *adj* stoïque

sto·i·cism ['stəʊɪsɪzm] stoïcisme *m*

stole [stəʊl] *pret* → **steal**

stol·en ['stəʊlən] *pp* → **steal**

stom·ach ['stʌmək] **1** *n (insides)* estomac *m*; *(abdomen)* ventre *m* **2** *v/t (tolerate)* supporter

'stom·ach·ache douleur *f* à l'estomac

stone [stəʊn] *n material, (precious ~)* pierre *f*; *(pebble)* caillou *m*; *in fruit* noyau *m*

stoned [stəʊnd] *adj* F *on drugs* défoncé F

stone-'deaf *adj* sourd comme un pot

'stone·wall *v/i* F atermoyer

ston·y ['stəʊnɪ] *adj ground, path* pierreux*

stood [stʊd] *pret & pp* → **stand**

stool [stuːl] *seat* tabouret *m*

stoop¹ [stuːp] **1** *n* dos *m* voûté **2** *v/i (bend down)* se pencher

stoop² [stuːp] *n (porch)* perron *m*

stop [stɑːp] **1** *n for train, bus* arrêt *m*; **come to a ~** s'arrêter; **put a ~ to** arrêter **2** *v/t (pret & pp -ped)* arrêter; *(prevent)* empêcher; **~ doing sth** arrêter de faire qch; **~ to do sth** s'arrêter pour faire qch; **it has ~ped raining** il s'est arrêté de pleuvoir; **I ~ped her from leaving** je l'ai empêchée

de partir; **~ a check** faire opposition à un chèque **3** *v/i (pret & pp -ped) (come to a halt)* s'arrêter

♦ **stop by** *v/i (visit)* passer

♦ **stop off** *v/i* faire étape

♦ **stop over** *v/i* faire escale

♦ **stop up** *v/t sink* boucher

'stop·gap bouche-trou *m*; 'stop·light *(traffic light)* feu *m* rouge; *(brake light)* stop *m*; 'stop·o·ver étape *f*

stop·per ['stɑːpər] *for bottle* bouchon *m*

'stop sign stop *m*

'stop·watch chronomètre *m*

stor·age ['stɔːrɪdʒ] COMM emmagasinage *m*; *in house* rangement *m*; **in ~** en dépôt

'stor·age ca·pac·i·ty COMPUT capacité *f* de stockage

'stor·age space espace *m* de rangement

store [stɔːr] **1** *n* magasin *m*; *(stock)* provision *f*; *(~house)* entrepôt *m* **2** *v/t* entreposer; COMPUT stocker

'store·front devanture *f* de magasin; 'store·house entrepôt *m*; 'store·keep·er ['stɔːrkiːpər] commerçant(e) *m(f)*; 'store·room réserve *f*

sto·rey ['stɔːrɪ] *Br* → **story²**

stork [stɔːrk] cigogne *f*

storm [stɔːrm] *n with rain, wind* tempête *f*; *(thunder~)* orage *m*

'storm drain égout *m* pluvial; 'storm warn·ing avis *m* de tempête; 'storm win·dow fenêtre *f* extérieure

storm·y *adj weather, relationship* orageux*

sto·ry¹ ['stɔːrɪ] *(tale, account*, F: *lie)* histoire *f*; *recounted by victim* récit *m*; *(newspaper article)* article *m*

sto·ry² ['stɔːrɪ] *of building* étage *m*

stout [staʊt] *adj person* corpulent, costaud; *boots* solide; *defender* acharné

stove [stəʊv] *for cooking* cuisinière *f*; *for heating* poêle *m*

stow [stəʊ] *v/t* ranger

♦ **stow away** *v/i* s'embarquer clandestinement

'stow·a·way passager clandestin *m*, passagère clandestine *f*

strag·gler ['stræglər] retardataire *m/f*

S

straight [streɪt] **1** adj line, back, knees droit; hair raide; (honest, direct) franc*; (not criminal) honnête; whiskey etc sec*; (tidy) en ordre; (conservative) sérieux*; (not homosexual) hétéro F; **be a ~ A student** être un étudiant excellent; **keep a ~ face** garder son sérieux **2** adv (in a straight line) droit; (directly, immediately) directement; **think ~** avoir les idées claires; **I can't think ~ any more!** je n'arrive pas à me concentrer!; **stand up ~!** tiens-toi droit!; **look s.o.. ~ in the eye** regarder qn droit dans les yeux; **go ~** F of criminal revenir dans le droit chemin; **give it to me ~** F dites-le moi franchement; **~ ahead** be situated, walk, drive, look tout droit; **carry ~ on** of driver etc continuer tout droit; **~ away, ~ off** tout de suite; **~ out** très clairement; **~ up** without ice sans glace

straight·en ['streɪtn] v/t redresser
♦ **straighten out 1** v/t situation arranger; F person remettre dans le droit chemin **2** v/i of road redevenir droit
♦ **straighten up** v/i se redresser

straight'for·ward adj (honest, direct) direct; (simple) simple

strain[1] [streɪn] **1** n on rope, engine tension f; on heart pression f; **suffer from ~** souffrir de tension nerveuse **2** v/t back se fouler; eyes s'abîmer; fig: finances, budget grever

strain[2] [streɪn] v/t vegetables faire égoutter; oil, fat etc filtrer

strain[3] [streɪn] n of virus etc souche f

strained [streɪnd] adj relations tendu

strain·er ['streɪnər] for vegetables etc passoire f

strait [streɪt] GEOG détroit m

strait·laced [streɪt'leɪst] adj collet monté inv

Straits of 'Dover Pas m de Calais

strand[1] [strænd] n of hair mèche f; of wool, thread brin m

strand[2] [strænd] v/t abandonner à son sort; **be ~ed** se retrouver bloqué

strange [streɪndʒ] adj (odd, curious) étrange, bizarre; (unknown, foreign) inconnu

strange·ly ['streɪndʒlɪ] adv (oddly) bizarrement; **~ enough, ...** c'est bizarre, mais …

strang·er ['streɪndʒər] étranger(-ère) m(f); **he's a complete ~** je ne le connais pas du tout; **I'm a ~ here myself** moi non plus je ne suis pas d'ici

stran·gle ['stræŋgl] v/t person étrangler

strap [stræp] n of purse, shoe lanière f; of brassiere, dress bretelle f; of watch bracelet m
♦ **strap in** v/t (pret & pp **-ped**) attacher
♦ **strap on** v/t attacher

strap·less ['stræplɪs] adj sans bretelles

stra·te·gic [strə'tiːdʒɪk] adj stratégique

strat·e·gy ['strætədʒɪ] stratégie f

straw [strɔː] **1** n material, for drink paille f; **that is the last ~** F c'est la goutte d'eau qui fait déborder le vase **2** adj hat, bag, mat de paille; seat en paille

straw·ber·ry ['strɔːberɪ] fraise f

stray [streɪ] **1** adj animal, bullet perdu **2** n animal m errant **3** v/i of animal vagabonder; of child s'égarer; fig: of eyes, thoughts errer (**to** vers)

streak [striːk] **1** n of dirt, paint traînée f; in hair mèche f; fig: of nastiness etc pointe f **2** v/i move quickly filer **3** v/t: **be ~ed with** être strié de

streak·y ['striːkɪ] adj window etc couvert de traces

stream [striːm] **1** n ruisseau m; fig: of people, complaints flot m; **come on ~** of new car etc entrer en production; of power plant être mis en service **2** v/i: **people ~ed out of the building** des flots de gens sortaient du bâtiment; **tears were ~ing down my face** mon visage ruisselait de larmes; **sunlight ~ed into the room** le soleil entrait à flots dans la pièce

stream·er ['striːmər] for party serpentin m

'**stream·line** v/t fig rationaliser

'**stream·lined** adj car, plane caréné; fig: organization rationalisé

street [striːt] rue f

'**street·car** tramway *m*; '**street cred** [kred] F image *f* de marque; '**street-light** réverbère *m*; '**street peo·ple** *npl* sans-abri *mpl*; '**street val·ue** *of drugs* prix *m* à la revente; '**street-walk·er** F racoleuse *f*; '**street-wise** *adj* débrouillard; *this kid is totally* ~ ce gamin est un vrai gavroche

strength [streŋθ] force *f*; (*strong point*) point *m* fort

strength·en ['streŋθn] **1** *v/t body* fortifier; *bridge, currency, bonds etc* consolider **2** *v/i* se consolider

stren·u·ous ['strenjʊəs] *adj climb, walk etc* fatigant; *effort* acharné

stren·u·ous·ly ['strenjʊəslɪ] *adv deny* vigoureusement

stress [stres] **1** *n* (*emphasis*) accent *m*; (*tension*) stress *m*; *be under* ~ souffrir de stress **2** *v/t syllable* accentuer; *importance etc* souligner; *I must* ~ *that* ... je dois souligner que ...

stressed 'out [strest] *adj* F stressé

stress·ful ['stresfʊl] *adj* stressant

stretch [stretʃ] **1** *n of land, water* étendue *f*; *of road* partie *f*; *at a* ~ (*non-stop*) d'affilée **2** *adj fabric* extensible **3** *v/t material* tendre; *small income* tirer le maximum de; F *rules* assouplir; *he* ~*ed out his hand* il tendit la main; *a job that* ~*es me* un métier qui me pousse à donner le meilleur de moi-même **4** *v/i to relax muscles, to reach sth* s'étirer; (*spread*) s'étendre (*from* de; *to* jusqu'à); *of fabric*: *give* être extensible; *of fabric*: *sag* s'élargir

stretch·er ['stretʃər] brancard *m*

strict [strɪkt] *adj* strict

strict·ly ['strɪktlɪ] *adv* strictement; *it is* ~ *forbidden* c'est strictement défendu

strict·ness ['strɪktnəs] sévérité *f*

strid·den ['strɪdn] *pp* → *stride*

stride [straɪd] **1** *n* (*grand*) pas *m*; *take sth in one's* ~ ne pas se laisser troubler par qch; *make great* ~*s fig* faire de grands progrès **2** *v/i* (*pret strode*, *pp stridden*) marcher à grandes enjambées

stri·dent ['straɪdnt] *adj* strident; *fig*: *demands* véhément

strike [straɪk] **1** *n of workers* grève *f*; *in baseball* balle *f* manquée; *of oil* découverte *f*; *be on* ~ être en grève; *go on* ~ faire grève **2** *v/i* (*pret & pp struck*) *of workers* faire grève; (*attack*: *of wild animal*) attaquer; *of killer* frapper; *of disaster* arriver; *of clock* sonner **3** *v/t* (*pret & pp struck*) *also fig* frapper; *match* allumer; *oil* découvrir; *he struck his head against the table* il s'est cogné la tête contre la table; *she struck me as being* ... elle m'a fait l'impression d'être ...; *the thought struck me that* ... l'idée que ... m'est venue à l'esprit

♦ **strike out** *v/t delete* rayer

♦ **strike·break·er** ['straɪkbreɪkər] briseur(-euse) *m(f)* de grève

strik·er ['straɪkər] (*person on strike*) gréviste *m/f*; *in soccer* buteur *m*

strik·ing ['straɪkɪŋ] *adj* (*marked, eye-catching*) frappant

string [strɪŋ] *n* ficelle *f*; *of violin, tennis racket* corde *f*; *the* ~*s musicians* les cordes; *pull* ~*s* user de son influence; *a* ~ *of* (*series*) une série de

♦ **string along** (*pret & pp strung*) F **1** *v/i*: *do you mind if I string along?* est-ce que je peux vous suivre? **2** *v/t*: *string s.o. along* tromper qn, faire marcher qn

♦ **string up** *v/t* F pendre

stringed 'in·stru·ment [strɪŋd] instrument *m* à cordes

strin·gent ['strɪndʒnt] *adj* rigoureux*

'**string play·er** joueur(-euse) *m(f)* d'un instrument à cordes

strip [strɪp] **1** *n* bande *f*; (*comic* ~) bande *f* dessinée; *of soccer team* tenue *f* **2** *v/t* (*pret & pp -ped*) *paint, sheets* enlever; *of wind* arracher; (*undress*) déshabiller; ~ *s.o. of sth* enlever qch à qn **3** *v/i* (*pret & pp -ped*) (*undress*) se déshabiller; *of stripper* faire du strip-tease

'**strip club** boîte *f* de strip-tease

stripe [straɪp] rayure *f*; MIL galon *m*

striped [straɪpt] *adj* rayé

'**strip mall** centre *m* commercial (*linéaire*)

strip·per ['strɪpər] **1** strip-teaseuse *f*;

male ~ strip-teaseuser *m*

'**strip show** strip-tease *m*

strip'tease strip-tease *m*

strive [straɪv] *v/i* (*pret* **strove**, *pp* **striven**): ~ *to do sth* s'efforcer de faire qch; *over a period of time* lutter *or* se battre pour faire qch; ~ *for* essayer d'obtenir

striv·en ['strɪvn] *pp* → **strive**

strobe, 'strobe light [stroʊb] lumière *f* stroboscopique

strode [stroʊd] *pret* → **stride**

stroke [stroʊk] **1** *n* MED attaque *f*; *in writing* trait *m* de plume; *in painting* coup *m* de pinceau; *style of swimming* nage *f*; *a* ~ *of luck* un coup de chance; *she never does a* ~ *(of work)* elle ne fait jamais rien **2** *v/t* caresser

stroll [stroʊl] **1** *n*: *go for* or *take a* ~ aller faire une balade **2** *v/i* flâner; *he just ~ed into the room* il est entré dans la pièce sans se presser

stroll·er ['stroʊlər] *for baby* poussette *f*

strong [strɒŋ] *adj* fort; *structure* solide; *candidate* sérieux*; *support, supporter* vigoureux*

'**strong·hold** *fig* bastion *m*

strong·ly ['strɒŋlɪ] *adv* fortement; *she feels very* ~ *about it* cela lui tient très à cœur

strong-mind·ed [strɒŋ'maɪndɪd] *adj*: *be* ~ avoir de la volonté; '**strong point** point *m* fort; '**strong-room** chambre *f* forte; **strong-willed** [strɒŋ'wɪld] *adj* qui sait ce qu'il veut

strove [stroʊv] *pret* → **strive**

struck [strʌk] *pret & pp* → **strike**

struc·tur·al ['strʌktʃərl] *adj damage* de structure; *fault, problems, steel* de construction

struc·ture ['strʌktʃər] **1** *n* (*something built*) construction *f*; *fig: of novel, poem etc* structure *f* **2** *v/t* structurer

strug·gle ['strʌgl] **1** *n* (*fight*) lutte *f*; *it was a* ~ *at times* ça a été très dur par moments **2** *v/i with a person* se battre; ~ *to do sth* or *for sth* avoir du mal à faire qch / à obtenir qch

strum [strʌm] *v/t* (*pret & pp* **-med**) *guitar* pincer les cordes de

strung [strʌŋ] *pret & pp* → **string**

strut [strʌt] *v/i* (*pret & pp* **-ted**) se pavaner

stub [stʌb] **1** *n of cigarette* mégot *m*; *of check, ticket* souche *f* **2** *v/t* (*pret & pp* **-bed**): ~ *one's toe* se cogner le pied (*on* contre)

♦ **stub out** *v/t* écraser

stub·ble ['stʌbl] *on face* barbe *f* piquante

stub·born ['stʌbərn] *adj person, refusal etc* entêté; *defense* farouche

stub·by ['stʌbɪ] *adj fingers* boudiné

stuck [stʌk] **1** *pret & pp* → **stick 2** *adj* F: *be* ~ *on s.o.* être fou* de qn

stuck-'up *adj* F snob *inv*

stu·dent ['stuːdnt] *at high school* élève *m/f*; *at college, university* étudiant(e) *m(f)*; **stu·dent 'driv·er** apprenti(e) conducteur(-trice) *m(f)*; **stu·dent 'nurse** élève-infirmier *m*, élève-infirmière *f*; **stu·dent 'teach·er** professeur *m/f* stagiaire

stu·di·o ['stuːdɪoʊ] *of artist* atelier *m*; (*film* ~, *TV* ~, *recording* ~) studio *m*

stu·di·ous ['stuːdɪəs] *adj* studieux*

stud·y ['stʌdɪ] **1** *n room* bureau *m*; (*learning*) études *fpl*; (*investigation*) étude *f* **2** *v/t* (*pret & pp* **-ied**) *at school, university* étudier; (*examine*) examiner **3** *v/i* (*pret & pp* **-ied**) étudier

stuff [stʌf] **1** *n* (*things*) trucs *mpl*; *substance, powder etc* truc *m*; (*belongings*) affaires *fpl* **2** *v/t turkey* farcir; ~ *sth into sth* fourrer qch dans qch

stuff·ing ['stʌfɪŋ] *for turkey* farce *f*; *in chair, teddy bear* rembourrage *m*

stuff·y ['stʌfɪ] *adj room* mal aéré; *person* vieux jeu *inv*

stum·ble ['stʌmbl] *v/i* trébucher

♦ **stumble across** *v/t* trouver par hasard

♦ **stumble over** *v/t object, words* trébucher sur

stum·bling block ['stʌmblɪŋ] pierre *f* d'achoppement

stump [stʌmp] **1** *n of tree* souche *f* **2** *v/t*: *I'm ~ed* je colle F

♦ **stump up** *v/t* F (*pay*) cracher F

stun [stʌn] *v/t* (*pret & pp* **-ned**) étourdir; *animal* assommer; *fig* (*shock*) abasourdir

stung [stʌŋ] pret & pp → **sting**

stunk [stʌŋk] pp → **stink**

stun·ning ['stʌnɪŋ] adj (amazing) stupéfiant; (very beautiful) épatant

stunt [stʌnt] for publicity coup m de publicité; in movie cascade f

'**stunt·man** in movie cascadeur m

stu·pe·fy ['stu:pɪfaɪ] v/t (pret & pp **-ied**) stupéfier

stu·pen·dous [stu:'pendəs] adj prodigieux*

stu·pid ['stu:pɪd] adj stupide

stu·pid·i·ty [stu:'pɪdətɪ] stupidité f

stu·por ['stu:pər] stupeur f

stur·dy ['stɜːrdɪ] adj robuste

stut·ter ['stʌtər] v/i bégayer

style [staɪl] n (method, manner) style m; (fashion) mode f; (fashionable elegance) classe f; **in** ~ à la mode; **go out of** ~ passer de mode

styl·ish ['staɪlɪʃ] adj qui a de la classe

styl·ist ['staɪlɪst] (hair ~, interior designer) styliste m/f

sub·com·mit·tee ['sʌbkəmɪtɪ] sous-comité m

sub·con·scious [sʌb'kɑːnʃəs] adj subconscient; **the** ~ **mind** le subconscient

sub·con·scious·ly [sʌb'kɑːnʃəslɪ] adv subconsciemment

sub·con·tract [sʌbkən'trækt] v/t sous-traiter

sub·con·trac·tor [sʌbkən'træktər] sous-traitant m

sub·di·vide [sʌbdɪ'vaɪd] v/t sous-diviser

sub·due [səb'du:] v/t rebellion, mob contenir

sub·dued [səb'du:d] adj person réservé; lighting doux*

sub·head·ing ['sʌbhedɪŋ] sous-titre m

sub·hu·man [sʌb'hju:mən] adj sous-humain

sub·ject ['sʌbdʒɪkt] **1** n of country, GRAM, (topic) sujet m; (branch of learning) matière f; **change the** ~ changer de sujet **2** adj: **be** ~ **to** être sujet à; ~ **to availability** tickets dans la limite des places disponibles; goods dans la limite des stocks disponibles **3** v/t [səb'dʒekt] soumettre (**to** à)

sub·jec·tive [səb'dʒektɪv] adj subjectif*

sub·junc·tive [səb'dʒʌŋktɪv] n GRAM subjonctif m

sub·let ['sʌblet] v/t (pret & pp **-let**) sous-louer

sub·ma·chine gun [sʌbmə'ʃi:ngʌn] mitraillette f

sub·ma·rine ['sʌbməri:n] sous-marin m

sub·merge [səb'mɜːrdʒ] **1** v/t in sth immerger (**in** dans); **be** ~**d** of rocks, iceberg être submergé **2** v/i of submarine plonger

sub·mis·sion [səb'mɪʃn] (surrender), to committee etc soumission f

sub·mis·sive [səb'mɪsɪv] adj soumis

sub·mit [səb'mɪt] (pret & pp **-ted**) **1** v/t plan, proposal soumettre **2** v/i se soumettre

sub·or·di·nate [sə'bɔːrdɪnət] **1** adj employee, position subalterne **2** n subordonné(e) m(f)

sub·poe·na [sə'pi:nə] LAW **1** n assignation f **2** v/t person assigner à comparaître

♦ **subscribe to** [səb'skraɪb] v/t magazine etc s'abonner à; theory souscrire à

sub·scrib·er [səb'skraɪbər] to magazine abonné(e) m(f)

sub·scrip·tion [səb'skrɪpʃn] abonnement m

sub·se·quent ['sʌbsɪkwənt] adj ultérieur

sub·se·quent·ly ['sʌbsɪkwəntlɪ] adv par la suite

sub·side [səb'saɪd] v/i of flood waters baisser; of high winds se calmer; of building s'affaisser; of fears, panic s'apaiser

sub·sid·i·a·ry [səb'sɪdɪrɪ] n filiale f

sub·si·dize ['sʌbsɪdaɪz] v/t subventionner

sub·si·dy ['sʌbsɪdɪ] subvention f

♦ **subsist on** [səb'sɪst] v/t subsister de

sub·sis·tence lev·el: live at ~ vivre à la limite de la subsistance

sub·stance ['sʌbstəns] (matter) substance *f*

sub·stan·dard [sʌb'stændərd] *adj* de qualité inférieure

sub·stan·tial [səb'stænʃl] *adj (considerable)* considérable; *meal* consistant

sub·stan·tial·ly [səb'stænʃlɪ] *adv (considerably)* considérablement; *(in essence)* de manière générale

sub·stan·ti·ate [səb'stænʃɪeɪt] *v/t* confirmer

sub·stan·tive [səb'stæntɪv] *adj* réel*

sub·sti·tute ['sʌbstɪtuːt] **1** *n for commodity* substitut *m (for* de); SP remplaçant(e) *m(f) (for* de) **2** *v/t* remplacer; ~ **X for Y** remplacer Y par X **3** *v/i*: ~ **for s.o.** remplacer qn

sub·sti·tu·tion [sʌbstɪ'tuːʃn] *act* remplacement *m*; **make a ~** SP faire un remplacement

sub·ti·tle ['sʌbtaɪtl] *n* sous-titre *m*; **with ~s** sous-titré

sub·tle ['sʌtl] *adj* subtil

sub·tract [səb'trækt] *v/t number* soustraire

sub·urb ['sʌbɜːrb] banlieue *f*, **the ~s** la banlieue

sub·ur·ban [sə'bɜːrbən] *adj* typique de la banlieue; *pej*: *attitudes etc* de banlieusards

sub·ver·sive [səb'vɜːrsɪv] **1** *adj* subversif* **2** *n* personne *f* subversive

sub·way ['sʌbweɪ] métro *m*

sub·ze·ro [sʌb'zɪːroʊ] *adj temperature* en-dessous de zéro

suc·ceed [sək'siːd] **1** *v/i (be successful)* réussir; ~ **in doing sth** réussir à faire qch; *to throne, presidency* succéder à, hériter de **2** *v/t (come after)* succéder à

suc·ceed·ing [sək'siːdɪŋ] *adj* suivant

suc·cess [sək'ses] réussite *f*; **be a ~** avoir du succès

suc·cess·ful [sək'sesfʊl] *adj person* qui a réussi; *talks, operation, marriage* réussi; **be ~ in doing sth** réussir à faire qch

suc·cess·ful·ly [sək'sesfʊlɪ] *adv* avec succès

suc·ces·sion [sək'seʃn] *(sequence), to office* succession *f*; **in ~** d'affilée

suc·ces·sive [sək'sesɪv] *adj* succes-

sif*; **on three ~ days** trois jours de suite

suc·ces·sor [sək'sesər] successeur *m*

suc·cinct [sək'sɪŋkt] *adj* succinct

suc·cu·lent ['sʌkjʊlənt] *adj* succulent

suc·cumb [sə'kʌm] *v/i (give in)* succomber; ~ **to temptation** succomber à la tentation

such [sʌtʃ] **1** *adj*: ~ **a** *(so much of a)* un tel, une telle; **it was ~ a surprise** c'était une telle surprise

◊ *(of that kind)*: ~ **as** tel / telle que; **there is no ~ word as ...** le mot ... n'existe pas; ~ **people are ...** de telles personnes sont ...

2 *adv* tellement; ~ **an easy question** une question tellement facile; **as ~** en tant que tel

suck [sʌk] **1** *v/t candy etc* sucer; ~ **one's thumb** sucer son pouce **2** *v/i* P: **it ~s** c'est merdique P

♦ **suck up** *v/t moisture* absorber

♦ **suck up to** *v/t* F lécher les bottes à

suck·er ['sʌkər] F *person* niais(e) *m(f)*; F *(lollipop)* sucette *f*

suc·tion ['sʌkʃn] succion *f*

sud·den ['sʌdn] *adj* soudain; **all of a ~** tout d'un coup

sud·den·ly ['sʌdnlɪ] *adv* tout à coup, soudain, soudainement; **so ~** tellement vite

suds [sʌdz] *npl (soap ~)* mousse *f* de savon

sue [suː] *v/t* poursuivre en justice

suede [sweɪd] *n* daim *m*

suf·fer ['sʌfər] **1** *v/i* souffrir; **be ~ing from** souffrir de **2** *v/t experience* subir

suf·fer·ing ['sʌfərɪŋ] *n* souffrance *f*

suf·fi·cient [sə'fɪʃnt] *adj* suffisant; **not have ~ funds / time** ne pas avoir assez d'argent / de temps; **just one hour will be ~** une heure suffira

suf·fi·cient·ly [sə'fɪʃntlɪ] *adv* suffisamment

suf·fo·cate ['sʌfəkeɪt] **1** *v/i* s'étouffer **2** *v/t* étouffer

suf·fo·ca·tion [sʌfə'keɪʃn] étouffement *m*

sug·ar ['ʃʊgər] **1** *n* sucre *m* **2** *v/t* sucrer

'sug·ar bowl sucrier *m*

'sug·ar cane canne *f* à sucre

sug·gest [sə'dʒest] *v/t* suggérer

sug·ges·tion [sə'dʒestʃən] suggestion *f*

su·i·cide ['suːɪsaɪd] *also fig* suicide *m*; **commit ~** se suicider

'**su·i·cide bomb at·tack** attentat *m* suicide; '**su·i·cide bomb·er** kamikaze *m/f*; '**su·i·cide pact** accord passé entre deux personnes pour se suicider ensemble

suit [suːt] **1** *n for man* costume *m*; *for woman* tailleur *m*; *in cards* couleur *f* **2** *v/t of clothes, color* aller à; **red ~s you** le rouge te va bien; **~ yourself!** *F* fais comme tu veux!; **be ~ed for sth** être fait pour qch

sui·ta·ble ['suːtəbl] *adj* approprié, convenable

sui·ta·bly ['suːtəblɪ] *adv* convenablement

'**suit·case** valise *f*

suite [swiːt] *of rooms* suite *f*; *furniture* salon *m* trois pièces; MUS suite *m*

sul·fur ['sʌlfər] soufre *m*

sul·fur·ic ac·id [sʌl'fjuːrɪk] acide *m* sulfurique

sulk [sʌlk] *v/i* bouder

sulk·y ['sʌlkɪ] *adj* boudeur*

sul·len ['sʌlən] *adj* maussade

sul·phur *etc Br* → **sulfur** *etc*

sul·try ['sʌltrɪ] *adj climate* lourd; *sexually* sulfureux*

sum [sʌm] *(total, amount)* somme *f*; *in arithmetic* calcul *m*; **a large ~ of money** une grosse somme d'argent; **~ insured** montant assuré; **the ~ total of his efforts** la somme de ses efforts

♦ **sum up** *(pret & pp -med)* **1** *v/t (summarize)* résumer; *(assess)* se faire une idée de; **that just about sums him up** c'est tout à fait lui **2** *v/i* LAW résumer les débats

sum·ma·rize ['sʌməraɪz] *v/t* résumer

sum·ma·ry ['sʌmərɪ] *n* résumé *m*

sum·mer ['sʌmər] été *f*

sum·mit ['sʌmɪt] *of mountain*, POL sommet *m*

'**sum·mit meet·ing** → **summit**

sum·mon ['sʌmən] *v/t staff, meeting* convoquer

♦ **summon up** *v/t strength* faire appel à

sum·mons ['sʌmənz] *nsg* LAW assignation *f* (à comparaître)

sump [sʌmp] *for oil* carter *m*

sun [sʌn] soleil *m*; **in the ~** au soleil; **out of the ~** à l'ombre; **he has had too much ~** il s'est trop exposé au soleil

'**sun·bathe** *v/i* prendre un bain de soleil; '**sun·bed** lit *m* à ultraviolets; '**sun·block** écran *m* solaire; '**sun·burn** coup *m* de soleil; '**sun·burnt** *adj*: **be ~** avoir des coups de soleil

Sun·day ['sʌndeɪ] dimanche *m*

'**sun·di·al** cadran *m* solaire

sun·dries ['sʌndrɪz] *npl expenses* frais *mpl* divers; *items* articles *mpl* divers

sung [sʌŋ] *pp* → **sing**

'**sun·glass·es** *npl* lunettes *fpl* de soleil

sunk [sʌŋk] *pp* → **sink**

sunk·en ['sʌŋkn] *adj cheeks* creux*

sun·ny ['sʌnɪ] *adj day* ensoleillé; *disposition* gai; **it's ~** il y a du soleil

'**sun·rise** lever *m* du soleil; '**sun·set** coucher *m* du soleil; '**sun·shade** *handheld* ombrelle *f*; *over table* parasol *m*; '**sun·shine** soleil *m*; '**sun·stroke** insolation *f*; '**sun·tan** bronzage *m*; **get a ~** bronzer

su·per ['suːpər] **1** *adj* F super *inv* F **2** *n (janitor)* concierge *m/f*

su·perb [su'pɜːrb] *adj* excellent

su·per·fi·cial [suːpər'fɪʃl] *adj* superficiel*

su·per·flu·ous [su'pɜːrfluəs] *adj* superflu

su·per·hu·man *adj efforts* surhumain

su·per·in·tend·ent [suːpərɪn'tendənt] *of apartment block* concierge *m/f*

su·pe·ri·or [su'pɪrɪər] **1** *adj quality, hotel, attitude* supérieur **2** *n in organization, society* supérieur *m*

su·per·la·tive [su'pɜːrlətɪv] **1** *adj (superb)* excellent **2** *n* GRAM superlatif *m*

'**su·per·mar·ket** supermarché *m*

'**su·per·mod·el** top model *m*

su·per·nat·u·ral 1 *adj powers* surnaturel* **2** *n*: **the ~** le surnaturel

'**su·per·pow·er** POL superpuissance *f*

su·per·son·ic [su:pər'sɑ:nɪk] *adj flight, aircraft* supersonique

su·per·sti·tion [su:pər'stɪʃn] superstition *f*

su·per·sti·tious [su:pər'stɪʃəs] *adj person* superstitieux*

su·per·vise ['su:pərvaɪz] *v/t children activities etc* surveiller; *workers* superviser

su·per·vi·sor ['su:pərvaɪzər] *at work* superviseur *m*

sup·per ['sʌpər] dîner *m*

sup·ple ['sʌpl] *adj* souple

sup·ple·ment ['sʌplɪmənt] *n (extra payment)* supplément *m*

sup·pli·er [sə'plaɪr] COMM fournisseur (-euse) *m(f)*

sup·ply [sə'plaɪ] **1** *n of electricity, water etc* alimentation *f* (**of** en); **~ and de·mand** l'offre et la demande; **sup·plies** *of food* provisions *fpl*; **office sup·plies** fournitures *fpl* de bureau **2** *v/t (pret & pp -ied) goods* fournir; **~ s.o. with sth** fournir qch à qn; **be supplied with …** être pourvu de …

sup·port [sə'pɔːrt] **1** *n for structure* support *m*; *(backing)* soutien *m* **2** *v/t building, structure* supporter; *financially* entretenir; *(back)* soutenir

sup·port·er [sə'pɔːrtər] *of politician, football team* supporteur(-trice) *m(f)*; *of theory* partisan(e) *m(f)*

sup·port·ive [sə'pɔːrtɪv] *adj attitude* de soutien; *person* qui soutient; **be ~ of s.o.** beaucoup soutenir qn

sup·pose [sə'pouz] *v/t (imagine)* supposer; **I ~ so** je suppose que oui; **be ~d to do sth** *(be meant to, said to)* être censé faire qch; **supposing …** (et) si …

sup·pos·ed·ly [sə'pouzɪdlɪ] *adv:* **this is ~ the …** c'est soi-disant *or* apparemment le …

sup·pos·i·to·ry [sə'pɑːzɪtɔːrɪ] MED suppositoire *m*

sup·press [sə'pres] *v/t rebellion etc* réprimer

sup·pres·sion [sə'preʃn] répression *f*

su·prem·a·cy [su:'preməsɪ] suprématie *f*

su·preme [su:'priːm] *adj* suprême

sur·charge ['sɜːrtʃɑːrdʒ] surcharge *f*

sure [ʃʊr] **1** *adj* sûr; **I'm ~** *as answer* j'en suis sûr; **be ~ that** être sûr que; **be ~ about sth** être sûr de qch; **make ~ that …** s'assurer que … **2** *adv:* **~ enough** en effet; **it ~ is hot today** F il fait vraiment chaud aujourd'hui; **~!** F mais oui, bien sûr!

sure·ly ['ʃʊrlɪ] *adv with negatives* quand même; *(gladly)* avec plaisir; **~ there is someone here who …** il doit y avoir quelqu'un ici qui …

sure·ty ['ʃʊrətɪ] *for loan* garant(e) *m(f)*

surf [sɜːrf] **1** *n on sea* écume *f* **2** *v/t the Net* surfer sur

sur·face ['sɜːrfɪs] **1** *n of table, water etc* surface *f*; **on the ~** *fig* en surface **2** *v/i of swimmer, submarine* faire surface; *(appear)* refaire surface

'sur·face mail courrier *m* par voie terrestre ou maritime

'surf·board planche *f* de surf

surf·er ['sɜːrfər] *on sea* surfeur(-euse) *m(f)*

surf·ing ['sɜːrfɪŋ] surf *m*; **go ~** aller faire du surf

surge [sɜːrdʒ] *n in electric current* surtension *f*; *in demand, interest, growth etc* poussée *f*

♦ **surge forward** *v/i of crowd* s'élancer en masse

sur·geon ['sɜːrdʒən] chirurgien *m(f)*

sur·ge·ry ['sɜːrdʒərɪ] chirurgie *f*; **un·der·go ~** subir une opération (chirurgicale)

sur·gi·cal ['sɜːrdʒɪkl] *adj* chirurgical

sur·gi·cal·ly ['sɜːrdʒɪklɪ] *adv remove* par opération chirurgicale

sur·ly ['sɜːrlɪ] *adj* revêche

sur·mount [sər'maunt] *v/t difficulties* surmonter

sur·name ['sɜːrneɪm] nom *m* de famille

sur·pass [sər'pæs] *v/t* dépasser

sur·plus ['sɜːrpləs] **1** *n* surplus *m* **2** *adj* en surplus

sur·prise [sər'praɪz] **1** *n* surprise *f* **2** *v/t* étonner; **be / look ~d** être / avoir l'air surpris

sur·pris·ing [sər'praızıŋ] *adj* étonnant

sur·pris·ing·ly [sər'praızıŋlı] *adv* étonnamment; ***not ~, ...*** comme on pouvait s'y attendre, ...

sur·ren·der [sə'rendər] **1** *v/i of army* se rendre **2** *v/t weapons etc* rendre **3** *n* capitulation *f*, *(handing in)* reddition *f*

sur·ro·gate moth·er ['sʌrəgət] mère *f* porteuse

sur·round [sə'raʊnd] **1** *v/t* entourer; ***be ~ed by*** être entouré par **2** *n of picture etc* bordure *f*

sur·round·ing [sə'raʊndıŋ] *adj* environnant

sur·round·ings [sə'raʊndıŋz] *npl* environs *mpl*; *setting* cadre *m*

sur·vey [*'sɜːrveɪ*] *n of modern literature etc* étude *f*; *of building* inspection *f*, *(poll)* sondage *m* **2** *v/t* [sər'veɪ] *(look at)* contempler; *building* inspecter

sur·vey·or [sɜːr'veɪr] expert *m*

sur·viv·al [sər'vaɪvl] survie *f*

sur·vive [sər'vaɪv] **1** *v/i* survivre; ***how are you?*** ***I'm surviving*** comment ça va? - pas trop mal; ***his two surviving daughters*** ses deux filles encore en vie **2** *v/t accident, operation, (outlive)* survivre à

sur·vi·vor [sər'vaɪvər] survivant(e) *m(f)*; ***he's a ~*** *fig* c'est un battant

sus·cep·ti·ble [sə'septəbl] *adj emotionally* influençable; ***be ~ to the cold*** être frileux*; ***be ~ to the heat*** être sensible à la chaleur

sus·pect ['sʌspekt] **1** *n* suspect(e) *m(f)* **2** *v/t* [sə'spekt] *person* soupçonner; *(suppose)* croire

sus·pect·ed [sə'spektıd] *adj murderer* soupçonné; *cause, heart attack etc* présumé

sus·pend [sə'spend] *v/t (hang), from office* suspendre

sus·pend·ers [sə'spendərz] *npl for pants* bretelles *fpl*; *Br* porte-jarretelles *m*

sus·pense [sə'spens] suspense *m*

sus·pen·sion [sə'spenʃn] *in vehicle, from duty* suspension *f*

sus·pen·sion bridge pont *m* suspendu

sus·pi·cion [sə'spıʃn] soupçon *m*

sus·pi·cious [sə'spıʃəs] *adj (causing suspicion)* suspect; *(feeling suspicion)* méfiant; ***be ~ of s.o.*** se méfier de qn

sus·pi·cious·ly [sə'spıʃəslı] *adv behave* de manière suspecte; *ask* avec méfiance

sus·tain [sə'steın] *v/t* soutenir

sus·tain·a·ble [sə'steınəbl] *adj economic growth* durable

swab [swɑːb] *n* tampon *m*

swag·ger ['swægər] *n* démarche *f* crâneuse

swal·low[1] ['swɑːloʊ] *v/t & v/i* avaler

swal·low[2] ['swɑːloʊ] *n bird* hirondelle *f*

swam [swæm] *pret* → **swim**

swamp [swɑːmp] **1** *n* marécage *m* **2** *v/t*: ***be ~ed with*** *with letters, work etc* être submergé de

swamp·y ['swɑːmpı] *adj ground* marécageux*

swan [swɑːn] cygne *m*

swap [swɑːp] *(pret & pp -ped)* **1** *v/t* échanger; ***~ sth for sth*** échanger qch contre qch **2** *v/i* échanger

swarm [swɔːrm] **1** *n of bees* essaim *m* **2** *v/i of ants, tourists etc* grouiller; ***the town was ~ing with ...*** la ville grouillait de ...; ***the crowd ~ed out of the stadium*** la foule est sortie en masse du stade

swar·thy ['swɔːrðı] *adj face, complexion* basané

swat [swɑːt] *v/t (pret & pp -ted) insect* écraser

sway [sweı] **1** *n (influence, power)* emprise *f* **2** *v/i in wind* se balancer; *because drunk, ill* tituber

swear [swer] *(pret* ***swore**, *pp* **sworn)** **1** *v/i (use swearword)* jurer; ***~ at s.o.*** injurier qn **2** *v/t* LAW, *(promise)* jurer *(to do sth* jurer qch)

♦ **swear in** *v/t witnesses etc* faire prêter serment à

'swear·word juron *m*

sweat [swet] **1** *n* sueur *f*; ***covered in ~*** trempé de sueur **2** *v/i* transpirer, suer

'sweat band bandeau *m* en éponge

sweat·er ['swetər] pull *m*

sweats [swets] *npl* SP survêtement *m*

'**sweat-shirt** sweat(-shirt) *m*

sweat-y ['sweti] *adj* hands, forehead plein de sueur

Swede [swi:d] Suédois(e) *m(f)*

Swe-den ['swi:dn] Suède *f*

Swe-dish ['swi:dɪʃ] **1** *adj* suédois **2** *n* suédois *m*

sweep [swi:p] **1** *v/t* (*pret & pp* **swept**) floor, leaves balayer **2** *n* (*long curve*) courbe *f*

♦ **sweep up** *v/t* mess, crumbs balayer

sweep-ing ['swi:pɪŋ] *adj* statement hâtif*; *changes radical

sweet [swi:t] *adj* taste, tea sucré; F (*kind*) gentil*; F (*cute*) mignon*

sweet and 'sour *adj* aigre-doux*

'**sweet-corn** maïs *m*

sweet-en ['swi:tn] *v/t* drink, food sucrer

sweet-en-er ['swi:tnər] *for drink* édulcorant *m*

'**sweet-heart** amoureux(-euse) *m(f)*

swell [swel] **1** *v/i* (*pp* **swollen**) of wound, limb enfler **2** *adj* F (*good*) super F *inv* **3** *n* of the sea houle *f*

swell-ing ['swelɪŋ] *n* MED enflure *f*

swel-ter-ing ['sweltərɪŋ] *adj* heat, day étouffant

swept [swept] *pret & pp →* ***sweep***

swerve [swɜːrv] *v/i* of driver, car s'écarter brusquement

swift [swɪft] *adj* rapide

swim [swɪm] **1** *v/i* (*pret* **swam**, *pp* **swum**) nager; **go ~ming** aller nager; **my head is ~ming** j'ai la tête qui tourne **2** *n* baignade *f*; **go for a ~** aller nager, aller se baigner

swim-mer ['swɪmər] nageur(-euse) *m(f)*

swim-ming ['swɪmɪŋ] natation *f*

'**swim-ming pool** piscine *f*

'**swim-suit** maillot *m* de bain

swin-dle ['swɪndl] **1** *n* escroquerie *f* **2** *v/t* person escroquer; **~ s.o. out of sth** escroquer qch à qn

swine [swaɪn] F person salaud *m* P

swing [swɪŋ] **1** *n* oscillation *f*; for child balançoire *f*; **~ to the Democrats** revirement *m* d'opinion en faveur des démocrates **2** *v/t* (*pret & pp* **swung**)

object in hand, hips balancer **3** *v/i* (*pret & pp* **swung**) se balancer; (*turn*) tourner; of public opinion etc virer

swing-'door porte *f* battante

Swiss [swɪs] **1** *adj* suisse **2** *n* person Suisse *m/f*; **the ~** les Suisses *mpl*

switch [swɪtʃ] **1** *n* for light bouton *m*; (*change*) changement *m* **2** *v/t* (*change*) changer de **3** *v/i* (*change*) passer (**to** à)

♦ **switch off** *v/t* lights, engine, PC éteindre; engine arrêter

♦ **switch on** *v/t* lights, engine, PC allumer; engine démarrer

'**switch-board** standard *m*

'**switch-o-ver** to new system passage *m*

Swit-zer-land ['swɪtsərlənd] Suisse *f*

swiv-el ['swɪvl] *v/i* (*pret & pp* **-ed**, Br **-led**) of chair, monitor pivoter

swol-len ['swoulən] **1** *pp →* ***swell* 2** *adj* stomach ballonné; ankles, face, cheek enflé

swoop [swu:p] *v/i* of bird descendre

♦ **swoop down on** *v/t* prey fondre sur

♦ **swoop on** *v/t* nightclub, hideout faire une descente dans

sword [sɔːrd] épée *f*

swore [swɔːr] *pret →* ***swear***

sworn [swɔːrn] *pp →* ***swear***

swum [swʌm] *pp →* ***swim***

swung [swʌŋ] *pret & pp →* ***swing***

syc-a-more ['sɪkəmɔːr] sycomore *m*

syl-la-ble ['sɪləbl] syllabe *f*

syl-la-bus ['sɪləbəs] programme *m*

sym-bol ['sɪmbəl] symbole *m*

sym-bol-ic [sɪm'bɑːlɪk] *adj* symbolique

sym-bol-ism ['sɪmbəlɪzm] in poetry, art symbolisme *m*

sym-bol-ist ['sɪmbəlɪst] symboliste *m/f*

sym-bol-ize ['sɪmbəlaɪz] *v/t* symboliser

sym-met-ri-cal [sɪ'metrɪkl] *adj* symétrique

sym-me-try ['sɪmətrɪ] symétrie

sym-pa-thet-ic [sɪmpə'θetɪk] *adj* (*showing pity*) compatissant; (*understanding*) compréhensif*; **be ~ toward** person être compréhensif envers; idea avoir des sympathies pour

♦ **sym-pa-thize with** ['sɪmpəθaɪz] *v/t*

person compatir avec; *views* avoir des sympathies pour

sym·pa·thiz·er ['sɪmpəθaɪzər] POL sympathisant(e) *m(f)*

sym·pa·thy ['sɪmpəθɪ] (*pity*) compassion *f*; (*understanding*) compréhension *f*; **you have our deepest ~ on bereavement** nous vous présentons toutes nos condoléances; **don't expect any ~ from me!** ne t'attends pas à ce que j'aie pitié de toi!

sym·pho·ny ['sɪmfənɪ] symphonie *f*

'**sym·pho·ny or·ches·tra** orchestre *m* symphonique

symp·tom ['sɪmptəm] MED, *fig* symptôme *m*

symp·to·mat·ic [sɪmptə'mætɪk] *adj*: **be ~ of** *fig* être symptomatique de

syn·chro·nize ['sɪŋkrənaɪz] *v/t* synchroniser

syn·o·nym ['sɪnənɪm] synonyme *m*

sy·non·y·mous [sɪ'nɑːnɪməs] *adj* synonyme; **be ~ with** *fig* être synonyme

de

syn·tax ['sɪntæks] syntaxe *f*

syn·the·siz·er ['sɪnθəsaɪzər] MUS synthétiseur *m*

syn·thet·ic [sɪn'θetɪk] *adj* synthétique

syph·i·lis ['sɪfɪlɪs] *nsg* syphilis *f*

Syr·i·a ['sɪrɪə] Syrie *f*

Syr·i·an ['sɪrɪən] **1** *adj* syrien* **2** *n* Syrien(ne) *m(f)*

sy·ringe ['sɪrɪndʒ] *n* seringue *f*

syr·up ['sɪrəp] sirop *m*

sys·tem ['sɪstəm] système *m*; (*orderliness*) ordre *m*; (*computer*) ordinateur *m*; **~ crash** COMPUT panne *f* du système; **the digestive ~** l'appareil *m* digestif

sys·te·mat·ic [sɪstə'mætɪk] *adj* approach, *person* systématique

sys·tem·at·i·cal·ly [sɪstə'mætɪklɪ] *adv* systématiquement

sys·tems an·a·lyst ['sɪstəmz] COMPUT analyste-programmeur (-euse) *m(f)*

T

tab [tæb] *n for pulling* languette *f*; *in text* tabulation *f*; **pick up the ~** régler la note

ta·ble ['teɪbl] *n* table *f*; *of figures* tableau *m*

'**ta·ble·cloth** nappe *f*; '**ta·ble lamp** petite lampe *f*; **ta·ble of 'con·tents** table *f* des matières; '**ta·ble·spoon** cuillère *f* à soupe

tab·let ['tæblɪt] MED comprimé *m*

'**ta·ble ten·nis** tennis *m* de table

tab·loid ['tæblɔɪd] *n newspaper* journal *m* à sensation; **the ~s** la presse à sensation

ta·boo [tə'buː] *adj* tabou *inv in feminine*

tac·it ['tæsɪt] *adj* tacite

tac·i·turn ['tæsɪtɜːrn] *adj* taciturne

tack [tæk] **1** *n* nail clou *m* **2** *v/t in sewing* bâtir **3** *v/i of yacht* louvoyer

tack·le ['tækl] **1** *n* (*equipment*) attirail *m*; SP tacle *m*; *in rugby* plaquage *m* **2** *v/t* SP tacler; *in rugby* plaquer; *problem* s'attaquer à; (*confront*) confronter; *physically* s'opposer à

tack·y ['tækɪ] *adj paint, glue* collant; F (*cheap, poor quality*) minable F

tact [tækt] tact *m*

tact·ful ['tæktfʊl] *adj* diplomate

tact·ful·ly ['tæktflɪ] *adv* avec tact

tac·ti·cal ['tæktɪkl] *adj* tactique

tac·tics ['tæktɪks] *npl* tactique *f*

tact·less ['tæktlɪs] *adj* qui manque de tact, peu délicat

tad·pole ['tædpoʊl] têtard *m*

tag [tæg] *n* (*label*) étiquette *f*

♦ **tag along** *v/i* (*pret & pp* **-ged**) venir aussi

tail [teɪl] *n* queue *f*

'**tail-back** *Br. in traffic* bouchon *m*

'**tail light** feu *m* arrière

tai-lor ['teɪlər] *n* tailleur *m*

tai-lor-made [teɪlər'meɪd] *adj also fig* fait sur mesure

'**tail pipe** *of car* tuyau *m* d'échappement

'**tail wind** vent *m* arrière

taint-ed ['teɪntɪd] *adj food* avarié; *atmosphere* gâté

Tai-wan [taɪ'wɑːn] Taïwan

Tai-wan-ese [taɪwɑːn'iːz] **1** *adj* taïwanais **2** *n* Taïwanais(e) *m(f)*

take [teɪk] *v/t* (*pret* **took**, *pp* **taken**) prendre; (*transport, accompany*) amener; *subject at school, photograph, photocopy, stroll* faire; *exam* passer; (*endure*) supporter; (*require: courage etc*) demander; ~ **s.o. home** ramener qn chez lui; *how long does it ~?* *journey, order* combien de temps est-ce que cela prend?; *how long will it ~ you to …?* combien de temps est-ce que tu vas mettre pour …?

◆ **take after** *v/t* ressembler à

◆ **take apart** *v/t* (*dismantle*) démonter; F (*criticize*) démolir F; F *in fight, game* battre à plates coutures

◆ **take away** *v/t object* enlever; *pain* faire disparaître; MATH soustraire (*from* de); *15 take away 5 is 10* 15 moins 5 égalent 10; *take sth away from s.o. driver's license etc* retirer qch à qn; *toys, knife etc* confisquer qch à qn

◆ **take back** *v/t object* rapporter; *person to a place* ramener; *that takes me back of music, thought etc* ça me rappelle le bon vieux temps; *she wouldn't take him back husband* elle ne voulait pas qu'il revienne

◆ **take down** *v/t from shelf, wall* enlever; *scaffolding* démonter; *pants* baisser; (*write down*) noter

◆ **take in** *v/t* (*take indoors*) rentrer; (*give accommodation to*) héberger; (*make narrower*) reprendre; (*deceive*) duper; (*include*) inclure

◆ **take off 1** *v/t clothes, hat* enlever; *10% etc* faire une réduction de; (*mimic*) imiter; *can you take a bit off here? to hairdresser* est-ce que vous pouvez couper un peu là?; *take a day / week off* prendre un jour / une semaine de congé **2** *v/i of airplane* décoller; (*become popular*) réussir

◆ **take on** *v/t job* accepter; *staff* embaucher

◆ **take out** *v/t from bag, pocket* sortir (*from* de); *appendix, tooth, word from text* enlever; *money from bank* retirer; *to dinner, theater etc* emmener; *dog* sortir; *kids* emmener quelque part; *insurance policy* souscrire à; *he's taking her out* (*dating*) il sort avec elle; *take it out on s.o.* en faire pâtir qn

◆ **take over 1** *v/t company etc* reprendre; *tourists take over the town* les touristes prennent la ville d'assaut **2** *v/i* POL arriver au pouvoir; *of new director* prendre ses fonctions; (*do sth in s.o.'s place*) prendre la relève; *take over from s.o.* remplacer qn

◆ **take to** *v/t: she didn't take to him / the idea* (*like*) il / l'idée ne lui a pas plu; *take to doing sth* (*form habit of*) se mettre à faire qch; *she took to drink* elle s'est mise à boire

◆ **take up** *v/t carpet etc* enlever; (*carry up*) monter; *dress etc* raccourcir; *judo, Spanish etc* se mettre à; *new job* commencer; *space, time* prendre; *I'll take you up on your offer* j'accepterai votre offre

'**take-home pay** salaire *m* net

tak-en ['teɪkən] *pp* → **take**

'**take-off** *of airplane* décollage *m*; (*impersonation*) imitation *f*; '**take-o-ver** COMM rachat *m*; '**take-o-ver bid** offre *f* publique d'achat, OPA *f*

ta-kings ['teɪkɪŋz] *npl* recette *f*

tal-cum pow-der ['tælkəmpaʊdər] talc *m*

tale [teɪl] histoire *f*

tal-ent ['tælənt] talent *m*

tal-ent-ed ['tæləntɪd] *adj* doué

'**tal-ent scout** dénicheur(-euse) *m(f)* de talents

talk [tɔːk] **1** *v/i* parler; *can I ~ to …?*

est-ce que je pourrais parler à …? **2**
v/t English etc parler; **~ business /
politics** parler affaires / politique;
~ s.o. into doing sth persuader qn
de faire qch **3** *n* (*conversation*) conversation *f*; (*lecture*) exposé *m*; **give a ~**
faire un exposé; **he's all ~** il ne
fait que parler; **~s** (*negotiations*)
pourparlers *mpl*

♦ **talk back** *v/i* répondre
♦ **talk down to** *v/t* prendre de haut
♦ **talk over** *v/t* discuter

talk-a-tive ['tɔ:kətɪv] *adj* bavard
talk-ing-to ['tɔ:kɪŋtu:] savon *m* F;
give s.o. a ~ passer un savon à qn F
'talk show talk-show *m*
tall [tɔ:l] *adj* grand
tall 'or-der: that's a ~ c'est beaucoup
demander
tall 'tale histoire *f* à dormir debout
tal-ly ['tælɪ] **1** *n* compte *m* **2** *v/i* (*pret &
pp* **-ied**) correspondre; *of stories*
concorder
♦ **tally with** *v/t* correspondre à; *of stories* concorder avec
tame [teɪm] *adj* *which has been tamed*
apprivoisé; *not wild* pas sauvage; *joke
etc* fade
♦ **tam-per with** ['tæmpər] *v/t* toucher à
tam-pon ['tæmpɑːn] tampon *m*
tan [tæn] **1** *n* *from sun* bronzage; *color*
marron *m* clair **2** *v/i* (*pret & pp* **-ned**)
in sun bronzer **3** *v/t* (*pret & pp* **-ned**)
leather tanner
tan-dem ['tændəm] *bike* tandem *m*
tan-gent ['tændʒənt] MATH tangente *f*
tan-ge-rine [tændʒə'ri:n] *fruit* mandarine *f*
tan-gi-ble ['tændʒɪbl] *adj* tangible
tan-gle ['tæŋgl] *n* enchevêtrement *m*
♦ **tangle up** *v/t*: **get tangled up** *of
string etc* s'emmêler
tan-go ['tæŋgoʊ] *n* tango *m*
tank [tæŋk] MOT, *for water* réservoir
m; *for fish* aquarium *m*; MIL char
m; *for skin diver* bonbonne *f* d'oxygène
tank-er ['tæŋkər] (*oil ~*) pétrolier *m*;
truck camion-citerne *m*
'tank top débardeur *m*
tanned [tænd] *adj* bronzé

Tan-noy® ['tænɔɪ] système *m* de hauts-
-parleurs; **over the ~** dans le haut-
-parleur
tan-ta-liz-ing ['tæntəlaɪzɪŋ] *adj* alléchant
tan-ta-mount ['tæntəmaʊnt]: **be ~ to**
équivaloir à
tan-trum ['tæntrəm] caprice *m*
tap [tæp] **1** *n* *Br* (*faucet*) robinet *m* **2** *v/t*
(*pret & pp* **-ped**) (*knock*) taper; *phone*
mettre sur écoute
♦ **tap into** *v/t* *resources* commencer à
exploiter
tap dance *n* claquettes *fpl*
tape [teɪp] **1** *n* *for recording* bande *f*;
recording cassette *f*; *sticky* ruban *m*
adhésif **2** *v/t* *conversation etc* enregistrer; *with sticky tape* scotcher
'tape deck platine *f* cassettes; **'tape
drive** COMPUT lecteur *m* de bandes;
'tape meas-ure mètre *m* ruban
♦ **taper off** *v/i* diminuer peu à peu
'tape re-cord-er magnétophone *m*
'tape re-cord-ing enregistrement *m*
tap-es-try ['tæpɪstrɪ] tapisserie *f*
tar [tɑːr] *n* goudron *m*
tar-dy ['tɑːrdɪ] *adj* *reply, arrival* tardif*
tar-get ['tɑːrgɪt] **1** *n* *in shooting* cible *f*;
fig objectif *m* **2** *v/t* *market* cibler
'tar-get au-di-ence public *m* cible;
'tar-get date date *f* visée; **'tar-get
fig-ure** objectif *m*; **'tar-get group**
COMM groupe *m* cible; **'tar-get
mar-ket** marché *m* cible
tar-iff ['tærɪf] (*customs ~*) taxe *f*;
(*prices*) tarif *m*
tar-mac ['tɑːrmæk] *at airport* tarmac *m*
tar-nish ['tɑːrnɪʃ] *v/t* ternir
tar-pau-lin [tɑːr'pɔːlɪn] bâche *f*
tart [tɑːrt] *n* tarte *f*
tar-tan ['tɑːrtn] tartan *m*
task [tæsk] *n* tâche *f*
'task force commission *f*; MIL corps *m*
expéditionnaire
tas-sel ['tæsl] gland *m*
taste [teɪst] **1** *n* goût *m*; **he has no ~** il
n'a pas de goût **2** *v/t* goûter; (*perceive
taste of*) sentir; *try, fig* goûter à **3** *v/i*: **it
~s like …** ça a un (un) goût de …; **it ~s**

very nice c'est très bon

taste·ful ['teɪstfl] *adj* de bon goût

taste·ful·ly ['teɪstflɪ] *adv* avec goût

taste·less ['teɪstlɪs] *adj food* fade; *remark, décor* de mauvais goût

tast·ing ['teɪstɪŋ] *of wine* dégustation *f*

tast·y ['teɪstɪ] *adj* délicieux*

tat·tered ['tætərd] *adj* en lambeaux

tat·ters ['tætərz]: **in ~** en lambeaux; *fig* ruiné

tat·too [tə'tu:] *n* tatouage *m*

tat·ty ['tætɪ] *adj Br F* miteux*

taught [tɔ:t] *pret & pp* → **teach**

taunt [tɔ:nt] **1** *n* raillerie *f* **2** *v/t* se moquer de

Tau·rus ['tɔ:rəs] ASTROL Taureau *m*

taut [tɔ:t] *adj* tendu

taw·dry ['tɔ:drɪ] *adj* clinquant

tax [tæks] **1** *n on income* impôt *m*; *on goods, services* taxe *f*; **before / after ~** brut / net, avant / après déductions **2** *v/t income* imposer; *goods, services* taxer

tax·a·ble 'in·come revenu *m* imposable

tax·a·tion [tæk'seɪʃn] *act* imposition *f*; *(taxes)* charges *fpl* fiscales

'tax a·void·ance évasion *f* fiscale; **'tax brack·et** fourchette *f* d'impôts; **'tax-de·duct·i·ble** *adj* déductible des impôts; **'tax e·va·sion** fraude *f* fiscale; **'tax-free** *adj goods* hors taxe; **'tax ha·ven** paradis *m* fiscal

tax·i ['tæksɪ] *n* taxi *m*

'tax·i driv·er chauffeur *m* de taxi

tax·ing ['tæksɪŋ] *adj* exténuant

'tax·i stand, *Br* **'tax·i rank** station *f* de taxis

'tax·pay·er contribuable *m/f*; **'tax re·turn** *form* déclaration *f* d'impôts; **'tax year** année *f* fiscale

TB [ti:'bi:] *abbr* (= **tuberculosis**) tuberculose *f*

tea [ti:] *drink* thé *m*

tea·bag ['ti:bæg] sachet *m* de thé

teach [ti:tʃ] **1** *v/t* (*pret & pp* **taught**); *subject* enseigner; *person, student* enseigner à; **~ s.o. sth** enseigner qch à qn; **~ s.o. to do sth** apprendre à qn à faire qch; *who taught you?* qui était ton prof? **2** *v/i* (*pret & pp* **taught**) en-

seigner

teach·er ['ti:tʃər] professeur *m/f*; *in elementary school* instituteur(-trice) *m(f)*

'teach·ers' lounge salle *f* des professeurs

teach·er 'train·ing formation *f* pédagogique

teach·ing ['ti:tʃɪŋ] *profession* enseignement *m*

'teach·ing aid outil *m* pédagogique

'tea·cup tasse *f* à thé

teak [ti:k] tek *m*

'tea leaves *npl* feuilles *fpl* de thé

team [ti:m] équipe *f*

'team mate coéquipier(-ière) *m(f)*

team 'spir·it esprit *m* d'équipe

team·ster ['ti:mstər] camionneur (-euse) *m(f)*

'team·work travail *m* d'équipe

tea·pot ['ti:pɑ:t] théière *f*

tear[1] [ter] **1** *n in cloth etc* déchirure *f* **2** *v/t* (*pret* **tore,** *pp* **torn**) *paper, cloth* déchirer; **be torn (between two alternatives)** être tiraillé (entre deux possibilités) **3** *v/i* (*pret* **tore,** *pp* **torn**) (*run fast, drive fast*): *she tore down the street* elle a descendu la rue en trombe

♦ **tear down** *v/t poster* arracher; *building* démolir

♦ **tear out** *v/t* arracher (*from* de)

♦ **tear up** *v/t* déchirer; *fig: contract etc* annuler

tear[2] [tɪr] *n in eye* larme *f*; **burst into ~s** fondre en larmes; **be in ~s** être en larmes

tear·drop ['tɪrdrɑ:p] larme *f*

tear·ful ['tɪrfl] *adj look* plein de larmes; **be ~** *person* être en larmes

'tear gas gaz *m* lacrymogène

tea·room ['ti:ru:m] salon *m* de thé

tease [ti:z] *v/t* taquiner

'tea·spoon cuillère *f* à café

teat [ti:t] *of animal* tétine *f*

tech·ni·cal ['teknɪkl] *adj* technique

tech·ni·cal·i·ty [teknɪ'kælətɪ] (*technical nature*) technicité *f*; LAW point *m* de droit; *that's just a ~* c'est juste un détail

tech·ni·cal·ly ['teknɪklɪ] *adv* (*strictly*

speaking) en théorie; *written* en termes techniques

tech·ni·cian [tek'nɪʃn] technicien(ne) *m(f)*

tech·nique [tek'niːk] technique *f*

tech·no·log·i·cal [teknə'lɑːdʒɪkl] *adj* technologique

tech·nol·o·gy [tek'nɑːlədʒɪ] technologie *f*

tech·no·pho·bi·a [teknə'foʊbɪə] technophobie *f*

ted·dy bear ['tedɪber] ours *m* en peluche

te·di·ous ['tiːdɪəs] *adj* ennuyeux*

tee [tiː] *n* in golf tee *m*

teem [tiːm] *v/i*: **be ~ing with rain** pleuvoir des cordes; **be ~ing with tourists / ants** grouiller de touristes / fourmis

teen·age ['tiːneɪdʒ] *adj magazines, fashion* pour adolescents; **~ boy / girl** adolescent / adolescente

teen·ag·er ['tiːneɪdʒər] adolescent(e) *m(f)*

teens [tiːnz] *npl* adolescence *f*; **be in one's ~** être adolescent; **reach one's ~** devenir adolescent

tee·ny ['tiːnɪ] *adj* F tout petit

teeth [tiːθ] *pl* → **tooth**

teethe [tiːð] *v/i* faire ses dents

teeth·ing prob·lems ['tiːðɪŋ] *npl* problèmes *mpl* initiaux

tee·to·tal [tiː'toʊtl] *adj* qui ne boit jamais d'alcool

tee·to·tal·er [tiː'toʊtlər] personne qui ne boit jamais d'alcool

tel·e·com·mu·ni·ca·tions [telɪkəm-juːnɪ'keɪʃnz] télécommunications *fpl*

tel·e·gram ['telɪɡræm] télégramme *m*

tel·e·graph pole ['telɪɡræfpoʊl] Br poteau *m* télégraphique

tel·e·path·ic [telɪ'pæθɪk] *adj* télépathique; **you must be ~!** vous devez avoir le don de télépathie!

te·lep·a·thy [tɪ'lepəθɪ] télépathie *f*

tel·e·phone ['telɪfoʊn] **1** *n* téléphone *m*; **be on the ~** (*be speaking*) être au téléphone; (*possess a phone*) avoir le téléphone **2** *v/t person* téléphoner à **3** *v/i* téléphoner

'tel·e·phone bill facture *f* de télé-

phone; **'tel·e·phone book** annuaire *m*; **'tel·e·phone booth** cabine *f* téléphonique; **'tel·e·phone call** appel *m* téléphonique; **'tel·e·phone con·ver·sa·tion** conversation *f* téléphonique; **'tel·e·phone di·rec·to·ry** annuaire *m*; **'tel·e·phone ex·change** central *m* téléphonique; **'tel·e·phone mes·sage** message *m* téléphonique; **'tel·e·phone num·ber** numéro *m* de téléphone

tel·e·pho·to lens [telɪ'foʊtoʊlenz] téléobjectif *m*

tel·e·sales ['telɪseɪlz] *npl or nsg* télévente *f*

tel·e·scope ['telɪskoʊp] télescope *m*

tel·e·scop·ic [telɪ'skɑːpɪk] *adj* télescopique

tel·e·thon ['telɪθɑːn] téléthon *m*

tel·e·vise ['telɪvaɪz] *v/t* téléviser

tel·e·vi·sion ['telɪvɪʒn] *also set* télévision *f*; **on ~** à la télévision; **watch ~** regarder la télévision

'tel·e·vi·sion au·di·ence audience *f* de téléspectateurs; **'tel·e·vi·sion pro·gram** émission *f* télévisée; **'tel·e·vi·sion set** poste *m* de télévision; **'tel·e·vi·sion stu·di·o** studio *m* de télévision

tell [tel] **1** *v/t* (*pret & pp* **told**) *story* raconter; *lie* dire; **I can't ~ the difference** je n'arrive pas à faire la différence; **~ s.o. sth** dire qch à qn; **don't ~ Mom** ne le dis pas à maman; **could you ~ me the way to …?** pourriez-vous m'indiquer où se trouve …?; **~ s.o. to do sth** dire à qn de faire qch; **you're ~ing me!** F tu l'as dit! F **2** *v/i* (*have effect*) se faire sentir; **the heat is ~ing on him** il ressent les effets de la chaleur; **time will ~** qui vivra verra

♦ **tell off** *v/t* F (*reprimand*) remonter les bretelles à F

tell·er [telər] *in bank* guichetier(-ière) *m(f)*

tell·ing ['telɪŋ] *adj blow* percutant; *sign* révélateur*

tell·ing 'off F: **get a ~** se faire remonter les bretelles F

tell·tale ['telteɪl] **1** *adj signs* révélateur* **2** *n* rapporteur(-euse) *m(f)*

temp [temp] **1** *n employee* intérimaire *m/f* **2** *v/i* faire de l'intérim

tem·per ['tempər] *character* caractère *m*; (*bad* ~) mauvaise humeur *f*; **have a terrible** ~ être coléreux*; **now then,** ~**!** maintenant, on se calme!; **be in a** ~ être en colère; **keep one's** ~ garder son calme; **lose one's** ~ se mettre en colère

tem·per·a·ment ['tempramant] tempérament *m*

tem·per·a·men·tal [tempra'mentl] *adj* (*moody*) capricieux*

tem·per·ate ['tempərət] *adj* tempéré

tem·per·a·ture ['temprətfər] température *f*

tem·ple¹ ['templ] REL temple *m*

tem·ple² ['templ] ANAT tempe *f*

tem·po ['tempou] MUS tempo *m*; *of work* rythme *m*

tem·po·rar·i·ly [tempə'rerılı] *adv* temporairement

tem·po·rar·y ['tempərerı] *adj* temporaire

tempt [tempt] *v/t* tenter

temp·ta·tion [temp'teıʃn] tentation *f*

tempt·ing ['temptıŋ] *adj* tentant

ten [ten] dix

te·na·cious [tı'neıʃəs] *adj* tenace

te·nac·i·ty [tı'næsıtı] ténacité *f*

ten·ant ['tenənt] locataire *m/f*

tend¹ [tend] *v/t lawn* entretenir; *sheep* garder; *the sick* soigner

tend² [tend] *v/i*: ~ **to do sth** avoir tendance à faire qch; ~ **toward sth** pencher vers qch

tend·en·cy ['tendənsı] tendance *f*

ten·der¹ ['tendər] *adj* (*sore*) sensible; (*affectionate*), *steak* tendre

ten·der² ['tendər] *n* COMM offre *f*

ten·der·ness ['tendənıs] *of kiss etc* tendresse *f*; *of steak* tendreté *f*

ten·don ['tendən] tendon *m*

ten·nis ['tenıs] tennis *m*

'ten·nis ball balle *f* de tennis; **'ten·nis court** court *m* de tennis; **'ten·nis play·er** joueur(-euse) *m(f)* de tennis; **'ten·nis rack·et** raquette *f* de tennis

ten·or ['tenər] *n* MUS ténor *m*

tense¹ [tens] *n* GRAM temps *m*

tense² [tens] *adj* tendu

♦ **tense up** *v/i* se crisper

ten·sion ['tenʃn] tension *f*

tent [tent] tente *f*

ten·ta·cle ['tentəkl] tentacule *m*

ten·ta·tive ['tentətıv] *adj smile, steps* hésitant; *conclusion, offer* provisoire

ten·ter·hooks ['tentərhuks]: **be on** ~ être sur des charbons ardents

tenth [tenθ] dixième; → **fifth**

tep·id ['tepıd] *adj also fig* tiède

term [tɜːrm] (*period, word*) terme *m*; EDU trimestre *m*; (*condition*) condition *f*; **be on good / bad** ~**s with s.o.** être en bons / mauvais termes avec qn; **in the long / short** ~ à long / court terme; **come to** ~**s with sth** accepter qch

ter·mi·nal ['tɜːrmınl] **1** *n at airport* aérogare *m*; *for buses* terminus *m*; *for containers*, COMPUT terminal *m*; ELEC borne *f* **2** *adj illness* incurable

ter·mi·nal·ly ['tɜːrmınəlı] *adv*: ~ **ill** en phase terminale

ter·mi·nate ['tɜːrmıneıt] **1** *v/t* mettre fin à; ~ **a pregnancy** interrompre une grossesse **2** *v/i* se terminer

ter·mi·na·tion [tɜːrmı'neıʃn] *of contract* résiliation *f*; *in pregnancy* interruption *f* volontaire de grossesse

ter·mi·nol·o·gy [tɜːrmı'nɑːlədʒı] terminologie *f*

ter·mi·nus ['tɜːrmınəs] terminus *m*

ter·race ['terəs] *on hillside*, (*patio*) terrasse *f*

ter·ra cot·ta [terə'kɑːtə] *adj* en terre cuite

ter·rain [te'reın] terrain *m*

ter·res·tri·al [te'restrıəl] **1** *adj television* terrestre **2** *n* terrien(ne) *m(f)*

ter·ri·ble ['terəbl] *adj* horrible, affreux*

ter·ri·bly ['terəblı] *adv* (*very*) très

ter·rif·ic [tə'rıfık] *adj* génial

ter·rif·i·cal·ly [tə'rıfıklı] *adv* (*very*) extrêmement, vachement F

ter·ri·fy ['terıfaı] *v/t* (*pret & pp* **-ied**) terrifier; **be terrified** être terrifié

ter·ri·fy·ing ['terıfaıŋ] *adj* terrifiant

ter·ri·to·ri·al [terə'tɔːrıəl] *adj* territorial

ter·ri·to·ri·al 'wa·ters *npl* eaux *fpl* territoriales

ter·ri·to·ry ['terɪtɔːrɪ] territoire *m*; *fig* domaine *m*

ter·ror ['terər] terreur *f*

ter·ror·ism ['terərɪzm] terrorisme *m*

ter·ror·ist ['terərɪst] terroriste *m/f*

'ter·ror·ist at·tack attentat *m* terroriste

'ter·ror·ist or·gan·i·za·tion organisation *f* terroriste

ter·ror·ize ['terəraɪz] *v/t* terroriser

terse [tɜːrs] *adj* laconique

test [test] **1** *n scientific, technical* test *m*; *academic, for driving* examen *m*; *put sth to the* ~ mettre qch à l'épreuve **2** *v/t person, machine, theory* tester, mettre à l'épreuve; ~ *s.o. on a subject* interroger qn sur une matière

tes·ta·ment ['testəmənt] *to s.o.'s life* témoignage *m* (*to* de); *Old / New Testament* REL Ancien / Nouveau Testament *m*

test-drive ['testdraɪv] *v/t* (*pret* -*drove*, *pp* -*driven*) *car* essayer

tes·ti·cle ['testɪkl] testicule *m*

tes·ti·fy ['testɪfaɪ] *v/i* (*pret & pp* -*ied*) LAW témoigner

tes·ti·mo·ni·al [testɪ'moʊnɪəl] références *fpl*

tes·ti·mo·ny ['testɪmənɪ] LAW témoignage *m*

'test tube éprouvette *f*

'test-tube ba·by bébé-éprouvette *m*

tes·ty ['testɪ] *adj* irritable

te·ta·nus ['tetənəs] tétanos *m*

teth·er ['teðər] **1** *v/t horse* attacher **2** *n*: *be at the end of one's* ~ être au bout du rouleau

text [tekst] **1** *n* texte *m*; *message* texto *m*, SMS *m* **2** *v/t* envoyer un texto à

'text·book manuel *m*

tex·tile ['tekstaɪl] textile *m*

'text mes·sage texto *m*, SMS *m*

tex·ture ['tekstʃər] texture *f*

Thai [taɪ] **1** *adj* thaïlandais **2** *n person* Thaïlandais(e) *m(f)*; *language* thaï *m*

Thai·land ['taɪlænd] Thaïlande *f*

than [ðæn] *adv* que; *with numbers* de; *faster* ~ *me* plus rapide que moi; *more than 50* plus de 50

thank [θæŋk] *v/t* remercier; ~ *you* mer-

ci; *no* ~ *you* (non) merci

thank·ful ['θæŋkfl] *adj* reconnaissant

thank·ful·ly ['θæŋkfulɪ] *adv* avec reconnaissance; (*luckily*) heureusement

thank·less ['θæŋklɪs] *adj task* ingrat

thanks [θæŋks] *npl* remerciements *mpl*; ~*!* merci!; ~ *to* grâce à

Thanks·giv·ing (Day) [θæŋks'gɪvɪŋ (deɪ)] jour *m* de l'action de grâces, Thanksgiving *m* (*fête célébrée le 4ème jeudi de novembre*)

that [ðæt] **1** *adj* ce, cette; *masculine before vowel* cet; ~ *one* celui-là, celle-là **2** *pron* ◊ cela, ça; *give me* ~ donne-moi ça

◊ : ~*'s mine* c'est à moi; ~*'s tea* c'est du thé; ~*'s very kind* c'est très gentil; *what is* ~*?* qu'est-ce que c'est que ça?; *who is* ~*?* qui est-ce? **3** *relative pron* que; *the person / car* ~ *you see* la personne / voiture que vous voyez **4** *adv* (*so*) aussi; ~ *big / expensive* aussi grand / cher **5** *conj* que; *I think* ~ ... je pense que ...

thaw [θɔː] *v/i of snow* fondre; *of frozen food* se décongeler

the [ðə] le, la; *pl* les; *to the station / theater* à la gare / au théâtre; ~ *more I try* plus j'essaie

the·a·ter ['θɪətər] théâtre *m*

'the·a·ter crit·ic critique *m/f* de théâtre

the·a·tre *Br* → **theater**

the·at·ri·cal [θɪ'ætrɪkl] *adj also fig* théâtral

theft [θeft] vol *m*

their [ðer] *adj* leur; *pl* leurs; (*his or her*) son, sa; *pl* ses; *everybody has* ~ *favorite* tout le monde a son favori

theirs [ðerz] *pron* le leur, la leur, les leurs; *it's* ~ c'est à eux / elles

them [ðem] *pron* ◊ *object* les; *indirect object* leur; *with prep* eux, elles; *I know* ~ je les connais; *I gave* ~ *a dollar* je leur ai donné un dollar; *this is for* ~ c'est pour eux / elles; *who?* - ~ qui? - eux / elles

◊ (*him or her*) le, l'; *indirect object, with prep* lui; *if someone asks you should help* ~ si quelqu'un de-

mande tu devrais l'aider; **does anyone have a pen with ~?** est-ce que
quelqu'un a un crayon sur lui?
theme [θiːm] thème *m*
'theme park parc *m* à thème
'theme song chanson *f* titre d'un film
them·selves [ðem'selvz] *pron* eux-
-mêmes, elles-mêmes; *reflexive* se;
after prep eux, elles; **they gave ~ a
holiday** ils se sont offerts des vacances; **by ~** *(alone)* tout seuls, toutes
seules
then [ðen] *adv (at that time)* à l'époque;
(after that) ensuite; *deducing* alors; **by
~** alors; **he'll be dead by ~** il sera
mort d'ici là
the·o·lo·gi·an [θɪə'loʊdʒɪən] théolo-
gien(-ne) *m(f)*
the·ol·o·gy [θɪ'ɑːlədʒɪ] théologie *f*
the·o·ret·i·cal [θɪə'retɪkl] *adj* théorique
the·o·ret·i·cal·ly [θɪə'retɪklɪ] *adv* en
théorie
the·o·ry ['θɪrɪ] théorie *f*; **in ~** en théorie
ther·a·peu·tic [θerə'pjuːtɪk] *adj* thérapeutique
ther·a·pist ['θerəpɪst] thérapeute *m/f*
ther·a·py ['θerəpɪ] thérapie *f*
there [ðer] *adv* là; **over ~ / down ~** là-
-bas; **~ is / are ...** il y a ...; **is / are
... ?** est-ce qu'il y a ...?, y a-t-il ...?; **~
is / are not ...** il n'y a pas ...; **~ you
are** voilà; **~ and back** aller et retour;
~ he is! le voilà!; **~, ~!** allons, allons;
we went ~ yesterday nous y som-
mes allés hier
there·a·bouts [ðerə'baʊts] *adv*: **$500
or ~** environ 500 $
there·fore ['ðerfɔːr] *adv* donc
ther·mom·e·ter [θər'mɑːmɪtər] thermomètre *m*
ther·mos flask ['θɜːrməsflæsk] thermos *m*
ther·mo·stat ['θɜːrməstæt] thermostat *m*
these [ðiːz] **1** *adj* ces **2** *pron* ceux-ci,
celles-ci
the·sis ['θiːsɪs] *(pl* **theses** ['θiːsiːz]*)*
thèse *f*
they [ðeɪ] *pron* ◇ ils, elles; *stressed* eux,

elles; **~ were the ones who ...** c'était
eux / elles qui ...; **there ~ are** les voilà
◇ *(he or she)* il; **if anyone looks at
this ~ will see that ...** si quelqu'un
regarde ça il verra que ...; **~ say that
... **on dit que ...; **~ are changing the
law** la loi va être changée
thick [θɪk] *adj* épais*; F *(stupid)* lourd;
it's 3 cm ~ ça fait 3 cm d'épaisseur
thick·en ['θɪkən] *v/t* sauce épaissir
thick·set ['θɪkset] *adj* trapu
thick-skinned ['θɪkskɪnd] *adj fig* qui a
la peau dure
thief [θiːf] *(pl* **thieves** [θiːvz]*)* voleur
(-euse) *m(f)*
thigh [θaɪ] cuisse *f*
thim·ble ['θɪmbl] dé *m* à coudre
thin [θɪn] *adj material* léger*, fin; *layer*
mince; *person* maigre; *line* fin; *soup*
liquide; **his hair's getting ~** il perd
ses cheveux
thing [θɪŋ] chose *f*; **~s** *(belongings)* affaires *fpl*; **how are ~s?** comment ça
va?; **it's a good ~ you told me** tu as
bien fait de me le dire; **that's a
strange ~ to say** c'est bizarre de dire
ça
thing·um·a·jig ['θɪŋʌmədʒɪg] F machin *m* F
think [θɪŋk] **1** *v/i (pret & pp* **thought***)*
penser; **I ~ so** je pense que oui; **I
don't ~ so** je ne pense pas; **I ~ so
too** je le pense aussi; **~ hard!**
creuse-toi la tête! F; **I'm ~ing about
emigrating** j'envisage d'émigrer; **I'll
~ about it** *offer* je vais y réfléchir **2** *v/t
(pret & pp* **thought***)* penser; **what do
you ~ (of it)?** qu'est-ce que tu en
penses?
♦**think over** *v/t* réfléchir à
♦**think through** *v/t* bien examiner
♦**think up** *v/t plan* concevoir
'think tank comité *m* d'experts
thin-skinned ['θɪnskɪnd] *adj fig* susceptible
third [θɜːrd] troisième; *(fraction)* tiers
m; → **fifth**
third·ly ['θɜːrdlɪ] *adv* troisièmement
third-'par·ty tiers *m*; **third-par·ty in'-**

sur·ance Br assurance f au tiers;
third 'per·son GRAM troisième personne f; **'third-rate** adj de dernier ordre; **'Third World** Tiers-Monde m
thirst [θɜːrst] soif f
thirst·y ['θɜːrstɪ] adj assoiffé; **be ~** avoir soif
thir·teen [θɜːr'tiːn] treize
thir·teenth [θɜːr'tiːnθ] treizième; →
fifth
thir·ti·eth ['θɜːrtɪɪθ] trentième
thir·ty ['θɜːrtɪ] trente
this [ðɪs] **1** adj ce, cette; masculine before vowel cet; **~ one** celui-ci, celle-ci **2** pron cela, ça; **~ is good** c'est bien; **~ is ...** c'est ...; introducing s.o. je vous présente ... **3** adv: **~ big / high** grand / haut comme ça
thorn [θɔːrn] épine f
thorn·y ['θɔːrnɪ] adj also fig épineux*
thor·ough ['θʌroʊ] adj search, knowledge approfondi; person méticuleux*
thor·ough·bred ['θʌrəbred] n horse pur-sang m
thor·ough·ly ['θʌrəlɪ] adv spoilt, ashamed, agree complètement; clean, search for, know à fond
those [ðoʊz] **1** adj ces **2** pron ceux-là, celles-là
though [ðoʊ] **1** conj (although) bien que (+subj), quoique (+subj); **as ~** comme si; **it sounds as ~ you've understood** on dirait que vous avez compris **2** adv pourtant; **it's not finished ~** mais ce n'est pas fini
thought[1] [θɔːt] n pensée f
thought[2] [θɔːt] pret & pp → **think**
thought·ful ['θɔːtfʊl] adj (pensive) pensif*; book profond; (considerate) attentionné
thought·ful·ly ['θɔːtflɪ] adv (pensively) pensivement; (considerately) de manière attentionnée
thought·less ['θɔːtlɪs] adj inconsidéré
thought·less·ly ['θɔːtlɪslɪ] adv de façon inconsidérée
thou·sand ['θaʊznd] mille m; **~s of** des milliers mpl de; exaggerating des millions de
thou·sandth ['θaʊzndθ] millième

thrash [θræʃ] v/t rouer de coups; SP battre à plates coutures
♦ **thrash about** v/i with arms etc se débattre
♦ **thrash out** v/t solution parvenir à
thrash·ing ['θræʃɪŋ] volée f de coups; **get a ~** SP se faire battre à plates coutures
thread [θred] **1** n for sewing fil m; of screw filetage m **2** v/t needle, beads enfiler
thread·bare ['θredber] adj usé jusqu'à la corde
threat [θret] menace f
threat·en ['θretn] v/t menacer
threat·en·ing ['θretnɪŋ] adj gesture, letter, sky menaçant
three [θriː] trois
three-'quar·ters toule les trois-quarts mpl
thresh·old ['θreʃhoʊld] of house, new era seuil m
threw [θruː] pret → **throw**
thrift [θrɪft] économie f
thrift·y ['θrɪftɪ] adj économe
thrill [θrɪl] **1** n frisson m **2** v/t: **be ~ed** être ravi
thrill·er ['θrɪlər] thriller m
thrill·ing ['θrɪlɪŋ] adj palpitant
thrive [θraɪv] v/i of plants bien pousser; of business, economy prospérer
throat [θroʊt] gorge f
'throat loz·enge pastille f pour la gorge
throb [θrɑːb] **1** n of heart pulsation f; of music vibration f **2** v/i (pret & pp **-bed**) of heart battre fort; of music vibrer
throm·bo·sis [θrɑːm'boʊsɪs] thrombose f
throne [θroʊn] trône m
throng [θrɑːŋ] n foule f
throt·tle ['θrɑːtl] **1** n on motorbike, boat papillon m des gaz **2** v/t (strangle) étrangler
♦ **throttle back** v/i fermer les gaz
through [θruː] **1** prep ◇ (across) à travers; **go ~ the city** traverser la ville ◇ (during) pendant; **all ~ the night** toute la nuit; **Monday ~ Friday** du lundi au vendredi (inclus)
◇ (by means of) par; **arranged ~ an**

agency organisé par l'intermédiaire d'une agence **2** *adv*: **wet ~** mouillé jusqu'aux os; **watch a film / read a book ~** regarder un film / lire un livre en entier **3** *adj*: **be ~** (*have arrived: of news etc*) être parvenu; **you're ~** TELEC vous êtes connecté; **we're ~** *of couple* c'est fini entre nous; **be ~ with s.o. / sth** en avoir fini avec qn / qch

'through flight vol *m* direct

through-out [θruː'aut] **1** *prep* tout au long de, pendant tout(e); **~ the novel** dans tout le roman **2** *adv* (*in all parts*) partout

'through train train *m* direct

throw [θrəʊ] **1** *v/t* (*pret* **threw**, *pp* **thrown**) jeter, lancer; *of horse* désarçonner; (*disconcert*) déconcerter; *party* organiser **2** *n* jet *m*; **it's your ~** c'est à toi de lancer

♦ throw away *v/t* jeter

♦ throw off *v/t jacket etc* enlever à toute vitesse; *cold etc* se débarrasser de

♦ throw on *v/t clothes* enfiler à toute vitesse

♦ throw out *v/t old things* jeter; *from bar, home* jeter dehors, mettre à la porte; *from country* expulser; *plan* rejeter

♦ throw up **1** *v/t ball* jeter en l'air; (*vomit*) vomir; **throw up one's hands** lever les mains en l'air **2** *v/i* (*vomit*) vomir

throw-a-way ['θrəʊweɪ] *adj* (*disposable*) jetable; **a ~ remark** une remarque en l'air

'throw-in SP remise *f* en jeu

thrown [θrəʊn] *pp* → **throw**

thru [θruː] → **through**

thrush [θrʌʃ] *bird* grive *f*

thrust [θrʌst] *v/t* (*pret & pp* **thrust**) (*push hard*) enfoncer; **~ one's way through the crowd** se frayer un chemin à travers la foule

thud [θʌd] *n* bruit *m* sourd

thug [θʌg] brute *f*

thumb [θʌm] **1** *n* pouce *m* **2** *v/t*: **~ a ride** faire de l'auto-stop

thumb-tack ['θʌmtæk] punaise *f*

thump [θʌmp] **1** *n* *blow* coup *m* de poing; *noise* bruit *m* sourd **2** *v/t person* cogner; **~ one's fist on the table** cogner du poing sur la table **3** *v/i of heart* battre la chamade; **~ on the door** cogner sur la porte

thun-der ['θʌndər] *n* tonnerre *m*

thun-der-ous ['θʌndərəs] *adj applause* tonitruant

thun-der-storm ['θʌndərstɔːrm] orage *m*

thun-der-struck *adj* abasourdi

thun-der-y ['θʌndərɪ] *adj weather* orageux*

Thurs-day ['θɜːrzdeɪ] jeudi *m*

thus [ðʌs] *adv* ainsi

thwart [θwɔːrt] *v/t person, plans* contrarier

thyme [taɪm] thym *m*

thy-roid gland ['θaɪrɔɪdglænd] thyroïde *f*

tick [tɪk] **1** *n of clock* tic-tac *m*; (*checkmark*) coche *f* **2** *v/i* faire tic-tac

tick-et ['tɪkɪt] *for bus, museum* ticket *m*; *for train, airplane, theater, concert, lottery* billet *m*; *for speeding, illegal parking* P.V. *m*

'tick-et col-lec-tor contrôleur(-euse) *m(f)*; 'tick-et in-spec-tor contrôleur(-euse) *m(f)*; 'tick-et ma-chine distributeur *m* de billets; 'tick-et of-fice billetterie *f*

tick-ing ['tɪkɪŋ] *noise* tic-tac *m*

tick-le ['tɪkl] *v/t & v/i* chatouiller

tick-lish ['tɪklɪʃ] *adj person* chatouilleux*

tid-al wave ['taɪdlweɪv] raz-de-marée *m*

tide [taɪd] marée *f*; **high / low ~** marée haute / basse; **the ~ is in / out** la marée monte / descend

♦ tide over *v/t* dépanner

ti-di-ness ['taɪdɪnɪs] ordre *m*

ti-dy ['taɪdɪ] *adj person, habits* ordonné; *room, house, desk* en ordre

♦ tidy away *v/t* (*pret & pp* **-ied**) ranger

♦ tidy up **1** *v/t room, shelves* ranger; **tidy o.s. up** remettre de l'ordre dans sa tenue **2** *v/i* ranger

tie [taɪ] **1** *n* (*necktie*) cravate *f*; SP (*even result*) match *m* à égalité; **he doesn't**

have any ~s il n'a aucune attache **2** *v/t laces* nouer; *knot* faire; *hands* lier; **~ sth to sth** attacher qch à qch; **~ two ropes together** lier deux cordes entre elles **3** *v/i* SP *of teams* faire match nul; *of runner* finir ex æquo

♦ **tie down** *v/t* with rope attacher; *fig (restrict)* restreindre

♦ **tie up** *v/t hair* attacher; *person* ligoter; *boat* amarrer; ***I'm tied up tomorrow*** (busy) je suis pris demain

tier [tɪr] *of hierarchy* niveau *m*; *of seats* gradin *m*

ti-ger ['taɪɡər] tigre *m*

tight [taɪt] **1** *adj clothes, knot, screw* serré; *shoes* trop petit; *(properly shut)* bien fermé; *not leaving much time* juste; *security* strict; F *(drunk)* bourré F **2** *adv hold fort*; *shut* bien

tight-en ['taɪtn] *v/t control, security* renforcer; *screw* serrer; *(make tighter)* resserrer

tight-fist-ed [taɪt'fɪstɪd] *adj* radin

tight-ly *adv* → **tight** *adv*

tight-rope ['taɪtroʊp] corde *f* raide

tights [taɪts] *npl Br* collant *m*

tile [taɪl] *n on floor, wall* carreau *m*; *on roof* tuile *f*

till[1] [tɪl] *prep, conj* → **until**

till[2] [tɪl] *n (cash register)* caisse *f*

till[3] [tɪl] *v/t soil* labourer

tilt [tɪlt] *v/t & v/i* pencher

tim-ber ['tɪmbər] bois *m*

time [taɪm] **1** *n* temps *m*; *(occasion)* fois *f*; ***for the ~ being*** pour l'instant; ***have a good ~*** bien s'amuser; ***have a good ~!*** amusez-vous bien!; ***what's the ~?***, ***what ~ is it?*** quelle heure est-il?; ***the first ~*** la première fois; ***four ~s*** quatre fois; ***~ and again*** cent fois; ***all the ~*** pendant tout ce temps; ***he knew all the ~ that …*** il savait depuis le début que …; ***two / three at a ~*** deux par deux / trois par trois; ***at the same ~*** *speak, reply etc*, *(however)* en même temps; ***in ~*** à temps; ***on ~*** à l'heure; ***in no ~ in the past*** en un rien de temps; *in the future* dans un rien de temps **2** *v/t* chronométrer

'time bomb bombe *f* à retardement;

'time clock *in factory* horloge *f* pointeuse; **'time-con-sum-ing** *adj task* de longue haleine; **'time dif-fer-ence** décalage *m* horaire; **'time-lag** laps *m* de temps; **'time lim-it** limite *f* dans le temps

time-ly ['taɪmlɪ] *adj* opportun

'time out SP temps *m* mort

tim-er ['taɪmər] *device* minuteur *m*

'time-sav-ing économie *f* de temps; **'time-scale** *of project* durée *f*; **'time switch** minuterie *f*; **'time-warp** changement *m* subit d'époque; **'time zone** fuseau *m* horaire

tim-id ['tɪmɪd] *adj* timide

tim-id-ly ['tɪmɪdlɪ] *adv* timidement

tim-ing ['taɪmɪŋ] *of actor, dancer* synchronisation *f*; ***the ~ of the announcement was perfect*** l'annonce est venue au parfait moment

tin [tɪn] *metal* étain *m*

tin-foil ['tɪnfɔɪl] papier *m* aluminium

tinge [tɪndʒ] *n* soupçon *m*

tin-gle ['tɪŋɡl] *v/i* picoter

♦ **tin-ker** ['tɪŋkər] *v/t engine* bricoler; ***stop tinkering with it!*** arrête de toucher à ça!

tin-kle ['tɪŋkl] *n of bell* tintement *m*

tin-sel ['tɪnsl] guirlandes *fpl* de Noël

tint [tɪnt] **1** *n of color* teinte *f*; *for hair* couleur *f* **2** *v/t*: **~ one's hair** se faire une coloration

tint-ed ['tɪntɪd] *adj eyeglasses* teinté; *paper* de couleur pastel

ti-ny ['taɪnɪ] *adj* minuscule

tip[1] [tɪp] *n (end)* bout *m*

tip[2] [tɪp] **1** *n advice* conseil *m*, truc *m* F; *money* pourboire *m* **2** *v/t (pret & pp -ped) waiter etc* donner un pourboire à

♦ **tip off** *v/t* informer

♦ **tip over** *v/t* renverser

'tip-off renseignement *m*, tuyau *m* F; ***have a ~ that …*** être informé que …

tipped [tɪpt] *adj cigarettes* à bout filtre

tip-py-toe ['tɪpɪtoʊ]: **on ~** sur la pointe des pieds

tip-sy ['tɪpsɪ] *adj* éméché

tire[1] ['taɪr] *n* pneu *m*

tire[2] ['taɪr] **1** *v/t* fatiguer **2** *v/i* se fatiguer; ***he never ~s of it*** il ne s'en lasse pas

tired ['taɪrd] *adj* fatigué; **be ~ of s.o. / sth** en avoir assez de qn / qch

tired·ness ['taɪrdnɪs] fatigue *f*

tire·less ['taɪrlɪs] *adj* efforts infatigable

tire·some ['taɪrsəm] *adj* (*annoying*) fatigant

tir·ing ['taɪrɪŋ] *adj* fatigant

tis·sue ['tɪʃuː] ANAT tissu *m*; *handkerchief* mouchoir *m* en papier

'tis·sue pa·per papier *m* de soie

tit[1] [tɪt] *bird* mésange *f*

tit[2] [tɪt]: **give s.o. ~ for tat** rendre la pareille à qn

tit[3] [tɪt] V (*breast*) nichon *m* V; **get on s.o.'s ~s** P casser les pieds de qn F

ti·tle ['taɪtl] *of novel, person etc* titre *m*; LAW titre *m* de propriét é (**to**) de)

'ti·tle-hold·er SP tenant(e) *m(f)* du titre

'ti·tle role rôle *m* éponyme

tit·ter ['tɪtər] *v/i* rire bêtement

to [tuː], *unstressed* [tə] **1** *prep* à; **~ Japan** au Japon; **~ Chicago** à Chicago; **let's go ~ my place** allons chez moi; **walk ~ the station** aller à la gare à pied; **~ the north / south of** au nord / sud de; **give sth ~ s.o.** donner qch à qn; **from Monday ~ Wednesday** once à de lundi à mercredi; *regularly* du lundi au mercredi; **from 10 ~ 15 people** de 10 à 15 personnes; **5 minutes ~ 10** *esp Br* 10 heures moins 5 **2** *with verbs:* **~ speak, ~ shout** parler, crier; **learn ~ drive** apprendre à conduire; **nice ~ eat** bon à manger; **too heavy ~ carry** trop lourd à porter; **~ be honest with you, …** pour être sincère, … **3** *adv:* **~ and fro** *walk, pace* de long en large; **go ~ and fro between …** *of ferry* faire la navette entre …

toad [toʊd] crapaud *m*

toad·stool ['toʊdstuːl] champignon *m* vénéneux

toast [toʊst] **1** *n for eating* pain *m* grillé; *when drinking* toast *m*; **propose a ~ to s.o.** porter un toast à qn **2** *v/t when drinking* porter un toast à

to·bac·co [tə'bækoʊ] tabac *m*

to·bog·gan [tə'bɑːgən] *n* luge *f*

to·day [tə'deɪ] *adv* aujourd'hui

tod·dle ['tɑːdl] *v/i of child* faire ses premiers pas

tod·dler ['tɑːdlər] jeune enfant *m*, bambin *m* F

to-do [tə'duː] F remue-ménage *m*

toe [toʊ] **1** *n* orteil *m*; *of sock, shoe* bout *m* **2** *v/t:* **~ the line** se mettre au pas; **~ the party line** suivre la ligne du parti

toe·nail ['toʊneɪl] ongle *m* de pied

to·geth·er [tə'geðər] *adv* ensemble; *(at the same time)* en même temps

toil [tɔɪl] *n* labeur *m*

toi·let ['tɔɪlɪt] toilettes *fpl*; **go to the ~** aller aux toilettes

'toi·let pa·per papier *m* hygiénique

toi·let·ries ['tɔɪlɪtrɪz] *npl* articles *mpl* de toilette

'toi·let roll rouleau *m* de papier hygiénique

to·ken ['toʊkən] *sign* témoignage *m*; *(gift ~)* bon *m* d'achat; *instead of coin* jeton *m*

told [toʊld] *pret & pp* → **tell**

tol·er·a·ble ['tɑːlərəbl] *adj* pain etc tolérable; *(quite good)* acceptable

tol·er·ance ['tɑːlərəns] tolérance *f*

tol·er·ant ['tɑːlərənt] *adj* tolérant

tol·er·ate ['tɑːləreɪt] *v/t* tolérer; **I won't ~ it!** je ne tolérerai pas ça!

toll[1] [toʊl] *v/i of bell* sonner

toll[2] [toʊl] *n (deaths)* bilan *m*

toll[3] [toʊl] *n for bridge, road* péage *m*

'toll booth poste *m* de péage; **'toll-free** *adj* TELEC gratuit; **~ number** numéro *m* vert; **'toll road** route *f* à péage

to·ma·to [tə'meɪtoʊ] tomate *f*

to·ma·to 'ketch·up ketchup *m*

to·ma·to 'sauce *for pasta etc* sauce *f* tomate

tomb [tuːm] tombe *f*

tom·boy ['tɑːmbɔɪ] garçon *m* manqué

tomb·stone ['tuːmstoʊn] pierre *f* tombale

tom·cat ['tɑːmkæt] matou *m*

to·mor·row [tə'mɔːroʊ] **1** *n* demain *m*; **the day after ~** après-demain **2** *adv* demain; **~ morning** demain matin

ton [tʌn] tonne *f* courte (= *907 kg*)

tone [toʊn] *of color, conversation* ton *m*; *of musical instrument* timbre *m*; *of neighborhood* classe *f*; **~ of voice** ton *m*

♦ **tone down** *v/t demands* réduire; *criticism* atténuer

ton·er ['toʊnər] toner *m*

tongs [tɑːŋz] *npl* pince *f*; (*curling ~*) fer *m* à friser

tongue [tʌŋ] langue *f*

ton·ic ['tɑːnɪk] MED fortifiant *m*

'ton·ic (wa·ter) Schweppes® *m*, tonic *m*

to·night [təˈnaɪt] *adv* ce soir; *sleep* cette nuit

ton·sil·li·tis [tɑːnsəˈlaɪtɪs] angine *f*

ton·sils ['tɑːnslz] *npl* amygdales *fpl*

too [tuː] *adv* (*also*) aussi; (*excessively*) trop; **me ~** moi aussi; **~ big / hot** trop grand / chaud; **~ much rice** trop de riz; **eat ~ much** manger trop

took [tʊk] *pret* → **take**

tool [tuːl] outil *m*

toot [tuːt] *v/t* F: **~ the horn** klaxonner

tooth [tuːθ] (*pl* **teeth** [tiːθ]) dent *f*

'tooth·ache mal *m* de dents

'tooth·brush brosse *f* à dents

tooth·less ['tuːθlɪs] *adj* édenté

'tooth·paste dentifrice *m*

'tooth·pick cure-dents *m*

top [tɑːp] **1** *n also clothing* haut *m*; (*lid: of bottle etc*) bouchon *m*; *of pen* capuchon *m*; *of the class, league* premier (-ère) *m(f)*; MOT: **gear** quatrième *f* / cinquième *f*; **on ~ of** sur; **be at the ~ of** être en haut de; *league* être premier *de*; **get to the ~** *of company, mountain etc* arriver au sommet; **be over the ~** *Br* (*exaggerated*) être exagéré **2** *adj branches* du haut; *floor* dernier*; *player etc* meilleur; *speed* maximum *inv in feminine*; *note* le plus élevé; **~ management** les cadres *mpl* supérieurs; **~ official** haut fonctionnaire *m* **3** *v/t* (*pret & pp* **-ped**): **~ped with cream** surmonté de crème chantilly

top 'hat chapeau *m* haut de forme

top 'heav·y *adj* déséquilibré

top·ic ['tɑːpɪk] sujet *m*

top·i·cal ['tɑːpɪkl] *adj* d'actualité

top·less ['tɑːplɪs] *adj waitress* aux seins nus

top·most ['tɑːpmoʊst] *adj branch* le plus haut; *floor* dernier*

top·ping ['tɑːpɪŋ] *on pizza* garniture *f*

top·ple ['tɑːpl] **1** *v/i* s'écrouler **2** *v/t government* renverser

top 'se·cret *adj* top secret *inv*

top·sy·tur·vy [tɑːpsɪˈtɜːrvɪ] *adj* sens dessus dessous

torch [tɔːrtʃ] *n with flame* flambeau *m*; *Br* lampe *f* de poche

tore [tɔːr] *pret* → **tear**

tor·ment ['tɔːrment] **1** *n* tourment *m* **2** *v/t* [tɔːrˈment] *person, animal* harceler; **~ed by doubt** tourmenté par le doute

torn [tɔːrn] *pp* → **tear**

tor·na·do [tɔːrˈneɪdoʊ] tornade *f*

tor·pe·do [tɔːrˈpiːdoʊ] **1** *n* torpille *f* **2** *v/t also fig* torpiller

tor·rent ['tɑːrənt] *also fig* torrent *m*

tor·ren·tial [təˈrenʃl] *adj rain* torrentiel*

tor·toise ['tɔːrtəs] tortue *f* (terrestre)

tor·ture ['tɔːrtʃər] **1** *n* torture *f* **2** *v/t* torturer

toss [tɑːs] **1** *v/t ball* lancer; *rider* désarçonner; *salad* remuer; **~ a coin** jouer à pile ou face **2** *v/i*: **~ and turn** se tourner et se retourner

to·tal ['toʊtl] **1** *adj sum, amount* total; *disaster* complet*; *idiot* fini; **he's a ~ stranger** c'est un parfait inconnu **2** *n* total *m* **3** *v/t* (*pret & pp* **-ed**, *Br* **-led**) F *car* bousiller F

to·tal·i·tar·i·an [toʊtælɪˈteriən] *adj* totalitaire

to·tal·ly ['toʊtlɪ] *adv* totalement

tote bag ['toʊtbæg] fourre-tout *m*

tot·ter ['tɑːtər] *v/i of person* tituber

touch [tʌtʃ] **1** *n sense* toucher *m*; **a ~ of** (*a little*) un soupçon de; **lose ~ with s.o.** perdre contact avec qn; **keep in ~ with s.o.** rester en contact avec qn; **in ~** SP en touche; **be out of ~ (with sth)** ne pas être au courant (de qch); **be out of ~ with s.o.** avoir perdu le contact avec qn **2** *v/t also emotionally* toucher; *exhibits etc* tou-

cher à **3** v/i of two things se toucher; **don't ~** ne touche pas à ça
♦ **touch down** v/i of airplane atterrir; SP faire un touché-en-but
♦ **touch on** v/t (mention) effleurer
♦ **touch up** v/t photo retoucher
touch-down ['tʌʃdaun] n of airplane atterrissage m; SP touché-en-but; **score a ~** SP faire un touché-en-but
touch-ing ['tʌʃɪŋ] adj emotionally touchant
'**touch-line** SP ligne f de touche
'**touch screen** écran m tactile
touch-y ['tʌʃɪ] adj person susceptible
tough [tʌf] adj person, material résistant; meat, question, exam, punishment dur
♦ **tough-en up** ['tʌfn] v/t person endurcir
'**tough guy** F dur m F
tour [tur] **1** n visite f (of de); as part of package circuit m (of dans); of band, theater company tournée f **2** v/t area visiter **3** v/i of tourist faire du tourisme; of band être en tournée
'**tour guide** accompagnateur(-trice) m(f)
tour-ism ['turɪzm] tourisme m
tour-ist ['turɪst] touriste m/f
'**tour-ist at-trac-tion** attraction f touristique; '**tour-ist in-dus-try** industrie f touristique; **tour-ist in-for-'ma-tion of-fice** syndicat m d'initiative, office m de tourisme; '**tour-ist sea-son** saison f touristique
tour-na-ment ['turnəmənt] tournoi m
'**tour op-er-a-tor** tour-opérateur m, voyagiste m
tou-sled ['tauzld] adj hair ébouriffé
tow [tou] **1** v/t car, boat remorquer **2** n: **give s.o. a ~** remorquer qn
♦ **tow away** v/t car emmener à la fourrière
to-wards [tə'wɔːdz], Br **to-ward** [tə'wɔːd] prep in space vers; with attitude, feelings etc envers; aiming at en vue de; **work ~ a solution** essayer de trouver une solution
tow-el ['tauəl] serviette f
tow-er ['tauər] tour f
♦ **tower over** v/t building surplomber;

person être beaucoup plus grand que
town [taun] ville f
town 'cen-ter, Br **town 'centre** centre-ville m; **town 'coun-cil** conseil m municipal; **town 'hall** hôtel m de ville
tow-rope ['touroup] câble m de remorquage
tox-ic ['tɑːksɪk] adj toxique
tox-ic 'waste déchets mpl toxiques
tox-in ['tɑːksɪn] BIOL toxine f
toy [tɔɪ] jouet m
♦ **toy with** v/t jouer avec; idea caresser
'**toy store** magasin m de jouets
trace [treɪs] **1** n of substance trace f **2** v/t (find) retrouver; draw tracer
track [træk] n path, (racecourse) piste f; motor racing circuit m; on record, CD morceau m; RAIL voie f (ferrée); **~ 10** RAIL voie 10; **keep ~ of sth** suivre qch
♦ **track down** v/t person retrouver; criminal dépister; object dénicher
track-suit ['træksuːt] survêtement m
trac-tor ['træktər] tracteur m
trade [treɪd] **1** n (commerce) commerce m; (profession, craft) métier m **2** v/i (do business) faire du commerce; **~ in sth** faire du commerce dans qch **3** v/t (exchange) échanger (for contre)
♦ **trade in** v/t when buying donner en reprise
'**trade fair** foire f commerciale; '**trade-mark** marque f de commerce; '**trade mis-sion** mission f commerciale
trad-er ['treɪdər] commerçant(e) m(f)
trade 'se-cret secret m commercial
tra-di-tion [trə'dɪʃn] tradition f
tra-di-tion-al [trə'dɪʃnl] adj traditionnel*
tra-di-tion-al-ly [trə'dɪʃnlɪ] adv traditionnellement
traf-fic ['træfɪk] n on roads circulation f; at airport, in drugs trafic m
♦ **traffic in** v/t (pret & pp **-ked**) drugs faire du trafic de
'**traf-fic cir-cle** rond-point m; '**traf-fic cop** F agent m de la circulation; '**traf-fic is-land** refuge m; '**traf-fic**

jam embouteillage *m*; **'traf·fic light** feux *mpl* de signalisation; **'traf·fic po·lice** police *f* de la route; **'traf·fic sign** panneau *m* de signalisation

trag·e·dy ['trædʒədɪ] tragédie *f*

trag·ic ['trædʒɪk] *adj* tragique

trail [treɪl] **1** *n (path)* sentier *m*; *of blood* traînée *f* **2** *v/t (follow)* suivre à la trace; *(tow)* remorquer **3** *v/i (lag behind: of person)* traîner; *of team* se traîner

trail·er ['treɪlər] *pulled by vehicle* remorque *f*; *(mobile home)* caravane *f*; *of movie* bande-annonce *f*

train[1] [treɪn] *n* train *m*; **go by ~** aller en train

train[2] [treɪn] **1** *v/t* entraîner; *dog* dresser; *employee* former **2** *v/i of team, athlete* s'entraîner; *of teacher etc* faire sa formation; **~ as a doctor** faire des études de médecine

train·ee [treɪ'ni:] stagiaire *m/f*

train·er ['treɪnər] SP entraîneur(-euse) *m(f)*; *of dog* dresseur(-euse) *m(f)*

train·ers ['treɪnərz] *npl Br. shoes* tennis *mpl*

train·ing [treɪnɪŋ] *of new staff* formation *f*; SP entraînement *m*; **be in ~** SP être bien entraîné; **be out of ~** SP avoir perdu la forme

'train·ing course cours *m* de formation

'train·ing scheme programme *m* de formation

'train sta·tion gare *f*

trait [treɪt] trait *m*

trai·tor ['treɪtər] traître *m*, traîtresse *f*

tramp[1] [træmp] *v/i* marcher à pas lourds

tramp[2] [træmp] *pej* femme *f* facile; *Br* clochard *m*

tram·ple ['træmpl] *v/t*: **be ~d to death** mourir piétiné; **be ~d underfoot** être piétiné

♦ **trample on** *v/t person, object* piétiner

tram·po·line ['træmpəli:n] trampoline *m*

trance [træns] transe *f*; **go into a ~** entrer en transe

tran·quil ['trænkwɪl] *adj* tranquille

tran·quil·i·ty [træn'kwɪlətɪ] tranquil-

lité *f*

tran·quil·iz·er, *Br* **tran·quil·liz·er** ['trænkwɪlaɪzər] tranquillisant *m*

trans·act [træn'zækt] *v/t deal, business* faire

trans·ac·tion [træn'zækʃn] *of business* conduite *f*; *piece of business* transaction *f*

trans·at·lan·tic [trænzət'læntɪk] *adj* transatlantique

tran·scen·den·tal [trænsen'dentl] *adj* transcendental

tran·script ['trænskrɪpt] transcription *f*

trans·fer [træns'fɜːr] **1** *v/t (pret & pp -red)* transférer **2** *v/i (pret & pp -red) when traveling* changer; *in job* être muté **(to** à) **3** *n* ['trænsfɜːr] *of money, in job, in travel* transfert *m*

trans·fer·a·ble [træns'fɜːrəbl] *adj ticket* transférable

'trans·fer fee *for sportsman* prix *m* de transfert

trans·form [træns'fɔːrm] *v/t* transformer

trans·for·ma·tion [trænsfər'meɪʃn] transformation *f*

trans·form·er [træns'fɔːrmər] ELEC transformateur *m*

trans·fu·sion [træns'fjuːʒn] transfusion *f*

tran·sis·tor [træn'zɪstər] *also radio* transistor *m*

trans·it ['trænzɪt] transit *m*; **in ~** en transit

tran·si·tion [træn'zɪʒn] transition *f*

tran·si·tion·al [træn'zɪʒnl] *adj* de transition

'trans·it lounge *at airport* salle *f* de transit

'trans·it pas·sen·ger passager(-ère) *m(f)* en transit

trans·late [træns'leɪt] *v/t& v/i* traduire

trans·la·tion [træns'leɪʃn] traduction *f*

trans·la·tor [træns'leɪtər] traducteur (-trice) *m(f)*

trans·mis·sion [trænz'mɪʃn] TV, MOT transmission *f*

trans·mit [trænz'mɪt] *v/t (pret & pp -ted) news, program* diffuser; *disease* transmettre

trans·mit·ter [trænz'mɪtər] RAD, TV émetteur *m*

trans·par·en·cy [træns'pærənsɪ] PHOT diapositive *f*

trans·par·ent [træns'pærənt] *adj* transparent; (*obvious*) évident; *he is so* ~ c'est tellement facile de lire dans ses pensées

trans·plant ['trænsplænt] **1** *n* MED transplantation *f*; *organ transplanted* transplant *m* **2** *v/t* [træns'plænt] MED transplanter

trans·port ['trænspɔːrt] **1** *n of goods, people* transport *m* **2** *v/t* [træn'spɔːrt] *goods, people* transporter

trans·por·ta·tion [trænspɔːr'teɪʃn] *of goods, people* transport *m*; *means of* ~ moyen *m* de transport; *public* ~ transports *mpl* en commun; *Department of Transportation* ministère *m* des Transports

trans·ves·tite [træns'vestaɪt] travesti *m*

trap [træp] **1** *n also fig* piège *m*; *set a* ~ *for s.o.* tendre un piège à qn **2** *v/t* (*pret & pp* *-ped*) *also fig* piéger; *be* ~*ped by enemy, flames, landslide etc* être pris au piège

trap·door ['træpdɔːr] trappe *f*

tra·peze [trə'piːz] trapèze *m*

trap·pings ['træpɪŋz] *npl of power* signes extérieurs *mpl*

trash [træʃ] **1** *n* (*garbage*) ordures *fpl*; F *goods etc* camelote *f* F; *fig: person* vermine *f* **2** *v/t* jeter; (*criticize*) démolir; *bar, apartment etc* saccager, vandaliser

'trash can poubelle *f*

trash·y ['træʃɪ] *adj goods* de pacotille; *novel* de bas étage

trau·ma ['trɔːmə] traumatisme *m*

trau·mat·ic [trɑː'mætɪk] *adj* traumatisant

trau·ma·tize ['trɑːmətaɪz] *v/t* traumatiser

trav·el ['trævl] **1** *n* voyages *mpl*; ~*s* voyages *mpl* **2** *v/i* (*pret & pp* *-ed*, *Br* *-led*) voyager **3** *v/t* (*pret & pp* *-ed*, *Br* *-led*) *miles* parcourir

'trav·el a·gen·cy agence *f* de voyages;
'trav·el a·gent agent *m* de voyages;

'trav·el bag sac *m* de voyage

trav·el·er ['trævələr] voyageur(-euse) *m(f)*

'trav·el·er's check chèque-voyage *m*

'trav·el ex·pen·ses *npl* frais *mpl* de déplacement

'trav·el in·sur·ance assurance-voyage *f*

trav·el·ler *Br* → **traveler**

'trav·el pro·gram, **'trav·el pro·gramme** *Br* programme *m* de voyages

'trav·el sick·ness mal *m* des transports

trawl·er ['trɔːlər] chalutier *m*

tray [treɪ] *for food, photocopier* plateau *m*; *to go in oven* plaque *f*

treach·er·ous ['tretʃərəs] *adj* traître

treach·er·y ['tretʃərɪ] traîtrise *f*

tread [tred] **1** *n* pas *m*; *of staircase* dessus *m* des marches; *of tire* bande *f* de roulement **2** *v/i* (*pret* **trod**, *pp* **trodden**) marcher; *mind where you* ~ fais attention où tu mets les pieds
♦ **tread on** *v/t person's foot* marcher sur

trea·son ['triːzn] trahison *f*

treas·ure ['treʒər] **1** *n* trésor *m* **2** *v/t gift etc* chérir

treas·ur·er ['treʒərər] trésorier(-ière) *m(f)*

Treas·ur·y De·part·ment ['treʒərɪ] ministère *m* des Finances

treat [triːt] **1** *n* plaisir *m*; *it was a real* ~ c'était un vrai bonheur; *I have a* ~ *for you* j'ai une surprise pour toi; *it's my* ~ (*I'm paying*) c'est moi qui paie **2** *v/t materials, illness, person* traiter; ~ *s.o. to sth* offrir qch à qn

treat·ment ['triːtmənt] traitement *m*

trea·ty ['triːtɪ] traité *m*

tre·ble[1] ['trebl] *n* MUS soprano *m* (*de jeune garçon*)

tre·ble[2] ['trebl] **1** *adv:* ~ *the price* le triple du prix **2** *v/i* tripler

tree [triː] arbre *m*

trem·ble ['trembl] *v/i* trembler

tre·men·dous [trɪ'mendəs] *adj* (*very good*) formidable; (*enormous*) énorme

tre·men·dous·ly [trɪ'mendəslɪ] *adv*

(*very*) extrêmement; (*a lot*) énormément

trem·or ['tremər] *of earth* secousse *f* (sismique)

trench [trentʃ] tranchée *f*

trend [trend] tendance *f*; (*fashion*) mode *f*

trend·y ['trendɪ] *adj* branché

tres·pass ['trespæs] *v/i* entrer sans autorisation; *no ~ing* défense d'entrer

♦ **trespass on** *v/t land* entrer sans autorisation sur; *s.o.'s rights* violer; *s.o.'s time* abuser de

tres·pass·er ['trespæsər] *personne qui viole la propriété d'une autre*; **~s will be prosecuted** défense d'entrer sous peine de poursuites

tri·al ['traɪəl] LAW procès *m*; *of equipment* essai *m*; **be on ~** LAW passer en justice; **have sth on ~** *equipment* essayer qch, acheter qch à l'essai

tri·al 'pe·ri·od période *f* d'essai

tri·an·gle ['traɪæŋgl] triangle *m*

tri·an·gu·lar [traɪ'æŋgjʊlər] *adj* triangulaire

tribe [traɪb] tribu *f*

tri·bu·nal [traɪ'bjuːnl] tribunal *m*

trib·u·ta·ry ['trɪbjətərɪ] *of river* affluent *m*

trick [trɪk] **1** *n to deceive* tour *m*; (*knack*) truc *m*; **just the ~** F juste ce qu'il me faut; *hedge* tailler; **play a ~ on s.o.** jouer un tour à qn **2** *v/t* rouler; **be ~ed** se faire avoir

trick·e·ry ['trɪkərɪ] tromperie *f*

trick·le ['trɪkl] **1** *n* filet *m*; *fig* tout petit peu *m* **2** *v/i* couler goutte à goutte

trick·ster ['trɪkstər] escroc *m*

trick·y ['trɪkɪ] *adj* (*difficult*) délicat

tri·cy·cle ['traɪsɪkl] tricycle *m*

tri·fle ['traɪfl] *n* (*triviality*) bagatelle *f*

tri·fling ['traɪflɪŋ] *adj* insignifiant

trig·ger ['trɪgər] *n on gun* détente *f*; *on camcorder* déclencheur *m*

♦ **trigger off** *v/t* déclencher

trim [trɪm] **1** *adj* (*neat*) bien entretenu; *figure* svelte **2** *v/t* (*pret & pp* -**med**) *hair* couper un peu; *hedge* tailler; *budget, costs* réduire; (*decorate: dress*) garnir **3** *n cut* taille *f*; **in good ~** en bon état; *boxer* en forme

tri·mes·ter ['trɪmestər] trimestre *m*

trim·ming ['trɪmɪŋ] *on clothes* garniture *f*; **with all the ~s** avec toutes les options

trin·ket ['trɪŋkɪt] babiole *f*

tri·o ['triːoʊ] MUS trio *m*

trip [trɪp] **1** *n* (*journey*) voyage *m*; (*outing*) excursion *f*; **go on a ~ to Vannes** aller visiter Vannes **2** *v/i* (*pret & pp* -**ped**) (*stumble*) trébucher **3** *v/t* (*pret & pp* -**ped**) (*make fall*) faire un croche-pied à

♦ **trip up 1** *v/t* (*make fall*) faire un croche-pied à; (*cause to go wrong*) faire trébucher **2** *v/i* (*stumble*) trébucher; (*make a mistake*) faire une erreur

tri·ple ['trɪpl] → **treble**

tri·plets ['trɪplɪts] *npl* triplé(e)s *m(f)pl*

tri·pod ['traɪpɑd] PHOT trépied *m*

trite [traɪt] *adj* banal

tri·umph ['traɪʌmf] *n* triomphe *m*

triv·i·al ['trɪvɪəl] *adj* insignifiant

triv·i·al·i·ty [trɪvɪ'ælətɪ] banalité *f*

trod [trɑd] *pret* → **tread**

trod·den ['trɑdn] *pp* → **tread**

trol·ley ['trɑːlɪ] (*streetcar*) tramway *m*

trom·bone [trɑːm'boʊn] trombone *m*

troops [truːps] *npl* troupes *fpl*

tro·phy ['troʊfɪ] trophée *m*

trop·ic ['trɑːpɪk] GEOG tropique *m*

trop·i·cal ['trɑːpɪkl] *adj* tropical

trop·ics ['trɑːpɪks] *npl* tropiques *mpl*

trot [trɑːt] *v/i* (*pret & pp* -**ted**) trotter

trou·ble ['trʌbl] **1** *n* (*difficulties*) problèmes *mpl*; (*inconvenience*) dérangement *m*; (*disturbance*) affrontements *mpl*; **sorry to put you to any ~** désolé de vous déranger; **go to a lot of ~ to do sth** se donner beaucoup de mal pour faire qch; **no ~!** pas de problème!; **get into ~** s'attirer des ennuis **2** *v/t* (*worry*) inquiéter; (*bother, disturb*) déranger; *of back, liver etc* faire souffrir

'trou·ble-free *adj* sans problème; **'trou·ble-mak·er** fauteur(-trice) *m(f)* de troubles; **'trou·ble-shoot·er** conciliateur(-trice) *m(f)*; **'trou·ble-shoot·ing** dépannage *m*

trou·ble·some ['trʌblsəm] *adj* pénible

trou·sers ['traʊzərz] *npl Br* pantalon

m

trout [traʊt] (*pl* **trout**) truite *f*

truce [truːs] trêve *f*

truck [trʌk] camion *m*

'**truck driv·er** camionneur(-euse) *m(f)*; '**truck farm** jardin *m* maraîcher; '**truck farm·er** maraîcher(-ère) *m(f)*; '**truck stop** routier *m*

trudge [trʌdʒ] **1** *v/i* se traîner **2** *n* marche *f* pénible

true [truː] *adj* vrai; *friend, American* véritable; **come ~** *of hopes, dream* se réaliser

tru·ly ['truːlɪ] *adv* vraiment; *Yours ~* je vous prie d'agréer mes sentiments distingués

trum·pet ['trʌmpɪt] *n* trompette *f*

trum·pet·er ['trʌmpɪtər] trompettiste *m/f*

trunk [trʌŋk] *of tree, body* tronc *m*; *of elephant* trompe *f*; (*large suitcase*) malle *f*; *of car* coffre *m*

trust [trʌst] **1** *n* confiance *f*; FIN fidéi-commis *m* **2** *v/t* faire confiance à; *I ~ you* je te fais confiance

trust·ed ['trʌstɪd] *adj* éprouvé

trust·ee [trʌs'tiː] fidéicommissaire *m/f*

trust·ful, trust·ing ['trʌstfl, 'trʌstɪŋ] *adj* confiant

trust·wor·thy ['trʌstwɜːrðɪ] *adj* fiable

truth [truːθ] vérité *f*

truth·ful ['truːθfl] *adj* honnête

try [traɪ] **1** *v/t* (*pret & pp -ied*) essayer; LAW juger; *~ to do sth* essayer de faire qch; *why don't you ~ changing suppliers?* pourquoi tu ne changes pas de fournisseur? **2** *v/i* (*pret & pp -ied*) essayer; *you must ~ harder* tu dois faire plus d'efforts **3** *n* essai *m*; *can I have a ~?* of food est-ce que je peux goûter?; *at doing sth* est-ce que je peux essayer?

♦ **try on** *v/t clothes* essayer

♦ **try out** *v/t* essayer

try·ing ['traɪɪŋ] *adj* (*annoying*) éprouvant

T-shirt ['tiːʃɜːrt] tee-shirt *m*

tub [tʌb] (*bath*) baignoire *f*; *for liquid* bac *m*; *for yoghurt, ice cream* pot *m*

tub·by ['tʌbɪ] *adj* boulot*

tube [tuːb] (*pipe*) tuyau *m*; *of tooth-paste, ointment* tube *m*

tube·less ['tuːblɪs] *adj* tire sans chambre à air

tu·ber·cu·lo·sis [tuːbɜːrkjə'loʊsɪs] tuberculose *f*

tuck [tʌk] **1** *n in dress* pli *m* **2** *v/t* (*put*) mettre

♦ **tuck away** *v/t* (*put away*) ranger; (*eat quickly*) bouffer F

♦ **tuck in 1** *v/t children* border; *tuck the sheets in* border un lit **2** *v/i* (*start eating*) y aller

♦ **tuck up** *v/t sleeves etc* retrousser; *tuck s.o. up in bed* border qn

Tues·day ['tuːzdeɪ] mardi *m*

tuft [tʌft] touffe *f*

tug[1] [tʌg] **1** *n* (*pull*): *I felt a ~ at my sleeve* j'ai senti qu'on me tirait la manche **2** *v/t* (*pret & pp -ged*) (*pull*) tirer

tug[2] NAUT remorqueur *m*

tu·i·tion [tuː'ɪʃn] cours *mpl*

tu·lip ['tuːlɪp] tulipe *f*

tum·ble ['tʌmbl] *v/i* tomber

tum·ble·down ['tʌmbldaʊn] *adj* qui tombe en ruines

tum·bler ['tʌmblər] *for drink* verre *m*; *in circus* acrobate *m/f*

tum·my ['tʌmɪ] F ventre *m*

'**tum·my ache** mal *m* de ventre

tu·mor ['tuːmər] tumeur *f*

tu·mult ['tuːmʌlt] tumulte *m*

tu·mul·tu·ous [tuː'mʌltuəs] *adj* tumultueux*

tu·na ['tuːnə] thon *m*; *~ sandwich* sandwich *m* au thon

tune [tuːn] **1** *n air m*; *in ~ instrument* (bien) accordé; *sing in ~* chanter juste; *out of ~ instrument* désaccordé; *sing out of ~* chanter faux **2** *v/t instrument* accorder

♦ **tune in** *v/i* RAD, TV se mettre à l'écoute

♦ **tune in to** *v/t* RAD, TV se brancher sur

♦ **tune up 1** *v/i of orchestra, players* s'accorder **2** *v/t engine* régler

tune·ful ['tuːnfl] *adj* harmonieux*

tun·er ['tuːnər] *of hi-fi* tuner *m*

tune-up ['tuːnʌp] *of engine* règlement

m

tun·nel ['tʌnl] *n* tunnel *m*

tur·bine ['tɜːrbaɪn] turbine *f*

tur·bu·lence ['tɜːrbjələns] *in air travel* turbulences *fpl*

tur·bu·lent ['tɜːrbjələnt] *adj* agité

turf [tɜːrf] gazon *m*; *piece* motte *f* de gazon

Turk [tɜːrk] Turc *m*, Turque *f*

Tur·key ['tɜːrkɪ] Turquie *f*

tur·key ['tɜːrkɪ] dinde *f*

Turk·ish ['tɜːrkɪʃ] **1** *adj* turc* **2** *n language* turc *m*

tur·moil ['tɜːrmɔɪl] confusion *f*

turn [tɜːrn] **1** *n* (*rotation*) tour *m*; *in road* virage *m*; *in vaudeville* numéro *m*; *the second ~ on the right* la deuxième (route) à droite; *take ~s doing sth* faire qch à tour de rôle; *it's my ~* c'est à moi; *it's not your ~ yet* ce n'est pas encore à toi; *take a ~ at the wheel* conduire à son tour; *do s.o. a good ~* rendre service à qn **2** *v/t wheel* tourner; *~ the corner* tourner au coin de la rue; *~ one's back on s.o. also fig* tourner le dos à qn **3** *v/i of driver, car, wheel* tourner; *of person* se retourner; *~ right / left here* tournez à droite / gauche ici; *it has ~ed sour / cold* ça s'est aigri / refroidi; *he has ~ed 40* il a passé les 40 ans

♦ **turn around 1** *v/t object* tourner; *company* remettre sur pied; COMM *order* traiter **2** *v/i* se retourner; *with a car* faire demi-tour

♦ **turn away 1** *v/t* (*send away*) renvoyer **2** *v/i* (*walk away*) s'en aller; (*look away*) détourner le regard

♦ **turn back 1** *v/t edges, sheets* replier **2** *v/i of walkers etc, in course of action* faire demi-tour

♦ **turn down** *v/t offer, invitation* rejeter; *volume, TV, heating* baisser; *edge, collar* replier

♦ **turn in 1** *v/i* (*go to bed*) aller se coucher **2** *v/t to police* livrer

♦ **turn off 1** *v/t radio, TV, computer, heater* éteindre; *faucet* fermer; *engine* arrêter; F *sexually* couper l'envie à **2** *v/i of car, driver* tourner; *of machine* s'éteindre

♦ **turn on 1** *v/t radio, TV, computer, heater* allumer; *faucet* ouvrir; *engine* mettre en marche; F *sexually* exciter **2** *v/i of machine* s'allumer

♦ **turn out 1** *v/t lights* éteindre **2** *v/i*: *as it turned out* en l'occurence; *it turned out well* cela s'est bien fini; *he turned out to be ...* il s'est avéré être ...

♦ **turn over 1** *v/i in bed* se retourner; *of vehicle* se renverser **2** *v/t* (*put upside down*) renverser; *page* tourner; FIN avoir un chiffre d'affaires de

♦ **turn up 1** *v/t collar* remonter; *volume* augmenter; *heating* monter **2** *v/i* (*arrive*) arriver, se pointer F

turn·ing ['tɜːrnɪŋ] *in road* virage *m*

'turn·ing point tournant *m*

tur·nip ['tɜːrnɪp] navet *m*

'turn·out *at game etc* nombre *m* de spectateurs; **'turn·o·ver** FIN chiffre *m* d'affaires; **'turn·pike** autoroute *f* payante; **'turn sig·nal** MOT clignotant *m*; **'turn·stile** tourniquet *m*; **'turn·ta·ble** *of record player* platine *f*

tur·quoise ['tɜːrkwɔɪz] *adj* turquoise

tur·ret ['tʌrɪt] *of castle, tank* tourelle *f*

tur·tle ['tɜːrtl] tortue *f*

tur·tle·neck 'sweat·er pull *m* à col cheminée

tusk [tʌsk] défense *f*

tu·tor ['tuːtər] Br: *at university* professeur *m/f*; (*private*) ~ professeur *m* particulier

tux·e·do [tʌk'siːdoʊ] smoking *m*

TV [tiː'viː] télé *f*; *on ~* à la télé

TV din·ner plateau-repas *m*; **TV guide** guide *m* de télé; **TV pro·gram** programme *m* télé

twang [twæŋ] **1** *n in voice* accent *m* nasillard **2** *v/t guitar string* pincer

tweez·ers ['twiːzərz] *npl* pince *f* à épiler

twelfth [twelfθ] douzième; → *fifth*

twelve [twelv] douze

twen·ti·eth ['twentɪɪθ] vingtième; → *fifth*

twen·ty ['twentɪ] vingt; **~-four seven** 24 heures/24, 7 jours/7

twice [twaɪs] *adv* deux fois; *~ as*

much deux fois plus

twid·dle ['twɪdl] *v/t* tripoter; **~ one's thumbs** se tourner les pouces

twig [twɪg] *n* brindille *f*

twi·light ['twaɪlaɪt] crépuscule *m*

twin [twɪn] jumeau *m*, jumelle *f*

'twin beds *npl* lits *mpl* jumeaux

twinge [twɪndʒ] *of pain* élancement *m*

twin·kle ['twɪŋkl] *v/i* scintiller

twin 'room chambre *f* à lits jumeaux

'twin town ville *f* jumelée

twirl [twɜːrl] **1** *v/t* faire tourbillonner; *mustache* tortiller **2** *n of cream etc* spirale *f*

twist [twɪst] **1** *v/t* tordre; **~ one's ankle** se tordre la cheville **2** *v/i of road* faire des méandres; *of river* faire des lacets **3** *n in rope* entortillement *m*; *in road* lacet *m*; *in plot, story* dénouement *m* inattendu

twist·y ['twɪstɪ] *adj road* qui fait des lacets

twit [twɪt] *Br F* bêta *m F*, bêtasse *f F*

twitch [twɪtʃ] **1** *n nervous* tic *m* **2** *v/i* (*jerk*) faire des petits mouvements saccadés

twit·ter ['twɪtər] *v/i of birds* gazouiller

two [tuː] deux; **the ~ of them** les deux

two-faced ['tuːfeɪst] *adj* hypocrite; **'two-stroke** *adj engine* à deux temps; **two-way 'traf·fic** circulation *f* à double sens

ty·coon [taɪˈkuːn] magnat *m*

type [taɪp] **1** *n* (*sort*) type *m*; **what ~ of ...?** quel genre de ...? **2** *v/i* (*use a keyboard*) taper **3** *v/t with a typewriter* taper à la machine

type·writ·er ['taɪpraɪtər] machine *f* à écrire

ty·phoid ['taɪfɔɪd] typhoïde *f*

ty·phoon [taɪˈfuːn] typhon *m*

ty·phus ['taɪfəs] typhus *m*

typ·i·cal ['tɪpɪkl] *adj* typique; **that's ~ of you / him!** c'est bien de vous / lui!

typ·i·cal·ly ['tɪpɪklɪ] *adv* typiquement; **~, he was late** il était en retard comme d'habitude; **~ American** typiquement américain

typ·ist ['taɪpɪst] dactylo *m/f*

ty·po ['taɪpoʊ] coquille *f*

tyr·an·ni·cal [tɪˈrænɪkl] *adj* tyrannique

tyr·an·nize [tɪˈrænaɪz] *v/t* tyranniser

tyr·an·ny ['tɪrənɪ] tyrannie *f*

ty·rant ['taɪrənt] tyran *m*

tyre *Br* → **tire**[1]

U

ug·ly ['ʌglɪ] *adj* laid

UK [juːˈkeɪ] *abbr* (= **United Kingdom**) R.-U. *m* (= Royaume-Uni)

ul·cer ['ʌlsər] ulcère *m*

ul·ti·mate ['ʌltɪmət] *adj* (*best, definitive*) meilleur possible; (*final*) final; (*fundamental*) fondamental

ul·ti·mate·ly ['ʌltɪmətlɪ] *adv* (*in the end*) en fin de compte

ul·ti·ma·tum [ʌltɪˈmeɪtəm] ultimatum *m*

ul·tra·sound ['ʌltrəsaʊnd] MED ultrason *m*

ul·tra·vi·o·let [ʌltrəˈvaɪələt] *adj* ultra-

violet*

um·bil·i·cal cord [ʌmˈbɪlɪkl] cordon *m* ombilical

um·brel·la [ʌmˈbrelə] parapluie *m*

um·pire ['ʌmpaɪr] *n* arbitre *m/f*

ump·teen [ʌmpˈtiːn] *adj* F des centaines de

UN [juːˈen] *abbr*(= **United Nations**) O.N.U. *f* (= Organisation des Nations unies)

un·a·ble [ʌnˈeɪbl] *adj*: **be ~ to do sth** *not know how to* ne pas savoir faire qch; *not be in a position to* ne pas pouvoir faire qch

un·ac·cept·a·ble [ʌnək'septəbl] *adj* inacceptable

un·ac·count·a·ble [ʌnə'kauntəbl] *adj* inexplicable

un·ac·cus·tomed [ʌnə'kʌstəmd] *adj:* **be ~ to sth** ne pas être habitué à qch

un·a·dul·ter·at·ed [ʌnə'dʌltəreitid] *adj fig (absolute)* à l'état pur

un-A·mer·i·can [ʌnə'merikən] *adj (not fitting)* antiaméricain; **it's ~ to run down your country** un Américain ne défine pas son pays

u·nan·i·mous [ju:'næniməs] *adj verdict* unanime

u·nan·i·mous·ly [ju:'næniməsli] *adv vote, decide* à l'unanimité

un·ap·proach·a·ble [ʌnə'prouʃəbl] *adj person* d'un abord difficile

un·armed [ʌn'ɑ:rmd] *adj person* non armé; **~ combat** combat *m* à mains nues

un·as·sum·ing [ʌnə'su:miŋ] *adj* modeste

un·at·tached [ʌnə'tætʃt] *adj without a partner* sans attaches

un·at·tend·ed [ʌnə'tendid] *adj* laissé sans surveillance; **leave sth ~** laisser qch sans surveillance

un·au·thor·ized [ʌn'ɒːθəraizd] *adj* non autorisé

un·a·void·a·ble [ʌnə'vɔidəbl] *adj* inévitable

un·a·void·a·bly [ʌnə'vɔidəbli] *adv:* **be ~ detained** être dans l'impossibilité absolue de venir

un·a·ware [ʌnə'wer] *adj:* **be ~ of** ne pas avoir conscience de

un·a·wares [ʌnə'werz] *adv:* **catch s.o. ~** prendre qn au dépourvu

un·bal·anced [ʌn'bælənst] *adj also PSYCH* déséquilibré

un·bear·a·ble [ʌn'berəbl] *adj* insupportable

un·beat·a·ble [ʌn'biːtəbl] *adj* imbattable

un·beat·en [ʌn'biːtn] *adj team* invaincu

un·be·knownst [ʌnbi'nounst] *adv:* **~ to** à l'insu de; **~ to me** à mon insu

un·be·lie·va·ble [ʌnbi'liːvəbl] *adj also F* incroyable

un·bi·as(s)ed [ʌn'baiəst] *adj* impartial

un·block [ʌn'blɒːk] *v/t pipe* déboucher

un·born [ʌn'bɔːrn] *adj generations, child* à naître

un·break·a·ble [ʌn'breikəbl] *adj* incassable

un·but·ton [ʌn'bʌtn] *v/t* déboutonner

un·called-for [ʌn'kɒːldfɔːr] *adj* déplacé

un·can·ny [ʌn'kæni] *adj* étrange, mystérieux*

un·ceas·ing [ʌn'siːsiŋ] *adj* incessant

un·cer·tain [ʌn'sɜːrtn] *adj* incertain; **be ~ about sth** avoir des doutes à propos de qch

un·cer·tain·ty [ʌn'sɜːrtnti] *of the future* caractère *m* incertain; **there is still ~ about ...** des incertitudes demeurent quant à ...

un·checked [ʌn'tʃekt] *adj:* **let sth go ~** ne rien faire pour empêcher qch

un·cle ['ʌŋkl] *oncle m*

un·com·for·ta·ble [ʌn'kʌmftəbl] *adj* inconfortable; **feel ~ about sth** être gêné par qch; **I feel ~ with him** je suis mal à l'aise avec lui

un·com·mon [ʌn'kɑːmən] *adj* inhabituel*

un·com·pro·mis·ing [ʌn'kɑːmprə-maiziŋ] *adj* intransigeant

un·con·cerned [ʌnkən'sɜːrnd] *adj:* **be ~ about s.o. / sth** ne pas se soucier de qn / qch

un·con·di·tion·al [ʌnkən'diʃnl] *adj* sans conditions

un·con·scious [ʌn'kɑːnʃəs] *adj MED, PSYCH* inconscient; **knock s.o. ~** assommer qn; **be ~ of sth** *(not aware)* ne pas avoir conscience de qch

un·con·trol·la·ble [ʌnkən'trouləbl] *adj* incontrôlable

un·con·ven·tion·al [ʌnkən'venʃnl] *adj* non conventionnel

un·co·op·er·a·tive [ʌnkou'ɑːpərətiv] *adj* peu coopératif*

un·cork [ʌn'kɔːrk] *v/t bottle* déboucher

un·cov·er [ʌn'kʌvər] *v/t* découvrir

un·dam·aged [ʌn'dæmidʒd] *adj* intact

un·daunt·ed [ʌn'dɒːntid] *adv:* **carry on ~** continuer sans se laisser décou-

U

rager

un·de·cid·ed [ʌndɪˈsaɪdɪd] *adj question* laissé en suspens; *be ~ about s.o. / sth* être indécis à propos de qn / qch

un·de·ni·a·ble [ʌndɪˈnaɪəbl] *adj* indéniable

un·de·ni·a·bly [ʌndɪˈnaɪəblɪ] *adv* indéniablement

un·der [ˈʌndər] **1** *prep (beneath)* sous; *(less than)* moins de; *he is ~ 30* il a moins de 30 ans; *it is ~ review / investigation* cela fait l'objet d'un examen / d'une enquête **2** *adv (anesthetized)* inconscient

un·der·age *adj* mineur; *~ drinking* la consommation d'alcool par les mineurs

'un·der·arm *adv throw* par en-dessous

'un·der·car·riage train *m* d'atterrissage

'un·der·cov·er *adj* clandestin; *~ agent* agent *m* secret

un·der'cut *v/t (pret & pp -cut)* COMM: *~ the competition* vendre moins cher que la concurrence

'un·der·dog outsider *m*

un·der'done *adj meat* pas trop cuit; *pej* pas assez cuit

un·der·es·ti·mate *v/t person, skills, task* sous-estimer

un·der·ex'posed *adj* PHOT sous-exposé

un·der'fed *adj* mal nourri

un·der'go *v/t (pret -went, pp -gone)* subir

un·der'grad·u·ate *Br* étudiant(e) *(de D.E.U.G. ou de licence)*

'un·der·ground 1 *adj passages etc* souterrain; POL *resistance, newpaper etc* clandestin **2** *adv work* sous terre; *go ~* POL passer dans la clandestinité

'un·der·growth sous-bois *m*

un·der'hand *adj (devious)* sournois; *do sth ~* faire qch en sous-main

un·der'lie *v/t (pret -lay, pp -lain)* sous-tendre

un·der'line *v/t text* souligner

un·der'ly·ing *adj causes, problems* sous-jacent

un·der'mine *v/t* saper

un·der·neath [ʌndərˈniːθ] **1** *prep* sous

2 *adv* dessous

'un·der·pants *npl* slip *m*

'un·der·pass *for pedestrians* passage *m* souterrain

un·der·priv·i·leged [ʌndərˈprɪvɪlɪdʒd] *adj* défavorisé

un·der'rate *v/t* sous-estimer

'un·der·shirt maillot *m* de corps

un·der·sized [ʌndərˈsaɪzd] *adj* trop petit

'un·der·skirt jupon *m*

un·der·staffed [ʌndərˈstæft] *adj* en manque de personnel

un·der·stand [ʌndərˈstænd] **1** *v/t (pret & pp -stood)* comprendre; *they are understood to be in Canada* on pense qu'ils sont au Canada **2** *v/i* comprendre

un·der·stand·a·ble [ʌndərˈstændəbl] *adj* compréhensible

un·der·stand·a·bly [ʌndərˈstændəblɪ] *adv* naturellement

un·der·stand·ing [ʌndərˈstændɪŋ] **1** *adj person* compréhensif* **2** *n of problem, situation* compréhension *f; (agreement)* accord *m; my ~ of the situation is that ...* ce que je comprends dans cette situation, c'est que ...; *we have an ~ that ...* il y a un accord entre nous selon lequel ...; *on the ~ that ...* à condition que ...

'un·der·state·ment euphémisme *m*

un·der'take *v/t (pret -took, pp -taken)* task entreprendre; *~ to do sth (agree to)* s'engager à faire qch

un·der·tak·er [ˈʌndərteɪkər] *Br* entrepreneur(-euse) des pompes funèbres

'un·der·tak·ing *(enterprise)* entreprise *f; (promise)* engagement *m*

un·der'val·ue *v/t* sous-estimer

'un·der·wear sous-vêtements *mpl*

un·der'weight *adj* en-dessous de son poids normal

'un·der·world *criminal* monde *m* du crime organisé

un·der'write *v/t (pret -wrote, pp -written)* FIN souscrire

un·de·served [ʌndɪˈzɜːrvd] *adj* non mérité

un·de·sir·a·ble [ʌndɪˈzaɪrəbl] *adj* indésirable; **~ element** *person* élément *m* indésirable

un·dis·put·ed [ʌndɪˈspjuːtɪd] *adj champion, leader* incontestable

un·do [ʌnˈduː] *v/t (pret* **-did**, *pp* **-done**) défaire

un·doubt·ed·ly [ʌnˈdaʊtɪdlɪ] *adv* à n'en pas douter

un·dreamt-of [ʌnˈdremtəv] *adj riches* inouï

un·dress [ʌnˈdres] **1** *v/t* déshabiller; **get ~ed** se déshabiller **2** *v/i* se déshabiller

un·due [ʌnˈduː] *adj (excessive)* excessif*

un·du·ly [ʌnˈduːlɪ] *adv (excessively)* excessivement

un·earth [ʌnˈɜːθ] *v/t also fig* déterrer

un·earth·ly [ʌnˈɜːθlɪ] *adj:* **at this ~ hour** à cette heure impossible

un·eas·y [ʌnˈiːzɪ] *adj relationship, peace* incertain; **feel ~ about** avoir des doutes sur; **I feel ~ about signing this** je ne suis pas sûr de vouloir signer cela

un·eat·a·ble [ʌnˈiːtəbl] *adj* immangeable

un·e·co·nom·ic [ʌniːkəˈnɒmɪk] *adj* pas rentable

un·ed·u·cat·ed [ʌnˈedʒəkeɪtɪd] *adj* sans instruction

un·em·ployed [ʌnɪmˈplɔɪd] **1** *adj* au chômage **2** *npl:* **the ~** les chômeurs(-euses)

un·em·ploy·ment [ʌnɪmˈplɔɪmənt] chômage *m*

un·end·ing [ʌnˈendɪŋ] *adj* sans fin

un·e·qual [ʌnˈiːkwəl] *adj* inégal; **be ~ to the task** ne pas être à la hauteur de la tâche

un·er·ring [ʌnˈɜːrɪŋ] *adj judgment, instinct* infaillible

un·e·ven [ʌnˈiːvn] *adj surface, ground* irrégulier*

un·e·ven·ly [ʌnˈiːvnlɪ] *adv distributed, applied* inégalement; **be ~ matched** *of two contestants* être mal assorti

un·event·ful [ʌnɪˈventfl] *adj day, journey* sans événement

un·ex·pec·ted [ʌnɪkˈspektɪd] *adj* inattendu

un·ex·pec·ted·ly [ʌnɪkˈspektɪdlɪ] *adv* inopinément

un·fair [ʌnˈfer] *adj* injuste

un·faith·ful [ʌnˈfeɪθfl] *adj husband, wife* infidèle; **be ~ to s.o.** tromper qn

un·fa·mil·i·ar [ʌnfəˈmɪljər] *adj* peu familier*; **be ~ with sth** ne pas (bien) connaître qch

un·fas·ten [ʌnˈfæsn] *v/t belt* défaire

un·fa·vo·ra·ble [ʌnˈfeɪvərəbl] *adj* défavorable

un·feel·ing [ʌnˈfiːlɪŋ] *adj person* dur

un·fin·ished [ʌnˈfɪnɪʃt] *adj* inachevé

un·fit [ʌnˈfɪt] *adj physically* peu en forme; *morally* indigne; **be ~ to eat / drink** être impropre à la consommation

un·fix [ʌnˈfɪks] *v/t part* détacher

un·flap·pa·ble [ʌnˈflæpəbl] *adj* imperturbable

un·fold [ʌnˈfoʊld] **1** *v/t sheets, letter* déplier; *one's arms* ouvrir **2** *v/i of story etc* se dérouler; *of view* se déployer

un·fore·seen [ʌnfɔːrˈsiːn] *adj* imprévu

un·for·get·ta·ble [ʌnfərˈgetəbl] *adj* inoubliable

un·for·giv·a·ble [ʌnfərˈgɪvəbl] *adj* impardonnable; **that was ~ of you** c'était impardonnable de votre part

un·for·tu·nate [ʌnˈfɔːrtʃənət] *adj* malheureux*; **that's ~ for you** c'est dommage pour vous

un·for·tu·nate·ly [ʌnˈfɔːrtʃənətlɪ] *adv* malheureusement

un·found·ed [ʌnˈfaʊndɪd] *adj* non fondé

un·friend·ly [ʌnˈfrendlɪ] *adj person, welcome, hotel* froid; *software* rébarbatif*

un·fur·nished [ʌnˈfɜːrnɪʃt] *adj* non meublé

un·god·ly [ʌnˈgɑːdlɪ] *adj:* **at this ~ hour** à cette heure impossible

un·grate·ful [ʌnˈgreɪtfl] *adj* ingrat

un·hap·pi·ness [ʌnˈhæpɪnɪs] chagrin *m*

un·hap·py [ʌnˈhæpɪ] *adj* malheureux*; *customers etc* mécontent (**with** de)

un·harmed [ʌnˈhɑːrmd] *adj* indemne

un·health·y [ʌnˈhelθɪ] *adj person* en

mauvaise santé; *food, atmosphere* malsain; *economy, finances* qui se porte mal

un-heard-of [ʌnˈhɜːrdəv] *adj*: **be ~** ne s'être jamais vu; *it was ~ for a woman to be in the police force* personne n'avait jamais vu une femme dans la police

un-hurt [ʌnˈhɜːrt] *adj* indemne

un-hy-gi-en-ic [ʌnhaɪˈdʒiːnɪk] insalubre

u-ni-fi-ca-tion [juːnɪfɪˈkeɪʃn] unification *f*

u-ni-form [ˈjuːnɪfɔːrm] **1** *n* uniforme *m* **2** *adj* uniforme

u-ni-fy [ˈjuːnɪfaɪ] *v/t (pret & pp -ied)* unifier

u-ni-lat-er-al [juːnɪˈlætərəl] *adj* unilatéral

u-ni-lat-er-al-ly [juːnɪˈlætərəli] *adv* unilatéralement

un-i-ma-gi-na-ble [ʌnɪˈmædʒɪnəbl] *adj* inimaginable

un-i-ma-gi-na-tive [ʌnɪˈmædʒɪnətɪv] *adj* qui manque d'imagination

un-im-por-tant [ʌnɪmˈpɔːrtənt] *adj* sans importance

un-in-hab-i-ta-ble [ʌnɪnˈhæbɪtəbl] *adj building, region* inhabitable

un-in-hab-it-ed [ʌnɪnˈhæbɪtɪd] *adj* inhabité

un-in-jured [ʌnˈɪndʒərd] *adj* indemne

un-in-tel-li-gi-ble [ʌnɪnˈtelɪdʒəbl] *adj* inintelligible

un-in-ten-tion-al [ʌnɪnˈtenʃnl] *adj* non intentionnel*; *that was ~* ce n'était pas voulu

un-in-ten-tion-al-ly [ʌnɪnˈtenʃnli] *adv* sans le vouloir

un-in-te-rest-ing [ʌnˈɪntrəstɪŋ] *adj* inintéressant

un-in-ter-rupt-ed [ʌnɪntəˈrʌptɪd] *adj sleep, two hours' work* ininterrompu

u-nion [ˈjuːnjən] POL union *f*; *(labor ~)* syndicat *m*

u-nique [juːˈniːk] *adj also* F *(very good)* unique

u-nit [ˈjuːnɪt] unité *f*

u-nit 'cost COMM coût *m* à l'unité

u-nite [juːˈnaɪt] **1** *v/t* unir **2** *v/i* s'unir

u-nit-ed [juːˈnaɪtɪd] *adj* uni; *efforts* conjoint

U-nit-ed 'King-dom Royaume-Uni *m*

U-nit-ed 'Na-tions Nations *fpl* Unies

U-nit-ed States (of A-mer-i-ca) États--Unis *mpl* (d'Amérique)

u-ni-ty [ˈjuːnətɪ] unité *f*

u-ni-ver-sal [juːnɪˈvɜːrsl] *adj* universel*

u-ni-ver-sal-ly [juːnɪˈvɜːrsəli] *adv* universellement

u-ni-verse [ˈjuːnɪvɜːrs] univers *m*

u-ni-ver-si-ty [juːnɪˈvɜːrsətɪ] **1** *n* université *f*; *he's at ~* il est à l'université **2** *adj* d'université

un-just [ʌnˈdʒʌst] *adj* injuste

un-kempt [ʌnˈkempt] *adj* négligé

un-kind [ʌnˈkaɪnd] *adj* méchant, désagréable

un-known [ʌnˈnoun] **1** *adj* inconnu **2** *n*: *a journey into the ~* un voyage dans l'inconnu

un-lead-ed [ʌnˈledɪd] *adj gas* sans plomb

un-less [ənˈles] *conj* à moins que *(+subj)*; *don't say anything ~ you are sure* ne dites rien si vous n'êtes pas sûr

un-like [ʌnˈlaɪk] *prep*: *the photograph was completely ~ her* la photographie ne lui ressemblait pas du tout; *it's ~ him to drink so much* cela ne lui ressemble pas de boire autant

un-like-ly [ʌnˈlaɪklɪ] *adj* improbable; *he is ~ to win* il a peu de chances de gagner; *it is ~ that ...* il est improbable que ... *(+subj)*

un-lim-it-ed [ʌnˈlɪmɪtɪd] *adj* illimité

un-list-ed [ʌnˈlɪstɪd] *adj* TELEC sur liste rouge

un-load [ʌnˈloud] *v/t* décharger

un-lock [ʌnˈlɑːk] *v/t* ouvrir (avec une clef)

un-luck-i-ly [ʌnˈlʌkɪlɪ] *adv* malheureusement

un-luck-y [ʌnˈlʌkɪ] *adj day* de malchance; *choice* malheureux*; *person* malchanceux*; *that was so ~ for you!* tu n'as vraiment pas eu de chance!

un-made-up [ʌnmeɪdˈʌp] *adj face* non

maquillé

un·manned [ʌn'mænd] *adj spacecraft* sans équipage

un·mar·ried [ʌn'mærɪd] *adj* non marié

un·mis·ta·ka·ble [ʌnmɪ'steɪkəbl] *adj handwriting* reconnaissable entre mille

un·moved [ʌn'muːvd] *adj emotionally* pas touché

un·mu·si·cal [ʌn'mjuːzɪkl] *adj person* pas musicien*; *sounds* discordant

un·nat·u·ral [ʌn'nætʃrəl] *adj* contre nature; *it's not ~ to be annoyed* il n'est pas anormal d'être agacé

un·ne·ces·sa·ry [ʌn'nesəserɪ] *adj* non nécessaire

un·nerv·ing [ʌn'nɜːrvɪŋ] *adj* déstabilisant

un·no·ticed [ʌn'noʊtɪst] *adj*: *it went ~* c'est passé inaperçu

un·ob·tain·a·ble [ʌnəb'teɪnəbl] *adj goods* qu'on ne peut se procurer; TELEC hors service

un·ob·tru·sive [ʌnəb'truːsɪv] *adj* discret

un·oc·cu·pied [ʌn'ɑːkjʊpaɪd] *adj* (*empty*) vide; *position* vacant; *person* désœuvré

un·of·fi·cial [ʌnə'fɪʃl] *adj* non officiel*

un·of·fi·cial·ly [ʌnə'fɪʃlɪ] *adv* non officiellement

un·pack [ʌn'pæk] **1** *v/t case* défaire; *boxes* déballer, vider **2** *v/i* défaire sa valise

un·paid [ʌn'peɪd] *adj work* non rémunéré

un·pleas·ant [ʌn'pleznt] *adj* désagréable; *he was very ~ to her* il a été très désagréable avec elle

un·plug [ʌn'plʌg] *v/t* (*pret & pp* **-ged**) *TV, computer* débrancher

un·pop·u·lar [ʌn'pɑːpjələr] *adj* impopulaire

un·pre·ce·den·ted [ʌn'presɪdentɪd] *adj* sans précédent

un·pre·dict·a·ble [ʌnprɪ'dɪktəbl] *adj person, weather* imprévisible

un·pre·ten·tious [ʌnprɪ'tenʃəs] *adj person, style, hotel* modeste

un·prin·ci·pled [ʌn'prɪnsɪpld] *adj* sans scrupules

un·pro·duc·tive [ʌnprə'dʌktɪv] *adj meeting, discussion, land* improductif*

un·pro·fes·sion·al [ʌnprə'feʃnl] *adj person, behavior* non professionnel*; *workmanship* peu professionnel; *it's very ~ not to …* ce n'est pas du tout professionnel de ne pas …

un·prof·i·ta·ble [ʌn'prɑːfɪtəbl] *adj* non profitable

un·pro·nounce·a·ble [ʌnprə'naʊnsəbl] *adj* imprononçable

un·pro·tect·ed [ʌnprə'tektɪd] *adj* sans protection; *~ sex* rapports *mpl* sexuels non protégés

un·pro·voked [ʌnprə'voʊkt] *adj attack* non provoqué

un·qual·i·fied [ʌn'kwɑːlɪfaɪd] *adj* non qualifié; *acceptance* inconditionnel*

un·ques·tion·a·bly [ʌn'kwestʃnəblɪ] *adv* (*without doubt*) sans aucun doute

un·ques·tion·ing [ʌn'kwestʃnɪŋ] *adj attitude, loyalty* aveugle

un·rav·el [ʌn'rævl] *v/t* (*pret & pp* **-ed**, *Br* **-led**) *knitting etc* défaire; *mystery, complexities* résoudre

un·read·a·ble [ʌn'riːdəbl] *adj book* illisible

un·re·al [ʌn'rɪəl] *adj* irréel*; *this is ~!* F je crois rêver!

un·re·a·lis·tic [ʌnrɪə'lɪstɪk] *adj* irréaliste

un·rea·so·na·ble [ʌn'riːznəbl] *adj* déraisonnable

un·re·lat·ed [ʌnrɪ'leɪtɪd] *adj* sans relation (*to* avec)

un·re·lent·ing [ʌnrɪ'lentɪŋ] *adj* incessant

un·re·li·a·ble [ʌnrɪ'laɪəbl] *adj* pas fiable

un·rest [ʌn'rest] agitation *f*

un·re·strained [ʌnrɪ'streɪnd] *adj emotions* non contenu

un·road·wor·thy [ʌn'roʊdwɜːrðɪ] *adj* qui n'est pas en état de rouler

un·roll [ʌn'roʊl] *v/t carpet* dérouler

un·ru·ly [ʌn'ruːlɪ] *adj* indiscipliné

un·safe [ʌn'seɪf] *adj* dangereux*

un·san·i·tar·y [ʌn'sænɪterɪ] *adj conditions, drains* insalubre

un·sat·is·fac·to·ry [ʌnsætɪs'fæktərɪ] *adj* insatisfaisant; (*unacceptable*) inac-

U

ceptable

un·sa·vo·ry [ʌnˈseɪvərɪ] *adj* louche

un·scathed [ʌnˈskeɪðd] *adj* (*not injured*) indemne; (*not damaged*) intact

un·screw [ʌnˈskru:] *v/t sth screwed on* dévisser; *top* décapsuler

un·scru·pu·lous [ʌnˈskru:pjələs] *adj* peu scrupuleux*

un·self·ish [ʌnˈselfɪʃ] *adj* désintéressé

un·set·tled [ʌnˈsetld] *adj on* incertain; *lifestyle* instable; *bills* non réglé; *issue, question* non décidé

un·shav·en [ʌnˈʃeɪvn] *adj* mal rasé

un·sight·ly [ʌnˈsaɪtlɪ] *adj* affreux*

un·skilled [ʌnˈskɪld] *adj worker* non qualifié

un·so·cia·ble [ʌnˈsouʃəbl] *adj* peu sociable

un·so·phis·ti·cat·ed [ʌnsəˈfɪstɪkeɪtɪd] *adj person, beliefs, equipment* peu sophistiqué

un·sta·ble [ʌnˈsteɪbl] *adj* instable

un·stead·y [ʌnˈstedɪ] *adj on one's feet* chancelant; *ladder* branlant

un·stint·ing [ʌnˈstɪntɪŋ] *adj* sans restriction; **be ~ in one's efforts** ne pas ménager sa peine (**to** pour)

un·stuck [ʌnˈstʌk] *adj*: **come ~** *of notice etc* se détacher; *F of plan etc* tomber à l'eau F

un·suc·cess·ful [ʌnsəkˈsesfl] *adj attempt* infructueux*; *artist, writer* qui n'a pas de succès; *candidate, marriage* malheureux*; **it was ~** c'était un échec; **he tried but was ~** il a essayé mais n'a pas réussi

un·suc·cess·ful·ly [ʌnsəkˈsesflɪ] *adv try, apply* sans succès

un·suit·a·ble [ʌnˈsu:təbl] *adj* inapproprié; **the movie is ~ for children** le film ne convient pas aux enfants

un·sus·pect·ing [ʌnsəˈpektɪŋ] *adj* qui ne se doute de rien

un·swerv·ing [ʌnˈswɜ:rvɪŋ] *adj loyalty, devotion* inébranlable

un·think·a·ble [ʌnˈθɪŋkəbl] *adj* impensable

un·ti·dy [ʌnˈtaɪdɪ] *adj* en désordre

un·tie [ʌnˈtaɪ] *v/t laces, knot* défaire; *prisoner, hands* détacher

un·til [ənˈtɪl] **1** *prep* jusqu'à; **from**

Monday ~ Friday de lundi à vendredi; **not ~ Friday** pas avant vendredi; **it won't be finished ~ July** ce ne sera pas fini avant le mois de juillet **2** *conj* jusqu'à ce que; **can you wait ~ I'm ready?** est-ce que vous pouvez attendre que je sois prêt?; **they won't do anything ~ you say so** ils ne feront rien jusqu'à ce que tu le leur dises

un·time·ly [ʌnˈtaɪmlɪ] *adj death* prématuré

un·tir·ing [ʌnˈtaɪrɪŋ] *adj efforts* infatigable

un·told [ʌnˈtould] *adj riches, suffering* inouï; *story* inédit

un·trans·lat·a·ble [ʌntrænsˈleɪtəbl] *adj* intraduisible

un·true [ʌnˈtru:] *adj* faux*

un·used[1] [ʌnˈju:zd] *adj goods* non utilisé

un·used[2] [ʌnˈju:st] *adj*: **be ~ to sth** ne pas être habitué à qch; **be ~ to doing sth** ne pas être habitué à faire qch

un·u·su·al [ʌnˈju:ʒl] *adj* inhabituel*; (*strange*) bizarre; *story* insolite; *not the standard* hors norme; **it's ~ for him to ...** il est rare qu'il ... (+*subj*)

un·u·su·al·ly [ʌnˈju:ʒəlɪ] *adv* anormalement, exceptionnellement

un·veil [ʌnˈveɪl] *v/t memorial, statue etc* dévoiler

un·well [ʌnˈwel] *adj* malade

un·will·ing [ʌnˈwɪlɪŋ] *adj*: **be ~ to do sth** refuser de faire qch

un·will·ing·ly [ʌnˈwɪlɪŋlɪ] *adv* à contre-cœur

un·wind [ʌnˈwaɪnd] **1** *v/t* (*pret & pp* **-wound**) *tape* dérouler **2** *v/i of tape, story* se dérouler; (*relax*) se détendre

un·wise [ʌnˈwaɪz] *adj* malavisé

un·wrap [ʌnˈræp] *v/t* (*pret & pp* **-ped**) *gift* déballer

un·writ·ten [ʌnˈrɪtn] *adj law, rule* tacite

un·zip [ʌnˈzɪp] *v/t* (*pret & pp* **-ped**) *dress etc* descendre la fermeture-éclair de; COMPUT décompresser

up [ʌp] **1** *adv*: **~ in the sky / on the roof** dans le ciel / sur le toit; **~ here** ici; **~ there** là-haut; **be ~** (*out of bed*) être debout; *of sun* être levé; (*built*) être construit; *of shelves* être en place; *of prices, temperature* avoir augmenté; (*have expired*) être expiré; *what's ~?* F qu'est-ce qu'il y a?; *~ to 1989* jusqu'à 1989; *he came ~ to me* il s'est approché de moi; *what are you ~ to these days?* qu'est-ce que tu fais en ce moment?; *what are those kids ~ to?* que font ces enfants?; *be ~ to something* être sur un mauvais coup; *I don't feel ~ to it* je ne m'en sens pas le courage; *it's ~ to you* c'est toi qui décides; *it's ~ to them to solve it* c'est à eux de le résoudre; *be ~ and about* *after illness* être de nouveau sur pied **2** *prep*: *further ~ the mountain* un peu plus haut sur la montagne; *he climbed ~ a tree* il est monté à un arbre; *they ran ~ the street* ils ont remonté la rue en courant; *the water goes ~ this pipe* l'eau monte par ce tuyau; *we traveled ~ to Paris* nous sommes montés à Paris **3** *n*: *~s and downs* hauts *mpl* et bas

'up·bring·ing éducation *f*

'up·com·ing *adj* (*forthcoming*) en perspective

up·date¹ ['ʌpdeɪt] *v/t file, records* mettre à jour; *~ s.o. on sth* mettre / tenir qn au courant de qch

'up·date² *n* *of files, records, software* mise *f* à jour

'up·grade *v/t computers etc*, (*replace with new versions*) moderniser; *ticket etc* surclasser; *product* améliorer

up·heav·al [ʌp'hi:vl] bouleversement *m*

up·hill [ʌp'hɪl] **1** *adv*: *walk / go ~* monter **2** *adj*: ['ʌphɪl] : *~ walk* montée *f*; *it was an ~ struggle* ça a été très difficile

up·hold *v/t* (*pret & pp* **-held**) *traditions, rights, decision* maintenir

up·hol·ster·y [ʌp'hoʊlstərɪ] *fabric* garniture *f*; *padding* rembourrage *m*

'up·keep *of buildings etc* maintien *m*

'up·load *v/t* COMPUT transférer

up·mar·ket *adj Br: restaurant, hotel* chic *inv*; *product* haut de gamme

up·on [ə'pɑːn] *prep* → **on**

up·per ['ʌpər] *adj part of sth* supérieur; *~ atmosphere* partie *f* supérieure de l'atmosphère

up·per-'class *adj accent, family* aristocratique, de la haute F

up·per 'clas·ses *npl* aristocratie *f*

'up·right **1** *adj* citizen droit **2** *adv* sit (bien) droit **3** *n* (*also: ~ piano*) piano *f* droit

up·ris·ing ['ʌpraɪzɪŋ] soulèvement *m*

'up·roar vacarme *m*; *fig* protestations *fpl*

'up·scale *adj restaurant, hotel* chic *inv*; *product* haut de gamme

up·set **1** *v/t* (*pret & pp* **-set**) *drink, glass* renverser; *emotionally* contrarier **2** *adj emotionally* contrarié, vexé; *get ~ about sth* être contrarié par qch; *why's she ~?* qu'est-ce qu'elle a?; *have an ~ stomach* avoir l'estomac dérangé

up·set·ting *adj* contrariant

'up·shot (*result, outcome*) résultat *m*

up·side 'down *adv* à l'envers; *car* renversé; *turn sth ~* tourner qch à l'envers

up·stairs **1** *adv* en haut; *~ from us* au-dessus de chez nous **2** *adj room* d'en haut

'up·start arriviste *m/f*

up·stream *adv* en remontant le courant

'up·take: *be quick / slow on the ~* F piger rapidement / lentement F

up·tight *adj* F (*nervous*) tendu; (*inhibited*) coincé

up-to-'date *adj* à jour

'up·turn *in economy* reprise *f*

up·ward ['ʌpwərd] *adv*: *fly ~* s'élever dans le ciel; *move sth ~* élever qch; *~ of 10,000* au-delà de 10 000

u·ra·ni·um [juˈreɪnɪəm] uranium *m*

ur·ban ['ɜːrbən] *adj* urbain

ur·ban·i·za·tion [ɜːrbənərˈzeɪʃn] urbanisation *f*

ur·chin ['ɜːrtʃɪn] gamin *m*

urge [ɜːrdʒ] **1** *n* (forte) envie *f* **2** *v/t*: *~ s.o. to do sth* encourager qn à faire qch

♦ urge on *v/t* (*encourage*) encourager

ur·gen·cy ['ɜːrdʒənsɪ] *of situation* ur-

U

gence f

ur·gent ['ɜːrdʒənt] *adj* urgent

u·ri·nate ['jʊrəneɪt] *v/i* uriner

u·rine ['jʊrɪn] urine *f*

urn [ɜːrn] urne *f*

US [juː'es] *abbr* (= **United States**) USA *mpl*

us [ʌs] *pron* nous; **he knows ~** il nous connaît; **he gave ~ a dollar** il nous a donné un dollar; **that's for ~** c'est pour nous; **who's that? - it's ~** qui est-ce? - c'est nous

USA [juːes'eɪ] *abbr* (= **United States of America**) USA *mpl*

us·a·ble ['juːzəbl] *adj* utilisable

us·age ['juːzɪdʒ] *linguistic* usage *m*

use 1 *v/t* [juːz] *also pej: person* utiliser; **I could ~ a drink** F j'ai besoin d'un verre **2** *n* [juːs] utilisation *f*; **be of great ~ to s.o.** servir beaucoup à qn; **that's of no ~ to me** cela ne me sert à rien; **is that of any ~?** est-ce que cela vous sert?; **it's no ~** ce n'est pas la peine; **it's no ~ try·ing / waiting** ce n'est pas la peine d'essayer / d'attendre

♦ **use up** *v/t* épuiser

used¹ [juːzd] *adj car etc* d'occasion

used² [juːst] *adj*: **be ~ to s.o. / sth** être habitué à qn / qch; **get ~ to s.o. / sth** s'habituer à qn / qch; **be ~ to doing sth** être habitué à faire qch; **get ~ to doing sth** s'habituer à faire qch

used³ [juːst]: **I ~ to work there** je tra-

vaillais là-bas avant; **I ~ to know him well** je l'ai bien connu autrefois

use·ful ['juːsfəl] *adj* utile

use·ful·ness ['juːsfəlnɪs] utilité *f*

use·less ['juːslɪs] *adj* inutile; F (*no good*) nul F; **it's ~ trying** ce n'est pas la peine d'essayer

us·er ['juːzər] *of product* utilisateur (-trice) *m(f)*

us·er-'friend·li·ness facilité *f* d'utilisation; COMPUT convivialité *f*

us·er-'friend·ly *adj* facile à utiliser; COMPUT convivial

ush·er ['ʌʃər] *n at wedding* placeur *m*

♦ **usher in** *v/t new era* marquer le début de

u·su·al ['juːʒl] *adj* habituel*; **as ~** comme d'habitude; **the ~, please** comme d'habitude, s'il vous plaît

u·su·al·ly ['juːʒəlɪ] *adv* d'habitude

u·ten·sil [juː'tensl] ustensile *m*

u·te·rus ['juːtərəs] utérus *m*

u·til·i·ty [juː'tɪlətɪ] (*usefulness*) utilité *f*; **public utilities** services *mpl* publics

u'til·i·ty pole poteau *m* télégraphique

u·til·ize ['juːtɪlaɪz] *v/t* utiliser

ut·most ['ʌtmoust] **1** *adj* le plus grand **2** *n*: **do one's ~** faire tout son possible

ut·ter ['ʌtər] **1** *adj* total **2** *v/t sound* prononcer

ut·ter·ly ['ʌtərlɪ] *adv* totalement

U-turn ['juːtɜːrn] MOT demi-tour *m*; *fig* revirement *m*

V

va·can·cy ['veɪkənsɪ] *Br: at work* poste *m* vacant, poste *m* à pourvoir

va·cant ['veɪkənt] *adj building* inoccupé; *look, expression* vide, absent; *Br: position* vacant, à pourvoir

va·cant·ly ['veɪkəntlɪ] *adv stare* d'un air absent

va·cate [veɪ'keɪt] *v/t room* libérer

va·ca·tion [veɪ'keɪʃn] *n* vacances *fpl*; **be on ~** être en vacances; **go to Egypt / Paris on ~** passer ses vacances en Égypte / à Paris, aller en vacances en Égypte / à Paris

va·ca·tion·er [veɪ'keɪʃənər] vacancier

m

vac·cin·ate ['væksineit] *v/t* vacciner; **be ~d against sth** être vacciné contre qch

vac·cin·a·tion [væksı'neıʃn] vaccination *f*

vac·cine ['væksi:n] vaccin *m*

vac·u·um ['vækjuəm] **1** *n* vide *m* **2** *v/t floors* passer l'aspirateur sur

'vac·u·um clean·er aspirateur *m*; **'vac·u·um flask** thermos *m or f*; **vac·u·um-'packed** *adj* emballé sous vide

va·gi·na [və'dʒaınə] vagin *m*

va·gi·nal ['vædʒınl] *adj* vaginal

va·grant ['veıgrənt] vagabond *m*

vague [veig] *adj* vague

vague·ly ['veıglı] *adv* vaguement

vain [vein] **1** *adj person* vaniteux*; *hope* vain **2** *n*: **in ~** en vain, vainement; **their efforts were in ~** leurs efforts n'ont servi à rien

val·en·tine ['væləntaın] *card* carte *f* de la Saint-Valentin; **Valentine's Day** la Saint-Valentin

val·et ['væleı] **1** *n person* valet *m* de chambre **2** *v/t* ['vælət] nettoyer; **have one's car ~ed** faire nettoyer sa voiture

'val·et ser·vice *for clothes, cars* service *m* de nettoyage

val·iant ['væljənt] *adj* courageux*, vaillant

val·iant·ly ['væljəntlı] *adv* courageusement, vaillamment

val·id ['vælıd] *adj* valable

val·i·date ['vælıdeıt] *v/t with official stamp* valider; *claim, theory* confirmer

va·lid·i·ty [və'lıdətı] validité *f*; *of argument* justesse *f*, pertinence *f*; *of claim* bien-fondé *m*

val·ley ['vælı] vallée *f*

val·u·a·ble ['væljubl] **1** *adj ring, asset* de valeur, précieux*; *colleague, help, advice* précieux* **2** *npl*: **~s** objets *mpl* de valeur

val·u·a·tion [vælju'eıʃn] estimation *f*, expertise *f*

val·ue ['vælju:] **1** *n* valeur *f*; **be good ~** offrir un bon rapport qualité-prix; **you got good ~** tu as fait une bonne

affaire; **get ~ for money** en avoir pour son argent; **rise / fall in ~** prendre / perdre de la valeur **2** *v/t* tenir à, attacher un grand prix à; **have an object ~d** faire estimer un objet

valve [vælv] *in machine* soupape *f*, valve *f*; *in heart* valvule *f*

van [væn] *small* camionnette *f*; *large* fourgon *m*

van·dal ['vændl] vandale *m*

van·dal·ism ['vændəlızm] vandalisme *m*

van·dal·ize ['vændəlaız] *v/t* vandaliser, saccager

van·guard ['vængɑ:rd]: **be in the ~ of** *fig* être à l'avant-garde de

va·nil·la [və'nılə] **1** *n* vanille *f* **2** *adj* à la vanille

van·ish ['vænıʃ] *v/i* disparaître; *of clouds, sadness* se dissiper

van·i·ty ['vænətı] *of person* vanité *f*

'van·i·ty case vanity(-case) *m*

'van·tage point ['væntıdʒ] position *f* dominante

va·por ['veıpər] vapeur *f*

va·por·ize ['veıpəraız] *v/t of atomic bomb, explosion* pulvériser

'va·por trail *of airplane* traînée *f* de condensation

va·pour *Br →* **vapor**

var·i·a·ble ['veriəbl] **1** *adj* variable; *moods* changeant **2** *n* MATH, COMPUT variable *f*

var·i·ant ['veriənt] *n* variante *f*

var·i·a·tion [veri'eıʃn] variation *f*

var·i·cose vein ['værıkous] varice *f*

var·ied ['verıd] *adj* varié

va·ri·e·ty [və'raıətı] variété *f*; **a ~ of things to do** un grand nombre de choses à faire; **for a whole ~ of reasons** pour de multiples raisons

var·i·ous ['veriəs] *adj (several)* divers, plusieurs; *(different)* divers, différent

var·nish ['vɑ:rnıʃ] **1** *n* vernis *m* **2** *v/t* vernir

var·y ['verı] **1** *v/i (pret & pp -ied)* varier, changer; **it varies** ça dépend; **with ~ing degrees of success** avec plus ou moins de succès **2** *v/t* varier, diversifier; *temperature* faire varier

vase [veız] vase *m*

V

vas·ec·to·my [vəˈsektəmɪ] vasectomie f

vast [væst] adj vaste; improvement, difference considérable

vast·ly [ˈvæstlɪ] adv improve etc considérablement; different complètement

Vat·i·can [ˈvætɪkən]: the ~ le Vatican

vau·de·ville [ˈvɔːdvɪl] variétés fpl

vault¹ [vɔːlt] n in roof voûte f; ~s of bank salle f des coffres

vault² [vɔːlt] 1 n SP saut m 2 v/t beam etc sauter

VCR [viːsiːˈɑːr] abbr (= video cassette recorder) magnétoscope m

veal [viːl] veau m

veer [vɪr] v/i virer; of wind tourner

ve·gan [ˈviːgn] 1 n végétalien(ne) m(f) 2 adj végétalien*

vege·ta·ble [ˈvedʒtəbl] légume m

ve·ge·tar·i·an [vedʒɪˈterɪən] 1 n végétarien(ne) m(f) 2 adj végétarien*

veg·e·ta·tion [vedʒɪˈteɪʃn] végétation f

ve·he·mence [ˈviːəməns] véhémence f

ve·he·ment [ˈviːəmənt] adj véhément

ve·he·ment·ly [ˈviːəməntlɪ] adv avec véhémence

ve·hi·cle [ˈviːɪkl] véhicule m; for information etc véhicule m, moyen m

veil [veɪl] 1 n voile m 2 v/t voiler

vein [veɪn] ANAT veine f; in this ~ fig dans cet esprit

Vel·cro® [ˈvelkrəʊ] velcro® m

ve·loc·i·ty [vɪˈlɑːsətɪ] vélocité f

vel·vet [ˈvelvɪt] n velours m

vel·vet·y [ˈvelvɪtɪ] adj velouté

ven·det·ta [venˈdetə] vendetta f

vend·ing ma·chine [ˈvendɪŋ] distributeur m automatique

vend·or [ˈvendər] LAW vendeur(-euse) m(f)

ve·neer [vəˈnɪr] n placage m; of politeness, civilization vernis m

ven·e·ra·ble [ˈvenərəbl] adj vénérable

ven·e·rate [ˈvenəreɪt] v/t vénérer

ven·e·ra·tion [venəˈreɪʃn] vénération f

ven·e·re·al dis·ease [vəˈnɪrɪəl] M.S.T. f, maladie f sexuellement transmissible

ve·ne·tian blind [vəˈniːʃn] store m vénitien

ven·geance [ˈvendʒəns] vengeance f; with a ~ pour de bon

ven·i·son [ˈvenɪsn] venaison f, chevreuil m

ven·om [ˈvenəm] venin m

ven·om·ous [ˈvenəməs] adj also fig venimeux*

vent [vent] n for air bouche f d'aération; give ~ to feelings, emotions donner libre cours à, exprimer

ven·ti·late [ˈventɪleɪt] v/t ventiler, aérer

ven·ti·la·tion [ventɪˈleɪʃn] ventilation f, aération f

ven·ti·la·tion shaft conduit m d'aération

ven·ti·la·tor [ˈventɪleɪtər] ventilateur m; MED respirateur m

ven·tril·o·quist [venˈtrɪləkwɪst] ventriloque m/f

ven·ture [ˈventʃər] 1 n (undertaking) entreprise f; COMM tentative f 2 v/i s'aventurer

ven·ue [ˈvenjuː] for meeting, concert etc lieu m; hall also salle f

ve·ran·da [vəˈrændə] véranda f

verb [vɜːrb] verbe m

verb·al [ˈvɜːrbl] adj (spoken) oral, verbal; GRAM verbal

verb·al·ly [ˈvɜːrbəlɪ] adv oralement, verbalement

ver·ba·tim [vɜːrˈbeɪtɪm] adv repeat textuellement, mot pour mot

ver·dict [ˈvɜːrdɪkt] LAW verdict m; (opinion, judgment) avis m, jugement m; bring in a ~ of guilty / not guilty rendre un verdict de culpabilité / d'acquittement

verge [vɜːrdʒ] n of road accotement m, bas-côté m; be on the ~ of ... être au bord de ...

♦ **verge on** v/t friser

ver·i·fi·ca·tion [verɪfɪˈkeɪʃn] (check) vérification f

ver·i·fy [ˈverɪfaɪ] v/t (pret & pp -ied) (check) vérifier, contrôler; (confirm) confirmer

ver·min [ˈvɜːrmɪn] npl (insects) vermine f, parasites mpl; (rats etc) animaux *mpl* nuisibles

ver·mouth [vər'mu:θ] vermouth *m*

ver·nac·u·lar [vər'nækjələr] *n* langue *f* usuelle

ver·sa·tile ['vɜːrsətəl] *adj person* plein de ressources, polyvalent; *piece of equipment* multiusages; *mind* souple

ver·sa·til·i·ty [vɜːrsə'tɪlətɪ] *of person* adaptabilité *f*, polyvalence *f*; *of piece of equipment* souplesse *f* d'emploi

verse [vɜːrs] *(poetry)* vers *mpl*, poésie *f*; *of poem* strophe *f*; *of song* couplet *m*

versed [vɜːrst] *adj*: **be well ~ in a subject** être versé dans une matière

ver·sion ['vɜːrʃn] version *f*

ver·sus ['vɜːrsəs] *prep* SP, LAW contre

ver·te·bra ['vɜːrtɪbrə] vertèbre *f*

ver·te·brate ['vɜːrtɪbreɪt] *n* vertébré *m*

ver·ti·cal ['vɜːrtɪkl] *adj* vertical

ver·ti·go ['vɜːrtɪɡoʊ] vertige *m*

ver·y ['verɪ] **1** *adv* très; *was it cold? - not ~* faisait-il froid? - non, pas tellement; *the ~ best* le meilleur **2** *adj* même; *at that ~ moment* à cet instant même, à ce moment précis; *in the ~ act* en flagrant délit; *that's the ~ thing I need* c'est exactement ce dont j'ai besoin; *the ~ thought of it makes me ...* rien que d'y penser, je ...; *right at the ~ top / bottom* tout en haut / bas

ves·sel ['vesl] NAUT bateau *m*, navire *m*

vest [vest] gilet *m Br. undershirt* maillot *m* (de corps)

ves·tige ['vestɪdʒ] vestige *m*; *fig* once *f*

vet[1] [vet] *n (veterinarian)* vétérinaire *m/f*, véto *m/f*

vet[2] [vet] *v/t (pret & pp -ted) applicants etc* examiner

vet[3] [vet] *n* MIL F ancien combattant *m*

vet·e·ran ['vetərən] **1** *n* vétéran *m*; *(war veteran)* ancien combattant *m*, vétéran *m* **2** *adj (old)* antique; *(old and experienced)* aguerri, chevronné

vet·e·ri·nar·i·an [vetərə'nerɪən] vétérinaire *m/f*

ve·to ['vi:toʊ] **1** *n* veto *m inv* **2** *v/t* opposer son veto à

vex [veks] *v/t (concern, worry)* préoc-

cuper

vexed [vekst] *adj (worried)* inquiet, préoccupé; *a ~ question* une question épineuse

vi·a ['vaɪə] *prep* par

vi·a·ble ['vaɪəbl] *adj* viable

vi·brate [vaɪ'breɪt] *v/i* vibrer

vi·bra·tion [vaɪ'breɪʃn] vibration *f*

vice[1] [vaɪs] vice *m*

vice[2] [vaɪs] *Br* → **vise**

vice 'pres·i·dent vice-président *m*

'vice squad brigade *f* des mœurs

vi·ce 'ver·sa [vaɪs'vɜːrsə] *adv* vice versa

vi·cin·i·ty [vɪ'sɪnətɪ] voisinage *m*, environs *mpl*; *in the ~ of ...* place à proximité de ...; *amount* aux alentours de ...

vi·cious ['vɪʃəs] *adj* vicieux*; *dog* méchant; *person, temper* cruel*; *attack* brutal

vi·cious 'cir·cle cercle *m* vicieux

vi·cious·ly ['vɪʃəslɪ] *adv* brutalement, violemment

vic·tim ['vɪktɪm] victime *f*

vic·tim·ize ['vɪktɪmaɪz] *v/t* persécuter

vic·tor ['vɪktər] vainqueur *m*

vic·to·ri·ous [vɪk'tɔ:rɪəs] *adj* victorieux*

vic·to·ry ['vɪktərɪ] victoire *f*; *win a ~ over* remporter une victoire sur

vid·e·o ['vɪdɪoʊ] **1** *n* vidéo *f*; *actual object* cassette *f* vidéo; *have sth on ~* avoir qch en vidéo **2** *v/t* filmer; *tape off TV* enregistrer

'vid·e·o cam·e·ra caméra *f* vidéo; **vid·e·o cas'sette** cassette *f* vidéo; **vid·e·o 'con·fer·ence** TELEC vidéoconférence *f*, vidéoconférence *f*; **'vid·e·o game** jeu *m* vidéo; **'vid·e·o·phone** visiophone *m*; **'vid·e·o re·cord·er** magnétoscope *m*; **'vid·e·o re·cord·ing** enregistrement *m* vidéo; **'vid·e·o·tape** bande *f* vidéo

vie [vaɪ] *v/i* rivaliser

Vi·et·nam [vɪet'næm] Vietnam *m*

Vi·et·nam·ese [vɪetnə'mi:z] **1** *adj* vietnamien* **2** *n* Vietnamien(ne) *m(f)*; *language* vietnamien *m*

view [vju:] **1** *n* vue *f*; *(assessment, opinion)* opinion *f*, avis *m*; *in ~ of*

V

compte tenu de, étant donné; **he did it in full ~ of his parents** il l'a fait sous les yeux de ses parents; **be on ~ of paintings** être exposé; **with a ~ to** en vue de, afin de **2** v/t events, situation considérer, envisager; TV program regarder; house for sale visiter **3** v/i (watch TV) regarder la télévision

view-er ['vjuːər] TV téléspectateur (-trice) m(f)

view-find-er ['vjuːfaɪndər] PHOT viseur m

'view-point point m de vue

vig-or ['vɪɡər] vigueur f, énergie f

vig-or-ous ['vɪɡərəs] adj vigoureux*

vig-or-ous-ly ['vɪɡərəslɪ] adv vigoureusement

vig-our Br → **vigor**

vile [vaɪl] adj smell etc abominable; action, person ignoble

vil-la ['vɪlə] villa f

vil-lage ['vɪlɪdʒ] village m

vil-lag-er ['vɪlɪdʒər] villageois(e) m(f)

vil-lain ['vɪlən] escroc m; in drama, literature méchant m

vin-di-cate ['vɪndɪkeɪt] v/t (prove correct) confirmer, justifier; (prove innocent) innocenter; **I feel ~d** cela m'a donné raison

vin-dic-tive [vɪn'dɪktɪv] adj vindicatif f

vin-dic-tive-ly [vɪn'dɪktɪvlɪ] adv vindicativement

vine [vaɪn] vigne f

vin-e-gar ['vɪnɪɡər] vinaigre m

vine-yard ['vɪnjɑːrd] vignoble m

vin-tage ['vɪntɪdʒ] **1** n of wine millésime m **2** adj (classic) classique; **this film is ~ Charlie Chaplin** ce film est un classique de Charlie Chaplin

vi-o-la [vɪ'oʊlə] MUS alto m

vi-o-late ['vaɪəleɪt] v/t violer

vi-o-la-tion [vaɪə'leɪʃn] violation f; (traffic ~) infraction f au code de la route

vi-o-lence ['vaɪələns] violence f; **outbreak of ~** flambée f de violence

vi-o-lent ['vaɪələnt] adj violent; **have a ~ temper** être d'un naturel violent

vi-o-lent-ly ['vaɪələntlɪ] adv violemment; **fall ~ in love with s.o.** tomber follement amoureux* de qn

vi-o-let ['vaɪələt] n color violet m; plant violette f

vi-o-lin [vaɪə'lɪn] violon m

vi-o-lin-ist [vaɪə'lɪnɪst] violoniste m/f

VIP [viːaɪ'piː] abbr (= **very important person**) V.I.P. m inv F, personnalité f de marque

vi-per ['vaɪpər] snake vipère f

vi-ral ['vaɪrəl] adj infection viral

vir-gin ['vɜːrdʒɪn] vierge f; male puceau m F; **be a ~** être vierge

vir-gin-i-ty [vɜːr'dʒɪnətɪ] virginité f; **lose one's ~** perdre sa virginité

Vir-go ['vɜːrɡoʊ] ASTROL Vierge f

vir-ile ['vɪrəl] adj viril; fig vigoureux*

vi-ril-i-ty [vɪ'rɪlətɪ] virilité f

vir-tu-al ['vɜːrtʃʊəl] adj quasi-; COMPUT virtuel*; **he became the ~ leader of the party** en pratique, il est devenu chef du parti

vir-tu-al-ly ['vɜːrtʃʊəlɪ] adv (almost) pratiquement, presque

vir-tu-al re-al-i-ty réalité f virtuelle

vir-tue ['vɜːrtʃuː] vertu f; **in ~ of** en vertu ou raison de

vir-tu-o-so [vɜːrtʊ'oʊzoʊ] MUS virtuose m/f; **give a ~ performance** jouer en virtuose

vir-tu-ous ['vɜːrtʃʊəs] adj vertueux*

vir-u-lent ['vɪrʊlənt] adj disease virulent

vi-rus ['vaɪrəs] MED, COMPUT virus m

vi-sa ['viːzə] visa m

vise [vaɪz] étau m

vis-i-bil-i-ty [vɪzə'bɪlətɪ] visibilité f

vis-i-ble ['vɪzəbl] adj visible; **not ~ to the naked eye** invisible à l'œil nu

vis-i-bly ['vɪzəblɪ] adv visiblement; **he was ~ moved** il était visiblement ému

vi-sion ['vɪʒn] (eyesight) vue f; REL vision f, apparition f

vis-it ['vɪzɪt] **1** n visite f; (stay) séjour m; **pay s.o. a ~** rendre visite à qn; **pay a ~ to the doctor / dentist** aller chez le médecin / dentiste **2** v/t person aller voir, rendre visite à; doctor, dentist aller voir; city, country aller à / en; castle, museum visiter; website consulter

♦ **visit with** v/t bavarder avec

vis·it·ing card ['vɪzɪtɪŋ] carte *f* de visite

'vis·it·ing hours *npl at hospital* heures *fpl* de visite

vis·it·or ['vɪzɪtər] (*guest*) invité *m*; (*tourist*) visiteur *m*

vi·sor ['vaɪzər] visière *f*

vis·u·al ['vɪʒʊəl] *adj* visuel*

vis·u·al 'aid support *m* visuel; **'vis·u·al arts** *npl* arts *mpl* plastiques; **vis·u·al dis'play u·nit** écran *m* de visualisation

vis·u·al·ize ['vɪʒʊəlaɪz] *v/t* (*imagine*) (s')imaginer; (*foresee*) envisager, prévoir

vis·u·al·ly ['vɪʒʊlɪ] *adv* visuellement; **~, the movie was superb** d'un point de vue visuel, le film était superbe

vis·u·al·ly im'paired *adj* qui a des problèmes de vue, malvoyant

vi·tal ['vaɪtl] *adj* (*essential*) vital, essentiel*; **it is ~ that ...** il faut absolument que ...

vi·tal·i·ty [vaɪ'tælətɪ] *of person, city etc* vitalité *f*

vi·tal·ly ['vaɪtəlɪ] *adv*: **~ important** d'une importance capitale

vi·tal 'or·gans *npl* organes *mpl* vitaux

vi·tal sta'tis·tics *npl of woman* mensurations *fpl*

vit·a·min ['vaɪtəmɪn] vitamine *f*

'vit·a·min pill comprimé *m* de vitamines

vit·ri·ol·ic [vɪtrɪ'ɑːlɪk] *adj* au vitriol; *attack* violent; *humor* caustique

vi·va·cious [vɪ'veɪʃəs] *adj* plein de vivacité, vif*

vi·vac·i·ty [vɪ'væsətɪ] vivacité *f*

viv·id ['vɪvɪd] *adj* vif*; *description* vivant

viv·id·ly ['vɪvɪdlɪ] *adv* vivement; *remember* clairement; *describe* de façon vivante; **~ colored** aux couleurs vives

V-neck ['viːnek] col *m* en V

vo·cab·u·la·ry [voʊ'kæbjʊlərɪ] vocabulaire *m*; (*list of words*) glossaire *m*, lexique *m*

vo·cal ['voʊkl] *adj* vocal; **teachers are becoming more ~** les enseignants se font de plus en plus entendre

'vo·cal cords *npl* cordes *fpl* vocales

'vo·cal group MUS groupe *m* vocal

vo·cal·ist ['voʊkəlɪst] MUS chanteur (-euse) *m(f)*

vo·ca·tion [və'keɪʃn] vocation *f*

vo·ca·tion·al [və'keɪʃnl] *adj* guidance professionnel*

vod·ka ['vɑːdkə] vodka *f*

vogue [voʊg] mode *f*, vogue *f*; **be in ~** être à la mode *or* en vogue

voice [vɔɪs] **1** *n* voix *f* **2** *v/t* opinions exprimer

'voice·mail messagerie *f* vocale

'voice·o·ver voix *f* hors champ

void [vɔɪd] **1** *n* vide *m* **2** *adj*: **~ of** dénué de, dépourvu de

vol·a·tile ['vɑːlətəl] *adj* personality, moods lunatique, versatile

vol·ca·no [vɑːl'keɪnoʊ] volcan *m*

vol·ley ['vɑːlɪ] *n* volée *f*

'vol·ley·ball volley(-ball) *m*

volt [voʊlt] volt *m*

volt·age ['voʊltɪdʒ] tension *f*

vol·ume ['vɑːljəm] volume *m*

'vol·ume con·trol (bouton *m* de) réglage *m* du volume

vol·un·tar·i·ly [vɑːlən'terɪlɪ] *adv* de son plein gré, volontairement

vol·un·ta·ry ['vɑːlənterɪ] *adj* volontaire; *worker, work* bénévole

vol·un·teer [vɑːlən'tɪr] **1** *n* volontaire *m/f*; (*unpaid worker*) bénévole *m/f* **2** *v/i* se porter volontaire

vo·lup·tu·ous [və'lʌptʃʊəs] *adj* woman, figure voluptueux*

vom·it ['vɑːmət] **1** *n* vomi *m*, vomissure *f* **2** *v/i* vomir

♦ **vomit up** *v/t* vomir

vo·ra·cious [və'reɪʃəs] *adj* vorace; *reader* avide

vo·ra·cious·ly [və'reɪʃəslɪ] *adv* avec voracité; *read* avec avidité

vote [voʊt] **1** *n* vote *m*; **have the ~** avoir le droit de vote **2** *v/i* POL voter (**for** pour; **against** contre) **3** *v/t*: **they ~d him President** ils l'ont élu président; **they ~d to stay** ils ont décidé de rester

♦ **vote in** *v/t* new member élire

♦ **vote on** *v/t* issue soumettre qch au vote

V

- ◆ **vote out** *v/t of office* ne pas réélire
- **vot·er** ['vəʊtər] POL électeur *m*
- **vot·ing** ['vəʊtɪŋ] POL vote *m*
- **'vot·ing booth** isoloir *m*
- ◆ **vouch for** [vaʊtʃ] *v/t truth, person* se porter garant de
- **vouch·er** ['vaʊtʃər] bon *m*
- **vow** [vaʊ] **1** *n* vœu *m*, serment *m* **2** *v/t*:

~ to do sth jurer de faire qch
vow·el ['vaʊəl] voyelle *f*
voy·age ['vɔɪdʒ] *n* voyage *m*
vul·gar ['vʌlɡər] *adj person, language* vulgaire
vul·ne·ra·ble ['vʌlnərəbl] *adj* vulnérable
vul·ture ['vʌltʃər] *also fig* vautour *m*

W

- **wad** [wɑːd] *n of paper, absorbent cotton etc* tampon *m*; *a ~ of $100 bills* une liasse de billets de 100 $
- **wad·dle** ['wɑːdl] *v/i* se dandiner
- **wade** [weɪd] *v/i* patauger
- ◆ **wade through** *v/t*: *I'm wading through …* j'essaie péniblement de venir à bout de …
- **wa·fer** ['weɪfər] *cookie* gaufrette *f*; REL hostie *f*
- **'wa·fer-thin** *adj* très fin
- **waf·fle**[1] ['wɑːfl] *n to eat* gaufre *f*
- **waf·fle**[2] ['wɑːfl] *v/i* parler pour ne rien dire
- **wag** [wæɡ] *v/t & v/i* (*pret & pp **-ged***) remuer
- **wage**[1] [weɪdʒ] *v/t*: *~ war* faire la guerre
- **wage**[2] [weɪdʒ] *n* salaire *m*
- **wage earn·er** ['weɪdʒɜːrnər] salarié(e) *m(f)*; **'wage freeze** gel *m* des salaires; **'wage ne·go·ti·a·tions** *npl* négociations *fpl* salariales; **'wage pack·et** *fig* salaire *m*
- **wag·gle** ['wæɡl] *v/t* remuer
- **wag·on**, *Br* **wag·gon** ['wæɡən] RAIL wagon *m*; **covered ~** chariot *m* (bâché); **be on the ~** F être au régime sec
- **wail** [weɪl] **1** *n* hurlement *m* **2** *v/i* hurler
- **waist** [weɪst] taille *f*
- **'waist·coat** *Br* gilet *m*
- **'waist·line** *of person* tour *m* de taille; *of dress* taille *f*
- **wait** [weɪt] **1** *n* attente *f* **2** *v/i* attendre **2** *v/t*: **don't ~ supper for me** ne m'attendez pas pour le dîner; **~ table** servir à manger
- ◆ **wait for** *v/t* attendre; **wait for me!** attends-moi!
- ◆ **wait on** *v/t* (*serve*) servir
- ◆ **wait up** *v/i*: **don't wait up (for me)** ne m'attends pas pour aller te coucher
- **wait·er** ['weɪtər] serveur *m*; **~!** garçon!
- **wait·ing** ['weɪtɪŋ] attente *f*
- **'wait·ing list** liste *f* d'attente
- **'wait·ing room** salle *f* d'attente
- **wait·ress** ['weɪtrɪs] serveuse *f*
- **waive** [weɪv] *v/t* renoncer à
- **wake**[1] [weɪk] **1** *v/i* (*pret* **woke**, *pp* **woken**): **~ (up)** se réveiller **2** *v/t person* réveiller
- **wake**[2] [weɪk] *n of ship* sillage *m*; *in the ~ of fig* à la suite de; *follow in the ~ of* venir à la suite de
- **'wake-up call**: **have a ~** se faire réveiller par téléphone
- **Wales** [weɪlz] pays *m* de Galles
- **walk** [wɔːk] **1** *n* marche *f*; (*path*) allée *f*; **it's a long / short ~ to the office** le bureau est loin / n'est pas loin à pied; **go for a ~** aller se promener, aller faire un tour **2** *v/i* marcher; *as opposed to taking the car, bus etc* aller à pied; (*hike*) faire de la marche **3** *v/t dog* promener; **~ the streets** (*walk around*) parcourir les rues

675   **warranty**

♦ **walk out** *v/i of spouse* prendre la porte; *of theater etc* partir; *(go on strike)* se mettre en grève

♦ **walk out on** *v/t family* abandonner; *partner, boyfriend, wife* quitter

walk·er ['wɔ:kər] *(hiker)* randonneur (-euse) *m(f)*; *for baby* trotte-bébé *m*; *for old person* déambulateur *m*; **be a slow / fast ~** marcher lentement / vite

walk-in 'clos·et placard *m* de plain-pied

walk·ing ['wɔ:kɪŋ] *as opposed to driving* marche *f*; *(hiking)* randonnée *f*; **be within ~ distance** ne pas être loin à pied

'**walk·ing stick** canne *f*

'**Walk·man**® walkman *m*; '**walk·out** *(strike)* grève *f*; '**walk·o·ver** *(easy win)* victoire *f* facile; '**walk·up** appartement dans un immeuble sans ascenseur

wall [wɔ:l] mur *m*; **go to the ~** *of company* faire faillite; **drive s.o. up the ~** F rendre qn fou

wal·let ['wɑ:lɪt] *(billfold)* portefeuille *m*

'**wall·pa·per 1** *n also* COMPUT papier *m* peint **2** *v/t* tapisser

'**Wall Street** Wall Street

wal·nut ['wɔ:lnʌt] *nut* noix *f*; *tree, wood* noyer *m*

waltz [wɔ:lts] *n* valse *f*

wan [wɑ:n] *adj* face pâlot*

wan·der ['wɑ:ndər] *v/i (roam)* errer; *(stray)* s'égarer

♦ **wander around** *v/i* déambuler

wane [weɪn] *v/i of moon* décroître; *of interest, enthusiasm* diminuer

wan·gle ['wæŋgl] *v/t* F réussir à obtenir (par une combine)

want [wɑ:nt] **1** *n*: **for ~ of** par manque de, faute de **2** *v/t* vouloir; *(need)* avoir besoin de; **~ to do sth** vouloir faire qch; **I ~ to stay here** je veux rester ici; **I don't ~ to** je ne veux pas; **she ~s you to go back** elle veut que tu reviennes *(subj)*; **he ~s a haircut** *(needs)* il a besoin d'une coupe de cheveux; **you ~ to be more careful** il faut que tu fasses *(subj)* plus attention **3** *v/i*: **~ for nothing** ne manquer de rien

'**want ad** petite annonce *f*

want·ed ['wɑ:ntɪd] *adj by police* recherché

want·ing ['wɑ:ntɪŋ] *adj*: **be ~ in** manquer de

wan·ton ['wɑ:ntən] *adj* gratuit

war [wɔ:r] guerre *f*; *fig: between competitors* lutte *f*; **the ~ on drugs / unemployment** la lutte antidrogue / contre le chômage; **be at ~** être en guerre

war·ble ['wɔ:rbl] *v/i of bird* gazouiller

ward [wɔ:rd] *Br: in hospital* salle *f*; *child* pupille *m/f*

♦ **ward off** *v/t* éviter

war·den ['wɔ:rdn] *of prison* gardien (ne) *m(f)*

'**ward·robe** *for clothes* armoire *f*; *(clothes)* garde-robe *f*

'**ware·house** ['werhaus] entrepôt *m*

'**war·fare** ['wɔ:rfer] guerre *f*

'**war·head** ogive *f*

war·i·ly ['werɪlɪ] *adv* avec méfiance

warm [wɔ:rm] *adj* chaud; *fig: welcome, smile* chaleureux*; **be ~** *of person* avoir chaud

♦ **warm up 1** *v/t* réchauffer **2** *v/i* se réchauffer; *of athlete etc* s'échauffer

warm-heart·ed ['wɔ:rmhɑ:rtɪd] *adj* chaleureux*

warm·ly ['wɔ:rmlɪ] *adv* chaudement; *fig: welcome, smile* chaleureusement

warmth [wɔ:rmθ] *also fig* chaleur *f*

'**warm-up** SP échauffement *m*

warn [wɔ:rn] *v/t* prévenir

warn·ing ['wɔ:rnɪŋ] avertissement *m*; **without ~ start to rain etc** tout à coup; *leave s.o. etc* sans prévenir

'**warn·ing light** voyant *m* (d'avertissement)

warp [wɔ:rp] **1** *v/t wood* gauchir; *fig: character* pervertir **2** *v/i of wood* gauchir

warped [wɔ:rpt] *adj fig* tordu

'**war·plane** avion *m* de guerre

war·rant ['wɔ:rənt] **1** *n* mandat *m* **2** *v/t (deserve, call for)* justifier

war·ran·ty ['wɔ:rəntɪ] *(guarantee)* garantie *f*; **be under ~** être sous garan-

W

tie

war·ri·or ['wɔːrɪər] guerrier(-ière) *m(f)*

'war·ship navire *m* de guerre

wart [wɔːrt] verrue *f*

'war·time temps *m* de guerre

war·y ['werɪ] *adj* méfiant; **be ~ of** se méfier de

was [wʌz] *pret* → **be**

wash [wɑːʃ] **1** *n*: **have a ~** se laver; **that shirt needs a ~** cette chemise a besoin d'être lavée **2** *v/t clothes, dishes* laver; **~ the dishes** faire la vaisselle; **~ one's hands** se laver les mains **3** *v/i* se laver

♦ **wash up** *v/i* (*wash one's hands and face*) se débarbouiller

wash·a·ble ['wɑːʃəbl] *adj* lavable

'wash·ba·sin, 'wash·bowl lavabo *m*

'wash·cloth gant *m* de toilette

washed out [wɑːʃt'aʊt] *adj* (*tired*) usé

wash·er ['wɑːʃər] *for faucet etc* rondelle *f*; → **wash·ing ma·chine**

wash·ing ['wɑːʃɪŋ] lessive *f*; **do the ~** faire la lessive

'wash·ing ma·chine machine *f* à laver

'wash·room toilettes *fpl*

wasp [wɑːsp] *insect* guêpe *f*

waste [weɪst] **1** *n* gaspillage *m*; *from industrial process* déchets *mpl*; **it's a ~ of time / money** c'est une perte de temps / d'argent **2** *adj* non utilisé **3** *v/t* gaspiller

♦ **waste away** *v/i* dépérir

'waste bas·ket corbeille *f* à papier

'waste dis·pos·al (u·nit) broyeur *m* d'ordures

waste·ful ['weɪstfʊl] *adj person, society* gaspilleur*

'waste·land désert *m*; **waste 'pa·per** papier(s) *m(pl)* (*jeté(s)*) *à la poubelle*); **'waste pipe** tuyau *m* d'écoulement; **'waste prod·uct** déchets *mpl*

watch [wɑːtʃ] **1** *n timepiece* montre *f*; **keep ~** monter la garde **2** *v/t* regarder; (*look after*) surveiller; (*spy on*) épier; **~ what you say** fais attention à ce que tu dis **3** *v/i* regarder

♦ **watch for** *v/t* attendre

♦ **watch out** *v/i* faire attention; **watch**

out! fais attention!

♦ **watch out for** *v/t* (*be careful of*) faire attention à

watch·ful ['wɑːtʃfʊl] *adj* vigilant

'watch·mak·er horloger(-ère) *m(f)*

wa·ter ['wɔːtər] **1** *n* eau *f*; **~s** *pl* NAUT eaux *f* **2** *v/t plant, garden* arroser **3** *v/i of eyes* pleurer; **my eyes were ~ing** j'avais les yeux qui pleuraient; **my mouth is ~ing** j'ai l'eau à la bouche

♦ **water down** *v/t drink* diluer

'wa·ter can·non canon *m* à eau

'wa·ter·col·or, *Br* **'wa·ter·col·our** aquarelle *f*

wa·ter·cress ['wɔːtərkres] cresson *m*

wa·tered down ['wɔːtərd] *adj fig* atténué

'wa·ter·fall chute *f* d'eau

'wa·ter·ing can ['wɔːtərɪŋ] arrosoir *m*

'wa·ter·ing hole *hum* bar *m*

'wa·ter lev·el niveau *m* de l'eau; **'wa·ter lil·y** nénuphar *m*; **'wa·ter·line** ligne *f* de flottaison; **wa·ter·logged** ['wɔːtərlɑːgd] *adj earth, field* détrempé; *boat* plein d'eau; **'wa·ter main** conduite *f* d'eau; **'wa·ter·mark** filigrane *m*; **'wa·ter·mel·on** pastèque *f*; **'wa·ter pol·lu·tion** pollution *f* de l'eau; **'wa·ter po·lo** water polo *m*; **'wa·ter·proof** *adj* imperméable; **'wa·ter·shed** *fig* tournant *m*; **'wa·ter·side** *n* bord *m* de l'eau; **at the ~** au bord de l'eau; **'wa·ter·ski·ing** ski *m* nautique; **'wa·ter·tight** *adj compartiment* étanche; *fig: alibi* parfait; **'wa·ter·way** voie *f* d'eau; **'wa·ter·wings** *npl* flotteurs *mpl*; **'wa·ter·works** F: **turn on the ~** se mettre à pleurer

wa·ter·y ['wɔːtərɪ] *adj soup, sauce* trop clair; *coffee* trop léger*

watt [wɑːt] watt *m*

wave[1] [weɪv] *n in sea* vague *f*

wave[2] [weɪv] **1** *n of hand* signe *m* **2** *v/i with hand* saluer; *of flag* flotter; **~ to s.o.** saluer qn (de la main) **3** *v/t flag etc* agiter

'wave·length RAD longueur *f* d'onde; **be on the same ~** *fig* être sur la même longueur d'onde

wa·ver ['weɪvər] *v/i* hésiter

wav·y ['weɪvɪ] *adj* ondulé

wax[1] [wæks] *n* cire *f*

wax[2] [wæks] *v/i of moon* croître

way [weɪ] **1** *n* (*method, manner*) façon *f*; (*route*) chemin *m* (**to** de); ***the ~ he behaves*** la façon dont il se comporte; ***this ~*** (*like this*) comme ça; (*in this direction*) par ici; ***by the ~*** (*incidentally*) au fait; ***by ~ of*** (*via*) par; (*in the form of*) en guise de; ***in a ~*** (*in certain respects*) d'une certaine façon; ***be under ~*** être en cours; ***be well under ~*** être bien avancé; ***give ~*** (*collapse*) s'écrouler; ***give ~ to*** (*be replaced by*) être remplacé par; ***want to have one's (own) ~*** n'en faire qu'à sa tête; ***he always had his own ~*** il a toujours fait ce qu'il voulait; ***OK, we'll do it your ~*** O.K., on va le faire à votre façon; ***lead the ~*** passer en premier; *fig* être le premier; ***lose one's ~*** se perdre; ***be in the ~*** (*be an obstruction*) gêner le passage; (*disturb*) gêner; ***it's on the ~ to the station*** c'est sur le chemin de la gare; ***I was on my ~ to the station*** je me rendais à la gare; ***it's a long ~*** c'est loin; ***no ~!*** pas question!; ***there's no ~ he can do it*** il ne peut absolument pas le faire **2** *adv* F (*much*): ***it's ~ too soon to decide*** c'est bien trop tôt pour décider; ***they're ~ behind with their work*** ils sont très en retard dans leur travail

way 'in entrée *f*; **way of 'life** mode *m* de vie; **way 'out** sortie *f*; *fig* issue *f*

we [wiː] *pron* nous

weak [wiːk] *adj government, currency, person* faible; *tea, coffee* léger*

weak·en ['wiːkn] **1** *v/t* affaiblir **2** *v/i of currency, person* s'affaiblir; *in negotiation etc* faiblir

weak·ling ['wiːklɪŋ] faible *m/f*

weak·ness ['wiːknɪs] faiblesse *f*; ***have a ~ for sth*** (*liking*) avoir un faible pour qch

wealth [welθ] richesse *f*; ***a ~ of*** une abondance de

wealth·y ['welθɪ] *adj* riche

weap·on ['wepən] arme *f*

wear [wer] **1** *n*: **~** (**and tear**) usure *f*; ***this coat has had a lot of ~*** cette veste est très usée; ***clothes for everyday / evening ~*** vêtements de tous les jours / du soir **2** *v/t* (*pret* **wore**, *pp* **worn**) (*have on*) porter; (*damage*) user; ***what are you ~ing to the party?*** comment t'habilles-tu pour la soirée?; ***what was he ~ing?*** comment était-il habillé? **3** *v/i* (*pret* **wore**, *pp* **worn**) (**~ out**) s'user; **~ well** (*last*) faire bon usage

♦ **wear away 1** *v/i* s'effacer **2** *v/t* user

♦ **wear down** *v/t* user; **wear s.o. down** make s.o. change their mind avoir qn à l'usure

♦ **wear off** *v/i of effect, feeling* se dissiper

♦ **wear out 1** *v/t* (*tire*) épuiser; *shoes, carpet* user **2** *v/i of shoes, carpet* s'user

wea·ri·ly ['wɪrɪlɪ] *adv* avec lassitude

wear·ing ['werɪŋ] *adj* (*tiring*) lassant

wear·y ['wɪrɪ] *adj* las*

weath·er ['weðər] **1** *n* temps *m*; ***be feeling under the ~*** ne pas être très en forme **2** *v/t crisis* survivre à

'weath·er-beat·en *adj* hâlé; **'weath·er chart** carte *f* météorologique; **'weath·er fore·cast** prévisions météorologiques *fpl*, météo *f*; **'weath·er·man** présentateur *m* météo

weave [wiːv] **1** *v/t* (*pret* **wove**, *pp* **wo·ven**) *cloth* tisser; *basket* tresser **2** *v/i* (*pret* **weaved**, *pp* **weaved**) *of driver, cyclist* se faufiler

Web [web]: ***the ~*** COMPUT le Web

web [web] *of spider* toile *f*

webbed 'feet [webd] *npl* pieds *mpl* palmés

'web page page *f* de Web

'web site site *m* de Web

wed·ding ['wedɪŋ] mariage *m*

'wed·ding an·ni·ver·sa·ry anniversaire *m* de mariage; **'wed·ding cake** gâteau *m* de noces; **'wed·ding day** jour *m* de mariage; ***on my ~*** le jour de mon mariage; **'wed·ding dress** robe *f* de mariée; **'wed·ding ring** alliance *f*

wedge [wedʒ] **1** *n to hold sth in place* cale *f*; *of cheese etc* morceau *m* **2** *v/t*: **~**

W

open maintenir ouvert avec une cale

Wed·nes·day ['wenzdeɪ] mercredi *m*

weed [wiːd] **1** *n* mauvaise herbe *f* **2** *v/t* désherber

♦ **weed out** *v/t (remove)* éliminer

'weed·kill·er herbicide *f*

weed·y ['wiːdɪ] *adj* F chétif*

week [wiːk] semaine *f*; *a ~ tomorrow* demain en huit

'week·day jour *m* de la semaine

'week·end week-end *m*; *on the ~ (on this ~)* ce week-end; *(on every ~)* le week-end

week·ly ['wiːklɪ] **1** *adj* hebdomadaire **2** *n magazine* hebdomadaire *m* **3** *adv be published* toutes les semaines; *be paid* à la semaine

weep [wiːp] *v/i (pret & pp wept)* pleurer

weep·y ['wiːpɪ] *adj*: *be ~* pleurer facilement

wee-wee ['wiːwiː] *n* F pipi *m* F; *do a ~* faire pipi

weigh [weɪ] **1** *v/t* peser; *~ anchor* lever l'ancre **2** *v/i* peser

♦ **weigh down** *v/t*: *be weighed down with* être alourdi par; *fig: with cares* être accablé de

♦ **weigh on** *v/t* inquiéter

♦ **weigh up** *v/t (assess)* juger

weight [weɪt] *of person, object* poids *m*; *put on ~* grossir; *lose ~* maigrir

♦ **weight down** *v/t* maintenir en place avec un poids

weight·less·ness ['weɪtlɪsnɪs] apesanteur *f*

weight·lift·er ['weɪtlɪftər] haltérophile *m/f*

weight·lift·ing ['weɪtlɪftɪŋ] haltérophilie *f*

weight·y ['weɪtɪ] *adj fig (important)* sérieux*

weir [wɪr] barrage *m*

weird [wɪrd] *adj* bizarre

weird·ly ['wɪrdlɪ] *adv* bizarrement

weird·o ['wɪrdoʊ] F cinglé(e) *m(f)* F

wel·come ['welkəm] **1** *adj* bienvenu; *make s.o. ~* faire bon accueil à qn; *you're ~!* je vous en prie!; *you're ~ to try some* si vous voulez en essayer, vous êtes le bienvenu **2** *n also*

fig: to news, announcements accueil *m* **3** *v/t* accueillir; *fig: news, announcement* se réjouir de; *opportunity* saisir

weld [weld] *v/t* souder

weld·er ['weldər] soudeur(-euse) *m(f)*

wel·fare ['welfer] bien-être *m*; *financial assistance* sécurité *f* sociale; *be on ~* toucher les allocations

'wel·fare check chèque *m* d'allocations; **wel·fare 'state** État *m* providence; **'wel·fare work** assistance *f* sociale; **'wel·fare work·er** assistant social *m*, assistante sociale *f*

well[1] [wel] *n for water, oil* puits *m*

well[2] **1** *adv* bien; *you did ~ in the exam* tu as bien réussi l'examen; *~ done!* bien!; *as ~ (too)* aussi; *(in addition to)* en plus de; *it's just as ~ you told me* tu as bien fait de me le dire; *very ~ acknowledging order* entendu; *reluctantly agreeing* très bien; *~, ~! surprise* tiens, tiens!; *~ ... uncertainty, thinking* eh bien ... **2** *adj*: *be ~* aller bien; *feel ~* se sentir bien; *get ~ soon!* remets-toi vite!

well-'bal·anced *adj person, meal, diet* équilibré; **well-be·haved** [welbɪ'heɪvd] *adj* bien élevé; **well-'be·ing** bien-être *m*; **well-'built** *adj also euph (fat)* bien bâti; **well-'done** *adj meat* bien cuit; **well-'dressed** [wel'drest] *adj* bien habillé; **well-'earned** [wel'ɜːrnd] *adj* bien mérité; **well-'heeled** [wel'hiːld] *adj* F cossu; **well-in-formed** [wel'ɪnfɔːrmd] *adj* bien informé; *be ~ (knowledgeable)* être bien informé; **well-'known** *adj* connu; **well-'made** *adj* bien fait; **well-man·nered** [wel'mænərd] *adj* bien élevé; **well-'mean·ing** *adj* plein de bonnes intentions; **well-'off** *adj* riche; **well-'paid** *adj* bien payé; **well-read** [wel'red] *adj* cultivé; **well-'timed** [wel'taɪmd] *adj* bien calculé; **well-to-'do** *adj* riche; **well-'wish·er** ['welwɪʃər] personne *f* apportant son soutien; *a ~ at end of anonymous letter* un ami qui vous veut du bien; **well-'worn** *adj* usé

Welsh [welʃ] **1** *adj* gallois **2** *n language* gallois *m*; *the ~* les Gallois *mpl*

went [went] *pret* → **go**

wept [wept] *pret & pp* → **weep**

were [wɜːr] *pret pl* → **be**

West [west]: *the* ~ POL *Western nations* l'Occident *m*; *part of a country* l'Ouest *m*

west [west] **1** *n* ouest *m*; *to the* ~ *of* à l'ouest de **2** *adj* ouest *inv*; *wind* d'ouest; ~ *Chicago* l'ouest de Chicago; ~ *Africa* l'Afrique de l'Ouest **3** *adv travel* vers l'ouest; ~ *of* à l'ouest de

West 'Coast *of USA* la côte ouest

west·er·ly ['westərlɪ] *adj wind* d'ouest; *direction* vers l'ouest

West·ern ['westərn] *adj* occidental

west·ern ['westərn] **1** *adj* de l'Ouest **2** *n movie* western *m*

West·ern·er ['westərnər] occidental (e)

west·ern·ized ['westərnaɪzd] *adj* occidentalisé

west·ward ['westwərd] *adv* vers l'ouest

wet [wet] *adj* mouillé; *(rainy)* humide; *get* ~ se mouiller, se faire tremper *F*; *it's* ~ *today* il fait humide aujourd'hui; *be* ~ *through* être complètement trempé; ~ *paint as sign* peinture fraîche

wet 'blan·ket *F* rabat-joie *m*

'**wet suit** *for diving* combinaison *f* de plongée

whack [wæk] **1** *n F (blow)* coup *m* **2** *v/t F* frapper

whacked [wækt] *adj Br F* crevé *F*

whack·o ['wækou] *F* dingue *m/f*

whack·y ['wækɪ] *adj F* déjanté *F*

whale [weɪl] baleine *f*

whal·ing ['weɪlɪŋ] chasse *f* à la baleine

wharf [wɔːrf] *Br* quai *m*

what [wɑːt] **1** *pron* ◇ : ~ ? quoi?; ~ *for? (why?)* pourquoi?; *so* ~? et alors?
◇ *as object* que; *before vowel* qu'; ~ *did he say?* qu'est-ce qu'il a dit?, qu'a-t-il dit?; ~ *is that?* qu'est-ce que c'est?; ~ *is it? (what do you want?)* qu'est-ce qu'il y a?
◇ *as subject* qu'est-ce qui; ~ *just fell off?* qu'est-ce qui vient de tomber?
◇ *relative as object* ce que; *that's not*

~ *I meant* ce n'est pas ce que je voulais dire; *I did* ~ *I could* j'ai fait ce que j'ai pu; *I don't know* ~ *you're talking about* je ne vois pas de quoi tu parles; *take* ~ *you need* prends ce dont tu as besoin
◇ *relative as subject* ce qui; *I didn't see* ~ *happened* je n'ai pas vu ce qui s'est passé
◇ *suggestions*: ~ *about heading home?* et si nous rentrions?; ~ *about some lunch?* et si on allait déjeuner?
2 *adj* quel, quelle; *pl* quels, quelles; ~ *color is the car?* de quelle couleur est la voiture?

what·ev·er [wɑːt'evər] **1** *pron* ◇ *as subject* tout ce qui; *as object* tout ce que; ~ *is left alive* tout ce qui est encore vivant; *he eats* ~ *you give him* il mange tout ce qu'on lui donne
◇ *(no matter what) with noun* quel(le) que soit; *with clause* quoi que (+*subj*); ~ *the season* quelle que soit la saison; ~ *you do* quoi que tu fasses
◇ : ~ *gave you that idea?* qu'est-ce qui t'a donné cette idée?; *ok,* ~ *F* ok, si vous le dites
2 *adj* n'importe quel(le); *you have no reason* ~ *to worry* tu n'as absolument aucune raison de t'inquiéter

wheat [wiːt] blé *m*

whee·dle ['wiːdl] *v/t*: ~ *sth out of s.o.* soutirer qch de qn par des cajoleries

wheel [wiːl] **1** *n* roue *f*; *(steering* ~*)* volant *m* **2** *v/t bicycle, cart* pousser **3** *v/i of birds* tournoyer

♦ **wheel around** *v/i* se retourner (brusquement)

'**wheel·bar·row** brouette *f*; '**wheel·chair** fauteuil *m* roulant; '**wheel clamp** *Br* sabot *m* de Denver

wheeze [wiːz] *v/i* respirer péniblement

when [wen] **1** *adv* quand; ~ *do you open?* quand est-ce que vous ouvrez?; *I don't know* ~ *I'll be back* je ne sais pas quand je serai de retour **2** *conj* quand; *esp with past tense also* lorsque; ~ *I was a child* quand *or* lorsque j'étais enfant; *on the day* ~

W

... le jour où ...

when·ev·er [wen'evər] *adv each time* chaque fois que; *regardless of when* n'importe quand

where [wer] **1** *adv* où; **~ from?** d'où?; **~ to?** où? **2** *conj* où; *this is ~ I used to live* c'est là que j'habitais

where·a·bouts [werə'bauts] **1** *adv* où **2** *npl: nothing is known of his ~* personne ne sait où il est

where·as *conj* tandis que

wher·ev·er [wer'evər] **1** *conj* partout où; **~ you go, don't forget to ...** où que tu ailles (*subj*), n'oublies pas de ...; *sit ~ you like* assieds-toi où tu veux **2** *adv* où (donc); *~ can it be?* où peut-il bien être?

whet [wet] *v/t* (*pret & pp* **-ted**) *appetite* aiguiser

wheth·er ['weðər] *conj* (*if*) si; *I don't know ~ to tell him or not* je ne sais pas si je dois lui dire ou pas; *~ you approve or not* que tu sois (*subj*) d'accord ou pas

which [wıtʃ] **1** *adj* quel, quelle; *pl* quels, quelles; *~ boy / girl?* quel garçon / quelle fille?

2 *pron* ◊ *interrogative* lequel, laquelle; *pl* lesquels, lesquelles; *~ are your favorites?* lesquels préférez-vous?; *take one, it doesn't matter ~* prends-en un, n'importe lequel

◊ *relative: subject* qui; *object* que; *after prep* lequel, laquelle; *pl* lesquels, lesquelles; *the mistake ~ is more serious* l'erreur qui est plus grave; *the mistake ~ you're making* l'erreur que tu fais; *the house in ~ ...* la maison dans laquelle ...

which·ev·er [wıtʃ'evər] **1** *adj* quel(le) que soit; *pl* quels / quelles que soient; *~ flight you take* quel que soit le vol que vous prenez; *choose ~ color you like* choisis la couleur que tu veux

2 *pron subject* celui / celle qui; *object* celui / celle que; *you can have ~ you want* tu peux avoir celui / celle que tu veux

◊ *no matter which* n'importe lequel / laquelle; *~ you choose* quel que soit

celui / quelle que soit celle que vous choississez

whiff [wıf]: *catch a ~ of sth* sentir qch

while [waıl] **1** *conj* pendant que; (*although*) bien que (+*subj*) **2** *n: a long ~* longtemps; *it's been a long ~ since we last met* ça fait longtemps qu'on ne s'est pas vu; *for a ~* pendant un moment; *I'll wait a ~ longer* je vais attendre un peu plus longtemps

♦ **while away** *v/t time* passer

whim [wım] caprice *m*; *on a ~* sur un coup de tête

whim·per ['wımpər] **1** *n* pleurnichement *m*; *of animal* geignement *m* **2** *v/i* pleurnicher; *of animal* geindre

whine [waın] *v/i of dog etc* gémir; F (*complain*) pleurnicher

whip [wıp] **1** *n* fouet *m* **2** *v/t* (*pret & pp* **-ped**) (*beat*) fouetter; *cream* battre; F (*defeat*) battre à plates coutures

♦ **whip out** *v/t* F (*take out*) sortir en un tour de main

♦ **whip up** *v/t crowds* galvaniser; *hatred* attiser

whipped cream ['wıptkri:m] crème *f* fouettée

whip·ping ['wıpıŋ] (*beating*) correction *f*; F (*defeat*) défaite *f* à plates coutures

whirl [wɜːrl] **1** *n: my mind is in a ~* la tête me tourne **2** *v/i of leaves* tourbillonner; *of propeller* tourner

♦ **whirl around** *v/i of person* se retourner brusquement

'whirl·pool *in river* tourbillon *m*; *for relaxation* bain *m* à remous

'whirl·wind tourbillon *m*

whirr [wɜːr] *v/i* ronfler

whisk [wısk] **1** *n* fouet *m* **2** *v/t eggs* battre

♦ **whisk away** *v/t plates etc* enlever rapidement

whis·kers ['wıskərz] *npl of man* favoris *mpl*; *of animal* moustaches *fpl*

whis·key, *Br* **whis·ky** ['wıskı] whisky *m*

whis·per ['wıspər] **1** *n* chuchotement *m*; (*rumor*) bruit *m* **2** *v/t & v/i* chuchoter

whis·tle ['wɪsl] **1** *n sound* sifflement *m*; *device* sifflet *m* **2** *v/t & v/i* siffler

whis·tle-blow·er ['wɪslbloʊər] F personne *f* qui vend la mèche

white [waɪt] **1** *n color, of egg* blanc *m*; *person* Blanc *m*, Blanche *f* **2** *adj* blanc*; **go ~** *of face* devenir pâle; *of hair, person* blanchir

white 'Christ·mas Noël *m* blanc; **white-col·lar 'work·er** col *m* blanc; **'White House** Maison *f* Blanche; **white 'lie** pieux mensonge *m*; **'white meat** viande *f* blanche; **'white-out** *in snow* visibilité *f* nulle à cause de la neige; *for text* fluide *m* correcteur; **'white·wash 1** *n* blanc *m* de chaux; *fig* maquillage *m* de la vérité **2** *v/t* blanchir à la chaux; **'white wine** vin *m* blanc

whit·tle ['wɪtl] *v/t wood* tailler au couteau

♦ **whittle down** *v/t* réduire (**to** à)

whizz [wɪz] *n*: **be a ~ at** F être un crack en F

♦ **whizz by, whizz past** *v/i of time, car* filer

'whizz-kid F prodige *m*

who [huː] *pron* ◊ *interrogative* qui; **~ was that?** c'était qui?, qui étaitce? ◊ *relative*: *subject* qui; *object* que; **the woman ~ saved the boy** la femme qui a sauvé le garçon; **the woman ~ you saw** la femme que tu as vue; **the man ~ she was speaking to** l'homme auquel elle parlait

who·dun·nit [huːˈdʌnɪt] roman *m* policier

who·ev·er [huːˈevər] *pron* ◊ qui que ce soit; **you can tell ~ you like** tu peux le dire à qui tu veux; **~ gets the right answer …** celui / celle qui trouve la bonne réponse … ◊ : **~ can that be?** qui cela peut-il bien être?

whole [hoʊl] **1** *adj* entier*; **the ~ …** tout le (toute la) …; **the ~ town** toute la ville; **he drank / ate the ~ lot** il a tout bu / mangé; **it's a ~ lot easier / better** c'est bien plus facile / bien mieux **2** *n* tout *m*, ensemble *m*; **the**

~ of the United States l'ensemble *m* des États-Unis; **on the ~** dans l'ensemble

whole-heart·ed [hoʊlˈhɑːrtɪd] *adj* inconditionnel*; **whole-heart·ed·ly** [hoʊlˈhɑːrtɪdlɪ] *adv* sans réserve; **'whole-meal bread** *Br* pain *m* complet; **'whole-sale 1** *adj* de gros; *fig* en masse **2** *adv* au prix de gros; **whole·sal·er** ['hoʊlseɪlər] grossiste *m/f*; **whole·some** ['hoʊlsəm] *adj* sain; **'whole wheat bread** pain *m* complet

whol·ly ['hoʊlɪ] *adv* totalement

whol·ly owned sub·sid·i·ar·y filiale *f* à 100%

whom [huːm] *pron fml* qui

whoop·ing cough ['huːpɪŋ] coqueluche *f*

whop·ping ['wɑːpɪŋ] *adj* F énorme

whore [hɔːr] *n* putain *f*

whose [huːz] **1** *pron* ◊ *interrogative* à qui; **~ is this?** à qui c'est? ◊ *relative* dont; **a man ~ wife …** un homme dont la femme …; **a country ~ economy is booming** un pays dont l'économie prospère **2** *adj* à qui; **~ bike is that?** à qui est ce vélo?; **~ car are we taking?** on prend la voiture de qui?; **~ fault is it then?** à qui la faute alors?

why [waɪ] *adv* pourquoi; **that's ~** voilà pourquoi; **~ not?** pourquoi pas?; **the reason ~ I'm late** la raison pour laquelle je suis en retard

wick [wɪk] mèche *f*

wick·ed ['wɪkɪd] *adj* méchant; (*mischievous*) malicieux*; P (*great*) tip top F

wick·er ['wɪkər] *adj* osier *m*

wick·er 'chair chaise *f* en osier

wick·et ['wɪkɪt] *in station, bank etc* guichet *m*

wide [waɪd] *adj street, field* large; *experience, range* vaste; **be 12 foot ~** faire 3 mètres et demi de large

wide-a'wake *adj* complètement éveillé

wide·ly ['waɪdlɪ] *adv* largement; **~ known** très connu; **it is ~ believed that …** on pense généralement

W

que …

wid·en ['waɪdn] **1** v/t élargir **2** v/i s'élargir

wide-'o·pen adj grand ouvert

wide-rang·ing [waɪd'reɪndʒɪŋ] adj de vaste portée

'wide·spread adj hunger, poverty, belief répandu

wid·ow ['wɪdou] n veuve f

wid·ow·er ['wɪdouər] veuf m

width [wɪdθ] largeur f

wield [wiːld] v/t weapon manier; power exercer

wife [waɪf] (pl wives [waɪvz]) femme f

wig [wɪg] perruque f

wig·gle ['wɪgl] v/t loose screw, tooth remuer; hips tortiller

wild [waɪld] **1** adj animal, flowers sauvage; teenager rebelle; party fou*; scheme délirant; applause frénétique; **be ~ about** enthusiastic être dingue de F; **go ~** devenir déchaîné; (become angry) se mettre en rage; **run ~ of** children faire tout et n'importe quoi; of plants pousser dans tous les sens **2** npl: **the ~s** les régions reculées

wil·der·ness ['wɪldərnɪs] désert m; fig: garden etc jungle f

'wild·fire: spread like ~ se répandre comme une traînée de poudre; **wild-'goose chase** recherche f inutile; **'wild·life** faune f et flore f; **~ pro·gram** émission f sur la nature

wild·ly ['waɪldlɪ] adv applaud, kick frénétiquement; F extremely follement

wil·ful Br → **willful**

will·ful ['wɪlfl] adj person, refusal volontaire

will[1] [wɪl] n LAW testament m

will[2] [wɪl] n (willpower) volonté f

will[3] [wɪl] v/aux: **I ~ let you know to-morrow** je vous le dirai demain; **~ you be there?** est-ce que tu seras là?; **I won't be back until late** je ne reviendrai qu'assez tard; **you ~ call me, won't you?** tu m'appelleras, n'est-ce pas?; **I'll pay for this - no you won't** je vais payer - non; **the car won't start** la voiture ne veut pas démarrer; **~ you tell her that …?** est-ce que tu pourrais lui dire que

…?; **~ you have some more cof-fee?** est-ce que vous voulez encore du café?; **~ you stop that!** veux-tu arrêter!

will·ing ['wɪlɪŋ] adj helper de bonne volonté; **be ~ to do sth** être prêt à faire qch

will·ing·ly ['wɪlɪŋlɪ] adv (with pleasure) volontiers

will·ing·ness ['wɪlɪŋnɪs] empressement m (**to do** à faire)

wil·low ['wɪlou] saule m

'will·pow·er volonté f

wil·ly-nil·ly [wɪlɪ'nɪlɪ] adv (at random) au petit bonheur la chance

wilt [wɪlt] v/i of plant se faner

wi·ly ['waɪlɪ] adj rusé

wimp [wɪmp] F poule f mouillée

win [wɪn] **1** n victoire f **2** v/t & v/i (pret & pp **won**) gagner; prize remporter

♦ **win back** v/t money, trust, voters regagner

wince [wɪns] v/i tressaillir

winch [wɪntʃ] n treuil m

wind[1] [wɪnd] **1** n vent m; (flatulence) gaz m; **get ~ of …** avoir vent de … **2** v/t: **be ~ed** by ball etc avoir le souffle coupé

wind[2] [waɪnd] **1** v/i (pret & pp **wound**) of path, river serpenter; of staircase monter en colimaçon; of ivy s'enrouler **2** v/t (pret & pp **wound**) enrouler

♦ **wind down 1** v/i of party etc tirer à sa fin **2** v/t car window baisser; business réduire progressivement

♦ **wind up 1** v/t clock, car window remonter; speech, presentation terminer; affairs conclure; company liquider **2** v/i (finish) finir; **wind up in the hospital** finir à l'hôpital

'wind·bag F moulin m à paroles F; **'wind·fall** fig aubaine f; **'wind farm** champ m d'éoliennes

wind·ing ['waɪndɪŋ] adj path qui serpente

'wind in·stru·ment instrument m à vent

'wind·mill moulin m (à vent)

win·dow ['wɪndou] also COMPUT fenêtre f; of airplane, boat hublot m; of store vitrine f; **in the ~ of** store dans la vitrine

'win·dow box jardinière *f*; **'win·dow clean·er** *person* laveur(-euse) *m(f)* de vitres; **'win·dow-pane** vitre *f*; **'win·dow seat** *on train* place *f* côté fenêtre; *on airplane* place côté hublot; **'win·dow-shop·ping: go ~** faire du lèche-vitrines; **win·dow-sill** ['wɪndoʊsɪl] rebord *m* de fenêtre

'wind·pipe trachée *f*; **'wind·screen** *Br* **'wind·shield** pare-brise *m*; **'wind·shield wip·er** essuie-glace *m*; **'wind·surf·er** véliplanchiste *m/f*; **'wind·surf·ing** planche *f* à voile; **'wind tur·bine** éolienne *f*

wind·y ['wɪndɪ] *adj weather, day* venteux*; *it's so ~* il y a tellement de vent; *it's getting ~* le vent se lève

wine [waɪn] vin *m*

'wine bar bar *m* à vin; **'wine cel·lar** cave *f* (à vin); **'wine glass** verre *m* à vin; **'wine list** carte *f* des vins; **'wine mak·er** vigneron(ne) *m(f)*; **'wine mer·chant** marchand *m* de vin

win·er·y ['waɪnərɪ] établissement *m* viticole

wing [wɪŋ] *of bird, airplane*, SP aile *f*

'wing·span envergure *f*

wink [wɪŋk] **1** *n* clin *m* d'œil; *I didn't sleep a ~* F je n'ai pas fermé l'œil de la nuit **2** *v/i of person* cligner des yeux; *~ at s.o.* faire un clin d'œil à qn

win·ner ['wɪnər] gagnant(e) *m(f)*

win·ning ['wɪnɪŋ] *adj* gagnant

'win·ning post poteau *m* d'arrivée

win·nings ['wɪnɪŋz] *npl* gains *mpl*

win·ter ['wɪntər] *n* hiver *m*

win·ter 'sports *npl* sports *mpl* d'hiver

win·try ['wɪntrɪ] *adj* d'hiver

wipe [waɪp] *v/t* essuyer; *tape* effacer; *~ one's eyes / feet* s'essuyer les yeux / les pieds

◆ **wipe out** *v/t* (*kill, destroy*) détruire; *debt* amortir

wip·er ['waɪpər] → **windshield wiper**

wire [waɪr] *n* fil *m* de fer; *electrical* fil *m* électrique

wire·less ['waɪrlɪs] **1** *n* radio *f* **2** *adj* sans fil

wire net·ting [waɪr'netɪŋ] grillage *m*

wir·ing ['waɪrɪŋ] ELEC installation *f* électrique

wir·y ['waɪrɪ] *adj person* nerveux*

wis·dom ['wɪzdəm] sagesse *f*

'wis·dom tooth dent *f* de sagesse

wise [waɪz] *adj* sage

'wise·crack F raillerie *f* F

'wise guy *pej* petit malin *m*

wise·ly ['waɪzlɪ] *adv act* sagement

wish [wɪʃ] **1** *n* vœu *m*; *make a ~* faire un vœu; *my ~ came true* mon vœu s'est réalisé; *against s.o.'s ~es* contre l'avis de qn; *best ~es* cordialement; *for birthday, Christmas* meilleurs vœux **2** *v/t* souhaiter; *I ~ that you didn't have to go* je regrette que tu doives partir; *I ~ that I could stay here for ever* j'aimerais rester ici pour toujours; *I ~ him well* je lui souhaite bien de la chance; *I ~ I could* si seulement je pouvais

◆ **wish for** *v/t* vouloir

'wish·bone fourchette *f*

wish·ful ['wɪʃfl] *adj*: *that's ~ thinking* c'est prendre ses désirs pour des réalités

wish·y-wash·y ['wɪʃɪwɑːʃɪ] *adj person* mollasse; *color* délavé

wisp [wɪsp] *of hair* mèche *m*; *of smoke* traînée *f*

wist·ful ['wɪstfl] *adj* nostalgique

wist·ful·ly ['wɪstflɪ] *adv* avec nostalgie

wit [wɪt] (*humor*) esprit *m*; *person* homme *m*/femme *f* d'esprit; *be at one's ~s' end* ne plus savoir que faire; *keep one's ~s about one* garder sa présence d'esprit; *be scared out of one's ~s* avoir une peur bleue

witch [wɪtʃ] sorcière *f*

'witch-hunt *fig* chasse *f* aux sorcières

with [wɪð] *prep* ◇ avec; *~ a smile / a wave* en souriant / faisant un signe de la main; *are you ~ me?* (*do you understand?*) est-ce que vous me suivez?; *~ no money* sans argent

◇ *agency, cause* de; *tired ~ waiting* fatigué d'attendre

◇ *characteristics* à; *the woman ~ blue eyes* la femme aux yeux bleus; *s.o. ~ experience* une personne d'expérience

W

◊ *at the house of* chez; *I live ~ my aunt* je vis chez ma tante

with·draw [wɪðˈdrɔː] **1** *v/t* (*pret* **-drew**, *pp* **-drawn**) retirer **2** *v/i* (*pret* **-drew**, *pp* **-drawn**) se retirer

with·draw·al [wɪðˈdrɔːəl] retrait *m*

with'draw·al symp·toms *npl* (symptômes *mpl* de) manque *m*

with·drawn [wɪðˈdrɔːn] *adj person* renfermé

with·er [ˈwɪðər] *v/i* se faner

with·hold *v/t* (*pret & pp* **-held**) *information, name, payment* retenir; *consent* refuser

with·in *prep* (*inside*) dans; *in expressions of time* en moins de; *in expressions of distance* à moins de; *is it ~ walking distance?* est-ce qu'on peut y aller à pied?; *we kept ~ the budget* nous avons respecté le budget; *~ my power / my capabilities* dans mon pouvoir / mes capacités; *~ reach* à portée de la main

with·out *prep* sans; *~ looking / asking* sans regarder / demander; *~ an umbrella* sans parapluie

with·stand *v/t* (*pret & pp* **-stood**) résister à

wit·ness [ˈwɪtnɪs] **1** *n* témoin *m* **2** *v/t* être témoin de

'wit·ness stand barre *f* des témoins

wit·ti·cism [ˈwɪtɪsɪzm] mot *m* d'esprit

wit·ty [ˈwɪtɪ] *adj* plein d'esprit

wob·ble [ˈwɑːbl] *v/i* osciller

wob·bly [ˈwɑːblɪ] *adj* bancal; *tooth* qui bouge; *voice* chevrotant

woke [wəʊk] *pret → wake*

wok·en [ˈwəʊkn] *pp → wake*

wolf [wʊlf] **1** *n* (*pl* **wolves**) loup *m*; (*fig: womanizer*) coureur *m* de jupons **2** *v/t: ~ (down)* engloutir

'wolf whis·tle *n* sifflement *m* (au passage d'une fille)

wom·an [ˈwʊmən] (*pl* **women** [ˈwɪmɪn]) femme *f*

wom·an 'doc·tor femme *f* médecin

wom·an 'driv·er conductrice *f*

wom·an·iz·er [ˈwʊmənaɪzər] coureur *m* de femmes

wom·an·ly [ˈwʊmənlɪ] *adj* féminin

wom·an 'priest prêtresse *f*

womb [wuːm] utérus *m*; *in his mother's ~* dans le ventre de sa mère

wom·en [ˈwɪmɪn] *pl → woman*

wom·en's lib [wɪmɪnzˈlɪb] libération *f* des femmes

wom·en's lib·ber [wɪmɪnzˈlɪbər] militante *f* des droits de la femme

won [wʌn] *pret & pp → win*

won·der [ˈwʌndər] **1** *n* (*amazement*) émerveillement *m*; *no ~!* pas étonnant!; *it's a ~ that ...* c'est étonnant que ... (*+subj*) **2** *v/i* se poser des questions **3** *v/t* se demander; *I ~ if you could help* je me demandais si vous pouviez m'aider

won·der·ful [ˈwʌndərfʊl] *adj* merveilleux*

won·der·ful·ly [ˈwʌndərflɪ] *adv* (*extremely*) merveilleusement

won't [wəʊnt] *→ will not*

wood [wʊd] bois *m*

wood·ed [ˈwʊdɪd] *adj* boisé

wood·en [ˈwʊdn] *adj* (*made of wood*) en bois

wood·peck·er [ˈwʊdpekər] pic *m*; **'wood·wind** MUS bois *m*; **'wood·work** *parts made of wood* charpente *f*; *activity* menuiserie *f*

wool [wʊl] laine *f*

wool·en [ˈwʊlən] **1** *adj* en laine **2** *n* lainage *m*

wool·len *Br → woolen*

word [wɜːrd] **1** *n* mot *m*; *of song*, (*promise*) parole *f*; (*news*) nouvelle *f*; *is there any ~ from ...?* est-ce qu'il y a des nouvelles de ...?; *you have my ~* vous avez ma parole; *have ~s* (*argue*) se disputer; *have a ~ with s.o.* en parler à qn **2** *v/t article, letter* formuler

word·ing [ˈwɜːrdɪŋ] formulation *f*

word 'pro·cess·ing traitement *m* de texte

word 'pro·ces·sor *software* traitement *m* de texte

wore [wɔːr] *pret → wear*

work [wɜːrk] **1** *n* travail *m*; *out of ~* au chômage; *be at ~* être au travail **2** *v/i of person* travailler; *of machine*, (*succeed*) marcher **3** *v/t employee* faire travailler; *machine* faire marcher

◆ **work off** *v/t excess weight* perdre; *hangover, bad mood* faire passer

◆ **work out 1** *v/t solution, (find out)* trouver; *problem* résoudre **2** *v/i at gym* s'entraîner; *of relationship, arrangement etc* bien marcher

◆ **work out to** *v/t (add up to)* faire

◆ **work up** *v/t:* **work up enthusiasm** s'enthousiasmer; **work up an appetite** s'ouvrir l'appétit; **get worked up** *angry* se fâcher; *nervous* se mettre dans tous ses états

work·a·ble ['wɜːrkəbl] *adj solution* possible

worka·hol·ic [wɜːrkə'hɑːlɪk] F bourreau *m* de travail

'work·day (*hours of work*) journée *f* de travail; (*not weekend*) jour *m* de travail

work·er ['wɜːrkər] travailleur(-euse) *m(f)*; **she's a good ~** elle travaille bien

'work·force main-d'œuvre *f*

'work hours *npl* heures *fpl* de travail

work·ing ['wɜːrkɪŋ] *adj day, week* de travail

'work·ing class classe *f* ouvrière; **'work·ing-class** *adj* ouvrier*; **'work·ing con·di·tions** *npl* conditions *fpl* de travail; **work·ing 'day** → **workday**; **'work·ing hours** → **work hours**; **work·ing 'knowledge** connaissances *fpl* suffisantes; **work·ing 'moth·er** mère *f* qui travaille

'work·load quantité *f* de travail; **'work·man** ouvrier *m*; **'work·man·like** *adj* de professionnel*; **'work·man·ship** fabrication *f*; **work of 'art** œuvre *f* d'art; **'work·out** séance *f* d'entraînement; **'work per·mit** permis *m* de travail; **'work·shop** *also seminar* atelier *m*; **'work sta·tion** station *f* de travail; **'work·top** plan *m* de travail

world [wɜːrld] monde *m*; **the ~ of computers / the theater** le monde des ordinateurs / du théâtre; **out of this ~** F extraordinaire

world-'class *adj* de niveau mondial; **World 'Cup** *in soccer* Coupe *f* du monde; **world-'fa·mous** *adj* mondialement connu

world·ly ['wɜːrldlɪ] *adj* du monde; *person* qui a l'expérience du monde

world 'pow·er puissance *f* mondiale; **world 're·cord** record *m* mondial; **world 'war** guerre *f* mondiale; **'world·wide 1** *adj* mondial **2** *adv* dans le monde entier

worm [wɜːrm] *n* ver *m*

worn [wɔːrn] *pp* → **wear**

worn-'out *adj shoes, carpet* trop usé; *person* éreinté

wor·ried ['wʌrɪd] *adj* inquiet*

wor·ried·ly ['wʌrɪdlɪ] *adv* avec inquiétude

wor·ry ['wʌrɪ] **1** *n* souci *m* **2** *v/t (pret & pp -ied)* inquiéter **3** *v/i (pret & pp -ied)* s'inquiéter

wor·ry·ing ['wʌrɪɪŋ] *adj* inquiétant

worse [wɜːrs] **1** *adj* pire **2** *adv play, perform, feel* plus mal

wors·en ['wɜːrsn] *v/i* empirer

wor·ship ['wɜːrʃɪp] **1** *n* culte *m* **2** *v/t (pret & pp -ped) God* honorer; *fig: person, money* vénérer

worst [wɜːrst] **1** *adj* pire **2** *adv:* **the areas ~ affected** les régions les plus (gravement) touchées; **we came off ~** nous sommes sortis perdants **3** *n:* **the ~** le pire; **if (the) ~ comes to (the) ~** dans le pire des cas

worst-case scen·a·ri·o scénario *m* catastrophe

worth [wɜːrθ] *adj:* **$20 ~ of gas** 20 $ de gaz; **be ~ ... in monetary terms** valoir; **it's ~ reading / seeing** cela vaut la peine d'être lu / vu; **be ~ it** valoir la peine

worth·less ['wɜːrθlɪs] *adj object* sans valeur; *person* bon à rien

worth'while *adj cause* bon*; **be ~** (*beneficial, useful*) être utile; **it's not ~ waiting** cela ne vaut pas la peine d'attendre

worth·y ['wɜːrðɪ] *adj person, cause* digne; **be ~ of sth** (*deserve*) être digne de qch

would [wʊd] *v/aux:* **I ~ help if I could** je vous aiderais si je pouvais; **I said that I ~ go** j'ai dit que je viendrais;

W

~ you like to go to the movies? est-ce que tu voudrais aller au cinéma?; **~ you tell her that ...?** pourriez-vous lui dire que ...?; **I ~ not have** *or* **~n't have been so angry if ...** je n'aurais pas été aussi en colère si ...

wound[1] [wuːnd] **1** *n* blessure *f* **2** *v/t with weapon, words* blesser

wound[2] [waʊnd] *pret & pp* → **wind**[1]

wove [woʊv] *pret* → **weave**

wo·ven ['woʊvn] *pp* → **weave**

wow [waʊ] *int* oh là là!

wrap [ræp] *v/t* (*pret & pp* **-ped**) *parcel, gift* envelopper; *scarf etc* enrouler

◆ **wrap up** *v/i against the cold* s'emmitoufler

wrap·per ['ræpər] emballage *m*; *for candy* papier *m*

wrap·ping ['ræpɪŋ] emballage *m*

'**wrap·ping pa·per** papier *m* d'emballage

wrath [ræθ] colère *f*

wreath [riːθ] couronne *f*

wreck [rek] **1** *n of ship* navire *m* naufragé; *of car, person* épave *f*; **be a nervous ~** avoir les nerfs détraqués **2** *v/t* détruire

wreck·age ['rekɪdʒ] *of ship* épave *m*; *of airplane* débris *mpl*; *fig: of marriage, career* restes *mpl*

wreck·er ['rekər] *truck* dépanneuse *f*

wreck·ing com·pa·ny ['rekɪŋ] compagnie *f* de dépannage

wrench [rentʃ] **1** *n tool* clef *f* **2** *v/t injure* fouler; (*pull*) arracher; **~ one's shoulder** se fouler l'épaule; **he ~ed it away from me** il me l'a arraché

wres·tle ['resl] *v/i* lutter

◆ **wrestle with** *v/t fig* lutter contre

wres·tler ['reslər] lutteur(-euse) *m(f)*

wres·tling ['reslɪŋ] lutte *f*

'**wres·tling con·test** combat *m* de lutte

wrig·gle ['rɪgl] *v/i* (*squirm*) se tortiller

◆ **wriggle out of** *v/t* se soustraire à

◆ **wring out** [rɪŋ] *v/t* (*pret & pp* **wrung**) *cloth* essorer

wrin·kle ['rɪŋkl] **1** *n in skin* ride *f*; *in clothes* pli *m* **2** *v/t clothes* froisser **3** *v/i of clothes* se froisser

wrist [rɪst] poignet *m*

'**wrist·watch** montre *f*

write [raɪt] *v/t* (*pret* **wrote**, *pp* **written**) écrire; *check* faire **2** *v/i* (*pret* **wrote**, *pp* **written**) écrire

◆ **write down** *v/t* écrire

◆ **write off** *v/t debt* amortir; *car* bousiller F

writ·er ['raɪtər] *of letter, book, song* auteur *m/f*; *of book* écrivain *m/f*

'**write-up** F critique *f*

writhe [raɪð] *v/i* se tordre

writ·ing ['raɪtɪŋ] (*handwriting, script*) écriture *f*; (*words*) inscription *f*; **in ~** par écrit; **~s of author** écrits *mpl*

'**writ·ing pa·per** papier *m* à lettres

writ·ten ['rɪtn] *pp* → **write**

wrong [rɔːŋ] **1** *adj information, decision, side* mauvais; *answer also* faux*; **be ~ of person** avoir tort; *of answer* être mauvais; *morally* être mal; **get the ~ train** se tromper de train; **what's ~?** qu'est-ce qu'il y a?; **there is something ~ with the car** la voiture a un problème **2** *adv* mal; **go ~ of person** se tromper; *of marriage, plan etc* mal tourner **3** *n* mal *m*; *injustice* injustice *f*; **be in the ~** avoir tort

wrong·ful ['rɔːŋfl] *adj* injuste

wrong·ly ['rɔːŋlɪ] *adv* à tort

wrong 'num·ber faux numéro *m*

wrote [roʊt] *pret* → **write**

wrought 'i·ron [rɔːt] fer *m* forgé

wrung [rʌŋ] *pret & pp* → **wring**

wry [raɪ] *adj* ironique

WWW [dʌbljuːdʌbljuː'dʌbljuː] *abbr* (= **Worldwide Web**) réseau *m* mondial des serveurs multimédias, web *m*

W

X

xen·o·pho·bi·a [zenou'foubiə] xénophobie *f*
X·mas ['krɪsməs, 'eksməs] *abbr* (= **Christmas**) Noël *m*

X-ray ['eksreɪ] **1** *n* radio *f* **2** *v/t* radiographier
xy·lo·phone [zaɪləˈfoun] xylophone *m*

Y

yacht [jɑːt] *n* yacht *m*
yacht·ing ['jɑːtɪŋ] voile *f*
yachts·man ['jɑːtsmən] yachtsman *m*
Yank [jæŋk] F Ricain(e) *m(f)* F
yank [jæŋk] *v/t* tirer violemment
yap [jæp] *v/i* (*pret & pp* **-ped**) *of small dog* japper; F (*talk a lot*) jacasser
yard¹ [jɑːrd] *of prison, institution etc* cour *f*; *behind house* jardin *m*; *for storage* dépôt *m*
yard² [jɑːrd] *measurement* yard *m*
'yard·stick point *m* de référence
yarn [jɑːrn] *n* (*thread*) fil *m*; F (*story*) (longue) histoire *f*
yawn [jɔːn] **1** *n* bâillement *m* **2** *v/i* bâiller
yeah [je] *adv* F ouais F
year [jɪr] année; **for ~s** depuis des années; **be six ~s old** avoir six ans
year·ly ['jɪrlɪ] **1** *adj* annuel* **2** *adv* tous les ans
yearn [jɜːrn] *v/i* languir
♦ **yearn for** *v/t* avoir très envie de
yeast [jiːst] levure *f*
yell [jel] **1** *n* hurlement *m* **2** *v/t & v/i* hurler
yel·low ['jeloʊ] **1** *n* jaune *m* **2** *adj* jaune
yel·low 'pag·es pages *fpl* jaunes
yelp [jelp] **1** *n of animal* jappement *m*; *of person* glapissement *m* **2** *v/i of animal* japper; *of person* glapir

yes [jes] *int* oui; *after negative question* si; **you didn't say that! - ~ (, I did)** tu n'as pas dit ça - si (je l'ai dit)
'yes·man *pej* béni-oui-oui *m* F
yes·ter·day ['jestərdeɪ] **1** *adv* hier **2** *n* hier *m*; **the day before ~** avant-hier
yet [jet] **1** *adv*: **the best ~** le meilleur jusqu'ici; **as ~** pour le moment; **have you finished ~?** as-tu (déjà) fini?; **is he here ~? - not ~** est-ce qu'il est (déjà) là? - non, pas encore; **~ bigger** encore plus grand **2** *conj* cependant, néanmoins; **~ I'm not sure** néanmoins, je ne suis pas sûr
yield [jiːld] **1** *n from crops, investment etc* rendement *m* **2** *v/t fruit, good harvest* produire; *interest* rapporter **3** *v/i* (*give way*) céder; MOT céder la priorité
yo·ga ['jougə] yoga *m*
yog·hurt ['jougərt] yaourt *m*
yolk [jouk] jaune *m* (d'œuf)
you [juː] *pron* ◊ *familiar singular: subject* tu; *object* te; *before vowels* t'; *after prep* toi; **he knows ~** il te connaît; **for ~** pour toi
◊ *polite singular, familiar plural and polite plural, all uses* vous
◊ *indefinite* on; **~ never know** on ne

sait jamais; **if ~ have your passport with ~** si on a son passeport sur soi

young [jʌŋ] *adj* jeune

young·ster ['jʌŋstər] jeune *m/f*; *child* petit(e) *m(f)*

your [jʊr] *adj familiar* ton, ta; *pl* tes; *polite* votre; *pl familiar and polite* vos

yours [jʊrz] *pron familiar* le tien, la tienne; *pl* les tiens, les tiennes; *polite* le / la vôtre; *pl* les vôtres; **a friend of ~** un(e) de tes ami(e)s; un(e) de vos ami(e)s; **~ ...** *at end of letter* bien amicalement; **~** *truly* *at end of letter* je vous prie d'agréer mes sentiments distingués

your·self *pron familiar* toi-même; *po-*

lite vous-même; *reflexive* te; *polite* se; *after prep* toi; *polite* vous; **did you hurt ~?** est-ce que tu t'es fait mal / est-ce que vous vous êtes fait mal?; **by ~** tout(e) seul(e)

your·selves *pron* vous-mêmes; *reflexive* se; *after prep* vous; **did you hurt ~?** est-ce que vous vous êtes fait mal?; **by ~** tout seuls, toutes seules

youth [ju:θ] *age* jeunesse *f*; *(young man)* jeune homme *m*; *(young people)* jeunes *mpl*

'youth club centre *m* pour les jeunes

youth·ful ['ju:θfʊl] *adj* juvénile

'youth hos·tel auberge *f* de jeunesse

yup·pie ['jʌpɪ] F yuppie *m/f*

Z

zap [zæp] *v/t* (*pret & pp* **-ped**) F COMPUT (*delete*) effacer; (*kill*) éliminer; (*hit*) donner un coup à; (*send*) envoyer vite fait

♦ **zap along** *v/i* F (*move fast*) filer; *of work* avancer vite

zapped [zæpt] *adj* F (*exhausted*) crevé F

zap·py ['zæpɪ] *adj* F *car, pace* rapide; *prose, style* vivant

zeal [zi:l] zèle *m*

ze·bra ['zebrə] zèbre *m*

ze·ro ['zɪroʊ] zéro *m*; **10 below ~** 10 degrés au-dessous de zéro

♦ **zero in on** *v/t* (*identify*) mettre le doigt sur

ze·ro 'growth croissance *f* zéro

zest [zest] *enjoyment* enthousiasme *m*; **~ for life** goût *m* de la vie

zig·zag ['zɪgzæg] **1** *n* zigzag *m* **2** *v/i* (*pret & pp* **-ged**) zigzaguer

zilch [zɪltʃ] F que dalle F

zinc [zɪŋk] zinc *m*

♦ **zip up** *v/t* (*pret & pp* **-ped**) *dress, jack*

et remonter la fermeture éclair de; COMPUT compresser

'zip code code *m* postal

zip·per ['zɪpər] fermeture *f* éclair

zit [zɪt] F *on face* bouton *m*

zo·di·ac ['zoʊdɪæk] zodiaque *m*; **signs of the ~** signes *mpl* du zodiaque

zom·bie ['zɑːmbɪ] F zombie *m/f*

zone [zoʊn] zone *f*

zonked [zɑːŋkt] *adj* P (*exhausted*) crevé F

zoo [zu:] zoo *m*

zo·o·log·i·cal [zu:ə'lɑːdʒɪkl] *adj* zoologique

zo·ol·o·gist [zu:'ɑːlədʒɪst] zoologiste *m/f*

zo·ol·o·gy [zu:'ɑːlədʒɪ] zoologie *f*

zoom [zu:m] *v/i* F (*move fast*) filer (à toute vitesse) F

♦ **zoom in on** *v/t* PHOT faire un zoom avant sur

'zoom lens zoom *m*

zuc·chi·ni [zu:'ki:nɪ] courgette *f*

Remarques sur le verbe anglais

a) Conjugaison

Indicatif

1. **Le présent** conserve la même forme que l'infinitif à toutes les personnes, à l'exception de la troisième personne du singulier, pour laquelle on ajoute un -*s* à la forme infinitive, par ex. *he brings*. Si l'infinitif se termine par une sifflante (ch, sh, ss, zz), on ajoute -*es*, comme dans *he passes*. Ce *s* peut être prononcé de deux manières différentes : après une consonne sourde, il se prononce de manière sourde, par ex. *he paints* [peɪnts] ; après une consonne sonore, il se prononce de manière sonore, par ex. *he sends* [sendz]. De plus, -*es* se prononce de manière sonore lorsque le *e* fait partie de la désinence ou est la dernière lettre de l'infinitif, par ex. *he washes* ['wɑːʃɪz], *he urges* ['ɜːrdʒɪz]. Dans le cas des verbes se terminant par -*y*, la troisième personne se forme en substituant -*ies* au *y* (*he worries*, *he tries*). Les verbes se terminant, à l'infinitif, par un -*y* précédé d'une voyelle sont tous réguliers (*he plays*). Le verbe *to be* est irrégulier à toutes les personnes : *I am, you are, he is, we are, you are, they are*. Trois autres verbes ont des formes particulières à la troisième personne du singulier : *do – he does, go – he goes, have – he has*.

   Aux autres temps, les verbes restent invariables à toutes les personnes. **Le prétérit** et **le participe passé** se forment en ajoutant -*ed* à la forme infinitive (*I passed, passed*), ou bien en ajoutant uniquement -*d* au verbe se terminant par un -*e* à l'infinitif, par ex. *I faced, faced*. (Il existe de nombreux verbes irréguliers ; voir ci-après). Cette désinence -(e)*d* se prononce généralement [t] : *passed* [pæst], *faced* [feɪst] ; cependant, lorsqu'il s'agit d'un verbe dont l'infinitif se termine par une consonne sonore, un son consonantique sonore ou un *r*, elle se prononce [d] : *warmed* [wɔːrmd], *moved* [muːvd], *feared* [fɪrd]. Lorsque l'infinitif se termine par -*d* ou -*t*, la désinence -*ed* se prononce [ɪd]. Lorsque l'infinitif se termine par un -*y*, ce dernier est remplacé par -*ie*, à quoi on ajoute ensuite le -*d* : *try – tried* [traɪd], *pity – pitied* ['pɪtiːd]. **Les temps composés du passé** sont formés avec l'auxiliaire *to have* et le participe passé : **passé composé** *I have faced*, **plus-que-parfait** *I had faced*. On forme **le futur** avec l'auxiliaire *will*, par ex. *I will face* ; **le conditionnel** se forme avec l'auxiliaire *would*, par ex. *I would face*.

   De plus, il existe pour chaque temps une forme progressive, qui est formée avec le verbe *to be* (= être) et le participe présent (voir ci-après) : *I am going, I was writing, I had been staying, I will be waiting*, etc.

2. En anglais, **le subjonctif** n'est pratiquement plus utilisé, à l'exception de quelques cas particuliers (*if I were you, so be it, it is proposed that a vote be taken*, etc.). Le subjonctif présent conserve la forme infinitive à toutes les personnes : *that I go, that he go*, etc.

3. En anglais, **le participe présent** et **le gérondif** ont la même forme et se construisent en ajoutant la désinence *-ing* à la forme infinitive : *painting, sending*. Toutefois : 1) lorsque l'infinitif d'un verbe se termine par un *-e* muet, ce dernier disparaît lors de l'ajout de la désinence, par ex. *love - loving, write - writing* (exceptions à cette règle : *dye - dyeing, singe - singeing*, qui conservent le *-e* final de l'infinitif) ; 2) le participe présent des verbes *die, lie, vie* etc., s'écrit *dying, lying, vying*, etc.

4. Il existe une catégorie de verbes partiellement irréguliers, se terminant par une seule consonne précédée d'une voyelle unique accentuée. Pour ces verbes, on double la consonne finale avant d'ajouter les désinences *-ing* ou *-ed* :

lob	lob*bed*	lob*bing*	compel	compel*led*	compel*ling*
wed	wed*ded*	wed*ding*	control	control*led*	control*ling*
beg	beg*ged*	beg*ging*	bar	bar*red*	bar*ring*
step	step*ped*	step*ping*	stir	stir*red*	stir*ring*

Dans le cas des verbes se terminant par un *-l* précédé d'une voyelle inaccentuée, l'orthographe britannique double cette consonne au participe passé et au participe présent, mais pas l'orthographe américaine :

  travel travel*led*, *Am* travel*ed* travel*ling*, *Am* travel*ing*

Lorsqu'un verbe se termine par *-c*, on substitue *-ck* au *c*, puis on ajoute la désinence *-ed* ou *-ing* :

  traffic traffic*ked* traffic*king*

5. **La voix passive** se forme exactement de la même manière qu'en français, avec le verbe *to be* et le participe passé : *I am obliged, he was fined, they will be moved*, etc.

6. Lorsque l'on s'adresse, en anglais, à une ou plusieurs autres personnes, on n'emploie que le pronom *you*, qui peut se traduire à la fois par le *tu* et le *vous* du français.

b) Verbes irréguliers anglais

Vous trouverez ci-après les trois formes principales de chaque verbe : l'infinitif, le prétérit et le participe passé.

arise – arose – arisen
awake – awoke – awoken, awaked
be (am, is, are) – was (were) – been
bear – bore – borne (1)
beat – beat – beaten
become – became – become
begin – began – begun

behold – beheld – beheld
bend – bent – bent
beseech – besought, beseeched – besought, beseeched
bet – bet, betted – bet, betted
bid – bid – bid
bind – bound – bound

bite – bit – bitten
bleed – bled – bled
blow – blew – blown
break – broke – broken
breed – bred – bred
bring – brought – brought
broadcast – broadcast – broadcast
build – built – built
burn – burnt, burned – burnt, burned
burst – burst – burst
bust – bust(ed) – bust(ed)
buy – bought – bought
cast – cast – cast
catch – caught – caught
choose – chose – chosen
cleave (*cut*) – clove, cleft – cloven, cleft
cleave (*adhere*) – cleaved – cleaved
cling – clung – clung
come – came – come
cost (*v/i*) – cost – cost
creep – crept – crept
crow – crowed, crew – crowed
cut – cut – cut
deal – dealt – dealt
dig – dug – dug
dive – dived, dove [douv] (2) – dived
do – did – done
draw – drew – drawn
dream – dreamt, dreamed – dreamt, dreamed
drink – drank – drunk
drive – drove – driven
dwell – dwelt, dwelled – dwelt, dwelled
eat – ate – eaten
fall – fell – fallen
feed – fed – fed
feel – felt – felt
fight – fought – fought
find – found – found
flee – fled – fled
fling – flung – flung
fly – flew – flown
forbear – forbore – forborne
forbid – forbad(e) – forbidden

forecast – forecast(ed) – forecast(ed)
forget – forgot – forgotten
forgive – forgave – forgiven
forsake – forsook – forsaken
freeze – froze – frozen
get – got – got, gotten (3)
give – gave – given
go – went – gone
grind – ground – ground
grow – grew – grown
hang – hung, hanged – hung, hanged (4)
have – had – had
hear – heard – heard
heave – heaved, naut hove – heaved, naut hove
hew – hewed – hewed, hewn
hide – hid – hidden
hit – hit – hit
hold – held – held
hurt – hurt – hurt
keep – kept – kept
kneel – knelt, kneeled – knelt, kneeled
know – knew – known
lay – laid – laid
lead – led – led
lean – leaned, leant – leaned, leant (5)
leap – leaped, leapt – leaped, leapt (5)
learn – learned, learnt – learned, learnt (5)
leave – left – left
lend – lent – lent
let – let – let
lie – lay – lain
light – lighted, lit – lighted, lit
lose – lost – lost
make – made – made
mean – meant – meant
meet – met – met
mow – mowed – mowed, mown
pay – paid – paid
plead – pleaded, pled – pleaded, pled (6)
prove – proved – proved, proven
put – put – put

quit – quit(ted) – quit(ted)
read – read [red] – read [red]
rend – rent – rent
rid – rid – rid
ride – rode – ridden
ring – rang – rung
rise – rose – risen
run – ran – run
saw – sawed – sawn, sawed
say – said – said
see – saw – seen
seek – sought – sought
sell – sold – sold
send – sent – sent
set – set – set
sew – sewed – sewed, sewn
shake – shook – shaken
shear – sheared – sheared, shorn
shed – shed – shed
shine – shone – shone
shit – shit(ted), shat – shit(ted), shat
shoe – shod – shod
shoot – shot – shot
show – showed – shown
shrink – shrank – shrunk
shut – shut – shut
sing – sang – sung
sink – sank – sunk
sit – sat – sat
slay – slew – slain
sleep – slept – slept
slide – slid – slid
sling – slung – slung
slink – slunk – slunk
slit – slit – slit
smell – smelt, smelled – smelt, smelled
smite – smote – smitten
sneak – sneaked, snuck – sneaked, snuck (7)
sow – sowed – sown, sowed
speak – spoke – spoken
speed – sped, speeded – sped, speeded (8)
spell – spelt, spelled – spelt, spelled (5)
spend – spent – spent
spill – spilt, spilled – spilt, spilled

spin – spun, span – spun
spit – spat – spat
split – split – split
spoil – spoiled, spoilt – spoiled, spoilt
spread – spread – spread
spring – sprang, sprung – sprung
stand – stood – stood
stave – staved, stove – staved, stove
steal – stole – stolen
stick – stuck – stuck
sting – stung – stung
stink – stunk, stank – stunk
strew – strewed – strewed, strewn
stride – strode – stridden
strike – struck – struck
string – strung – strung
strive – strove, strived – striven, strived
swear – swore – sworn
sweep – swept – swept
swell – swelled – swollen
swim – swam – swum
swing – swung – swung
take – took – taken
teach – taught – taught
tear – tore – torn
tell – told – told
think – thought – thought
thrive – throve – thriven, thrived (9)
throw – threw – thrown
thrust – thrust – thrust
tread – trod – trodden
understand – understood – understood
wake – woke, waked – woken, waked
wear – wore – worn
weave – wove – woven (10)
wed – wed(ded) – wed(ded)
weep – wept – wept
wet – wet(ted) – wet(ted)
win – won – won
wind – wound – wound
wring – wrung – wrung
write – wrote – written

(1) mais **be born** *naître*

(2) **dove** n'est pas utilisé en anglais britannique

(3) **gotten** n'est pas utilisé en anglais britannique

(4) **hung** pour les tableaux mais **hanged** pour les meurtriers

(5) l'anglais américain n'emploie normalement que la forme en **-ed**

(6) **pled** s'emploie en anglais américain ou écossais

(7) la forme **snuck** ne s'emploie que comme forme alternative familière en anglais américain

(8) avec **speed up** la seule forme possible est **speeded up**

(9) la forme **thrived** est plus courante

(10) mais **weaved** au sens de *se faufiler*

French verb conjugations

The verb forms given on the following pages are to be seen as models for conjugation patterns. In the French-English dictionary you will find a code given with each verb (*1a*, *2b*, *3c*, *4d* etc). The codes refer to these conjugation models.

Alphabetical list of the conjugation patterns given

abréger 1g	couvrir 2f	manger 1l	rire 4r
acheter 1e	croire 4v	menacer 1k	saluer 1n
acquérir 2l	croître 4w	mettre 4p	savoir 3g
aimer 1b	cueillir 2c	moudre 4y	sentir 2b
aller 1o	déchoir 3m	mourir 2k	seoir 3k
appeler 1c	dire 4m	mouvoir 3d	suivre 4h
asseoir 3l	échoir 3m	naître 4g	traire 4s
avoir 1	écrire 4f	paraître 4z	vaincre 4i
blâmer 1a	employer 1h	payer 1i	valoir 3h
boire 4u	envoyer 1p	peindre 4b	vendre 4a
bouillir 2e	être 1	plaire 4aa	venir 2h
clore 4k	faillir 2n	pleuvoir 3e	vêtir 2g
conclure 4l	faire 4n	pouvoir 3f	vivre 4e
conduire 4c	falloir 3c	prendre 4q	voir 3b
confire 4o	fuir 2d	punir 2a	vouloir 3i
conjuguer 1m	geler 1d	recevoir 3a	
coudre 4d	haïr 2m	régner 1f	
courir 2i	lire 4x	résoudre 4bb	

Note:

1. The *Imparfait* and the *Participe présent* can always be derived from the 1st person plural of the present indicative, eg:. nous trou**vons**; je trou**vais** *etc*, trou**vant**

2. The *Passé simple* is nowadays normally replaced by the *Passé composé* in spoken French.

3. The *Imparfait du subjonctif* is nowadays almost only used in the 3rd person singular, whether in spoken or in written French. It is normally replaced by the *Présent du subjonctif*.

(1) avoir

Auxiliaries

A. Indicatif

I. Simple forms

Présent

sg.	j'ai	
	tu as	
	il a	
pl.	nous avons	
	vous avez	
	ils ont	

Imparfait

sg.	j'avais
	tu avais
	il avait
pl.	nous avions
	vous aviez
	ils avaient

Passé simple

sg.	j'eus
	tu eus
	il eut
pl.	nous eûmes
	vous eûtes
	ils eurent

Futur simple

sg.	j'aurai
	tu auras
	il aura
pl.	nous aurons
	vous aurez
	ils auront

Conditionnel présent

sg.	j'aurais
	tu aurais
	il aurait
pl.	nous aurions
	vous auriez
	ils auraient

Participe présent

ayant

Participe passé

eu (f. eue)

II. Compound forms

Passé composé

j'ai eu

Plus-que-parfait

j'avais eu

Passé antérieur

j'eus eu

Futur antérieur

j'aurai eu

Conditionnel passé

j'aurais eu

Participe composé

ayant eu

Infinitif passé

avoir eu

B. Subjonctif

I. Simple forms

Présent

sg.	que j'aie
	que tu aies
	qu'il ait
pl.	que nous ayons
	que vous ayez
	qu'ils aient

Imparfait

sg.	que j'eusse
	que tu eusses
	qu'il eût
pl.	que nous eussions
	que vous eussiez
	qu'ils eussent

Impératif

aie – ayons – ayez

II. Compound forms

Passé

que j'aie eu

Plus-que-parfait

que j'eusse eu

Auxiliaries

(1) être

A. Indicatif

I. Simple forms

Présent

sg. je suis
tu es
il est

pl. nous sommes
vous êtes
ils sont

Imparfait

sg. j'étais
tu étais
il était

pl. nous étions
vous étiez
ils étaient

Passé simple

sg. je fus
tu fus
il fut

pl. nous fûmes
vous fûtes
ils furent

Futur simple

sg. je serai
tu seras
il sera

pl. nous serons
vous serez
ils seront

Conditionnel présent

sg. je serais
tu serais
il serait

pl. nous serions
vous seriez
ils seraient

Participe présent

étant

Participe passé

été

II. Compound forms

Passé composé

j'ai été

Plus-que-parfait

j'avais été

Passé antérieur

j'eus été

Futur antérieur

j'aurai été

Conditionnel passé

j'aurais été

Participe composé

ayant été

Infinitif passé

avoir été

B. Subjonctif

I. Simple forms

Présent

sg. que je sois
que tu sois
qu'il soit

pl. que nous soyons
que vous soyez
qu'ils soient

Imparfait

sg. que je fusse
que tu fusses
qu'il fût

pl. que nous fussions
que vous fussiez
qu'ils fussent

Impératif

sois – soyons – soyez

II. Compound forms

Passé: que j'aie été

Plus-que-parfait

que j'eusse été

(1a) blâmer

First conjugation

I. Simple forms

Présent
sg. je blâme
tu blâmes
il blâme[1]

pl. nous blâmons
vous blâmez
ils blâment

Passé simple
sg. je blâmai
tu blâmas
il blâma

pl. nous blâmâmes
vous blâmâtes
ils blâmèrent

Participe passé
blâmé(e)

Infinitif présent
blâmer

Impératif
blâme - blâmons - blâmez
NB. blâmes-en (-y)

Imparfait
sg. je blâmais
tu blâmais
il blâmait

pl. nous blâmions
vous blâmiez
ils blâmaient

Participe présent
blâmant

Futur
sg. je blâmerai
tu blâmeras
il blâmera

pl. nous blâmerons
vous blâmerez
ils blâmeront

Conditionnel
sg. je blâmerais
tu blâmerais
il blâmerait

pl. nous blâmerions
vous blâmeriez
ils blâmeraient

Subjonctif présent
sg. que je blâme
que tu blâmes
qu'il blâme

pl. que nous blâmions
que vous blâmiez
qu'ils blâment

Subjonctif imparfait
sg. que je blâmasse
que tu blâmasses
qu'il blâmât

pl. que nous blâmassions
que vous blâmassiez
qu'ils blâmassent

II. Compound forms

Using the *Participe passé* together with **avoir** and **être**

1. Active
Passé composé: j'ai blâmé
Plus-que-parfait: j'avais blâmé
Passé antérieur: j'eus blâmé
Futur antérieur: j'aurai blâmé
Conditionnel passé: j'aurais blâmé

2. Passive
Présent: je suis blâmé
Imparfait: j'étais blâmé
Passé simple: je fus blâmé
Passé composé: j'ai été blâmé
Plus-que-parf.: j'avais été blâmé
Passé antérieur: j'eus été blâmé
Futur: je serai blâmé
Futur antérieur: j'aurai été blâmé
Conditionnel: je serais blâmé
Conditionnel passé: j'aurais été blâmé
Impératif: sois blâmé
Participe présent: étant blâmé
Participe passé: ayant été blâmé
Infinitif présent: être blâmé
Infinitif passé: avoir été blâmé

[1](blâme-t-il?)

Infinitif	Notes	Présent de l'indicatif	Présent du subjonctif	Passé simple	Futur	Impératif	Participe passé
(1b) aimer	When the second syllable is not silent the **ai** is often pronounced as an open **e** [ɛ]: **aime** [ɛm] but **aimons** [emõ].	aime	aime	aimai	aimerai		aimé(e)
		aimes	aimes	aimas	aimeras	aime	
		aime	aime	aima	aimera	aimons	
		aimons	aimions	aimâmes	aimerons	aimez	
		aimez	aimiez	aimâtes	aimerez		
		aiment	aiment	aimèrent	aimeront		
(1c) appeler	Note the consonant doubling.	apelle	appelle	appelai	appellerai	appelle	appelé(e)
		appelles	appelles	appelas	appelleras	appelons	
		appelle	appelle	appela	appellera	appelez	
		appelons	appelions	appelâmes	appellerons		
		appelez	appeliez	appelâtes	appellerez		
		appellent	appellent	appelèrent	appelleront		
(1d) geler	Note the switch from **e** to **è**.	gèle	gèle	gelai	gèlerai	gèle	gelé(e)
		gèles	gèles	gelas	gèleras	gelons	
		gèle	gèle	gela	gèlera	gelez	
		gelons	gelions	gelâmes	gèlerons		
		gelez	geliez	gelâtes	gèlerez		
		gèlent	gèlent	gelèrent	gèleront		
(1e) acheter	Note the **è**.	achète	achète	achetai	achèterai	achète	acheté(e)
		achètes	achètes	achetas	achèteras	achetons	
		achète	achète	acheta	achètera	achetez	
		achetons	achetions	achetâmes	achèterons		
		achetez	achetiez	achetâtes	achèterez		
		achètent	achètent	achetèrent	achèteront		

Infinitif	Notes	Présent de l'indicatif	Présent du subjonctif	Passé simple	Futur	Impératif	Participe passé
(1f) régner	Note that the **é** becomes **è** only in the *prés.* and *impér.*, not in the *fut.* or *cond.*	règne règnes règne régnons régnez règnent	règne règnes règne régnions régniez règnent	régnai régnas régna régnâmes régnâtes régnèrent	régnerai régneras régnera régnerons régnerez régneront	règne régnons régnez	régné (*inv*)
(1g) abréger	Note that **é** becomes **è** only in the *prés.* and *impér.*, not in the *fut.* or *cond.* A silent **e** is inserted after a **g** coming before **a** and **o**.	abrège abrèges abrège abrégeons abrégez abrègent	abrège abrèges abrège abrégions abrégiez abrègent	abrégeai abrégea abrégeâmes abrégeâtes abrégèrent	abrégerai abrégeras abrégera abrégerons abrégerez abrégeront	abrège abrégeons abrégez	abrégé(e)
(1h) employer	Note the switch from **y** to **i**.	emploie emploies emploie employons employez emploient	emploie emploies emploie employions employiez emploient	employai employas employa employâmes employâtes employèrent	emploierai emploieras emploiera emploierons emploierez emploieront	emploie employons employez	employé(e)
(1i) payer	Where both the **y** and the **i** spelling are possible, the spelling with **i** is preferred.	paie, paye paies, payes paie, paye payons payez paient, -yent	paie, paye paies, payes paie, paye payions payiez paient, -yent	payai payas paya payâmes payâtes payèrent	paierai, paye- paieras paiera paierons paierez paieront	paie, paye payons payez	payé(e)

Infinitif	Notes	Présent de l'indicatif	Présent du subjonctif	Passé simple	Futur	Impératif	Participe passé
(1k) menacer	c takes a cedilla (ç) before a and o so as to retain the [s] sound.	menace	menace	menaçai	menacerai		menacé(e)
		menaces	menaces	menaças	menaceras	menace	
		menace	menace	menaça	menacera	menaçons	
		menaçons	menacions	menaçâmes	menacerons	menacez	
		menacez	menaciez	menaçâtes	menacerez		
		menacent	menacent	menacèrent	menaceront		
(1l) manger	A silent e is inserted after the g and before an a or o so as to keep the g soft.	*mange*	mange	mangeai	mangerai		mangé(e)
		manges	manges	mangeas	mangeras	mange	
		mange	mange	mangea	mangera	mangeons	
		mangeons	mangions	mangeâmes	mangerons	mangez	
		mangez	mangiez	mangeâtes	mangerez		
		mangent	mangent	mangèrent	mangeront		
(1m) conjuguer	The silent u is always kept, even before a and o.	conjugue	conjugue	conjuguai	conjuguerai		conjugué(e)
		conjugues	conjugues	conjuguas	conjugueras	conjugue	
		conjugue	conjugue	conjugua	conjuguera	conjuguons	
		conjuguons	conjuguions	conjuguâmes	conjuguerons	conjuguez	
		conjuguez	conjuguiez	conjuguâtes	conjuguerez		
		conjuguent	conjuguent	conjuguèrent	conjugueront		
(1n) saluer	u is pronounced shorter when another syllable follows: **salue** [saly] but **saluons** [salɥɔ̃].	salue	salue	saluai	saluerai		salué(e)
		salues	salues	saluas	salueras	salue	
		salue	salue	salua	saluera	saluons	
		saluons	saluions	saluâmes	saluerons	saluez	
		saluez	saluiez	saluâtes	saluerez		
		saluent	saluent	saluèrent	salueront		

Infinitif	Notes	Présent de l'indicatif	Présent du subjonctif	Passé simple	Futur	Impératif	Participe passé
(1o) aller	Not every form uses the stem **all**.	vais vas va allons allez vont	aille ailles aille allions alliez aillent	allai allas alla allâmes allâtes allèrent	irai iras ira irons irez iront	va (vas-y; but: va-t'en) allons allez	allé(e)
(1p) envoyer	As (1h) but with an irregular *fut.* and *cond.*	envoie envoies envoie envoyons envoyez envoient	envoie envoies envoie envoyions envoyiez envoient	envoyai envoyas envoya envoyâmes envoyâtes envoyèrent	enverrai enverras enverra enverrons enverrez enverront	envoie envoyons envoyez	envoyé(e)

Second conjugation

(2a) punir*

The second, regular conjugation, characterized by ...iss...

1. Simple forms

Présent

sg. je punis
tu punis
il punit

pl. nous punissons
vous punissez
ils punissent

Impératif

punis
punissons
punissez

Imparfait

sg. je punissais
tu punissais
il punissait

pl. nous punissions
vous punissiez
ils punissaient

Passé simple

sg. je punis
tu punis
il punit

pl. nous punîmes
vous punîtes
ils punirent

Participe présent

punissant

Participe passé

puni(e)

Infinitif présent

punir

Futur

sg. je punirai
tu puniras
il punira

pl. nous punirons
vous punirez
ils puniront

Conditionel

sg. je punirais
tu punirais
il punirait

pl. nous punirions
vous puniriez
ils puniraient

Subjonctif présent

sg. que je punisse
que tu punisses
qu'il punisse

pl. que nous punissions
que vous punissiez
qu'ils punissent

Subjonctif imparfait

sg. que je punisse
que tu punisses
qu'il punît

pl. que nous punissions
que vous punissiez
qu'ils punissent

II. Compound forms

Using the *Participe passé* with **avoir** and **être**; see (1a)

* **fleurir** in the figurative sense normally has as *Participe présent* **florissant** and as *Imparfait* **florissait**

Infinitif	Notes	Présent de l'indicatif	Présent du subjonctif	Passé simple	Futur	Impératif	Participe passé
(2b) sentir	No ...iss...	sens sens sent sentons sentez sentent	sente sentes sente sentions sentiez sentent	sentis sentis sentit sentîmes sentîtes sentirent	sentirai sentiras sentira sentirons sentirez sentiront	sens sentons sentez	senti(e)
(2c) cueillir	*prés, fut.* and *cond.* as in the first conjugation	cueille cueilles cueille cueillons cueillez cueillent	cueille cueilles cueille cueillions cueilliez cueillent	cueillis cueillis cueillit cueillîmes cueillîtes cueillirent	cueillerai cueilleras cueillera cueillerons cueillerez cueilleront	cueille cueillons cueillez	cueilli(e)
(2d) fuir	No ...iss... Note the switch between **y** and **i**.	fuis fuis fuit fuyons fuyez fuient	fuie fuies fuie fuyions fuyiez fuient	fuis fuis fuit fuîmes fuîtes fuirent	fuirai fuiras fuira fuirons fuirez fuiront	fuis fuyons fuyez	fui(e)
(2e) bouillir	*prés. ind.* and derived forms as in the fourth conjugation	bous bous bout bouillons bouillez bouillent	bouille bouilles bouille bouillions bouilliez bouillent	bouillis bouillis bouillit bouillîmes bouillîtes bouillirent	bouillirai bouilliras bouillira bouillirons bouillirez bouilliront	bous bouillons bouillez	bouilli(e)

Infinitif	Notes	Présent de l'indicatif	Présent du subjonctif	Passé simple	Futur	Impératif	Participe passé
(2f) couvrir	*prés. ind.* and derived forms as in the first conjugation; *p.p.* ends in **-ert**.	couvre couvres couvre couvrons couvrez couvrent	couvre couvres couvre couvrions couvriez couvrent	couvris couvris couvrit couvrîmes couvrîtes couvrirent	couvrirai couvriras couvrira couvrirons couvrirez couvriront	couvre couvrons couvrez	couvert(e)
(2g) vêtir	Follows (2b) apart from *p.p.* **vêtir** is rarely used other than in the form **vêtu**.	vêts vêts vêt vêtons vêtez vêtent	vête vêtes vête vêtions vêtiez vêtent	vêtis vêtis vêtit vêtîmes vêtîtes vêtirent	vêtirai vêtiras vêtira vêtirons vêtirez vêtiront	vêts vêtons vêtez	vêtu(e)
(2h) venir	*prés. ind., fut., p.p.* and derived forms as fourth conjugation. Vowel change in the *passé simple*; note the added **-d-** in the the *fut.* and *cond.*	viens viens vient venons venez viennent	vienne viennes vienne venions veniez viennent	vins vins vint vînmes vîntes vinrent	viendrai viendras viendra viendrons viendrez viendront	viens venons venez	venu(e)
(2i) courir	*prés. ind., p.p., fut.* and and derived forms as in the fourth conjugation. *passé simple* as in the third conjugation; **-rr-** in *fut.* and *cond.*	cours cours court courons courez courent	coure coures coure courions couriez courent	courus courus courut courûmes courûtes coururent	courrai courras courra courrons courrez courront	cours courons courez	couru

Infinitif	Notes	Présent de l'indicatif	Présent du subjonctif	Passé simple	Futur	Impératif	Participe passé
(2k) mourir	*prés. ind.* and derived forms as in the fourth conjugation, but note vowel shift to **eu** from **ou**; *passé simple* as in the third conjugation.	**meurs** **meurs** **meurt** mourons mourez **meurent**	**meure** **meures** **meure** mourions mouriez **meurent**	mourus mourus mourut mourûmes mourûtes moururent	mourrai mourras mourra mourrons mourrez mourront	**meurs** mourons mourez	mort(*e*)
(2l) acquérir	*pres. ind.* and derived forms as in the fourth conjugation with an **i** inserted before **e**; *p.p.* with **-s**; **-err-** in *fut.* and *cond.*	acquiers acquiers acquiert acquérons acquérez acquièrent	acquière acquières acquière acquérions acquériez acquièrent	acquis acquis acquit acquîmes acquîtes acquirent	acquerrai acquerras acquerra acquerrons acquerrez acquerront	acquiers acquérons acquérez	acquis(*e*)
(2m) haïr	Follows (2a); but in *sg. prés. ind.* and *impér.* the dieresis on the **i** is dropped.	hais [e] hais hait haïssons haïssez haïssent	haïsse haïsses haïsse haïssions haïssiez haïssent	haïs [a'i] haïs haït haïmes haïtes haïrent	haïrai haïras haïra haïrons haïrez haïront	hais haïssons haïssez	haï(*e*)
(2n) faillir	defective verb			faillis faillis faillit faillîmes faillîtes faillirent	faillirai failliras faillira faillirons faillirez failliront		failli

Third conjugation

I. Simple forms

(3a) recebir

Présent
sg.
- je reçois
- tu reçois
- il reçoit

pl.
- nous recevons
- vous recevez
- ils reçoivent

Impératif
- reçois
- recevons
- recevez

Futur
sg.
- je recevrai
- tu recevras
- il recevra

pl.
- nous recevrons
- vous recevrez
- ils recevront

Subjonctif présent
sg.
- que je reçoive
- que tu reçoives
- qu'il reçoive

pl.
- que nous recevions
- que vous receviez
- qu'ils reçoivent

Imparfait
sg.
- je recevais
- tu recevais
- il recevait

pl.
- nous recevions
- vous receviez
- ils recevaient

Conditionnel
sg.
- je recevrais
- tu recevrais
- il recevrait

pl.
- nous recevrions
- vous recevriez
- ils recevraient

Subjonctif imparfait
sg.
- que je reçusse
- que tu reçusses
- qu'il reçût

pl.
- que nous reçussions
- que vous reçussiez
- qu'ils reçussent

Passé simple
sg.
- je reçus
- tu reçus
- il reçut

pl.
- nous reçûmes
- vous reçûtes
- ils reçurent

Participe présent
recevant

Participe passé
reçu(e)

Infinitif présent
recevoir

II. Compound forms

Using the *Participe passé* together with **avoir** and **être**

707

Infinitif	Notes	Présent de l'indicatif	Présent du subjonctif	Passé simple	Futur	Impératif	Participe passé
(3b) voir	Switch between **i** and **y** as in (2d). Derived forms regular, but with **-err-** (instead of **-oir-**) in *fut.* and *cond.*	vois vois voit **voyons** **voyez** voient	voie voies voie **voyions** **voyiez** voient	*vis* *pourvoir:* je *pourvus*	verrai *pourvoir:* je *pourvoirai;* *prévoir:* je *prévoirai*	vois voyons voyez	vu(e)
(3c) falloir	Only used in the third person singular.	il faut	qu'il faille	il *fallut*	il faudra		fallu (*inv*)
(3d) mouvoir	Note the switch between **eu** and **ou**.	meus meus meut mouvons mouvez meuvent	meuve meuves meuve mouvions mouviez meuvent	*mus* *mus* *mut* *mûmes* *mûtes* *murent*	mouvrai mouvras mouvra mouvrons mouvrez mouvront	meus mouvons mouvez	mû, mue
(3e) pleuvoir		il pleut	qu'il pleuve	il *plut*	il pleuvra		plu (*inv*)
(3f) pouvoir	In the *prés. ind.* sometimes also **je puis**; interrogative **puis-je?**	peux peux peut pouvons pouvez peuvent	puisse puisses puisse puissions puissiez puissent	*pus* *pus* *put* *pûmes* *pûtes* *purent*	pourrai pourras pourra pourrons pourrez pourront		pu (*inv*)

Infinitif	Notes	Présent de l'indicatif	Présent du subjonctif	Passé simple	Futur	Impératif	Participe passé
(3g) savoir	p.pr. **sachant**	sais sais sait savons savez savent	sache saches sache sachions sachiez sachent	sus sus sut sûmes sûtes surent	saurai sauras saura saurons saurez sauront	sache sachons sachez	su(e)
(3h) valoir	**prévaloir** is regular in the *prés. subj.*: **que je prévale** etc.	vaux vaux vaut valons valez valent	vaille vailles vaille valions valiez vaillent	valus valus valut valûmes valûtes valurent	vaudrai vaudras vaudra vaudrons vaudrez vaudront		valu(e)
(3i) vouloir	Note the switch between **eu** and **ou**. In the *fut.* a **-d-** is inserted.	veux veux veut voulons voulez veulent	veuille veuilles veuille voulions vouliez veuillent	voulus voulus voulut voulûmes voulûtes voulurent	voudrai voudras voudra voudrons voudrez voudront	veuille veuillons veuillez	voulu(e)
(3k) seoir	Restricted usage: *p.pr.* **seyant**; *impf.* **seyait**; *cond.* **siérait**	il sied					

Infinitif	Notes	Présent de l'indicatif	Présent du subjonctif	Passé simple	Futur	Impératif	Participe passé
(3l) asseoir	Apart from in the *passé simple* and *p.p.* (**assis**), there are two forms. *Impf.* **asseyais** or **assoyais**. However it is not common to use the **oi** or **oy** forms with either **vous** or **nous**.	asseyons asseyez asseyent	asseye asseyes asseye asseyions asseyiez asseyent	assis assis assit assîmes assîtes assirent	assiérai assiéras assiéra assiérons assiérez assiéront	assieds asseyons asseyez	assis(e)
	surseoir forms **je sursois, nous sursoyons** etc, *fut.* **je surseoirai**.	*or* assois assois assoit assoyons assoyez assoient	*or* assoie assoies assoie assoyions assoyiez assoient		*or* assoirai assoiras assoira assoirons assoirez assoiront	*or* assois assoyons assoyez	
(3m) déchoir		déchois déchois déchoit déchoyons déchoyez déchoient	déchoie déchoies déchoie déchoyions déchoyiez déchoient	déchus déchus déchut déchûmes déchûtes déchurent	déchoirai déchoiras déchoira déchoirons déchoirez déchoiront		déchu(e)
échoir	defective verb	il échoit ils échoient	qu'il échoie qu'ils échoient	il échut ils échurent	il échoira ils échoiront		échu(e)

Fourth conjugation

(4a) vendre

Regular fourth conjugation, no change to stem

I. Simple forms

Présent

sg.
je vend**s***
tu vend**s***
il vend*

pl.
nous vendons
vous vendez
ils vendent

Participe passé

vendu(e)

Futur

sg.
je vendrai
tu vendras
il vendra

pl.
nous vendrons
vous vendrez
ils vendront

Subjonctif présent

sg.
que je vende
que tu vendes
qu'il vende

pl.
que nous vendions
que vous vendiez
qu'ils vendent

Impératif

vends
vendons
vendez

Conditionnel

sg.
je vendrais
tu vendrais
il vendrait

pl.
nous vendrions
vous vendriez
ils vendraient

Imparfait

sg.
je vendais
tu vendais
il vendait

pl.
nous vendions
vous vendiez
ils vendaient

Subjonctif imparfait

sg.
que je vendisse
que tu vendisses
qu'il vendît

pl.
que nous vendissions
que vous vendissiez
qu'ils vendissent

Passé simple

sg.
je vendis
tu vendis
il vendit

pl.
nous vendîmes
vous vendîtes
ils vendirent

Infinitif présent

vendre

Participe présent

vendant

II. Compound forms

Using the *Participe passé* together with **avoir** and **être**, see (1a)

* **rompre** has: il rompit; **battre** has: je (tu) bats, il bat; **foutre** has: je (tu) fous.

Infinitif	Notes	Présent de l'indicatif	Présent du subjonctif	Passé simple	Futur	Impératif	Participe passé
(4b) peindre	Switch between nasal **n** und palatalated **n** (**gn**); **-d-** only before **r** in the *inf.*, *fut.* and *cond.*	peins peins peint peignons peignez peignent	peigne peignes peigne peignions peigniez peignent	peignis peignis peignit peignîmes peignîtes peignirent	peindrai peindras peindra peindrons peindrez peindront	peins peignons peignez	peint(e)
(4c) conduire	**Luire, reluire, nuire** do not take a **t** in the *p.p.*	conduis conduis conduit conduisons conduisez conduisent	conduise conduises conduise conduisions conduisiez conduisent	conduisis conduisis conduisit conduisîmes conduisîtes conduisirent	conduirai conduiras conduira conduirons conduirez conduiront	conduis conduisons conduisez	conduit(e)
(4d) coudre	**-d-** is replaced by **-s-** before endings which start with a vowel.	couds couds coud cousons cousez cousent	couse couses couse cousions cousiez cousent	cousis cousis cousit cousîmes cousîtes cousirent	coudrai coudras coudra coudrons coudrez coudront	couds cousons cousez	cousu(e)
(4e) vivre	Final **-v** of the stem is dropped in the *sg.* *prés. ind.*; *passé simple* **vécus**; *p.p.* **vécu**	vis vis vit vivons vivez vivent	vive vives vive vivions viviez vivent	vécus vécus vécut vécûmes vécûtes vécurent	vivrai vivras vivra vivrons vivrez vivront	vis vivons vivez	vécu(e)

Infinitif	Présent de l'indicatif	Présent du subjonctif	Passé simple	Futur	Impératif	Participe passé	Notes
(4f) écrire	écris écris écrit écrivons écrivez écrivent	écrive écrives écrive écrivions écriviez écrivent	écrivis écrivis écrivit écrivîmes écrivîtes écrivirent	écrirai écriras écrira écrirons écrirez écriront	écris écrivons écrivez	écrit(e)	Before a vowel the old Latin v remains.
(4g) naître	nais nais naît naissons naissez naissent	naisse naisses naisse naissions naissiez naissent	naquis naquis naquit naquîmes naquîtes naquirent	naîtrai naîtras naîtra naîtrons naîtrez naîtront	nais naissons naissez	né(e)	-ss- in the pl. prés. ind. and derived forms; in the sg. prés. ind. i before t becomes î.
(4h) suivre	suis suis suit suivons suivez suivent	suive suives suive suivions suiviez suivent	suivis suivis suivit suivîmes suivîtes suivirent	suivrai suivras suivra suivrons suivrez suivront	suis suivons suivez	suivi(e)	p.p. as in the second conjugation
(4i) vaincre	vaincs vaincs vainc vainquons vainquez vainquent	vainque vainques vainque vainquions vainquiez vainquent	vainquis vainquis vainquit vainquîmes vainquîtes vainquirent	vaincrai vaincras vaincra vaincrons vaincrez vaincront	vaincs vainquons vainquez	vaincu(e)	No t in the third person sg. prés. ind.; switch from c to qu before vowels (exception: vaincu)

Infinitif	Notes	Présent de l'indicatif	Présent du subjonctif	Passé simple	Futur	Impératif	Participe passé
(4k) clore	prés. third person pl. **closent**; likewise prés. subj.; third person sg. prés. ind. in **...ôt**.	je clos tu clos ils closent	que je close		je clorai	clos	clos(e)
éclore	Only used in the third person.	il éclôt ils éclosent	qu'il éclose qu'ils éclosent		il éclora ils écloront		éclos(e)
(4) conclure	passé simple follows the third conjugation. **Reclure** has **reclus(e)** in p.p.; likewise: **inclus(e)**; but note: **exclu(e)**.	conclus conclus conclut concluons concluez concluent	conclue conclues conclue concluions concluiez concluent	conclus conclus conclut conclûmes conclûtes conclurent	conclurai concluras conclura conclurons conclurez concluront	conclus concluons concluez	conclu(e)
(4m) dire	**Redire** is conjugated like **dire**. Other compounds have **...disez** in the prés. with the exception of **maudire**, which follows the second conjugation, except for **maudit** in the p.p.	dis dis dit disons dites disent	dise dises dise disions disiez disent	dis dis dit dîmes dîtes dirent	dirai diras dira dirons direz diront	dis disons dites	dit(e)

Infinitif	Notes	Présent de l'indicatif	Présent du subjonctif	Passé simple	Futur	Impératif	Participe passé
(4n) faire	Frequent vowel shifts in the stem. [fə-] in all *fut.* forms.	fais [fɛ] fais [fɛ] fait [fɛ] faisons [fəzõ] faites [fɛt] font	fasse fasses fasse fassions fassiez fassent	fis fis fit fîmes fîtes firent	ferai feras fera ferons ferez feront	fais faisons faites	fait(e)
(4o) confire	**suffire** has **suffi** (*inv*) in the *p.p.*	confis confis confit confisons confisez confisent	confise confises confise confisions confisiez confisent	confis confis confit confîmes confîtes confirent	confirai confiras confira confirons confirez confiront	confis confisons confisez	confit(e)
(4p) mettre	Only one **t** in the *sg. prés. ind.* first three persons.	mets mets met mettons mettez mettent	mette mettes mette mettions mettiez mettent	mis mis mit mîmes mîtes mirent	mettrai mettras mettra mettrons mettrez mettront	mets mettons mettez	mis(e)
(4q) prendre	Omission of **d** in some forms.	prends prends prend prenons prenez prennent	prenne prennes prenne prenions preniez prennent	pris pris prit prîmes prîtes prirent	prendrai prendras prendra prendrons prendrez prendront	prends prenons prenez	pris(e)

Infinitif	Notes	Présent de l'indicatif	Présent du subjonctif	Passé simple	Futur	Impératif	Participe passé
(4r) rire	*p.p.* as in the second conjugation.	ris ris rit rions riez rient	rie ries rie riions riiez rient	ris ris rit rîmes rîtes rirent	rirai riras rira rirons rirez riront	ris rions riez	ri (*inv*)
(4s) traire	There is no *passé simple*.	trais trais trait trayons trayez traient	traie traies traie trayions trayiez traient		trairai trairas traira trairons trairez trairont	trais trayons trayez	trait(e)
(4u) boire	Note the **v** before a vowel (from the old Latin **b**); *passé simple* follows the third conjugation.	bois bois boit buvons buvez boivent	boive boives boive buvions buviez boivent	bus bus but bûmes bûtes burent	boirai boiras boira boirons boirez boiront	bois buvons buvez	bu(e)

Infinitif	Notes	Présent de l'indicatif	Présent du subjonctif	Passé simple	Futur	Impératif	Participe passé
(4v) croire	*passé simple* as in the third conjugation	crois crois croit croyons croyez croient	croie croies croie croyions croyiez croient	crus crus crut crûmes crûtes crurent	croirai croiras croira croirons croirez croiront	crois croyons croyez	cru(e)
(4w) croître	**î** in the *sg. pres. ind.* and the *sg. imper.; passé simple* as in the third conjugation	croîs croîs croît croissons croissez croissent	croisse croisses croisse croissions croissiez croissent	crûs crûs crût crûmes crûtes crûrent	croîtrai croîtras croîtra croîtrons croîtrez croîtront	croîs croissons croissez	crû, crue
(4x) lire	*passé simple* as in the third conjugation	lis lis lit lisons lisez lisent	lise lises lise lisions lisiez lisent	lus lus lut lûmes lûtes lurent	lirai liras lira lirons lirez liront	lis lisons lisez	lu(e)
(4y) moudre	*passé simple* as in the third conjugation	mouds mouds moud moulons moulez moulent	moule moules moule moulions mouliez moulent	moulus moulus moulut moulûmes moulûtes moulurent	moudrai moudras moudra moudrons moudrez moudront	mouds moulons moulez	

Infinitif	Notes	Présent de l'indicatif	Présent du subjonctif	Passé simple	Futur	Impératif	Participe passé
(4z) paraître	i before **t**; *passé simple* as in the third conjugation	parais parais paraît paraissons paraissez paraissent	paraisse paraisses paraisse paraissions paraissiez paraissent	parus parus parut parûmes parûtes parurent	paraîtrai paraîtras paraîtra paraîtrons paraîtrez paraîtront	parais paraissons paraissez	paru(e)
(4aa) plaire	*passé simple* as in the third conjugation; **taire** has **il tait** (without the circumflex)	plais plais plaît plaisons plaisez plaisent	plaise plaises plaise plaisions plaisiez plaisent	plus plus plut plûmes plûtes plurent	plairai plairas plaira plairons plairez plairont	plais plaisons plaisez	plu *(inv)*
(4bb) résoudre	**absoudre** has **no** *passé simple*, *participe passé* **absous, absoute.**	résous résous résout résolvons résolvez résolvent	résolve résolves résolve résolvions résolviez résolvent	résolus résolus résolut résolûmes résolûtes résolurent	résoudrai résoudras résoudra résoudrons résoudrez résoudront	résous résolvons résolvez	résolu(e)

Numbers / Les nombres
Cardinal Numbers / Les nombres cardinaux

0	zero, *Br aussi* nought *zéro*
1	one *un*
2	two *deux*
3	three *trois*
4	four *quatre*
5	five *cinq*
6	six *six*
7	seven *sept*
8	eight *huit*
9	nine *neuf*
10	ten *dix*
11	eleven *onze*
12	twelve *douze*
13	thirteen *treize*
14	fourteen *quatorze*
15	fifteen *quinze*
16	sixteen *seize*
17	seventeen *dix-sept*
18	eighteen *dix-huit*
19	nineteen *dix-neuf*
20	twenty *vingt*
21	twenty-one *vingt et un*
22	twenty-two *vingt-deux*
30	thirty *trente*
31	thirty-one *trente et un*
40	forty *quarante*
50	fifty *cinquante*
60	sixty *soixante*
70	seventy *soixante-dix*
71	seventy-one *soixante et onze*
72	seventy-two *soixante-douze*
79	seventy-nine *soixante-dix-neuf*
80	eighty *quatre-vingts*
81	eighty-one *quatre-vingt-un*
90	ninety *quatre-vingt-dix*
91	ninety-one *quatre-vingt-onze*
100	a hundred, one hundred *cent*
101	a hundred and one *cent un*
200	two hundred *deux cents*
300	three hundred *trois cents*
324	three hundred and twenty-four *trois cent vingt-quatre*
1000	a thousand, one thousand *mille*
2000	two thousand *deux mille*
1959	one thousand nine hundred and fifty-nine *mille neuf cent cinquante-neuf*

2000	two thousand *deux mille*		
1 000 000	a million, one million *un million*		
2 000 000	two million *deux millions*		
1 000 000 000	a billion, one billion *un milliard*		

Notes / Remarques:

i) **vingt** and **cent** take an -s when preceded by another number, except if there is another number following.

ii) If **un** is used with a following noun, then it is the only number to agree (one man **un homme**; one woman **une femme**).

iii) 1.25 (one point two five) = 1,25 (un virgule vingt-cinq)

iv) 1,000,000 (en anglais) = 1 000 000 ou 1.000.000 (in French)

Ordinal Numbers / Les nombres ordinaux

1st	first	$1^{er}/1^{ère}$	*premier / première*
2nd	second	2^e	*deuxième*
3rd	third	3^e	*troisième*
4th	fourth	4^e	*quatrième*
5th	fifth	5^e	*cinquième*
6th	sixth	6^e	*sixième*
7th	seventh	7^e	*septième*
8th	eighth	8^e	*huitième*
9th	ninth	9^e	*neuvième*
10th	tenth	10^e	*dixième*
11th	eleventh	11^e	*onzième*
12th	twelfth	12^e	*douzième*
13th	thirteenth	13^e	*treizième*
14th	fourteenth	14^e	*quatorzième*
15th	fifteenth	15^e	*quinzième*
16th	sixteenth	16^e	*seizième*
17th	seventeenth	17^e	*dix-septième*
18th	eighteenth	18^e	*dix-huitième*
19th	nineteenth	19^e	*dix-neuvième*
20th	twentieth	20^e	*vingtième*
21st	twenty-first	21^e	*vingt et unième*
22nd	twenty-second	22^e	*vingt-deuxième*
30th	thirtieth	30^e	*trentième*
31st	thirty-first	31^e	*trente et unième*
40th	fortieth	40^e	*quarantième*
50th	fiftieth	50^e	*cinquantième*
60th	sixtieth	60^e	*soixantième*
70th	seventieth	70^e	*soixante-dixième*
71st	seventy-first	71^e	*soixante et onzième*
80th	eightieth	80^e	*quatre-vingtième*
90th	ninetieth	90^e	*quatre-vingt-dixième*
100th	hundredth	100^e	*centième*
101st	hundred and first	101^e	*cent unième*

1000th	thousandth	1000ᵉ	*millième*
2000th	two thousandth	2000ᵉ	*deux millième*
1,000,000th	millionth	1 000 000ᵉ	*millionième*
1,000,000,000th	billionth	1 000 000 000ᵉ	*milliardième*

Fractions and other Numbers
Les fractions et autres nombres

¹/₂	one half, a half	*un demi, une demie*
1¹/₂	one and a half	*un et demi*
¹/₃	one third, a third	*un tiers*
²/₃	two thirds	*deux tiers*
¹/₄	one quarter, a quarter	*un quart*
³/₄	three quarters	*trois quarts*
¹/₅	one fifth, a fifth	*un cinquième*
3⁴/₅	three and four fifths	*trois et quatre cinquièmes*
¹/₁₁	one eleventh, an eleventh	*un onzième*
	seven times as big,	*sept fois plus grand*
	seven times bigger	
	twelve times more	*douze fois plus*
	first(ly)	*premièrement*
	second(ly)	*deuxièmement*
7 + 8 = 15	seven and (*or* plus) eight	*sept plus huit égalent quinze*
	are (*or* is) fifteen	
10 − 3 = 7	ten minus three is seven,	*dix moins trois égalent sept,*
	three from ten leaves seven	*trois ôté de dix il reste sept*
2 x 3 = 6	two times three is six	*deux fois trois égalent six*
20 ÷ 4 = 5	twenty divided by four is	*vingt divisé par quatre égalent*
	five	*cinq*

Dates / Les dates

1996	nineteen ninety-six	*mille neuf cent quatre-vingt-seize*
2005	two thousand (and) five	*deux mille cinq*

November 10/11 (ten, eleven), *Br* **the 10th/11th of November**
le dix/onze novembre

March 1 (first), *Br* **the 1st of March**
le premier mars

Headword in blue	**bloop•er** ['bluːpər] F gaffe *f*
Entrée en bleu	
	con•flict ['kɑːnflɪkt] **1** *n* (*disagreement*) conflit *m* **2** *v/i* [kən'flɪkt] (*clash*) s'opposer, être en conflit; *of dates* coïncider
International Phonetic Alphabet	
Alphabet phonétique international	**clip•pers** ['klɪpərz] *npl for hair* tondeuse *f*; *for nails* pince *f* à ongles; *for gardening* sécateur *m*
Translation in normal characters with gender shown in *italics*	**as•sai•lant** [ə'seɪlənt] assaillant(e) *m(f)*
Traduction en caractères normaux et genre en *italique*	
Hyphenation points	**flam•ma•ble** ['flæməbl] *adj* inflammable
Points de coupure de mot	**fly•ing 'sau•cer** soucoupe *f* volante
Stress shown in headwords	**di•scrim•i•nate** [dɪ'skrɪmɪneɪt] *v/i*: **~ against** pratiquer une discrimination contre; **be ~d against** être victime de discrimination; **~ between sth and sth** distinguer qch de qch
Accent indiqué dans les entrées	
Examples and phrases in **bold italics**	**en•try** ['entrɪ] (*way in, admission*) entrée *f*; *for competition: person* participant(e) *m(f)*; *in diary, accounts* inscription *f*; *in reference book* article *m*
Exemples et locutions en **gras et italique**	
Indicating words in *italics*	**du•ress** [dʊ'res]: **under ~** sous la contrainte
Indicateurs contextuels et sémantiques en *italique*	
Swung dash replaces the entire headword	**ea•gle-eyed** [iːgl'aɪd] *adj*: **be ~** avoir des yeux d'aigle
Le tilde (~) remplace l'entrée en entier.	
Compounds	**'brown-nose** *v/t* P lécher le cul à P; **brown 'pa•per** papier *m* d'emballage, papier *m* kraft; **brown pa•per 'bag** sac *m* en papier kraft; **brown 'sug•ar** sucre *m* roux
Mots composés	